Lecture Notes in Computer Science 11141

More information about this series at http://www.springer.com/series/7407

Věra Kůrková · Yannis Manolopoulos
Barbara Hammer · Lazaros Iliadis
Ilias Maglogiannis (Eds.)

Artificial Neural Networks and Machine Learning – ICANN 2018

27th International Conference on Artificial Neural Networks
Rhodes, Greece, October 4–7, 2018
Proceedings, Part III

Editors
Věra Kůrková
Czech Academy of Sciences
Prague 8
Czech Republic

Lazaros Iliadis
Democritus University of Thrace
Xanthi
Greece

Yannis Manolopoulos
Open University of Cyprus
Latsia
Cyprus

Ilias Maglogiannis
University of Piraeus
Piraeus
Greece

Barbara Hammer
CITEC Bielefeld University
Bielefeld
Germany

ISSN 0302-9743 ISSN 1611-3349 (electronic)
Lecture Notes in Computer Science
ISBN 978-3-030-01423-0 ISBN 978-3-030-01424-7 (eBook)
https://doi.org/10.1007/978-3-030-01424-7

Library of Congress Control Number: 2018955577

LNCS Sublibrary: SL1 – Theoretical Computer Science and General Issues

This Springer imprint is published by the registered company Springer Nature Switzerland AG
The registered company address is: Gewerbestrasse 11, 6330 Cham, Switzerland

Preface

Technological advances in artificial intelligence (AI) are leading the rapidly changing world of the twenty-first century. We have already passed from machine learning to deep learning with numerous applications. The contribution of AI so far to the improvement of our quality of life is profound. Major challenges but also risks and threats are here. Brain-inspired computing explores, simulates, and imitates the structure and the function of the human brain, achieving high-performance modeling plus visualization capabilities.

The International Conference on Artificial Neural Networks (ICANN) is the annual flagship conference of the European Neural Network Society (ENNS). It features the main tracks "Brain-Inspired Computing" and "Machine Learning Research," with strong cross-disciplinary interactions and applications. All research fields dealing with neural networks are present.

The 27th ICANN was held during October 4–7, 2018, at the Aldemar Amilia Mare five-star resort and conference center in Rhodes, Greece. The previous ICANN events were held in Helsinki, Finland (1991), Brighton, UK (1992), Amsterdam, The Netherlands (1993), Sorrento, Italy (1994), Paris, France (1995), Bochum, Germany (1996), Lausanne, Switzerland (1997), Skovde, Sweden (1998), Edinburgh, UK (1999), Como, Italy (2000), Vienna, Austria (2001), Madrid, Spain (2002), Istanbul, Turkey (2003), Budapest, Hungary (2004), Warsaw, Poland (2005), Athens, Greece (2006), Porto, Portugal (2007), Prague, Czech Republic (2008), Limassol, Cyprus (2009), Thessaloniki, Greece (2010), Espoo-Helsinki, Finland (2011), Lausanne, Switzerland (2012), Sofia, Bulgaria (2013), Hamburg, Germany (2014), Barcelona, Spain (2016), and Alghero, Italy (2017).

Following a long-standing tradition, these Springer volumes belong to the *Lecture Notes in Computer Science Springer* series. They contain the papers that were accepted to be presented orally or as posters during the 27th ICANN conference. The 27th ICANN Program Committee was delighted by the overwhelming response to the call for papers. All papers went through a peer-review process by at least two and many times by three or four independent academic referees to resolve any conflicts. In total, 360 papers were submitted to the 27th ICANN. Of these, 139 (38.3%) were accepted as full papers for oral presentation of 20 minutes with a maximum length of 10 pages, whereas 28 of them were accepted as short contributions to be presented orally in 15 minutes and for inclusion in the proceedings with 8 pages. Also, 41 papers (11.4%) were accepted as full papers for poster presentation (up to 10 pages long), whereas 11 were accepted as short papers for poster presentation (maximum length of 8 pages).

The accepted papers of the 27th ICANN conference are related to the following thematic topics:

AI and Bioinformatics
Bayesian and Echo State Networks
Brain-Inspired Computing

Chaotic Complex Models
Clustering, Mining, Exploratory Analysis
Coding Architectures
Complex Firing Patterns
Convolutional Neural Networks
Deep Learning (DL)

- DL in Real Time Systems
- DL and Big Data Analytics
- DL and Big Data
- DL and Forensics
- DL and Cybersecurity
- DL and Social Networks

Evolving Systems – Optimization
Extreme Learning Machines
From Neurons to Neuromorphism
From Sensation to Perception
From Single Neurons to Networks
Fuzzy Modeling
Hierarchical ANN
Inference and Recognition
Information and Optimization
Interacting with the Brain
Machine Learning (ML)

- ML for Bio-Medical Systems
- ML and Video-Image Processing
- ML and Forensics
- ML and Cybersecurity
- ML and Social Media
- ML in Engineering

Movement and Motion Detection
Multilayer Perceptrons and Kernel Networks
Natural Language
Object and Face Recognition
Recurrent Neural Networks and Reservoir Computing
Reinforcement Learning
Reservoir Computing
Self-Organizing Maps
Spiking Dynamics/Spiking ANN
Support Vector Machines
Swarm Intelligence and Decision-Making
Text Mining
Theoretical Neural Computation
Time Series and Forecasting
Training and Learning

The authors of submitted papers came from 34 different countries from all over the globe, namely: Belgium, Brazil, Bulgaria, Canada, China, Czech Republic, Cyprus, Egypt, Finland, France, Germany, Greece, India, Iran, Ireland, Israel, Italy, Japan, Luxembourg, The Netherlands, Norway, Oman, Pakistan, Poland, Portugal, Romania, Russia, Slovakia, Spain, Switzerland, Tunisia, Turkey, UK, USA.

Four keynote speakers were invited, and they gave lectures on timely aspects of AI.

We hope that these proceedings will help researchers worldwide to understand and to be aware of timely evolutions in AI and more specifically in artificial neural networks. We believe that they will be of major interest for scientists over the globe and that they will stimulate further research.

October 2018

Věra Kůrková
Yannis Manolopoulos
Barbara Hammer
Lazaros Iliadis
Ilias Maglogiannis

Organization

General Chairs

Věra Kůrková	Czech Academy of Sciences, Czech Republic
Yannis Manolopoulos	Open University of Cyprus, Cyprus

Program Co-chairs

Barbara Hammer	Bielefeld University, Germany
Lazaros Iliadis	Democritus University of Thrace, Greece
Ilias Maglogiannis	University of Piraeus, Greece

Steering Committee

Vera Kurkova (President of ENNS)	Czech Academy of Sciences, Czech Republic
Cesare Alippi	Università della Svizzera Italiana, Switzerland
Guillem Antó i Coma	Pompeu Fabra University, Barcelona, Spain
Jeremie Cabessa	Université Paris 2 Panthéon-Assas, France
Wlodzislaw Duch	Nicolaus Copernicus University, Poland
Petia Koprinkova-Hristova	Bulgarian Academy of Sciences, Bulgaria
Jaakko Peltonen	University of Tampere, Finland
Yifat Prut	The Hebrew University, Israel
Bernardete Ribeiro	University of Coimbra, Portugal
Stefano Rovetta	University of Genoa, Italy
Igor Tetko	German Research Center for Environmental Health, Munich, Germany
Alessandro Villa	University of Lausanne, Switzerland
Paco Zamora-Martínez	das-Nano, Spain

Publication Chair

Antonis Papaleonidas	Democritus University of Thrace, Greece

Communication Chair

Paolo Masulli	Technical University of Denmark, Denmark

Program Committee

Najem Abdennour	Higher Institute of Computer Science and Multimedia (ISIMG), Gabes, Tunisia

Tetiana Aksenova	Atomic Energy Commission (CEA), Grenoble, France
Zakhriya Alhassan	Durham University, UK
Tayfun Alpay	University of Hamburg, Germany
Ioannis Anagnostopoulos	University of Thessaly, Greece
Cesar Analide	University of Minho, Portugal
Annushree Bablani	National Institute of Technology Goa, India
Costin Badica	University of Craiova, Romania
Pablo Barros	University of Hamburg, Germany
Adam Barton	University of Ostrava, Czech Republic
Lluís Belanche	Polytechnic University of Catalonia, Spain
Bartlomiej Beliczynski	Warsaw University of Technology, Poland
Kostas Berberidis	University of Patras, Greece
Ege Beyazit	University of Louisiana at Lafayette, USA
Francisco Elanio Bezerra	University Ninth of July, Sao Paolo, Brazil
Varun Bhatt	Indian Institute of Technology, Bombay, India
Marcin Blachnik	Silesian University of Technology, Poland
Sander Bohte	National Research Institute for Mathematics and Computer Science (CWI), The Netherlands
Simone Bonechi	University of Siena, Italy
Farah Bouakrif	University of Jijel, Algeria
Meftah Boudjelal	Mascara University, Algeria
Andreas Bougiouklis	National Technical University of Athens, Greece
Martin Butz	University of Tübingen, Germany
Jeremie Cabessa	Université Paris 2, France
Paulo Vitor Campos Souza	Federal Center for Technological Education of Minas Gerais, Brazil
Angelo Cangelosi	Plymouth University, UK
Yanan Cao	Chinese Academy of Sciences, China
Francisco Carvalho	Federal University of Pernambuco, Brazil
Giovanna Castellano	University of Bari, Italy
Jheymesson Cavalcanti	University of Pernambuco, Brazil
Amit Chaulwar	Technical University Ingolstadt, Germany
Sylvain Chevallier	University of Versailles St. Quentin, France
Stephane Cholet	University of Antilles, Guadeloupe
Mark Collier	Trinity College, Ireland
Jorg Conradt	Technical University of Munich, Germany
Adriana Mihaela Coroiu	Babes-Bolyai University, Romania
Paulo Cortez	University of Minho, Portugal
David Coufal	Czech Academy of Sciences, Czech Republic
Juarez Da Silva	University of Vale do Rio dos Sinos, Brazil
Vilson Luiz Dalle Mole	Federal University of Technology Parana, Brazil
Debasmit Das	Purdue University, USA
Bodhisattva Dash	International Institute of Information Technology, Bhubaneswar, India
Eli David	Bar-Ilan University, Israel
Konstantinos Demertzis	Democritus University of Thrace, Greece

Antreas Dionysiou	University of Cyprus, Cyprus
Sergey Dolenko	Lomonosov Moscow State University, Russia
Xiao Dong	Chinese Academy of Sciences, China
Shirin Dora	University of Amsterdam, The Netherlands
Jose Dorronsoro	Autonomous University of Madrid, Spain
Ziad Doughan	Beirut Arab University, Lebanon
Wlodzislaw Duch	Nicolaus Copernicus University, Poland
Gerrit Ecke	University of Tübingen, Germany
Alexander Efitorov	Lomonosov Moscow State University, Russia
Manfred Eppe	University of Hamburg, Germany
Deniz Erdogmus	Northeastern University, USA
Rodrigo Exterkoetter	LTrace Geophysical Solutions, Florianopolis, Brazil
Yingruo Fan	The University of Hong Kong, SAR China
Maurizio Fiasché	Polytechnic University of Milan, Italy
Lydia Fischer	Honda Research Institute Europe, Germany
Andreas Fischer	University of Fribourg, Germany
Qinbing Fu	University of Lincoln, UK
Ninnart Fuengfusin	Kyushu Institute of Technology, Japan
Madhukar Rao G.	Indian Institute of Technology, Dhanbad, India
Mauro Gaggero	National Research Council, Genoa, Italy
Claudio Gallicchio	University of Pisa, Italy
Shuai Gao	University of Science and Technology of China, China
Artur Garcez	City University of London, UK
Michael Garcia Ortiz	Aldebaran Robotics, France
Angelo Genovese	University of Milan, Italy
Christos Georgiadis	University of Macedonia, Thessaloniki, Greece
Alexander Gepperth	HAW Fulda, Germany
Peter Gergel'	Comenius University in Bratislava, Slovakia
Daniel Gibert	University of Lleida, Spain
Eleonora Giunchiglia	University of Genoa, Italy
Jan Philip Goepfert	Bielefeld University, Germany
George Gravanis	Democritus University of Thrace, Greece
Ingrid Grenet	University of Côte d'Azur, France
Jiri Grim	Czech Academy of Sciences, Czech Republic
Xiaodong Gu	Fudan University, China
Alberto Guillén	University of Granada, Spain
Tatiana Valentine Guy	Czech Academy of Sciences, Czech Republic
Myrianthi Hadjicharalambous	KIOS Research and Innovation Centre of Excellence, Cyprus
Petr Hajek	University of Pardubice, Czech Republic
Xue Han	China University of Geosciences, China
Liping Han	Nanjing University of Information Science and Technology, China
Wang Haotian	National University of Defense Technology, China
Kazuyuki Hara	Nihon University, Japan
Ioannis Hatzilygeroudis	University of Patras, Greece

Stefan Heinrich	University of Hamburg, Germany
Tim Heinz	University of Siegen, Germany
Catalina Hernandez	District University of Bogota, Colombia
Alex Hernández García	University of Osnabrück, Germany
Adrian Horzyk	AGH University of Science and Technology in Krakow, Poland
Wenjun Hou	China Agricultural University, China
Jian Hou	Bohai University, China
Haigen Hu	Zhejiang University of Technology, China
Amir Hussain	University of Stirling, UK
Nantia Iakovidou	King's College London, UK
Yahaya Isah Shehu	Coventry University, UK
Sylvain Jaume	Saint Peter's University, Jersey City, USA
Noman Javed	Namal College Mianwali, Pakistan
Maciej Jedynak	University of Grenoble Alpes, France
Qinglin Jia	Peking University, China
Na Jiang	Beihang University, China
Wenbin Jiang	Huazhong University of Science and Technology, China
Zongze Jin	Chinese Academy of Sciences, China
Jacek Kabziński	Lodz University of Technology, Poland
Antonios Kalampakas	American University of the Middle East, Kuwait
Jan Kalina	Czech Academy of Sciences, Czech Republic
Ryotaro Kamimura	Tokai University, Japan
Andreas Kanavos	University of Patras, Greece
Savvas Karatsiolis	University of Cyprus, Cyprus
Kostas Karatzas	Aristotle University of Thessaloniki, Greece
Ioannis Karydis	Ionian University, Greece
Petros Kefalas	University of Sheffield, International Faculty City College, Thessaloniki, Greece
Nadia Masood Khan	University of Engineering and Technology Peshawar, Pakistan
Gul Muhammad Khan	University of Engineering and Technology, Peshawar, Pakistan
Sophie Klecker	University of Luxembourg, Luxembourg
Taisuke Kobayashi	Nara Institute of Science and Technology, Japan
Mario Koeppen	Kyushu Institute of Technology, Japan
Mikko Kolehmainen	University of Eastern Finland, Finland
Stefanos Kollias	University of Lincoln, UK
Ekaterina Komendantskaya	Heriot-Watt University, UK
Petia Koprinkova-Hristova	Bulgarian Academy of Sciences, Bulgaria
Irena Koprinska	University of Sydney, Australia
Dimitrios Kosmopoulos	University of Patras, Greece
Costas Kotropoulos	Aristotle University of Thessaloniki, Greece
Athanasios Koutras	TEI of Western Greece, Greece
Konstantinos Koutroumbas	National Observatory of Athens, Greece

Giancarlo La Camera	Stony Brook University, USA
Jarkko Lagus	University of Helsinki, Finland
Luis Lamb	Federal University of Rio Grande, Brazil
Ángel Lareo	Autonomous University of Madrid, Spain
René Larisch	Chemnitz University of Technology, Germany
Nikos Laskaris	Aristotle University of Thessaloniki, Greece
Ivano Lauriola	University of Padua, Italy
David Lenz	Justus Liebig University, Giessen, Germany
Florin Leon	Technical University of Iasi, Romania
Guangli Li	Chinese Academy of Sciences, China
Yang Li	Peking University, China
Hongyu Li	Zhongan Technology, Shanghai, China
Diego Ettore Liberati	National Research Council, Rome, Italy
Aristidis Likas	University of Ioannina, Greece
Annika Lindh	Dublin Institute of Technology, Ireland
Junyu Liu	Huiying Medical Technology, China
Ji Liu	Beihang University, China
Doina Logofatu	Frankfurt University of Applied Sciences, Germany
Vilson Luiz Dalle Mole	Federal University of Technology – Paraná (UTFPR), Campus Toledo, Spain
Sven Magg	University of Hamburg, Germany
Ilias Maglogiannis	University of Piraeus, Greece
George Magoulas	Birkbeck College, London, UK
Christos Makris	University of Patras, Greece
Kleanthis Malialis	University of Cyprus, Cyprus
Kristína Malinovská	Comenius University in Bratislava, Slovakia
Konstantinos Margaritis	University of Macedonia, Thessaloniki, Greece
Thomas Martinetz	University of Lübeck, Germany
Gonzalo Martínez-Muñoz	Autonomous University of Madrid, Spain
Boudjelal Meftah	University Mustapha Stambouli, Mascara, Algeria
Stefano Melacci	University of Siena, Italy
Nikolaos Mitianoudis	Democritus University of Thrace, Greece
Hebatallah Mohamed	Roma Tre University, Italy
Francesco Carlo Morabito	Mediterranean University of Reggio Calabria, Italy
Giorgio Morales	National Telecommunications Research and Training Institute (INICTEL), Peru
Antonio Moran	University of Leon, Spain
Dimitrios Moschou	Aristotle University of Thessaloniki, Greece
Cristhian Motoche	National Polytechnic School, Ecuador
Phivos Mylonas	Ionian University, Greece
Anton Nemchenko	UCLA, USA
Roman Neruda	Czech Academy of Sciences, Czech Republic
Amy Nesky	University of Michigan, USA
Hoang Minh Nguyen	Korea Advanced Institute of Science and Technology, South Korea
Giannis Nikolentzos	Ecole Polytechnique, Palaiseau, France

Dimitri Nowicki	National Academy of Sciences, Ukraine
Stavros Ntalampiras	University of Milan, Italy
Luca Oneto	University of Genoa, Italy
Mihaela Oprea	University Petroleum-Gas of Ploiesti, Romania
Sebastian Otte	University of Tubingen, Germany
Jun Ou	Beijing University of Technology, China
Basil Papadopoulos	Democritus University of Thrace, Greece
Harris Papadopoulos	Frederick University, Cyprus
Antonios Papaleonidas	Democritus University of Thrace, Greece
Krzysztof Patan	University of Zielona Góra, Poland
Jaakko Peltonen	University of Tampere, Finland
Isidoros Perikos	University of Patras, Greece
Alfredo Petrosino	University of Naples Parthenope, Italy
Duc-Hong Pham	Vietnam National University, Vietnam
Elias Pimenidis	University of the West of England, UK
Vincenzo Piuri	University of Milan, Italy
Mirko Polato	University of Padua, Italy
Yifat Prut	The Hebrew University, Israel
Jielin Qiu	Shanghai Jiao Tong University, China
Chhavi Rana	Maharshi Dayanand University, India
Marina Resta	University of Genoa, Italy
Bernardete Ribeiro	University of Coimbra, Portugal
Riccardo Rizzo	National Research Council, Rome, Italy
Manuel Roveri	Polytechnic University of Milan, Italy
Stefano Rovetta	University of Genoa, Italy
Araceli Sanchis de Miguel	Charles III University of Madrid, Spain
Marcello Sanguineti	University of Genoa, Italy
Kyrill Schmid	University of Munich, Germany
Thomas Schmid	University of Leipzig, Germany
Friedhelm Schwenker	Ulm University, Germany
Neslihan Serap	Sengor Istanbul Technical University, Turkey
Will Serrano	Imperial College London, UK
Jivitesh Sharma	University of Agder, Norway
Rafet Sifa	Fraunhofer IAIS, Germany
Sotir Sotirov	University Prof. Dr. Asen Zlatarov, Burgas, Bulgaria
Andreas Stafylopatis	National Technical University of Athens, Greece
Antonino Staiano	University of Naples Parthenope, Italy
Ioannis Stephanakis	Hellenic Telecommunications Organisation, Greece
Michael Stiber	University of Washington Bothell, USA
Catalin Stoean	University of Craiova, Romania
Rudolf Szadkowski	Czech Technical University, Czech Republic
Mandar Tabib	SINTEF, Norway
Kazuhiko Takahashi	Doshisha University, Japan
Igor Tetko	Helmholtz Center Munich, Germany
Yancho Todorov	Aalto University, Espoo, Finland

César Torres-Huitzil	National Polytechnic Institute, Victoria, Tamaulipas, Mexico
Athanasios Tsadiras	Aristotle University of Thessaloniki, Greece
Nicolas Tsapatsoulis	Cyprus University of Technology, Cyprus
George Tsekouras	University of the Aegean, Greece
Matus Tuna	Comenius University in Bratislava, Slovakia
Theodoros Tzouramanis	University of the Aegean, Greece
Juan Camilo Vasquez Tieck	FZI, Karlsruhe, Germany
Nikolaos Vassilas	ATEI of Athens, Greece
Petra Vidnerová	Czech Academy of Sciences, Czech Republic
Alessandro Villa	University of Lausanne, Switzerland
Panagiotis Vlamos	Ionian University, Greece
Thanos Voulodimos	National Technical University of Athens, Greece
Roseli Wedemann	Rio de Janeiro State University, Brazil
Stefan Wermter	University of Hamburg, Germany
Zhihao Ye	Guangdong University of Technology, China
Hujun Yin	University of Manchester, UK
Francisco Zamora-Martinez	Veridas Digital Authentication Solutions, Spain
Yongxiang Zhang	Sun Yat-Sen University, China
Liu Zhongji	Chinese Academy of Sciences, China
Rabiaa Zitouni	Tunis El Manar University, Tunisia
Sarah Zouinina	Université Paris 13, France

Keynote Talks

Cognitive Phase Transitions in the Cerebral Cortex – *John Taylor Memorial Lecture*

Robert Kozma

University of Massachusetts Amherst

Abstract. Everyday subjective experience of the stream of consciousness suggests continuous cognitive processing in time and smooth underlying brain dynamics. Brain monitoring techniques with markedly improved spatio-temporal resolution, however, show that relatively smooth periods in brain dynamics are frequently interrupted by sudden changes and intermittent discontinuities, evidencing singularities. There are frequent transitions between periods of large-scale synchronization and intermittent desynchronization at alpha-theta rates. These observations support the hypothesis about the cinematic model of cognitive processing, according to which higher cognition can be viewed as multiple movies superimposed in time and space. The metastable spatial patterns of field potentials manifest the frames, and the rapid transitions provide the shutter from each pattern to the next. Recent experimental evidence indicates that the observed discontinuities are not merely important aspects of cognition; they are key attributes of intelligent behavior representing the cognitive "Aha" moment of sudden insight and deep understanding in humans and animals. The discontinuities can be characterized as phase transitions in graphs and networks. We introduce computational models to implement these insights in a new generation of devices with robust artificial intelligence, including oscillatory neuromorphic memories, and self-developing autonomous robots.

On the Deep Learning Revolution in Computer Vision

Nathan Netanyahu

Bar-Ilan University, Israel

Abstract. Computer Vision (CV) is an interdisciplinary field of Artificial Intelligence (AI), which is concerned with the embedding of human visual capabilities in a computerized system. The main thrust, essentially, of CV is to generate an "intelligent" high-level description of the world for a given scene, such that when interfaced with other thought processes can elicit, ultimately, appropriate action. In this talk we will review several central CV tasks and traditional approaches taken for handling these tasks for over 50 years. Noting the limited performance of standard methods applied, we briefly survey the evolution of artificial neural networks (ANN) during this extended period, and focus, specifically, on the ongoing revolutionary performance of deep learning (DL) techniques for the above CV tasks during the past few years. In particular, we provide also an overview of our DL activities, in the context of CV, at Bar-Ilan University. Finally, we discuss future research and development challenges in CV in light of further employment of prospective DL innovations.

From Machine Learning to Machine Diagnostics

Marios Polycarpou

University of Cyprus

Abstract. During the last few years, there have has been remarkable progress in utilizing machine learning methods in several applications that benefit from deriving useful patterns among large volumes of data. These advances have attracted significant attention from industry due to the prospective of reducing the cost of predicting future events and making intelligent decisions based on data from past experiences. In this context, a key area that can benefit greatly from the use of machine learning is the task of detecting and diagnosing abnormal behaviour in dynamical systems, especially in safety-critical, large-scale applications. The goal of this presentation is to provide insight into the problem of detecting, isolating and self-correcting abnormal or faulty behaviour in large-scale dynamical systems, to present some design methodologies based on machine learning and to show some illustrative examples. The ultimate goal is to develop the foundation of the concept of machine diagnostics, which would empower smart software algorithms to continuously monitor the health of dynamical systems during the lifetime of their operation.

Multimodal Deep Learning in Biomedical Image Analysis

Sotirios Tsaftaris

University of Edinburgh, UK

Abstract. Nowadays images are typically accompanied by additional information. At the same time, for example, magnetic resonance imaging exams typically contain more than one image modality: they show the same anatomy under different acquisition strategies revealing various pathophysiological information. The detection of disease, segmentation of anatomy and other classical analysis tasks, can benefit from a multimodal view to analysis that leverages shared information across the sources yet preserves unique information. It is without surprise that radiologists analyze data in this fashion, reviewing the exam as a whole. Yet, when aiming to automate analysis tasks, we still treat different image modalities in isolation and tend to ignore additional information. In this talk, I will present recent work in learning with deep neural networks, latent embeddings suitable for multimodal processing, and highlight opportunities and challenges in this area.

Contents – Part III

Deep Learning

Brain Neurocomputing Modeling

Robotics/Motion Detection

Social Media

Social Media

Recurrent ANN

Policy Learning Using SPSA

R. Ramamurthy[1,2(✉)], C. Bauckhage[1,2], R. Sifa[1,2], and S. Wrobel[1,2]

[1] Department of Computer Science, University of Bonn, Bonn, Germany
ramamurt@iai.uni-bonn.de

[2] Fraunhofer Center for Machine Learning, Sankt Augustin, Germany

Abstract. We analyze the use of simultaneous perturbation stochastic approximation (SPSA), a stochastic optimization technique, for solving reinforcement learning problems. In particular, we consider settings of partial observability and leverage the short-term memory capabilities of echo state networks (ESNs) to learn parameterized control policies. Using SPSA, we propose three different variants to adapt the weight matrices of an ESN to the task at hand. Experimental results on classic control problems with both discrete and continuous action spaces reveal that ESNs trained using SPSA approaches outperform conventional ESNs trained using temporal difference and policy gradient methods.

Keywords: Echo state networks · Recurrent neural networks
Reinforcement learning · Stochastic optimization

1 Introduction

Creating systems that learn to solve complex tasks from interactions with their environment is one of the primary goals of artificial intelligence research. Recently, much progress has been made in this regard, mainly achieved through modern reinforcement learning (RL) techniques [1,21]. Examples of recent successes include systems which exceed human level performance in playing console-based Atari games [12] or can navigate 3D virtual environments [11], and AlphaGo Zero [17] became the first program to beat world class GO players by learning from self-play only. Function approximators such as deep neural networks, when used with off-policy and bootstrapping methods such as Q-learning, which used to be unstable and were referred to as a "deadly-triad" [20], have now been proven to be a competent approach using techniques such as experience replay [8] which stabilize learning with the help of a large replay memory.

Spurred by these successes, another line of recent research has considered alternative approaches to RL using black-box optimization methods which do not require back propagation of gradient computations. Corresponding contributions include systems [10,14] that are trained using so called evolution strategies which achieve competitive performance in playing Atari games. Similar performance was obtained in [19] where genetic algorithms were found to scale better than evolution strategies. This revived interest in black-box methods for solving

V. Kůrková et al. (Eds.): ICANN 2018, LNCS 11141, pp. 3–12, 2018.
https://doi.org/10.1007/978-3-030-01424-7_1

RL problems as these can be parallelized when using modern distributed architectures. However, most real-world systems must deal with limited and noisy state information resulting in partial observability as encountered in partially observable Markov decision processes (POMDPs). To learn policies under such circumstances, systems need to have internal memory. Therefore, recurrent RL methods to cope with partial observability have recently been investigated but were found to be difficult to train [4].

In this paper, we focus on these kind of problems and consider RL in partially observable environments. Since echo state networks [5] are known for their simple architecture and short-term memorization capabilities, we choose them in order to train parameterized control policies. In particular, we propose to use simultaneous perturbation stochastic optimization (SPSA), a gradient approximation technique, as a training algorithm, which at each iteration requires only two evaluations of objective function regardless of dimension of the parameter. Using SPSA, we devise three types of ESN training that differ in how the weight matrices are chosen in each iteration. Finally, we use such ESNs to learn policies and test them against baselines on classic control problems.

Previous work on black-box methods for training echo state networks seeks to combine genetic algorithms to train internal weights of the reservoir and stochastic gradient descent to train the output weights [3,15]. Similar work was done in [6] where output weights and spectral radii of internal weight matrices were evolved. Alternatively, more recent work [16] concerning different learning strategy focused on using hebbian learning rules to adapt reservoir matrices. An interesting hybrid of using hebbian learning and temporal difference learning was later proposed in [7] to adapt actor-critic ESNs. In contrast to these previous approaches, we use SPSA to optimize the entire network weights which has several noteworthy properties: (i) it requires only two loss measurements at each iteration, (ii) it does not require back propagation of gradients, (iii) it does not require any maintenance of candidate solutions as in genetic algorithms, and (iv) it can handle stochastic returns and hence does not require averaging over multiple measurements to account for the noisy returns.

2 Simultaneous Perturbation Stochastic Approximation

In this short section, we briefly recall the main ideas behind simultaneous perturbation stochastic approximation (SPSA) for derivative free optimization; readers familiar with this technique may safely skip ahead.

Consider the general problem of maximizing a differentiable objective function $f(\boldsymbol{\theta}) : \mathbb{R}^d \rightarrow \mathbb{R}$, that is, consider the problem of finding $\boldsymbol{\theta}^* = \operatorname{argmax}_{\boldsymbol{\theta}} f(\boldsymbol{\theta})$.

For many complex systems, the gradient $\partial f / \partial \boldsymbol{\theta}$ cannot be computed directly so that $\partial f / \partial \boldsymbol{\theta} = \mathbf{0}$ can often not be solved. It is, however, typically possible to evaluate $f(\boldsymbol{\theta})$ at various values of $\boldsymbol{\theta}$ which, in turn, allows, for computing stochastic approximations of the gradient. One method in this regard is SPSA due to Spall [18] which iteratively updates estimates of the optimal $\boldsymbol{\theta}$ as

$$\boldsymbol{\theta}_{k+1} = \boldsymbol{\theta}_k + l_k \hat{\boldsymbol{g}}_k(\boldsymbol{\theta}_k) \tag{1}$$

where $\hat{\boldsymbol{g}}_k(\boldsymbol{\theta}_k)$ is an estimator of the gradient at $\boldsymbol{\theta}_k$ and l_k is the learning rate in iteration k. To estimate the gradient, two perturbations are generated, namely $(\boldsymbol{\theta}_k + c_k\,\boldsymbol{\delta}_k)$ and $(\boldsymbol{\theta}_k - c_k\,\boldsymbol{\delta}_k)$ where $\boldsymbol{\delta}_k$ is a perturbation vector and c_k is a scaling parameter. Then, the possibly noisy objective function $F(\cdot) = f(\cdot) + noise$ is measured at $F(\boldsymbol{\theta}_k + c_k\,\boldsymbol{\delta}_k)$ and $F(\boldsymbol{\theta}_k - c_k\,\boldsymbol{\delta}_k)$ and the gradient is estimated using a two-sided gradient approximation

$$\hat{\boldsymbol{g}}_k(\boldsymbol{\theta}_k) = \frac{F(\boldsymbol{\theta}_k + c_k\,\boldsymbol{\delta}_k) - F(\boldsymbol{\theta}_k - c_k\,\boldsymbol{\delta}_k)}{2\,c_k\,\boldsymbol{\delta}_k}. \tag{2}$$

The convergence of the SPSA algorithm critically depends on the choice of its parameters l_k, c_k and $\boldsymbol{\delta}_k$. In particular, the learning rate l_k must meet the Robbins-Monro conditions [13], namely $l_k > 0$ and $\sum_{k=1}^{\infty} l_k = \infty$, and a common choice in practice therefore is $l_k = \frac{l}{(L+k)^{\alpha}}$ where $l, \alpha, L > 0$. Similarly, the scaling factor c_k must satisfy $\sum_{k=1}^{\infty} \left(\frac{l_k}{c_k}\right)^2 < \infty$ so that a good choice amounts to $c_k = \frac{c}{k^{\gamma}}$ where $c, \gamma > 0$. And, essentially, each element of the perturbation vector $\boldsymbol{\delta}_k$ is sampled from a uniform distribution over the set $\{-1, +1\}$.

3 Learning Policies Using Echo State Networks

In this section, we first briefly review policy learning under partial observability as well as echo state networks and then introduce our approach towards policy learning using echo state networks trained via SPSA.

3.1 Partial Observability

Consider an agent interacting with an environment. At any time t, the agent observes the state $\boldsymbol{s}_t$ of the environment and performs an action a_t by following a policy $\pi(a_t|\boldsymbol{s}_t)$ which is a mapping of state $\boldsymbol{s}_t$ to the probability of choosing action a at time t. In return, the environment responds with a reward r_t and finds itself in a new state $\boldsymbol{s}_{t+1}$.

However, in environments that are only partially observable, the agent does not receive all relevant state information because of limited sensory inputs. In this case, the state $\boldsymbol{s}_t$ does not satisfy the Markov property because it does not summarize what has happened in the past so that an informed decision cannot be taken. For such non-Markovian states, it is necessary to make the policy dependent on a history of states $h_t = \{\boldsymbol{s}_t, \boldsymbol{s}_{t-1}, \ldots\}$ rather than on the current state $\boldsymbol{s}_t$ only. Hence, the policy becomes $\pi(a_t|h_t)$.

This, however, becomes impractical to compute whenever different tasks require arbitrary lengths of histories. In situations like these, an echo state network can be used to integrate the required history in its reservoir states. In this way, we are able to parameterize the policy with weights of an echo state network $\boldsymbol{\theta}$ as $\pi(a_t|\boldsymbol{s}_t, \boldsymbol{\theta})$ which takes the current state $\boldsymbol{s}_t$ as the input and returns probabilities of actions by compacting the history of input states in the reservoir memory.

3.2 Echo State Networks

We next briefly recall the notion of echo state networks. These belong to reservoir computing paradigm in which a large reservoir of recurrently interconnected neurons processes sequential input data. In our setup, given that the state of the environment $\boldsymbol{s}_t \in \mathbb{R}^{n_s}$ is given as the input to the network, the hidden states and output of our policy network are given by $\boldsymbol{h}_t \in \mathbb{R}^{n_h}$ and $\boldsymbol{\pi}_t \in \mathbb{R}^{n_a}$, respectively. The temporal evolution of such a network is governed by the following, non-linear dynamical system

$$\boldsymbol{h}_t = (1-\beta)\,\boldsymbol{h}_{t-1} + \beta\, f_h\big(\boldsymbol{W}^h \boldsymbol{h}_{t-1} + \boldsymbol{W}^s \boldsymbol{s}_t\big) \tag{3}$$

$$\boldsymbol{\pi}_t = f_\pi\big(\boldsymbol{W}^a \boldsymbol{h}_t\big) \tag{4}$$

where $\beta \in [0,1]$ is called the leaking rate and $\boldsymbol{W}^s$, $\boldsymbol{W}^h$, and $\boldsymbol{W}^a$ are the input, reservoir, and output weight matrices, respectively. The function $f_h(\cdot)$ is understood to act component-wise on its argument and is typically a sigmoidal activation function. For the output layer, however, $f_\pi(\cdot)$ is usually just a linear or softmax function depending on the application context.

3.3 Policy Learning Using Echo State Networks

At any time, the goal of the agent is to maximize the expected cumulative reward or the return received over a period of time which is defined as $R_T = \sum_{t=1}^{T} r_t$.

Hence, the objective function that is to be maximized is $f(\boldsymbol{\theta}) = \mathbb{E}_{\pi_\theta}\big[R_T\big]$ and finding an optimal policy amounts to finding $\boldsymbol{\theta}^* = \operatorname{argmax}_{\boldsymbol{\theta}} f(\boldsymbol{\theta})$ where we now write $\boldsymbol{\theta}$ to denote the set of weights of an echo state network used to approximate the policy $\pi(a_t|\boldsymbol{s}_t, \boldsymbol{\theta})$.

According to our discussion in Sect. 2, we can then iteratively learn an optimal $\boldsymbol{\theta}$ according to a stochastic gradient ascent rule that follows the gradient $\nabla_\theta \mathbb{E}_{\pi_\theta}\big[R_T\big]$. In particular, we can resort to SPSA in order to approximate this gradient as

$$\nabla_\theta \mathbb{E}_{\pi_\theta}\big[R_T\big] \approx \frac{F(\boldsymbol{\theta}+\epsilon) - F(\boldsymbol{\theta}-\epsilon)}{2\epsilon} \tag{5}$$

where $F(\cdot)$ is the stochastic return from the environment by running an episode where, in each step, the agent follows the policy $\pi(a_t|\boldsymbol{s}_t, \boldsymbol{\theta})$ approximated by the ESN and where $\boldsymbol{\epsilon}$ is the perturbation generated by SPSA. A summary of this learning method can be found in Algorithm 1.

3.4 Deterministic and Stochastic Policies

An agent's policy can either be deterministic or stochastic. In a discrete action space, the agent may apply a deterministic, greedy, "winner-takes-all" strategy to select an action, i.e. $a_t = \operatorname{argmax}_a \pi(a|\boldsymbol{s}_t, \boldsymbol{\theta})$. However, in order to encourage exploration, the agent can follow a stochastic softmax policy in which actions are sampled based on action probabilities according to the policy $\pi(a_t|\boldsymbol{s}_t, \boldsymbol{\theta})$, i.e. $a_t \sim f_\pi$ where f_π is the softmax function. In a continuous action space, the agent's actions are sampled from a Gaussian policy parameterized by mean and variance neurons, that is f_π is considered a Gaussian probability distribution.

Simple Recurrent Neural Networks for Support Vector Machine Training

Rafet Sifa[1,2,3(✉)], Daniel Paurat[1,2], Daniel Trabold[1,2], and Christian Bauckhage[1,2,3]

[1] Fraunhofer Center for Machine Learning, Sankt Augustin, Germany
[2] Fraunhofer IAIS, Sankt Augustin, Germany
{rafet.sifa,daniel.paurat,daniel.trabold, christian.bauckhage}@iais.fraunhofer.de
[3] B-IT, University of Bonn, Bonn, Germany

Abstract. We show how to implement a simple procedure for support vector machine training as a recurrent neural network. Invoking the fact that support vector machines can be trained using Frank-Wolfe optimization which in turn can be seen as a form of reservoir computing, we obtain a model that is of simpler structure and can be implemented more easily than those proposed in previous contributions.

1 Introduction

Support vector machines can be seen as neural networks with a single hidden layer (see Fig. 1). Since this insight is not new but dates back to work by Cortes and Vapnik [6], it seems odd that the literature on neurocomputing approaches towards SVM training is rather scarce [1,7,11,13,16–18]. Moreover, while these contributions show that SVMs can be trained using recurrent neural networks, they are mainly concerned with continuous dynamical systems and, curiously, how to implement those in electronic circuits.

In this paper, we propose to train support vector machines by means of much simpler, time-discrete recurrent neural networks. We base our arguments on recent work in [2] where it was shown that recurrent neural networks can implement the Frank-Wolfe algorithm [8] for constrained convex optimization. That is, we show how the Frank-Wolfe algorithm allows for SVM training and how this approach can be interpreted in terms of neural reservoir computation. For mathematical convenience, we focus on L_2 support vector machines [12]; not because our approach would not work for classical SVMs, but because the equations for the dual problem of L_2 SVM training are particularly easy to work with.

We begin our presentation with a brief review of L_2 support vector machines for binary classification; in particular, we point out differences between L_2- and classical L_1 SVMs and clarify to what extent SVMs can be understood as neural networks. We then show how the Frank-Wolfe algorithm can train SVMs

V. Kůrková et al. (Eds.): ICANN 2018, LNCS 11141, pp. 13–22, 2018.
https://doi.org/10.1007/978-3-030-01424-7_2

and how this process can be implemented by means of recurrent neural networks. We present and discuss didactic practical examples to illustrate this idea and conclude with a discussion of implications and suggestions for practical implementations.

2 L_2 Support Vector Machines

Next, we briefly review the idea of L_2 support vector machines for binary classification. The likely unfamiliar matrix-vector notation we introduce in passing is intended to simplify our subsequent discussion.

Consider a set of labeled training data $\{(\boldsymbol{x}_i, y_i)\}_{i=1}^n$ where the data $\boldsymbol{x}_i \in \mathbb{R}^m$ have been sampled from two distinct classes and the labels $y_i \in \{-1, +1\}$ indicate class membership. Training a linear L_2 support vector classifier

$$y(\boldsymbol{x}) = \operatorname{sign}\big(\boldsymbol{x}^\intercal \boldsymbol{w} - \theta\big) \tag{1}$$

is to determine suitable parameters $\boldsymbol{w}$ and θ. In its *primal* form, this problem consists in solving

$$\begin{aligned} \underset{\boldsymbol{w},\theta,\boldsymbol{\xi}}{\operatorname{argmin}} \;& \boldsymbol{w}^\intercal \boldsymbol{w} + \theta^2 - \rho + C \sum_{i=1}^{n} \xi_i^2 \\ \text{s.t.} \;& y_i\big(\boldsymbol{w}^\intercal \boldsymbol{x}_i - \theta\big) \geq \rho - \xi_i \end{aligned} \tag{2}$$

and we note that, contrary to classical L_1 SVMs [6], the slack variables ξ_i enter the objective in squared form. While this may improve generalization [12,15] our interest in L_2 SVMs mainly stems from the fact that their Lagrangian duals are easy to work with.

Introducing a data matrix $\boldsymbol{X} = [\boldsymbol{x}_1, \ldots, \boldsymbol{x}_n]$, a label vector $\boldsymbol{y} = [y_1, \ldots, y_n]^\intercal$, and three $n \times n$ matrices

$$\boldsymbol{Y} = \operatorname{diag}(\boldsymbol{y}) \tag{3}$$

$$\boldsymbol{Z} = \boldsymbol{Y}^\intercal \boldsymbol{X}^\intercal \boldsymbol{X} \boldsymbol{Y} \qquad \Leftrightarrow \; Z_{ij} = y_i\, \boldsymbol{x}_i^\intercal \boldsymbol{x}_j\, y_j, \tag{4}$$

$$\boldsymbol{M} = \boldsymbol{Z} + \boldsymbol{y}\boldsymbol{y}^\intercal + \tfrac{1}{C}\boldsymbol{I} \tag{5}$$

it is straightforward to see [3] that—when written as a minimization problem—the *dual* problem to the one in (2) consists in solving

$$\begin{aligned} \underset{\boldsymbol{\alpha}}{\operatorname{argmin}} \;& \boldsymbol{\alpha}^\intercal \boldsymbol{M} \boldsymbol{\alpha} \\ \text{s.t.} \;& \mathbf{1}^\intercal \boldsymbol{\alpha} = 1 \\ & \boldsymbol{\alpha} \geq \mathbf{0} \end{aligned} \tag{6}$$

where $\boldsymbol{\alpha} = [\alpha_1, \ldots, \alpha_n]^\intercal$ is a vector of Lagrange multipliers. Once (6) has been solved, those elements α_s of $\boldsymbol{\alpha}$ that exceed zero identify the support vectors in $\boldsymbol{X}$ and thus allow for computing both parameters of the support vector machine

$$\boldsymbol{w} = \sum_{\alpha_s > 0} \alpha_s\, y_s\, \boldsymbol{x}_s = \boldsymbol{X}\boldsymbol{Y}\boldsymbol{\alpha} \tag{7}$$

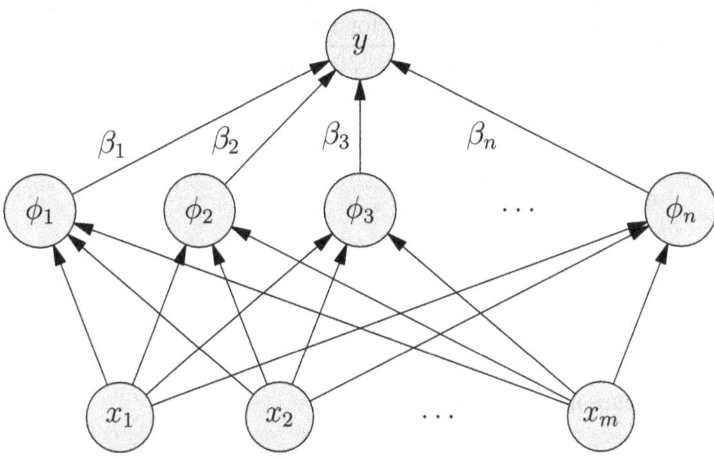

Fig. 1. Support vector machines are specific basis function networks. For an input vector $\boldsymbol{x} \in \mathbb{R}^m$, they compute $y(\boldsymbol{x}) = \operatorname{sign}\bigl(\sum_{i=1}^n \beta_i \, \phi_i(\boldsymbol{x})\bigr)$ using basis functions $\phi_i(\boldsymbol{x}) = k(\boldsymbol{x}, \boldsymbol{x}_i)+1$ where $k(\boldsymbol{x}, \boldsymbol{x}_i)$ is a linear or non-linear kernel function. In either case, the $\boldsymbol{x}_i$ denote training data and the weight vector $\boldsymbol{\beta} = \boldsymbol{Y}\boldsymbol{\alpha}$ results from training the machine on this data.

$$\theta = -\sum_{\alpha_s > 0} \alpha_s \, y_s = -\mathbf{1}^\intercal \boldsymbol{Y}\boldsymbol{\alpha}. \tag{8}$$

Plugging these training results into (1) provides a classifier which, written in the matrix-vector notation introduced above, reads

$$y(\boldsymbol{x}) = \operatorname{sign}\bigl(\boldsymbol{x}^\intercal \boldsymbol{X}\boldsymbol{Y}\boldsymbol{\alpha} + \mathbf{1}^\intercal \boldsymbol{Y}\boldsymbol{\alpha}\bigr) = \operatorname{sign}\Bigl(\bigl(\boldsymbol{x}^\intercal \boldsymbol{X} + \mathbf{1}^\intercal\bigr)\boldsymbol{Y}\boldsymbol{\alpha}\Bigr). \tag{9}$$

Introducing the shorthand $\boldsymbol{\beta} = \boldsymbol{Y}\boldsymbol{\alpha}$, we can think of this classifier as a basis function network [4]. In other words, writing (9) as

$$y(\boldsymbol{x}) = \operatorname{sign}\left(\sum_{i=1}^{n} \beta_i \, \phi_i(\boldsymbol{x})\right) \tag{10}$$

we recognize it as an instance of the neural architecture in Fig. 1 where the basis functions in the hidden layer in our case are given by $\phi_i(\boldsymbol{x}) = \boldsymbol{x}^\intercal \boldsymbol{x}_i + 1$.

We further observe that, during training and application of this machine, i.e. in the expressions $\boldsymbol{Z} = \boldsymbol{Y}^\intercal \boldsymbol{X}^\intercal \boldsymbol{X}\boldsymbol{Y}$ and $\boldsymbol{x}^\intercal \boldsymbol{w} = \boldsymbol{x}^\intercal \boldsymbol{X}\boldsymbol{Y}\boldsymbol{\alpha}$, all (training) data vectors occur in form of inner products. This of course allows for invoking the kernel trick where inner products are replaced by kernel evaluations so that the approach becomes applicable to non-linear settings.

In other words, given an appropriate Mercer kernel $k : \mathbb{R}^m \times \mathbb{R}^m \to \mathbb{R}$, a non-linear L_2 support vector classifier can be trained by letting $\boldsymbol{Z} = \boldsymbol{Y}^\intercal \boldsymbol{K}\boldsymbol{Y}$

Algorithm 1. Frank-Wolfe algorithm for iteratively solving (6)

guess an initial, feasible point $\boldsymbol{\alpha}_0 \in \Delta^{n-1}$, for instance, $\boldsymbol{\alpha}_0 = \frac{1}{n}\mathbf{1}$
for $t = 0, \ldots, t_{\max}$ **do**
determine

$$\begin{aligned} \boldsymbol{s}_t &= \underset{\boldsymbol{s} \in \Delta^{n-1}}{\operatorname{argmin}}\ \boldsymbol{s}^\intercal \nabla f(\boldsymbol{\alpha}_t) \\ &= \underset{\boldsymbol{s} \in \Delta^{n-1}}{\operatorname{argmin}}\ \boldsymbol{s}^\intercal \boldsymbol{M} \boldsymbol{\alpha}_t \end{aligned}$$

update the learning rate

$$\eta_t = \tfrac{2}{t+2}$$

update the current estimate

$$\boldsymbol{\alpha}_{t+1} = \boldsymbol{\alpha}_t + \eta_t \left(\boldsymbol{s}_t - \boldsymbol{\alpha}_t\right)$$

---

where $K_{ij} = k(\boldsymbol{x}_i, \boldsymbol{x}_j)$ and the trained classifier becomes

$$y(\boldsymbol{x}) = \operatorname{sign}\left(\sum_{\alpha_s > 0} k(\boldsymbol{x}, \boldsymbol{x}_s)\, y_s\, \alpha_s - \theta\right) = \operatorname{sign}\left(\boldsymbol{k}^\intercal(\boldsymbol{x}) \boldsymbol{Y} \boldsymbol{\alpha} + \mathbf{1}^\intercal \boldsymbol{Y} \boldsymbol{\alpha}\right) \tag{11}$$

$$= \operatorname{sign}\left(\left(\boldsymbol{k}^\intercal(\boldsymbol{x}) + \mathbf{1}^\intercal\right) \boldsymbol{Y} \boldsymbol{\alpha}\right) \tag{12}$$

where $k_i(\boldsymbol{x}) = k(\boldsymbol{x}, \boldsymbol{x}_i)$. Using $\boldsymbol{\beta} = \boldsymbol{Y}\boldsymbol{\alpha}$ and $\phi_i(\boldsymbol{x}) = k(\boldsymbol{x}, \boldsymbol{x}_i) + 1$, this classifier, too, can be expressed as in (10) and therefore is nothing but another instance of the neural network shown in Fig. 1.

Finally, we note that a linear SVM is a kernel SVM where $\boldsymbol{K} = \boldsymbol{X}^\intercal \boldsymbol{X}$ and $\boldsymbol{k}(\boldsymbol{x}) = \boldsymbol{X}^\intercal \boldsymbol{x}$. Henceforth, we will thus drop this distinction and only discuss the kernel case.

3 Frank-Wolfe Training of Support Vector Machines

One of the favorable properties of L_2 support vector machines is that the dual training problem in (6) is of comparatively simple nature.

Just as in the case of L_1 SVMs, the minimization objective $f(\boldsymbol{\alpha}) = \boldsymbol{\alpha}^\intercal \boldsymbol{M}\, \boldsymbol{\alpha}$ is a quadratic form. However, in contrast to L_1 SVMs, the two constraints $\mathbf{1}^\intercal \boldsymbol{\alpha} = 1$ and $\boldsymbol{\alpha} \geq \mathbf{0}$ constitute a simplicial - rather than a box constraint. That is, the feasible set of the L_2 SVM training problem in (6) is the standard simplex

$$\Delta^{n-1} = \left\{\boldsymbol{\alpha} \in \mathbb{R}^n \;\middle|\; \mathbf{1}^\intercal \boldsymbol{\alpha} = 1 \wedge \boldsymbol{\alpha} \geq \mathbf{0}\right\}. \tag{13}$$

In other words, we are dealing with a quadratic minimization problem over an arguably simple compact convex set.

The Frank-Wolfe algorithm shown in Algorithm 1 is an efficient iterative solver for this kind of problems. Given an initial feasible guess $\boldsymbol{\alpha}_{t=0} = \frac{1}{n}\mathbf{1}$

for the solution, the basic idea in our setting is to determine the $\boldsymbol{s}_t \in \Delta^{n-1}$ that minimizes $\boldsymbol{s}^\intercal \nabla f(\boldsymbol{\alpha}_t)$ and to apply conditional gradient updates $\boldsymbol{\alpha}_{t+1} = \boldsymbol{\alpha}_t + \eta_t \, (\boldsymbol{s}_t - \boldsymbol{\alpha}_t)$ where the learning rate $\eta_t \in [0,1]$ decreases over time. This guarantees that updates will not leave the feasible set and the efficiency of the algorithm stems from the fact that it turns a quadratic optimization problem into a series of simple linear optimization problems. Moreover, one can show that after t iterations the current estimate $\boldsymbol{\alpha}_t$ is $O(1/t)$ from the optimal solution [5] which provides a convenient criterion for choosing the number $t_{\max}$ of iterations to be performed. For further details on the Frank-Wolfe algorithm, its properties and applications, we refer to [10] and [14].

4 Neural Training of Support Vector Machines

For the gradient of the objective function in (6), we simply have $\nabla f(\boldsymbol{\alpha}) = 2\,\boldsymbol{M}\boldsymbol{\alpha}$ so that each iteration of the Frank-Wolfe algorithm has to compute

$$\boldsymbol{s}_t = \underset{\boldsymbol{s} \in \Delta^{n-1}}{\operatorname{argmin}} \; \boldsymbol{s}^\intercal \boldsymbol{M} \, \boldsymbol{\alpha}_t \tag{14}$$

where we dropped the factor 2 as it exerts no influence on the outcome of argmin.

Clearly, the expression on the right of (14) is linear in $\boldsymbol{s}$ and needs to be minimized over a compact convex set. Since the minima of a linear function over a compact convex sets are necessarily attained at a vertex of that set, $\boldsymbol{s}_t$ on the left of (14) must coincide with a vertex of Δ^{n-1}. Hence, as the vertices of the standard simplex in $\mathbb{R}^n$ correspond to the standard basis vectors $\boldsymbol{e}_j \in \mathbb{R}^n$, we can rewrite (14) as

$$\begin{aligned} \boldsymbol{s}_t &= \underset{\boldsymbol{e}_j}{\operatorname{argmin}} \, \boldsymbol{e}_j^\intercal \boldsymbol{M} \, \boldsymbol{\alpha}_t && (15) \\ &\approx \boldsymbol{\sigma}\big(\boldsymbol{M} \, \boldsymbol{\alpha}_t\big). && (16) \end{aligned}$$

Here, the non-linear, vector-valued function $\boldsymbol{\sigma}(\boldsymbol{z})$ introduced in (16) denotes the softmin operator whose components are given by

$$\boldsymbol{\sigma}(\boldsymbol{z})_i = \frac{e^{-\beta z_i}}{\sum_j e^{-\beta z_j}} \tag{17}$$

and we note that

$$\lim_{\beta \to \infty} \boldsymbol{\sigma}(\boldsymbol{z}) = \boldsymbol{e}_i = \underset{\boldsymbol{e}_j}{\operatorname{argmin}} \, \boldsymbol{e}_j^\intercal \boldsymbol{z}. \tag{18}$$

Given the relaxed optimization step in (16), we can rewrite the Frank-Wolfe updates for our problem as

$$\begin{aligned} \boldsymbol{\alpha}_{t+1} &= \boldsymbol{\alpha}_t + \eta_t \, \big(\boldsymbol{s}_t - \boldsymbol{\alpha}_t\big) && (19) \\ &= (1 - \eta_t) \, \boldsymbol{\alpha}_t + \eta_t \, \boldsymbol{s}_t && (20) \\ &\approx (1 - \eta_t) \, \boldsymbol{\alpha}_t + \eta_t \, \boldsymbol{\sigma}\big(\boldsymbol{M} \, \boldsymbol{\alpha}_t\big). && (21) \end{aligned}$$

But this is then to say that—by choosing an appropriate parameter β for the softmin function—the following non-linear dynamical system

$$\boldsymbol{\alpha}_{t+1} = (1 - \eta_t)\,\boldsymbol{\alpha}_t + \eta_t\,\boldsymbol{\sigma}\Big(\big(\boldsymbol{Y}^\intercal \boldsymbol{K} \boldsymbol{Y} + \boldsymbol{y}\boldsymbol{y}^\intercal + \tfrac{1}{C}\boldsymbol{I}\big)\,\boldsymbol{\alpha}_t\Big) \tag{22}$$

$$\boldsymbol{\beta}_t = \boldsymbol{Y}\boldsymbol{\alpha}_t \tag{23}$$

mimics the Frank-Wolfe algorithm up to arbitrary precision and can therefore accomplish support vector machine training.

The equivalence of the Frank-Wolfe algorithm for SVM training and the non-linear dynamical system in (22), (23) is the main result of this paper. From the point of view of neural network research, the system in (22), (23) is of interest because it is structurally equivalent to the governing equations of the simple recurrent architectures considered in the area of reservoir computing [9]. In other words, we can think of this system in terms of a reservoir of n neurons whose synaptic connections are encoded in the matrix $\boldsymbol{Y}^\intercal \boldsymbol{K} \boldsymbol{Y} + \boldsymbol{y}\boldsymbol{y}^\intercal + \frac{1}{C}\boldsymbol{I}$. The system evolves without inputs, its output weights are given by $\boldsymbol{Y}$, and the learning rate η_t assumes the role of the leaking rate of the reservoir. At each time t, the next internal state $\boldsymbol{\alpha}_{t+1}$ of the network is a convex combination of the current state and a nonlinear transformation of the synaptically weighted current state. Since η_t decays towards zero, states will stabilize and the output is guaranteed to approach a fixed point $\boldsymbol{\alpha}^* = \lim_{t\to\infty} \boldsymbol{\alpha}_t$.

What is further worth noting about the system in (22), (23) is that the weight matrices $\boldsymbol{Y}^\intercal \boldsymbol{K} \boldsymbol{Y} + \boldsymbol{y}\boldsymbol{y}^\intercal + \frac{1}{C}\boldsymbol{I}$, and $\boldsymbol{Y}$ depend on the training data for the problem under consideration. From the point of view of a learning system, they could thus be interpreted as a form of short term memory. At the beginning of a learning episode, data is loaded into this memory and used to determine crucial properties (support vectors) of the problem at hand. At the end of a learning episode, only those data points and labels required for decision making, i.e. those $\boldsymbol{x}_s$ and y_s for which $\alpha_s > 0$, need to be persisted in a long term memory to be able to compute the decision function in (11). In order for this memorization to be efficient it would thus be desirable if $\boldsymbol{\alpha}$ was sparse because then only a few basis functions ϕ_i and weights β_i could solve the problem satisfactory.

5 Practical Examples

In this section, we consider several examples to investigate the behavior of the system in (22), (23) for training support vector machines. Note that, in order for these examples to be intuitive and interpretable, they are deliberately simple.

Figure 2 shows three training sets of 200 two-dimensional data points each. It also visualizes how a support vector machine with a Gaussian kernel solves the corresponding classification problem after having been trained using the Frank-Wolfe algorithm or, equivalently, the system in (22), (23) if the parameter of the softmin activation function of the reservoir neurons is set to $\beta = \infty$.

Figures 3 and 4 illustrate intermediate steps in learning such decision functions. Here, we considered a polynomial kernel and a Gaussian kernel and also replaced the sign function in the output of the classifier by tanh so as to see more clearly, how class regions and margins evolve over time. What is noticeable is that, in either case, the simple recurrent neural network model discussed in this paper is able to train robust classifiers in only moderately many, i.e 100, iterations.

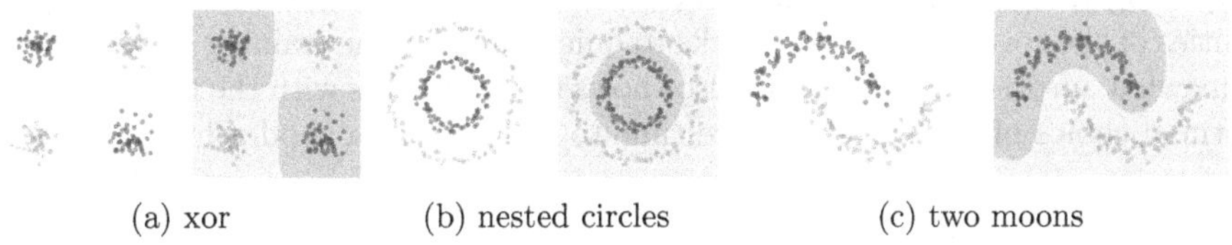

(a) xor (b) nested circles (c) two moons

Fig. 2. Didactic data sets and support vector classifiers using Gaussian kernels.

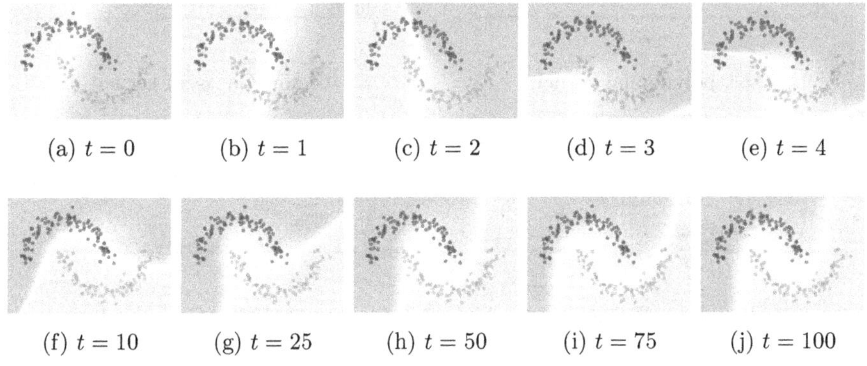

(a) $t = 0$ (b) $t = 1$ (c) $t = 2$ (d) $t = 3$ (e) $t = 4$

(f) $t = 10$ (g) $t = 25$ (h) $t = 50$ (i) $t = 75$ (j) $t = 100$

Fig. 3. Evolution of a support vector classifier over 100 iterations of the system in (22), (23) using a 5th-degree polynomial kernel $k(\boldsymbol{x}, \boldsymbol{x}_i) = \left(\boldsymbol{x}^\intercal \boldsymbol{x}_i + 1\right)^5$.

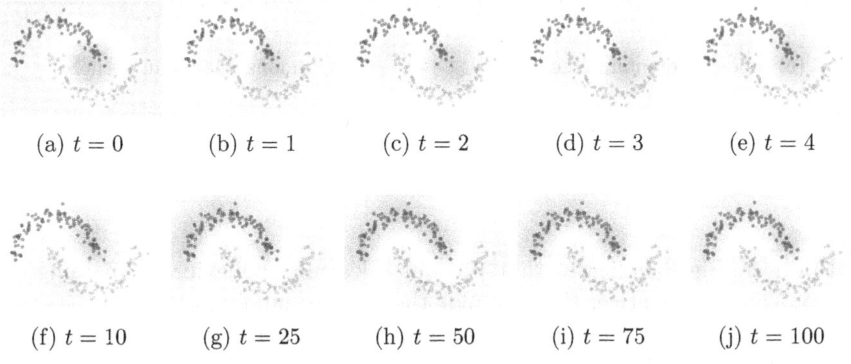

(a) $t = 0$ (b) $t = 1$ (c) $t = 2$ (d) $t = 3$ (e) $t = 4$

(f) $t = 10$ (g) $t = 25$ (h) $t = 50$ (i) $t = 75$ (j) $t = 100$

Fig. 4. Evolution of a support vector classifier over 100 iterations of the system in (22), (23) using a Gaussian kernel $k(\boldsymbol{x}, \boldsymbol{x}_i) = \exp\left(-\frac{1}{2\sigma^2}\|\boldsymbol{x} - \boldsymbol{x}_i\|^2\right)$ where $\sigma = 1/2$.

A natural question to ask is then: how sensitive is neural SVM training to different choices of the parameter β of the reservoir activation function? To investigate this, we randomly created 1000 different training sets for the xor, nested circles, and two moons problems, used the system in (22), (23) to train SVMs with polynomial and Gaussian kernels, and plotted the average training error (measured in terms of 0–1 loss) over 100 training iterations. Somewhat surprisingly, we observe in Fig. 5 that the choice of β does not impact the capabilities of the corresponding networks to quickly reduce the training error. Again somewhat surprisingly, the figure also shows that networks with the theoretically optimal choice of $\beta = \infty$ need more time to converge to a good solution.

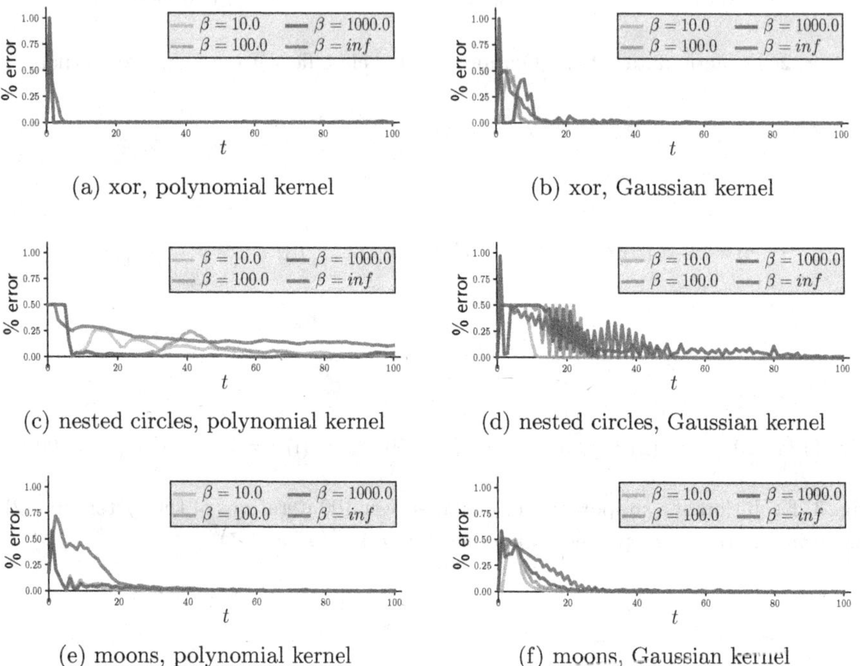

(a) xor, polynomial kernel

(b) xor, Gaussian kernel

(c) nested circles, polynomial kernel

(d) nested circles, Gaussian kernel

(e) moons, polynomial kernel

(f) moons, Gaussian kernel

Fig. 5. Evolution of average training errors over 100 iterations of the system in (22), (23). Regardless of the choice of softmin activation parameter β, training errors decrease quickly.

However, Fig. 6 indicates that the quick learning behavior for parameters $\beta \ll \infty$ comes at a price. Here we plot the average number of support vectors (in percentage of all training data) identified in each iteration of the training process. What is noticeable is that running the recurrent network in (22), (23) using larger values of β yields sparser solutions and letting $\beta = \infty$ yields much sparser solutions and thus more efficient classifiers.

All in all, these experiments illustrate that the simple dynamical system in (22), (23) or, equivalently, rather simple recurrent neural network models known from reservoir computing can train SVMs. This appears to be independent of the choice of kernel function but care needs to be exercised when choosing the activation function of the neuron in the reservoir.

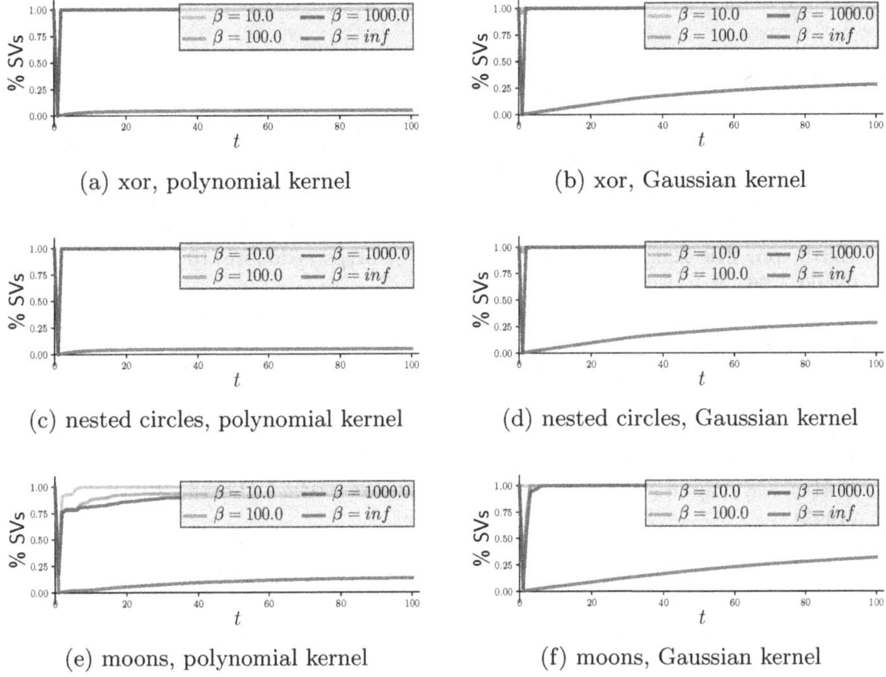

(a) xor, polynomial kernel (b) xor, Gaussian kernel

(c) nested circles, polynomial kernel (d) nested circles, Gaussian kernel

(e) moons, polynomial kernel (f) moons, Gaussian kernel

Fig. 6. Evolution of the average number (percentage of training data) of support vectors identified in 100 iterations of the system in (22), (23).

6 Conclusion

Building on work in [2], we considered Frank-Wolfe optimization for the task of training support vector machines and showed how to interpret this as a form of reservoir computing. In other words, we showed that a recurrent reservoir of neurons governed by simple dynamics can identify support vectors.

Since support vector machines themselves are basis function networks, our results underline that both training and running an SVM are forms of neurcomputing. Moreover, the mechanism discussed in this paper is interpretable in terms of short- and long-term memory processes. At the beginning of a learning episode, data is encoded in the weights of a neural architecture for training; upon convergence of a learning episode, crucial information is persisted in the basis functions and weights of a neural architecture for classification.

With respect to practical application, we note that our experimental results were obtained from direct implementations of the matrix-vector equations and softmin activations discussed throughout the text. However, we mainly used this notation because it seamlessly reveals that to train an SVM is to run a dynamical system. For real world applications, training will be more efficient when using (15) rather than (16). Likewise, implementations of the resulting classifier should use the equation in the middle of (11) rather than Eq. (12).

References

1. Anguita, D., Boni, A.: Improved neural network for SVM learning. IEEE Trans. Neural Netw. **13**(2), 1243–1244 (2002)
2. Bauckhage, C.: A neural network implementation of Frank-Wolfe optimization. In: Lintas, A., Rovetta, S., Verschure, P., Villa, A. (eds.) ICANN 2017. LNCS, vol. 10613, pp. 219–226. Springer, Cham (2017). https://doi.org/10.1007/978-3-319-68600-4_26
3. Bauckhage, C.: The dual problem of L_2 SVM training. Technical report, ResearchGate (2018)
4. Bishop, C.: Neural Networks for Pattern Recognition. Oxford University Press, Oxford (1995)
5. Clarkson, K.: Coresets, sparse greedy approximation, and the Frank-Wolfe algorithm. ACM Trans. Algorithms **6**(4), 63:1–63:30 (2010)
6. Cortes, C., Vapnik, V.: Support vector networks. Mach. Learn. **20**(3), 273–297 (1995)
7. Duch, W.: Support vector neural training. In: Duch, W., Kacprzyk, J., Oja, E., Zadrożny, S. (eds.) ICANN 2005. LNCS, vol. 3697, pp. 67–72. Springer, Heidelberg (2005). https://doi.org/10.1007/11550907_11
8. Frank, M., Wolfe, P.: An algorithm for quadratic programming. Nav. Res. Logist. Q. **3**(1–2), 95–110 (1956)
9. Jäger, H., Haas, H.: Harnessing nonlinearity: predicting chaotic systems and saving energy in wireless communication. Science **304**(5667), 78–80 (2004)
10. Jaggi, M.: Revisiting Frank-Wolfe: projection-free sparse convex optimization. J. Mach. Learn. Res. **28**(1), 427–435 (2013)
11. Jändel, M.: Biologically relevant neural network architectures for support vector machines. Neural Netw. **49**, 39–50 (2014)
12. Koshiba, Y., Abe, S.: Comparison of L1 and L2 support vector machines. In: Proceedings IJCNN (2003)
13. Perfetti, R., Ricci, E.: Analogue neural network for support vector machine learning. IEEE Trans. Neural Netw. **17**(4), 1085–1091 (2006)
14. Sifa, R.: An overview of Frank-Wolfe optimization for stochasticity constrained interpretable matrix and tensor factorization. In: ICANN 2018 (2018)
15. Tang, Y.: Deep Learning using Linear Support Vector Machines. arXiv:1306.0239 [cs.LG] (2013)
16. Vincent, P., Bengio, Y.: A neural support vector network architecture with adaptive kernels. In: Proceedings IJCNN (2000)
17. Xia, Y.: A new neural network for solving linear and quadratic programming problems. IEEE Trans. Neural Netw. **7**(6), 1544–1547 (1996)
18. Yang, Y., He, Q., Hu, X.: A compact neural network for training support vector machines. Neurocomputing **86**, 193–198 (2012)

RNN-SURV: A Deep Recurrent Model for Survival Analysis

Eleonora Giunchiglia[1(✉)], Anton Nemchenko[2], and Mihaela van der Schaar[2,3,4]

[1] DIBRIS, Università di Genova, Genova, Italy
eleonora.giunchiglia@icloud.com
[2] Department of Electrical and Computer Engineering, UCLA, Los Angeles, USA
[3] Department of Engineering Science, University of Oxford, Oxford, UK
[4] Alan Turing Institute, London, UK

Abstract. Current medical practice is driven by clinical guidelines which are designed for the "average" patient. Deep learning is enabling medicine to become personalized to the patient at hand. In this paper we present a new recurrent neural network model for personalized survival analysis called RNN-SURV. Our model is able to exploit censored data to compute both the risk score and the survival function of each patient. At each time step, the network takes as input the features characterizing the patient and the identifier of the time step, creates an embedding, and outputs the value of the survival function in that time step. Finally, the values of the survival function are linearly combined to compute the unique risk score. Thanks to the model structure and the training designed to exploit two loss functions, our model gets better concordance index (C-index) than the state of the art approaches.

1 Introduction

Healthcare is moving from a population-based model, in which the decision making process is targeted to the "average" patient, to an individual-based model, in which each diagnosis is based on the features characterizing the given patient. This process has been boosted by the recent developments in the Deep Learning field, which has been proven to not only get impressive results in its traditional areas, but also to perform very well in medical tasks.

In particular, in the medical field, the study of the *time-to-event*, i.e., the expected duration of time until one or more events happen, such as death or recurrence of a disease, is of vital importance. Nevertheless, it is often made more complicated by the presence of *censored data*, i.e., data in which the information about the time-to-event is incomplete, as it happens, e.g., when a patient drops a clinical trial. Traditionally, these issues are tackled in a field called Survival Analysis, a branch of statistics in which special models have been proposed to predict the time-to-event exploiting censored data, while only a few deep learning approaches have such an ability (e.g., [13,28]). About the latter, it is interesting to note that most of the encountered deep learning approaches are

V. Kůrková et al. (Eds.): ICANN 2018, LNCS 11141, pp. 23–32, 2018.
https://doi.org/10.1007/978-3-030-01424-7_3

based on feedforward neural networks and, at least so far, there does not seem to exist published results deploying recurrent neural networks despite the sequential nature of the problem.

In this paper we present a new recurrent neural network model handling censored data and computing, for each patient, both a survival function and a unique risk score. The survival function is computed by considering a series of binary classifications problems each leading to the estimation of the survival probability in a given interval of time, while the risk score is obtained through the linear combination of the estimates. RNN-SURV three main features are:

1. its ability to model the possible time-variant effects of the covariates,
2. its ability to model the fact that the survival probability estimate at time t is function of each survival probability estimate at $t' : t' < t$, and
3. its ability to compute a highly interpretable risk score.

The first two are given by the recurrent structure, while the last is given by the linear combination of the estimates.

RNN-SURV is tested on three small publicly available datasets and on two large heart transplantation datasets. On these datasets RNN-SURV performs significantly better than the state of the art models, always resulting in a higher C-index than the state of the art models (up to 28.4%). We further show that if we simplify the model we always get worse performances, hence showing the significance of RNN-SURV different features.

This paper is structured as follows. We start with the analysis of the related work (Sect. 2), followed by the background about Survival Analysis (Sect. 3). Then, we present of our model (Sect. 4), followed by the experimental analysis (Sect. 5), and finally the conclusions (Sect. 6).

2 Related Work

The problem of survival analysis has attracted the attention of many machine learning scientists, giving birth to models such as random survival forest [11], dependent logistic regressors [26], multi-task learning model for survival analysis [17], semi-proportional hazard model [27] and support vector regressor for censored data [21], all of which not based on neural networks.

Considering the works that have been done in the field of Survival Analysis using Deep Learning techniques, these can be divided in three main subcategories, that stemmed from just as many seminal papers:

(1) Faraggi and Simon [7] generalized Cox Proportional Hazards model (CPH) [5] allowing non-linear functions instead of the traditional linear combinations of covariates by modeling the relationship between the input covariates and the corresponding risk with a single hidden layer feedforward neural network. This work has been later resumed in [13] and [28]. Contrarily to RNN-SURV, CPH and the models [13] and [28] assume time-invariant effects of the covariates.

(2) Liestbl, Andersen and Andersen [18] subdivided time into K intervals, assumed the hazard to be constant in each interval and proposed a feed-forward neural network with a single hidden layer that for each patient outputs the conditional event probabilities $p_k = P(T \geq t_k | T \geq t_{k-1})$ for $k = 1, ..., K$, T being the time-to-event of the given patient. This work was then expanded in [2], but even in this later work the value of the estimate p_{k-1} for a given patient is not exploited for the computation of the estimate p_k for the same patient. On the contrary, RNN-SURV, thanks to the presence of recurrent layers, is able to capture the intrinsic sequential nature of the problem.

(3) Buckley and James [4] developed a linear regression model that deals with each censored data by computing its most likely value on the basis of the available data. This approach was then generalized using neural networks in various ways (e.g., [6]). Unlike RNN-SURV, in [4] and in the following ones, estimated and known data are treated in the same way during the regression phase.

3 Background on Survival Analysis

Consider a patient i, we are interested in estimating the duration T_i of the interval in between the event of interest for i and the time t_0 at which we start to measure time for i. We allow for *right censored* data, namely, data for which we do not know when the event occurred, but only that it did not occur before a censoring time C_i. The *observed time* Y_i is defined as $Y_i = \min(T_i, C_i)$, and each datapoint corresponds to the pair (Y_i, δ_i) where $\delta_i = 0$ if the event is censored (in which case $Y_i = C_i$) and $\delta_i = 1$ otherwise.

In Survival Analysis, the standard functions used to describe T_i are the survival function and the hazard function [15].

1. The *survival function* $S_i(t)$ is defined as:

$$S_i(t) = Pr(T_i > t) \tag{1}$$

with $S_i(t_0) = 1$.

2. The *hazard function* $h_i(t)$ is defined as:

$$h_i(t) = \lim_{dt \to 0} \frac{Pr(t \leq T_i < t + dt \mid T_i \geq t)}{dt}. \tag{2}$$

Further, in order to offer a fast understanding of the conditions of the patient, a common practice of the field is to create a risk score r_i for each patient i: the higher the score the higher the risk of the occurrence of the event of interest.

4 RNN-SURV

In order to transform the survival analysis problem in a series of binary decision problems, we assume that the maximal observed time is divided into K

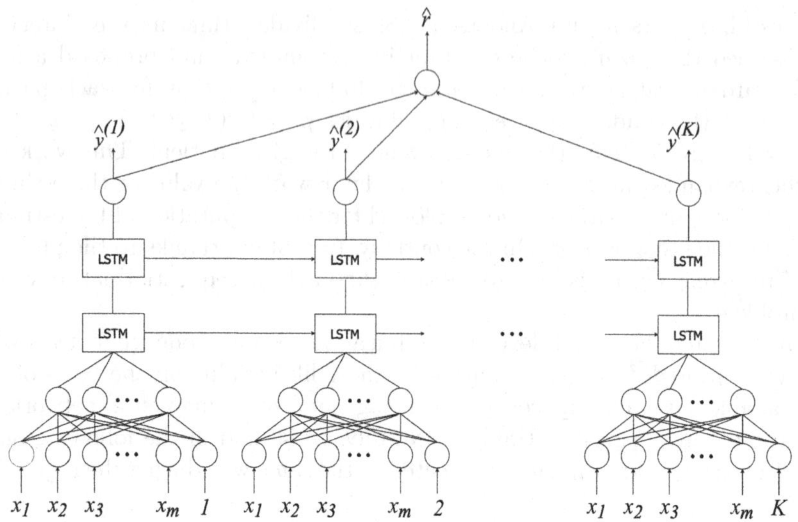

Fig. 1. RNN-SURV with $N_1 = 2$ feedforward layers, followed by $N_2 = 2$ recurrent layers.

intervals $(t_0, t_1], \ldots, (t_{K-1}, t_K]$ and that the characteristic function modeling T_i is constant within each interval $(t_{k-1}, t_k]$ with $k = 1, \ldots, K$. Given a patient i, the purpose of our model is to output both an estimate $\hat{y}_i^{(k)}$ of the survival probability S_i for the kth time interval and a risk score r_i.

4.1 The Structure of the Model

The overall structure of RNN-SURV is represented in Fig. 1 and is described and motivated below:

1. the input of each layer is given by the features $\mathbf{x}_i$ of each patient i together with the time interval identifier k. Thanks to this input, RNN-SURV is able to capture the time-variant effect of each feature over time,
2. taking the idea from the natural language processing field, the input is then elaborated by N_1 embedding layers. Thanks to the embeddings we are able to create a more meaningful representation of our data, and
3. the output of the embedding layers is then passed through N_2 recurrent layers and a sigmoid non-linearity. This generates the estimates $\hat{y}_i^{(1)}, \ldots, \hat{y}_i^{(K)}$ from which we can compute the risk score with the following equation:

$$\hat{r}_i = \sum_{k=1}^{K} w_k \hat{y}_i^{(k)} \tag{3}$$

where w_k for $k = 1, \ldots, K$ are the parameters of the last layer of RNN-SURV. Thanks to the linear combination, the risk score, whose quality is evaluated with the C-index [9], is highly interpretable.

Further, in order to handle the vanishing gradient problem, the feedforward layers use the ReLU non-linearity [19], while the recurrent layers are constituted of LSTM cells [10], which are defined as:

$$\begin{aligned}
\begin{pmatrix} \mathbf{i}_t \\ \mathbf{f}_t \\ \mathbf{o}_t \\ \mathbf{g}_t \end{pmatrix} &= \begin{pmatrix} \sigma(\mathbf{W}_i[\mathbf{w}_t, \mathbf{h}_{t-1}] + \mathbf{b}_i) \\ \sigma(\mathbf{W}_f[\mathbf{w}_t, \mathbf{h}_{t-1}] + \mathbf{b}_f) \\ \sigma(\mathbf{W}_o[\mathbf{w}_t, \mathbf{h}_{t-1}] + \mathbf{b}_o) \\ f(\mathbf{W}_g[\mathbf{w}_t, \mathbf{h}_{t-1}] + \mathbf{b}_g) \end{pmatrix} \\
\mathbf{c}_t &= \mathbf{f}_t * \mathbf{c}_{t-1} + \mathbf{i}_t * \mathbf{g}_t \\
\mathbf{h}_t &= \mathbf{o}_t * f(\mathbf{c}_t).
\end{aligned} \tag{4}$$

4.2 Training

Since the neural network predicts both the discrete survival function and the risk score for each datapoint, it is trained to jointly minimize two different loss functions:

1. The first one is a modified cross-entropy function able to take into account the censored data, defined as:
$$\mathcal{L}_1 = -\sum_{k=1}^{K} \sum_{i \in U_k} \left[\mathbb{I}(Y_i > t_k) \log \hat{y}_i^{(k)} + (1 - \mathbb{I}(Y_i > t_k)) \log(1 - \hat{y}_i^{(k)}) \right] \tag{5}$$
where $U_k = \{i \mid \delta_i = 1 \text{ or } C_i > t_k\}$ represents the set of individuals that are uncensored throughout the entire observation time or for which censoring has not yet happened at the end of the kth time interval.
2. The second one is an upper bound of the negative C-index [23] defined as:
$$\mathcal{L}_2 = -\frac{1}{|\mathcal{C}|} \sum_{(i,j) \in \mathcal{C}} \left[1 + \left(\frac{\log \sigma(\hat{r}_j - \hat{r}_i)}{\log 2} \right) \right] \tag{6}$$
where $\mathcal{C}$ is the set of pairs $\{(i,j) \mid \delta_i = 1 \text{ and } (Y_i \leq Y_j)\}$. The advantage of minimizing (6) instead of the negative C-index is that the former still leads to good results [23], and the latter is far more expensive to compute and would have made the experimental evaluation impractical.

The two losses $\mathcal{L}_1$ and $\mathcal{L}_2$ are then linearly combined, with the hyperparameters of the sum optimized during the validation phase.

In order to avoid overfitting, we apply dropout to both the feedforward layers [22] and to the recurrent layers [8], together with a holdout-based early stopping as described in [20]. Further, we add $L2$-regularization to the linear combination of the losses. The entire neural network is trained using mini-batching and Adam optimizer [14].

5 Experimental Analysis

All our experiments are conducted on two large datasets, UNOS Transplant and UNOS Waitlist, from the United Network for Organ Sharing (UNOS)[1] and on

[1] https://www.unos.org/data/.

three publicly available, small datasets, AIDS2, FLCHAIN, NWTCO.[2] In each experiment we deploy 60/20/20 division into training, validation and test sets and the early stopping is configured as a no validation gain for 25 consecutive epochs. The main characteristics of these datasets are shown in Table 1, while the structure of RNN-SURV for each dataset is shown in Table 2. The performances of our model are measured using the C-index [9].[3]

Table 1. Datasets description

Dataset	Num. features	Num. patients	(%) Censored	Missing data
UNOS Transplant	53	60400	51.3	Yes
UNOS Waitlist	27	36329	48.9	Yes
NWTCO	9	4028	85.8	No
FLCHAIN	26	7874	72.5	Yes
AIDS2	12	2843	38.1	No

Table 2. Structure of the model for each experiment.

	UNOS Transplant	UNOS Waitlist	NWTCO	FLCHAIN	AIDS2
# FF layers	2	2	3	3	2
# recurrent layers	2	2	2	2	2
# neurons I FF layer	53	33	18	45	22
# neurons II FF layer	51	35	18	40	25
# neurons III FF layer	-	-	18	35	-
LSTM state size	55	26	17	32	15

5.1 Preprocessing

Our datasets present missing data and thus they require a preprocessing phase. UNOS Transplant and UNOS Waitlist contain data about patients that registered in order to undergo heart transplantation during the years from 1985 to 2015. In particular UNOS Transplant contains data about patients who have already undergone the surgery, while UNOS Waitlist contains data about patients who are still waitlisted. From the complete datasets, we discard 12 features that can be obtained only after transplantation and all the features for which more than 10% of the patients have missing information. In order to deal with the missing data on the remaining 53 and 27 features, we conduct 10 multiple imputations using Multiple Imputation by Chained Equations (MICE) [24].

The three small datasets contain data about:

1. NWTCO: contains data from the National Wilm's Tumor Study [3],
2. FLCHAIN: contains half of the data collected during a study [16] about the possible relationship between serum FLC and mortality, and
3. AIDS2: contains data on patients diagnosed with AIDS in Australia [25].

[2] https://vincentarelbundock.github.io/Rdatasets/datasets.html/.
[3] Implementation by LIFELINES package.

Table 3. Performances, in terms of C-index, of RNN-SURV, CPH, AAH, DEEP-SURV, RFS and MTLSA together with the 95% confidence interval for the mean C-index. The * indicates a p-value < 0.05 while ** < 0.01.

	UNOS Transp.	UNOS Waitlist	NWTCO	FLCHAIN	AIDS2
CPH	0.566** (0.565–0.567)	0.642** (0.637–0.647)	0.706 (0.687–0.725)	0.883* (0.879–0.887)	0.558 (0.546–0.570)
AAH	0.561** (0.557–0.565)	0.636** (0.632–0.640)	0.710 (0.601–0.719)	0.885 (0.879–0.891)	0.557 (0.542–0.572)
DEEP-SURV	0.566** (0.560–0.572)	0.645* (0.638–0.652)	0.706 (0.686–0.726)	0.835 (0.774–0.896)	0.558 (0.532–0.584)
RFS	0.563** (0.561–0.565)	0.646* (0.642–0.650)	0.663* (0.648–0.678)	0.828 (0.765–0.891)	0.501** (0.489–0.513)
MTLSA	0.484** (0.480–0.488)	0.529** (0.525–0.533)	0.595* (0.567–0.623)	0.696** (0.688–0.704)	0.520* (0.500–0.540)
RNN-SURV	**0.587 (0.583–0.591)**	**0.656 (0.652–0.660)**	**0.724 (0.697–0.751)**	**0.894 (0.886–0.902)**	**0.573 (0.553–0.593)**

For these datasets, we complete the missing data using the mean value for the continuous features and using the most recurrent value for the categorical ones. Once complete the missing data, we then use one-hot encoding for the categorical features and we standardize each feature so that each has mean $\mu = 0$ and variance $\sigma = 1$.

5.2 Comparison with Other Models

We have compared RNN-SURV with the two traditional Survival Analysis models, CPH and Aalen Additive Hazards model (AAH) [1], and with three recent models that try to conjugate Machine Learning with Survival Analysis: RFS [11], DEEP-SURV [13] and MTLSA [17]. Both CPH and AAH have been implemented using the LIFELINES package[4], while we deployed the RANDOMFORESTSRC package[5] for RFS, the DEEPSURV package[6] for DEEP-SURV and the MTLSA package[7] for MTLSA. The results shown in Table 3 are obtained using k-fold cross validation (with $k = 5$). As it can be seen from the table, RNN-SURV outperforms the other models in all the datasets. In particular, the biggest improvements are obtained with respect to MTLSA, with a peak of 28.4% on the FLCHAIN dataset.

5.3 Estimating the Survival Curves

To further demonstrate the good results obtained by RNN-SURV, in Fig. 2 we show some of the survival curves obtained in largest dataset available, the UNOS Transplant dataset.

Figure 2 shows that our model is able to capture the average trend of the survival curves, both for the whole population and for subsets of it. Further,

[4] https://github.com/CamDavidsonPilon/lifelines/.
[5] https://cran.r-project.org/web/packages/randomForestSRC/.
[6] https://github.com/jaredleekatzman/DeepSurv/.
[7] https://github.com/yanlirock/MTLSA/.

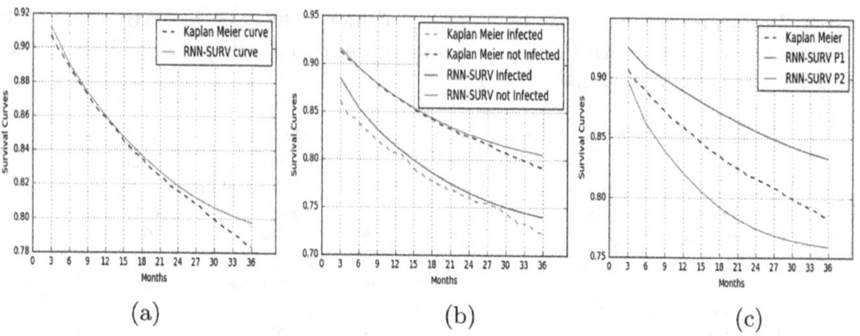

(a) (b) (c)

Fig. 2. Performances of RNN-SURV on UNOS Transplant dataset on a 36 months horizon on the test set. (a) average Survival Function obtained with RNN-SURV and Kaplan-Meier curve [12]. (b) average Survival Functions obtained with RNN-SURV and Kaplan-Meier curves for two subgroups of patients: patients who experienced an infection and patients who did not. (c) Kaplan-Meier curve together with the survival curves of two different patients (P1: Patient 1, P2: Patient 2).

RNN-SURV demonstrates to have a great discriminative power: it is able to plot a unique survival function for each patient and, as it is shown in Fig. 2(c), the survival curves can be very different one from another and from the average survival curve.

5.4 Analysis of the Model

We now analyze how the different main components of RNN-SURV contribute to its good performances. In particular, we consider the model without the three main features of the model:

1. We first consider the case in which we do not have the feedforward layers, i.e., with $N_1 = 0$;
2. Then the case in which the interval identifier k as input to the feedforward layer is always set to 1;
3. Finally the case in which the model has only one likelihood, i.e., $\mathcal{L}_2$.

The C-index of the various versions and of the complete model on the different datasets are shown in Table 4. In the Table the best results are in bold, while the worst results are underlined. As it can be seen, the best performances are always obtained by the complete model, meaning that all the different components have a positive contribution. Interestingly, the worst performances are obtained when we disable the $\mathcal{L}_1$ score on the large datasets and the feedforward layers in the small ones. The explanation for the very positive contribution of using both the $\mathcal{L}_1$ and $\mathcal{L}_2$ scores on the two large datasets is that $\mathcal{L}_1$ allows to take into account the intermediate performances of the network when computing $\hat{y}_i^{(1)}, \ldots, \hat{y}_i^{(K)}$. On the other hand, for the small datasets, the positive contribution of using the two scores is superseded by the feedforward layers and this can be explained by the characteristics of the datasets presenting a majority of discrete features.

This design of the capsule allows more capabilities in representing its features. Capsule Networks are also translation equivariance, which means they consider the spatial position of key features.

3 Dataset

In this comparison the database GTSRB [16] is used because it has different problems between its classes which are explained later. The images were cut from a sequence recorded from a vehicle, leading to many similar data.

3.1 Preparation

The images in the dataset appear in different scales and aspect ratios. To feed the images through the network they are resized to 48 × 48 px. At this point no normalization was performed on the images. The networks use batch-normalization instead. The original dataset has a widely spread number of samples per class. The distribution is visualized in Fig. 1.

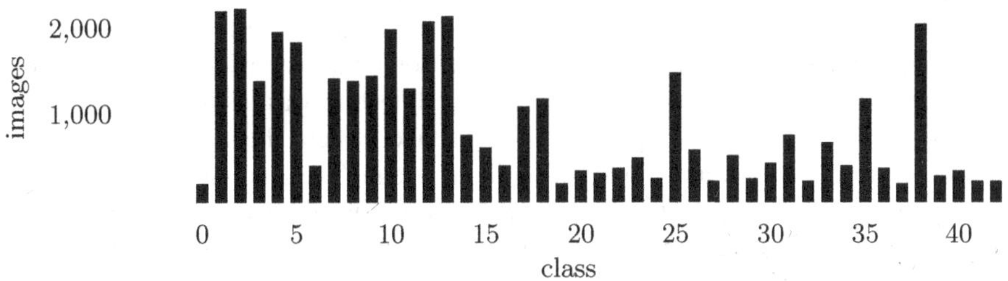

Fig. 1. Amount of images in each class of the original GTSRB dataset.

This gives a high a priori probability of the class existence to the network. The network might learn that some classes are more important than others, which can be a big problem if the distribution does not correlate with the real world distribution of the data or the input data is not very good distinguishable between two classes. Multiple datasets based on the original trainingset were created.

- **Original** (Or): Only images from the original dataset.
- **A priori** (Ap): Original images were copied to achieve the same amount of images in each class.
- **Augmented** (Au): Each class contains the same number of images, but there are new images generated based on the original ones.

Lawrence et al. [9] described the problem of having an uneven balance of the individual classes. Buda et al. [1] presented different methods of addressing this issue.

3.2 Augmentation

To create the augmented images their Rotation, Brightness, Color and Contrast were randomly changed. It is important to not change these parameters too much to prevent getting completely black or white images and not to loose the effect of augmentation as mentioned by Shijie et al. [14].

To not mix the classes *Keep left* and *Keep right* the images were not rotated more than 40° in each direction.

4 Approach

Given the three different datasets the three networks were trained using TensorFlow.

The convolutional network uses three convolution layer, where the first one is used for normalizing the color. It uses the ReLU activation function. Except for the fully connected layer only small filter were selected to fit the number of parameters to the capsule network. This network contains a total number of 148.635 trainable parameters. The network uses several regularization techniques like dropout and the batches are normalized after each convolution. The learning rate was set to decay exponential starting from 0.001. The Capsule Network was adapted from a project by Neveu [11]. The code was modified to work with the three different datasets. Also slight changes to the hyperparameters were made resulting in a total number of 207.947 trainable parameters. The Spatial Transformer Networks architecture was inspired by the CNN. The biggest difference is the spatial transform layer where the network learns the translation, scale, rotation and clutter of an input image. The amount of parameters is close to the CNN. Currently the training process of capsule networks is very slow. Running on the same machine this network runs about 5 times longer than the CNN.

5 Results

In this section several parameters are evaluated. In Sect. 5.1 the overall performance on the different training- and testsets is compared. In Sect. 5.2 the rotation robustness of some classes is appraised. The figures refer (if not mentioned) to the original training- and testdata.

5.1 Accuracy

With the convolutional network the results mentioned in Table 1 can be accomplished when running for 30 epochs.

These are not state-of-the-Art results for the testset, but they show how much the accuracy drops if the augmented testset is evaluated with the network. When being trained on the augmented trainingset the network becomes much more robust against the augmented testset. Stallkamp et al. [16] measured the human performance on the dataset with 98.97%. Sermanet et al. [13] got a performance of 98.31% using their Multi-Scale CNN. Therefore they selected features from not only the last layer for

2.4 General Networks

We have shown above that MLPs, CNNs, and RNNs can be written as MLP ArbNets associated with different hash functions. Since deep networks are built using a combination of these three primitive networks, it follows that deep networks can be expressed as MLP ArbNets. This shows the generality of the ArbNet framework.

Fully connected layers do not share any weights, while convolutional layers share weights within a layer in a very specific pattern resulting in sparse Toeplitz matrices when flattened out, and recurrent layers share the exact same weights across layers. The design space of potential neural networks is extremely big, and one could conceive of effective weight-sharing strategies that deviate from these three standard patterns of weight-sharing.

In general, since any neural network, not just MLPs, can be augmented with a hash table, ArbNets are a powerful mechanism for studying weight-sharing in neural networks. The problem of studying weight-sharing in neural networks can then be reduced to the problem of studying the properties of the associated hash functions.

3 Related Work

Chen et al. [1] proposed HashedNets for neural network compression, which is an MLP ArbNet where the hash function is computed layer-wise using `xxHash` prior to the start of training. Han et al. [4] also made use of the same layer-wise hashing strategy for the purposes of network compression, but hashed according to clusters found by a K-means algorithm run on the weights of a trained network. Our work generalizes this technique, and uses it as an experimental tool to study the role of weight-sharing.

Besides hard weight-sharing, it is also possible to do soft weight-sharing, where two different weights in a network are not forced to be equal, but are related to each other. Nowlan et al. [7] implemented a soft weight-sharing strategy for the purposes of regularization where the weights are drawn from a Gaussian mixture model. Ullrich et al. [9] also used Gaussian mixture models as soft weight-sharing for doing network compression.

Another soft weight-sharing strategy called HyperNetworks [3] involves using a LSTM controller as a meta-learning algorithm to generate the weights of another network.

4 Experimental Setup

In this paper, we limit our attention to studying certain properties of MLP ArbNets as tested on the MNIST and CIFAR10 image classification tasks. Our aim is not to best any existing benchmarks, but to show the differences in test accuracy as a result of changing various properties of the hash function associated with the MLP ArbNet.

4.1 Balance of the Hash Table

The balance of the hash table can be measured by Shannon entropy:

$$H = -\sum_i p_i \log p_i \tag{7}$$

where p_i is the probability that the ith table entry will be used on a forward pass in the network. We propose to control this with a Dirichlet hash, which involves sampling from a symmetric Dirichlet distribution and using the output as the parameters of a multinomial distribution which we will use as the hash function. The symmetric Dirichlet distribution has the following probability density function:

$$P(X) = \frac{\Gamma(\alpha N)}{\Gamma(\alpha)^N} \prod_{i=1}^{N} x_i^{\alpha-1} \tag{8}$$

where the x_i lie on the $N-1$ simplex. The Dirichlet hash can be given by the following function:

$$w_i = table_{Multinomial_\alpha(n)} \tag{9}$$

A high α leads to a balanced distribution (high Shannon entropy), and a low α

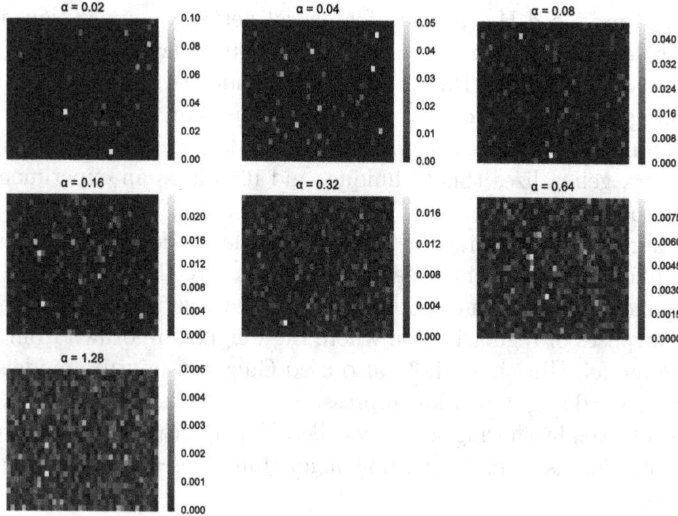

Fig. 1. Heatmap of multinomial parameters drawn from different values of α

leads to an unbalanced distribution (low Shannon entropy). The limiting case of $\alpha \to \infty$ results in a uniform distribution, which has maximum Shannon entropy. See Fig. 1 for a visualization of the effects of α on a hash table with 1000 entries.

4.2 Noise in the Hash Function

A modulus hash and a uniform hash both have the property that the expected load of all the entries in the hash table is the same. Hence, in expectation, both of them will be balanced the same way, i.e. have the same expected Shannon entropy. But the former is entirely deterministic while the latter is entirely random. In this case, it is interesting to think about the effects of this source of noise, if any, on the performance of the neural network. We propose to investigate this with a Neighborhood hash, which involves the composition of a modulus hash and a uniform distribution around a specified *radius*. This is given by the following hash function:

$$w_i = table_{(i+Uniform([-radius,\ radius]))\ \mathrm{mod}\ n} \tag{10}$$

When the *radius* is 0, the Neighborhood hash reduces to the modulus hash, and when the radius is at least half the size of the hash table, it reduces to the uniform hash. Controlling the radius thus allows us to control the intuitive notion of 'noise' in the specific setting where the expected load of all the table entries is the same.

4.3 Network Specification

On MNIST, our ArbNet is a three layer MLP (200-ELU-BN-200-ELU-BN-10-ELU-BN) with exponential linear units [2] and batch normalization [6].

On CIFAR10, our ArbNet is a six layer MLP (2000-ELU-BN-2000-ELU-BN-2000-ELU-BN-2000-ELU-BN-2000-ELU-BN-10-ELU-BN) with exponential linear units and batch normalization.

We trained both networks using SGD with learning rate 0.1 and momentum 0.9, and a learning rate scheduler that reduces the learning rate 10x every four epochs if there is no improvement in training accuracy. No validation set was used.

5 Results and Discussion

5.1 Dirichlet Hash

We observe in Fig. 2 that on the MNIST dataset, increasing α has a direct positive effect on test accuracy, across different levels of sparsity. On the CIFAR10 dataset, when the weights are sparse, increasing α has a small positive effect, but at lower levels of sparsity, it has a huge positive effect. This finding seems to indicate that it is more likely for SGD to get stuck in local minima when the weights are both non-sparse and shared unevenly.

We can conclude that balance helps with network performance, but it is unclear if it brings diminishing returns. Re-plotting the MNIST graph in Fig. 2 with the x-axis replaced with Shannon Entropy (Eq. 7) instead of α in Fig. 3 gives us a better sense of scale. Note that in this case, a uniform distribution on 1000 entries would have a Shannon entropy of 6.91. The results shown by Fig. 3 suggest a linear trend at high sparsity and a concave trend at low sparsity, but more evidence is required to come to a conclusion.

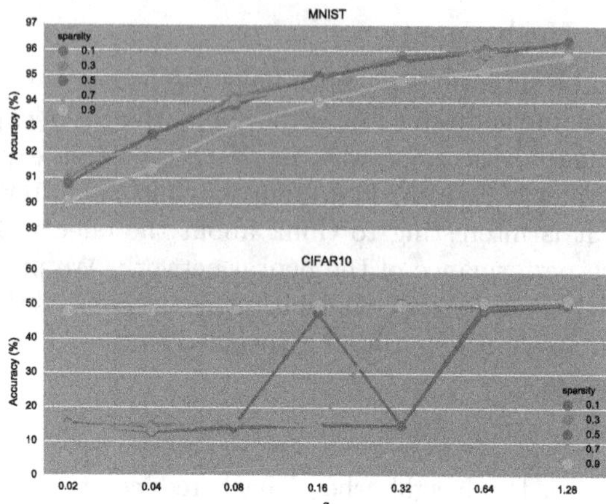

Fig. 2. Effect of α (balance) in Dirichlet hash on network accuracy across different levels of sparsity

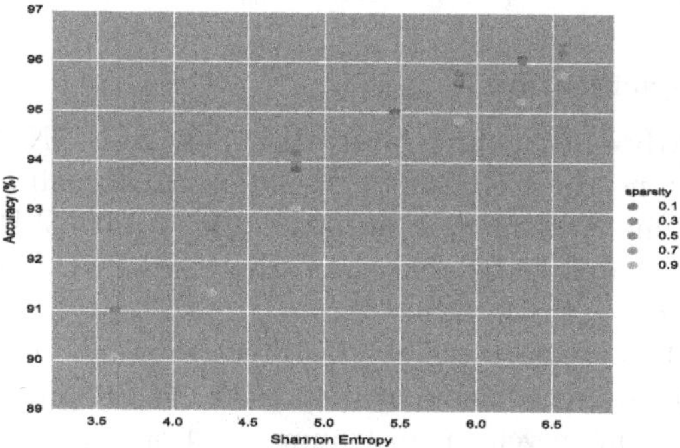

Fig. 3. Effect of Shannon entropy (balance) in Dirichlet hash on network accuracy across different levels of sparsity

5.2 Neighborhood Hash

The trends in Fig. 4 are noisier, but it seems like an increase in *radius* has the overall effect of diminishing test accuracy. On MNIST, we notice that higher levels of sparsity result in a smaller drop in accuracy. The same effect seems to be present but not as pronounced in CIFAR10, where we note an outlier in the case of sparsity 0.1, *radius* 0. We hypothesize that this effect occurs because the increase in noise leads to the increased probability of two geometrically distant weights in the network being forced to share the same weights. This is undesirable in the task of image classification, where local weight-sharing is proven to be advantageous, and perhaps essential to the task. When the network is sparse, the positive effect of local weight-sharing is not prominent, and hence the noise does not affect network performance as much.

Thus, we can conclude that making the ArbNet hash more deterministic (equivalently, less noisy) boosts network performance, but less so when it is sparse.

We notice that convolutional layers, when written as an MLP ArbNet as in Eq. 6, have a hash function that is both balanced (all the weights are used with the same probability) and deterministic (the hash function does not have any noise in it). This helps to explain the role weight-sharing plays in the success of convolutional neural networks.

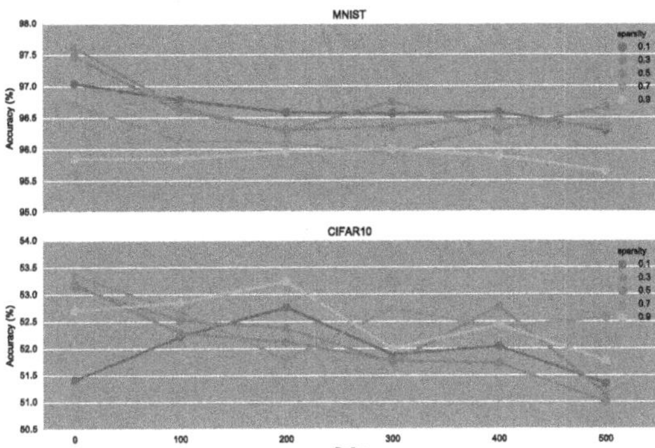

Fig. 4. Effect of *radius* (noise) in Neighborhood hash on network accuracy across different levels of sparsity

6 Conclusion

Weight-sharing is very important to the success of deep neural networks. We proposed the use of ArbNets as a general framework under which weight-sharing can be studied, and investigated experimentally, for the first time, how balance and noise affects neural network performance in the specific case of an MLP ArbNet and two image classification datasets.

References

1. Chen, W., Wilson, J.T., Tyree, S., Weinberger, K.Q., Chen, Y.: Compressing neural networks with the hashing trick, vol. 37 (2015)
2. Clevert, D.A., Unterthiner, T., Hochreiter, S.: Fast and accurate deep network learning by exponential linear units (ELUs) (2016)
3. Ha, D., Dai, A.M., Le, Q.V.: Hypernetworks (2017)
4. Han, S., Mao, H., Dally, W.J.: Deep compression: compressing deep neural networks with pruning, trained quantization and Huffman coding (2016)
5. Inan, H., Khosravi, K., Socher, R.: Tying word vectors and word classifiers: a loss framework for language modeling (2017)
6. Ioffe, S., Szegedy, C.: Batch normalization: accelerating deep network training by reducing internal covariate shift, vol. 37 (2015)

7. Nowlan, S.J., Hinton, G.E.: Simplifying neural networks by soft weight-sharing. Neural Comput. **4**, 473–493 (1992)
8. Roweis, S.: EM algorithms for PCA and SPCA. In: Neural Information Processing Systems, vol. 10 (1997)
9. Ullrich, K., Meeds, E., Welling, M.: Soft weight-sharing for neural network compression (2017)
10. Zhang, C., Bengio, S., Hardt, M., Recht, B., Vinyals, O.: Understanding deep learning requires re-thinking generalization (2017)

Neural Networks with Block Diagonal Inner Product Layers

Amy Nesky(✉) and Quentin F. Stout

Computer Science and Engineering, University of Michigan,
Ann Arbor, MI 48109, USA
{anesky,qstout}@umich.edu

Abstract. We consider a modified version of the fully connected layer we call a block diagonal inner product layer. These modified layers have weight matrices that are block diagonal, turning a single fully connected layer into a set of densely connected neuron groups. This idea is a natural extension of group, or depthwise separable, convolutional layers applied to the fully connected layers. Block diagonal inner product layers can be achieved by either initializing a purely block diagonal weight matrix or by iteratively pruning off diagonal block entries. This method condenses network storage and speeds up the run time without significant adverse effect on the testing accuracy.

Keywords: Neural networks · Block diagonal · Structured sparsity

1 Introduction

Ideally, efforts to reduce the memory requirements of neural networks would also lessen their computational demand, but often these competing interests force a trade-off. Fully connected layers are unwieldy, yet they continue to be present in the most successful networks [13,23,28]. Our work addresses both memory and computational efficiency without compromise. Focusing our attention on the fully connected layers, we decrease network memory footprint and improve network runtime.

There are a variety of methods to condense large networks without much harm to their accuracy. One such technique that has gained popularity is pruning [3,4,21], but traditional pruning has disadvantages related to network runtime. Most existing pruning processes slow down network training, and the resulting condensed network is usually significantly slower to execute [3]. Sparse format operations require additional overhead that can greatly slow down performance unless one prunes nearly all weight entries, which can damage network accuracy.

Localized memory access patterns can be computed faster than non-localized lookups. By implementing block diagonal inner product layers in place of fully connected layers, we condense neural networks in a structured manner that

V. Kůrková et al. (Eds.): ICANN 2018, LNCS 11141, pp. 51–61, 2018.
https://doi.org/10.1007/978-3-030-01424-7_6

speeds up the final runtime and does little harm to the final accuracy. Block diagonal inner product layers can be implemented by either initializing a purely block diagonal weight matrix or by initializing a fully connected layer and focusing pruning efforts off the diagonal blocks to coax the dense weight matrix into structured sparsity. The first method reduces the gradient computation time and hence the overall training time. The latter method retains higher accuracy and supports the robustness of networks to *shaping*. That is, pruning can be used as a mapping between architectures—in particular, a mapping to more convenient architectures. Depending on how many iterations the pruning process takes, this method may also speed up training.

We have converted a single fully connected layer into a ensemble of smaller inner product learners whose combined efforts form a stronger learner, in essence boosting the layer. These methods also bring artificial neural networks closer to the architecture of biological mammalian brains, which have more local connectivity [6].

2 Related Work

There is an assortment of criteria by which one may choose which weights to prune. With any pruning method, the result is a sparse network that takes less storage space than its fully connected counterpart. Han et al. iteratively prune a network using the penalty method by adding a mask that disregards pruned parameters for each weight tensor [4]. This means that the number of required floating point operations decreases, but the number performed stays the same. Furthermore, masking out updates takes additional time. Han et al. report the average time spent on a forward propagation after pruning is complete and the resulting sparse layers have been converted to CSR format; for batch sizes larger than one, the sparse computations are significantly slower than the dense calculations [3].

More recently, there has been momentum in the direction of structured reduction of network architecture. Node pruning preserves some structure, but drastic node pruning can harm the network accuracy and requires additional weight fine-tuning [5,25]. Other approaches include storing a low rank approximation for a layer's weight matrix [22] and training smaller models on outputs of larger models (distillation) [7]. Group lasso expands the concept of node pruning to convolutional filters [14,26,27]. That is, group lasso applies L_1-norm regularization to entire filters. Sidhawani et al. propose structured parameter matrices characterized by low displacement rank that yield high compression rate as well as fast forward and gradient evaluation [24]. Their work focuses on toeplitz-related transforms of the fully connected layer weight matrix. However, speedup is generally only seen for compression of large weight matrices. According to their Fig. 3, for displacement rank higher than 1.5×10^{-3} times the matrix dimension the forward pass is slowed down, and backward pass is slowed down for displacement rank higher than 9×10^{-4} times the matrix dimension.

Group, or depthwise separable, convolutions have been used in recent CNN architectures with great success [2,8,29]. In group convolutions, a particular filter does not see all of the channels of the previous layer. Block diagonal inner product layers apply this idea of separable neuron groups to the fully connected layers. This method transforms a fully connected layer into an ensemble of smaller fully connected neuron groups that boost the layer.

3 Methodology

We consider two methods for implementing block diagonal inner product layers:

1. We initialize a layer with a purely block diagonal weight matrix and keep the number of connections constant throughout training.
2. We initialize a fully connected layer and iteratively prune entries off the diagonal blocks to achieve a block substructure.

Within a layer, all blocks have the same size. Method 2 is accomplished in three phases: a dense phase, an iterative pruning phase and a block diagonal phase. In the dense phase a fully connected layer is initialized and trained in the standard way. During the iterative pruning phase, focused pruning is applied to entries off the diagonal blocks using the weight decay method with L_1-norm. That is, if W is the weight matrix for a fully connected layer we wish to push toward block diagonal, we add

$$\alpha \sum_{i,j} |\mathbb{1}_{i,j} W_{i,j}| \tag{1}$$

to the loss function during the iterative pruning phase, where α is a tuning parameter and $\mathbb{1}_{i,j}$ indicates whether $W_{i,j}$ is off the diagonal blocks in W. The frequencies of regularization and pruning during this phase are additional hyperparameters. During this phase, masking out updates for pruned entries is more efficient than maintaining sparse format. When pruning is complete, to maximize speedup it is best to reformat the weight matrix once such that the blocks are condensed and adjacent in memory.[1] Batched smaller dense calculations for the blocks use cuBLAS strided batched multiplication [20]. There is a lot of flexibility in method 2 that can be tuned for specific user needs. More pruning iterations may increase the total training time but can yield higher accuracy and reduce overfitting.

4 Experiments: Speedup and Accuracy

Our goal is to reduce memory storage of the inner product layers while maintaining or reducing the final execution time of the network with minimal loss in accuracy. We will also see the reduction of total training time in some cases. All experiments are run on the Bridges' NVIDIA P100 GPUs through the Pittsburgh Supercomputing Center.

[1] When using block diagonal layers, one should alter the output format of the previous layer and the expected input format of the following layer accordingly, in particular to row major ordering.

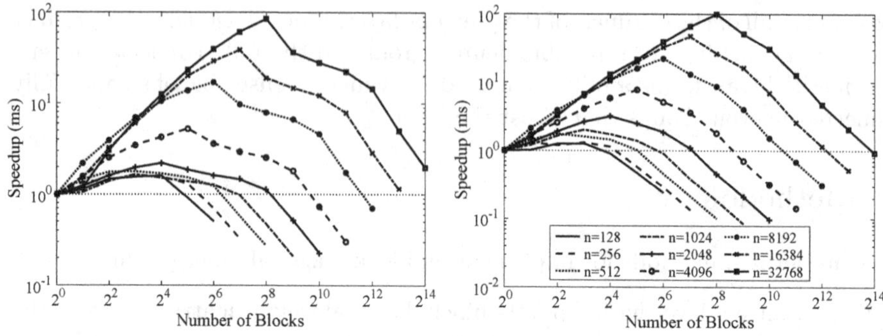

Fig. 1. Speedup when performing matrix multiplication using an $n \times n$ weight matrix and batch size 100. (Left) Speedup when performing only one forward matrix product. (Right) Speedup when performing all three matrix products involved in the forward and backward pass in gradient descent. Both images in this figure share the same key.

For speedup analysis we timed block diagonal multiplications using $n \times n$ matrices with varying dimension sizes and varying numbers of blocks; we considered the forward pass and gradient updates. We also calculate an upper bound on the ratio of the number of pruning iterations to the number of pure block iterations that will yield speedup when using block diagonal method 2. For accuracy results, we ran experiments on the MNIST [16] dataset using a LeNet-5 [15] network, and the SVHN [19] and CIFAR10 [10] datasets using Krizhevsky's cuda-convnet [11]. Cuda-convnet does not produce state-of-art accuracies for SVHN or CIFAR10, but demonstrates the performance differences between our methods and others. We implement our work in Caffe, which provides these architectures; Caffe's MNIST example uses LeNet-5 and cuda-convnet can be found in Caffe's CIFAR10 "quick" example.

4.1 Speedup

Figure 1 shows the speedup when performing matrix multiplication using an $n \times n$ weight matrix and batch size 100 when the weight matrix is purely block diagonal. The speedup when performing only the forward-pass matrix product is shown in the left pane, and the speedup when performing all gradient descent products is shown in the right pane. As the number of blocks increases, the overhead to perform cuBLAS strided batched multiplication can become noticeable; this library is not yet well optimized for performing many small matrix products [17]. However, with specialized batched multiplications for many small matrices, Jhurani et al. attain up to 6 fold speedup [9]. Using cuBLAS strided batched multiplication, maximum speedup is achieved when the number of blocks is $1/2^7$ times the matrix dimension. When only timing the forward pass, the speedup is always greater than 1 when the number of blocks is at most $1/2^5$ times the matrix dimension. When timing the forward and backward pass, the speedup is always greater than 1 when the number of blocks is at most $1/2^6$ times the matrix dimension.

For a given inner product layer, using block diagonal method 2 we would see speedup during training if

$$\frac{T(\mathrm{FC}) - T(\mathrm{Block})}{T(\mathrm{Prune})} > \frac{y}{x} \tag{2}$$

where $T(\cdot)$ is the combined time to perform the forward and backward passes of an inner product layer in the input state, x is the number of pure block iterations, and y is the number of pruning iterations. $T(\mathrm{Prune})$ is the time to regularize and apply a mask to the off diagonal block layer weights, which happens once in a training iteration. Figure 2 plots the upper bound in ratio 2 against the number of blocks for a layer with an $n \times n$ weight matrix and batch size 100.

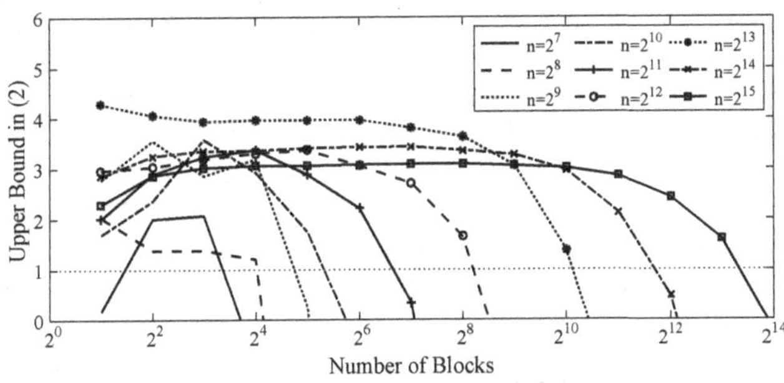

Fig. 2. Using batch size 100, upper bound on the ratio of the number of pruning iterations to the number of pure block iterations that will result in an overall training speedup when using block diagonal method 2.

Figure 3 shows timing results for the inner product layers in Lenet-5 (Left) and cuda-convnet (Right), which both have two inner product layers. We plot the forward time per inner product layer when the layers are purely block diagonal, the combined forward and backward time to do the three matrix products involved in gradient descent training when the layers are purely block diagonal, and the runtime of sparse matrix multiplication with random entries in CSR format using cuSPARSE [20]. For brevity we refer to a block diagonal network architecture as $(b_1, \ldots, b_n)$-BD; $b_i = 1$ indicates that the ith inner product layer is fully connected. FC is short for all inner product layers being fully connected. The points at which the forward sparse and forward block curves meet in each plot in Fig. 3 indicate the fully connected dense forward runtimes for each layer; these are made clearer with dotted, black, vertical lines. In Lenet-5 (Left), the first inner product layer, ip1, has a 500×800 weight matrix, and the second has a 10×500 weight matrix, so the (b_1, b_2)-BD architecture has $(800 \times 500)/b_1 + (500 \times 10)/b_2$ nonzero weights across both inner

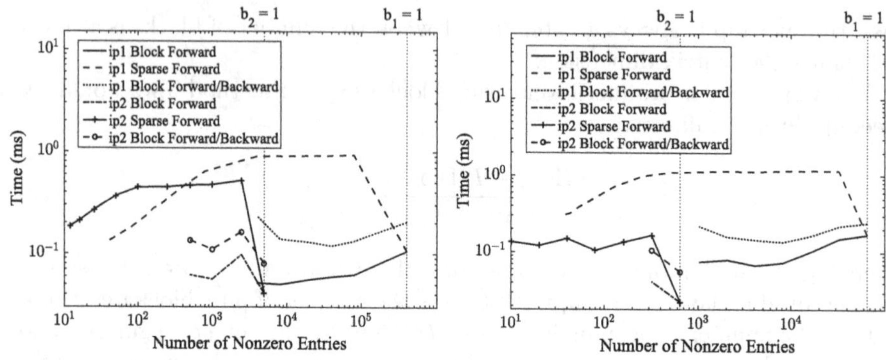

Fig. 3. For each inner product layer in Lenet-5 (Left) and cuda-convnet (Right): forward runtimes of block diagonal and CSR sparse formats, combined forward and backward runtimes of block diagonal format. Lenet-5 uses batch size 64, and cuda-convnet uses batch size 100.

product layers. There is $\geq$1.4$\times$ speedup for $b_1 \leq 50$, or 8000 nonzero entries, when timing both forward and backward matrix products, and 1.6$\times$ speedup when $b_1 = 100$, or 4000 nonzero entries, in the forward only case. In cuda-convnet (Right), the first inner product layer, ip1, has a 64×1024 weight matrix, and the second has a 10×64 weight matrix. The (b_1, b_2)-BD architecture has $(1024 \times 64)/b_1 + (64 \times 10)/b_2$ nonzero entries across both inner product layers. In the ip1 layer, there is $\geq$1.26$\times$ speedup for $b_1 \leq 32$, or 2048 nonzero entries, when timing both forward and backward matrix products, and $\geq$1.65$\times$ speedup for $b_1 \leq 64$, or 1024 nonzero entries, in the forward only case. In both plots we see sparse format performs poorly until there are less than 50 nonzero entries.

4.2 Accuracy Results

All hyperparameters and initialization distributions provided by Caffe's example architectures are left unchanged. Training is done with batched gradient descent using the cross-entropy loss function on the softmax of the output layer. In our experiments we performed only manual hyperparameter tuning of new hyperparameters introduced by block diagonal method 2 like the coefficient of the new regularization term (see Eq. 1) and the pruning modulus cutoff.

In ShuffleNet, Zhang et al. note that when multiple group convolutions are stacked together this can block information flow between channel groups and weaken representation [29]. To correct for this, they suggest dividing the channels in each group into subgroups, and shuffling the outputs of the subgroups in this layer before feeding them to the next layer. Applying this approach to block inner product layers requires either moving entries in memory or doing more, smaller matrix products. Both of these options would hurt efficiency. Using pruning to achieve the block diagonal structure, as in method 2, also addresses information flow. Pruning does add some work to the training iterations, but, unlike the

ShuffleNet method, does not add work to the final execution of the trained network. After pruning is complete, the learned weights are the result of a more complete picture; while the information flow has been constrained, it is preserved like a ghost in the remaining weights. Another alternative is to randomly shuffle whole blocks each pass like in the "random sparse convolution" layer in the CNN library *cuda-convnet* [12]. We found that for the inner product layers in LeNet-5 and Krizhevsky's Cuda-convnet, the ShuffleNet method did not show as much improvement in accuracy as randomly shuffling the whole blocks, so we do not include results using the ShuffleNet method.

Table 1 shows the accuracy results for block diagonal method 1, method 1 with random block shuffling, method 2 and traditional iterative pruning, which uses the penalty method to prune weight entries not subject to any confinement or organization. We show accuracy results for the most condensed net with block diagonal inner product layers and the net with the fastest speedup in the inner product layers.

Table 1. Accuracy results on MNIST, SVHN, and CIFAR10 datasets.

	Method 1	Rand. shuff	Method 2	Trad. it. prune
MNIST (99.11% accurate when using FC)				
(10, 1)-BD	98.83%	98.81%	99.02%	99.04%
(100, 10)-BD	98.39%	98.42%	98.65%	98.55%
SVHN (91.96% accurate when using FC)				
(8, 1)-BD	91.39%	91.46%	91.88%	91.15%
(64, 2)-BD	89.21%	89.69%	90.02%	90.93%
CIFAR10 (76.29% accurate when using FC)				
(8, 1)-BD	75.07%	75.09%	76.05%	75.64%
(64, 2)-BD	72.7%	73.45%	74.81%	75.18%

MNIST. We experimented on the MNIST dataset with the LeNet-5 framework [15] using a training batch size of 64 for 10000 iterations. LeNet-5 has two convolutional layers with pooling followed by two inner product layers with ReLU activation. FC achieves a final accuracy of 99.11%. In all cases testing accuracy remains within 1% of FC accuracy.

Using traditional iterative pruning with L_2 regularization, as suggested in [4], pruning until 4000 and 500 nonzero entries survived in ip1 and ip2 respectively gave an accuracy of 98.55%, but the forward multiplication was more than 8 times slower than the dense fully connected case (See Fig. 3 Left). Implementing $(100, 10)$-BD method 2 with pruning using 15 dense iterations and 350 pruning iterations gave a final accuracy of 98.65%. (10, 1)-BD yielded $\approx$1.4$\times$ speedup for all gradient descent matrix products in both inner product layers after any pruning is complete, and (100, 10)-BD condensed the inner product layers in LeNet-5 $\approx$81 fold.

SVHN. We experimented on the SVHN dataset with Krizhevsky's cuda-convnet [11] using batch size 100 for 9000 iterations. Cuda-convnet has three convolutional layers with ReLu activation and pooling, followed by two fully connected layers with no activation. (8, 1)-BD yielded ≈1.5× speedup for all gradient descent matrix products in both inner product layers when purely block diagonal, and (64, 2)-BD condensed the inner product layers in Cuda-convnet ≈47 fold.

Using FC we obtained a final accuracy of 91.96%. Table 1 shows all methods stayed under a 2.5% drop in accuracy. Using traditional iterative pruning with L_2 regularization until 1024 and 320 nonzero entries survived in the final two inner product layers respectively gave an accuracy of 90.93%, but the forward multiplication was more than 8 times slower than the dense fully connected computation. On the other hand, implementing (64, 2)-BD method 2 with pruning, which has corresponding numbers of nonzero entries, with 500 dense iterations and <1000 pruning iterations gave a final accuracy of 90.02%. This is ≈47 fold compression of the inner product layer parameters with only a 2% drop in accuracy when compared to FC.

CIFAR10. We experimented on the CIFAR10 dataset with Krizhevsky's cuda-convnet [11] using batch size 100 for 9000 iterations. Using FC we obtained a final accuracy of 76.29%. Table 1 shows all methods stayed within a 4% drop in accuracy. Using traditional iterative pruning with L_2 regularization until 1024 and 320 nonzero entries survived in the final two inner product layers gave an accuracy of 75.18%, but again the forward multiplication was more than 8 times slower than the dense fully connected computation. On the other hand, implementing (64, 2)-BD method 2 with pruning, which has corresponding numbers of nonzero entries, with 500 dense iterations and <1000 pruning iterations gave a final accuracy of 74.81%. This is ≈47 fold compression of the inner product layer parameters with only a 1.5% drop in accuracy. The total forward runtime of ip1 and ip2 in (64, 2)-BD is 1.6 times faster than in FC. To achieve comparable speed with sparse format we used traditional iterative pruning to leave 37 and 40 nonzero entries in the final inner product layers giving an accuracy of 73.01%. Thus implementing block diagonal layers with pruning yields comparable accuracy and memory condensation to traditional iterative pruning with faster final execution time.

Whole node pruning decreases the accuracy more than corresponding reductions in the block diagonal setting. Node pruning until ip1 had only 2 outputs, i.e. a 1024×2 weight matrix, and ip2 had a 2×10 weight matrix for a total of 2068 weights between the two layers gave a final accuracy of 59.67%. (64, 2)-BD has a total of 1344 weights between the two inner product layers and had a final accuracy 15.14% higher with pruning.

The final accuracy on an independent test set was 76.29% on CIFAR10 using the FC net while the final accuracy on the training set itself was 83.32%. Using the (64, 2)-BD net without pruning, the accuracy on an independent test set was 72.49%, but on the training set was 75.63%. With pruning, the accuracy of

(64, 2)-BD on an independent test set was 74.81%, but on the training set was 76.85%. Both block diagonal methods decrease overfitting; the block diagonal method with pruning decreases overfitting slightly more.

5 Conclusion

We have shown that block diagonal inner product layers can reduce network size, training time and final execution time without significant harm to the network performance.

While traditional iterative pruning can reduce storage, the scattered surviving weights make sparse computation inefficient, slowing down both training and final execution time. Our block diagonal methods address this inefficiency by confining dense regions to blocks along the diagonal. Without pruning, block diagonal method 1 allows for faster training time. Method 2 preserves the learning with focused, structured pruning that reduces computation for speedup during execution. In our experiments, method 2 saw higher accuracy than the purely block diagonal method. The success of method 2 supports the use of pruning as a mapping from large dense architectures to more efficient, smaller, dense architectures. Both methods make larger network architectures more feasible to train and use since they convert a fully connected layer into a collection of smaller inner product learners working jointly to form a stronger learner. In particular, GPU memory constraints become less constricting.

There is a lot of room for additional speedup with block diagonal layers. Dependency between layers poses a noteworthy bottleneck in network parallelization. With structured sparsity like ours, one no longer needs a full barrier between layers. Additional speedup would be seen in software optimized to support weight matrices with organized sparse form, such as blocks, rather than being optimized for dense matrices. For example, for many small blocks, one can reach up to 6 fold speedup with specialized batched matrix multiplication [9]. Hardware has been developing to better support sparse operations. Block format may be especially suitable for training on evolving architectures such as neuromorphic systems. These systems, which are far more efficient than GPUs at simulating mammalian brains, have a pronounced 2-D structure and are ill-suited to large dense matrix calculations [1,18].

Acknowledgments. This material is based upon work supported by the National Science Foundation Graduate Research Fellowship under Grant No. DGE-1256260. This work used the Extreme Science and Engineering Discovery Environment (XSEDE), which is supported by National Science Foundation grant number OCI-1053575. Specifically, it used the Bridges system, which is supported by NSF award number ACI-1445606, at the Pittsburgh Supercomputing Center (PSC).

References

1. Boahen, K.: Neurogrid: a mixed-analog-digital multichip system for large-scale neural simulations. Proc. IEEE **102**(5), 699–716 (2014)
2. Chollet, F.: Xception: deep learning with depthwise separable convolutions. arXiv:1610.02357 (2017)
3. Han, S., et al.: Deep compression: compressing deep neural networks with pruning, trained quantization and Huffman coding. In: ICLR (2015)
4. Han, S., et al.: Learning both weights and connections for efficient neural networks. In: NIPS, pp. 1135–1143 (2015)
5. He, T., et al.: Reshaping deep neural network for fast decoding by node-pruning. In: IEEE ICASSP, pp. 245–249 (2014)
6. Herculano-Houzel, S.: The remarkable, yet not extraordinary, human brain as a scaled-up primate brain and its associated cost. PNAS **109**(Supplement 1), 10661–10668 (2012)
7. Hinton, G., et al.: Distilling the knowledge in a neural network. In: NIPS (2014)
8. Ioannou, Y., et al.: Deep Roots: improving CNN efficiency with hierarchical filter groups. In: CVPR (2017)
9. Jhurani, C., et al.: A GEMM interface and implementation on NVIDIA GPUs for multiple small matrices. J. Parallel Distrib. Comput. **75**, 133–140 (2015)
10. Krizhevsky, A.: Learning multiple layers of features from tiny images. Technical report, Computer Science, University of Toronto (2009)
11. Krizhevsky, A.: Cuda-convnet. Technical report, Computer Science, University of Toronto (2012)
12. Krizhevsky, A.: Cuda-convnet: high-performance C++/CUDA implementation of convolutional neural networks (2012)
13. Krizhevsky, A., et al.: Imagenet classification with deep convolutional neural networks. In: NIPS, pp. 1106–1114 (2012)
14. Lebedev, V., et al.: Fast convnets using group-wise brain damage. In: CVPR (2016)
15. LeCun, Y., et al.: Gradient-based learning applied to document recognition. Proc. IEEE **86**(11), 2278–2324 (1998)
16. LeCun, Y., et al.: The MNIST database of handwritten digits. Technical report
17. Masliah, I., et al.: High-performance matrix-matrix multiplications of very small matrices. In: Dutot, P.-F., Trystram, D. (eds.) Euro-Par 2016. LNCS, vol. 9833, pp. 659–671. Springer, Cham (2016). https://doi.org/10.1007/978-3-319-43659-3_48
18. Merolla, P.A., et al.: A million spiking-neuron integrated circuit with a scalable communication network and interface. Science **345**(6197), 668–673 (2014)
19. Netzer, Y., et al.: Reading digits in natural images with unsupervised feature learning. In: NIPS (2011)
20. Nickolls, J., et al.: Scalable parallel programming with CUDA. ACM Queue **6**(2), 40–53 (2008)
21. Reed, R.: Pruning algorithms-a survey. IEEE Trans. Neural Netw. **4**(5), 740–747 (1993)
22. Sainath, T.N., et al.: Low-rank matrix factorization for deep neural network training with high-dimensional output targets. In: IEEE ICASSP (2013)
23. Simonyan, K., et al.: Very deep convolutional networks for large-scale image recognition. arXiv:1409.1556 (2014)
24. Sindhwani, V., et al.: Structured transforms for small-footprint deep learning. In: NIPS, pp. 3088–3096 (2015)

25. Srinivas, S., et al.: Data-free parameter pruning for deep neural networks. arXiv:1507.06149 (2015)
26. Wen, W., et al.: Learning structured sparsity in deep neural networks. In: NIPS, pp. 2074–2082 (2016)
27. Yuan, M., et al.: Model selection and estimation in regression with grouped variables. J. Royal Stat. Soc. Ser. B **68**(1), 49–67 (2006)
28. Zeiler, M.D., et al.: Visualizing and understanding convolutional networks. arXiv:1311.2901 (2013)
29. Zhang, X., et al.: ShuffleNet: an extremely efficient convolutional neural network for mobile devices. arXiv:1707.01083 (2017)

Training Neural Networks Using Predictor-Corrector Gradient Descent

Amy Nesky(✉) and Quentin F. Stout

Computer Science and Engineering, University of Michigan,
Ann Arbor, MI 48109, USA
{anesky,qstout}@umich.edu

Abstract. We improve the training time of deep feedforward neural networks using a modified version of gradient descent we call Predictor-Corrector Gradient Descent (PCGD). PCGD uses predictor-corrector inspired techniques to enhance gradient descent. This method uses a sparse history of network parameter values to make periodic predictions of future parameter values in an effort to skip unnecessary training iterations. This method can cut the number of training epochs needed for a network to reach a particular testing accuracy by nearly one half when compared to stochastic gradient descent (SGD). PCGD can also outperform, with some trade-offs, Nesterov's Accelerated Gradient (NAG).

Keywords: Neural networks · Accelerated gradient methods

1 Introduction

The immense expressional power of artificial neural networks has advanced machine learning and data science a great deal. Large networks can achieve unprecedented accuracy in intricate learning problems, yet their size consumes significant computational resources and, consequently, time [13]. Advances in compute power allow neural networks with millions of parameters to be trained on enormous, complex data sets, and the use of GPUs has decreased training time drastically, but new techniques for reducing network training time must arise for deep learning to progress.

In this work, we propose a new training technique called Predictor-Corrector Gradient Descent (PCGD) that reduces the number of iterations required to learn. In PCGD we monitor the trend of the parameters as the network learns with gradient descent, and periodically adjust each parameter by inferring future values from the trend. A number of standard gradient descent iterations between predictions act to refine the predicted approximations. This alternating process works in much the same way that predictor-corrector methods for solving ordinary differential equations work. We will show that incorporating prediction into the training process of networks makes learning significantly more efficient.

The human brain already utilizes predictions. Predictions are crucial to survival because they allow us to respond more appropriately to our surroundings

V. Kůrková et al. (Eds.): ICANN 2018, LNCS 11141, pp. 62–72, 2018.
https://doi.org/10.1007/978-3-030-01424-7_7

and they improve reaction time. Perception is also impacted by brain predictions: our perceptions are a combination of expectations and sensory information [7,14]. Thus, if we wish to improve artificial neural network efficiency, integrating prediction into training is a natural modification.[1]

2 Related Work

There is a plethora of work that supplements standard gradient descent in hopes of improving neural network training. Gradient noise and stale gradients have been successful adaptations to gradient descent [8,15]. Adaptive Gradient techniques give frequently occurring features low learning rates and infrequent features high learning rates; these methods use the information theoretic idea that infrequent features carry more information about the data distribution [5,6,10,23,24]. Momentum and Nesterov's Accelerated Gradient (NAG) accumulate a descent direction across iterations to alleviate zig-zagging and accelerate convergence [17,19] . There are also meta-learning methods that allow networks to be trained jointly with their learning algorithm. Meta-methods may intelligently adjust hyperparameters like the learning rate, or learn the entire update term perhaps as a function of the batched gradient [1,4]. Each of these techniques complement gradient descent to improve network learning and can be used in conjunction with our methods.

Prediction-correction methods are traditionally used in numerical analysis to integrate ordinary differential equations [22]. Since their inception, predictor-corrector methods have been used in a variety of fields that require optimization like theoretical study of chemical reactions and time-varying convex optimization [9,21]. Prediction-correction has been incorporated into neural network training in the past by convolving a pair of neural networks, a prediction network and a correction network [25,26].

Scieur et al. propose a related learning algorithm to the one presented in this paper called Regularized Nonlinear Acceleration (RNA) [20]. RNA computes estimates of the optimum from a nonlinear average of a history of iterations produced by an optimization method like gradient descent. Like in RNA, the prediction step in PCGD is based on a history of parameter values obtained with gradient descent. However, our predictions use parameter specific linear regression rather than a nonlinear average of complete historical iterations. Making parameter specific predictions with linear regression allows our method to update predictions incrementally, which removes the need to keep all historical iterations relevant to a particular prediction. RNA must store the entire iteration history relevant to a particular prediction, which makes this method unfeasible for training large neural networks.

[1] One caution ought to be mentioned here: brain predictions also enable prejudices, so one must be careful how much trust is placed in predictions.

3 Methodology

PCGD uses best fit predictions and stochastic gradient descent in tandem. When estimating the trend in the network parameters through training, we will use fit functions for which the least squares problem has a closed form solution using the normal equations. One could use more complex fit functions, but we want to avoid needing an extra iterative process. Using only least squares problems with closed form solutions to make parameter predictions also saves memory because they can be solved incrementally, avoiding the need to store a long history of network snapshots.

We will define the algorithm around the gradient descent iterations. We will make parameter predictions every p gradient descent iterations and collect snapshots of the network parameters every s^{th} gradient descent iteration where $p > s$ and $s|p$. Parameter predictions only consider the previous p/s network snapshots. Since $p > s$, only a sparse history of snapshots are considered. We'll call p the prediction increment and s the snapshot increment. For the remainder of this paper, the variables p and s will retain this definition.

Suppose our network has n weight and bias parameters. Let $f(\boldsymbol{a}, x) : \mathbb{R}^c \times \mathbb{R} \to \mathbb{R}$ be our chosen fit function class for parameter prediction. For each network parameter, θ, we aim to solve for $\boldsymbol{a}$, such that $f(\boldsymbol{a}, x)$ estimates a future value of θ for a chosen prediction length x. $f(\boldsymbol{a}, x)$ has c unknowns where $c \le p/s$. Define $F(A, x) : \mathbb{R}^{c\times n} \times \mathbb{R} \to \mathbb{R}^n$ such that the ith entry of $F(A, x)$ is $f(\boldsymbol{a}_i, x)$ where $\boldsymbol{a}_i$ is the ith column of A. When using PCGD, network parameter vector $\boldsymbol{\theta} \in \mathbb{R}^n$ receives the update,

$$\begin{aligned} \boldsymbol{v}_t &= -\,\epsilon \nabla L(\boldsymbol{\theta}_t) \\ \boldsymbol{\theta}_{t+1} &= \begin{cases} F(A_{t+1}, l_{t+1}) & \text{if } t+1 \equiv 0 \mod p \\ \boldsymbol{\theta}_t + \boldsymbol{v}_t & \text{otherwise} \end{cases} \end{aligned} \tag{1}$$

where L is the desired loss function, ϵ is some learning rate, $l_{t+1} \ge p/s$ is an increasing prediction length and $A_{t+1} \in \mathbb{R}^{c\times n}$, minimizes the L_2-norms of the columns of $JA_{t+1} - \Theta_{t+1}$. Here, $J \in \mathbb{R}^{(p/s)\times c}$ has entries $J_{i,j} = \partial f(\boldsymbol{a}, i)/\partial a_j$, and the ith row of Θ_{t+1} is the vector $\boldsymbol{\theta}_{t+1-p+is}^{\top}$ for $i < p/s$ and $\boldsymbol{\theta}_t^{\top} + \boldsymbol{v}_t^{\top}$ for $i = p/s$.[2] Note that the columns of A_{t+1} each solve independent least squares problems for particular network parameters; the systems are overdetermined if $c < p/s$. We use one fit function class, f, but calculate network-parameter specific fit function variables. One could easily add regularizers or momentum to the velocity term, $\boldsymbol{v}_t$. l_{t+1} is an increasing prediction length dependent on the gradient descent iteration, but one could also consider an adaptive, or parameter specific prediction length. Iterations, t, in which $t \equiv 0 \mod p$ constitute the 'predictive' step in PCGD, and all other gradient descent iterations comprise the 'corrective' step.

We solve for prediction fit function variables A_{t+1} incrementally so as to minimize the extra storage required to perform PCGD. Fit function variables

[2] Note that the jacobian, J, is not specific to the column of A_{t+1}.

are updated at snapshot intervals. Let $\Theta_{t+1}^{(i)}$ denote the shorter matrix containing only the first i rows of Θ_{t+1}. Similarly, $J^{(i)}$ is the shorter matrix containing only the first i rows of J. When c snapshots have been recorded, we solve $J^{(c)}A_{t+1} = \Theta_{t+1}^{(c)}$ for the fit function variable matrix A_{t+1}; with c snapshots $J^{(c)}A_{t+1} = \Theta_{t+1}^{(c)}$ is a determined system. After this initial solve, only A_{t+1} must still be stored, $\Theta_{t+1}^{(c)}$ is no longer needed. At snapshot intervals $c+1$ through p/s we update the fit function variable matrix using the incremental least squares algorithm found in [3]. That is, for $i \in [c+1, p/s]$, we update,

$$A_{t+1} \leftarrow A_{t+1} + \boldsymbol{y}_i \left(\left(\boldsymbol{\theta}_{t+1}^{(i)} \right)^\top - \boldsymbol{j}_i^\top A_{t+1} \right) \tag{2}$$

where $\left(\boldsymbol{\theta}_{t+1}^{(i)}\right)^\top$ is the ith row in Θ_{t+1}, $\boldsymbol{j}_i^\top$ is the ith row of J, and $\boldsymbol{y}_i$ is the solution to $\left(J^{(i)}\right)^\top J^{(i)}\boldsymbol{y}_i = \boldsymbol{j}_i$.

This process then repeats writing over old fit function variables and parameter history in memory. Since fit functions variables are parameter specific, they can be updated layer-wise. If a network has n total parameters, PCGD requires storing at most an additional $O(cn)$ values in memory at any one time during training when using a fit function with c unknowns. The size of the extra storage is c times the size of layers not being currently being updated plus at most $2c$ times the size of the layer currently being updated.

By using an incremental least squares approach and solving for parameter specific best fit functions, we are able to conserve memory during training; without this approach one would need to store np/s parameter history values. This makes PCGD a feasible technique for training large networks provided c is small. Given the same history, RNA would solve for p/s coefficients for p/s entire network snapshots to obtain a nonlinear average of the whole snapshots [20]. Hence, RNA would require storing all np/s parameter history values. However, for the memory conservation afforded by incrementally updating fix functions, one pays a little extra work. Rather than solving for A_{t+1} directly, one must perform $p/s - c + 1$ incremental updates to A_{t+1}.

It should be noted that this is a general adaptation to stochastic gradient descent that is not specific to neural networks. This method may also appropriate for other high dimensional optimization problems.

4 Relationship to Nesterov's Accelerated Gradient

One could make predictions every iteration, which would bring our method closer to some existing accelerated gradient schemes. If one made predictions every iteration using a linear fit function our algorithm could be written,

$$\boldsymbol{z}_t = \begin{cases} \boldsymbol{\theta}_t & \text{if } t < p \\ A_t^\top \begin{bmatrix} 1 \; l_t \end{bmatrix}^\top & \text{otherwise} \end{cases}$$
$$\boldsymbol{\theta}_{t+1} = \boldsymbol{z}_t - \epsilon \nabla L(\boldsymbol{z}_t)$$

where A_t minimizes the L_2-norms of the columns of $JA_t - \Theta_t$. Here, $J \in \mathbb{R}^{(p/s)\times 2}$ has $\begin{bmatrix} 1^{i-1} \; 2^{i-1} \cdots (p/s)^{i-1} \end{bmatrix}^\top$ for its ith column vector, and $\Theta_t \in \mathbb{R}^{(p/s)\times n}$ has $\boldsymbol{\theta}_{t-p+is}^\top$ for its ith row vector. With $p = 2$ and $s = 1$, this begins to look quite a bit like NAG algorithm which makes the update,

$$\boldsymbol{z}_t = (1 - \gamma_{t-1})\boldsymbol{\theta}_t + \gamma_{t-1}\boldsymbol{\theta}_{t-1} \qquad \text{with } \boldsymbol{z}_0 = \boldsymbol{\theta}_0$$
$$\boldsymbol{\theta}_{t+1} = \boldsymbol{z}_t - \epsilon \nabla L(\boldsymbol{z}_t)$$

for specifically chosen series $\{\gamma_t\}_{t=0}^{\infty}$. With $l_t = 2 - \gamma_{t-1}$ these methods are identical. For continuously differentiable, smooth, convex loss functions NAG can achieve a global convergence rate of $O(1/t^2)$ [2,17]. A natural extension of NAG incorporates a history of three points such that the update is

$$\lambda_t = \left(1 + \sqrt{1 + 4\lambda_{t-r}^2}\right) \Big/ 2$$
$$\boldsymbol{z}_t = \begin{cases} \frac{\lambda_{t-1}}{\lambda_t}\boldsymbol{\theta}_t + \frac{(\lambda_t - 1)}{\lambda_t}\boldsymbol{\theta}_{t-r+1} - \frac{(\lambda_{t-1} - 1)}{\lambda_t}\boldsymbol{\theta}_{t-r} & \text{if } t > r \\ \boldsymbol{\theta}_t & \text{otherwise} \end{cases} \tag{3}$$
$$\boldsymbol{\theta}_{t+1} = \boldsymbol{z}_t - \epsilon \nabla L(\boldsymbol{z}_t)$$

where $\lambda_0, \cdots, \lambda_{r-1} = 0$ and $r \in \mathbb{Z}^{>0}$.

Theorem 1. *Let L be a convex, continuously differentiable and β-smooth function that admits a minimizer $\boldsymbol{\theta}^* \in \mathbb{R}^n$. Given an arbitrary initialization $\boldsymbol{\theta}_0 \in \mathbb{R}^n$, for $T > r$ and $\epsilon = 1/\beta$, update scheme (3) satisfies,*

$$\sum_{t=T-r}^{T} \lfloor (t+1)/r \rfloor^2 \left(L(\boldsymbol{\theta}_{t+1}) - L(\boldsymbol{\theta}^*)\right) \leq 2\beta \|\boldsymbol{z}_r - \boldsymbol{\theta}^*\|_2^2.$$

When $r = 1$ this reduces to NAG . If in addition we assume strong convexity of our objective function L the convergence rate becomes clearer.

Corollary 1. *Let L be strongly convex with parameter $m > 0$, continuously differentiable and β-smooth function that admits a minimizer $\boldsymbol{\theta}^* \in \mathbb{R}^n$. Given an arbitrary initialization $\boldsymbol{\theta}_0 \in \mathbb{R}^n$, for $T > r$ and $\epsilon = 1/\beta$, update scheme (3) satisfies,*

$$\sum_{t=T-r}^{T} \lfloor (t+1)/r \rfloor^2 \left(L(\boldsymbol{\theta}_{t+1}) - L(\boldsymbol{\theta}^*)\right) \leq \frac{\beta^2 \|\boldsymbol{\theta}_0 - \boldsymbol{\theta}^*\|_2^2}{mr}.$$

The order of r in the denominator on each side of the above inequality is the same. Hence, for $m = \beta$, $\min_{t\in\{T-r,\cdots,T\}}\{L(\boldsymbol{\theta}_{t+1}) - L(\boldsymbol{\theta}^*)\}$ converges at the same rate as NAG. The proof of Theorem 1 and Corollary 1 can be found in Appendix A [16].

In this well-behaved, theoretical environment, updating based on a linear combination of older values maintains the convergence rate of NAG. However, update method (3) is not practical for deep learning because it requires $r\times$ the memory to save a history of network parameter values. Instead, making parameter predictions every p^{th} iteration, as in update method (1), makes the additional memory requirement significantly more practical. In the setting of neural network parameters, update method (1) has the capacity to outperform NAG. Considering an evenly distributed history of values extending further in the past allows one to de-noise trends. By incorporating a longer history, method (1) can afford to make predictions further into the future while minimizing additional memory requirements.

In comparison to NAG, employing update scheme (1) requires more memory for the fit function variables A_t, but performs less work as snapshot increment s and prediction increment p increase since fit function updates and parameter predictions happen less often. One must strike a balance though: for large p and large p/s one should be able to predict network parameters with more confidence provided the chosen fit function is well suited for the trend, but large p will exhibit delayed performance. Method (1) introduces a number of new hyperparameters that can be tuned for a particular task.

5 Experimental Results

The goal of our approach is to decrease the number of training epochs needed for a network to reach a particular testing accuracy. To test this, we ran experiments on the SVHN [18], and CIFAR10 [11] datasets using Krizhevsky's cuda-convnet with 4 hidden layers [12]. This net does not produce state-of-art accuracies for these datasets, but rather highlights the improvement seen by PCGD when compared to SGD. We implement our work in Caffe, which provides this architecture in their CIFAR10 "quick" example. We trained using batch size 100. Unless otherwise specified, hyperparameters and initialization distributions provided by Caffe's "quick" architecture are left unchanged. All experiments are run on the Bridges' NVIDIA P100 GPUs through the Pittsburgh Supercomputing Center. Training is done with batched gradient descent using the cross-entropy loss function on the softmax of the output layer.

In this paper we will only use linear fit functions to make parameter predictions. That is, the fit function class is $f(\boldsymbol{a}, x) = a_1 + a_2 x$ and the number of fit function variables to solve for each network parameter is $c = 2$. In this case, a network with n parameters requires storing an additional $2n$ values. If m is the maximum number of iterations we will train, p is the prediction increment and s is the snapshot increment, define $g_{(d,\boldsymbol{u})}(\boldsymbol{b}, t) = b_1 + b_2\,(t/p)^d$ where and $\boldsymbol{b}$ is chosen such that $g_{(d,\boldsymbol{u})}(\boldsymbol{b}, 0) = p/s + u_1$ and $g_{(d,\boldsymbol{u})}(\boldsymbol{b}, m) = p/s + u_2$

for some $u_1, u_2 \in [0, 2p/s]$, $u_1 < u_2$. We chose our prediction length such that $l_t = g_{(d,u)}(\boldsymbol{b}, t)$. This means that at iteration p, PCGD tries to predict what the network weights will be at iteration $p + su_1$ and sets the weights to those predicted values. Similarly, at iteration m, PCGD *would* try to predict what the network weights would be at iteration $m + su_2$, but we do not make the last, or last few, predictions because immediately after predicting there is often a slight drop in accuracy that needs to be corrected by some gradient descent steps. This slight drop after predicting could be minimized by less aggressive predictions or better fit function choices, but we chose to simply leave out the last few predictions. It is a good idea to have u_1 small because parameter trends can alter and we do not want to be over-influenced by start-up trends.[1]

We will compare PCGD with NAG and SGD. We also consider a hybrid method combining NAG and PCGD, abbreviated as NAG-PCGD. To combine the two methods we nest NAG updates inside PCGD updates; the update scheme for NAG-PCGD is written out explicitly in Appendix B [16]. When training with PCGD and NAG-PCGD, we use prediction increment $p = 150$, snapshot increment $s = 15$ for all of our experiments. When plotting accuracy results, we will plot the maximum testing accuracy seen so far by that training iteration against iterations. While training, testing accuracy is usually noisy, which can obscure differences in performance when comparing different methods. Plotting the maximum testing accuracy seen so far displays these differences more clearly. There was no noticeable difference in the amount of noise seen in the testing accuracy for the various methods in our experiments.

5.1 SVHN

We experimented on the SVHN dataset with Krizhevsky's cuda-convnet [12]. The base learning rate was 0.001 and dropped by a factor of 10 after 4,000 iterations. Testing took place every 50 training iterations. When training with PCGD and NAG-PCGD, we use prediction length $l_t = g_{(6,[5,10])}(\boldsymbol{b}, t)$.

Figure 1 (Left) plots the maximum accuracy seen so far against iterations using standard SGD, NAG, PCGD and NAG-PCGD. Figure 1 (Right) plots the slopes of the curves in Fig. 1 (Left) versus iteration. We show the iterations of steepest accuracy increase to highlight the difference in convergence rates of the various methods. NAG and NAG-PCGD initially increase at nearly the same rate which is $\approx 4\times$ faster than PCGD and SGD. Around iteration 450 PCGD leaves behind SGD, begins to catch up to NAG and eventually supersedes it. NAG-PCGD tends to hug the top of all the other curves exhibiting the benefits of both sub-methods. Confined to 2000 iterations, NAG-PCGD gives the best results. At iterations 4000 when the learning rate decreases by a factor of 10, there is another jump in accuracy where we can see the difference in convergence rates again on a smaller scale.

After 9000 iterations, the network trained using traditional SGD achieves a final accuracy of 91.96%, NAG has a final accuracy of 92.38%, PCGD has a final accuracy of 92.42%, and NAG-PCGD has a final accuracy of 92.34%. SGD hit a maximum testing accuracy of 92.06% at iteration 8600, NAG took

4700 iterations to reach this accuracy level, PCGD also took 4700 iterations and NAG-PCGD took 5100 iterations. That is, PCGD reached SGD's testing maximum in just over half the number of training iterations that SGD took.

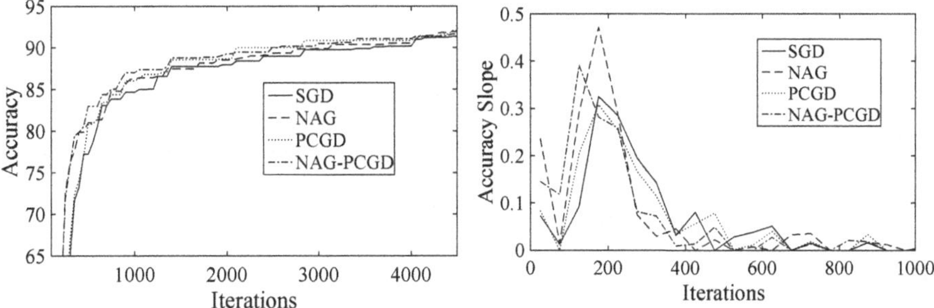

Fig. 1. (Left) Maximum accuracy results on the SVHN data set. Testing takes place every 50 training iterations (Right) slope of left figure versus iterations.

5.2 CIFAR10

We also trained Krizhevsky's cuda-convnet on the CIFAR10 for 195,000 iterations. The base learning rate was 0.001. We dropped the learning rate by a factor of 10 after 60,000 iterations and again after 125,000 iterations. Testing took place every 250 training iterations. We used $l_t = g_{(4,[5,10])}(\boldsymbol{b}, t)$ for our prediction length at prediction intervals.

Figure 2 (Left) shows maximum accuracy results through training using SGD, NAG, PCGD and NAG-PCGD. Again, we show only the iterations of steepest accuracy increase. Here, the testing increment is larger than our prediction increment which may hide any initial convergence advantage of NAG over PCGD. Given more time to excel, PCGD shows performance advantages over NAG; NAG does not even consistently outperform SGD per iteration. At any one time, NAG is at most 3.18% more accurate than SGD, PCGD is at most 3.91% more accurate than SGD, and NAG-PCGD is at most 6.49% more accurate than SGD.

Figure 2 (Right) shows, for a given accuracy, the percent of SGD iterations each method took to reach that accuracy. That is, if it took SGD x iterations to reach a particular accuracy for the first time, and PCGD took y iterations to reach that accuracy for the first time, then the value plotted for PCGD at that accuracy is $100 \times y/x$. This figure shows PCGD generally reaching particular accuracies before SGD and NAG-PCGD generally reaching accuracies before PCGD. SGD took 114,000 iterations to become 81.7% accurate. Training with NAG yielded 81.7% accuracy in 73% of the iterations required by SGD to reach this accuracy, training with PCGD yielded 81.7% accuracy in 56% of the iterations required by SGD and training with NAG-PCGD yielded 81.7% accuracy in 50% of the iterations required by SGD. That is, PCGD took only 77% of the iterations required by NAG to reach 81.7% accuracy.

For these values of s and p, using PCGD does not noticeably increase the average iteration runtime when compared with SGD. For both methods, the average forward-backward pass took ≈46 ms when using batch size 100 on Bridges' NVIDIA P100 GPU; time was measured using caffe time benchmarks.

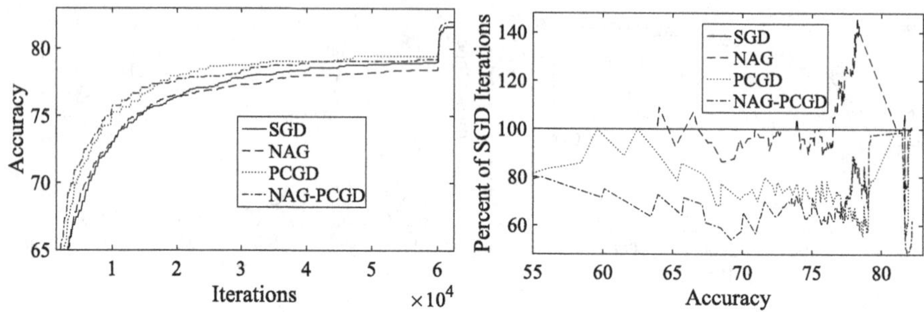

Fig. 2. Results on the CIFAR10 data set. (Left) Maximum accuracy versus iterations. Testing takes place every 250 training iterations. (Right) Percent of SGD iterations each method took to reach a particular accuracy.

6 Conclusion

We have developed a general adaptation to gradient descent and considered the impact in the case of training neural networks. Predictor-Corrector Gradient Descent reduces the number of iterations required to learn by incorporating traditional predictor-corrector inspired ideas into classic gradient descent.

We have shown that PCGD can significantly decreases the number of training epochs needed for a network to reach a particular testing accuracy when compared to stochastic gradient descent. On both datasets considered, PCGD reduced the number of required iterations to reach SGD maximum accuracy by nearly one half. When two identical networks are allowed to train for the same number of iterations, the networks trained using PCGD regularly outperforms the network trained using SGD. We have also shown that PCGD can outperform Nesterov's Accelerated Gradient for more complex learning problems requiring more training. By substantially reducing the number of iterations required to reach a particular accuracy, PCGD can make training large networks more feasible in cases where one can afford to increase the training storage by a small constant multiple.

We have also considered the theoretical case of a strongly convex, continuously differentiable and smooth objective function and showed that updating parameters as a linear combination of historical values preserves the convergence rate of NAG. Although our experimental environment is far from this hypothetical one, this theory holds true when using PCGD to train neural networks. After an initial delay, we found PCGD can outperform NAG.

In this work, we only used linear fit functions and a single prediction length for every network parameter. These choices worked well, but there is room for additional exploration. One may see further improvement by using a dynamic value for the prediction interval p.

Acknowledgments. This material is based upon work supported by the National Science Foundation Graduate Research Fellowship under Grant No. DGE-1256260. This work used the Extreme Science and Engineering Discovery Environment, which is supported by National Science Foundation grant number OCI-1053575. Specifically, it used the Bridges system, which is supported by NSF award number ACI-1445606, at the Pittsburgh Supercomputing Center.

References

1. Andrychowicz, M., et al.: Learning to learn by gradient descent by gradient descent. In: NIPS (2016)
2. Beck, A., et al.: A fast iterative shrinkage-thresholding algorithm for linear inverse problems. SIAM J. Imaging Sci. **2**(1), 183–202 (2009)
3. Cassioli, A., et al.: An incremental least squares algorithm for large scale linear classification. Eur. J. Oper. Res. **224**(3), 560–565 (2013)
4. Daniel, C., et al.: Learning step size controllers for robust neural network training. In: AAAI (2016)
5. Dozat, T.: Incorporating Nesterov momentum into Adam. In: ICLR Workshop (2016)
6. Duchi, J., et al.: Adaptive subgradient methods for online learning and stochastic optimization. JMLR **12**, 2121–2159 (2011)
7. Heeger, D.J.: Theory of cortical function. Proc. Natl. Acad. Sci. USA **114**(8), 1773–1782 (2016)
8. Ho, Q., et al.: More effective distributed ML via a stale synchronous parallel parameter server. In: NIPS, pp. 1223–1231 (2013)
9. Hratchian, H., et al.: Steepest descent reaction path integration using a first-order predictor-corrector method. J. Chem. Phys. **133**(22), 224101 (2010)
10. Kingma, D., et al.: Adam: a method for stochastic optimization. In: ICLR (2015)
11. Krizhevsky, A.: Learning multiple layers of features from tiny images. Technical report, Computer Science, University of Toronto (2009)
12. Krizhevsky, A.: cuda-convnet. Technical report, Computer Science, University of Toronto (2012)
13. Krizhevsky, A., et al.: ImageNet classification with deep convolutional neural networks. In: NIPS, pp. 1106–1114 (2012)
14. Luca, M.D., et al.: Optimal perceived timing: integrating sensory information with dynamically updated expectations. Sci. Rep. **6**, 28563 (2016)
15. Neelakantan, A., et al.: Adding gradient noise improves learning for very deep networks. arXiv:1511.06807 (2015)
16. Nesky, A., et al.: Training neural networks using predictor-corrector gradient descent: Appendix (2018). http://www-personal.umich.edu/~anesky/PCGD_appendix.pdf
17. Nesterov, Y.: A method of solving a convex programming problem with convergence rate o(1/sqr(k)). Soviet Mathematics Doklady **27**, 372–376 (1983)

18. Netzer, Y., et al.: Reading digits in natural images with unsupervised feature learning. In: NIPS Workshop on Deep Learning and Unsupervised Feature Learning (2011)
19. Polyak, B.: Some methods of speeding up the convergence of iteration methods. USSR Comput. Math. Math. Phys. **4**(5), 1–17 (1964)
20. Scieur, D., et al.: Regularized nonlinear acceleration. In: NIPS (2016)
21. Simonetto, A., et al.: Prediction-correction methods for time-varying convex optimization. In: IEEE Asilomar Conference on Signals, Systems and Computers (2015)
22. Süli, E., et al.: An Introduction to Numerical Analysis, pp. 325–329 (2003)
23. Tieleman, T., et al.: Lecture 6a - rmsprop. COURSERA: Neural Networks for Machine Learning (2012)
24. Zeiler, M.D.: ADADELTA: an adaptive learning rate method. arXiv:1212.5701 (2012)
25. Zhang, Y., et al.: Prediction-adaptation-correction recurrent neural networks for low-resource language speech recognition. arXiv:1510.08985 (2015)
26. Zhang, Y., et al.: Speech recognition with prediction-adaptation-correction recurrent neural networks. In: IEEE ICASSP (2015)

Investigating the Role of Astrocyte Units in a Feedforward Neural Network

Peter Gergel'(✉) and Igor Farkaš

Faculty of Mathematics, Physics and Informatics, Comenius University in Bratislava
Mlynská dolina, 84248 Bratislava, Slovak Republic
peter.gergel@gmail.com, farkas@fmph.uniba.sk
http://cogsci.fmph.uniba.sk

Abstract. Current research in neuroscience has begun to shift perspective from neurons as sole information processors to including the astrocytes as equal and cooperating units in this function. Recent evidence sheds new light on astrocytes and presents them as important regulators of neuronal activity and synaptic plasticity. In this paper, we present a multi-layer perceptron (MLP) with artificial astrocyte units which listen to and regulate hidden neurons based on their activity. We test the behavior and performance of this bio-inspired model on two classification tasks, N-parity problem and the two-spirals problem and show that proposed models outperform the standard MLP. Interestingly, we have also discovered multiple regimes of astrocyte activity depending on the complexity of the problem.

Keywords: Glial cells · Astrocytes · MLP · Classification
Computational model

1 Introduction

Glial cells, predominantly astrocytes, have gained a lot of attention in neuroscience during the last few decades, as compelling evidence has shown that these cells are no longer considered as passive and supportive but are actively involved in neuronal regulation and synaptic plasticity [1,12]. The classical view on astrocytes supports the idea that they are inevitable in the development of the central nervous system, providing metabolic and physical support to other neural cells, or maintaining homeostasis. It was assumed that astrocytes were not able to generate actions potentials similar to neurons, or be involved in brain functions such as information transfer and processing, learning, and plasticity, i.e. functions attributed solely to neurons.

However, recent research has challenged this view as it was discovered that astrocytes were characterized as having resting membrane potential of $\sim-80\,\text{mV}$, pairing $\sim$1.4 astrocytes for every neuron in the human cortex [3] and encapsulating $\sim10^5$ synapses [5]. This led to a novel concept of an intimate connection between neurons and astrocytes named the *tripartite synapse.* Moreover, astrocytes release gliotransmitters to local neurons and propagate Ca^{2+} waves using

V. Kůrková et al. (Eds.): ICANN 2018, LNCS 11141, pp. 73–83, 2018.
https://doi.org/10.1007/978-3-030-01424-7_8

a cellular network called *glial syncytium*, although the signalization occurs on a much slower time scale ranging from seconds to minutes, as opposed to neurons whose time scale is milliseconds. This implies the existence of a bidirectional communication between astrocytes and neurons whose importance is still not well understood.

Still, it is assumed that the brain function and possibly higher cognition emerge from the coordinated activity of astrocytes and neurons in neuron–glia networks [11]. A better understanding of astrocyte–neuron coupling may lead to providing building blocks for studying the regulatory capability of astrocytic networks on a larger scale. Computational models of neural networks extended with artificial glia may not only be used as an interesting novel concept, but mainly to provide space for hypotheses for the potential roles of glial cells in biological neuronal circuits and networks.

In this paper we propose a model of a MLP extended with artificial astrocytes whose role is to regulate neuronal activity. For evaluating the model performance we chose the classification task using two datasets: N-parity and two spirals. The paper is organized as follows. Section 2 includes the related work. In Sect. 3, we describe various versions of the investigated model. In Sect. 4, we provide the experimental results. Section 5 concludes the paper.

2 Related Work

In computational neuroscience two modeling paradigms have so far been considered: (1) biophysical with the focus on low–level physical and chemical properties of a biological system or (2) connectionist which does not try to model every single aspect of a system, but instead focuses on abstractions. Despite the plethora of biophysical models of astrocytes, connectionist modeling is still in a pre-mature state.

The concept of artificial astrocytes in connectionist systems was first introduced in [6] where authors augmented the hidden layer of an MLP with an astrocytic network whose function was to generate chaotic noise according to the given tent map formula as a means of avoiding local minima during gradient optimization. On the two-spirals problem the model achieved better performance than the regular MLP. Later, the same authors presented multiple works including impulse astrocytes with active listening and regulation of neurons based on their activity [7], Hopfield network augmented with astrocytes [9], or neurogenesis driven by astrocytes [8].

Similar approach was taken in [13] and [2] where instead of modeling the neuronal regulation, the authors focused on modeling synaptic plasticity driven solely by astrocytes. Using an MLP with combination of evolutionary algorithms they showed that the model with artificial astrocytes was superior to the model without them. Using computer simulations they demonstrated that the model was able to learn various problems despite the fact that no gradient-based method was used for training neural networks.

Finally, in [10], the authors presented a model, SONG-Net, that combines an MLP, a self-organizing map (SOM) and neuron–glial interactions. By evaluating the performance on four tasks, they showed that the proposed model achieved faster convergence up to twelve times with a lower error rate. However, the authors did not present glia as individual functional units, but instead they were used only as an inspiration for the concept of neuronal regulation.

3 Proposed Models

Here we present multiple models, all based on an MLP combined with artificial astrocytes. We start with a simplest model to allow faster in–depth exploration, and we gradually move toward adding more complex, yet biologically plausible mechanisms.

3.1 A-MLP

Since the human cortex contains on average 1.4 astrocytes for each neuron, we simplify this notion and present a model with the ratio of astrocyte to neuron being 1:1. Inspired by [7] we combine the hidden layer of an MLP with impulse astrocytes that listen to and modulate neuronal activity of hidden neurons (Fig. 1).

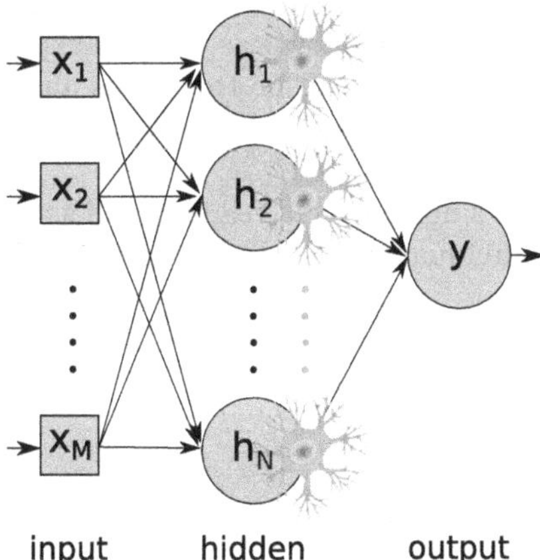

Fig. 1. Basic MLP architecture with astrocyte units (A-MLP). Each hidden neuron is paired with an astrocyte that listens to and regulates its regime based on activity. Since we consider binary classification problems, only one output unit is used.

The output of i-th hidden neuron is given by the following formula

$$h_i(t+1) = f(\sum_{j=0}^{M} w_{ij}x_j(t) + \alpha\psi_i(t)) \tag{1}$$

where the activation function is

$$f(net) = \frac{1}{1 + \exp(-net)} \tag{2}$$

and the astrocyte activity is modified as

$$\psi_i(t) = \begin{cases} 1, & \text{if } \theta < h_i(t-1) \\ \gamma\psi_i(t-1), & \text{otherwise} \end{cases} \tag{3}$$

Each astrocyte contributes, with a weight α, to the activity of the hidden neuron (Eq. 1). When the neuron output exceeds the given threshold θ, the astrocyte activation is set to 1 and then starts to decay by a factor γ, where $0 < \gamma < 1$.

Note that the model consists of three free hyperparameters whose optimal values have to be found experimentally. Since each problem requires a different set of optimal parameters, finding them requires time-intensive computations. We try to solve these issues by replacing constant parameters with modifiable versions.

3.2 A-MLP(α)

Traditionally in supervised model learning, the neuron weights are updated using a gradient descent method, better known as error backpropagation algorithm. Since the astrocytic weight in Eq. 1 can be treated as any other weight, we can apply the same optimization method for its update (derivation of the formula is provided in appendix).

Next, instead of using a single mutual weight for all astrocytes, we equip each astrocyte unit with an individual weight. The activation rule for the hidden unit then becomes

$$h_i(t+1) = f(\sum_{j=0}^{M} w_{ij}x_j(t) + \alpha_i\psi_i(t)) \tag{4}$$

3.3 A-MLP(θ)

Since we cannot directly update the parameter θ (Eq. 3) using a gradient-based method, we propose an unsupervised learning rule. It is relatively common that during training some neurons may get trapped in one of the two extremes, by becoming either dead or permanently active. The weight update of such neurons becomes problematic, because the gradient is close to zero and no errors would propagate through a dead neuron, therefore no update would occur. On the other hand, weights might grow into large values affecting other neurons in the network, making the model unstable.

The same issue may happen in artificial astrocytes when the threshold θ is set too low, making the astrocytes fire all the time, or too high, preventing the neighboring neurons from exceeding the required activation. Moreover, since each neuron in the neural network develops its own role in the classification task, single shared θ for all neurons may become more of a burden than benefit.

To solve these problems, we propose an individual θ_i for each astrocyte and two variations of an update rule. In order to stabilize the astrocytic regime, we can set the threshold θ either directly to the mean value $\langle . \rangle_t$ (Eq. 5) of an astrocyte unit or only shift the threshold slightly closer to the mean value (Eq. 6) using the learning speed η_θ. This forces the astrocyte to move only within its mean values avoiding the critical values of 0 and 1. With a higher θ it becomes harder for the neuron to overpass, thus the activity decays and vice versa. Hence, the update rules are

$$\theta_i(t+1) = \langle \psi_i(t) \rangle_t \tag{5}$$

and

$$\theta_i(t+1) = \theta_i(t) + \eta_\theta(\langle \psi_i(t) \rangle_t - \theta_i(t)) \tag{6}$$

introducing another free parameter, namely the length of an averaging window.

3.4 A-MLP(γ)

Hyperparameter γ can be updated based on the same principle as explained in the previous section. This time we update γ to achieve inverse correlation with the mean value of the astrocytic activity

$$\gamma_i(t+1) = 1 - \langle \psi_i(t) \rangle_t \tag{7}$$

$$\gamma_i(t+1) = \gamma_i(t) + \eta_\gamma(1 - \langle \psi_i(t) \rangle_t - \gamma_i(t)) \tag{8}$$

Higher values of γ are achieved during a lower activity, thus a hypo-excited astrocyte holds its activation value for a longer period. On the other hand, lower γ triggers faster output decay forcing the astrocyte to avoid excessive simulation.

3.5 A-MLP(γ, θ), A-MLP(α, γ, θ)

Finally, the last two models are simple combinations of previous ideas. A-MLP (γ, θ) combines models with dynamic θs and γs and A-MLP(α, γ, θ) includes dynamic αs as well.

4 Experiments

We assess the performance of all six proposed models and standard MLP (without astrocyte units) as a baseline, on two difficult classification tasks: (1) N-parity problem and (2) two spirals problem. All results are averaged over 100 simulations with different initial setups. The learning rate in backpropagation algorithm is set to $\eta = 0.1$.

4.1 N-parity Problem

The task is to determine whether a binary input vector has even or odd number of ones. More formally, an input vector has the form $[x_1, \ldots, x_N], x_i = \{0, 1\}$ and the target $y = (1 + \sum_{i=1}^{N} x_i) \mod 2$. Since the problem is notoriously difficult to generalize to unseen patterns for machine learning algorithms, we train the models on full dataset (no train/test split) whose total size is 2^N.

Starting with MLP, we chose the hidden layer with N neurons (a higher amount did not yield better results) and output layer of only single neuron (0 = odd input vector, 1 = even input vector). Proposed models with astrocyte units had the following values for fixed hyperparameters: $\alpha = -0.5, \gamma = 0.5, \theta = 0.5$ (previously found using the grid search). In Table 1 we present performance of all models and although we see models with astrocyte units lead on average to better performance, the differences are not statistically significant ($p > 0.1$).

Next, in order to get insight into learned parameters, we displayed the distributions of astrocyte activities (shown in Fig. 2). It can be seen that astrocytes develop various regimes depending on the problem complexity. With lower N it is possible to clearly detect N astrocyte regimes, but with higher N the profiles gradually lose their multimodality, albeit remaining non uniformly distributed.

Table 1. Mean squared error (MSE) + standard deviation of 100 instances on three parity problems trained for 10000 epochs. Models with astrocyte units yield lower error rate although no statistical significance was found. In each task, the best model is denoted with $*$.

Model	4-parity	6-parity	8-parity
MLP	0.081 ± 0.060	0.065 ± 0.035	0.046 ± 0.070
A-MLP	0.083 ± 0.086	$0.059 \pm 0.034*$	0.039 ± 0.023
A-MLP(α)	0.080 ± 0.065	0.072 ± 0.054	0.073 ± 0.069
A-MLP(θ)	0.083 ± 0.075	0.065 ± 0.036	$0.037 \pm 0.021*$
A-MLP(γ)	0.087 ± 0.065	0.062 ± 0.034	0.042 ± 0.026
A-MLP(γ, θ)	$0.074 \pm 0.051*$	0.063 ± 0.055	0.042 ± 0.027
A-MLP(α, γ, θ)	0.092 ± 0.072	0.078 ± 0.056	0.056 ± 0.028

4.2 Two-Spirals Problem

The two spirals consist of two interleaved sets of points in 2D space (Fig. 3). The problem is, given point (x, y), to decide whether it belongs to the first or the second spiral. This is considered a complex nonlinear problem and hard for a standard MLP due to a high number of local minima which are generally rather problematic for gradient-based models.

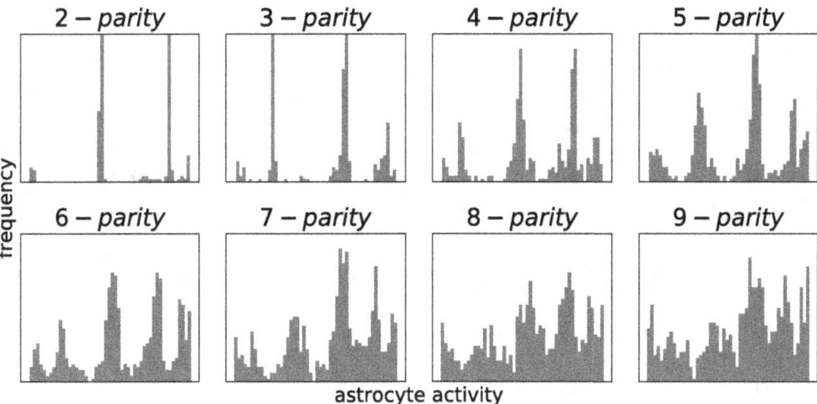

Fig. 2. Distributions of astrocyte activity (across 100 simulations) after being fully trained on a parity problem. With lower N it is possible to detect N peaks assuming that each astrocyte handles a single bit from an input vector. On the other hand, with higher N, the peaks become less visible.

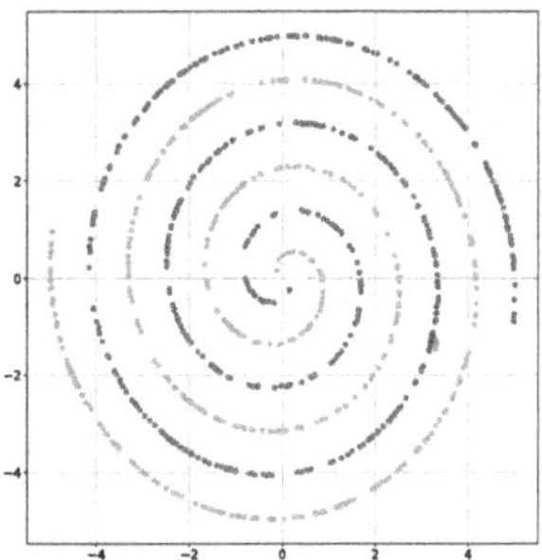

Fig. 3. Two-spirals problem where the task is to separate the interleaved classes.

For the simulations we firstly found optimal hyperparameter values for MLP and then used them in models with astrocyte units. We used $N = 30$ hidden neurons (more units did not produce better results), 5000 training epochs and train/test dataset split in ratio 80:20. For models with astrocytes we found optimal hyperparameters using grid search (presented in Fig. 4) and hence used the values: $\alpha = -0.1$, $\gamma = 0.5$, $\theta = 0.1$.

Results averaged over 100 simulations are in Table 2 with A-MLP(γ, θ) being the best model yielding 50% lower error rate compared to the standard MLP. Similarly we looked at astrocyte activities of the fully trained network and observed normal distribution shown in Fig. 6.

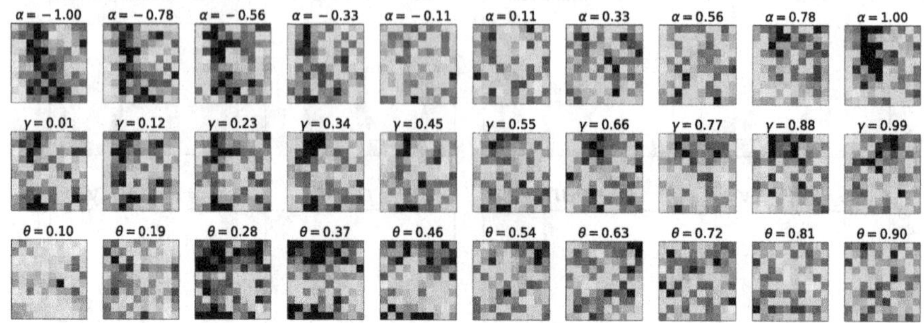

Fig. 4. Grid search for optimal values of hyperparameters. Each heatmap uses a fixed single parameter (shown in the title) and displays all combinations for the other two parameters. Each cell in every heatmap is averaged over 5 simulations with lighter color denoting better performance.

Table 2. Mean-squared error + standard deviation over 100 instances on the two-spirals task trained for 5000 epochs. The best model, A-MLP(γ, θ), yields 50% lower error rate compared to the MLP with statistical significance ($p < 0.001$) (Fig. 5).

Model	Train	Test
MLP	0.075 ± 0.067	0.094 ± 0.066
A-MLP	0.073 ± 0.067	0.088 ± 0.068
A-MLP(α)	0.050 ± 0.049	0.078 ± 0.050
A-MLP(θ)	0.034 ± 0.045	0.049 ± 0.046
A-MLP(γ)	0.068 ± 0.065	0.085 ± 0.063
A-MLP(γ, θ)	$0.030 \pm 0.035*$	$0.051 \pm 0.041*$
A-MLP(α, γ, θ)	0.060 ± 0.051	0.095 ± 0.051

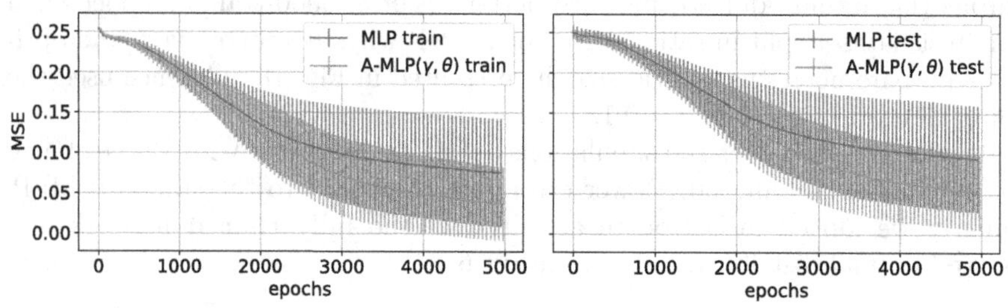

Fig. 5. Performance of the best model, A-MLP(γ, θ), compared to MLP on both training and testing sets.

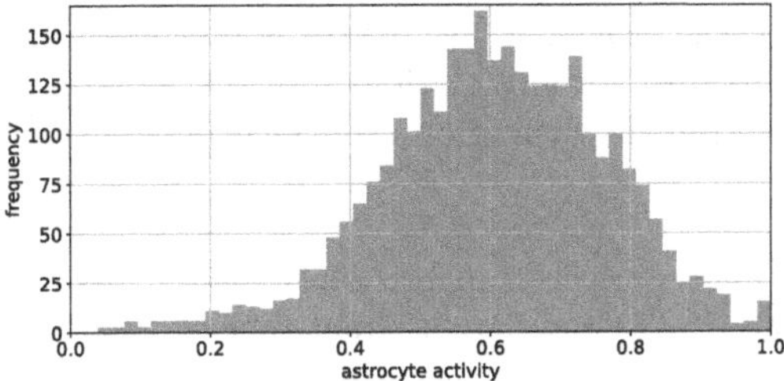

Fig. 6. Normal distribution of astrocyte activity ($N = 30$) at the end of training, accumulated over 100 simulations.

5 Conclusion

Inspired by [7] and the recent findings from biological research of astrocyte physiology and their interactions with surrounding neurons, we proposed artificial astrocyte units to be integrated in a MLP.

It is known that astrocytes in CNS form networks in which they communicate using Ca^{2+} waves whose purpose according to current knowledge is to regulate neuronal activity and synaptic plasticity. In this paper we focused exclusively on neuronal regulation using separate astrocytes each maintaining a single neuron. Astrocytes contribute in neuronal summation formula (Eq. 4) weighted by the factor α_i which was either constant or dynamic. However, the dynamic change of a weight along the negative gradient of the loss function does not always provide better results (as in N-parity problem). We also proposed two methods for dynamic update of both the astrocyte threshold and the decay (Eqs. 5–8) with the second formula performing better than the first one which we used in all our simulations.

We chose two classification problems, N-parity and two spirals, which are known to be rather problematic for machine learning algorithms, so we used them for analysis of the performance and behavior of our models. For both problems we first selected an MLP with optimal parameters (the number of hidden neurons, the learning rate, initial weight distribution) and then used them in models with astrocyte units. The results obtained for N-parity did not outperform MLP, assuming that all models already converged to the global minimum. However, for the two spirals all our models performed better in terms of the lower errors with statistical significance ($p < 0.001$). Both problems developed unique astrocyte regimes in terms of output distributions whose shape depended on the number of astrocytes in case of N-parity problem and was gaussian in the two spirals task. Understanding of this phenomenon requires further investigations.

For our future research we would like to focus on a different set of problems trying to explain why astrocyte regimes develop and how important they are for the given problem. We only focused on feedforward models, but it makes sense to apply the very same idea to recurrent neural networks. Another issue worth investigation would be to adjust the dynamics of astrocytes. In our models, astrocyte parameters were updated at the same speed as weights, but it is known that the dynamics of the biological astrocytes is much slower [4]. Last but not least, since we only focused on modulations of single neurons, we would like to connect astrocytes within the syncytium and incorporate their role in synaptic plasticity.

Acknowledgments. This work was supported by grant UK/256/2018 from Comenius University in Bratislava (P.G.) and Slovak Grant Agency for Science, project VEGA 1/0796/18 (I.F.)

Appendix: Derivation of the update formula

Here we derive formula for stochastic (online) update of astrocyte weights α_i in models A-MLP(α) and A-MLP(α, θ, γ). The goal is to minimize the loss function $E(w) = 1/2(d - y(x))^2$, by moving the astrocytic weights along the negative gradient, i.e. $\Delta\alpha_i = -\partial E(w)/\partial\alpha_i$. Since E is differentiable with respect to α_i, we can write using the chain rule,

$$\Delta\alpha_i = -\frac{\partial E}{\partial y}\frac{\partial y}{\partial net_y}\frac{\partial net_y}{\partial h_i}\frac{\partial h_i}{\partial net_{hi}}\frac{\partial net_{hi}}{\partial \alpha_i} \tag{9}$$

$$\Delta\alpha_i = -\overbrace{(d - y(x))y(x)(1 - y(x))}^{\delta_y}\, w_{yh_i} h_i(1 - h_i)\psi_i \tag{10}$$

$$\Delta\alpha_i = -\overbrace{\delta_y w_{yh_i} h_i(1 - h_i)}^{\delta_i}\,\psi_i \tag{11}$$

which yields the final formula:

$$\Delta\alpha_i = -\delta_i\psi_i \tag{12}$$

References

1. Allen, N.J., Barres, B.A.: Signaling between glia and neurons: focus on synaptic plasticity. Curr. Opin. Neurobiol. **15**(5), 542–548 (2005)
2. Alvarellos-González, A., Pazos, A., Porto-Pazos, A.B.: Computational models of neuron-astrocyte interactions lead to improved efficacy in the performance of neural networks. Comput. Math. Methods Med. (2012). https://doi.org/10.1155/2012/476324
3. Bass, N.H., Hess, H.H., Pope, A., Thalheimer, C.: Quantitative cytoarchitectonic distribution of neurons, glia, and DNA in rat cerebral cortex. J. Comp. Neurol. **143**(4), 481–490 (1971)
4. Cornell-Bell, A.H., Finkbeiner, S.M., Cooper, M.S., Smith, S.J.: Glutamate induces calcium waves in cultured astrocytes: long-range glial signaling. Science **247**(4941), 470–473 (1990)
5. Halassa, M.M., Fellin, T., Takano, H., Dong, J.H., Haydon, P.G.: Synaptic islands defined by the territory of a single astrocyte. J. Neurosci. **27**(24), 6473–6477 (2007)

6. Ikuta, C., Uwate, Y., Nishio, Y.: Multi-layer perceptron with chaos glial network. In: IEEE Workshop on Nonlinear Circuit, Networks, pp. 11–13 (2009)
7. Ikuta, C., Uwate, Y., Nishio, Y.: Multi-layer perceptron with impulse glial network. In: IEEE Workshop on Nonlinear Circuit, Networks, pp. 9–11 (2010)
8. Ikuta, C., Uwate, Y., Nishio, Y.: Investigation of multi-layer perceptron with pulse glial chain including neurogenesis. In: IEEE Workshop on Nonlinear Circuit, Networks, pp. 70–72 (2014)
9. Ikuta, C., Uwate, Y., Nishio, Y., Yang, G.: Hopfield neural network with glial network. In: International Workshop on Nonlinear Circuits, pp. 369–372 (2012)
10. Marzouki, K.: Neuro-glial interaction: SONG-Net. In: Arik, S., Huang, T., Lai, W.K., Liu, Q. (eds.) ICONIP 2015. LNCS, vol. 9491, pp. 619–626. Springer, Cham (2015). https://doi.org/10.1007/978-3-319-26555-1_70
11. Nedergaard, M., Ransom, B., Goldman, S.A.: New roles for astrocytes: redefining the functional architecture of the brain. Trends Neurosci. **26**(10), 523–530 (2003)
12. Parpura, V., Basarsky, T.A., Liu, F., Jeftinija, K., Jeftinija, S., Haydon, P.G.: Glutamate-mediated astrocyte-neuron signalling. Nature **369**(6483), 744 (1994)
13. Porto-Pazos, A.B., et al.: Artificial astrocytes improve neural network performance. PLoS ONE **6**(4), e19109 (2011)

Interactive Area Topics Extraction with Policy Gradient

Jingfei Han[1], Wenge Rong[1(✉)], Fang Zhang[2], Yutao Zhang[2], Jie Tang[2], and Zhang Xiong[1]

[1] School of Computer Science and Engineering, Beihang University, Beijing, China
{jfhan,w.rong,xiongz}@buaa.edu.cn
[2] Department of Computer Science and Technology, Tsinghua University, Beijing, China
{fang-zha15,yt-zhang13}@mails.tsinghua.edu.cn, jietang@tsinghua.edu.cn

Abstract. Extracting representative topics and improving the extraction performance is rather challenging. In this work, we formulate a novel problem, called *Interactive Area Topics Extraction*, and propose a learning interactive topics extraction (LITE) model to regard this problem as a sequential decision making process and construct an end-to-end framework to use interaction with users. In particular, we use recurrent neural network (RNN) decoder to address the problem and policy gradient method to tune the model parameters considering user feedback. Experimental result has shown the effectiveness of the proposed framework.

Keywords: Interactive area topics extraction · RNN decoder
Policy gradient

1 Introduction

Extracting representative topics of an area plays an increasingly important role in trend analysis or historical analysis. It can help researchers learn overview of some disciplines or areas, grasp the development trend, and discover the potential research points [20]. In addition, the newcomers to an area can be guided to find hot topics by the topics extraction of the area.

Much attention has been paid to extracting hypernym-hyponym relationship from big corpora or knowledge base [10,18]. In academic vocabulary, extracting hypernym-hyponym relationship is equivalent to the topic of a given area [1]. However, there are too many topics in an area according to the automatic extraction from text. For example, the hypernym "AI" (Artificial Intelligence) includes many coarse-grained hyponym such as "Machine Learning" and fine-grained hyponym such as "Support Vector Machine". It is necessary to extract the representative topics of a given area automatically because people cannot gain useful information from too many hypernym-hyponym relationship. Earlier works [2,12] mainly focused on topics extraction from documents but not areas.

V. Kůrková et al. (Eds.): ICANN 2018, LNCS 11141, pp. 84–93, 2018.
https://doi.org/10.1007/978-3-030-01424-7_9

Recently, Zhang et al. [20] tried extract topics for areas based on knowledge base [14], while the overall performance is greatly affected by the knowledge base. Hence, we try to use additional information such as user feedback to improve the extraction performance.

Interactive area topics extraction has rarely been explored. The major challenges lie in formally formulating the problem, extracting the representative topics with user feedback, and designing experiments and evaluation to prove the method's effectiveness. To address the aforementioned challenges, we design a Learning Interactive Topics Extraction (LITE) to consider topics sequences extraction of a given area and user feedback and map it into an end-to-end framework. The major contributions of this paper include: (1) We formulate interactive area topics extraction as a sequential decision making problem, and model interaction with users. (2) We propose an LITE, which applies a recurrent decoder to model the topics generation of a given area and uses policy gradient based reinforcement learning method to introduce user feedback or interaction. (3) We design experiments on synthetic dataset to evaluate the proposed model. Experimental results prove the effectiveness of the proposed model.

2 Related Work

Various approaches have been proposed to extract topics from document and knowledge base, including topic model and keyphrase extraction. As to topic model, Blei et al. [2] proposed Latent Dirichlet Allocation (LDA), whose main idea is that each document consists of many topics and the probability of each word appearing in the topic is different. The topic's probability provides an explicit representation of a specific document. However, it is hard to identify what topics stand for because topics in LDA are multinomial distributions over words. We need to label the topics if we need this information. Although many researchers have conducted extensive research on automation of LDA [9,11], there is a clear gap between automatic labeling and manual labeling.

Keyphrase extraction mainly includes two approaches: supervised learning and unsupervised learning. In supervised learning, Jiang et al. [7] sort candidate keyword set by features. They regard the problem as a ranking problem and use Ranking SVM to address this problem. In unsupervised learning, Hasan et al. divide unsupervised learning researches into four groups [6]: graph-based ranking, topic-based clustering, simultaneous learning, and language modeling. In addition, Zhang et al. [20] propose a FastKATE model feed knowledge bases into the model to extract topics of a given area. However, it is difficult to generate or gain a clean taxonomy. Hence, we try to introduce interaction with users to improve the performance of extraction.

Many researchers also try to introduce user feedback to improve performance for their tasks. Yang et al. [19] predict a user's intention based on user's feedback for some questions by their proposed model in order to understand user intention interactively. Carlson et al. [3] design a knowledge base called NELL, which can make an iterative learning by interacting with a human for 10–15 min each day.

Deldjoo et al. [5] use interactive information to alter the recommendation results so that the recommendation can increase the user satisfaction.

3 Methodology

3.1 Problem Formulation

Firstly we give formal definition of the basic terms in this research. **Concept** in the following section refers to a set of all knowledge entities, like a vocabulary list. It contains any knowledge from coarse-grained concept such as "Computer Science" to fine-grained concept such as "Backpropagation". **Area** is a subset of concept, whose elements include hyponym concept. **Topic** is also a subset of concept, but all topic's elements have hypernym concept. Let $\mathcal{C}$ denote concept space, $\mathcal{X}$ denote area space and $\mathcal{Y}$ denote topic space where $\mathcal{X} \subset \mathcal{C}$ and $\mathcal{Y} \subset \mathcal{C}$, and an area can be regarded as a topic.

Now the problem we are solving in this research can be formally defined as follows: Given an specific area $x \in \mathcal{X}$ and an integer $K \in Z^+$, we can extract a topic set $y = \{y_1, y_2, \ldots, y_K\}$, which can represent the given area, where $y \subset \mathcal{Y}$. Intuitively, we hope that the extraction result will be closer to the feedback of most users by tuning our model's output.

User feedback U will be provided and u_{ik} represents the ith user's evaluation for the topics extraction of a given area x_i. When considering user feedback, our target is to improve extraction performance with feedback. Thus, a mapping function f can be learnt, which is formally defined as follows:

$$f : \{x, y, u_{*x} | x \in \mathcal{X}, y \subset \mathcal{Y}, u_{*x} \in U\} \mapsto \{\hat{y} = \{\hat{y}_i | \hat{y}_i \in \mathcal{Y}, i = 1, 2, \ldots, K\}\} \quad (1)$$

where u_{*x} refers to all feedback of the area x.

3.2 LITE Model

In this research a learning interactive topics extraction (LITE) model is proposed to obtain topics with user feedback. The model is divided into two steps, i.e., pre-training step and updating step, as shown in Fig. 1.

Pre-training. Considering that the length of the topics sequence of a given area is K, a mapping function from x to $\{y_1, y_2, \ldots, y_K\}$ need to be learnt. Assume we extracted part of results $\{y_1, y_2, \ldots, y_{k-1}\}$, as such we should consider the area x and the part of extraction when extracting the kth topic. Here we use recurrent neural network (RNN) decoder model, which use RNN to generate topics sequence of a given area, to address the problem and we define the input and output space (IO space) $\mathcal{V} = \mathcal{X} \cup \mathcal{Y}$.

The left part of Fig. 1 is the pre-training step of area topics extraction and here we set $K = 4$ for just illustration. Given an area x, which is from the user

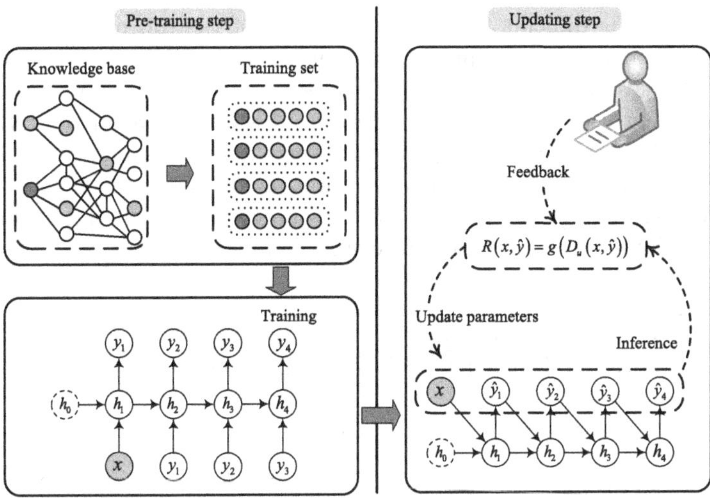

Fig. 1. An overview of LITE model framework. x indicates a given area. Dash node indicates a virtual hidden state, which is usually initialized to zero vector.

input in real application, the model can generate topic sequence one by one. Formally, the conditional distribution of y given x can be written as:

$$p(y|x;\theta) = \prod_{k=1}^{K} p(y_k|x, y_1, y_2, \ldots, y_{k-1};\theta) \tag{2}$$

where y_i is the ith topic extracted from the IO space $\mathcal{V}$. We define $y_0 = x$ to simplify the formula. The area and topic representation is one hot vector, and $x, y \in \mathbb{R}^{|\mathcal{V}|}$, where $|\mathcal{V}|$ is the size of IO space.

Let $h_k \in \mathbb{R}^d$ be a hidden state at the kth step extraction. We have $h_k = g_1(h_{k-1}, y_{k-1})$, where $k = 1, 2, \ldots, K$. g_1 is an activation function such as tanh, ReLU, or a more complicated structure like GRU unit [4]. The conditional distribution of the kth topic is

$$p(y_k|y_{k-1}, y_{k-2}, \ldots, y_1, y_0;\theta) = g_2(h_k;\theta) \tag{3}$$

where g_2 must produce valid probabilities such as softmax. Thus, the extraction at step k is

$$y_k^* = \mathop{\arg\max}_{y_0, y_1, \ldots, y_{k-1} \in \mathcal{V}} g_2(h_k;\theta) \tag{4}$$

We first train this model and find an optimal parameter θ by maximizing the conditional log-probability on a training set S. Then we infer the topics sequence for every user's query, which is regarded as an area input. In other words, we divide the pre-trained model into two phases: training and inference.

In the training phrase, we need a training set to find optimal solution from the large space. We use the training set to pre-train model for the following two reasons. First, it is difficult to converge because of the too many parameters. Second, we hope to improve performance using user feedback. Therefore our model should have ability of generating diverse results so as to adjust the model parameters using user feedback. Hence, we use K-Nearest Neighbors (KNN) to generate a fixed sort of topics sequence of every area and shuffle the extracted topics. In particular, we try to add noise into raw distance, which can be measured by word2vec [13]. The training set can be generated as Algorithm 1. Kd tree can be adopted in Line 8 to reduce time complexity [16].

Algorithm 1. Generate training set using K-Nearest Neighbor.

Input: Topic space $\mathcal{X}$, the number of shuffle data for one area T, output size K
Output: Training set S
1: Initialize training set $S = \phi$
2: **for** each $x \in \mathcal{X}$ **do**
3:     *tuple* ← ComputeDistance(x)
4:     $y \leftarrow tuple[0]$
5:     $distance \leftarrow tuple[1]$
6:     **for** each $t \in [1, T]$ **do**
7:         $newDistance \leftarrow distance + noise$
8:         $sample \leftarrow$ SORTED$(y, key = newDistance, descending = True)[1 : K]$
9:         Append *sample* into S
10:    **end for**
11: **end for**
12: **return** S

In the inference phrase, when we make inference using the pre-trained model, we hope to find the optimal topics sequence $\hat{y}^* = \{\hat{y}_1^*, \hat{y}_2^*, \ldots, \hat{y}_K^*\}$ and the probability of each extraction step $\hat{y}_k^*$ depends on the input area x and the previously extracted sequence $\{\hat{y}_1^*, \hat{y}_2^*, \ldots, \hat{y}_{k-1}^*\}$. However, finding the global optimal is intractable. Thus, we try to make inference one by one. It means that we choose the current topic with the highest probability using input and previous output, which is similar with text generation. Thus, k^{th} topic for the given area x and previous output $\{\hat{y}_1^*, \hat{y}_2^*, \ldots, \hat{y}_{k-1}^*\}$ is

$$\hat{y}_k^* = \arg\max_{y_k \in \mathcal{Y}} \log p(y_k | x, \hat{y}_1^*, \hat{y}_2^*, \ldots, \hat{y}_{k-1}^*) \tag{5}$$

Updating. The pre-trained model can extract a topics sequence by training in lots of samples. However, the performance depends on training set, which is from an existing knowledge base and text corpus. Through analysis of popular knowledge base such as Wiki Taxonomy and Microsoft Field of Study, which will be introduced in Sect. 4.1, there is a lot of noise in the existing knowledge base. What's more, the representative hypernym-hyponym relationship itself is subjective and we cannot capture all users' thoughts by a static knowledge base. Hence, we try to improve performance by interaction with users. The user feedback matrix $D_U(x, y)$ denotes how well (x, y) pair considering user feedback, where y is the inference results for area x. Given that, we can define the reward as a function of user feedback, which can be written as: $R(x, y) = g(D_U(x, y))$, where g is a function mapping feedback into reward. Our current goal is to maximize the expected reward: $J(\theta|x) = E_{y \sim P(y|x;\theta)}[R(x, y)]$ We use policy gradient [17] to maximize $J(\theta|x)$, and the gradient of $J(\theta|x)$ can be written as follows:

$$\nabla_\theta J(\theta|x) = E_{y \sim P(y|x;\theta)}[R(x, y)\nabla_\theta \log p(y|x;\theta)] \tag{6}$$

We then update parameters using Stochastic Gradient Descent (SGD) or other advanced optimization algorithms such as Adam, RMSProp [15]. In summary, the algorithm can be described as Algorithm 2.

Algorithm 2. An overview of LITE model using SGD.

```
Input: Training set S, user feedback D_U(x, y)
Output: Model parameters θ
Compute p(y|x; θ) using pre-trained model
for each user u_i from all users U do
    Collect area query x of u_i
    Sample topics extraction y for the given x according to p(y|x; θ)
    Calculate R(x, y) according to D_{u_i}(x, y)
    Calculate gradient ∇_θ J(θ|x) by Eq. (6)
    θ ← θ + α∇_θ J(θ|x)
end for
return θ
```

4 Experimental Study

4.1 Experiment Configuration

Computer Science Taxonomy Knowledge Base. We use three knowledge bases to gain concepts, including Wiki Taxonomy tree[1], ACM CCS classification tree[2], and Microsoft Field of Study[3]. We extract all concepts from "Computer Science" and merge them into a new CS taxonomy knowledge base, called Computer Science Taxonomy Knowledge Base (CSTKB), where $|\mathcal{C}| = 13,738$. We define $\mathcal{Y} = \mathcal{C}$. Then we extract some concepts, which include more than *threshold* hyponyms (*threshold* = 100 in our experiments), and regard them as areas. Finally, we select 100 of them. I.e. $|\mathcal{X}| = 100$.

[1] https://dumps.wikimedia.org.

[2] https://www.acm.org/publications/class-2012.

[3] https://www.microsoft.com/en-us/research/project/microsoft-academic-graph/.

Synthetic Interaction Data. We need user feedback to update our model. There are two reasons why we use synthetic user feedback to evaluate performance of our model. Firstly, everyone may have different opinions for the same pair (x, y) because feedback is subjective. Secondly, We need label the specific data by crowdsourcing and annotators must have domain knowledge if we try to evaluate the performance of the proposed model. There is a huge cost to collect huge user feedback in short time. Hence, we try to generate Synthetic Interaction Data according a fixed rule. Every user has an ideal topics sequence y, called *user ideal list.* We assume all users ideal lists are samples of groundtruth. For example, we define area x has a best topics extraction y^*, which is groundtruth, y_i^* denotes the ith topic in y^*. For user u_1, his or her top-3 ideal list may be $<y_3^*, y_1^*, y_4^*>$, and $<y_1^*, y_5^*, y_2^*>$ for user u_2. We can gain the groundtruth if we count enough users ideal lists statistically.

Evaluation Metrics. When we measure the effect of extraction, we need to remove the individual difference of each user. Hence, we evaluate the result by comparing them with groundtruth.

(1) **P@k** P refers to precision. We define the number of topics extraction for a given area is the same as groundtruth. Given an area $x \in \mathcal{X}$, a model's output sequence will be compared with groundtruth. $P@k$ measures accuracy of the first k topics of the models output compared with groundtruth.

$$P@k = \frac{\{y_1, y_2, \dots, y_k\} \cap l}{k} \quad (7)$$

where l is the set of groundtruth. Since the topics order is also important, we introduce MAP as follows.

(2) **MAP@k.** Average Precision (AP) emphasizes ranking right topics higher.

$$AP@k = \frac{\sum_{r=1}^{k}(P@r \times rel(r)}{k} \quad (8)$$

where $rel(i)$ is a binary function on the relevence of a topics sequence. When AP is used to measure the score from users, l denotes the user ideal list. $MAP@k$ denotes the mean $AP@k$ of every user feedback.

Baseline Methods. We compare our method with the following baselines.

(1) **KNN.** We use KNN to generate training set for pre-training the model. Hence, KNN is the best result before introducing user feedback.
(2) **Counting.** Considering user feedback, an intuitive method is to adjust results by users' click. However, we only get the score of entire topics sequence. Thus, we assume that we can get all forms of user feedback in the method.
(3) **ϵ-greedy.** This method can explore the better topics in candidate set and exploit current experience. However, we only replace a topic that is selected randomly because we only get the score of entire topics sequence, not of each topic in output sequence. We set $\epsilon = 0.1$ in our experiments.

4.2 Results and Discussion

In Algorithm 1, we set $T = 100, K = 10$. Assuming groundtruth is generated only considering the first layer's topics in the CSTKB, the user ideal lists can be generated by adding noise into groundtruth. User feedback can be collected from clicking every right topic, or giving a score considering the entire sequence. We choose the latter because users can give a comprehensive evaluation based on the order and accuracy. We regard $AP@K$ as the score by users.

Table 1. Quantitative results comparing several methods.

Methods	P@3	P@5	P@10	MAP@3	MAP@5	MAP@10
KNN	0.2267	0.2080	0.1810	0.1833	0.1490	0.1086
ϵ-greedy	0.2067	0.1660	0.1450	0.1722	0.1267	0.0906
Counting	0.4633	0.3380	0.1810	0.4633	0.3380	0.1810
LITE	**0.7700**	**0.6280**	**0.3590**	**0.7656**	**0.6202**	**0.3506**

Table 1 demonstrates that LITE model outperforms all other baseline methods, which proves LITE model can adjust the pre-training model by interaction with users. The performance of ϵ-greedy is inferior to KNN, because the solution space is huge and we only update the part of value from any topic samples.

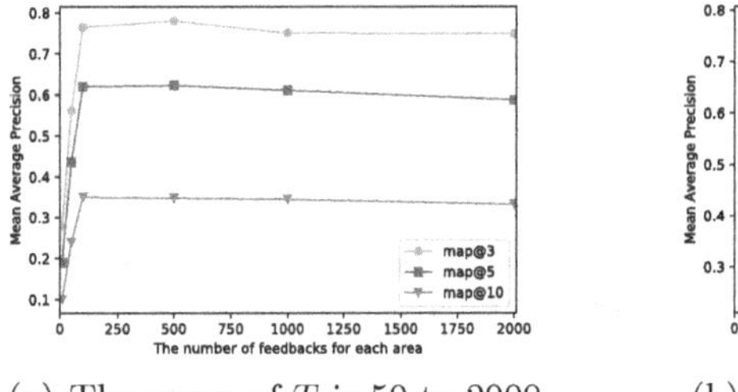

(a) The range of T is 50 to 2000

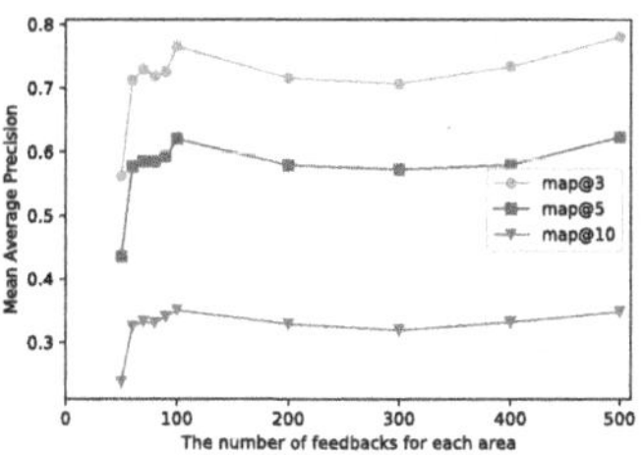

(b) The range of T is 50 to 500

Fig. 2. MAP w.r.t the number of user feedback of one area.

In the experiments, we collect 100 users' feedback of each given area $x \in \mathcal{X}, |\mathcal{X}| = 100$ to improve pre-training model's performance. We change the number of user feedback and observe the performance. Assuming we have T feedback for one area, Fig. 2 illustrates the performance with respect to the number of user feedback of one area and $T = 100$ can get the best performance. However, we cannot get global optimal parameters but local optimal parameters because of the huge solution space. The performance may not be significantly improved even though we collect more feedback because the extraction results may fluctuate near the local optimal solution and we can improve performance using better initialization parameters. We list the top-10 topics extraction by three methods. As a case, Table 2 presents the extracted topics in "Data Mining" area.

Table 2. Top-10 topics in "Data Mining" area using different methods, where bold items represent the same as groundtruth.

ϵ-greedy	Counting	LITE
Data Warehouse	**Data Visualization**	**Data Visualization**
Business Intelligence	**Big Data**	**Big Data**
Data Management	**Text Mining**	**Information Extraction**
Big Data	**Business Intelligence**	**Sentiment Analysis**
Expert System	Machine Learning	**Text Mining**
Machine Learning	Data Analysis	**Business Analytics**
Natural Language Processing	Information Retrieval	**Decision Support System**
Analytics	Data Integration	**Business Intelligence**
Data Visualization	Data Management	Deep Learning
Data Analysis	Data Warehousing	Data Integration

5 Conclusion

In this paper, we propose LITE, an end to end framework, aiming to extract topics extraction of given area with interaction. We did experiments on real knowledge base and synthetic interaction data. Experimental results prove the effectiveness of the proposed method. We deployed the proposed model in Aminer system[4] and collect user feedback to improve extraction performance. A/B test [8] can be used to evaluate the performance and we leave this to our future work.

References

1. Al-Zaidy, R.A., Giles, C.L.: Extracting semantic relations for scholarly knowledge base construction. In: Proceedings of 12th IEEE International Conference on Semantic Computing, pp. 56–63 (2018)
2. Blei, D.M., Ng, A.Y., Jordan, M.I.: Latent Dirichlet allocation. J. Mach. Learn. Res. **3**, 993–1022 (2003)
3. Carlson, A., Betteridge, J., Kisiel, B., Settles, B., Hruschka Jr., E.R., Mitchell, T.M.: Toward an architecture for never-ending language learning. In: Proceedings of 24th AAAI Conference on Artificial Intelligence, pp. 1306–1313 (2010)
4. Cho, K., et al.: Learning phrase representations using RNN encoder-decoder for statistical machine translation. In: Proceedings of 2014 Conference on Empirical Methods in Natural Language Processing, pp. 1724–1734 (2014)
5. Deldjoo, Y., Frà, C., Valla, M., Cremonesi, P.: Letting users assist what to watch: an interactive query-by-example movie recommendation system. In: Proceedings of 8th Italian Information Retrieval Workshop, pp. 63–66 (2017)
6. Hasan, K.S., Ng, V.: Automatic keyphrase extraction: a survey of the state of the art. In: Proceedings of 52nd Annual Meeting of the Association for Computational Linguistics, pp. 1262–1273 (2014)

[4] https://aminer.org.

7. Jiang, X., Hu, Y., Li, H.: A ranking approach to keyphrase extraction. In: Proceedings of 32nd Annual International ACM SIGIR Conference on Research and Development in Information Retrieval, pp. 756–757 (2009)
8. Kohavi, R., Longbotham, R., Sommerfield, D., Henne, R.M.: Controlled experiments on the web: survey and practical guide. Data Min. Knowl. Discov. **18**(1), 140–181 (2009)
9. Lau, J.H., Grieser, K., Newman, D., Baldwin, T.: Automatic labelling of topic models. In: Proceedings of 49th Annual Meeting of the Association for Computational Linguistics, pp. 1536–1545 (2011)
10. Liang, J., Zhang, Y., Xiao, Y., Wang, H., Wang, W., Zhu, P.: On the transitivity of hypernym-hyponym relations in data-driven lexical taxonomies. In: Proceedings of 31st AAAI Conference on Artificial Intelligence, pp. 1185–1191 (2017)
11. Mei, Q., Shen, X., Zhai, C.: Automatic labeling of multinomial topic models. In: Proceedings of 13th ACM SIGKDD International Conference on Knowledge Discovery and Data Mining, pp. 490–499 (2007)
12. Mihalcea, R., Tarau, P.: Textrank: Bringing order into text. In: Proceedings of the 2004 Conference on Empirical Methods in Natural Language Processing (2004)
13. Mikolov, T., Sutskever, I., Chen, K., Corrado, G.S., Dean, J.: Distributed representations of words and phrases and their compositionality. In: Proceedings of 27th Annual Conference on Neural Information Processing Systems, pp. 3111–3119 (2013)
14. Ponzetto, S.P., Strube, M.: Wikitaxonomy: a large scale knowledge resource. In: Proceedings of 18th European Conference on Artificial Intelligence, pp. 751–752 (2008)
15. Ruder, S.: An overview of gradient descent optimization algorithms. CoRR abs/1609.04747 (2016)
16. Samet, H.: The Design and Analysis of Spatial Data Structures. Addison-Wesley, Boston (1990)
17. Sutton, R.S., McAllester, D.A., Singh, S.P., Mansour, Y.: Policy gradient methods for reinforcement learning with function approximation. In: Proceedings of 1999 Annual Conference on Neural Information Processing Systems, pp. 1057–1063 (1999)
18. Wang, C., Fan, Y., He, X., Zhou, A.: Predicting hypernym-hyponym relations for Chinese taxonomy learning. Knowl. Inf. Syst. 1–26 (2018, in press)
19. Yang, Y., Tang, J.: Beyond query: interactive user intention understanding. In: Proceedings of 2015 IEEE International Conference on Data Mining, pp. 519–528 (2015)
20. Zhang, F., Wang, X., Han, J., Wang, S.: Fast top-k area topics extraction with knowledge base. In: Proceedings of 2018 IEEE International Conference on Data Science in Cyberspace (2018)

Implementing Neural Turing Machines

Mark Collier(✉) and Joeran Beel(✉)

Trinity College Dublin, Dublin, Ireland
{mcollier,joeran.beel}@tcd.ie

Abstract. Neural Turing Machines (NTMs) are an instance of Memory Augmented Neural Networks, a new class of recurrent neural networks which decouple computation from memory by introducing an external memory unit. NTMs have demonstrated superior performance over Long Short-Term Memory Cells in several sequence learning tasks. A number of open source implementations of NTMs exist but are unstable during training and/or fail to replicate the reported performance of NTMs. This paper presents the details of our successful implementation of a NTM. Our implementation learns to solve three sequential learning tasks from the original NTM paper. We find that the choice of memory contents initialization scheme is crucial in successfully implementing a NTM. Networks with memory contents initialized to small constant values converge on average 2 times faster than the next best memory contents initialization scheme.

Keywords: Neural Turing Machines
Memory Augmented Neural Networks

1 Introduction

Neural Turing Machines (**NTMs**) [4] are one instance of several new neural network architectures [4,5,11] classified as Memory Augmented Neural Networks (**MANNs**). MANNs defining attribute is the existence of an external memory unit. This contrasts with gated recurrent neural networks such as Long Short-Term Memory Cells (**LSTMs**) [7] whose memory is an internal vector maintained over time. LSTMs have achieved state-of-the-art performance in many commercially important sequence learning tasks, such as handwriting recognition [2], machine translation [12] and speech recognition [3]. But, MANNs have been shown to outperform LSTMs on several artificial sequence learning tasks that require a large memory and/or complicated memory access patterns, for example memorization of long sequences and graph traversal [4–6,11].

V. Kůrková et al. (Eds.): ICANN 2018, LNCS 11141, pp. 94–104, 2018.
https://doi.org/10.1007/978-3-030-01424-7_10

The authors of the original NTM paper, did not provide source code for their implementation. Open source implementations of NTMs exist[1,2,3,4,5,6,7] but a number of these implementations (See footnote 5, 6 and 7) report that the gradients of their implementation sometimes become NaN during training, causing training to fail. While others report slow convergence or do not report the speed of learning of their implementation. The lack of a stable open source implementation of NTMs makes it more difficult for practitioners to apply NTMs to new problems and for researchers to improve upon the NTM architecture.

In this paper we define a successful NTM implementation[8] which learns to solve three benchmark sequential learning tasks [4]. We specify the set of choices governing our NTM implementation. We conduct an empirical comparison of a number of memory contents initialization schemes identified in other open source NTM implementations. We find that the choice of how to initialize the contents of memory in a NTM is a key factor in a successful NTM implementation. Our Tensorflow implementation is available publicly under an open source license (See footnote 8).

2 Neural Turing Machines

NTMs consist of a controller network which can be a feed-forward neural network or a recurrent neural network and an external memory unit which is a $N * W$ memory matrix, where N represents the number of memory locations and W the dimension of each memory cell. Whether the controller is a recurrent neural network or not, the entire architecture is recurrent as the contents of the memory matrix are maintained over time. The controller has read and write heads which access the memory matrix. The effect of a read or write operation on a particular memory cell is weighted by a soft attentional mechanism. This addressing mechanism is similar to attention mechanisms used in neural machine translation [1,9] except that it combines location based addressing with the content based addressing found in these attention mechanisms.

In particular for a NTM, at each timestep (t), for each read and write head the controller outputs a set of parameters: $\mathbf{k}_t$, $\beta_t \geq 0$, $g_t \in [0,1]$, $\mathbf{s}_t$ (s.t. $\sum_k s_t(k) = 1$ and $\forall k \; s_t(k) \geq 0$) and $\gamma_t \geq 1$ which are used to compute the weighting $\mathbf{w}_t$ over the N memory locations in the memory matrix $\mathbf{M}_t$ as follows:

$$w_t^c(i) \leftarrow \frac{exp(\beta_t K[\mathbf{k}_t, \mathbf{M}_t(i)])}{\sum_{j=0}^{N-1} exp(\beta_t K[\mathbf{k}_t, \mathbf{M}_t(j)])} \tag{1}$$

[1] https://github.com/snowkylin/ntm.
[2] https://github.com/chiggum/Neural-Turing-Machines.
[3] https://github.com/yeoedward/Neural-Turing-Machine.
[4] https://github.com/loudinthecloud/pytorch-ntm.
[5] https://github.com/camigord/Neural-Turing-Machine.
[6] https://github.com/snipsco/ntm-lasagne.
[7] https://github.com/carpedm20/NTM-tensorflow.
[8] Source code at: https://github.com/MarkPKCollier/NeuralTuringMachine.

$\mathbf{w}_t^c$ allows for content based addressing where $\mathbf{k}_t$ represents a lookup key into memory and K is some similarity measure such as cosine similarity:

$$K[\mathbf{u}, \mathbf{v}] = \frac{\mathbf{u} \cdot \mathbf{v}}{\|\mathbf{u}\| \cdot \|\mathbf{v}\|} \tag{2}$$

Through a series of operations NTMs also enable iteration from current or previously computed memory weights as follows:

$$\mathbf{w}_t^g \leftarrow g_t \mathbf{w}_t^c + (1 - g_t)\mathbf{w}_{t-1} \tag{3}$$

$$\tilde{w}_t(i) \leftarrow \sum_{j=0}^{N-1} w_t^g(j) s_t(i - j) \tag{4}$$

$$w_t(i) \leftarrow \frac{\tilde{w}_t(i)^{\gamma_t}}{\sum_{j=0}^{N-1} \tilde{w}_t(j)^{\gamma_t}} \tag{5}$$

where (3) enables the network to choose whether to use the current content based weights or the previous weight vector, (4) enables iteration through memory by convolving the current weighting by a 1-D convolutional shift kernel and (5) corrects for any blurring occurring as a result of the convolution operation.

The vector $\mathbf{r}_t$ read by a particular read head at timestep t is computed as:

$$\mathbf{r}_t \leftarrow \sum_{i=0}^{N-1} w_t(i)\mathbf{M}_t(i) \tag{6}$$

Each write head modifies the memory matrix at timestep t by outputting additional erase ($\mathbf{e}_t$) and add ($\mathbf{a}_t$) vectors:

$$\tilde{\mathbf{M}}_t(i) \leftarrow \mathbf{M}_{t-1}(i)[\mathbf{1} - w_t(i)\mathbf{e}_t] \tag{7}$$

$$\mathbf{M}_t(i) \leftarrow \tilde{\mathbf{M}}_t(i) + w_t(i)\mathbf{a}_t \tag{8}$$

Equations (1) to (8) define how addresses are computed and used to read and write from memory in a NTM, but many implementation details of a NTM are open to choice. In particular the choice of the similarity measure K, the initial weightings $\mathbf{w}_0$ for all read and write heads, the initial state of the memory matrix $\mathbf{M}_0$, the choice of non-linearity to apply to the parameters outputted by each read and write head and the initial read vector $\mathbf{r}_0$ are all undefined in a NTM's specification.

While any choices for these satisfying the constraints on the parameters outputted by the controller would be a valid NTM, in practice these choices have a significant effect on the ability of a NTM to learn.

3 Our Implementation

Memory contents initialization - We hypothesize that how the memory contents of a NTM are initialized may be a defining factor in the success of a NTM implementation. We compare the three memory contents initialization schemes that we identified in open source implementations of NTMs. In particular, we compare *constant initialization* where all memory locations are initialized to 10^{-6}, *learned initialization* where we backpropagate through initialization and *random initialization* where each memory location is initialized to a value drawn from a truncated Normal distribution with mean 0 and standard deviation 0.5. We note that five of the seven implementations (See footnote 1, 2, 3, 4 and 5) we identified randomly initialize the NTM's memory contents. We also identified an implementation which initialized memory contents to a small constant value (See footnote 6) and an implementation where the memory initialization was learned (See footnote 7).

Constant initialization has the advantage of requiring no additional parameters and providing a stable known memory initialization during inference. *Learned initialization* has the potential advantage of learning an initialization that would enable complex non-linear addressing schemes [6] while also providing stable initialization after training. This comes at the cost of $N * W$ extra parameters. *Random initialization* has the potential advantage of acting as a regularizer, but it is possible that during inference memory contents may be in a space not encountered during training.

Other parameter initialization - Instead of initializing the previously read vectors $\mathbf{r}_0$ and address weights $\mathbf{w}_0$ to bias values as per [4] we backpropagate through their initialization and thus initialize them to a learned bias vector. We argue that this initialization scheme provides sufficient generality for tasks that require more flexible initialization with little cost in extra parameters (the number of additional parameters is $W * H_r + N * (H_r + H_w)$ where H_r is the number of read heads and H_w is the number of write heads). For example, if a NTM with multiple write heads wishes to write to different memory locations at timestep 1 using location based addressing then $\mathbf{w}_0$ must be initialized differently for each write head. Having to hard code this for each task is an added burden on the engineer, particularly when the need for such addressing may not be known a priori for a given task, thus we allow the network to learn this initialization.

Similarity measure - For K, we follow [4] in using cosine similarity (2) which scales the dot product into the fixed range $[-1, 1]$.

Controller inputs - At each timestep the controller is fed the concatenation of the input coming externally into the NTM $\mathbf{x}_t$ and the previously read vectors $\mathbf{r}_{t-1}$ from all of the read heads of the NTM. We note that such a setup has achieved performance gains for attentional encoder-decoders in neural machine translation [9].

Parameter non-linearities - Similarly to a LSTM we force the contents of the memory matrix to be in the range $[-1, 1]$, by applying the tanh function to the outputs of the controller corresponding to $\mathbf{k}_t$ and $\mathbf{a}_t$ while we apply the sigmoid function to the corresponding erase vector $\mathbf{e}_t$. We apply the function $softplus(x) \leftarrow \log(\exp(x) + 1)$ to satisfy the constraint $\beta_t \geq 0$. We apply the logistic sigmoid function to satisfy the constraint $g_t \in [0, 1]$. In order to make the convolutional shift vector $\mathbf{s}_t$ a valid probability distribution we apply the softmax function. In order to satisfy $\gamma_t \geq 1$ we first apply the *softplus* function and then add 1.

4 Methodology

4.1 Tasks

We test our NTM implementation on three of the five artificial sequence learning tasks described in the original NTM paper [4].

Copy - for the Copy task, the network is fed a sequence of random bit vectors followed by an end of sequence marker. The network must then output the input sequence. This requires the network to store the input sequence and then read it back from memory. In our experiments we train and test our networks on 8-bit random vectors with sequences of length sampled uniformly from $[1, 20]$.

Repeat Copy - similarly to the Copy task, with Repeat Copy the network is fed an input sequence of random bit vectors. Unlike the Copy task, this is followed by a scalar that indicates how many times the network should repeat the input sequence in its output sequence. We train and test our networks on 8-bit random vectors with sequences of length sampled uniformly from $[1, 10]$ and number of repeats also sampled uniformly from $[1, 10]$.

Associative Recall - Associative Recall is also a sequence learning problem with sequences consisting of random bit vectors. In this case the inputs are divided into items, with each item consisting of 3×6-dimensional vectors. After being fed a sequence of items and an end of sequence marker, the network is then fed a query item which is an item from the input sequence. The correct output is the next item in the input sequence after the query item. We train and test our networks on sequences with the number of items sampled uniformly from $[2, 6]$.

4.2 Experiments

We first run a set of experiments to establish the best memory contents initialization scheme. We compare the *constant*, *random* and *learned* initialization schemes on the above three tasks. We demonstrate below (Sect. 5) that the best such scheme is the *constant initialization* scheme. We then compare the NTM implementation described above (Sect. 3) under the *constant initialization* scheme to two other architectures on the Copy, Repeat Copy and Associative

Recall tasks. We follow the NTM authors [4] in comparing our NTM implementation to a LSTM network. As no official NTM implementation has been made open source, as a further benchmark, we compare our NTM implementation to the official implementation[9] of a Differentiable Neural Computer (**DNC**) [5], a successor to the NTM. This provides a guide as to how a stable MANN implementation performs on the above tasks.

In all of our experiments for each network we run training 10 times from different random initializations. To measure the learning speed, every 200 steps during training we evaluate the network on a validation set of 640 examples with the same distribution as the training set.

For all tasks the MANNs had 1 read and 1 write head, with an external memory unit of size 128×20 and a LSTM controller with 100 units. The controller outputs were clipped elementwise to the range $(-20, 20)$. The LSTM networks were all a stack of 3×256 units. All networks were trained with the Adam optimizer [8] with learning rate 0.001 and on the backward pass gradients were clipped to a maximum gradient norm of 50 as described in [10].

5 Results

5.1 Memory Initialization Comparison

We hypothesized that how the memory contents of a NTM were initialized would be a key factor in a successful NTM implementation. We compare the three memory initialization schemes we identified in open source NTM implementations. We then use the best identified memory contents initialization scheme as the default for our NTM implementation.

Copy - Our NTM initialized according the *constant initialization* scheme converges to near zero error approximately 3.5 times faster than the *learned initialization* scheme, while the *random initialization* scheme fails to solve the Copy task in the allotted time (Fig. 1). The learning curves suggest that initializing the memory contents to small constant values offers a substantial speed-up in convergence over the other two memory initialization schemes for the Copy task.

Repeat Copy - A NTM initialized according the *constant initialization* scheme converges to near zero error approximately 1.43 times faster than the *learned initialization* scheme and 1.35 times faster than the *random initialization* scheme (Fig. 2). The relative speed of convergence between *learned* and *random* initialization is reversed as compared with the Copy task, but again the *constant initialization* scheme demonstrates substantially faster learning than either alternative.

Associative Recall - A NTM initialized according the *constant initialization* scheme converges to near zero error approximately 1.15 times faster than the *learned initialization* scheme and 5.3 times faster than the *random initialization* scheme (Fig. 3).

[9] https://github.com/deepmind/dnc.

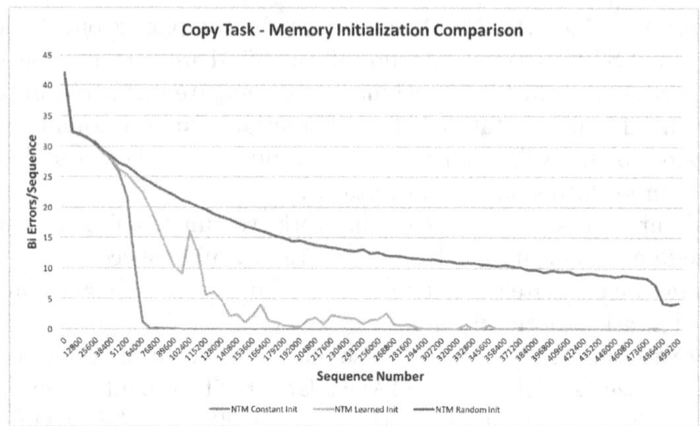

Fig. 1. Copy task memory initialization comparison - learning curves. Median error on 10 training runs (each) for a NTM initialized according to the *constant*, *learned* and *random* initialization schemes.

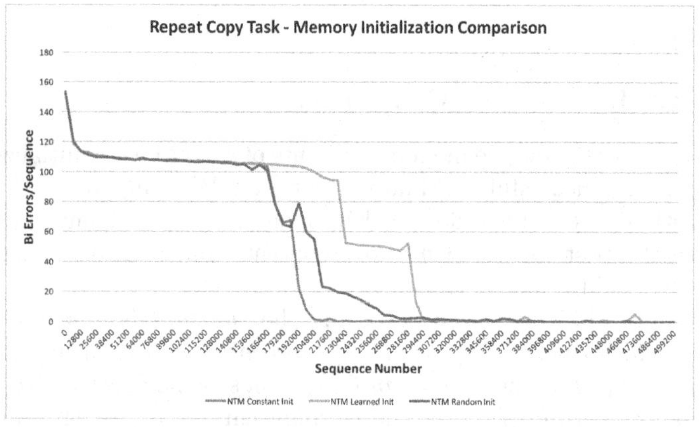

Fig. 2. Repeat Copy task memory initialization comparison - learning curves. Median error on 10 training runs (each) for a NTM initialized according to the *constant*, *learned* and *random* initialization schemes.

The *constant initialization* scheme demonstrates fastest convergence to near zero error on all three tasks. We conclude that initializing the memory contents of a NTM to small constant values results in faster learning than backpropagating through memory contents initialization or randomly initializing memory contents. Thus, we use the *constant initialization* scheme as the default scheme for our NTM implementation.

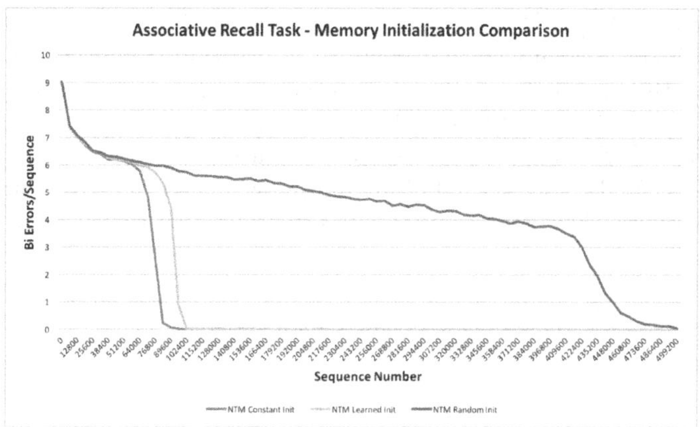

Fig. 3. Associative Recall task memory initialization comparison - learning curves. Median error on 10 training runs (each) for a NTM initialized according to the *constant*, *learned* and *random* initialization schemes.

5.2 Architecture Comparison

Now that we have established the best memory contents initialization scheme is *constant initialization* we wish to test whether our NTM implementation using this scheme is stable and has similar speed of learning and generalization ability as claimed in the original NTM paper. We compare the performance of our NTM to a LSTM and a DNC on the same three tasks as for our memory contents initialization experiments.

Copy - Our NTM implementation converges to zero error in a number of steps comparable to the best published results on this task [4] (Fig. 4). Our NTM converges to zero error 1.2 times slower than the DNC and as expected both MANNs learn substantially faster (4–5 times) than a LSTM.

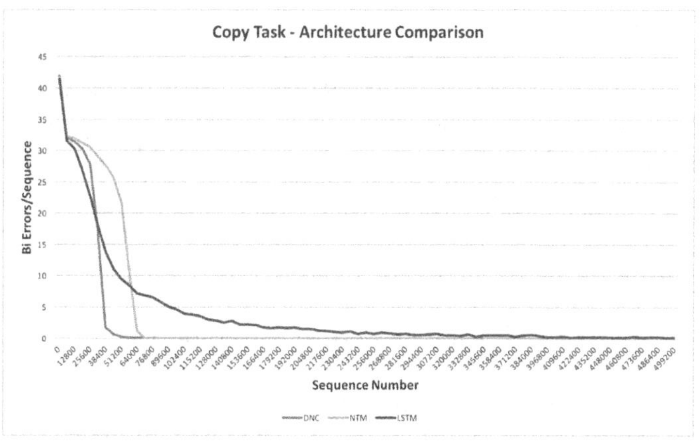

Fig. 4. Copy task architecture comparison - learning curves. Median error on 10 training runs (each) for a DNC, NTM and LSTM.

Repeat Copy - As per [4], we also find that the LSTM performs better relative to the MANNs on Repeat Copy compared to the Copy task, converging only 1.44 times slower than a NTM, perhaps due to the shorter input sequences involved (Fig. 5). While both the DNC and the NTM demonstrate slow learning during the first third of training both architectures then rapidly fall to near zero error before the LSTM. Despite the NTM learning slower than the DNC during early training, the DNC converges to near zero error just 1.06 times faster than the NTM.

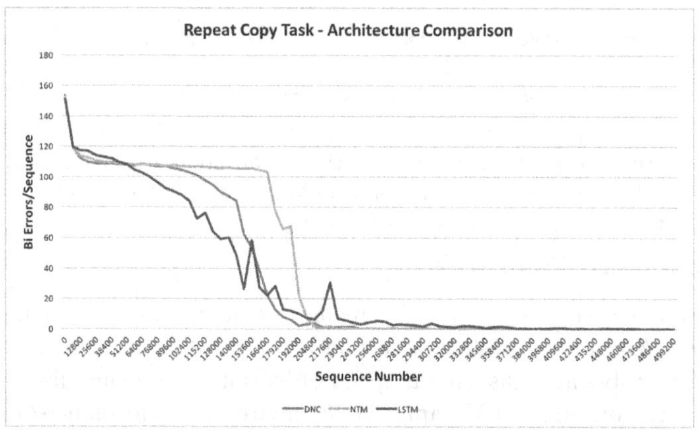

Fig. 5. Repeat Copy task architecture comparison - learning curves. Median error on 10 training runs (each) for a DNC, NTM and LSTM.

Associative Recall - Our NTM implementation converges to zero error in a number of steps almost identical to the best published results on this task [4] and at the same rate as the DNC (Fig. 6). The LSTM network fails to solve the task in the time provided.

Our NTM implementation learns to solve all three of the five tasks proposed in the original NTM paper [4] that we tested. Our implementation's speed to convergence and relative performance to LSTMs is similar to the results reported in the NTM paper. Speed to convergence for our NTM is only slightly slower than a DNC - another MANN. We conclude that our NTM implementation can be used reliably in new applications of MANNs.

6 Summary

NTMs are an exciting new neural network architecture that achieve impressive performance on a range of artificial tasks. But the specification of a NTM leaves many free choices to the implementor and no source code is provided that makes these choices and replicates the published NTM results. In practice the choices left to the implementor have a significant impact on the ability of a NTM to learn. We observe great diversity in how these choices are made amongst open source

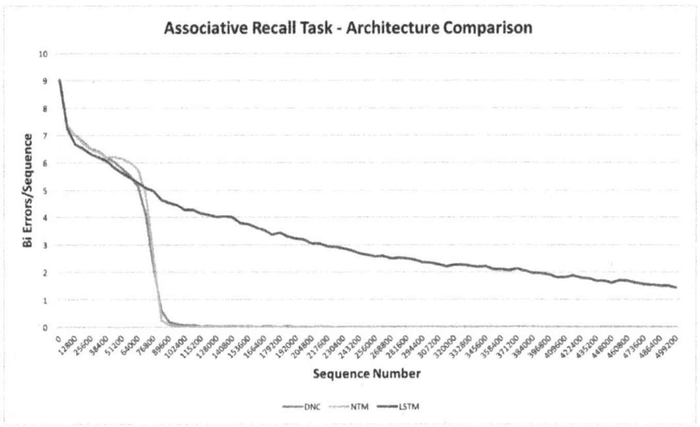

Fig. 6. Associative Recall task architecture comparison - learning curves. Median error on 10 training runs (each) for a DNC, NTM and LSTM.

efforts to implement a NTM, many of which fail to replicate these published results.

We have demonstrated that the choice of memory contents initialization scheme is crucial to successfully implementing a NTM. We conclude from the learning curves on three sequential learning tasks that learning is fastest under the *constant initialization* scheme. We note that the *random initialization* scheme which was used in five of the seven identified open source implementations was the slowest to converge on two of the three tasks and the second slowest on the Repeat Copy task.

We have made our NTM implementation with the *constant initialization* scheme open source. Our implementation has learned the Copy, Repeat Copy and Associative Recall tasks at a comparable speed to previously published results and the official implementation of a DNC. Training of our NTM is stable and does not suffer from problems such as gradients becoming NaN reported in other implementations. Our implementation can be reliably used for new applications of NTMs. Additionally, further research on NTMs will be aided by a stable, performant open source NTM implementation.

References

1. Bahdanau, D., Cho, K., Bengio, Y.: Neural machine translation by jointly learning to align and translate. arXiv preprint arXiv:1409.0473 (2014)
2. Graves, A., Liwicki, M., Fernández, S., Bertolami, R., Bunke, H., Schmidhuber, J.: A novel connectionist system for unconstrained handwriting recognition. IEEE Trans. Pattern Anal. Mach. Intell. **31**(5), 855–868 (2009)
3. Graves, A., Mohamed, A.R., Hinton, G.: Speech recognition with deep recurrent neural networks. In: 2013 IEEE International Conference on Acoustics, speech and Signal Processing (ICASSP), pp. 6645–6649. IEEE (2013)

4. Graves, A., Wayne, G., Danihelka, I.: Neural Turing machines. arXiv preprint arXiv:1410.5401 (2014)
5. Graves, A., et al.: Hybrid computing using a neural network with dynamic external memory. Nature **538**(7626), 471 (2016)
6. Gulcehre, C., Chandar, S., Cho, K., Bengio, Y.: Dynamic neural Turing machine with soft and hard addressing schemes. arXiv preprint arXiv:1607.00036 (2016)
7. Hochreiter, S., Schmidhuber, J.: Long short-term memory. Neural Comput. **9**(8), 1735–1780 (1997)
8. Kingma, D.P., Ba, J.: Adam: a method for stochastic optimization. arXiv preprint arXiv:1412.6980 (2014)
9. Luong, T., Pham, H., Manning, C.D.: Effective approaches to attention-based neural machine translation. In: Proceedings of the 2015 Conference on Empirical Methods in Natural Language Processing, pp. 1412–1421 (2015)
10. Pascanu, R., Mikolov, T., Bengio, Y.: On the difficulty of training recurrent neural networks. In: International Conference on Machine Learning, pp. 1310–1318 (2013)
11. Sukhbaatar, S., Weston, J., Fergus, R.: End-to-end memory networks. In: Advances in Neural Information Processing Systems, pp. 2440–2448 (2015)
12. Wu, Y., et al.: Google's neural machine translation system: bridging the gap between human and machine translation. arXiv preprint arXiv:1609.08144 (2016)

A RNN-Based Multi-factors Model for Repeat Consumption Prediction

Zengwei Zheng[1], Yanzhen Zhou[1,2], Lin Sun[1(✉)], and Jianping Cai[1]

[1] Hangzhou Key Laboratory for IoT Technology and Application, Zhejiang University City College, Hangzhou, China
{zhengzw,sunl,jpcai}@zucc.edu.com

[2] College of Computer Science and Technology, Zhejiang University, Hangzhou, China
zhouyanzhen@zju.edu.com

Abstract. Consumption is a common activity in people's daily life, and some reports show that repeat consumption even accounts for a greater portion of people's observed activities compared with novelty-seeking consumption. Therefore, modeling repeat consumption is a very important study to understand human behavior. In this paper, we proposed a multi-factors RNN (MF-RNN) model to predict the users' repeat consumption behavior. We analysed some factors which can influence customers' daily repeat consumption and introduced those factor in MF-RNN model to predict the users' repeat consumption behavior. An empirical study on real-world data sets shows encouraging results on our approach. In the real-world dataset, the MF-RNN gets good prediction performance, better than Most Frequent, HMM, Recency, DYRC and LSTM methods. We compared the effect of different factors on the customers' repeat consumption behavior, and found that the MF-RNN gets better performance than non-factor RNN. Besides, we analyzed the differences in consumption behaviors between different cities and different regions in China.

Keywords: Repeat consumption · Recurrent Neural Network (RNN) Multi-factors

1 Introduction

Nowadays, with the rapid development of mobile payment technology, people can make payment in an store by smartphones apps (such as Alipay, WeChat pay and Apple pay etc.) instead of by cash. Therefore, how to use previous consumption record and model user's repeat consumption behavior to predict which store the user likely to go in future time is very important. The study of consumption behavior is to know the way an individual spends his resources in the process of consuming items. This is an approach that comprises of studies of the items that they buy and the reason for buying and the timing. It is also about where

V. Kůrková et al. (Eds.): ICANN 2018, LNCS 11141, pp. 105–115, 2018.
https://doi.org/10.1007/978-3-030-01424-7_11

they make the purchase and how frequently. Due to the fact that people prefer the things they are familiar with, they may repeatedly interact with same items overtime. Therefore, users always like to visit the same stores that they have purchased previously, such as shopping at a same fruit shop and eating regularly at a same restaurant. For the reason of that, repeat consumption accounts for a major portion of people's daily consumption behavior, and we focus on the repeat consumption behavior study in this paper.

In real life, some factors can affect peoples' daily activities. For instance, we usually visit some places in the vicinity of our office during the workdays, but usually visit some places near our home in holidays; we probably go out for some outdoor activities when the weather is nice but stay indoor when the weather is terrible; we like to take cool drinks in summer day but choose some hot things in winter instead. Therefore, we believe that peoples' daily repeat consumption behavior can be affected by some factors too. In this paper, we proposed an MF-RNN model which is based on RNN and introduce some factors to predict peoples' repeat consumption behavior. Through analysis, we selected three factors as influential factors: holiday factor, weather factor and temperature factor. An empirical study on real-world dataset shows encouraging results on our approach. The MF-RNN gets encouraging performance for repeat consumption behavior prediction, better than MF, HMM, Recency, DYRC and LSTM model. And the MF-RNN with all three factors gets better performance than without any factors.

2 Related Works

Consumption behavior is an approach to know the way that an individual spends his resources in the process of consuming items. Consumption behavior analysis is critically extending the domain of behavior analysis and behavioral economics into marketing theory. In past, the ways of predicting the consumers' behavior involved Content-based recommendation, collaborative filtering-based recommendation, time series analysis and data mining. Content-based recommender systems are based on the idea that the features of items are useful in suggesting relevant and interesting items for users [1]. Collaborative filtering-based recommender systems identify users whose tastes are similar to that of a target user and then recommend items that the others have liked [2,3]. Time series analysis and data mining method used the historical data to extra some feature to model the user's consumption behavior [4].

But the study of repeat consumption behavior is a bit different of consumption behavior, it focuses on predicting whether or not the user will repeat purchase items which he has consumed in previous time. The problems of how and why users repeatedly consume certain items have been approached from several angles in various discipline [5]. Some of the earliest works focus on understanding repeat behavior on the web, like re-searching queries and website revisitation. Adar, Teevan and Fumais [6] carried out a large-scale analysis of revisitation, and classified websites into different groups based in how often they attract revisitors. Then, those researchers explored the relationship between the content change in web pages and people's revisition to these pages [7]. Teevan et al. [8] studied query logs to find repeat queries in web research, and that more than 40% of the queries are repeat queries. Then, many methods have been proposed to predict people's repeated consumption behavior. Anderson et al. [9] analyzed the dynamics of repeat consumption. They studied the pattern by which a user consumes the same item repeatedly over time, in some wide variety domains ranging from check-ins at the same business location to re-watches of the same video, and found that recency of consumption is the strong predictor consumption. Chen et al. [10] formulate the problem of recommendation for repeat consumption with user implicit feedback, then proposed a time-sensitive personalized pairwise ranking (TS-PPR) method based on user behavioral features. Rafailidis and Nanopoulos [11] present the CTF model and W-CTF model for recommend items with repeat consumption, by capturing the rate with which the current preferences of each user shift over time and by exploiting side information in a coupled tensor factorization technique. Zhang et al. [12] proposes a dining recommender system termed NDRS, which gives associated recommendation strategies according to different novelty-seeking statuses. They first designed a CRF (Conditional Random Field) with constrains to infer novelty-seeking status, then proposed a context-aware collaborative filtering method and a HMM (Hidden Markov Model) with temporal regularity method are proposed for novel and regular restaurant recommendation. Christina and Lars [13] developed the multinomial SVM (Support Vector Machine) item recommender system MN-SVM-IR to calculate personalized item recommendation for a repeat-buying scenario. Although there are many methods for predicting repeated consumption behavior, most methods focus on the features of the consumers or the items and rarely care about other relevant informations.

3 Methodolody

Recurrent Neural Network (RNN) is a type of feedforward neural network whose output is not only depend on the weight of the current input, but also depend on the present state of the network. Augmented by the inclusion of recurrent edges that span adjacent time steps, the RNN introducing a notion of time to the model [14]. In other words, the feedback from the hidden layer not only goes to the output, but also goes into the next time step hidden layer. Thus, the RNN has some memory. In the previous research, RNN proved to be very useful in sequence learning problem. RNN can be employed in text processing, image captioning, machine translation, video captioning and handwriting recognition. In this paper, we proposed a prediction model based on RNN and combine with several other influential factors to predict the users' repeat consumption behavior.

3.1 RNN-based Multi-factors Prediction Model

As mentioned above, we selected 3 different factors as the influential factors in the repeat consumption behavior prediction case. Then, we defined the MF-RNN model which is a three-layers network include input layer, hidden layer and output layer, shown in Fig. 1.

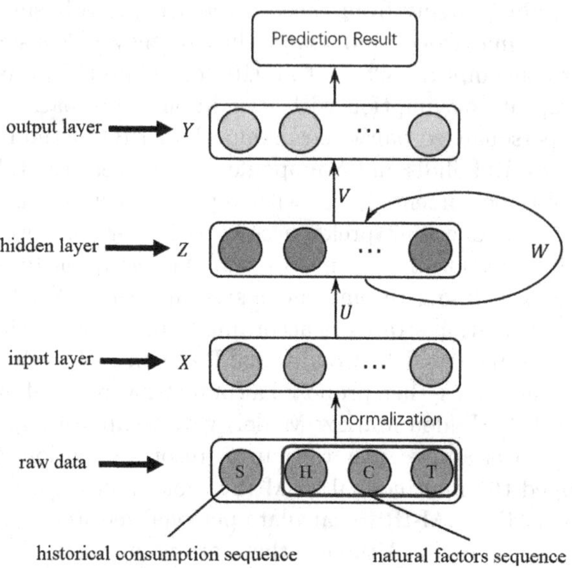

Fig. 1. The framework of MF-RNN.

Input Layer: The input layer X is a vector consists of four normalized input data as Eq. (1): S is visited offline store sequence, H is the holiday factor sequence, C is the weather factor sequence, T is the temperature factor sequence. The output data Y is the prediction result represent the offline store which this customer will visit in the next time.

$$X = [SHCT] \tag{1}$$

Hidden Layer: Z is hidden layer, its state in time t z_t is affected by the current input x_t and the state of the previous time step hidden layer z_{t-1}:

$$z_t = f(Ux_t + Wz_{t-1} + b_z) \tag{2}$$

where U is the weight between the input and hidden layers, W is the recurrent weight between the hidden layers at adjacent time steps, b_z is the bias in hidden layer.

Output Layer: The output layer Y is the prediction result represent offline stores the user will visit at next times. The output in time t calculate as Eq. (3), and V is the weight between the output and hidden layers, g is an activation function and b_y is the bias in output layer.

$$y_t = g(Vz_t + b_y) \tag{3}$$

Then, we used the historical data to training this network. A Back Propagation Through Time (BPTT) algorithm is employed in the training process to calculate the parameters U V W and b_z b_y. The loss function of the networks defined as Eq. (4), and e_t is the loss at each step.

$$E = \sum_t e_t \tag{4}$$

The gradient of V calculate as Eq. (5), y_t' is the supervision information at time step t.

$$\nabla V = \frac{\partial E}{\partial V} = \sum_t (y_t - y_t') \otimes z_t \tag{5}$$

Then we defined two operator δ_t^z as Eq. (6) and δ_t^y as Eq. (7), and calculate the gradient of U, W as Eqs. (8) and (9), finally calculate the gradient of two bias as Eqs. (10) and (11). After parameters training process, we got a trained network to calculate the output data Y, then to predict user's repeat consumption behavior in future time.

$$\delta_t^z = \frac{\partial E}{\partial (f(Ux_t + Wz_{t-1} + b_z))} \tag{6}$$

$$\delta_t^y = \frac{\partial E}{\partial (g(Vz_t + b_y))} \tag{7}$$

$$\nabla U = \frac{\partial E}{\partial U} = \sum_t \frac{\partial e_t}{\partial U} = \sum_t \delta_t^z \times x_t \tag{8}$$

$$\nabla W = \frac{\partial E}{\partial W} = \sum_t \frac{\partial e_t}{\partial W} = \sum_t \delta_t^z \times z_{t-1} \tag{9}$$

$$\Delta b_z = \frac{\partial E}{\partial b_z} = \sum_t \frac{\partial e_t}{\partial b_z} = \sum_t \delta_t^z \tag{10}$$

$$\Delta b_y = \frac{\partial E}{\partial b_y} = \sum_t \frac{\partial e_t}{\partial b_y} = \sum_t \delta_t^y \tag{11}$$

3.2 Influential Factors Selection

Holiday Factor: There is a big difference between peoples' daily activities on holidays and on workdays. For example, people prefer to choose the restaurant near their office room to have lunch on workdays but choose the restaurant near home to have lunch on holidays, and people can often visit supermarket during holidays but can't do it when they are at work. Therefore, the holiday factor will affect peoples' repeat consumption behavior. In this paper, according to Chinese statutory holiday arrangements, we generate a holiday sequence for each user, 1 represent holiday and 0 represent workday.

Weather Factor: Weather can also affect peoples' daily activities. For instance, people can do some outdoor activities like go to a playground and visit the park when the weather is good, but they always stay indoors when rainy and snowy. Then, we choose the weather as an influential factor in this repeat consumption study. The types of weather are diverse, including sunny, cloudy, rainy, snowy and etc. In this paper, we classify the weather into the following categories based on the types and the severity of the weather, and give them different labels, as shown in Table 1.

Temperature Factor: In addition to holiday factor and weather factor, temperature can also influence peoples' daily consumption behavior. When the temperature is very high, people may buy some cool drink or ice-cream. And when the temperature is low, people may prefer to buy some hot tea or hot coffee. We generate two temperature sequence including the highest and lowest temperature in each day for each user.

Table 1. Different weather conditions and their labels.

Weather type	Label
Sunny	0
Light Rain	−0.5
Heavy Rain	−1
Light Snow	−1.5
Heavy Snow	−2

4 Experiment

4.1 Dataset

The dataset we used in this study is a real-world dataset [15]. It's the consumption record of consumer to use Alipay at offline stores. This dataset includes 2000 shops in different city over the country. The dataset time covers from July 1st 2015 to October 31th 2016. We selected 1057 consumers who consumed more than 120 times and more than 3 different stores.

We calculated the information entropy of user's consumption sequence according to Eq. (12).

$$H(x) = E(log_2(1/p(x_i))] = -\sum(p(x_i)log_2(1/p(x_i))), (i = 1, 2, \ldots, n) \quad (12)$$

$P(x_i)$ in Eq. (12) represent the probability of random variables event x_i. The information entropy can be used to measure the uncertainty of random variables events. The higher the information entropy of the user's consumption record sequence, the more complex and unpredictable of consumer's consumption behavior is. Then we divided the all consumer to 3 groups by the information entropy, show in Table 2. The users' consumption behavior in Group3 is most unpredictable.

Table 2. Consumers grouping according to their consumption record sequence information entropy.

	Group1	Group2	Group3
Information entropy	0∼0.5	0.5∼1.0	>1.0
Numbers of consumer	448	296	313

4.2 Baselines Comparison

In this paper, we compared the performance of the proposed method with some other baselines. These methods are:

Most Frequent (MF): We considerate the consumption frequency is a particular aspect of people's consumption behavior, so we choose the most frequent as the baseline of our data experiment.

Hidden Markov Model (HMM): HMM is a powerful statistical tool for modeling generative sequences that can be characterized by an underlying process generating an observable sequence. It's one of the most basic and extensively used statistical tools for modeling the discrete time series.

Recency [9]**:** This baseline assumes that the recently consumed items are more likely to be reconsumed.

DYRC [16]**:** This method proposes a mixed weighted scheme to recommend repeat items based on item popularity and recency effect.

Long Short-Term Memory (LSTM): LSTM introducing a memory cell and generating a unit of computation to replace traditional artificial neurons in the hidden layer of a network. With these memory cells, networks are able to overcome some difficulties with training encountered in earlier recurrent nets.

In the experiment, we set 50 hidden units in the networks, and choose MAE(Mean Absolute Error) as loss function and Adam as optimizer to train this networks. A linear function was selected as the activation function in this network. In all six methods, we set 60 as the length of training sequence. The Fig. 2 illustrates the prediction accuracy of all the baselines and MF-RNN model on the whole three groups of customers. The MF method undoubtedly got the lowest prediction accuracy, nearly to the HMM. And we can find that the neural network method has a great performance improvement over the other four methods. Finally, the model we proposed gets 83.5% prediction accuracy on the most unpredictable group and win the best perform among all six methods. The MF-RNN improve 26.0% than MF on Group3, 23.8% than HMM, 24.1% than Recency, 21.8% than DYRC, and 6.8% than LSTM.

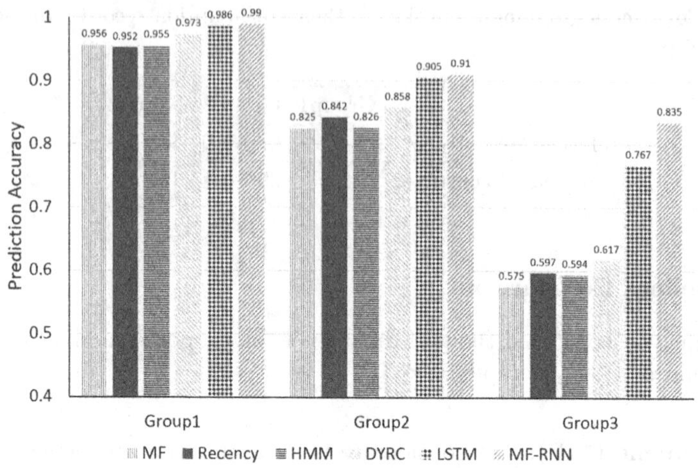

Fig. 2. Prediction accuracy comparison among six methods.

4.3 Influential Factor Analyze

In order to understand which factor has the greatest impact on consumer behavior, we compared the prediction accuracy of different influential factors on MF-RNN model. The experiment on Group3 customers shown in Table 3. We can find that the prediction model with all three factor has the best performance on the real-world dataset. The MF-RNN improve 2.5% than the RNN without any factors. This shows that the introduction of nature influential factors can improve the performance of the prediction model. The MF-RNN improve 1.8% than the non-factor RNN by introducing holiday factor, improve 1.3% by introducing weather factor, and improve 1.7% by introducing temperature factor.

Table 3. Prediction result of different influential factors on Group3.

	Non-factor (RNN)	+Holiday factor	+Weather factor	+Temperature factor	+All factor
Prediction accuracy	0.810	0.828	0.823	0.827	**0.835**

In general, consumers in different cities may have different lifestyles and lead to different daily activities. Thence, we made some data experiment to compare the repeat consumption behavior in cities of different level. We divided 313 customers in Group3 into two groups according to the city they living in. The first group includes 219 users who lives in the first and second tier cities, such as Beijing, Shanghai, Hangzhou and etc. And the second group includes 94 user who lives in other small cities. We compared the differences in repeat consumption behavior between these two groups of users. The result shows in Table 4. We can find that holiday factor has the greatest impact on users in first and second tier cities. We think this is because the pace of life in these cities is fast and most of the users in those big cities are office workers. Those users' daily consumption behavior between workdays and holidays are different. But the lifestyles in small cities are different. From the results, it can be seen that not holiday factor but the weather factor is the most important factor for the consumers in small cities.

Table 4. Prediction accuracy comparison between very large cities and small cities on Group3.

	+Holiday factor	+Weather factor	+Temperature factor
Very large cities	**0.837**	0.820	0.826
Other small cities	0.808	**0.810**	0.806

Besides, we try to analyze the consumption behavior differences in different regions. We divided the customers in Group3 into south group and north group according to their location. The south group includes 255 customers and the north group includes 58 customers. We compared the differences in consumption behavior between these two groups of users. The result shows in Table 5. It illustrates that the North China group is most sensitive to temperature factor, probably because of the extreme temperature changes in the northern China regions. And weather factor has a greater impact on South group than on north group.

Table 5. Prediction accuracy comparison between south China and north China on Group3.

	+Holiday factor	+Weather factor	+Temperature factor
South China	**0.826**	0.820	0.824
North China	0.838	0.837	**0.840**

5 Conclusion

In this paper, we proposed a prediction framework that based on MF-RNN to predict the customer's repeat consumption behavior. This method uses an three-layer RNN structure, and introduce three factors include holiday factor, weather factor and temperature factor to model customer's repeat consumption behavior. We compared the method with some other baseline methods. The experiment result shows that our MF-RNN gets better performance than MF, HMM, Recency, DYRC and LSTM. Then we compared the effect of different factors on the customers' repeat consumption behavior. And the result shows that after introduced three factors the MF-RNN get better performance, the prediction accuracy improved 2.5% than RNN without any factors. Finally, we found there is a large difference in consumption behavior between different cities and regions in China. Therefore, to a certain extent, our research has practical significance for predicting the repeat consumption behavior.

Acknowledgement. This work was supported by Zhejiang Provincial Natural Science Foundation of China (NO. LY17F020008).

References

1. Ricci, F.: Recommender Systems Handbook. Springer, New York (2011). https://doi.org/10.1007/978-1-4899-7637-6
2. Herlocker, J.L., Konstan, J.A., Borchers, A., et al.: An algorithmic framework for performing collaborative filtering. In: 22nd Annual International ACM SIGIR Conference on Research and Development in Information Retrieval, pp. 230–237. ACM (1999)
3. Ekstrand, M.D., Riedl, J.T., Konstan, J.A.: Collaborative filtering recommender systems. Foundations and trends? Hum. Comput. Interact. **4**(2), 81–173 (2011)
4. Yi, Z., Wang, D., Hu, K., et al.: Purchase behavior prediction in M-commerce with an optimized sampling methods. In: IEEE International Conference on Data Mining Workshop, pp. 1085–1092. IEEE Computer Society (2015)
5. Russell, C.A., Levy, S.J.: The temporal and focal dynamics of volitional reconsumption: a phenomenological investigation of repeated hedonic experiences. J. Consum. Res. **39**(2), 341–359 (2011)
6. Adar, E., Teevan, J., Dumais, S.T.: Large scale analysis of web revisitation patterns. In: SIGCHI Conference on Human Factors in Computing Systems, pp. 1197–2008. ACM (2008)
7. Adar, E., Teevan, J., Dumais, S.T.: Resonance on the web: web dynamics and revisitation patterns. In: SIGCHI Conference on Human Factors in Computing Systems, pp. 1381–1390. ACM (2009)
8. Teevan, J., Adar, E., Jones, R., et al.: Information re-retrieval: repeat queries in Yahoo's logs. In 30th Annual International ACM SIGIR Conference on Research and Development in Information Retrieval, pp. 151–158. ACM (2007)
9. Anderson, A., Kumar, R., Tomkins, A., et al.: The dynamics of repeat consumption. In: Proceedings of the 23rd International Conference on World Wide Web, pp. 419–430. International World Wide Conference Committee (2014)
10. Chen, J., Wang, C., Wang, J.: Recommendation for repeat consumption from user implicit feedback. IEEE Trans. Knowl. Data Eng. **28**(11), 3083–3097 (2016)
11. Rafailidis, D., Nanopoulos, A.: Repeat consumption recommendation based on users preference dynamics and side information. In 24th International Conference on World Wide Web, pp. 99–100. ACM (2015)
12. Zhang, F., Zheng, K., Yuan, N.J., et al.: A novelty-seeking based dining recommender system. In: 24th International Conference on World Wide Web, pp. 1362–1372. International World Wide Conference Committee (2015)
13. Lichtenthäler, C., Schmidt-Thieme, L.: Multinomial SVM item recommender for repeat-buying scenarios. In: Spiliopoulou, M., Schmidt-Thieme, L., Janning, R. (eds.) Data Analysis, Machine Learning and Knowledge Discovery. SCDAKO, pp. 189–197. Springer, Cham (2014). https://doi.org/10.1007/978-3-319-01595-8_21

14. Lipton, Z.C., Berkowitz, J., Elkan, C.: A critical review of recurrent neural networks for sequence learning. Comput. Sci. (2015)
15. Tianchi big data contest. https://tianchi.aliyun.com/competition/index.htm. Accessed 2 May 2018
16. Benson, A.R., Kumar, R., Tomkins, A.: Modeling user consumption sequences. In: 25th International Conference on World Wide Web, pp. 519–529. International World Wide Conference Committee (2016)

Practical Fractional-Order Neuron Dynamics for Reservoir Computing

Taisuke Kobayashi(✉)

Division of Information Science, Graduate School of Science and Technology, Nara Institute of Science and Technology, Nara, Japan
kobayashi@is.naist.jp

Abstract. This paper proposes a practical reservoir computing with fractional-order leaky integrator neurons, which yield longer memory capacity rather than normal leaky integrator. In general, fractional-order derivative needs all memories leading to the current state from the initial state. Although this feature is useful as a viewpoint of memory capacity, to keep all memories is intractable, in particular, for reservoir computing with many neurons. A reasonable approximation to the fractional-order neuron dynamics is therefore introduced, thereby deriving a model that exponentially decays past memories before threshold. This derivation is regarded as natural extension of reservoir computing with leaky integrator that has been used most commonly. The proposed method is compared with reservoir computing methods with normal neurons and leaky integrator neurons by solving four kinds of regression and classification problems with time-series data. As a result, the proposed method shows superior results in all of problems.

Keywords: Reservoir computing · Fractional-order leaky integrator Regression and classification

1 Introduction

Recently, recurrent neural network (RNN) is a general approach to predict and classify time-series data, coupled with recent deep learning technology [6]. RNN is one of the neural networks with recursive connections in hidden layer, which enables to store past inputs for a certain period as internal states, which are useful in solving real problems that does not have a Markov process. Let us call "memory capacity" how much past inputs (and outputs) can be reflected on the next outputs. The long memory capacity is suitable to handle the time-series data. As a means to improve the memory capacity, long-short term memory (LSTM) and its relatives [3,7] have been major proposals, and actually, they have achieved excellent results. For embedded systems, however, backpropagation through time (BPTT) in RNN is sometimes intractable in terms of calculation cost since its calculation graph grows with time. A method to update LSTM

V. Kůrková et al. (Eds.): ICANN 2018, LNCS 11141, pp. 116–125, 2018.
https://doi.org/10.1007/978-3-030-01424-7_12

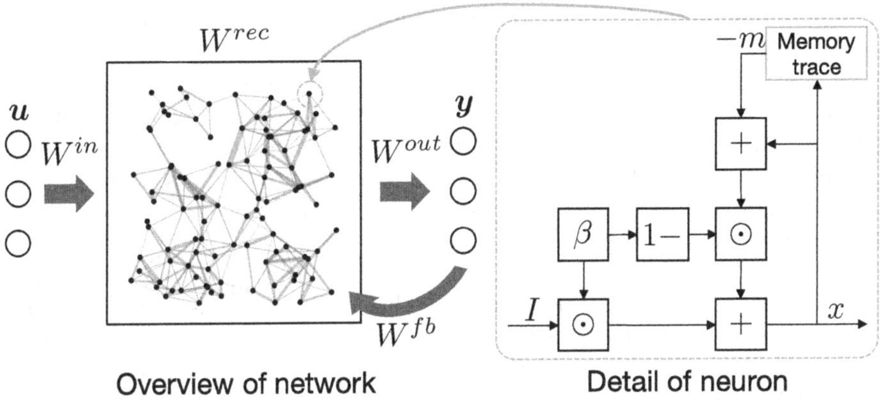

Fig. 1. Concept of reservoir computing with fractional-order leaky integrator: reservoir layer consists of fractional-order leaky integrator neurons; each neuron has a practical memory trace, which approximates the original one for computing with constant cost, to improve the memory capacity.

parameters using evolutionary algorithm instead of BPTT was proposed [18], but sufficient computational resources are still needed.

Under such circumstances, reservoir computing (RC) [11], typified by echo state network (ESN) [8] and liquid state machine (LSM) [13], has been proposed as a special case of RNN (see the left side of Fig. 1). As well as RNN, RC has recursive connections in hidden layer (called reservoir layer), although the connections are sparsely given in general. The decisive difference between RNN and RC is the weights to be learned: in RC, only readout weights to generate outputs from the internal states of the reservoir layer. The other weights, i.e., inputs and reservoir weights, are randomly given as constants. That is, BPTT is no longer required in RC, and instead, RC is learned easily in a linear regression manner. Even in terms of performance to predict or classify the time-series data, it is known that RC is not inferior to RNN. In addition, since learning parameters increased only linearly with respect to the number of neurons, a huge number of neurons would easily be set in the reservoir layer like cerebellum [23].

To improve the memory capacity in RC, two important dynamics should be considered: (i) network dynamics of the reservoir layer [5,17] and; (ii) neuron dynamics in the reservoir layer [9,12,15,21]. Note that these combination has been reported to be remarkable improvement of memory capacity [22]. Although each summary is described in the below, a new method for (ii) the neuron dynamics is proposed in this paper.

With regard to (i) the network dynamics, the reservoir layer, which is randomly given in general, has been structured explicitly. For instance, Rodan and Tino showed that several network models with minimal recursive connections have sufficient performance for prediction [17]. Gallicchio et al. achieved longer memory capacity by deepening the reservoir layer [5]. These results are, however, gained through trial-and-error (or heuristic) design based on the intuition of researchers, namely not derived mathematically.

On the other hand, (ii) the neuron dynamics often employs firing models of a neuron of organism. In particular, leaky integrator has shown utility in LSM [21]. After that, it has been diverted to ESN, which does not directly deal with neuron firing, by Jaeger et al., and has improved the memory capacity [9]. Recently, Lun et al. extended the leaky integrator to the one, which holds past internal states with different leaking rates for a certain period [12]. This model actually improved the performance of RC, while it is heuristically designed. Teka et al. have proposed a new leaky integrator that explicitly holds all past internal states according to a mathematically sophisticated approach, i.e., fractional-order derivative [19,20]. The fractional-order leaky integrator has recently been introduced to ESN by Pahnehkolaei et al. [15]. However, to hold all past internal states in memory is practically infeasible, in particular in RC with many neurons.

Hence, this paper proposes the RC with practical fractional-order leaky integrators (FLRC), a block diagram of which is shown in the right side of Fig. 1. That is, a reasonable approximation is given to the fractional-order neurons so as to calculate their dynamics with a constant cost. With this approximation, the past internal states before threshold are treated in a recursive manner without holding their values explicitly. FLRC is also regarded as the extension of the RC with leaky integrator (LRC) by introducing a new parameter, named fractional rate. In this paper, the proposed FLRC was evaluated via four kinds of time-series data prepared as benchmarks for regression or classification problems. We found that the proposed FLRC outperformed the conventional RC and LRC in all benchmarks.

2 Preliminaries

2.1 Reservoir Computing with Leaky Integrator Neurons

RC is one of the recurrent neural networks, which updates only readout weights, W^{out}. Other weights, i.e., inputs weights, W^{in}, feedback weights, W^{fb}, and recursive weights, W^{rec}, are randomly given to be constants. Regarding W^{rec}, however, the magnitude of eigenvalues is limited to satisfy the echo state property. This paper employs $\rho(|W^{rec}|) = 0.999$, where $\rho(\cdot)$ gives the maximum eigenvalue, as the echo state property according to ref. [24].

RC dynamics with N leaky integrator neurons is given as follows:

$$\boldsymbol{I}_t = f(W^{rec}\boldsymbol{x}_{t-1} + W^{in}\boldsymbol{u}_t + W^{fb}\boldsymbol{y}_{t-1}) \tag{1}$$

$$\boldsymbol{x}_t = (1 - a\beta)\boldsymbol{x}_{t-1} + \beta\boldsymbol{I}_t \tag{2}$$

$$\boldsymbol{y}_t = g(W^{out}[\boldsymbol{x}_t^\top, \boldsymbol{u}_t^\top]^\top) \tag{3}$$

where $\boldsymbol{x}$ are internal states of respective neurons, $\boldsymbol{u}$ and $\boldsymbol{y}$ are inputs and outputs of this system, respectively. $f(\cdot)$ is the activation function (hyperbolic tangent in general), and $g(\cdot)$ is task-dependent function: linear function in regression and softmax function in classification. a is usually given to be 1 for simplicity. Note that, when $\beta = 1$, the above equations match the basic RC.

β is generally a scalar, but in this paper, it is vectorized so as to have different time constants for each neuron. In addition, W^{fb} and direct inputs to outputs are ignored for simplicity. That is, the LRC dynamics in this paper is defined as follows:

$$\boldsymbol{I}_t = f(W^{rec}\boldsymbol{x}_{t-1} + W^{in}\boldsymbol{u}_t) \tag{4}$$

$$\boldsymbol{x}_t = (1 - \boldsymbol{\beta}) \odot \boldsymbol{x}_{t-1} + \boldsymbol{\beta}\boldsymbol{I}_t \tag{5}$$

$$\boldsymbol{y}_t = g(W^{out}\boldsymbol{x}_t) \tag{6}$$

2.2 Learning of Readout Weights

Let us introduce the way to update readout weights, W^{out}. Depending on the conducted task (regression or classification), loss function is defined as follows:

$$\mathcal{L} = \begin{cases} \sum_{i=1}^{n_b} \frac{1}{2}\|\boldsymbol{y}_i - \boldsymbol{t}_i\|_2^2 & \text{Regression} \\ -\sum_{i=1}^{n_b} \ln(\boldsymbol{y}_i)^\top \boldsymbol{t}_i & \text{Classification} \end{cases} \tag{7}$$

where n_b is the size of mini batch and $\boldsymbol{t}$ are supervisory signals. W^{out} is updated to minimize $\mathcal{L}$ generally by recursive least square method for linear regressor. In this paper, however, stochastic gradient decent (SGD) is employed since the latest SGD (Adam [10] with L2 regularization in this paper) can generate a stable gradient every time step. Note that learning rate η is given as $10^{-3}/N$.

3 Fractional-Order Neuron Dynamics

3.1 Derivation of Fractional-Order Leaky Integrator

In this section, the practical dynamics of fractional-order leaky integrator neurons are derived. Although derivation process is basically in accordance with refs. [19,20], it is noticed that the way to handle discrete time is partially corrected. In addition, the dynamics for single neuron is derived for simplicity of description.

First of all, the derivative of fractional-order leaky integrator neuron is defined as follows:

$$\frac{d^\alpha x_t}{dt^\alpha} = (-x_t + I_t)\tau^{-1} \tag{8}$$

where $\tau > 0$ is the time constant, and $\alpha \in (0, 1]$ is the order of the fractional derivative, named fractional rate. The left side of the above equation can be approximated by the following numerical integration using the L1 scheme of the Caputo fractional derivative [4].

$$\frac{d^\alpha x_t}{dt^\alpha} \simeq \frac{\delta^{-\alpha}}{\Gamma(2-\alpha)} \left[\sum_{k=0}^{t-1} (x_{k+1} - x_k) \left\{ (t-k)^{1-\alpha} - (t-1-k)^{1-\alpha} \right\} \right] \tag{9}$$

where δ is time step and $\Gamma(\cdot)$ is gamma function.

When $\delta^\alpha \tau^{-1} \Gamma(2-\alpha)$ is replaced as C, the above two equations are merged as follows:

$$\begin{aligned} C(-x_t + I_t) &= x_t - x_{t-1} \\ &+ \sum_{k=0}^{t-2} (x_{k+1} - x_k) \left\{ (t-k)^{1-\alpha} - (t-1-k)^{1-\alpha} \right\} \end{aligned} \quad (10)$$

The last term on the right side of the above equation is defined as m_{t-1}, named a memory trace.

$$m_{t-1} := \sum_{k=0}^{t-2} (x_{k+1} - x_k) \left\{ (t-k)^{1-\alpha} - (t-1-k)^{1-\alpha} \right\} \quad (11)$$

In that case, x_t is derived in a recursive manner.

$$\begin{aligned} (1+C)x_t &= x_{t-1} + CI_t - m_{t-1} \\ x_t &= \frac{1}{1+C}(x_{t-1} - m_{t-1}) + \frac{C}{1+C} I_t \\ \therefore x_t &= (1-\beta)(x_{t-1} - m_{t-1}) + \beta I_t \end{aligned} \quad (12)$$

where β replaces $C/(1+C)$.

As can be seen in Eq. (12), (5) is extended to it by adding the memory trace. When $\alpha = 1$, this equation is equivalent to Eq. (5) since the memory trace is no longer stored (see Eq. (11)). In addition, when $\beta = 1$, the memory trace does not affect the internal state, thereby matching the basic RC. In the original derivation in refs. [19,20], $(1-\beta)$ was not multiplied with the memory trace, which could always affect the internal state unless $\alpha = 1$.

3.2 Approximation to Memory Trace

However, the memory trace defined in Eq. (11) is intractable to calculate numerically because it requires all internal states from the initial time 0 to the current time t. A single neuron still has room for computing, but it is infeasible in RC with many neurons. A reasonable approximation is therefore applied to calculate the memory trace feasibly.

Now, a parameter, $n \in \mathbb{N}$, is introduced for approximation. The memory trace m_t is divided by using n as follows:

$$\begin{aligned} m_t = &\sum_{k=0}^{t-1-n} (x_{k+1} - x_k) \left\{ (t+1-n-k)^{1-\alpha} - (t-n-k)^{1-\alpha} \right\} \\ &\times \frac{(t+1-k)^{1-\alpha} - (t-k)^{1-\alpha}}{(t+1-n-k)^{1-\alpha} - (t-n-k)^{1-\alpha}} \\ &+ \sum_{k=t-n}^{t-1} (x_{k+1} - x_k) \left\{ (t+1-k)^{1-\alpha} - (t-k)^{1-\alpha} \right\} \end{aligned} \quad (13)$$

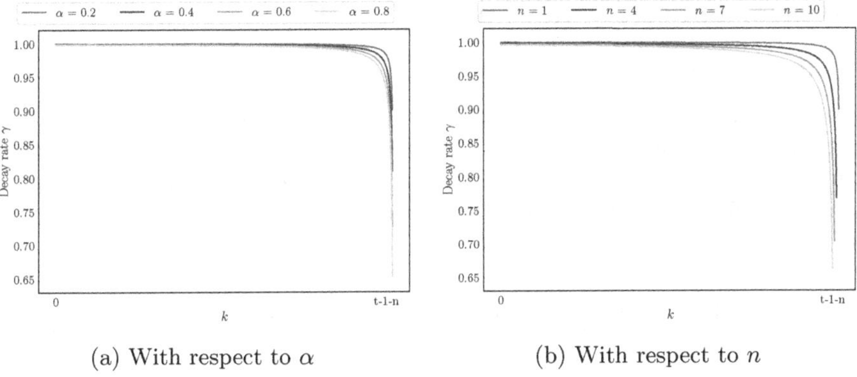

(a) With respect to α (b) With respect to n

Fig. 2. Decay rate $\gamma(\alpha, n, t, k)$: t is fixed with 500; as α and n increase, the approximation accuracy is expected to worsen; note that n yields the precise memory trace up to n, although this fact cannot be shown in this figure.

The latter summation can be computed with a constant cost, and an efficient solver has been proposed in ref. [14]. The former summation matches m_{t-n} if the multiplied coefficients, named decay rates, are excluded. It is therefore approximated as a value unrelated to k.

$$\frac{(t+1-k)^{1-\alpha} - (t-k)^{1-\alpha}}{(t+1-n-k)^{1-\alpha} - (t-n-k)^{1-\alpha}} =: \gamma(\alpha, n, t, k) \simeq \gamma(\alpha, n) \tag{14}$$

Since $\gamma(\alpha, n)$ is independent on k, it can be putted out of the summation. Namely, m_t is approximated in a recursive manner as follows:

$$m_t \simeq \gamma(\alpha, n) m_{t-n} + \sum_{k=t-n}^{t-1} (x_{k+1} - x_k) \left\{ (t+1-k)^{1-\alpha} - (t-k)^{1-\alpha} \right\} \tag{15}$$

Note that, even after this approximation, the memory trace is 0 when $\alpha = 1$.

The effect of this approximation can be confirmed from plots of the decay rate $\gamma(\alpha, n, t, k)$ summarized in Fig. 2. The smaller α yields quicker convergence to 1, which makes it easier to improve the approximation accuracy. The smaller n also improves the approximation accuracy, while the latest memory trace up to n can be calculated without the approximation. Then, to prioritize minimization of cost, $n = 1$ is employed in this paper.

$$m_t \simeq \gamma(\alpha, 1) m_{t-1} + (x_t - x_{t-1})(2^{1-\alpha} - 1) \tag{16}$$

As approximation methods of γ, several methods are considered: an optimistic method by approximating $\gamma(\alpha, n) = 1$; a worst-used method by approximating $\gamma(\alpha, n)$ with a minimum decay rate in a range of approximation; and a method mixing them. In the mixed method with mixing rate ζ (= 0.1, in this paper), $\gamma(\alpha, 1)$ is given as follows:

$$\gamma(\alpha, 1) = \zeta + (1 - \zeta) \frac{3^{1-\alpha} - 2^{1-\alpha}}{2^{1-\alpha} - 1} \tag{17}$$

4 Performance Evaluation

4.1 Benchmark Problems

10th NARMA System (NARMA). The task in the nonlinear auto-regressive moving average (NARMA) system [1] is to predict the next output from the current input and output. The input s is generated uniformly from an interval $[0, 0.5]$. The output in the 10th order system, y, is given by the following equation.

$$y(t+1) = 0.3y(t) + 0.05y(t)\sum_{i=0}^{9} y(t-i) + 1.5s(t-9)s(t) + 0.1 \tag{18}$$

That is, long memory capacity is required to predict the output since inputs and outputs up to 10 steps before are necessary. In this paper, 500 steps have been generated as one sequence, and 50 sequences are prepared as a dataset.

Inverse Kinematics for Two-Link Arm (IK). The task in the two-link arm, which has links ℓ_1 and ℓ_2 with 0.5 m, is to predict the joint angles and their angular velocities, (θ_1, θ_2) and $(\dot{\theta}_1, \dot{\theta}_2)$, from the reference of the tip of arm, (x, y). The reference trajectory is generated by sine waves with several frequencies for respective axes. This inverse kinematics can be solved analytically as follows:

$$\begin{aligned} \theta_1 &= \mathrm{atan2}(y, x) - \mathrm{atan2}\left(\sqrt{x^2 + y^2 - d_1^2}, d_1\right) \\ \theta_2 &= -\theta_1 + \mathrm{atan2}(y, x) + \mathrm{atan2}\left(\sqrt{x^2 + y^2 - d_2^2}, d_2\right) \end{aligned} \tag{19}$$

$$\text{where } d_1 = (x^2 + y^2 + \ell_1^2 - \ell_2^2)/(2\ell_1),\ d_2 = (x^2 + y^2 - \ell_1^2 + \ell_2^2)/(2\ell_2)$$

Their angular velocities are given as backward difference. In this paper, 500 steps have been generated from the specific reference trajectory as one sequence, and 50 sequences are prepared as a dataset.

Walking Path Classification (MovementAAL). This dataset is provided by ref. [2]. The task in this paper is to classify walking path into six paths according to the current four radio signal strengths (RSS). Although classification task with time-series data is generally evaluated by classifications for one sequence, it is evaluated by classifications at respective times in this paper. This setting is harder than general one and leads to clarifying the performance of the classifiers. Note that the size of mini batch is smaller than the other datasets ($n_b = 5$ in this dataset and $n_b = 50$ in the other datasets) due to the shorter sequences.

Activity Classification (AReM). This dataset is provided by ref. [16]. Seven activity, i.e., bending1, bending2 cycling, lying, sitting, standing, and walking, are classified from six inputs, i.e., respective means and variances of three RSS. As well as the walking path classification, this task is also evaluated by the classification results at respective times.

4.2 Evaluation Criteria

The prepared dataset is divided into training data with 75% and test data with 25%. Note that this division conducted 10 patterns for statistics. After learning 20 epochs with the training data, each method is evaluated with the test data. Evaluation differs between regression problems (first two benchmarks) and classification problems (remaining two). In the regression problems, criterion is given as normalized mean square error (NMSE).

$$\mathrm{NMSE} = \frac{\|\boldsymbol{y} - \boldsymbol{t}\|_2^2}{\|\boldsymbol{t}\|_2^2} \tag{20}$$

A smaller value means higher regression performance. The classification criterion is given as accuracy (ACC) of classification at each time.

$$\mathrm{ACC} = \frac{T_{cor}}{T_{all}} \tag{21}$$

where T_{cor} is the cumulative time successfully classified and T_{all} is the total time of dataset. A larger value means higher classification performance.

4.3 Results

Three methods, i.e., RC with $\boldsymbol{\alpha}, \boldsymbol{\beta} = 1$, LRC with $\boldsymbol{\alpha} = 1$ and $\boldsymbol{\beta} \in (0, 1)$, and FLRC (proposal) with $\boldsymbol{\alpha}, \boldsymbol{\beta} \in (0, 1)$, were compared in terms of the evaluation criteria. Note that $\boldsymbol{\alpha}$ and $\boldsymbol{\beta}$ were generated uniformly (or fixed to 1) for respective neurons, although they are usually scalars, which is specialized for a task to be learned. This design aims to eliminate the task-dependent optimization and to improve generalization. Except for $\boldsymbol{\alpha}$ and $\boldsymbol{\beta}$, all other network constants, such as W^{rec}, are commonly used.

Table 1. Means and standard deviations of evaluation results: in each benchmark, the best results were shown in bold; the means of FLRC with $N = 500$ outperformed the other methods in all benchmarks.

Benchmark	RC		LRC		FLRC (proposal)	
	$N = 100$	$N = 500$	$N = 100$	$N = 500$	$N = 100$	$N = 500$
NARMA (NMSE $\times 10^3$)	37.8 ± 0.6	55.2 ± 1.3	37.0 ± 0.5	35.0 ± 0.4	35.9 ± 0.5	**33.2 ± 0.5**
IK (NMSE $\times 10^2$)	13.3 ± 1.7	13.3 ± 1.7	12.4 ± 1.6	12.2 ± 1.6	12.3 ± 1.6	**12.0 ± 1.6**
MovementAAL (ACC%)	38.4 ± 3.5	38.7 ± 3.0	52.6 ± 4.8	54.6 ± 4.2	58.6 ± 3.5	**60.6 ± 3.4**
AReM (ACC%)	63.0 ± 4.1	62.8 ± 4.2	68.2 ± 4.6	68.8 ± 4.8	68.7 ± 4.7	**69.8 ± 4.7**

Results were shown in Fig. 3(a) and (b) and Table 1. As can be seen in them, FLRC outperformed the conventional RC and LRC in all benchmarks. In NARMA and MovementAAL, significant superiorities were confirmed, although the remaining two had no significances. This is because the former two benchmarks required the longer memory capacity rather than the latter two. In particular, NARMA absolutely needs the longer memory capacity in accordance with Eq. (18), while LRC is enough to predict the trajectory of the two-link arm from the current states and the next references in IK (see Eq. (19)).

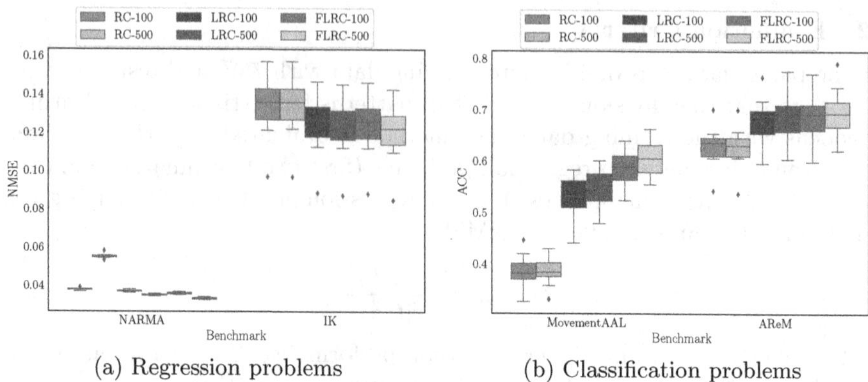

(a) Regression problems (b) Classification problems

Fig. 3. Box plots of evaluation results: the number behind the names of methods represented the number of neurons N, which basically improved the performance to some extent; FLRC outperformed the conventional methods, namely RC and LRC, in all benchmarks, although its superiorities in IK and AReM were not so significant.

5 Conclusion

This paper proposed a practical fractional-order leaky integrator neurons for RC, named FLRC, which yielded the long memory capacity. Although fractional-order derivative generally needs all memories leading to the current state from the initial state and this feature is intractable for RC with many neurons, a reasonable approximation to the fractional-order neuron dynamics derives the model that exponentially decays past memories before threshold. This derivation is regarded as natural extension of the normal leaky integrator. FLRC was compared with the conventional RC and LRC by solving four kinds of regression and classification problems with time-series data. As a result, FLRC achieved superior results in all of problems.

Future work of this study is to analyze the optimal design of α and β. Alternatively, they will be dynamically optimized according to SGD.

References

1. Atiya, A.F., Parlos, A.G.: New results on recurrent network training: unifying the algorithms and accelerating convergence. IEEE Trans. Neural Netw. **11**(3), 697–709 (2000)
2. Bacciu, D., Barsocchi, P., Chessa, S., Gallicchio, C., Micheli, A.: An experimental characterization of reservoir computing in ambient assisted living applications. Neural Comput. Appl. **24**(6), 1451–1464 (2014)
3. Chung, J., Gulcehre, C., Cho, K., Bengio, Y.: Empirical evaluation of gated recurrent neural networks on sequence modeling. arXiv preprint arXiv:1412.3555 (2014)
4. Diethelm, K., Ford, N.J., Freed, A.D., Luchko, Y.: Algorithms for the fractional calculus: a selection of numerical methods. Comput. Methods Appl. Mech. Eng. **194**(6–8), 743–773 (2005)

5. Gallicchio, C., Micheli, A., Pedrelli, L.: Deep reservoir computing: a critical experimental analysis. Neurocomputing **268**, 87–99 (2017)
6. Hermans, M., Schrauwen, B.: Training and analysing deep recurrent neural networks. In: Advances in Neural Information Processing Systems, pp. 190–198 (2013)
7. Hochreiter, S., Schmidhuber, J.: Long short-term memory. Neural Comput. **9**(8), 1735–1780 (1997)
8. Jaeger, H., Haas, H.: Harnessing nonlinearity: predicting chaotic systems and saving energy in wireless communication. Science **304**(5667), 78–80 (2004)
9. Jaeger, H., Lukoševičius, M., Popovici, D., Siewert, U.: Optimization and applications of echo state networks with leaky-integrator neurons. Neural Netw. **20**(3), 335–352 (2007)
10. Kingma, D., Ba, J.: Adam: a method for stochastic optimization. In: International Conference for Learning Representations, pp. 1–15 (2015)
11. Lukoševičius, M., Jaeger, H.: Reservoir computing approaches to recurrent neural network training. Comput. Sci. Rev. **3**(3), 127–149 (2009)
12. Lun, S.x., Yao, X.s., Hu, H.f.: A new echo state network with variable memory length. Inf. Sci. **370**, 103–119 (2016)
13. Maass, W., Markram, H.: On the computational power of circuits of spiking neurons. J. Comput. Syst. Sci. **69**(4), 593–616 (2004)
14. Marinov, T., Ramirez, N., Santamaria, F.: Fractional integration toolbox. Fract. Calc. Appl. Anal. **16**(3), 670–681 (2013)
15. Pahnehkolaei, S.M.A., Alfi, A., Machado, J.T.: Uniform stability of fractional order leaky integrator echo state neural network with multiple time delays. Inf. Sci. **418**, 703–716 (2017)
16. Palumbo, F., Gallicchio, C., Pucci, R., Micheli, A.: Human activity recognition using multisensor data fusion based on reservoir computing. J. Ambient. Intell. Smart Environ. **8**(2), 87–107 (2016)
17. Rodan, A., Tino, P.: Minimum complexity echo state network. IEEE Trans. Neural Netw. **22**(1), 131–144 (2011)
18. Schmidhuber, J., Wierstra, D., Gagliolo, M., Gomez, F.: Training recurrent networks by evolino. Neural Comput. **19**(3), 757–779 (2007)
19. Teka, W., Marinov, T.M., Santamaria, F.: Neuronal spike timing adaptation described with a fractional leaky integrate-and-fire model. PLoS Comput. Biol. **10**(3), e1003526 (2014)
20. Teka, W.W., Upadhyay, R.K., Mondal, A.: Fractional-order leaky integrate-and-fire model with long-term memory and power law dynamics. Neural Netw. **93**, 110–125 (2017)
21. Verstraeten, D., Schrauwen, B., Stroobandt, D., Van Campenhout, J.: Isolated word recognition with the liquid state machine: a case study. Inf. Process. Lett. **95**(6), 521–528 (2005)
22. Xue, F., Li, Q., Li, X.: The combination of circle topology and leaky integrator neurons remarkably improves the performance of echo state network on time series prediction. PloS one **12**(7), e0181816 (2017)
23. Yamazaki, T., Igarashi, J.: Realtime cerebellum: a large-scale spiking network model of the cerebellum that runs in realtime using a graphics processing unit. Neural Netw. **47**, 103–111 (2013)
24. Yildiz, I.B., Jaeger, H., Kiebel, S.J.: Re-visiting the echo state property. Neural Netw. **35**, 1–9 (2012)

An Unsupervised Character-Aware Neural Approach to Word and Context Representation Learning

Giuseppe Marra[1,2(✉)], Andrea Zugarini[1,2], Stefano Melacci[2], and Marco Maggini[2]

[1] DINFO, University of Firenze, Florence, Italy
{g.marra,andrea.zugarini}@unifi.it
[2] DIISM, University of Siena, Siena, Italy
mela@diism.unisi.it, marco.maggini@unisi.it

Abstract. In the last few years, neural networks have been intensively used to develop meaningful distributed representations of words and contexts around them. When these representations, also known as "embeddings", are learned from unsupervised large corpora, they can be transferred to different tasks with positive effects in terms of performances, especially when only a few supervisions are available. In this work, we further extend this concept, and we present an unsupervised neural architecture that jointly learns word and context embeddings, processing words as sequences of characters. This allows our model to spot the regularities that are due to the word morphology, and to avoid the need of a fixed-sized input vocabulary of words. We show that we can learn compact encoders that, despite the relatively small number of parameters, reach high-level performances in downstream tasks, comparing them with related state-of-the-art approaches or with fully supervised methods.

Keywords: Recurrent Neural Networks · Unsupervised learning
Word and context embeddings · Natural Language Processing
Deep learning

1 Introduction

Recent advances in Natural Language Processing (NLP) are characterized by the development of techniques that compute powerful word embeddings and by the extensive use of neural language models. Word Embeddings (WEs) aim at representing individual words in a low-dimensional continuous space, in order to exploit its topological properties to model semantic or grammatical relationships between different words. In particular, they are based on the assumption that functionally or semantically related words appear in similar contexts.

Despite the idea of continuous word representations was proposed a several years ago [4], their importance became strongly popular mostly after the work of Mikolov et al. [13], when the CBOW and Skip-Gram models were introduced as

V. Kůrková et al. (Eds.): ICANN 2018, LNCS 11141, pp. 126–136, 2018.
https://doi.org/10.1007/978-3-030-01424-7_13

implementations of the *word2vec* idea. Key features of these models are the unsupervised scheme of the learning process and the simplicity of the computation that allows a highly efficient training from very large unlabeled corpora. Moreover, the learning objective function is task-independent, such that it allows the development of embeddings suitable for several NLP tasks. WEs are generally constituted by a single vector to represent each specific word in a vocabulary V of $N = |V|$ words. The requirement of a predefined vocabulary is an important limitation for every NLP model. Rare and Out-Of-Vocabulary (OOV) words will not have a meaningful vector representation. Moreover, WEs do not take into account morphological properties of words. For instance, the same suffix *ing* may suggest that two words have some functional similarity. Hence, the information conveyed by the sequence of characters representing a word may be useful to tackle both the problem of unseen words and the modelling of morphology for in-vocabulary tokens. For instance, the character structure of tokens can also help to detect Named Entities, usually treated as OOV elements, recognizing proper nouns, by means of capital letters, or acronyms. Furthermore, a character-based model can deal with noise caused by typos, slang, etc., that are common issues in open-domain systems such as conversational agents or sentiment analysis tools.

There are several NLP tasks in which it is useful to generate vectorial representations of contexts too. In fact, polysemy and homonymy cause inherent semantic ambiguities in language interpretation, that can only be resolved by looking at the surrounding context, that is the goal of the Word Sense Disambiguation (WSD) task. Neural approaches have been developed to learn context embeddings, such as *context2vec* [12].

In this work we propose a character-based unsupervised model to learn both context and word embeddings from generic text. The model consists in a hierarchy of two distinct Bidirectional Long Short Term Memories (Bi-LSTMs) [18], to encode words as sequences of characters and word-level contextual representations, respectively. Our unsupervised learning approach, despite being more compact than other related algorithms, yields generic embeddings with features that can be efficiently exploited in different NLP tasks requiring either word or context embeddings, such as chunking and WSD, as we show in our comparisons.

The paper is structured as follows. First, in Sect. 2 the related work is summarized. Then, we describe the proposed model in Sect. 3. Section 4 reports our experimental results and Sect. 5 draws our conclusions and the directions for future work.

2 Related Work

Our unsupervised computational scheme follows the one of the CBOW instance of the *word2vec* algorithm [13]. The method we propose in this paper is inspired by the ideas behind *context2vec* [12], that we extend with a bidirectional recurrent neural model that processes words as sequence of characters. We also focus on a single encoder that we use both to represent words alone and words belonging to a context.

There are several approaches that jointly learn task-oriented (supervised) word and character-based representations, that are subsequently either concatenated or combined by a non-linear function. In [14] a gate adaptively decides how to mix the two representations, whereas the models proposed in [16,17] exploit the concatenation of word embeddings and character representations to address Part-Of-Speech (POS) Tagging and Named Entity Recognition (NER), respectively. Differently, our work focusses on a single character-level encoder that is trained in an unsupervised manner.

There exists a number of different approaches that extract vectorial representations directly from the character sequences of words, mostly focused on Language Modeling (LM) or Character Language Modeling (CLM). These representations are generally computed by either Convolutional Neural Networks (CNNs) or Recurrent Neural Networks (RNNs) - mostly LSTMs [5]. Ling et al. [11] applied Bidirectional LSTMs [18] to learn task-dependent character level features for Language Modeling and POS tagging, showing particular improvements in morphologically rich languages such as Turkish. A multi-layered Hierarchical Recurrent Neural Network was applied in [7] to solve CLM. Differently from our approach, the output of this model is a distribution over characters, while we exploit word level predictions. The character-aware model of [10], is based on a highway-network on top of 1-d convolutional filters processing input characters. The resulting output is then handled by a LSTM for a LM task. The highway-network output does provide the distributed representation of a word. In [9] different architectures, mostly based on CNNs, are studied in LM tasks. The proposed approach differs from most of the previous ones (1) for the learning mechanism, that is completely unsupervised on large text corpora, thus allowing the development of task-independent representations, and (2) for the architecture that is aimed at obtaining character-aware representations of both contexts and words, that are suitable for a large variety of NLP applications.

3 The Character-Aware Neural Model

The proposed model is organized as a hierarchical architecture based on Bi-LSTMs processing sentences. Each sentence is first split into a sequence of words using space characters (i.e. whitespaces, tabs, newlines, etc.) as separators. Words are further split into sequences of characters, such that there is no need to specify a vocabulary in advance. Then, the character sequence of an input word x is processed to obtain its vectorial representation (word embedding), while the character sequences of the surrounding words are used to encode the context to which x belongs (context embedding). Given the current sentence, the context of x comprises the words that precede and follow x. Inspired by the CBOW scheme [13], our model is trained to predict the current word given its context. In the following we describe each layer of the proposed architecture.

3.1 Word and Context Embeddings

We consider an input sentence s composed of n words, $s = (x_1, \ldots, x_n)$, where each word is a sequence of characters $x_i = (c_{i,1}, \ldots, c_{i,|x_i|})$, being $|x_i|$ the length of the sequence x_i. Each character c_{ij} is encoded as an index in a dictionary of C characters and it is mapped to a real vector $\hat{c}_{ij} \in \mathbb{R}^{d_c}$ as

$$\hat{c}_{ij} = W_c \cdot 1(c_{ij}), \tag{1}$$

where $W_c \in \mathbb{R}^{C \times d_c}$ is the matrix of the learnable character representations, each of them of size d_c, while $1(\cdot)$ is a function returning a one-hot representation of its integer input. Note that C is quite small, in the order of hundreds, compared to common word vocabularies, whose size is in the order of hundreds of thousands.

For each input word x_i, the first layer of the model extracts a *word embedding* e_i, using a bidirectional recurrent neural network with LSTM cells (Bi-LSTM) [2]. Let $\overrightarrow{r_c}$ and $\overleftarrow{r_c}$ be the forward and backward components of a Bi-LSTM taking a sequence of character embeddings as input and returning their internal states $\overrightarrow{h_c}$ and $\overleftarrow{h_c}$ after the entire sequence has been processed. The embeddings e_i of the word x_i is then the concatenation of $\overrightarrow{h_c}$ and $\overleftarrow{h_c}$:

$$e_i = [\overrightarrow{h_c}, \overleftarrow{h_c}] = [\overrightarrow{r_c}(\hat{c}_{i,1} \ldots \hat{c}_{i,|x_i|}), \overleftarrow{r_c}(\hat{c}_{i,|x_i|} \cdots \hat{c}_{i,1})], \tag{2}$$

where we indicated with $[\cdot\,,\cdot]$ the concatenation operation and we emphasized the backward nature of $\overleftarrow{r_c}$ by showing the character sequence in reverse order.

The second layer follows a similar scheme to compute the *contextual embedding* $\hat{e}_i$ of the word x_i in the sentence s. Let $\overrightarrow{r_e}$ and $\overleftarrow{r_e}$ be the forward and backward components of a Bi-LSTM taking as inputs the embeddings of left context of x_i (i.e. $[e_1, \ldots, e_{i-1}]$) and of the right context of x_i (i.e. $[e_{i+1}, \ldots, e_n]$), respectively. Given the Bi-LSTM internal states $\overrightarrow{h_e}$ and $\overleftarrow{h_e}$ obtained after processing the input left and right context sequences, the contextual embedding $\hat{e}_i$ of the word x_i is then obtained by projecting the concatenation of $\overrightarrow{h_e}$ and $\overleftarrow{h_e}$ into a lower-dimensional space by means of a Multi-Layer Perceptron (MLP), with the goal of merging and compressing the left and right context representations,

$$\hat{e}_i = MLP([\overrightarrow{h_e}, \overleftarrow{h_e}]) = MLP([\overrightarrow{r_e}(e_1 \ldots, e_{i-1}), \overleftarrow{r_e}(e_n \ldots e_{i+1})]). \tag{3}$$

The overall architecture is sketched in Fig. 1. Notice that e_i is the embedding of word x_i, whereas $\hat{e}_i$ is the representation of x_i in the context of s without including x_i itself. Hence, the model computes at the same time word (Eq. (2)) and context (Eq. (3)) embeddings for a specific word.

3.2 Learning Algorithm

Both word and context representations are learned following the unsupervised approach used in CBOW [12,13]. Given a corpus of textual data, the objective of our model is to predict each word given the representation of its surrounding context (Eq. (3)). In particular, the context embedding of Eq. (3) is projected into the space of the corpus vocabulary using a linear projection. Instead of performing a softmax activation and minimizing the cross-entropy (as commonly done in LM tasks), the whole network is trained by minimizing the Noise Contrastive Estimation (NCE) loss function [3]. NCE belongs to a family of classification algorithms, which approximate a softmax regression by means of sampling methods. NCE is particularly helpful in all those cases in which the number of output units is prohibitively high, as it is for our (and related) model.

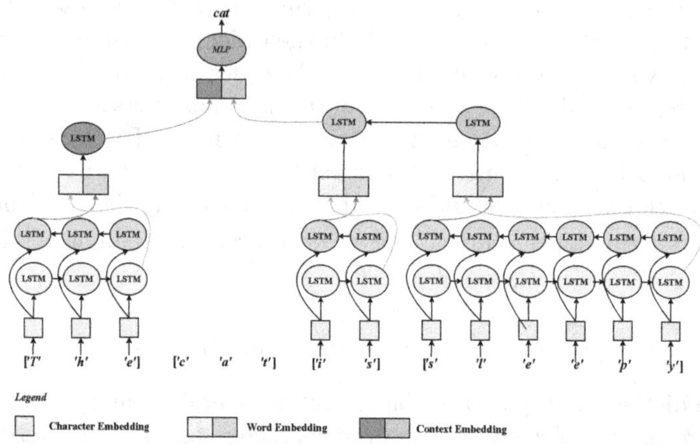

Fig. 1. The sentence "*The cat is sleepy*" is fed to our model, with target word *cat*. The sequence of character embeddings (orange squares on the bottom) are processed by the word-level Bi-LSTM yielding the word embeddings (yellow-red squares in the middle). The context-level Bi-LSTM processes the word embeddings in the left and right contexts of *cat*, to compute a representation of the whole context (blue-green squares on the top). Such representation is used to predict the target word *cat*, after having projected it by means of a MLP. (Color figure online)

One could argue that a vocabulary of words is still needed, since it is required to make the aforementioned word prediction. However, this is not a limitation, since it is only necessary at training time, while it is not needed when deploying the model. In principle, a different approach would be feasible, where the context representation of Eq. (3) is decoded into a sequence of characters that represent the word to predict. We tried both approaches and we found the word level prediction to give the best results. Thanks to the dynamic behaviour of the context-level RNNs, our model can deal with contexts of any length. In this work, the state of the RNN r_e is reset at the beginning of a new sentence, to reduce the variability of the contexts.

4 Experimental Results

We conducted different experiments to evaluate the word and context representations developed by the proposed model. In particular, we first trained our model on a large corpora. Then, we detached the learned word and context encoders and considered the tasks of Chunking and Word Sense Disambiguation (WSD), exploiting our word and context embeddings as features for each task-specific classifier, as shown in Fig. 2. Depending on the problem at hand, it may be useful to use either both the word and context embeddings or only one of them. Any other additional features can also be concatenated to these representations to obtain a richer input vector. We also evaluated the robustness of our model to character-level noise. Hence, we considered the WSD task when the input words are perturbed by typos modelled as random replacements of single characters. Finally we report some qualitative examples, showing the nearest neighbours for both word and context representations of a set of sample words.

Model Setup. Our model has been trained on the ukWaC corpus[1] (2 billion words). The size d_c of the character embeddings is set to 50, whereas word and context embeddings are of sizes 1000 and 600, respectively. The MLP, that maps the RNN states into the context embeddings, has one hidden layer of 1200 units with ReLU activation functions. These settings are inspired by those used in the *context2vec* architecture [12] (the structure of the last projection layer described in Subsect. 3.2 is the same). The complete encoding model has around 7 million trainable parameters, which is about 16 TIMES SMALLER than the *context2vec* model in [12]; this is due to the fact that words are encoded using a RNN that does not depend on the vocabulary size.

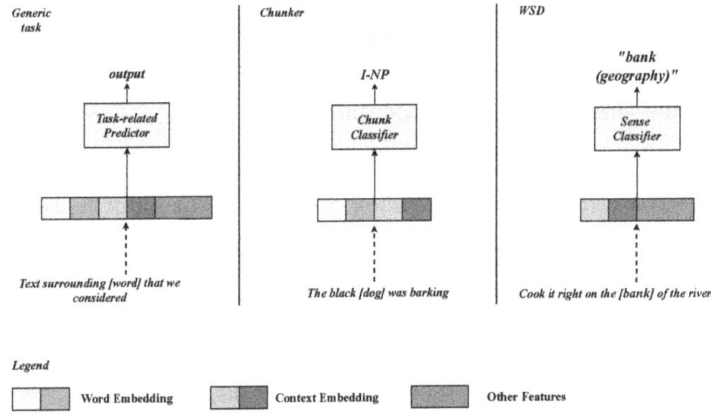

Fig. 2. Examples of how word and context embeddings can be used in a generic task, and in the cases of Chunking and WSD of this paper.

Chunking. Chunking is a classical NLP problem whose goal is to tag text segments with labels defining their syntactic roles, e.g. noun phrase (NP) or verbal

[1] http://wacky.sslmit.unibo.it/doku.php?id=corpora

phrase (VP). Each word is uniquely associated with a single tag expressing the segment class and its position within the phrase. An instance of Chunking classification is shown in Fig. 2, where the word *dog* is marked with the label *I-NP*, standing for Inside-chunk Noun Phrase. A standard benchmark for Chunking is the CoNLL 2000 dataset that contains 211,727 tokens in the training set and 47,377 tokens in the test set. The chunk tag is predicted by training a classifier that receives as input only the concatenation of the word and context embeddings computed by the model. This vector is projected onto a 600 dimensional space, and further processed by a Bi-LSTM that outputs vectors of size 500 that are finally mapped to the space of 23 classes, representing the chunk tags. Weights are updated using Adam Optimizer with default hyper-parameters and weight decay regularization with a factor of 0.001. We compared several variants of the proposed model and the resulting F1 scores are shown in Table 1. We report results when using only Word Embeddings (WE), only Context Embeddings (CE), and both of them (WE+CE). In this case we also considered WE and CE that are not generated by our model, but that are variables of the whole architecture trained with the task-level supervision. Both the feature types (WE and CE) are needed to achieve better performances, as expected. This experiment highlights the importance of using embeddings that are pre-trained with our model, that allows us to obtain the best F1 score of 93.30. This value can be compared with the results reported by Collobert et al. [1] (94.32) and by Huang et al. [6] (94.46), taking into account that in our case we did not make use of any hand-crafted feature nor of any kind of post-processing to adjust incoherent predictions. Moreover, when adding POS tagging features, our model reaches the same performances (93.94) of the state-of-the-art architecture [6] without Conditional Random Fields. Hence, we can conclude that the proposed architecture provides word and context embeddings that convey enough information to reach competitive performances. Furthermore, it should be considered that the number of parameters in the model is dramatically reduced with respect to such competitors, since there is no word vocabulary.

Table 1. Results on the Chunking task - different input features.

Input features	F1 %
Our WE only	89.68
Our CE only	89.59
Our WE + Our CE	**93.30**
WE + CE trained on task	89.83

Word Sense Disambiguation. Experiments on WSD were carried out within the evaluation framework proposed in [15], that collects multiple benchmarks (Senseval*, SemEval*, and a merged collection - ALL). The goal of WSD is to identify the correct sense of words. We followed the commonly used IMS approach [19], that is based on an SVM classifier on top of conventional WSD features. We compare our method against the original IMS model and other instances of it in which the WSD features are augmented with different context embeddings. We report the results in Tables 2 and 3. Our embeddings outperform both the IMS with only conventional features and *word2vec* embeddings, opportunely averaged [8], moreover it is competitive with *context2vec* representations. It is also worth to mention that, to the best of our knowledge, the use of *context2vec* features as input of the IMS is a novel attempt in the literature.

Table 2. Word Sense Disambiguation in the benchmarks collected in [15]. The best results (F1 %) are obtained by the *contex2Vec* model that however has 16 TIMES MORE PARAMETERS THAN THE PROPOSED MODEL and no capability to deal with OOV tokens.

Model	Senseval2	Senseval3	SemEval2007	SemEval2013	SemEval2015	ALL
IMS	70.2	68.8	62.2	65.3	69.3	68.1
IMS+word2vec	72.2	69.9	62.9	66.2	71.9	69.6
IMS+context2vec	**73.8**	**71.9**	**63.3**	**68.1**	**72.7**	**71.1**
IMS+Our CE	72.8	70.5	62.0	66.2	71.9	69.9

Table 3. Overall results (F1%) grouped by Part of Speech (ALL benchmark [15]).

Model	Noun	Adjective	Verb	Adverb
IMS	70.0	75.2	56.0	83.2
IMS+word2vec	71.8	76.1	57.4	83.5
IMS+context2vec	**73.1**	**77.0**	**60.5**	83.5
IMS+Our CE	71.3	76.6	58.1	**83.8**

Robustness to Typos. Many NLP applications should deal with noisy textual data. Indeed, misspelled words are likely to be set as OOV in models based on word dictionaries. We compare the proposed model against *context2vec* on a WSD task (ALL benchmark), when introducing an increasing probability to randomly perturb a character of a word. Conventional WSD features are completely removed for both the models, that only use context-level representations. Figure 3 shows how the F1 score decreases with the increase of the noise probability. Both the models suffer for word perturbations, but the character-aware embeddings yield a slower degradation in performances, that allows it to outperforms *context2vec* for high levels of noise.

Qualitative Evaluation. One of the most intriguing properties of embeddings is their capability to capture semantic and syntactic similarities into the topology of the embedding space. Such characteristic is illustrated by means of examples for both the representations (word and context) obtained by the proposed model. Distance between the distributed representations are computed by the cosine

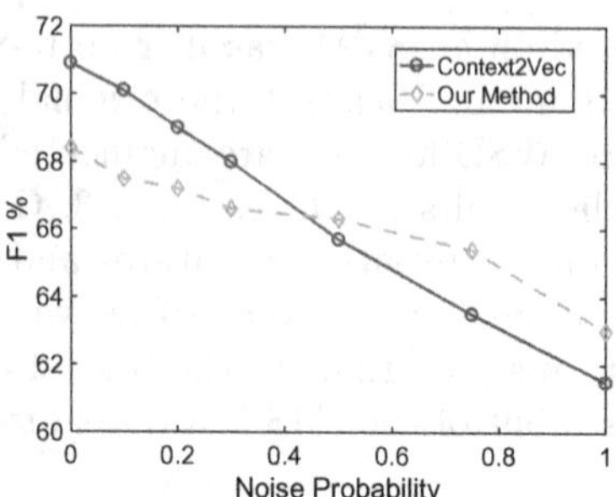

Fig. 3. Robustness to typos in a WSD task (ALL benchmark [15]). The "noise probability" represents the probability of having a typo in a word.

similarity. In Table 4 we show the 5 nearest neighbours for some given words. The examples show that the character based model is capable of capturing both morphological and semantic similarities.

Table 4. Top-5 closest words for a given target word.

Turkish	Sometimes	Usually	Happiness
Danish	Somehow	Normally	Weirdness
Welsh	Altogether	Basically	Fairness
French	Perhaps	Barely	Deformity
Kurdish	Nonetheless	Typically	Ripeness
Swedish	Heretofore	Formerly	Smoothness

For the evaluation of context representations, we considered 8 sentences related to 2 different topics (4 sentences each): capitals of states and pizza. A context embedding is obtained by considering the tokens around the word *capital* or *pizza*. Then, a random sentence is chosen as query, and the remaining

Table 5. Some contexts sorted by descending cosine similarity with respect to the query context *"I like eating [ ] with cheese and ham"* of (unused) target word *pizza*.

	Query: *I like eating [ ] with cheese and ham.*	pizza
Contexts sorted by descending cosine similarity	Do you like to eat [ ] with cheese and salami?	pizza
	Did you eat [ ] at lunch?	pizza
	What is the best [ ] i can eat here?	pizza
	Paris is the [ ] and most populous city in France ...	capital
	London is the [ ] and most populous city of England ...	capital
	Rome is the [ ] of Italian Republic	capital
	Washington , D.C. , ... , is the [ ] of the United States	capital

sentences are sorted according to the distance between the query context embedding and their vectors. An example is shown in Table 5, where it is clear that all the contexts related to *pizza* instances are closer to the query than sentences concerning *capitals*.

5 Conclusions

We presented an unsupervised neural model that can develop task-independent word and context representations using character-level inputs. We trained our model on a 2 billion word corpus, and the resulting word and context encoders were used to produce robust input features to approach some popular NLP tasks (Chunking, WSD). The proposed model has shown the capability of building powerful representations that are competitive to state-of-the-art embeddings generated by models with a significantly larger number of parameters. Our future work will include applications of this model to conversational systems.

References

1. Collobert, R., Weston, J., Bottou, L., Karlen, M., Kavukcuoglu, K., Kuksa, P.: Natural language processing (almost) from scratch. J. Mach. Learn. Res. **12**, 2493–2537 (2011)
2. Graves, A., Schmidhuber, J.: Framewise phoneme classification with bidirectional LSTM and other neural network architectures. Neural Netw. **18**(5–6), 602–610 (2005)
3. Gutmann, M., Hyvärinen, A.: Noise-contrastive estimation: a new estimation principle for unnormalized statistical models. In: AISTATS, pp. 297–304 (2010)
4. Hinton, G.E., Mcclelland, J.L., Rumelhart, D.E.: Distributed Representations, Parallel Distributed Processing: Explorations in the Microstructure of Cognition, vol. 1: foundations (1986)
5. Hochreiter, S., Schmidhuber, J.: Long short-term memory. Neural Comput. **9**(8), 1735–1780 (1997)
6. Huang, Z., Xu, W., Yu, K.: Bidirectional LSTM-CRF models for sequence tagging. arXiv preprint arXiv:1508.01991 (2015)
7. Hwang, K., Sung, W.: Character-level language modeling with hierarchical recurrent neural networks. In: 2017 IEEE International Conference on Acoustics, Speech and Signal Processing (ICASSP), pp. 5720–5724. IEEE (2017)
8. Iacobacci, I., Pilehvar, M.T., Navigli, R.: Embeddings for word sense disambiguation: an evaluation study. In: ACL (Volume 1: Long Papers), pp. 897–907 (2016)
9. Jozefowicz, R., Vinyals, O., Schuster, M., Shazeer, N., Wu, Y.: Exploring the limits of language modeling. arXiv preprint arXiv:1602.02410 (2016)
10. Kim, Y., Jernite, Y., Sontag, D., Rush, A.M.: Character-aware neural language models. In: AAAI, pp. 2741–2749 (2016)
11. Ling, W., et al.: Finding function in form: compositional character models for open vocabulary word representation. In: EMNLP, pp. 1520–1530 (2015)
12. Melamud, O., Goldberger, J., Dagan, I.: context2vec: learning generic context embedding with bidirectional LSTM. In: Proceedings of the 20th SIGNLL Conference on Computational Natural Language Learning, pp. 51–61 (2016)

13. Mikolov, T., Chen, K., Corrado, G., Dean, J.: Efficient estimation of word representations in vector space. arXiv preprint arXiv:1301.3781 (2013)
14. Miyamoto, Y., Cho, K.: Gated word-character recurrent language model. In: Proceedings of the 2016 Conference on EMNLP, pp. 1992–1997 (2016)
15. Raganato, A., Camacho-Collados, J., Navigli, R.: Word sense disambiguation: a unified evaluation framework and empirical comparison. In: EACL (2017)
16. Santos, C.D., Zadrozny, B.: Learning character-level representations for part-of-speech tagging. In: ICML, pp. 1818–1826 (2014)
17. Santos, C.N.d., Guimaraes, V.: Boosting named entity recognition with neural character embeddings. arXiv preprint arXiv:1505.05008 (2015)
18. Schuster, M., Paliwal, K.K.: Bidirectional recurrent neural networks. IEEE Trans. Signal Process. **45**(11), 2673–2681 (1997)
19. Zhong, Z., Ng, H.T.: It makes sense: a wide-coverage word sense disambiguation system for free text. In: ACL, pp. 78–83 (2010)

Towards End-to-End Raw Audio Music Synthesis

Manfred Eppe(✉), Tayfun Alpay, and Stefan Wermter

Knowledge Technology, Department of Informatics, University of Hamburg, Vogt-Koelln-Str. 30, 22527 Hamburg, Germany
{eppe,alpay,wermter}@informatik.uni-hamburg.de
http://www.informatik.uni-hamburg.de/WTM/

Abstract. In this paper, we address the problem of automated music synthesis using deep neural networks and ask whether neural networks are capable of realizing timing, pitch accuracy and pattern generalization for automated music generation when processing raw audio data. To this end, we present a proof of concept and build a recurrent neural network architecture capable of generalizing appropriate musical raw audio tracks.

Keywords: Music synthesis · Recurrent neural networks

1 Introduction

Most contemporary music synthesis tools generate symbolic musical representations, such as MIDI messages, Piano Roll, or ABC notation. These representations are later transformed into audio signals by using a synthesizer [8,12,16]. Symbol-based approaches have the advantage of offering relatively small problem spaces compared to approaches that use the raw audio waveform. A problem with symbol-based approaches is, however, that fine nuances in music, such as timbre and microtiming must be explicitly represented as part of the symbolic model. Established standards like MIDI allow only a limited representation which restricts the expressiveness and hence also the producible audio output.

An alternative is to directly process raw audio data for music synthesis. This is independent of any restrictions imposed by the underlying representation, and, therefore, offers a flexible basis for realizing fine tempo changes, differences in timbre even for individual instruments, or for the invention of completely novel sounds. The disadvantage of such approaches is, however, that the representation space is continuous, which makes them prone to generating noise and other inappropriate audio signals.

In this work, we provide a proof of concept towards filling this gap and develop a baseline system to investigate how problematic the large continuous representation space of raw audio music synthesis actually is. We hypothesize

V. Kůrková et al. (Eds.): ICANN 2018, LNCS 11141, pp. 137–146, 2018.
https://doi.org/10.1007/978-3-030-01424-7_14

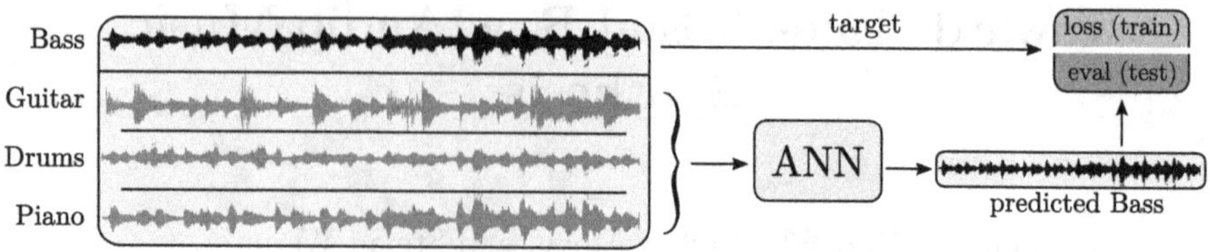

Fig. 1. The practical application and workflow of our system.

that a recurrent network architecture is capable of synthesizing non-trivial musical patterns directly in wave form while maintaining an appropriate quality in terms of pitch, timbre, and timing.

The practical context in which we situate our system is depicted in Fig. 1. Our system is supposed to take a specific musical role in an ensemble, such as generating a bassline, lead melody, harmony or rhythm and to automatically generate appropriate audio tracks given the audio signals from the other performers in the ensemble. To achieve this goal, we train a recurrent artificial neural network (ANN) architecture (described in Fig. 2) to learn to synthesize a well-sounding single instrument track that fits an ensemble of multiple other instruments. For example, in the context of a classic rock ensemble, we often find a composition of lead melody, harmony, bass line, and drums. Our proposed system will learn to synthesize one of these tracks, say bass, given the others, i.e., lead melody, harmony and drums. Herein, we do not expect the resulting system to be able to fully replace a human musician, but rather focus on specific measurable aspects. Specifically, we investigate:

1. Timing and beat alignment, i.e., the ability to play a sequence of notes that are temporally aligned correctly to the song's beat.
2. Pitch alignment, i.e., the ability to generate a sequence of notes that is correct in pitch.
3. Pattern generalization and variation, i.e., the ability to learn general musical patterns, such as alternating the root and the 5th in a bass line, and to apply these patterns in previously unheard songs.

We hypothesize that our baseline model offers these capabilities to a fair degree.

2 Related Work

An example for a symbolic approach for music generation, melody invention and harmonization has been presented by Eppe et al. [4,6], who build on *concept blending* to realize the harmonization of common jazz patterns. The work by Liang et al. [12], employs a symbol-based approach with recurrent neural networks (RNNs) to generate music in the style of Bach chorales. The authors demonstrate that their system is capable of generalizing appropriate musical patterns and applying them to previously unheard input. An advanced general artistic framework that also offers symbol-based melody generation is Magenta [16]. Magenta's Performance-RNN module is able to generate complex polyphonic musical patterns. It also supports micro timing and advanced dynamics, but the underlying representation is still symbolic, which implies that the producible audio data is restricted. For example, novel timbre nuances cannot be generated from scratch. As another example, consider the work by Hung et al. [8], who demonstrate an end-to-end approach for automated music generation using a MIDI representation and Piano Roll representation.

Contemporary approaches for raw audio generation usually lack the generalization capability for higher-level musical patterns. For example, the Magenta framework also involves NSynth [3], a neural synthesizer tool focusing on high timbre quality of individual notes of various instruments. The NSynth framework itself is, however, not capable of generating sequences of notes, i.e., melodies or harmonies, and the combination with the Performance-RNN Magenta melody generation tool [16] still uses an intermediate symbolic musical representation which restricts the produced audio signal. Audio generation has also been investigated in-depth in the field of speech synthesis. For example, the WaveNet architecture [15] is a general-purpose audio-synthesis tool that has mostly been employed in the speech domain. It has inspired the Tacotron text-to-speech framework which provides expressive results in speech synthesis [18]. To the best of our knowledge, however, WaveNet, or derivatives of it, have not yet been demonstrated to be capable of generalizing higher-level musical patterns in the context of generating a musical track that fits other given tracks. There exist some recent approaches to sound generation operating on raw waveforms without any external knowledge about musical structure, chords or instruments. A simple approach is to perform regression in the frequency domain using RNNs and to use a seed sequence after training to generate novel sequences [9,14]. We are, however, not aware of existing work that has been evaluated with appropriate empirical metrics. In our work, we perform such an evaluation and determine the quality of the produced audio signals in terms of pitch and timing accuracy.

3 A Baseline Neural Model for Raw Audio Synthesis

For this proof of concept we employ a simple baseline core model consisting of two Gated Recurrent Unit (GRU) [2] layers that encode 80 Mel spectra into a dense bottleneck representation and then decode this bottleneck representation back to 80 Mel spectra (see Fig. 2). Similar neural architectures have proven to be very successful for various other audio processing tasks in robotics and signal processing (e.g. [5]), and we have experimented with several alternative architectures using also dropout and convolutional layers but found that these variations did not improve the pitch and timing accuracy significantly. We also performed hyperparameter optimization using a Tree-Parzen estimator [1] to determine the optimal number of layers and number of units in each layer. We found that for most experiments two GRU layers of 128 units each for the encoder and the decoder, and a Dense layer consisting of 80 units as a bottleneck representation produced the best results. The dense bottleneck layer is useful because it forces the neural network to learn a Markovian compressed representation of the input signal, where each generated vector of dense activations is independent of the previous ones. This restricts the signals produced during the testing phase of the system, such that they are close to the signals that the system learned from during the training phase.

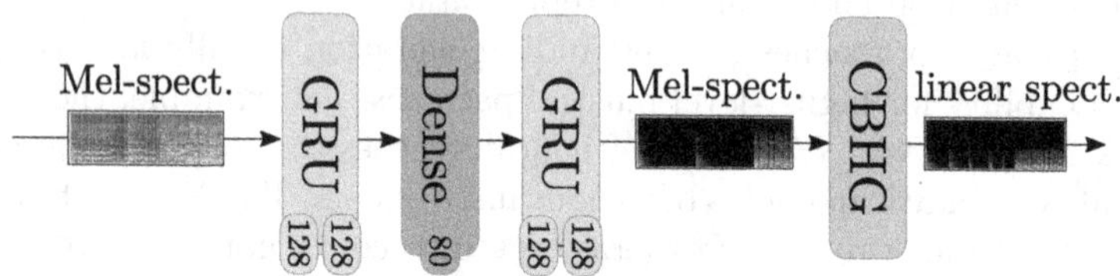

Fig. 2. Our proposed network for mapping the Mel spectra to a dense bottleneck representation, back to Mel spectra, and then to linear frequency spectra.

To transform the Mel spectra generated by the decoding GRU layers back into an audio signal, we combine our model with techniques known from speech synthesis that have been demonstrated to generate high-quality signals [15]. Specifically, instead of using a Griffin-Lim algorithm [7] to transform the Mel spectra into audio signals, we use a CBHG network to transform the 80 Mel coefficients into 1000 linear frequency coefficients, which are then transformed into an audio signal using Griffin-Lim. The CBHG network [11] is composed of a **C**onvolutional filter **B**ank, a **H**ighway layer, and a bidirectional **G**RU. It acts as a sequence transducer with feature learning capabilities. This module has been demonstrated to be very efficient within the Tacotron model for speech recognition [18], in the sense that fewer Mel coefficients, and therefore fewer network parameters, are required to produce high-quality signals [15]. Our loss function is also inspired by the recent work on speech synthesis, specifically the Tacotron [18] architecture: We employ a joint loss function that involves an L1 loss on the Mel coefficients plus a modified L1 loss on the linear frequency spectra where low frequencies are prioritized.

4 Data Generation

To generate the training and testing audio samples, we use a publicly available collection of around 130,000 midi files[1]. The dataset includes various kinds of musical genres including pop, rock, rap, electronic music, and classical music. Each MIDI file consists of several tracks that contain sequences of messages that indicate which notes are played, how hard they are played, and on which channel they are played. Each channel is assigned one or more instruments. A problem with this dataset is that it is only very loosely annotated and very diverse in

[1] https://redd.it/3ajwe4, accessed 18/01/18.

terms of musical genre, musical complexity, and instrument distribution. We do not expect our proof of concept system to be able to cope with the full diversity of the dataset and, therefore, only select those files that meet the following criteria:

1. They contain between 4 and 6 different channels, and each channel must be assigned exactly one instrument.
2. They are from a similar musical genre. For this work, we select classical pop and rock from the 60s and 70s and select only songs from the following artists: The Beatles, The Kinks, The Beach Boys, Simon and Garfunkel, Johnny Cash, The Rolling Stones, Bob Dylan, Tom Petty, Abba.
3. We eliminate duplicate songs.
4. They contain exactly one channel with the specific instrument to extract.

For this work, we consider bass, reed, and guitar as instruments to extract. The bass channel is representing a rhythm instrument that is present in most of the songs, yielding large amounts of data. The reed channel is often used for lead melody, and guitar tracks often contain chords consisting of three ore more notes. As a result, we obtain 78 songs with an extracted guitar channel, 61 songs with an extracted reed channel, and 128 songs with an extracted bass channel. We split the songs such that 80% are used for training and 20% for testing for each instrument. For each file, we extract the channel with the instrument that we want to synthesize, generate a raw audio (.wav) file from that channel, and chunk the resulting file into sliding windows of 11.5 s, with a window step size of 6 s. We then discard those samples which contain a low amplitude audio signal with an average root-mean-square energy of less than 0.2.

5 Results and Evaluation

To obtain results, we trained the system for 40,000 steps with a batch size of 32 samples and generated a separate model for each instrument. For the training, we used an Adam optimizer [10] with an adaptive learning rate. We evaluate the system empirically by developing appropriate metrics for pitch, timing and variation, and we also perform a qualitative evaluation in terms of generalization capabilities of the system. We furthermore present selected samples of the system output and describe qualitatively in how far the system is able to produce high-level musical patterns.

5.1 Empirical Evaluation

For the empirical evaluation, we use a metric that compares the audio signals of a generated track with the original audio track for each song in the test subset of the dataset. The metric considers three factors: timing accuracy, pitch accuracy, and variation.

Timing Accuracy. For the evaluation of the timing of a generated track, we compute the onsets of each track and compare them with the beat times obtained from the MIDI data. Onset estimation is realized by locating note onset events by picking peaks in an onset strength envelope [13]. The timing error is estimated as the mean time difference between the detected onsets and the nearest 32nd notes. Results are illustrated in Fig. 3 for bass, guitar and reed track generation. The histograms show that there exists a difference in the timing error between the generated and the original tracks, specifically for the generated bass tracks. Hence, we conclude that the neural architecture is very accurate in timing. This coincides with our subjective impression that we gain from the individual samples depicted in Sect. 5.2. The computed mean error is between 20 ms and 40ms, which is the same for the original track. Since the onset estimation sometimes generates wrong onsets (cf. the double onsets in the original track of *Ob-La-Di, Ob-La-Da*, Sect. 5.2), we hypothesize that the error results from this inaccuracy rather than from inaccurate timing.

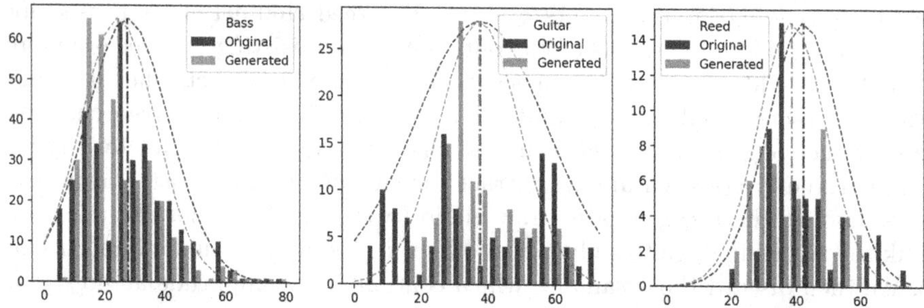

Fig. 3. Timing results for bass, guitar and reed track generation. The x-axis denotes the average error in ms and the y-axis the number of samples in a histogram bin.

Pitch Accuracy. We measure the pitch accuracy of the generated audio track by determining the base frequency of consecutive audio frames of 50ms. Determining the base frequency is realized by quadratically interpolated FFT [17], and we compare it to the closest frequency of the 12 semitones in the chromatographic scale over seven octaves. The resulting error is normalized w.r.t. the frequency interval between the two nearest semitones, and averaged over all windows for each audio sample. The results (Fig. 4) show that that the system is relatively accurate in pitch, with a mean error of 11%, 7%, and 5.5% of the frequency interval between the nearest two semitones for bass, guitar, and reed respectively. However, in particular for the bass, this is a significantly larger error than the error of the original track. The samples depicted in Sect. 5.2 confirm these results subjectively, as the produced sound is generally much less clean than the MIDI-generated data, and there are several noisy artifacts and chunks that are clearly outside of the chromatographic frequency spectrum.

Variation. To measure variation appropriateness, we consider the number of tones and the number of different notes in each sample. However, in contrast to pitch and timing, it is not possible to compute an objective error for the

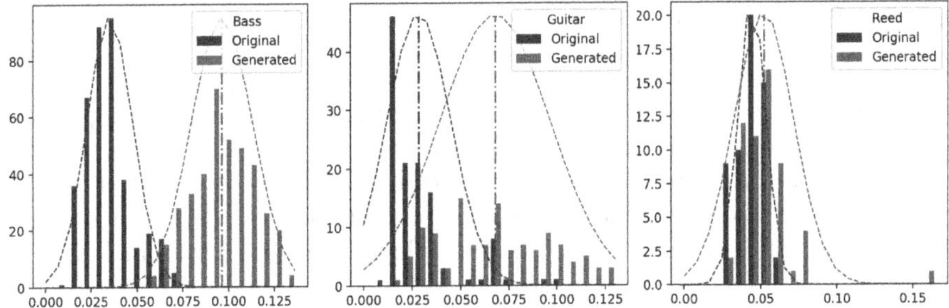

Fig. 4. Pitch accuracy results for bass, guitar and reed track generation; The x-axis denotes the average pitch error in fractions of the half interval between the two closest semitone frequencies.

amount of variation in a musical piece. Hence, we directly compare the variation in the generated samples with the variation in the original samples and assume implicitly that the original target track has a perfect amount of notes and tones. Hence, to compute the variation appropriateness v we compare the number of original notes (n_{orig}) and tones (t_{orig}) with the number of generated notes (n_{gen}) and tones (t_{gen}), as described in Eq. 1.

$$
\begin{gathered}
v = v_{\text{notes}} \cdot v_{\text{tones}} \quad \text{with} \\
v_{\text{tones}} = \begin{cases} \frac{\mathrm{t}_{orig}}{\mathrm{t}_{gen}} & \text{if } \mathrm{t}_{orig} < \mathrm{t}_{gen} \\ \frac{\mathrm{t}_{gen}}{\mathrm{t}_{orig}} & \text{otherwise} \end{cases} \quad v_{\text{notes}} = \begin{cases} \frac{\mathrm{n}_{orig}}{\mathrm{n}_{gen}} & \text{if } \mathrm{n}_{orig} < \mathrm{n}_{gen} \\ \frac{\mathrm{n}_{gen}}{\mathrm{n}_{orig}} & \text{otherwise} \end{cases}
\end{gathered} \tag{1}
$$

Results are illustrated in Fig. 5. The histograms show that there are several cases where the system produces the same amount of variation as the original tracks. The average variation value is approximately 0.5 for all instruments. However, we do not consider this value as a strict criterion for the quality of the generated tracks, but rather as an indicator to demonstrate that the system is able to produce tracks that are not too different from the original tracks.

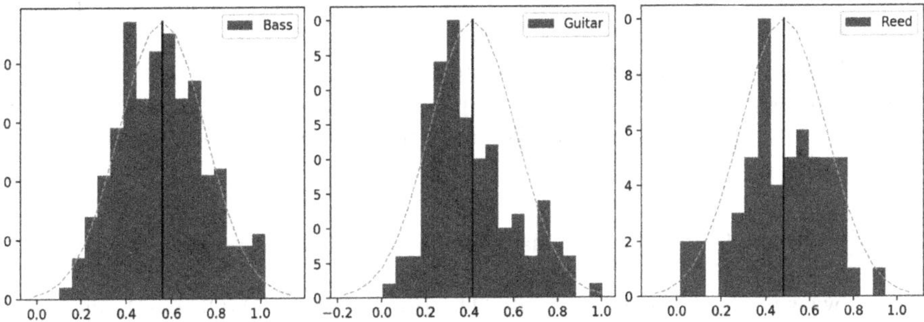

Fig. 5. Variation of generated tracks compared to the original track for three different instruments.

5.2 Qualitative Evaluation

To evaluate the generated audio files qualitatively, we investigate the musical patterns of the generated examples. The patterns that we found range from simple sequences of quarter notes over salient accentuations and breaks to common musical patterns like minor and major triads. In the following, analyze two examples of generated bass lines and, to demonstrate how the approach generalizes over different instruments, also one example of a generated flute melody. We visualize the samples using beat-synchronous chromagrams with indicated onsets (vertical while lines). The upper chromagrams represent the original melodies and the lower chromagrams the generated ones. Audio samples where the original tracks are replaced by the generated ones are linked with the song titles.

Op. 74 No. 15 Andantino Grazioso - Mauro Giuliano.[2] The piece has been written for guitar and flute, and we obtained this result by training the network on all files in our dataset that contain these two instruments. The newly generated flute track differs significantly from the original one although style and timbre are very similar. All notes of the generated track are played in D major scale, same as the original track. The beat is also the same even though the network generates more onsets overall. Near the end of the track, the flute plays a suspended C# which dissolves itself correctly into the tonic chord D. This shows how the network successfully emulates harmonic progression from the original.

The Beatles - Ob-La-Di, Ob-La-Da.[3] Most generated samples are similar to the illustrated one from *The Beatles - Ob-La-Di, Ob-La-Da*, where the generated notes are in the same key of the original composition, including the timings of chord changes. In some places, however, alternative note sequences have formed as can be seen in the first section of the chromagram, where the F-G is replaced by an D-G pattern, and in the middle section of the chromagram, where the D is exchanged with an A for two beats.

Bob Dylan - Positively 4th Street.[4] In some instances, the generated track contains melodies that are also played by other instruments (e.g. the left hand of the piano often mirrors the bassline). For these cases, we observed that the network has learned to imitate the key tones of other instruments. This results in generated tracks that are nearly identical to the original tracks, as illustrated in the following chromagram of *Positively 4th Street.*

However, while the original bass sequence has been generated by a MIDI synthesizer, the new sample sounds much more bass-like and realistic. This

[2] http://www.publications.eppe.eu/data/Giuliani_Op74_No15_Andantino_grazioso_merged

[3] http://www.publications.eppe.eu/data/The_Beatles_Ob-La-Di_Ob-La-Da_merged.wav

[4] http://www.publications.eppe.eu/data/Bob_Dylan_Positively_4th_Street_merged.wav

means that our system can effectively be used to synthesize an accurate virtual instrument, which can exploited as a general mechanism to re-synthesize specific tracks.

6 Conclusion

We have presented a neural architecture for raw audio music generation, and we have evaluated the system in terms of pitch, timing, variation, and pattern generalization. The metrics that we applied are sufficiently appropriate to determine whether our base line neural network architecture, or future extensions of it, have the potential to synthesize music directly in wave form, instead of using symbolic representations that restrict the possible outcome. We found that this is indeed the case, as the system is very exact in terms of timing, relatively exact in pitch, and because it generates a similar amount of variation as original music. We also conclude that the system applies appropriate musical standard patterns, such as playing common cadences. Examples like *Positively 4th Street* also show that our system is potentially usable as a synthesizer to enrich and replace MIDI-generated tracks.

As future work, we also want to investigate in how far the system implicitly learns high-level musical features and patterns like cadences and triads, and how it uses such patterns to generate appropriate musical audio data.

Acknowledgments. The authors gratefully acknowledge partial support from the German Research Foundation DFG under project CML (TRR 169), the European Union under project SECURE (No 642667).

References

1. Bergstra, J., Yamins, D., Cox, D.: Making a science of model search: hyperparameter optimization in hundreds of dimensions for vision architectures. In: International Conference on Machine Learning (ICML) (2013)
2. Chung, J., Gulcehre, C., Cho, K., Bengio, Y.: Empirical evaluation of gated recurrent neural networks on sequence modeling. In: Neural Information Processing Systems (NIPS) (2014)
3. Engel, J., et al.: Neural audio synthesis of musical notes with WaveNet autoencoders. Technical report (2017). http://arxiv.org/abs/1704.01279
4. Eppe, M., et al.: Computational invention of cadences and chord progressions by conceptual chord-blending. In: Proceedings of the 24th International Joint Conference on Artificial Intelligence (IJCAI), pp. 2445–2451 (2015)
5. Eppe, M., Kerzel, M., Strahl, E.: Deep neural object analysis by interactive auditory exploration with a humanoid robot. In: International Conference on Intelligent Robots and Systems (IROS) (2018)
6. Eppe, M., et al.: A computational framework for concept blending. Artif. Intell. **256**(3), 105–129 (2018)
7. Griffin, D., Lim, J.: Signal estimation from modified short-time Fourier transform. IEEE Trans. Acoust. Speech Signal Process. **32**(2), 236–243 (1984)

8. Huang, A., Wu, R.: Deep learning for music. Technical report (2016). https://arxiv.org/pdf/1606.04930.pdf
9. Kalingeri, V., Grandhe, S.: Music generation using deep learning. Technical report (2016). https://arxiv.org/pdf/1612.04928.pdf
10. Kingma, D.P., Ba, J.L.: Adam: a method for stochastic optimization. In: International Conference on Learning Representations (ICLR) (2015)
11. Lee, J., Cho, K., Hofmann, T.: Fully character-level neural machine translation without explicit segmentation. Trans. Assoc. Comput. Linguist. **5**, 365–378 (2017)
12. Liang, F., Gotham, M., Johnson, M., Shotton, J.: Automatic stylistic composition of bach chorales with deep LSTM. In: Proceedings of the 18th International Society for Music Information Retrieval Conference, pp. 449–456 (2017)
13. Mcfee, B., et al.: librosa: audio and music signal analysis in Python. In: Python in Science Conference (SciPy) (2015)
14. Nayebi, A., Vitelli, M.: GRUV: algorithmic music generation using recurrent neural networks. Stanford University, Technical report (2015)
15. van den Oord, A., et al.: WaveNet: a generative model for raw audio. Technical report (2016). http://arxiv.org/abs/1609.03499
16. Simon, I., Oore, S.: Performance RNN: generating music with expressive timing and dynamics (2017). https://magenta.tensorflow.org/performance-rnn
17. Smith, J.O.: Spectral Audio Signal Processing. W3K Publishing (2011)
18. Wang, Y., et al.: Tacotron: towards end-to-end speech synthesis. Technical report, Google, Inc. (2017). http://arxiv.org/abs/1703.10135

Real-Time Hand Prosthesis Biomimetic Movement Based on Electromyography Sensory Signals Treatment and Sensors Fusion

João Olegário de Oliveira de Souza(✉),
José Vicente Canto dos Santos, Rodrigo Marques de Figueiredo,
and Gustavo Pessin

UNISINOS University, Sao Leopoldo, Brazil
jolegario@unisinos.br

Abstract. The hand of the human being is a very sophisticated and useful instrument, being essential for all types of tasks, from delicate manipulations and of high precision, to tasks that require a lot of force. For a long time researchers have been studying the biomechanics of the human hand, to reproduce it in robotic hands to be used as a prosthesis in humans, in the replacement of limbs lost or used in robots. In this study, we present the implementation (electronics project, acquisition, treatment, processing and control) of different sensors in the control of prostheses. The sensors studied and implemented are: inertial, electromyography (EMG), force and slip. The tests showed reasonable results due to sliding and dropping of some objects. These sensors will be used in a more complex system that will approach the fusion of sensors through Artificial Neural Networks (ANNs) and new tests should be performed for different scenarios.

Keywords: Sensors fusion · Prosthesis biomimetic
Artificial neural networks (ANN)

1 Introduction

Human being can make a lot of activities using the hands. Hence, the loss of the hand will limit the capabilities of realizing the daily activities of any person. In a psychological way, it is also very difficult for any one to accept any member amputation [1]. About 30% of the whole world 4 millions amputees society has the superior member loss [2]. Hand prosthesis are solutions to help people who has superior member loss. In order to diminish the psychological damage emerged the aesthetics prosthesis to hide the deficiency, but with no movements. The development of digital systems integrated to new prosthesis designs allowed movement function utilities. Every day situations, such as handle objects, are possible to amputated people when the movement prosthesis are available. However, nowadays, a simple and limited movement prosthesis is very expensive. Thus, the research of new technologies of biomimetic prosthesis becomes necessary.

V. Kůrková et al. (Eds.): ICANN 2018, LNCS 11141, pp. 147–156, 2018.
https://doi.org/10.1007/978-3-030-01424-7_15

The interface between patient muscles and the acquisition system is a critical part of this project. The measure of the muscle signals and understand the useful information from it is very challenging. The system for prosthesis control are based on sensor-fusion by an trained artificial neural network, and it will allow to implement new movement features any time. The artificial neural network will be trained with the data measured from the muscle (EMG sensor) and accelerometer, force and slipper sensors connected in the prothesis.

The intension of this project is to build a hand prosthesis functional prototype with a set of possible movements, such as, pinch, catch and hold objects, and make social gestures like point and wave. First, the tests will run on non amputated people and after that, this prototype will be ready to be tested on real amputated people. This proposal aims a product with a low cost production and, therefore, provide it to a larger number of amputated persons.

We already have a first version of the hand prosthesis. We used an open-source project and printed at a 3D printer. With a preliminary hardware and software, the first prototype of the prosthetic hand already have simple movements. The pressure of the five fingers can be monitored when it holds an object and it can detect when an object is slipping. These results will be presented forward.

2 Methodology

This project focuses in two main points in the study of robotics systems: electromyographic signal data acquisition and selective interpretation of those signals to be used on robotic devices operation.

Another feature of the project is to apply artificial intelligence by using embedded artificial neural networks for electromyographic pattern recognition. The system will also learn and adapt to the environment habit changes and other behavior modifica-

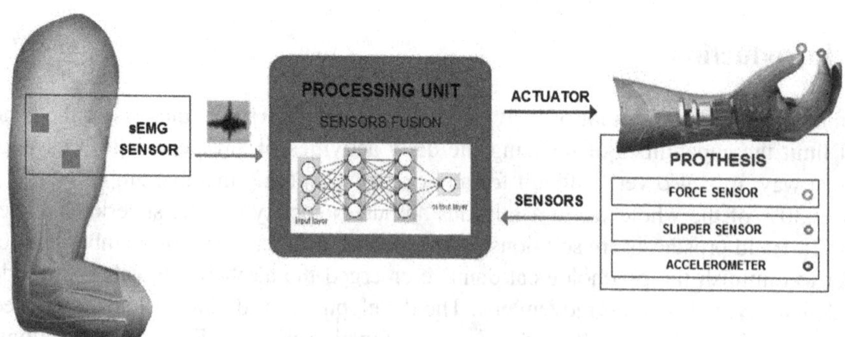

Fig. 1. Proposed system architecture

tions. Figure 1 shows the proposed workflow for the threetier system (sensors, processing and operation).

2.1 Electromyography (EMG)

Electromyography (EMG) is a monitoring technique for evaluating the electric activity produced by the skeletal muscles. The final result of these measures are the potential difference between two or more sensors applied to the patient skin versus time. Many relevant information are contained on timing EMG signals, such as, the total time of the muscle activation, the intensity of movement and the behavior variation in every repetitive movement.

2.2 EMG Acquisition

The EMG signal is a continuous time information obtained through an sensor applied to the patient near the muscles whose measurement we are interested. There are two kind of sensors: surface and intramuscular. In this project we choose to use the surface ones for a practical and non-invasive process. According to SENIAM (Surface EMG for the Non-Invasive Assessment of Muscles) [3] the Ag-AgCl surface sensors should be used with an conductor gel to an stable measurement along time and avoid undesirable noise.

The EMG signal is obtained by the potential difference between two (or more) surface sensors and it can be divided into mono-polar or multi-polar systems [4]. The mono-polar configuration require an reference sensor and it is typically placed very far from the sensor we want to measure, in order to acquire simple signals. In the multi-polar configuration the potential difference is acquired through three or more points: a reference point and two or more signal points in relation to the reference, and the potential difference is obtained by subtracting these signals. In this project the bipolar sensor was used for better information acquisition from different muscle movements. Figure 2 shows the fixation of the electrodes on the arm for the tests of this work.

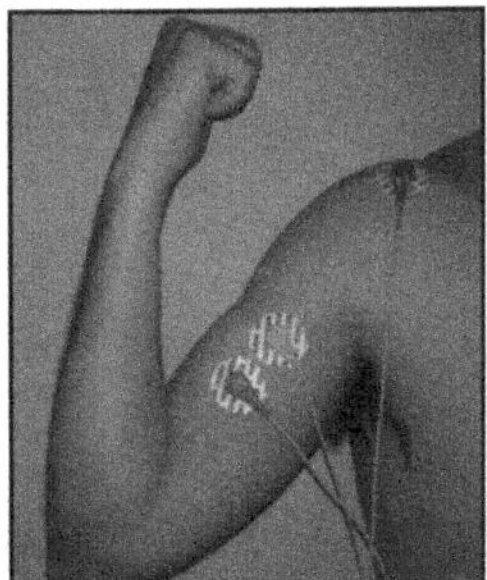

Fig. 2. Fixation of the electrodes on the arm

2.3 Signal Treatment

Typically EMG signal are represented in low frequencies from 70 Hz to 500 Hz [5]. However, it is not so easy to extract useful information from the signal without an electronic circuit that separates the real data of the muscle movement from noise. Noise is any other signal out of EMG information, such as, cardiac beatings, neighbor muscles or electric coupling between wires and sensors. The electronic circuit was developed with different technologies of frequency active filters in order to catch the real data from the EMG.

After a good filtering, the signal should be converted to discrete time. With the data correctly sampled it is possible to evaluate the behavior of the signal in time domain or even in the frequency domain. Many tools like digital filters or Fourier analysis are useful to extract important information and proceed a good data mining.

And after the choice of the analog-digital converter device, we have almost all data captured from muscle movements ready to be stored in a database. As will be explained forward, this database is the information to, in the first step, train an artificial neural network that is the main process core of this project. After a good training, this neural network will be embedded into the main core that will control other actuators to move the prosthetic hand. An electronic circuit was developed to real time sampling the analogical signal and supply the main core, already programmed, to move the prosthetic hand.

2.4 The Prosthetic Hand

The prototype developed of the hand prosthesis (Fig. 3) was based on the InMoov [6] open source design for full size 3D printer. The material used for the construction of its mechanical structure was ABS and the hand has 16 degrees of freedom. Each finger moves with a plastic coated steel cable and a servomotor (Towerpro, MG995). The finger returns to the rest position is done with a rubber band attached to each one. The five servomotors are located in the forearm of the prosthesis and the electric drive was realized by an ATmega2560 microcontroller embedded on an Arduino. This first prototype has many issues, like gaps and non precise movements, and a better one should be build.

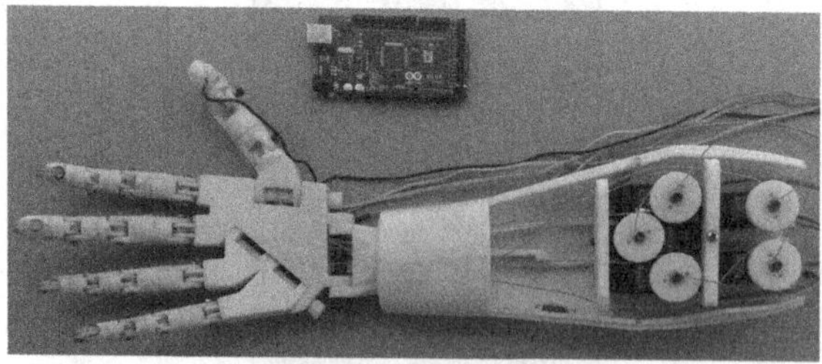

Fig. 3. Test holding the plastic cup with minimal force

At this stage of the work, the pressure of the five fingers from the prosthetic hand are monitored when it holds an object and it can detect when an object is slipping. For this monitoring, force and slippery sensors are used and each finger has its own servomotor. The myoelectric signal, from a human arm is used to open and close the fingers of the prosthetic hand. For the signal capture, non-invasive superficial electrodes were used. To measure the force applied, the force sensor FSR400 from Interlink Electronics was used (Fig. 4). The slippery sensor (Fig. 5) used was the LDT0-028K from Measurement Specialties [7]. The slippery sensor is responsible to detect if an object is slipping from the fingers.

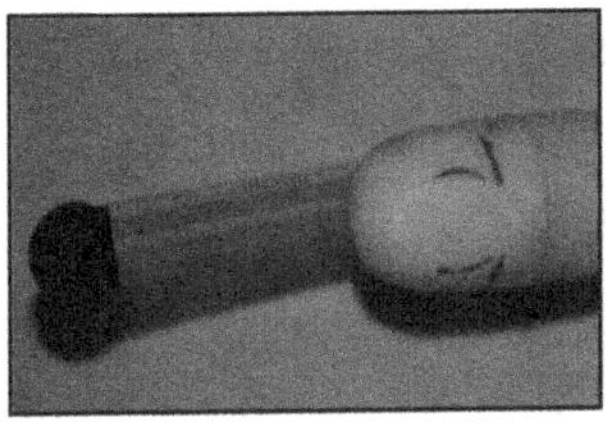
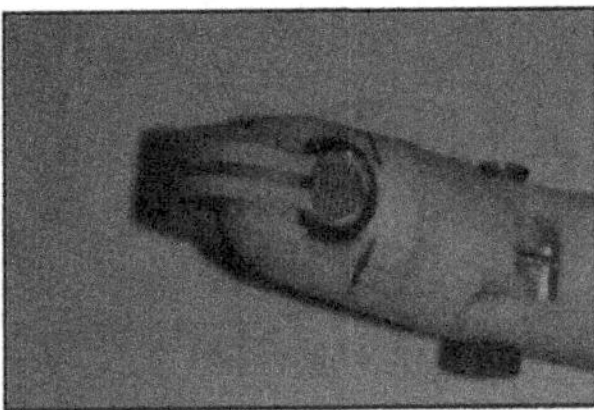

Fig. 4. Sensor force FSR400 and fixation

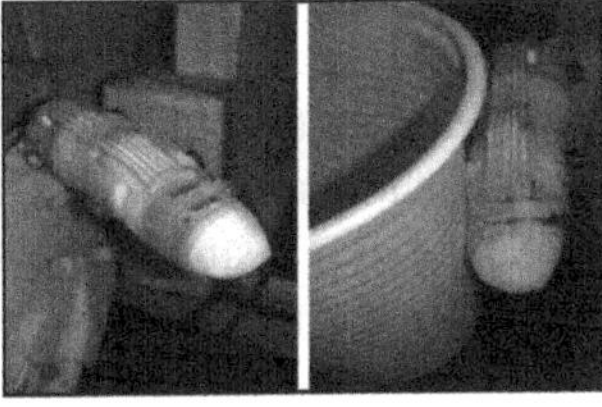

Fig. 5. Slippery sensor LDT0-028K

2.5 Database and Artificial Neural Networks

Artificial neural networks (ANNs) are often used to determine these relationships because the artificial neurons can learn nonlinear behaviors [8–10]. The artificial neuron arrangement increases the ANN learning capacity [11, 12]. ANNs are regularly used for correlating stochastic variables in other fields, such as weather forecasting [13], load forecasting in electric systems [14], satellite imaging classification [15] and others. ANNs are also used in industrial applications and academic studies [14, 16]. Massively parallel distributed ANNs can process generic behaviors and mimic patterns [17]. They are based on processing units called artificial neurons [18].

There are different types of neural networks exist in the literature, as feedforward neural networks. Feedforward neural networks consist of layers that are input, hidden and output layers (Fig. 6).

MLP and RBF networks, are the two most commonly used types of feedforward neural networks. They differ in the way that the hidden layer performs its computation. The MLP use inner products and training is done through Backpropagation. In RBF, each neuron in the hidden layer computes the Euclidean distance between an input vector and a point in the neuron which can be viewed as a centre vector [19]. After the first tests of Prosthetic Hand, different Multilayer Perceptron (MLP) and Radial Basis Function (RBF) neural network techniques will be used and compared to control the movements of the prosthesis.

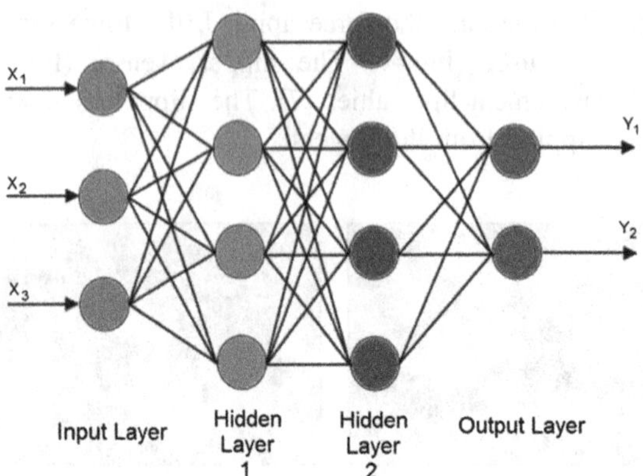

Fig. 6. A feedforward neural network

2.6 Sensors Fusion

Using two different sensors to acquire data information, instead of one, bring best and more accurate results, the sensor fusion algorithms are based on this idea [20]. Despite the principle behind the idea is simple, the implementation needs a functional algorithm to be able to implement, this algorithm to fuse the information from two or more sensors can be done based on optimal estimation [21].

The combination of the sensor information and the subsequent state estimation can be done in a coherent way, so that the uncertainty is reduced. The Kalman Filter is a state-estimator algorithm widely used to optimally estimate the unknown state of a linear dynamic system from noise-corrupted measurements [22]. In this work, after the first tests, an Artificial Neural Network will be used as an algorithm to fuse the information from the EMG, slip, force and accelerometer sensors.

3 Preliminary Results

For the system kick-start and preliminary tests, the InMoov [6] open-source project was used. The prosthetic hand was prototyped using a 3D printer at the University. On this first version, an Arduino was used to acquire the input signals (myoelectric and other sensors) and for the operation of the servomotor that controls the fingers of the prosthetic hand. On the current status of the project, the neural network was not yet implemented. To analyze the results, a video of each test was recorded and then checked frame by frame through video analysis software called Tracker. The objects used in the tests were: a plastic cup, a tennis ball and a whiteboard eraser.

At first test with the cup (Fig. 7), the prosthetic hand only applied minimal force to the object to hold it. It doesn't monitored slippery (used EMG and force sensors) applying the minimum force on the object. In Fig. 9(a) we can verify that the glass moved 44.8 mm down, in relation to its initial position.

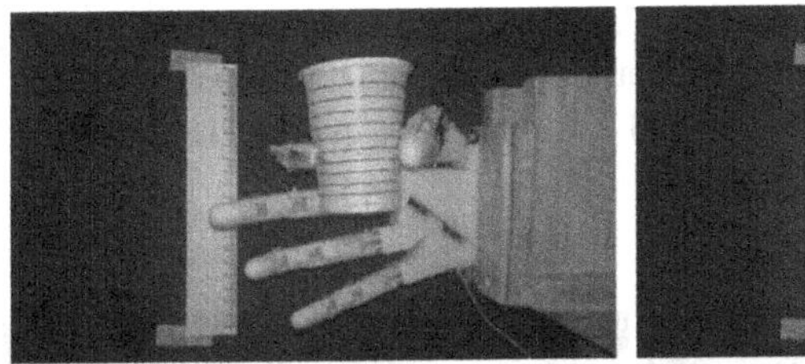
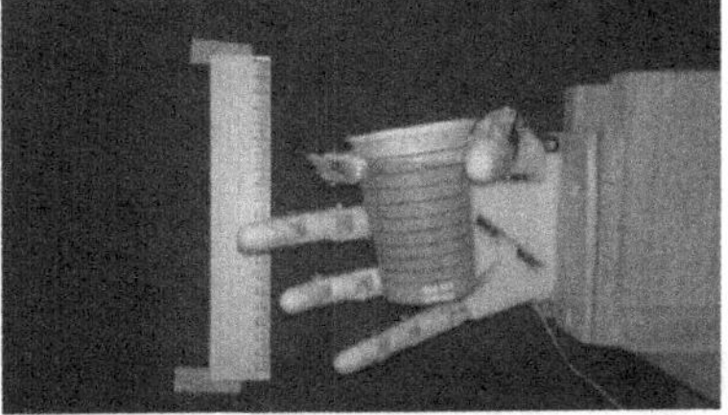

Fig. 7. Holding and slipping test of the plastic cup

Then, at second stage the test (Fig. 8), the prosthetic hand monitored the slippery and applied more force when it detected that the object started to slip.

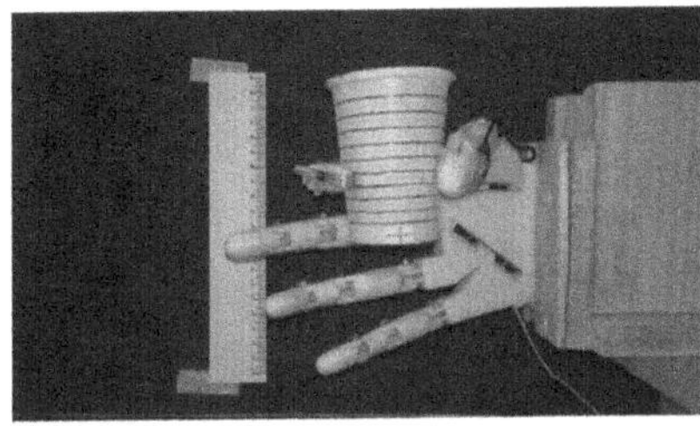
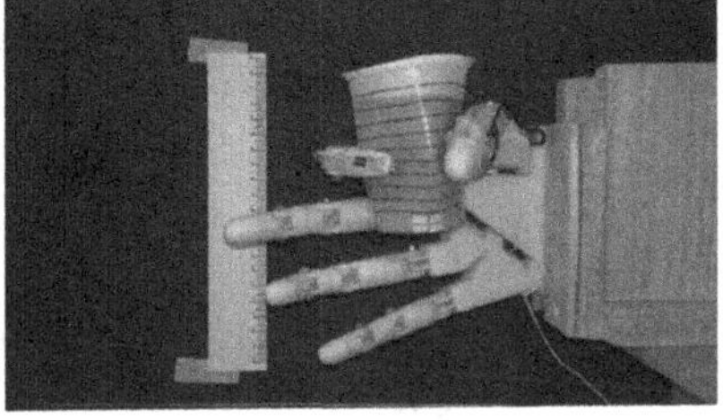

Fig. 8. Holding and slipping test of the plastic cup

The prosthetic hand was tested ten times. It was possible to observe in the Fig. 9(b) that the object slid less than in the previous test.

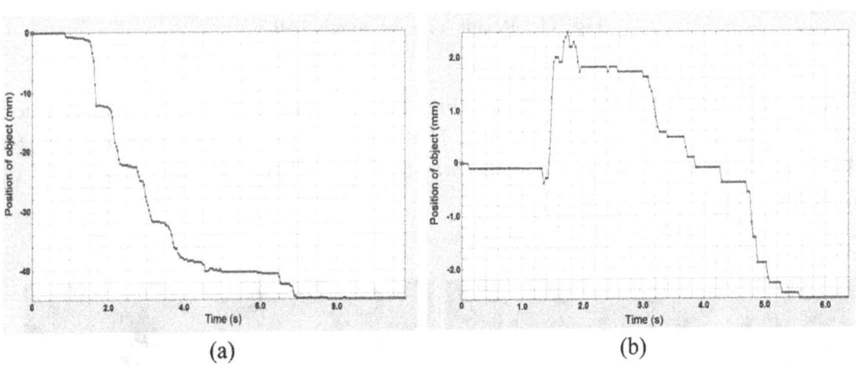

Fig. 9. Results with the tennis ball - (a) without slip sensor and (b) all sensors.

The third test was with the tennis ball (Fig. 10). The system monitored the slippery and applied more force when it detected that the object started to slip. The system was tested ten times and on average the ball slid 2.5 mm down. In Fig. 11, one of the tests completed.

Fig. 10. Holding and slipping test of the tennis ball

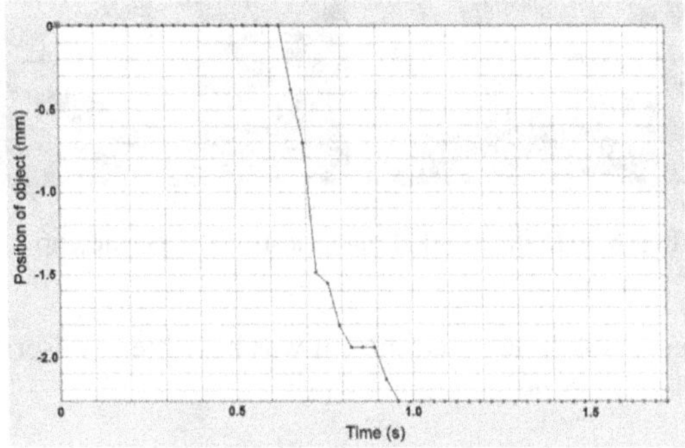

Fig. 11. Result with the tennis ball

As a final test, a whiteboard eraser (Fig. 12). The prosthetic hand was tested ten times with this object and it did not fall. The lowest value was 1.63 mm, the highest value was 18.75 mm and the mean slip was 5.63 mm. Figure 13 shows the result of one of the tests.

Fig. 12. Holding and slipping test of the whiteboard eraser

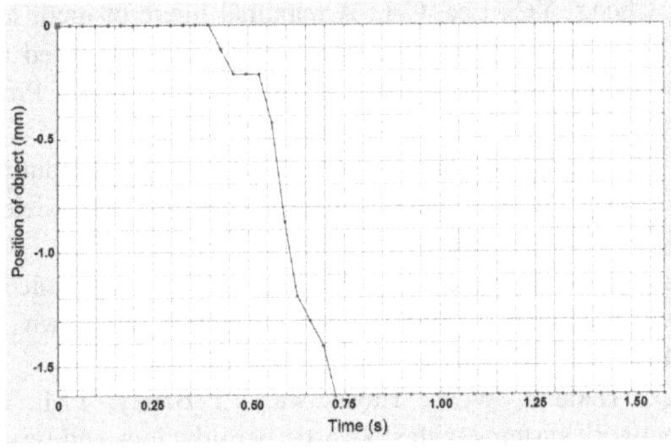

Fig. 13. Result with the whiteboard eraser

4 Conclusion

This study was focused on performing a set of experiments of one Prosthetic Hand to grasp different objects by EMG, force and slip sensors. This work contributes with the thesis that only simulation is not sufficient to evaluate the characteristics of real systems, since some behaviors can not be predicted. Future works can be made to use fusion sensor techniques to improve the Prosthetic Hand. Having more accurate sensors techniques, different tests with various different objects can be used to best performance comparison of the systems.

References

1. Pillet, J., Didierjean-Pillet, A.: Aesthetic hand prosthesis: gadget or therapy? Presentation of a new classification. J. Hand Surg. **26**(6), 523–528 (2001)
2. Toledo, C., Leija, L., Munoz, R., Vera, A., Ramirez, A.: Upper limb prostheses for amputations above elbow: a review. In: Health Care Exchanges, PAHCE 2009, Pan American, pp. 104–108. IEEE (2009)
3. Hermens, H.J., Freriks, B., Disselhorst-Klug, C., Rau, G.: Development of recommendations for SEMG sensors and sensor placement procedures. J. Electromyogr. Kinesiol. **10**(5), 361–374 (2000)
4. Duchêne, J., Goubel, F.: Surface electromyogram during voluntary contraction: processing tools and relation to physiological. Crit. Rev. Biomed. Eng. **21**(4), 313–397 (1993)
5. Delsys Homepage. Neuromuscular Research Center. Boston University. http://www.delsys.com/library/papers. Accessed 31 Mar 2018
6. Langevin, G.: Inmov | Open-Source 3d Printed Life-Size Robot (2015). http://inmoov.fr/project/. Accessed 15 Sept 2017
7. LDT with Crimps Vibration Sensor/Switch. Measurement Specialties (2015). https://www.variohm.com/images/datasheets/ENG_DS_LDT_with_Crimps_A.pdf. Accessed 25 Sept 2017
8. Philip Chen, C.L., Liu, Y.J., Wen, G.X.: Fuzzy neural network-based adaptive control for a class of uncertain nonlinear stochastic systems. IEEE Trans. Cybern. **44**(5), 583–593 (2014)

9. Li, K., Huang, Z., Cheng, YC., Lee, CH.: A maximal figure-of-merit learning approach to maximizing mean average precision with deep neural network based classifiers. In: 2014 IEEE International Conference on Acoustics, Speech and Signal Processing (ICASSP), pp. 4503–4507 (2014)
10. Tong, S., Wang, T., Li, Y., Zhang, H.: Adaptive neural network output feedback control for stochastic nonlinear systems with unknown dead-zone and unmodeled dynamics. IEEE Trans. Cybern. **44**(6), 910–921 (2014)
11. Yu, Z., Li, S.: Neural-network-based output-feedback adaptive dynamic surface control for a class of stochastic nonlinear time-delay systems with unknown control directions. Neurocomputing **129**, 540–547 (2014)
12. Zeng, X., Hui, Q., Haddad, W.M., Hayakawa, T., Bailey, J.M.: Synchronization of biological neural network systems with stochastic perturbations and time delays. J. Franklin Inst. **351**(3), 1205–1225 (2014)
13. Culclasure, A.: Using neural networks to provide local weather forecasts. Electronic Theses & Dissertations, Jack N. Averitt College of Graduate Studies (COGS) (2013)
14. Hayati, M., Shirvany, Y.: Artificial neural network approach for short term load forecasting for Illam region. World Acad. Sci. Eng. Technol. **28**, 280–284 (2007)
15. Piscini, A., et al.: A neural network approach for the simultaneous retrieval of volcanic ash parameters and SO2 using modis data. Atmos. Meas. Tech. **7**(12), 4023 (2014)
16. Krizhevsky, A., Hinton, G.: Learning multiple layers of features from tiny images. Master's thesis. Department of Computer Science University of Toronto (2009)
17. Shamir, R.R., et al.: A Method for Predicting the Outcomes of Combined Pharmacologic and Deep Brain Stimulation Therapy for Parkinson's Disease. In: Golland, P., Hata, N., Barillot, C., Hornegger, J., Howe, R. (eds.) MICCAI 2014. LNCS, vol. 8674, pp. 188–195. Springer, Cham (2014). https://doi.org/10.1007/978-3-319-10470-6_24
18. Haykin, S.: Neural Networks and Learning Machines, vol. 3. Pearson Education, Upper Saddle River (2009)
19. Sereno, F., Marques de Sá, J.P., Matos, A., Bernardes, J.: A comparative study of MLP and RBF neural nets in the estimation of the fetal weight and length. In: Campilho, A., Mendonça, A. (eds.) Proceedings of RECPAD 2000 - 11th Portuguese Conference on Pattern Recognition, University of Porto (2000)
20. Waltz, E., Llinas, J.: Multisensor Data Fusion, vol. 685. Artech House, Norwood (1990)
21. Surachai, P., Afzulpurkar, N.: Sensor Fusion Techniques in Navigation Application for Mobile Robot. INTECH Open Access Publisher (2011)
22. Manyika, J., Durrant-Whyte, H.: Data Fusion and Sensor Management: A Decentralized Information - Theoretic Approach. Ellis Horwood, London (1994)

An Exploration of Dropout with RNNs for Natural Language Inference

Amit Gajbhiye[1(✉)], Sardar Jaf[1], Noura Al Moubayed[1], A. Stephen McGough[2], and Steven Bradley[1]

[1] Department of Computer Science, Durham University, Durham, UK
{amit.gajbhiye,sardar.jaf,noura.al-moubayed,s.p.bradley}@durham.ac.uk
[2] School of Computing, Newcastle University, Newcastle upon Tyne, UK
stephen.mcgough@ncl.ac.uk

Abstract. Dropout is a crucial regularization technique for the Recurrent Neural Network (RNN) models of Natural Language Inference (NLI). However, dropout has not been evaluated for the effectiveness at different layers and dropout rates in NLI models. In this paper, we propose a novel RNN model for NLI and empirically evaluate the effect of applying dropout at different layers in the model. We also investigate the impact of varying dropout rates at these layers. Our empirical evaluation on a large (Stanford Natural Language Inference (SNLI)) and a small (SciTail) dataset suggest that dropout at each feed-forward connection severely affects the model accuracy at increasing dropout rates. We also show that regularizing the embedding layer is efficient for SNLI whereas regularizing the recurrent layer improves the accuracy for SciTail. Our model achieved an accuracy 86.14% on the SNLI dataset and 77.05% on SciTail.

Keywords: Neural networks · Dropout · Natural Language Inference

1 Introduction

Natural Language Understanding (NLU) is the process to enable computers to understand the semantics of natural language text. The inherent complexities and ambiguities in natural language text make NLU challenging for computers. Natural Language Inference (NLI) is a fundamental step towards NLU [14]. NLI involves logically inferring a hypothesis sentence from a given premise sentence.

The recent release of a large public dataset the Stanford Natural Language Inference (SNLI) [2] has made it feasible to train complex neural network models for NLI. Recurrent Neural Networks (RNNs), particularly bidirectional LSTMs (BiLSTMs) have shown state-of-the-art results on the SNLI dataset [9]. However, RNNs are susceptible to overfitting – the case when a neural network learns the exact patterns present in the training data but fails to generalize to unseen data [21]. In NLI models, regularization techniques such as early stopping [4], L2 regularization and dropout [20] are used to prevent overfitting.

V. Kůrková et al. (Eds.): ICANN 2018, LNCS 11141, pp. 157–167, 2018.
https://doi.org/10.1007/978-3-030-01424-7_16

For RNNs, dropout is an effective regularization technique [21]. The idea of dropout is to randomly omit computing units in a neural network during training but to keep all of them for testing. Dropout consists of element-wise multiplication of the neural network layer activations with a zero-one mask (r_j) during training. Each element of the zero-one mask is drawn independently from $r_j \sim \text{Bernoulli}(p)$, where p is the probability with which the units are retained in the network. During testing, activations of the layer are multiplied by p [19].

Dropout is a crucial regularization technique for NLI [9,20]. However, the location of dropout varies considerably between NLI models and is based on trail-and-error experiments with different locations in the network. To the best of our knowledge no prior work has been performed to evaluate the effectiveness of dropout location and rates in the RNN NLI models.

In this paper, we study the effect of applying dropout at different locations in an RNN model for NLI. We also investigate the effect of varying the dropout rate. Our results suggest that applying dropout for every feed forward connection, especially at higher dropout rates degrades the performance of RNN. Our best model achieves an accuracy of 86.14% on the SNLI dataset and an accuracy of 77.05% on SciTail dataset.

To the best of our knowledge this research is the first exploratory analysis of dropout for NLI. The main contributions of this paper are as follows: (1) A RNN model based on BiLSTMs for NLI. (2) A comparative analysis of different locations and dropout rates in the proposed RNN NLI model. (3) Recommendations for the usage of dropout in the RNN models for NLI task.

The layout of the paper is as follows. In Sect. 2, we describe the related work. In Sect. 3, we discuss the proposed RNN based NLI model. Experiments and the results are presented in Sect. 4. Recommendations for the application of dropouts are presented in Sect. 5. We conclude in Sect. 6.

2 Related Work

The RNN NLI models follow a general architecture. It consists of: (1) an embedding layer that take as input the word embeddings of premise and hypothesis (2) a sentence encoding layer which is generally an RNN that generates representations of the input (3) an aggregation layer that combines the representations and; (4) a classifier layer that classifies the relationship (entailment, contradiction or neutral) between premise and hypothesis.

Different NLI models apply dropout at different layers in general NLI architecture. NLI models proposed by Ghaeini et al. [9] and Tay et al. [20] apply dropout to each feed-forward layer in the network whereas others have applied dropout only to the final classifier layer [13]. Bowman et al. [2] apply dropout only to the input and output of sentence encoding layers. The models proposed by Bowman et al. [3] and Choi et al. [7] applied dropout to the output of embedding layer and to the input and output of classifier layer. Chen et al. [4] and Cheng et al. [6] use dropout but they do not elaborate on the location.

Dropout rates are also crucial for the NLI models [15]. Even the models which apply dropout at the same locations vary dropout rates.

Previous research on dropout for RNNs on the applications such as neural language models [16], handwriting recognition [18] and machine translation [21] have established that recurrent connection dropout should not be applied to RNNs as it affects the long term dependencies in sequential data.

Bluche et al. [1] studied dropout at different places with respect to the LSTM units in the network proposed in [18] for handwriting recognition. The results show that significant performance difference is observed when dropout is applied to distinct places. They concluded that applying dropout only after recurrent layers (as applied by Pham et al. [18]) or between every feed-forward layer (as done by Zaremba et al. [21]) does not always yield good results. Cheng et al. [5], investigated the effect of applying dropout in LSTMs. They randomly switch off the outputs of various gates of LSTM, achieving an optimal word error rate when dropout is applied to output, forget and input gates of the LSTM.

Evaluations in previous research were conducted on datasets with fewer samples. We evaluate the RNN model on a large, SNLI dataset (570,000 data samples) as well as on a smaller SciTail dataset (27,000 data samples). Furthermore, previous studies concentrate only on the location of dropout in the network with fixed dropout rate. We further investigate the effect of varying dropout rates. We focus on the application of widely used conventional dropout [19] to non-recurrent connection in RNNs.

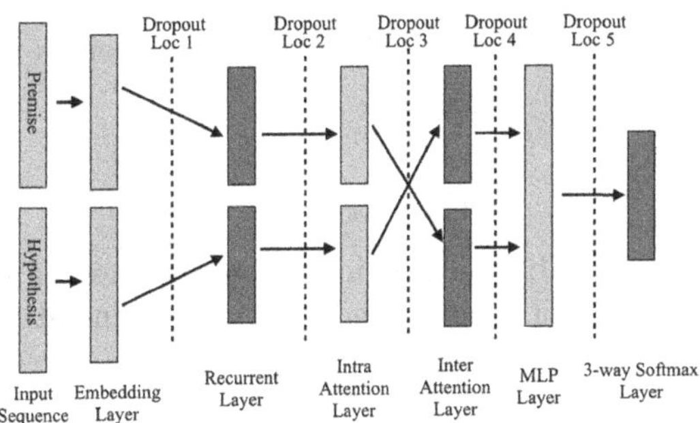

Fig. 1. The Recurrent Neural Network model with possible dropout locations

3 Recurrent Neural Network Model for NLI Task

The RNN NLI model that we have developed follows the general architecture of NLI models and is depicted in Fig. 1. The model combines the intra-attention model [13] with soft-attention mechanism [11]. The embedding layer takes as input word embeddings in the sentence of length L. The recurrent layer with BiLSTM units encodes the sentence. Next, the intra-attention layer generates the attention weighted sentence representation following the Eqs. (1)–(3)

$$M = \tanh\left(W^y Y + W^h R_{avg} \otimes e_L\right) \tag{1}$$

$$\alpha = softmax\left(w^T M\right) \tag{2}$$

$$R = Y\alpha^T \tag{3}$$

where, W^y, W^h are trained projection matrices, w^T is the transpose of trained parameter vector w, Y is the matrix of hidden output vectors of the BiLSTM layer, R_{avg} is obtained from the average pooling of Y, $e_L \in \mathbb{R}^L$ is a vector of 1s, α is a vector of attention weights and R is the attention weighted sequence representation. The attention weighted sequence representation is generated for premise and hypothesis and is denoted as R_p and R_h. The attention weighted representation gives more importance to the words which are important to the semantics of the sequence and also captures its global context.

The interaction between R_p and R_h is performed by inter-attention layer, following the Eqs. (4)–(6).

$$I_v = R_p^T R_h \tag{4}$$

$$\tilde{R_p} = softmax(I_v)R_h \tag{5}$$

$$\tilde{R_h} = softmax(I_v)R_p \tag{6}$$

where, I_v is the interaction vector. $\tilde{R_p}$ contains the words which are relevant based on the content of sequence R_h. Similarly, $\tilde{R_h}$ contains words which are important with respect to the content of sequence R_p. The final sequence encoding is obtained from the element-wise multiplication of intra-attention weighted representation and inter-attention weighted representation as follows:

$$F_p = \tilde{R_p} \odot R_p \tag{7}$$

$$F_h = \tilde{R_h} \odot R_h \tag{8}$$

To classify the relationship between premise and hypothesis a relation vector is formed from the encoding of premise and hypothesis generated in Eqs. (7) and (8), as follows:

$$\mathrm{v}_{p,avg} = \mathrm{averagepooling}(F_p), \mathrm{v}_{p,max} = \mathrm{maxpooling}(F_p) \tag{9}$$

$$\mathrm{v}_{h,avg} = \mathrm{averagepooling}(F_h), \mathrm{v}_{h,max} = \mathrm{maxpooling}(F_h) \tag{10}$$

$$F_{relation} = \left[\mathrm{v}_{p,avg}; \mathrm{v}_{p,max}; \mathrm{v}_{h,avg}; \mathrm{v}_{h,max}\right] \tag{11}$$

where v is a vector of length L. The relation vector ($F_{relation}$) is fed to the MLP layer. The three-way softmax layer outputs the probability for each class of NLI.

4 Experiments and Results

4.1 Experimental Setup

The standard train, validation and test splits of SNLI [2] and SciTail [10] are used in empirical evaluations. The validation set is used for hyper-parameter tuning. The non-regularized model is our baseline model. The parameters for the baseline model are selected separately for SNLI and SciTail dataset by a grid search from the combination of L2 regularization [$1e-4, 1e-5, 1e-6$], batch size [$32, 64, 256, 512$] and learning rate [$0.001, 0.0003, 0.0004$]. The Adam [12] optimizer with first momentum set to 0.9 and the second to 0.999 is used. The word embeddings are initialized with pre-trained 300-D Glove 840B vectors [17]. Extensive experiments with dropout locations and hidden units were conducted however we show only the best results for brevity and space limits.

4.2 Dropout at Different Layers for NLI Model

Table 1 presents the models with different combinations of layers to the output of which dropout are applied in our model depicted in Fig. 1. Table 2. shows the results for the models in Table 1. Each model is evaluated with dropout rates ranging from 0.1 to 0.5 with a granularity of 0.1.

Table 1. Models with corresponding layers to the outputs of which dropout is applied.

Model	Layer
Model 1	No Dropout (Baseline)
Model 2	Embedding
Model 3	Recurrent
Model 4	Embedding and Recurrent
Model 5	Recurrent and Intra-Attention
Model 6	Inter-Attention and MLP
Model 7	Recurrent, Inter-Attention and MLP
Model 8	Embedding, Inter-Attention and MLP
Model 9	Embedding, Recurrent, Inter-Attention and MLP
Model 10	Recurrent, Intra-Attention, Inter-Attention and MLP
Model 11	Embedding, Intra-Attention, Inter-Attention and MLP
Model 12	Embedding, Recurrent, Intra-Attention, Inter-Attention and MLP
Model 13	Embedding, Recurrent, Inter-Attention and MLP

Dropout at Individual Layers. We first apply dropout at each layer including the embedding layer. Although the embedding layer is the largest layer it is often not regularized for many language applications [8]. However, we observe the benefit of regularizing it. For SNLI, the highest accuracy is achieved when the embedding layer is regularized (Model 2, DR 0.4).

For SciTail, the highest accuracy is obtained when the recurrent layer is regularized (Model 3, DR 0.1). The dropout injected noise at lower layers prevents higher fully connected layers from overfitting. We further experimented regularizing higher fully connected layers (Intra-Attention, Inter-Attention and MLP) individually, however no significant performance gains were observed.

Table 2. Model accuracy with varying dropout rates for SNLI and SciTail datasets. Bold numbers shows the highest accuracy for the model within the dropout range.

Models	Dataset	Dropout Rate (DR)				
		0.1	0.2	0.3	0.4	0.5
Model 1	SNLI	84.45				
	SciTail	74.18				
Model 2	SNLI	84.56	84.59	84.42	**86.14**	84.85
	SciTail	**75.45**	75.12	74.22	73.10	74.08
Model 3	SNLI	84.12	**84.21**	83.76	81.04	79.63
	SciTail	**76.15**	75.78	73.50	73.19	75.26
Model 4	SNLI	83.83	**85.22**	84.34	80.82	79.92
	SciTail	74.65	**76.08**	74.22	74.46	73.19
Model 5	SNLI	**84.72**	83.43	72.89	70.49	62.13
	SciTail	**75.87**	75.13	75.26	73.71	72.25
Model 6	SNLI	84.17	**84.32**	83.71	82.79	81.68
	SciTail	73.85	**75.68**	75.26	73.95	73.28
Model 7	SNLI	**84.33**	82.97	82.00	81.15	79.25
	SciTail	73.75	**75.02**	74.37	73.37	73.42
Model 8	SNLI	84.67	**85.82**	84.60	84.14	83.94
	SciTail	73.80	73.52	69.29	**75.82**	73.89
Model 9	SNLI	**84.44**	83.05	82.09	81.64	79.62
	SciTail	75.68	**76.11**	75.96	70.84	74.55
Model 10	SNLI	**84.45**	80.95	75.31	70.81	69.34
	SciTail	73.30	**75.21**	74.98	74.65	71.59
Model 11	SNLI	**84.31**	82.43	78.94	74.93	70.54
	SciTail	**75.63**	73.47	74.93	74.93	70.32
Model 12	SNLI	**84.32**	82.60	73.36	71.53	66.67
	SciTail	73.47	**75.63**	74.74	73.42	74.40

Dropout at Multiple Layers. We next explore the effect of applying dropout at multiple layers. For SNLI and SciTail, the models achieve higher performance when dropout is applied to embedding and recurrent layer (Model 4, DR 0.2). This supports the importance of regularizing embedding and recurrent layer as shown for individual layers.

It is interesting to note that regularizing the recurrent layer helps SciTail (Model 7, DR 0.2) whereas regularizing the embedding layer helps SNLI (Model 8, DR 0.2). A possible explanation to this is that for the smaller SciTail dataset the model can not afford to lose information in the input, whereas for the larger SNLI dataset the model has a chance to learn even with the loss of information in input. Also, the results from models 7 and 8 suggests that applying dropout at a single lower layer (Embedding or Recurrent; depending on the amount of training data) and to the inputs and outputs of MLP layer improves performance.

We can infer from models 9, 10, 11 and 12 that applying dropout to each feed forward connection helps preventing the model overfit for SciTail (DR 0.1 and 0.2). However, for both the datasets with different dropout locations the performance of the model decreases as the dropout rate increases (Sect. 4.4).

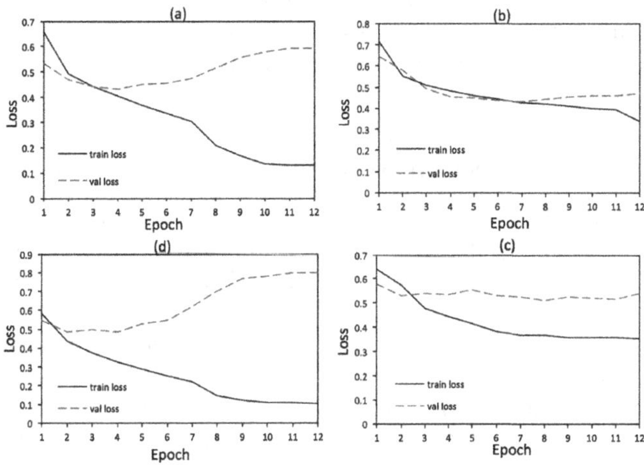

Fig. 2. Convergence Curves: (a) Baseline Model for SNLI (Model 1), (b) Best Model for SNLI (Model 2, DR 0.4), (c) 100 Unit Model for SciTail (Model 13 DR 0.4), (d) 300 Unit Model for SciTail (Model 9 DR 0.2).

4.3 The Effectiveness of Dropout for Overfitting

We study the efficacy of dropout on overfitting. The main results are shown in Fig. 2. For SNLI, Fig. 2(a)–(b), shows the convergence curves for the baseline model and the model achieving the highest accuracy (Model 2, DR 0.4). The convergence curves show that dropout is very effective in preventing overfitting. However, for the smaller SciTail dataset when regularizing multiple layers, we observe that the highest accuracy achieving model (Model 9, DP 0.2), overfits significantly (Fig. 2(d)). This overfitting is due to the large model size. With limited training data of SciTail, our model with higher number of hidden units learns the relationship between the premise and the hypothesis most accurately (Fig. 2(d)). However, these relationships are not representative of the validation set data and thus the model does not generalize well. When we reduced the model size (50, 100 and 200 hidden units) we achieved the best accuracy for SciTail at 100 hidden units (Table 3). The convergence curve (Fig. 2(c)) shows that dropout effectively prevents overfitting in the model with 100 hidden units in comparison to 300 units. Furthermore, for SciTail dataset, the model with 100 units achieved higher accuracy for almost all the experiments when compared to models with 50, 200 and 300 hidden units.

Table 3. Accuracy of 100 unit model for SciTail dataset

Models	Dataset	Dropout Rate (DR)				
		0.1	0.2	0.3	0.4	0.5
Model 13	SciTail	76.72	76.25	**<u>77.05</u>**	72.58	74.22

The results of this experiment suggest that given the high learning capacity of RNNs an appropriate model size selection according to the amount of training data is essential. Dropout may independently be insufficient to prevent overfitting in such scenarios.

4.4 Dropout Rate Effect on Accuracy and Dropout Location

We next investigate the effect of varying dropout rates on the accuracy of the models and on various dropout locations. Figure 3 illustrates varying dropout rates and the corresponding test accuracy for SNLI. We observe some distinct trends from the plot. First, the dropout rate and location does not affect the accuracy of the models 2 and 8 over the baseline. Second, in the dropout range [0.2–0.5], the dropout locations affect the accuracy of the models significantly. Increasing the dropout rate from 0.2 to 0.5 the accuracy of models 5 and 12 decreases significantly by 21.3% and 15.9% respectively. For most of the models (3, 4, 6, 7, 9 and 10) the dropout rate of 0.5 decreases accuracy.

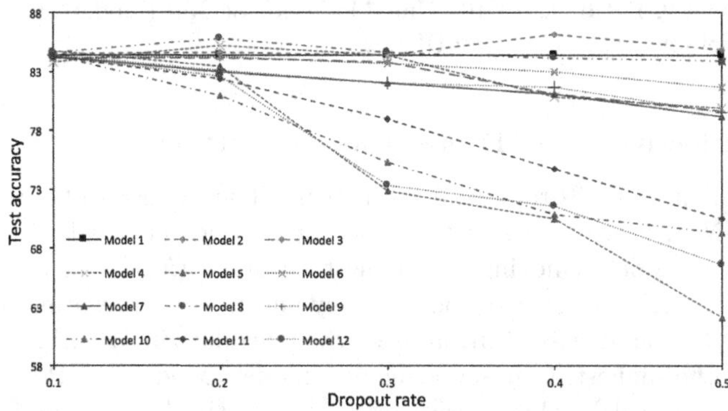

Fig. 3. Plot showing the variation of test accuracy across the dropout range for SNLI.

From the experiments on SciTail dataset (Fig. 4), we observed that the dropout rate and its location do not have a significant effect on most of the models, with the exception of model 8 (which shows erratic performance). Finally, for almost all the experiments a large dropout rate (0.5) decreases the accuracy of the models. The dropout rate of 0.5 works for a wide range of neural networks and tasks [19]. However, our results show that this is not desirable for RNN models of NLI. Based on our evaluations a dropout range of [0.2–0.4] is advised.

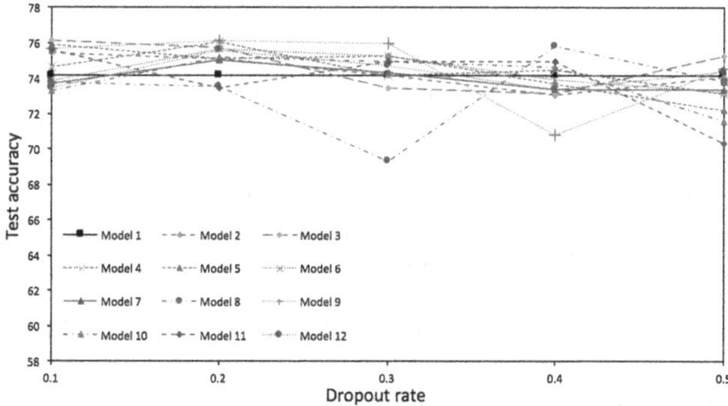

Fig. 4. Plot showing the variation of test accuracy across the dropout range for SciTail.

5 Recommendations for Dropout Application

Based on our empirical evaluations, the following is recommended for regularizing a RNN model for NLI task: (1) Embedding layer should be regularized for large datasets like SNLI. For smaller datasets such as SciTail regularizing recurrent layer is an efficient option. The dropout injected noise at these layers prevents the higher fully connected layers from overfitting. (2) When regularizing multiple layers, regularizing a lower layer (embedding or recurrent; depending on the amount of data) with the inputs and outputs of MLP layer should be considered. The performance of our model decreased when dropout is applied at each intermediate feed-forward connection. (3) When dropout is applied at multiple feed forward connections, it is almost always better to apply it at lower rate – [0.2 – 0.4]. (4) Given the high learning capacity of RNNs, an appropriate model size selection according to the amount of training data is essential. Dropout may independently be insufficient to prevent overfitting in the scenarios otherwise.

6 Conclusions

In this paper, we reported the outcome of experiments conducted to investigate the effect of applying dropout at different layers in an RNN model for the NLI task. Based on our empirical evaluations we recommended the probable locations of dropouts to gain high performance on NLI task. Through extensive exploration, for the correct dropout location in our model, we achieved the accuracies of 86.14% on SNLI and 77.05% on SciTail datasets. In future research, we aim to investigate the effect of different dropout rates at distinct layers.

References

1. Bluche, T., Kermorvant, C., Louradour, J.: Where to apply dropout in recurrent neural networks for handwriting recognition? In: 2015 13th International Conference on Document Analysis and Recognition (ICDAR), pp. 681–685. IEEE (2015)
2. Bowman, S.R., Angeli, G., Potts, C., Manning, C.D.: A large annotated corpus for learning natural language inference. In: Proceedings of the 2015 Conference on Empirical Methods in Natural Language Processing, pp. 632–642. Association for Computational Linguistics (2015)
3. Bowman, S.R., Gauthier, J., Rastogi, A., Gupta, R., Manning, C.D., Potts, C.: A fast unified model for parsing and sentence understanding. In: Proceedings of the 54th Annual Meeting of the Association for Computational Linguistics (Volume 1: Long Papers), vol. 1, pp. 1466–1477 (2016)
4. Chen, Q., Zhu, X., Ling, Z.H., Inkpen, D.: Natural language inference with external knowledge. arXiv preprint arXiv:1711.04289 (2017)
5. Cheng, G., Peddinti, V., Povey, D., Manohar, V., Khudanpur, S., Yan, Y.: An exploration of dropout with LSTMs. In: Proceedings of Interspeech (2017)
6. Cheng, J., Dong, L., Lapata, M.: Long short-term memory-networks for machine reading. In: Proceedings of the 2016 Conference on Empirical Methods in Natural Language Processing, pp. 551–561 (2016)
7. Choi, J., Yoo, K.M., Lee, S.G.: Learning to Compose Task-specific Tree Structures. AAAI (2017)
8. Gal, Y., Ghahramani, Z.: A theoretically grounded application of dropout in recurrent neural networks. In: Advances in Neural Information Processing Systems, pp. 1019–1027 (2016)
9. Ghaeini, R., et al.: Dr-bilstm: Dependent reading bidirectional LSTM for natural language inference. arXiv preprint arXiv:1802.05577 (2018)
10. Khot, T., Sabharwal, A., Clark, P.: SciTail: a textual entailment dataset from science question answering. In: Proceedings of AAAI (2018)
11. Kim, Y., Denton, C., Hoang, L., Rush, A.M.: Neural machine translation by jointly learning to align and translate. In: Proceedings of ICLR (2017)
12. Kingma, D.P., Ba, J.: Adam: a method for stochastic optimization. arXiv preprint arXiv:1412.6980 (2014)
13. Liu, Y., Sun, C., Lin, L., Wang, X.: Learning natural language inference using bidirectional LSTM model and inner-attention. CoRR abs/1605.09090 (2016)
14. MacCartney, B.: Natural language inference. Stanford University (2009)
15. Munkhdalai, T., Yu, H.: Neural tree indexers for text understanding. In: Proceedings of the Conference, Association for Computational Linguistics, Meeting, vol. 1, p. 11. NIH Public Access (2017)
16. Pachitariu, M., Sahani, M.: Regularization and nonlinearities for neural language models: when are they needed? arXiv preprint arXiv:1301.5650 (2013)
17. Pennington, J., Socher, R., Manning, C.: GloVe: global vectors for word representation. In: Proceedings of the 2014 Conference on Empirical Methods in Natural Language Processing (EMNLP), pp. 1532–1543 (2014)
18. Pham, V., Bluche, T., Kermorvant, C., Louradour, J.: Dropout improves recurrent neural networks for handwriting recognition. In: 2014 14th International Conference on Frontiers in Handwriting Recognition (ICFHR), pp. 285–290. IEEE (2014)

19. Srivastava, N., Hinton, G., Krizhevsky, A., Sutskever, I., Salakhutdinov, R.: Dropout: a simple way to prevent neural networks from overfitting. J. Mach. Learn. Res. **15**(1), 1929–1958 (2014)
20. Tay, Y., Tuan, L.A., Hui, S.C.: A compare-propagate architecture with alignment factorization for natural language inference. arXiv preprint arXiv:1801.00102 (2017)
21. Zaremba, W., Sutskever, I., Vinyals, O.: Recurrent neural network regularization. arXiv preprint arXiv:1409.2329 (2014)

Neural Model for the Visual Recognition of Animacy and Social Interaction

Mohammad Hovaidi-Ardestani[1,2], Nitin Saini[1,2], Aleix M. Martinez[3], and Martin A. Giese[1(✉)]

[1] Section of Computational Sensomotorics, Department of Cognitive Neurology, CIN and HIH, University Clinic Tübingen, Ottfried-Müller-Str. 25, 72076 Tübingen, Germany
martin.giese@uni-tuebingen.de

[2] IMPRS for Cognitive and Systems Neuroscience, Tübingen, Germany

[3] Department of Electrical and Computer Engineering, The Ohio State University, Columbus, OH 43210, USA

Abstract. Humans reliably attribute social interpretations and agency to highly impoverished stimuli, such as interacting geometrical shapes. While it has been proposed that this capability is based on high-level cognitive processes, such as probabilistic reasoning, we demonstrate that it might be accounted for also by rather simple physiologically plausible neural mechanisms. Our model is a hierarchical neural network architecture with two pathways that analyze form and motion features. The highest hierarchy level contains neurons that have learned combinations of relative position-, motion-, and body-axis features. The model reproduces psychophysical results on the dependence of perceived animacy on motion smoothness and the orientation of the body axis. In addition, the model correctly classifies six categories of social interactions that have been frequently tested in the psychophysical literature. For the generation of training data we propose a novel algorithm that is derived from dynamic human navigation models, and which allows to generate arbitrary numbers of abstract social interaction stimuli by self-organization.

Keywords: Hierarchy · Neural network model · Animacy
Social interaction perception

1 Introduction

Humans spontaneously can decode animacy and social interactions from strongly impoverished stimuli. A classical study by Heider and Simmel [1] demonstrated that humans derived very consistently interpretations in terms of social interactions from simple geometrical figures that moved around in the two-dimensional plain. The figures were interpreted as living agents, to which even personality traits were attributed. More recent studies have characterized in more detail which critical features of simple stimuli affect the perception of animacy, that

V. Kůrková et al. (Eds.): ICANN 2018, LNCS 11141, pp. 168–177, 2018.
https://doi.org/10.1007/978-3-030-01424-7_17

is whether the object is perceived as alive [2–4]. Furthermore, detailed studies have focused on the perception of social interactions between multiple moving shapes, e.g. focusing on 'chasing' or 'fighting' [5,6]. Six interaction types have been used in a number of studies [7–9], McAleer and Pollick [9] showed that these categories can be reliably classified from stimuli showing moving circular disks whose movements were derived from real interactions.

Coarse neural substrates of the processing of such stimuli have been identified in fMRI studies. Animacy has been studied, modulating the movement parameters of individual moving shapes [10–12], and stimuli similar to the ones by Heider & Simmel have been frequently used in studies addressing Theory of Mind [13,14]. In fMRI and monkey studies regions like the superior temporal sulcus (STS) and human area TPJ were found to be selective for these stimuli [15–18]. In spite of this localization of relevant cortical areas, the underlying exact neural circuits of this processing remain entirely unclear. Some theories have associated the processing of such abstract stimuli with probabilistic reasoning [19,20], while others have linked them to lower-level visual processing [6]. So far no ideas exist how such functions could be accounted for by physiologically plausible neural circuits.

The goal of this paper is to present a simple neural model that reproduces some of the key observations in psychophysical experiments about the perception of animacy and social interactions from simple abstract stimuli. The model in its present form is simple, but in principle extendable for the processing of more complex stimuli that require also the processing of shape details or shapes in clutter. The model is an extension of classical models of the visual processing stream that account for the processing of object shape and actions [21–24]. However, such models never have been applied to account for the perception of animacy or social interaction. Our attempt to use these types of architectures is motivated by recent work that showed that models of this type for the recognition of hand actions also account for the perception of causality from simple stimulus displays that consist of moving disks [25]. This modeling work predicted also the existence of neurons in macaque cortex that are specifically involved in the visual perception of causality [26]. Here we show that a model based on similar principles accounts for the perception of animacy and social interactions.

In the following section, we first describe how we generated a stimulus set for training of the neural model, devising a generative model for social interaction stimuli that is based on a dynamical systems approach. We then describe the architecture of the model. The following section describes the results, followed by a brief discussion.

2 Stimulus Synthesis

For the training of neural network models a sufficient set of stimuli is required. The problem is that from the classical psychophysical studies only a rather small set of stimuli is publicly available. For a meaningful application of learning-based neural networks approaches thus a sufficiently large training data set with similar properties needs to be generated. In our study we used movies showing individual moving agents, and interaction of 2 agents (chasing, playing, following, flirting, guarding, fighting) described in psychophisical studies [7–9].

In order to model the interaction of two moving agents we exploited a dynamical systems approach, which before was used very successfully for the modeling of human navigation [27]. The underlying idea, originally derived from robotics [28], is to define a dynamical systems or differential equations for the heading directions ϕ_i and the instantaneous propagation speeds v_i of the interacting agents (in our case $i = 1, 2$). The specified movement is dependent on goal and obstacle points in the two dimensional plain, where the other agent can also act as goal or obstacle as well. We modified a model for human steering behavior during walking [29] to reproduce the movements during social interactions.

The resulting dynamics is given by the following differential equations for the heading direction:

$$\ddot{\phi}_i = -b\dot{\phi}_i - k_g(\phi_i - \psi_{\mathrm{g},i})(e^{-c_1 d_{\mathrm{g},i}} + c_2) + k_o \sum_{n=1}^{N_{\mathrm{obst}}} (\phi_i - \psi_{\mathrm{o},ni})(e^{-c_3|\phi_i - \psi_{\mathrm{o},ni}|})(e^{-c_4 d_{\mathrm{o},ni}}). \tag{1}$$

The variables $\psi_{\mathrm{g},i}$ and $d_{\mathrm{g},i}$ signify the absolute direction of the actual goal point and the distance of the goal from the agent in the 2D plain. Likewise, $\psi_{\mathrm{o},ni}$ and $d_{\mathrm{o},ni}$ signify the absolute direction and distance from obstacle number n from the agent, where N_{obst} is the number of relevant obstacles, and where k_m and c_m signify constants. The forward speed of the agents is specified by the two stochastic differential equations

$$\tau \dot{v}_i = -v_i + F_i(d_{\mathrm{g},i}) + k_\epsilon \epsilon_i(t), \tag{2}$$

where $\epsilon_i(t)$ is Gaussian white noise. The two functions F_i that specify the distance dependence of the speed dynamics are different for the two agents:

$$F_1(d) = \frac{1}{1 + e^{-c_5(d - c_6)}} - c_7 e^{-kd} \tag{3}$$

$$F_2(d) = \frac{c_8}{1 + e^{-c_9(d - c_{10})}} - c_{11} e^{-kd} + c_{12}. \tag{4}$$

The goal point of the second agent was typically the first agent. The goal points for the first agent was given by a sequence of fixed positions, which were randomly generated by uniformly sampling from the 2D plain and rejecting the samples that were closer than a fixed distance from the last sample. Since it turned out that the influence of the obstacle terms was rather low for the speed dynamics, we dropped the obstacle terms from the speed control dynamics. Table 1 provides an overview of the model parameters for the six simulated behaviors. We generated 50 stimuli for each interaction class. Figure 1 shows examples paths of the agents for the different behaviors for typical simulations.

Table 1. Parameters of simulation algorithm.

	Agent 1					Agent 2						
	k_ε	C_5	C_6	C_7	k	k_ε	C_8	C_9	C_{10}	C_{11}	C_{12}	k
Guarding (Gu)	0	1	5	0	0	0	1	1	3	0	0.5	0
Following (FO)	0	10	7	0	0	0	1	4	4	0	0	0
Fighting (FI)	1	1	3	1	0.1	1	1	1	3	1	0	0.1
Chasing (CH)	0	10	7	0	0	0	1	1	7	0	0	0
Flirting (FL)	0	1	5	0	0	1	0.6	1	2	1	0	0.5
Playing (PL)	0	1	5	0	0	1	1	1	10	0	0.5	0

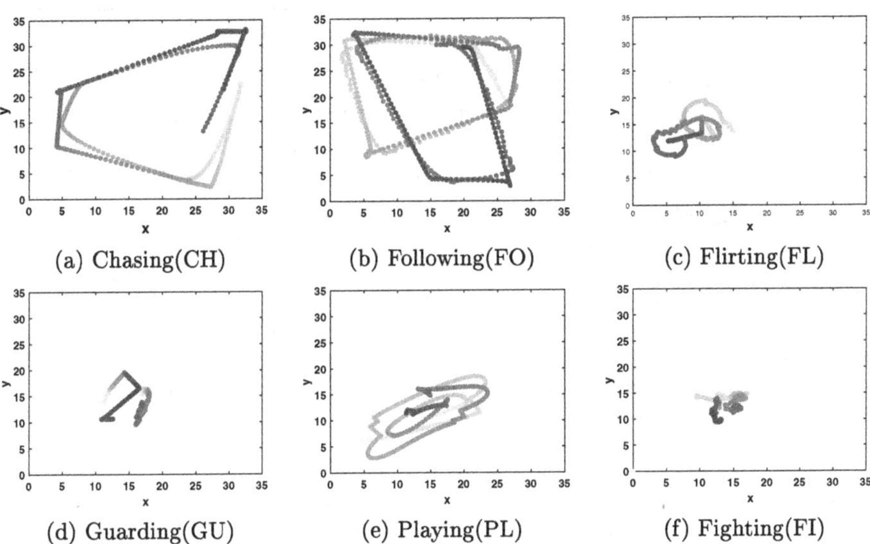

(a) Chasing(CH) (b) Following(FO) (c) Flirting(FL)

(d) Guarding(GU) (e) Playing(PL) (f) Fighting(FI)

Fig. 1. Sample trajectories for 6 different social interactions. Colors indicate the positions of the two agents (agent 1: blue, agent 2: red). Color saturation indicates time, the color fading out after long times. (Color figure online)

3 Model Architecture

An overview of the model architecture is shown in Fig. 2. Building on classical biologically-inspired models for shape and action processing [21,22], the model comprises a form and a motion pathway, each consisting of a hierarchy of feature detectors. Presently, these pathways were modelled following these classical papers, which was sufficient for the tested simple stimuli.

Form Pathway: The form pathway of the simple model implementation here comprises only three hierarchy layers. The first is composed from (even and uneven) Gabor filters with 8 different orientations (cf. [22]), whose centers were placed in a grid of 120 by 120 points across the pixel image. The outputs of

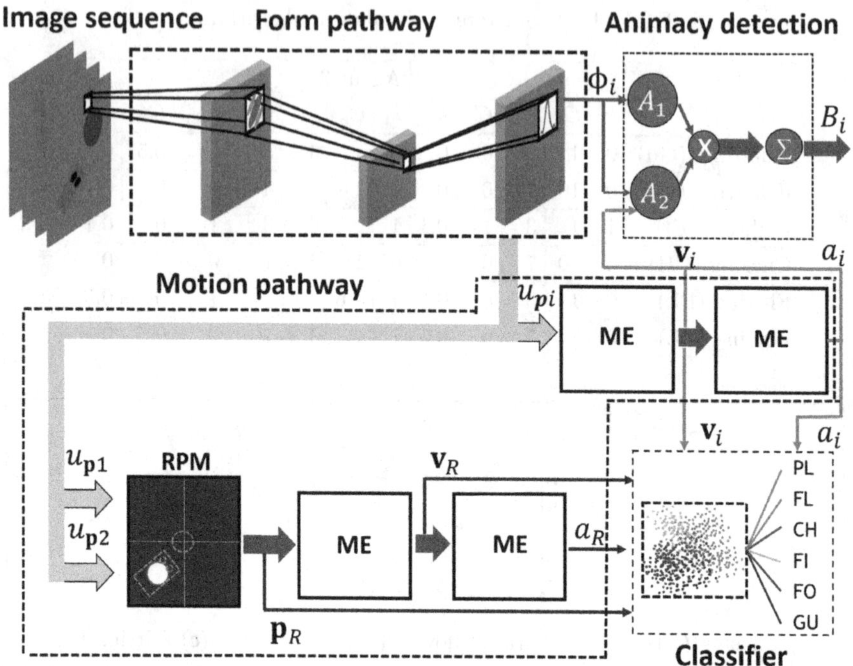

Fig. 2. Model consisting of a form and a motion pathway. ME signifies a layer of motion energy detectors, and RPM the relative position map. The top level of the model is formed by neural detectors for the perceived animacy, and a network that classifies six different types of interactions. (See text for details.)

this Gabor filter array are pooled by the next layer using a maximum operation over a grid of 41 by 41 filters, separately for the different orientations, in order to increase the position-invariance of the representation. The highest layer of the form pathway is formed by Gaussian radial basis function, which are trained with the shapes of the agents in different 2D orientations. Opposed to many other object recognition architectures, these shape-selective neurons have receptive fields of limited size (about 20% of the width of the image), which is consistent with neural data from area IT [30]. The outputs of this layer provide thus information about the identity of the agents, their positions, and their orientation in the image plain. The signal $u_k(\phi, x, y)$ is the output activity of the neural detectors detecting shape k at the 2D position (x, y). Summing this signal over all ϕ provides a neural activity distribution $u_{\mathbf{p}_k}(x, y)$ whose peak signals the position of agent k in the image. This signal is used to compute the velocity and the relative positions of the moving elements or animate objects. Similarly, by summing over the positions one obtains a activity distribution $u_{\phi_k}(\phi)$ over the directions with a peak at ϕ_k.vadjust

Motion Pathway: It analyzes the 2D motion and the relative motion of the moving agents. As input we use the time-dependent signals $u_{\mathbf{p}_k}(x, y)$ for each agent as input to a field of standard motion energy detectors (ME in Fig. 2), resulting in an output that encodes the motion energy in terms of a four-dimensional neural activity distribution (dropping the index k in the following) $u_{\mathbf{v}}(x, y, v_x, v_y, t)$, where $\mathbf{v} = (v_x, v_y)$ is the preferred velocity vector of the motion energy detector. Pooling this output activity distribution over all spatial positions using a maximum operation, a position-invariant neural representation of velocity is obtained. From this a neural representation of motion direction is obtained by pooling this activity distribution over all neurons with the same (similar) motion direction, resulting in a one-dimensional activity distribution $u_\theta(\theta, t)$ over the motion direction θ, from which the direction can be easily estimated by computing a population vector[1]. The same applies to the length of the velocity vector[2] $v = |\mathbf{v}|$. In order to compute also the acceleration of the agents, we transmit the position-invariant activity distribution $u_{\mathbf{v}}(v_x, v_y, t)$ as input to another field of motion energy detectors, which computes from this an energy distribution $u_{\mathbf{a}}(x, y, a_x, a_y, t)$ over the acceleration vectors $\mathbf{a} = (a_x, a_y)$. By pooling over directions, from this an activity distribution over the length of these vectors $a = |\mathbf{a}|$) is computed, and again this parameter can be estimated by a simple population vector. The population estimates of θ, $\mathbf{v}$ and a enter the animacy computation (s.b.).

For analyzing the relative motion of the two agents, following [22], the output distributions $u_{\mathbf{p}_k}(x, y)$ of the form pathway are also fed into a gain field network that computes a representation of the position of the second agent in a coordinate frame that is centered on the first. Its output is computed as convolution-like integral of the form $u_{\mathbf{p}_R}(x, y) = \int_{x',y'} u_{\mathbf{p}_1}(x', y') u_{\mathbf{p}_2}(x + x', y + y')\, \mathrm{d}x'\mathrm{d}y'$. This output defines a neural *relative position map* that represents the position of agent 2 as an activity peak in a coordinate frame that is centered on the first. The integral is taken over a finite region of shifts $|(x, y)| < D$, implying that situations where the agents have a distance substantially larger than D will not produce an output peak. This makes sense since agents that are too distant do not produce the percept of a social interaction. The activity distribution $u_{\mathbf{p}_R}(x, y, t)$ is again processed by a cascade of two levels of motion energy detectors in order to compute the relative speed and acceleration of the two agents. Population estimates of the relative distance $d_R = |\mathbf{p}_R|$, velocity $\mathbf{v}_R$, and the acceleration a_R enter the interaction classifier.

Recognition Level: The highest level of the model consists of a circuit that derives the perceived animacy of the two agents, and another one that classifies the perceived interaction class. The neurons detecting instantaneous animacy (dropping again the index k and time) multiply two input derived from the signal of both pathways signals $B = A_1 A_2$. The first signal measures the alignment of

[1] A simple estimate of the encoded angle is given by $\hat{\theta} = \arg\big((\sum_m \exp(i\theta_m)\, u_\theta(\theta_m, t))/(\sum_m u_\theta(\theta_m, t))\big)$, where the θ_m are the preferred directions of the neurons.

[2] Here the estimator is $\hat{v} = \arg\big((\sum_m v_m u_v(v_m, t))/(\sum_m u_v(v_m, t))\big)$, where the v_m are the preferred speeds of the neurons.

the body axis of the moving agent with its direction of its motion. It is just given by the scalar product of the activity distributions over the body axis of the agent $u_\phi(\phi)$ and the motion direction of the agent $u_\theta(\theta)$ in the form $A_1 = \sum_n u_\phi(\theta_n)u_\theta(\theta_n)$. The second signal A_2 linearly combines information about the speed, and the magnitude changes and angular changes of speed, which are given by a and the angular component of $\mathbf{a}$. The linear mixing weights of the animacy neurons were estimated by fitting the psychophysical results from [2]. Final animacy responses were computed as time averages over the whole trajectories.

The second circuit at the top level of the model classifies the different interaction types based on the following features: speeds $\mathbf{v}_i$ and acceleration a_i of the agents, and relative position $\mathbf{p}_R$, velocity $\mathbf{v}_R$, and acceleration a_R of the agents. These features served as inputs of different classifier models, We tested a multi-layer perceptron, linear and nonlinear discriminant analysis (see also [31]), k-nearest neighbor classification, and a linear and a nonlinear support vector machine.

4 Results

Results on animacy detection are shown in Fig. 3. The model reproduces at least qualitatively the dependence of animacy ratings on directions and speed changes [2]. In these experiments an agent shape moved along a straight line and then suddenly changed speed or direction by different amounts. In addition, the model reproduces the fact that a moving figure that has a body axis, like a rectangle, results in stronger perceived animacy than a circle if the movement, and that the rating is highest if the body axis is aligned with the motion than if it is not aligned [2].

Figure 4 shows example results from the application of the different classifier models for the 6 interaction behaviors in the study [9]. The classifiers were trained on movies generated with the stimulus generation algorithm described in Sect. 2. The linear SVM classifier achieves 99% correct classifications on this data set. See Table 2 for the results with the other classifiers. Most importantly, the model achieved also 100 % correct classifications on the example videos from [9], even though these movies were not used for training.

Table 2. Classification results with different classifiers (6 interaction types).

Classifier	Accuracy
Linear SVM	99.0%
Gaussian kernel SVM	96.3%
LDA	94.7%
KNN	94.7%
Nonlinear LDA	94.3%
Neural Network	94.0%

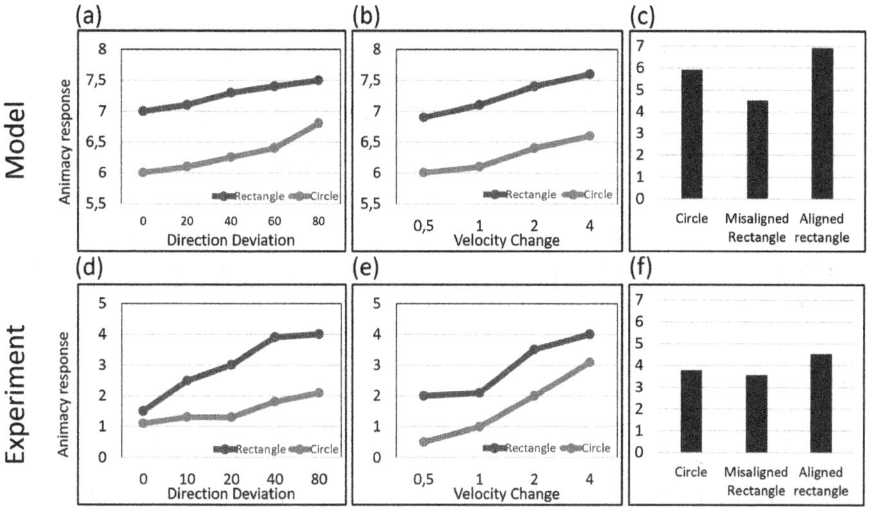

Fig. 3. Simulation results for animacy perception in comparison with experimental results. (a), (d): Dependence of animacy ratings on size of direction change. (b), (e): Dependence of animacy rating on size of speed change. (c), (f): Effect of alignment of body axis with motion direction, compared with moving circle (no body axis).

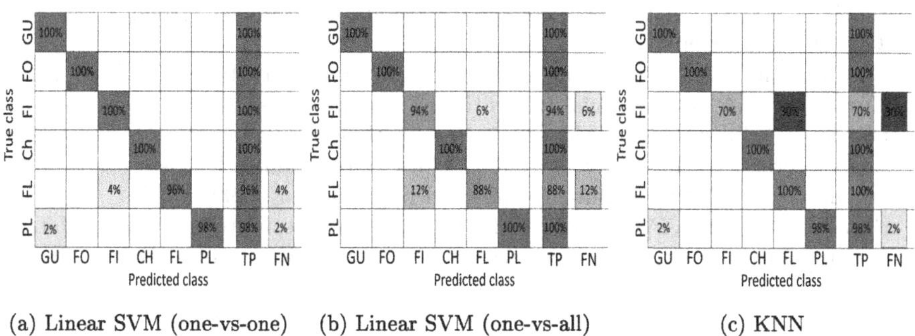

(a) Linear SVM (one-vs-one) (b) Linear SVM (one-vs-all) (c) KNN

Fig. 4. Confusion matrices for the best (Linear SVM) and the worst (KNN) classifier; TP: true positive rate, FN stands for false negative rate. 50 videos per class.

5 Conclusion

Our model accounts by combination of very elementary neural mechanisms for a number of classical results from animacy and social interaction perception from abstract figures. To our knowledge this is the first neural model that can account for such results. Evidently the model is only a proof-of-concept with many shortcomings, a major one being that the accuracy of the form and motion pathway that provide input to the animacy and interaction detection have to be improved. Since the model is in principle consistent with deep architectures for form and action recognition that can achieve high performance level it seems likely that it can be extended to the processing of much more challenging stimulus material. Even in its simple form the model proves that animacy and social interaction judgements partly might be derived by very elementary operations in hierarchical neural vision systems, without a need of sophisticated or accurate probabilistic inference.

Acknowledgments. This work was supported by: HFSP RGP0036/2016; the European Commission HBP FP7-ICT2013-FET-F/604102 and COGIMON H2020-644727, the DFG KA 1258/15-1, and BMBF CRNC FK: 01CQ1704.

References

1. Heider, F., Simmel, M.: An experimental study of apparent behavior. Am. J. Psychol. **57**(2), 243–259 (1944)
2. Tremoulet, P.D., Feldman, J.: Perception of animacy from the motion of a single object. Perception **29**, 943–951 (2000)
3. Tremoulet, P.D., Feldman, J.: The influence of spatial context and the role of intentionality in the interpretation of animacy from motion. Percept. Psychophys. **68**(6), 1047–1058 (2006)
4. Hernik, M., Fearon, P., Csibra, G.: Action anticipation in human infants reveals assumptions about anteroposterior body structure and action. In: Proceedings, Biological Sciences (2014)
5. Scholl, B.J., Tremoulet, P.D.: Perceptual causality and animacy. Trends Cogn. Sci. **4**(8), 299–309 (2000)
6. Gao, T., Scholl, B.J.: Perceiving animacy and intentionality. In: Rutherford, M.D., Kuhlmeier, V.A., (eds.) Social Perception. The MIT Press (2013)
7. Blythe, P., Miller, G.F., Todd, P.M.: How motion reveals intention: categorizing social interactions. In: Gigerenzer, G., Todd, P. (eds.) Simple heuristics that make us smart, pp. 257–285. Oxford University Press, London (1999)
8. Barrett, H.C., Todd, P.M., Miller, G.F., Blythe, P.W.: Accurate judgments of intention from motion cues alone: a cross-cultural study. Evol. Hum. Behav. **26**(4), 313–331 (2005)
9. McAleer, P., Pollick, F.E.: Understanding intention from minimal displays of human activity. Behav. Res. Methods **40**, 830–839 (2008)
10. Schultz, J., Friston, K.J., O'Doherty, J., Wolpert, D.M., Frith, C.D.: Activation in posterior superior temporal sulcus parallels parameter inducing the percept of animacy. Neuron **45**(4), 625–635 (2005)
11. Morito, Y., Tanabe, H.C., Kochiyama, T., Sadato, N.: Neural representation of animacy in the early visual areas: a functional MRI study. Brain Res. Bull. **79**(5), 271–280 (2009)
12. Shultz, S., McCarthy, G.: Perceived animacy influences the processing of human-like surface features in the fusiform gyrus. Neuropsychologia **60**, 115–120 (2014)
13. Blakemore, S.-J., Boyer, P., Pachot-Clouard, M., Meltzoff, A., Segebarth, C., Decety, J.: The detection of contingency and animacy from simple animations in the human brain. Cereb. Cortex **13**(8), 837–844 (2003)
14. Yang, D.Y.-J., Rosenblau, G., Keifer, C., Pelphrey, K.A.: An integrative neural model of social perception, action observation, and theory of mind. Neurosci. Biobehav. Rev. **51**, 263–275 (2015)

15. Lahnakoski, J.M., et al.: Naturalistic FMRI mapping reveals superior temporal sulcus as the hub for the distributed brain network for social perception. Front. Hum. Neurosci. **6**, 233 (2012)
16. Isik, L., Koldewyn, K., Beeler, D., Kanwisher, N.: Perceiving social interactions in the posterior superior temporal sulcus. PNAS **114**, E9145–E9152 (2017)
17. Sliwa, J., Freiwald, W.A.: A dedicated network for social interaction processing in the primate brain. Science **356**(6339), 745–749 (2017)
18. Walbrin, J., Downing, P., Koldewyn, K.: Neural responses to visually observed social interactions. Neuropsychologia **112**, 31–39 (2018)
19. Baker, C.L., Saxe, R., Tenenbaum, J.B.: Action understanding as inverse planning. Cogn. Reinf. Learn. High. Cogn. **113**, 329–349 (2009)
20. Shu, T., Peng, Y., Fan, L., Lu, H., Zhu, S.-C.: Perception of human interaction based on motion trajectories: from aerial videos to decontextualized animations. Top. Cogn. Sci. **10**(1), 225–241 (2018)
21. Riesenhuber, M., Poggio, T.: Hierarchical models of object recognition in cortex. Nat. Neurosci. **2**, 1019–1025 (1999)
22. Giese, M.A., Poggio, T.: Neural mechanisms for the recognition of biological movements. Nat. Rev. Neurosci. **4**, 179–192 (2003)
23. Jhuang, H., Serre, T., Wolf, L., Poggio, T.: A biologically inspired system for action recognition. In: IEEE 11th International Conference on Computer Vision (2007)
24. Fleischer, F., Caggiano, V., Thier, P., Giese, M.A.: Physiologically inspired model for the visual recognition of transitive hand actions. J. Neurosci. **15**(33), 6563–80 (2013)
25. Fleischer, F., Christensen, A., Caggiano, V., Thier, P., Giese, M.A.: Neural theory for the perception of causal actions. Psychol. Res. **76**(4), 476–493 (2012)
26. Caggiano, V., Fleischer, F., Pomper, J.K., Giese, M.A., Thier, P.: Mirror neurons in Monkey premotor area F5 show tuning for critical features of visual causality perception. Current Biology **26**(22), 3077–3082 (2016)
27. Warren, W.H.: The dynamics of perception and action. Psychol. Rev. **113**(2), 358–389 (2006)
28. Schner, G., Dose, M.: A dynamical systems approach to task-level system integration used to plan and control autonomous vehicle motion. Robot. Auton. Syst. **10**(4), 253–267 (1992)
29. Fajen, B.R., Warren, W.H.: Behavioral dynamics of steering, obstacle avoidance, and route selection. J. Exp. Psychology Hum. Percept. Perform. **1**(3), 184–184 (2003)
30. di Carlo, J.J., Zoccolan, D., Rust, N.C.: How does the brain solve visual object recognition? Neuron **73**(3), 415–434 (2012)
31. You, D., Hamsici, O.C., Martinez, A.M.: Kernel optimization in discriminant analysis. IEEE Trans. Pattern Anal. Mach. Intell. **33**(3), 631–638 (2011)

Attention-Based RNN Model for Joint Extraction of Intent and Word Slot Based on a Tagging Strategy

Dongjie Zhang[1,2], Zheng Fang[1,2], Yanan Cao[2(✉)], Yanbing Liu[2], Xiaojun Chen[2], and Jianlong Tan[2]

[1] School of Cyber Security, University of Chinese Academy of Sciences, Beijing, China
[2] Institute of Information Engineering, Chinese Academy of Sciences, Beijing, China
{zhangdongjie, fangzheng, caoyanan, liuyanbing, chenxiaojun, tanjianlong}@iie.ac.cn

Abstract. In this paper, we proposed an attention-based recurrent neural network model based on a tagging strategy for intent detection and word slot extraction. Unlike other joint models dividing the joint task into two sub-models by sharing parameters, we explore a tagging strategy to incorporate the intent detection task and word slot extraction task in a sequence labeling model. We implemented experiments on a public dataset and the results show that the tagging strategy methods outperform most of the existing pipelined and joint methods. Our tagging strategy model obtained 97.65% accuracy rate on intent detection task and 95.15% F1 score on word slot extraction task.

Keywords: Intent detection · Word slot extraction · Joint model
Attention mechanism · Tagging strategy

1 Introduction

Intent detection and word slot extraction are two basic issues in the field of Natural Language Understanding and these two tasks are usually handled separately [19]. Intent detection and word slot extraction can be regarded as a sentence classification and sequence tagging task respectively. Traditionally, we solve these problems in a sequential order, extracting the word slots first and then detecting the intent of the given sentence. This separated framework makes the task easy to handle and can deal with different subtask issues more flexibly. It is assumed that these two tasks have no correlation between them which enables them to be treated as an independent model, however, in many cases this is not true. Thus, the results of the word slot extraction can affect the outcome of the intent detection by the propagation of errors.

Compared with the pipeline models, the joint learning framework handles the two tasks using a single model [2]. The joint model can integrate the information of word slots and of intent by sharing collective parameters and it has been shown to perform well on the joint extraction task [20]. These joint models can make the intent detection

V. Kůrková et al. (Eds.): ICANN 2018, LNCS 11141, pp. 178–188, 2018.
https://doi.org/10.1007/978-3-030-01424-7_18

and word slot extraction process simpler as we only need to train one model to fine-tune the tasks.

Although the aforementioned joint methods can handle the two subtasks in a single model, they can also produce redundant information by extracting word slots and intents separately. Generally, these frameworks need two classifiers which have separate label collections: one for intent extraction and another for word slot labeling. So the total number of labels is the combined size of the two label collections. However, this may produce redundant labeling results, that is, if there is a slot s that never appears in the intent i, the model may still give the result of labeling a word as word slot s along with the intention i. In addition, it's inevitable to propagate the error of two classifiers to each other during training the joint model. In our work, we model the relation of word slots and intent directly by using only one sequential label classifier instead of extracting the word slots and intents separately. We redefined a set of tags containing the information of word slot and the intent of the whole sentence. Based on this tagging strategy, the joint extraction of word slot and intent can be converted into a sequence tagging problem. With this strategy, we can easily use sequence-to-sequence models to handle the two tasks simultaneously without complicated feature engineering.

However, one word slot may have various intents in different sentences and the words indicating the intent of the sentence may locate far away from the current input word. Many sequence labeling model are capable of capturing long-distance dependence information but they still strongly focus on the parts around the current input word. The attention mechanism which has made satisfactory effect in the field of machine translation [1] can effectively learn global attention information of the sequence by emphasizing the influence of key words on the model results. Specially, we wonder if the attention mechanism can be utilized in and improve our joint tagging model. So we implemented the attention mechanism on our joint model to make it more sensitive to key information, especially the long-distance information indicating the intent.

In this paper, we focus on resolving the issue of redundant labeling results, propagation of interactions intrinsically in the pipeline as well as the traditional joint training models on word slot extraction task and intent detection task. Based on the motivation, we applied a tagging strategy accompanied with an end-to-end model to settle the problem by transforming the joint extraction task into a sequence tagging problem. In order to solve the influence of the diversified relation between word slots and intentions, we introduce global sentence information through attention mechanism to enhance the effect of sentence intent. Experiments on ATIS data set show that our joint model significantly outperforms pipeline and traditional joint models.

The rest of our paper is organized as follows. In Sect. 2, we introduce the related works of RNN sequence labeling model and the attention mechanism for sequence labeling. In Sect. 3, we describe our labeling strategy and end-to-end RNN extraction models in detail. In Sect. 4 we mainly show the settings and results of our experiments. Finally, we conclude the work in Sect. 5.

2 Related Works

Intent detection and word slot extraction are corresponded to two fundamental problems–text classification and sequence labeling, which are the basis of many natural language applications and are usually solved in a pipeline manner. For Intent detection, Support Vector machines (SVMs) [3], deep neural network methods [14] and Convolutional Neural Networks (CNNs) [7] have been widely used. The boosting method [16] and its improved method with dependency parsing-based sentence simplification [17] can handle the complex, longer and natural utterances more effectively. The adaptation of the recursive neural network also achieved competitive performance on the intent detection task [2]. In case of word slot extraction, few of the most popular methods include Maximum Entropy Markov Models (MEMMs) [10], Conditional Random Fields (CRFs) [13] and Recurrent Neural Networks (RNNs) [11]. Label dependency is beneficial for word slot extraction task by feeding previous output label [9]. The RNN-CRF networks can also be used in word slot extraction task [5]. In general, simple Recurrent Neural Networks and Convolutional Neural Networks have shown to significantly outperform the previous state-of-the-art Maximum Entropy Markov Models and Conditional Random Fields and the deep Long Short-Term Memories (LSTMs) was emphatically proposed to be applied to the word slot extraction task [20]. In addition, the joint training model has become a research hotspot. The joint model of Recursive Neural Networks integrated two subtasks into one compositional model by providing an elegant mechanism for incorporating both discrete syntactic structure and continuous-space word and phrase representations [2]. The CNN-CRF model can be jointly trained by extracting features automatically from CNN layers and sharing with the intent model [19].

Recently, a novel tagging strategy has been proposed in joint extraction of entities and relations [22]. Results show that the tagging methods are better than most of the existing pipelined and joint learning methods without identifying entities and relations separately. This task mainly focuses on extracting a triplet consisting of two entities and the relation of the two entities. Unlike traditional models, this work proposed a tagging strategy that label triples directly rather than extracting entities and relationships separately. To implement this tagging strategy, a new set of labels containing information about the entities and the relation between them has been designed. With this tagging strategy, the joint extraction of entities and relations can be transformed into a sequence labeling problem. In this way, the sequence labeling model can be conveniently used to handle the joint task without complex feature engineering. However, this tagging strategy still has deficiencies in identifying overlapping relationships and the diversity association between two corresponding entities still needs to be refined.

3 Proposed Methods

3.1 The Tagging Strategy

Traditional model labels the intent and the words slot separately as Table 1 shows. The labels of intent and word slot are divided into two collections.

Table 1. The word slots and intent of a sentence instance in ATIS corpus.

Sentence	Flights	From	Boston	To	Kansas	City	On	Friday
Word slot	O	O	B-fromloc	O	B-toloc	I-toloc	O	B-depart time
Intent	Flight							

In order to avoid the redundant labeling results and propagation interaction, we adopt a new tagging strategy. How the results are tagged is shown in Fig. 1. Based on our tagging strategy, each word is assigned to a tag that contains three parts: the word position in word slot, the word slot type, and the intent of the whole sentence. With the symbol "O" at the head of the tag, this represents the "Other" tag, which means that the corresponding word is not in any of the word slots. In addition to symbol "O", we apply the "BIES" symbol to represent the position information in word slot. The word slot type is obtained from a predefined set. The intent type symbol can also get from a predefined set but the intention of all words in a given sequence is exactly the same. Thus, the total number of tags is $N_t = N_p * N_s * N_i - \Phi$, where N_p is the number of the "BIES" position information symbol, N_s is the size of the word slot set, N_i is the number of all intents and Φ is the number of redundant labels.

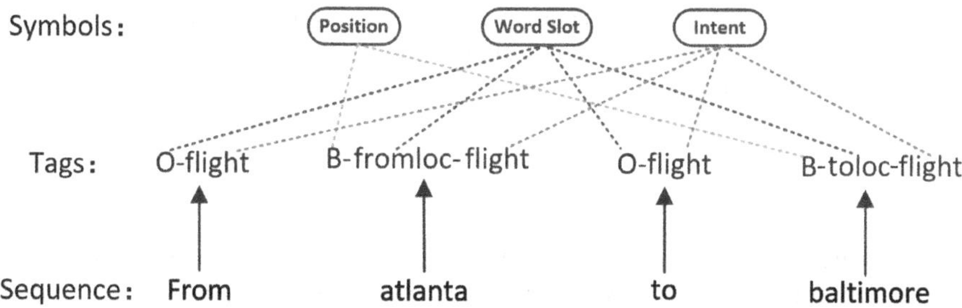

Fig. 1. The instance of our tagging strategy. The word slot symbol "fromloc" and "toloc" represent the departure and destination of the flight. the "flight" symbol expresses the intent of asking for flight information.

As is shown in Fig. 1, the word "atlanta" is signed the tag "B-fromloc-flight". The position information is marked as "B", the word slot type is marked as "fromloc", the intent type is marked as "flight" and the three parts of the tag are connected by the symbol "-". The intent of a sentence is obtained from the majority intent symbols of all the words.

3.2 Attention-Based RNN Model

In recent years, end-to-end model based on recurrent neural network has been widely used in sequence labeling task [12, 20]. In this paper, we investigate an end-to-end model to produce the extraction results as Fig. 2 shows. It contains an embedding layer, a bi-directional RNN layer and a hidden layer with attention mechanism.

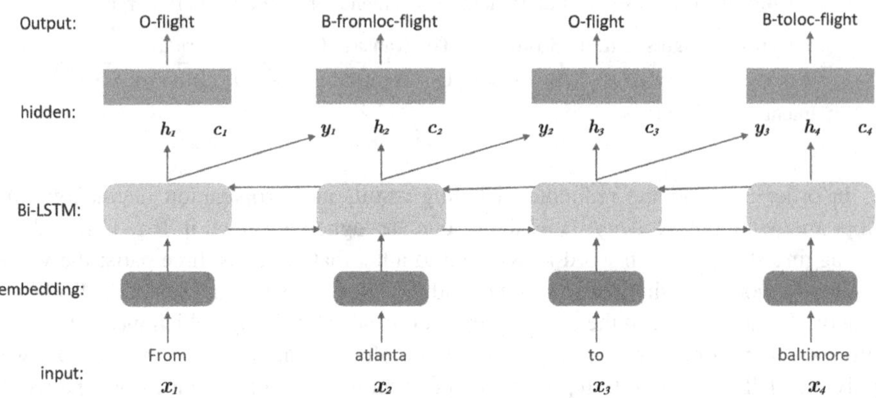

Fig. 2. The illustration of our model with a word embedding layer, a bi-LSTM layer and a hidden layer. y_i is the hidden layer output, h_i is the hidden layer state and c_i is the attention context vector.

The Bi-RNN Layer. In the sequence labeling task, we generally learn a function $f : X \rightarrow Y$ that maps the input sequence to its corresponding label sequence explicitly aligned to the given the input sequence $X(x_1, x_2, \cdots, x_T)$ and its corresponding label sequence $Y(y_1, y_2, \cdots, y_T)$. In our joint task, we want to find the best label sequence Y given input words X such that:

$$\hat{y} = \arg max \, P(Y|X) \tag{1}$$

The bidirectional RNN model has been proven to capture the semantic and sequential information for each word effectively in sequence tagging task by reading sentences bidirectionally. In our proposed model, we use a bidirectional RNN layer reading the input sequence in both forward and backward directions. The forward RNN reading the input sequence in its original order generates a hidden state fh_i at each time step i. Similarly, the backward RNN reading the input sequence in its reverse order generates a sequence of hidden states $[bh_1, bh_2, \cdots, bh_T]$. The bidirectional RNN layer hidden state h_i at each time step i is combined of the forward state fh_i and backward state bh_i, $h_i = [fh_i, bh_i]$. Each hidden state h_i carries information of the entire input sequence with strong focus on the parts around the i th word. The hidden state h and the bi-RNN output y are then combined with an attention context vector c to produce the label distribution.

The Attention Mechanism. Attention mechanism can be regarded as the process of selectively filtering a small amount of important information from all the provided information ignoring most of the non-important information [18]. The process can be reflected in the calculation of the weight coefficient. The greater the weight is, the more it focuses on its corresponding value. The weight represents the importance and the value is its corresponding information. In the joint extraction task, the attention mechanism can provide the classifier with global attention information by giving different weights to the words.

The attention mechanism is applied in a hidden layer above the bi-RNN layer. We initialize the hidden layer state using the last hidden state of the bi-RNN layer following the approach in [2]. At each time step i, the hidden layer state s_i is calculated as a function of the previous bi-RNN output y_{i-1}, the bi-RNN hidden state h_i and the attention context vector c_i:

$$s_i = f(y_{i-1}, h_i, c_i) \tag{2}$$

The attention context distribution c is generated by the hidden state h of the bidirectional RNN. In detail, c_i is calculated as the weighted sum of the bi-RNN states $h = (h_1, h_2, \cdots, h_T)$ [2]:

$$c_i = \sum\nolimits_{j=1}^{T} \alpha_{i,j} h_j \tag{3}$$

$$\alpha_{i,j} h_j = \frac{exp(e_{i,j})}{\sum\nolimits_{k=1}^{T} exp(e_{i,k})} \tag{4}$$

$$e_{i,k} = g(s_{i-1}, h_k) \tag{5}$$

where g is a feed-forward neural network. The attention context vector c_i provides additional information to the hidden layer that can be viewed as weighted sequential features of the RNN hidden layer states $(h_1, h_2, \cdots, h_T)$. In this way, the attention mechanism can provide global weighted information to generate labels.

The Bias Loss Function. In order to enhance the influence of word slots we tried to use the RMSprop optimization method [15] by defining the loss function as:

$$L = max \sum\nolimits_{j=1}^{|D|} \sum\nolimits_{i=1}^{T} (1 + \alpha I(O)) log(p_i = y_i | x_i, \theta) \tag{6}$$

$$p_i^{(j)} = \frac{exp\left(o_i^{(j)}\right)}{\sum\nolimits_{k=1}^{N_t} exp\left(o_i^{(k)}\right)} \tag{7}$$

Where $|D|$ is the size of the data set, T is the length of the sequence, y_i is the label of the i th word, p_i is the normalized probability of the tags which is defined in formula 7. N_t is the total number of tags, o_i is the output of the i th word, α is the bias weight of the loss function. The larger α is, the more influence the corresponding tag has. $I(O)$ is a binary function that distinguishes the loss of tag "O" and word slot tags and it was defined as follows:

$$I(O) = \begin{cases} 0, & \text{tag} = \text{O} \\ 1, & \text{tag} \neq \text{O} \end{cases}$$

4 Experiments

For a better comparison with previous methods and presenting the effect of our method, we carried out experiments on the Air Travel Information System (ATIS) pilot corpus. Then our model was compared with the previous pipeline and joint training models to demonstrate the performance in both independent and joint tasks.

4.1 Experimental Settings

Dataset. ATIS (Airline Travel Information Systems) data set [4] is widely used in intent detection and word slot extraction task. The data set contains the conversation text of persons who made the flight reservation. In this work, we follow the ATIS corpus setup used in [9, 11, 16, 19]. There are 4978 conversation text from the ATIS-2 and ATIS-3 corpora in the training set and 893 conversation text from the ATIS-3 NOV93 and DEC94 data sets in the test set. The total number of word slot labels is 127 and the size of intent types is 18. We use the F1 score to evaluate the results on word slot extraction and evaluate the performance of intent detection by using classification accuracy rate.

Hyperparameters. In our experiments, LSTM cell is used as the basic RNN unit. Our LSTM implementation follows the design in [21]. The number of cells in the LSTM layer is 128. We set the initial LSTM forget gate bias as 1 [6]. In our model, there is only one LSTM layer and the multilayer LSTM will be explored in future work. The word embeddings dimension is set to 128. We randomly initialize the word embeddings and fine-tuned during backward propagation. The training batch size is 16. Dropout rate on the fully connected network is set to 0.5 for regularization [21]. To prevent the gradient from exploding, the maximum value of gradient clipping is set to 5. The bias of the loss function is set to 10 and the number of headers of the attention is set to 10. We apply Adam optimization to our model following the settings in [8].

4.2 Intent Detection Task Results

We first report the results on independent tasks of intent detection and word slot extraction. We used the bi-LSTM model as our baseline and compared the performance of our proposed model with previously reported methods on intent detection task and illustrate the results in Table 2.

As we can see, our joint methods performs better than pipelined methods on intent detection. The attention-based bi-LSTM joint model and the bi-LSTM joint model with

Table 2. The results on independent task of intent detection

Model	Intent accuracy (%)
Recursive NN [2]	95.40
Boosting [16]	95.62
Boosting + Simplified sentences [17]	96.98
bi-LSTM	97.14
bi-LSTM with attention	97.31
bi-LSTM with bias loss function	97.20
bi-LSTM with attention-bias loss function	**97.65**

bias loss function advances the bi-LSTM model. Moreover, the bi-LSTM model combined with attention mechanism and bias loss function achieved the best accuracy of intent detection. This could be attributed to the combination of attention mechanism and bias loss function that allows the model to learn the sequence level information more efficiently.

While training the attenuation model, we found the attention mechanism is helpful to enhance the influence of long-distance keywords when the intent of words is been labeling. As shown in Fig. 3, We can find that the attention weights at the beginning of the sentence are higher when we label the last word "thursday". The word slot of "thursday" is a date slot which may appear in many sentences with different intents. So we should know the intent of the sentence as well as the slot of the word "thursday" and then label the word with "B-depart_date-flight". Obviously, the beginning words carry most information of the intent and the attention mechanism can find additional long-distance information effectively to solve multiple intent issues. This may explain one side of the reason for the good performance of our joint model on intent detect task.

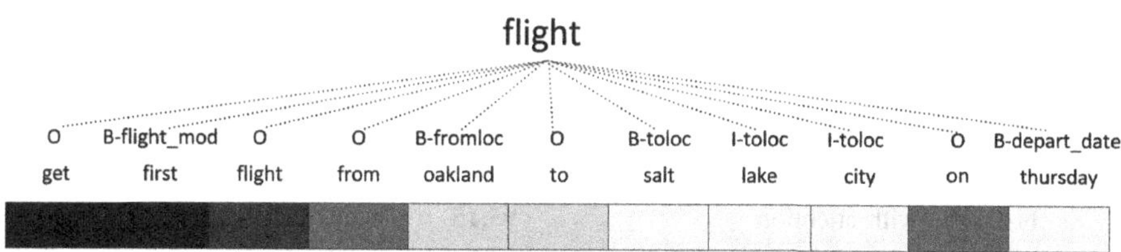

Fig. 3. The distribution of the attention weights when labeling the last word "thursday" with the intent "flight" of the sentence. The darker shade is the higher attention weight is.

4.3 Word Slot Extraction Task Results

Table 3 shows the performance of our proposed model for word slot extraction and previously reported results. Once again, the joint model performs better than the pipeline method. Besides, the attention-based model gives slightly better F1 score than the non-attention-based models. The reason could be the attention mechanism seeking to find other supporting information from input word sequence for the word slot label prediction. Overall, attention-based RNN Models outperform the ones without attention mechanism and the bias loss function is helpful for the word slot extraction.

When we combine attention mechanism and bias loss function on bi-LSTM model we find the F1 score gets slight reduction. We think the weight of bias loss function may disrupt the weight of attention during backpropagation. As the bias is manually set, it is difficult to select a perfectly suitable hyperparameter, which may lead to human errors affecting the training process. In the next work, we will try to optimize the bias by setting it as a parameter of the model.

Table 3. The results on independent task of word slot extraction

Model	F1 score (%)
CNN-CRF [19]	94.35
RNN with Label Sampling [9]	94.89
Hybrid RNN [11]	95.06
Deep LSTM [20]	95.08
bi-LSTM	94.89
bi-LSTM with attention	**95.15**
bi-LSTM with bias loss function	95.13
bi-LSTM with attention-bias loss function	95.05

4.4 Joint Task Results

Table 4 shows our tagging model's performance on joint extraction task of intent and word slots comparing to previously reported results.

Table 4. The results of joint task on intent detection and word slot extraction

Model	F1 score (%)	Intent accuracy(%)
RecNN [2]	93.22	95.40
RecNN + Viterbi [2]	93.96	95.40
bi-LSTM	94.89	97.09
bi-LSTM with attention	**95.15**	**97.20**
bi-LSTM with bias loss function	95.13	96.89
bi-LSTM with attention-bias loss function	95.05	97.09

As shown in this table, the joint model using tagging strategy achieved promising performance on both intent detection and word slot extraction. The attention based bi-LSTM get the best performance during our experiments. However, the combination model based on attention mechanism and bias loss function still have much room for improvement.

We checked the badcase in the results, most of which were caused by the word "UNK" which represents low frequency words. Besides, many word slots are also infrequent in the mislabeling results. It can be speculated that due to the limit of the data size, the training data could not cover all the cases well, especially for words and word slots with low frequency. In future missions, we will scale the size of the data set and adopt a deeper RNN model to further improve the performance of our model.

The experimental results show the effectiveness of our proposed method. But it still has shortcoming on identifying multiple tags. In the next work, we will replace the softmax function in the output layer with multiple classifier, so that a word can be labeled multiple tags. In this way, the word tagging process can be transformed into a multi-classification problem, which can solve the problem of multiple tags. Although, our model can enhance the effect of word slot words, the associations between word slots and sentence intent still require refinement in next works.

5 Conclusion

In this paper, we explored a tagging strategy and investigated the end-to-end RNN models to jointly extract of intent and word slots. We further improved our joint tagging strategy model with the attention mechanism to solve the problem of diversified relationship between word slots and intentions. Based on our tagging strategy model, the joint task of intent detection and word slot extraction is greatly simplified as only one sequence tagging model needs to be trained and deployed. We conduct experiments on a public dataset and the experimental results show that our joint model achieved better performance on the benchmark ATIS task compared with most of the existing pipelined and joint models for both independent and joint extraction task.

Acknowledgement. This work was supported by the National Key Research and Development program of China (No. 2018YFB1004703).

References

1. Bahdanau, D., Cho, K., Bengio, Y.: Neural machine translation by jointly learning to align and translate. arXiv preprint arXiv:1409.0473 (2014)
2. Guo, D., Tur, G., Yih, W., Zweig, G.: Joint semantic utterance classification and slot filling with recursive neural networks. In: 2014 IEEE Spoken Language Technology Workshop (SLT), pp. 554–559. IEEE (2014)
3. Haffner, P., Tur, G., Wright, J.H.: Optimizing SVMs for complex call classification. In: 2003 IEEE International Conference on Acoustics, Speech, and Signal Processing. Proceedings (ICASSP 2003), vol. 1, pp. I–I. IEEE (2003)
4. Hemphill, C.T., Godfrey, J.J., Doddington, G.R.: The ATIS spoken language systems pilot corpus. In: Speech and Natural Language: Proceedings of a Workshop Held at Hidden Valley, Pennsylvania, 24–27 June 1990 (1990)
5. Huang, Z., Xu, W., Yu, K.: Bidirectional LSTM-CRF models for sequence tagging. arXiv preprint arXiv:1508.01991 (2015)

6. Jozefowicz, R., Zaremba, W., Sutskever, I.: An empirical exploration of recurrent network architectures. In: International Conference on Machine Learning, pp. 2342–2350 (2015)
7. Kim, Y.: Convolutional neural networks for sentence classification. arXiv preprint arXiv: 1408.5882 (2014)
8. Kingma, D.P., Ba, J.: Adam: a method for stochastic optimization. arXiv preprint arXiv: 1412.6980 (2014)
9. Liu, B., Lane, I.: Recurrent neural network structured output prediction for spoken language understanding. In: Proceedings of the NIPS Workshop on Machine Learning for Spoken Language Understanding and Interactions (2015)
10. McCallum, A., Freitag, D., Pereira, F.C.: Maximum entropy markov models for information extraction and segmentation. In: ICML, vol. 17, pp. 591–598 (2000)
11. Mesnil, G., et al.: Using recurrent neural networks for slot filling in spoken language understanding. IEEE/ACM Trans. Audio Speech Lang. Process. **23**(3), 530–539 (2015)
12. Mikolov, T., Kombrink, S., Burget, L., Černocký, J., Khudanpur, S.: Extensions of recurrent neural network language model. In: 2011 IEEE International Conference on Acoustics, Speech and Signal Processing (ICASSP), pp. 5528–5531. IEEE (2011)
13. Raymond, C., Riccardi, G.: Generative and discriminative algorithms for spoken language understanding. In: Eighth Annual Conference of the International Speech Communication Association (2007)
14. Sarikaya, R., Hinton, G.E., Ramabhadran, B.: Deep belief nets for natural language call-routing. In: 2011 IEEE International Conference on Acoustics, Speech and Signal Processing (ICASSP), pp. 5680–5683. IEEE (2011)
15. Tieleman, T., Hinton, G.: Lecture 6.5-rmsprop: divide the gradient by a running average of its recent magnitude. COURSERA Neural Netw. Mach. Learn. **4**(2), 26–31 (2012)
16. Tur, G., Hakkani-Tür, D., Heck, L.: What is left to be understood in ATIS? In: 2010 IEEE Spoken Language Technology Workshop (SLT), pp. 19–24. IEEE (2010)
17. Tur, G., Hakkani-Tür, D., Heck, L., Parthasarathy, S.: Sentence simplification for spoken language understanding. In: 2011 IEEE International Conference on Acoustics, Speech and Signal Processing (ICASSP), pp. 5628–5631. IEEE (2011)
18. Vaswani, A., et al.: Attention is all you need. In: Advances in Neural Information Processing Systems, pp. 6000–6010 (2017)
19. Xu, P., Sarikaya, R.: Convolutional neural network based triangular CRF for joint intent detection and slot filling. In: 2013 IEEE Workshop on Automatic Speech Recognition and Understanding (ASRU), pp. 78–83. IEEE (2013)
20. Yao, K., Peng, B., Zhang, Y., Yu, D., Zweig, G., Shi, Y.: Spoken language understanding using long short-term memory neural networks. In: 2014 IEEE Spoken Language Technology Workshop (SLT), pp. 189–194. IEEE (2014)
21. Zaremba, W., Sutskever, I., Vinyals, O.: Recurrent neural network regularization. arXiv preprint arXiv:1409.2329 (2014)
22. Zheng, S., Wang, F., Bao, H., Hao, Y., Zhou, P., Xu, B.: Joint extraction of entities and relations based on a novel tagging scheme. arXiv preprint arXiv:1706.05075 (2017)

Using Regular Languages to Explore the Representational Capacity of Recurrent Neural Architectures

Abhijit Mahalunkar(✉) and John D. Kelleher

Dublin Institute of Technology, Dublin, Ireland
abhijit.mahalunkar@mydit.ie, john.d.kelleher@dit.ie

Abstract. The presence of Long Distance Dependencies (LDDs) in sequential data poses significant challenges for computational models. Various recurrent neural architectures have been designed to mitigate this issue. In order to test these state-of-the-art architectures, there is growing need for rich benchmarking datasets. However, one of the drawbacks of existing datasets is the lack of experimental control with regards to the presence and/or degree of LDDs. This lack of control limits the analysis of model performance in relation to the specific challenge posed by LDDs. One way to address this is to use synthetic data having the properties of subregular languages. The degree of LDDs within the generated data can be controlled through the k parameter, length of the generated strings, and by choosing appropriate *forbidden strings*. In this paper, we explore the capacity of different RNN extensions to model LDDs, by evaluating these models on a sequence of SPk synthesized datasets, where each subsequent dataset exhibits a longer degree of LDD. Even though SPk are simple languages, the presence of LDDs does have significant impact on the performance of recurrent neural architectures, thus making them prime candidate in benchmarking tasks.

Keywords: Sequential models · Long distance dependency
Recurrent neural networks · Regular languages
Strictly piecewise languages

1 Introduction

A Recurrent Neural Network (RNN) is able to model temporal data efficiently [1]. In theory, RNNs are capable of modeling infinitely long dependencies. A long distance dependency (LDD) describes a contingency (or interaction) between two (or more) elements in a sequence that are separated by an arbitrary number of positions. LDDs often occur in natural language, for example in English there is a requirement for subjects and verbs to agree, compare: "*The **dog** in that house **is** aggressive*" with "*The **dogs** in that house **are** aggressive*". However, in practice successfully training an RNN to model LDDs is still extremely difficult, due in-part to exploding or vanishing gradients [2,3]. There have been

V. Kůrková et al. (Eds.): ICANN 2018, LNCS 11141, pp. 189–198, 2018.
https://doi.org/10.1007/978-3-030-01424-7_19

significant advances in this domain, and various architectures have been developed to address the issue of LDDs [4–11]. Indeed, the fact that a number of RNN extensions are specifically designed to address the problem of modeling LDDs is a testament to the fundamental importance of the challenge posed by LDDs.

In order to test the representational capacity of these models and aide in future development of new models, there is a growing need for large datasets which manifest various degrees of LDDs. Various benchmarking datasets and tasks which exhibit such properties are currently being employed [4,7,12,13]. However, using them provides no experimental control over the degree of LDD these datasets exhibit. Although, the copy and add task [4] does have control over this factor, the dataset generated via this scheme does not possess comparable complexity with datasets sampled from real world sequential processes.

Strictly k-Piecewise (SPk) languages, as studied by Rogers et al. [14], are proper subclasses of piecewise testable languages [15]. SPk languages are natural and can express some of the kinds of LDDs found in natural languages [16,18]. In relation to research on LDDs, SPk languages are particularly interesting because by controlling the parameter k and the length of the strings, one can control the maximum LDD in the dataset, and by choosing appropriate *forbidden strings*, it is possible to simulate a natural dataset exhibiting a certain degree of LDD. These properties make SPk languages prime candidate for benchmarking tasks.

Contribution: This research used a finite-state implementation of an SP*2* grammar to generate strings of varying length, from 2 to 500. SP*2* is analogous to subject-verb agreement in English language, thus using this grammar generates LDDs of similar complexity, and controlling the length of the strings generated controls the maximum LDD span in the dataset. Appropriate *forbidden strings* were chosen. State-of-the-art sequential data models were trained to predict the next character for every generated dataset. It was observed that as the length of the strings in the datasets increased the perplexity of the models increased. This is due in-part to the limitations of the representational capacity of these models. However, of the models tested it was observed that Recurrent Highway Networks display the lowest perplexity on character prediction task for large sequences exhibiting very high LDDs.

2 Recurrent Neural Architectures for LDDs

The focus of this paper is to experimentally evaluate the ability of modern RNN architectures to model LDDs by testing current state-of-the-art models on datasets of SPk sequences which exhibit LDDs of varying lengths. For our experiments we chose the following architectures as the relevant representatives of RNNs: Long Short Term Memory [4], Recurrent Highway Networks [9] and Orthogonal RNNs [10]. This choice of networks was based on the fact that (a) each of these networks were specifically designed to address performance issue of the standard RNN while modeling LDD datasets, and (b) taken together the set of selected models provide coverage of the different approaches found in the literature to the problem of LDDs.

LSTMs were an early effort in addressing the vanishing gradient effect by introducing *"constant error carousels"*, which enforced *constant error flow through* thereby bridging minimal time lags in excess of 1000 discrete steps. Neural Turing Machines are memory augmented networks. They are composed of a network *controller* and a memory bank. These components allowed the network to provide attention to different memory locations. Recurrent Highway Networks (RHNs) extended the LSTM architecture to allow step-to-step transition depths larger than one. Orthogonal RNNs (ORNNs) extend the standard RNN architecture by enforcing soft or hard orthogonality on the weight matrix.

3 Benchmarking Datasets

There is a relatively small number of datasets that are popular for testing the representational capacity of RNNs. Most of these datasets are known to exhibit LDDs, which is a necessary criteria for their selection as a benchmarking dataset. The *Penn Treebank* [12] (PTB) is one of these datasets. It consists of over 4.5 million words of American English and was constructed by sampling English sentences from a range of sources. The *WikiText* language modeling dataset [7] was released in 2016 and has become a popular choice for language modeling experiments. It is a collection of over 100 million tokens extracted from various Wikipedia articles. This dataset is much larger than the PTB, which is the primary reason that it is preferred to the PTB in recent works. Although, the PTB and WikiText differ in terms of the sources that the sentences they contain are sampled from, both dataset exclusively contain English language sentences. Hence both the datasets are constrained by English language grammar, and therefore will exhibit similar LDD characteristics. Moreover, it is unclear what these LDDs are because the data is sampled from a natural process (the English language) the LDD characteristics of which are not accurately estimated.

The difficulty of using naturally occurring datasets to investigate LDDs has been recognized and several synthetic benchmarks have been used to test the ability of RNNs to learn LDDs in sequential data. The copy and adding tasks, introduced in [4], is one such example. The task entails remembering an input sequence followed by a string of blank inputs. The sequence is terminated using a delimiter after which the network must produce the input sequence, ignoring the string of blanks inputs that follow the original sequence [10]. This task provides an experimenter with a great degree of control over the length of LDD in the dataset they synthesize in order to train and test their models.

Another method of testing models on simulated LDDs, is to train them to learn the MNIST image classes [13]. This is achieved by sequentially feeding all the 784 pixels of a MNIST image to the model under test and then training the network to classify MNIST image category. Every image is fed to the network pixel by pixel, starting from the top left pixel and finishing at the bottom right pixel. This simulates LDDs of length 784 as the network has to remember all the 784 pixels in order to classify the images.

Formal languages, have previously been used to train RNNs and investigate their inner workings. The *Reber grammar* [19] was used to train various first order

RNNs [21,22]. The Reber grammar was also used as a benchmarking dataset in the original work on LSTM models [4]. Regular languages, studied by Tomita [20], were used to train RNNs to learn grammatical structures of the string. A very recent example of research using formal languages to evaluate RNNs is Avcu et al. [17]. The work presented in this paper falls within this tradition of analysis, however it extends the previous research on using formal languages by: (a) broadening the variety of LDDs within the generated datasets, (b) evaluating a broader variety of models, and (c) using language model perplexity as the evaluation metric.

4 Formal Language Theory and Regular Languages

Formal Language Theory (FLT) finds its use in various domains of science. Primarily developed to study the computational basis of human language, FLT is now being used to extensively analyze any rule-governed system [23–25]. Regular languages are the simplest grammars (type-3 grammars) within the Chomsky hierarchy which are driven by regular expressions. Subregular languages, e.g. Strictly k-Piecewise or Strictly k-Local, are subclasses of regular languages. These languages can be identified by mechanisms much less complicated than Finite-State Automata. Many aspects of human language such as local and non local dependencies are similar to subregular languages [26], and there are certain types of LDDs in human language which allow finite-state characterization [18]. These types of LDD can be modeled using Strictly k-Piecewise languages.

4.1 Strictly Piecewise Languages

In order to explain how we used SPk languages to generate datasets appropriate to our experimental goals it is first necessary to present an explanation of these languages. Following [14,16,17], a language L is described by a finite set of symbols, i.e. an alphabet, denoted by Σ. The symbols are analogous to words or characters in English, music notes in music theory, genes in genomics, etc. A set Σ^* is a *free monoid*, a set of finite sequences of zero or more elements from Σ. For example, for $\Sigma = \{a, b, c\}$, its Σ^* contains all concatenations of a, b, and c: $\{\lambda, a, ab, ba, cac, acbabc, ...\}$. The string of length zero is denoted by λ. w_i is the ith word/string (w) of L. The length of a string u is denoted $|u|$. A stringset (or Formal Language) is a subset of Σ^*.

If u and v are strings, uv denotes their concatenation. For all u, v, w, x $\in \Sigma^*$, if $x = uwv$, then w is a *substring* of x. For example, bc is a *substring* of $abcd$, as concatenating a, bc, d yields $abcd$. Similarly, a string v is a *subsequence* of string w iff $v = \sigma_1\sigma_2...\sigma_n$ and $w \in \Sigma^*\sigma_1\Sigma^*\sigma_2\Sigma^*...\Sigma^*\sigma_n\Sigma^*$, where $\sigma \in \Sigma$. For example, string bd is a *subsequence* of length $k = 2$ of $abcd$, acd is a subsequence of length $k = 3$ of the same string $abcd$, but string db is *not a subsequence* of $abcd$. A *subsequence* of length k is called a *k-subsequence*. Let $\text{subseq}_k(w)$ denote the set of subsequences of w up to length k.

A Strictly Piecewise grammar can be defined as a set of permissible subsequences. The grammar G is simply all strings whose k-long *subsequences* are permissible according to G. Consider a language L, consisting of $\Sigma = \{a, b, c, d\}$. The grammar, $G_{SP2} = \{aa, ac, ad, ba, bb, bc, bd, ca, cb, cc, cd, da, db, dc, dd\}$ are comprised of these permissible *subsequences* of length $k = 2$. Note, however, that although $\{ab\}$ is a logically possible subsequence of length k, it is not in the grammar. Subsequences which are not in the grammar are called *forbidden strings.* The string $u = [bbcbdd]$, where $|u| = 6$ belongs to G_{SP2}, because it is composed of subsequences that are in that grammar. Similarly, the string $v = [bbdbbbcbddaa]$, where $|v| = 12$ belongs to G_{SP2}. However, the string $w = [bbabbbcbdd]$ does not because $\{ab\}$ is a forbidden subsequence as it is not part of the grammar. This condition applies for any string x for $|x| \in \mathbb{Z}$. One can also define an SP grammar for k = 3 and k = 4 for $\Sigma = \{a, b\}$ as $\mathrm{G_{SP3}}$ and $\mathrm{G_{SP4}}$ respectively. For example, $\mathrm{G_{SP3}} = \{aaa,\ aab,\ abb,\ baa,\ bab,\ bba,\ bbb\}$, with $\{aba\}$ as *forbidden string.* A string $[aaaaaaab]$ of length 8 is a valid G_{SP3} string and $[aaaaabaa]$ is invalid. Thus, an appropriate grammar reflecting the dataset one intends to simulate can be designed by selecting appropriate permissible strings in the grammar. For the specific language, *forbidden strings* can be computed[1]. Note, to define an SPk grammar it is necessary to specify at least one *forbidden string.*

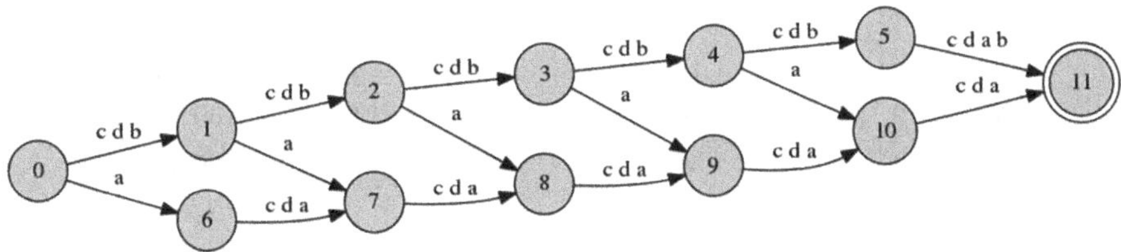

Fig. 1. The automaton for G_{SP2} $(k = 2)$ which generates strings of length = 6

Figure 1 illustrates the finite-state diagram of a G_{SP2} for strings of length 6 with *forbidden string* $\{ab\}$. Traversing a path from state 1 until state 11 will generate valid G_{SP2} strings of length 6, e.g. $\{accdda,\ caaaaa\}$. It can also be noted that there is no path which generates a string which has an $\{ab\}$ subsequence e.g. $\{abcccc\}$. Using the above described methodology, of choosing strings of appropriate length, one can simulate appropriate LDDs in a dataset. One can also control the number of dependent elements by choosing an appropriate k. *Forbidden strings* allow for elimination of certain combinations in generated datasets, which can be useful when one is trying to simulate real world datasets.

[1] Refer Sect. 5.2 *Finding the shortest forbidden subsequences* in [16] for method to compute *forbidden sequences* for a particular SP language.

5 Experiment

In this experiment, we generate 4 datasets of SP*2* language. For each dataset we train an LSTM, an ORNN, and a RHN, and evaluate and compare the performance of the models.

5.1 Generating SP*2* dataset

For our experiment, $\Sigma = \{a, b, c, d\}$ was selected. *Forbidden strings* for this language were selected as $\{ab, bc\}$. In order to introduce various degrees of LDDs, strings with lengths l were generated in random order, where $2 \leq l \leq 500$. For every l, the number of strings per l is n_l. For this experiment, $n_l \leq 1,000,000$. This allowed for uniform distribution of strings of all lengths. These strings were grouped in 4 datasets as described in Table 1. Within each dataset, strings were randomly ordered to avoid biased gradients. For training the neural networks, a subset of these generated datasets were used due to the size of each dataset.

Table 1. Datasets of SP*2* language

Dataset	Min length	Max length	Max LDDs	Original	Sample
Dataset 1	2	20	20	15 MB	15 MB
Dataset 2	21	100	100	470 MB	50 MB
Dataset 3	101	200	200	1.5 GB	100 MB
Dataset 4	201	500	500	9.9 GB	200 MB

The strings were generated using the tool *foma* [27]. A post processing *python* script was developed to select the small sample from the original datasets 1, 2, 3 and 4 as described in Table 1. Every dataset is made up of strings of varying l. The *python script* was also used to randomize the order of strings (as per the length), so as not to bias the models[2].

5.2 Training Task

All the networks were trained on a character prediction task. For each network type (LSTM, ORNN, RHN) a network was trained on each of the 4 SP*2* datasets, and also on a standard dataset of English language. The English language datasets were included in the experiments to provide a comparison for model performance when the vocabulary and type of data was varied. For the LSTM and ORNN the PTB was used as the standard English language dataset, and for the RHN the Text8 dataset was used. Note, that the experimental task was kept constant across all datasets, so although the PTB and Text8 datasets

[2] Source code available at https://github.com/silentknight/ICANN2018.

are often used as part of a word-prediction task, in these experiments the networks were trained and evaluated on character prediction on the PTB and Text8 datasets. For SPk languages, the generated datasets were split into training (60%), validation (20%) and test (20%) sets. The LSTM[3] with dropout models were trained as advised in [28]; the ORNN[4] models were trained as recommended in [10]; and, the RHN[5] models were trained following [9].

The performance of all the three network types was measured by computing the perplexity of the network after each epoch. The performance curve for the LSTM model is plotted in Fig. 2a, the performance of ORNN model is plotted in Fig. 2b, and the performance curve of RHN is plotted in Fig. 2c.

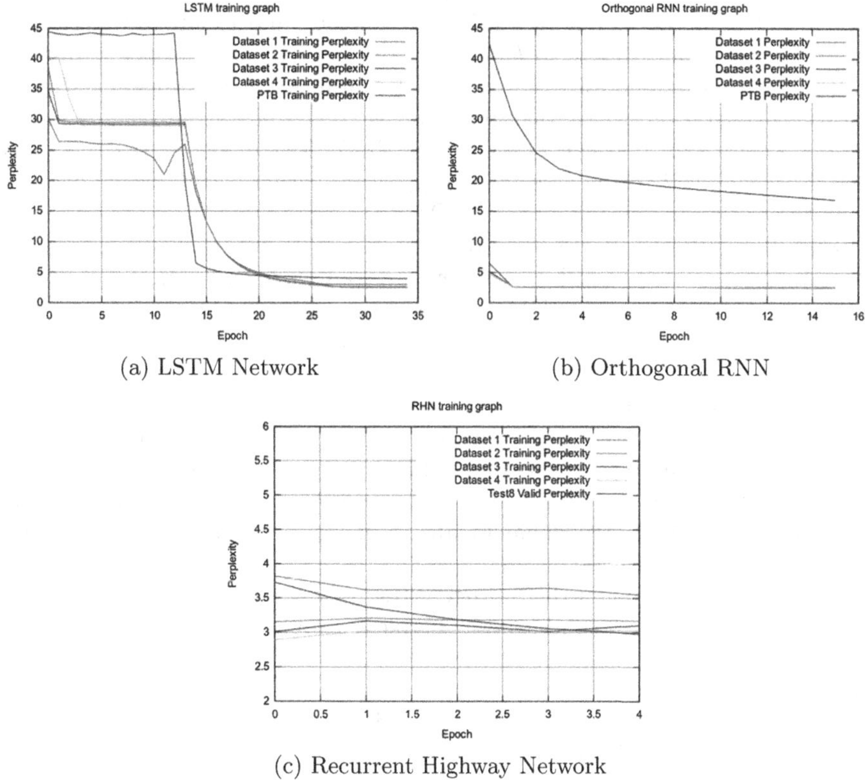

(a) LSTM Network

(b) Orthogonal RNN

(c) Recurrent Highway Network

Fig. 2. Perplexity vs training epoch for recurrent neural architectures.

[3] LSTM source https://github.com/tensorflow/models/blob/master/tutorials/rnn/ptb/ptb_word_lm.py.

[4] ORNN Source https://github.com/veugene/spectre_release.

[5] RHN source https://github.com/julian121266/RecurrentHighwayNetworks.

6 Analysis

In Fig. 2, we visualize the impact of increasing LDDs while training all the three architectures. Our results show that during the initial phase of the training, the LSTM network displayed perplexity directly proportional to the degree of LDDs present in the dataset. It is seen that dataset 4 (LDD order of around 500) presents higher perplexity as compared to the other datasets. However, every dataset eventually exhibits lower perplexity after epoch 20. When compared with the PTB task, one can observe lower perplexity by LSTM network in modeling datasets 1, 2, 3 and 4 during the initial phase of training. This is due in-part to the small vocabulary size in the SP*2* datasets ($\Sigma = \{a,b,c,d\}$). A small vocabulary size tends to lower entropy in a sequence. The PTB has much larger vocabulary thus increasing the entropy and eventually increasing perplexity. Selection of more *forbidden strings* leads to much richer grammar. SPk languages generated for this experiment contained only 2 *forbidden strings*, this led to generation of less rich grammar as compared to the PTB (English grammar). However, one can observe that the LSTM model learns the PTB much faster than SP*2* languages (the graph drops earlier). This can be directly attributed to the presence of longer LDDs in the SP*2* datasets.

Orthogonal RNNs enforce soft orthogonality to address vanishing gradient problem. When compared with LSTM network training of the PTB, it is observed that the perplexity of both architectures is very similar during the initial training phase, but ORNNs performance does not improve with more training as compared to LSTM. The impact of vocabulary size is also evident in this case (the perplexity for PTB is much higher than for the SP*2* datasets). However, it can be seen that ORNNs trained with datasets 1 and 2 present higher perplexity as compared to datasets 3 and 4 (longer LDDs) suggesting that ORNN models overfit datasets 1 and 2 and are able to generalize on datasets 3 and 4. This could be attributed to orthogonal weight initializations which makes learning longer dependencies easier.

Focusing on the graph for the Recurrent Highway Networks it can be observed that the model tended to exhibit lower perplexity on SP*2* datasets with higher degrees of LDDs. This could be attributed to the architecture of the network. Due to increased depth in recurrent transitions in these networks, it was possible for the model to achieve good performance on datasets with long LDDs. However, on datasets with lower degrees of LDDs these models tend to overfit and, thus, exhibit higher perplexity. Furthermore, comparing the RHN graph on the Text8 dataset with the LSTM and ORNN graphs on the PTB it is apparent that RHNs are better at handling larger vocabularies: the RHN graph for Text8 is lower than the LSTM and ORNN graphs on the PTB.

7 Conclusion

In this paper, we used SPk languages to generate benchmarking datasets for LDDs. We trained various RNNs with the generated datasets and analyzed their performance. The analysis revealed that SPk languages are able to generate datasets with varying degree of LDDs. Consequently, using SPk languages gives experimental control over the generation of rich datasets by controlling the k, the length of the strings, the vocabulary of the generated language, and by choosing appropriate *forbidden strings*. The analysis also revealed that RHNs have a much better capability (as compared with LSTMs and ORNNs) to model LDDs.

Acknowledgements. This research was partly supported by the ADAPT Research Centre, funded under the SFI Research Centres Programme (Grant 13/RC/2106) and is co-funded under the European Regional Development Funds. The research was also supported by an IBM Shared University Research Award. We also, gratefully, acknowledge the support of NVIDIA Corporation with the donation of the Titan Xp GPU under NVIDIA GPU Grant used for this research.

References

1. Elman, J.L.: Finding structure in time. Cogn. Sci. **14**, 179–211 (1990)
2. Hochreiter. S.: Untersuchungen zu dynamischen neuronalen Netzen. Diploma thesis, TU Munich (1991)
3. Yoshua, B., Simard, P., Frasconi, P.: Learning long-term dependencies with gradient descent is difficult. IEEE Trans. Neural Netw. **5**(2), 157–166 (1994)
4. Hochreiter, S., Schmidhuber, J.: Long short-term memory. Neural Comput. **9**(8), 1735–1780 (1997)
5. Graves, A., Wayne, G., Danihelka, I.: Neural Turing Machines. CoRR (2014)
6. Salton, G.D., Ross, R.J., Kelleher, J.D.: Attentive language models. In: Proceedings of the 8th International Joint Conference on Natural Language Processing, pp. 441–450 (2017)
7. Merity, S., Xiong, C., Bradbury, J., Socher, R.: Pointer sentinel mixture models. In: ICLR 2016 (2016)
8. Chang, S. et al.: Dilated recurrent neural networks. In: Guyon, I., et al. (eds.) Advances in Neural Information Processing Systems, vol. 30, pp. 77–87. Curran Associates, Inc. (2017)
9. Zilly, J.G., Srivastava, R.K., Koutnk, J., Schmidhuber, J.: Recurrent highway networks. In: Proceedings of the 34th International Conference on Machine Learning, Sydney, Australia, PMLR, vol. 70 (2017)
10. Vorontsov, E., Trabelsi, C., Kadoury, S., Pal, C.: On orthogonality and learning recurrent networks with long term dependencies. In: Proceeding of ICML 2017 (2017)
11. Henaff, M., Szlam, A., LeCun, Y.: Recurrent orthogonal networks and long-memory tasks. In: Proceedings of the 33rd International Conference on Machine Learning, PMLR, vol. 48, pp. 2034–2042 (2016)
12. Marcus, M.P., Marcinkiewicz, M.A., Santorini, B.: Building a large annotated corpus of English: The Penn Treebank. Comput. Linguist. **19**(2), 313–330 (1993). ISSN 0891–2017
13. LeCun, Y., Bottou, L., Bengio, Y., Haffner, P.: Gradient-based learning applied to document recognition. Proc. IEEE **86**(11), 2278–2324 (1998)
14. Rogers, J., et al.: On languages piecewise testable in the strict sense. In: Ebert, C., Jäger, G., Michaelis, J. (eds.) MOL 2007/2009. LNCS (LNAI), vol. 6149, pp. 255–265. Springer, Heidelberg (2010). https://doi.org/10.1007/978-3-642-14322-9_19

15. Simon, I.: Piecewise testable events. In: Brakhage, H. (ed.) GI-Fachtagung 1975. LNCS, vol. 33, pp. 214–222. Springer, Heidelberg (1975). https://doi.org/10.1007/3-540-07407-4_23
16. Ogihara, M., Tarui, J. (eds.): TAMC 2011. LNCS, vol. 6648. Springer, Heidelberg (2011). https://doi.org/10.1007/978-3-642-20877-5
17. Avcu, E., Shibata, C., Heinz, J.: Subregular complexity and deep learning. In: Proceedings of the Conference on Logic and Machine Learning in Natural Language (LaML 2017), vol. 1, pp. 20–33 (2017)
18. Heinz. J., Rogers, J.: Estimating strictly piecewise distributions. In: Proceedings of the 48th Annual Meeting of the Association for Computational Linguistics, pp. 886–896 (2010)
19. Reber, A.S.: Implicit learning of artificial grammars. J. Verbal Learn. Verbal Behav. **6**(6), 855–863 (1967)
20. Tomita, M.: Learning of construction of finite automata from examples using hill-climbing. In: Proceedings of Fourth International Cognitive Science Conference, pp. 105–108 (1982)
21. Casey, M.: The dynamics of discrete-time computation, with application to recurrent neural networks and finite statemachine extraction. Neural Comput. **8**(6), 1135–1178 (1996)
22. Smith, A.W., Zipser, D.: Encoding sequential structure: experience with the real-time recurrent learning algorithm. Proc. IJCNN **I**, 645–648 (1989)
23. Chomsky, N.: Three models for the description of language. IRE Trans. Inf. Theory **2**, 113–124 (1956)
24. Chomsky, N.: On certain formal properties of grammars. Inf. Control. **2**, 137–167 (1959)
25. Fitch, W.T., Friederici, A.D.: Artificial grammar learning meets formal language theory: an overview. Philos. Trans. R. Soc. B Biol. Sci. **367**(1598), 1933–1955 (2012)
26. Jager, G., Rogers, J.: Formal language theory: refining the Chomsky hierarchy. Philos. Trans. R. Soc. B Biol. Sci. **367**(1598), 1956–1970 (2012)
27. Hulden, M.: Foma: a finite-state compiler and library. In: Proceedings of the 12th Conference of the European Chapter of the Association for Computational Linguistics, pp. 29–32 (2009)
28. Zaremba, W., Sutskever, I., Vinyals, O.: Recurrent neural network regularization. In: Proceedings of ICRL (2015)

Learning Trends on the Fly in Time Series Data Using Plastic CGP Evolved Recurrent Neural Networks

Gul Mummad Khan[1(✉)] and Durr-e-Nayab[2]

[1] Electrical Engineering Department, UET Peshawar, Peshawar, Pakistan
gk502@uetpeshawar.edu.pk

[2] Computer System Engineering Department, UET Peshawar, Peshawar, Pakistan
nayaab_khan@nwfpuet.edu.pk

Abstract. An approach of Direct Online Learning (DOL) to incorporate developmental plasticity in Recurrent Neural Networks termed as Plastic Cartesian Genetic Programming evolved Recurrent Neural Network (PCGPRNN), is proposed to exploit the trends in the data of the foreign currency to forecast the future currency rates, while reshaping its connectivity, biasing factors and selecting various parameters from the input vector 'on the fly' according to the traversed trends. The developed model learns in real time and exhibits the optimum topology for the best possible output using neuro-evolution. The network performance is observed in a range of scenarios with varying network parameters and various currencies and trading indexes obtaining competitive results. Networks trained to predict single instances are further explored in independent scenarios to predict various time intervals in advance, achieving remarkable results.

Keywords: Cartesian genetic programming · Developmental plasticity
Foreign currency exchange · Neuro evolution · Recurrent Neural Networks

1 Introduction

Plasticity in neural networks is an efficient phenomenon that exists in biological neural networks [19]. In artificial neural networks (ANNs) plasticity is attained by ability to change the aspects of the network in response to environmental conditions [15–17]. Due to their natural capacity they are turning more famous to study in variable work environments. They are becoming more known due to their essential ability to train live in the variable task environment. Similarly, systems with memory (i.e. recurrent) neural networks have tremendous fast learning ability that makes them efficient for dealing with challenging scenarios [8]. The developmental plastic neural networks when incorporated with the capabilities of the feedback give rise to a novel neural network approach which combines the capabilities of the developmental plasticity and recurrent networks. In this work, it is applied to evolve for prediction of foreign currency exchange rates. This mechanism is called Plastic Cartesian Genetic Programming evolved Recurrent Neural Network (PCGPRNN). The proposed dynamic ANN creates new neural sub-systems when they witness dynamic learning scheme and have

V. Kůrková et al. (Eds.): ICANN 2018, LNCS 11141, pp. 199–207, 2018.
https://doi.org/10.1007/978-3-030-01424-7_20

premiere performance due to feedback mechanism. The plasticity allows the network to customize its aspects while the problem domain is evolving and solves multiple linear/nonlinear issues without adversity from the damaging interference. Catastrophic interference or catastrophic forgetting occurs when a neural network trained on one problem forgets how to solve it when trained on another problem [2, 18]. The feedback mechanism of the network is both constructive and destructive and proves to be useful and convenient for the unsteady financial time series data because of its quick learning ability [8]. PCGPRNN is an exceptional technique because of the existence of a feedback mechanism in the network which takes the system status inputs into consideration while continuously converting the morphology at runtime. PCGPRNN as opposed to feed-forward can measure random sequence inputs because of its ability of exploiting the internal memory [8]. Through this task our target is to seek a neural network technique which integrates bio-inspired developmental measures using feedback. The Plastic Cartesian Genetic Programming based Recurrent Neural Network (PCGPRNN) proposed in this work is obtained for a dynamic network with capability to regularly fix its design and weights in response to external environment. Foreign Exchange (Forex) rates are directly influenced by many macro and micro economic factors collectively besides international relations and global state of business. Likewise the inflation rate, rate of interest, Per capita income, role of speculations, cost of manufacturing, industry, economic growth in terms of Gross Domestic Income, Political Stability and Relative Strength Index (RSI) of the stocks and the economization of other countries changes the worth of a currency instantaneously as well as in long run [23].

With linear data sets the traditional statistical models shows better performance compare to that of the performance with non-linear data sets where it shows some limitations, for example stock indices [6]. Time series forecasting [1] was used for Hidden Markov model (HMM) which shows susceptibility to external factors like stock indices making it ambiguous and immutable. A support vector machine used in [27] learnt progression of volatility levels of forex data predicted by Hidden Markov Model & predicted approximations of the level. Improved outputs were obtained by executing numerical measure of actual data. The two ANN schemes Multilayer Perceptron (MLP) and Volterra mentioned in [4] are also exploited for time series forecasting. Multi-neural ANN evolved comprising a master with three sub networks [15] that forecasted US Dollar and Taiwan Dollar (TWD) exchange rates, their predisposition on five macro-economic factors. The MLP forecasting model produces efficient and accurate results of three (3) days' ahead USD/Euro exchange rates but its performance plunged with intrusion of external factors [11]. In [24] an extension of the traditional application of Genetic Programming was proposed in the domain of daily currency exchange rates predictions, in conjunction with trigonometric operators. High-order statistical functions to analyze each system performance using daily returns of the British Pound and Japanese Yen were proposed with a unique representation. It was presented that using high-order statistical functions with integration of trigonometric functions outperformed the traditional models.

The trend of Genetic Programming based prediction model for Forex rate prediction started recently [24–26]. Before this, statistical models [22], ANN and data mining concepts were employed [21].

2 Literature Review

Generative and developmental approaches of artificial neural networks dynamically changes the aspects of the network continuously during problem solving phase. Nolfi introduced indirect mapping of ANN model [17]. In [10] a similar network was proposed where a single cell utilizes the process of mitosis and migration forming a 2-D neural network. The plastic neural model introduced in [12] could develop itself at run time influenced by changes in the environment. In [14], Floreano et al. explored the behavioral sturdiness of synaptic plasticity evolving neuro-controllers to solve light switching scenario having no reward mechanism. The HyperNEAT encoding scheme in [5] is exploited for evolution of synaptic weights and learning rules parameter set with poor testing results in the T-maze foraging bee scenario. The learning capability of the agents was enhanced later on [7]. In [18] developmental model of neurons, comprising of seven chromosomes encoding various computational functions of biological neuron is presented to demonstrate learning with development. In [20] the interaction of Hebbian homo-synaptic with fast non-hebbian hetero-synaptic plasticity is demonstrated to be sufficient for assembly formation. The reminiscence don't forget in a spiking recurrent network model with excitatory and inhibitory neurons. Blocking any component of plasticity averted strong functioning as a memory network.

The work here uses Cartesian Genetic Programming to obtain suitable computational functions for internal processing and developmental rules. To solve the time series forecasting scenario of currency exchange learning potential of the system is evaluated. Promising results are obtained in this work demonstrating robustness to deal with the dynamic scenarios. Miller pioneered Cartesian Genetic Programming (CGP) for evolution of digital circuits in 1999 [13]. It comprises of a 2D-two dimensional graphical architecture unlike the traditional tree based structure of genetic programming, having function nodes arranged in Cartesian format interconnected in a feed-forward manner. CGP has been evaluated in diverse fields of application generating fascinating and competitive results [13].

3 Plastic Cartesian Genetic Programming Evolved Recurrent Neural Network

Plasticity in the form of dynamic weights, topology and complexity of the network is incorporated in Cartesian Genetic Programming (CGP) based Recurrent Neural Network (RNN) to explore the ability of online learning at runtime. RNN provide the state information to be part of the input parameters thus making the network markovian [8]. Plasticity is introduced by providing additional genes to make the developmental decisions [9]. The CGPRNN is having feedback mechanism, which feeds one or more system outputs back to the system. The general approach of Plastic CGPRNN is depicted in Fig. 1. Figure 1 shows the basic CGPRNN block illustrating the network parameters developmental gene to introduce plasticity in the network.

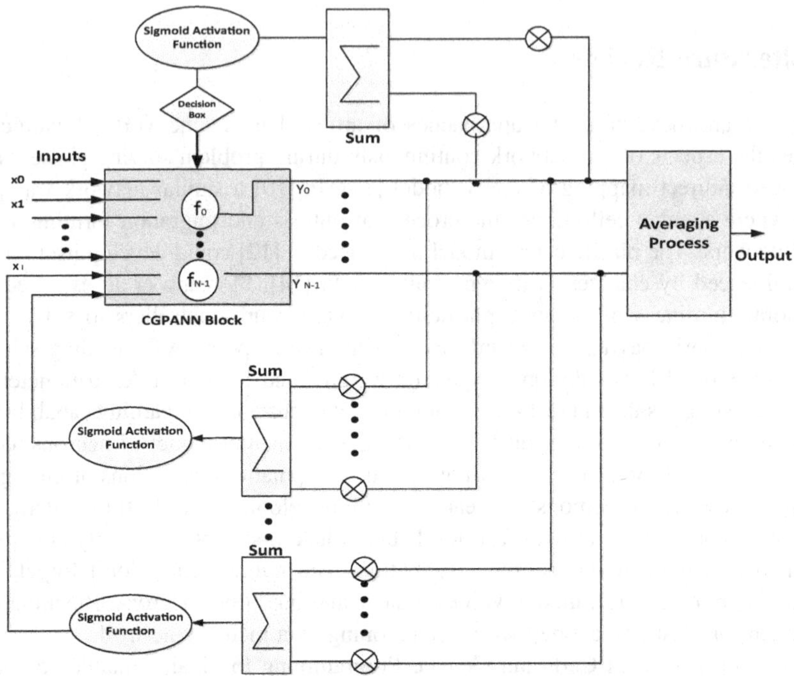

Fig. 1. A generalized approach of PCGPRNN

Development in the network occurs as a reflection of the system weighted output passed through a log-sigmoid function. The uniqueness of the approach is that changes in the network take place in real time related to the flow of data in the network, modifying its architecture, topology, complexity and weights.

4 Experimental Setup

The PCGPRNN currency forecaster model introduced here exploits the currency exchange rates data acquired from the Australian Reserved Bank (ARB) for training and testing of the model. Daily exchange rates of US Dollars are considered for up to 500 days to train the model. Testing is performed on independent set of exchange rates data of 1000 days, for ten currencies namely: Korean Won (KW), Indonesian Rupiah (IDR), Canadian Dollars (CAD), Singapore Dollars (SGD), New Zealand Dollars (NZD), Taiwanese Dollars (TWD), Great Britain Pounds (GBP), Euros (EUR), Swiss Franc (CHF), Japanese Yen (YEN) and Malaysian Ringgits (MR). Initially random populations of PCGPRNN networks are produced for training purposes, these networks develop during the run time of a particular generation. Ten independent networks having different genotype sizes and each working on five independent random seeds are introduced for training purposes. Maximum numbers of generations are restricted to one million in each training phase. The optimal trained networks are then evaluated on ten different currencies for their performance. Five inputs are allowed per neuron, log-sigmoid being used as activation function, system inputs are ten (10) in numbers, the mutation rate (μ_r) is set at 10%. The evolutionary strategy used is $1 + \lambda$, with λ set to 9, representing the number of offspring. These parameters are based on the previous performance of CGPANN and CGPRNN [2, 3, 8].

5 Results and Analysis

Experimentation is performed on offline historical data and performance is obtained from the difference of estimated and actual values during training and testing processes. The system takes ten days daily averaged currency values as input and the eleventh days' currency value is estimated. Once the optimal system is achieved during training phase, it is tested with the new data sets keeping the output historical values hidden from the system. The system predicts the unknown eleventh days' exchange rate and is compared with the actual exchange rate to assess the system enactment. The experiments are carried out for the mentioned network architecture and the results are shown in Tables 1, 2, 3 and 4. Table 1 enlists results of the PCGPRNN forecaster model during training phase in terms of Mean Absolute Percentage Error (MAPE) values. The performance of the network is analyzed and the preeminent performance is attained with 150 nodes network securing the MAPE value of **1.537**. Table 2 shows the performance of the PCGPRNN model during the testing phase. The results show that the best results are accomplished with Korean Won (KW) data set for the network of **150** nodes securing the MAPE value of **1.1315**.

Table 1. Training phase results of PCGPRNN

Nodes	MAPE
50	1.715
100	1.698
150	**1.537**
200	1.700
250	2.928
300	1.621
350	1.571
400	1.574
450	2.010
500	1.541

Table 2. Testing phase results of PCGPRNN model

Data	50	100	150	200	250	300	350	400	450	500
SDR	1.71	1.69	1.53	1.70	2.92	1.62	1.57	1.57	2.01	1.54
CNY	2.45	2.21	2.28	2.25	3.21	2.40	2.26	2.26	3.07	2.29
IDR	1.89	1.61	1.56	1.69	3.18	1.80	1.55	1.63	2.59	1.57
KW	1.79	1.18	**1.13**	1.23	3.91	3.60	1.14	1.40	2.82	1.13
TD	2.34	1.50	1.45	1.59	5.14	4.13	1.45	1.80	3.84	1.45
MR	1.90	1.68	1.62	1.75	3.10	7.32	1.62	1.68	2.48	1.63
HKD	1.87	1.58	1.53	1.67	3.11	7.58	1.52	1.61	2.57	1.54
CAD	1.98	1.62	1.59	1.74	3.22	7.99	1.57	1.67	2.79	1.61
NZD	5.08	1.76	1.68	1.85	5.55	3.93	1.69	2.05	4.10	1.68
CHF	7.38	1.85	1.73	1.98	8.22	3.63	1.75	2.19	4.52	1.73
GBP	15. 9	1.84	1.74	1.94	26.4	7.48	1.73	1.85	2.87	1.75
EUR	15.1	1.82	1.73	1.87	25.6	7.14	1.73	1.78	2.51	1.73
TWI	12.1	2.24	2.11	2.27	21.4	5.97	2.11	2.22	3.33	2.11
YEN	17.2	1.56	1.52	1.68	28.2	8.03	1.51	1.59	2.58	1.54
Avg	11.5	1.36	1.30	1.43	20.9	5.59	1.29	1.49	2.75	1.31

Table 3 highlights a comparison between the accuracy of PCGPRNN forecaster model with the contemporary ANN models introduced previously for similar exchange rates. PCGPRNN with **98.87%** seems to outperform all. Note that all other networks are static, whereas PCGPRNN continue to change at runtime in response to the input data patterns.

Table 3. Comparison of PCGPRNN with contemporary ann models

Network	Accuracy
Multi Layer Perceptron [4]	72
Volterra Network [4]	76
AFERFM [1]	81.2
HFERFM [1]	69.9
Back Propagation Network [15]	62.27
Multi Neural Network [15]	66.82
CGPANN [2]	98.84
PCGPRNN (Proposed)	**98.87**

Learning with Development

In order to evaluate 'learning on the fly' capability of the network, we have tested the network for its performance in a completely new scenario. We have evaluated the performance of PCGPRNN to predict more days (i.e. 7, 10, 15, 30, 60) rather than single day. Table 4 shows the MAPE values of the proposed PCGPRNN model for multiple days' prediction. It can be observed the proposed model performs better in the advance prediction scenarios as well.

Table 4. Testing results of PCGPRNN model

Currency	7	10	15	30	60
SDR	3.8298	3.9776	4.5585	5.8555	7.9523
CNY	3.0987	3.4626	4.0178	5.3280	7.5935
IDR	**2.2317**	**2.5736**	**3.3274**	**4.7754**	**7.2544**
KW	2.9470	3.2516	3.9662	5.8721	9.3758
TD	3.1521	3.5315	4.1070	5.6000	7.9183
MR	3.0304	3.3461	3.8826	5.1105	7.2978
HKD	3.1586	3.4931	3.9919	5.2200	7.1626
CAD	3.2143	3.9818	4.8699	6.2117	8.8012
NZD	3.8877	4.4869	5.4938	6.5251	9.9959
CHF	3.4591	4.3415	5.3881	7.0680	8.6958
GBP	3.3462	4.0830	4.8516	5.5046	8.0757
EUR	4.2062	5.0777	6.4202	7.9186	9.8737
TWI	2.9801	3.3947	3.8889	5.0798	6.6557
YEN	2.7573	3.1262	3.8094	4.8327	6.2890

6 Conclusion and Future Enhancements

We have enhanced the forecasting of foreign currency volatility in the global market using the power of neuro evolution and its amalgamation with DOL to its next station. The recurrent models, that are used in work exhibit self-modifying and orientation capabilities. Cartesian Genetic Programming is explored to encode the dynamic computational networks and is evolved for its learning behavior at runtime in the proposed system. It incorporates synaptic as well as developmental plasticity in Recurrent Neural Networks. Plastic Cartesian Genetic Programming evolved Recurrent Neural Network (PCGPRNN), the model exploits the trends in foreign exchange to predict the upcoming currency exchange rates, while developing its topology, synaptic connectivity and other architectural component including input vector ‘on the fly’. The results demonstrated the system to be robust and able to learn on the fly to predict the volatile nature of foreign exchange rates.

References

1. Philip, A.A., Tofiki, A.A., Bidemi, A.A.: Artificial neural network model for forecasting foreign exchange rate. World Comput. Sci. Inf. Technol. J. **1**(3), 110–118 (2011)
2. Khan, G.M., Nayab, D., Mehmud, S.A., Zafar, M.H.: Evolving dynamic forecasting model for foreign currency exchange rates using plastic neural networks. In: IEEE 12th International Conference on Machine Learning and Applications ICMLA (2013)
3. Nayab, D., Muhammad Khan, G., Mahmud, S.A.: Prediction of foreign currency exchange rates using CGPANN. In: Iliadis, L., Papadopoulos, H., Jayne, C. (eds.) EANN 2013. CCIS, vol. 383, pp. 91–101. Springer, Heidelberg (2013). https://doi.org/10.1007/978-3-642-41013-0_10

4. Kryuchin, O.V., Arzamastsev, A.A., Troitzsch, K.G.: The prediction of currency exchange rates using artificial neural networks. Exch. Organ. Behav. Teach. J., no. 4 (2011)
5. Risi, S., Stanley, Kenneth O.: Indirectly encoding neural plasticity as a pattern of local rules. In: Doncieux, S., Girard, B., Guillot, A., Hallam, J., Meyer, J.-A., Mouret, J.-B. (eds.) SAB 2010. LNCS (LNAI), vol. 6226, pp. 533–543. Springer, Heidelberg (2010). https://doi.org/10.1007/978-3-642-15193-4_50
6. Kadilar, C., Alada, H.: Forecasting the exchange rate series with ANN: the case of Turkey. Econ. Stat. Chang. **9**, 17–29 (2009)
7. Galeshchuk, S., Mukherjee, S.: Deep networks for predicting direction of change in foreign exchange rates. Intell. Syst. Account., Financ. Manag. **24**, 100–110 (2017)
8. Khan, M.M., Khan, G.M., Miller, J.F.: Efficient representation of recurrent neural networks for Markovian/non-Markovian non-linear control problems. In: International Conference on Intelligent Systems Design and Applications, pp. 615–620 (2010)
9. Khan, M.M., Khan, G.M., Miller, J.F.: Developmental plasticity in cartesian genetic programming artificial neural networks. In: Proceedings of the International Conference on Informatics in Control, Automation and Robotics, pp. 449–458 (2011)
10. Cangelosi, A., Nolfi, S., Parisi, D.: Cell division and migration in a 'genotype' for neural networks. Netw. Comput. Neural Syst. **5**, 497–515 (1994)
11. Pacelli, V., Bavelacqua, V., Azzollini, M.: An artificial neural network model to forecast exchange rates. J. Int. Learn. Syst. Appl. **3**(2A), 57–69 (2011)
12. Upegui, A., Perez-Uribe, A., Thoma, Y., Sanchez, E.: Neural development on the Ubichip by means of dynamic routing mechanisms. In: Hornby, G.S., Sekanina, L., Haddow, P.C. (eds.) ICES 2008. LNCS, vol. 5216, pp. 392–401. Springer, Heidelberg (2008). https://doi.org/10.1007/978-3-540-85857-7_35
13. Miller, J.F.: Cartesian Genetic Programming. Natural Computing Series. Springer, Heidelberg (2011). https://doi.org/10.1007/978-3-642-17310-3
14. Floreano, D., Urzelai, J.: Evolutionary robots with on-line self-organization and behavioral fitness. Neural Netw. **13**(4), 431–443 (2000)
15. Chen, A.P., Hsu, Y.C., Hu, K.F.: A hybrid forecasting model for foreign exchange rate based on a multi-neural network. In: Fourth International Conference on Natural Computation, ICNC, vol. 5, pp. 293–298 (2008)
16. Coleman, O.J., Blair, A.D.: Evolving plastic neural networks for online learning: review and future directions. In: Thielscher, M., Zhang, D. (eds.) AI 2012. LNCS (LNAI), vol. 7691, pp. 326–337. Springer, Heidelberg (2012). https://doi.org/10.1007/978-3-642-35101-3_28
17. Nolfi, S., Miglino, O., Parisi, D.: Phenotypic plasticity in evolving neural networks. In: Proceedings of the International Conference from Perception to Action, pp. 146–157. IEEE Press (1994)
18. Khan, G.M., Miller, J.F., Halliday, D.M.: A developmental model of neural computation using cartesian genetic programming. In: Proceedings of the Genetic and Evolutionary Computation (Companion), pp. 2535–2542. ACM (2007)
19. Massobrio, P., et al.: In vitro studies of neuronal networks and synaptic plasticity in invertebrates and in mammals using multielectrode arrays. Neural Plast. (2015)
20. Zenke, F., Agnes, E.J., Gerstner, W.: Diverse synaptic plasticity mechanisms orchestrated to form and retrieve memories in spiking neural networks. Nat. Commun. **21**(6), 6922 (2015)
21. Ravi, V., Lal, R., Kiran, N.R.: Foreign exchange rate prediction using computational intelligence methods. Int. J. Comput. Inf. Syst. Ind. Manag. Appl. **4**, 659–670 (2012)
22. FOREX Tutorial: Economic Theories, Models, Feeds & Data Available: http://www.investopedia.com/university/forexmarket/forex5.asp.Accessed:September. Accessed Sep 2017

23. Patel, P.J., Patel, N.J., Patel, A.R.: Factors affecting currency exchange rate, economical formulas and prediction models. International Journal of Application or Innovation in Engineering Managment. **3**, 53–56 (2014)
24. Schwaerzel, R., Bylander, T.: Predicting currency exchange rates by genetic programming with trigonometric functions and high-order statistics. In: Proceedings of the 8th Annual Conference on Genetic and Evolutionary Computation. ACM (2006)
25. Alvarez Diaz, M.: Speculative strategies in the foreign exchange market based on genetic programming predictions. Appl. Financ. Econ. **20**(6), 465–476 (2010)
26. Shylajan, C.S., Sreejesh, S., Suresh, K.G.: Rupee-dollar exchange rate and macroeconomic fundamentals: an empirical analysis using flexible-price monetary model. J. Int. Bus. Econ. **12**(2), 89–105 (2011)
27. Shioda, K., Deng, S., Sakurai, A.: Prediction of foreign exchange market states with support vector machine. In: 2011 10th International Conference on Machine Learning and Applications and Workshops (ICMLA), vol. 1. IEEE (2011)

Noise Masking Recurrent Neural Network for Respiratory Sound Classification

Kirill Kochetov(✉), Evgeny Putin, Maksim Balashov, Andrey Filchenkov, and Anatoly Shalyto

Computer Technologies Lab, ITMO University, 49 Kronverksky Pr, 197101 St. Petersburg, Russia
{kskochetov,eoputin,balashov,afilchenkov,shalyto}@corp.ifmo.ru

Abstract. In this paper, we propose a novel architecture called noise masking recurrent neural network (NMRNN) for lung sound classification. The model jointly learns to extract only important respiratory-like frames without redundant noise and then by exploiting this information is trained to classify lung sounds into four categories: normal, containing wheezes, crackles and both wheezes and crackles. We compare the performance of our model with machine learning based models. As a result, the NMRNN model reaches state-of-the-art performance on recently introduced publicly available respiratory sound database.

Keywords: Respiratory sound classification
Recurrent neural networks · Deep learning

1 Introduction

In the last decades many machine learning (ML) approaches have been introduced to analyze respiratory cycle sounds including crackles, coughs, wheezes [1–6]. However almost all conventional ML models solely rely on hand-crafted features. Furthermore, highly complex preprocessing steps are required to make use of designed features [4–6]. Thus, merely ML-based models may not be robust to external/internal noises in lung sounds and may not generalize their performance across different softwares and measuring devices. However, to be used in clinics respiratory tracking systems have to reach high classification accuracy.

From that perspective deep learning (DL) models [7] have gained a lot of attention in the community. DL-based models primary rely on high abstract representation of data that are learned through the training of models. Due to this fact, DL models reach state-of-the-art performance on the range of tasks including image recognition [8], speech recognition [9], time series forecasting [10].

In this work, we propose an architecture of recurrent neural network (RNN) called NMRNN that is trained in end-to-end manner to simultaneously detect noise in respiratory cycles and to classify lung sounds into several categories such as: normal, wheezes, crackles or wheezes and crackles. In other words, our model

V. Kůrková et al. (Eds.): ICANN 2018, LNCS 11141, pp. 208–217, 2018.
https://doi.org/10.1007/978-3-030-01424-7_21

itself decides what information and from what time points it should use to make effective prediction of respiratory sounds. The crucial feature of the model is that it is trained without applying any hand preprocessing stages like slicing of individual respiratory cycles. Through extensive testing, the proposed model has reached state-of-the-art performance on recently published large open database of lung sound records [11].

The rest of the paper is organized as follows. In Sect. 2, we review several notable works in respiratory sounds classification using ML and DL based models. Detailed description of NMRNN is given in Sect. 3. Sections 4 and 5 presents results and comparative study with solely ML-based models. Conclusions are presented in Sect. 6.

2 Related Work

Recently a comprehensive comparative study of applying different ML models to automatic wheeze detection was done in [4]. Authors used a lot of models including feed-forward neural network, random forest (RF), support vector machine (SVM) and trained them on two datasets: phonopneumogram samples and the Dubrovnik General Hospital (DGH) dataset. To reduce the influence of cardiovascular and muscular noise, they applied Yule-Walker filter followed by STFT procedure. Then, two types of features were extracted from the lung sounds: MFCC (Mel-frequency cepstral coefficients) features and some statistical features. The authors reported that their best model with statistical features got 93.62% and 91.77% accuracy on phonopneumograms and DGH datasets, accordingly. Meanwhile, based on MFCC features SVM model reached 99% accuracy on both datasets.

In [12], authors proposed to use hidden Markov models (HMM) coupled with Gaussian mixture models (GMM) for classification of respiratory sounds into four categories: normal, containing wheezes, crackles and both crackles and wheezes. The main idea behind applying HMM was that it is able to take into account frame position in a sequence which leads to better accuracy comparing to GMM. To tackle with noise in sound records, they applied spectral subtraction technique [13]. MFCC extracted from the records were used as input features to the model. In addition to MFCC features obtained in range from 50 Hz to 2000 Hz, the first time derivatives of MFCCs were used to track feature dynamics and to decorrelate feature vectors resulting in feature set with size 30. As a result, the ensemble model of 28 HMMs with 5 states and 1 Gaussian per state achieved 0.495 and 0.396 scores on the cross-validation and second evaluation score respectively. In both experiments different patients were used for training and testing, so it was honest validation, and we can compare these results with ours.

One of the most successful attempts of applying DL models to the field of respiratory sound classification was done in [14]. Authors used convolutional neural networks (CNN) to detect wheezes in lung sound records. Firstly, respiratory records were augmented by biasing sound sample in several time frames.

Then, STFT features were computed followed by standard normalization. Lastly, obtained normalized spectrograms of lung sounds were used to train 2D CNN. The final model received 99% accuracy and 0.96 AUC on the dataset.

3 Method

RNNs are a class of artificial neural networks (ANNs), which are able to process temporal data, such as sound and text. RNNs can use their internal state (memory) and feedback to process sequences of inputs.

LSTM (Long short-term memory) and GRU (gated recurrent unit) networks [15,16] are popular variants of RNN. They are show unprecedented performance on sequence-related tasks such as NLP (Natural Language Processing) [17] and speech recognition [18].

We use both LSTM and GRU units for our experiments. NMRNN is based on three main ideas:

1. Adapt RNNs, which are designed for time-scale data and can consider all information from sequential frames of input signal.
2. Distinguish noise and content automatically during training.
3. Make predictions using only breath (without noise), because noise can include biased anomalies similar to wheezes or crackles.

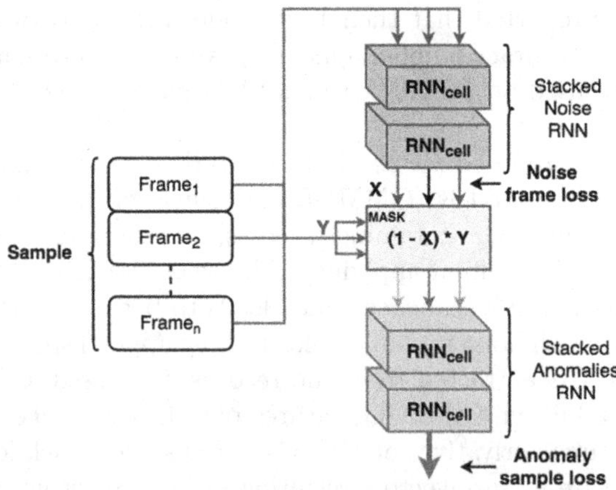

Fig. 1. MNRNN architecture. Stacked Noise RNN predicts one noise label per frame using original MFCC data. MASK block adds attention mechanism of the most important frames with respiratory cycles. Stacked Anomalies RNN predicts one anomaly label per sample using highlighted data from the MASK block.

The MNRNN model consists of three parts: noise classifier, respiratory (or anomaly) classifier and some kind of attention called MASK. Schematic overview of the model is shown in Fig. 1.

First of all, before model training each sound sample was split on frames with equal length. There is only one anomaly label for sound sample and one noise label for each frame.

Noise classifier is a stacked RNN called NRNN, which predicts noise label for every frame from the sample. NRNN optimizes a cross-entropy loss calculated for each output during training

$$L_{CE}(p,q) = -\sum p(x) \times \log(q(x)). \tag{1}$$

Then predicted noise labels propagates through masking layer called MASK, where original frames multiplies with masking coefficient $(1 - X) \times Y$, where X is the predicted noise label ($X = 1$ for noise frame) and Y is a frame.

Anomaly classifier is a stacked RNN called ARNN, which predicts one anomaly label for one sample (all frames). ARNN takes highlighted frames from MASK block as input data and optimize cross-entropy loss for one label per sample.

The final loss of the proposed architecture is following:

$$L_{model} = a_1 \times L_{CEnoise} + a_2 \times L_{CEanom}. \tag{2}$$

Values of coefficients a_1 and a_2 are based on the idea that the main goal of the model is anomaly classification, not noise classification.

The proposed MASK mechanism is simple and efficient and was inspired by gating technique used in GRU cell, where memory needs to be rewritten on each time step using only important information from the input. NRNN parameters were optimized using both NRNN and ARNN losses, so together NRNN and MASK mechanisms allow not only to mask noise frames, but to highlight useful subsamples with respiratory-like content. Attention mechanism used in current model is not the same as usually used for seq2seq models [19]. The main difference is that seq2seq attention mechanism commonly create context vector with weighted sum of encoder hidden states and maps it with current decoder hidden state. So attention in seq2seq extends sight of decoder during sequence prediction. Our MASK layer relies on both predicted noise and anomaly labels, because it receives gradients from both RNN blocks. We conducted additional experiment to show that model with MASK mechanism outperforms model without it in terms of classification metrics.

The main feature of MNRNN method is the ability to perform end-to-end classification without using any manual preprocessing steps like slicing breath on separate cycles. The only commonly used preprocessing step that we did was splitting data to equal frames. The amount of frames does not affect on model training and testing too.

4 Experiments

In the study, logistic regression (LR), random forest (RF), gradient boosting machine (GBM), SVM-based classifier [20] and standard RNN were used as baselines for comparison with the NMRNN model. For baseline experiments, we used the same preprocessing as provided in [4].

4.1 Database

For training and evaluation the ICBHI Scientific Challenge database was used [11]. The database contains audio samples, collected independently by two research teams in two different countries over several years. The database consists of 920 annotated audio samples from 126 patients. It includes 6898 different respiratory cycles with 1864 crackles, 886 wheezes and 506 crackles and wheezes. The database summary is presented in Table 1.

There are a lot of noise in sounds: 1840 noise cycles in all data and 1366 in AKGC417L data. It simulates real life conditions and made the classification algorithm more robust and stable for noise attack.

Table 1. Database summary. Recordings columns includes statistics about separate sound recordings data. Cycles columns includes statistics about individual respiratory cycles

Num of	Recordings		Cycles	
	All equipment	AKGC417L	All equipment	AKGC417L
Patients	126	56	126	56
Samples	920	683	6898	4697
Normal breath	287	196	3642	2226
Wheezes	134	77	886	512
Crackles	297	252	1864	1578
Wheezes and Crackles	202	158	506	381

4.2 Experiments Setup

In this work, we conducted several experiments. Different data and preprocessing steps were used for them. The key idea of all experiments is to compare proposed approach with other machine learning models in different situations in terms of performance and robustness.

1. Simple noise binary classification experiment for initial model checking.
2. 4-class anomalies classification using individual respiratory cycle as input.
3. 4-class anomalies classification using sound samples with several respiratory cycles in each (end-to-end classification).

The aim of the first experiment is to check RNN and NMRNN ability to learn respiratory and noise cycle interval lengths and frequencies. The second experiment should compare our baseline models with recently proposed method [12].

The second experiment is demonstrative, but it has one critical limitation: it is not end-to-end experiment, because first of all we need to split lung sounds on respiratory cycles, but there is no automatic universal solution for this task yet. So, for each new lung sound record we need to manually split it into respiratory cycles.

For this reason, the third experiment was conducted. The aim of this experiment is to check the abilities of the models to find what input information is important and where it is located in multidimensional feature space. Model as end-to-end classifier needs to find respiratory-dependent features in the data by itself.

Also, there are two variations of data for each experiment. We use all available data and data recorded only on AKGC417L microphone. The main idea of using second data type is to show that the models can achieve better performance using only one unbiased data source.

All experiments were conducted on a computer with Intel Core i7-6900 CPU with 128GB of RAM and NVIDIA GTX 1080Ti GPU.

4.3 Result Evaluation

Due to the unbalanced data set, we used sensitivity and specificity as statistical indicators of the models performance. Sensitivity, specificity and overall score were proposed in the original data set paper [11,12].

Overall evaluation score can be formulated as:

$$Score = \frac{Sensitivity + Specificity}{2}. \tag{3}$$

We used 5-fold cross-validation over patients to evaluate the results and it is important to note that there is no patients from the train set in the test set on each split. So, we used honest real-oriented division of the data for validation.

4.4 Preprocessing

To remove sounds caused by heartbeats, the signal components at low frequencies have to be suppressed. We use the high pass finite impulse response (FIR) filter with cutoff frequency $fc = 100$ Hz for remove sounds caused by heartbeat [12].

In this work, MFCC was used as feature extractor. The lower and upper frequencies of processed content were cut to 50 and 2000 Hz respectively, because wheezes and crackles are in this interval [12]. Parameters frame length and frame step were both chosen equal to 0.05 s using grid search optimization [21].

Every sound sample from original database was sliced on pieces called frames with length of 0.5 s each. Every frame was split on 10 non-overlapping frames. Both frame length and frame step are 0.05 s. One MFCC set (13 values) was extracted from each frame. So, every piece is described by 130 MFCC features. Each frame and sample corresponds to a breathing (presence of anomaly) and noise label. There are four breathing classes in the database: normal breathing, breathing with wheezes, crackles and with both wheezes and crackles.

During anomaly classification using all frames (one label per sound) or subset of frames (one label per respiratory cycle) we want to predict existence of anomalies in the overall sound sample or in the only one respiratory cycle respectively. So, for baseline models each sound sample or respiratory cycle was reshaped into a single flattened array. Taking into account different audio lengths, final data samples were cut or filled using standard padding technique. Also, augmentation technique (was proposed in [14]) with shifting was used for solving the problem of respiratory cycles localization. PCA (Principal Component Analysis) was used for dimensionality reduction (only for baseline models).

5 Results

For noise binary classification task NMRNN achieved 0.89 evaluation score compared with the best baseline model GBM, which reached only 0.53 score. It can be explained by the ability of RNN to learn cycle and noise intervals length and frequency and use this additional information during prediction.

Table 2. Results of 4-class classification of each respiratory cycle. Metrics of Jakovljevic HMM was not provided with AKGC417L data

	All equipment			AKGC417L		
Model	Sens	Spec	Score	Sens	Spec	Score
GBM	0.476	0.554	0.515	0.534	0.568	0.551
LR	0.425	0.508	0.466	0.426	0.51	0.468
RF	0.438	0.538	0.488	0.483	0.521	0.502
SVM	0.49	0.502	0.496	0.502	0.518	0.51
Jakovljevic [12]	0.423	0.567	0.495	-	-	-
RNN (ours)	0.584	0.73	**0.657**	0.617	0.741	0.679

Results of 4-class classification of each respiratory cycle are presented in Table 2. There is a comparison of our baseline and NMRNN models with HMM-based method proposed by Jakovljevic. All models were trained on MFCC features. Performance of our models is similar with performance of Jakovljevic HMM [12], except for NMRNN, which outperforms competitors. So, it is correct to compare presented baseline models with proposed RNN-based approach in the next experiment. Also, models trained only on AKGC417L data show better scores as expected due to reduced bias of data distribution. The second experiment is less complex than the third one, because of data manually sliced on respiratory cycles before training.

Results of end-to-end classification are provided in Table 3. NMRNN definitely outperforms other methods with respect to the chosen criterion. The main reason is that RNN was designed to process such kind of data with temporal dependencies. Another models face with problems of large dimensionality

Table 3. Results of 4-class classification of each sound sample

	All equipment			AKGC417L		
Model	Sens	Spec	Score	Sens	Spec	Score
GBM	0.362	0.142	0.252	0.348	0.174	0.261
LR	0.348	0.184	0.266	0.366	0.236	0.301
RF	0.433	0.054	0.244	0.451	0.079	0.265
SVM	0.313	0.251	0.282	0.278	0.256	0.267
RNN (ours)	0.511	0.717	0.614	0.572	0.728	0.65
NMRNN (ours)	0.56	0.736	**0.648**	0.62	0.75	**0.685**

and localization of respiratory cycles. So, neither PCA or augmentation do not help to solve these problems, because the baseline models are not adapted for unstable data with floating content such as sound with several respiratory cycles.

MASK block with noise classification increases performance on about 0.035 in terms of score. It can be explained by ability of the final model to concentrate only on frames with respiratory cycles, not with noise. Also MASK block helps to distinguish false positive anomalies (biased noise) with real anomalies (crackles or wheezes) as justified on Fig. 2.

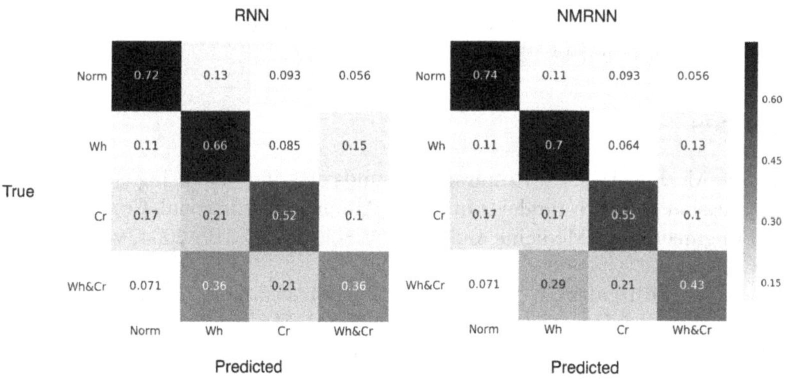

Fig. 2. Confusion matrices of RNN and NMRNN. MASK block helps to clarify some samples similarity by masking false positive anomalies detected in noise frames. Due to that both sensitivity and specificity was improved.

Models trained only on AKGC417L data show performance as in the previous experiments. This proves that the model can be adapted for single source and can in theory boost performance with increasing of amount of unbiased data for training.

We used grid search [21] as optimization algorithm for finding best hyper-parameters for baseline and RNN-based models. So the best RNN-based model with MASK block consists of 2-layer RNNs as both NRNN and ARNN parts with GRU cells with 256 units in each. Coefficients a_1 and a_2 from Eq. 2 are 0.3 and 0.7 respectively, which corresponds to the main task of the model (anomaly classification). Overall model architecture was trained using Adam [22] optimizer with $learning\_rate = 0.0001$.

6 Conclusion

In this paper, we proposed RNN-based end-to-end model architecture called NMRNN to detect different anomalies in lung sound data with masking of noise. MASK block is very powerful, so it allows the model to consider only relevant frames during classification. We assume, that the trained MASK mechanism is a superior direction of further improvement.

The main contribution of this approach is that it is trained without applying any manual preprocessing steps using respiratory records of any lengths. NMRNN reaches state-of-the-art performance in comparison with another ML models on respiratory sound classification task and, including recently proposed [12], on individual respiratory cycle classification task.

Also, this study shows the ability of the model to learn cycle and the lengths of noise intervals and frequencies. Experiments with AKGC417L microphone motivate to concentrate on single data source during creation of approach applicable in real life conditions.

Acknowledgements. This work was financially supported by the Government of the Russian Federation, Grant 08-08.

References

1. Bahoura, M., Pelletier, C.: Respiratory sounds classification using cepstral analysis and Gaussian mixture models. In: 26th Annual International Conference of the IEEE Engineering in Medicine and Biology Society, IEMBS 2004, vol. 1, pp. 9–12. IEEE (2004)
2. Mayorga, P., Druzgalski, C., Morelos, R.L., Gonzalez, O.H., Vidales, J.: Acoustics based assessment of respiratory diseases using GMM classification. In: 2010 Annual International Conference of the IEEE Engineering in Medicine and Biology Society (EMBC), pp. 6312–6316. IEEE (2010)
3. Palaniappan, R., Sundaraj, K., Sundaraj, S.: A comparative study of the SVM and K-NN machine learning algorithms for the diagnosis of respiratory pathologies using pulmonary acoustic signals. BMC Bioinform. **15**(1), 223 (2014)
4. Milicevic, M., Mazic, I., Bonkovic, M.: Classification accuracy comparison of asthmatic wheezing sounds recorded under ideal and real-world conditions. In: 15th International Conference on Artificial Intelligence, Knowledge Engineering and Databases (AIKED 2016), Venice (2016)
5. Rocha, B.M., Mendes, L., Chouvarda, I., Carvalho, P., Paiva, R.P.: Detection of cough and adventitious respiratory sounds in audio recordings by internal sound analysis. In: Maglaveras, N., Chouvarda, I., de Carvalho, P. (eds.) Precision Medicine Powered by pHealth and Connected Health. IP, vol. 66, pp. 51–55. Springer, Singapore (2018). https://doi.org/10.1007/978-981-10-7419-6_9

6. Serbes, G., Ulukaya, S., Kahya, Y.P.: An automated lung sound preprocessing and classification system based onspectral analysis methods. In: Maglaveras, N., Chouvarda, I., de Carvalho, P. (eds.) Precision Medicine Powered by pHealth and Connected Health. IP, vol. 66, pp. 45–49. Springer, Singapore (2018). https://doi.org/10.1007/978-981-10-7419-6_8
7. LeCun, Y., Bengio, Y., Hinton, G.: Deep learning. Nature **521**(7553), 436 (2015)
8. Szegedy, C., Ioffe, S., Vanhoucke, V., Alemi, A.A.: Inception-v4, inception-resnet and the impact of residual connections on learning. In: AAAI, vol. 4, p. 12 (2017)
9. Palaz, D., Magimai-Doss, M., Collobert, R.: Analysis of CNN-based speech recognition system using raw speech as input. Technical report, Idiap (2015)
10. Weigend, A.S.: Time Series Prediction: Forecasting the Future and Understanding the Past. Routledge, New York (2018)
11. Rocha, B.M., et al.: A respiratory sound database for the development of automated classification. In: Maglaveras, N., Chouvarda, I., de Carvalho, P. (eds.) Precision Medicine Powered by pHealth and Connected Health. IP, vol. 66, pp. 33–37. Springer, Singapore (2018). https://doi.org/10.1007/978-981-10-7419-6_6
12. Jakovljević, N., Lončar-Turukalo, T.: Hidden Markov model based respiratory sound classification. In: Maglaveras, N., Chouvarda, I., de Carvalho, P. (eds.) Precision Medicine Powered by pHealth and Connected Health. IP, vol. 66, pp. 39–43. Springer, Singapore (2018). https://doi.org/10.1007/978-981-10-7419-6_7
13. Berouti, M., Schwartz, R., Makhoul, J.: Enhancement of speech corrupted by acoustic noise. In: IEEE International Conference on Acoustics, Speech, and Signal Processing, ICASSP 1979, vol. 4, pp. 208–211. IEEE (1979)
14. Kochetov, K., Putin, E., Azizov, S., Skorobogatov, I., Filchenkov, A.: Wheeze detection using convolutional neural networks. In: Oliveira, E., Gama, J., Vale, Z., Lopes Cardoso, H. (eds.) EPIA 2017. LNCS (LNAI), vol. 10423, pp. 162–173. Springer, Cham (2017). https://doi.org/10.1007/978-3-319-65340-2_14
15. Hochreiter, S., Schmidhuber, J.: Long short-term memory. Neural Comput. **9**(8), 1735–1780 (1997)
16. Cho, K., Van Merriënboer, B., Bahdanau, D., Bengio, Y.: On the properties of neural machine translation: encoder-decoder approaches. arXiv preprint arXiv:1409.1259 (2014)
17. Sundermeyer, M., Schlüter, R., Ney, H.: LSTM neural networks for language modeling. In: Thirteenth Annual Conference of the International Speech Communication Association (2012)
18. Graves, A., Mohamed, A., Hinton, G.: Speech recognition with deep recurrent neural networks. In: 2013 IEEE international conference on Acoustics, speech and signal processing (ICASSP), pp. 6645–6649. IEEE (2013)
19. Luong, M.-T., Pham, H., Manning, C.D.: Effective approaches to attention-based neural machine translation. arXiv preprint arXiv:1508.04025 (2015)
20. Hastie, T., Tibshirani, R., Friedman, J.: The Elements of Statistical Learning. SSS. Springer, New York (2009). https://doi.org/10.1007/978-0-387-84858-7
21. Bergstra, J., Bengio, Y.: Random search for hyper-parameter optimization. J. Mach. Learn. Res. **13**, 281–305 (2012)
22. Kingma, D.P., Ba, J.: Adam: a method for stochastic optimization. arXiv preprint arXiv:1412.6980 (2014)

Lightweight Neural Programming: The GRPU

Felipe Carregosa[1(✉)], Aline Paes[2], and Gerson Zaverucha[1]

[1] Department of Systems Engineering and Computer Science, Universidade Federal do Rio de Janeiro, Rio de Janeiro, RJ, Brazil
{fborda,gerson}@cos.ufrj.br

[2] Department of Computer Science, Institute of Computing, Universidade Federal Fluminense, Niterói, RJ, Brazil
alinepaes@ic.uff.br

Abstract. Deep Learning techniques have achieved impressive results over the last few years. However, they still have difficulty in producing understandable results that clearly show the embedded logic behind the inductive process. One step in this direction is the recent development of Neural Differentiable Programmers. In this paper, we designed a neural programmer that can be easily integrated into existing deep learning architectures, with similar amount of parameters to a single commonly used Recurrent Neural Network. Tests conducted with the proposal suggest that it has the potential to induce algorithms even without any kind of special optimization, achieving competitive results in problems handled by more complex RNN architectures.

Keywords: Recurrent Neural Networks
Neural Differentiable Programmers

1 Introduction

Recently there has been a renewed interest in merging traditional programming and Neural Networks (NNs), particularly thanks to more advanced Automatic Differentiation (AD) tools [8]. These new tools can evaluate functions written in the host languages idiomatic structures, allowing programmers to easily and efficiently obtain the gradient of varied units of code with respect to their arguments. This enables augmenting the programming toolset with the Machine Learning capabilities.

With a similar goal, Neural Differentiable Programmers (NDPs) [9,11] have been developed to allow NNs to compose algorithms in more traditional ways. This allows them to potentially tackle hard problems, involving complex arithmetic and logical reasoning. Thus, in order to model the input-output relationship, instead of applying a series of transformations directly over the input, NDPs

The authors would like to thank the Brazilian Research Agencies CNPq and CAPES for partially finance this research.

V. Kůrková et al. (Eds.): ICANN 2018, LNCS 11141, pp. 218–227, 2018.
https://doi.org/10.1007/978-3-030-01424-7_22

choose a sequence of transformations from a predefined instruction set, yielding an explicit algorithm to transform the input into the solution. Furthermore, they can also decouple its learned logic from the specific input values, allowing for better generalization and re-usability in different contexts. However, current NDP models focus on end-to-end solutions for specific contexts and problems, instead of being easily integrated into current Deep Learning models.

In this paper, we propose The Gated Recurrent Programmer Unit (GRPU), a NDP technique that can be easily integrated into any current model that uses a Recurrent Neural Network (RNN). Moreover, GRPU uses around the same amount of parameters as a simple Gated Recurrent Unit (GRU) [4], is agnostic in terms of external memory structure and data inputs, and can be extended in similar ways to RNNs, like stacking and soft attention strategies. This way it can provide a lightweight way of augmenting Deep Learning models with the induction of more traditional programs.

The rest of the paper is organized as follows. The next section briefly explains the GRU and the most known NDPs in the literature. The 3rd section details the model devised in this work. The 4th section brings the experiments we have conducted in this work, and the last section is the conclusion.

2 Preliminaries

Here we briefly explain the GRUs, by which our model is inspired, and the most relevant neural programmers found in the related literature.

2.1 Gated Recurrent Unit (GRU)

Recently, a new, simpler, architecture for RNNs has been developed, the *Gated Recurrent Unit* (GRU) [4]. GRUs present comparative performance to the traditionally used *Long Short-Term Memory* (LSTM) [5], while using fewer parameters, as they have only two interacting layers instead of three: the *update gate* and the *reset gate*. When the value computed at the reset gate is close to 0, the corresponding previous hidden state is erased and, therefore, ignored when creating the new state. This allows the GRU to drop information judged irrelevant. The update gate, on the other hand, controls how much information from the previous hidden state should be directly carried over to the current hidden state. This shortcut between the previous state and the following one allows information to be kept untouched indefinitely, helping with the Vanishing Gradient Problem [3].

The value of the current hidden state is computed as $h_t = (1 - u_t) * h_{t-1} + u_t * \tilde{h}_t$, where **u** and **r** stands for the update and reset gates, respectively, and $\tilde{h}_t$, the new candidate state: $\tilde{h}_t = \tanh(W.[r_t * h_{t-1}, x_t] + b)$. The values of the update and reset gates are defined with their own set of parameters, where the update gate is computed as $u_t = \sigma(W_z.[h_{t-1}, x_t] + b_u)$ and the reset gate as $r_t = \sigma(W_r.[h_{t-1}, x_t] + b_r)$.

2.2 Related Work: Neural Programmers

Neural Differentiable Programming (NDP) techniques try to combine the pattern matching and universal approximation nature of the neural networks with the discrete series of operations from traditional algorithms [9]. Fundamentally, neural networks are simply a chain of geometric transformations, and finding one of such transformations that can fully generalize each traditional operation, such as arithmetic and logic operations, is hard and require potentially large amounts of data. For example, even a simple sum or product of numbers is not a trivial task for a neural network to learn, especially considering the distortion caused by the non linear transformations that occur at each step.

Integrating algorithmic-like aspects has been a tendency since the success of the attention models [12]. They allow the network to learn to choose the data it wants to access in a completely differentiable way. NDPs go one step further and not only apply the selection to the input data, but also to the operation applied to the data. For that, they comprise a selection of differentiable operations, and through soft attention they are able to select an operation for each step, and the results of each step can then become the input of the following step. They possess, then, the ability to induce algorithms that transform the original input into the desired output through the multiple steps. The selection operation usually has the form $result = oplist(args)^T softmax(opcode)$, where *oplist* is an N-sized vector in which each field is an operation like sum or multiplication, and *opcode* is a vector with N values, generated by a RNN at each step.

Some of the most notable neural programmers are:

- The *Neural Programmer* [9] is a table query based model that, given an input question, selects a series of aggregate operations and a series of columns from the input table for each operation to be applied. The training phase involves finding the operations and column arguments that minimizes the error towards the given output, using two LSTMs and two softmax layers.
- The Neural Programmer Interpreter [10] is composed of a single LSTM and a domain specific encoder for the state of the environment. The LSTM has three selector units to choose the next operation, its arguments, and when the subprogram terminates. It predicts the next step of a program only, and not the full program at once, requiring the program trace as input.
- The *Neural Random Access Machines* [7] is a sequence-to-sequence programmer model, in which every data register of the virtual machine it implements contains a pointer (a probability distribution) that can be transformed into new pointers through look-up-table based operations. Each pointer can be used to read or write from a memory tape using attention.

3 The Gated Recurrent Programmer Unit

We introduce a novel neural differentiable programmer architecture that focuses on low footprint and easy integration with other neural architectures. It has considerably fewer parameters than the models described in the previous section, and it does not require a complex input in both training and execution (such as tables, preprocessed lists or programs traces). Additionally, unlike the previous models, the GRPU instructions can have any number of arguments, due to not requiring softmax selection, and of operations transforming those arguments in a single step.

3.1 The Architecture

Figure 1 exhibits the GRPU architecture, which is built upon the structure of a regular GRU. GRPU is not only easily exchangeable wherever a GRU can be used, enabling traditional algorithmic manipulation of it's inputs, but it can also be implemented with just a few lines of codes over the GRU. The fundamental difference between the two models is the way the new state is produced, but this small difference also affects how everything else is interpreted.

Thus, in GRPU, the affine transformation is replaced by an *Arithmetic and Logic Unit* (ALU), a module that executes one operation for each set of fields of the hidden state to produce the next state values. The *Virtual Machine* (VM) state, which replaces the hidden state in the GRU, is $h^{vm} \in \mathcal{R}^N$, where N is both the ALU's operation's outputs sizes summed and the argument's sizes summed. In other words, the VM state is both the arguments for the ALU, and the outputs of the ALU.

The ALU receives the previous VM state and returns a new candidate for the next state from the results of each operation. The reset gate, in this context, operates as the argument selector, responsible for determining which arguments will be fed to the ALU, turning the ones that should be ignored to zero. The update gate defines which operations have their results kept and which ones are ignored. In this last case, the previous values of the VM state are restored, and the operation is replaced by a *NOP*, *No Operation*. The algorithm is, therefore produced by producing the GRU gates $[u_t, r_t]$ based on the inputs, which is equivalent to producing the opcode $[operations, operands]_t$. Calculating every step gives the final algorithm, like the example displayed in Fig. 2.

Unlike with GRUs though, the hidden state, or the VM state, shouldn't be used in the creation of the gates output, and therefore in the creation of the instructions. This is done so the model can learn generic algorithms, that can automatically deal with data not seen in the training base. In the current

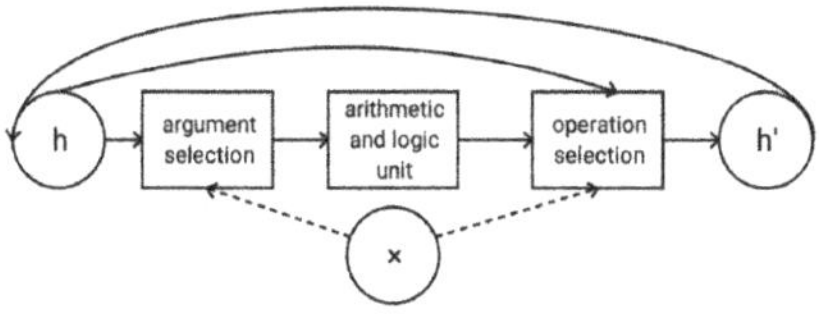

Fig. 1. The basic Gated Recurrent Programmer Unit. Dashed lines are the input of the gates, normal lines are the hidden (VM) state path.

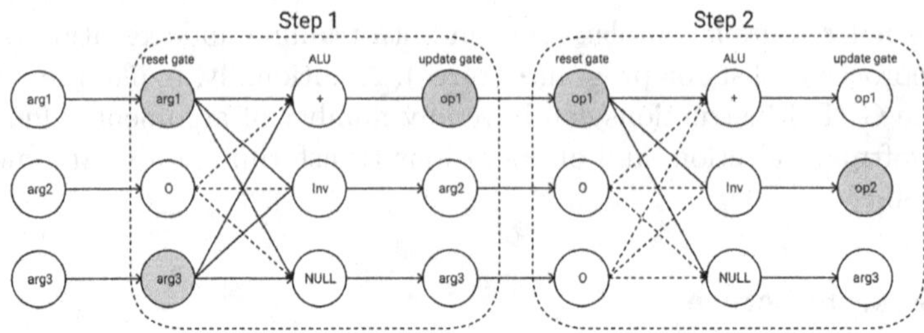

Fig. 2. Example of a two step algorithm: -(arg1+arg3). Each row has one argument and one operation throughout two recurrent steps. The reset gate selects the arguments for the ALU operations (grayed in the image with solid lines), while the update gate selects which operation results or arguments will be kept (grayed operation results).

architecture it means that there is a direct mapping between the current input and the respective instruction.

While this behavior is sometimes enough, we would like the model to use past information for creating the algorithm, and, for that reason, we include an additional *controller* unit, which acts in parallel to the programmer and has the same structure as the GRU. The complete model is depicted in Fig. 3, and represented by the following set of equations (from Eqs. 2 to 5):

$$r_t = \sigma(W_r.[h^c_{t-1}, x_t] + b_r) \tag{1}$$

$$u_t = \sigma(W_u.[h^c_{t-1}, x_t] + b_u) \tag{2}$$

$$\widetilde{h^c_t} = \tanh(W.[r^c_t * h^c_{t-1}, x_t] + b) \tag{3}$$

$$\widetilde{h^{vm}_t}[i] = ALU(r^{vm}_t, h^{vm}_{t-1}, external_t, operation[i]) \tag{4}$$

$$h_t = (1 - u_t) * h_{t-1} + u_t * \tilde{h}_t \tag{5}$$

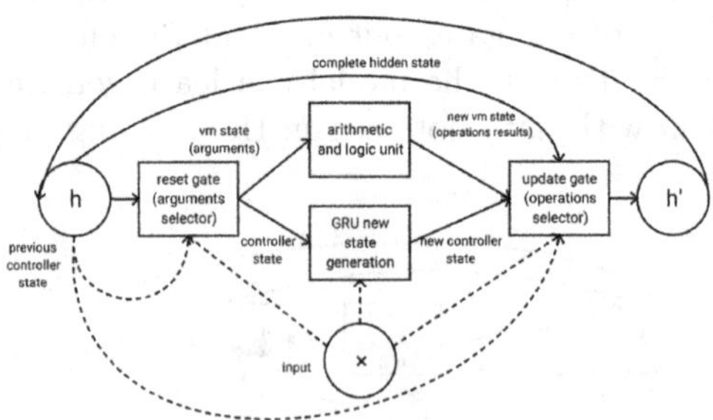

Fig. 3. The Gated Recurrent Programmer Unit. The upper part is the virtual machine, which executes the instruction according to the selections made by the gates. The lower part is the controller, which encodes a representation of all past inputs for the gates, producing instructions that aren't just a mapping of the current input.

Where vm defines the Virtual Machine (VM) section and c the controller section of the state and gate outputs, $h_t = [h_t^{vm}, h_t^c]$, $r_t = [r_t^{vm}, r_t^c]$ and $u_t = [h_t^{vm}, h_t^c]$ are the hidden state (formed by the concatenation of VM and controller states), reset gate (which assumes the task of argument selector for the VM state) and update gate (which assumes the task of the operation selector for the VM state), respectively. $\widetilde{h}_t = [\widetilde{h}_t^{vm}, \widetilde{h}_t^c]$ is the next state candidate. The ALU is a function that receives the VM state (arguments), the argument selection (reset gate output), any external data or differentiable memory that can be read/write through specific operations, and the list of operations to apply to the arguments.

3.2 The Arithmetic and Logic Unit (ALU)

The ALU natively supports n-ary operations, with the arguments selected directly with the argument selector. But one aspect that must be considered is what is the neutral element in the operation. The argument selector rejects arguments by multiplying them by zero. This behavior does not influence operations such as summation and the logical *or*. In other cases, though, such as the product or the logical *and*, a zero valued (rejected) argument would guarantee that the result is zero or False, respectively. To solve this issue, we introduce a transformation that makes rejected arguments (in which $r_t[i] = 0$) to have value one, instead of zero, and selected arguments to have the argument value itself, which may include zero. Table 1 shows the output we would like the both cases have.

Table 1. Target inputs for operations with neutral element 0 and 1.

Input (i)	Selector (r)	Neutral 0	Neutral 1	Input (i)	Selector (r)	Neutral 0	Neutral 1
0	0	0	1	x	0	0	1
0	1	0	0	x	1	x	x

An additional complication is that the argument selector gate is not restricted to binary outputs, but instead, covers the entire space between 0 and 1. To handle that we need to work on a superset of the Boolean algebra, like the Fuzzy Logic [6]. In particular, we choose the following generalized form for the basic logic operators, though other options are also possible: x AND $y = x * y$, x OR $y = 1 - (1 - x) * (1 - y) = x + y - x * y$ and NOT $x = 1 - x$.

Converting the neutral 1 column in terms of i and r in the truth Table 1 into a sum of products representation (where "." is the logical *and*, "+" is the logical *or*, and "$\overline{x}$" is the logical negation of x) we get $i.r + i.\overline{r} + \overline{i}.\overline{r}$. Next, by factoring $\overline{r}$ on the last two terms, we reach $\overline{r}.(i + \overline{i}) + i.r$, and by applying the identity $i + \overline{i} = 1$), we reach Eq. 6.

$$\overline{r} + i.r \tag{6}$$

Then, replacing the boolean operators for the fuzzy operators in the form of (NOT r) OR (i AND r), we get $(1-r)$ OR $(i*r) = (1-r)+(i*r)-(1-r)*(i*r) = 1 - r + i * r - i * r + i * r^2$, which brings us the Eq. 7.

$$1 - r + i * r^2 \tag{7}$$

Similarly, the sum of product form for the neutral 0 in Table 1 is simply $i \ AND \ r$, and, therefore in the generalized operators it is defined as $i * r$, which is already how the reset gate output is applied to the hidden state.

Thus, for any operation wherein the neutral element is zero we do $i * r$ and for any operation wherein the neutral element is one we apply Eq. 7 as its input.

For lesser arity operations, it's possible to simply eliminate some of the connections to the arguments (for example a toggle operation only needs a connection to it's previous result), and/or to use aggregate functions. By averaging the reset gate outputs before multiplying the VM state, it's also possible to have a soft selection equivalent to the softmax.

Besides the operations that map arguments to results, algorithms also require testing and flow control, and for that we first have to define *comparison operations*. Comparison operations typically have arity two (such as equal, not equal, less than, greater than), or one (equal to zero, not equal to zero, etc.) and return one if the condition is true, or zero otherwise. The way we implement the differentiable *not equal* (and the *equal*, by simply subtracting it from 1) is by having $|arg1 - arg2|/(|arg1 - arg2| + \epsilon)$ where ϵ is a constant to avoid division by zero. $Greater\ than$ and $less - than$ can be implemented with a shifted sigmoid (logistic) function, approximating the Heaviside step function.

With the comparison operator, we can implement an element of control flow in the differentiable machine, the *conditional operation*. It makes the instruction to be executed only if the condition determined by a comparison operation, or a combination of them through logical operators, is met, and otherwise all the instruction is rejected. This is implemented by changing the operation selection mechanism according to Table 2, in which $\widetilde{u}_{cond}$ is the operation selector value (update gate value) for the conditional operation, $\widetilde{u}_{op}$ is the operation selector value for the target normal operation, h_{cond} is the result of the comparison used for the conditional, and u_{op} is the final operation selector values (the value of the operation or a NOP, or No Operation, equivalent to the update gate rejecting the operation). Simplifying the table like with the neutral element above:

$$u_{op} = \widetilde{u}_{op} \text{ AND } ((\text{ NOT } \widetilde{u}_{cond}) \text{ OR } \widetilde{h}_{cond}) \tag{8}$$

And using the same transformation inspired by Fuzzy Logic we discussed above, we arrive in the Eq. 9 below:

$$u_{op} = u_{op} * (1 + \widetilde{u}_{cond} * (\widetilde{h}_{cond} - 1)) \tag{9}$$

And for integrating it within the model equations, with u_t being the final output of the update gate for using in Eq. 5, $\widetilde{u}_t^c$ the controller section and $\widetilde{u}_t^{vm}$ the VM section of the update gate calculated in Eq. 2:

$$u_t = [\widetilde{u}_t^{vm}, \widetilde{u}_t^{vm} * (1 + u_{cond} * (\widetilde{h}_{cond} - 1))] \tag{10}$$

If the rejection condition happens, the whole programmer section of the update gate is multiplied by a scalar zero, and the new VM state becomes h_{t-1}^{vm}, and, therefore, the algorithm does not produce any effect in that step.

Table 2. Desired output when accepting or rejecting the input.

u_{cond}	$\widetilde{h}_{cond}$	$\widetilde{u}_{op}$	u_{op}	u_{cond}	$\widetilde{h}_{cond}$	$\widetilde{u}_{op}$	u_{op}
0 (-)	0 (-)	0 (-)	0 (nop)	1 (if)	0 (false)	0 (-)	0 (nop)
0 (-)	0 (-)	1 (do op)	1 (op)	1 (if)	0 (false)	1 (do op)	0 (nop)
0 (-)	1 (-)	0 (-)	0 (nop)	1 (if)	1 (true)	0 (-)	0 (nop)
0 (-)	1 (-)	1 (do op)	1 (op)	1 (if)	1 (true)	1 (do op)	1 (op)

3.3 Expanding the Model

Since the GRPU is similar in structure to a GRU, it can be extended in similar ways. For instance, by stacking a number of GRPUs it is possible to have different control flows, executing multiple operations per step, according to the number and order of transformations over the VM state. Another possibility is to use the encoder-decoder with soft attention [2] as inspiration, allowing the model to learn its own sequencing through the input, while also decoupling the input size from the program size.

4 Experimental Results

To produce the results presented here, we run all the tests with Tensorflow [1] on a single GPU, Adam optimization, learning rate 10^{-4}, and, otherwise, default parameters and no regularization. The controller hidden state has size 100.

4.1 The Adding Problem

To evaluate the potential to learn long algorithms, we use a variant of the RNN Adding Problem described in [13]. In each step the network is fed with a control value of either -1, 0 or 1 and an input value ranged $[0, 1]$. If the control is 1, which always happens in exactly two of the steps, then the corresponding input value should be one of the operands in the sum. There are between 50 and 55 steps. With a 10,000 samples training set and a 1,000 samples test set, batch size of 100, and using a bidirectional GRU with the outputs connected to a fully connected linear regression layer, the cited author achieves the mean squared error of 0.0041 on the test set.

Using the GRPU, we feed only the control vector to the controller unit to avoid dependence between the induction of the algorithm and the processed data. The ALU also contains 3 operations, a READ operator that returns the control vector, an ADD operator and a PRODUCT operator. This means that each step has to choose to store the result of each of the 3 possible operations, or keep the previous argument, and to choose any combination of the 3 previous results as input for the operations, creating a very large search space with a program up to 55 instructions long. The output of the model is the result of the sum.

Table 3. Experiments. *Bidirectional GRU results from [13]

Configuration	1,000 epochs (training)	1,000 epochs (test)
Bidirectional GRU - batch 100 - 1,000 samples*	N/A	0.0041
GRPU - batch 100 - 10,000 samples	0.247	0.759
GRPU - batch 32 - 32,000 samples	0.0089	0.00699
GRPU - batch 10 - 10,000 samples	0.0000387	0.00709
GRPU - batch 10 - 10,000 samples - Varying number of steps	0.000426	0.000696
GRPU - batch 10 - 10,000 samples - (Multiplication Variant)	0.00616	0.0166
GRPU - batch 10 - 10,000 samples (Conditional Variant)	0.06	0.06

Table 3 shows that using the same batch size leads to very poor performance, indicating that the model is more prone to getting stuck in local minima. Either increasing the number of samples or reducing the batch size, which increases the stochastic effect, brings the results much closer to the more complex traditional model. Starting with just 10 steps and increasing the number up to the target throughout the epochs yields the best generalization.

4.2 Other Variations

Just changing the example above from addition to product, and changed the input range to $[0.5, 1.5]$, to prevent values frequently close to zero, allow us to evaluate the logic for the operations with neutral element one. The network behaved similarly, reducing the error to adequate levels after the 1,000 epochs, as seen on the Multiplication Variant on Table 3.

To test the conditional, we moved the control vector of the Adding Problem to the virtual machine, to be read on a second READ operator. It's also added a conditional operation that checks if it's input is 1, and if otherwise it forces a NOP in the step. This adds to 5 operations in the ALU, and the controller in this variation has no input besides it's state, and it's therefore incapable of choosing on it's own when to select the ADD operation and when to skip. This variation converges very fast, but gets easily stuck in a local minima worse than the original variant.

5 Conclusions and Future Work

Here, we presented a novel Neural Programming architecture that can help building a framework connecting neural networks and traditional programming. It has the potential of helping both models that write programs autonomously and users to integrate their logic within the neural network operation. The experiments have found some of the issues of previous neural programmer works: the convergence of such models is not trivial, possibly since the higher restriction on the search space may conduct to more local minima. More research in this area could provide better insights on the model behavior during training.

A number of further tests could be conducted in future works to better understand the potential of our model, such as tuning the hyper-parameters and ALU settings, adding regularization, experimenting with transfer learning and domain adaptation using the added transparency, evaluating deep GRPU models, and also techniques to extract efficient discrete algorithms.

References

1. Abadi, M., et al.: TensorFlow: large-scale machine learning on heterogeneous systems (2015). https://www.tensorflow.org/
2. Bahdanau, D., Cho, K., Bengio, Y.: Neural machine translation by jointly learning to align and translate. arXiv preprint arXiv:1409.0473 (2014)
3. Bengio, Y., Simard, P.Y., Frasconi, P.: Learning long-term dependencies with gradient descent is difficult. IEEE Trans. Neural Netw. **5**(2), 157–166 (1994)
4. Cho, K., et al.: Learning phrase representations using RNN encoder-decoder for statistical machine translation. In: Proceedings of the 2014 Conference on Empirical Methods in Natural Language Processing, pp. 1724–1734. ACL (2014)
5. Hochreiter, S., Schmidhuber, J.: Long short-term memory. Neural Comput. **9**(8), 1735–1780 (1997)
6. Klir, G.J., Yuan, B.: Fuzzy Sets and Fuzzy Logic: Theory and Applications. Prentice Hall, Upper Saddle River (1995)
7. Kurach, K., Andrychowicz, M., Sutskever, I.: Neural random access machines. ERCIM News **2016**(107) (2016)
8. Maclaurin, D., Duvenaud, D., Adams, R.P.: Autograd: effortless gradients in numpy (2015)
9. Neelakantan, A., Le, Q.V., Sutskever, I.: Neural programmer: inducing latent programs with gradient descent. CoRR abs/1511.04834 (2015). http://arxiv.org/abs/1511.04834
10. Reed, S.E., de Freitas, N.: Neural programmer-interpreters. CoRR abs/1511.06279 (2015). http://arxiv.org/abs/1511.06279
11. Vinyals, O., Fortunato, M., Jaitly, N.: Pointer networks. In: Advances in Neural Information Processing Systems (NIPS 2015), vol. 28, pp. 2692–2700 (2015)
12. Xu, K., et al.: Show, attend and tell: neural image caption generation with visual attention. In: Proceedings of the 32nd International Conference on Machine Learning, pp. 2048–2057 (2015)
13. Zhou, G.B., Wu, J., Zhang, C.L., Zhou, Z.H.: Minimal gated unit for recurrent neural networks. Int. J. Autom. Comput. **13**(3), 226–234 (2016)

Towards More Biologically Plausible Error-Driven Learning for Artificial Neural Networks

Kristína Malinovská(✉), Ľudovít Malinovský, and Igor Farkaš

Faculty of Mathematics, Physics and Informatics, Comenius University in Bratislava, Bratislava, Slovakia
{malinovska,farkas}@fmph.uniba.sk
http://cogsci.fmph.uniba.sk/cnc/

Abstract. Since the standard error backpropagation algorithm for supervised learning was shown biologically implausible, alternative models of training that use only local activation variables have been proposed. In this paper we present a novel algorithm called UBAL, inspired by the GeneRec model. We shortly describe the model and show the performance of the algorithm for XOR and 4-2-4 problems.

Keywords: Error-driven learning · Biological plausibility

In search for an alternative to error backpropagation [5], considered to be biologically implausible [1], O'Reilly proposed the GeneRec model [4]. Instead of propagating error values, neuron activation is propagated in GeneRec bidirectionally. The weight update is based on the difference in the net activation in the minus phase (producing output from input) and the plus phase (desired value is "clamped" on the output layer and the activation spread back to the hidden layer). Building on this principle, we proposed the BAL model [3] for bidirectional heteroassociative mappings, but failed to reach 100% convergence on the canonical 4-2-4 encoder task despite extensive experimental tuning [2]. As an improvement, we propose the Universal Bidirectional Activation-based Learning (UBAL) algorithm with additional learning parameters enabling the model to perform also unidirectional association tasks such as classification. As GeneRec, our model uses activation state differences, but with separate weight matrices M and W for each direction of activation flow. The activation is propagated in four phases (Fig. 1).
As outlined in Table 1, in the forward prediction phase FP, the input is presented to layer p and the activation spreads to layer q and vice versa for the backward prediction BP. Additionally, there are echo activation phases (FE and BE) in which the network's previous outputs q^{FP} and p^{BP} are echoed back to p and q through weights M and W, respectively.

The learning rule in Eqs. 1 and 2 takes as inputs intermediate terms t (target) and e (estimate) from Table 2.

V. Kůrková et al. (Eds.): ICANN 2018, LNCS 11141, pp. 228–231, 2018.
https://doi.org/10.1007/978-3-030-01424-7_23

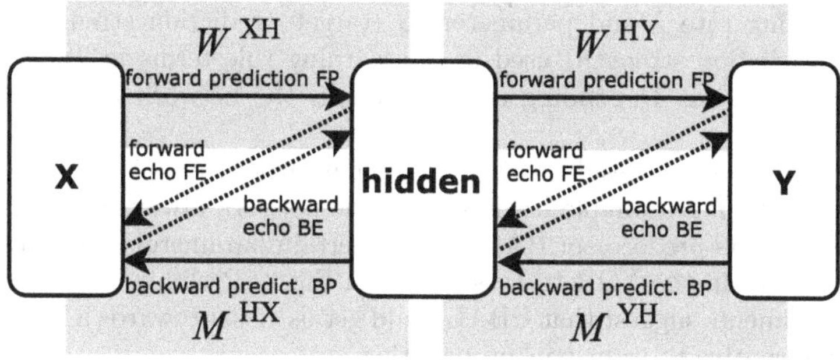

Fig. 1. Activation propagation in a network with input-output layers **x** and **y** and one hidden layer.

Table 1. Activation propagation rules, p and q denote two layers of the network connected by weight matrices W and M. Symbols b and d denote the biases and σ stands for the standard logistic activation function.

Direction and phase	Term	Value
Forward prediction	q_j^{FP}	$\sigma(\sum_i w_{ij} p_i^{\mathrm{FP}} + b_j)$
Forward echo	p_i^{FE}	$\sigma(\sum_j m_{ji} q_j^{\mathrm{FP}} + d_i)$
Backward prediction	p_i^{BP}	$\sigma(\sum_j m_{ji} q_j^{\mathrm{BP}} + d_i)$
Backward echo	q_j^{BE}	$\sigma(\sum_i w_{ij} p_i^{\mathrm{BP}} + b_j)$

Table 2. Definition of terms used in the learning rule.

Term name	Term	Value
Forward target	t_j^{F}	$\beta_q^{\mathrm{F}} q_j^{\mathrm{FP}} + (1 - \beta_q^{\mathrm{F}}) q_j^{\mathrm{BP}}$
Forward estimate	e_j^{F}	$\gamma_q^{\mathrm{F}} q_j^{\mathrm{FP}} + (1 - \gamma_q^{\mathrm{F}}) q_j^{\mathrm{BE}}$
Backward target	t_i^{B}	$\beta_p^{\mathrm{B}} p_i^{\mathrm{BP}} + (1 - \beta_p^{\mathrm{B}}) p_i^{\mathrm{FP}}$
Backward estimate	e_i^{B}	$\gamma_p^{\mathrm{B}} p_i^{\mathrm{BP}} + (1 - \gamma_p^{\mathrm{B}}) p_i^{\mathrm{FE}}$

$$\Delta w_{ij} = \lambda\ t_i^{\mathrm{B}} (t_j^{\mathrm{F}} - e_j^{\mathrm{F}}) \quad (1)$$

$$\Delta m_{ij} = \lambda\ t_j^{\mathrm{F}} (t_i^{\mathrm{B}} - e_i^{\mathrm{B}}) \quad (2)$$

The learning rate λ and parameters β (target prediction strength) and γ (estimate prediction strength) used in the learning rule terms in Table 2 drive the network learning. Depending on their values the network can accomplish different tasks.

In Fig. 2 we present results from experiments with the 4-2-4 encoder indicating that using a reasonable learning rate the network always converges to a solution. Unlike its predecessor BAL, given a certain parameter setup (Table 3), UBAL converges in the XOR task as shown in Fig. 3. Preliminary results from further experiments suggest that UBAL could get us closer towards a biologically plausible alternative to error backpropagation.

Table 3. Parameters β a γ in our experiments, $\beta^B = 1 - \beta^F$.

	4-2-4 Encoder	XOR
	X — H — Y	X — H — Y
β^{F}	1.0 – 0.5 – 0.0	0.01 – 1.0 – 0.0
γ^{F}	0.5 – 0.5	0.0 – 0.0
γ^{B}	0.5 – 0.5	0.0 – 0.0

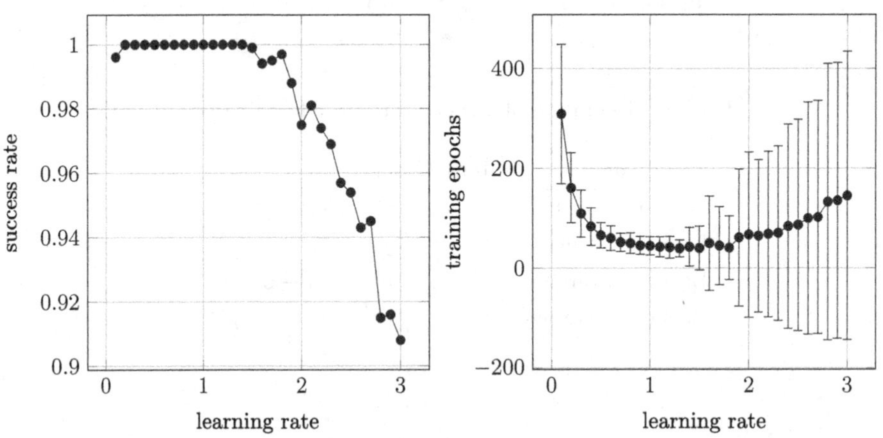

Fig. 2. Results from 4-2-4 encoder experiments with varying λ (1000 nets). Success rate indicates how many networks were able to learn the task with 100% accuracy.

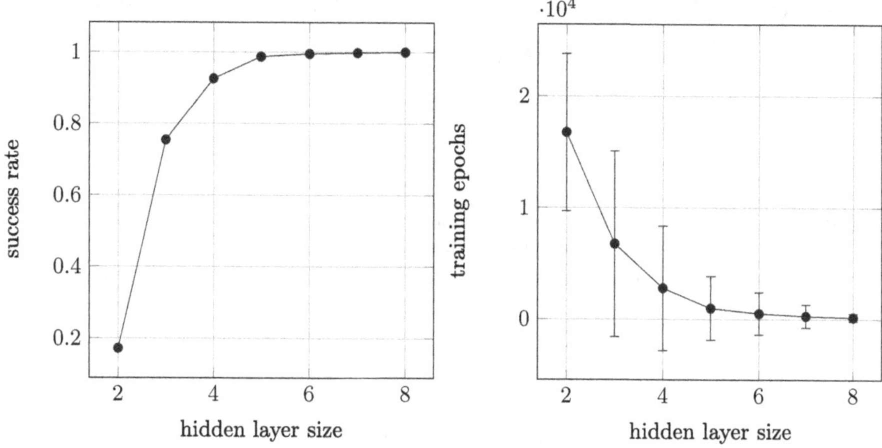

Fig. 3. Results from XOR experiments with varying hidden layer size (1000 nets) and $\lambda = 0.2$. Maximum training epochs: 20000.

Acknowledgment. This work was supported by grants VEGA 1/0796/18 and KEGA 017UK-4/2016.

References

1. Crick, F.: The recent excitement about neural networks. Nature **337**(6203), 129–132 (1989)
2. Csiba, P., Farkaš, I.: Computational analysis of the bidirectional activation-based learning in autoencoder task. In: International Joint Conference on Neural Networks (IJCNN), pp. 1–6. IEEE (2015)
3. Farkaš, I., Rebrová, K.: Bidirectional activation-based neural network learning algorithm. In: Mladenov, V., Koprinkova-Hristova, P., Palm, G., Villa, A.E.P., Appollini, B., Kasabov, N. (eds.) ICANN 2013. LNCS, vol. 8131, pp. 154–161. Springer, Heidelberg (2013). https://doi.org/10.1007/978-3-642-40728-4_20
4. O'Reilly, R.: Biologically plausible error-driven learning using local activation differences: the generalized recirculation algorithm. Neural Comput. **8**(5), 895–938 (1996)
5. Rumelhart, D., Hinton, G., Williams, R.: Learning Internal Representations by Error Propagation, pp. 318–362. no. 1. The MIT Press, Cambridge (1986)

Online Carry Mode Detection for Mobile Devices with Compact RNNs

Philipp Kuhlmann(✉), Paul Sanzenbacher, and Sebastian Otte

Cognitive Modeling Group Computer Science Department, University of Tübingen, Sand 14, 72076 Tübingen, Germany
kuhlmann.ph+icann18@gmail.com, sebastian.otte@uni-tuebingen.de

Abstract. Nowadays mobile devices are an essential part of our daily life. Especially fitness tracking application, which record our daily actions or exercise sessions, require a robust carry mode detection of the device. For a detailed and accurate analysis of the acquired data it is essential to know the relative position and thus the expected movement of the phone relative to the performed actions. On the other hand, it is important that such a detection is as energy-efficient as possible, which eliminates common deep convolutional approaches in advance. The contribution of this paper is twofold. First, we provide a mobile device carry mode data set, which currently consists of 6 h and 28 min of labeled accelerometer recordings. Second, we developed a robust online method to estimate the carry mode of such a device, which allows robust classification of long sequences of data based on compact Recurrent Neural Networks (RNNs), particularly Long Short-Term Memories (LSTMs). Our approach is generally applicable due to only requiring data from an accelerometer and is lightweight enough to run on small embedded devices. Specifically, we demonstrate that LSTMs can almost perfectly distinguish between the carry modes hand, bag and pocket.

Keywords: Mobile devices · RNN · LSTM · Carry mode detection

1 Introduction

Modern mobile devices contain a variety of sensors including accelerometer, gyroscope, magnetometer and GPS, to name just a few. While single sensors or combinations thereof fulfill essential functions such as estimating location or orientation of the device, they are also increasingly used in exercising or health applications. The broad availability of sensor data from a huge variety of sensors also allows for using machine learning techniques to extract all kinds of information. In particular, sequentially recorded sensor data can be processed using recurrent neural networks. We present an approach for classifying the carry mode of a mobile device using accelerometer data. The carry mode is classified into one of three categories *hands*, *bag* and *pocket* using a LSTM-based recurrent neural network [3]. Knowing the current carry mode can be useful for several

V. Kůrková et al. (Eds.): ICANN 2018, LNCS 11141, pp. 232–241, 2018.
https://doi.org/10.1007/978-3-030-01424-7_24

applications. For example, the time required to pick up the phone when it starts ringing depends on its location that is directly related to the carry mode. The carry mode information can therefore be used to notify the calling party so they can decide if it is worth waiting for the call to be picked up. Another example application is to use the carry mode as a safety measure. While a certain safety mode is activated, the phone is assumed to be in the bag or pocket. As soon as the hand carry mode is detected in that safety mode, an alarm can be triggered if somebody is trying to steal the device.

Previous works already explored the possibilities of using accelerometer measurements to estimate or classify external conditions. Hernandez et al. [2] used the accelerometer measurements to monitor physiological conditions like the heart or breath rate of the person carrying the devices. Additionally, they proved that the measurement is possible regardless of the carry mode of the phone but with significantly varying accuracy. Otte et al. [5] have demonstrated the potential of LSTM-based RNNs to classify the terrain type on which a mobile robot is driving by only evaluating the vibrations of the robot platform on the different terrain types. The aim of this paper, however, is to evaluate if and how well RNNs, particularly ones with relatively few parameters, are able to detect the current carry mode of the device in an online fashion, that is, without a time-window incrementally classifying each new time step of input data.

The paper is organized as follows. First, in Sect. 2 the dataset that we used in our experiments is introduced. Second, the applied RNN architecture is motivated and sketched out in Sect. 3. Third, our experimental results are presented and discussed in Sect. 4. Finally, Sect. 5 recapitulates this study and gives ideas for the next research steps.

2 Dataset

Alongside our work, we recorded our own extensive dataset[1] for training and verification purposes. The complete dataset was recorded by multiple persons using different mobile devices. A detailed composition of the recorded data is shown in Table 1.

Table 1. Composition of our recorded dataset that is used for training and verification.

Phone	# Datapoints	Total length	# Recordings by class		
			Pocket	Hands	Bag
Sony Xperia ZX1	555028	4:43:29	21	7	5
HTC M8 One	60087	36:04	5	4	2
OnePlus 5T	106782	58:35	4	3	0
Total	721897	6:28:09	30	14	7

[1] Available under: http://cm.inf.uni-tuebingen.de.

2.1 Acquisition

For recording of the training and validation sequences, an Android application is used that offers the user the possibility to select the carry mode and add an optional comment in case there are some unexpected irregularities in the recording. A single sequence is created by pressing a start button at the beginning and a stop button at the end. After a sequence is recorded, the application encodes the data as JSON object and uploads it to a server, where it is stored in a database. If the upload fails, e.g., due to missing internet connectivity, the data is stored on-device and can be re-uploaded as soon as a connection is established again.

The recorded data includes the raw accelerometer data, consisting of the x, y, z acceleration of the mobile device in the device's local coordinate system and the time-stamp of each sample. The time-stamp is used to detect and account for deviations from the requested sampling rate of 50 Hz.

Each recording is tagged with the associated carry mode. We distinguish between *bag*, *hands*, and *pocket*, which are the most commonly used methods for carrying a mobile device and which have significantly different characteristics.

Most of the data was recorded during the everyday usage of the mobile devices, while some recordings were specially crafted to cover edge cases. To prevent over-fitting we tried to vary the device's orientation and location between each recording. Figure 1 shows example extracts from different recordings.

2.2 Dataset Preparation

For training, sequences of length 100 or 200 were extracted from the recordings. Since especially for the *pocket* and *bag* carry modes the mobile device is not carried in the expected mode at the beginning and at the end of the recorded sequence, it is cut at both ends by three seconds.

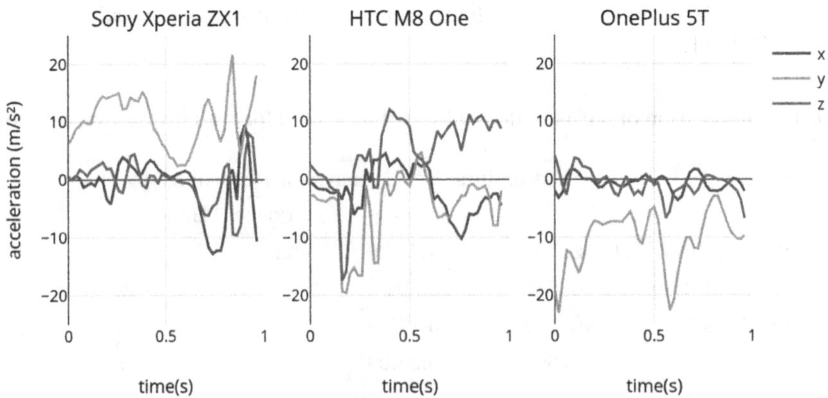

Fig. 1. Extracts of sequences recorded in carry mode *pocket* for three different devices. All extracts contain 50 samples which corresponds to one second.

3 Recurrent Neural Networks

Due to their cyclic connections RNNs are able to learn temporal dependencies in data sequences, whereas feed-forward networks can only learn static pattern mappings. In contrast to traditional RNNs, the before mentioned LSTM model [3], which can be seen as a differentiable memory cell, overcomes the problem of vanishing gradients. LSTMs are capable to handle even very long time lags up to 10 000 time steps. Due to this and other capabilities, e.g., precise timing, precise value reproduction, or counting, LSTM-like RNNs unleash an impressive learning potential and are the de-facto standard for sequential learning tasks. Note that we applied specific RNN regularization [8]. Prior to classification we may optionally apply some preprocessing steps to prepare the data for the network.

3.1 Data Preprocessing

The preprocessing consists of multiple steps depending on the mode of operation. First of all the input data is split into multiple sequences of length n. The value of n depends on whether we are training or evaluating the model. When evaluating the model we use $n = N$, where N is the total length of the recording.

The second step is an optional dimensionality reduction via principle component analysis. The reduction was intended to prevent over-fitting on the device orientation, which can normally be detected due to the gravity acceleration. Nevertheless the evaluation has shown that the network does not over-fit on the data and the dimensionality reduction significantly reduces the information for the network.

Lastly, we have to take care of all three classification categories to be equally represented in the training dataset in order to prevent over-fitting on one category. Therefore we select only an equally sized subset of sequences for each category from the available input data.

3.2 RNN Architecture

The input is fed into three convolution layers with kernel sizes $k = 1, 3, 5$, performing a convolution along the temporal axis of our input data stream. The outputs of the convolutional layers are concatenated and then used as input to each cell of our LSTM block, resulting in a sequence of 9 samples per time step. Each sample of the concatenated sequence is fed into an LSTM block consisting of $c = 50$ parallel independent LSTM cells. Also the only recurrent connections are within this block. Each LSTM cell receives the concatenated input and the recurrent output from every other cell. The output from each LSTM cell is connected to a fully connected layer with 20 neurons that uses a leaky ReLU activation function. The category mapping is achieved through a final fully connected layer with a softmax output function, resulting in a probability for each output category. An overview over the complete network structure is shown in Fig. 2. The network comprises a total of 13,173 trainable parameters.

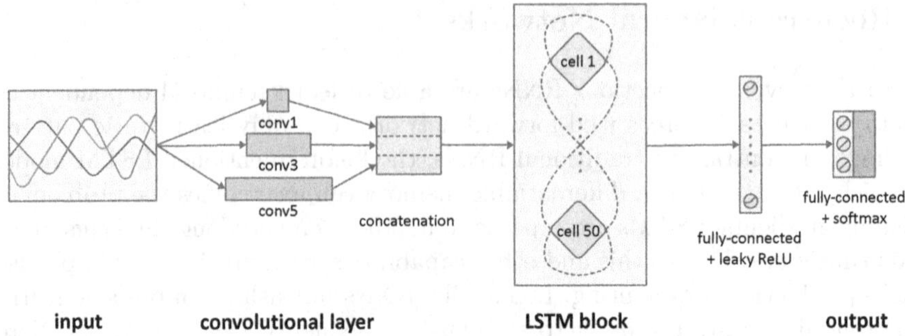

Fig. 2. Network architecture consisting of multiple parallel temporal convolutions of different size, an LSTM block with multiple independent LSTM cells, and a fully-connected layer followed by a softmax function.

3.3 Training

Given the ground-truth one-hot vectors for each input sequence, the cross-entropy is minimized between the ground truth and the output of the network via Back-Propagation Through Time (BPTT) [6]. For optimization, we use the Adam optimizer [4] with a constant learning rate of $\eta = 10^{-5}$ and default parameters $\beta_1 = 0.9$, $\beta_2 = 0.999$, and $\varepsilon = 10^{-3}$.

3.4 Implementation Details

The network architecture as well as the training and testing procedures are implemented in TensorFlow [1] and using Tensorpack as a training interface [7]. Although TensorFlow is not particularly efficient when it comes to training recurrent neural networks with low-dimensional sequences, it allows for fast prototyping and for models to be exported and run on mobile devices using TensorFlow Lite[2]. The preprocessing is performed online, as it does not require much computation time.

4 Experimental Results

4.1 Network Configurations

In order to find a suitable network architecture for achieving a high accuracy and fast convergence, several network components were added and explored. Using a single LSTM block is sufficient for achieving a high validation accuracy, whereas using two successive blocks drastically slows down the training process without increasing the overall accuracy. Appending additional fully-connected layers after the LSTM block can increase the convergence speed. However, they do in general not increase the final accuracy. Applying several parallel convolutional

[2] https://www.tensorflow.org/mobile/tflite/.

layers with different sizes of receptive fields allows the network to extract the most important local information from the input sequences and can also help to smoothen out high-frequency noise. We found out that the convolutional layers are especially helpful when training the architecture using data from multiple different devices, as the acceleration sensors in the devices have different noise characteristics.

4.2 Results

The network architecture (see Fig. 2) was trained on two datasets containing sequences from three devices and one single device respectively. The training results and accuracies are listed in Table 2.

Table 2. Accuracies for different datasets and number of sequences on the training and validation set.

Dataset	Devices	Size	Training accuracy	Validation accuracy
1	3	1497 Sequences	0.994	0.984
2	1	753 Sequences	0.998	0.987

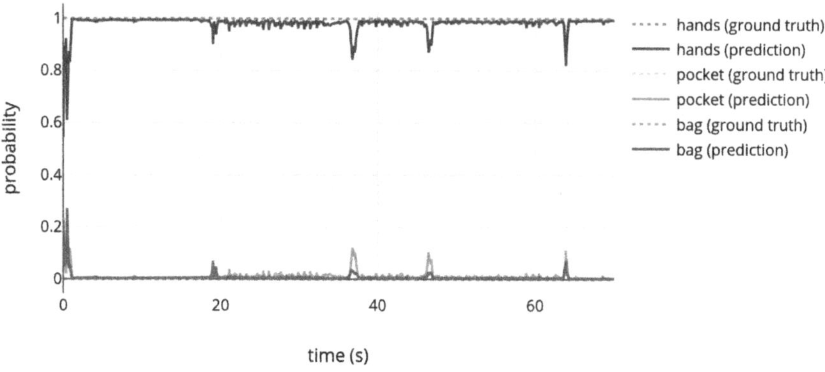

Fig. 3. Classification example of a sequence of the *hands* class.

Since the acceleration sensors in mobile devices have different signal characteristics, it is important to have a uniform distribution of training data across the different devices and carry modes in order for the model to generalize adequately. We can show that training the network on data from a single device can further increase the classification accuracy, as it can adapt to these specific sensor characteristics. Another significant observation we made is that the hand carry mode is detected a lot better than the other carry modes. This is because

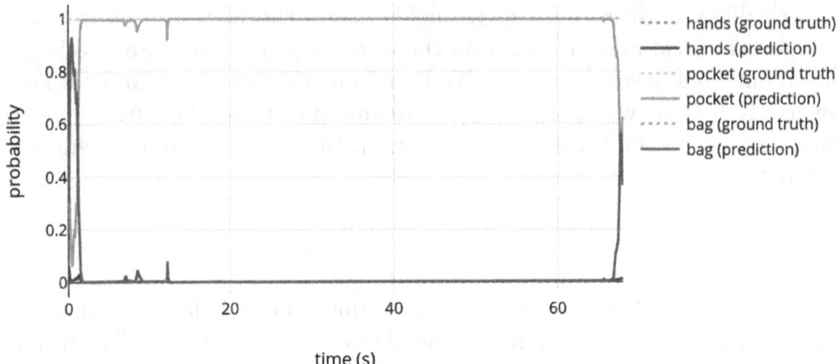

Fig. 4. Classification example of a sequence of the *pocket* class.

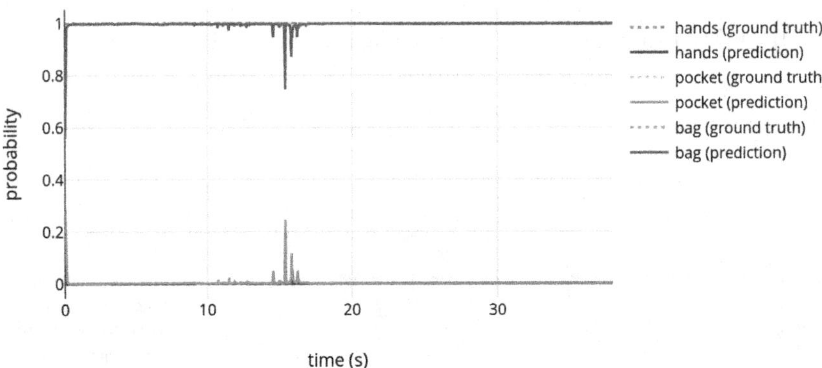

Fig. 5. Classification example of an sequence of the *bag* class. Although the classification is generally correct, the noise level is much higher than the results for the other two classes.

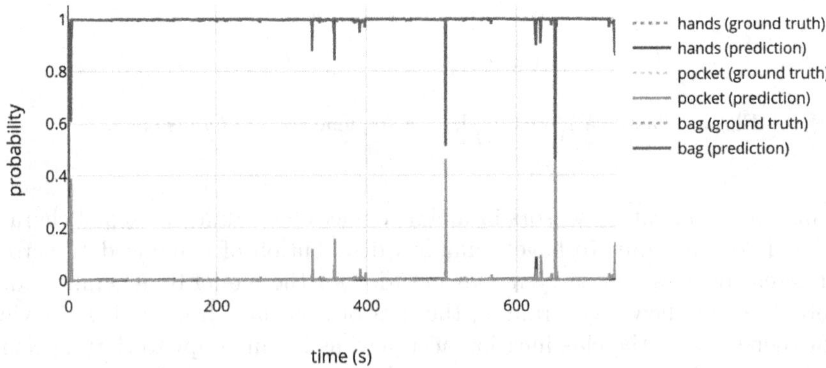

Fig. 6. Classification example of an sequence of the *bag* class, which shows that the classification remains stable despite the long sequence length of over 10 min with over 36000 samples.

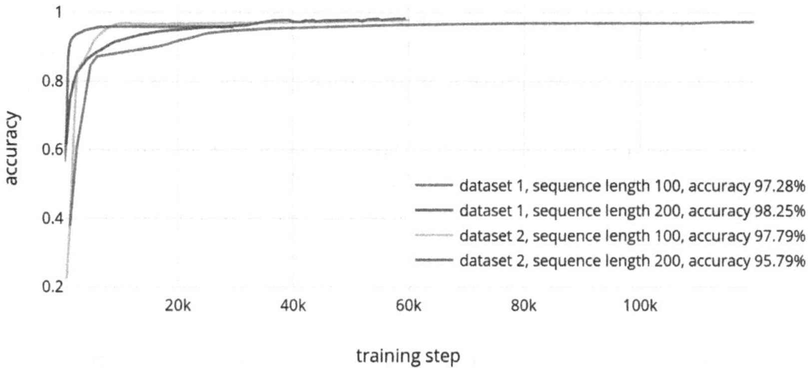

Fig. 7. Comparison of convergence rates of the two datasets with different training sequence lengths. The different sample sizes for each curve result from the dataset sizes as well as from the number of epochs depending on the sequence length.

the transition between the bag and the pocket carry mode is not as clear as between the hand carry mode and the others. While the mobile device follows a characteristic movement pattern when carried in a pocket or a bag, the movement is damped when carried in the hands. Classified example sequences for each class are shown in Figs. 3, 4, and 5. Figure 6 shows that the classification remains stable even when processing long sequences.

We tested several different options for the sequence length for our training input, where 100 and 200 proved to yield the best results. On the one hand, the longer sequence length with a length of 200 time steps achieves significantly better results on the diverse dataset 1 that contains data captured from multiple devices. On the other hand, if the data is relatively uniform a longer sequence length does not improve the results. Nonetheless, the final accuracy is lower, but the convergence is still faster. The convergence rates can be seen in Fig. 7.

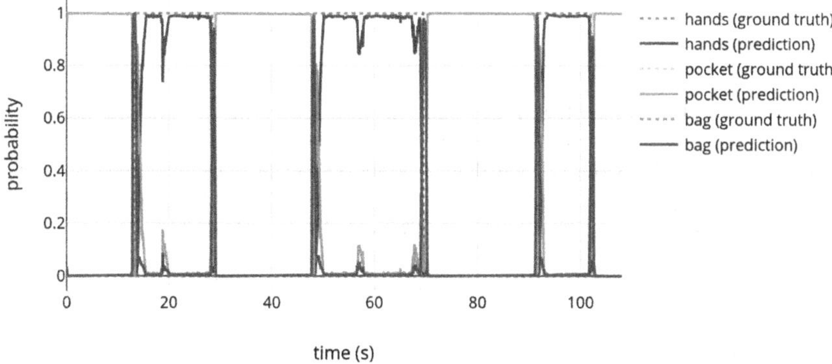

Fig. 8. Classification output of the RNN facing altering class transitions.

Finally, we investigated the behavior at class transitions, which is an important aspect when using RNNs in a continuous classification scenario without clear class boundaries. We found that in any case the RNNs were able to catch the class transitions successfully. We think that this might run out-of-the-box because of the applied regularization [8]. Figure 8 exemplary shows that the reference network is clearly able to detect the transitions between the altering classes hands and pocket rapidly. Note that the ability of catching class transitions

5 Conclusion

We have shown that LSTM-based RNNs are a robust and easily implementable way to reliably detect the carry mode of mobile devices. The results indicate that this task is heavily impacted by the device model.

Compared to other possible (deep learning) approaches our specific network architecture is relatively lightweight (≈13,000 parameters) but still achieved a very high detection rate of nearly 99 % on our carry mode dataset with three classes. We also proved that a step-by-step online detection is feasible for which no large time-window (as e.g. for spectral transformation-based approaches) is necessary.

Further work can explore a more diverse set of carry modes and try to stabilize long input sequences, which are generally a weak point of generic LSTM networks. Nonetheless our architecture kept stable even over 10,000 s time-steps of continuous classification.

Additionally, the work can be extended to also estimate the actual movement performed by the person carrying the devices with the help of the predicted carry mode. It is also thinkable to randomly skip time-steps in order to further improve the energy efficiency.

Acknowledgements. We would like to thank Denis Heid and Florian Grimm for testing the dataset recording application and for their effort in collecting a diverse dataset in many different real-life scenarios.

References

1. Abadi, M., et al.: TensorFlow: large-scale machine learning on heterogeneous systems (2015). https://www.tensorflow.org/
2. Hernandez, J., McDuff, D.J., Picard, R.W.: Biophone: physiology monitoring from peripheral smartphone motions. In: 2015 37th Annual International Conference of the IEEE Engineering in Medicine and Biology Society (EMBC), pp. 7180–7183. IEEE (2015)
3. Hochreiter, S., Schmidhuber, J.: Long short-term memory. Neural Comput. **9**(8), 1735–1780 (1997). https://doi.org/10.1162/neco.1997.9.8.1735
4. Kingma, D.P., Ba, J.L.: Adam: a method for stochastic optimization. In: 3rd International Conference for Learning Representations (2015)

5. Otte, S., Weiss, C., Scherer, T., Zell, A.: Recurrent neural networks for fast and robust vibration-based ground classification on mobile robots. In: 2016 IEEE International Conference on Robotics and Automation (ICRA), pp. 5603–5608. IEEE (2016)
6. Werbos, P.J.: Backpropagation through time: what it does and how to do it. Proc. IEEE **78**(10), 1550–1560 (1990)
7. Wu, Y., et al.: Tensorpack (2016). https://github.com/tensorpack/
8. Zaremba, W., Sutskever, I., Vinyals, O.: Recurrent neural network regularization. arXiv preprint arXiv:1409.2329 (2014)

Deep Learning

Deep CNN-ELM Hybrid Models for Fire Detection in Images

Jivitesh Sharma(✉), Ole-Christopher Granmo, and Morten Goodwin

Center for Artificial Intelligence Research, University of Agder, Jon Lilletuns vei 9, 4879 Grimstad, Norway
{jivitesh.sharma,ole.granmo,morten.goodwin}@uia.no

Abstract. In this paper, we propose a hybrid model consisting of a Deep Convolutional feature extractor followed by a fast and accurate classifier, the Extreme Learning Machine, for the purpose of fire detection in images. The reason behind using such a model is that Deep CNNs used for image classification take a very long time to train. Even with pre-trained models, the fully connected layers need to be trained with backpropagation, which can be very slow. In contrast, we propose to employ the Extreme Learning Machine (ELM) as the final classifier trained on pre-trained Deep CNN feature extractor. We apply this hybrid model on the problem of fire detection in images. We use state of the art Deep CNNs: VGG16 and Resnet50 and replace the softmax classifier with the ELM classifier. For both the VGG16 and Resnet50, the number of fully connected layers is also reduced. Especially in VGG16, which has 3 fully connected layers of 4096 neurons each followed by a softmax classifier, we replace two of these with an ELM classifier. The difference in convergence rate between fine-tuning the fully connected layers of pre-trained models and training an ELM classifier are enormous, around 20x to 51x speed-up. Also, we show that using an ELM classifier increases the accuracy of the system by 2.8% to 7.1% depending on the CNN feature extractor. We also compare our hybrid architecture with another hybrid architecture, i.e. the CNN-SVM model. Using SVM as the classifier does improve accuracy compared to state-of-the-art deep CNNs. But our Deep CNN-ELM model is able to outperform the Deep CNN-SVM models. (Preliminary version of some of the results of this paper appear in "Deep Convolutional Neural Networks for Fire Detection in Images", Springer Proceedings Engineering Applications of Neural Networks 2017 (EANN'17), Athens, Greece, 25–27 August).

Keywords: Deep convolutional neural networks
Extreme learning machine · Image classification · Fire detection

1 Introduction

The problem of fire detection in images has received a lot of attention in the past by researchers from computer vision, image processing and deep learning.

V. Kůrková et al. (Eds.): ICANN 2018, LNCS 11141, pp. 245–259, 2018.
https://doi.org/10.1007/978-3-030-01424-7_25

This is a problem that needs to be solved without any compromise. Fire can cause massive and irrevocable damage to health, life and property. It has led to over a 1000 deaths a year in the US alone, with property damage in access of one billion dollars. Besides, the fire detectors currently in use require different kinds of expensive hardware equipment for different types of fire [27].

What makes this problem even more interesting is the changing background environment due to varying luminous intensity of the fire, fire of different shades, different sizes etc. Also, the false alarms due to the environment resembling fire pixels, like room with bright red/orange background and bright lights. Furthermore, the probability of occurrence of fire is quite low, so the system must be trained to handle imbalance classification.

Various techniques have been used to classify between images that contain fire and images that do not. The state-of-the-art vision-based techniques for fire and smoke detection have been comprehensively evaluated and compared in [39]. The colour analysis technique has been widely used in the literature to detect and analyse fire in images and videos [4,24,31,37]. On top of colour analysis, many novel methods have been used to extract high level features from fire images like texture analysis [4], dynamic temporal analysis with pixel-level filtering and spatial analysis with envelope decomposition and object labelling [40], fire flicker and irregular fire shape detection with wavelet transform [37], etc.

These techniques give adequate performance but are currently outperformed by Machine Learning techniques. A comparative analysis between colour-based models for extraction of rules and a Machine Learning algorithm is done for the fire detection problem in [36]. The machine learning technique used in [36] is Logistic Regression which is one of the simplest techniques in Machine Learning and still outperforms the colour-based algorithms in almost all scenarios. These scenarios consist of images containing different fire pixel colours of different intensities, with and without smoke.

Instead of explicitly designing features by using image processing techniques, deep neural networks can be used to extract and learn relevant features from images. The Convolutional Neural Networks (CNNs) are the most suitable choice for the task of image processing and classification.

In this paper, we employ state-of-the-art Deep CNNs for fire detection and then propose to use hybrid CNN-ELM and CNN-SVM models to outperform Deep CNNs. Such hybrid models have been used in the past for image classification, but the novelty of our approach lies in using state-of-the-art Deep CNNs like VGG16 and Resnet50 as feature extractors and then remove some/all fully connected layers with an ELM classifier. This models outperform Deep CNNs in terms of accuracy, training time and size of the network. We also compare the CNN-ELM model with another hybrid model, CNN-SVM and show that the CNN-ELM model gives the best performance.

The rest of the paper is organized in the following manner: Sect. 2 briefly describes the related work with CNNs for fire detection and Hybrid models for image classification. Section 3 explains our work in detail and Sect. 4 gives details of our experiments and presents the results. Section 5 summarizes and concludes our work.

2 Related Work

In this paper, we integrate state-of-the-art CNN hybrid models and apply it to the problem of fire detection in images. To the best of our knowledge, hybrid models have never been applied to fire detection. So, we present a brief overview of previous research done in CNNs used for fire detection and hybrid models separately in the next two sub-sections.

2.1 CNNs for Fire Detection

There have been many significant contributions from various researchers in developing a system that can accurately detect fire in the surrounding environment. But, the most notable research in this field involves Deep Convolutional Neural Networks (Deep CNN). Deep CNN models are currently among the most successful image classification models which makes them ideal for a task such as Fire detection in images. This has been demonstrated by previous research published in this area.

In [7], the authors use CNN for detection of fire and smoke in videos. A simple sequential CNN architecture, similar to LeNet-5 [18], is used for classification. The authors quote a testing accuracy of 97.9% with a satisfactory false positive rate.

Whereas in [43], a very innovative cascaded CNN technique is used to detect fire in an image, followed by fine-grained localisation of patches in the image that contain the fire pixels. The cascaded CNN consists of AlexNet CNN architecture [17] with pre-trained ImageNet weights [28] and another small network after the final pooling layer which extracts patch features and labels the patches which contain fire. Different patch classifiers are compared.

The AlexNet architecture is also used in [34] which is used to detect smoke in images. It is trained on a fairly large dataset containing smoke and non-smoke images for a considerably long time. The quoted accuracies for large and small datasets are 96.88% and 99.4% respectively with relatively low false positive rates.

Another paper that uses the AlexNet architecture is [23]. This paper builds its own fire image and video dataset by simulating fire in images and videos using Blender. It adds fire to frames by adding fire properties like shadow, fore-ground fire, mask etc. separately. The animated fire and video frames are composited using OpenCV [2]. The model is tested on real world images. The results show reasonable accuracy with high false positive rate.

As opposed to CNNs which extract features directly from raw images, in some methods image/video features are extracted using image processing techniques and then given as input to a neural network. Such an approach has been used in [6]. The fire regions from video frames are obtained by threshold values in the HSV colour space. The general characteristics of fire are computed using these values from five continuous frames and their mean and standard deviation is given as input to a neural network which is trained using back propagation to identify forest fire regions. This method performs segmentation of images very accurately and the results show high accuracy and low false positive rates.

In [11], a neural network is used to extract fire features based on the HSI colour model which gives the fire area in the image as output. The next step is fire area segmentation where the fire areas are roughly segmented and spurious fire areas like fire shadows and fire-like objects are removed by image difference. After this the change in shape of fire is estimated by taking contour image difference and white pixel ratio to estimate the burning degree of fire, i.e. no-fire, small, medium and large. The experimental results show that the method is able to detect different fire scenarios with relatively good accuracy.

2.2 Hybrid Models for Image Classification

The classifier part in a Deep CNN is a simple fully connected perceptron with a softmax layer at the end to output probabilities for each class. This section of the CNN has a high scope for improvement. Since it consists of three to four fully connected layers containing thousands of neurons, it becomes harder and slower to train it. Even with pre-trained models that require fine tuning of these layers. This has led to the development of hybrid CNN models, which consist of a specialist classifier at the end.

Some of the researchers have employed the Support Vector Machine (SVM) as the final stage classifier [1,21,25,33,38]. In [25], the CNN-SVM hybrid model is applied to many different problems like object classification, scene classification, bird sub-categorization, flower recognition etc. A linear SVM is fed 'off the shelf convolutional features' from the last layer of the CNN. This paper uses the OverFeat network [30] which is a state-of-the-art object classification model. The paper shows, with exhaustive experimentation, that extraction of convolutional features by a deep CNN is the best way to obtain relevant characteristics that distinguishes an entity from another.

The CNN-SVM model is used in [21] and successfully applied to visual learning and recognition for multi-robot systems and problems like human-swarm interaction and gesture recognition. This hybrid model has also been applied to gender recognition in [38]. The CNN used here is the AlexNet [17] pre-trained with ImageNet weights. The features extracted from the entire AlexNet are fed to an SVM classifier. A similar kind of research is done in [33], where the softmax layer and the cross-entropy loss are replaced by a linear SVM and margin loss. This model is tested on some of the most well known benchmark datasets like CIFAR-10, MNIST and Facial Expression Recognition challenge. The results show that this model outperforms the conventional Deep CNNs.

In 2006, G.B. Huang introduced a new learning algorithm for a single hidden layer feedforward neural network called the Extreme Learning Machine [13,14]. This technique was many times faster than backpropagation and SVM, and outperformed them on various tasks. The ELM randomly initializes the input weights and analytically determines the output weights. It produces a minimum norm least squares solution which always achieves lowest training accuracy, if there are enough number of hidden neurons. There have been many variants of ELM depending upon a specific application, which have been summarised in [12].

This led to the advent of CNN-ELM hybrid models, which were able to outperform the CNN-SVM models on various applications. The major advantage of CNN-ELM models is the speed of convergence. In [29], the CNN-ELM model is used for Wireless Capsule Endoscopy (WCE) image classification. The softmax classifier of a CNN is replaced by an ELM classifier and trained on the feature extracted by the CNN feature extractor. This model is able to outperform CNN-based classifiers.

The CNN-ELM model has also been used for handwritten digit classification [19,22]. In [19], a 'shallow' CNN is used for feature extraction and ELM for classification. The shallow CNN together with ELM speeds up the training process. Also, various weight initialization strategies have been tested for ELM with different receptive fields. Finally, two strategies, namely the Constrained ELM (C-ELM) [44] and Computed Input Weights ELM (CIW-ELM) [35] are combined in a two layer ELM structure with receptive fields. This model was tested on the MNIST dataset and achieved 0.83% testing error. In [22], a deep CNN is used for the same application and tested on the USPS dataset.

A shallow CNN with ELM is tested on some benchmark datasets like MNIST, NORB-small, CIFAR-10 and SVHN with various hyper parameter configurations in [20]. Another similar hybrid model that uses CNN features and Kernel ELM as classifier is used in [9] for age estimation using facial features. Another application where a CNN-ELM hybrid model has been applied is the traffic sign recognition [41].

A different strategy of combining CNN feature extraction and ELM learning is proposed in [15]. Here, an ELM with single hidden layer is inserted after every convolution and pooling layer and at the end as classifier. The ELM is trained by borrowing values from the next convolutional layer and each ELM is updated after every iteration using backpropagation. This interesting architecture is applied to the application of lane detection and achieves excellent performance.

A comparative analysis of the CNN-ELM and CNN-SVM hybrid models for object recognition from ImageNet has been illustrated in [42]. Both these models were tested for object recognition from different sources like Amazon, Webcam, Caltech and DSLR. The final results show that the CNN-ELM model outperforms the CNN-SVM model on all datasets and using Kernel ELM further increases accuracy.

Using ELM as a final stage classifier does not end at image classification with CNNs. They have also been used with DBNs for various applications [3,26].

3 The Fire Detector

In this paper, we propose to employ hybrid deep CNN models to perform fire detection. The AlexNet has been used by researchers in the past for fire detection which has produced satisfactory results. We propose to use two Deep CNN architectures that have outperformed the AlexNet on the ImageNet dataset, namely VGG16 [32] and Resnet50 [10]. We use these models with pre-trained ImageNet weights. This helps greatly when there is lack of training data. So, we fine-tune the ELM classifier on our dataset, which is fed the features extracted by the Deep CNNs.

3.1 Deep ConvNet Models

The Convolutional Neural Network was first introduced in 1980 by Kunihiko Fukushima [8]. The CNN is designed to take advantage of two dimensional structures like 2D Images and capture local spatial patterns. This is achieved with local connections and tied weights. It consists of one or more convolution layers with pooling layers between them, followed by one or more fully connected layers, as in a standard multilayer perceptron. CNNs are easier to train compared to Deep Neural Networks because they have fewer parameters and local receptive fields.

In CNNs, kernels/filters are used to see where particular features are present in an image by convolution with the image. The size of the filters gives rise to locally connected structure which are each convolved with the image to produce feature maps. The feature maps are usually sub-sampled using mean or max pooling. The reduction in parameters is due to the fact that convolution layers share weights.

The reason behind parameter sharing is that we make an assumption, that the statistics of a patch of a natural image are the same as any other patch of the image. This suggests that features learned at one location can also be learned for other locations. So, we can apply this learned feature detector anywhere in the image. This makes CNNs ideal feature extractors for images.

The CNNs with many layers have been used for various applications especially image classification. In this paper, we use two state-of-the-art Deep CNNs that have achieved one of the lowest error rates in image classification tasks.

In this work, we use VGG16 and Resnet50, pre-trained on the ImageNet dataset, along with a few modifications. We also compare our modified and hybrid models with the original ones. The VGG16 architecture was proposed by the Visual Geometry Group at the University of Oxford [32], which was deep, simple, sequential network whereas the Resnet50, proposed by Microsoft research [10], was an extremely deep graphical network with residual connections (which avoids the vanishing gradients problem and residual functions are easier to train).

We also test slightly modified versions of both these networks by adding a fully-connected layer and fine-tuning on our dataset. We also tested with more fully connected layers but the increase in accuracy was overshadowed by the increase in training time.

3.2 The Hybrid Model

We propose to use a hybrid architecture for fire detection in images. In this paper, instead of using a simple CNN as feature extractor, we employ state-of-the-art Deep CNNs like the VGG16 and Resnet50.

Figure 1(a) and (b) show the architecture of the VGG16-ELM and Resnet50-ELM hybrid models respectively. Usually, only the softmax classifier is replaced by another classifier (ELM or SVM) in a CNN to create a hybrid model. But, we go one step further by replacing the entire fully connected multi-layer perceptron with a single hidden layer ELM. This decreases the complexity of the model even further.

The Theory of Extreme Learning Machine: The Extreme Learning Machine is a supervised learning algorithm [13]. The input to the ELM, in this case, are the features extracted by the CNNs. Let it be represented as x_i, t_i, where x_i is the input feature instance and t_i is the corresponding class of the image. The inputs are connected to the hidden layer by randomly assigned weights w. The product of the inputs and their corresponding weights act as inputs to the hidden layer activation function. The hidden layer activation function is a non-linear non-constant bounded continuous infinitely differentiable function that maps the input data to the feature space. There is a catalogue of activation functions from which we can choose according to the problem at hand. We ran experiments for all activation functions and the best performance was achieved with the multiquadratics function:

$$f(x) = \sqrt{\|x_i - \mu_i\|^2 + a^2} \tag{1}$$

The hidden layer and the output layer are connected via weights β, which are to be analytically determined. The mapping from the feature space to the output space is linear. Now, with the inputs, hidden neurons, their activation functions, the weights connecting the inputs to the hidden layer and the output weights produce the final output function:

$$\sum_{i=1}^{L} \beta_i g(w_i.x_j + b_i) = o_j \tag{2}$$

The output in Matrix form is:

$$H\beta = T \tag{3}$$

The error function used in Extreme Learning Machine is the Mean Squared error function, written as:

$$E = \sum_{j=1}^{N} (\sum_{i=1}^{L} \beta_i g(w_i.x_j + b_i) - t_j)^2 \tag{4}$$

To minimize the error, we need to get the least-squares solution of the above linear system.

$$\|H\beta^* - T\| = min_\beta \|H\beta - T\| \tag{5}$$

The minimum norm least-squares solution to the above linear system is given by:

$$\hat{\beta} = H^{\dagger}T \tag{6}$$

Properties of the above solution:

1. *Minimum Training Error:* The following equation provides the least-squares solution, which means the solution for $\|H\beta - T\|$, i.e. the error is minimum. $\|H\beta^{*} - T\| = min_{\beta}\|H\beta - T\|$
2. *Smallest Norm of Weights:* The minimum norm of least-squares solution is given by the Moore-Penrose pseudo inverse of H. $\hat{\beta} = H^{\dagger}T$
3. *Unique Solution:* The minimum norm least-squares solution of $H\beta = T$ is unique, which is: $\hat{\beta} = H^{\dagger}T$

Detailed mathematical proofs of these properties and the ELM algorithm can be found in [14]. Both the VGG16 and Resnet50 extract rich features from the images. These features are fed to the ELM classifier which finds the minimum norm least squares solution. With enough number of hidden neurons, the ELM outperforms the original VGG16 and Resnet50 networks. Both VGG16 and Resnet50 are pre-trained with ImageNet weights. So, only the ELM classifier is trained on the features extracted by the CNNs.

Apart from fast training and accurate classification, there is another advantage of this model. This hybrid model does not require large training data. In fact, our dataset consists of just 651 images, out of which the ELM is trained on 60% of images only. This shows its robustness towards lack of training data. A normal Deep CNN would require much higher amount of training data to fine-tune its fully-connected layers and the softmax classifier. Even the pre-trained VGG16 and Resnet50 models required at least 80% training data to fine-tune their fully-connected layers.

And, as we will show in the next section, a hybrid CNN-ELM trained with 60% training data outperforms pre-trained VGG16 and Resnet50, fine-tuned on 80% training data.

3.3 Paper Contributions

1. The previous hybrid models have used simple CNNs for feature extraction. We employ state-of-the-art Deep CNNs to make feature extraction more efficient and obtain relevant features since the dataset is difficult to classify.
2. Other hybrid models simply replace the softmax classifier with SVM or sometimes ELM. We completely remove the fully connected layers to increase speed of convergence since no fine-tuning is needed and also reduce the complexity of the architecture. Since VGG16 and Resnet50 extract rich features and the ELM is an accurate classifier, we do not need the fully-connected layers. This decreases the number of layers by 2 in VGG16 and by 1 in Resnet50, which is 8192 and 4096 neurons respectively.

3. The above point also justifies the use of complex features extractors like VGG16 and Resnet50. If we used a simple CNN then, we might not be able to remove the fully-connected layers since the features might not be rich enough. Due to this, the fully-connected layers would have to be fine-tuned on the dataset which would increase training time and network complexity.
4. Also, we see that the data required for training the ELM classifier is lower than the data required for fine-tuning the fully-connected layers of a pre-trained Deep CNN.
5. We apply our hybrid model on the problem of fire detection in images (on our own dataset). And, to the best of our knowledge, this is the first time a hybrid ELM model has been applied to this problem.

4 Experiments

We conducted our experiments to compare training and testing accuracies and execution times of: the VGG16 and Resnet50 models including modifications, Hybrid VGG16 and Resnet50 models with ELM classifier. We also compare our hybrid VGG16-ELM and Resnet50-ELM models with VGG16-SVM and Resnet50-SVM as well. We used pre-trained Keras [5] models and fine-tune the fully-connected layers on our dataset. The training of the models was done on the following hardware specifications: Intel i5 2.5 GHz, 8 GB RAM and Nvidia Geforce GTX 820 2 GB GPU. Each model was trained on the dataset for 10 training epochs. The ADAM optimizer [16] with default parameters $\alpha = 0.001$, $\beta_1 = 0.9$, $\beta_2 = 0.999$ and $\epsilon = 10^{-8}$ was used to fine-tune the fully-connected layers for VGG16 and Resnet50 and their modified versions. The details of the dataset are given in the next subsection.

4.1 The Real World Fire Dataset

Since there is no benchmark dataset for fire detection in images, we created our own dataset by handpicking images from the internet.[1] This dataset consists of 651 images which is quite small in size but it enables us to test the generalization capabilities and the effectiveness and efficiency of models to extract relevant features from images when training data is scarce. The dataset is divided into training and testing sets. The training set consists of 549 images: 59 fire images and 490 non-fire images. The imbalance is deliberate to replicate real world situations, as the probability of occurrence of fire hazards is quite small. The datasets used in previous papers have been balanced which does not imitate the real world environment. The testing set contains 102 images: 51 images each of fire and non-fire classes. As the training set is highly unbalanced and the testing set is exactly balanced, it makes a good test to see whether the models are able to generalize well or not. For a model with good accuracy, it must be able to extract the distinguishing features from the small amount of fire images. To

[1] The dataset is available here: https://github.com/UIA-CAIR/Fire-Detection-Image-Dataset.

Fig. 1. Examples of fire images

extract such features from small amount of data the model must be deep enough. A poor model would just label all images as non-fire, which is exemplified in the results.

Apart from being unbalanced, there are a few images that are very hard to classify. The dataset contains images from all scenarios like fire in a house, room, office, forest fire, with different illumination intensity and different shades of red, yellow and orange, small and big fires, fire at night, fire in the morning. Non-fire images contain a few images that are hard to distinguish from fire images like a bright red room with high illumination, sunset, red coloured houses and vehicles, bright lights with different shades of yellow and red etc.

The Figs. 1(a) to (f) show fire images in different environments: indoor, outdoor, daytime, nighttime, forest fire, big and small fire. And the Figs. 2(a) to (f) show the non-fire images that are difficult to classify. Considering these characteristics of our dataset, detecting fire can be a difficult task. We have made the dataset available online so that it can be used for future research in this area.

4.2 Results

Our ELM hybrid models are tested on our dataset and compared with SVM hybrid models and the original VGG16 and Resnet50 Deep CNN models. Tables 1 and 2 show the results of the experiments. The dataset was randomly split into training and testing sets. Two cases were considered depending on the amount of training data. The Deep CNN models (VGG16 and Resnet50) were trained only on 80% training data, since 60% is too less for these models. All the hybrid models have been trained on both 60% and 80% of training data.

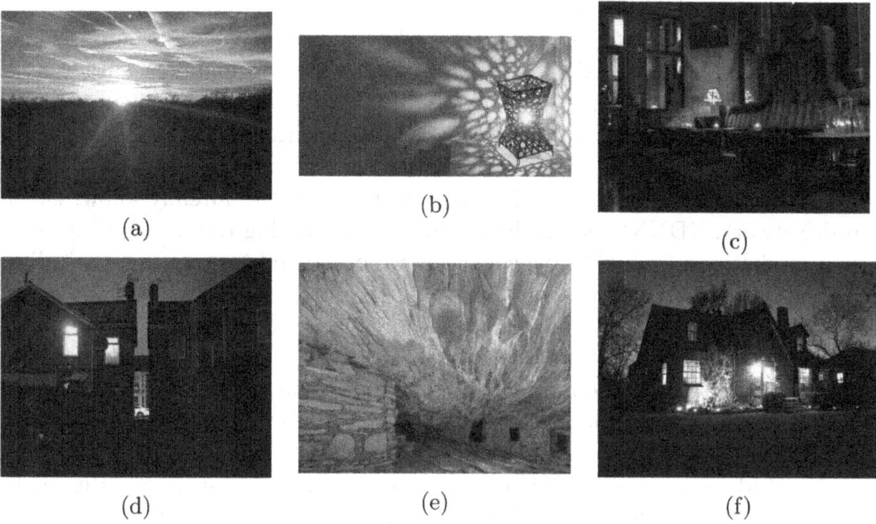

Fig. 2. Examples of non-fire images that are difficult to classify

Table 1. Accuracy and execution time

Model	D_T	Acc_{train}	T_{train}	T^C_{train}	Acc_{test}	T_{test}
VGG16 (pre-trained)	80	100	7149	6089	90.19	121
VGG16 (modified)	80	100	7320	6260	91.176	122
Resnet50 (pre-trained)	80	100	15995	13916	91.176	105
Resnet50 (modified)	80	100	16098	13919	92.15	107
VGG16+SVM	60	99.6	2411	1352	87.4	89
VGG16+SVM	80	100	2843	1784	93.9	81
VGG16+ELM	60	100	1340	281	93.9	24
VGG16+ELM	80	100	1356	297	96.15	21
Resnet50+SVM	60	100	3524	1345	88.7	97
Resnet50+SVM	80	100	4039	1860	94.6	86
Resnet50+ELM	60	100	2430	251	98.9	32
Resnet50+ELM	80	100	2452	272	99.2	26

D_T is the percentage of total data used for training the models.
Acc_{train} and Acc_{test} are the training and testing accuracies respectively.
T_{train} and T_{test} are the training and testing times for the models.
T^C_{train} is the time required to train the classifier part of the models

One point to be noted here is that, the SVM hybrid models contain an additional fully-connected layer of 4096 neurons, while the ELM is directly connected to the last pooling layer.

The results in Table 1 show that the ELM hybrid models outperform the VGG16, Resnet50 and SVM hybrid models by achieving higher accuracy and learning much faster. In general, we can see that the hybrid models outperform the state-of-the-art Deep CNNs in terms of both accuracy and training time.

Apart from accuracy and training time, another important point drawn from the results is the amount of training data required. As we already know, Deep Neural Networks (DNN) require huge amount of training data. So, using pre-trained models can be highly beneficial, as we only need to fine-tune the fully-connected layers. But, with models like VGG16 and Resnet50 which have large fully-connected layers, even fine-tuning requires large amount of training data. We had to train the VGG16 and Resnet50 on at least 80% training data otherwise they were overfitting on the majority class, resulting in 50% accuracy.

But in case of hybrid models, especially ELM hybrid models, the amount of training data required is much less. Even after being trained on 60% training data, the ELM models were able to outperform the original VGG16 and Resnet50 models which were trained on 80% training data. This shows that reducing the fully-connected layers, or replacing them with a better classifier can reduce the amount of training data required. Also, the ELM is more robust towards lack of training data which adds to this advantage.

Among the hybrid models, the ELM hybrid models outperform the SVM hybrid models both in terms of testing accuracy and training time. Also, we can see that the hybrid models with Resnet50 as the feature extractor achieves better results than the hybrid models with VGG16 as the feature extractor. This is due to the depth and the residual connections in Resnet50 in contrast to the simple, shallower (compared to Resnet50) and sequential nature of VGG16.

Table 2 compares results between different number of hidden neurons used by ELM. The accuracy increases as the number of hidden neurons increase. The models are tested for 2^{12}, 2^{13} and 2^{14} number of neurons. The testing accuracy starts to decrease for 2^{14} neurons, which means the model overfits. All the tests in Table 2 were conducted with 60% training data.

Table 2. Number of hidden neurons in ELM

CNN features	# Hidden neurons	Testing accuracy
VGG16 feature extractor	4096	93.9
VGG16 feature extractor	8192	94.2
VGG16 feature extractor	16384	91.1 (Overfitting)
Resnet50 feature extractor	4096	98.9
Resnet50 feature extractor	8192	99.2
Resnet50 feature extractor	16384	96.9 (Overfitting)

5 Conclusion

In this paper, we have proposed a hybrid model for fire detection. The hybrid model combines the feature extraction capabilities of Deep CNNs and the classification ability of ELM. The Deep CNNs used for creating the hybrid models are the VGG16 and Resnet50 instead of a simple Deep CNN. The fully connected layers are removed completely and replaced by a single hidden layer feedforward neural network trained using the ELM algorithm. This decreases complexity of the network and increases speed of convergence. We test our model on our own dataset which has been created to replicate a realistic view of the environment which includes different scenarios, imbalance due to lower likelihood of occurrence of fire. The dataset is small in size to check the robustness of models towards lack of training data, since deep networks require a considerable amount of training data. Our hybrid model is compared with the original VGG16 and Resnet50 models and also with SVM hybrid models. Our Deep CNN-ELM model is able to outperform all other models in terms of accuracy by 2.8% to 7.1% and training time by a speed up of 20x to 51x and requires less training data to achieve higher accuracy for the problem of fire detection.

References

1. Azizpour, H., Razavian, A.S., Sullivan, J., Maki, A., Carlsson, S.: From generic to specific deep representations for visual recognition. CoRR, abs/1406.5774 (2014)
2. Bradski, G.: OpenCV. Dr. Dobb's J. Soft. Tools **25**, 120–126 (2000)
3. Cao, L., Huang, W., Sun, F.: A deep and stable extreme learning approach for classification and regression. In: Cao, J., Mao, K., Cambria, E., Man, Z., Toh, K.-A. (eds.) Proceedings of ELM-2014 Volume 1. PALO, vol. 3, pp. 141–150. Springer, Cham (2015). https://doi.org/10.1007/978-3-319-14063-6_13
4. Chino, D.Y.T., Avalhais, L.P.S., Rodrigues Jr., J.F., Traina, A.J.M.: BoWFire: detection of fire in still images by integrating pixel color and texture analysis. CoRR, abs/1506.03495 (2015)
5. Chollet, F.: Keras (2015)
6. Zhao, J., et al.: Image based forest fire detection using dynamic characteristics with artificial neural networks. In: 2009 International Joint Conference on Artificial Intelligence, pp. 290–293, April 2009
7. Frizzi, S., Kaabi, R., Bouchouicha, M., Ginoux, J.M., Moreau, E., Fnaiech, F.: Convolutional neural network for video fire and smoke detection. In: IECON 2016–42nd Annual Conference of the IEEE Industrial Electronics Society, pp. 877–882, October 2016
8. Fukushima, K.: Neocognitron: a self-organizing neural network model for a mechanism of pattern recognition unaffected by shift in position. Biol. Cybern. **36**(4), 193–202 (1980)
9. Gürpinar, F., Kaya, H., Dibeklioglu, H., Salah, A.A.: Kernel ELM and CNN based facial age estimation. In: 2016 IEEE Conference on Computer Vision and Pattern Recognition Workshops (CVPRW), pp. 785–791, June 2016
10. He, K., Zhang, X., Ren, S., Sun, J.: Deep residual learning for image recognition. In: The IEEE Conference on Computer Vision and Pattern Recognition (CVPR), June 2016

11. Horng, W.-B., Peng, J.-W.: Image-based fire detection using neural networks. In: JCIS (2006)
12. Huang, G., Huang, G.-B., Song, S., You, K.: Trends in extreme learning machines: a review. Neural Netw. **61**, 32–48 (2015)
13. Huang, G.-B., Zhu, Q.-Y., Siew, C.-K.: Extreme learning machine: a new learning scheme of feedforward neural networks. In: 2004 IEEE International Joint Conference on Neural Networks, Proceedings, vol. 2, pp. 985–990. IEEE (2004)
14. Huang, G.-B., Zhu, Q.-Y., Siew, C.-K.: Extreme learning machine: theory and applications. Neurocomputing **70**(1), 489–501 (2006)
15. Kim, J., Kim, J., Jang, G.-J., Lee, M.: Fast learning method for convolutional neural networks using extreme learning machine and its application to lane detection. Neural Netw. **87**, 109–121 (2017)
16. Kingma, D.P., Ba, J.: Adam: a method for stochastic optimization. CoRR, abs/1412.6980 (2014)
17. Krizhevsky, A., Sutskever, I., Hinton, G.E.: Imagenet classification with deep convolutional neural networks. In: Pereira, F., Burges, C.J.C., Bottou, L., Weinberger, K.Q. (eds.) Advances in Neural Information Processing Systems 25, pp. 1097–1105. Curran Associates Inc (2012)
18. Lecun, Y., Bottou, L., Bengio, Y., Haffner, P.: Gradient-based learning applied to document recognition. Proc. IEEE **86**(11), 2278–2324 (1998)
19. McDonnell, M.D., Tissera, M.D., van Schaik, A., Tapson, J.: Fast, simple and accurate handwritten digit classification using extreme learning machines with shaped input-weights. CoRR, abs/1412.8307 (2014)
20. McDonnell, M.D., Vladusich, T.: Enhanced image classification with a fast-learning shallow convolutional neural network. CoRR, abs/1503.04596 (2015)
21. Nagi, J., Di Caro, G.A., Giusti, A., Nagi, F., Gambardella, L.M.: Convolutional neural support vector machines: hybrid visual pattern classifiers for multi-robot systems. In: ICMLA, no. 1, pp. 27–32. IEEE (2012)
22. Pang, S., Yang, X.: Deep convolutional extreme learning machine and its application in handwritten digit classification. Intell. Neurosci. **2016** (2016)
23. Tomas Polednik, Bc.: Detection of fire in images and video using CNN. Excel@FIT (2015)
24. Poobalan, K., Liew, S.C.: Fire detection algorithm using image processing techniques. In: 3rd International Conference on Artificial Intelligence and Computer Science (AICS2015), Ocotober 2015
25. Razavian, A.S., Azizpour, H., Sullivan, J., Carlsson, S.: CNN features off-the-shelf: an astounding baseline for recognition. CoRR, abs/1403.6382 (2014)
26. Ribeiro, B., Lopes, N.: Extreme learning classifier with deep concepts. In: Ruiz-Shulcloper, J., Sanniti di Baja, G. (eds.) CIARP 2013. LNCS, vol. 8258, pp. 182–189. Springer, Heidelberg (2013). https://doi.org/10.1007/978-3-642-41822-8_23
27. Custer, R.B.R.: Fire detection: the state of the art. NBS Technical Note, US Department of Commerce (1974)
28. Russakovsky, O., et al.: ImageNet large scale visual recognition challenge. Int. J. Comput. Vis. (IJCV) **115**(3), 211–252 (2015)
29. Yu, J.S., Chen, J., Xiang, Z.Q., Zou, Y.X.: A hybrid convolutional neural networks with extreme learning machine for WCE image classification. In: 2015 IEEE International Conference on Robotics and Biomimetics (ROBIO), pp. 1822–1827, December 2015
30. Sermanet, P., Eigen, D., Zhang, X., Mathieu, M., Fergus, R., LeCun, Y.: OverFeat: integrated recognition, localization and detection using convolutional networks. CoRR, abs/1312.6229 (2013)

31. Shao, J., Wang, G., Guo, W.: An image-based fire detection method using color analysis. In: 2012 International Conference on Computer Science and Information Processing (CSIP), pp. 1008–1011, August 2012
32. Simonyan, K., Zisserman, A.: Very deep convolutional networks for large-scale image recognition. CoRR, abs/1409.1556 (2014)
33. Tang, Y.: Deep learning using support vector machines. CoRR, abs/1306.0239 (2013)
34. Tao, C., Zhang, J., Wang, P.: Smoke detection based on deep convolutional neural networks. In: 2016 International Conference on Industrial Informatics - Computing Technology, Intelligent Technology, Industrial Information Integration (ICIICII), pp. 150–153, December 2016
35. Tapson, J., de Chazal, P., van Schaik, A.: Explicit computation of input weights in extreme learning machines. CoRR, abs/1406.2889 (2014)
36. Toulouse, T., Rossi, L., Celik, T., Akhloufi, M.: Automatic fire pixel detection using image processing: a comparative analysis of rule-based and machine learning-based methods. Sig. Image Video Process. **10**(4), 647–654 (2016)
37. Töreyin, B.U., Dedeoğlu, Y., Güdükbay, U., Çetin, A.E.: Computer vision based method for real-time fire and flame detection. Patt. Recogn. Lett. **27**(1), 49–58 (2006)
38. Wolfshaar, J.V.D., Karaaba, M.F., Wiering, M.A.: Deep convolutional neural networks and support vector machines for gender recognition. In: 2015 IEEE Symposium Series on Computational Intelligence, pp. 188–195, December 2015
39. Verstockt, S., Lambert, P., Van de Walle, R., Merci, B., Sette, B.L State of the art in vision-based fire and smoke dectection. In: Luck, H., Willms, I. (eds.) 14th International Conference on Automatic Fire Detection, Proceedings, vol. 2, pp. 285–292. University of Duisburg-Essen. Department of Communication Systems (2009)
40. Vicente, J., Guillemant, P.: An image processing technique for automatically detecting forest fire. Int. J. Therm. Sci. **41**(12), 1113–1120 (2002)
41. Zeng, Y., Xu, X., Fang, Y., Zhao, K.: Traffic sign recognition using deep convolutional networks and extreme learning machine. In: He, X., et al. (eds.) IScIDE 2015. LNCS, vol. 9242, pp. 272–280. Springer, Cham (2015). https://doi.org/10.1007/978-3-319-23989-7_28
42. Zhang, L., Zhang, D.: SVM and ELM: who wins? object recognition with deep convolutional features from imagenet. CoRR, abs/1506.02509 (2015)
43. Zhang, Q., Xu, J., Xu, L., Guo, H.: Deep convolutional neural networks for forest fire detection, February 2016
44. Zhu, W., Miao, J., Qing, L.: Constrained extreme learning machine: a novel highly discriminative random feedforward neural network. In: 2014 International Joint Conference on Neural Networks (IJCNN), pp. 800–807, July 2014

Siamese Survival Analysis with Competing Risks

Anton Nemchenko[1(✉)], Trent Kyono[1], and Mihaela Van Der Schaar[1,2,3]

[1] University of California, Los Angeles, Los Angeles, CA 90095, USA
santon834@g.ucla.edu
[2] University of Oxford, Oxford OX1 2JD, UK
[3] Alan Turing Institute, 96 Euston Rd, Kings Cross, London NW1 2DB, UK

Abstract. Survival analysis in the presence of multiple possible adverse events, i.e., competing risks, is a pervasive problem in many industries (healthcare, finance, etc.). Since only one event is typically observed, the incidence of an event of interest is often obscured by other related competing events. This nonidentifiability, or inability to estimate true cause-specific survival curves from empirical data, further complicates competing risk survival analysis. We introduce Siamese Survival Prognosis Network (SSPN), a novel deep learning architecture for estimating personalized risk scores in the presence of competing risks. SSPN circumvents the nonidentifiability problem by avoiding the estimation of cause-specific survival curves and instead determines pairwise concordant time-dependent risks, where longer event times are assigned lower risks. Furthermore, SSPN is able to directly optimize an approximation to the C-discrimination index, rather than relying on well-known metrics which are unable to capture the unique requirements of survival analysis with competing risks.

Keywords: Survival analysis · Competing risks
Siamese neural networks · C-index

1 Introduction

1.1 Motivation

Survival analysis is a method for analyzing data where the outcome variable is the time to the occurrence of an event (death, disease, stock liquidation, mechanical failure, etc.) of interest. Competing risks are additional possible events or outcomes that "compete" with and may preclude or interfere with the desired event observation. Though survival analysis is practiced across many disciplines (epidemiology, econometrics, manufacturing, etc.), this paper focuses on healthcare applications, where competing risk analysis has recently emerged as an important analytical tool in medical prognosis [9,22,26]. With an increasing aging population, the presence of multiple coexisting chronic diseases (multimorbidities) is on the rise, with more than two-thirds of people aged over 65

V. Kůrková et al. (Eds.): ICANN 2018, LNCS 11141, pp. 260–269, 2018.
https://doi.org/10.1007/978-3-030-01424-7_26

considered multimorbid. Developing optimal treatment plans for these patients with multimorbidities is a challenging problem, where the best treatment or intervention for a patient may depend upon the existence and susceptibility to other competing risks. Consider oncology and cardiovascular medicine, where the risk of a cardiac disease may alter the decision on whether a cancer patient should undergo chemotherapy or surgery. Countless examples like this involving competing risks are pervasive throughout the healthcare industry and insufficiently addressed in it's current state.

1.2 Related Works

Previous work on classical survival analysis has demonstrated the advantages of deep learning over statistical methods [14,18,27]. Cox proportional hazards model [6] is the baseline statistical model for survival analysis, but is limited since the dependent risk function is the product of a linear covariate function and a time dependent function, which is insufficient for modeling complex non-linear medical data. [14] replaced the linear covariate function with a feed-forward neural network as input for the Cox PH model and demonstrated improved performance. The current literature addresses competing risks based on statistical methods (the Fine Gray model [8]), classical machine learning (Random Survival Forest [12,13]), multi-task learning [1]) etc., with limited success. These existing competing risk models are challenged by computational scalability issues for datasets with many patients and multiple covariates. To address this challenge, we propose a deep learning architecture for survival analysis with competing risks to optimize the time-dependent discrimination index. This is not trivial and will be elaborated in the next section.

1.3 Contributions

In both machine learning and statistics, predictive models are compared in terms of the area under the receiver operating characteristic (ROC) curve or the time-dependent discrimination index (in the survival analysis literature). The equivalence of the two metrics was established in [11]. Numerous works on supervised learning [4,19,20,23] have shown that training the models to directly optimize the AUC improves out-of-sample (generalization) performance (in terms of AUC) rather than optimizing the error rate (or the accuracy). In this work, we adopt and apply this idea to survival analysis with competing risks. We develop a novel Siamese feed-forward neural network [3] designed to optimize concordance and account for competing risks by specifically targeting the time-dependent discrimination index [2]. This is achieved by estimating risks in a relative fashion so that the risk for the "true" event of a patient (i.e. the event which actually took place) must be higher than: all other risks for the same patient and the risks for the same true event of other patients that experienced it at a later time. Furthermore, the risks for all the causes are estimated jointly in an effort to generate a unified representation capturing the latent structure of the data and estimating cause-specific risks. Because our neural network issues a joint risk for all competing events, it compares different risks for the different events at different times and arranges them in a concordant fashion (earlier time means higher risk for any pair of patients).

Unlike previous Siamese neural networks architectures [3,5,25] developed for purposes such as learning the pairwise similarity between different inputs, our architecture aims to maximize the distance between output risks for the different inputs. We overcome the discontinuity problem of the above metric by introducing a continuous approximation of the time-dependent discrimination function. This approximation is only evaluated at the survival times observed in the dataset. However, training a neural network only over the observed survival times will result in poor generalization and undesirable out-of-sample performance (in terms of discrimination index computed at different times). In response to this, we add a loss term (to the loss function) which for any pair of patients, penalizes cases where the longer event time does not receive lower risk.

The nonidentifiability problem in competing risks arises from the inability to estimate the true cause-specific survival curves from empirical data [24]. We address this issue by bypassing and avoiding the estimation of the individual cause-specific survival curves and utilize concordant risks instead. Our implementation is agnostic to any underlying causal assumptions and therefore immune to nonidentifiability.

We report statistically significant improvements over state-of-the-art competing risk survival analysis methods on both synthetic and real medical data.

2 Problem Formulation

We consider a dataset $\mathcal{H}$ comprising of time-to-event information about N subjects who are followed up for a finite amount of time. Each subject (patient) experiences an event $D \in \{0, 1, .., M\}$, where D is the event type. $D = 0$ means the subject is censored (lost in follow-up or study ended). If $D \in \{1, .., M\}$, then the subject experiences one of the events of interest (for instance, subject develops cardiac disease). We assume that a subject can only experience one of the above events and that the censorship times are independent of them [7,8,10,17,22,24]. T is defined as the time-to-event, where we assume that time is discrete $T \in \{t_1, ..., t_K\}$ and $t_1 = 0$ (t_i denotes the elapsed time since t_1). Let $\mathcal{H} = \{T_i, D_i, x_i\}_{i=1}^N$, where T_i is the time-to-event for subject i, D_i is the event experienced by the subject i and $x_i \in \mathbb{R}^S$ are the covariates of the subject (the covariates are measured at baseline, which may include age, gender, genetic information etc.).

The Cumulative Incidence Function (CIF) [8] computed at time t for a certain event D is the probability of occurrence of a particular event D before time t conditioned on the covariates of a subject x, and is given as $F(t, D|x) = Pr(T \leq t, D|x)$. The cumulative incidence function evaluated at a certain point can be understood as the risk of experiencing a certain event before a specified time.

In this work, our goal is to develop a neural network that can learn the complex interactions in the data specifically addressing competing risks survival analysis. In determining our loss function, we consider that the time-dependent discrimination index is the most commonly used metric for evaluating models in survival analysis [2]. Multiple publications in the supervised learning literature demonstrate that approximating the area under the curve (AUC) directly and training a classifier leads to better generalization performance in terms of the AUC (see e.g. [4,19,20,23]). However, these ideas were not explored in the context of survival analysis with competing risks. We will follow the same principles to construct an approximation of the time-dependent discrimination index to train our neural network. We first describe the time-dependent discrimination index below.

Consider an ordered pair of two subjects (i, j) in the dataset. If the subject i experiences event m, i.e., $D_i \neq 0$ and if subject j's time-to-event exceeds the time-to-event of subject i, i.e., $T_j > T_i$, then the pair (i, j) is a comparable pair. The set of all such comparable pairs is defined as the comparable set for event m, and is denoted as X^m.

A model outputs the risk of the subject x for experiencing the event m before time t, which is given as $R^m(t, x) = F(t, D = m|x)$. The time-dependent discrimination index for a certain cause m is the probability that a model accurately orders the risks of the comparable pairs of subjects in the comparable set for event m. The time-dependent discrimination index [2] for cause m is defined as

$$C_t(m) = \frac{\sum_{k=1}^{K} AUC^m(t_k) w^m(t_k)}{\sum_{k=1}^{K} w^m(t_k)} \,. \tag{1}$$

where

$$AUC^m(t_k) = Pr\{R^m(t_k, x_i) > R^m(t_k, x_j) | T_i = t_k, T_j > t_k, D_i = m\} \,, \tag{2}$$

$$w^m(t_k) = Pr\{T_i = t_k, T_j > t_k, D_i = m\} \,. \tag{3}$$

The discrimination index in (1) cannot be computed exactly since the distribution that generates the data is unknown. However, the discrimination index can be estimated using a standard estimator, which takes as input the risk values associated with subjects in the dataset. [2] defines the estimator for (1) as

$$\hat{C}_t(m) = \frac{\sum_{i,j=1}^{N} \mathbf{1}\{R^m(T_i, x_i) > R^m(T_i, x_j)\} \cdot \mathbf{1}\{T_j > T_i, D_i = m\}}{\sum_{i,j=1}^{N} \mathbf{1}\{T_j > T_i, D_i = m\}} \,. \tag{4}$$

Note that in the above (4) only the numerator depends on the model. Henceforth, we will only consider the quantity in the numerator and we write it as

$$\bar{C}_t(m) = \sum_{i,j=1}^{N} \mathbf{1}\{R^m(T_i, x_i) > R^m(T_i, x_j)\} \cdot \mathbf{1}\{T_j > T_i, D_i = m\} \,. \tag{5}$$

The above equation can be simplified as

$$\bar{C}_t(m) = \sum_{i=1}^{|X^m|} \mathbf{1}\{R^m(T_i(\text{left}), X_i^m(\text{left})) > R^m(T_i(\text{left}), X_i^m(\text{right}))\} \,. \tag{6}$$

where $\mathbf{1}(x)$ is the indicator function, $X_i^m(\text{left})$ ($X_i^m(\text{right})$) is the left (right) element of the ith comparable pair in the set X^m and $T_i(\text{left})$ ($T_i(\text{right})$) is the respective time-to-event. In the next section, we will use the above simplification (6) to construct the loss function for the neural network.

3 Siamese Survival Prognosis Network

In this section, we will describe the architecture of the network and the loss functions that we propose to train the network.

Denote H as a feed-forward neural network which is visualized in Fig. 1. It is composed of a sequence of L fully connected hidden layers with "scaled exponential linear units" (SELU) activation. The last hidden layer is fed to M layers of width K. Each neuron in the latter M layers estimates the probability that a subject x experiences cause m occurs in a time interval t_k, which is given as $Pr^m(t_k, x)$. For an input covariate x the output from all the neurons is a vector of probabilities given as $\left\{\left[Pr^m(t_k, x)\right]_{k=1}^{K}\right\}_{m=1}^{M}$.

The estimate of cumulative incidence function computed for cause m at time t_k is given as $\tilde{R}^m(t_k, x) = \sum_{i=1}^{k} Pr^m(t_i, x)$. The final output of the neural network for input x is vector of estimates of the cumulative incidence function given as $H(x) = \left\{\left[\tilde{R}^m(t_k, x)\right]_{k=1}^{K}\right\}_{m=1}^{M}$.

The loss function is composed of three terms: discrimination, accuracy, and a loss term.

We cannot use the metric in (6) directly to train the network because it is a discontinuous function (composed of indicators), which can impede training. We overcome this problem by approximating the indicator function using a scaled sigmoid function $\sigma(\alpha x) = \frac{1}{1+exp(-\alpha x)}$. The approximated discrimination index is given as

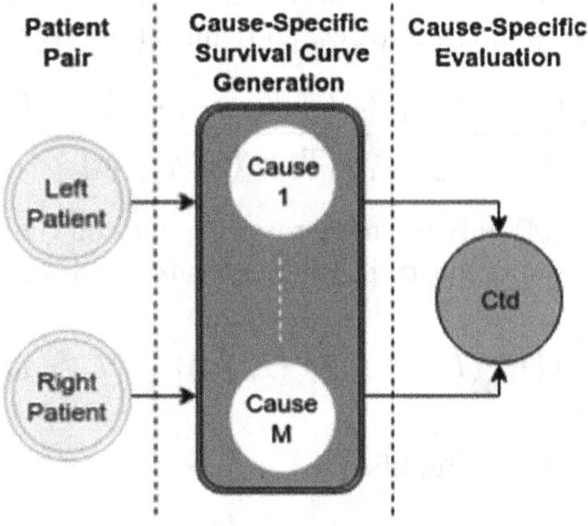

Fig. 1. Illustration of the architecture.

$$\hat{\hat{C}}_{\text{t}}(m) = \sum_{i=1}^{|X^m|} \sigma\Big[\alpha\big[\tilde{R}^m(T_i(\text{left}), X_i^m(\text{left})) - \tilde{R}^m(T_i(\text{left}), X_i^m(\text{right}))\big]\Big] . \quad (7)$$

The scaling parameter α determines the sensitivity of the loss function to discrimination. If the value of α is high, then the penalty for error in discrimination is also very high. Therefore, higher values of alpha guarantee that the subjects in a comparable pair are assigned concordant risk values.

The discrimination part defined above captures a model's ability to discriminate subjects for each cause separately. We also need to ensure that the model can predict the cause accurately. We define the accuracy of a model in terms of a scaled sigmoid function with scaling parameter κ as follows

$$L^1 = \sum_{i=1}^{|X^m|} \sigma\Big[\kappa\big(\tilde{R}^{D(\text{left})}(T_i(\text{left}), X_i^m(\text{left})) - \sum_{m \neq D(\text{left})} \tilde{R}^m(T_i(\text{left}), X_i^m(\text{left}))\big)\Big] . \quad (8)$$

The accuracy term penalizes the risk functions only at the event times of the left subjects in comparable pairs. However, it is important that the neural network is optimized to produce risk values that interpolate well to other time intervals as well. Therefore, we introduce a loss term below

$$L^2 = \beta \sum_{m=1}^{M} \sum_{i=1}^{|X^m|} \sum_{t_k < T_i(\text{left})} R^m(t_k, X_i^m(\text{right}))^2 . \quad (9)$$

The loss term ensures that the risk of each right subject is minimized for all the times before time-to-event of the left subject in the respective comparable pair. Intuitively, the loss term can be justified as follows. The right subjects do not experience an event before the time $T_i(\text{left})$. Hence, the probability that they experience an event before $T_i(\text{left})$ should take a small value.

The final loss function is the sum of the discrimination terms (described above), the accuracy and the loss terms, and is given as

$$\sum_{m=1}^{M} \hat{\hat{C}}_{\text{t}}(m) + L^1 + L^2 . \quad (10)$$

Finally, we adjust for the event imbalance and the time interval imbalance caused by the unequal number of pairs for each event and time interval with inverse propensity weights. These weights are the frequency of the occurrence of the various events at the various times and are multiplying the loss functions of the corresponding comparable pairs.

We train the feed-forward network using the above loss function (10) and regularize it using SELU dropout [16]. Since the loss function involves the discrimination term, each term in the loss function involves a pairwise comparison. This makes the network training similar to a Siamese network [3]. The backpropagation terms now depend on each comparable pair.

4 Experiments

This section includes a discussion of hyper-parameter optimization followed by competing risk and survival analysis experiments[1]. We compare against Fine-Gray model ("cmprsk" R package), Competing Random Forest (CRF) ("randomForestSRC" R package) and the cause-specific (cs) extension of two single event (non-competing risks) methods, Cox PH model and [14]. In cause-specific extension of single event models, we mark the occurrence of any event apart from the event of interest as censorship and decouple the problem into separate single event problem (one for each cause); this is a standard way of extending single-event models to competing risk models. In the following results we refer to our method with the acronym SSPN.

4.1 Hyper-Parameter Optimization

Optimization was performed using a 5-fold cross-validation with fixed censorship rates in each fold. We choose 60-20-20 division for training, validation and testing sets. A standard grid search was used to determine the batch size, number of hidden layers, width of the hidden layers and the dropout rate. The optimal values of α and β were consistently 500 and 0.01 for all datasets. As previously mentioned, the sets are comprised of patient pairs. In each training iteration, a batch size of pairs was sampled with replacement from the training set which reduces convergence speed but doesn't lower performance relative to regular batches [21]. We note that the training sets are commonly in the tens of million pairs with patients appearing multiple times in both sides of the pair. A standard definition of an epoch would compose of a single iteration over all patient. However, in our case, we not only learn patient specific characteristics but also patient comparison relationships, which means an epoch with a number of iterations equal to the number of patients is not sufficient. On the other hand, an epoch definition as an iteration over all pairs is impractical. Our best empirical results were attained after 100 K iterations with Tensorflow on 8-core Xeon E3-1240, Adam optimizer [15] and a decaying learning rate, $LR^{-1}(i) = 10^{-3} + i$. Table 1 summarizes the optimal hyper-parameters.

4.2 SEER

The Surveillance, Epidemiology, and End Results Program (SEER) dataset provides information on breast cancer patients during the years 1992–2007. A total

Table 1. Summary of hyper-parameters

Parameter	Batch size	# Hidden layers	Hidden layers width	Dropout rate
SEER	2048	3	50	0.4
Synthetic data	2048	2	40	0.35

[1] Code available at https://github.com/santon834/Siamese-Competing-Risks

Table 2. Summary of competing C_{t} index on SEER.

Dataset	CVD	Breast cancer	Other
cs-Cox PH	0.656 [0.629–0.682]	0.634 [0.626–0.642]	0.695 [0.675–0.714]
cs-[14]	0.645 [0.625–0.664]	0.697 [0.686–0.708]	0.675 [0.644–0.706]
Fine-Gray	0.659 [0.605–0.714]	0.636 [0.622–0.650]	0.691 [0.673–0.708]
CRF	0.601 [0.565–0.637]	0.705 [0.692–0.718]	0.636 [0.624–0.648]
SSPN	**0.663 [0.625–0.701]**	**0.735 [0.678–0.793]**	**0.699 [0.681–0.716]**

*p-value < 0.05

of 72,809 patients experienced breast cancer, cardiovascular disease (CVD), other diseases, or were right-censored. The cohort consists of 23 features, including age, race, gender, morphology information, diagnostic information, therapy information, tumor size, tumor type, etc. Missing values were replaced by mean value for real-valued features and by the mode for categorical features. 1.3% of the patients experienced CVD and 15.6% experienced breast cancer. Table 2 displays the results for this dataset. We notice that for the infrequent adverse event, CVD, the performance gain is negligible while for the frequent breast cancer event, the gain is significant. However, we wish to remind the reader that our focus is on healthcare where even minor gains have the potential to save lives. Considering there are 72,809 patients, a performance improvement even as low as 0.1% has the potential to save multiple lives and should not be disregarded.

4.3 Synthetic Data

Due to the relative scarcity of competing risks datasets and methods, we have created an additional synthetic dataset to further validate the performance of our method. We have constructed two stochastic processes with parameters and the event times as follows

$$x_i^1, x_i^2, x_i^3 \sim \mathcal{N}(0, \mathbf{I}),\ T_i^1 \sim \exp\left((x_i^3)^2 + x_i^1\right),\ T_i^2 \sim \exp\left((x_i^3)^2 + x_i^2\right)\ . \tag{11}$$

where (x_i^1, x_i^2, x_i^3) is the vector of features for patient i. For $k = 1, 2$, the features x^k only have an effect on the event time for event k, while x^3 has an effect on the

Table 3. Summary of competing C_{t} index on synthetic data.

Method	Cause 1	Cause 2
cs-Cox PH	0.571 [0.554–0.588]	0.581 [0.570–0.591]
cs-[14]	0.580 [0.556–0.603]	0.593 [0.576–0.611]
Fine-Gray	0.574 [0.559–0.590]	0.586 [0.577–0.594]
Competing random forest	0.591 [0.575–0.606]	0.573 [0.557–0.588]
SSPN	**0.603 [0.593–0.613]**	**0.613 [0.598–0.627]**

*p-value < 0.05

event times of both events. Note that we assume event times are exponentially distributed with a mean parameter depending on both linear and non-linear (quadratic) function of features. Given the parameters, we first produced 30,000 patients; among those, we randomly selected 15,000 patients (50%) to be right-censored at a time randomly drawn from the uniform distribution on the interval $[0, \min\{T_i^1, T_i^2\}]$. (This censoring fraction was chosen to be roughly the same censoring fraction as in the real datasets, and hence to present the same difficulty as found in those datasets). Table 3 displays the results for the above dataset. We demonstrate the same consistent performance gain as in the previous case.

5 Conclusion

Competing risks settings are pervasive in healthcare. They are encountered in cardiovascular diseases, in cancer, and in the geriatric population suffering from multiple diseases. To solve the challenging problem of learning the model parameters from time-to-event data while handling right censoring, we have developed a novel deep learning architecture for estimating personalized risk scores in the presence of competing risks based on the well-known Siamese network architecture. Our method is able to capture complex non-linear representations missed by classical machine learning and statistical models. Experimental results show that our method is able to outperform existing competing risk methods by successfully learning representations which flexibly describe non-proportional hazard rates with complex interactions between covariates and survival times that are common in many diseases with heterogeneous phenotypes.

References

1. Alaa, A.M., van der Schaar, M.: Deep multi-task Gaussian processes for survival analysis with competing risks (2017)
2. Antolini, L., Boracchi, P., Biganzoli, E.: A time-dependent discrimination index for survival data. Stat. Med. **24**(24), 3927–3944 (2005)
3. Bromley, J., Guyon, I., LeCun, Y., Säckinger, E., Shah, R.: Signature verification using a "siamese" time delay neural network. In: Advances in Neural Information Processing Systems, pp. 737–744 (1994)
4. Chen, Y., Jia, Z., Mercola, D., Xie, X.: A gradient boosting algorithm for survival analysis via direct optimization of concordance index. Comput. Math. Methods Med. **2013**, 8 (2013). https://doi.org/10.1155/2013/873595. Article ID 873595
5. Chopra, S., Hadsell, R., LeCun, Y.: Learning a similarity metric discriminatively, with application to face verification. In: 2005 IEEE Computer Society Conference on Computer Vision and Pattern Recognition, CVPR 2005, vol. 1, pp. 539–546. IEEE (2005)
6. Cox, D.R.: Models and life-tables regression. JR Stat. Soc. Ser. B **34**, 187–220 (1972)
7. Crowder, M.J.: Classical Competing Risks. CRC Press, London (2001)
8. Fine, J.P., Gray, R.J.: A proportional hazards model for the subdistribution of a competing risk. J. Am. Stat. Assoc. **94**(446), 496–509 (1999)

9. Glynn, R.J., Rosner, B.: Comparison of risk factors for the competing risks of coronary heart disease, stroke, and venous thromboembolism. Am. J. Epidemiol. **162**(10), 975–982 (2005)
10. Gooley, T.A., Leisenring, W., Crowley, J., Storer, B.E.: Estimation of failure probabilities in the presence of competing risks: new representations of old estimators. Stat. Med. **18**(6), 695–706 (1999)
11. Heagerty, P.J., Zheng, Y.: Survival model predictive accuracy and ROC curves. Biometrics **61**(1), 92–105 (2005)
12. Ishwaran, H., Gerds, T.A., Kogalur, U.B., Moore, R.D., Gange, S.J., Lau, B.M.: Random survival forests for competing risks. Biostatistics **15**(4), 757–773 (2014)
13. Ishwaran, H., Kogalur, U.B., Blackstone, E.H., Lauer, M.S.: Random survival forests. Ann. Appl. Stat. **2**, 841–860 (2008)
14. Katzman, J., Shaham, U., Bates, J., Cloninger, A., Jiang, T., Kluger, Y.: Deep survival: a deep cox proportional hazards network. arXiv preprint arXiv:1606.00931 (2016)
15. Kingma, D., Ba, J.: Adam: a method for stochastic optimization. arXiv preprint arXiv:1412.6980 (2014)
16. Klambauer, G., Unterthiner, T., Mayr, A., Hochreiter, S.: Self-normalizing neural networks. arXiv preprint arXiv:1706.02515 (2017)
17. Lambert, P., Dickman, P., Nelson, C., Royston, P.: Estimating the crude probability of death due to cancer and other causes using relative survival models. Stat. Med. **29**(7–8), 885–895 (2010)
18. Luck, M., Sylvain, T., Cardinal, H., Lodi, A., Bengio, Y.: Deep learning for patient-specific kidney graft survival analysis. arXiv preprint arXiv:1705.10245 (2017)
19. Mayr, A., Hofner, B., Schmid, M.: Boosting the discriminatory power of sparse survival models via optimization of the concordance index and stability selection. BMC Bioinform. **17**(1), 288 (2016)
20. Mayr, A., Schmid, M.: Boosting the concordance index for survival data-a unified framework to derive and evaluate biomarker combinations. PloS ONE **9**(1), e84483 (2014)
21. Recht, B., Re, C.: Beneath the valley of the noncommutative arithmetic-geometric mean inequality: conjectures, case-studies, and consequences (2012)
22. Satagopan, J., Ben-Porat, L., Berwick, M., Robson, M., Kutler, D., Auerbach, A.: A note on competing risks in survival data analysis. Br. J. Cancer **91**(7), 1229–1235 (2004)
23. Schmid, M., Wright, M.N., Ziegler, A.: On the use of harrell's c for clinical risk prediction via random survival forests. Exp. Syst. Appl. **63**, 450–459 (2016)
24. Tsiatis, A.: A nonidentifiability aspect of the problem of competing risks. Proc. Nat. Acad. Sci. **72**(1), 20–22 (1975)
25. Wang, J., Fang, Z., Lang, N., Yuan, H., Su, M.Y., Baldi, P.: A multi-resolution approach for spinal metastasis detection using deep siamese neural networks. Comput. Biol. Med. **84**, 137–146 (2017)
26. Wolbers, M., Koller, M.T., Witteman, J.C., Steyerberg, E.W.: Prognostic models with competing risks: methods and application to coronary risk prediction. Epidemiology **20**(4), 555–561 (2009)
27. Yousefi, S., et al.: Predicting clinical outcomes from large scale cancer genomic profiles with deep survival models. bioRxiv, p. 131367 (2017)

A Survey on Deep Transfer Learning

Chuanqi Tan(✉), Fuchun Sun, Tao Kong, Wenchang Zhang, Chao Yang, and Chunfang Liu

State Key Laboratory of Intelligent Technology and Systems, Tsinghua National Laboratory for Information Science and Technology (TNList), Department of Computer Science and Technology, Tsinghua University, Beijing, China

{tcq15,kt14,zhangwc14,yang-c15}@mails.tsinghua.edu.cn, {fcsun,cfliu1985}@tsinghua.edu.cn

Abstract. As a new classification platform, deep learning has recently received increasing attention from researchers and has been successfully applied to many domains. In some domains, like bioinformatics and robotics, it is very difficult to construct a large-scale well-annotated dataset due to the expense of data acquisition and costly annotation, which limits its development. Transfer learning relaxes the hypothesis that the training data must be independent and identically distributed (i.i.d.) with the test data, which motivates us to use transfer learning to solve the problem of insufficient training data. This survey focuses on reviewing the current researches of transfer learning by using deep neural network and its applications. We defined deep transfer learning, category and review the recent research works based on the techniques used in deep transfer learning.

Keywords: Deep transfer learning · Transfer learning · Survey

1 Introduction

Deep learning has recently received increasing attention from researchers and has been successfully applied to numerous real-world applications. Deep learning algorithms attempt to learn high-level features from mass data, which make deep learning beyond traditional machine learning. It can automatic extract data features by unsupervised or semi-supervised feature learning algorithm and hierarchical feature extraction. In contrast, traditional machine learning methods need to design features manually that seriously increases the burden on users. It can be said that deep learning is an representation learning algorithm based on large-scale data in machine learning.

Data dependence is one of the most serious problem in deep learning. Deep learning has a very strong dependence on massive training data compared to traditional machine learning methods, because it need a large amount of data to understand the latent patterns of data. An interesting phenomenon can be

V. Kůrková et al. (Eds.): ICANN 2018, LNCS 11141, pp. 270–279, 2018.
https://doi.org/10.1007/978-3-030-01424-7_27

found that the scale of the model and the size of the required amount of data has a almost linear relationship. An acceptable explanation is that for a particular problem, the expressive space of the model must be large enough to discover the patterns under the data. The pre-order layers in the model can identify high-level features of training data, and the subsequent layers can identify the information needed to help make the final decision.

Insufficient training data is a inescapable problem in some special domains. The collection of data is complex and expensive that make it is extremely difficult to build a large-scale, high-quality annotated dataset. For example, each sample in bioinformatics dataset often demonstration a clinical trial or a painful patient. In addition, even we obtain training dataset by paid an expensive price, it is very easy to get out of date and thus cannot be effectively applied in the new tasks.

Transfer learning relaxes the hypothesis that the training data must be independent and identically distributed (i.i.d.) with the test data, which motivates us to use transfer learning to against the problem of insufficient training data. In transfer learning, the training data and test data are not required to be i.i.d., and the model in target domain is not need to trained from scratch, which can significantly reduce the demand of training data and training time in the target domain.

In the past, most studies of transfer learning were conducted in traditional machine learning methods. Due to the dominance position of deep learning in modern machine learning methods, a survey on deep transfer learning and its applications is particularly important. The **contributions** of this survey paper are as follows:

- We define the deep transfer learning and categorizing it into four categories for the first time.
- We reviewing the current research works on each category of deep transfer learning, and given a standardized description and sketch map of every category.

2 Deep Transfer Learning

Transfer learning is an important tool in machine learning to solve the basic problem of insufficient training data. It try to transfer the knowledge from the source domain to the target domain by relaxing the assumption that the training data and the test data must be i.i.d. This will leads to a great positive effect on many domains that are difficult to improve because of insufficient training data. The learning process of transfer learning illustrated in the Fig. 1.

Some notations used in this survey need to be clearly defined. First of all, we give the definitions of a domain and a task respectively: A domain can be represented by $\mathcal{D} = \{\chi, P(X)\}$, which contains two parts: the feature space χ and the edge probability distribution $P(X)$ where $X = \{x_1, ..., x_n\} \in \chi$. A task can be represented by $\mathcal{T} = \{y, f(x)\}$. It consists of two parts: label space y and target prediction function $f(x)$. $f(x)$ can also be regarded as a conditional probability function $P(y|x)$. Then, the transfer learning can be formal defined as follows:

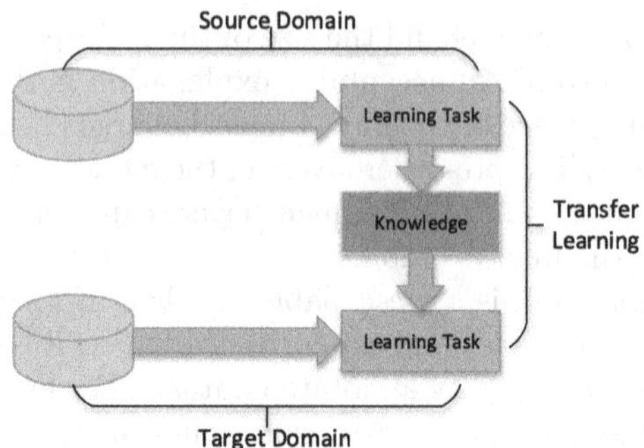

Fig. 1. Learning process of transfer learning.

Definition 1 *(Transfer Learning). Given a learning task $\mathcal{T}_t$ based on $\mathcal{D}_t$, and we can get the help from $\mathcal{D}_s$ for the learning task $\mathcal{T}_s$. Transfer learning aims to improve the performance of predictive function $f_{\mathcal{T}}(\cdot)$ for learning task $\mathcal{T}_t$ by discover and transfer latent knowledge from $\mathcal{D}_s$ and $\mathcal{T}_s$, where $\mathcal{D}_s \neq \mathcal{D}_t$ and/or $\mathcal{T}_s \neq \mathcal{T}_t$. In addition, in the most case, the size of $\mathcal{D}_s$ is much larger than the size of $\mathcal{D}_t$, $N_s \gg N_t$.*

Surveys [19,25] divide the transfer learning methods into three major categories with the relationship between the source domain and the target domain, which has been widely accepted. These surveys are good summary of the past works on transfer learning, which introduced a number of classic transfer learning methods. Further more, many newer and better methods have been proposed recently. In recent years, transfer learning research community are mainly focused on the following two aspects: domain adaption and multi-source domains transfer.

Nowadays, deep learning has achieved dominating situation in many research fields in recent years. It is important to find how to effectively transfer knowledge by deep neural network, which called deep transfer learning that defined as follows:

Definition 2 *(Deep Transfer Learning). Given a transfer learning task defined by $\langle \mathcal{D}_s, \mathcal{T}_s, \mathcal{D}_t, \mathcal{T}_t, f_{\mathcal{T}}(\cdot) \rangle$. It is a deep transfer learning task where $f_{\mathcal{T}}(\cdot)$ is a non-linear function that reflected a deep neural network.*

3 Categories

Deep transfer learning studies how to utilize knowledge from other fields by deep neural networks. Since deep neural networks have become popular in various fields, a considerable amount of deep transfer learning methods have been proposed that it is very important to classify and summarize them. Based on the techniques used in deep transfer learning, this paper classifies deep transfer learning into four categories: instances-based deep transfer learning, mapping-based

Table 1. Categorizing of deep transfer learning.

Approach category	Brief description	Some related works
Instances-based	Utilize instances in source domain by appropriate weight	[4, 10, 11, 20, 24, 26, 27]
Mapping-based	Mapping instances from two domains into a new data space with better similarity	[2, 8, 12, 14, 23]
Network-based	Reuse the partial of network pre-trained in the source domain	[3, 6, 9, 15, 17, 28, 30]
Adversarial-based	Use adversarial technology to find transferable features that both suitable for two domains	[1, 5, 13, 16, 21, 22]

deep transfer learning, network-based deep transfer learning, and adversarial-based deep transfer learning, which are shown in Table 1.

3.1 Instances-Based Deep Transfer Learning

Instances-based deep transfer learning refers to use a specific weight adjustment strategy, select partial instances from the source domain as supplements to the training set in the target domain by assigning appropriate weight values to these selected instances. It is based on the assumption that "*Although there are different between two domains, partial instances in the source domain can be utilized by the target domain with appropriate weights*". The sketch map of instances-based deep transfer learning are shown in Fig. 2.

TrAdaBoost proposed by [4] use AdaBoost-based technology to filter out instances that are dissimilar to the target domain in source domains. Re-weighted instances in source domain to compose a distribution similar to target domain. Finally, training model by using the re-weighted instances from source domain and origin instances from target domain. It can reduce the weighted training error on different distribution domains that preserving the properties of AdaBoost. TaskTrAdaBoost proposed by [27] is a fast algorithm promote rapid retraining over new targets. Unlike TrAdaBoost is designed for classification problems, ExpBoost.R2 and TrAdaBoost.R2 were proposed by [20] to cover the

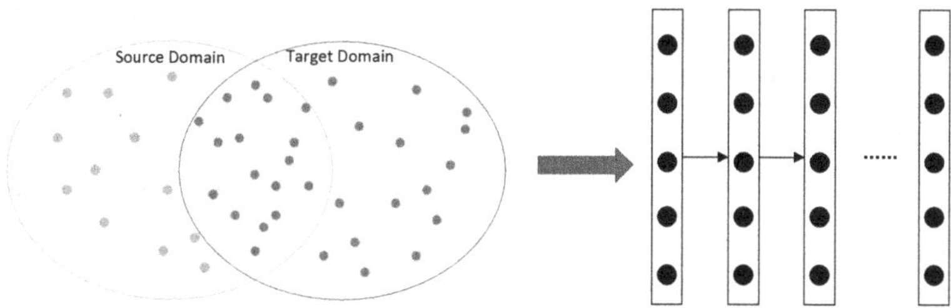

Fig. 2. Sketch map of instances-based deep transfer learning. Instances with light blue color in source domain meanings dissimilar with target domain are exclude from training dataset; Instances with dark blue color in source domain meanings similar with target domain are include in training dataset with appropriate weight.

regression problem. Bi-weighting domain adaptation (BIW) proposed [24] can aligns the feature spaces of two domains into the common coordinate system, and then assign an appropriate weight of the instances from source domain. [10] propose a enhanced TrAdaBoost to handle the problem of interregional sandstone microscopic image classification. [26] propose a metric transfer learning framework to learn instance weights and a distance of two different domains in a parallel framework to make knowledge transfer across domains more effective. [11] introduce an ensemble transfer learning to deep neural network that can utilize instances from source domain.

3.2 Mapping-Based Deep Transfer Learning

Mapping-based deep transfer learning refers to mapping instances from the source domain and target domain into a new data space. In this new data space, instances from two domains are similarly and suitable for a union deep neural network. It is based on the assumption that "*Although there are different between two origin domains, they can be more similarly in an elaborate new data space.*". The sketch map of instances-based deep transfer learning are shown in Fig. 3.

Transfer component analysis (TCA) introduced by [18] and TCA-based methods [29] had been widely used in many applications of traditional transfer learning. A natural idea is extend the TCA method to deep neural network. [23] extend MMD to comparing distributions in a deep neural network, by introduces an adaptation layer and an additional domain confusion loss to learn a representation that is both semantically meaningful and domain invariant. The MMD distance used in this work is defined as

$$D_{\mathcal{MMD}}(X_S, X_T) = \left\| \frac{1}{|X_S|} \sum_{x_s \in X_S} \phi(x_s) - \frac{1}{|X_T|} \sum_{x_t \in X_T} \phi(x_t) \right\| \quad (1)$$

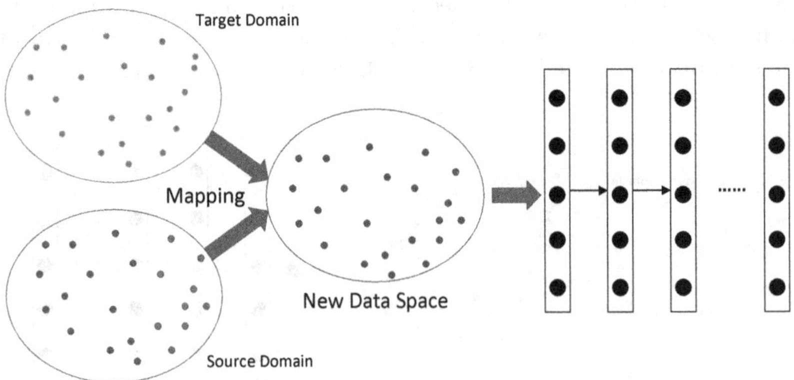

Fig. 3. Sketch map of mapping-based deep transfer learning. Simultaneously, instances from source domain and target domain are mapping to a new data space with more similarly. Consider all instances in the new data space as the training set of the neural network.

and the loss function is defined as

$$\mathcal{L} = \mathcal{L}_C(X_L, y) + \lambda D^2_{\mathcal{MMD}}(X_S, X_T). \quad (2)$$

[12] improved previous work by replace MMD distance with multiple kernel variant MMD (MK-MMD) distance proposed by [8]. The hidden layer related with the learning task in the convolutional neural networks (CNN) is mapped into the reproducing kernel Hilbert space (RKHS), and the distance between different domains is minimized by the multi-core optimization method. [14] propose joint maximum mean discrepancy (JMMD) to measurement the relationship of joint distribution. JMMD was used to generalize the transfer learning ability of the deep neural networks (DNN) to adapt the data distribution in different domain and improved the previous works. Wasserstein distance proposed by [2] can be used as a new distance measurement of domains to find better mapping.

3.3 Network-Based Deep Transfer Learning

Network-based deep transfer learning refers to the reuse the partial network that pre-trained in the source domain, including its network structure and connection parameters, transfer it to be a part of deep neural network which used in target domain. It is based on the assumption that "*Neural network is similar to the processing mechanism of the human brain, and it is an iterative and continuous abstraction process. The front-layers of the network can be treated as a feature extractor, and the extracted features are versatile*". The sketch map of network-based deep transfer learning are shown in Fig. 4.

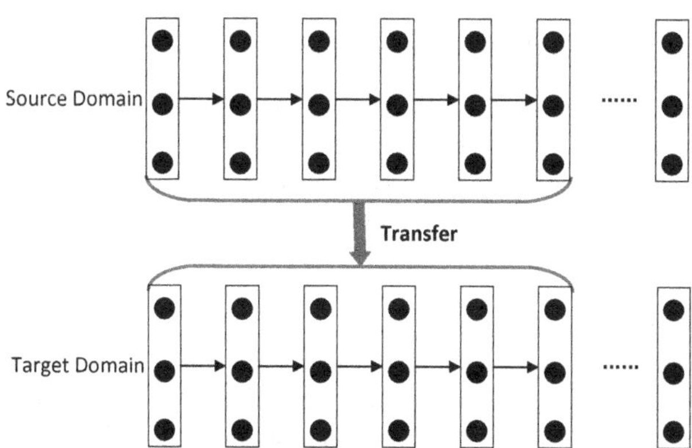

Fig. 4. Sketch map of network-based deep transfer learning. First, network was trained in source domain with large-scale training dataset. Second, partial of network pre-trained for source domain are transfer to be a part of new network designed for target domain. Finally, the transfered sub-network may be updated in fine-tune strategy.

[9] divide the network into two parts, the former part is the language-independent feature transform and the last layer is the language-relative classifier. The language-independent feature transform can be transfer between multi

languages. [17] reuse front-layers trained by CNN on the ImageNet dataset to compute intermediate image representation for images in other datasets, CNN are trained to learning image representations that can be efficiently transferred to other visual recognition tasks with limited amount of training data. [15] proposed a approach to jointly learn adaptive classifiers and transferable features from labeled data in the source domain and unlabeled data in the target domain, which explicitly learn the residual function with reference to the target classifier by plugging several layers into deep network. [30] learning domain adaptation and deep hash features simultaneously in a DNN. [3] proposed a novel multi-scale convolutional sparse coding method. This method can automatically learns filter banks at different scales in a joint fashion with enforced scale-specificity of learned patterns, and provides an unsupervised solution for learning transferable base knowledge and fine-tuning it towards target tasks. [6] apply deep transfer learning to transfer knowledge from real-world object recognition tasks to glitch classifier for the detector of multiple gravitational wave signals. It demonstrate that DNN can be used as excellent feature extractors for unsupervised clustering methods to identify new classes based on their morphology, without any labeled examples.

Another very noteworthy result is that [28] point out the relationship between network structure and transferability. It demonstrated that some modules may not influence in-domain accuracy but influence the transferability. It point out what features are transferable in deep networks and which type of networks are more suitable for transfer. Given an conclusion that LeNet, AlexNet, VGG, Inception, ResNet are good chooses in network-based deep transfer learning.

3.4 Adversarial-Based Deep Transfer Learning

Adversarial-based deep transfer learning refers to introduce adversarial technology inspired by generative adversarial nets (GAN) [7] to find transferable representations that is applicable to both the source domain and the target domain. It is based on the assumption that "*For effective transfer, good representation should be discriminative for the main learning task and indiscriminate between the source domain and target domain*". The sketch map of adversarial-based deep transfer learning are shown in Fig. 5.

The adversarial-based deep transfer learning has obtained the flourishing development in recent years due to its good effect and strong practicality. [1] introduce adversarial technology to transfer learning for domain adaption, by using a domain adaptation regularization term in the loss function. [5] proposed an adversarial training method that suitable for most any feed-forward neural model by augmenting it with few standard layers and a simple new gradient reversal layer. [21] proposed a approach transfer knowledge cross-domain and cross-task simultaneity for sparsely labeled target domain data. A special joint loss function was used in this work to force CNN to optimize both the distance between domains which defined as $\mathcal{L}_D = \mathcal{L}_c + \lambda\mathcal{L}_{adver}$, where $\mathcal{L}_c$ is classification loss, $\mathcal{L}_{adver}$ is domain adversarial loss. Because the two losses stand in direct opposition to one another, an iterative optimize algorithm are introduced to

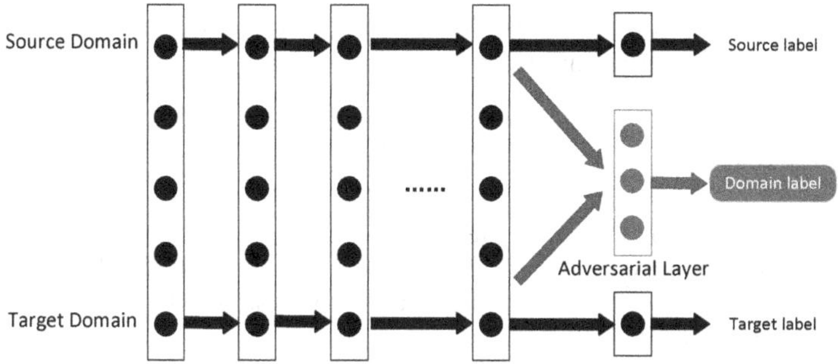

Fig. 5. Sketch map of adversarial-based deep transfer learning. In the training process on large-scale dataset in the source domain, the front-layers of network is regarded as a feature extractor. It extracting features from two domains and sent them to adversarial layer. The adversarial layer try to discriminates the origin of the features. If the adversarial network achieves worse performance, it means a small difference between the two types of feature and better transferability, and vice versa. In the following training process, the performance of the adversarial layer will be considered to force the transfer network discover general features with more transferability.

update one loss when fixed another. [22] proposed a new GAN loss and combine with discriminative modeling to a new domain adaptation method. [13] proposed a randomized multi-linear adversarial networks to exploit multiple feature layers and the classifier layer based on a randomized multi-linear adversary to enable both deep and discriminative adversarial adaptation. [16] utilize a domain adversarial loss, and generalizes the embedding to novel task using a metric learning-based approach to find more tractable features in deep transfer learning.

4 Conclusion

In this survey paper, we have review and category current researches of deep transfer learning. Deep transfer learning is classified into four categories for the first time: instances-based deep transfer learning, mapping-based deep transfer learning, network-based deep transfer learning, and adversarial-based deep transfer learning. In most practical applications, the above multiple technologies are often used in combination to achieve better results. Most current researches focuses on supervised learning, how to transfer knowledge in unsupervised or semi-supervised learning by deep neural network may attract more and more attention in the future. Negative transfer and transferability measures are important issues in traditional transfer learning. The impact of these two issues in deep transfer learning also requires us to conduct further research. In addition, a very attractive research area is to find a stronger physical support for transfer knowledge in deep neural network, which requires the cooperation of physicists, neuroscientists and computer scientists. It can be predicted that deep transfer learning will be widely applied to solve many challenging problems with the development of deep neural network.

References

1. Ajakan, H., Germain, P., Larochelle, H., Laviolette, F., Marchand, M.: Domain-adversarial neural networks. arXiv preprint arXiv:1412.4446 (2014)
2. Arjovsky, M., Chintala, S., Bottou, L.: Wasserstein GAN. arXiv preprint arXiv:1701.07875 (2017)
3. Chang, H., Han, J., Zhong, C., Snijders, A., Mao, J.H.: Unsupervised transfer learning via multi-scale convolutional sparse coding for biomedical applications. IEEE Trans. Patt. Anal. Mach. Intell. **40**(5), 1182–1194 (2017)
4. Dai, W., Yang, Q., Xue, G.R., Yu, Y.: Boosting for transfer learning. In: Proceedings of the 24th International Conference on Machine Learning, pp. 193–200. ACM (2007)
5. Ganin, Y., Lempitsky, V.: Unsupervised domain adaptation by backpropagation. arXiv preprint arXiv:1409.7495 (2014)
6. George, D., Shen, H., Huerta, E.: Deep transfer learning: a new deep learning glitch classification method for advanced LIGO. arXiv preprint arXiv:1706.07446 (2017)
7. Goodfellow, I., et al.: Generative adversarial nets. In: Advances in Neural Information Processing Systems, pp. 2672–2680 (2014)
8. Gretton, A., et al.: Optimal kernel choice for large-scale two-sample tests. In: Advances in Neural Information Processing Systems, pp. 1205–1213 (2012)
9. Huang, J.T., Li, J., Yu, D., Deng, L., Gong, Y.: Cross-language knowledge transfer using multilingual deep neural network with shared hidden layers. In: 2013 IEEE International Conference on Acoustics, Speech and Signal Processing (ICASSP), pp. 7304–7308. IEEE (2013)
10. Li, N., Hao, H., Gu, Q., Wang, D., Hu, X.: A transfer learning method for automatic identification of sandstone microscopic images. Comput. Geosci. **103**, 111–121 (2017)
11. Liu, X., Liu, Z., Wang, G., Cai, Z., Zhang, H.: Ensemble transfer learning algorithm. IEEE Access **6**, 2389–2396 (2018)
12. Long, M., Cao, Y., Wang, J., Jordan, M.: Learning transferable features with deep adaptation networks. In: International Conference on Machine Learning, pp. 97–105 (2015)
13. Long, M., Cao, Z., Wang, J., Jordan, M.I.: Domain adaptation with randomized multilinear adversarial networks. arXiv preprint arXiv:1705.10667 (2017)
14. Long, M., Wang, J., Jordan, M.I.: Deep transfer learning with joint adaptation networks. arXiv preprint arXiv:1605.06636 (2016)
15. Long, M., Zhu, H., Wang, J., Jordan, M.I.: Unsupervised domain adaptation with residual transfer networks. In: Advances in Neural Information Processing Systems, pp. 136–144 (2016)
16. Luo, Z., Zou, Y., Hoffman, J., Fei-Fei, L.F.: Label efficient learning of transferable representations acrosss domains and tasks. In: Advances in Neural Information Processing Systems, pp. 164–176 (2017)
17. Oquab, M., Bottou, L., Laptev, I., Sivic, J.: Learning and transferring mid-level image representations using convolutional neural networks. In: 2014 IEEE Conference on Computer Vision and Pattern Recognition (CVPR), pp. 1717–1724. IEEE (2014)

18. Pan, S.J., Tsang, I.W., Kwok, J.T., Yang, Q.: Domain adaptation via transfer component analysis. IEEE Trans. Neural Netw. **22**(2), 199–210 (2011)
19. Pan, S.J., Yang, Q.: A survey on transfer learning. IEEE Trans. Knowl. Data Eng. **22**(10), 1345–1359 (2010)
20. Pardoe, D., Stone, P.: Boosting for regression transfer. In: Proceedings of the 27th International Conference on International Conference on Machine Learning, pp. 863–870. Omnipress (2010)
21. Tzeng, E., Hoffman, J., Darrell, T., Saenko, K.: Simultaneous deep transfer across domains and tasks. In: 2015 IEEE International Conference on Computer Vision (ICCV), pp. 4068–4076. IEEE (2015)
22. Tzeng, E., Hoffman, J., Saenko, K., Darrell, T.: Adversarial discriminative domain adaptation. In: Computer Vision and Pattern Recognition (CVPR), vol. 1, p. 4 (2017)
23. Tzeng, E., Hoffman, J., Zhang, N., Saenko, K., Darrell, T.: Deep domain confusion: maximizing for domain invariance. arXiv preprint arXiv:1412.3474 (2014)
24. Wan, C., Pan, R., Li, J.: Bi-weighting domain adaptation for cross-language text classification. In: IJCAI Proceedings of International Joint Conference on Artificial Intelligence, vol. 22, p. 1535 (2011)
25. Weiss, K., Khoshgoftaar, T.M., Wang, D.: A survey of transfer learning. J. Big Data **3**(1), 9 (2016)
26. Xu, Y., et al.: A unified framework for metric transfer learning. IEEE Trans. Knowl. Data Eng. **29**(6), 1158–1171 (2017)
27. Yao, Y., Doretto, G.: Boosting for transfer learning with multiple sources. In: 2010 IEEE Conference on Computer Vision and Pattern Recognition (CVPR), pp. 1855–1862. IEEE (2010)
28. Yosinski, J., Clune, J., Bengio, Y., Lipson, H.: How transferable are features in deep neural networks? In: Advances in Neural Information Processing Systems, pp. 3320–3328 (2014)
29. Zhang, J., Li, W., Ogunbona, P.: Joint geometrical and statistical alignment for visual domain adaptation. In: CVPR (2017)
30. Zhu, H., Long, M., Wang, J., Cao, Y.: Deep hashing network for efficient similarity retrieval. In: AAAI, pp. 2415–2421 (2016)

Cloud Detection in High-Resolution Multispectral Satellite Imagery Using Deep Learning

Giorgio Morales(✉), Samuel G. Huamán, and Joel Telles

National Institute of Research and Training in Telecommunications (INICTEL-UNI), National University of Engineering, San Luis 1771, 15021 Lima, Peru
{gmorales,shuaman,jtelles}@inictel.edu.pe

Abstract. Cloud detection in high-resolution satellite images is a critical step for many remote sensing applications, but also a challenge, as such images have limited spectral bands. The contribution of this paper is twofold: We present a dataset called CloudPeru as well as a methodology for cloud detection in multispectral satellite images (approximately 2.8 meters per pixel) using deep learning. We prove that an agile Convolutional Neural Network (CNN) is able to distinguish between non-clouds and different types of clouds, including thin and very small ones, and achieve a classification accuracy of 99.94%. Each image is subdivided into superpixels by the SLICO algorithm, which are then processed by the trained CNN. Finally, we obtain the cloud mask by applying a threshold of 0.5 on the probability map. The results are compared with manually annotated images, showing a Kappa coefficient of 0.944, which is higher than that of compared methods.

Keywords: Cloud detection · High-resolution
Convolutional neural networks · Deep learning

1 Introduction

Today, there are many operational high-resolution satellites, and they have multiple applications in agriculture, surveillance and environmental monitoring. The images acquired by these satellites require common procedures such as geometric and atmospheric corrections and cloud detection.

Previous works have addressed cloud detection from different perspectives. The simplest are the threshold-based methods [1–3], which tend to ignore additional features such as object texture and shape and, consequently, show problems in highly reflective non-cloud regions with little detail.

Other methods attempt to explicitly extract and combine local features such as reflectance and texture descriptors that allow the differentiation of cloud and non-cloud regions through intelligent classifiers such as support vector machines or neural networks [4–7]. These methods work well for some types of clouds and

V. Kůrková et al. (Eds.): ICANN 2018, LNCS 11141, pp. 280–288, 2018.
https://doi.org/10.1007/978-3-030-01424-7_28

certain types of territories; however, they usually fail to identify thin or semi-transparent clouds. Given that previously used features are manually selected, some of them prove not to be sufficient for the detection of a wide range of cloud types, which is why methods such as [8,9] propose the use of Convolutional Neural Networks (CNN), an efficient end-to-end deep hierarchical feature learning model that can capture the intrinsic features of high-resolution satellite images.

In this paper, we propose a new efficient method to detect clouds in high-resolution multispectral satellite images from PERUSAT-1, a Peruvian satellite managed and supervised by the Space Agency of Peru (CONIDA). This and other agencies, such as the Peruvian Ministry of Environment (MINAM), require to develop tools for this kind of tasks that work properly in the many Peruvian geographies (e.g. coast, mountains, rainforest, dry forest). As a first step, we used the SLICO algorithm [10] to divide the image into small homogenous regions called superpixels. Then, we generated 27×27-pixel patches around the center of each superpixel and process them in the CNN, as previously trained in the CloudPeru dataset. We take previous works on cloud detection with deep learning as main reference, but extend them to the use of multispectral images and smaller image patches for the CNN input, thus expecting to improve the classification accuracy and the final Kappa coefficient.

2 Proposed Method

2.1 CloudPeru Dataset

A PERUSAT-1 scene has four spectral bands: red (0.63–0.7 m), green (0.53–0.59 m), blue (0.45–0.50 m) and NIR (0.752–0.885 m). The spatial resolution of the multispectral bands is 2.8 m per pixel and that of the panchromatic band is 0.7 m per pixel. We used 15 PERUSAT-1 scenes of different area and from different geographies to create the training, validation and test set in order to train and select the optimal Convolutional Neural Network (CNN), and 15 additional scenes to extract 30 test images of 1000×1000 pixels to validate the proposed method and compare it with others.

Each of the 15 selected images was adjusted to reflectance values. An image labeling tool developed as part of this study was used to manually extract and label cloud and non-cloud patches. Firstly, each scene was divided into homogeneous regions called superpixels with the SLICO algorithm using only the RGB channels, setting the size to approximately 150 pixels and the compactness to 0.1. This is done because some cloud regions, especially thin clouds, have very irregular shape, and a low compactness value encourages the SLICO algorithm to create more irregular superpixels. Then, after choosing a labeling option (cloud or non-cloud), the user selects multiple superpixels, thus creating a patch for each one and taking a 27×27 - pixel window around its center. Using this method, we created the CloudPeru dataset[1], conformed by 476,422 image patches, of which 207,963 are clouds and 268,459 are non-clouds. We split 95%

[1] The CloudPeru dataset is available at the web link [11].

Fig. 1. Color corrected sample images from CloudPeru dataset for visualization.

of the data to create the training set, 2.5% to create the validation set and 2.5% to create the test set. A sample of images from the dataset is shown in Fig. 1.

2.2 Neural Network Training

Figure 2 shows the architecture of our CNN model. It consists of four convolutional and two fully-connected layers, similar to the one presented in [8]. All the convolutional blocks, denoted as "CONV", use 3×3 filters with a stride of "s". Blocks marked with "V" are valid padded, which means that the input patch is reduced accordingly to the filter and stride sizes; if they are marked with "S", it means that the output is the same size as the input. "MAXPOOL" represents a max pooling layer and "BN" a batch normalization layer. The first fully-connected layer has 128 units with a PRelu activation function [12] and the second one has one unit with a sigmoid activation function. The CNN was trained using an Adam optimizer [13] with a learning rate of 0.0001, a momentum term β_1 of 0.9, a momentum term β_2 of 0.999 and a mini-batch size of 512. Figures 3 and 4 show the evolution of the accuracy and the loss, respectively, over training time.

Additionally, to select the optimal window size, we created two more databases: the first with 493,460 four-channel image patches of 21×21 pixels and the second with 288,478 three-channel image patches (RGB) of 55×55 pixels, as used in [8,9]. We split the data in the same proportions as we previously did and use the same architecture to train a new CNN for each dataset.

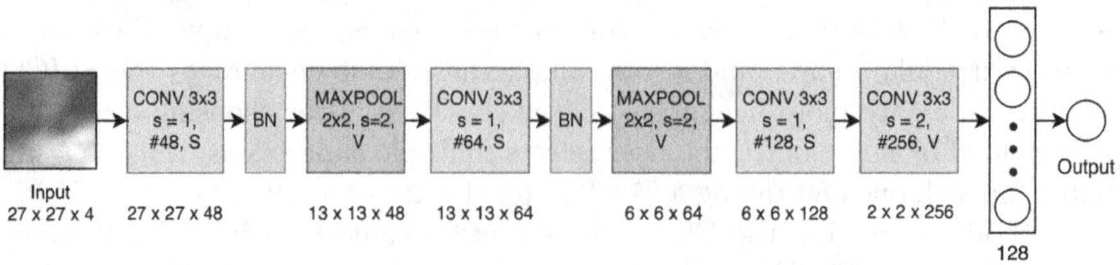

Fig. 2. The proposed CNN model architecture.

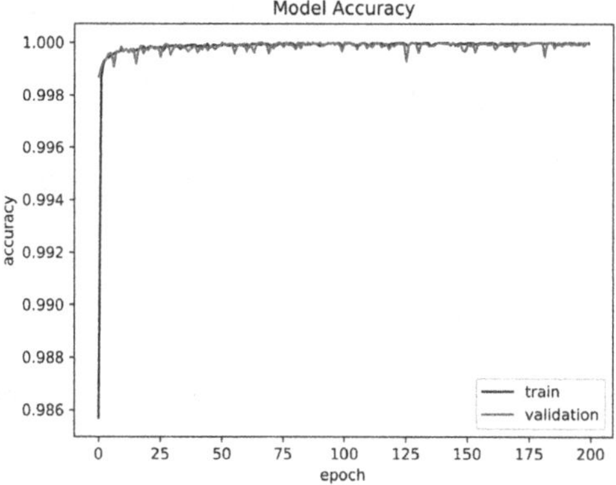

Fig. 3. Epochs vs. Accuracy for training in the CloudPeru dataset.

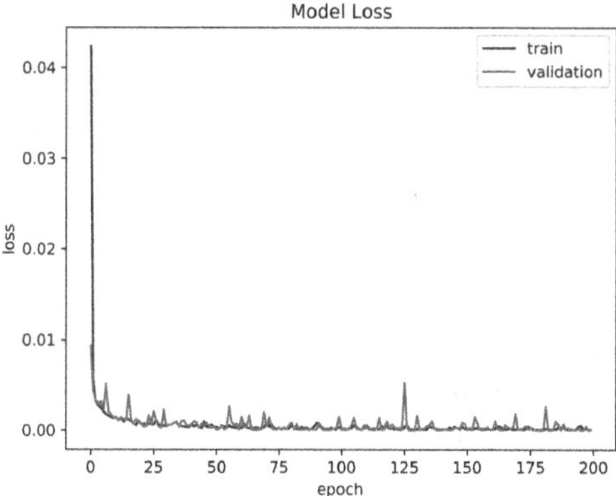

Fig. 4. Epochs vs. Loss for training in the CloudPeru dataset.

The evaluation consists of comparison of metrics between the results obtained with each validation set, as shown in Table 1, proving that the optimal patch size is 27×27 pixels, which is why it was selected to create the CloudPeru dataset.

In addition, Table 2 compares the selected network, CNN1 (Fig. 3), with two other networks. The first one, CNN2, has only three convolutional blocks and can be described as $CONV1(27 \times 27 \times 48) \rightarrow BN1 \rightarrow MAXP1 \rightarrow CONV2(13 \times 13 \times 96) \rightarrow CONV3(6 \times 6 \times 128) \rightarrow FC4(128) \rightarrow FC5(1)$, while the second one, CNN3, is more complex and has five convolutional blocks, which can be described as $CONV1(27 \times 27 \times 32) \rightarrow BN1 \rightarrow MAXP1 \rightarrow CONV2(13 \times 13 \times 64) \rightarrow BN2 \rightarrow MAXP2 \rightarrow CONV3(6 \times 6 \times 128) \rightarrow BN3 \rightarrow CONV4(6 \times 6 \times 256) \rightarrow CONV5(2 \times 2 \times 512) \rightarrow FC6(128) \rightarrow FC7(1)$. Each model is trained for 200 epochs approximately, using an early stopping criteria considering $1e-05$ as the minimum change in loss quantity (binary cross-entropy) to qualify as an improvement. Therefore, Table 2 proves that the selected network CNN1 has

Table 1. Comparison of metrics beteen the results obtained with the three datasets.

Patch size	Accuracy (%)	Precision (%)	Recall (%)	Specificity (%)
21 × 21	99.508	99.357	99.451	99.548
27 × 27	99.990	99.837	99.942	99.873
55 × 55	99.823	99.801	99.843	99.810

Table 2. Comparison of metrics beteen different architectures.

Network	Accuracy (%)	Precision (%)	Recall (%)	Specificity (%)
CNN1	99.990	99.837	99.942	99.873
CNN2	99.714	99.423	99.924	99.550
CNN3	99.874	99.810	99.905	99.850

the best performance. When evaluating on the test set, it shows an accuracy of 99.945%, a precision of 99.952%, a recall of 99.923% and a specificity of 99.962%.

3 Results

The proposed algorithm was implemented using Python 3.6 on a PC with Intel CPU i7-7000 at 3.6 GHz and a NVIDIA GeForce GTX 1070 GPU. As explained in Sect. 2.1, we use 30 test images of 1000 × 1000 pixels extracted from 15 PERUSAT-1 scenes of different geographies, such as coast, tropical forest, desert, urban areas and agricultural areas.

We first apply the SLICO algorithm for each test image using the same previously mentioned parameters (Fig. 5b). Then, we generated a four-channel patch of 27 × 27 pixels around the center of each super pixel, which is processed by the trained CNN, whose output is taken as the probability of said super pixel to be considered as a cloud, so that we are able to create a probability map as shown in Fig. 5c. After that, we apply a threshold of 0.5 over the probability map in order to create the final cloud mask (Fig. 5d).

To assess the performance of our method, we compared the results with hand-drawn ground truth images. In addition, we compared the ground truth with other four cloud detection methods. The first method uses a CNN and three-channel 55 × 55 image patches [8]; the second method uses texture and spectral descriptors processed by an artificial neural network and a false positive discard method based on Hough descriptors over a panchromatic fusion [7]; the third method uses a progressive refinement scheme [2] and, finally, there is the segmentation method of K-means [14]. The visual comparison of all mentioned methods is shown in Fig. 6. In addition, in Table 3 we included the results reported in [9], which consist on using two CNNs in order to perform multilevel cloud detection extracting patches of 55 × 55 and 111 × 111.

Likewise, we quantitatively compare all methods with respect to the ground truth using five metrics: accuracy (ACC), precision (PREC), recall/sensitivity (SN), specificity (SP) and Kappa coefficient, as shown in Table 3. The ACC ratio indicates the correctly predicted observations against total observations; the PREC ratio indicates the correctly predicted positive observations against the total predicted positive observations; the SN ratio indicates the correctly predicted positive observations against the total actual positive observations, and the SP ratio indicates the correctly predicted negative observations against the total actual negative observations. Meanwhile, the Kappa coefficient yields the numerical rating of the degree of agreement between a detection result and the ground truth.

In Table 3 we note that the Kappa coefficient of our method (94.4%) is greater than its successor (88.2%) by more than 6 % points, which demonstrates its outstanding advantage and means that our results are more similar to the ground truth masks. Besides, the accuracy of the other four methods is around 95%, while ours is greater than 97%. On the other hand, while the precision and specificity of the method in [7] is superior to ours by approximately one percentage value, which is not concluding, the sensitivity of our method is greater than that of the method in [7] by approximately ten percentage points, i.e., our approach has greater capacity to avoid false positives, like the ones made by [7], mainly in

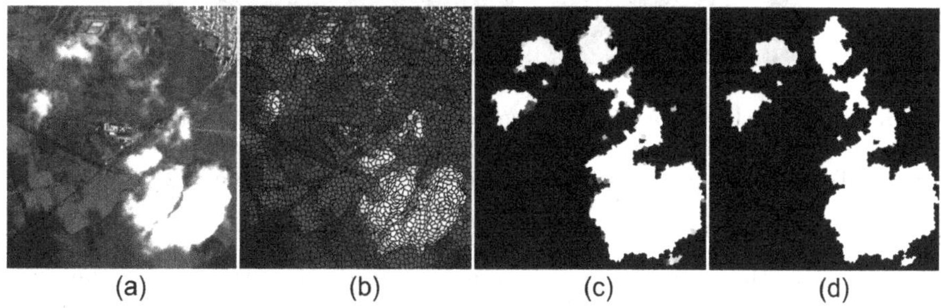

Fig. 5. Cloud detection using our trained CNN. (a) Original image (b) Result of SLICO (c) Probability map (d) Cloud mask.

Table 3. Comparison of performance metrics from different cloud detection methods.

Method	Metric				
	ACC (%)	PREC (%)	SN (%)	SP (%)	Kappa (%)
K-means	95.133	84.538	66.702	95.019	81.671
Progressive refinement	95.227	80.973	71.447	92.799	82.848
ANN [7]	94.862	**98.165**	85.709	**99.234**	87.855
CNN RGB [8]	95.283	93.475	91.818	96.938	88.169
Multilevel CNN RGB [9]	-	90.39	94.54	-	-
Proposed method	**97.569**	96.999	**95.431**	98.589	**94.419**

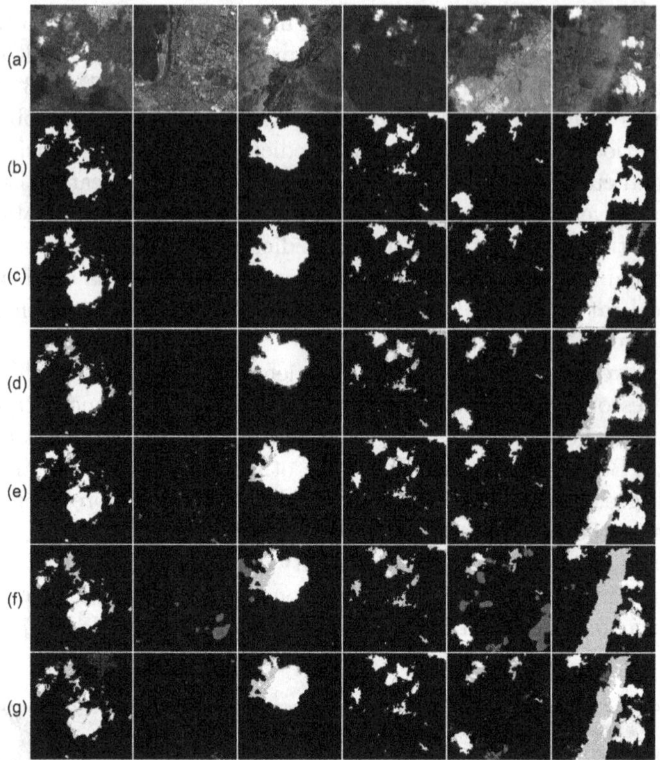

Fig. 6. Cloud detection using different methods. Green color represents False Negatives and red color, False Positives. (a) Original image (b) Ground truth (c) Our proposed method (d) Method of [8] (e) Method of [7] (f) Progressive refinement [2] (g) K-means.

urban areas, as shown in the second picture of Fig. 6e. This is important because misclassifying an area as a cloud involves losing useful information.

Moreover, the CNN trained with three-channel patches of 55×55 pixels, as in [8,9], shows a poorer performance due to two facts: First, the patch size is too big to detect very small and thin clouds and it presents errors in some patches corresponding to the semitransparent borders of some clouds (as can be seen in the first, fourth and fifth pictures of Fig. 6d) and, secondly, it lacks the additional spectral information of the NIR channel. Nevertheless, the precision obtained for this CNN is superior to the one presented in [9] by more than 6 % points, which demonstrates that the changes made to the architecture, such as changing the Local Response Normalization layers for Batch Normalization layers, changing the Relu activations for PRelu activations and using the Adam optimizer instead of the Stochastic Gradient Descent, were of great significance.

4 Conclusions

The inclusion of the NIR band and an optimal patch size for superpixels improved the performance of the CNN model used. The comparison of metrics showed that the proposed method presents a high percentage of accuracy and Kappa coefficient. Likewise, such percentages are higher than those of the other three methods used for performance comparison. Consequently, we can conclude that the proposed method is very efficient for cloud detection in high-resolution multispectral satellite images.

Acknowledgements. The authors would like to thank the National Commission for Aerospace Research and Development (CONIDA) and the National Institute of Research and Training in Telecommunications of the National University of Engineering (INICTEL-UNI) for the support provided.

References

1. Marais, I.V.Z., Du Preez, J.A., Steyn, W.H.: An optimal image transform for threshold-based cloud detection. Int. J. Remote Sens. **32**(6), 1713–1729 (2011)
2. Zhang, Q., Xiao, C.: Cloud detection of RGB color aerial photographs by progressive refinement scheme. IEEE Trans. Geosci. Remote Sens. **52**(11), 7264–7275 (2014)
3. Hang, Y., Kim, B., Kim, Y., Lee, W.H.: Automatic cloud detection for high spatial resolution multi-temporal. Remote Sens. Lett. **5**(7), 601–608 (2014)
4. Li, P., Dong, L., Xiao, H., Xu, M.: A cloud image detection method based on SVM vector machine. Neurocomputing **169**, 34–42 (2015)
5. Yuan, Y., Hu, X.: Bag-of-words and object-based classification for cloud extraction from satellite imagery. IEEE J. Sel. Topics Appl. Earth Observations Remote Sens. **8**(8), 4197–4205 (2015)
6. Bai, T., Deren, L., Sun, K., Chen, Y., Wenzhuo, L.: Cloud detection for high-resolution satellite imagery using machine learning and multi-feature fusion. Remote Sens. **8**(9), 715 (2016)
7. Morales, G., Huamán, S., Telles, J.: Cloud detection for PERUSAT-1 imagery using spectral and texture descriptors, ANN and panchromatic fusion. In: Proceedings of the 3rd Brazilian Technology Symposium - Emerging Trends and Challenges in Technology (BTSym). Springer, Campinas (2018, in press)
8. Shi, M., Xie, F., Zi, Y., Yin, J.: Cloud detection of remote sensing images by deep learning. In: 2016 IEEE International Geoscience and Remote Sensing Symposium (IGARSS), pp. 701–704. IEEE Press, Beijing (2016)
9. Xie, F., Shi, M., Shi, Z.: Multilevel cloud detection in remote sensing images based on deep learning. IEEE J. Sel. Topics Appl. Earth Observations Remote Sens. **10**(8), 3631–3640 (2017)
10. Achanta, R., Shaji, A., Smith, K., Lucchi, A., Fua, P., Süsstrunck, S.: SLIC superpixels compared to state-of-the-art superpixel methods. IEEE Trans. Patt. Anal. Mach. Intell. **34**(11), 2274–2282 (2012)
11. CloudPeru Dataset. http://didt.inictel-uni.edu.pe/dataset/CloudPeru.hdf5
12. He, K., Zhang, X., Ren, S., Sun, J.: Delving deep into rectifiers: surpassing human-level performance on ImageNet classification. In: Proceedings of the IEEE International Conference on Computer Vision (ICCV), pp. 1026–1034. IEEE Press, Vancouver (2015)

13. Kingma, D., Ba, J.: Adam: a method for stochastic optimization. In: International Conference on Learning Representations (ICLR), San Diego (2015)
14. Kanungo, T., Mount, D.M., Netanyahu, N.S., Piatko, C.D., Silverman, R., Wu, A.Y.: An efficient k-means clustering algorithm: analysis and implementation. IEEE Trans. Patt. Anal. Mach. Intell. **24**(7), 881–892 (2002)

Metric Embedding Autoencoders for Unsupervised Cross-Dataset Transfer Learning

Alexey Potapov[1,3(✉)], Sergey Rodionov[1,2], Hugo Latapie[4], and Enzo Fenoglio[4]

[1] SingularityNET Foundation, Amsterdam, Netherlands
pas.aicv@gmail.com, astroseger@gmail.com
[2] Novamente LLC, Rockville, USA
[3] ITMO University, St. Petersburg, Russia
[4] Chief Technology and Architecture Office, Cisco, San Jose, USA
{hlatapie,efenogli}@cisco.com

Abstract. Cross-dataset transfer learning is an important problem in person re-identification (Re-ID). Unfortunately, not too many deep transfer Re-ID models exist for realistic settings of practical Re-ID systems. We propose a purely deep transfer Re-ID model consisting of a deep convolutional neural network and an autoencoder. The latent code is divided into metric embedding and nuisance variables. We then utilize an unsupervised training method that does not rely on co-training with non-deep models. Our experiments show improvements over both the baseline and competitors' transfer learning models.

Keywords: Transfer learning · DCNN · Autoencoder · Triplet loss

1 Introduction

Transfer learning is essential to most applications of deep learning in computer vision because of the scarcity of data available to train large networks in many tasks. The common practice is to take deep convolutional neural networks (DCNNs) such as ResNet-50 [8] or MobileNet [11] pre-trained on ImageNet [4] and fine-tune for the specific task by supervised learning on a subset of annotated samples. Actually, this practice can be considered as transferring features learned on a broad class of images from ImageNet to a more restricted domain.

However, it may be necessary to transfer a model, pre-trained via unsupervised learning, to a domain for which no labels are available. Person re-identification (Re-ID) can be considered as a motivating example as it consists of matching humans across cameras with non-overlapping fields of view. This task is challenging because of high variations in background, illumination, human poses, etc., and the absence of tight space-time constraints on candidate IDs such as in tracking, in addiction to re-identify persons absent in the training set. Even worse, it is usually necessary to deploy a person Re-ID system to a new camera

V. Kůrková et al. (Eds.): ICANN 2018, LNCS 11141, pp. 289–299, 2018.
https://doi.org/10.1007/978-3-030-01424-7_29

Fig. 1. Pairs of images of same IDs from different cameras from different datasets: Market-1501 [21], CUHK03 [14], Duke [22], VIPeR [7], WARD [16].

set for which a large labeled training set is expensive or impossible to acquire, thus further motivating the use of pre-trained models for real-world applications. Unfortunately, if a model is trained on one dataset and tested on another, performances drop significantly below the level of hand-crafted features [5], since variations between datasets are too large (see Fig. 1). For example, Rank-1 score can decrease from 0.762 to 0.361 on Market-1501 [21] test set if the training is performed on DukeMTMC-reID [22] training set instead of Market-1501 training set. Thus, it is essential to perform online unsupervised fine-tuning of pre-trained models. Generative models can provide a nice theoretical solution to the problem of unsupervised learning and transfer learning by constructing a generative model with the latent code containing different parts. The generative model can be fine-tuned in an unsupervised manner by marginalizing over unknown factors of variation.

State-of-the-art results in different tasks are usually achieved with discriminative models. Metric embedding learning [9] or Siamese DCNNs [19] are successfully used in the Re-ID task, although without any capabilities of transferring to new camera sets. Generative models are not as *deep* as discriminative models, and are not pre-trained on large datasets. Actually, they are tested on simple domains, such as MNIST, [2,15] with limited practical applicability. Moreover, these models can utilize additional simplifications such as explicit one-hot coding of IDs [15], which are not applicable in the Re-ID task. As a result, heuristic methods for unsupervised fine-tuning of the state-of-the-art discriminative models, such as the Progressive Unsupervised Learning (PUL) method applied to classification features [5]), are still beneficial.

2 Related Work

2.1 Deep Re-ID Methods

Success of DCNNs in different applications of computer vision did not achieve acceptable performance on the task of person Re-ID, and a number of deep Re-ID models based on DCNNs have been proposed in recent years [1,14,20]. The most popular approach is a deep metric learning with pairwise verification loss. In particular, Siamese DCNNs initially proposed in [20] for Re-ID are frequently used [1,18,19] for this purpose. This approach requires executing a model on each pair of a query and an image gallery. A more scalable approach is to learn a metric embedding (using triplet loss) which maps each image in the feature space where semantic similarity between images can be calculated using simple metrics. A number of models has been developed, [3,12], but cannot compare well with the models trained with classification and verification losses. However, Hermans et al. [9] achieve state-of-the-art results using metric embedding which we have also chosen for practical reasons. Many original Re-ID models exist, but they are out of scope since the focus of our work is on the problem of transferring models to new domains.

2.2 Deep Transfer Learning for Re-ID

There are different approaches to cross-dataset transfer learning for Re-ID. Some utilize dictionary learning methods [17] and l_1 graph learning [13], which are not deep. In these papers, the results are usually demonstrated on cases of transferring models to small datasets to show their advantages in comparison to deep learning models, which usually require large datasets. However, the work of Geng et al. [6] which uses co-training of a DCNN model and a graph regularised subspace learning model for unsupervised transfer learning, shows the potential to fine-tune DCNNs on the same small datasets (e.g. VIPeR [7] or PRID [10]) in order to achieve better performance. Real Re-ID systems can gather a large unlabeled amount of data quickly. A recent work by Fan et al. [5] describes a PUL method consisting of simultaneous improvement of the DCNN model and person clustering, and conducted experimental validations on larger modern datasets including Market-1501 [21] and Duke [22]. We consider Fan et al. [5] more practical and realistic for our purposes, while assuming PUL a baseline for our comparison. The contributions of our work are as follows:

- A new, purely deep neural architecture is developed for cross-dataset transfer learning, consisting of a DCNN and an autoencoder, which latent code is divided into embedding and nuisance variables.

- A method for training the proposed model is described, which preserves the properties of metric embedding during autoencoder unsupervised pre-training and fine-tuning.
- Experiments are conducted showing considerable improvements over the baseline method.

3 Metric Embedding Learning

3.1 Loss Function

For person Re-ID, it is usually assumed that bounding boxes (BBs) around humans are already extracted. BBs are usually resized to a fixed size. Each BB yields a pattern (image) in an initial space of raw features $\mathbf{x} \in \mathbb{R}^N$. BBs containing certain IDs can be tracked by each camera, forming *tracklets*, and in practice, it is better to compare tracklets instead of separate BBs. Each image $\mathbf{x}$ corresponds to a certain ID y, and the task is to identify which images from different cameras have the same ID. The IDs can be considered surrogate of classes, where the number of classes is large and unknown while the number of images in each class is small. Therefore, it is inefficient to cast the Re-ID task as a traditional pattern recognition problem. One way to solve this problem is to train a model with a Siamese network that accepts two images as input and infers whether the two have the same ID. In this approach, the model is run for one query image for each gallery image. Another option is to train a classification model with an DCNNs for a fixed set of IDs known for a training set, cut off the fully connected (classification) layers, and compare images using high-level convolutional features which were useful for the classification. Similarity between images can be calculated directly as distance between latent features with acceptable performance in the practical cases. However, in the non-linear space of features useful for classification, images with the same ID will not be necessarily closer together than images with different ID. An additional step of metric learning is mandatory to improve the overall performance. Actually, what we want to learn is a metric embedding, i.e. a mapping $f(\mathbf{x}|\boldsymbol{\theta})\colon \mathbb{R}^N \to \mathbb{R}^M$ that transforms semantically similar images onto metrically close points in $\mathbb{R}^M$, and semantically dissimilar images onto metrically distant points, i.e. $D_{i,j} = D(f(\mathbf{x}_i|\boldsymbol{\theta}), f(\mathbf{x}_j|\boldsymbol{\theta}))$ is small if $y_i = y_j$ and large otherwise, where D is some metric distance measure (e.g. Euclidean [9]). One can try to learn this mapping directly without learning the surrogate classification model, if an appropriate loss function is specified. In this case, the following triplet loss function can be used [9]:

$$\mathcal{L}_{tri} = \sum_{\substack{a,p,n \\ y_a = y_p \neq y_n}} [m + D_{a,p} - D_{a,n}]_+ \tag{1}$$

where m is some margin by which positive and negative examples should be separated. That is, different triplets of images are considered – one is the anchor image with index a, the other is a positive example $y_p = y_a$ with index p, and the last one is a negative example $y_n \neq y_a$ with index n. We want the distance $D_{a,p}$ to be smaller than the distance $D_{a,n}$ by m. Softplus $ln(1+exp(x))$ is proposed in place of the hinge function $[m + \bullet]_+$ in [9], since in Re-ID we want to pull images with the same ID, even after the margin m is reached. Hard positive samples and hard negative samples shall be selected to make embedding learning with the triplet loss successful. Computationally efficient selection of hard samples can be done with the use of *Batch Hard* loss function [9]. The idea is to form batches using P randomly selected classes (IDs) with randomly sampled K images per class, and to select the hardest positive and negative samples within the batch to form the triplets for the loss function [9].

3.2 Network Architecture

We implemented the same network architecture as in [9] with a few differences. Instead of ResNet-50, we used MobileNet [11], since we found that the performance is very similar, while MobileNet is much faster. We also discarded the last classification layer and added two fully connected layers to map high-level convolutional features to the embedding space. Similarly, see Hermans et al. [9], we used the first dense layer with 1024 units with ReLU activation function, while the second (output) layer had 128 units corresponding to the embedding dimension. We also used batch normalization between layers.

3.3 Embedding Training

For the metric embedding training, we used ADAM optimizer with default parameters ($\beta_1 = 0.9, \beta_2 = 0.999$). The learning rate was set to 10^{-4} during the first 100 epochs, and during the next 300 epochs we exponentially decayed the learning rate to 10^{-7}. The number of steps per epoch was somewhat arbitrarily defined as N_{total}/N_{batch}, where N_{total} is the total number of images in the datasets used, and $N_{batch} = K{*}P$ is the batch size. We used $K = 4$ and $P = 18$ in all experiments. We also applied embedding training on multiple datasets. Instead of simply merging the datasets together, we trained an embedding in such a way that the network never *sees* images from different datasets simultaneously. We achieved this by forming each batch with images from only one dataset, and we continuously switched between them during training. This was done to prevent the model from simply pushing images from different datasets apart. Instead, this approach forced the model to search for invariant features, which will generalize to other datasets as well.

4 Unsupervised Transfer Learning of Embedding

The problem with purely discriminative models to transfer learning is that we do not have a criterion for fine-tuning unlabeled datasets. That is why a method such as PUL [5] uses a pre-trained model or some additional inputs to guess the reliability of positive and negative samples to use them with the same loss of supervised pre-training. To enable unsupervised transfer learning, we introduce a generative model describing the joint probability distribution $p(\mathbf{x}, \mathbf{z}_{id}, \mathbf{z}_{nui}, \mathbf{z}_{cam}|\boldsymbol{\theta})$, where $\mathbf{z}_{id}$ is the part of the latent code describing a specific person, $\mathbf{z}_{cam}$ describes a specific camera, $\mathbf{z}_{nui}$ is the vector of the rest nuisance variables (person pose and appearance, illumination conditions, etc.), and $\boldsymbol{\theta}$ is the parameter of the model. Since only few cameras are available and we do not have sufficient data to train this generative model, we consider a model with camera-dependent parameters, i.e. $p(\mathbf{x}, \mathbf{z}_{id}, \mathbf{z}_{nui}|\boldsymbol{\theta}(\text{cam}))$. We want to train this model marginalizing over latent variables on several datasets to get the parameters $\boldsymbol{\theta}(\text{cam})$, which will be applicable (non-optimally) to different cameras, and then fine-tune (specialize) for a specific camera without labeled data. Using a generative model for Re-ID, we want the latent code $\mathbf{z}_{id}$ for IDs to be a metric embedding. One option is to train a generative model, e.g. Adversarial Autoencoders (AAE) [15], using an additional update for $\mathbf{z}_{id}$ with the triplet loss. Unfortunately, the quality of embedding drops because the updates for the adversarial and reconstruction losses spoil it. If we take the embedding trained independently, we will not know the corresponding priors $p(\mathbf{z}_{id})$, and we cannot directly use this embedding within a generative model. Therefore, we performed an unsupervised fine-tuning of the embedding without knowing or enforcing the corresponding priors $p(\mathbf{z}_{id})$ and $p(\mathbf{z}_{nui})$.

4.1 Our Solution

For practical considerations, we show improvements on the state-of-the-art Re-ID model. The first step of our method is to train the embedding model $\mathbf{z}_{id} = f_{emb}(\mathbf{x}|\boldsymbol{\theta}_{emb})$ as described in Sect. 3. We supplement this mapping with the mappings $\mathbf{z}_{nui} = f_{nui}(\mathbf{x}|\boldsymbol{\theta}_{nui})$ and $\mathbf{x} = f_{dec}(\mathbf{z}_{id}, \mathbf{z}_{nui}|\boldsymbol{\theta}_{dec})$. Here, (f_{emb}, f_{nui}) is an encoder with the latent code consisting of two parts – $\mathbf{z}_{id}$ and $\mathbf{z}_{nui}$, and f_{dec} is a decoder constituting together an autoencoder. In the second step of our method we train the autoencoder using the same available labeled datasets, on which the embedding was trained. Here, weights $\boldsymbol{\theta}_{emb}$ are kept frozen, and $\boldsymbol{\theta}_{nui}$ and $\boldsymbol{\theta}_{dec}$ are optimized to minimize the reconstruction loss. This gives the pre-trained autoencoder, i.e. one part of the latent code to which corresponds the state-of-the-art embedding mapping. We will call this model EmbAE. However, the parameters of the autoencoder are not optimized for the target cameras, for which only unlabeled data is available. Thus, the third step should be the unsupervised fine-tuning. We can try to learn the parameters of all parts of the model, including $\boldsymbol{\theta}_{emb}$, $\boldsymbol{\theta}_{nui}$ and, $\boldsymbol{\theta}_{dec}$. Even such straightforward fine-tuning of the whole autoencoder improves scores of the model on new datasets, but it is not the best approach since nothing prevents $\mathbf{z}_{id}$ and $\mathbf{z}_{nui}$ from mixing within it. A layman approach to prevent this, is to freeze $\boldsymbol{\theta}_{nui}$ on the unsupervised fine-tuning step. This method works in practice even though $\boldsymbol{\theta}_{nui}$ should also depend on the dataset. We call this model EmbAE-fix$\boldsymbol{\theta}_{nui}$. It is possible to prevent $\mathbf{z}_{id}$ and $\mathbf{z}_{nui}$ from mixing by optimizing $\boldsymbol{\theta}_{emb}$ and $\boldsymbol{\theta}_{nui}$ separately. We developed the following two-step fine-tuning procedure: first, discard pre-trained $\boldsymbol{\theta}_{nui}$ and optimize it with reconstruction loss with fixed $\boldsymbol{\theta}_{emb}$ and $\boldsymbol{\theta}_{dec}$. Second, we optimize $\boldsymbol{\theta}_{emb}$ and $\boldsymbol{\theta}_{dec}$ using fixed new $\boldsymbol{\theta}_{nui}$. We call this model EmbAE-new$\boldsymbol{\theta}_{nui}$. It appears that the mapping parameters $\boldsymbol{\theta}_{nui}$ are considerably different for different datasets. We also considered a model which has its own mapping $f_{nui}(\mathbf{x}|\boldsymbol{\theta}_{nui})$ for each dataset. It is fine-tuned similarly to EmbAE-new$\boldsymbol{\theta}_{nui}$, but during pre-training on multiple datasets it also maintains different values of $\boldsymbol{\theta}_{nui}$ for each of them. However, this model is outperformed by the model, in which different $\boldsymbol{\theta}_{nui}$ is learned for each camera and each dataset. We call this model EmbAE-cam$\boldsymbol{\theta}_{nui}$. The method consists in the following steps:

- Offline training of the embedding with the triplet loss on one or several labeled datasets.
- Offline training of the EmbAE with common or individual (for each camera) encoder part $f_{nui}(\mathbf{x}|\boldsymbol{\theta}_{nui})$.
- Unsupervised fine-tuning with frozen or re-trained $\boldsymbol{\theta}_{nui}$.

4.2 Model Details

The architecture for $f_{nui}(\mathbf{x}|\boldsymbol{\theta}_{nui})$ is the same as for $f_{emb}(\mathbf{x}|\boldsymbol{\theta}_{emb})$. Moreover, they share the same convolutional features of MobileNet. Only dense layers are independent, but with the same structure: dense layer with 1024 units and ReLU activations followed by batch normalization followed by dense layer with 128 units with linear activations. The decoder consists of the dense layer with 1024 units with ReLU activation followed by one more dense layer with the number of units corresponding to the number of highest-level convolutional features in MobileNet, the reconstruction loss is calculated for the MobileNet features. Our model network architecture (see Fig. 2) can be treated as an autoencoder with a truncated decoder, or in other words, that EmbAE is built on top of MobileNet: it accepts convolutional features from MobileNet, and reconstructs these features – not the original images.

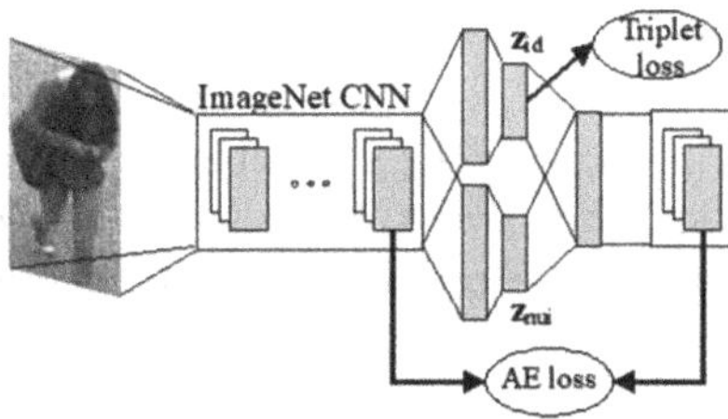

Fig. 2. Deep Re-ID network architecture with unsupervised fine-tuning.

5 Experiments

We tested our approach using standard datasets CUHK03 [14], Duke [22], VIPeR [7], WARD [16] for training and Market-1501 [21] for evaluation.

Pre-training on a single dataset was used for comparison. Training on multiple datasets also helped to achieve higher scores. In our base architecture, we used one encoder for all images. In some cases, we used different encoders for images from different cameras of each dataset as described above. In all cases, we used only one embedding and one decoder.

5.1 Score Computation

To evaluate the models, we used Rank-1 and mAP scores. For each image from the query set we searched the corresponding images in the test set. We let ID_q and C_q respectively be the image identity and the camera for a given query image q. Then, all images with ID_q from camera C_q are ignored and only images of ID_q on cameras different from C_q are assumed positive examples. Images with ID_s different from ID_q are assumed negative samples, including images from camera C_q. In addition to the usual metrics, we consider scores calculated ignoring all the images from camera C_q. We refer to these scores as Rank-1-nd and mAP-nd. We use this score, because in real situations we will search only for images on other cameras, so negative examples from the same camera C_q will not be considered. In our experiments, we used test-time data augmentation (see [9] for details) in the score calculation. All networks were trained and tuned on data augmented by horizontal flip. We also used embedding normalization, i.e. we normalize $\mathbf{z}_{id}$ by its length: $\mathbf{z}_{id}/|\mathbf{z}_{id}|$ to increase the quality of models after unsupervised fine-tuning, because optimizing the reconstruction loss can distort the embedding space. The normalization was used only for score calculation.

5.2 Single Dataset Pre-training

Our first experiment was carried out for the models pre-trained on Duke dataset [22]. Tests were performed on a different non-overlapping dataset, namely, Market-1501 [21]. Table 1 shows the results of the evaluation of different proposed architectures in comparison with the baseline model. The model with different encoders for different cameras provided the best results, and the improvement is rather large. EmbAE-new$\boldsymbol{\theta}_{nui}$ is no better than EmbAE-fix$\boldsymbol{\theta}_{nui}$. Thus, the better performance of EmbAE-cam$\boldsymbol{\theta}_{nui}$ is not simply resulting from the optimization of $\boldsymbol{\theta}_{nui}$ for the specific dataset, but also to the increase of invariance of embedding w.r.t. cameras that helped to move all camera-variant features into $f_{nui}(\mathbf{x}|\boldsymbol{\theta}_{nui})$.

5.3 Multiple Dataset Pre-training

We pre-trained our models using four datasets: Duke [22], CUHK03 [14], VIPeR [7], WARD [16]. Table 2 shows the results of evaluation of these models in comparison with the baseline model. The model with different $\boldsymbol{\theta}_{nui}$ for each camera has the best scores. Although the improvements due to unsupervised fine-tuning became smaller, the final scores were much higher because the models properly pre-trained on several datasets were already considerably better.

Table 1. Re-ID accuracy of EmbAE trained on one dataset.

Model	Rank-1		Rank-1-nd		mAP		mAP-nd	
Baseline	0.421		0.485		0.177		0.211	
EmbAE-fix$\boldsymbol{\theta}_{nui}$	0.553	(+0.132)	0.661	(+0.176)	0.275	(+0.098)	0.339	(+0.128)
EmbAE-new$\boldsymbol{\theta}_{nui}$	0.556	(+0.135)	0.650	(+0.165)	0.280	(+0.103)	0.337	(+0.126)
EmbAE-cam$\boldsymbol{\theta}_{nui}$	0.585	(+0.164)	0.669	(+0.184)	0.294	(+0.117)	0.345	(+0.134)

Table 2. Re-ID accuracy of EmbAE trained on one dataset.

Model	Rank-1		Rank-1-nd		mAP		mAP-nd	
Baseline	0.528		0.607		0.273		0.322	
EmbAE-fix$\boldsymbol{\theta}_{nui}$	0.596	(+0.068)	0.712	(+0.105)	0.329	(+0.056)	0.399	(+0.077)
EmbAE-new$\boldsymbol{\theta}_{nui}$	0.606	(+0.078)	0.707	(+0.1)	0.342	(+0.069)	0.404	(+0.082)
EmbAE-cam$\boldsymbol{\theta}_{nui}$	0.643	(+0.115)	0.729	(+0.122)	0.357	(+0.084)	0.414	(+0.092)

5.4 Comparison with PUL

We are interested in training our model on a large high-quality dataset like Duke [22] and also evaluating on other large datasets. We compare the scores achieved by our model with PUL method [5], for which the results of transferring from both Duke and multiple datasets to Market-1501 [21] are available. Tables 3 and 4 show the results of this comparison, including the results obtained with the baseline models without transfer learning and improvements over these models from fine-tuning. Despite that PUL uses an additional parameter (number of IDs in the new dataset), and that it was applied to improve the worse model,

Table 3. Re-ID accuracy of PUL and EmbAE methods pre-trained on Duke.

Model	Rank-1		mAP	
Baseline PUL	0.361		0.142	
Fine-Tuned PUL	0.447	(+0.086)	0.201	(+0.059)
Baseline embedding	0.421		0.273	
EmbAE-cam$\boldsymbol{\theta}_{nui}$	0.585	(+0.164)	0.294	(+0.117)

Table 4. Re-ID accuracy of PUL/EmbAE pre-trained on multiple datasets.

Model	Rank-1		mAP	
Baseline PUL	0.400		0.170	
Fine-Tuned PUL	0.455	(+0.055)	0.205	(+0.035)
Baseline embedding	0.528		0.273	
EmbAE-cam$\boldsymbol{\theta}_{nui}$	0.643	(+0.115)	0.357	(+0.084)

both the final scores and the improvements over the baseline models are better for our model, although still less than the models trained in supervised manner and tested on Market-1501, which Rank-1 score can exceed 85%.

6 Conclusion

We have proposed a deep architecture for unsupervised cross-dataset transfer learning for person re-ID. This architecture is based on metric embedding learning with triplet loss function, which achieves state-of-the-art results [9]. For transfer learning, metric embedding is incorporated into autoencoders. Special methods for pre-training and fine-tuning of autoencoders, which have a part of the latent code corresponding to metric embedding, have been proposed. These methods preserve embedding and prevent it from mixing with nuisance variables during unsupervised fine-tuning. Our experiments show improvements over competitors' transfer learning models using the recent Progressive Unsupervised Learning method [5], both in absolute scores and over the baseline models.

References

1. Ahmed, E., Jones, M.J., Marks, T.K.: An improved deep learning architecture for person re-identification. In: CVPR (2015)
2. Chen, X., et al.: InfoGAN: interpretable representation learning by information maximizing generative adversarial nets. CoRR abs/1606.03657 (2016)
3. Cheng, D., Gong, Y., Zhou, S., Wang, J., Zheng, N.: Person re-identification by multi-channel parts-based CNN with improved triplet loss function. In: CVPR (2016)
4. Deng, J., Dong, W., Socher, R., Li, L., Li, K., Li, F.: ImageNet: a large-scale hierarchical image database. In: CVPR (2009)
5. Fan, H., Zheng, L., Yang, Y.: Unsupervised person re-identification: clustering and fine-tuning. CoRR abs/1705.10444 (2017)
6. Geng, M., Wang, Y., Xiang, T., Tian, Y.: Deep transfer learning for person re-identification. CoRR abs/1611.05244 (2016)
7. Gray, D., Tao, H.: Viewpoint invariant pedestrian recognition with an ensemble of localized features. In: Forsyth, D., Torr, P., Zisserman, A. (eds.) ECCV 2008. LNCS, vol. 5302, pp. 262–275. Springer, Heidelberg (2008). https://doi.org/10.1007/978-3-540-88682-2_21
8. He, K., Zhang, X., Ren, S., Sun, J.: Deep residual learning for image recognition. CoRR abs/1512.03385 (2015)
9. Hermans, A., Beyer, L., Leibe, B.: In defense of the triplet loss for person re-identification. CoRR abs/1703.07737 (2017)
10. Hirzer, M., Beleznai, C., Roth, P.M., Bischof, H.: Person re-identification by descriptive and discriminative classification. In: Heyden, A., Kahl, F. (eds.) SCIA 2011. LNCS, vol. 6688, pp. 91–102. Springer, Heidelberg (2011). https://doi.org/10.1007/978-3-642-21227-7_9
11. Howard, A.G., et al.: MobileNets: efficient convolutional neural networks for mobile vision applications. CoRR abs/1704.04861 (2017)

12. Khamis, S., Kuo, C.-H., Singh, V.K., Shet, V.D., Davis, L.S.: Joint learning for attribute-consistent person re-identification. In: Agapito, L., Bronstein, M.M., Rother, C. (eds.) ECCV 2014. LNCS, vol. 8927, pp. 134–146. Springer, Cham (2015). https://doi.org/10.1007/978-3-319-16199-0_10
13. Kodirov, E., Xiang, T., Fu, Z., Gong, S.: Person re-identification by unsupervised ℓ_1 graph learning. In: Leibe, B., Matas, J., Sebe, N., Welling, M. (eds.) ECCV 2016. LNCS, vol. 9905, pp. 178–195. Springer, Cham (2016). https://doi.org/10.1007/978-3-319-46448-0_11
14. Li, W., Zhao, R., Xiao, T., Wang, X.: DeepReID: deep filter pairing neural network for person re-identification. In: CVPR (2014)
15. Makhzani, A., Shlens, J., Jaitly, N., Goodfellow, I.J.: Adversarial autoencoders. CoRR abs/1511.05644 (2015)
16. Martinel, N., Micheloni, C.: Re-identify people in wide area camera network. In: CVPR (2012)
17. Peng, P., et al.: Unsupervised cross-dataset transfer learning for person re-identification. In: CVPR (2016)
18. Shi, H., et al.: Embedding deep metric for person re-identification: a study against large variations. In: Leibe, Bastian, Matas, Jiri, Sebe, Nicu, Welling, Max (eds.) ECCV 2016. LNCS, vol. 9905, pp. 732–748. Springer, Cham (2016). https://doi.org/10.1007/978-3-319-46448-0_44
19. Varior, R.R., Haloi, M., Wang, G.: Gated siamese convolutional neural network architecture for human re-identification. CoRR abs/1607.08378
20. Yi, D., Lei, Z., Liao, S., Li, S.Z.: Deep metric learning for person re-identification. In: 22nd International Conference on Pattern Recognition, ICPR (2014)
21. Zheng, L., Shen, L., Tian, L., Wang, S., Wang, J., Tian, Q.: Scalable person re-identification: a benchmark. In: ICCV (2015)
22. Zheng, Z., Zheng, L., Yang, Y.: Unlabeled samples generated by GAN improve the person re-identification baseline in vitro. CoRR abs/1701.07717 (2017)

Classification of MRI Migraine Medical Data Using 3D Convolutional Neural Network

Hwei Geok Ng[1(✉)], Matthias Kerzel[1(✉)], Jan Mehnert[2(✉)], Arne May[2(✉)], and Stefan Wermter[1(✉)]

[1] Department of Informatics, Knowledge Technology, Universität Hamburg, Vogt-Kölln-Str. 30, 22527 Hamburg, Germany
{5ng,kerzel,wermter}@informatik.uni-hamburg.de
[2] Institut für Systemische Neurowissenschaften, Universitätsklinikum Hamburg-Eppendorf, Martinistraße 52, 20246 Hamburg, Germany
{j.mehnert,a.may}@uke.de

Abstract. While statistical approaches are being implemented in medical data analyses because of their high accuracy and efficiency, the use of deep learning computations can potentially provide out-of-the-box insights, especially when statistical approaches did not yield a good result. In this paper we classify migraine and non-migraine magnetic resonance imaging (MRI) data, using a deep learning method named convolutional neural network (CNN). 198 MRI scans, which were obtained equally from both data groups, resulted in the maximum classification test accuracy of 85% (validation accuracy: $\bar{x} = 0.69$, $\sigma = 0.06$), compared to the baseline statistical accuracy of 50%. We then used class activation mapping (CAM) method to visualize brain regions that the CNN model took to distinguish one data group from the other and the visualization pointed at the parietal lobe, corpus callosum, brain stem and anterior cingulate cortex, of which the brain stem was mentioned in the medical findings for white matter abnormalities. Our findings suggest that CNN and CAM combined can be a useful image-based data analysis tool to add inspiration or discussion in the medical problem-solving process.

Keywords: Convolutional neural network
Class activation mapping · Migraine · Magnetic resonance imaging

1 Introduction

Statistical approaches are used in medical data analyses because they are efficient to be implemented and return precise results. Nevertheless, given sufficient meaningful data and computational power, deep learning approaches can also assist in

The authors from Universität Hamburg gratefully acknowledge partial support from the German Research Foundation DFG under project CML (TRR 169).

V. Kůrková et al. (Eds.): ICANN 2018, LNCS 11141, pp. 300–309, 2018.
https://doi.org/10.1007/978-3-030-01424-7_30

the data analytics process. Convolutional neural networks (CNNs) are a useful deep learning approach, known for their high accuracy in learning relevant features for arbitrary classification tasks, especially for image classification. CNNs have been utilized in solving numerous medical data problems, such as multiple sclerosis lesion detection [9], Alzheimer's disease recognition [4] and neuronal structure segmentation [3]. Given a balanced dataset, deep learning approaches provide insights that are unbiased to the medical domain knowledge and potentially suggest out-of-the-box findings. Besides, in situations where conventional statistical analyses did not yield good results, deep learning approaches can be a helpful alternative in getting suggestions and inspiration in the problem-solving process.

A trained CNN classification model can be further combined with the class activation mapping (CAM) approach to visualize discriminative regions, which contributed to the classification of the given data. CAM utilizes the learned spatial information of the CNN model and displays discriminative regions of a given image with respect to a chosen class label. The resulted map shows the locations of discriminative features of the image, which the model used to make the classification decision. For an example, a small part of an image showing a toothbrush can be identified as having the strongest contribution to the image being classified as 'brushing teeth' [10]. Applying CNN for classification means that we get to know 'what' is in the image and applying CAM for feature localisation means that we get to know 'where' in the image are the relevant parts that contributed to the classification.

CNN and CAM combined as a medical data analysis tool can be applied to any image-based data. In this paper, we evaluated the classification performance of a CNN specifically on migraine magnetic resonance imaging (MRI) data and used CAM to point out respective discriminative regions. Migraine is a common headache disorder that originates in the trigeminal nervous system which influences 12–14% of the world's human population [6]. Nevertheless there is no clear evidence which cortical structures are causing the disorder. MRI image analysis of migraineurs might give a hint of which structures are involved in the development of a migraine as well as providing insights into long-term structural changes caused by migraine.

198 white matter MRIs were obtained equally from migraine and non-migraine participants and preprocessed by the authors from the medical domain. The data was then analyzed using CNN and CAM by the authors from the computer science domain. The CNN classification result was evaluated by executing the best-performing model ten times with random data shuffling. The frequently-occurred and sample-based CAMs were reported. We aim to explore whether an outcome that is free from medical knowledge bias could bring insight to the current medical research as well as to foster scientific exchange and collaborations between medical and computer science domains.

Section 2 explains the experimental setup and methodologies used. Section 3 reports the classification and feature localisation results of the best model.

Section 4 discusses the experiment outcome and concludes the study with suggestions for future work.

2 Experimental Setup and Neural Network Architecture

The experimental setup was divided into three stages: (1) dataset acquisition and data preprocessing, (2) CNN training, optimising and testing, and (3) CAM visualization of discriminative regions. The raw MRI images were preprocessed by isolating only white matter regions and discarding all other parts of the images. A three-dimensional CNN architecture was implemented and hyperparameters were modified to get the most optimised validation and test accuracies. The best CNN model was executed ten times with random data shuffling and its accuracy was evaluated. The weights from the best trial were further used for activation maps generation. The regions of activation maps were reported and discussed.

2.1 Dataset Acquisition and Data Preprocessing

The MRI dataset is provided by the authors from the Headache and Pain Research Group at the University Medical Center Hamburg-Eppendorf (UKE). All migraineurs were categorized by a team of trained physicians at the Headache Ambulance of the UKE, while healthy controls reported neither psychiatric nor neurological disorder and no headache disorder in first degree relatives. Raw structural (MPRAGE) images were preprocessed using the Computational Anatomy Toolbox (CAT12[1]) for SPM12 which was implemented in MATLAB. Hereby, each image was segmented into its compartments (grey matter, white matter and cerebrospinal fluid) and normalized to a standardized template space (Montreal Neurological Institute space), as shown in Fig. 1. The images were modulated to keep the volumetric information during this non-linear transformation. The chosen 'mwc2' dataset consisted of 99 white matter MRIs respectively from different migraine patients and the same number from non-migraine people, making a total of 198 images in NIfTI[2] format. Each sample was warped to the same dimensions of (x:121, y:145, z:121).

The preprocessed dataset was handed over to the authors from the Knowledge Technology Group, University of Hamburg, for CNN and CAM implementation. An initial visual inspection showed that every sample looked different from each other, yet there was no obvious feature to distinguish the dataset into the migraine and non-migraine categories, as shown in Fig. 2. A preliminary statistical t-processing done by the medical authors has found no discriminant feature from the dataset, therefore we assumed a baseline accuracy of 50% from the t-test. That means any result from this study that yielded a higher-than-random baseline accuracy can be seen as an improvement to the statistical approach.

[1] http://www.neuro.uni-jena.de/cat/.

[2] https://nifti.nimh.nih.gov/.

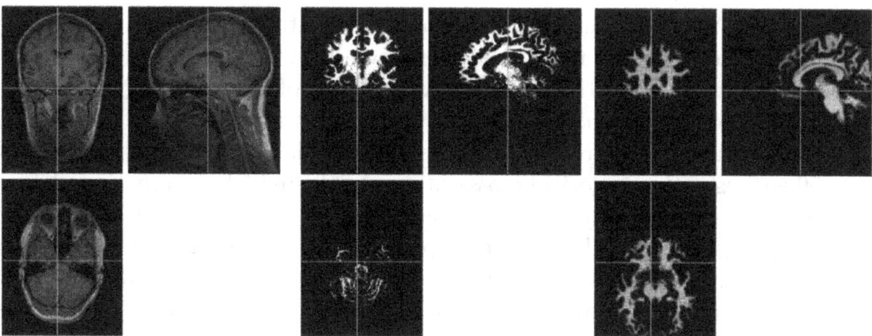

Fig. 1. An example of MRI data: (left) original image sample, (middle) white matter segment and (right) modulated and normalized white matter compartment.

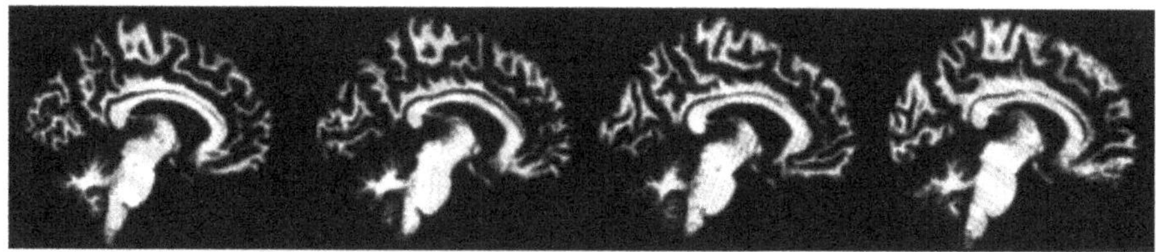

Fig. 2. Four different MRI samples sliced at X: 66/121, Y: 73/145, Z:59/121. Two MRIs from the left are of non-migraineurs and two MRIs from the right are of migraineurs. From visual inspection, all images have different structures but there is no obvious feature to categorise them into migraine and non-migraine groups.

The Nibabel[3] Python library was used to load the NIfTI dataset as multidimensional arrays. The arrays from both the migraine and non-migraine classes were assigned to their respective labels. The arrays were then shuffled within their own classes, before being assigned to the train, validation and test sets. An approximation of 80%, 10% and 10% data proportion were assigned: 158 images to the train set, 20 images to the validation set and 20 images to the test set, with equal data proportion from both the classes to achieve an unbiased outcome. The arrays were then shuffled again, separately within each set.

2.2 Network Architecture

A CNN was implemented in Keras[4] with Tensorflow[5] as backend, trained with two 8GB Nvidia GeForce GTX 1080 GPUs. Figure 3 shows the final network architecture and hyperparameter configuration for the CNN after extensive testing and principled grid search for hyperparameters.

[3] http://nipy.org/nibabel/.

[4] https://keras.io/.

[5] https://www.tensorflow.org/install/.

The search range for the best hyperparameters started by taking the minimum values that made the network converge, up until the maximum values that could be allocated by the GPU memory. A batch size of two was assigned to cope with the limited GPU memory. A larger batch size with a smaller network did not yield good accuracies from empirical analyses. The CNN training phase was set to 50 epochs with categorical cross-entropy as the model loss function, Adam [2] with 0.0001 learning rate as the optimizing function and categorical accuracy as the accuracy measure. The input shape for the first convolutional layer was (2, 121, 145, 121). All convolutional layers have a filter size of (3,3,3) with zero padding, rectified linear units as the activation function and glorot uniform as the kernel initializer. The small filter size was used to retain many low-level features from the input. The number of filters differs in each convolutional layer: 20, 10 and 5 in ascending layer order. Max-pooling layers were only applied to the second and third convolutional layer. The reason not to pool the first layer was to retain as much information as possible from the input to the first feature maps. Each max-pooling layer has the same pool size and pool stride of (2,2,2) to decrease the size of network parameters. The dense layers have rectified linear units as the activation function, with the first and the second dense layers having 300 and 100 units respectively. The output layer has two units indicating a two-classes classification and softmax was used as the non-linearity function.

2.3 Discriminative Regions Visualization

The CNN model that achieved the best validation and testing accuracies was further examined with CAM. The steps to generate discriminative activation maps from the original approach by Zhou et al. [10] are: (1) pass an input image to a CNN, which has no dense layers, (2) the feature maps of the final convolutional layer are global-average-pooled (GAP) and influence the output layer prediction, (3) get a classification prediction, (4) the weights between the GAP and the output layer are multiplied with their respective feature maps to identify important regions, (5) sum all the feature maps into one class activation map, and (6) transform the map into heatmaps. The reason to replace the dense layers with a GAP was that the learned spatial information in a CNN will be lost in the dense layers.

A slight modification was done to the CAM approach that we apply in this paper to preserve the dense layers in our network architecture: feature maps from the final convolutional layer were obtained, summed, normalized and transformed into heatmaps, as shown in Fig. 3. This implied that we did not use the weights between the GAP and the output layer. The reason why the modification did not affect the discriminative region accuracy was because of the binary-class CNN classification. Without relying on the weights, the discriminative regions shown from activation maps were class-invariant. It might be problematic for a multi-classes type classification as each class has different features to prioritize. However, for a binary migraine/non-migraine classification, the discriminative regions showed in any activation map separate one class from another: the same region distinguishes migraine from non-migraine class and vice versa.

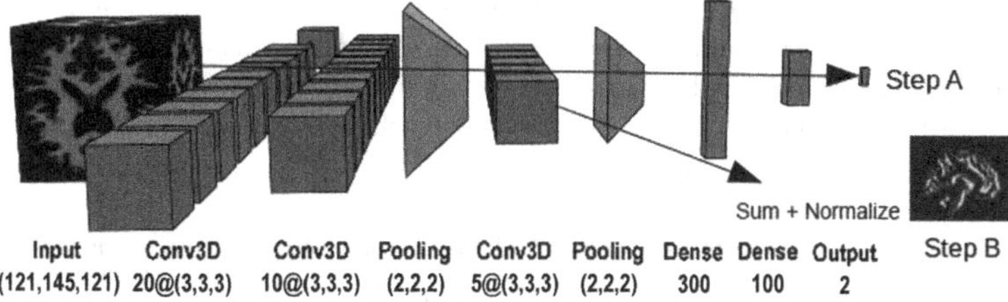

Fig. 3. The three-dimensional CNN architecture and hyperparameter configuration: three convolutional layers, two max-pooling layers, two dense layers and one output layer. Step A: the normal network architecture with dense layers producing a classification prediction. Step B: a modified version of class activation maps. At the final convolutional layer, the feature maps were obtained, summed and normalized to form a class-invariant activation map out of a binary classification.

The final convolutional layer was chosen for CAM visualisation as its activations contain the most detailed features compared to the earlier convolutional layers. For each test sample and each activation unit of a convolutional layer, a three-dimensional activation map was generated by summing and normalizing the activations across activation units. Each map was sliced at the x-axis (sagittal brain section) to obtain 60 slices of two-dimensional activation maps. Each slice was resized to five times its current dimensions for better visual inspection. Overall, the total number of generated activation maps was 20 test samples x 60 slices = 1,200 activation maps. The maps visualized how much a given voxel contributed to the classification result: the blue regions indicate a low contribution while the red regions indicate a high contribution. For an example, Fig. 5 shows discriminative features marked in red colour.

3 Experimental Results

The experimental setup in Sect. 2.2 was evaluated for its CNN classification performance and the best performing model was used to display discriminative regions using CAM.

3.1 Classification Result of CNN

The CNN configuration was validated ten times with random data shuffling and the result is shown in Table 1. The highest test accuracy was 85% (validation accuracy: $\bar{x} = 0.69$, $\sigma = 0.06$) and the lowest test accuracy was 40% (validation accuracy: $\bar{x} = 0.60$, $\sigma = 0.07$). In contrast with established CNN architectures from vision processing, which usually have an ascending number of convolutional filters [7], the number of convolutional filters of this study was descending over the layers (20-10-5 convolutional units). Through extensive empirical testing, we found the model that has an ascending number of filters performed better than the model that has a descending number of filters (5-10-20 convolutional

Table 1. Ten evaluations of the best configuration with random data shuffling. From left: trials, test loss, test accuracy, mean ($\bar{x}$) and standard deviation (σ) of validation loss, mean ($\bar{x}$) and standard deviation (σ) of validation accuracy. Run 7 achieved the best mean validation accuracy of 69% ($\sigma = 0.06$), which led itself to have the best test accuracy of 85%.

Run	Test loss	Test accuracy	Val loss ($\bar{x}$, σ)	Val accuracy ($\bar{x}$, σ)
1	1.06	0.55	1.61, 0.42	0.36, 0.06
2	0.87	0.70	1.16, 0.19	0.49, 0.05
3	0.91	0.65	1.14, 0.21	0.38, 0.05
4	1.31	0.55	0.98, 0.13	0.47, 0.04
5	1.89	0.45	1.36, 0.34	0.46, 0.04
6	1.79	0.40	0.85, 0.08	0.60, 0.05
7	**0.68**	**0.85**	**0.68, 0.04**	**0.69, 0.06**
8	0.77	0.60	0.92, 0.13	0.59, 0.04
9	2.00	0.55	0.91, 0.10	0.53, 0.04
10	1.66	0.40	1.15, 0.20	0.60, 0.07

units). The latter yielded only 35% test accuracy. Understanding that the first convolutional layer needed some minimum amount of units in order to extract useful low-level features for good classification accuracy, the 20-10-5 architecture was used to optimally utilize the limited GPU memory. Three layers achieved the best result compared to other numbers of convolutional layers.

Figure 4 shows the losses and accuracies from the best model, Run 7, which achieved 85% test accuracy (validation accuracy: $\bar{x} = 0.69$, $\sigma = 0.06$). From the twelfth epoch onwards, the training loss decreased to 0.0 while the validation loss slowly increased to 0.75 over time. From the ninth epoch onwards, the training accuracy increased to 1.0 while the validation accuracy slowly increased to 0.75 over time. The losses indicated overfitting of the model as the training loss decreased while the validation loss increased over time. There were further attempts to alter the network architecture to decrease overfitting. Nevertheless, this was the best result with the available data size. Although the validation loss increased over time, the increased validation accuracy indicated that the network did learn relevant features for the classification.

3.2 Visualisation Result of CAM

The best model from the CNN classification (Run 7) was further analysed with CAM to visualize relevant areas that contributed to the classification. The model with the highest test accuracy was used because the features it has learned were the most accurate to separate the data into two classes. 1,200 two-dimensional activation maps were generated from 20 test samples and each map was visually inspected and analyzed. The most common regions that appeared in all test samples are the parietal lobe and the corpus callosum, as shown in Fig. 5 (top).

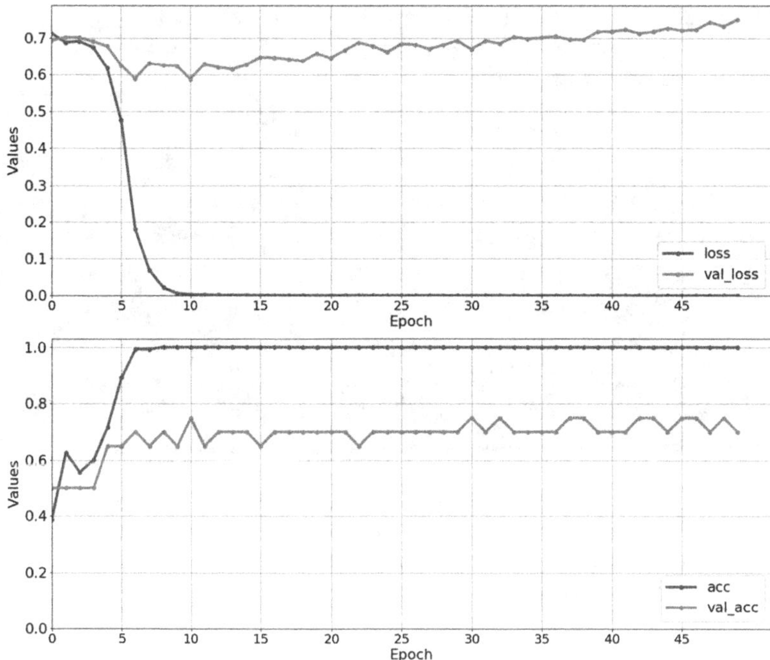

Fig. 4. (Top) The training and validation losses of Run 7: the training loss decreased while the validation loss increased over time, indicating an expected network overfitting because of the small dataset and large data dimensions. (Bottom) The training and validation accuracies of Run 7: both the training and validation accuracies increased over time. Although the validation accuracy was not as good as the training accuracy, the increased accuracies indicated that useful features were learned for the classification.

Although the extent of distinction (red areas) was different for each test sample, these three regions were highly discriminative in every test sample, indicating that the model regarded these areas as important in classifying migraine and non-migraine MRIs. The discriminative regions that appeared specifically in certain test samples were also visualised at the bottom of the same figure, which highlight the brain stem, the corpus callosum and the anterior cingulate cortex.

There are many medical research methods that aim to identify the differences of migraine and non-migraine brains, such as using functional, grey matter and white matter MRI data. These studies report different brain regions which were distinct in showing the differences between migraine and non-migraine brains, such as activation in the brainstem [8], decrease of grey matter in the cingulate cortex [5] and white matter abnormalities in the brain stem and other areas [1]. As we used white matter MRI data for CNN and CAM computations, the CAMs which pointed as discriminative areas at the brainstem showed that these regions were also regarded as important for CNN classification and the other regions suggested by CAMs might be worth further exploration for migraine study.

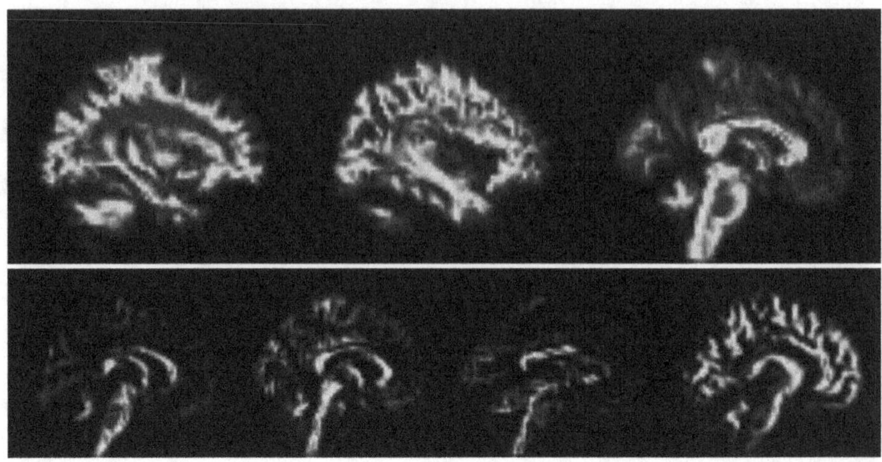

Fig. 5. (Top) Three highly discriminative regions (marked in red) appeared in every test data. From left: left parietal lobe, right parietal lobe and corpus callosum. (Bottom) Four CAMs detected from certain test samples. From left: brain stem (area 1), brain stem (area 2), corpus callosum and anterior cingulate cortex. (Color figure online)

4 Discussion, Conclusion and Future Work

This paper described the classification of migraine MRI data using a CNN and the discriminative areas visualization using CAM. The challenge for the chosen dataset was that the preliminary statistical t-processing returned no discriminative feature. Compared to thousands or millions of images used for general CNN visual recognition tasks, we were dealing with a small dataset (198 samples) with high-dimensional data (x:121, y:145, z:121), which made the neural network prone to overfitting. Slicing dimensions and adding noise variants to increase the data size did not seem appropriate since without professional medical knowledge we might introduce errors. Nevertheless, one main contribution of the paper is the classification performance, which yielded 85% maximum test accuracy (validation accuracy: $\bar{x} = 0.69$, $\sigma = 0.06$), higher than the 50% baseline statistical result and the approach suggested areas that the deep learning model made a distinction for data classification. Some areas such as the brain stem was mentioned in the medical literature fro white matter abnormalities [1], while some areas such as the parietal lobe and the corpus callosum are not mentioned.

Migraine MRI data is challenging to be analysed because the differences between migraine and non-migraine classes are subtle, unlike other MRI data such as Alzheimer's disease, which displays distinguishable structural change between MRIs of patients and the control group [4]. From the medical perspective, the classification and localisation accuracies are yet to be improved, nevertheless, this is a good milestone with the limited number of samples available. Our intention is to provide a useful pipeline to assist in medical discussions as a recommender system from the point of view of a computation system - which feature the CNN used to make the classification decision. For future work, we look forward to improving results even further when more data and more powerful GPUs become available.

There are many challenges in the medical domain to which neural network approaches can potentially contribute. It is important for researchers to gain interdisciplinary knowledge and to design efficient data acquisition processes that help in the performance of neural networks. Fostering collaboration between experts from both computer science and medical domains, more medical-related problems could potentially be solved by combining expertise from both sides.

References

1. Bashir, A., Lipton, R.B., Ashina, S., Ashina, M.: Migraine and structural changes in the brain: a systematic review and meta-analysis. Neurology **81**(14), 1260–1268 (2013)
2. Kingma, D.P., Ba, J.: Adam: a method for stochastic optimization. arXiv preprint arXiv:1412.6980 (2014)
3. Ronneberger, O., Fischer, P., Brox, T.: U-Net: convolutional networks for biomedical image segmentation. In: Navab, N., Hornegger, J., Wells, W.M., Frangi, A.F. (eds.) MICCAI 2015. LNCS, vol. 9351, pp. 234–241. Springer, Cham (2015). https://doi.org/10.1007/978-3-319-24574-4_28
4. Sarraf, S., Tofighi, G.: Deep learning-based pipeline to recognize Alzheimer's disease using fMRI data. In: Future Technologies Conference (FTC), pp. 816–820. IEEE (2016)
5. Schmidt-Wilcke, T., Gänßbauer, S., Neuner, T., Bogdahn, U., May, A.: Subtle grey matter changes between migraine patients and healthy controls. Cephalalgia **28**(1), 1–4 (2007). https://doi.org/10.1111/j.1468-2982.2007.01428.x
6. Schulte, L.H., May, A.: The migraine generator revisited: continuous scanning of the migraine cycle over 30 days and three spontaneous attacks. Brain **139**(7), 1987–1993 (2016). https://doi.org/10.1093/brain/aww097
7. Simonyan, K., Zisserman, A.: Very deep convolutional networks for large-scale image recognition. arXiv preprint arXiv:1409.1556 (2014)
8. Sprenger, T., May, A.: Advanced neuroimaging for the study of migraine pathophysiology. Pain Clin. Updates **20**(6), 1–7 (2012). https://www.iasp-pain.org/files/Content/ContentFolders/Publications2/PainClinicalUpdates/Archives/PCU_20-6_web.pdf. Accessed 14 July 2018
9. Valverde, S., et al.: Improving automated multiple sclerosis lesion segmentation with a cascaded 3D convolutional neural network approach. NeuroImage **155**, 159–168 (2017)
10. Zhou, B., Khosla, A., Lapedriza, A., Oliva, A., Torralba, A.: Learning deep features for discriminative localization. In: Proceedings of the IEEE Conference on Computer Vision and Pattern Recognition, pp. 2921–2929 (2016)

Deep 3D Pose Dictionary: 3D Human Pose Estimation from Single RGB Image Using Deep Convolutional Neural Network

Reda Elbasiony[1,2,4(✉)], Walid Gomaa[1,3], and Tetsuya Ogata[4]

[1] Cyber-Physical Systems Lab, Egypt-Japan University of Science and Technology, New Borg El Arab, Egypt
walid.gomaa@ejust.edu.eg
[2] Faculty of Engineering, Tanta University, Tanta, Egypt
Reda@f-eng.tanta.edu.eg
[3] Faculty of Engineering, Alexandria University, Alexandria, Egypt
[4] Graduate School of Fundamental Science and Engineering, Waseda University, Tokyo, Japan
ogata@waseda.jp

Abstract. In this work, we propose a new approach for 3D human pose estimation from a single monocular RGB image based on a deep convolutional neural network (CNN). The proposed method depends on reducing the huge search space of the continuous-valued 3D human poses by discretizing and approximating these continuous poses into many discrete key-poses. These key-poses constitute more restricted search space and then can be considered as multiple-class candidates of 3D human poses.

Thus, a suitable classification technique is trained using a set of 3D key-poses and their corresponding RGB images to build a model to predict the 3D pose class of an input monocular RGB image. We use deep CNN as a suitable classifier because it is proven to be the most accurate technique for RGB image classification. Our approach is proven to achieve good accuracy which is comparable to the state-of-the-art methods.

Keywords: 3D pose estimation · CNN · Deep learning · Human3.6m

1 Introduction

3D human pose estimation has gained a lot of research interest in the last few years. The more challenging and worthy problem is the estimation of the 3D human pose from a monocular RGB image. It is mainly challenging because of the absence of depth information in RGB images which makes it difficult to predict the 3D information of human joints. However, this confusion can be relieved by considering two factors. The first is the natural anatomy of the human skeleton which restricts the ranges of motion and the relative positions of body joints. The second is that the structure of human

V. Kůrková et al. (Eds.): ICANN 2018, LNCS 11141, pp. 310–320, 2018.
https://doi.org/10.1007/978-3-030-01424-7_31

skeleton is the same for all people, which leads to a high degree of similarity between poses of different adult people.

In the last three years, there are two types of methods that are used: (1) optimization-based methods and (2) regression-based methods. The first approach deals with the 3D human pose estimation issue as an optimization problem, i.e. trying to find the optimal parameters for a scoring function which is responsible for finding the most suitable 3D pose for an input image [1]. However, the most appropriate 3D pose is found by searching all the possible poses in the pose space, which is a computationally intensive process and consumes a lot of computational time.

The second approach depends on learning a regression model which represents a mapping between the input RGB image and the output 3D human pose such as [2]. However, this method ignores the natural anatomy and joint constraints of the human body. Some other researchers tried to consider the body structure by mapping both the input and the output to higher dimensional spaces and then learning a mapping between these spaces such as [3]. Although this modification solves the problem of not considering the body structure, regression-based methods still suffer from the problem of predicting only a single output. However, multiple outputs might be valid for the input image because of the ambiguity resulted from the absence of depth data and the occlusion of the input RGB images.

In this paper, we propose a simple yet efficient approach which overcomes many drawbacks of the previous approaches and outperforms their accuracy. Our approach exploits the structure of AlexNet [4], a well-known deep CNN [5], to build a classification model which is trained to classify a single RGB image into a predefined 3D key-pose. In the training phase, a training set consists of multiple records of human pose images with the corresponding 3D key-poses, i.e. classes, is provided to AlexNet to train a classification model. The key-poses are chosen from a dataset containing many records of RGB images for multiple poses and their corresponding exact 3D poses using a clustering technique. The resulted cluster centers are used as the key-poses for the main CNN-based classification process.

Thus, the contribution of this paper is to show that, for 3D human pose estimation from RGB images, using CNN in classification is more accurate than regression. The usage of classification solves two main problems appearing in regression based methods. The first problem is the negligence of the natural structure of the body and the relationship between joints. In our classification-based method, the relationship between body joints are taken into consideration implicitly because the output 3D key-poses are already selected among a pool of real 3D human poses. The second problem in regression-based solutions is the inability to suggest multiple outputs for the same RGB image to consider the ambiguity in pose images, while classification predicts all the recommended classes and their probabilities. Then, we can select top-n classes to represent the pose image which can lead to higher estimation accuracy.

The rest of this paper is organized as follows. Section 2 discusses some of the relevant previous work. In Sect. 3 we explain the proposed approach in more details. Section 4 shows the experimental results. Finally, Sect. 5 concludes the paper and shows some trends to be researched in the future.

2 Related Work

3D human pose estimation from monocular images has been studied several years ago. Recently, Deep Learning has been widely used for 3D human pose estimation. In [2], the authors used CNNs to predict 3D human pose directly from monocular RGB images through regression. They proved the efficiency of using CNNs in 3D human pose estimation by achieving a very high estimation accuracy compared with the old methods. The authors did not take the correlation between human body parts into consideration explicitly and claimed that the network learned them automatically.

However, authors in [1]. focused more on the dependencies between joint locations. They made an integration between maximum-margin structured learning and CNNs by taking both RGB image and a 3D pose as inputs and learning a score function to output a score value representing the degree of matching between the inputs (an RGB image and a 3D pose). Yet, to estimate the best 3D pose for an image, a computationally expensive optimization problem is required.

In [6], the authors proposed an approach which depends on dual-data-source. The first data source is a set of images with defined 2D joint locations, and the second source is a set of 3D motion capture data. Then the two sources are integrated together by learning a regression model to estimate 2D pose from the image data. Then, the nearest 3D pose is retrieved to finally estimate a mapping between 3D poses and image data through 2D poses.

In [3], a method which considers the correlation between joints in a more efficient way is proposed. Authors proposed an integration between CNNs and auto-encoders, where the auto-encoder is mainly used to account for human body structure by projecting joint positions to a high-dimensional space. However, the overall method is still suffering from the drawback of the regression based methods as discussed above.

Many researchers have been attracted by the big success achieved by CNNs in solving the problem of 2D human pose estimation from a single RGB Image. So, a new trend depending on 2-step based methods has arisen. The first step is using a CNN to detect the 2D positions of the body joints from a single RGB image, and the second step depends on using the predicted 2D information to infer 3D joint locations. The methods proposed in [7–10] are considered as examples on these 2-step based methods.

Another method which combines localization, classification, and regression techniques using CNN has been proposed in [11]. The probable regions in the image where human exists are first estimated, then, some predefined anchor poses are placed into the estimated regions, finally, the placed anchor poses are scored using a classification based method and refined using a regression based method. In [12], the authors improved the end-to-end learning paradigm by proposing two main contributions. First, they proposed a fine discretization method of the 3D pose by forming the problem as a 3D keypoint localization problem. Second, they employed a coarse-to-fine prediction method based on multiple convolutional components to gradually refine the initial estimates. Using this method, they succeeded to achieve state-of-the-art estimation accuracy.

3 Proposed Approach

In this work, we propose a new approach for estimating 3D human pose directly from a single monocular RGB image. The proposed approach exploits both the K-Medoids [13] clustering method and the CNN in the training process in order to learn a CNN-based classifier. The predicted 3D pose is represented by the 3D locations of 31 human body joints which are measured relative to the Hips joint. To the best of our knowledge, none of the previous methods used direct classification to solve the problem of 3D human pose estimation due to the enormous search space; instead they use regression. However, direct regression alone does not produce high detection accuracy due to the problem of the ignorance of human body structure. This issue is required to be treated using additional methods such as in [1, 3]. Also, the issue of being unable to address self-occlusion affects the estimation accuracy highly. This problem is solved in our method by giving multiple probable solutions for the same input image as discussed above.

In our method, we solve the problem of continuous and enormous search space by exploiting a simple discretization method using the K-Medoids clustering algorithm, which produces a set of key-poses which substitute the continuous search space efficiently and at the same time, considers the dependencies between body joints implicitly. Then, the problem can be treated as a classification problem by training a CNN to learn a mapping between the input images and the corresponding key-poses which represent the output classes. Figure 1 shows the steps of the proposed method.

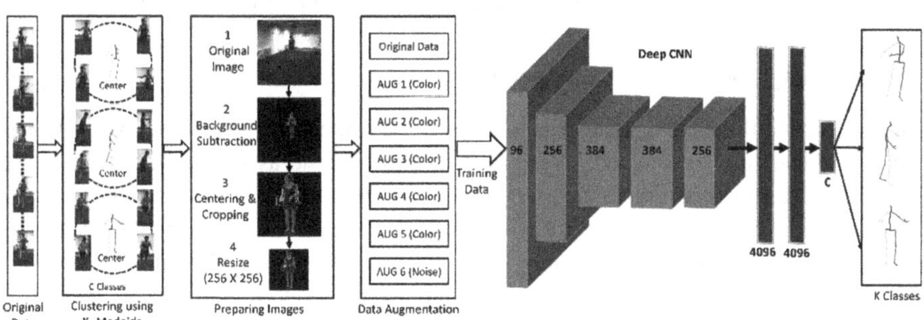

Fig. 1. Training process of the proposed approach.

3.1 Building the 3D Pose Dictionary

The first step in the proposed method is to prepare the training dataset to be suitable for the classification process. All the available datasets which can be used in the training process consist of multiple pairs of RGB pose image and its corresponding 3D joints positions. The dataset on this form cannot be used for classification because joint positions are continuous values. A proposed method for discretization is to replace the continuous 3D poses by a set of key-poses selected from the same continuous data by applying a clustering process.

Thus, the clustering process divides the set of 3D poses into many clusters, where the number of clusters is determined empirically according to the overall clustering accuracy. So, the 3D pose which is selected as the center of the cluster can approximate the whole cluster as a key-pose. The K-Medoids algorithm is selected to perform the clustering task because it uses the data points themselves as cluster centers, this means that the selected key-pose will be a real 3D pose from the dataset, not just a calculated mean such as K-Means, which may not be a real nor an available human pose. The output of this step is a 3D pose-image dictionary. The dictionary contains a predefined number of sets; each set contains multiple RGB pose images resulted from the clustering process and is represented by a single 3D key-pose (the cluster center). Thus, we can build a classification model to map between each set of images and the corresponding 3D key-pose using CNN.

3.2 Preprocessing and Augmentation

A necessary preprocessing step has to be applied before training the CNN. The image background is removed with the help of the background subtraction mask provided with the dataset. Then, the subject is centered in the image, and it is cropped around the subject. Finally, the image is resized to fixed dimensions.

Data augmentation is also an essential step. We used two methods to perform data augmentation: color jittering and noise addition. Color jittering is mainly used to make the method robust against color hue and saturation changes. The noise addition process is important to make the system robust against noise existence. The detailed augmentation process will be explained later in the experimental results section.

3.3 Training AlexNet for Classification

The structure of the CNN used in this method is the same structure as AlexNet [4]. The size of the last fully connected layer is set to be the same as the number of clusters selected in the previous clustering step *K*. *We formulate the 3D pose estimation as a classification problem*. Thus, the 3D pose-image dictionary resulted from the clustering process is used in this step for training the CNN classifier where the input is the pose RGB images and the output is the corresponding key-pose, which is dealt with as a discrete class not a set of continuous values of 3D joint locations. So, the job of the trained model is to map between a pose RGB image and a certain key-pose from the set of the predefined classes. This mapping guarantees that the predicted 3D joint locations will formulate a valid 3D human pose preserving the proper human body structure and relations between joints.

The role of the output softmax layer in the CNN is to calculate the probabilities of the all possible classes of the input RGB image. So, the probability-based descending-ordered classes can be considered as multiple candidates for the estimated 3D pose. The most accurate solution can be selected from the highest probability n classes, where $n \ll K$. This assumption can be used to enhance the estimation accuracy later.

4 Experimental Results

We used the Human3.6m dataset [14] to evaluate our method. Human3.6m contains 3.6 million images and the corresponding 3D poses. The data is organized as 50 frames/sec videos for 15 motions (Eating, Walking, Sitting, ...) acted by 11 actors. The original resolution of each frame is 1000 × 1000 pixels. It formulates the 3D pose as a skeleton of 32 joints. The dataset creators also provide accurate mask for background subtraction and persons bounding boxes.

$$MPJPE = \frac{1}{F}\frac{1}{N}\sum_{f=1}^{F}\sum_{n=1}^{N}\left\| \left(J_n^{(f)} - J_{Hips}^{(f)}\right) - \left(\hat{j}_n^{(f)} - \hat{j}_{Hips}^{(f)}\right) \right\|_2 \tag{1}$$

where $J_n^{(f)}$ and $\hat{j}_n^{(f)}$ are the real and the predicted joint 3D positions in frame f respectively, $J_{Hips}^{(f)}$ and $\hat{j}_{Hips}^{(f)}$ are the 3D positions of the real and the predicted root joints in the frame f.

To compare our results with the previous work we use the same training and testing procedures. So, we trained and tested each action separately. We used five subjects for training (S1, S5, S6, S7, S8) and two other subjects for testing (S9, S11). We formulate the 3D pose as a skeleton of 17 joints like previous works. We trained and tested CNNs for all the 15 actions of the dataset using the two sub-actions of each action available in the original dataset.

We used the K-Medoids clustering algorithm implemented by MATLAB® to construct the 3D deep-pose dictionary. We chose the number of clusters K based on the "Elbow method" [15] by calculating the sum of squared errors (SSE) inside each cluster between the cluster center and the associated poses for different values of K ranging from 100 to 1000 clusters. A number of 500 clusters was a good candidate for the value of K.

In the Image preprocessing step, the RGB images are background-subtracted and cropped using bound boxes provided with the dataset. Then, the images are resized to 256 × 256 pixels. Then, six augmentation processes are performed on the data. Five processes for color augmentation after converting the images from RGB to HSV, and one noise augmentation is performed by adding noise of the form of a random number of square shapes (between 150 and 200) of random sizes (between 1 and 5 pixels) and random RGB colors. Thus, the number of the training images is multiplied by 7 (original data plus six augmentation sets). Table 1 describes the augmentation process.

To evaluate our proposed method against the previous methods, we use the metric of *mean per joint position error* (MPJPE) [14]. For a set of frames F; each frame contains an N-joints' skeleton, the relative MPJPE is calculated as follows: For the training CNN process, the Caffe framework is used to implement and train the network [18]. We used the ADAM optimization method [19] with a learning rate of $1e^{-6}$ and a batch size of 128. Training is stopped after about 25 epochs. The training and testing processes are carried out on a workstation with an NVIDIA Quadro K4200 GPU under Windows® 10 platform. The training procedure takes from 50 to 60 h for one action. Figure 2 shows the effect of considering the top-5 solutions on MPJPE. As illustrated in the figure, just

Table 1. Details of data augmentation and its effect on a sample image.

Data	Modifications	Description
Aug #1	$S_{Aug1} = S_{Im}^{0.4}$ $V_{Aug1} = V_{Im}^{0.4}$	Raising Saturation and Value of the original image to a power of 0.4
Aug #2	$S_{Aug2} = S_{Im}^{2}$ $V_{Aug2} = V_{Im}^{2}$	Raising Saturation and Value of the original image to a power of 2
Aug #3	$S_{Aug3} = S_{Aug1}*1.5 + 0.1$ $V_{Aug3} = V_{Aug1}*1.5 + 0.1$	Multiplying Aug1 Saturation and Value by a factor of 1.5 and adding 0.1
Aug #4	$H_{Aug4} = H_{Im} + 0.1$	Adding 0.1 to the Hue of original image
Aug #5	$H_{Aug5} = H_{Im} - 0.02$	Subtracting 0.02 from Hue of original image
Aug #6	Adding random number between *150* and *200* square shapes of random color and random sizes between *1* and *5* pixels	

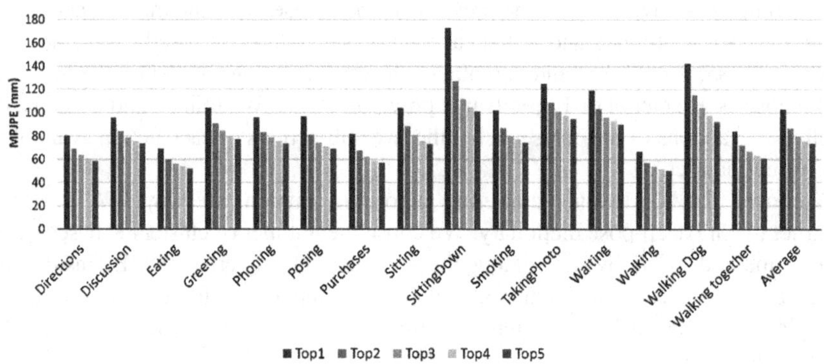

Fig. 2. Top-5 MPJPEs achieved by our proposed method for all actions.

considering the top-2 candidates reduces the error by about 15% which can be exploited by additional selection method to reduce the final estimation error.

Table 2 shows a comparison between our proposed method and the similar previous methods based on MPJPE in millimeters for the tested actions. We calculated the MPJPEs for two cases, the first case is when considering that the solution is the predicted top-1 scores. The second case is when selecting the best class within the predicted top-5 scores (top 1% predicted classes). As shown in the table, we achieve a top-1 average accuracy better than the first 8 methods in the table ([14], [2], [1], [3], [16], [17], [7], and [8]). The next 3 methods ([10], [11], and [9]) achieved higher average accuracy than our top-1 average accuracy, however, our top-5 average accuracy is higher than these 3 methods. Finally, regarding the method proposed by Pavlakos et al. [12] which achieved the state-of-the-art results till now, our achieved top-5 accuracy of individual actions is better than them in 6 actions, and the average top-5 accuracy achieved by our method occupies the second stage after their method

Table 2. A comparison between MPJPE of our method and previous methods using the same test procedure on the Human3.6m dataset

	Direct.	Discuss.	Eating	Greeting	Phoning	Posing	Purchase	Sitting
LinKDE [14]	132.71	183.55	132.37	164.39	162.12	150.61	171.31	151.57
Li and Chan [2]	-	148.79	104.01	127.17	-	-	-	-
Li et al. [1]	-	136.88	96.94	124.74	-	-	-	-
Tekin et al. [3]	-	129.06	91.43	121.68	-	-	-	-
Tekin et al. [16]	102.41	147.72	88.83	125.28	118.02	112.38	129.17	138.89
Zhou et al. [17]	87.36	109.31	87.05	103.16	116.18	106.88	99.78	124.52
Park et al. [7]	100.34	116.19	89.96	116.49	115.34	117.57	106.94	137.21
Chen and Ramanan [8]	89.87	97.57	89.98	107.87	107.31	93.56	136.09	133.14
Tome et al. [10]	64.98	73.47	76.82	86.43	86.28	68.93	74.79	110.19
Rogez et al. [11]	76.2	80.2	75.8	83.3	92.2	79	71.7	105.9
Moreno [9]	67.48	79.01	76.48	83.12	97.43	74.58	71.96	102.4
Pavlakos et al. [12]	**67.38$^{(2)}$**	**71.95$^{(1)}$**	**66.7$^{(2)}$**	**69.07$^{(1)}$**	**71.95$^{(1)}$**	**65.03$^{(1)}$**	**68.3$^{(2)}$**	**83.66$^{(2)}$**
Our Method (Top 1)	80.12	95.5	69	104.3	96.04	96.4	81.57	103.9
Our Method (Top 5)	**58.68$^{(1)}$**	**73.32$^{(2)}$**	**52.1$^{(1)}$**	**77.5$^{(2)}$**	**73.4$^{(2)}$**	**68.8$^{(2)}$**	**57.08$^{(1)}$**	**73.1$^{(1)}$**
	Sit. Down	Smoke	photo	Wait	Walk	W. Dog	W. Together	Avg
LinKDE [14]	243.03	162.14	205.94	170	96.6	177.13	127.88	162.14
Li and Chan [2]	-	-	189.08	-	77.6	146.59	-	-
Li et al. [1]	-	-	168.68	-	69.97	132.17	-	-
Tekin et al. [3]	-	-	162.17	-	65.75	130.53	-	-
Tekin et al. [16]	224.9	118.42	182.73	138.75	55.07	126.29	65.76	124.97
Zhou et al. [17]	199.23	107.42	143.32	118.09	79.39	114.23	97.7	113.01
Park et al. [7]	190.82	105.78	149.55	125.12	62.64	131.9	96.18	117.34
Chen and Ramanan [8]	240.12	106.65	139.17	106.21	87.03	114.05	90.55	114.18
Tome et al. [10]	173.91	84.95	110.67	85.78	71.36	86.26	73.14	88.39
Rogez et al. [11]	127.1	88	105.7	**83.7$^{(2)}$**	64.9	86.6	84	87.7
Moreno [9]	116.68	87.7	100.37	94.57	75.21	**82.72$^{(2)}$**	74.92	85.64
Pavlakos et al. [12]	**96.51$^{(1)}$**	**71.74$^{(1)}$**	**76.97$^{(1)}$**	**65.83$^{(1)}$**	**59.11$^{(2)}$**	**74.89$^{(1)}$**	**63.24$^{(2)}$**	**71.9$^{(1)}$**
Our Method (Top 1)	172.6	101.7	124.9	119.12	66.5	142.3	83.6	102.5
Our Method (Top 5)	**101.3$^{(2)}$**	**74.5$^{(2)}$**	**94.8$^{(2)}$**	89.81	**50.5$^{(1)}$**	92.4	**60.9$^{(1)}$**	**73.24$^{(2)}$**

with only a very small difference (1.3 mm). Figure 3 shows some selected results for both subjects 9 and 11 while acting different actions.

4.1 Discussion

The strength of our method lies in its ability to identify and select 3D poses from the training dataset which have the highest similarity to the test 3D pose. However, the estimation accuracy of individual actions depends on the degree of similarity between the training and the test 3D poses of the action itself. This truth is almost tangible for our achieved results stated in Table 2 where the estimation accuracy for actions (Directions, Eating, Purchases, Walking, and Walking Together) are relatively high compared to the estimation accuracy for the other actions.

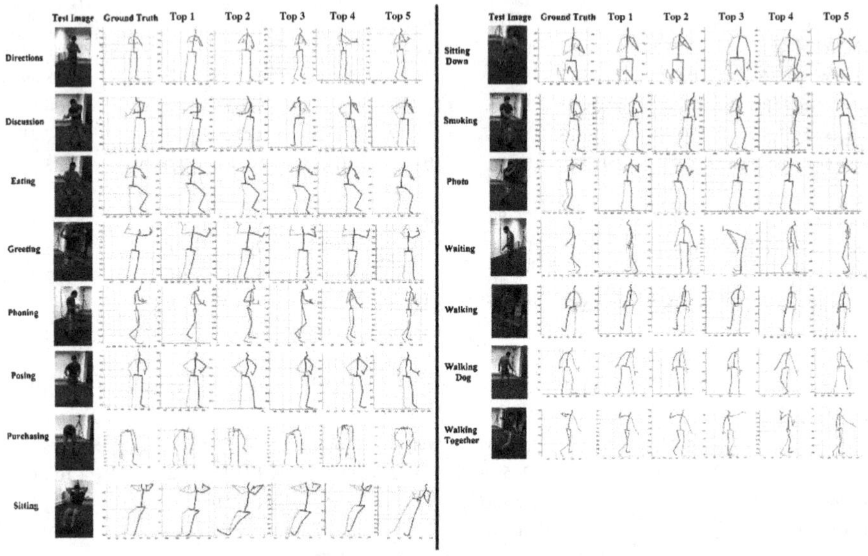

Fig. 3. Samples of the ground truth and all the Top-5 predicted 3D poses.

To prove this assumption, we measured the similarity between all test and training 3D poses for all actions through calculating the average of the minimum 3D pose distances between each test frame and all training frames for every single action by applying the following equation to the ground truth 3D poses.

$$D = \frac{1}{S}\sum_{s=1}^{S} min_{r=1}^{R}\left[\sum_{n=1}^{N}\left\|\left(J_n^{(s)} - J_{Hips}^{(s)}\right) - \left(J_n^{(r)} - J_{Hips}^{(r)}\right)\right\|_2\right] \tag{2}$$

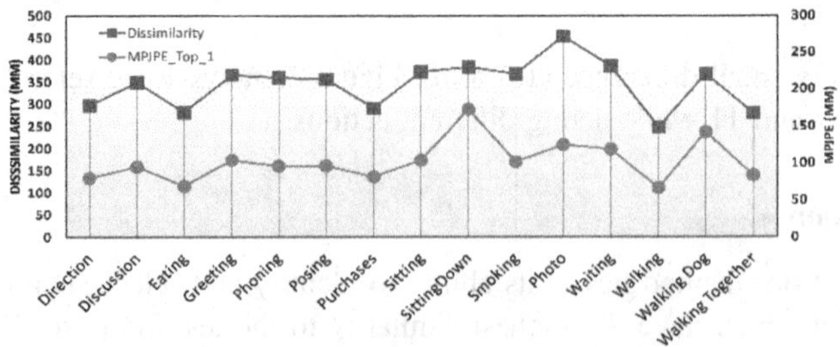

Fig. 4. The relationship between test and training frames dissimilarity and the estimated MPJPE

Where D is the average distance which represents the dissimilarity between test and training data for the selected action, S is the number of test frames, and R is the number of training frames. Figure 4 shows the relationship between the dissimilarity measure and the estimated top-1 MPJPE where the MPJPE is directly proportional with the dissimilarity measure.

5 Conclusions

We have introduced a novel approach for 3D human pose estimation from a single RGB image. The proposed method formulates the 3D pose estimation as a classification problem which classifies the input RGB images into corresponding pre-defined 3D *key-poses*. The target key-poses are extracted from the training dataset using K-Medoids clustering algorithm as a discretization method. Although the search space for 3D human poses is huge, the proposed method exploits the power of convolutional neural networks (CNN) to classify RGB images into a significant number of classes efficiently. The proposed method achieved a prediction accuracy which is comparable to the state-of-the-art methods.

Acknowledgments. The corresponding author would like to thank Intelligent Dynamics Representation Laboratory (Prof. Ogata's Laboratory), School of Fundamental Science and Engineering, Waseda University, Japan for providing technical support for this research work.

References

1. Li, S., Zhang, W., Chan, A.B.: Maximum-margin structured learning with deep networks for 3d human pose estimation. In: Proceedings of the IEEE International Conference on Computer Vision, pp. 2848–2856 (2015)
2. Li, S., Chan, Antoni B.: 3D human pose estimation from monocular images with deep convolutional neural network. In: Cremers, D., Reid, I., Saito, H., Yang, M.-H. (eds.) ACCV 2014. LNCS, vol. 9004, pp. 332–347. Springer, Cham (2015). https://doi.org/10.1007/978-3-319-16808-1_23
3. Tekin, B., Katircioglu, I., Salzmann, M., Lepetit, V., Fua, P.: Structured prediction of 3d human pose with deep neural networks. In: Proceedings of the British Machine Vision Conference (BMVC), pp. 130.1–130.11, September 2016
4. Krizhevsky, A., Sutskever, I., Hinton, G.E.: ImageNet classification with deep convolutional neural networks. In: Advances in Neural Information Processing Systems, pp. 1097–1105 (2012)
5. Zeiler, M.D., Fergus, R.: Visualizing and understanding convolutional networks. In: Fleet, D., Pajdla, T., Schiele, B., Tuytelaars, T. (eds.) ECCV 2014. LNCS, vol. 8689, pp. 818–833. Springer, Cham (2014). https://doi.org/10.1007/978-3-319-10590-1_53
6. Yasin, H., Iqbal, U., Kruger, B., Weber, A., Gall, J.: A dual-source approach for 3d pose estimation from a single image. In: Proceedings of the IEEE Conference on Computer Vision and Pattern Recognition, pp. 4948–4956 (2016)
7. Park, S., Hwang, J., Kwak, N.: 3D human pose estimation using convolutional neural networks with 2D pose information. In: Hua, G., Jégou, H. (eds.) ECCV 2016. LNCS, vol. 9915, pp. 156–169. Springer, Cham (2016). https://doi.org/10.1007/978-3-319-49409-8_15

8. Chen, C.H., Ramanan, D.: 3d human pose estimation = 2d pose estimation + matching. In: 2017 IEEE Conference on Computer Vision and Pattern Recognition (CVPR), pp. 5759–5767, July 2017
9. Moreno-Noguer, F.: 3d human pose estimation from a single image via distance matrix regression. In: 2017 IEEE Conference on Computer Vision and Pattern Recognition (CVPR), pp. 1561–1570, July 2017
10. Tome, D., Russell, C., Agapito, L.: Lifting from the deep: convolutional 3d pose estimation from a single image. In: 2017 IEEE Conference on Computer Vision and Pattern Recognition (CVPR), pp. 5689–5698, July 2017
11. Rogez, G., Weinzaepfel, P., Schmid, C.: LCR-Net: localization-classification-regression for human pose. In: 2017 IEEE Conference on Computer Vision and Pattern Recognition (CVPR), pp. 1216–1224, July 2017
12. Pavlakos, G., Zhou, X., Derpanis, K.G., Daniilidis, K.: Coarse-to-Fine volumetric prediction for single-image 3d human pose. In: 2017 IEEE Conference on Computer Vision and Pattern Recognition (CVPR), pp. 1263–1272, July 2017
13. Kaufman, L., Rousseeuw, P.: Clustering by Means of Medoids. North-Holland, Amsterdam (1987)
14. Ionescu, C., Papava, D., Olaru, V., Sminchisescu, C.: Human3.6m: Large scale datasets and predictive methods for 3d human sensing in natural environments. IEEE Trans. Pattern Anal. Mach. Intell. **36**(7), 1325–1339 (2014)
15. Thorndike, R.L.: Who belongs in the family? Psychometrika **18**(4), 267–276 (1953)
16. Tekin, B., Rozantsev, A., Lepetit, V., Fua, P.: Direct prediction of 3d body poses from motion compensated sequences. In: Proceedings of the IEEE Conference on Computer Vision and Pattern Recognition, pp. 991–1000 (2016)
17. Zhou, X., Zhu, M., Leonardos, S., Derpanis, K.G., Daniilidis, K.: Sparseness meets deepness: 3d human pose estimation from monocular video. In: Proceedings of the IEEE Conference on Computer Vision and Pattern Recognition, pp. 4966–4975 (2016)
18. Jia, Y., et al.: Caffe: convolutional architecture for fast feature embedding. In: Proceedings of the 22nd ACM International Conference on Multimedia, pp. 675–678. ACM (2014)
19. Kingma, D., Ba, J.: Adam: a method for stochastic optimization. arXiv preprint arXiv:1412. 6980 (2014)

FiLayer: A Novel Fine-Grained Layer-Wise Parallelism Strategy for Deep Neural Networks

Wenbin Jiang(✉), Yangsong Zhang, Pai Liu, Geyan Ye, and Hai Jin

Services Computing Technology and System Lab, Cluster and Grid Computing Lab, Big Data Technology and System Lab, School of Computer Science and Technology, Huazhong University of Science and Technology, Wuhan 430074, China
{wenbinjiang,zhangyangsong,liunxpaisley,gyye,hjin}@hust.edu.cn

Abstract. Data parallelism and model parallelism are regarded as two major parallelism strategies for *deep neural networks* (DNNs). However, the two methodologies achieve acceleration mainly by applying coarse-grained network-model-based parallelization. Neither methodology can fully tap into the potentials of the parallelism of network models and many-core systems (such as GPUs). In this work, we propose a novel fine-grained parallelism strategy based on layer-wise parallelization (named FiLayer), which includes inter-layer parallelism and intra-layer parallelism. The former allows several adjacent layers in a network model to be processed in a pipelined manner. The latter divides the operations in one layer into several parts and processes them in parallel. CUDA streams are applied to realize the above fine-grained parallelisms. FiLayer is implemented by extending Caffe. Several typical datasets are used for the performance evaluation. The experimental results indicate that FiLayer can help Caffe achieve speedups of 1.58×–2.19×.

Keywords: Deep learning · Fined-grained parallelism · CUDA stream

1 Introduction

In recent years, deep learning [11] (also known as *deep neural networks* (DNNs)) has made various breakthroughs in numerous areas such as speech recognition, text processing, and image processing. A variety of open-source projects, including Caffe [7], MXNet [3], and TensorFlow [1], have continuously been presented. Various deep learning network models, such as AlexNet [10], GoogLeNet [14], and ResNet-50 [5], are also springing up.

To train a good deep learning network model, large amounts of time and energy are necessary (e.g. [10,14]). If we can parallelize the training process of network models, substantial time and energy savings can be achieved. This is a matter worth investigating further. Currently, there are two main strategies for parallelizing DNNs: data parallelism (e.g. [3]) and model parallelism (e.g. [1]). Both data parallelism and model parallelism can be sped up by increasing

V. Kůrková et al. (Eds.): ICANN 2018, LNCS 11141, pp. 321–330, 2018.
https://doi.org/10.1007/978-3-030-01424-7_32

the number of training workers. This coarse-grained parallelism strategy significantly accelerates the training of network models, but certain flaws remain. First, communications for synchronizing between multiple training workers represent a large part of the time required during the training process. Therefore, it is difficult to achieve linear acceleration. Actually, the training speed of a single training worker is decreased instead of being increased. Second, GPUs are not fully utilized, especially for smaller datasets. A large amount of GPU computation and memory resources are often left idle. Additionally, this coarse-grained parallelism strategy is difficult to extend for many researchers who want to use deep learning systems. The main reasons include the expensive GPUs and the technical difficulties in extending the systems.

To address the above problems facing the two parallelism strategies and exploit the potential of a single GPU fully, we propose a new fine-grained layer-wise parallelism strategy (named FiLayer), which includes inter-layer and intra-layer parallelisms. Both of them aim to parallelize the training of network models at the layer level inside a GPU-based training worker. The benefit of FiLayer is twofold. First, instead of adding more hardware resources such as more training workers that speed up the model training through data and model parallelisms, it fully exploits the parallelism potential within network and improves the training speed in a single GPU. Second, it has good compatibility with other parallelism methods. In other words, FiLayer can be used in situations characterized by data parallelism and model parallelism with minimal modification and achieve further speedups. CUDA stream technology is used here to implement the parallelism strategies. We design and implement FiLayer by extending Caffe, and name the FiLayer-based system as LP-Caffe. The experimental results show that speedups of 1.58×–2.19× are achieved by FiLayer compared with Caffe. The contributions of this study can be summarized as follows.

- A fine-grained layer-wise concept for DNN parallelism, which is a meaningful extension of data and model parallelism. CUDA streams are applied to realize the concept.
- An inter-layer parallelism strategy for adjacent layers of deep neural network models. The mini-batch for a model is split into several fragments so that different fragments from different mini-batches can be processed by different adjacent layers in a pipeline manner.
- An intra-layer parallelism strategy for convolution layers. The strategy divides the operations in one convolution layer into several parts and runs them in parallel.

2 Related Works

Numerous works on training neural network models in parallel have been conducted by researchers. Most of them achieve their acceleration by coarse-grained data and model parallelism strategies and by more acceleration hardwares. The following are some representative works.

FireCaffe [6] trains GoogLeNet and *Network-in-Network* (NIN) [8] on ImageNet [13] on a cluster of 128 GPUs, and achieves a speedup of 47× and 39× respectively, compared with the original Caffe. Ammar et al. design S-Caffe system [2] that uses data parallelism to train GoogLeNet on a GPU cluster. It achieves a speedup of 2.5× when increasing the number of GPUs from 32 to 160.

The above works have a similarity in that they obtain their speedups by leveraging more acceleration hardwares. They have difficulties realizing the ideal linear acceleration based on this coarse-grained parallelism strategy. Some research works have paid their attention to lower parallelism granularity level of DNNs. MXNet proposes an idea of dividing LSTM network model into several GPUs by layer. Inter-GPU can perform the computation of layers in a pipelined manner. However, layers in the same GPU still cannot be processed in parallel.

CuDNN [4] is library for optimizing computational functions (e.g. convolution, pooling, and sigmod) for deep learning, which focuses on refining the process inside each layers of neural networks. According to [4], the majority of functions in cuDNN have a straightforward implementation, however, the convolution implementation related to matrix multiplication is not obvious. Since it is not open-source, we can not get more details about its low-level implementation. It is also worth noting that, cuDNN only concerns intra-layer optimization, without considering any optimization approach for inter-layer issue, which is exactly what we want to do in this paper.

Generally, few researches have been done for fine-grained layer-wise parallelism for DNNs by considering both inter-layer and intra-layer issues.

3 Inter-layer Parallelism

3.1 Problem Analysis of Mini-batch Gradient Descent

Mini-batch gradient descent (MBGD) is regarded as one of the main optimization algorithms used in deep learning systems, it consumes less memory and has a high convergence speed. However, limited by the inherent sequentiality of MBGD caused by the data dependency between layers, it is difficult to parallelize the computations between multiple layers.

3.2 Data Pipeline Algorithm

Inspired by the concept of instruction pipeline algorithms, we propose a new algorithm for the processes between multiple layers of neural network models: *Data Pipeline Algorithm* (DPA). The aim of the DPA is to overcome the limitation of the inherent order of MBGD and enables the computations of layers to be executed in parallel. Therefore, more resources can be used for the training process, which can speed up the training process of models. The main ideas of this algorithm are described in the remaining parts. See Fig. 1 for a depiction of the DPA, and see Algorithm 1 for its detailed procedure.

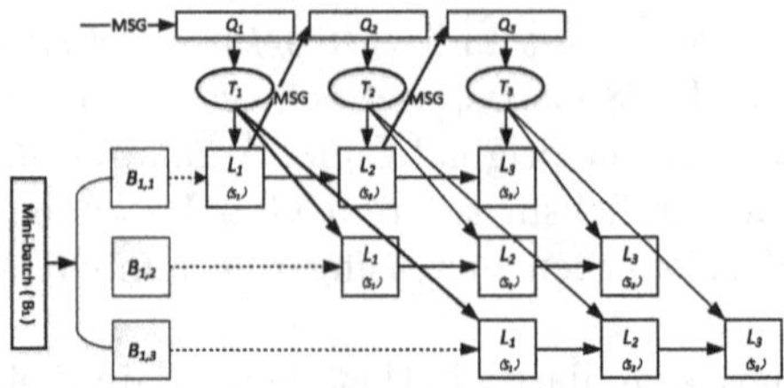

Fig. 1. Depiction of Data Pipeline Algorithm. L_i devotes a part of a model, T_i denotes a thread, Q_i denotes a message queue, B_i, B_j denotes a fragment, S_i denotes a CUDA stream.

First, we divide a neural network model with N layers into N parts by layer (Line 2 in Algorithm 1). Each part consists of one layer, and is controlled by one CPU thread, which maintains a message queue to exchange messages with other threads. During the algorithm's operation, each thread monitors its own message queue and performs different computation operations according to different messages (Lines 11–18). These messages include the forward propagation message (FM), the backward propagation message (BM), and the exit message (EM). Figure 1 shows a schematic diagram of the algorithm.

Second, we split each mini-batch into F fragments to reduce the data dependency between layers (Line 4). Each fragment has the same size, and the data dependency is reduced from a mini-batch to a fragment. At a given moment, each fragment is processed by only one layer. However, different layers can process different fragments concurrently. The former can ensure the correctness of the network model training, whereas the latter is designed to reduce the training time of the network model. Specifically, in the ith iteration process, the first task is to divide one mini-batch into F fragments: $B_{i,1}, B_{i,2}, ..., B_{i,F}$. Next, during the process of forward propagation of the network model, after L_i finishes computing $B_{i,f}$, L_i immediately informs L_{i+1} to enable the latter to compute the fragment $B_{i,f}$ at once. Simultaneously, L_i starts to compute $B_{i,f+1}$, allowing L_i and L_{i+1} to compute different fragments in parallel. The process of the backward propagation of the network model is also done the same as the style of the forward propagation, but inversely.

Third, we create N CUDA streams for each thread and issue different operations into different CUDA streams to ensure different operations can be executed in parallel (Lines 15–16). A stream in CUDA is a sequence of operations that execute on the device in the order in which they are issued by the host code. While operations within a stream are guaranteed to be executed in the prescribed order, operations in different streams can be interleaved, and when possible, they can even run concurrently. Considering the computation operations in different streams are executed asynchronously, CUDA API *cudaStreamSynchronize* is called to synchronize S_i to ensure the logic correctness of the algorithm after L_i finishes the computation operation in S_i, and before it notifies the next layer L_{i+1} to continue.

Based on the above ideas, the DPA can be performed on a GPU in parallel.

Algorithm 1. Data Pipeline Algorithm

Input: *mini_batch*
Output: *network_params*

function TrainModel
  create T_1, T_2, ... ,T_N threads, T_i runs PIPELINE(i);
  for iteration $i = 1 \rightarrow ITER$ **do**
    $B_i \rightarrow B_{i,1}, B_{i,2}, ..., B_{i,F}$;
    $Q_1.push(FM_1,\ FM_2,\ ...\ ,FM_F)$, then $wait()$;
    $Q_N.push(BM_1,\ BM_2,\ ...\ ,BM_F)$, then $wait()$;
    $update(network\_params)$;
  for layer $j = 1 \rightarrow N$ **do**
    $Q_j.push(EM)$;
return *network_params*
function PIPELINE(i)
  $flag$=true; // the controller of **while** statement
  while $flag$ **do**
    $msg \leftarrow Q_i.pop()$; $B_{i,f} \leftarrow B_i$;
    if ($msg = FM$), $L_i.forward(B_{i,f}, S_i)$;
    if ($msg = BM$), $L_i.backward(B_{i,f}, S_i)$;
    if ($msg = EM$), $flag$=false, and $L_i.exit()$;
    $notify\_TrainModel\_thread()$;

4 Intra-layer Parallelism

DPA only realizes the inter-layer parallelism of a DNN. Actually, inside certain special layers, there is still great parallelism potential to be exploited. The convolution layer that is realized based on matrix multiplication is such a type of layer. In this section, we present a fine-grained intra-layer parallelism strategy by parallelizing the processing of the convolution layer.

4.1 Analysis of Convolution Operation

Figure 2(a) shows the forward propagation of a convolution layer in Caffe, where the size of the mini-batch of input data is six. Because all the input images are submitted to the default CUDA stream, the algorithm eventually is performed in a completely serialized form for all the input data. There is also a similar problem in the backward propagation of the convolution layer. Obviously, this type of realization leads to a serious waste of the computational resources of the GPU even if it can support massive parallel computations. Inevitably, the training time of the entire network model increases. In the following subsection, we show how to optimize this algorithm by parallelizing the convolution operations based on CUDA streams.

4.2 Parallelization of Convolution Layer

Figure 2(b) shows the parallelization of the forward propagation of the convolution layer under an ideal situation, where we assume that operations in different streams can be performed concurrently and where the process time of each image is equal. However, in practical situations, operations in different streams cannot completely run concurrently, and the computation times of each image may be unequal. Figure 2(c) shows such a situation, and Algorithm 2 presents more details.

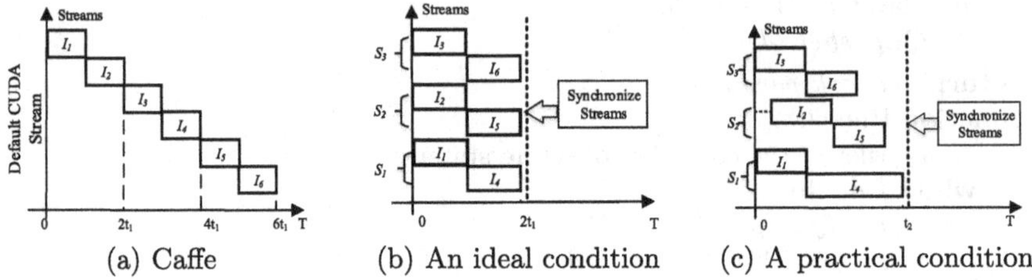

Fig. 2. The forward propagation of a convolution layer. Here, for convenience of discussion, the batch size of the input data is set to 6, and the number of CUDA streams used in (b) and (c) is set to 3. I_i denotes the forward propagation of the ith image of one mini-batch. S_s denotes the sth CUDA stream created by users.

Algorithm 2. The parallelization forward propagation of the convolution layer

---

Input: Btm, Top, W // Btm, Top, and W denote the bottom data, the top data, and the weight of the neural network model, respectively.
Output: Top

1: **function Parallelization_Forward**
2: get S CUDA streams $Streams$;
3: **for** batch_size $n = 1 \rightarrow BS$ **do**
4: $i \leftarrow n \cdot TopDim$; //get the offset of the nth image in Top.
5: $j \leftarrow n \cdot BtmDim$; //get the offset of the nth image in Btm.
6: $s \leftarrow n \mod S$; //get the index of the sth stream.
7: //convert the nth image into a matrix(bf_s).
8: $Input2Matrix(Btm_j, bf_s, Streams_s)$;
9: //execute convolution operation in $Streams_s$.
10: $Conv(bf_s, Top_i, W, Streams_s)$;
11: **for** stream $s = 1 \rightarrow S$ **do**
12: $Sync(Streams_s)$; //synchronize the sth stream.
13: **return** Top

The main idea of Algorithm 2 is to assign different images to different CUDA streams, and to process these images in parallel by utilizing the concurrency of the streams. Specifically, we first get S CUDA streams created in advance (Line

2 in Algorithm 2). Second, during the forward propagation, we need to calculate the offset of the nth image stored in the top data, and the offset of the nth image stored in the bottom data (Lines 4–6). Then, we convert the nth image into a matrix and submit its convolution operation to the sth stream (Lines 7–10). To ensure the correctness of the process, we need to perform the following two steps. First, to guarantee the data for different streams to be independent, we allocate a buffer(bf) used to convert an image into a matrix for each stream. Second, because multiple streams run concurrently (Fig. 2(b)), we need to synchronize all the streams before starting the next operation (Lines 11–12). In the back propagation of the convolution layer, we take a similar strategy to parallelize the convolution operations. Due to space constraints, it will not be shown here.

5 Experimental Results

5.1 Datasets and Environments

We use four typical image classification datasets and three different hardware environments for the performance evaluation. The datasets include MNIST [12],CIFAR10 [9], CIFAR100 [9], and ImageNet [13]. The specific experimental environment is shown in Table 1.

Table 1. Experimental environment

Machine/OS	CPUs/machine	GPUs/machine	GPU Memory	CUDA Version
M1/Ubuntu 14.04	1 × (i7 920)	1 × Titan Z (only one GPU used)	12 GB (6 GB used)	CUDA7.5
M2/Ubuntu 14.04	1 × (Xeon E5-2620)	1 × Tesla K40m	12 GB	CUDA7.5
M3/Ubuntu 14.04	1 × (Xeon E5-2680)	1 × Tesla P100	16 GB	CUDA7.5

5.2 Evaluating Inter-layer Parallelism

In this subsection, we evaluate the inter-layer parallelism strategy. Specifically, for different datasets, we analyze the effects of different F on the convergence speed of the network model in different hardware environments. We choose the result of the original Caffe as the benchmark. We take the experimental results of CIFAR10 trained on M1 as an example. The more detailed experimental results are given in Table 2.

From Table 2, we notice that different F values have different effects on the convergence speed of the network model. When F is 1, which means that the mini-batch is not split into fragments, the model training time is greater than that of the benchmark because of the additional scheduling overhead associated with the DPA. When F is 6, the network model achieves the highest convergence speed, and the speedup SP is 1.51. The convergence speed begins to decrease when F increases further. When F increases to 10, the convergence speed of the

Table 2. The experimental results of the inter-layer parallelism

M	CIFAR10			MNIST			CIFAR100			ImageNet		
M1	F	Images/S (I/S)	Speedup (SP)	F	I/S	SP	F	I/S	SP	F	I/S	SP
	-	1224	1.00×	-	2425	1.00×	-	1150	1.00×	-	129	1.00×
	1	1194	0.98×	1	2341	0.97×	1	1095	0.95×	1	121	0.94×
	2	1571	1.28×	2	2853	1.18×	2	1517	1.32×	**2**	**153**	**1.19**×
	4	1760	1.44×	4	2990	1.23×	**4**	**1815**	**1.58**×	4	140	1.09×
	6	**1851**	**1.51**×	**6**	**2998**	**1.24**×	6	1808	1.57×	6	123	0.96×
	8	1831	1.50×	8	2942	1.21×	8	1739	1.51×	8	115	0.89×
	10	1763	1.44×	10	2857	1.18×	10	1674	1.46×	10	103	0.80×

M denotes machines. F denotes the number of fragments. Rows where F equals '-' denote the experimental results for the original Caffe, and its speedup SP is set to one.

network model becomes lower than that with F_6, and the speedup SP decreases to 1.44. The following reasons can account for the above result. First, GPUs are more suitable for handling larger mini-batches, and when a mini-batch is divided into F fragments, the number of iterations of each mini-batch becomes F. Therefore, the total time for the GPU to compute the F fragments is more than the time for the integral mini-batch. Second, whether the operation can be actually executed in parallel is also decided by the amount of computation resources on the GPU. When the value of F reaches a certain threshold, all the computational resources of the GPU are allocated. Then, even if the value of F is further increased, the time for the training process cannot be reduced further. Conversely, because of the increase of the border overheads, the time will deteriorate as F further increases.

The experimental results of other datasets are also given in Table 2. Due to limited space, experimental data for M2 and M3 are not shown in details here. We can draw similar conclusion from the experimental results on M2 and M3.

5.3 Evaluating Intra-layer Parallelism

In this subsection, we evaluate the performance of the proposed intra-layer parallelism strategy based on inter-layer parallelism. Specifically, when the values of F are optimal, we analyze the effects of different S on the convergence speed of the network model in different hardware environments. A detailed overview of the experimental results is given in Table 3. Here, we also take the experimental results of CIFAR10 trained on M1 as an example for detailed explanation.

From Table 3, we can see that the convergence speed of the network model firstly increases and then decreases with increasing S. When S is 6, the speedup SP achieves the maximum value of 2.19. With further increases in S, the value of SP begins to decrease. The major reason for the above result is that the GPU cannot support too many CUDA streams in parallel because of its limited resources. The second factor is the GPU resources (memory, registers, and blocks) assigned to a single stream. When the value of S reaches a certain threshold, the GPU resources are completely consumed. At this time, even if the value

Table 3. The experimental results of the intra-layer parallelism

M	CIFAR10			MNIST			CIFAR100			ImageNet		
M1	S	Images/s (I/S)	Speedup (SP)	S	I/S	SP	S	I/S	SP	S	I/S	SP
	F6			F6			F4			F6		
	-	1224	1.00×	-	2429	1.00×	-	1150	1.00×	-	129	1.00×
	2	2435	1.99×	2	3999	1.65×	2	2022	1.76×	2	161	1.19×
	4	2646	2.16×	4	4211	1.73×	**4**	**2048**	**1.78**×	4	164	1.26×
	6	**2677**	**2.19**×	6	4194	1.73×	6	2046	1.78×	**6**	**172**	**1.33**×
	8	2643	2.16×	**8**	**4223**	**1.74**×	8	2038	1.77×	8	167	1.29×
	10	2612	2.13×	10	4147	1.71×	10	2021	1.76×	10	160	1.24×
	12	2586	2.11×	12	4104	1.69×	12	2011	1.75×	12	159	1.23×

S denotes the number of CUDA streams. Rows where S equals '-' denote the experimental results for the original Caffe, and the speedup (SP) is set to one.

of S is increased further, the processing time cannot be further reduced. The above two factors show that more CUDA streams do not mean gaining further higher speedups. We also can draw similar conclusion from the experimental results on M2 and M3.

6 Conclusions and Future Works

In this work, we propose FiLayer, a fine-grained layer-wise parallelism strategy for deep neural networks, including inter-layer parallelism and intra-layer parallelism. FiLayer is implemented by extending Caffe. We call the FiLayer-based system LP-Caffe. To realize inter-layer parallelism, we propose a fine-grained pipeline algorithm, DPA, which allows several adjacent layers in a network model to be processed in a pipelined manner. For the intra-layer parallelism, we focus on the convolution process. CUDA stream technology is applied to realize the above two fine-grained parallelism strategies. However, we cannot deploy FiLayer over cuDNN yet, because of some confliction between the CUDA stream mechanism of cuDNN and that of the inter-layer parallelism strategy of FiLayer. Since cuDNN is not open-source, we cannot overcome the conflict yet. Therefore, in our experiments, we choose the original Caffe as the benchmark. The experimental results indicate that our proposed FiLayer-based LP-Caffe achieves 1.58×–2.19× speedups compared with the benchmark. In the future, we will focus on combining FiLayer and cuDNN work together, as well as pushing FiLayer to the situations of multiple GPUs and multiple training workers.

Acknowledgments. This work is supported by National Natural Science Foundation of China under grant No. 61672250.

References

1. Abadi, M., et al.: Tensorflow: a system for large-scale machine learning. In: Proceedings of 12th USENIX Symposium on Operating Systems Design and Implementation (OSDI), pp. 265–283. USENIX, Berkeley (2016)
2. Awan, A.A., Hamidouche, K., Hashmi, J.M., Panda, D.K.: S-Caffe: co-designing MPI runtimes and Caffe for scalable deep learning on modern GPU clusters. In: Proceedings of the 22nd ACM SIGPLAN Symposium on Principles and Practice of Parallel Programming (PPoPP), pp. 193–205. ACM, New York (2017)
3. Chen, T., et al.: MXNet: a flexible and efficient machine learning library for heterogeneous distributed systems. arXiv preprint arXiv:1512.01274 (2015)
4. Chetlur, S., et al.: cuDNN: efficient primitives for deep learning. arXiv preprint arXiv:1410.0759 (2014)
5. He, K., Zhang, X., Ren, S., Sun, J.: Deep residual learning for image recognition. In: Proceedings of the 29th IEEE Conference on Computer Vision and Pattern Recognition (CVPR), pp. 770–778. IEEE, Piscataway (2016)
6. Iandola, F.N., Moskewicz, M.W., Ashraf, K., Keutzer, K.: FireCaffe: near-linear acceleration of deep neural network training on compute clusters. In: Proceedings of the 29th IEEE Conference on Computer Vision and Pattern Recognition (CVPR), pp. 2592–2600. IEEE, Piscataway (2016)
7. Jia, Y., et al.: Caffe: convolutional architecture for fast feature embedding. In: Proceedings of the 22nd ACM International Conference on Multimedia (ACM MM), pp. 675–678. ACM, New York (2014)
8. Jiang, H., Ruan, J.: The application of genetic neural network in network intrusion detection. J. Comput. **4**, 1276–1283 (2009)
9. Krizhevsky, A., Hinton, G.: Learning multiple layers of features from tiny images. Technical report, University of Toronto (2009)
10. Krizhevsky, A., Sutskever, I., Hinton, G.E.: ImageNet classification with deep convolutional neural networks. In: Proceedings of the 26th Annual Conference on Neural Information Processing Systems (NIPS), pp. 1097–1105. Curran Associates Inc., New York (2012)
11. LeCun, Y., Bengio, Y., Hinton, G.E.: Deep learning. Nature **521**, 436–444 (2015)
12. LeCun, Y., Bottou, L., Bengio, Y., Haffner, P.: Gradient-based learning applied to document recognition. Proc. IEEE **86**, 2278–2324 (1998)
13. Russakovsky, O., et al.: ImageNet large scale visual recognition challenge. Int. J. Comput. Vis. **115**, 211–252 (2015)
14. Szegedy, C., et al.: Going deeper with convolutions. In: Proceedings of the 28th IEEE Conference on Computer Vision and Pattern Recognition (CVPR), pp. 1–9. IEEE, Piscataway (2015)

DeepVol: Deep Fruit Volume Estimation

Hongyu Li(✉) and Tianqi Han(✉)

AI Lab, ZhongAn Information Technology Service Co., Ltd., Shanghai, China
{lihongyu,hantianqi}@zhongan.io

Abstract. Due to the variety of fruit, fruit volume estimation is quite challenging. In this paper, we present a deep neural network based approach, DeepVol, to joint detection and volume estimation in a framework. The proposed architecture consists two independent parts: SSD-based fruit detector and ResNet-based volume regressor. To train the network models, a fruit dataset involving fruit volume and images is collected as a benchmark to verify the volume estimation framework. This method is simple and convenient in practical applications, owing to its requiring no conventional camera calibration and only single image as input. Experimental results demonstrate that our approach is robust to different surroundings, and promising in calorie measurement and unmanned stores.

Keywords: Fruit volume estimation · Fruit detection · DeepVol
Deep neural network

1 Introduction

Mobile applications in calorie counting and diet are increasingly popular these years. To accurately count food calorie, it is crucial to measure food volume based on input food images [17]. Visual food volume measurement is extremely difficult and challenging since many foods have large variations in shape and appearance. Compared to other types of food, fruits deserve more concern for common consumers due to their stable shape. In addition, with the rapid development of unmanned stores, fruit volume estimation is urgently needed to compute the corresponding price.

To improve the accuracy of volume estimation, deep neural network (DNN) starts to be used in food volume measurement [10], which generally requires a large amount of images to train an estimation model. However, the available datasets for food volume estimation are in shortage due to the difficulty of collecting the ground truth of food volume. Fruits are relatively popular and easy to collect and measure the volume. Therefore, a fruit dataset involving fruit volume and images is collected as a benchmark to verify fruit volume estimation methods, which is publicly available from the website in [9].

Meanwhile, we propose a deep neural network based approach, named *DeepVol*, to predict the fruit volume after fruit detection. Inspired by dense multi-view

V. Kůrková et al. (Eds.): ICANN 2018, LNCS 11141, pp. 331–341, 2018.
https://doi.org/10.1007/978-3-030-01424-7_33

stereo methods [1] for uncalibrated images, *it is assumed that implicit features for camera calibration can be effectively extracted with deep learning techniques from large scale images.* Based on this assumption, the proposed method needs no reference for calibration, but requires a large number of fruit images for the DNN model training. In essence, the volume estimation in our approach is implemented through modifying deep residual net (ResNet [6]) as a regression model, where only single image is required as input for prediction. To reduce the effects of surroundings on estimation accuracy, and predict multiple fruits in an image, each fruit is first detected and only effective fruit regions are fed to the volume estimation model.

In contrast to the state-of-the-art methods, the proposed approach is simple and flexible in practical applications, owing to its requiring no conventional camera calibration and only single image as input. Experimental results demonstrate that our approach is robust to different surroundings, and promising in calorie measurement and unmanned stores.

2 Related Work

In recent ten years, some vision based methods emerged for food volume estimation. According to the difference of inputs, they can be grouped into two classes: single-view [7,14,18] or multi-view [2,5,15].

The single-view technique requires only single image and estimates food volume by using a reference for camera calibration after food portion segmentation and identification. In this case, a circular object (e.g., a dining plate or a bowl) is often used as a physical reference for calibration [18]. In addition, checkerboard [7], thumb [14], block [8] or card [12] is alternative to simplify calibration in food calorie measurement. However, the use of reference objects is inconvenient in real applications due to the difficulty of fetching them.

For multi-view volume estimation, at least two images are necessary for reconstructing three-dimensional (3D) models of food and calculating food portion size. In [2], the estimation approach requires a pair of stereo images to be captured from which a 3D model is built. The 3D model serves to estimate the volume of the different items. In [5], six images with different viewpoints are first selected from an input short video, and a point cloud is generated to model food after an interactive segmentation. In multi-view cases, either a checkerboard [5,15] or card [2] is used as ground reference for camera calibration in 3D reconstruction. Both multiple input images and reference objects seem too complicated for users in practical applications.

As an emerging and powerful technique in feature learning, deep learning has been widely used in the area of computer vision. To identify food portions more accurately, it is also adopted to increase the accuracy of food classification [8,13] and detection [10]. Food volume estimation, however, is not well studied with deep features due to the shortage of usable datasets.

To the best of our knowledge, there is only a study in [10] involving fruit volume estimation, where fruits are extracted through Faster R-CNN [16] and volume is calculated with a coin as a reference. In addition, [10] provides a fruit dataset with the ground truth volume, but there are only two views captured from side and top for each fruit, which makes this dataset unsuitable for training deep network models.

The main contribution of this work is to propose an efficient and effective framework, DeepVol, to jointly reason about fruit location, and fruit volume. Under this framework, it is feasible to avoid the fore-mentioned inconveniences, multiple input images and reference objects. The proposed framework can also be extended to other food types, provided that the related dataset is collected for the model training.

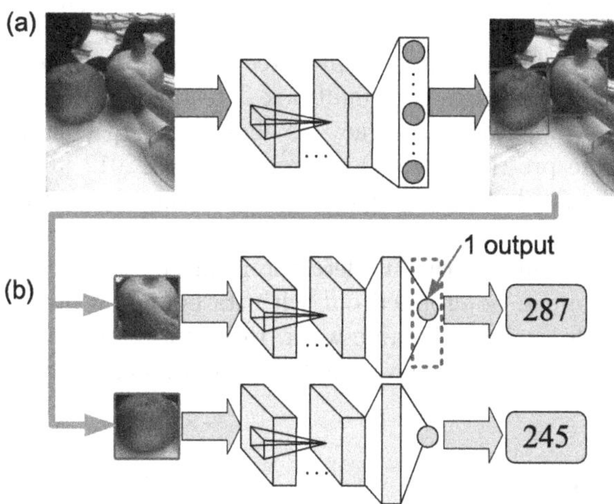

Fig. 1. Overview of the proposed framework: (a) fruit detection, (b) volume estimation. Given an image with multiple fruits, the DeepVol framework first finds each fruit and then estimates its volume separately.

3 DeepVol for Volume Estimation

The DeepVol approach is composed of two independent deep neural networks: detection and estimation, as illustrated in Fig. 1. The input image is first fed to the detection network for locating and extracting each fruit. The extracted subimages regarding fruits are then delivered to the estimation network respectively for predicting the volume of each fruit.

3.1 Fruit Detection

During fruit detection, we aim to separate an image with multiple fruits into subimages, each containing only one fruit. In this work, we make use of the

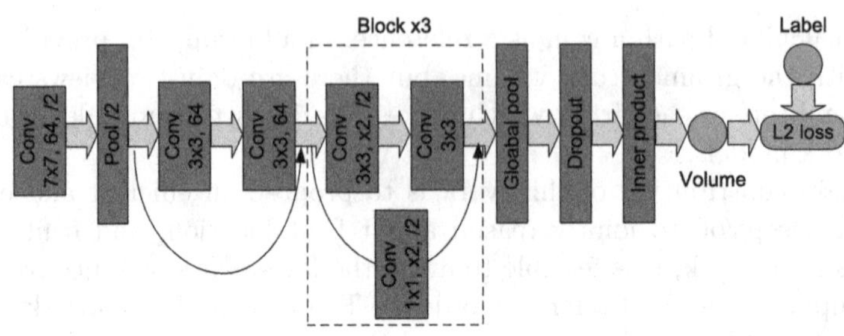

Fig. 2. The estimation network architecture composed of 12 convolutional layers and a regression layer.

deep neural network to generate a fruit detector. As a fast object detector for multiple categories, the single shot multibox detector (SSD) is simple and easy to train, and has competitive accuracy, as shown in [11]. Our detection model is finetuned on the pre-trained SSD network on VOC2012 [3], which uses the VGG-16 network as a base and adds auxiliary feature layers to the end of the base network.

Once a fruit is found with our detector from the input image, the corresponding subimage can be cropped out with its bounding box as the input of the subsequent volume estimation network. In this way, the disturbance of surroundings can be effectively removed and the eventual estimation accuracy will increase.

3.2 Volume Estimation

To predict food volume, it is straightforward to cast volume estimation as a regression problem since the estimation is essentially to predict a scalar. Motivated by the fact that deep features are effective in food classification [4], we utilize deep neural network to extract significant features for volume estimation.

In the estimation network, the early layers are based on a standard architecture truncated before the classification layers, where the extracted deep features are of 512 dimensions. An auxiliary regression layer, whose output is a neuron, is added after the early layers for estimation. In our method, the ResNet network [6] is adopted as a base due to its better performance in feature representation, but other networks should also produce good results. As shown in Fig. 2, the estimation network contains a total of 12 convolutional layers and a regression layer.

In practice, to prevent the overfitting of the estimation model, we need to collect a large amount of fruit images with volume for training large scale parameters. However, the number of training data is generally small, therefore we select for volume estimation a customized ResNet and pretrain it on ImageNet with a tiny number of parameters.

4 Training Details

In this section we describe the loss functions we employ as well as other details of our training procedure.

4.1 Loss Functions

In the detection network, the loss function is defined as the sum of two losses for detection: Softmax loss for the confidences and L1 loss on the bounding box coordinates. In the context of the detection, we solely need to determine whether the object is a fruit. As a result there are only two classes, fruit and background, to take into account in the confidence loss.

To predict fruit volume, the estimation loss adopts Euclidean loss for volume regression, which is stacked with the customized ResNet. Specifically, the loss is defined as

$$\mathcal{L}_{est} = \|\mathbf{V} - \overline{\mathbf{V}}\|_2^2, \tag{1}$$

where $\mathbf{V}$ and $\overline{\mathbf{V}}$ are respectively the predicted and ground truth volumes.

4.2 Training Strategy

As shown in Fig. 1, the detection and estimation networks are sequentially concatenated and are thus two separate models in our framework. This allows us to independently train each network with its own set of training parameters.

We first train the detection model using the annotated images with bounding boxes. The detection model is initialized using the pre-trained SSD weights on VOC2012, and then finetuned with a tiny amount of annotated images. We observed that thousands iterations are generally enough for training the detection network.

The estimation network is optimized with cropped images labeled with ground truth volumes. The convolutional layers of the estimation network are initialized using the ResNet weights pre-trained on ImageNet. The weights for the regression layer are randomly initialized under a uniform distribution in the range $(-0.1, 0.1)$.

4.3 Optimizer and Regularization

We use the SGD optimizer with a learning rate of $1e{-}3$ to train the detection network. A weight decay of $5e{-}4$ is applied to all layers in the detection network.

For the optimization of the estimation network, the Adam optimizer is utilized with a learning rate $1e{-}5$. A weight decay of $2e{-}4$ is applied to all layers and the dropout with probability 0.5 is used after global pooling in the estimation network.

5 Experimental Results

To train the estimation network, the annotated volume is required for a dataset of fruit images. So far, however, there are hardly any available fruit dataset providing volume labels except in [10]. Unfortunately, only several pairs of images from the side and top views of a fruit are taken in the dataset of [10], which does not make for deep neural network generally requiring a big amount of training data. Moreover, the background of fruit images is relatively simple and thus results in the small intra-class variations in this dataset, tending to overfit deep neural network. With these considerations, we collected a new dataset of fruit images with varied backgrounds and views. In addition, we performed our experimental evaluation on the collected and available datasets in this section.

Table 1. Dataset description

Type	Count	Volume	Image	Detected	Recall
Apple	17	160–750	5366	5170	96.3%
Pear	7	180–550	2100	2048	97.5%
Orange	2	240–270	627	591	94.3%
Mango	1	300	313	311	99.4%
Granate	1	250	275	267	97.1%
Total	28	160–750	8681	8387	96.6%

5.1 Dataset Collection

To validate the feasibility of the proposed framework, we collected a dataset containing 28 different fruits, as listed in Table 1, where the volume is manually measured with a counting cup. There are 8681 fruit images in total, each containing individual fruit, and around 300 images collected on average for each fruit.

To prevent the overfitting of the evaluation model, on the one hand, each fruit is captured with 10 diverse backgrounds, e.g., kitchen, office, street and park. On the other hand, some fruit models made of plastics are also used for collection to ensure the variety of albedo and reflection. To alleviate the effect of uncalibration on the evaluation and take advantage of deep features among multi-view images, for each background, about 30 different views are varied for shooting through rotating fruits or moving the camera. To decrease the effect of surroundings on the evaluation, we crop the subimage of each fruit from the raw images as the input for training.

It is worth noting that the collected dataset is not large enough to cover all types of fruits due to the difficulty of measuring the volume of each fruit. But it is effective for us to check the performance of the proposed framework. The framework is scalable and extensible to large-scale fruit data.

5.2 Performance Evaluation

Detection. For the detection network training, fruit images must be labelled with bounding boxes. In this work, we randomly picked and manually annotated 500 fruit images from the collected dataset, and then finetuned the detection network with these data. The finetuned detection network is used to test all the images in the collected data.

In the proposed framework, the objective of detection is to extract each fruit and obtain the corresponding bounding box from an input image. In this regard, we are mainly concerned with the *recall* capability of the detection network, i.e., the success rate of finding fruits from test images. The number of detected fruits and the detection recall are respectively listed in the last two columns of Table 1.

It is observed that the overall recall rate is over 96%, which is basically satisfactory to the framework. Note that the more the annotated images for training, the better the detection performance.

Table 2. Estimation error of different fruits on average

Type	Ground Truth	Estimation	Error
Apple model	368.75	333.05	−9.68%
Apple	225.56	230.15	2.04%
Pear	324.29	314.28	−3.09%
Orange	255	272.18	6.74%
Mango	300	257.17	−14.3%
Granate	250	282.97	13.2%

Volume Estimation. In the following experiments, we divided the collected dataset into 6 groups, each of which contains 4 or 5 different fruits. Each group is respectively picked out as the test data, and all the left groups are kept for training. In this way, the test fruits are unknown to the training data and are able to check the ability of generalization and robustness of the estimation network. In summary, 6 round experiments will be conducted to make sure that each fruit image is estimated at least once.

To evaluate the performance of the estimation network, we define an average relative error of estimated volumes for N images as,

$$E = \frac{1}{N}\sum_{k=1}^{N}\frac{V_k - \overline{V}_k}{\overline{V}_k}, \tag{2}$$

where V_k and $\overline{V}_k$ are the estimated and ground truth volumes respectively.

In this test, we computed an average volume of the images under different views for each background in the test data. It is observed from Table 2 that the estimation network has the good robustness to the variation of background, with all the relative errors less than 15%. Two worst cases, −14.3% for Mango and 13.2% for Granate, happen to be due to the shortage of training data. Experimental results in Fig. 3, show that the volumes predicted with the proposed framework are stable and robust once the shooting distance is greater than 15 cm, even if the surroundings are complex.

In fact, if we enlarged the training data in a way of uniform sampling in the volume range, the estimation error will be greatly decreased, even for the fruits with extremely large or small volumes. Unfortunately, however, since the extreme large and small fruits are scarce, we ddi not collect enough for training in the current dataset.

It is worth to note that fruit volume can be predicted in a good way although it is still unclear how deep features contribute to volume estimation. In our view, those intrinsic and extrinsic parameters for building geometric model of digital camera are well learned with deep neural network, so that the proposed method is effective even if the scale, translation or rotation transform comes up in the collected fruit images.

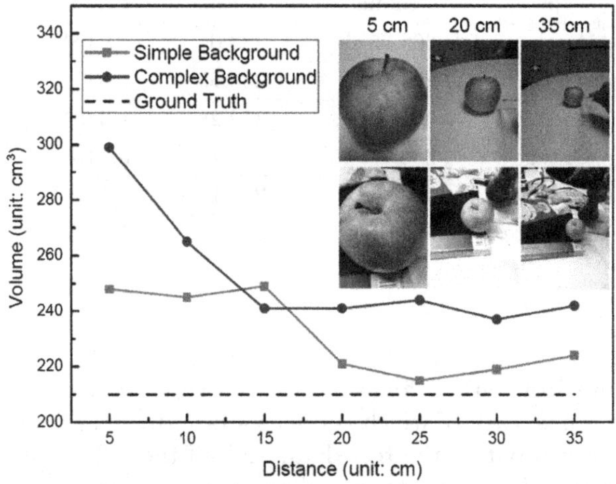

Fig. 3. Volume estimation under different shooting distances and background complexity

Comparison. There is only an available fruit dataset, the ECUSTFD data in [10], with labeled volume. We also tested the proposed DeepVol method on the ECUSTFD data and compare it with the method in [10]. The ECUSTFD data is completely different from ours in such factors as fruit types, backgrounds, and shooting conditions. Moreover, only two views are captured from side and top in the ECUSTFD data, which makes this dataset more challenging to the proposed method.

In this test, our method only requires a single-view image as the input and thus has more test images after detection while [10] needs two images from different views. As shown in Table 3, the estimation network performs well on new unknown data and shows the good capability of generalization. Specifically, the relative error of estimated volumes with the DeepVol method is 1.33% on apple images, lower than the result 3.65 % in [10]. The DeepVol method performs in a poor way on pear with a higher error as a result of the minor amount of training samples involving pear.

Table 3. Comparison between DeepVol and [10]

Type	Method	Ground truth	Estimation	Error
Apple	[10]	332.78	320.65	−3.65%
	DeepVol	318.95	323.20	1.33%
Pear	[10]	266.86	265.57	−0.48%
	DeepVol	250.00	268.62	7.45%

Multiple Fruits. To test the proposed method in dealing with images with multiple fruits, we randomly shot some pictures of two fruits under different views and backgrounds, as shown in Fig. 4(a). For example, the granate in Image #3 and the small apple in Image #4 are brandly new to the training data, and the *cartoon* background in Image #4 is unusual as well. Moreover, the shooting devices and conditions are completely changed to check the robustness of the learned detection and estimation models.

The volume estimation results in Fig. 4(b) demonstrate that the estimation error is not more than 15% even in the worst case where a strange granate appears in Image #3. In fact, the estimation accuracy can be further improved by simply increasing the training data.

Mobile Application. We also developed an application on a mobile device, which is based on a SaaS framework. In this application, the mobile end user first takes a photo of fruits with the mobile camera, and then transmits it to the server with NVIDIA GeForce GTX 1080Ti on which fruit detection and volume estimation are run. The proposed method spends, on average, about 53 ms in detecting multiple fruits and 7 ms in volume estimation of each fruit. In sum, the whole computational process usually requires less than 100 ms for an image with multiple fruits, which is acceptable and feasible in practical applications. The video demo involving the mobile application can be found in the supplemental material in [9], where the fruit samples did not appear in the collected dataset.

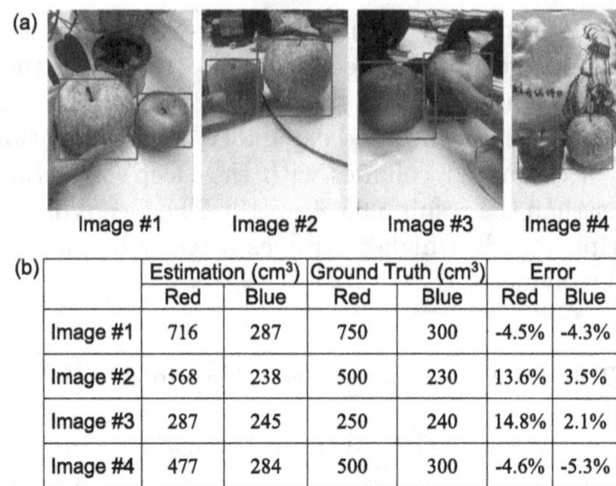

	Estimation (cm³)		Ground Truth (cm³)		Error	
	Red	Blue	Red	Blue	Red	Blue
Image #1	716	287	750	300	-4.5%	-4.3%
Image #2	568	238	500	230	13.6%	3.5%
Image #3	287	245	250	240	14.8%	2.1%
Image #4	477	284	500	300	-4.6%	-5.3%

Fig. 4. (a) detection results for multiple fruits. Each fruit is surrounded with a bounding box colored in red or blue. (b) volume estimation results for the above images. (Color figure online)

6 Conclusion

This paper proposes a deep neural network based approach for fruit volume estimation. In contrast to the state-of-the-art methods, the proposed approach is simple and flexible for practical applications, owing to its requiring no conventional camera calibration and only single image as input. It is easy to extend to other food types once the dataset with volume is collected for training.

References

1. Cui, P., Liu, Y., Wu, P., Li, J., Yi, S.: An effective multiview stereo method for uncalibrated images. In: Zha, H., Chen, X., Wang, L., Miao, Q. (eds.) CCCV 2015. CCIS, vol. 546, pp. 124–133. Springer, Heidelberg (2015). https://doi.org/10.1007/978-3-662-48558-3_13
2. Dehais, J., Anthimopoulos, M., Shevchik, S., Mougiakakou, S.: Two-view 3d reconstruction for food volume estimation. IEEE Trans. Multimed. **19**(5), 1090–1099 (2017)
3. Everingham, M., Eslami, S.M.A., Van Gool, L., Williams, C.K.I., Winn, J., Zisserman, A.: The pascal visual object classes challenge: a retrospective. Int. J. Comput. Vis. **111**(1), 98–136 (2015)
4. Fu, Z., Chen, D., Li, H.: ChinFood1000: a large benchmark dataset for Chinese food recognition. In: Huang, D.-S., Bevilacqua, V., Premaratne, P., Gupta, P. (eds.) ICIC 2017. LNCS, vol. 10361, pp. 273–281. Springer, Cham (2017). https://doi.org/10.1007/978-3-319-63309-1_25
5. Hassannejad, H., Matrella, G., Ciampolini, P., Munari, I.D., Mordonini, M., Cagnoni, S.: A new approach to image-based estimation of food volume. Algorithms **10**(2), 66 (2017)

6. He, K., Zhang, X., Ren, S., Sun, J.: Deep residual learning for image recognition. In: 2016 IEEE Conference on Computer Vision and Pattern Recognition (CVPR), pp. 770–778, June 2016
7. He, Y., Xu, C., Khanna, N., Boushey, C.J., Delp, E.J.: Food image analysis: segmentation, identification and weight estimation. In: 2013 IEEE International Conference on Multimedia and Expo (ICME), pp. 1–6, July 2013
8. Kuhad, P., Yassine, A., Shimohammadi, S.: Using distance estimation and deep learning to simplify calibration in food calorie measurement. In: 2015 IEEE International Conference on Computational Intelligence and Virtual Environments for Measurement Systems and Applications (CIVEMSA), pp. 1–6, June 2015
9. Li, H., Han, T.: ZA-Fruit Dataset and Video Demo (2018). https://pan.baidu.com/s/1tezw9Ok8-byNyTy6giSQqg#list/path=%2FDeepVol
10. Liang, Y., Li, J.: Computer vision-based food calorie estimation: dataset, method, and experiment. CoRR abs/1705.07632, http://arxiv.org/abs/1705.07632 (2017)
11. Liu, W., et al.: SSD: Single Shot MultiBox Detector. In: Leibe, B., Matas, J., Sebe, N., Welling, M. (eds.) ECCV 2016. LNCS, vol. 9905, pp. 21–37. Springer, Cham (2016). https://doi.org/10.1007/978-3-319-46448-0_2
12. Okamoto, K., Yanai, K.: An automatic calorie estimation system of food images on a smartphone. In: Proceedings of MADiMa 2016, pp. 63–70 (2016)
13. Pouladzadeh, P., Kuhad, P., Peddi, S.V.B., Yassine, A., Shirmohammadi, S.: Food calorie measurement using deep learning neural network. In: 2016 IEEE International Instrumentation and Measurement Technology Conference Proceedings, pp. 1–6, May 2016
14. Pouladzadeh, P., Shirmohammadi, S., Al-Maghrabi, R.: Measuring calorie and nutrition from food image. IEEE Trans. Instrum. Meas. **63**(8), 1947–1956 (2014)
15. Rahman, M.H., et al.: Food volume estimation in a mobile phone based dietary assessment system. In: 2012 Eighth International Conference on Signal Image Technology and Internet Based Systems, pp. 988–995, November 2012
16. Ren, S., He, K., Girshick, R., Sun, J.: Faster R-CNN: towards real-time object detection with region proposal networks. IEEE Trans. Pattern Anal. Mach. Intell. **39**(6), 1137–1149 (2015)
17. Xu, C., He, Y., Khannan, N., Parra, A., Boushey, C., Delp, E.: Image-based food volume estimation. In: Proceedings of the 5th International Workshop on Multimedia for Cooking and Eating Activities, CEA 2013, pp. 75–80 (2013)
18. Yue, Y., et al.: Food volume estimation using a circular reference in image-based dietary studies. In: Proceedings of the 2010 IEEE 36th Annual Northeast Bioengineering Conference (NEBEC), pp. 1–2, March 2010

Graph Matching and Pseudo-Label Guided Deep Unsupervised Domain Adaptation

Debasmit Das(✉) and C. S. George Lee

School of Electrical and Computer Engineering, Purdue University, West Lafayette, IN, USA
{das35,csglee}@purdue.edu

Abstract. The goal of domain adaptation is to train a high-performance predictive model on the target domain data by using knowledge from the source domain data, which has different but related data distribution. In this paper, we consider unsupervised domain adaptation where we have labelled source domain data but unlabelled target domain data. Our solution to unsupervised domain adaptation is to learn a domain-invariant representation that is also category discriminative. Domain-invariant representations are realized by minimizing the domain discrepancy. To minimize the domain discrepancy, we propose a novel graph-matching metric between the source and target domain representations. Minimizing this metric allows the source and target representations to be in support of each other. We further exploit confident unlabelled target domain samples and their pseudo-labels to refine our proposed model. We expect the refining step to improve the performance further. This is validated by performing experiments on standard image classification adaptation datasets. Results showed our proposed approach out-perform previous domain-invariant representation learning approaches.

Keywords: Unsupervised domain adaptation · Transfer learning
Graph matching · Pseudo-labels

1 Introduction

Unsupervised Domain Adaptation (UDA) defines the problem when the target domain is unlabelled and the source domain is fully labelled and these domains have different marginal distributions [15]. UDA tries to transfer knowledge from a source domain to help learning in a target domain. The assumption in UDA for the classification problem is that the source and target categories are the same. Because of shifting distributions and the lack of annotations, machine learning models trained in the source domain will fail to perform well in the target domain and hence UDA is necessary.

Most popular domain-adaptation methods involve feature transformation. Among these methods, asymmetric feature-based methods transform the features of one domain to more closely match another domain [3,10]. Symmetric

V. Kůrková et al. (Eds.): ICANN 2018, LNCS 11141, pp. 342–352, 2018.
https://doi.org/10.1007/978-3-030-01424-7_34

methods on the other hand transform the source and target domains to a common latent space where the distribution discrepancy is minimized. Deep-learning-based domain adaptation methods allow symmetric feature-based methods to be included in the form of learning a domain-invariant representation [7,13]. Among these methods, minimizing the maximum mean discrepancy (MMD) [9] is common. MMD is a non-parametric metric that measures the distribution divergence between the mean embeddings of two distributions in reproducing kernel Hilbert space (RKHS), and MMD has been used as a domain discrepancy metric between the deep activations of the source and target domains [13,20]. On the other hand, the correlation alignment (CORAL) method [17] aligns the covariances of the source and target distributions. They also extended their work to learn representations that align correlations of features extracted from the deep neural network [18]. A different class of symmetric feature-based methods uses an adversarial objective to reduce domain discrepancy. Domain adversarial neural network (DANN) [7] was proposed for learning domain-invariant representations by forcing a minimax game between the domain discriminator and the feature extractor. Tzeng et al. [19] generalized the idea of adversarial adaptation by choosing adversarial loss for the domain classifier and also proposed a weight sharing strategy. Shen et al. [16] also considers an adversarial adaptation method where it minimizes the empirical Wasserstein distance between source and target features. Previous work on using graph-matching on hand-crafted features for unsupervised domain adaptation was also proposed [4,5].

Our proposed method is a symmetric feature transformation method where both the source and target samples are transformed to a common space using the feature extractor of a deep neural network. This is done by carrying out domain-invariant representation learning that uses graph-matching (GM) loss as the domain discrepancy metric. The graph-matching loss considers the cost of matching the source and target graphs constructed from the corresponding representations. The matching consists of both node-to-node matching and edge-to-edge matching between the source and target representation graphs. This second-order matching of edges provides additional structural and geometric information about the representations that are absent on just using the first-order information [16]. The feature extraction network is iteratively optimized to minimize this graph matching loss along with minimizing the mis-classification loss using the source domain labelled data. Our proposed method adopts an iterative adversarial training scheme where the adversarial loss is a combination of first-order and second-order graph-based matchings between the source and target domain features. It is important to note that our matching approach is local and it considers matching between each instance of the source and target domain representations. On the other hand, methods like CORAL [18] and those based on MMD [13,20] are global moment-matching methods that match statistics of the source and target feature distributions.

After the learning has converged and the source and target representations lie in support of each other, we perform an additional refinement of the model. The pseudo-labels (PL) of the confident unlabelled target domain data are used to make sure that target samples lie further from the softmax decision boundary.

This allows better generalization to unseen target samples. Finally, to validate our approach, we perform experiments on standard domain adaptation datasets for image classification.

2 Proposed Approach

2.1 Problem Definition

For the unsupervised domain adaptation problem, we have n^s labelled samples, $\mathbf{X}^s = \{(\mathbf{x}_i^s, y_i^s)\}_{i=1}^{n^s}$ from the source domain $\mathcal{D}^s$. We also have n^t unlabelled samples $\mathbf{X}^t = \{\mathbf{x}_i^t\}_{i=1}^{n^t}$ from the target domain $\mathcal{D}^t$. We assume that the domains share the same feature and label space but follow different marginal data distributions; that is, $P(\mathbf{X}^s) \neq P(\mathbf{X}^t)$. The goal is to learn a transferable classifier $\mathbf{K}(\cdot)$ and a representation $\phi(\cdot)$ to minimize the target risk $\epsilon_t = P_{(\mathbf{x},y)\sim D_t}[\mathbf{K}(\phi(\mathbf{x})) \neq y]$.

2.2 Minimizing Domain Discrepancy with Graph Matching

Our goal is to learn domain-invariant representations by minimizing a graph matching loss between the source and target representations. In our case, we realize feature extraction using a neural network. We force the feature extractor to learn domain-invariant representations. Given an input sample $\mathbf{x} \in \mathbb{R}^n$ from a domain, the feature extractor learns a function $\phi : \mathbb{R}^n \rightarrow \mathbb{R}^d$ that maps an instance to a d-dimensional feature space. The parameters of the feature extractor can be represented by Θ_F. In order to minimize the discrepancy between the source and target domains, we minimize the graph matching loss between the source and target representations. To encounter excess discrepancy between the source and target domains, we allow an additional affine transformation on the source domain representations. Thus, we have a modified source domain representation $\phi'(\cdot)$ such that $\phi'^T(\mathbf{x}^s) = \phi^T(\mathbf{x}^s)\mathbf{W}_{map} + \mathbf{b}_{map}^T$, where $\mathbf{W}_{map} \in \mathbb{R}^{d\times d}$ and $\mathbf{b}_{map} \in \mathbb{R}^d$ are scaling matrix and bias, respectively. Superscript T indicates the transpose operation. The graph-matching loss considers minimizing a combination of first and second-order matching cost between graphs constructed from the source and target domains. So, if a mini-batch contains n_b^s, n_b^t source and target samples respectively, we represent the matching between the source and target representations through a matching matrix $\mathbf{C} \in \mathbb{R}^{n_b^s \times n_b^t}$. An element $[\mathbf{C}]_{ij}$ is a measure of matching between mini-batch source sample i and mini-batch target sample j. The source mini-batch features can be stacked to form a matrix $\Phi^s \in \mathbb{R}^{n_b^s \times d}$. Similarly, the target mini-batch features are stacked to form $\Phi^t \in \mathbb{R}^{n_b^t \times d}$. Accordingly, for the first-order matching we want the corresponding target representation to be close to the corresponding mapped source representation. Mathematically, this implies minimizing $||\mathbf{C}\Phi^t - \Phi'^s||_F^2$ where Φ'^s is the modified source domain feature matrix after affine transformation on Φ^s and $||\cdot||_F$ is the Frobenius norm. For the second-order matching, we try to minimize the discrepancy between the adjacency matrix of graphs constructed using the source and target mini-batches. Mathematically, this implies minimizing $||\mathbf{C}\mathbf{D}^t - r\mathbf{D}^s\mathbf{C}||_F^2$, where $\mathbf{D}^t \in \mathbb{R}^{n_b^t \times n_b^t}$ and $\mathbf{D}^s \in \mathbb{R}^{n_b^s \times n_b^s}$ are adjacency matrices constructed from Φ^t and Φ^s, respectively. We use the dot product for the similarity measure of the adjacency matrices and consequently $\mathbf{D}^t = \Phi^t \Phi^{tT}$ and $\mathbf{D}^s = \Phi^s \Phi^{sT}$, with diagonals set to 0. $r = \frac{n_b^t}{n_b^s}$ is a correction factor to account for the difference in the size of the source and target mini-batches. In addition, the constraints on $\mathbf{C}$ are as follows: $\mathbf{C} \geq \mathbf{0}$, $\mathbf{C}\mathbf{1}_{n_b^t} = \mathbf{1}_{n_b^s}$ and $\mathbf{C}^T\mathbf{1}_{n_b^s} = (\frac{n_b^s}{n_b^t})\mathbf{1}_{n_b^t}$. The equality constraint $\mathbf{C}\mathbf{1}_{n_b^t} = \mathbf{1}_{n_b^s}$ implies that the sum of the correspondences of all target samples to each source sample is one. The second equality constraint $\mathbf{C}^T\mathbf{1}_{n_b^s} = (\frac{n_b^s}{n_b^t})\mathbf{1}_{n_b^t}$ implies that the sum of correspondences of all source samples to each target sample should increase proportionately by $\frac{n_b^s}{n_b^t}$ to allow for multiple correspondences. Accordingly the optimization problem becomes

$$\min_{\mathbf{C},\mathbf{W}_{map},\mathbf{b}_{map}} \mathcal{L}_{0GM} = \frac{1}{(n_s d)}||\mathbf{C}\Phi^t - \Phi'^s||_F^2 + \lambda_s||\mathbf{C}\mathbf{D}^t - r\mathbf{D}^s\mathbf{C}||_F^2$$
$$s.t. \quad \mathbf{C} \geq \mathbf{0}, \quad \mathbf{C}\mathbf{1}_{n_b^t} = \mathbf{1}_{n_b^s}, \quad \mathbf{C}^T\mathbf{1}_{n_b^s} = (\frac{1}{r})\mathbf{1}_{n_b^t} \tag{1}$$

In the context of training neural networks, the above optimization problem can be solved using the projected gradient descent, where each iterate is projected onto the constraint set. Training neural networks generally requires a lot of time and further projection might increase the time complexity. As a result, we propose to reformulate the equality constraints as penalties in addition to the cost function. Thus our optimization problem becomes

$$\min_{\mathbf{C},\mathbf{W}_{map},\mathbf{b}_{map}} \mathcal{L}_{GM} = \frac{1}{(n_s d)}||\mathbf{C}\Phi^t - \Phi'^s||_F^2 + \lambda_s||\mathbf{C}\mathbf{D}^t - r\mathbf{D}^s\mathbf{C}||_F^2$$
$$+ \lambda_p(||\mathbf{C}\mathbf{1}_{n_b^t} - \mathbf{1}_{n_b^s}||_2^2 + ||\mathbf{C}^T\mathbf{1}_{n_b^s} - (\frac{1}{r})\mathbf{1}_{n_b^t}||_2^2) \quad s.t. \quad \mathbf{C} \geq \mathbf{0}, \tag{2}$$

where λ_p weighs the penalty terms. As a result, we can carry out gradient descent on $\mathcal{L}_{GM}$ and project it onto the set of positive matrices after each iteration.

In addition, we can exploit the labels of the source domain data to build a classifier on top of the feature extractor. We can add several layers as the classifier on top of the feature extraction network. Since the graph-matching loss ensures transferability of the learned representations, the shared classifier can be directly applied to the target domain. The objective of the classifier $\mathbf{K}(\cdot) : \mathbb{R}^d \to \mathbb{R}^l$ is to compute softmax prediction for the l classes. Let us denote the parameters of the classifier as Θ_K. The classifier loss function is the cross-entropy between the predicted probabilistic distribution and one-hot encoding of the class labels:

$$\mathcal{L}_c(\mathbf{x}^s, y^s) = -\frac{1}{n_b^s}\sum_{i=1}^{n_b^s}\sum_{k=1}^{l} 1(y_i^s = k)\log(\mathbf{K}(\phi'(\mathbf{x}_i^s))_k) \tag{3}$$

where $1(y_i^s = k)$ is a 0-1 indicator function and $\mathbf{K}(\phi'(\mathbf{x}_i^s))_k$ corresponds to the kth dimension value of the softmax output. Thus, the classification loss is combined with the graph matching loss to obtain the following objective function

$$\min_{\Theta_F,\Theta_K} \{\mathcal{L}_c + \lambda \min_{\mathbf{C}\geq\mathbf{0},\mathbf{W}_{map},\mathbf{b}_{map}} [\mathcal{L}_{GM}]\} \tag{4}$$

where λ is the coefficient controlling the balance between classification and graph matching loss. Note that the minimization is carried out using mini-batch gradient descent. As described in Algorithm 1, using a mini-batch containing labelled source data and unlabelled target data, $\mathcal{L}_{GM}$ is optimized with respect to $\mathbf{C}$ and after that iteratively projecting onto positive matrices. After the optimized matching matrix $\mathbf{C}^*$ is obtained, we solve for $\mathbf{W}_{map}, \mathbf{b}_{map}$, for which a closed form solution exists. The solution for $\mathbf{W}_{map}, \mathbf{b}_{map}$ can be obtained as follows:

$$\begin{bmatrix} \mathbf{W}_{map} \\ \mathbf{b}_{map}^T \end{bmatrix} = \left[\frac{1}{n_b^s d} \begin{bmatrix} \Phi^{sT} \\ \mathbf{1}^T \end{bmatrix} [\Phi^s \ \mathbf{1}] + \frac{\lambda_w}{d^2} \begin{bmatrix} \mathbf{I} & \mathbf{0} \\ \mathbf{0}^T & 0 \end{bmatrix} \right]^{-1} \left[\frac{1}{n_b^s d} \begin{bmatrix} \Phi^{sT} \\ \mathbf{1}^T \end{bmatrix} \mathbf{C}^* \Phi^t + \frac{\lambda_w}{d^2} \begin{bmatrix} \mathbf{I} \\ \mathbf{0}^T \end{bmatrix} \right] \quad (5)$$

Here λ_w regularizer is introduced to allow for a smooth mapping transformation. Subsequently, we optimize for the total loss as in Eq. (4) with respect to the parameters of the feature extractor and the classifier. The learned representations are domain invariant as well as target discriminative since the feature extractor parameter Θ_F receives gradients from both the graph matching and classification loss. The overall framework of our method is given in Fig. 1(a). The detailed algorithm of the training procedure is illustrated in Algorithm 1.

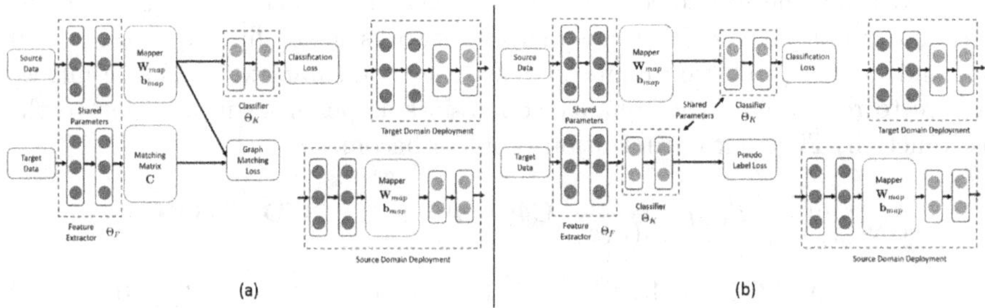

Fig. 1. The overall neural network framework for training using (a) Graph Matching (GM) Loss and (b) Pseudo-label (PL) Loss. On the right of (a) and (b), we see the model we should use for inference.

Algorithm 1. Graph-Matching-Guided Deep Domain Adaptation

Given : Source Labelled Data $\mathbf{X}^s$, $\mathbf{Y}^s$, Target Unlabelled Data $\mathbf{X}^t$
Parameters : $\lambda_s, \lambda_p, \lambda, m, T_i$ and learning rates
Randomly Initialize $\Theta_F, \Theta_K, \mathbf{C}, \mathbf{W}_{map}, \mathbf{b}_{map}$
Repeat
  Sample mini-batch $\{\mathbf{x}_i^s, y_i^s\}_{i=1}^m$, $\{\mathbf{x}_i^t\}_{i=1}^m$ from $\mathbf{X}^s$ and $\mathbf{X}^t$
  Use mini-batch to form Φ^t and Φ^s
  for $t_i = 1, 2, ...T_i$
    $\mathbf{C} \leftarrow \mathbf{C} - \alpha_1 \nabla_{\mathbf{C}} \mathcal{L}_{GM}(\Phi^t, \Phi^s)$
    $\mathbf{C} \leftarrow \max(\mathbf{C}, \mathbf{0})$
  end for
  Use Eq. (5) to obtain $\mathbf{W}_{map}$, $\mathbf{b}_{map}$
  $\Theta_K \leftarrow \Theta_K - \alpha_2 \nabla_{\Theta_K} \mathcal{L}_c(\mathbf{x}^s, y^s)$
  $\Theta_F \leftarrow \Theta_F - \alpha_3 \nabla_{\Theta_F} [\mathcal{L}_c(\mathbf{x}^s, y^s) + \lambda \mathcal{L}_{GM}(\Phi^t, \Phi^s)]$
Until Convergence

2.3 Refinement with Pseudo-labels

This is the second stage of our proposed unsupervised domain adaptation approach. Till now, we have the mapped source domain representations in support of the target domain representations. Since the domain discrepancy has been minimized, we can think of all the source and target representations belonging to a single domain. This single domain consists of labelled and unlabelled data. This is a semi-supervised learning setting that has been explored from a low-density separation, manifold regularization point of view [2]. In this paper, we propose a novel approach to exploit the confident unlabelled target domain data to further refine the classification decision boundary.

Initially, we select a subset of a mini-batch of the unlabelled target data that provide highly-confident labels as output. In other words, we select those samples whose maximum softmax probability output is greater than a threshold (t_h). Mathematically, we select those $\mathbf{x}_i^t$ for which $\max\{\mathbf{K}(\phi(\mathbf{x}_i^t))_k\} \geq t_h$ over all classes $k \in \{1, 2, ...l\}$ and we repeat this for all unlabelled target domain samples in the mini-batch $i \in \{1, 2, ...m\}$. The pseudo-labels for those selected samples would be $\underset{k}{\operatorname{argmax}}\{\mathbf{K}(\phi(\mathbf{x}_i^t))_k\}$. After that, we use the original labelled data $\{\mathbf{x}_i^s, y_i^s\}_{i=1}^m$ and the selected unlabelled samples as $\{\mathbf{x}_i^t\}_{i=1}^{m'}$, where $m' \leq m$ to further refine our model. The intuition for our method is that we want the unlabelled samples to be as far as possible from the decision boundaries. This would make it possible for unseen examples in the target domain to not be misclassified easily. As a result, we expect performance in the target domain to increase significantly.

In our model, we have a softmax classifier that returns probabilities of each class that the sample belongs to. Also pairwise relations between the probabilities give a measure of how far a sample is from a decision boundary between the corresponding pair of classes. For example, if the softmax classifier returns $(p_1, p_2, ...p_l)$ as outputs to input sample $\mathbf{x}$, $|p_i - p_j|$ is a measure of how far the sample $\mathbf{x}$ is from the decision boundary between class i and class j. If $p_i = p_j$, then the sample lies on the decision boundary between class i and class j. The general expression for maximizing the distance to the decision boundaries for all selected unlabelled samples and all classes is as follows:

$$\mathcal{L}_p(\mathbf{x}^t, \hat{y}^s) = \frac{1}{m'} \sum_{i=1}^{m'} \sum_{j,k} 1(\hat{y}_i^t = j \ OR \ \hat{y}_i^t = k)(p_j - p_k)^2. \tag{6}$$

Here, $p_j = \mathbf{K}(\phi(\mathbf{x}_i^t))_j$, and $\hat{y}_i^t$ is the pseudo-label corresponding to the input sample $\mathbf{x}_i^t$ as obtained using thresholding. When $\hat{y}_i^t = j$ or $\hat{y}_i^t = k$ is true, we have $1(\hat{y}_i^t = j \text{ OR } \hat{y}_i^t = k) = 1$, and 0 otherwise. We call $\mathcal{L}_p$ as the *Pseudo-Label* (PL) loss. We also use the classification loss $\mathcal{L}_c$ introduced in Eq. (3) to regularize $\mathcal{L}_p$. Hence, we need to solve the following optimization problem,

$$\min_{\Theta_F, \Theta_K} \{-\mathcal{L}_p + \gamma \mathcal{L}_c\}, \tag{7}$$

where γ weighs the classification cost term. In Fig. 1(b), we show the overall neural network framework for using the Pseudo-Label (PL) loss. Algorithm 2 outlines the detailed approach of the training procedure.

Algorithm 2. Pseudo-label-guided Deep Domain Adaptation

Given : Source Labelled Data $\mathbf{X}^s$, $\mathbf{Y}^s$, Target Unlabelled Data $\mathbf{X}^t$
Parameters : γ, t_h, m and learning rates
Restart $\Theta_F, \Theta_K, \mathbf{W}_{map}, \mathbf{b}_{map}$ obtained from Algorithm 1
Repeat
Sample mini-batch $\{\mathbf{x}_i^s, y_i^s\}_{i=1}^m$, $\{\mathbf{x}_i^t\}_{i=1}^m$ from $\mathbf{X}^s$ and $\mathbf{X}^t$
Obtain high-confidence samples and pseudo-labels $\{\mathbf{x}_i^t, \hat{y}_i^t\}_{i=1}^{m'}$ using t_h criterion and use those samples for parameter update as follows
$\Theta_K \leftarrow \Theta_K - \alpha_2 \nabla_{\Theta_K} [-\mathcal{L}_p(\mathbf{x}^t, \hat{y}^t) + \gamma \mathcal{L}_c(\mathbf{x}^s, y^s)]$
$\Theta_F \leftarrow \Theta_F - \alpha_3 \nabla_{\Theta_F} [-\mathcal{L}_p(\mathbf{x}^t, \hat{y}^t) + \gamma \mathcal{L}_c(\mathbf{x}^s, y^s)]$
Until Convergence

3 Experiments and Results

To evaluate the effectiveness of our proposed approach on standard domain adaptation datasets for image classification, we utilized the Office-Caltech dataset, a small-scale domain adaptation benchmark dataset, initially released by [8]. The dataset is composed of 10 common categories across 4 domains - Amazon (A), Webcam (W), DSLR (D) and Caltech (C). Each of these domains varies in terms of image quality, viewpoints, presence/absence of backgrounds, etc. For domain adaptation, we would have 12 tasks, where each task consists of a source domain and a target domain picked from the 4 domains. For our experiments, we use *Decaf* features as the input. These deep features [6] are 4096-dimensional FC7 hidden activations of the deep convolutional neural network AlexNet [12].

We compared our method to recent approaches in learning domain-invariant representations. As a lower bound on recognition accuracy, we also compare against the no-adaptation (NA) baseline which includes training the model using only the source data and directly testing on the target data. The methods that we compared against include: (a) DANN [7], (b) MMD [9], (c) CORAL [18] and (d) WDGRL [16]. These approaches have been described in the Introduction section. We have implemented our approach in Tensorflow [1] and the training was carried out using *Adam* [11] optimizer. We followed the standard protocol used in previous method as in [16]. Since hyper-parameter selection is not possible using deep unsupervised domain-adaptation methods, we reported the best results of each approach after carrying out grid search on their respective hyper-parameters. For training, we have used a batch size of 64 samples with 32 samples from each domain. The feature extractor is a 2-layer neural network with 500 and 100 nodes and a ReLU activation. We used this same feature extractor in all the methods for fair comparisons. For our method, we used the following values of the penalty parameter $\lambda_p = 10$, threshold $t_h = 0.8$, and mapping regularization $\lambda_w = 0.1$. We set λ_s, λ and γ as the tunable hyper-parameters over which we reported the best results averaged over 10 trials in Table 1. From Table 1, we see that in almost all cases our proposed graph-matching method (GM) is close to the previous best method. However, with the additional pseudo-labelling stage (PL), our proposed method produces better recognition accuracy in almost all the domain-adaptation tasks. Also, in almost all cases, the improvement of GM+PL over GM is 2–3%. This justifies the exploitation of labelled and unlabelled data after minimizing domain discrepancy, leading to an improvement in performance. For the task D→C, GM and eventually GM+PL do not produce the best result. This is possibly because the datasets D and C do not have enough structurally similar regions to be matched appropriately.

Table 1. Domain-adaptation results for object recognition using Office-Caltech datasets using Decaf features for a pair of source → target domain.

Task	NA	MMD	DANN	CORAL	WDGRL	GM	GM+PL
A→C	83.93	86.72	87.12	86.24	87.84	87.99	**89.48**
A→D	82.23	89.96	83.27	90.36	91.67	92.82	**95.73**
A→W	76.69	90.68	80.13	89.61	89.34	92.63	**94.23**
W→A	80.23	89.34	81.36	83.42	92.34	90.64	**94.68**
W→D	96.49	**100**	**100**	**100**	**100**	**100**	**100**
W→C	78.65	88.64	80.11	86.27	89.42	88.78	**91.31**
D→A	82.91	90.24	84.72	84.1	91.34	89.24	**92.34**
D→W	96.86	97.68	98.34	96.93	97.24	97.84	**99.83**
D→C	78.61	86.58	83.69	80.49	**90.24**	85.68	88.87
C→A	89.97	91.6	90.84	92.49	93.57	93.68	**95.83**
C→W	86.47	90.36	88.74	91.62	91.23	92.68	**94.21**
C→D	87.79	90.64	89.41	88.71	92.68	92.83	**94.51**

We chose a particular task A→W and studied the effect of varying hyper-parameters on recognition performance. In Fig. 2(a), we see that the performance reaches a peak at $\lambda_s = 10$. The red-dotted line is the base-line performance for $\lambda_s = 0$. So, the presence of the second-order matching term increases the performance over when it is not. Also, for $\lambda_s = 100$, the performance dips by a large amount, suggesting that putting excess weight on second-order term is not recommended. We saw a similar trend for the hyper-parameter λ in Fig. 2(b). λ weighs the graph-matching loss with respect to the classification loss. As expected, putting too much weight ($\lambda = 10$) ignores the classification loss in domain adaptation and produces a dip in performance. Recognition performance is comparatively less sensitive to γ as seen in Fig. 2(c). This is because domain discrepancy has already been minimized and the presence of classification loss on the source data does not affect target domain recognition rate much. Figure 2(d) shows the convergence of source and target error. We used GM stage for the first 2000 iterations followed by the PL stage in the next 2000 iterations. We noticed

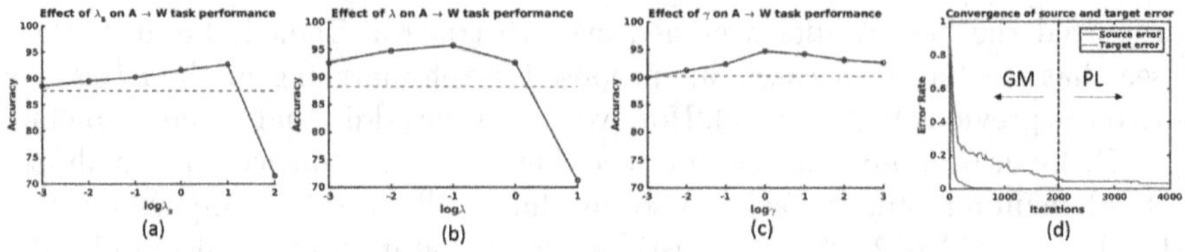

Fig. 2. Accuracy results on the A→W task due to change in (a) λ_s, (b) λ, (c) γ and (d) convergence results.

the drop in error rate when the PL stage was introduced after 2000 iterations. We also visualized the learned features using t-SNE [14] in Fig. 3. The clusters in the figure correspond to 10 classes. The blue and red points correspond to the source and target data respectively. For the un-adapted data in Fig. 3(a), the target domain classes do not form compact clusters. Also, there is a lot of discrepancy between the corresponding source and target clusters, causing a lot of mis-classification. For UDA, using only the GM procedure as in Fig. 3(b), the target domain classes form clusters but there are still some divergence between some of the corresponding source and target classes, which are reduced further using the PL stage as shown in Fig. 3(c).

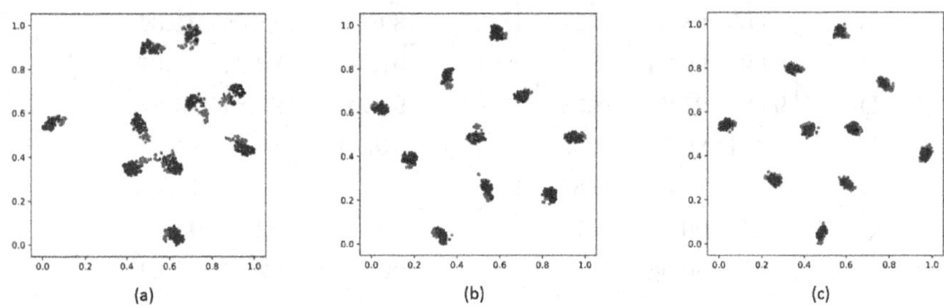

Fig. 3. Feature visualization for the A→W task for (a) no adaptation, (b) UDA with only Graph Matching and (c) UDA with Graph Matching and Pseudo-labelling. (Color figure online)

4 Conclusions

In this paper, we proposed a two-stage approach to learning domain-invariant-feature representations for unsupervised domain adaptation. In the first stage, we considered minimizing graph matching (GM) loss to minimize the discrepancy between source and target domains. The graph matching loss includes a second-order structural similarity term that allows us to consider structural similarity between two domains. For the second stage, we refined the feature/classifier using the confident pseudo-labels (PL) of the target domain data. Empirical results on image classification datasets demonstrated that our proposed GM+PL method outperforms previous domain-invariant representation learning approaches.

Acknowledgments. This work was supported in part by the National Science Foundation under Grant IIS-1813935. Any opinion, findings, and conclusions or recommendations expressed in this material are those of the authors and do not necessarily reflect the views of the National Science Foundation.

References

1. Abadi, M., et al.: TensorFlow: a system for large-scale machine learning. In: OSDI, pp. 265–283 (2016)
2. Chapelle, O., Schlkopf, B., Zien, A.: Semi-Supervised Learning, 1st edn. The MIT Press, Cambridge (2010)
3. Courty, N., Flamary, R., Tuia, D., Rakotomamonjy, A.: Optimal transport for domain adaptation. IEEE Trans. Pattern Anal. Mach. Intell. **39**(9), 1853–1865 (2017)
4. Das, D., Lee, C.S.G.: Sample-to-sample correspondence for unsupervised domain adaptation. Eng. Appl. Artif. Intell. **73**, 80–91 (2018)
5. Das, D., Lee, C.S.G.: Unsupervised domain adaptation using regularized hyper-graph matching. In: Proceedings of IEEE International Conference on Image Processing (2018, to appear)
6. Donahue, J., et al.: DECAF: a deep convolutional activation feature for generic visual recognition. In: International Conference on Machine Learning, pp. 647–655 (2014)
7. Ganin, Y., et al.: Domain-adversarial training of neural networks. J. Mach. Learn. Res. **17**(59), 1–35 (2016)
8. Gong, B., Shi, Y., Sha, F., Grauman, K.: Geodesic flow kernel for unsupervised domain adaptation. In: Proceedings of IEEE Conference on Computer Vision and Pattern Recognition (CVPR), pp. 2066–2073 (2012)
9. Gretton, A., Smola, A., Huang, J., Schmittfull, M., Borgwardt, K., Schölkopf, B.: Covariate shift by kernel mean matching. Dataset Shift Mach. Learn. **3**(4), 5 (2009)
10. Hoffman, J., Rodner, E., Donahue, J., Kulis, B., Saenko, K.: Asymmetric and category invariant feature transformations for domain adaptation. Int. J. Comput. Vis. **109**(1–2), 28–41 (2014)
11. Kingma, D.P., Ba, J.: Adam: a method for stochastic optimization. In: International Conference on Learning Representations (2015)
12. Krizhevsky, A., Sutskever, I., Hinton, G.E.: Imagenet classification with deep convolutional neural networks. In: Advances in Neural Information Processing Systems, pp. 1097–1105 (2012)
13. Long, M., Cao, Y., Wang, J., Jordan, M.I.: Learning transferable features with deep adaptation networks. In: International Conference on Machine Learning, pp. 97–105 (2015)
14. Maaten, L.V.D., Hinton, G.: Visualizing data using t-SNE. J. Mach. Learn. Res. **9**(Nov), 2579–2605 (2008)
15. Pan, S.J., Yang, Q.: A survey on transfer learning. IEEE Trans. Knowl. Data Engg. **22**(10), 1345–1359 (2010)
16. Shen, J., Qu, Y., Zhang, W., Yong, Y.: Wasserstein distance guided representation learning for domain adaptation. In: AAAI, pp. 3–9 (2018)
17. Sun, B., Feng, J., Saenko, K.: Return of frustratingly easy domain adaptation. In: Thirtieth AAAI Conference on Artificial Intelligence (2016)

18. Sun, B., Saenko, K.: Deep CORAL: correlation alignment for deep domain adaptation. In: Hua, G., Jégou, H. (eds.) ECCV 2016. LNCS, vol. 9915, pp. 443–450. Springer, Cham (2016). https://doi.org/10.1007/978-3-319-49409-8_35
19. Tzeng, E., Hoffman, J., Saenko, K., Darrell, T.: Adversarial discriminative domain adaptation. arXiv preprint arXiv:1702.05464 (2017)
20. Tzeng, E., Hoffman, J., Zhang, N., Saenko, K., Darrell, T.: Deep domain confusion: maximizing for domain invariance. arXiv preprint arXiv:1412.3474 (2014)

fNIRS-Based Brain–Computer Interface Using Deep Neural Networks for Classifying the Mental State of Drivers

Gauvain Huve[1], Kazuhiko Takahashi[2(✉)], and Masafumi Hashimoto[2]

[1] Graduate School of Doshisha University, Kyoto, Japan
[2] Doshisha University, Kyoto, Japan
{katakaha,mhashimo}@mail.doshisha.ac.jp, duq3103@mail4.doshisha.ac.jp

Abstract. Accidents on the road mostly occur because of human error. Understanding and predicting the manner in which the brain functions when driving can help in reduce fatalities. Particularly, with the recent development of auto-driving cars, it is important to ensure that the driver is ready to retake the control of the vehicle at all times in the event of a system failure. This study attempts to create a brain–computer interface (BCI) using signals obtained through functional near-infrared spectroscopy (fNIRS) to evaluate the impact of different external conditions on the driver's mental state: weather condition, type of road, including manual driving versus auto-pilot. A deep neural network (DNN) and a recurrent neural network (RNN) are employed for their ability of pattern recognition in the processing of fNIRS signals and are compared to other common classification methods. The results of the study demonstrated that both DNN and RNN offer the same performance. Furthermore, brain activity under different weather conditions cannot be classified by any of the proposed methods. Nevertheless, DNN and RNN have proven their effectiveness in the road type classification with 63% accuracy.

Keywords: Brain computer interface · fNIRS · Deep neural network
Recurrent neural network · Drive simulator

1 Introduction

According to a recent study by the National Highway Traffic Safety Administration, 94% of crashes are caused by human error [1]. While recent advances in automation should have an impact on this number, there will always be situations where the auto-pilot will be inadequate and a human would have to manually drive the car. A way of decreasing the number of accidents when a human is driving would be to develop brain–computer interfaces (BCIs) that can analyse the brain activity of the driver and help them in maintaining consistent attention.

V. Kůrková et al. (Eds.): ICANN 2018, LNCS 11141, pp. 353–362, 2018.
https://doi.org/10.1007/978-3-030-01424-7_35

The idea of a BCI is to transmit the user's intentions to an external device without any intervention from the user himself. This type of interface has been the focus of research for the past twenty years [2–4]. Depending on the area of the brain that the interface is linked to, it can be used in many different ways. For example, with the proper equipment, a BCI linked to the motor cortex of paraplegic patients could help them regain control of their limbs. To analyse the driver's mental state, the area of interest is the pre-frontal cortex, which is implicated in the thought process. There exist several methods of measuring brain activity for BCIs. Invasive methods have the highest quality signals but require surgery to implant captors. The most commonly used non-invasive method is electroencephalography (EEG), which directly measures the electrical activity of the brain. However, the focus has recently shifted towards functional near-infrared spectroscopy (fNIRS), a non-direct method [5]. fNIRS measures the concentration of two molecules in the blood (oxygenated haemoglobin (OxyHb) and deoxygenated haemoglobin (DeoxyHb)) by using differences in their absorption spectrum. It is then possible to deduce the variations in brain activity from the variations of the blood flow. For processing data obtained through fNRIS, various studies have tested different approaches, including linear discriminant analysis [6–9], support vector machines (SVMs) [10,11] and neural networks [10,12–15]. However, none of them has been found to be strictly better than the others when classifying diverse mental tasks.

fNIRS has various applications in the domain of driving. For instance, fNIRS could allow the activation/deactivation of the auto-pilot based functionality on the current driving ability of the driver or detect emergency braking before the driver even begins to move his foot towards the brake pedal. To analyse the driver's mental state, studies have been performed using different tasks [16]. Reference [17] used an n-back task to induce different workloads on patients while driving and presents a way of reliably using brain activity to quantify workload. In [18], researchers demonstrated the effectiveness of using fNIRS for detecting drowsiness in the patient, with a detection rate of almost 85%. Reference [19] analysed the effects of three modes of control during lane change on brain activity. Other tasks, such as overtaking and following [20], were also shown to have an impact on the activity in the pre-frontal cortex.

In this study, the brain activity in the pre-frontal cortex is recorded while using a drive simulator. Several experiments of specific external conditions are conducted. This study then attempts to determine which of those experiments generated any given brain activity signal. The chosen conditions include the weather conditions (clear weather versus rainy weather) and the type of roads (city driving versus highway driving). In light of the recent advancements in automated cars, this study also examines the differences in brain activity of the driver when driving manually compared with when the vehicle is on auto-pilot. For processing the fNIRS signals, this study uses both a deep neural network (DNN) and a recurrent neural network (RNN), and compares their accuracy to several other common methods.

Fig. 1. Drive simulator.

2 Methods

2.1 Equipment

The brain activity of patients was recorded in real time by an fNIRS-based headset (WOT-220, Hitachi, Ltd.) linked to a personal computer. The setup measures the blood flow in the prefrontal cortex, which is involved in the thinking process and recorded at 5 Hz. Equipped with eight transmitters and eight receptors, it evaluates the concentration of oxygenated haemoglobin (oxyHb) and deoxygenated haemoglobin (deoxyHb) in the blood flow at 22 different locations (channels) on the forehead. Because the device is sensitive to sudden movements, the patient is asked to refrain from making any head movements during the entire duration of the experiment.

To record brain activity during driving, a full-fledged Forum-8 drive simulator [21] shown in Fig. 1 was used. It features fully customisable roads, weather, traffic, and landscape. The simulator also provides access to real-time information, including vehicle speed, lateral position, pedals angle, and wheel angle. It enables external control of the vehicle through its API, which led to a fully functional auto-pilot system that can be turned on and off at will. The drive simulator uses automatic transmission.

2.2 Data Capture

The objective is to classify brain activity of the driver under various external conditions. The chosen categories include: weather (clear versus rainy), type of roads (city versus highway), and type of driving (manual versus auto-pilot). To ensure that other parameters are exactly identical, the data in all cases (except city driving) were recorded on a highway scenario with light traffic and clear weather (except for the rainy driving). The city driving scenario featured clear weather with heavier traffic.

The protocol consisted of driving the whole scenario under chosen external conditions. The duration of the drive was between 3 min and 20 s to 3 min and 50 s depending on the driving speed. The signals were then truncated at the

3 min mark to ensure that all signals were of the same length. In the manual versus auto-pilot case, two different protocols were used:

- In the first protocol, the car started in auto-pilot and switched to manual at a random moment between 30 s and 2 min and 30 s after the initiation of the drive. The driver then had to complete the scenario in manual mode.
- In the second protocol (denoted by "alt." afterwards), the car started in auto-pilot and alternated between the two modes every 20 s.

Once again, the duration of the drive lasted 3 min and 20 s to 3 min and 50 s and the obtained signals were truncated at the 3 min mark.

For each of the chosen category, both types of scenario were driven the same number of times every day the experiment was conducted to limit the effect of the variance in brain activity from one day to the other. During the data capture session, the scenarios were presented in random order to ensure that the effect of variations, resulting from fatigue, on the classification is at a minimum.

2.3 Pre-processing

The signals recorded for both the concentration of oxyHb and deoxyHb for each channel are then pre-processed to remove noise from biological sources (such as heartbeat) and noise from equipment, which are not representative of brain activity of the patient while driving. Two different types of pre-processing are used.

Filters [13]**:** The signals are passed through a Butterworth high-pass filter with a cut-off frequency of 0.01 Hz, and the fast variations are then removed by smoothing the signals using the least-square method.

Wavelet Reconstruction [22]**:** Using multi-resolution analysis, it is possible to decompose a signal into an approximation signal (low frequency) and several detailed signals (high frequency). In such a decomposition, the Daubechies wavelet with eight taps is used as the mother wavelet. The denoised signal is then reconstructed by adding the 4th, 5th and 6th detailed components.

Pre-processing is then followed by a calculation of the variations using the least-square method. The signals obtained after the first pre-processing steps and their variations are then standardised and used for classification, resulting in four signals for each channel in each experiment (concentration of oxyHb, concentration of deoxyHb and their variations).

2.4 Feature Extraction

The signals obtained after pre-processing are then cut into segments of 2 s and labeled by the type of driving at the corresponding time. For the case of manual versus auto-pilot (alt.), the first and last 2 s of each 20 s periods are removed because of a spike in activity arising from the sudden change in driving. Various inputs are created from the pre-processed signals and are classified separately.

Time Series: Each segment is directly placed in a one-dimensional vector of 880 points (22 channels of oxyHb, deoxyHb, and their variations, for 2 s at 5 Hz) and used as input for the classifier.

Pearson Correlation Coefficient: For every 2-s segment, the correlation coefficients between the signals of each channels are used as inputs. The correlation between the different oxyHb signals, between the different deoxyHb signals and the correlation between oxyHb and deoxyHb signals are calculated. The variation signals are not used. This results in a vector of $\binom{22+22}{2} = 946$ data points, which is used as an input for the classifier.

Spearman Rank Correlation Coefficient: In the same way, the Spearman rank correlation coefficients for the same signals are used, resulting in a vector of 946 data points.

2.5 Classifiers

This study attempts at evaluating the performance of DNNs and RNNs compared with other common classifiers. The objective of an RNN is to account for the temporal dimension of the input, and it does not make sense to use an RNN when the input is not a time series. As such, the RNN will only be used for time series inputs and not the correlation coefficients. For the RNN, the data structure of the inputs will be changed from a one-dimensional vector of 880 elements to a 10 × 88 points. After optimisation, the structure chosen for the DNN consists of 880 inputs, two layers of 300 neurons with a rectified linear unit activation function and a dropout probability of 50% and two output neurons. The structure used for the RNN includes 88 inputs, two layers of 70 long short-term memory units with a dropout probability of 50% and two output neurons.

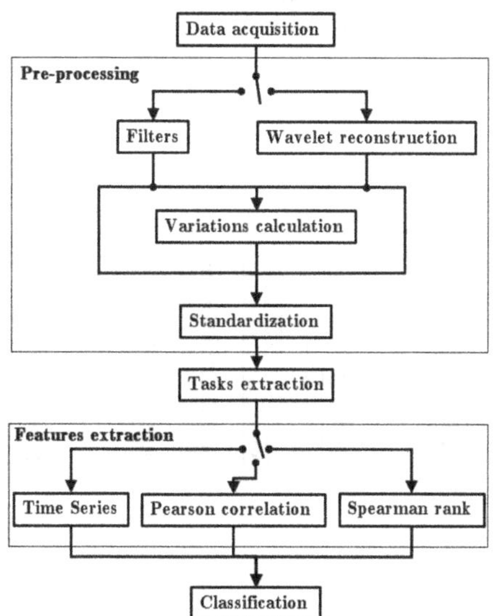

Fig. 2. Overview of the classification process.

These neural networks will be compared with the nearest neighbour algorithm (NNA), a simple feed-forward network (FFNN) with 300 hidden neurons, a linear support vector machine (LSVM), a non-linear support vector machine (NLSVM) with a radial basis function kernel, and a random algorithm. Because the amount of data available is not infinite, the accuracy of the random algorithm is not at 50%. To evaluate this accuracy, a binomial cumulative distribution model with a significance level of 5% was used [23].

An overview of classification process is depicted in Fig. 2.

3 Experimental Results

3.1 Comparison of DNN and RNN

The first results, obtained using time series inputs with filter pre-processing, is shown in Fig. 3(a) for the DNN, the RNN and the random algorithm in each classification. What appears immediately is that for both the DNN and the RNN, the average accuracy of the first two classifications is not significantly above the random algorithm, which implies that the neural networks cannot determine patterns characteristics of each class in the signals and cannot differentiate between the classes in the current setup. This is however not true for the classification of manual driving versus auto-pilot. When considering all cases, neither network appears to significantly outperform the other.

One possible origin of the errors in the weather and road type classification could be pre-processing. The chosen pre-processing procedures might be removing features of the signals that are characteristic of the task. To test this hypothesis, the pre-processing was changed to replace the filters with wavelet reconstruction, resulting in the average accuracies presented in Fig. 3(b). With this new pre-processing, the classification for city versus highway driving went from 49% up to 63% for both the DNN and the RNN, which is significantly

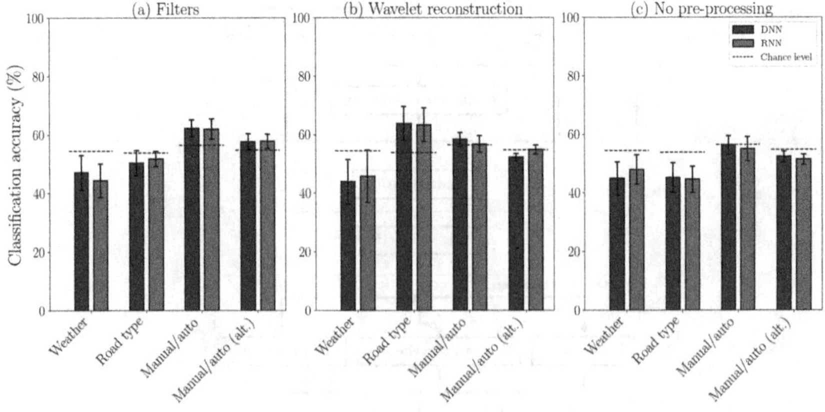

Fig. 3. Average accuracy of the DNN and the RNN for each type of pre-processing.

higher than the 53.8% of the random algorithm. However, the weather classification still performs poorly and the accuracy in both types of manual versus auto-pilot reduced, reaching accuracies that are not significantly better than the chance level. Nevertheless, just as in the previous case, both DNN and RNN offer the same performance. Only for manual versus auto-pilot (alt.) the RNN outperforms the DNN by a small margin, although still close to the chance level.

Given the difference when changing the pre-processing, the classification was performed without any kind of pre-processing in order to examine its effect. Directly using the signals themselves produces the results presented in Fig. 3(c). In every situation, the accuracy remains on the same level or even below the chance level.

3.2 Comparison with Common Classifiers

The previous results demonstrated that the pre-processing using filters was better suited for the classification of auto-pilot while the pre-processing using wavelet reconstruction increased the recognition rate for road type classification. In the case of weather recognition, however, the accuracy remained poor for both types of pre-processing. For that reason, classification with other methods is performed using the filter pre-processing, except for the road type classification where wavelet reconstruction is used.

The recognition rate of the DNN and the RNN are compared with that of FFNN, NNA, LSVM, and NLSVM. The values for each case are presented in Fig. 4. The first thing to notice is how none of the classifiers can differentiate between brain activity of the patient while driving under clear weather versus driving under rainy weather. The two tasks are possibly too close to each other. It does not really feel any different to drive under rain in the drive simulator compared with clear weather. In particular, after completing the scenario a few times the driver starts remembering the route, which reduces the effect of the reduced visibility because the driver already knows what comes next. In the

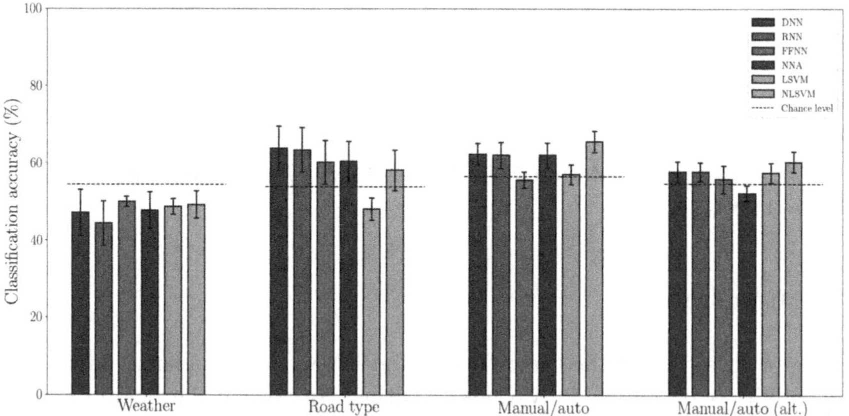

Fig. 4. Average accuracy of each classifier for each scenario.

road type classification, all classifiers except linear SVM outperform the random algorithm, with DNN having the highest accuracy among them. However, the NLSVM seems to outperform every other classifier when it comes to both scenarios of manual driving versus auto-pilot. In both types, the FFNN is unable to differentiate between the two classes, while the NNA can only make a distinction when the two tasks are not alternating.

3.3 Changing the Inputs

A way to improve the results would be to change the nature of the inputs to some statistical representation. This study attempts to use the Pearson's correlation coefficients and the Spearman rank correlation coefficients. The results for both are shown in Fig. 5(a) and (b) for the DNN and the NLSVM, which present better results than the DNN in some cases. Using the RNN for this type of input would not make sense because the time component was removed. For the Pearson's coefficient and the Spearman rank, the obtained average accuracy is not significantly better than the chance level in three of the four scenarios. For the road type scenario, the performance of both inputs is similar, with a prediction rate of about 60%, but remains below the accuracy in the case when time series inputs are used.

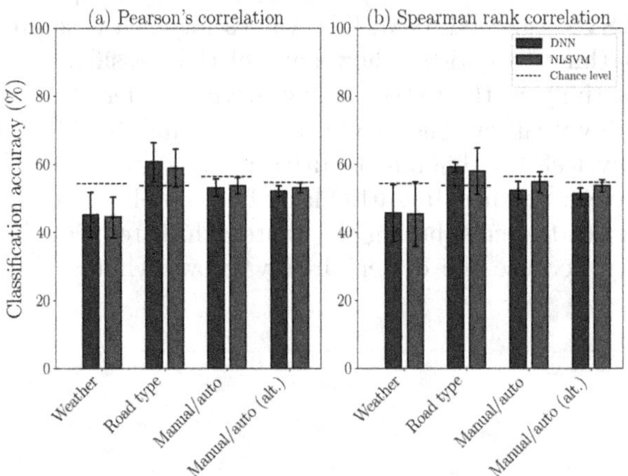

Fig. 5. Average accuracy of the DNN and the NLSVM when using correlation coefficients for inputs.

4 Conclusions

This paper investigated the use of DNNs and RNNs for recognising patterns in brain activity of drivers under various conditions. In none of the attempts, could the networks differentiate between driving under clear weather versus driving under rainy weather. A possible cause could be the similarity between the two tasks. One effect of rainy weather is reduced visibility, forcing the driver to drive at lower speeds. However, once the driver becomes accustomed to the scenario, this effect is greatly reduced. This results in a driving experience that is very close to driving under fair weather. For a comparison of driving in the city compared with driving on a highway, changing the pre-processing from using filters to using wavelet reconstruction increases the average accuracy from 50% to over 63% for both the DNN and the RNN when time series inputs are used. However, the same pre-processing reduces the accuracy in the case of the differences in manual driving versus auto-pilot. Using the better of the two types of pre-processing, the accuracy reaches 62% when the two tasks are separated, and 58% when they alternate. A possible cause of the difference could be that the concentration levels are limited by the insufficient time to return to a normal state when the tasks alternate. In any case, both the DNN and the RNN provide similar results. When compared with other common classification methods, the neural networks are outperformed by the NLSVM when it comes to classifying manual driving versus auto-pilot. Nevertheless, their average accuracy for the road type classification is among the highest for all tested classifiers.

Changing the inputs from time series data to correlation coefficients does not improve the results. However, this study uses 2 s of signal at 5 Hz, which comprises of only 10 data points. This low number might be insufficient for reliable correlation calculation. Using correlation coefficients with longer signals might result in higher accuracy. Given the significant differences when changing the pre-processing, a way to improve the results would be to optimise the pre-processing step. Changing the input from time series to a statistical representation such as the mean, peak, or variance, could also have an impact on classification accuracy.

Acknowledgement. This study was partially supported by the MEXT-Supported Program for the Strategic Research Foundation at Private Universities, 2014–2018, Ministry of Education, Culture, Sports, Science and Technology, Japan.

References

1. National Highway Traffic Safety Administration: Critical Reasons for Crashes Investigated in the National Motor Vehicle Crash Causation Survey. US Department of Transportation, Washington, DC (2015)
2. Nicolas-Alonso, L.F., Gomez-Gil, J.: Brain computer interfaces, a review. Sensors **12**, 1211–1279 (2012)
3. He, B., Gao, S., Yuan, H., Wolpaw, J.R.: Brain-computer interface. In: He, B. (ed.) Neural Engineering, pp. 87–151. Springer, Boston (2013). https://doi.org/10.1007/978-1-4614-5227-0
4. Ramadan, R.A., Vasilakos, A.V.: Brain computer interface: control signals review. Neurocomputing **223**, 26–44 (2017)
5. Ferrari, M., Quaresima, V.: A brief review on the history of human functional near-infrared spectroscopy (fNIRS) development and fields of application. NeuroImage **63**, 921–935 (2012)

6. Herff, C., Heger, D., Putze, F., Hennrich, J., Fortman, O., Schultz, T.: Classification of mental tasks in the prefrontal cortex using fNIRS. In: Proceedings of 35th Annual International Conference of the IEEE Engineering in Medicine and Biology Society, pp. 2160–2163 (2013)
7. Hong, K., Naseer, N., Kim, Y.: Classification of pre-frontal and motor cortex signals for three-class fNIRS-BCI. Neurosci. Lett. **587**, 87–92 (2015)
8. Herff, C., Heger, D., Fortmann, O., Hennrich, J., Putze, F., Schultz, T.: Mental workload during n-back task - quantified in the pre-frontal cortex using fNIRS. Hum. Neurosci. **7**, 935 (2014). https://doi.org/10.3389/fnhum.2013.00935
9. Naseer, N., Noori, F.M., Qureshi, N.K., Hong, K.: Determining optimal feature-combination for LDA classification of functional near-infrared spectroscopy signals in brain-computer interface application. Front. Hum. Neurosci. **10**, 237 (2016). https://doi.org/10.3389/fnhum.2016.00237
10. Kazuki, Y., Tsunashima, H.: Development of portable brain-computer interface using NIRS. In: Proceedings of IEEE International Conference on Control, pp. 702–707 (2014)
11. Hu, X., Hong, K., Ge, S.S.: fNIRS-based online deception decoding. J. Neural Eng. **9**(2), 026012 (2012)
12. Huve, G., Takahashi, K., Hashimoto, M.: Brain activity recognition with a wearable fNIRS using neural networks. In: Proceedings of IEEE International Conference on Mechatronics and Automation, pp. 1573–1578 (2017)
13. Huve, G., Takahashi, K., Hashimoto, M.: Brain-computer interface using deep neural network and its application to mobile robot control. In: Proceedings of IEEE International Workshop on Advanced Motion Control, pp. 169–174 (2018)
14. Hennrich, J., Herff, C., Heger, D., Schultz, T.: Investigating Deep Learning for fNIRS based BCI. In: Proceedings of 37th Annual International Conference of the IEEE Engineering in Medicine and Biology Society, pp. 2844–2847 (2015)
15. Lu, N., Ki, T., Ren, X., Miao, H.: A deep learning scheme for motor imagery classification based on restricted Boltzmann machines. IEEE Trans. Neural Syst. Rehabil. Eng. **25**(6), 566–576 (2017)
16. Liu, T., Pelowski, M., Pang, C., Zhou, Y., Cai, J.: Near-infrared spectroscopy as a tool for driving research. Ergonomics **59**(3), 368–379 (2016)
17. Unni, A., et al.: Brain activity measured with fNIRS for the prediction of cognitive workload. In: Proceedings of IEEE International Conference on Cognitive Infocommunications, pp. 349–354 (2015)
18. Khan, J., Hong, K.: Passive BCI based on drowsiness detection: an fNIRS study. Biomed. Opt. Express **6**(10), 4063–4078 (2015)
19. Sibi, S., Baiters, S., Mok, B., Steiner, M., Ju, W.: Assessing driver cortical activity under varying levels of automation with functional near infrared spectroscopy. In: Proceedings of IEEE Intelligent Vehicles Symposium, pp. 1509–1516 (2017)
20. Foy, H.J., Runham, P., Chapman, P.: Prefrontal cortex activation and young driver behaviour: a fNIRS study. PLoS ONE **11**(5), e0156512, 18 pages (2016). https://doi.org/10.1371/journal.pone.0156512
21. FORUM 8. http://www.forum8.co.jp/english/uc-win/road-drive-e.htm
22. Tsunashima, H., Yanagisawa, K.: Measurement of brain function of car driver using functional near-infrared spectroscopy (fNIRS). Comput. Intell. Neurosci. **2009**, 12 pages (2009). Article ID 164958. https://doi.org/10.1155/2009/164958
23. Combrisson, E., Jerbi, K.: Exceeding chance level by chance: the caveat of theoretical chance levels in brain signal classification and statistical assessment of decoding accuracy. J. Neurosci. Methods **250**, 126–136 (2015). https://doi.org/10.1016/j.jneumeth.2015.01.010

Research on Fight the Landlords' Single Card Guessing Based on Deep Learning

Saisai Li[1,2], Shuqin Li[1,2(✉)], Meng Ding[1,2], and Kun Meng[1,2]

[1] Computer Academy, Beijing Information Science & Technology University, Beijing, China
lishuqin_de@126.com
[2] Perception and Computation Intelligence Joint Lab, No. 35, North Fourth Ring Road, Chaoyang District, Beijing, China

Abstract. In the real world, most of the information is non-accurate and non-complete. The model which guesses the number of the cards is a predictive model based on incomplete information. Players need to know a relatively small amount of information on the card to make accurate predictions. Based on the deep learning method, this paper studies single card speculation method on Fight the landlords game. Located in the perspective of the landlord, the model based on a certain amount of historical card information extracts the dominant features, and makes a reasonable prediction for peasant players' hands. The algorithm uses the CNN model to design the game turn-based body, single player's history and the brand-out process of three players simultaneously in the model input matrix. It extracts the characteristics of the landlord playing cards, and predicts the situation of the hand of two peasant players up and down. The experimental results show that the result of single card guess basically accords with the habit of human playing cards.

Keywords: Deep learning · Fight the landlords · Guess cards
Incomplete · Information · Game

1 Introduction

AI has made some breakthroughs in recent years, and games are often taken as important milestones. Games can be further divided into complete information games (such as Go, Chess and Checkers) and incomplete information games (such as poker). The state information of non-complete information games is hidden behind one or more players and requires more complex reasoning than their perfect information. [1]

There is less research on Landlords in the world, usually the most incomplete information game research carrier for Texas Hold'em. In 2017, CMU-designed Libratus used endgame solving which is a more optimized sub-tree solution based on CFR, to refine the state space and strategy space and reach a higher level of intelligence in continuous self-improvement [2, 3]. In the incomplete information game, human lost to the AI. This paper mainly adopts the Convolutional neural network (CNN) model, based on landlord status, through the analysis of a small amount of players' information

V. Kůrková et al. (Eds.): ICANN 2018, LNCS 11141, pp. 363–372, 2018.
https://doi.org/10.1007/978-3-030-01424-7_36

on the cards, the number of single cards in the peasant's hand is guessed, and then the game under the incomplete information is studied.

2 Fight the Landlords Games Introduction

Fight the Landlord is a card game for three players. In each hand one player, the "landlord", plays alone and the others peasants a team. The landlord's aim is to be the first to play out all his cards in valid combinations, and the team wins if any one of them manages to play all their cards before the landlord.

A complete deck consists of 52 standard cards plus 2 jokers, red and black. The cards rank from high to low: R (Red Joker), B (Black joker), 2, A, K, Q, J, T(10), 9, 8, 7, 6, 5, 4, 3. Each rank of standard card has 4 cards. At the beginning of each round, the landlord has 20 cards and the others each get 17 cards. The landlord plays first, and may play a single card or any legal combination. Each subsequent player in anti-clockwise order must either pass (play no card) or beat the previous play by playing a higher combination of the same number of cards and same type. There are just two exceptions to this: a rocket can beat any combination, and a bomb can beat any combination except a higher bomb or rocket - see definitions below.

In this game, there are thirteen types of combination that can be played:

Single card: ranking from 3 (low) up to red joker (high) as explained above.
Pair: two cards of the same rank, from 3 (low) up to 2 (high), for example 3-3, A-A.
Triplet: three cards of the same rank, for example 9-9-9.
Triplet with an attached card: a triplet with a single card added, the single card must be different from the triplet, for example 6-6-6-8. These rank according to the rank of the triplet - so for example 9-9-9-3 beats 8-8-8-A.
Triplet with an attached pair: a triplet with a pair added, the ranking being determined by the rank of the triplet - for example Q-Q-Q-6-6 beats 10-10-10-K-K.
Sequence: at least five cards of consecutive rank, from 3 up to ace - for example 8-9-10-J-Q. 2 and jokers cannot be used.
Sequence of pairs: at least three pairs of consecutive ranks, from 3 up to A. 2 and jokers cannot be used. For example 10-10-J-J-Q-Q-K-K.
Sequence of triplets: at least two triplets of consecutive ranks from 3 up to A. 2 cannot be used. For example 4-4-4-5-5-5.
Sequence of triplets with attached cards: an extra card is added to each triplet. Only the triplets have to be in sequence, for example 7-7-7-8-8-8-3-6. The attached cards must be different from all the triplets and from each other.
Sequence of triplets with attached pairs: an extra pair is attached to each triplet. Only the triplets have to be in sequence - for example 8-8-8-9-9-9-4-4-J-J. The pairs must be different in rank from each other and from all the triplets. Although triplets of 2 cannot be included in the triplets sequence.
Bomb: four cards of the same rank. A bomb can beat everything except a rocket or a bomb with higher rank.
Rocket: a pair of jokers. It is the highest combination and beats anything else, including bombs.

Quadplex set: there are two types: a quad (four same cards) with two single cards of different ranks attached, such as 6-6-6-6-8-9, or a quad with two pairs of different ranks attached, such as J-J-J-J-9-9-Q-Q.

3 Model Overall Frame Design

Convolutional neural network (CNN) [4] is an important supervised learning method that proved to be a powerful model, and has made great progress in game AI. Since game participants all have private information, they cannot obtain all the status information of the current situation. Therefore, it is impossible to make a reasonable assessment of the game situation through artificial extraction of features, and it is difficult to determine the opponent's availability. The range of operations and the game tree of incomplete information games are extremely large. Among them, convolutional neural network occupies an important part in machine learning. As long as the design is reasonable, it will often produce unexpected results. Fight the landlord game players operate in sequence to form serialized game data. The combination of playing cards is a reasonable combination to fully reflect the characteristics of the game. Therefore, the player's hand can be predicted and the player's winning probability can be improved by setting reasonable parameters.

This paper uses a standard CNN network. First of all, we clean the original data of a large number of actual platforms, eliminate the noise data, and get the behavior data of all stages of the players. Secondly, we designed the structure of CNN, and the original data are combined into the input data of the model in a proper way. After the data is extracted through the network, the probability distribution of the number of single cards in the opponent's hand is obtained. Thus, the type of cards can be effectively predicted. Finally, a detailed evaluation method is used to evaluate the quality of the model. The overall framework is shown in Fig. 1.

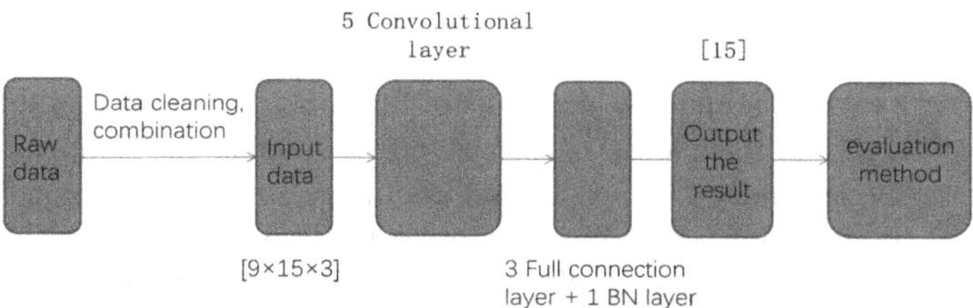

Fig. 1. The overall framework of model. Where $[9 \times 15 \times 3]$ is the input data dimension and [15] is the output prediction result dimension.

3.1 Data Cleaning

Data cleaning is to clean dirty data, improve data quality. The game logs come from Lianzhong (Beijing Lianzhong interactive Network Inc, http://www.ourgame.com/) platform. The raw data is not perfect. In order to maximize the interest of the players, there are often phenomena such as excessive power in one player's initial cards. At this time, the player plays all the cards within a very short turn, and there is no meaning for guessing cards.

In this paper, we rejects too few rounds of data. We randomly selected 240,000 innings data, after the first step of cleaning the game data. The number of rounds spent per game statistics and found that the majority of rounds concentrated in 6 to 12 rounds. As shown in Fig. 2. In Fight the landlords, the landlord first comes out as the start of the game. The order of the landlord, *pa* and *pb* is in turn for a round. Generally, if the game is over in six rounds, a player card is relatively large. The player will be able to play cards continuously but the other players cannot play cards. At this point, it is not possible to perform effective hand predictions for the players, and it is of no practical significance to make predictions on such situations because the purpose of this paper is to make hand predictions for opponents at the similar player levels and increase their own winning ratio. When the hand is too strong, players can easily win without predicting. So we remove the data that the game is over within six steps.

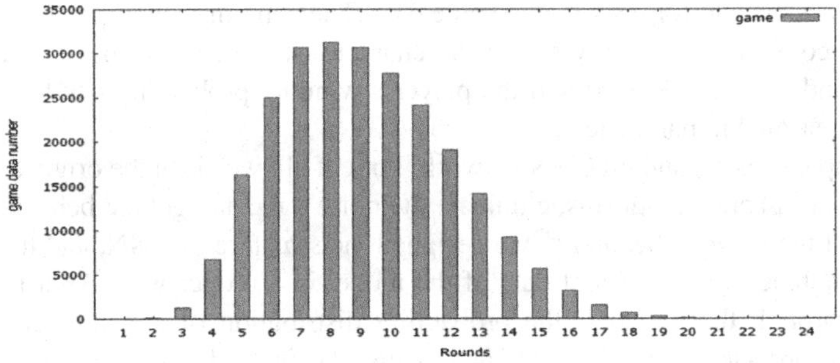

Fig. 2. The number of game data ending in a different number of rounds (240,000 data). If the player has a good hand, the game will end quickly.

3.2 CNN Network Input and Output

Input. It is very important and also the focus of this article that how to transform the game data of Fight the Landlords into data format suitable for CNN model. The speculation model designed in this paper predicts the peasant player's brand from the perspective of the landlord. Three channels are set to represent three players in the game. Each channel draws a single player all the cards features, including the total card, the landlord card, the remaining cards out of the landlord, the total card each round, multiple rounds of card data. We here only consider the first five rounds of the situation, a total of 9 features. As shown in Fig. 3.

Regardless of the card type, poker cards face a total of 13 cards from "A" to "K" and two jokers, for which purpose the dimensions of each card are set to 15, as shown in Fig. 4. We directly use the corresponding number to indicate the number of cards. In the round of card data, the data is combined in the same way as the card, the cards that have not been played are set to "0" as shown in Fig. 5.

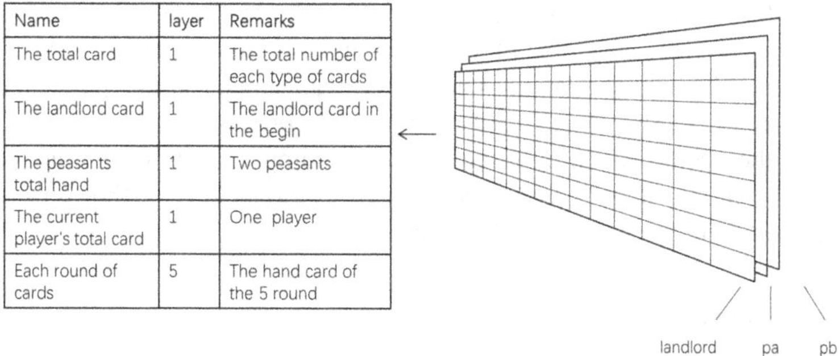

Name	layer	Remarks
The total card	1	The total number of each type of cards
The landlord card	1	The landlord card in the begin
The peasants total hand	1	Two peasants
The current player's total card	1	One player
Each round of cards	5	The hand card of the 5 round

Fig. 3. Model input design. The right side is the input matrix, the dimension is [9 × 15 × 3], and the left side is the game situation information contained in each dimension.

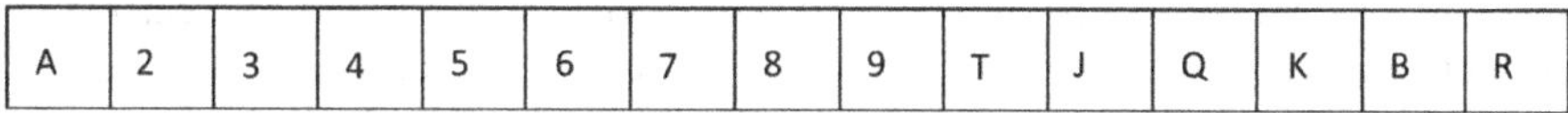

A	2	3	4	5	6	7	8	9	T	J	Q	K	B	R

Fig. 4. Each dimension card type meaning. It represents the number of each type of card

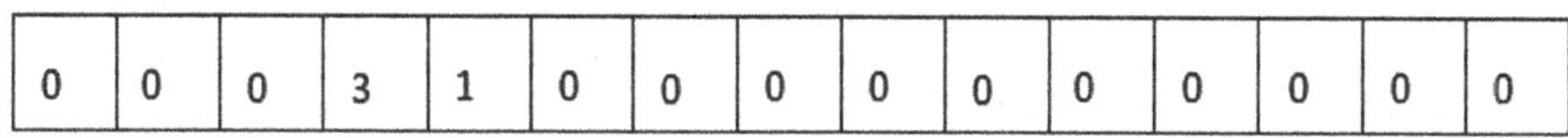

0	0	0	3	1	0	0	0	0	0	0	0	0	0	0

Fig. 5. Every round of playing cards. The total number of "A" to "K" is 4, while the number of the jokers is one. The figure shows the player playing the four cards with a "4445".

In the Fig. 4, the card type "10" is indicated by "T", the card type "Black joker" is indicated by "B", and the card type "Red joker" is indicated by "R".

In summary, the designed CNN input dimension is [9 × 15 × 3]. "3" represents three players, "9" represents all data information that the landlords can recognize, and "15" represents the digital representation dimension of each kind of data information.

Output. In the model output, it uses the classification method. The combination of the number of two peasant players (*pa* and *pb*) is set to 15 categories, as shown in Fig. 6. In the figure, "12" means that the number of the player *pb* is 1 and 2 for the player *pa*. The output of the fully connected layer on the last layer, through the Softmax activation function [5], obtains the probability distribution of the number of the 15 types of corresponding brand types. The most probable class is taken from the output as the model's prediction.

00	01	02	03	04	10	11	12	13	20	21	22	30	31	40

Fig. 6. Model output. The picture shows the predicted distribution of the number of one card type in the other two players.

Figure 6 shows the card combination of "13" and "31" of the player *pb* and the player *pa* belong to two cases. The player's combination must be completely guessed.

The network's input is as a landlord player's private hand, and as a public record of round cards. Round cards are recorded by a special combination of encoding. It not only includes the overall situation of the game, including its own hand, other players' total hand, etc., it also reflects the player's confrontational relationship on the input depth, and has a better description of the game.

3.3 The Use of CNN Model

Each round of playing cards will reduce the amount of private information, increase the amount of common information, and increase the accuracy of model predictions to a certain extent. This article only considers the 5 rounds of data model construction, corresponding to five convolutional layers. The first convolutional layer selects the convolution kernel of [9 × 5], in which "9" corresponds to the round data entered in the input data, the purpose of which is to consider a collective effect of all information. The 5-round data at all the same locations is convoluted together. Fight the Landlords consider the number of cards to play generally less than or equal to 5 accounted for the majority, that three belts (Triplet, Triplet with an attached card and Triplet with an attached pair) and 5 cards of Sequence will be included. Convolutional layer performs feature abstraction on game data in different dimensions. The remaining convolutional layers are all convolution kernels [5 × 5]. The adjustment of the output of the convolution kernel through the activation function of the Relu activation function can greatly speed up the convergence rate, as in

$$\mathrm{f(x)} = \max(0, \mathrm{x}) \tag{1}$$

It connects three fully connected layers after Convolution layer. To prevent the model from overfitting, a layer of BN [6] (Batch Normalization) is added after the second fully connected layer. The first two fully connected layers have 256 nodes; the last layer has 15 nodes. The weighted output passes through the softmax activation function and normalizes the output to the constraint of adding a value of 1 to output the probability of predicting the number of cards. The calculation trained throughout Gradient descent.

3.4 The Use of CNN Model Evaluation Program

Under a large number of game data, there will be some rules for players to play cards. However, when the status of data branches is huge, the data is complicated and there is some noise (In the face of similar game states, the player may make a difference, or even a long way to go, although this may be due to player level differences, but still affect the model's performance) in the data, we cannot evaluate whether the network is the same as the real label or not. The paper uses a more complex evaluation method.

In this paper, the model compared predicts result from the input data with the real result, and calculates the percentage of the correct data in the total data, which is called *acc* (the correct rate). In order to more intuitively and accurately reflect the intelligence level of the proposed method, this paper not only calculates the prediction accuracy of the whole data, but also divides the original data into more detailed ones to understand the excellent performance of the model in different situations. Specific refinement assessment method, the real card round data, some cards played a small number, while some may never appear. If the predicted card type all appears, it must be able to know which player in the hands of the card, the correct rate is 1, so the numbers of cards appear to refine the performance evaluation model separately is necessary. The specific refinement method will be described below.

4 Model Overall Frame Design Experimental Results and Analysis

The original data is the real playing record of the Lianzhong Fight the landlords platform. It gets 5 million appropriate game data, including each player's private hand situation and all round of the card record of the deal after cleaning the data. We can use this data to make neural network input data and tag data using the above method. Use these Fight the landlords' data to train the card network. A single-core Titan GPU can be used during model training. The training time is 8 h and it can converge to better results. The training Batchsize [7] is 100, the learning rate is 0.001, and the optimizer uses Adam [8]. Loss is the cross-entropy of the real data and the prediction result, as in

$$loss = -\frac{1}{n}\sum\nolimits_{x} [y \ln a + (1 - y)\ln(1 - a)] \tag{2}$$

The y represents the expected output, the a represents the actual output of the neuron, the x represents the sample, and the n represents the total number of samples in (2). The optimization goal is to minimize the loss. In training, a batchsize size data is entered each time, and it is recorded as an epoch. When the model training is to a certain extent, the model gradually fitted, the correct rate is no longer significantly improved. The following are the prediction experiments on single brand "8" and all single cards.

4.1 Single Card Prediction and Refinement Assessment Method

In all the cards of the Landlords, the "8" card is in the middle of the card power, and in the first experiment the paper set the tag data as the true result of the "8" card. In the overall accuracy rate, the correct rate of the training set is 97% and 83% on the test set. As shown in Figs. 7 and 8.

The ordinate in the diagram is the correct rate of the model and the abscissa is epoch. In the final stage of network training, the correct rate of guessing the number of '8' cards reached 83%.

In the thinning aspect, the status of each card is different when it reaches the 5 round. For example, in the landlord's position, for the card "8", it may not appear at the time when the model is predicted; and it is also possible that the peasant players play out one, and so on. In the absence of "8" in a case, it is the most difficult to predict the

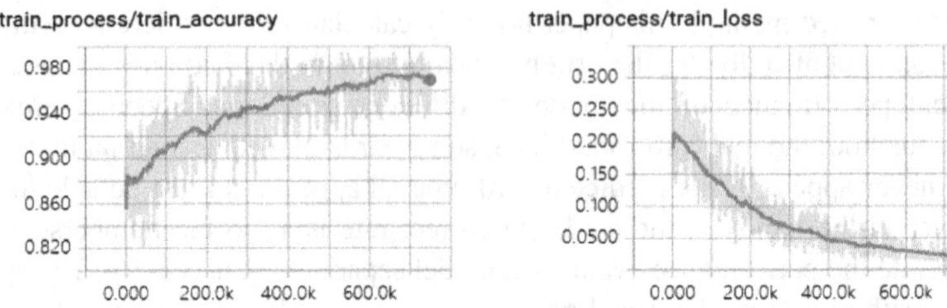

Fig. 7. Training process *acc* and *loss*. As the training progresses, the model gradually tends to fit in the training set. The number of forecasts cards is gradually accurate.

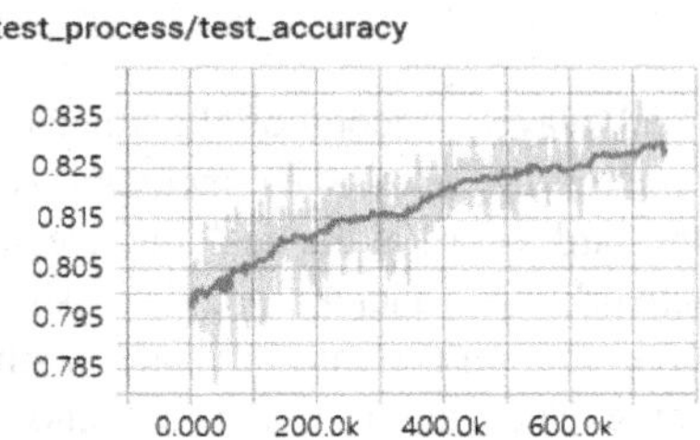

Fig. 8. Test process *acc*. Show better predictions in the test set.

number of the cards. With the increase of the number of "8", the degree of difficulty is gradually decreasing. Because the model considers the landlord's perspective to guess the hand of the peasant player, the landlord player has '8' in his hand, and even if it's not hit, he thinks "8" appears. The following tables are derived from the scale of the test set of 10000 bureaus, and the following results are generated.

In Table 1, the number of "8" cards is 4 which is not appear, that means there is no "8" in his hand and the opponent did not play out card "8".

Table 1. The correctness of the individual card '8'.

The number of rounds of entering test data (the first few rounds)	The number of cards that do not show up (remove the card the landlords hand and the Peasants played out)	The number of appeared game data (10000 data)	Acc (the correct rate) (%)
5 rounds	4	879	51.64
	3	1946	53.54
	2	2675	66.65
	1	2728	81.19
	0	1770	99.88

In the case of landlord guessing cards under incomplete information, the deep learning model can also show some good results. In the guess of the number of remaining cards 1 and 0, the correct rates were 81% and 99%. It shows that the model has learned some rules of Fight the landlords, such as the number of cards for each type is 4. When the number of "8" cards remains 4, two peasants have more combinations of cards, and their combination reaches five of "04", "40", "13", "31" and "22". When the model gets less information, the combination of '04' and '40' has greatly increased the difficulty of speculation, and it is more difficult to guess the player's hand.

4.2 All Card Prediction

In the single-card speculation, the effect of guessing cards is good, and this paper has trained 13 types of cards separately, as shown in Fig. 9.

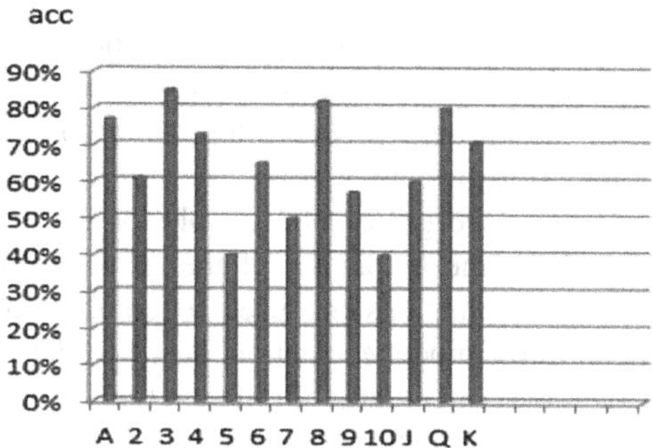

Fig. 9. Each card type correct rate. We tested the predictions for each card type, and only the '5', '7', and '10' cards predicted a correct rate of less than 50%. Other card type predictions can effectively estimate teammates' cards after a certain round of games.

In Fig. 9, the card type is 13 kinds of cards in poker (excluding jokers), and the correct rate is "acc" of the first evaluation method mentioned in the previous article. The result shows that the model has quite different predictions for different types of cards because the different types of cards have different probability of being played for the players and the resulting amount of information is different. It has a certain impact on the outcome of the game. In the equal card power (the size of the card) of the card type, the difficulty is different according to their different purposes. For example, "3" and "5" are usually combined into one sequence, but when the sequence does not hold and they become separate hands, "3" has a higher probability of being shot, so the accuracy of the prediction is a little different. In the cards "K" and "A", the power of the card is similar and the probability is close. When they are played out, they may be defeated by the card "2", so the accuracy of the cards is close. For the card '8', which is in the middle of the entire card type, When players played out various kinds of cards before and after the power of this card, such as sequence and triplet, it may bring more information about the card "8". For the model which be used to guesses its number, it can get a broader perspective.

In view of the lack of research on the game of Fight the landlord by computer games, this paper proposes the above two indicators that can evaluate the performance of the model, and provides a standard that can be weighed and compared to the next researchers in this field.

In summary, the different of card power will bring different information on the type of guessing, and also produced a different correct rate of the card. When the numbers of cards are predicted, it is still important for the player to have a total card number limit of 17 private hands and may have an impact on the end result. In the next experiment, we will try to use a regression method to show all the number combinations of the cards all at once.

5 Conclusion

In order to solve the AI problem of incomplete information game, the deep neural network is used to analyze the historical game records, extract features, and get the probability distribution of the player's private information combination. In the early stage of the game data multidimensional analysis, the data is scheduled to the appropriate format; In order to make the game data suitable for the model input, and to a certain extent, it is helpful for the extraction of the model features. In the testing process, a variety of data combinations are used to compare and select the most effective data arrangement. In the model evaluation, based on the situation of the cards which was played, we count the correct rates of different types of cards, which based on the number of non-appearing. This model can be used as a game AI module, in order to make a strong support for the subsequent AI's playing behavior.

Acknowledgment. This work is Supported by National Natural Science Foundation of China (No. 61502039), Supported by the special bidding project of teaching & education reform (2017JGZB08), and Supported by 2018 Beijing Information Science and Technology University Graduate Student Science and Technology Innovation Project.

References

1. Gilpin, A., Sandholm, T.: Lossless abstraction of imperfect information games. ACM (2007)
2. Moravčík, M., Schmid, M., Burch, N., et al.: DeepStack: expert-level artificial intelligence in heads-up no-limit poker. Science **356**(6337), 508 (2017)
3. Brown, N., Sandholm, T.: Libratus: the Superhuman AI for no-limit poker. In: Twenty-Sixth International Joint Conference on Artificial Intelligence, pp. 5226–5228 (2017)
4. Lecun, Y., Bengio, Y., Hinton, G.: Deep learning. Nature **521**(7553), 436–444 (2015)
5. Bishop, C.M.: Pattern Recognition and Machine Learning. Information Science and Statistics. Springer, New York (2006). 049901
6. Ioffe, S., Szegedy, C.: Batch normalization: accelerating deep network training by reducing internal covariate shift, pp. 448–456 (2015)
7. Ruder, S.: An overview of gradient descent optimization algorithms (2016)
8. Kingma, D.P., Ba, J.: Adam: a method for stochastic optimization. Computer Science (2014)

Short-Term Precipitation Prediction with Skip-Connected PredNet

Ryoma Sato(✉), Hisashi Kashima, and Takehiro Yamamoto

Kyoto University, Kyoto, Japan
r.sato@ml.ist.i.kyoto-u.ac.jp,
kashima@i.kyoto-u.ac.jp,
tyamamot@dl.kuis.kyoto-u.ac.jp

Abstract. Short-term forecasting of rainfall in a local area is called precipitation nowcasting, and it has been traditionally addressed using rule-based or numerical approaches. Recently, deep neural network models have started to be used for precipitation nowcasting; however, their utility has not been extensively explored yet. Especially, the existing efforts focus only on the choice of their building blocks and pay little attention to the design of the whole network structure. In this paper, we propose a new precipitation nowcasting model based on the PredNet network architecture, which was originally proposed for short-term video prediction tasks. The proposed model outperforms the state-of-the-art models in the MovingMNIST++ dataset in terms of MSE, and it also shows a good predictive performance on a real dataset of precipitation in Kyoto City.

Keywords: Nowcasting · Precipitation prediction · Deep neural network

1 Introduction

Precipitation nowcasting is the problem of predicting rainfall intensity in a local area (*e.g.*, a city) in a very short period of time (*e.g.*, several minutes to a few hours). It is quite beneficial not only for our daily decision making but also for companies and governments to plan safer flight schedules, to predict the number of customers of a store, and to warn people for evacuation in the area where a heavy rainfall is expected in the near future.

Over the years, many researchers have tackled the precipitation nowcasting problem. Traditional approaches are based on optical flows [1] and numerical simulation [8]; they are deterministic algorithms and only use the current rainfall information. Recently, data-driven approaches using Deep Neural Network (DNN) have started to be applied on precipitation nowcasting. These approaches utilize a large amount of past rainfall data to learn a prediction model. Such data-driven approaches include Convolutional LSTM (ConvLSTM) [9], Convolutional GRU (ConvGRU), and Trajectory GRU (TrajGRU) [10].

Their utility, however, has not been extensively explored yet. Especially, the existing approaches have only focused on designing new building blocks in the networks and paid little attention to designing the whole network structure such as the depth of the network and the connection between the blocks.

V. Kůrková et al. (Eds.): ICANN 2018, LNCS 11141, pp. 373–382, 2018.
https://doi.org/10.1007/978-3-030-01424-7_37

In this work, we propose a new precipitation nowcasting model based on the PredNet architecture. PredNet was originally proposed for the short-term video prediction, inspired by neuroscientific predictive coding concept, and is one of the state-of-the-art approaches in the field.

We investigate the effectiveness of our proposed model with the synthetic MovingMNIST++ benchmark [10] and a real precipitation dataset in Kyoto City. The experimental results demonstrate that our proposed model outperforms the state-of-the-art model in the MovingMNIST++ benchmark in terms of MSE and it also shows a good predictive performance on the real precipitation data, while our proposed model requires less GPU memory.

The rest of the paper is organized as follows: after the review of the existing work in Sects. 2 and 3 gives the definition of the precipitation nowcasting task and describe our proposed model. We then show its effectiveness with experiments in Sect. 4. Finally, we conclude our work and mention future work in the last section.

2 Related Work

2.1 Video Generation with DNN

Video generation is highly related to precipitation nowcasting because we can regard a rainfall map as a grayscale image and a sequence of rainfall maps as a video.

Video generation is a challenging task because videos are high dimensional and we need to extract the movement of each component correctly. It is, however, an essential task for robotics [3] and self-driving cars [2]. Many DNN models have been proposed and also achieved state-of-the-art performance in this task. The encoder-decoder model [11] is the most basic but powerful model. This kind of models is used in precipitation nowcasting task as well [9, 10]. The adversarial network model also performs well in video generation [13].

2.2 Network Architecture of DNN

Various network architectures have been proposed to train deeper networks efficiently and to reduce the number of parameters for image recognition tasks. These techniques help us design our model. ResNet [4] uses shortcut connections, which enable to train far deeper models and is applied to many other fields such as machine translation [15] and speech synthesis [14]. We also adopt a variant of skip connection in our model. Dilated Convolution [16] employs sparse connections in the convolutional layer which expands the receptive field with a small number of parameters, which is successfully applied in Wavenet [7]. We use this operation to reduce the number of parameters and expand the receptive field.

3 Model

In this section, we introduce the problem setting and propose our model. We also describe the building block and the loss functions for our model.

3.1 Problem Setting

Precipitation nowcasting can be regarded as an unsupervised video prediction task. Figure 1 illustrates an example of inputs and outputs of the precipitation nowcasting.

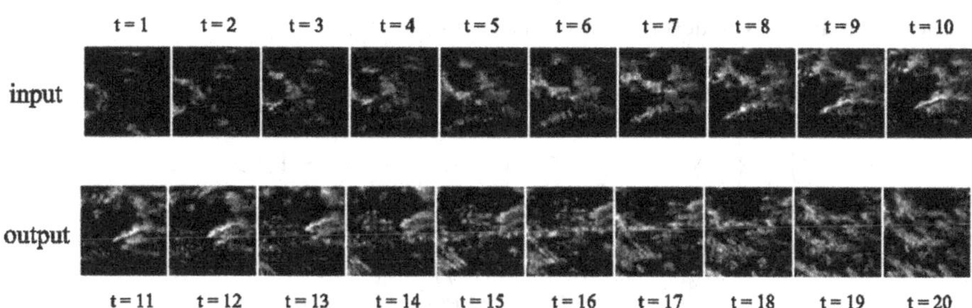

Fig. 1. Inputs and outputs of the precipitation nowcasting.

Formally, the input is previous precipitation matrices $x_1, x_2, \ldots, x_I \in \mathbb{R}^{H \times W}$, where the (i,j)-th value of x_t is the amount of rainfall at location (i,j) at time t. The output is the estimated values of subsequent matrices $\hat{x}_{I+1}, \hat{x}_{I+2}, \ldots, \hat{x}_{I+O} \in \mathbb{R}^{H \times W}$. We fix the number of input frames I and output frames O as $I = O = 10$, and the height of the matrices H and the width W as $H = W = 64$ throughout this paper.

3.2 Convolutional GRU

While PredNet consists of ConvLSTM in its original form, we adopt ConvGRU as the unit. The main advantage is its simplicity. ConvGRU is given as the equations:

$$Z_t = \sigma(W_{xz} * X_t + W_{hz} * H_{t-1}) \tag{1}$$

$$R_t = \sigma(W_{xr} * X_t + W_{hr} * H_{t-1}) \tag{2}$$

$$H_t^{'} = LReLU(W_{xh} * X_t + R_t \odot (W_{hh} * H_{t-1})) \tag{3}$$

$$H_t = (1 - Z) \odot H_t^{'} + Z \odot H_{t-1} \tag{4}$$

where σ is a sigmoid function, LReLU is the Leaky ReLU with slope rate 0.2, $*$ is the convolution operation with a bias term and $\odot$ is element-wise multiplication. We use the dilated convolution [16] where kernel size as $(3,3)$ and the dilation as $(2,2)$ throughout this paper.

3.3 Our Model

We make several modifications to the original PredNet for precipitation nowcasting. First, we add the skip connection in the error representation layer. The original idea of the skip connection is introduced by ResNet [4], although we used concatenation rather than addition. This connection helps deep networks stabilize their learning process. Next, we make the network deeper. While the original PredNet model has four or five blocks, we stack up to nine blocks. Such deep structure improves the performance as shown in the experiments. In addition, we change the input layer A_0^t to feedback the prediction $\hat{A}_0^t$ when $t > I$. This is because the original model predicts only the next frame, while our model predicts the next O frames.[1]Finally, we change the loss function, which we will describe in the next subsection.

Our modified PredNet is summarized as the following equations:

$$A_l^t = \begin{cases} x_t & (l = 1, t \leq I) \\ \hat{A}_l^t & (l = 1, t > I) \\ MaxPool(ReLU(Conv(E_l^t))) & (l > 1) \end{cases} \tag{5}$$

$$\hat{A}_l^t = \begin{cases} Clip(Conv(R_l^t)) & (l = 1) \\ ReLU(Conv(R_l^t)) & (l > 1) \end{cases} \tag{6}$$

$$E_l^t = \left[ReLU\left(A_l^t - \hat{A}_l^t\right), ReLU\left(\hat{A}_l^t - A_l^t\right), A_l^t\right] \tag{7}$$

$$R_l^t = \begin{cases} ConvGRU\left(\left[E_l^{t-1}, R_l^{t-1}, Upsample\left(R_{l+1}^t\right)\right]\right) & (l<L) \\ ConvGRU\left(\left[E_l^{t-1}, R_l^{t-1}\right]\right) & (l = L) \end{cases} \tag{8}$$

where Clip is the function to clip the input in $[0, 1]$. $A_l, R_l, \hat{A}_l, E_l$ are the input convolution layer, the recurrent representation layer, the prediction layer and the error representation layer, respectively. E_l and R_l are initialized to zero. Figure 2 shows the diagram of the building block used in our model, which is stacked up to nine times in our model.

3.4 Loss Functions

In the original PredNet model, the loss function is the sum of the error representation layer with some fixed weights. It uses not only the error values of output phase ($t > I$), but also during input phase ($t \leq I$); however, this loss function turned out not to work well in our problem setting. Instead, we mainly use the B-MSE [10] of the output frames, namely,

$$L = \frac{1}{OHW} \sum\nolimits_{t=I+1}^{I+O} \sum\nolimits_{i=1}^{H} \sum\nolimits_{j=1}^{W} w\left(x_{tij}\right) \cdot \left(\hat{A}_{1ij}^t - x_{tij}\right)^2, \tag{9}$$

[1] Actually, this modification is suggested in the appendix of the original paper [6].

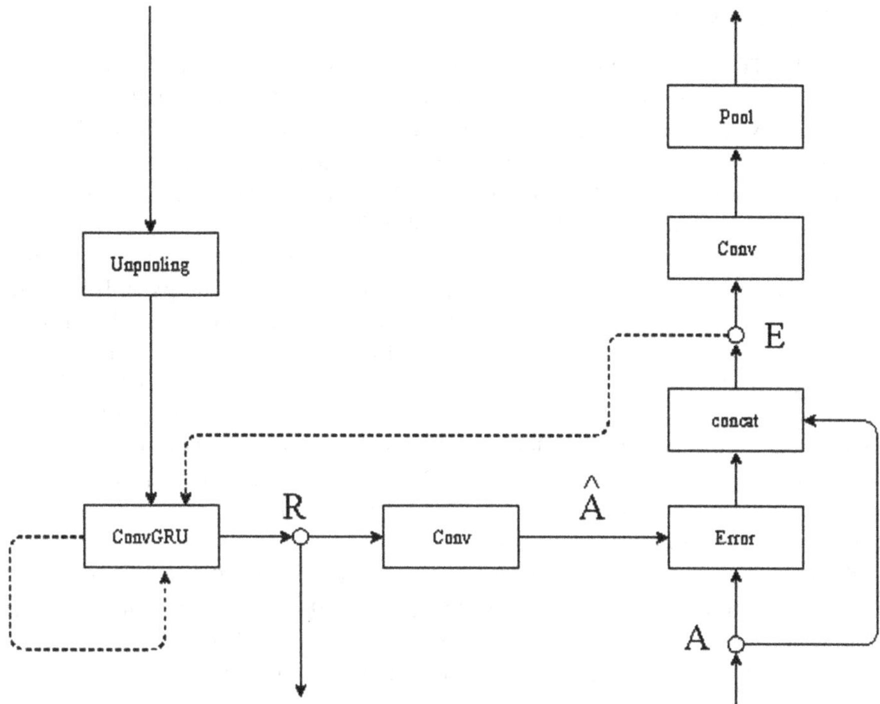

Fig. 2. The diagram of a building block in our model. The incoming and outgoing arrows stand for the inputs and output of the function, respectively. The dotted arrow means to use the previous value. For example, the ConvGRU unit on the lower left side corresponds to the Eq. (8). We stack this up to nine times.

where $w : \mathbb{R} \rightarrow \mathbb{R}$ is a weight function to adjust imbalance. We use $w(x) = 1$ (MSE) in MovingMNIST++ experiments (Sect. 4.1), and

$$w(x) = \begin{cases} 1 & (x < 2) \\ 2 & (2 \leq x < 5) \\ 5 & (5 \leq x < 10) \\ 10 & (10 \leq x < 30) \\ 30 & (30 \leq x) \end{cases} \tag{10}$$

in the Kyoto dataset (Sect. 4.2), following the existing paper [10].

4 Experiments

We carried out experiments on two datasets, the MovingMNIST++ dataset and the real precipitation data in Kyoto City. We first show the effectiveness of our model with the MovingMNIST++ dataset, and we then report the results with the real precipitation data, which shows the prediction performance in a more practical situation.

4.1 MovingMNIST++

MovingMNIST [11], which consists of parallel movement and reection of MNIST, is one of the most popular datasets in the video prediction field. MovingMNIST++ [10], which is an extension of MovingMNIST by allowing random rotations, scale changes, and illumination changes, has recently been proposed by Shi et al. for evaluating precipitation nowcasting models. Our model (SDPredNet) contains nine blocks, where the numbers of channels are $1, 32, 32, 64, 64, 128, 128, 256, 256$, respectively. We remove pooling and unpooling layers in the even-numbered blocks because pooling operation halves the image size and full pooling operation results in 1px $\times$ 1px image size in the 7th layer. The TrajGRU model [10] is the state-of-the-art model on precipitation nowcasting tasks. We set the number of links to $L = 17, 17, 17$. Also, we set the numbers of the channels of the encoder and the decoder as $1, 16, 64, 64, 96, 96, 96$ and $96, 96, 96, 96, 96, 64, 16, 1$, respectively, following the parameters reported in the original paper [10] that achieved the best MSE on the MovingMNIST++ dataset.

We also carried out ablation analysis. SPredNet is a five-blocks shallow model where the number of channels are $1, 32, 64, 128, 256$, respectively. NPredNet is SPredNet variant without skip connection.

We implemented these models with Chainer [12] and trained them with Adam [5]. We used the learning rate as 10^{-4}, β_1 as 0.5 and β_2 as 0.999. The minibatch size was set to 32 for NPredNet, SPredNet, SDPredNet, and 4 for TrajGRU.

Table 1 summarizes the MSE of the models on the MovingMNIST++ dataset. Note that the values reported in the table were obtained after the 150 k-th iteration due to the limitation of computational resources, whereas the value reported in the table as [10] trained the model with 200 k iterations.

From the table, we observe that deep model helps improve the accuracy, and skip connection is also effective.

The generated images with these models are shown in Fig. 3. Our model predicts more clearly and more accurately than TrajGRU, which also shows the effectiveness of our model.

4.2 Kyoto Dataset

We prepared the real precipitation data in Kyoto City to investigate the model efficiency in a more practical situation. The center of the observation point is Yoshida-honmachi, Sakyo-Ku, Kyoto, Japan. We collected the rainfall data ranging from 2013 to 2017 by using the Yahoo! Static Map API. The rainfall data (*i.e.*, frames) are recorded in every five minutes, and one pixel in a frame corresponds to 1 km^2. There are many data where all the input values are zero (*e.g.*, in a sunny day) in the raw data. We removed such data from the dataset since they contain no useful information. We used the $154,098$ data from 2013 to 2015 for training, the $50,244$ data in 2016 for validation, and the $57,403$ data in 2017 for testing.

One of the large difference of this dataset from the MovingMNIST++ dataset is the imbalanced frequency of data. Thus we use the B-MSE described in Sect. 3.4 as the loss functions for the SDPredNet and TrajGRU models.

Table 1. Results of different models on MovingMNIST++ dataset (Lowest value among models is in bold). Values are obtained at the 150 k-th iteration. Since we reimplemented the TrajGRU model with Chainer, we also provide the original MSE of TrajGRU on MovingMNIST ++ dataset reported in the original paper [10].

	Baselines		Proposed		
	[10]	TrajGRU	NPredNet	SPredNet	SDPredNet
MSE $\times 10^{-2}$	1.138	1.151	0.9308	0.8949	**0.7745**

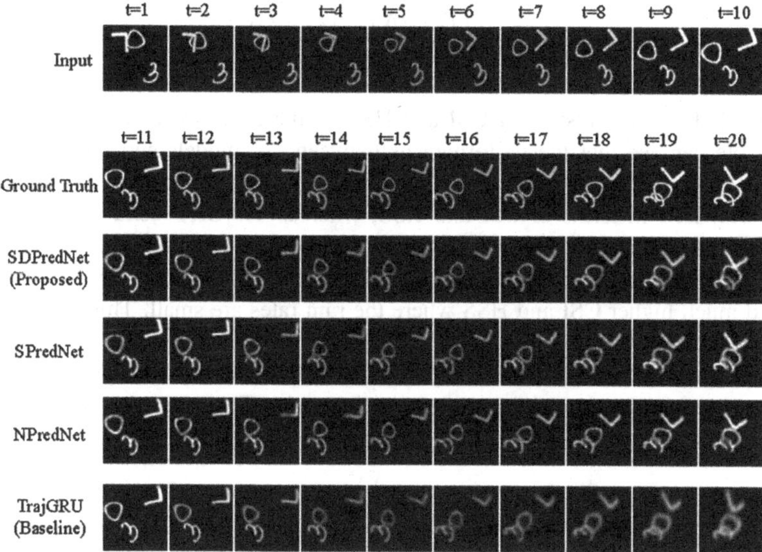

Fig. 3. Inputs, ground truth, and outputs of each model on MovingMNIST++ dataset.

We trained the SDPredNet and TrajGRU models on this dataset. For the SDPredNet model, the number of channels is set to $1, 32, 32, 64, 64, 128, 128, 256, 256$. For the TrajGRU model, the number of links is set to $L = 7, 5, 3$, and the numbers of channels of encoder and the decoder are set to $1, 8, 16, 16, 32, 32, 32$ and $32, 32, 32, 32, 32, 16, 8, 1$, respectively.

In addition to SDPredNet and TrajGRU, we trained classification variant of SDPredNet (SDPredNet-class) in this dataset. In this model, we split the data into 9 classes $[0, 1), [1, 2), [2, 4), [4, 8), [8, 12), [12, 16), [16, 24), [24, 32), [32, \infty)$ in mm/h. We used weighted cross entropy loss function, and set weights to w(lowest value in the class). (*e.g.*, the weights of class $[4, 8)$ is $w(4) = 2$.)

We trained the SDPredNet, SDPredNet-class and TrajGRU models with Adam, using the same learning rates as in the previous experiment. The minibatch size was set to 32, and we iterated $24,078$ mini batches in the training. In this setting, SDPredNet,

SDPredNet-class, and TrajGRU model consume 7,858, 9,524, and 12,658 MiB of GPU memory respectively. It shows GPU memory efficiency of our model. We consider this is because we adopt simple building blocks such as convGRU and dilated convolution with small kernel.

As for the evaluation metrics, we used CSI and Heidke Skill Score (HSS), following the existing paper [10]. CSI and HSS are calculated as follows:

$$CSI = \frac{TP}{TP + FN + FP} \tag{11}$$

$$HSS = \frac{(TP \cdot TN) - (FP \cdot FN)}{(TP + FN)(FN + TN) + (TP + FP)(FP + TN)} \tag{12}$$

Table 2 shows the results of CSI and HSS of the different models on the Kyoto dataset. We can see that the performances between our models and the baseline are comparable. For the thresholds of 2, 4, 8, 12, 16, and 24 mm/h, SDPredNet outperformed TrajGRU in terms of CSI and HSS, whereas TrajGRU achieved higher performances than SDPredNet in the thresholds of 1 and 32 mm/h. When we compare the results of SDPredNet and SDPredNet-class, we can see that the SDPredNet-class model achieved much higher CSI and HSS where the rain rates are small. This indicates that the classification model is beneficial when we want to roughly know the rainfall amount. Recalling that our model requires less GPU memory, our proposed model shows the usefulness of precipitation nowcasting tasks. The generated images of each model are shown Fig. 4.

Table 2. CSI and HSI of different models on Kyoto Dataset. Highest values among models are in bold, and second highest values are underlined.

Rain rate (mm/h)	CSI			HSI		
	Proposed		Baseline	Proposed		Baseline
	SDPredNet	SDPredNet-class	TrajGRU	SDPredNet	SDPredNet-class	TrajGRU
≥1	0.4950	**0.6316**	<u>0.5037</u>	0.2999	**0.3694**	<u>0.3005</u>
≥2	<u>0.4800</u>	**0.5613**	0.4680	<u>0.3033</u>	**0.3446**	0.2949
≥4	<u>0.4444</u>	**0.4950**	0.4344	<u>0.2942</u>	**0.3215**	0.2882
≥8	<u>0.3900</u>	**0.4217**	0.3886	<u>0.2733</u>	**0.2893**	0.2725
≥12	<u>0.3026</u>	**0.3321**	0.2999	<u>0.2283</u>	**0.2462**	0.2268
≥16	**0.2445**	0.2307	<u>0.2435</u>	**0.1941**	0.1854	<u>0.1935</u>
≥24	<u>0.1896</u>	**0.1940**	0.1889	<u>0.1581</u>	**0.1609**	0.1577
≥32	<u>0.1498</u>	0.1154	**0.1561**	<u>0.1297</u>	0.1025	**0.1345**

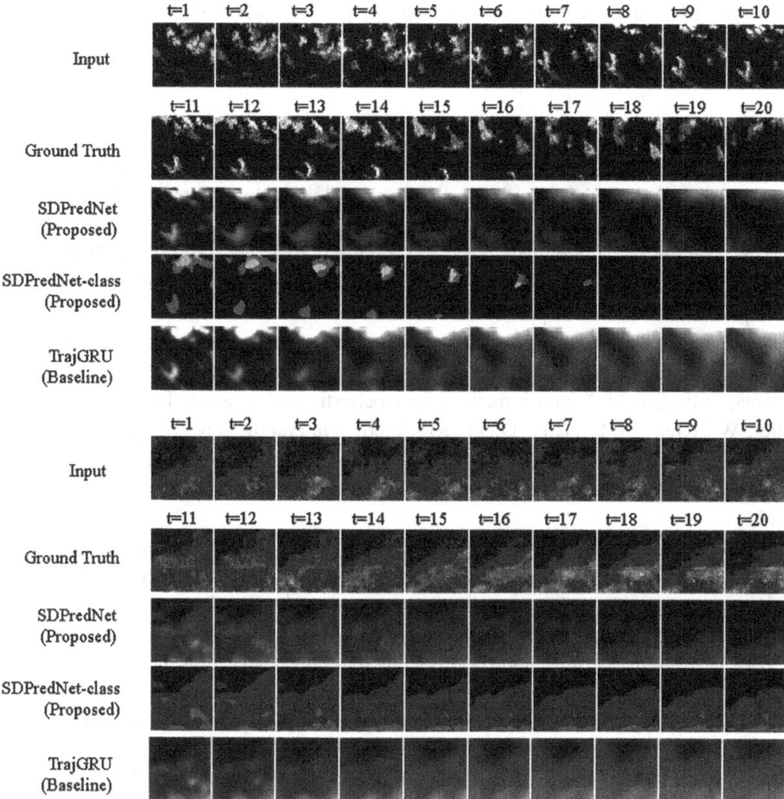

Fig. 4. Output frames predicted by each model on Kyoto dataset.

5 Conclusion

In this work, we proposed a new model for precipitation nowcasting based on the PredNet architecture. Our proposed model shows the state-of-the-art performance in the MovingMNIST++ benchmark in terms of MSE and a good predictive performance in the real precipitation dataset in Kyoto City. Our model consumes less GPU memory than the Trajectory GRU model, and this feature is beneficial especially in training with a large dataset.

In our experiment with the Kyoto dataset, the training data is limited to three years due to a restriction of the data provider. Recalling that our model greatly reduced the MSE from the current state-of-the-art in the MovingMNIST++ benchmark, we expect that our model would show better prediction performance on the real precipitation dataset when it uses more training data, which is an interesting future direction.

Finally, our model is general and can be applicable to other prediction tasks than precipitation nowcasting. We also plan to apply our model to other video prediction tasks.

Acknowledgment. This research was supported by JSPS KAKENHI Grant Numbers 15H01704, 18H03243.

References

1. Cheung, P., Yeung, H.Y.: Application of optical-flow technique to significant convection nowcast for terminal areas in Hong Kong. In: WSN, pp. 6–10 (2012)
2. Eder, S., George, H.: Learning a driving simulator. CoRR abs/1409.0473 (2016)
3. Finn, C., Goodfellow, I., Levine, S.: Unsupervised learning for physical interaction through video prediction. In: NIPS, pp. 64–72 (2016)
4. He, K., Zhang, X., Ren, S., Sun, J.: Deep residual learning for image recognition. In: CVPR. pp. 770–778 (2016)
5. Kingma, D.P., Ba, J.: Adam: a method for stochastic optimization. In: ICLR (2015)
6. Lotter, W., Kreiman, G., Cox, D.D.: Deep predictive coding networks for video prediction and unsupervised learning. In: ICLR (2017)
7. van den Oord, A., et al.: Wavenet: a generative model for raw audio. CoRR abs/1609.03499 (2016)
8. Sharif, H.O., Yates, D., Roberts, R., Mueller, C.: The use of an automated nowcasting system to forecast flash floods in an urban watershed. J. Hydrometeorol. **7**(1), 190–202 (2006)
9. Shi, X., Chen, Z., Wang, H., Yeung, D.Y., Wong, W.K., Woo, W.C.: Convolutional LSTM network: a machine learning approach for precipitation nowcasting. In: NIPS, pp. 802–810 (2015)
10. Shi, X., et al.: Deep learning for precipitation nowcasting: a benchmark and a new model. In: NIPS, pp. 5622–5632 (2017)
11. Srivastava, N., Mansimov, E., Salakhutdinov, R.: Unsupervised learning of video representations using LSTMS. In: ICML. pp. 843–852 (2015)
12. Tokui, S., Oono, K., Hido, S., Clayton, J.: Chainer: a next-generation open source framework for deep learning. In: Proceedings of Workshop on Machine Learning Systems (LearningSys) in The Twenty-ninth Annual Conference on Neural Information Processing Systems (NIPS) (2015)
13. Vondrick, C., Pirsiavash, H., Torralba, A.: Generating videos with scene dynamics. In: NIPS, pp. 613–621 (2016)
14. Wang, Y., et al.: Tacotron: towards end-to-end speech synthesis. In: Proceedings of Interspeech, pp. 4006–4010 (2017)
15. Wu, Y., et al.: Google's neural machine translation system: bridging the gap between human and machine translation. CoRR abs/1609.08144 (2016)
16. Yu, F., Koltun, V.: Multi-scale context aggregation by dilated convolutions. In: ICLR (2016)

An End-to-End Deep Learning Architecture for Classification of Malware's Binary Content

Daniel Gibert([✉]), Carles Mateu, and Jordi Planes

University of Lleida, Jaume II, 69, Lleida, Spain
{daniel.gibert, carlesm, jplanes}@diei.udl.cat

Abstract. In traditional machine learning techniques for malware detection and classification, significant efforts are expended on manually designing features based on expertise and domain-specific knowledge. These solutions perform feature engineering in order to extract features that provide an abstract view of the software program. Thus, the usefulness of the classifier is roughly dependent on the ability of the domain experts to extract a set of descriptive features. Instead, we introduce a file agnostic end-to-end deep learning approach for malware classification from raw byte sequences without extracting hand-crafted features. It consists of two key components: (1) a denoising autoencoder that learns a hidden representation of the malware's binary content; and (2) a dilated residual network as classifier. The experiments show an impressive performance, achieving almost 99% of accuracy classifying malware into families.

Keywords: Malware classification · Deep learning
Denoising autoencoders · Dilated residual networks

1 Introduction

During the last decade, there has been a lot of research and deployment of machine learning techniques to address the problem of malware detection and classification. Machine learning is an attractive signaturless approach to malware detection because of its ability to recognize never-before-seen malware by summarizing complex relationships among the input features and making decisions about it. In traditional machine learning approaches, efforts are spent on manually designing features based on expertise and domain-specific knowledge. These solutions perform feature engineering to extract features that provide an abstract view of malware that a classifier, e.g. neural network, decision tree, support vector machine, etc., use to make a decision. The most effective approaches in the literature are based on N-Gram analysis and entropy analysis. On the one hand, byte N-grams [7] and opcode N-grams [11] are continuous sequences of N items from a given sequence of bytes or opcodes, respectively. The main

V. Kůrková et al. (Eds.): ICANN 2018, LNCS 11141, pp. 383–391, 2018.
https://doi.org/10.1007/978-3-030-01424-7_38

drawback of N-gram based methods is that they are dependent on N and the number of possible combinations increases exponentially with N. To solve this limitation, Gibert et al. [3] proposed a convolutional neural network to automatically learn N-gram like patterns from raw sequences of opcodes, removing the need to exhausivelly enumerate a large number of N-grams. On the other hand, entropy analysis [8] has been used effectively to detect encrypted and compressed executables as they tend to have higher entropy. This characteristic has been exploited by Gibert [4] to group malware into families based on their structural entropy. However, these solutions depend almost entirely on the ability and knowledge of domain experts to extract a set of descriptive and discriminant features into which represent malware.

Instead, the approach presented in this paper neither relies on feature engineering nor on experts' knowledge of the domain. The main contribution of our work is the development of a file agnostic end-to-end deep learning system for malware classification from raw byte sequences. This is accomplished by using denoising autoencoders to learn an encoded representation of the malware's binary content that captures the main factors of variation in the bytes sequences. Afterwards, decisions about the input are made by a dilated residual network classifier that given the encoded representation of the malware's binary content it outputs the family it belongs. The suitability of our approach has been evaluated on a public benchmark provided by Microsoft for the Big-Data Innovators Gathering (BIG 2015) Anti-Malware Prediction Challenge [10]. Experiments demonstrate the greater predictive generalization performance of our approach with respect to the binary-based methods in the literature.

The rest of the paper is organized as follows. Section 2 presents our approach for malware classification. Section 3 describes the experiments and compares our approach with state-of-the-art methods in the literature. Lastly, Sect. 4 contains the concluding remarks and our future line of research.

2 Deep Learning for Malware Classification

In the present paper we describe a file agnostic deep learning system to successfully process and classify malware from raw byte inputs. The system can be summarized in two phases:

Step 1 Chunk Encoding. A given malware binary is divided into contiguous, non-overlapping chunks of fixed size. Afterwards, a denoising autoencoder takes as input every chunk of bytes values and projects it into a hidden representation of only on value that captures the main factors of variation in the data. The resulting output is a time series $m = \{m_1, m_2, ..., m_n\}$, where m_i corresponds to the encoding of the i-th chunk and n is the number of chunks into which a binary executable has been divided. The activation function of the encoding layer is the hyperbolic tangent. Figure 1 displays the encoded version of samples belonging to the Simda and Obfuscator.ACY malware families. You can observe that the encodings of samples belonging to the same family are similar while distinct from the encoding of samples belonging to a different family. This visual similarity is perhaps the result of reusing code to create new variants and the result of common obfuscation techniques. In consequence, by encoding an executable we can detect this local changes while retaining the global structure of the file.

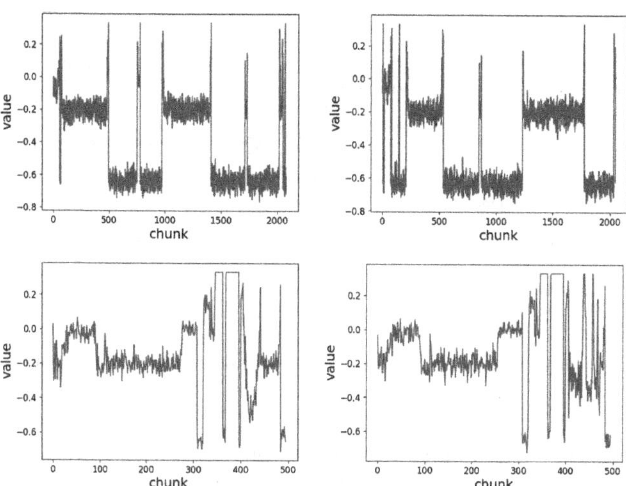

Fig. 1. Bytes encoding representation. Figures from the first and second row belong to the Simda and Obfuscator.ACY families, respectively

Step 2 Feature Extraction and Classification. The resulting time series is fed into a dilated residual network which learns descriptive patterns from the encoding of a bytes sequence and classifies a given malware binary into their corresponding family.

The overall architecture of the network is illustrated in Fig. 2. This architecture corresponds to the network that achieved a higher cross validation accuracy during evaluation. The hyperparameters of the network were selected using a grid search. The input is an univariate time series $m = m_1, m_2, ..., m_n$, where m_i corresponds to the encoding of the i-th chunk. The core of the network consists of 4 custom residual blocks [6] followed by one fully-connected layer and the output layer. The residual blocks perform feature learning while the later fully-connected layer combines the features learned. In particular, each residual block consists of a few stacked convolutional layers whose formulation is as follows:

$$h(x) = \sigma(W_2\sigma(W_1x + b_1) + b_2) + \sigma(W_3x + b_3) \quad (1)$$

where x and $h(x)$ are the input and output of the residual block, W_i and b_i are the weights and biases of the i-th convolutional layer and σ is the activation function.

The input of each convolutional layer goes through a 3-stage feature extractor which learns hierarchical features through convolution, activation and pooling

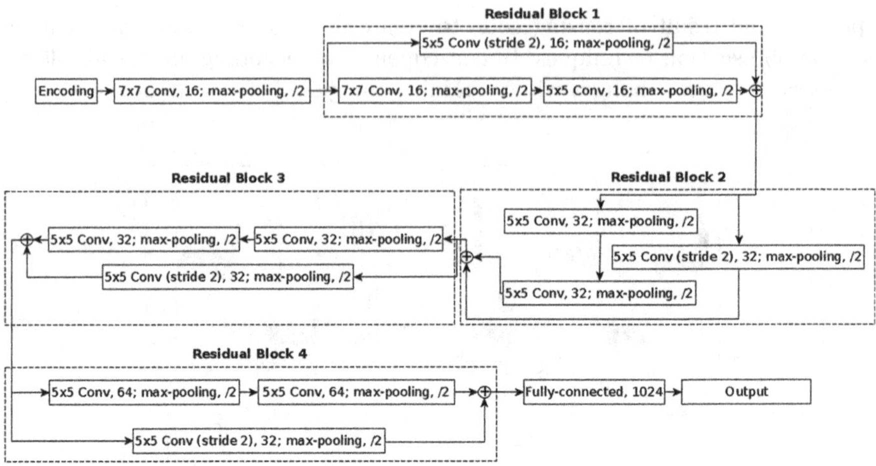

Fig. 2. Overall architecture of the dilated residual network.

layers. More specifically, in the place of the convolution operation, we calculated a dilated convolution [12]. The activation function adopted in all layers the Exponential Linear Unit. Lastly, the pooling operation of our choice has been the MAX operation.

Afterwards, the feature maps extracted by the residual blocks are combined and fed as the input of the subsequent fully-connected layer plus a softmax layer for classification. Additionally, Xavier's initialization [5] has been used to make sure weights are neither too small or big to propagate accurately the signals. To prevent overfitting we employed dropout, a regularization mechanism that randomly drops a proportion of p units during forward propagation and prevents the co-adaptation between neurons.

3 Evaluation

3.1 Microsoft Malware Classification Challenge

The system has been evaluated on the dataset released by Microsoft for the Big Data Innovators Gathering Anti-Malware Prediction Challenge [10]. The dataset consists of 10868 samples for training and 10873 samples for testing of 9 malware families. For each sample, it is provided a file containing the hexadecimal's representation of the binary content and its corresponding disassembled file generated with IDA Pro.

3.2 Experimental Setup

The generalization performance of our approach has been estimated using 10-fold cross validation. Additionally, the best model has been selected according to the macro-averaged F1 score, which is the average of the individual F1 scores obtained for each class.

$$macro\_F_1 = \frac{1}{q}\sum_{i=1}^{q} F_1^i \tag{2}$$

where q is the number of classes in the dataset and F_1^i is the F1 score of class i. Furthermore, the model has been evaluated on the test set using the multi-class logarithmic loss.

$$logloss = -\frac{1}{N}\sum_{i=1}^{N}\sum_{j=1}^{M}(y_{i,j}log(p_{i,j}) + (1 - y_{i,j})log(1 - p_{i,j})) \tag{3}$$

where N is the number of observations, M is the number of class labels, log is the natural logarithm, $y_{i,j}$ is 1 if the observation i is in class j and 0 otherwise, and $p_{i,j}$ is the predicted probability that observation i is in class j.

3.3 State-of-the-art Comparison

To assess the generalization performance of our approach, we compared our model with state-of-the-art methods in the literature that are based on features extracted from the hexadecimal representation of malware on the Microsoft benchmark. These methods can be divided into two groups, depending on how they represent the information of binary executables.

1. Entropy-based approaches. This group includes approaches that are based on the representation of executable files as a stream of entropy values or their structural entropy. Concretely, Gibert et al. [4] evaluated the performance of both convolutional neural networks and the K-nearest neighbor algorithm.
2. IMG-based approaches. This group includes approaches that represent the binary content of an executable as a gray scale image. Such images are generally constructed by treating each byte of the binary as a gray-scale pixel value. In particular, Ahmadi et al. [1] and Narayanan et al. [9] extracted Haralick and Local Binary Pattern (LBP) features, and Principal Component Analysis (PCA) features, respectively.

Table 1. 10-fold cross validation confusion matrix

Family	Ramnit	Lollipop	Kelihos_ver3	Vundo	Simda	Tracur	Kelihos_ver1	Obfuscator.ACY	Gatak
Ramnit	1520	4	0	0	0	1	1	11	4
Lollipop	7	2457	0	1	1	3	1	4	4
Kelihos_ver3	0	0	2940	0	0	1	0	1	0
Vundo	1	2	0	468	0	0	0	4	0
Simda	1	1	0	0	35	2	1	2	0
Tracur	2	2	1	5	1	726	1	7	6
Kelihos_ver1	1	1	0	0	0	0	394	1	1
Obfuscator.ACY	21	14	2	6	0	8	2	1172	3
Gatak	2	2	0	1	0	2	0	2	1005
Accuracy	10717 / 10868 = 0.9861					F1 score	0.9719		

Table 2. Performance comparison of state-of-the-art approaches based on the binary's content of an executable. The approach presented in this article is denoted "AE+DRN". "DTW+K-NN" refers to the K-nearest neighbor algorithm plus the dynamic time warping. "Haar approximation + DTW + K-NN" refers to the aforementioned method trained using the approximation time series obtained after applying the Haar Wavelet Transform to the entropy time series. "CNN entropy" and "CNN haar approximation & details" refer to the convolutional neural networks trained with the structural entropy of executables and the approximation and details coefficients obtained after applying the Haar Wavelet Transform to the structural entropy, respectively. "Haralick features + XGBoost" and "LBP features + XGBoost" refer to the models of Ahmadi et al. [1], which extracted Haralick and Local Binary Pattern features and trained boosted trees for classification. Moreover, Narayanan et al. [9] extracted PCA features and trained different models. "CNN IMG" refers to a convolutional neural network model trained on images of size 128×128 pixels. Those approaches that their authors have not tested their performance on the test set or didn't make public the training confusion matrix appear with a '-' mark. Approaches with a '*' mark indicate that they performed 5-fold cross validation instead of 10-fold cross validation.

	10-Fold accuracy	F1 score	Test logloss
Entropy-based approaches			
DTW + K-NN [4]	0.9894	0.9813	0.367724
Haar approximation + DTW + K-NN [4]	0.9870	0.9710	0.458191
CNN entropy [4]	0.9708	0.9314	0.134624
CNN haar approximation & details [4]	0.9828	0.9636	0.124431
IMG-based approaches			
Haralick features + XGBoost [1]*	0.955	-	-
LBP features + XGBoost [1]*	0.951	-	-
12 PCA features + 1-NN [9]	0.966	0.910	-
10 PCA features + SVM [9]	0.946	0.864	-
52 PCA features + SFN1 [9]	0.956	0.864	-
52 PCA features + SFN2 [9]	0.942	0.849	-
52 PCA features + DFN [9]	0.955	0.889	-
CNN IMG	0.975	0.940	0.184483
AE + DRN	0.9861	0.9719	0.106343

Table 1 presents the 10-fold cross validation accuracy and F1 score obtained on the training data. The major contributor to errors is the Obfuscator.ACY family which comprises malware that can have any purpose, whose code has been obfuscated and they couldn't be detected using their respective signatures and heuristics. This is produced because of the similarity in the encoding of some samples of the Obfuscator.ACY family and the rest. This issue affects the methods in the literature that are based on the hexadecimal representation of the binary content. Consequently, to correctly classify the remaining samples it might be necessary to use other type of features such as the assembly language instructions or the Windows API functions invoked.

Table 2 presents a comparison of the performance of state-of-the-art approaches based on the binary's content of an executable. The methods that are performing worse are those that represent the binary content of an executable as a gray scale image. This is because this kind of representation is counterintuitive. Binaries are not images and by constructing them you enforce non-existent 2D spatial correlations. Nevertheless, following recent trends in machine learning, it can be seen that deep learning aproaches outperform those that rely on the use of hand-designed feature extractors such as Haralick and LBP. On the other hand, the entropy-based convolutional neural network models outmatched the K-NN approaches on the test set and demonstrated a clear superior predictive power. Last but not least, our approach outperformed all the other methods on the test set and only the K-NN method achieved a greater macro-averaged F1 score on the training data, which as already mentioned, it failed to generalize to unseen data.

4 Conclusions

In this work we have described an end-to-end deep learning system for malware classification from raw byte sequences. This has been accomplished by learning an encoded representation of the malware's binary content using denoising autoencoders. Afterwards, a dilated residual network classifies the resulting malware's encoding into their corresponding family.

The proposed approach in this paper exhibits strong classification performance compared with the binary-based state-of-the-art methods in the literature. This is due to the exploitation of the visual similarity between malware samples belonging to the same family as the result of reusing code and using common obfuscation techniques to generate new samples. Therefore, the classifier learns descriptive and robust features through stacking various convolutional layers which are later used for classification purposes.

As far as we know, it is the first approach that applies deep learning for encoding malware's binary content. The main idea behind the encoding is to reduce the dimensionality of the input bytes sequence while being able to capture the main factors of variation in the data. The proposed solution has two major advantages with respect traditional machine learning approaches. First, it is file agnostic. That is, even that the solution has been evaluated on malware executables in Portable Executable format, it could be easily deployed for classifying malware in any other file format or targeting any other operative system. Second, it neither relies on costly feature engineering nor on expertise and domain-specific knowledge and thus, the extraction and prediction time are minimal.

4.1 Future Work

Even though machine learning solutions are a promising tool for detecting and classifying malware, they have their limitations. Specifically, they are susceptible to adversarial attacks that try to poison the training procedure or manipulate the binaries to bypass detection [2]. Due to the limitations of binary-based approaches, a future line of research might be studying how to transfer the features learned by the classifier as a subset of input features for M.L. models attempting to classify malware based on distinct types of file features.

Acknowledgments. This research has been partially funded by the Spanish MICINN Projects TIN2014-53234-C2-2-R, TIN2015-71799-C2-2-P, ENE2015-64117-C5-1-R, and is supported by the University of Lleida.

References

1. Ahmadi, M., Giacinto, G., Ulyanov, D., Semenov, S., Trofimov, M.: Novel feature extraction, selection and fusion for effective malware family classification. CoRR abs/1511.04317 (2015)
2. Anderson, H.S., Kharkar, A., Filar, B., Evans, D., Roth, P.: Learning to evade static PE machine learning malware models via reinforcement learning. CoRR abs/1801.08917 (2018), http://arxiv.org/abs/1801.08917
3. Gibert, D., Bejar, J., Mateu, C., Planes, J., Solis, D., Vicens, R.: Convolutional neural networks for classification of malware assembly code. In: International Conference of the Catalan Association for Artificial Intelligence, pp. 221–226, October 2017. https://doi.org/10.3233/978-1-61499-806-8-221, http://www.ebooks.iospress.com/volumearticle/47742
4. Gibert, D., Mateu, C., Planes, J., Vicens, R.: Classification of malware by using structural entropy on convolutional neural networks. In: Proceedings of the Innovative Applications of Artificial Intelligence Conference (IAAI 2018). Association for the Advancement of Artificial Intelligence (2018)
5. Glorot, X., Bengio, Y.: Understanding the difficulty of training deep feedforward neural networks. In: Proceedings of the International Conference on Artificial Intelligence and Statistics (AISTATS 2010). Society for Artificial Intelligence and Statistics (2010)
6. He, K., Zhang, X., Ren, S., Sun, J.: Deep residual learning for image recognition. CoRR abs/1512.03385 (2015). http://arxiv.org/abs/1512.03385
7. Jain, S., Meena, Y.K.: Byte level n–gram analysis for malware detection. In: Venugopal, K.R., Patnaik, L.M. (eds.) ICIP 2011. CCIS, vol. 157, pp. 51–59. Springer, Heidelberg (2011). https://doi.org/10.1007/978-3-642-22786-8_6
8. Lyda, R., Hamrock, J.: Using entropy analysis to find encrypted and packed malware. IEEE Secur. Anal. **5**, 40–45 (2007)
9. Narayanan, B.N., Djaneye-Boundjou, O., Kebede, T.M.: Performance analysis of machine learning and pattern recognition algorithms for malware classification. In: 2016 IEEE National Aerospace and Electronics Conference (NAECON) and Ohio Innovation Summit (OIS), pp. 338–342. IEEE (2016)

10. Ronen, R., Radu, M., Feuerstein, C., Yom-Tov, E., Ahmadi, M.: Microsoft Malware Classification Challenge. ArXiv e-prints, February 2018)
11. Santos, I., Brezo, F., Ugarte-Pedrero, X., Bringas, P.G.: Opcode sequences as representation of executables for data-mining-based unknown malware detection. Inf. Sci. **231**, 64–82 (2013). https://doi.org/10.1016/j.ins.2011.08.020. data Mining for Information Security
12. Yu, F., Koltun, V.: Multi-scale context aggregation by dilated convolutions. CoRR abs/1511.07122 (2015). http://arxiv.org/abs/1511.07122

Width of Minima Reached by Stochastic Gradient Descent is Influenced by Learning Rate to Batch Size Ratio

Stanislaw Jastrzębski[1,2,3](✉), Zachary Kenton[1,2], Devansh Arpit[2], Nicolas Ballas[3], Asja Fischer[4], Yoshua Bengio[2,5], and Amos Storkey[6]

[1] Jagiellonian University, Kraków, Poland
[2] MILA, Université de Montréal, Montreal, Canada
staszek.jastrzebski@gmail.com
[3] Facebook AI Research, Paris, France
[4] Faculty of Mathematics, Ruhr-University Bochum, Bochum, Germany
[5] CIFAR Senior Fellow, Toronto, Canada
[6] School of Informatics, University of Edinburgh, Edinburgh, Scotland

Abstract. We show that the dynamics and convergence properties of SGD are set by the ratio of learning rate to batch size. We observe that this ratio is a key determinant of the generalization error, which we suggest is mediated by controlling the width of the final minima found by SGD. We verify our analysis experimentally on a range of deep neural networks and datasets.

1 Introduction

Deep neural networks (DNNs) have demonstrated good generalization ability and achieved state-of-the-art performances in many application domains despite being massively over-parameterized, and despite the fact that modern neural networks are capable of getting an error close to zero on the training data [20]. What is the reason for their good generalization performance, remains an open question.

The standard way of training DNNs involves minimizing a loss function using stochastic gradient descent (SGD) and its variants [3]. Since the loss functions of DNNs are typically non-convex functions of the parameters, with complex structure and potentially multiple minima and saddle points, SGD generally converges to different regions of the parameter space, with different geometric and generalization properties, depending on optimization hyper-parameters and initialization.

Recently, several works [1,2,15] have investigated how SGD impacts the generalization of DNNs. It has been argued that wide minima tend to generalize better than sharp ones [6,15]. One paper [15] empirically showed that a larger batch size correlates with sharper minima and worse generalization performance.

S. Jastrzębski and Z. Kenton—Equally contributed.

V. Kůrková et al. (Eds.): ICANN 2018, LNCS 11141, pp. 392–402, 2018.
https://doi.org/10.1007/978-3-030-01424-7_39

In this paper we find that the critical control parameter for SGD is not the batch size alone, but the ratio of the learning rate (LR) to batch size (BS), i.e. LR/BS. SGD performs similarly for different batch sizes but a constant LR/BS. On the other hand higher values for LR/BS result in convergence to wider minima, which indeed seem to result in better generalization.

Our main contributions are as follows:

- We note that any SGD processes with the same LR/BS value is a discretization of the same stochastic differential equation (SDE).
- We derive a relation between LR/BS and the width of the minimum found by SGD.
- We verify experimentally that the SGD dynamics are similar when rescaling the LR and BS by the same amount.
- We demonstrate experimentally that a larger LR/BS correlates with a wider endpoint of SGD and better generalization.

2 Theory

Let us consider a model parameterized by $\boldsymbol{\theta}$ where the components are θ_i for $i \in \{1, \ldots, q\}$. For N training examples $\boldsymbol{x}_n, n \in \{1, ..., N\}$, the loss function, $L(\boldsymbol{\theta}) = \frac{1}{N}\sum_{n=1}^{N} l(\boldsymbol{\theta}, \boldsymbol{x}_n)$, and the corresponding gradient $\mathbf{g}(\boldsymbol{\theta}) = \frac{\partial L}{\partial \boldsymbol{\theta}}$, are defined based on the sum over the loss values for *all* training examples.

Stochastic gradients $\mathbf{g}^{(S)}(\boldsymbol{\theta})$ arise when we consider a minibatch $\mathcal{B}$ of size $S < N$ of random indices drawn uniformly from $\{1, ..., N\}$ and form an (unbiased) estimate of the gradient based on the corresponding subset of training examples $\mathbf{g}^{(S)}(\boldsymbol{\theta}) = \frac{1}{S}\sum_{n \in \mathcal{B}} \frac{\partial}{\partial \boldsymbol{\theta}} l(\boldsymbol{\theta}, \boldsymbol{x}_n)$.

We consider SGD with learning rate η, as defined by the update rule

$$\boldsymbol{\theta}_{k+1} = \boldsymbol{\theta}_k - \eta \boldsymbol{g}^{(S)}(\boldsymbol{\theta}_k), \tag{1}$$

where the index k enumerate the discrete update steps.

2.1 Learning Rate to Batch Size Ratio Determines SGD Dynamics

In this section we derive SGD as a discretization of an SDE in which the learning rate and batch size only enter in their ratio. Other SDEs which discretize to SGD have been considered in earlier work [11,12].

Stochastic Gradient Descent: We focus on SGD in the context of large datasets. Consider the loss gradient for a randomly chosen data point,

$$\boldsymbol{g}_n(\boldsymbol{\theta}) = \frac{\partial}{\partial \boldsymbol{\theta}} l(\boldsymbol{\theta}, \boldsymbol{x}_n). \tag{2}$$

Viewed as a random variable induced by the random sampling of the data items, $\boldsymbol{g}_n(\boldsymbol{\theta})$ is an unbiased estimator of the gradient $\boldsymbol{g}(\boldsymbol{\theta})$. For typical loss functions this estimator has finite covariance which we denote by $\mathbf{C}(\boldsymbol{\theta})$.

The batch estimate $\boldsymbol{g}^{(S)}(\boldsymbol{\theta})$ is the arithmetic mean of the components $\boldsymbol{g}_n(\boldsymbol{\theta})$. By the central limit theorem, for sufficient large batch size $\boldsymbol{g}^{(S)}(\boldsymbol{\theta})$ is approximately Gaussian distributed with mean $g(\boldsymbol{\theta})$ and variance $\boldsymbol{\Sigma}(\boldsymbol{\theta}) = (1/S)\mathbf{C}(\boldsymbol{\theta})$.

Stochastic gradient descent (1) can be written as

$$\boldsymbol{\theta}_{k+1} = \boldsymbol{\theta}_k - \eta \boldsymbol{g}(\boldsymbol{\theta}_k) + \eta(\boldsymbol{g}^{(S)}(\boldsymbol{\theta}_k) - \boldsymbol{g}(\boldsymbol{\theta}_k)), \tag{3}$$

where we have established that $(\boldsymbol{g}^{(S)}(\boldsymbol{\theta}_k) - \boldsymbol{g}(\boldsymbol{\theta}_k))$ is an additive zero mean Gaussian random noise with variance $\boldsymbol{\Sigma}(\boldsymbol{\theta}) = (1/S)\mathbf{C}(\boldsymbol{\theta})$. Hence we can rewrite (3) as

$$\boldsymbol{\theta}_{k+1} = \boldsymbol{\theta}_k - \eta \boldsymbol{g}(\boldsymbol{\theta}_k) + \frac{\eta}{\sqrt{S}}\boldsymbol{\epsilon}, \tag{4}$$

where $\boldsymbol{\epsilon}$ is a zero mean Gaussian random variable with covariance $\mathbf{C}(\boldsymbol{\theta})$.

Stochastic Differential Equation: Consider now a stochastic differential equation[1] of the form

$$d\boldsymbol{\theta} = -\mathbf{g}(\boldsymbol{\theta})dt + \sqrt{\frac{\eta}{S}}\mathbf{R}(\boldsymbol{\theta})d\boldsymbol{W}(t), \tag{5}$$

where $\mathbf{R}(\boldsymbol{\theta})\mathbf{R}(\boldsymbol{\theta})^T = \mathbf{C}(\boldsymbol{\theta})$, $\mathbf{R}(\boldsymbol{\theta}) = \mathbf{U}(\boldsymbol{\theta})\boldsymbol{\Lambda}(\boldsymbol{\theta})^{\frac{1}{2}}$, and the eigendecomposition of $\mathbf{C}(\boldsymbol{\theta})$ is given by $\mathbf{C}(\boldsymbol{\theta}) = \mathbf{U}(\boldsymbol{\theta})\boldsymbol{\Lambda}(\boldsymbol{\theta})\mathbf{U}(\boldsymbol{\theta})^T$, with diagonal matrix $\boldsymbol{\Lambda}(\boldsymbol{\theta})$ containing the eigenvalues and orthonormal matrix $\mathbf{U}(\boldsymbol{\theta})$ containing the eigenvectors of $\mathbf{C}(\boldsymbol{\theta})$.

This SDE can be discretized using the Euler-Maruyama (EuM) method[2] with stepsize η to obtain precisely the same equation as (4).

Hence we can say that SGD implements an EuM approximation[3] to the SDE (5). As much as the discretized approximation is valid, the SGD optimization process must inherit all the properties[4] of the underlying SDE. Specifically we note that in the underlying SDE the learning rate and batch size only appear in the ratio η/S, which we also refer to as the stochastic noise. This implies that these are not independent variables in SGD. Rather it is only their ratio that affects the path properties of the optimization process. The only independent effect of the learning rate η is to control the stepsize of the EuM method approximation, affecting only the per batch speed at which the discrete process follows the dynamics of the SDE. There are, however, more batches in an epoch for smaller batch sizes, so the per data-point speed is the same.

2.2 LR/BS Ratio Controls Trace of Hessian at a Minimum

We argue in this paper that there is a theoretical relationship between the expected loss value, the level of stochastic noise η/S in SGD and the width

[1] See [12] for a different SDE which also has a discretization equivalent to SGD.

[2] See e.g. [9].

[3] For a more formal analysis, not requiring central limit arguments, see an alternative approach [11] which also considers SGD as a discretization of an SDE. Note that the batch size is not present there.

[4] Including the paths of the dynamics, the equilibria, the shape of the learning curves.

of the minimum explored at this final stage of training. We derive that relationship in this section. We then go on to show in the next section that, empirically, SGD finds regions of equivalent expected loss for different values of the stochastic noise. Hence the stochastic noise must control the width of the minimum. Further experiments demonstrate that this is indeed the case and furthermore, this does indeed affect generalisation performance.

In talking about the width of a minimum, we will define it in terms of $Tr(\mathbf{H}(\boldsymbol{\theta}))$, the trace of the Hessian at the minimum: the lower the $Tr(\mathbf{H}(\boldsymbol{\theta}))$, the wider the minima. For notational convenience, in the rest of this section we drop dependence of $\mathbf{H}(\boldsymbol{\theta})$ and $\mathbf{C}(\boldsymbol{\theta})$ on $\boldsymbol{\theta}$.

In order to derive the required relationship, we will make the following assumptions in the final phase of training:

Assumption 1. As we expect the training to have arrived in a local minima, the loss surface can be approximated by a quadratic bowl, with minimum at zero loss (reflecting the ability of networks to fully fit the training data). Given this the training can be approximated by an Ornstein-Unhlenbeck process. This is a similar assumption to previous papers [12,13].

Assumption 2. The covariance of the gradients and the Hessian of the loss approximation are approximately equal, i.e. we can sufficiently assume $\mathbf{C} = \mathbf{H}$. A closeness of the Hessian and the covariance of the gradients in practical training of DNNs has been argued before [14,21].

Based on Assumptions 1 and 2, the Hessian is positive definite, and matches the covariance $\mathbf{C}$. Hence its eigendecomposition is $\mathbf{H} = \mathbf{C} = \mathbf{V}\boldsymbol{\Lambda}\mathbf{V}^T$, with $\boldsymbol{\Lambda}$ being the diagonal matrix of positive eigenvalues, and $\mathbf{V}$ an orthonormal matrix. We can reparameterize the model in terms of a new variable $\boldsymbol{z}$ defined by $\boldsymbol{z} \equiv \mathbf{V}^T(\boldsymbol{\theta} - \boldsymbol{\theta}_*)$ where $\boldsymbol{\theta}_*$ are the parameters at the minimum.

Starting from the SDE (5), and making the quadratic approximation of the loss $L(\theta) \approx (\boldsymbol{\theta} - \boldsymbol{\theta}_*)^T\mathbf{H}(\boldsymbol{\theta} - \boldsymbol{\theta}_*)$ and the change of variables, results in an Ornstein-Unhlenbeck (OU) process for $\boldsymbol{z}$

$$d\boldsymbol{z} = -\boldsymbol{\Lambda}\boldsymbol{z}dt + \sqrt{\frac{\eta}{S}}\boldsymbol{\Lambda}^{1/2}d\mathbf{W}(t) \ . \tag{6}$$

It is a standard result that the stationary distribution of an OU process of the form (6) is Gaussian with zero mean and covariance $\text{cov}(\boldsymbol{z}) = \mathbb{E}(\boldsymbol{z}\boldsymbol{z}^T) = \frac{\eta}{2S}\mathbf{I}$.

Moreover, in terms of the new parameters $\boldsymbol{z}$, the expected loss can be written as

$$\mathbb{E}(L) = \frac{1}{2}\sum_{i=1}^{q}\lambda_i\mathbb{E}(z_i^2) = \frac{\eta}{4S}\text{Tr}(\boldsymbol{\Lambda}) = \frac{\eta}{4S}\text{Tr}(\mathbf{H}) \tag{7}$$

where the second equality follows from the expression for the OU covariance.

We see from Eq. (7) that the learning rate to batch size ratio controls the trade-off between width and expected loss associated with SGD dynamics within a minimum centred at a point of zero loss, with $\frac{\mathbb{E}(L)}{Tr(\mathbf{H})} \propto \frac{\eta}{S}$. In the experiments which follow, we compare geometrical properties of minima with the same loss value (but different generalization properties) to empirically analyze this relationship between $Tr(\mathbf{H})$ and $\frac{\eta}{S}$.

As a special case, we note that if two runs of SGD, with different LR/BS ratios that have the same final average loss, $\mathbb{E}(L)$, then the SGD processes with the higher (η/S) ratio, must have had a smaller $\mathrm{Tr}(\mathbf{H})$, and hence must have found a different minima, and indeed one that is wider.

3 Experiments

We now present an empirical analysis motivated by the theory discussed in the previous section. In all experiments all models are initialized from the same distribution.

Learning Dynamics of SGD Depend on LR/BS. In this section we look experimentally at the approximation of SGD as an SDE given in Eq. (5), investigating how the dynamics are affected by the learning rate to batch size ratio.

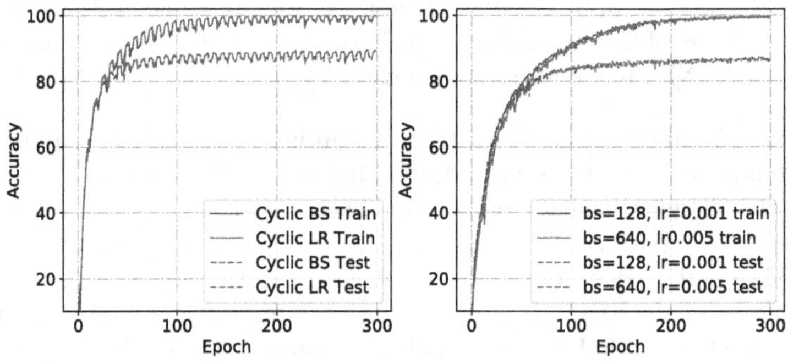

Fig. 1. VGG11 on CIFAR10. Left: cyclic schedules. Right: constant η, S. Red and blue curves match implies dynamics set by ratio of learning rate to batch size. (Color figure online)

We first look at the results of four experiments involving the VGG11 architecture[5] [16] on the CIFAR10 dataset, shown in Fig. 1[6]. The left plot compares two experimental settings: a cyclic batch size (CBS) schedule (blue) oscillating between 128 and 640 at fixed learning rate $\eta = 0.005$, compared to a cyclic learning rate (CLR) schedule (red) oscillating between 0.001 to 0.005 with a fixed batch size of $S = 128$. The right plot compares the results for two other experimental settings: a constant learning rate to batch size ratio of $\frac{\eta}{S} = \frac{0.001}{128}$ (blue) versus $\frac{\eta}{S} = \frac{0.005}{640}$ (red). We emphasize the similarity of the curves for

[5] We have adapted the final layers to be compatible with the CIFAR10 dataset.

[6] Each experiment was repeated for 5 different random initializations.

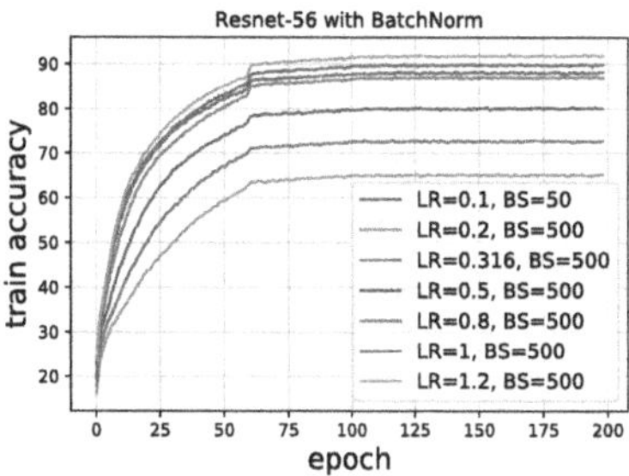

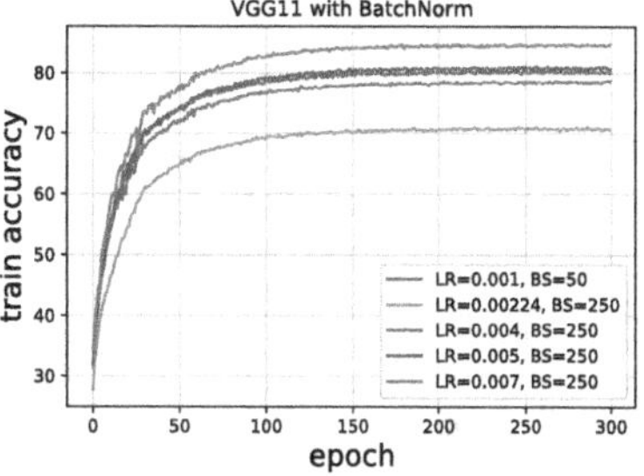

Fig. 2. ResNet (left) and VGG11 (right) on CIFAR10. Different learning rates trying to match learning curve of a small batch size (blue). Rescaling learning rate exactly with batch size (left, brown; right red) gives closest match to small-batch. (Color figure online)

each pair of experiments, demonstrating that the learning dynamics are approximately invariant under changes in learning rate or batch size that keep the ratio η/S constant.

We next ran experiments with other rescalings of the learning rate when going from a small batch size to a large one, to compare them against rescaling the learning rate exactly with the batch size. In Fig. 2 we show the results from two experiments on ResNet56 and VGG11, both trained with SGD and batch normalization on CIFAR10. In both settings the blue line corresponds to training with a small batch size of 50 and a small starting learning rate[7]. The other lines correspond to models trained with different learning rates and a larger batch size. It becomes visible that when rescaling η by the same amount as S (brown curve for ResNet, red for VGG11) the learning curve matches fairly closely the blue curve. Explaining the small difference is left for future work. Other rescaling strategies such as keeping the ratio $\eta/\sqrt{S}$ constant, as suggested by [7], (green curve for ResNet, orange for VGG) lead to larger differences in the learning curves.

Geometry and Generalization Depend on LR/BS. In this section we investigate experimentally the impact of learning rate to batch size ratio on the geometry of the region that SGD ends in. We trained a series of 4-layer batch-normalized ReLU MLPs on Fashion-MNIST [19] with different η, S[8]. To access the loss curvature at the end of training, we computed the largest eigenvalue and we approximated the Frobenius norm of the Hessian (higher values imply a sharper minimum) using the finite difference method. Figure 3a and b show the values of these quantities for minima obtained by SGD for different $\frac{\eta}{S}$, with $\eta \in [5e-3, 1e-1]$ and $S \in [25, 1000]$. As $\frac{\eta}{S}$ grows, the norm of the Hessian at the

[7] We used a adaptive learning rate schedule with η dropping by a factor of 10 on epochs 60, 100, 140, 180 for ResNet56 and by a factor of 2 every 25 epochs for VGG11.

[8] Each experiment was run for 200 epochs in which most models reached an accuracy of almost 100% on the training set.

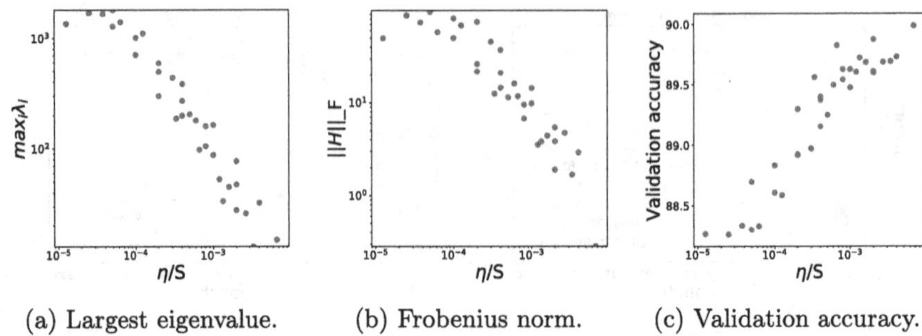

(a) Largest eigenvalue. (b) Frobenius norm. (c) Validation accuracy.

Fig. 3. Ratio of learning rate to batch size, η/S, for a grid of η, S for 4 layer ReLU MLP on FashionMNIST. Higher η/S correlates with lower Hessian maximum eigenvalue, lower Hessian Frobenius norm, i.e. wider minima, and better generalization. The validation accuracy is consistent for different batch sizes, and different learning rates, so long as the ratio is constant.

minimum decreases, suggesting that higher values of $\frac{\eta}{S}$ push the optimization towards flatter regions. Figure 3c shows the results from exploring the impact of $\frac{\eta}{S}$ on the final validation performance, which confirms that better generalization correlates with higher values of $\frac{\eta}{S}$. Taken together, Fig. 3a, b and c imply that as $\frac{\eta}{S}$ increases, SGD finds wider regions which correlate well with better generalization[9].

In Fig. 4 we qualitatively illustrate the behavior of SGD with different $\frac{\eta}{S}$. We follow [15] by investigating the loss on the line interpolating between the parameters of two models with interpolation coefficicent α. In Fig. 4(a,b) we consider Resnet56 models on CIFAR10 for different $\frac{\eta}{S}$. We see sharper regions on the right of each, for the lower $\frac{\eta}{S}$. In Fig. 4(c,d) we consider VGG-11 models on CIFAR10 for the same ratio, but different β, where $\frac{\eta=0.1\times\beta}{S=50\times\beta}$. We see the same sharpness for the same ratio. Experiments were repeated several times with different random initializations and qualitatively similar plots were achieved.

Breakdown of η/S Scaling. We expect discretization errors to become important when the learning rate gets large. We also expect our central limit theorem to break down for a large batch size and smaller dataset size.

We show this experimentally in Fig. 5, where similar learning dynamics and final performance can be observed when simultaneously multiplying the learning rate and batch size by a factor β up to a certain limit[10]. This is done for a smaller training set size in Fig. 5 (a) than in (b). The curves don't match when β gets too large as expected from our approximations.

[9] Assuming the network has enough capacity.

[10] Experiments are repeated 5 times with different random seeds. The graphs denote the mean validation accuracies and the numbers in the brackets denote the mean and standard deviation of the maximum validation accuracy across different runs. The * denotes at least one seed diverged.

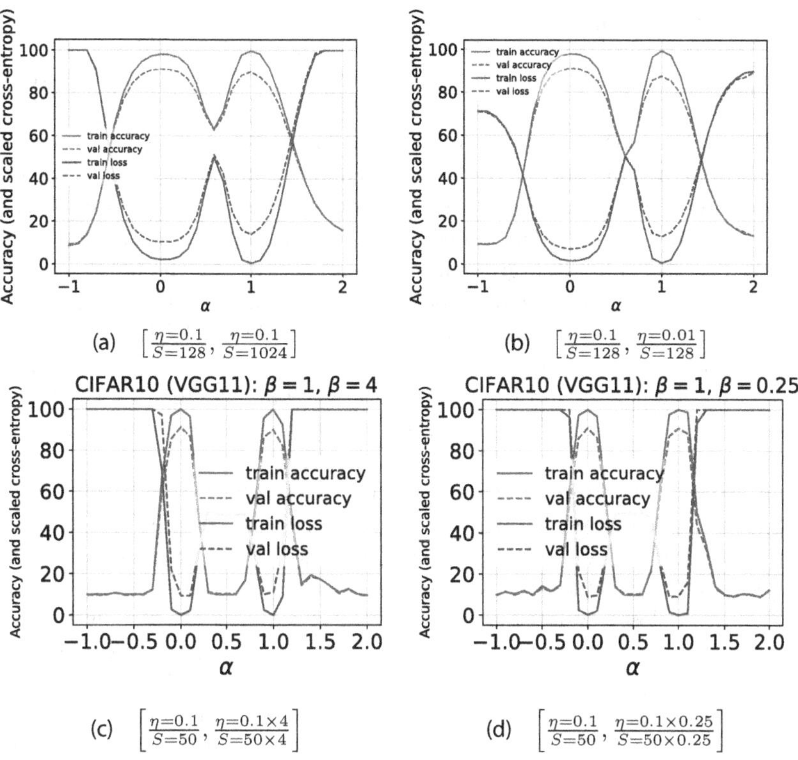

(a) $\left[\frac{\eta=0.1}{S=128}, \frac{\eta=0.1}{S=1024}\right]$ (b) $\left[\frac{\eta=0.1}{S=128}, \frac{\eta=0.01}{S=128}\right]$

(c) $\left[\frac{\eta=0.1}{S=50}, \frac{\eta=0.1\times 4}{S=50\times 4}\right]$ (d) $\left[\frac{\eta=0.1}{S=50}, \frac{\eta=0.1\times 0.25}{S=50\times 0.25}\right]$

Fig. 4. Interpolations between models with α interpolation coefficient. At $\alpha = 0$ there is one trained model (1st element of subcaption), at $\alpha = 1$ there is another (2nd element of subcaption). (a), (b): Resnet56 with different ratio $\frac{\eta}{S}$. (c), (d): VGG11 with the same ratio, but different η, S. Higher ratios give wider minima (a,b) as seen by the great width of the basin around $\alpha = 0$, whilst the same ratio gives the same width minima (c,d), despite differences in batch size and learning rate.

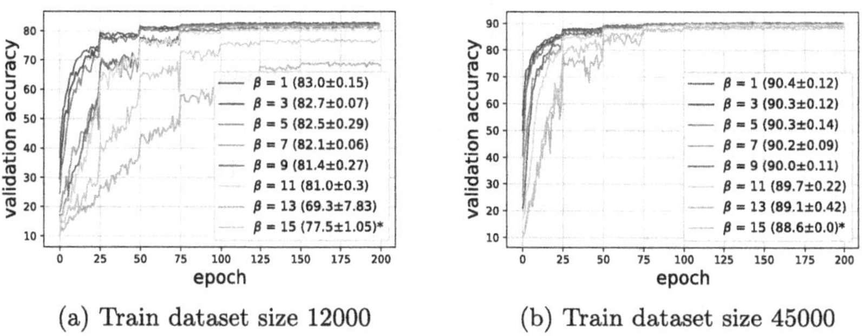

(a) Train dataset size 12000 (b) Train dataset size 45000

Fig. 5. Validation accuracy for different dataset sizes and different β values for fixed ratio $\frac{\beta\times(\eta=0.1)}{\beta\times(S=50)}$. The curves diverging from the blue shows the approximation of the SDE discretized to SGD breaking down for large β, which is magnified for smaller dataset size. (Color figure online)

4 Related Work

The analysis of SGD as an SDE is well established in the stochastic approximation literature, see e.g. [10]. It was shown by [11] that SGD can be approximated by an SDE in an order-one weak approximation. However, batch size does not enter their analysis. In contrast, our analysis makes the role of batch size evident and shows the dynamics are set by the ratio of learning rate to batch size. The work of [8] reproduce the SDE result of [11] and further show that the covariance matrix of the minibatch-gradient scales inversely with the batch size[11] and proportionally to the sample covariance matrix over all examples in the training set. The authors of [12] approximate SGD by a different SDE and show that SGD can be used as an approximate Bayesian posterior inference algorithm. In contrast, we show the ratio of learning rate over batch influences the width of the minima found by SGD. We then explore each of these experimentally linking also to generalization.

Many works have used stochastic gradients to sample from a posterior, see e.g. [18], using a decreasing learning rate to correctly sample from the actual posterior. In contrast, we consider SGD with a fixed learning rate and our focus is not on applying SGD to sample from the actual posterior.

Our work is closely related to the ongoing discussion about how batch size affects sharpness and generalization. Our work extends this by investigating the impact of both batch size and learning rate on sharpness and generalization. In [15] it's shown empirically that SGD ends up in a sharp minimum when using a large batch size. In [7] the learning rate is rescaled with the square root of the batch size, and more epochs are trained for to reach the same generalization with a large batch size. The empirical analysis of [5] demonstrated that rescaling the learning rate linearly with batch size can result in same generalization. Our work theoretically explains this empirical finding, and extends the experimental results on this.

Anisotropic noise in SGD was studied in [21]. It was found that the gradient covariance matrix is approximately the same as the Hessian, late on in training. In the work of [14], the Hessian is also related to the gradient covariance matrix, and both are found to be highly anisotropic. In contrast, our focus is on the importance of the scale of the noise, set by the learning rate to batch size ratio.

Concurrent with this work, [17] derive an analytical expression for the stochastic noise scale and – based on the trade-off between depth and width in the Bayesian evidence – find an optimal noise scale for optimizing the test accuracy. The work of [4] explores the stationary non-equilibrium solution for the SDE for non-isotropic gradient noise.

5 Conclusion

By approximating SGD as an SDE, we found that the learning rate to batch size ratio controls the dynamics. This ratio is a key determinant of generalization via

[11] This holds approximately, in the limit of small batch size compared to training set size.

the width of minima found by SGD. We experimentally explored this using a range of DNN models and datasets, confirming approximate invariance under rescaling of learning rate and batch size, and that the ratio of learning rate to batch size correlates with width and generalization with a higher ratio leading to wider minima and better generalization.

Acknowledgements. We thank NSERC, Canada Research Chairs, IVADO and CIFAR for funding. SJ was in part supported by Grant No. DI 2014/016644 and ETIUDA stipend No. 2017/24/T/ST6/00487. This project has received funding from the European Union's Horizon 2020 programme under grant agreement No 732204 and Swiss State Secretariat for Education,Research and Innovation under contract No. 16.0159.

References

1. Advani, M.S., Saxe, A.M.: High-dimensional dynamics of generalization error in neural networks. arXiv preprint arXiv:1710.03667 (2017)
2. Arpit, D., et al.: A closer look at memorization in deep networks. In: ICML (2017)
3. Bottou, L.: Online learning and stochastic approximations. On-line Learn. Neural netw. **17**(9), 142 (1998)
4. Chaudhari, P., Soatto, S.: Stochastic gradient descent performs variational inference, converges to limit cycles for deep networks. arXiv:1710.11029 (2017)
5. Goyal, P., et al.: Accurate, Large Minibatch SGD: Training ImageNet in 1 Hour. ArXiv e-prints (2017)
6. Hochreiter, S., Schmidhuber, J.: Flat minima. Neural Comput. **9**(1), 1–42 (1997)
7. Hoffer, E., et al.: Train longer, generalize better: closing the generalization gap in large batch training of neural networks. ArXiv e-prints, arxiv:1705.08741
8. Junchi Li, C., et al.: Batch Size Matters: A Diffusion Approximation Framework on Nonconvex Stochastic Gradient Descent. ArXiv e-prints (2017)
9. Kloeden, P.E., Platen, E.: Numerical Solution of Stochastic Differential Equations. Springer, Heidelberg (1992). https://doi.org/10.1007/978-3-662-12616-5
10. Kushner, H., Yin, G.: Stochastic Approximation and Recursive Algorithms and Applications (Stochastic Modelling and Applied Probability) (v. 35), 2nd edn. Springer (2003). http://www.amazon.com/exec/obidos/redirect?tag=citeulike07-20&path=ASIN/0387008942
11. Li, Q., Tai, C., E., W.: Stochastic modified equations and adaptive stochastic gradient algorithms. In: Proceedings of the 34th ICML (2017)
12. Mandt, S., Hoffman, M.D., Blei, D.M.: Stochastic gradient descent as approximate Bayesian inference. J. Mach. Learn. Res. **18**, 134:1–134:35 (2017)
13. Poggio, T., et al.: Theory of Deep Learning III: explaining the non-overfitting puzzle. ArXiv e-prints, ArXiv e-prints, arxiv:1801.00173 (2018)
14. Sagun, L., Evci, U., Ugur Guney, V., Dauphin, Y., Bottou, L.: Empirical Analysis Of The Hessian Of Over-parametrized Neural Networks. ArXiv e-prints (2017)
15. Shirish Keskar, N., Mudigere, D., Nocedal, J., Smelyanskiy, M., Tang, P.T.P.: On Large-Batch Training for Deep Learning: Generalization Gap and Sharp Minima. ArXiv e-prints (2016)
16. Simonyan, K., Zisserman, A.: Very deep convolutional networks for large-scale image recognition. arXiv preprint, arXiv:1409.1556 (2014)

17. Smith, S., Le, Q.: Understanding generalization and stochastic gradient descent. arXiv preprint, arXiv:1710.06451 (2017)
18. Welling, M., Teh, Y.W.: Bayesian learning via stochastic gradient Langevin dynamics. In: Proceedings of the 28th ICML, pp. 681–688 (2011)
19. Xiao, H., Rasul, K., Vollgraf, R.: Fashion-MNIST: a Novel Image Dataset for Benchmarking Machine Learning Algorithms. ArXiv e-prints (2017)
20. Zhang, C., Bengio, S., Hardt, M., Recht, B., Vinyals, O.: Understanding deep learning requires rethinking generalization. arXiv preprint, arXiv:1611.03530 (2016)
21. Zhu, Z., Wu, J., Yu, B., Wu, L., Ma, J.: The Regularization Effects of Anisotropic Noise in Stochastic Gradient Descent. ArXiv e-prints (2018)

Data Correction by a Generative Model with an Encoder and its Application to Structure Design

Takaya Ueda, Masataka Seo, and Ikuko Nishikawa(✉)

College of Information Science and Engineering, Ritsumeikan University, Kusatsu, Shiga 525-8577, Japan
nishi@ci.ritsumei.ac.jp

Abstract. An alternative training model is proposed for adversarial networks to correct a slightly defective data. Generator is first acquired by classical Generative Adversarial Networks, where the discriminator is trained only by feasible data. Then, both an encoder as the inverse mapping of the generator and a classifier which judges a feasibility of a generated data, are trained to lead the generator to correct an infeasible data by the minimum modification. The proposed method is applied to a housing member placement problem to satisfy every constraint for earthquake resistance, and evaluated by a rigorous structural calculation.

Keywords: Deep generative model · Encoder · Classifier
Data correction · Structural constraint

1 Introduction

Convolutional neural networks (CNN) have been effectively used for various tasks in pattern recognition and data generation. Among the generative models by deep CNNs, most notable models are Generative Adversarial Nets (GAN) proposed by Goodfellow et al. [1] and Variational Auto-Encoder (VAE) by Kingma et al. [2]. Generator in GAN implemented by a CNN is a mapping from an unknown latent space onto a high-dimensional data space. It learns not each data but a whole data distribution through the mutual and adversarial training with a discriminator, which learns to discriminate each given data whether it is sampled from a real data distribution or output from a generator. Autoencoder in VAE also acquires a distribution of a given data set on its coding space, or its latent space, through the training of each data with a probability distribution. After the training, the decoder part becomes a generator which is a mapping from a latent space onto a high-dimensional data space. The nature of the encoder sometimes enable us to interpret the meaning of several latent variables and the partial structure of the obtained latent space.

This paper proposes to use the generator as an auto-corrector of the input data, together with an encoder which learns the local structure of the latent space

V. Kůrková et al. (Eds.): ICANN 2018, LNCS 11141, pp. 403–413, 2018.
https://doi.org/10.1007/978-3-030-01424-7_40

of the generator. Generator is first trained via GAN to generate the acceptable data by the discriminator. Then, encoder is trained to search the optimal point in the latent space of the generator. If the input data to the encoder is acceptable and be able to be generated, then the encoder is trained to be an inverse mapping of the generator. On the other hand, if the input data to the encoder is not acceptable and therefore not be able to be generated, then the encoder is trained to find the point in the latent space which is mapped to the nearest data in the acceptable data set. In other words, when the latent space is trained to be a manifold which corresponds to the entire set of the acceptable data, then the encoder is trained to be the mapping onto the manifold. A point in the neighbor of the manifold is mapped onto the manifold through the encoder and generator, to be corrected to a similar but acceptable data.

In the followings, Sect. 2 briefly reviews the training in GAN and VAE, as the basis of our framework. Then, Sect. 3 explains our method to train the generator and encoder for the auto-correction of the slightly infeasible data. Section 4 shows the computer experiments of the proposed models. The first experiment is a toy example on simple two-dimensional data using the handwritten MNIST data. The second experiment is on complicated three-dimensional data to satisfy multiple physical constraints on a building structure design.

2 Generative Models by Neural Networks

This section introduces two representative models of the generator implemented by CNN, that is, GAN and VAE, as the basis of our proposed method.

2.1 Generative Adversarial Nets

GAN [1] is composed of two CNNs; a generator (hereinafter referred to as G) and a discriminator (referred to as D). $G(\boldsymbol{z})$ is a mapping from a low-dimensional latent space $\boldsymbol{z}$ to a data space $\boldsymbol{x}$, and $D(\boldsymbol{x})$ classifies an input data $\boldsymbol{x}$ whether it is sampled from a real data distribution $p_{\text{data}}(\boldsymbol{x})$ or generated by G, i.e. $\boldsymbol{x} = G(\boldsymbol{z})$. Objective function of both learning is given as:

$$V(G, D) = E_{\boldsymbol{x} \sim p_{\text{data}}(\boldsymbol{x})}[\log D(\boldsymbol{x})] + E_{\boldsymbol{z} \sim p(\boldsymbol{z})}[\log(1 - D(G(\boldsymbol{z}))], \qquad (1)$$

where $E[\cdot]$ is an expectation under a given distribution. Equation (1) should be minimized by G and maximized by D, therefore this simultaneous learning process is called adversarial. D measures Jensen-Shannon (JS) divergence between real data distribution $p_{\text{data}}(\boldsymbol{x})$ and generated 'fake' data distribution by the maximization of V. On the other hand, G acquires the real data distribution by the minimization of V.

2.2 Wasserstein GAN

Wasserstein GAN (WGAN) proposed by Arjovsky et al. [3] uses a different distance than the previous JS divergence as a measure for the distribution. D in

WGAN uses Earth Mover's Distance (or Wasserstein distance) between the distribution $p_{\text{data}}(\boldsymbol{x})$ and another distribution $p_g(\boldsymbol{x})$, a data distribution generated by G in the present case. Its definition is equivalently expressed in the following form as the upper limit:

$$W(p_{\text{data}}, p_g) = \sup_{||f_w||_L \leq 1} \left(E_{\boldsymbol{x} \sim p_{\text{data}}(\boldsymbol{x})}[f_w(\boldsymbol{x})] - E_{\boldsymbol{x} \sim p_g(\boldsymbol{x})}[f_w(\boldsymbol{x})] \right), \quad (2)$$

where f_w is an arbitrary function which is Lipschitz continuous with Lipschitz constant 1. Equation (2) leads to the following form of the objective function to be maximized by D:

$$E_{\boldsymbol{x} \sim p_{\text{data}}(\boldsymbol{x})}[D(\boldsymbol{x})] - E_{\boldsymbol{z} \sim p(\boldsymbol{z})}[D(G(\boldsymbol{z}))] . \quad (3)$$

Here D corresponds to function f_w in the original definition by Eq. (2), with the parameter $\boldsymbol{w}$ of CNN, and the training is expressed by the maximization to attain the upper limit, which is purely Wasserstein distance.

Lipschitz continuity constraint on f_w now becomes a constraint on D. Gulrajani et al. [4] add the following penalty term by the gradient of D for the continuity of the mapping:

$$E_{\hat{\boldsymbol{x}} \sim p(\hat{\boldsymbol{x}})} \left[(||\nabla_{\hat{\boldsymbol{x}}} D(\hat{\boldsymbol{x}})||_2 - 1)^2 \right], \quad (4)$$

where $\hat{\boldsymbol{x}} = \varepsilon \boldsymbol{x} + (1 - \varepsilon)\tilde{\boldsymbol{x}}$ with $\boldsymbol{x} \sim p_{\text{data}}, \tilde{\boldsymbol{x}} \sim p_g, \varepsilon \sim U[0, 1]$. This improved version with the gradient penalty (WGAN-GP) is used in the experiments in Sect. 4.

2.3 Variational Auto-Encoder

Auto-encoder is trained to output the same data as input with a smaller number of units in the middle layer. It is used for the dimension reduction of original data $\boldsymbol{x}$ to lower dimension $\boldsymbol{z}$ in the middle layer. Encoder part is a mapping from $\boldsymbol{x}$ to $\boldsymbol{z}$, while a decoder part is an inverse mapping from $\boldsymbol{z}$ to $\boldsymbol{x}$. In other words, two mappings correspond to recognition and generation, individually. Variational Auto-encoder proposed by Kingma et al. [2] considers a probability distribution $p(\boldsymbol{z})$ on $\boldsymbol{z}$ space. Encoder maps original data $\boldsymbol{x}$ to a certain distribution $p(\boldsymbol{z})$ as a normal distribution $N(\boldsymbol{\mu}, \boldsymbol{\sigma}^2)$. Whole network with encoder and decoder is trained to minimize both a reconstruction error to be an auto-encoder, and a regularization loss which is given by Kulback-Leibler divergence with a simple distribution on $\boldsymbol{z}$.

In general, the training of VAE is more stable compared with GAN where the mode collapse is often observed, while the generated data is less refine and rather blurred. Combined approaches to take the advantage of both VAE and GAN are found in VAE/GAN by Larsen et al. [5] and α-GAN by Rosca et al. [6], which use the reconstruction error in the generator training.

Besides the auto-encoder, there are several studies to obtain the inverse mapping of the generative network, from data $\boldsymbol{x}$ to a latent vector $\boldsymbol{z}$, as proposed by

Donahue et al. [7] and by Dumoulin et al. [8]. Metz et al. [9] and Lipton et al. [10] also propose a gradient-based method to obtain $\boldsymbol{z}$ from $\boldsymbol{x}$. We also propose to train an encoder as an inverse mapping of a generator, but not simply as an inverse mapping but also as a corrector for a defective data.

3 Proposed Model of GAN with an Encoder

The main idea of the present paper is to utilize the acquired low dimensional manifold $\boldsymbol{z}$ as an auto-corrector of defective data, which is slightly out of the manifold, by mapping onto the manifold. Encoder (referred to as E) is attached to the generator as shown in Fig. 1 to infer the latent space $\boldsymbol{z}$. G, D, E, and also a classifier (referred to as C), if any, are all implemented by CNNs with multiple layers. E is a variational version which outputs a probability distribution on $\boldsymbol{z}$ as described in Subsect. 2.3. The details will be explained in the following subsections for each model.

3.1 Basic Model of GAN with an Encoder

Generator G is first trained by GAN framework, where discriminator D is trained by a set of correct data $\boldsymbol{x}_{\text{ok}}$ under a certain criteria (Fig. 1 left). Obtained latent space $\boldsymbol{z}$ is expected to become a lower dimensional manifold expressing a whole set of correct data $\{\boldsymbol{x}_{\text{ok}}\}$. Next, an encoder $E : \boldsymbol{x} \to \boldsymbol{z}$ (shown in Fig. 1 right) is trained by an error minimization of the reconstruction through $G(\boldsymbol{z})$. When input $\boldsymbol{x}$ to E is a correct data, then E should be an inverse mapping G^{-1} to generate the original input $\boldsymbol{x}$. If input $\boldsymbol{x}$ to E is not a correct data, then E should find $\boldsymbol{z}$ which generates a correct data $G(\boldsymbol{z})$ with minimal difference with original $\boldsymbol{x}$. Here we assume a continuity of mapping G^{-1} out of but within a certain neighbor of manifold $G(\{\boldsymbol{z}\})$ in $\boldsymbol{x}$ space.

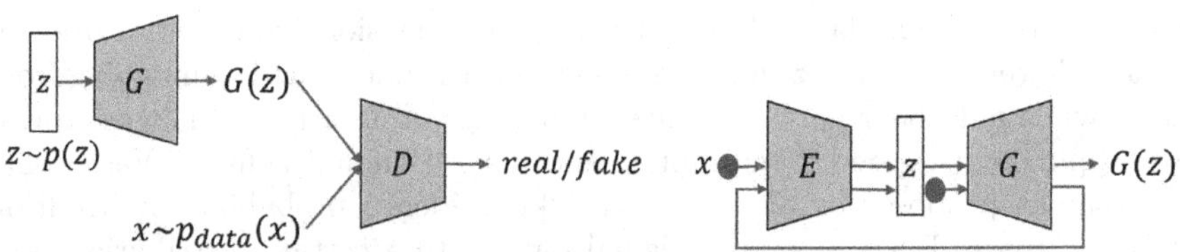

Fig. 1. Generator G is trained by GAN with correct data $\boldsymbol{x}$ fed to D in the first stage (left). Then, an encoder E is attached to G (right), as a mapping from data $\boldsymbol{x}$ to latent variable $\boldsymbol{z}$. In the second stage, E is trained to be an inverse mapping G^{-1} for a correct data $\boldsymbol{x}$, while to be an auto-corrector for a defective data $\boldsymbol{x}$.

E outputs the mean $\boldsymbol{\mu}$ and variance $\boldsymbol{\sigma}^2$ of a normal distribution in $\boldsymbol{z}$ as in VAE. Then, the reconstruction error is given by the following L_2 norm:

$$E_{\boldsymbol{z}\sim q_\phi(\boldsymbol{z}|\boldsymbol{x})}\left[||G(\boldsymbol{z}) - \boldsymbol{x}||_2\right], \tag{5}$$

where q_ϕ expresses encoder E as CNN with parameter ϕ.

3.2 Fine-Tuning with a Classifier on Data Space: Model 1

Basic model described in the previous subsection assumes that every data generated by G is correct after GAN training. Unfortunately, this is not always the case, as in the second example in Sect. 4, where correct data $\boldsymbol{x}_{\text{ok}}$ should satisfy a large number of physical constraints. To ensure G to generate only correct data, further fine-tuning stage is proposed by adding C as shown in Fig. 2.

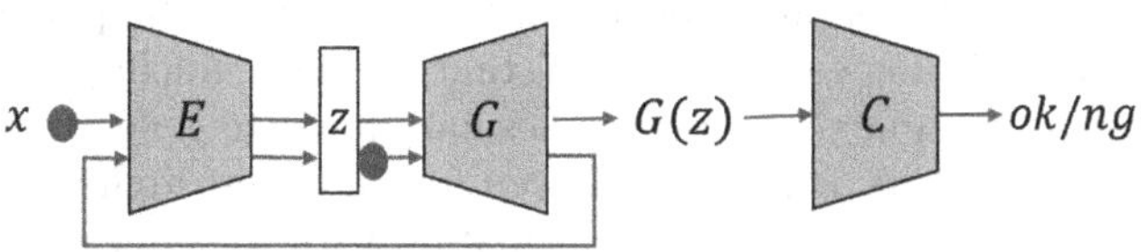

Fig. 2. Generator G is trained by GAN at the first stage. At the same time, classifier C is trained to discriminate whether data $\boldsymbol{x}$ is correct or not with the labeled data sets $\{\boldsymbol{x}_{\text{ok}}\}$ and $\{\boldsymbol{x}_{\text{ng}}\}$. In the second stage, both encoder E and C are attached to G, and E is trained to reconstruct an appropriate correct data, regardless of the correctness of the input, under the supervision of C.

Generator G is trained as in the previous model by GAN. Classifier C is acquired by the ordinary supervised training with labeled data sets $\{\boldsymbol{x}_{\text{ok}}\}$ and $\{\boldsymbol{x}_{\text{ng}}\}$. Then C is used in the second stage for the training of E. Loss function is modified from a single reconstruction error Eq. (5), to following Eq. (6) with an additional penalty term:

$$E_{\boldsymbol{z}\sim q_\phi(\boldsymbol{z}|\boldsymbol{x})}\left[||G(\boldsymbol{z})-\boldsymbol{x}||_2\right]+\alpha E_{\boldsymbol{x}_g\sim G(\boldsymbol{z}),\boldsymbol{z}\sim q_\phi(\boldsymbol{z}|\boldsymbol{x})}\left[\max(T-C(\boldsymbol{x}_g),0)\right], \tag{6}$$

where T is a threshold of classifier, under which a generated data $\boldsymbol{x}_g$ is classified as incorrect $\boldsymbol{x}_{\text{ng}}$, and thus E is penalized. α is a coefficient of the penalty term. Equation (6) forces E to find $\boldsymbol{z}$ which reconstructs a correct data, even G may generate an incorrect data.

Alternately with Eq. (6) during an iterative training, following loss is also used with a certain frequency to ensure E to be an inverse mapping G^{-1} on $\boldsymbol{z}$:

$$E_{\boldsymbol{z}\sim p(\boldsymbol{z})}\left[||E(G(\boldsymbol{z}))-\boldsymbol{z}||_2\right], \tag{7}$$

where $p(\boldsymbol{z})=N(\boldsymbol{z}|0,\boldsymbol{I})$.

3.3 Fine-Tuning with a Classifier on Latent Space: Model 2

Another variant of the classifier is the classifier on $\boldsymbol{z}$, to train E to reconstruct only a correct data. The framework is mostly the same as the previous model, but C classifies $\boldsymbol{z}$, therefore it is trained with labeled data sets $\{\boldsymbol{z}_{\text{ok}}\}$ and $\{\boldsymbol{z}_{\text{ng}}\}$.

4 Computer Experiments Using Real Building Data

Computer experiments of the proposed models are shown in this section. First Subsect. 4.1 shows a preliminary experiment using MNIST handwritten character. Trained G generates only correct data, where the correctness is judged by human recognition, and CNNs are also able to recognize and generate a character successfully. The second experiment is on real world problem in a housing construction. Given a three dimensional structure of a building, various kind of building members, such as pillar, beams and so on, should be placed to satisfy multiple legal criteria for earthquake resistance while reducing the amount of material as less as possible. Now, it becomes hard for G to generate only feasible data, where the feasibility is not trivial even for an expert architect but should be computed by a rigorous structural calculation with dynamical simulations.

4.1 MNIST Handwritten Digits

Handwritten digits dataset MNIST is widely used for the benchmark training in recognition and generation. Each data is 28 × 28 pixel gray scale image with a label of either digit from '0' to '9'. In the following, data with label '9' is used as correct $\boldsymbol{x}_{\text{ok}}$, while data with label '7' is used as incorrect $\boldsymbol{x}_{\text{ng}}$.

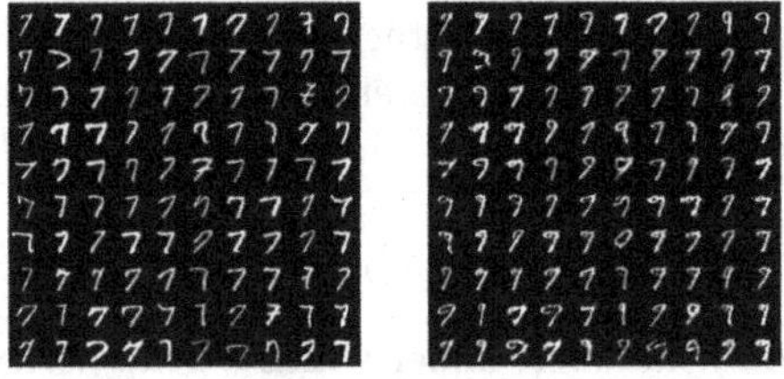

Fig. 3. 100 example pairs of an input '7' (left) and its corrected data (right). The position in 10 rows and 10 columns indicates a corresponding pair of input and output

Basic model without classifier
: 5000 data of '9' are used as $\{\boldsymbol{x}_{\text{ok}}\}$ for training of WGAN-GP. Dimension of the latent space $\boldsymbol{z}$ is set 16. 5000 data of '7' are used as $\{\boldsymbol{x}_{\text{ng}}\}$ for training of E. E is trained by the L_2 norm given by Eq. (5). After the training of 400 epoch with the batch of size 100, reconstruction error is successfully reduced. 'Correction' from '7' to '9' is shown in Fig. 3, for 100 randomly chosen examples. These data are not included in the training dataset.

Model 1 with classifier C_x
: Same '9' and '7' datasets are used for $\{\boldsymbol{x}_{\text{ok}}\}$ and $\{\boldsymbol{x}_{\text{ng}}\}$ as in the above model. Here, both are used for the training of WGAN-GP, to make G generate both. At the same time, classifier C_x is trained by the same datasets, to learn the classification of $\{\boldsymbol{x}_{\text{ok}}\}$ and $\{\boldsymbol{x}_{\text{ng}}\}$. Then E is trained in such a way so as to

minimize the loss functions given in Eq. (6) with $\alpha = 0.05, T = 0.5$ and in Eq. (7). Figure 4 for 25 randomly chosen examples shows that E becomes inverse mapping G^{-1} for correct data '9', while modifying to be '9' for an incorrect input '7' with minimal correction.

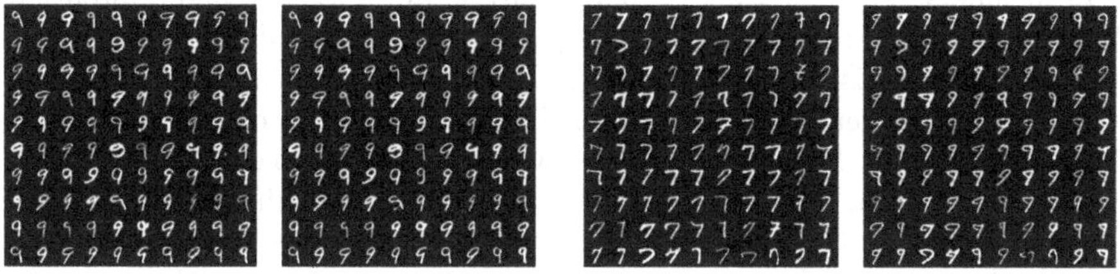

Fig. 4. Left: 100 example pairs for an input '9' and its identical output. Right: 100 example pairs for an input '7' and its corrected output

E in both models successfully corrects an input data, judging by a human recognition and classifier C obtained by a supervised training with labeled data. Thus CNNs is effective in this simple recognition and generation task. Next example has multiple physical criteria beyond a human recognition.

4.2 Building Members Placement

Target Problem. Construction of an ordinary house is considered. First, three dimensional structure of a building outline is given. Then, structural members, such as pillar, girder, beams and bearing wall, are placed in each horizontal and vertical frame of the building (Fig. 5).

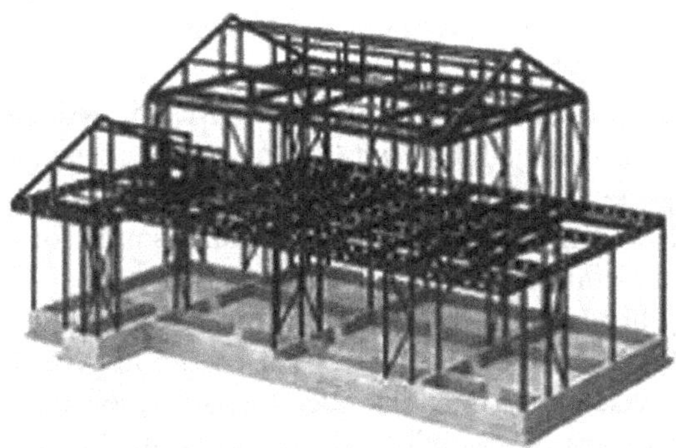

Fig. 5. Example of structural members placement for a two story house (from [11])

Planning of how many, which members, to place where, can be considered a combinatorial problem, especially for an industrialized housing with standardized members [11]. It is obligatory to satisfy earthquake resistance standards, which are described by hundreds of physical inequality constraints. Placement of more member in number and thickness may lead to stronger resistance in general, while a construction cost is reduced by lesser amount of total materials of members. Therefore, it is important to obtain a feasible and appropriate placement. Expert architect designs the placement plan based on the experience , and its feasibility is computed by a rigorous structural calculation.

Member placement plan for a given building outline is expressed as three dimensional data $\boldsymbol{x}$. Each data is easily switched from feasible $\boldsymbol{x}_{\mathrm{ok}}$ to infeasible $\boldsymbol{x}_{\mathrm{ng}}$, and vice versa, by a small shift or a small change in the thickness of one member. Therefore, it is hard for G to generate only feasible data. Moreover, it is not trivial for C to classify $\boldsymbol{x}_{\mathrm{ok}}$ and $\boldsymbol{x}_{\mathrm{ng}}$ without any structural calculation. Following subsections describe how each proposed model is applied to correct a placement design from $\boldsymbol{x}_{\mathrm{ng}}$ to $\boldsymbol{x}_{\mathrm{ok}}$.

Voxel Dataset for Each Model. Three dimensional data $\boldsymbol{x}$ used in the following experiments is a voxel data with size $15 \times 15 \times 15$ [cm^3]. Members placement for a three story house is expressed by voxels of 25(W) $\times$ 81(D) $\times$ 6(H), where the vertical data is compressed considering the vertical symmetry. Then, six vertical layers correspond to vertical and horizontal frames for three stories. The value of each voxel is the volume occupation ratio of member material, i.e. steel, normalized into [0,1]. Training data are prepared for each model as follows.

Basic model without classifier

15000 feasible placements are used as $\{\boldsymbol{x}_{\mathrm{ok}}\}$ for training of WGAN-GP. 15000 infeasible placements are used as $\{\boldsymbol{x}_{\mathrm{ng}}\}$ for training of E. All feasible and infeasible data are obtained through the evolutionary search processes for the placement optimization [11], and the rigorous feasibility is obtained by the structural calculation. All infeasible data are close to the feasible boundary, which slightly break few constraints. However, how to correct them is not trivial in most cases.

Stack GAN proposed by Zhang et al. [12] is used in WGAN-GP, where two pairs of G and D are trained in two steps. In the first stage, only partial placement is generated, then a whole placement is generated in the second stage. Dimension of the latent space $\boldsymbol{z}$ is set 100. Adam is used for the optimization, and Batch Normalization is used for each layer.

Model 1 with classifier $C_{\boldsymbol{x}}$

Same datasets $\{\boldsymbol{x}_{\mathrm{ok}}\}$ and $\{\boldsymbol{x}_{\mathrm{ng}}\}$ are used as the above , for GAN and E, respectively. At the same time, classifier $C_{\boldsymbol{x}}$ is trained by both datasets, to learn the classification of feasibility. Then E is trained in such a way so as to minimize the loss function given in Eq. (6) with the penalty term replaced by softmax function.

Model 2 with classifier $C_{\boldsymbol{z}}$

Instead of using $\{\boldsymbol{x}_{\mathrm{ok}}\}$ and $\{\boldsymbol{x}_{\mathrm{ng}}\}$ for the training of a classifier, dataset

of latent variable $\boldsymbol{z}$ are prepared for $C_{\boldsymbol{z}}$ with the feasibility label. $\boldsymbol{z}_{\text{ok}}$ is a feasible data which generates a feasible placement $G(\boldsymbol{z}_{\text{ok}})$, while $\boldsymbol{z}_{\text{ng}}$ is an infeasible data which generates an infeasible placement $G(\boldsymbol{z}_{\text{ng}})$, by the structural calculation.
As the structural calculation requires a considerable computational cost, it is not effective to randomly chose the training data from 100 dimensional $\boldsymbol{z}$ space. Instead, for the effective training of E, trained E_0 by the basic model is used to generate the training data. To be more precise, same 15000 infeasible placements $\{\boldsymbol{x}_{\text{ng}}\}$ as used in the above models are input to trained E_0, to obtain 15000 data $\{\boldsymbol{z}\}$. Those are then input to G which has been trained in the first stage. Finally, the structural calculation are executed on the 15000 outputs $G(E_0(\{\boldsymbol{x}_{\text{ng}}\}))$ to give the feasibility label to each $\boldsymbol{z}$. Obtained labeled datasets are rather imbalanced with more $\{\boldsymbol{z}_{\text{ng}}\}$ compared with $\{\boldsymbol{z}_{\text{ok}}\}$, which could obstruct the training of C, and then E.
Therefore, the additional loop for the training of C, together with E, is iterated. That is, after C, and then E using C, are trained, the output from E is examined by the structural calculation to give the correct label. Those labeled $\boldsymbol{z}$ are added to the training dataset, and the training of C and E is iterated in the next loop with newly added training data.

Results. After the training, 100 infeasible data $\boldsymbol{x}_{\text{ng}}$ are input to E as test data. Each resultant data generated by $G(E(\boldsymbol{x}_{\text{ng}}))$ is classified by $C_{\boldsymbol{x}}$ or $C_{\boldsymbol{z}}$,in model 1 or 2, respectively. As the result, all 100 data are classified as feasible in both models. In this sense, the correction results are successful.

However, the real judgment by a structural computation differs from the classifiers, as is shown in Table 1. For the computation, corrected data in a voxel format is transformed into the member placement format which is readable for the calculation algorithm. Data denoted uncomputable in the table does not possess the required format for the calculation (for example, there is no corresponding member.).

Table 1. Number of feasible and infeasible data by structural calculation for 100 infeasible input as the test data for each model after the training

Correction model	Corrected	Still infeasible	Incomputable
Basic model	38	53	9
Model 1	53	40	7
Model 2	57	28	15

The discrepancy between the trained classifier and the structural calculation simply means the imperfect accuracy of the classifier. This additional training for C and E is also applied in model 1. However, it does not work well for model 1, where the number of feasible data increases to 90, while the reconstruction error gets worse. Visualization by t-Distributed Stochastic Neighbor Embedding (t-SNE) [13] on $\boldsymbol{z}$ space indicates the generated data tends to converge to a similar $\boldsymbol{x}_{\mathrm{ok}}$ after the additional training. On the other hand, the result is improved in model 2 by the iterative loop, where the number of successfully corrected data is increased to 57 with keeping a low reconstruction error.

The obtained result indicates the limit of learning ability of the classifier in this target problem. Even if the voxel data possesses almost all information of the member placement, it is not trivial to learn which shape is earthquake-resistant against various kinds of loads from multiple directions. Moreover, the feasible solution set may not form a simply connected manifold. In addition, the mapping onto the manifold may need further information on the dynamics near the feasibility boundary.

An example of typical correction is shown in Fig. 6. A shift of a bearing wall, a removal, addition or shift of a beam are observed in each floor, and corresponding constraints become satisfied after the correction.

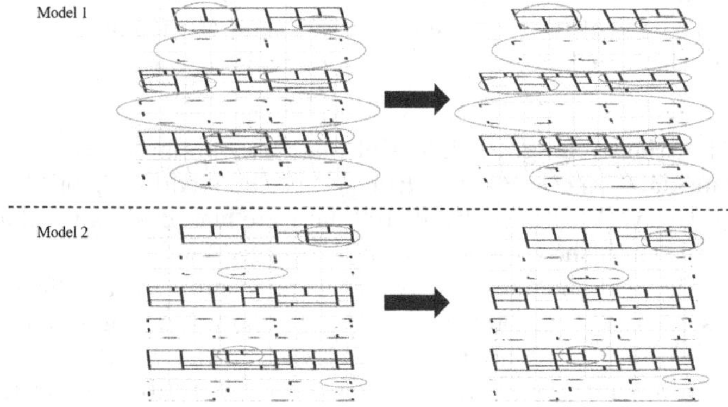

Fig. 6. An example of a infeasible placement (left) corrected by Models 1 (upper) and 2 (lower) to be feasible (right), which is verified by a structural calculation. Each corrected part is indicated by a circle, while a voxel with a member is colored.

5 Present Summary and Future Problems

Based on the generation ability of GAN, an encoder is added to infer the obtained latent space and to use it for the correction of slightly infeasible data. Classifier is also added for the fine-tuning for rigorous feasibility criteria. Computer experiments show the effectiveness of the proposed model for a simple recognition task, and a limit of CNN for a complex dynamical task.

Comprehensive framework of the training of generator, encoder and classifier is a future problem, together with the investigation of the training ability beyond a recognition task.

References

1. Goodfellow, I.J., et al.: Generative adversarial nets. In: Advances in Neural Information Processing Systems, pp. 2672–2680 (2014)
2. Kingma, D.P., Welling, M.: Auto-encoding variational bayes. In: Advances in Neural Information Processing Systems (2014)
3. Arjovsky, M., Chintala, S. and Bottou, L.: Wasserstein GAN. arXiv:1701.07875v2 (2017)
4. Gulrajani, I., Ahmed, F., Arjovsky, M., Dumoulin, V., Courville, A.: Improved training of Wasserstein GANs. arXiv preprint arXiv:1704.00028 (2017)
5. Larsen, A.B.L., Sønderby, S.K., Larochelle, H., Winther, O.: Autoencoding beyond pixels using a learned similarity metric. arXiv:1512.09300 (2016)
6. Rosca, M., Lakshminarayanan, B., Warde-Farley, D., Mohamed, S.: Variational Approaches for Auto-encoding Generative Adversarial Networks. arXiv:1706.04987 (2017)
7. Donahue, J., Krähenbühl, P., Darrell, T.: Adversarial Feature Learning. arXiv:1605.09782v7 (2017)
8. Dumoulin, V., et al.: Adversarially Learned Inference. arXiv:1606.00704v3 (2017)
9. Metz, D., Poole, B., Pfau, D., Sohl-Dickstein, J.: Unrolled Generative Adversarial Networks. arXiv:1611.02163v4 (2017)
10. Lipton, Z.C., Tripathi, S.: Precise Recovery of Latent Vectors from Generative Adversarial Networks. arXiv:1702.04782v2 (2017)
11. Yoshitomi, S., Nakagawa, D., Sada, T.: Research on structural optimization for steel industrialised housing. J. Struct. Constr. Eng. **80**(714), 1347–1355 (2015)
12. Zhang, H., et al.: Stack GAN: Text to Photo-realistic Image Synthesis with Stacked Generative Adversarial Networks. arXiv:1612.03242 (2016)
13. Van der Maaten, L., Hinton, G.: Visualizing data using t-SNE. J. Mach. Learn. Res. **9**, 2579–2605 (2008)

PMGAN: Paralleled Mix-Generator Generative Adversarial Networks with Balance Control

Xia Xiao(✉) and Sanguthevar Rajasekaran

Computer Science and Engineering Department, University of Connecticut, Storrs, CT 06269, USA
{xia.xiao, sanguthevar.rajasekaran}@uconn.edu

Abstract. A Generative Adversarial Network (GAN) is an unsupervised generative framework to generate a sample distribution that is identical to the data distribution. Recently, mix strategy multi-generator/discriminator GANs have been shown to outperform single pair GANs. However, the mixed model suffers from the problem of linearly growing training time. Also, imbalanced training among generators makes it difficult to parallelize. In this paper, we propose a balanced mix-generator GAN that works in parallel by mixing multiple disjoint generators to approximate the real distribution. The weights of the discriminator and the classifier are controlled by a balance strategy. We also present an efficient loss function, to force each generator to embrace few modes with a high probability. Our model is naturally adaptive to large parallel computation frameworks. Each generator can be trained on multiple GPUs asynchronously. We have performed extensive experiments on synthetic datasets, MNIST1000, CIFAR-10, and ImageNet. The results establish that our model can achieve the state-of-the-art performance (in terms of the modes coverage and the inception score), with significantly reduced training time. We also show that the missing mode problem can be relieved with a growing number of generators.

Keywords: Deep learning · Generative adversarial networks
Parallelization

1 Introduction

Generative Adversarial Networks were proposed by [8], where two neural networks, the generator and the discriminator, are trained to play a minimax game. The generator is trained to fool the discriminator while the discriminator is trained to distinguish fake data from real data. When Nash Equilibrium is reached, the generated distribution P_G will be identical to the real distribution P_{real}. Unlike Restricted Boltzmann Machine or Variational Auto-encoder that

This work has been supported in part by the NSF grants 1447711 and 1743418.

V. Kůrková et al. (Eds.): ICANN 2018, LNCS 11141, pp. 414–424, 2018.
https://doi.org/10.1007/978-3-030-01424-7_41

explicitly approximate data distribution, the approximation of GAN is implicit [7]. Training a GAN is challenging due to various potential problems such as gradient vanish [1], missing mode [5,10,11,15,16], mode collapse [2,7], equilibrium [3,4], etc.

Recently, the authors of [3,9] have used a set of generators to replace a single complex generator. Each generator only captures a part of the real distribution. In this case, the distance between the mix-generated distribution and the real distribution should be minimized. A new classifier is added to separate each pair of generators. The generated image using this approach obtained the highest score (Inception Score of about 15% better than the average of the second and the third competitors). Note that the overlapping penalty from the classifier and an unrealistic penalty from the discriminator may conflict during training. More specifically, we observe two problems in practice: (1) competition: multiple generators try to capture one mode, but are hampered by a strict boundary. The competition happens when the total number of generators K is greater than the actual number of modes of P_{real}. (2) One beats all: One or a few of the generators are too strong to capture all the modes, while the other generators are forced to move away from the data distribution since the penalty of the classifier is stronger than the penalty of the discriminator. In this paper, we offer novel and efficient techniques to solve the imbalance problems and effectively parallelize the multi-generator model.

Our idea is to dynamically balance between two penalties, based on the stage where each generator stands. To control this competition, we propose a balance term β, where all the training information from all the generators are collected, the current progress of each generator is evaluated, and a decision is made based on the overall stage of all the generators. To further improve and speed up the model, we propose a reverse KL divergence loss function instead of JS Divergence as the generator loss, to avoid mode collapse and improve the generator's ability to capture all the modes. Moreover, our model can allow parallelized training among generators, with synchronized or asynchronized updates for the discriminator, which significantly reduces the training time. Another advantage of our parallelization framework is robustness and extensibility. Increasing or decreasing the number of processors will not hamper the training process. The framework can dynamically adapt to the change. Experimental results show that our model can solve the missing mode problem and generate diverse images by adding generators into the model.

2 Related Works

Recently, many researchers have started focusing on designing a mixture of generators to beat the discriminator. The authors of [13] train different generators to capture different granularities of the image and generate a high-resolution image. The paper [17] uses the idea of Adaboost, where the weight of the misclassified data is increased, and the final model is a mixture of all the weak learners trained in previous steps. A mixture model where multiple generators are trained to play against the discriminator is given in [3]. Given enough number and complexity of generators, a Nash Equilibrium can also be achieved, and the discriminator tends to lose the game. The authors of [9] follow this idea and achieve the state-of-the-art generated quality (inception score). However, these two methods suffer from the imbalance and competition problems mentioned in the previous section. Our method extends this idea in a novel manner. We exploit the fact that given enough generators, with balance control, all the modes can be captured and the mixed generators can finally win.

To understand and solve the missing mode problem, [1] proves that any proxy loss function that contains the reverse Kullback Leibler divergence (KL divergence [12]) term tends to capture a single or few modes of P_{data}, while ignoring the other modes. It has been claimed that an imbalance in data points for different modes may cause the missing mode problem [5]. The generation manifold tends to move to modes with dominating data points while ignoring modes with only a few data points. Chey et al. [5] propose to use an autoencoder to map the data points back to the prior distribution z, and let the generator sample from the mapped distribution prior instead of a simple Gaussian. This paper also introduces an evaluation metric to measure both the generated quality and the ability to handle the missing mode problem, which is not highlighted in the traditional Inception Score measurement ([15]). Unrolled GAN, where copies of the discriminators are made, and back-propagation is done through all of the discriminators, while the generator is updated based on the gradient update of those discriminators has been presented in [10]. In [6], the authors propose a multi-discriminator model, where weak discriminators are trained using parts of the data, and the gradients from all the discriminators are passed to the generator. The authors of [16] have used another reconstructor network to learn the reverse mapping from generated distribution to prior noise. If the support of the mapped distribution is aggregated to a small portion, then the missing mode problem is detected. A dual discriminator model where KL and reverse KL divergence are controlled by two discriminators is offered in [11]. In this model, the weights of the two discriminators are controlled by a neural network.

3 Our Method

The original generative adversarial network was first proposed in [8], and can be formulated as a minimax game between a discriminator D and a generator G, where the loss function can be defined as:

$$\begin{aligned} \mathcal{J}_{\theta^D}^D &= \mathbb{E}_{x \sim P_{data}}[\log D(x)] + \mathbb{E}_{z \sim p_z(z)}[\log(1 - D(G(z)))] \\ \mathcal{J}_{\theta^G}^G &= \mathbb{E}_{z \sim p_z(z)}[\log(D(G(z)))] \\ \theta^G &= \underset{\theta^G}{\operatorname{argmin}} \max_{\theta^D} \mathcal{J}_{\theta^D}^D \end{aligned} \tag{1}$$

For the generator, the optimal discriminator at each step is $D^* = \frac{P_{data}}{P_{data}+P_g}$. When convergence is reached, we can obtain $P_g = P_{data}$. The procedure is equivalent to minimizing the Jensen Shannon Divergence $JSD(P_g||P_{data})$. As discussed in [1], the zero sum loss results in the gradient vanish problem where generator can learn nothing since the gradient is zero. Thus heuristic/proxy loss for the generator G is proposed. As is proved in [1], the gradient of the heuristic loss is equivalent to the gradient $\nabla_{\theta^G}[KL(P_g||P_{data}) + JSD(P_g||P_{data})]$.

3.1 Loss Functions

In our work, we design a multi-player game by dividing one generator into K generators, and adding another classifier to the original minimax game. The loss function for every single generator is:

$$\begin{aligned}
\mathcal{J}^D(G,D) &= \mathbb{E}_{x\sim P_{data}}[\log D(x)] + \mathbb{E}_{x\sim P_G}[\log(1-D(x))] \\
\mathcal{J}^C(G,C) &= \mathbb{E}_{x\sim P_{g_{-k}}}[\log C(x)] + \mathbb{E}_{x\sim P_{g_k}}[\log(1-C(x))] \\
\mathcal{J}^{G_k}(G_k,C,D) &= \mathbb{E}_{x\sim P_{g_k}}[1+\log D(x) - \log(1-D(x))] \\
&\quad - \beta_k\,\mathbb{E}_{x\sim P_{g_k}}[\log(1-C(x))]
\end{aligned} \tag{2}$$

Since the loss function $\mathcal{J}^{G_k}(G_k, C, D)$ is not bounded, we need to truncate $\mathcal{J}^{G_k}$ if $D > t$ to avoid the gradient explosion problem, where t is a threshold value. The goal is to solve the multi-player minimax game. If we take a closer look at the loss functions, we will notice that: (1) The discriminator loss $\mathcal{J}^D$ is nothing but the loss from the original GAN paper, which minimizes the Jensen-Shannon Divergence (JSD) between the mixture of generators and P_{real}; (2) the classifier loss $\mathcal{J}^C$ is actually another discriminator that treats G_{-k} as real samples, G_k as fake samples, and separates each generator G_k from all the other generators G_{-k} maximizing $JSD(G_k||G_{-k})$. The output of the classifier C is a softmax layer with size K; and (3) each generator is trained according to the gradient provided by both the discriminator D and a weighted classifier C.

We can show that the distance we are minimizing is $D_{KL}(P_{g_k}||P_{data})$ and $-D_{JSD}(P_{g_k}||P_{g_{-k}})$. From [8], the optimal discriminator, given the current generator G, has a close form $D^*_G = \frac{P_{data}(x)}{P_{data}(x)+P_g(x)}$. Since the loss function of C is fairly close to D, we can obtain the optimal C given that the current G is $C^*_G = \frac{P_{G_{-k}}(x)}{P_{G_{-k}}+P_g(x)}$. Next, we will analyze the loss of the generator when we fix $D = D^*$ and $C = C^*$.

Proposition 1. *Given optimal D^* and C^*, minimizing the loss for generator in Eq. 2 is equivalent to minimizing:*

$$D(P_{g_k}, P_{data}, P_{g_{-k}}) = D_{KL}(P_{g_k}||P_{data}) - \beta D_{JSD}(P_{g_k}||P_{g_{-k}}).$$

Proof. We first show that minimizing the first term is equivalent to minimizing $D_{KL}(P_{g_k}||P_{data})$. If we take the partial derivative of the reverse KL divergence:

$$\frac{\partial}{\partial\theta}D_{KL}(P_{g_k}(\theta)||P_{data}) = \frac{\partial}{\partial\theta}\int P_{g_k}(\theta)\log\frac{P_{g_k}(\theta)}{P_{data}}\,dx.$$

We can use Leibniz integral rule to switch integral and derivative, if we assume that the function inside the integral satisfies: 1. continuity, 2. continuous derivative, and 3. $\lim_{x\to\infty} f(x) = 0$. We obtain:

$$\frac{\partial}{\partial\theta} D_{KL}(P_{g_k}(\theta)||P_{data}) = \int \frac{\partial P_{g_k}(\theta)}{\partial\theta} \log \frac{P_{g_k}}{P_{data}} + P_{g_k} \frac{\partial P_{g_k}(\theta)}{\partial\theta}\, dx.$$

Substituting D with optimal D^*, $\mathcal{J}^{G_k}(G_k, C, D)$ can also be rewritten as:

$$\mathcal{J}^{G_k}(G_k, C, D^*) = \mathbb{E}_{x\sim P_G}[1 + \log(\frac{1-D^*}{D^*})] = \mathbb{E}_{x\sim P_G}[1 + \log \frac{P_{g_k}(\theta)}{P_{data}}]$$

$$= \frac{\partial}{\partial\theta} \int \log \frac{P_{g_k}}{P_{data}} P_{g_k}(\theta) + P_{g_k}(\theta)\, dx = \int \log \frac{P_{g_k}}{P_{data}} \frac{\partial P_{g_k}(\theta)}{\partial\theta} + P_{g_k} \frac{\partial \log P_{g_k}(\theta)}{\partial\theta}\, dx,$$

which is equivalent to the gradient of the reverse KL divergence. Note that we assume that $\frac{P_{g_k}}{P_{data}}$ is a constant when optimal D^* is obtained. The second term in the generator loss is the same as the zero-sum loss, which is equivalent to minimizing the Jensen Shannon Divergence $D_{JSD}(P_{g_k}||P_{g_{-k}})$. □

3.2 The Balance Term

For the loss function in the previous section, both the discriminator and the classifier provide gradient to the generator, i.e., the unrealistic error and overlapping error. Note that the two directions may conflict in practice. Based on the information gathered from all the other generators, one should decide whether to focus on minimizing the unrealistic error, or the overlapping error. The information includes: how the generator k performs against all the other generators; how the generator k performs against an ideal generator; and how much overlap is detected by the classifier C. We define these three terms as relative performance w , absolute bias d, and absolute overlap c for the generator k, assuming the total number of generators is K:

$$w_k = \frac{\exp \mathcal{J}_k^D}{\sum_{i=1}^K \exp \mathcal{J}_i^D},\ d_k = \sigma(\mathcal{J}_k^D),\ c_k = \mathcal{J}_k^C \tag{3}$$

The balance term β is constructed based on w, d and c, considering the intuition:

1. c_k and d_k are both high or both low, the generator k is either in the initial stage or in a stable stage, and there is no need to increase or decrease β.
2. c_k is low but d_k is high, the generator k runs outward in a wrong direction, β needs to be reduced to pull P_{G_k} back to P_{data}.
3. c_k is high but d_k is low, the generator k captures a certain mode of P_{data} while conflicting with another generator. β has to be increased to separate the two joint generators.

Synthesizing all the criteria above, we can construct β as:

$$\beta_k = w_k \exp(-(\frac{c}{d} - \lambda)) = \frac{\exp \mathcal{J}_k^D}{\sum_{i=1}^K \exp \mathcal{J}_i^D} \exp(-(\frac{\mathcal{J}_k^C}{\sigma(\mathcal{J}_k^D)} - \lambda)) \tag{4}$$

The final β will be renormalized using $\beta_k = \frac{\exp \beta_k}{\sum_{i=1}^{K} \exp \beta_i}$. Note that the sigmoid in the expression is to map the discriminator loss to $R^{(0,1)}$. λ can be interpreted as 'diversity factor' to control the separation among the generators. β will decrease sharply if $c/d > \lambda$. A higher λ will cause a higher penalty from overlapping error which results in a higher generated diversity.

In practice, we also multiply an extra term t decaying with time, where $t = \exp(-\alpha t)$, if the expected number of modes is small or the number of generators is high. Adding the term t forces the overlapping error shrink over time, and reduces the three players game back to two players game, where the convergence is guaranteed.

3.3 Structure of PMGAN

The structure of PMGAN is shown in Fig. 1. All generators and the classifier are connected by shared memory. The communication among them only happens through the shared memory. The shared memory has K slots, where K is the number of generators. Each slot contains three subslots: a sample part where the samples generated by the generator k are stored, a validation part where the value of the classifier is stored, and a progress part where the loss of the generator is stored. Thus the total size of the shared memory is $k(batchsize + 3)$. During training, generator k will store its generated sample in the sample part of kth slot, and continue training. Once the validation or progress slot is updated, the generator will recalculate the overlapping loss or β_k. Classifier C will update once all the sample slots are updated, and store the softmax output to validation slots for each k. Note that it is not necessary that the generator should stop and wait for the response from the classifier or progress from the others since the generator will not go far away from the previous update, and the training process is totally distributed and asynchronized.

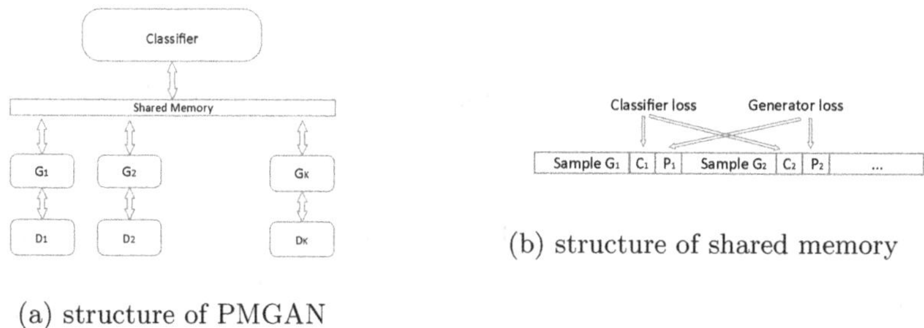

(a) structure of PMGAN

(b) structure of shared memory

Fig. 1. Illustration of our proposed PMGAN

4 Experiments

In this section, we demonstrate the practical effectiveness of our algorithm through experiments on synthetic datasets and real datasets. The set up for all the experiments is: (1) Learning rate = 0.0002, (2) Minibatch size = 128 for the generator, the discriminator, and the classifier, (3) Adam optimizer with first-order momentum = 0.5, (4) β is set to 1 at the beginning, with decay $\beta = \exp^{-\lambda t}$, and (5) Activation function is LeakyReLU, weight initialization is from DCGAN [14]. All the codes have been implemented in Pytorch (Inception Score in Tensorflow).

4.1 Synthetic Datasets

Synthetic datasets are a mixture of 8 Gaussians without any overlaps. We have used two settings: 8 generators and 10 generators. First, we train exactly 8 generators with random initialization. In Fig. 2, we show the results for every 5 K steps (discriminator steps).

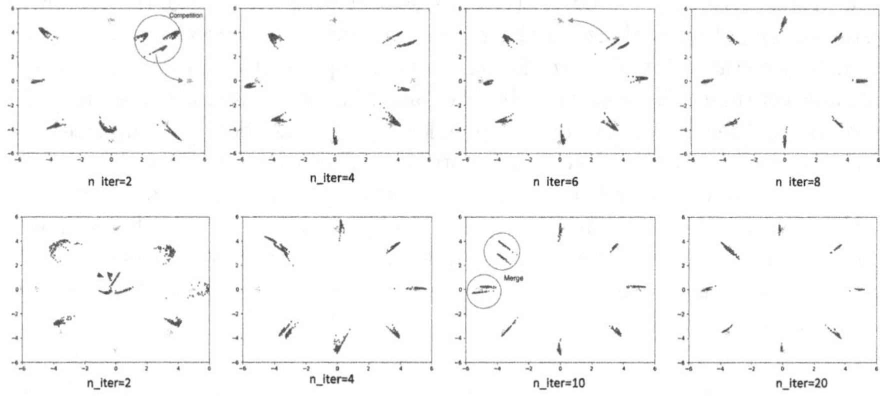

Fig. 2. Evaluation on synthetic datasets. Top: 8 generators, 8 modes. Bottom: 10 Generators, 8 modes

From the results, we see that all the generators are spread out at the beginning. The overlapping penalty and the generators proceeding in the same direction will be divided after certain number of steps. Since the number of modes is exactly the same as the number of generators, the property of the reverse KL divergence will keep each generator stay stationary. When competition happens, the other generators will be pushed to other un-captured modes. Finally, all the 8 modes are captured by different generators.

We have then increased the number of generators to 10. The result is shown in Fig. 3. In the beginning, the situation is the same as in the previous setting, but the strong penalty will hamper the mode captured by two generators.

The two generators are competing for the same mode. This illustrates that the function of the balance term with decay is to 'mediate' the competition among the generators. Two or more generators can collapse to the same mode and reach final convergence after several epochs(determined by the decay factor).

4.2 Real World Data

In this section, we use three popular datasets, MNIST1000, CIFAR-10 and Imagenet. Note that the difference between MNIST and MNIST1000 is that the latter one is constructed using $1,000$ channels to evaluate the missing mode of the model. To evaluate the quality of the generated samples, we use the Inception Score proposed in [15], where the score is calculated by the expectation of KL divergence $\mathbb{E}[D_{KL}p(y|x)||p(y)]$, where we calculate the distance between the conditional label and the real label.

MNIST1000 Dataset: The MNIST dataset contains $1,000$ classes. We ran our model with different numbers of generators ranging from 1 to 16. The result is shown in Tables 1 and 2. Note that by increasing the number of generators, the modes captured by the mixed generator increased, while the distance between generators decreased. Comparing to other models, our model captures all the $1,000$ modes, and obtains the lowest distance between the generated distribution and the real data distribution.

Table 1. MNIST-1000 results for different models

Missing mode evaluation				
Model	GAN	UnrolledGAN	DCGAN	PMGAN
Modes covered	628.0 ± 140.9	817.4 ± 37.9	849.6 ± 62.7	**1,000**
$D_{KL}(model\|\|data)$	2.58	1.43	0.73	**0.06**

Table 2. MNIST-1000 results for different numbers of generators

Num of generator	1	4	8	12	16
Mode covered	140	488	732	977	1,000

CIFAR-10 and ImageNet Dataset: We trained 1 to 20 generators for CIFAR-10 and ImageNetdataset. From the results, we can conclude that the inception score increases with the number of generators, while it gradually gets saturated. From our observation, the threshold depends on the complexity of the dataset, model capacity, and the classifier. The highest score we get is 8.17 and 9.08, with more than 12 generators, which is very close to the sequential MGAN model. See Table 3.

4.3 Training Time

The training time for the sequential mix generator model for CIFAR-10 dataset is 115.4 min in our setting. To obtain around the same score, the PMGAN with 4 generators takes 54% of the time, 8 generators takes 42%, 12 generators takes 37%, and 16 generators takes 35%. The inception scores are 7.02, 8.03, 8.73, 9.01, and 9.08, respectively. From Fig. 3(d), we can observe that with the significantly reduced training time, the inception scores remain unchanged(only with slightly decrease).

Table 3. Real world data results

Inception score		
Model	CIFAR-10	ImageNet
Real data	11.24 ± 0.16	25.78 ± 0.47
Wasserstein GAN [2]	3.82 ± 0.06	
MIX+WGAN [3]	4.04 ± 0.07	
DCGAN [14]	6.40 ± 0.05	7.89
D2GAN [11]	7.15 ± 0.07	8.25
MGAN [9]	$\mathbf{8.33 \pm 0.10}$	**9.22**
PMGAN(Our work)	$\mathbf{8.19 \pm 0.16}$	**9.08**

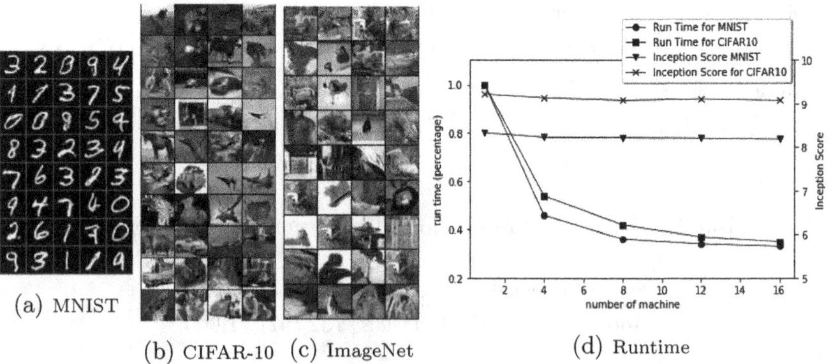

(a) MNIST (b) CIFAR-10 (c) ImageNet (d) Runtime

Fig. 3. (a): Random pick from the mix generator for MNIST dataset. (b): Random pick from the mix generator for CIFAR-10 dataset. (c):Inception score for mix generators and single generator for both datasets. (d): Runtimes and Inception Scores for different numbers of machines

5 Conclusions

In this paper, we propose a novel balanced mixed generator GAN. Our algorithm is parallelizable and can be scaled to large platforms. To resolve the competition and one-beat all problems in the mix generator model, we have designed the reverse KL divergence loss function, and a carefully designed balance term to produce a stable, converging, and fast training method. Experimental results show that we can handle the situation when the generators compete for the same mode even when the number of generators is greater than the number of modes. The empirical results reveal that our method achieves the state-of-the-art performance on the quality of the generated distribution (in terms of the inception score). Also, we show that our model solves the missing mode problem on the MNIST1000 dataset.

More works have to be done in this multi-player game. First, the balance method can also be improved if we can have a better heuristic for β. We can also train to learn β, and to achieve a balance between competition and convergence. The parallelization scheme that we propose can be utilized with other multi-generator models such as the one in [13], to generate better resolution and complex images.

References

1. Arjovsky, M., Bottou, L.: Towards principled methods for training generative adversarial networks. arXiv preprint arXiv:1701.04862 (2017)
2. Arjovsky, M., Chintala, S., Bottou, L.: Wasserstein gan. arXiv preprint arXiv:1701.07875 (2017)
3. Arora, S., Ge, R., Liang, Y., Ma, T., Zhang, Y.: Generalization and equilibrium in generative adversarial nets (gans). arXiv preprint arXiv:1703.00573 (2017)
4. Berthelot, D., Schumm, T., Metz, L.: Began: Boundary equilibrium generative adversarial networks. arXiv preprint arXiv:1703.10717 (2017)
5. Che, T., Li, Y., Jacob, A.P., Bengio, Y., Li, W.: Mode regularized generative adversarial networks. arXiv preprint arXiv:1612.02136 (2016)
6. Durugkar, I., Gemp, I., Mahadevan, S.: Generative multi-adversarial networks. arXiv preprint arXiv:1611.01673 (2016)
7. Goodfellow, I.: Nips 2016 tutorial: Generative adversarial networks. arXiv preprint arXiv:1701.00160 (2016)
8. Goodfellow, I., et al.: Generative adversarial nets. In: Advances in Neural Information Processing Systems, pp. 2672–2680 (2014)
9. Hoang, Q., Nguyen, T.D., Le, T., Phung, D.: Multi-generator gernerative adversarial nets. arXiv preprint arXiv:1708.02556 (2017)
10. Metz, L., Poole, B., Pfau, D., Sohl-Dickstein, J.: Unrolled generative adversarial networks. arXiv preprint arXiv:1611.02163 (2016)
11. Nguyen, T.D., Le, T., Vu, H., Phung, D.: Dual discriminator generative adversarial nets. arXiv preprint arXiv:1709.03831 (2017)
12. Nowozin, S., Cseke, B., Tomioka, R.: F-GAN: training generative neural samplers using variational divergence minimization. In: Advances in Neural Information Processing Systems, pp. 271–279 (2016)

13. Okadome, Y., Wei, W., Aizono, T.: Parallel-pathway generator for generative adversarial networks to generate high-resolution natural images. In: Lintas, A., Rovetta, S., Verschure, P.F.M.J., Villa, A.E.P. (eds.) ICANN 2017. LNCS, vol. 10614, pp. 655–662. Springer, Cham (2017). https://doi.org/10.1007/978-3-319-68612-7_74
14. Radford, A., Metz, L., Chintala, S.: Unsupervised representation learning with deep convolutional generative adversarial networks. arXiv preprint arXiv:1511.06434 (2015)
15. Salimans, T., Goodfellow, I., Zaremba, W., Cheung, V., Radford, A., Chen, X.: Improved techniques for training gans. In: Advances in Neural Information Processing Systems, pp. 2234–2242 (2016)
16. Srivastava, A., Valkov, L., Russell, C., Gutmann, M., Sutton, C.: Veegan: Reducing mode collapse in gans using implicit variational learning. arXiv preprint arXiv:1705.07761 (2017)
17. Tolstikhin, I., Gelly, S., Bousquet, O., Simon-Gabriel, C.J., Schölkopf, B.: Adagan: Boosting generative models. arXiv preprint arXiv:1701.02386 (2017)

Modular Domain-to-Domain Translation Network

Savvas Karatsiolis[1(✉)], Christos N. Schizas[1], and Nicolai Petkov[2]

[1] University of Cyprus, University Avenue 1, 2109 Aglantzia, Nicosia, Cyprus
karatsioliss@cytanet.com.cy

[2] Department of Intelligent Systems Group, Johann Bernoulli Institute for Mathematics and Computer Science, University of Groningen, 9712 CP Groningen, Netherlands

Abstract. We present a method for constructing and training a deep domain-to-domain translation network: two datasets describing the same classes (i.e. the source and target domains) are used to train a deep network that can translate a pattern coming from the source domain to its counterpart form in the target domain. We introduce the development of a hierarchical architecture that encapsulates information of the target domain by embedding individually trained networks. This deep hierarchical architecture is then trained as one unified deep network. Using this approach, we prove that samples from the original domain are translated to the target domain format for both the cases where there is a one-to-one correspondence in the samples of the two domains and also when this correspondence information is absent. In our experiments we get a good translation operation as long as the target domain dataset provides good classification results when trained alone. We use either some distorted version of the MNIST dataset or the SVHN dataset as the original domain for the translation task and the MNIST as the target domain. The translation from one information domain to the other is visualized and evaluated. We also discuss the proposed model's relation to the conditional Generative Adversarial Networks and we further argue that deep learning can benefit from such forms of strict hierarchical architectures.

Keywords: Unsupervised learning · Autoencoder · Feature mapping
Neural nets

1 Introduction

Deep Learning has taken pattern recognition into a new level during the past years. Some years ago, implementations that are now hugely favored by deep learning approaches were confined by shallow network architectures due to the lack of processing power that could deal with really deep models and of algorithms that could regularize and optimize learning across a much increased number of layers. The former problem is mitigated by the technological advances achieved by the technology of Graphical Processing Units (GPUs) that can execute a tremendous amount of calculations in a huge parallelized fashion while the latter problem was overcame with the discovery of powerful training algorithms like Batch Normalization [5], Dropout [14]

V. Kůrková et al. (Eds.): ICANN 2018, LNCS 11141, pp. 425–435, 2018.
https://doi.org/10.1007/978-3-030-01424-7_42

and Adam [7]. While Batch Normalization and Adam concentrate on a better optimization in terms of the objective function, Dropout focuses on the regularization of the model by combining the hypotheses of an ensemble of networks. Convolutional networks were highly favored by the advancement of deep learning in the sense that a large part of the machine learning research community working in the specific field is producing very interesting results. Recently, there is also an interest revitalization in the exploration of methods for applying knowledge transfer. The specific concept may be implemented in different flavors: domain adaptation, cross-domain information passing and feature preserving networks. Hinton et al. [4] studied a form of knowledge transfer from a cumbersome model to a smaller model and called this method knowledge distillation. The cumbersome model could be an ensemble of separately trained models or a single large model that is heavily trained. According to Hinton, knowledge transfer is implemented through training the smaller model to match the class probabilities as calculated from the cumbersome model in the form of higher entropy "soft targets. Another approach to knowledge transfer was introduced by Chen et al. [1] with their Net2Net function preserving transformations: Net2WiderNet and Net2DeeperNet. Using these transformations a working model can be expanded to a wider or a deeper network that is equivalent in the sense that the model function is kept unaltered. Using these transformations Chen et al. implemented the concept of knowledge transfer from a teacher network to an architecture enriched student network that was able to accomplish better accuracy and faster learning. The knowledge transfer research field could also be benefited by the increased interest in unsupervised and semi-supervised learning algorithms along with the recent discoveries of very promising generative models like the Generative Adversarial Network (GAN) [3]. Mirza and Osindero [9] implemented the conditional flavor of the original generative adversarial network algorithm by feeding the generator and the discriminator networks with an extra piece of information that enabled conditioning the generated output on some auxiliary data such as a class label vector. Denton et al. [2] used a Laplacian pyramid framework with conditional generative adversarial networks to construct a coarse-to-fine generative model producing CIFAR10 images that human evaluators mistaken for real images 40% of the time. Odena [10] modified the GAN discriminator in order not only to predict whether an image was real or came from the generator but also to provide the class of the real images. In other words, the discriminator had $K + 1$ classes instead of just 2 (real or fake image) which is advantageous for training a data efficient classifier and generating good quality images when trained in a semi-supervised fashion. Conditional adversarial Networks were also used by Isola et al. [10] to implement image to image translation and effectively synthesize photos from labels, reconstruct images from edge maps and colorize images. This work is notable because it illustrates that GANS can be trained with a mapping relating one image domain with another domain, without the need of hand-engineering these mappings. Cross-domain image generation has been studied by Taigman, Polyak and Wolf [15] - by implementing a modified multiclass GAN that they called Domain Transfer Network to produce an image that is relevant to an input image. Finally, Tim Salimans et al. [12] published a set of improved techniques for training GANs with their most interesting method being their semi-supervised learning using feature mapping.

2 The Proposed Model

The proposed model aims in the translation of patterns from a source domain to patterns belonging to a target domain. Both domains share the same problem categories and the target domain patterns should be able to train a well performing discriminator. For our experiments the MNIST domain represents the target domain, while the source domain is either the SVHN data or a distorted variant of the MNIST domain. Having a well- performing classifier for the target domain at hand is important to the proposed model because, during training, it provides the vital information for performing the translation from one domain to the other. Domain to domain translation may deal with two scenarios:

1. Cross-domain pattern information correspondence which is the case of having the same information expressed by very similar but still different domains (patterns have a 1:1 correspondence). For example, given an informational pattern x, the target domain may carry this information in its original form while the input domain may contain a modified version of this information x' which is obtained after x has been altered by a transformation t or distorted by a signal n, that is, $x' = t(x) + n$. Nevertheless, these operations are reversible and maintain a great deal of the original information.
2. Cross-domain pattern categorical correspondence which is the case of having samples from two quite different domains belonging to the same set of problem classes. This kind of relation will be referred to as 1:M correspondence because one sample from the target domain is related to many samples of the input domain simply because of categorical resemblance.

2.1 Deep Domain to Domain Translation Architecture

The proposed model's concept relies on building a deep architecture that comprises of three distinct components: the input domain to target domain representation network, the decoding of this representation back to the target domain and a well performing target domain classifier. All these stages (representation, decoding and classifier) are embedded into a deep architecture that is trained with back propagation to produce a translation network from the input domain to the target domain. However, the three distinct stages must be trained before being embedded in the final deep architecture. This pre-training strategy places the unified architecture in the vicinity of a good initial training state that maintains the objective function and prevents over fitting due to the increased number of model parameters. It also prevents under fitting due to the vanishing gradients phenomenon caused by the deep architecture. The detailed steps for the construction of the model are shown in Tables 1 and 2. Figure 1 shows the model architecture and the distinguishable stages that are trained before their unification to a deep network architecture. It must be noted that every distinct stage is not restricted to a specific architecture and can be shallow or deep according to the application complexity. However, the width and depth of every stage affects the final model size accordingly. As soon as the individual networks are constructed, they are embedded to a deep architecture and trained as a unified network with tiny learning rates for the final two stages in order to preserve the information transferred by the pre-training procedure.

Table 1. Steps for constructing the deep domain-to-domain translation network

Assuming an input domain dataset of the form $\{(z_1, y_1), (z_2, y_2), \ldots, (z_M, y_M)\}$ and a target domain dataset of the form $\{(x_1, y_1), (x_2, y_2), \ldots, (x_C, y_C)\}$.
For 1:1 pattern correspondence between Z and X, it should also hold that $M = C$.

- Construct an auto-encoder for the target domain such as $f: X \to L$, $g: L \to X$ with f being the encoder, g the decoder and $L \in \Re^K$ is the latent representation. The auto-encoder should use the sigmoid activation function to maintain a direct probabilistic interpretation for the latent representations.
- Train a representation network $T: Z \to R$ with the M input domain patterns with cross-entropy loss function. The training targets are binary vectors $\vec{r}_m$ sampled from the latent representations calculated in step (1) such as $r_m^k \in \{0,1\}$. The sampling is performed for every mini-batch of the training. Table2 describes this step in detail.
- Train a well performing classifier D for the target domain such as $D: X \to Y$.
- Create a deep architecture model by embedding the model from step (2), the decoder g from step (1) and the classifier D from step (3) in this exact order as shown in Figure 1.
- Train the unified model $F = \{T, g, D\}$ with tiny learning rates for stages g and D such as $F: Z \to Y$
- The final translation model S is formed by discarding the D stage and keeping $S = \{T, g\}$

Table 2. Training algorithm for the representation network

Assuming an input domain dataset of the form $\{z_1, z_2, z_3, z_4, \ldots, z_M\}$, the corresponding target domain latent representations $\{l_1, l_2, l_3, l_4, \ldots, l_M\}$ as calculated from step (1) of Table 1 and the binary form of these representations as the formal problem targets $\{t_1, t_2, \ldots, t_M\}$ such as

$$t_i = \begin{cases} 1 & l_i \geq 0.5 \\ 0 & l_i < 0.5 \end{cases}$$

Repeat until convergence

Repeat until the whole dataset is examined

- Sample a k-size mini batch such as $\{z_1, z_2, \ldots, z_k\}$ associated with binary targets $\{r_1, r_2, \ldots, r_k\}$ sampled from the probabilities $\{l_1, l_2, \ldots, l_k\}$ such as
- $r_i = \begin{cases} 1 & p \leq l_i \\ 0 & p > l_i \end{cases}, \quad p \sim U(0,1)$
- Perform batch-normalization training with cross-entropy loss on the current mini batch and $\{r_1, r_2, \ldots, r_k\}$ as targets.
- End
- Evaluate network for dataset $\{z_1, z_2, z_3, \ldots, z_M\}$ with targets $\{t_1, t_2, \ldots, t_M\}$.

End

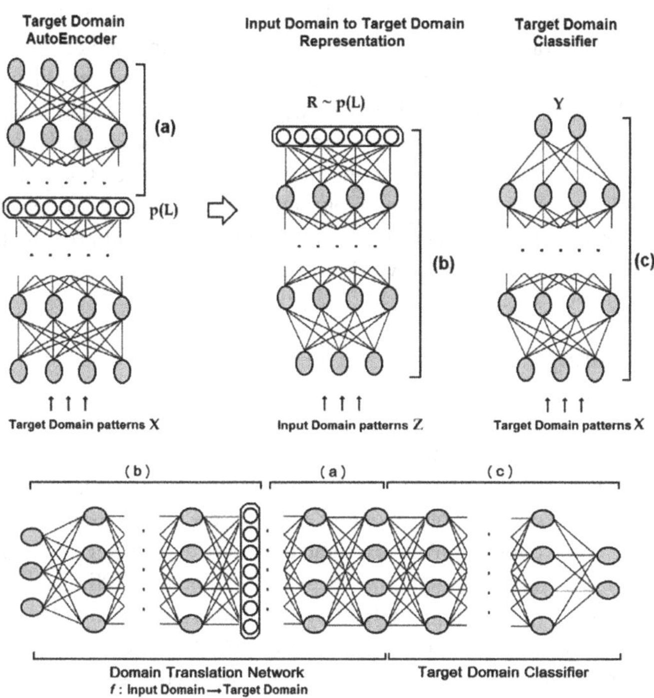

Fig. 1. The proposed model architecture. Three distinct networks are pre-trained and then placed into the final deep architecture: (a) a target domain auto-encoder (b) an input-domain to target-domain representation network trained on cross entropy loss of sampled binary values from the latent variables of the target domain auto-encoder and (c) a well performing pre trained classifier of the target domain. After these stages are placed as shown in the final deep architecture model, they are trained with very small learning rates in stages (a) and (c) in order to avoid destruction of the knowledge transferred from the target domain. The final model effectively consists of the domain translation network formed by stages (b) and (a). At the output of the domain translation network, just before the final classifier, it is expected to observe patterns belonging to the target domain.

If the target-domain-dependent stages are trained with anything but tiny learning rates, then the network will not necessarily maintain its prior knowledge. In the experiments these learning rates were assigned a value of $1e^{-8}$. Since the last stage was initialized to be a well-performing target-domain classifier allowed to undergo only slight changes due to a very small learning rate, it is expected to maintain a great portion of this ability after the training of the model is over. Furthermore, it is expected to guide (through the back propagation of its gradient information) the early stages of the unified architecture in adapting their feature mapping in such a way that the constructed features are a match for the last stage feature space. Consequently, this will drive the early stages of the architecture to figure out a way to construct features that are related to the target domain. The final model is not trained with batch normalization because this could destroy the pre-training and provoke the loss of the target domain information encapsulated in the network. Training the stages provided by the target domain with learning rates that are not tiny can have the same effect. In turn, the first three hidden layers are trained with a small learning rate while the next layers use a tiny learning rate. The final domain translation model's performance could be enhanced by adding the available target domain auto encoder as an extra stage at the output of the model. This approach produces sharper and more detailed images but is not applied in the experimental results because the main purpose is to evaluate the proposed model in its basic form. Performance enhancements and output image improvements may be explored and implemented in future work.

3 Problem Setup

Having two forms of information describing the same or similar observations is not a rare situation. For example, a digit recognition problem can be described by two datasets, the MNIST and the SVHN (Street View Home Numbers). In the case of the SVHN-MNIST pair every example in one of the datasets can be associated with many examples in the other dataset linked by their common class label. Thus, their correspondence is of a general nature (simply categorical) since it is difficult or meaningless to link the examples with a more detailed relation like style, orientation, displacement etc. In other words there is not a one-to-one correspondence between the examples of the MNIST dataset and the examples of the SVHN dataset (Fig. 2).

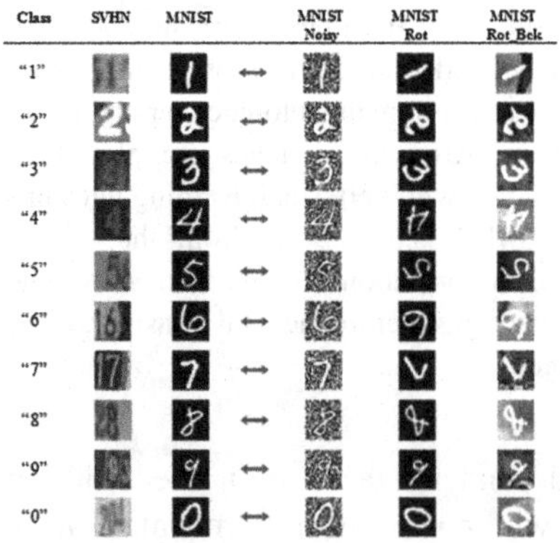

Fig. 2. Samples from the SVHN, MNIST, MNIST_Rot, MNIST_Noisy and MNIST_Rot_Back datasets. The arrows represent a 1:1 correspondence between the patterns of MNIST and its variants. This correspondence is not applicable when a domain translation from SVHN to MNIST domain is applied or vice versa.

In order to explore such a one-to-one correspondence between the examples of the two domains, we introduce three datasets which are corrupted versions of the original MNIST dataset. These MNIST variants are listed below:

- Rotated MNIST (MNIST_Rot): the original digits are rotated by an angle generated randomly in the range 0 *to* 2π.
- Noisy MNIST (MNIST_Noisy): each pixel in the original image is replaced with 20% probability by a random number uniformly sampled from the range 0 *to* 1.
- Rotated + Background image (MNIST_Rot_Bck): the digits are randomly rotated as in rotated MNIST and the background is replaced with a black and white image patch. These 28×28 patches are extracted from random nature pictures downloaded from the internet and screened for having a minimum level of pixel variation. More specifically, patches that have a variance less than 0.01 are discarded.

4 Experimental Results

Two experimental pathways are explored: domain translation with cross-domain pattern correspondence and domain translation without cross-domain pattern correspondence. Both pathways are studied with the MNIST variants translation to the MNIST domain while the translation of the SVHN domain to the MNIST domain is performed only according to the latter pathway. According to the proposed methodology the MNIST auto-encoder is trained making use of the whole 60000 available patterns in the dataset. Next, the MNIST dataset is expressed by the latent representation of the auto-encoder and all constant valued variables (1 or 0) are removed by making the necessary bias weights' adjustments for the decoder stage where necessary. Furthermore, for the case of the SVHN to MNIST translation model the mean latent representations per class are calculated. Finally, the individual stages defined by the proposed model are placed in a unified architecture which is trained with a tiny learning rate for the final stages. After the unified model is constructed by embedding the various stages, it is trained with mini batch gradient descent. According to the networks used to form the model, the final architecture for the MNIST variants is *784-2000-2000-922-784-800-800-10* and for the SVHN is *1024-2000-2000-922-784-800-800-10*. The results are particularly interesting for the SVHN to MNIST translation setup since the model learns implicitly an efficient way to reconstruct the MNIST form of the number in the middle of the image ignoring any numbers appearing at its sides. Additionally, this model trains itself on dealing with distorted digit images and many variations of the original patterns. During experimentation it was noted that the quality of the target domain auto-encoder and the training of the input domain representation network were more crucial for the performance of the final model than extreme tuning of the final stage classifier. Another, rather unexpected, observation extracted from the results, is the fact that cross-domain pattern correspondence is not as advantageous as expected. The resulted quality of both experimental pathways (1:1 correspondence and 1:M correspondence) is not that different which suggests that during training of the input domain representation model, an adequate approximation of the target domain manifold is sufficient in terms of enabling the unified architecture to learn how to perform the domain translation (Fig. 3).

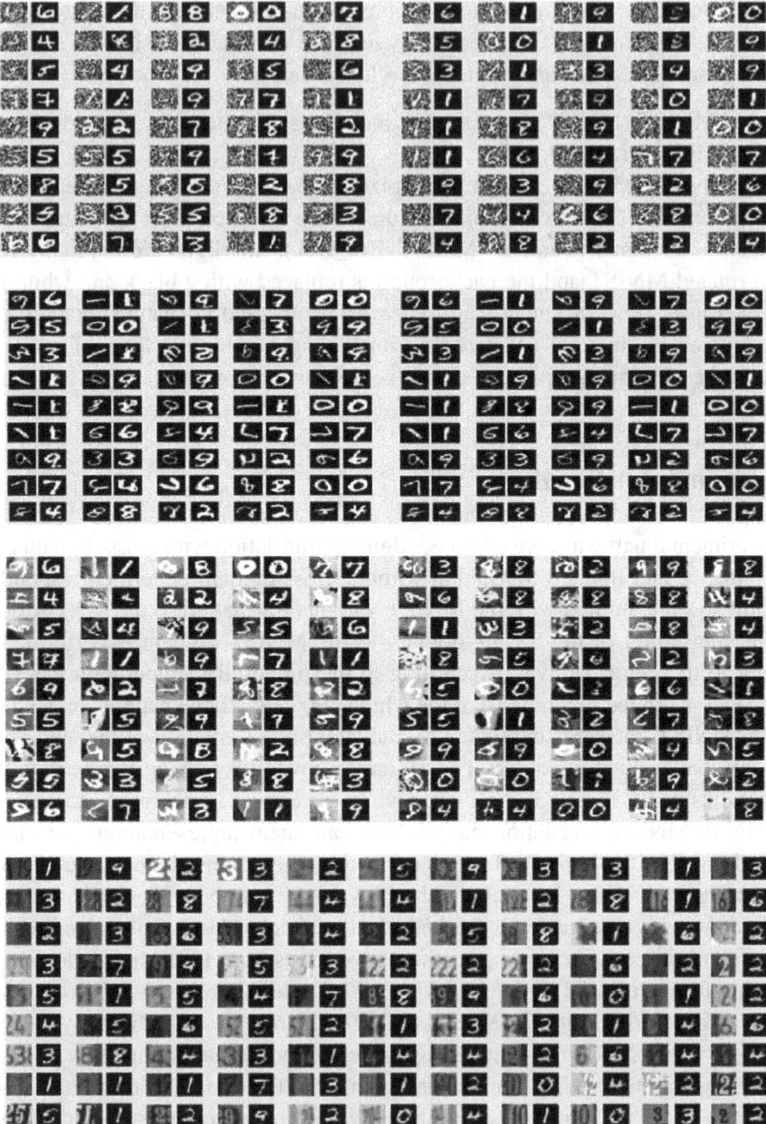

Fig. 3. From top to bottom: Random dataset samples for the MNIST_Noisy, MNIST_Rot, MNIST_RotBck and SVHN domain to the MNIST domain translation experiments. Each pair of images is formed by the input domain pattern on the left and the model's output on the right. The left side of the first three figures shows the 1:1 cross-domain pattern correspondence case while the right side shows the translation results for the 1:M case.

5 Conclusions

We have introduced a method for performing cross-domain pattern translation which transfers a pattern from one domain to a similar domain that spans the same classification categories. The results are also interesting from another point of view: the stages of the model that perform the domain translation and the classifier of the final model stage resemble the mechanisms of a conditional GAN. The former group of stages represents the GAN generator and the latter represents the GAN discriminator that outputs the K problem classes. In respect to Tim Salivans et al. semi-supervised GAN [12] which implements $K+1$ discriminator outputs, the proposed model omits the fake image output class. This output is rather safely omitted because the generator is pre-trained to produce images in the vicinity of the domain information format and is prevented from deviating away from it since the training gradients come from a well performing classifier acting on that domain. The concept served by the feature mapping property added to the objective function of Tim Salivan et al. method is also served by the pre-training of the input domain representation network proposed by our approach: instead of enforcing a similarity on how an intermediate layer of the discriminator is mapping real and generated information, our model consolidates this representation through the pre-training process, the embedding of the decoder stage of the target domain decoder and the tiny learning rate applied on this stage. Extending this rational, the proposed model is acting similarly to a conditional GAN with $K+1$ outputs, starting from an advanced training point, after the generator has started performing “reasonably” by producing images that should mostly be classified as belonging to one of the K problem classes. Hypothetically, the discriminator is constantly fooled by the generator in identifying one of the available K classes for every fake image it examines. Consequently, the fake output is omitted and not considered as an output option. Jost Tobias Springenber [13] also uses K output classes for training a GAN in an unsupervised or semi-supervised manner by omitting the fake image output. His strategy is to train an artificial image generator which produces fake images that seem real and uses a uniform distribution of samples in terms of their associating label. At the same time the discriminator must be trained to perform well on real data, to raise classification uncertainty when dealing with fake data and to choose the output class uniformly. By the requirements it is obviously assumed that the model deals with uniform class priors. Our model complies with all the requirements stated above both for the generator and the discriminator. Uniform distribution of sample generation is satisfied by the generator due to equal class priors. The discriminator also satisfies this requirement and the one for performing well on real data because of its pre-training on the target domain data. The raised uncertainty condition for the discriminator is naturally due to the noise injected during sampling of the latent probabilities. The proposed model also shares some theoretic principles with the semi-supervised GAN described by Odena [10] which uses $K+1$ discriminator outputs. An obvious modelling deviation of the proposed model from GANs is the absence of a noise generator at the input. Noise is important for the unconditional GAN for supplying the necessary variance at the input of the model. For conditional GANs, to which the proposed model is parallelized, this noise is not critical or even necessary since there is enough input variation due to the input domain images applied to the network and are acting like a condition for the generative process. This is supported by Isola et al. [6] and Mathieu et al. [8]. However, a great deal of noise is added to the proposed model during training because of the latent variables' sampling performed for each mini-batch. Besides the conditional GAN parallelization, there is another notable characteristic of the proposed model. It shows that deep networks perform well when the layers obey a hierarchy of functionality. Of course this is not a new idea since convolutional networks are built upon a function specific layer architecture with various types of layers (convolutional, pooling and fully connected layers). However, a stricter sectional embedding paradigm in the form proposed might worth further investigation and experimentation. Embedding domain information to a model in the form of whole network blocks, may produce networks that learn in a more efficient way. It could also provide the structural foundation of combining information from many similar domains to construct high level concepts that are transferable between these domains and are used to build more sophisticated models.

References

1. Chen, T., Goodfellow, I., Shlens, J.: Net2Net: accelerating learning via knowledge transfer. http://arxiv.org/abs/1511.05641 (2015)
2. Denton, E., Chintala, S., Szlam, A., Fergus, R.: Deep generative image models using a laplacian pyramid of adversarial networks. arxiv Preprint http://arxiv.org/abs/1506.05751, pp. 1–10 (2015)
3. Goodfellow, I., Pouget-Abadie, J., Mirza, M.: Generative adversarial networks. arXiv Preprint http://arxiv.org/abs/1406.2661, pp. 1–9 (2014)
4. Hinton, G., Vinyals, O., Dean, J.: Distilling the knowledge in a neural network. In: NIPS 2014 Deep Learning Workshop, pp. 1–9. https://doi.org/10.1063/1.4931082 (2015)
5. Ioffe, S., Szegedy, C.: Batch normalization: accelerating deep network training by reducing internal covariate shift, pp. 1–11 (2015). arXiv:1502.03167, https://doi.org/10.1007/s13398-014-0173-7.2
6. Isola, P., Zhu, J.-Y., Zhou, T., Efros, A.A.: Image-to-image translation with conditional adversarial networks. http://arxiv.org/abs/1611.07004 (2016)
7. Kingma, D., Ba, J.: Adam: a method for stochastic optimization. In: International Conference On Learning Representations, pp. 1–13. http://arxiv.org/abs/1412.6980 (2014)
8. Mathieu, M., Couprie, C., LeCun, Y.: Deep multi-scale video prediction beyond mean square error. In: ICLR, pp. 1–14. http://arxiv.org/abs/1511.05440 (2015)
9. Mirza, M., Osindero, S.: Conditional generative adversarial nets. CoRR, pp. 1–7. http://arxiv.org/abs/1411.1784 (2014)
10. Odena, A.: Semi-supervised learning with generative adversarial networks. In: ICML, pp. 1–3. http://arxiv.org/abs/1504.01391 (2016)
11. Rasmus, A., Berglund, M., Honkala, M., Valpola, H., Raiko, T.: Semi-supervised learning with ladder networks. In: Advances in Neural Information Processing Systems, pp. 3532–3540 (2015)
12. Salimans, T., Goodfellow, I., Zaremba, W., Cheung, V., Radford, A., Chen, X.: Improved Techniques for Training GANs. In: NIPS, pp. 1–10. http://arxiv.org/abs/1504.01391 (2016)
13. Springenberg, J.T.: Unsupervised and semi-supervised learning with categorical generative adversarial networks. http://arxiv.org/abs/1511.06390 (2015)

14. Srivastava, N., Hinton, G.E., Krizhevsky, A., Sutskever, I., Salakhutdinov, R.: Dropout: a simple way to prevent neural networks from overfitting. J. Mach. Learn. Res. (JMLR) **15**, 1929–1958 (2014). https://doi.org/10.1214/12-AOS1000
15. Taigman, Y., Polyak, A., Wolf, L.: Unsupervised cross-domain image generation. http://arxiv.org/abs/1611.02200 (2016)

OrieNet: A Regression System for Latent Fingerprint Orientation Field Extraction

Zhenshen Qu[1], Junyu Liu[1], Yang Liu[1(✉)], Qiuyu Guan[1], Chunyu Yang[2], and Yuxin Zhang[3]

[1] Department of Control Science and Engineering, HIT, Harbin, China
miraland@hit.edu.cn,
{17s004086,17s004024}@stu.hit.edu.cn
[2] Beijing Hisign Technology Co., Ltd., Beijing, China
[3] Cross-Strait Tsinghua Research Institute, Beijing, China

Abstract. Orientation field is an important characteristic of fingerprints. Many biometrics processing steps rely on its accurate estimation. Previous works on this task failed because of blurry fingerprint patterns and severe background noises. In this paper, a new algorithm system specific for fingerprint orientation estimation is proposed, combining domain knowledge of handcraft methods and the generalization ability of DNN. System's preprocessing part roughly extracts effective information of input image with specially designed traditional method combination, then a Deep Regression Neural Network (DRNN) is adopted to predict the orientations fields, showing much faster convergence speed during training process than classification networks with the same backbone structure. Novel structure for DNN design is proposed to solve problem of discontinuity around 0° and increase prediction accuracy. Experimental results on test database proves that proposed algorithm system defeats state-of-the-art fingerprint orientation estimation algorithms.

Keywords: Fingerprint · Orientation field · DRNN

1 Introduction

As a biometric identification technology, automatic fingerprint recognition is widely used in judicial, government, commercial and financial fields because of its advantages such as easy access, strong operability and high reliability. Automatic fingerprint identification system (AFIS) [1] generally includes: fingerprint acquisition, image enhancement, feature extraction, matching and other parts. Since the 1990s, algorithms of each part of AFIS have been continuously improved [2–4].Due to the importance of fingerprint orientation, a large number of scholars have conducted research in this field to improve the accuracy of fingerprint recognition.

One of the commonly used methods is a gradient-based algorithm, which performs a difference operation on the latent image. Therefore, it is very sensitive to image quality. Hong et al. [5] improved this method. They proposed to filter the directional field with a low-pass filter while correcting the isolated wrong direction. Another is the model-based approach. This method mainly uses the global constraints to model the

V. Kůrková et al. (Eds.): ICANN 2018, LNCS 11141, pp. 436–446, 2018.
https://doi.org/10.1007/978-3-030-01424-7_43

orientation field mathematically. Sherlock et al. [6] proposed a zero-pole model that models the fingerprint orientation field based on the location of singular points. However, this method fails when there is no singularity in the fingerprint.

A few dictionary-based approaches have been proposed to improve latent orientation field estimation. Feng et al. [7] proposed a novel fingerprint orientation field extraction algorithm based on prior knowledge of fingerprint structure. The dictionary is constructed using a set of ground truth orientation fields, and the compatibility constraint among neighboring orientation patches. The dictionary-based approach has better generalization ability than the model-based approach, but its performance relies on large and diverse dictionaries, and results in higher computational cost.

Recent years, deep learning has made remarkable achievements in the field of pattern recognition. Convolutional neural networks (CNN) are widely used in image classification, object recognition, object detection and other fields [8–10]. Cao et al. [11] proposed a learning-based approach to classify the orientation field of a latent patch as one of a set of representative orientation patterns using a ConvNet. However, the pattern set's quality is directly affected by the quality of database. In 2017, Yao et al. [12] proposed an end-to-end deep convolutional network combining domain knowledge and the representation ability of deep learning. In terms of orientation field, a classification network based on DeepLab v2 [13] is adopted. This pipeline achieves better results with expert network-marked labels, but it still meets with difficult in convergence and is easy to drop into local optimal solution.

Inspired by abundant achievements on semantic segmentation [14] in recent years, we propose an effective orientation extraction framework for latent fingerprint. Considering the poor quality of latent images, we first design preprocessing method combining local total variation (LTV) decomposition, band-pass filter and Gabor filter on latent fingerprints so that input condition of the network is improved. Processed images are passed to the proposed Convolutional Neural Network for high accuracy orientation field prediction. Experimental results on test database proves that proposed algorithm system defeats state-of-the-art fingerprint orientation estimation algorithms.

The contributions of this paper are summarized as follows:

1. A new algorithm system specific for fingerprint orientation estimation consisting of preprocessing and deep neural network part. Domain knowledge and the generalization ability of network are combined in this system.
2. Effective preprocess to enhance the potential ridge structure of poor quality fingerprints by specially designed algorithm combination.
3. A novel deep regression neural network(DRNN) is proposed, with higher accuracy, faster training speed and less difficulty during convergence.
4. A new structure sources from traditional boosting algorithm is introduced into proposed DRNN, solving label discontinuity problem and significantly improve network performance.

2 Proposed Method

2.1 Methods Overview

The basic idea is to build an algorithm system specific for fingerprint orientation estimation. Recent years, many works [12, 19, 20] show the necessity and tendency of combining domain knowledge of traditional image algorithms with deep learning. Along this way, we propose an algorithm consists of preprocessing part and full convolutional network part. Firstly, preprocessing part is introduced, which roughly extracts effective information of input images with designed traditional method combination, including cartoon-texture decomposition and Gabor filtration. Secondly, we discuss how to construct a deep neural network predicting the partial orientations, and make full use of preprocessed fingerprints (Fig. 1).

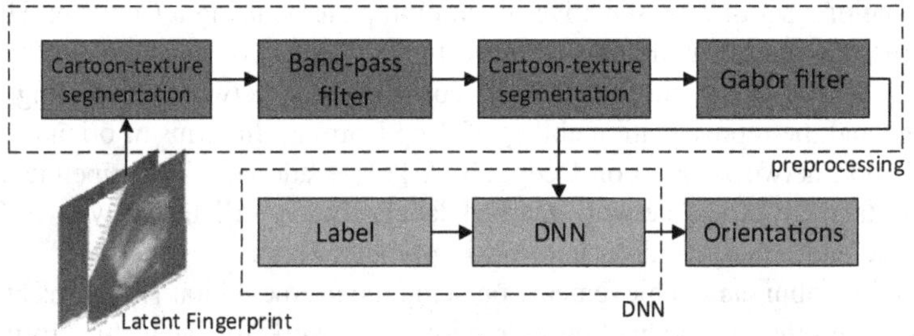

Fig. 1. The block diagram of the proposed method.

2.2 Latent Fingerprint Preprocessing

Firstly, the LTV model, a nonlinear filter pair which retains both the essential features of Meyer's models and the simplicity and rapidity of the linear model, is used to decompose images. Then, a Log-Gabor filter [15] is utilized to enhance the potential ridge structure in marked ROI. Each latent image is divided into non-overlapping blocks of 64 × 64 pixels. In order to avoid the edge effect of the filter, only 16 × 16 pixel in the center of the block is taken after filtering. In the frequency domain, two-dimensional Log-Gabor Transfer function is defined as two parts:

$$G(w) = exp\left(-[ln(w/w_0)]^2/2[ln(k/w_0)]^2\right) \tag{1}$$

$$G(\theta) = exp\left(-(\theta-\theta_0)^2/2\sigma_\theta^2\right) \tag{2}$$

The final Gabor filter can be obtained as follow:

$$G(w,\theta) = G(w)\cdot G(\theta) \tag{3}$$

Since the center frequency of Log-Gabor filter needs to be determined in advance, an automatic optimization method is used to find the appropriate frequency iteratively. Then, a set of 12 directional filters is generated which is used to obtain the responses in 12 directions, where two orientations with the highest responses are selected. Finally, the enhanced blocks are combined to generate the whole enhanced latent.

2.3 Deep Regression Neural Network

DRNN. Fingerprint orientation estimation can be regarded as a pixel level segmentation question after down-sampling. Instead of widely used classification networks for image segmentation [14], a deep regression neural network (DRNN) has been designed in this work. Outputs of the network are directly the predicted angles, allowing continuous value of estimation. Meanwhile, we find that with small sample and relatively large category quantity, it's hard for classification networks to convergence in practice. This is probably because in a segmentation network, the last layer divides every pixel into different classes. Structure of this layer can be regarded as an aggregation of classification outputs. The aggregation is much sparser than that of a single classification network. Suppose the aggregation's size is 20 * 20 * 90 (which is the condition in our network during training), then there will be 20 * 20 = 400 1 s in the aggrega-

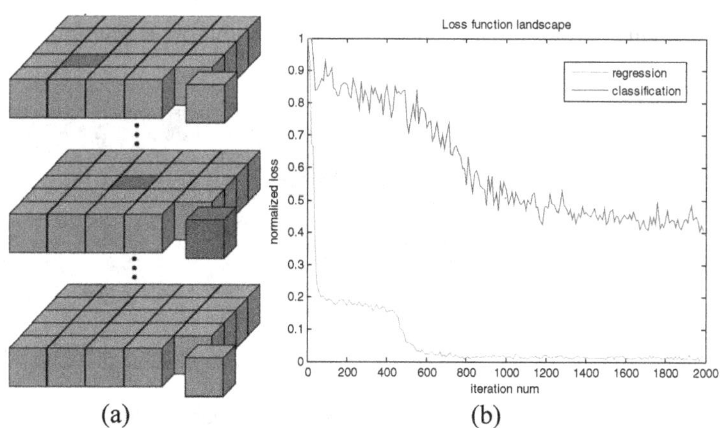

Fig. 2. (a) Demonstration of classification layer of segmentation network. It can be seen that positive samples (red) are much less than negative ones (blue), causing sample imbalance during training process. (b) Convergence curve of classification network (top) and regression network (bottom) with the same structure except the final output layer. X axis is number of training iterations and y axis is normalized loss. It can be seen that regression network's convergence speed is much faster. Loss of regression network tend to be stable after 800 iterations while that of classification network still keep on descending after 1800 iterations. It should be noticed that the final magnitude of losses don't represent two networks' performance (Color figure online).

tion, and 20 * 20 * 89 = 35600 zeros. Positive samples are far less than negative ones, which is demonstrated in Fig. 2. But a regression network has dense outputs. It can perfectly avoid this problem. Right one in Fig. 2 shows the loss decrease rate by training iteration of DRNN and classification network. Two networks are the same in backbone structures, and the only difference is the final layer.

Boosting Structure. Anew structure sources from traditional boosting algorithm is introduced into proposed DRNN's output part. Boosting is a general machine learning algorithm for improving the accuracy of any given learning algorithm [16]. Boosting algorithm requires different kinds of weak learning machines, and then fuse the output of all learning machines together with a certain strategy. As a result, boosting algorithm solves the problem of discontinuity around 0° and produce a much more accurate output.

Our expected outputs are angles range from 0 to 180°. Angles near 0 and those approaching 180° are continuous in physical meaning but have a huge gap in scale, which causes mutations in labels, as displayed in Fig. 3. This is the problem of discontinuity around 0°, and labels around 0° in physical meaning are called *bad zones* in rest of this paper. Convolutional layers have the property of smoothing neighborhood outputs, after which bad zone outputs will deviance. As shown in left one in Fig. 3, labels nearer to bad zone result in larger deviation in outputs. Output nearly changes 90° when label is close to 0°. For this reason, if the regression result is directly taken as final output, the proposed DRNN will be a weak learning machine in this situation. In this work, boosting algorithm is introduced to upgrade this weak learning machine.

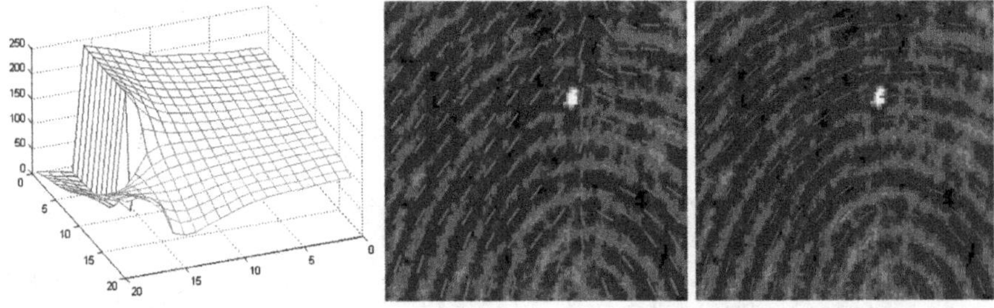

Fig. 3. Illustration of label discontinuity around 0° caused by angles' definition (left). Cliff-type descent is observed, which is extremely harmful for network performance. Example of network outputs with single pass way (middle) and after using boosting structure (right). It's clear that predictions biasing for around 90° in the middle are corrected by boosting structure.

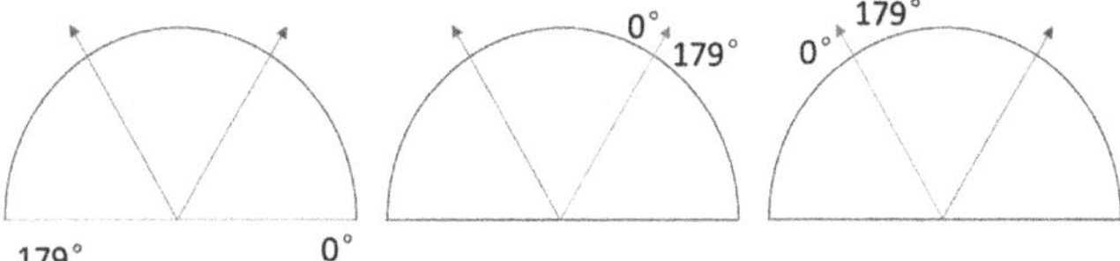

Fig. 4. Demonstration of angles' definitions in 3 pass ways. Angles increase along the counterclockwise. The last two pass ways' 0 and 180° are defined as the first one's 60° and 120° respectively.

Instead of only one layer of outputs (angles), the network has been adjusted to 3 the same pass ways, but each pass way has a different 0° definition. Figure 4 shows degree definitions of three pass ways, in which definitions for pass way 2 and 3 can be transformed from pass way 1 by (4) and (5). After this process, bad zone of 3 pass ways will not overlap.

$$x2' = \begin{cases} x2 + 120, x2 < 60 \\ x2 - 60, x2 \geq 60 \end{cases} \tag{4}$$

$$x3' = \begin{cases} x3 + 60, x3 < 120 \\ x3 - 120, x3 \geq 120 \end{cases} \tag{5}$$

Outputs of three pass ways are first reversed to normal definition, and output 1, 2, 3 are single results of three pass ways at the same position respectively. Then output strategy of this network is: if difference of output 1 and 2 is less than 10°, output is the average of first 2 output channels, or output will be the last one. Kindly sacrificing the simplicity of network, bad zones' impact have been eliminated, causing large improvement in output accuracy. Detailed data is displayed in experiments section.

Network Architecture. In practice, images of fingerprints are different in size and aspect ratio, so a full convolutional network has been proposed for this task. The first part of the network are 3 Conv-ReLu blocks. Instead of pooling, a Conv layer with stride 2 is used in each block to compress the variables, totally 8 times down-sampling. This is because pooling layers can create an invariance to small shifts and distortions [17], which is advantage in object detection tasks, but this task is sensitive to partial rotation. According to the results in [18], kernel size of the first part has been adjusted to 7 * 7, 5 * 5 and 3 * 3 respectively (Fig. 5).

Second part of the network used ASPP [13] layers of the same size in 3 parallel passing ways. In each passing way 2 atrous convolutional layers have been deployed with different sample rates. Both layers' feature maps are fused together. The final layer is the direct overlap of three pass ways' output. Implementing boosting algorithm, predicted orientation field is produced.

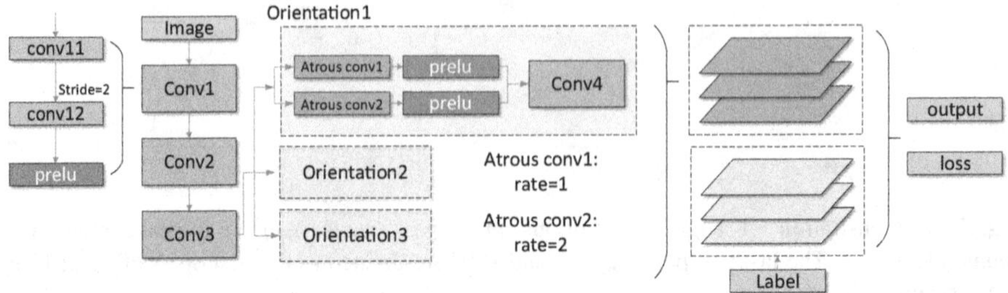

Fig. 5. Detailed network architecture. Pooling layers are replaced by striding 2 convolutional layers. Each passing way generates area information in two different scales. Three pass ways are the same in kernel sizes, consisting a whole boosting structure.

Label, Loss Function and Training. As second part of network has three pass ways, labels are also transformed to match the designed regression results. Instead of traditional quadratic error between label and regression results, the loss function is defined as:

$$loss = \frac{1}{NM}\sum((1 - \left(20 \cdot labels - 1)^2\right) \cdot 100\left(new\_labels - reg\_result)^2\right) \tag{6}$$

Where N is size of output orientation field, M is batch size, reg_result represents the regression result of network's second part, $labels$ is original labels, and new_labels means transformed labels. According to scale of loss, scale of labels can be adjusted by multiplying a constant. To some extent, DRNN's convergence speed can be controlled in this way. After experiments, rather than [0,180), we found smaller labels mapped into range [0, 0.01) help the network to convergence much easier. To improve the accuracy of results, a weight $((1 - \left(20 \cdot labels - 1)^2\right)$ is added to the loss function, thus bad zones get ignorable weights. We don't care what bad zones predict and only consider the accuracy of effective areas. To speed up training process and improve network performance, input images are all normalized and masked at first.

After reversing the regression result to one channel using the method in boosting structure, accuracy is defined like:

$$accuracy = 1 - \frac{\sum|labels - output|}{N} \tag{7}$$

In training process, to increase samples' number, we segmented the training images into overlapping 160 × 160 blocks. Latent fingerprints are straightly used as inputs. Labels' quality were worse than library fingerprints, but fingerprints' patterns were the same with required inputs. In testing process, we used test images directly as input because the input size of our system are not constrained, and impact of edge effect can be eliminated.

3 Experiments

3.1 Database

Database used in this paper is collected by *Beijing Hisign Technology Co., Ltd*, winner of FVC-Ongoing 2017. Fingerprints are divided into 2 groups: library fingerprints and latent fingerprints, every latent image has its matched library fingerprint image, totally 2164 pairs. 500 pairs are made into testing samples and the rest are used for training. Each latent fingerprint is 512 × 512 pixels in size and 500 ppi in this paper, and library fingerprints are 640 × 640 pixels and 500 ppi. Latent images' orientations are to be detected and used to enhance input latent fingerprints. Lacking of ground truth orientation information, labels are produced by fingerprint recognition SDK of *Beijing Hisign Technology Co., Ltd.*. Library fingerprints' labels are more accurate, while latent images' output labels will include more mistakes.

3.2 Identification Performance

To test the quality of our output orientations, an objective comparison with other methods is made. Gabor-based algorithm extracts orientation field on Gabor phase. Template -based algorithm extracts orientation fields by first clustering label block templates, then classifying fingerprint blocks into templates with a learned deep learning network. FingerNet is re-trained and tested using the same data set with ours. FingerNet extract orientation field with a learnt fully convolutional network based on DeepLab v2. As our labels were collected using Hisign SDK, SDK's performance is also considered. After getting the output orientation fields of each methods, the same reinforcement method has been used to fuse the orientation information and latent fingerprint images. Finally, Hisign SDK was used to get the matching accuracy of each method. Results are shown in Table 1.

Table 1. Matching results of each method on testing dataset

Method	Top1	Top5	Top20	Top50
Hisign SDK	425/500	456/500	472/500	479/500
Gabor	406/500	441/500	462/500	471/500
Cao et al.	239/500	275/500	296/500	304/500
FingerNet	419/500	449/500	469/500	478/500
Proposed	427/500	459/500	473/500	481/500
Proposed (no boosting)	279/500	306/500	322/500	327/500
Proposed (no preprocess)	421/500	452/500	470/500	478/500

The Cumulative Match Characteristic (CMC) curves of above seven methods on 500 latent images are shown in Fig. 6. Following the control variable principle, FingerNet(yellow) is re-trained and tested using the same data set with ours. For more convenient comparison, the results of some methods are placed separately in another figure shown below. Thus, we can see the trend of the curve of fingerprint recognition rate clearly.

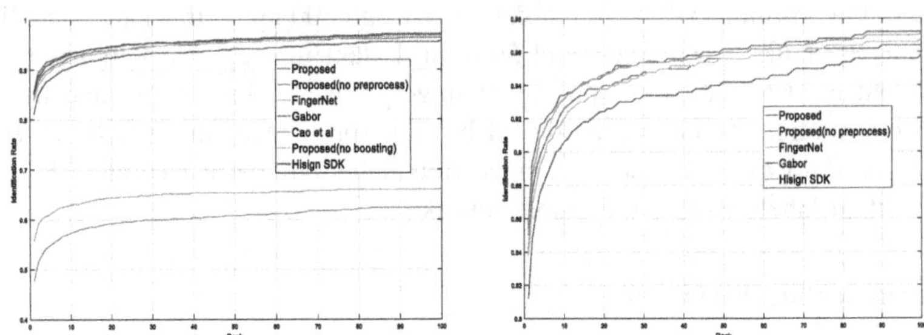

Fig. 6. Identification performance (CMC curves) of different algorithms on all 500 latents.

The results show our method made an accuracy of over 85% in top 1 matching test, which is undoubtedly better than Gabor or masking method. The result is also 1.6 percent higher than the result of FingerNet's outputs. Boosting algorithm and preprocess make clear contribution to the improvement of output quality. Comparing with SDK's result, our method get some increase in accuracy, which means the network has the ability of generalization and corrects some mistakes made by SDK.

Figure 7 shows threshold-recall curves of proposed method and FingerNet. Recall is defined as proportion of test images with average angular precision higher than threshold. It shows that proposed method gets results closer to labels than FingerNet. Figure 8 compares the orientation fields from top 2 algorithms on latent fingerprints visually while the original latent image is also given. We observe that the proposed algorithm outperforms the other algorithms on latent fingerprints.

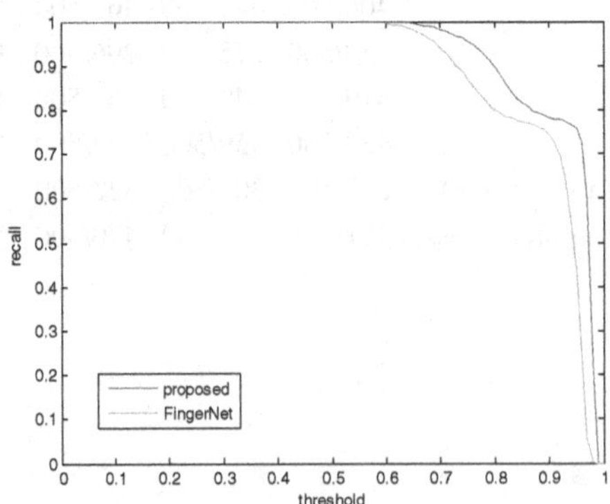

Fig. 7. Threshold-recall curves of proposed method and FingerNet.

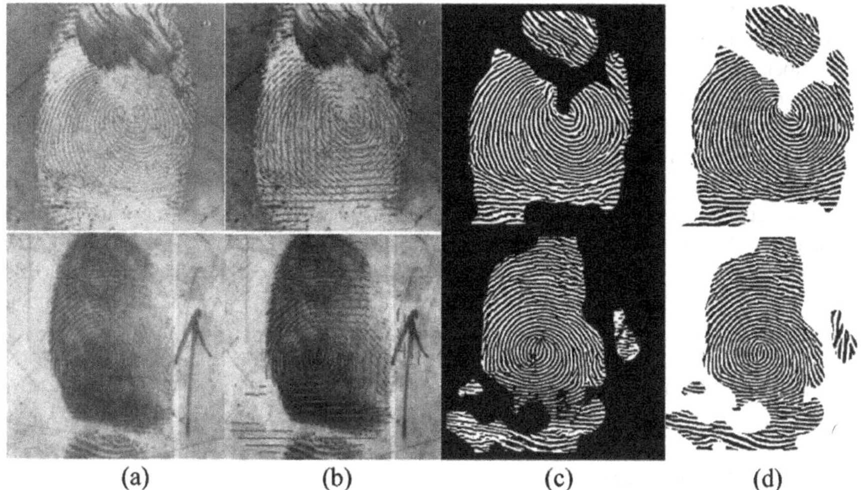

Fig. 8. Result comparison of different methods on different cropped latents shown in column (a). Original fingerprints (b) Orientation fields obtained by proposed method and (c)–(d) enhancement images obtained by proposed method and SDK method.

4 Conclusion and Future Work

We propose a whole system to produce more accuracy orientation fields of latent fingerprints, including preprocess and orientation estimation. This system has combined domain knowledge got from preprocess and contextual information generated by deep learning method to outperform other orientation estimation algorithms. For better and faster training of the network, not classification but regression network was designed to get the output orientation field. To eliminate error in bad zones, boosting algorithm and new structure is adopted in network design.

Future work will include (1) integration of the whole system, (2) optimization of the network and preprocess, (3) extending this system to reinforcement and matching.

Acknowledgement. We would like to thank *Beijing Hisign Technology Co., Ltd.* and *Cross-strait Tsinghua Research Institute* for providing essential resource and support to us.

References

1. Maltoni, D., Maio, D., Jain, A.K., Prabhakar, S.: Handbook of Fingerprint Recognition. Springer, London (2003). https://doi.org/10.1007/b97303
2. Jain, A.K., Feng, J., Nandakumar, K.: Fingerprint matching. Computer **43**(2), 36–44 (2010)
3. Conti, V., et al.: Fast fingerprints classification only using the directional image. In: Apolloni, B., Howlett, R.J., Jain, L. (eds.) KES 2007. LNCS (LNAI), vol. 4692, pp. 34–41. Springer, Heidelberg (2007). https://doi.org/10.1007/978-3-540-74819-9_5
4. Jiang, X., Liu, M., Kot, A.C.: Fingerprint retrieval for identification. IEEE Trans. Inf. Foren. Secur. **1**(4), 532–542 (2006)

5. Hong, L., Wan, Y., Jain, A.: Fingerprint image enhancement: algorithm and performance evaluation. IEEE Trans. Pattern Anal. Mach. Intell. **20**(8), 777–789 (1970)
6. Sherlock, B.G., Monro, D.M.: A model for interpreting fingerprint topology. Pattern Recogn. **26**(7), 1047–1055 (1993)
7. Feng, J., Zhou, J., Jain, A.K.: Orientation field estimation for latent fingerprint enhancement. IEEE Trans. Pattern Anal. Mach. Intell. **35**(4), 925–940 (2013)
8. Krizhevsky, A., Sutskever, I., Hinton, G.E.: ImageNet classification with deep convolutional neural networks. In: International Conference on Neural Information Processing Systems, pp. 1097–1105. Curran Associates Inc (2012)
9. Redmon, J., et al.: You only look once: unified, real-time object detection. In: IEEE Conference on Computer Vision and Pattern Recognition, pp. 779–788. IEEE Computer Society (2016)
10. Liu, W., et al.: SSD: single shot MultiBox detector. In: Leibe, B., Matas, J., Sebe, N., Welling, M. (eds.) ECCV 2016. LNCS, vol. 9905, pp. 21–37. Springer, Cham (2016). https://doi.org/10.1007/978-3-319-46448-0_2
11. Cao, K., Jain, A.K.: Latent orientation field estimation via convolutional neural network. In: International Conference on Biometrics, pp. 349–356. IEEE (2015)
12. Tang, Y., et al.: FingerNet: an unified deep network for fingerprint minutiae extraction. In: IEEE International Joint Conference on Biometrics, pp. 108–116. IEEE (2017)
13. Chen, L.C., Papandreou, G., Kokkinos, I., et al.: DeepLab: semantic image segmentation with deep convolutional nets, atrous convolution, and fully connected CRFs. IEEE Trans. Pattern Anal. Mach. Intell. **PP**(99), 1 (2017)
14. Shelhamer, E., Long, J., Darrell, T.: Fully convolutional networks for semantic segmentation. IEEE Trans. Pattern Anal. Mach. Intell. **39**(4), 640 (2014)
15. Buades, A., Le, T.M., Morel, J.M., et al.: Fast cartoon + texture image filters. IEEE Trans. Image Process. **19**(8), 1978 (2010)
16. Schapire, R.E.: The boosting approach to machine learning: an overview. In: Denison, D.D., Hansen, M.H., Holmes, C.C., Mallick, B., Yu, B. (eds.) Nonlinear Estimation and Classification. Lecture Notes in Statistics, vol. 171. Springer, New York (2003). https://doi.org/10.1007/978-0-387-21579-2_9
17. Lecun, Y., Bengio, Y., Hinton, G.: Deep learning. Nature **521**(7553), 436 (2015)
18. Simonyan, K., Zisserman, A.: Very deep convolutional networks for large-scale image recognition. In: Computer Science (2014)
19. Schuch, P., Schulz, S.-D., Busch, C.: ConvNet regression for fingerprint orientations. In: Sharma, P., Bianchi, F.M. (eds.) SCIA 2017. LNCS, vol. 10269, pp. 325–336. Springer, Cham (2017). https://doi.org/10.1007/978-3-319-59126-1_27
20. Liu, S., Pan, J., Yang, M.-H.: Learning recursive filters for low-level vision via a hybrid neural network. In: Leibe, B., Matas, J., Sebe, N., Welling, M. (eds.) ECCV 2016. LNCS, vol. 9908, pp. 560–576. Springer, Cham (2016). https://doi.org/10.1007/978-3-319-46493-0_34

Avoiding Degradation in Deep Feed-Forward Networks by Phasing Out Skip-Connections

Ricardo Pio Monti(✉), Sina Tootoonian, and Robin Cao

Gatsby Computational Neuroscience Unit, UCL, London W1T 4JG, UK
{r.monti,s.tootoonian,r.cao}@ucl.ac.uk

Abstract. A widely observed phenomenon in deep learning is the degradation problem: increasing the depth of a network leads to a decrease in performance on both test *and* training data. Novel architectures such as ResNets and Highway networks have addressed this issue by introducing various flavors of skip-connections or gating mechanisms. However, the degradation problem persists in the context of plain feed-forward networks. In this work we propose a simple method to address this issue. The proposed method poses the learning of weights in deep networks as a constrained optimization problem where the presence of skip-connections is penalized by Lagrange multipliers. This allows for skip-connections to be introduced during the early stages of training and subsequently phased out in a principled manner. We demonstrate the benefits of such an approach with experiments on MNIST, fashion-MNIST, CIFAR-10 and CIFAR-100 where the proposed method is shown to greatly decrease the degradation effect and is often competitive with ResNets.

Keywords: Degradation · Shattered/vanishing gradients
Skip-connections

1 Introduction

The *representation view* of deep learning suggests that neural networks learn an increasingly abstract representation of input data in a hierarchical fashion [7,8,25]. Such representations may then be exploited to perform various tasks such as image classification, machine translation and speech recognition.

A natural conclusion of the representation view is that deeper networks will learn more detailed and abstract representations as a result of their increased capacity. However, in the case of feed-forward networks it has been observed that performance deteriorates beyond a certain depth, even when the network is applied to training data. Recently, Residual Networks (ResNets; [10]) and Highway Networks [21] have demonstrated that introducing various flavors of skip-connections or gating mechanisms makes it possible to train increasingly deep networks. However, the aforementioned degradation problem persists in

V. Kůrková et al. (Eds.): ICANN 2018, LNCS 11141, pp. 447–456, 2018.
https://doi.org/10.1007/978-3-030-01424-7_44

the case of plain deep networks (i.e., networks without skip-connections of some form).

A widely held hypothesis explaining the success of ResNets is that the introduction of skip-connections serves to improve the conditioning of the optimization manifold as well as the statistical properties of gradients employed during training. [19,20] show that the introduction of specially designed skip-connections serves to diagonalize the Fisher information matrix, thereby bringing standard gradient steps closer to the natural gradient. More recently, [1] demonstrated that the introduction of skip-connections helps retain the correlation structure across gradients. This is contrary to the gradients of deep feed-forward networks, which resemble white noise. More generally, the skip-connections are seen to reduce the effects of vanishing gradients by introducing a linear term [11].

The goal of this work is to address the degradation issue in plain feed-forward networks by leveraging some of the desirable optimization properties of ResNets. We approach the task of learning parameters for a deep network under the framework of constrained optimization. This strategy allows us to introduce skip-connections penalized by Lagrange multipliers into the architecture of our network. In our setting, skip-connections play an important role during the initial training of the network and are subsequently removed in a principled manner. Throughout a series of experiments we demonstrate that such an approach leads to improvements in generalization error when compared to architectures without skip-connections and is competitive with ResNets in some cases. The contributions of this work are as follows:

- We propose an alternative training strategy for plain feed-forward networks which reduces the degradation in performance as the depth of the network increases. The proposed method introduces skip-connections which are penalized by Lagrange multipliers. This allows for the presence of skip-connections to be iteratively phased out during training in a principled manner. The proposed method is thereby able to enjoy the optimization benefits associated with skip-connections during the early stages of training.
- A number of benchmark datasets are used to demonstrate the empirical capabilities of the proposed method. In particular, the proposed method greatly reduces the degradation effect compared to plain networks and is on several occasions competitive with ResNets.

2 Related Work

The hierarchical nature of many feed-forward networks is loosely inspired by the structure of the visual cortex where neurons in early layers capture simple features (e.g., edges) which are subsequently aggregated in deeper layers [14]. This interpretation of neural networks suggests that the depth of a network should be maximized, thereby allowing the network to learn more abstract (and hopefully useful) representations [3]. However, a widely reported phenomenon is that deeper networks are more difficult to train. This is often termed the degradation effect in deep networks [10,21]. This effect has been partially attributed to optimization challenges such as vanishing and shattered gradients [1,12].

In the past these challenges have been partially addressed via the use of supervised and unsupervised pre-training [2] and more recently through careful parameter initialization [6,9] and batch normalization [15]. In the past couple of years further improvements have been obtained via the introduction of skip-connections. ResNets [10,11] introduce residual blocks consisting of a residual function $\mathcal{F}$ together with a skip-connection. Formally, the residual block is defined as:

$$\mathbf{x}_{l+1} = \mathcal{F}_l(\mathbf{x}_l, \mathbf{W}_l) + \mathbf{W}'_l \mathbf{x}_l \tag{1}$$

where $\mathcal{F}_l : \mathbb{R}^n \to \mathbb{R}^{n'}$ represents some combination of affine transformation, non-linearity and batch normalization parameterized by $\mathbf{W}_l$. The matrix $\mathbf{W}'_l$ parameterizes a linear projection to ensure the dimensions are aligned[1]. More generally, ResNets are closely related to Highway Networks [21] where the output of each layer is defined as:

$$\mathbf{x}_{l+1} = \mathcal{F}_l(\mathbf{x}_l, \mathbf{W}_l) \cdot \mathcal{T}(\mathbf{x}_l, \mathbf{H}_l) + \mathbf{x}_l \cdot (1 - \mathcal{T}(\mathbf{x}_l, \mathbf{H}_l)), \tag{2}$$

where $\cdot$ denotes element-wise multiplication. In Highway Networks the output of each layer is determined by a gating function:

$$\mathcal{T}(\mathbf{x}_l, \mathbf{H}_l) = \text{sigmoid}\ (\mathbf{H}_l \mathbf{x}_l)$$

inspired from LSTMs. We note that both ResNets and Highway Networks were introduced with the explicit goal of training deeper networks.

Recently, the goal of learning deep networks without skip-connections has begun to receive more attention. [24] propose a novel re-parameterization of weights in feed-forward networks which they call the Dirac parameterization. Instead of explicitly adding a skip-connection, they model the weights as a residual of the Dirac function, effectively moving the skip-connection inside the non-linearity. In related work, [1] propose to initialize weights in a CReLU activation function in order to preserve linearity during the initial phases of training. This is achieved by initializing the weights in a mirrored block structure. During training the weights are allowed to diverge, resulting in non-linear activations.

Finally, we note that while the aforementioned approaches have sought to train deeper networks via modifications to the network architecture (i.e., by adding skip-connections) success has also been obtained by modifying the non-linearities [5,16].

---

[1] Unless stated otherwise we will assume $\mathcal{F}$ retains the dimension of $\mathbf{x}_l$ and set $\mathbf{W}'_l$ to the identity.

3 Variable Activation Networks

The goal of this work is to train deep feed-forward networks without suffering from the degradation problem described in previous sections. To set notation, we denote $\mathbf{x}_0$ as the input and $\mathbf{x}_L$ as the output of a feed-forward network with L layers. Given training data $\{\mathbf{y}, \mathbf{x}_0\}$ it is possible to learn parameters $\{\mathbf{W}_l\}_{l=1}^L$ by locally minimizing some objective function

$$\{\hat{\mathbf{W}}_l\}_{l=1}^L = \arg\min\ \mathcal{C}\left(\mathbf{y}, \mathbf{x}_L; \{\mathbf{W}_l\}_{l=1}^L\right). \tag{3}$$

First-order methods are typically employed due to the complexity of the objective function in Eq. (3). However, directly minimizing the objective is not practical in the context of deep networks: beyond a certain depth performance quickly deteriorates on both test *and* training data. Such a phenomenon does not occur in the presence of skip-connections. Accordingly, we take inspiration from ResNets and propose to modify Eq. (1) in the following manner:

$$\mathbf{x}_{l+1} = \mathcal{F}_l(\mathbf{x}_l, \mathbf{W}_l) + (1 - \boldsymbol{\alpha}_l) \cdot \mathbf{x}_l \tag{4}$$

where $\boldsymbol{\alpha}_l \in [0,1]^n$ determines the weighting given to the skip-connection. More specifically, $\boldsymbol{\alpha}_l$ is a vector were the entry i dictates the presence and magnitude of a skip-connection for neuron i in layer l. Due to the variable nature of parameters $\boldsymbol{\alpha}_l$ in Eq. (4), we refer to networks employing such residual blocks as Variable Activation Networks (VAN).

The objective of the proposed method is to train a feed-forward network under the constraint that $\boldsymbol{\alpha}_l = \mathbf{1}$ for all layers, l. When the constraint is satisfied all skip-connections are removed. The advantage of such a strategy is that we only require $\boldsymbol{\alpha}_l = \mathbf{1}$ at the *end* of training. This allows us to initialize $\boldsymbol{\alpha}_l$ to some other value, thereby relaxing the optimization problem and obtaining the advantages associated with ResNets during the early stages of training. In particular, whenever $\boldsymbol{\alpha}_l \neq \mathbf{1}$ information is allowed to flow through the skip-connections, alleviating issues associated with shattered and vanishing gradients.

As a result of the equality constraint on $\boldsymbol{\alpha}_l$, the proposed activation function effectively does not introduce any additional parameters. All remaining weights can be trained by solving the following constrained optimization problem:

$$\{\hat{\mathbf{W}}_l\}_{l=1}^L = \operatorname{argmin} \mathcal{C}\left(\mathbf{y}, \mathbf{x}_L; \{\mathbf{W}_l, \boldsymbol{\alpha}_l\}_{l=1}^L\right) \text{ such that } \alpha_l = \mathbf{1} \text{ for } l = 1, \ldots, L. \tag{5}$$

The associated Lagrangian takes the following simple form [4]:

$$\mathcal{L} = \mathcal{C}\left(\mathbf{y}, \mathbf{x}_L; \{\mathbf{W}_l, \boldsymbol{\alpha}_l\}_{l=1}^L\right) + \sum_{l=1}^{L} \boldsymbol{\lambda}_l^T (\boldsymbol{\alpha}_l - \mathbf{1}), \tag{6}$$

where each $\boldsymbol{\lambda}_l \in \mathbb{R}^n$ are the Lagrange multipliers associated with the constraints on $\boldsymbol{\alpha}_l$. In practice, we iteratively update $\boldsymbol{\alpha}_l$ via stochastic gradients descent (SGD) steps of the form:

$$\boldsymbol{\alpha}_l \leftarrow \boldsymbol{\alpha}_l - \eta \left(\frac{\partial \mathcal{C}}{\partial \boldsymbol{\alpha}_l} + \boldsymbol{\lambda}_l \right) \tag{7}$$

where η is the step-size parameter for SGD. Throughout the experiments we will often take the non-linearity in $\mathcal{F}_l$ to be ReLU. Although not strictly required, we clip the values $\boldsymbol{\alpha}_l$ to ensure they remain in the interval $[0, 1]^n$.

From Eq. (6), we have that the gradients with respect to Lagrange multipliers are of the form:

$$\boldsymbol{\lambda}_l \leftarrow \boldsymbol{\lambda}_l + \eta' \left(\boldsymbol{\alpha}_l - \mathbf{1} \right), \tag{8}$$

We note that since we require $\boldsymbol{\alpha}_l \in [0, 1]^n$, the values of $\boldsymbol{\lambda}_l$ are monotonically decreasing. As the value of Lagrange multiplier decreases, this in turn pushes $\boldsymbol{\alpha}_l$ towards $\mathbf{1}$ in Eq. (7). We set the step-size for the Lagrange multipliers, η', to be a fraction of η. The motivation behind such a choice is to allow the network to adjust as we enforce the constraint on $\boldsymbol{\alpha}_l$.

4 Experiments

We present experiments to demonstrate that the proposed method is able to effectively alleviate the degradation problem in deep networks. We first demonstrate the capabilities of the proposed method using a simple, non-convolutional architecture on the MNIST and Fashion-MNIST datasets [22] in Sect. 4.1. More extensive comparisons are then considered on the CIFAR datasets [17] in Sect. 4.2.

4.1 MNIST and Fashion-MNIST

Networks of varying depths were trained on both MNIST and Fashion-MNIST datasets. Following [21] the networks employed in this section were *thin*, with each layer containing 50 hidden units. In all networks the first layer was a fully connected plain layer followed by l layers or residual blocks (depending on the architecture) and a final softmax layer. The proposed method is benchmarked against several popular architectures such as ResNets and Highway Networks as well as the recently proposed DiracNets [24]. Plain networks without skip-connections are also considered. Finally, we also considered VAN network where the constraint $\boldsymbol{\alpha}_l = \mathbf{1}$ was not enforced. This corresponds to the case where $\boldsymbol{\lambda}_l = 0$ for all l. This comparison is included in order to study the capacity and flexibility of VAN networks without the need to satisfy the constraint to remove skip-connections. For clarity, we refer to such networks as VAN ($\lambda = 0$) networks. For all architectures the ReLU activation function was employed together with batch-normalization. In the case of ResNets and VAN, the residual function consisted of batch-normalization followed by ReLU and a linear projection.

The depth of the network varied from $l = 1$ to $l = 30$ hidden layers. All networks were trained using SGD with momentum. The learning rate is fixed at $\eta = 0.001$ and the momentum parameter at 0.9. Training consisted of 50 epochs with a batch-size of 128. In the case of VAN networks the $\boldsymbol{\alpha}_l$ values were initialized to 0 for all layers. As such, during the initial stages of training VAN networks where equivalent to ResNets. The step-size parameter for Lagrange multipliers, η', was set to be one half of the SGD step-size, η. Finally, all Lagrange multipliers, $\boldsymbol{\lambda}_l$, are initialized to -1.

Results. The results are shown in Fig. 1 where the test accuracy is shown as a function of the network depth for both the MNIST and Fashion-MNIST datasets. In both cases we see clear evidence of the degradation effect: the performance of plain networks deteriorates significantly once the network depth exceeds some critical value (approximately 10 layers). As would be expected, this is not the case for ResNets, Highway Networks and DiracNets as such architectures have been explicitly designed to avoid this behavior. We note that VAN networks do not suffer such a pronounced degradation as the depth increases. This provides evidence that the gradual removal of skip-connections via Lagrange multipliers leads to improved generalization performance compared to plain networks. Finally, we note that VAN networks obtain competitive results across all depths. Further, we note that VAN ($\lambda = 0$) networks, where no constraint is placed on skip-connections, obtain competitive results across all depths.

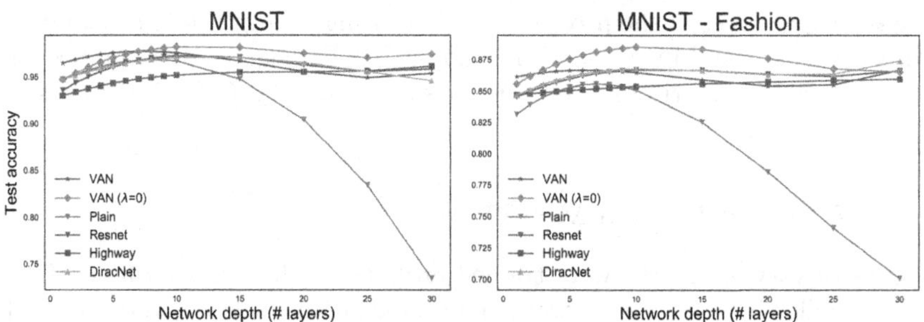

Fig. 1. Results on MNIST (left) and fashion-MNIST (right) for various different architectures as the depth of the network varies from 1 to 30. Mean average test accuracy over 10 independent training sessions is shown. We note that with the exception of plain networks, the performance of all remaining architectures is stable as the number of layers increases.

4.2 CIFAR

As a more challenging benchmark we consider the CIFAR-10 and CIFAR-100 datasets. These consist of 60000 32 × 32 pixel color images with 10 and 100 classes respectively. The datasets are divided into 50000 training images and 10000 test images.

We follow [10] and train deep convolutional networks consisting of four blocks each consisting of n residual layers, consisting of residual functions of the form `conv-BN-ReLU-conv-BN-ReLU`. This corresponds to the *pre-activation* function [11]. The convolutional layers consist of 3×3 filters with downsampling at the beginning of blocks 2, 3 and 4. The network ends with a fully connected softmax layer, resulting in a depth of $8n + 2$.

Networks were trained using SGD with momentum over 165 epochs. The learning rate was set to $\eta = 0.1$ and divided by 10 at the 82nd and 125th epoch. The momentum parameter was set to 0.9. Networks were trained using mini-batches of size 128. Data augmentation followed [18]: this involved random cropping and horizontal flips. Weights were initialized following [9]. As in Sect. 4.1, we initialize $\boldsymbol{\alpha}_l = 0$ for all layers. Furthermore, we set the step-size parameter for the Lagrange multipliers, η', to be one tenth of η and all Lagrange multipliers, $\boldsymbol{\lambda}_l$, are initialized to -1. On CIFAR-10 we ran experiments with $n \in \{1, 2, 3, 4, 5, 6, 8, 10\}$ yielding networks with depths ranging from 10 to 82. For CIFAR-100 experiments were run with $n \in \{1, 2, 3, 4\}$.

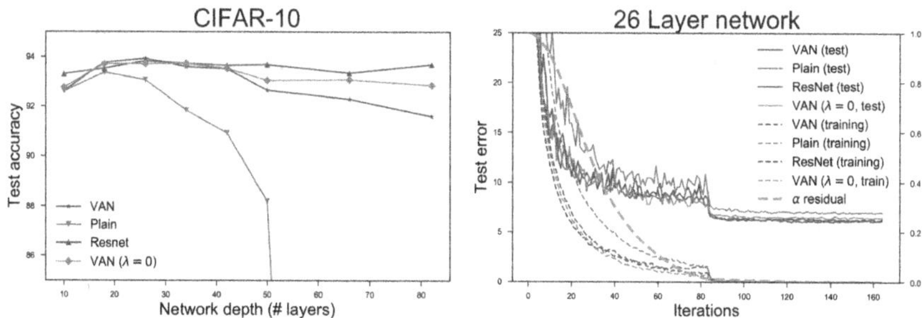

Fig. 2. Left: Results on CIFAR-10 dataset are shown as the depth of networks increase. We note that the performance of both VAN and plain networks deteriorates as the depth increases, but the effect is far less pronounced for VAN networks. **Right:** Training and test error curves are shown for networks with 26 layers. We also plot the mean α residuals: $\frac{1}{L}\sum_{l=1}^{L}(\mathbf{1} - \boldsymbol{\alpha}_l)^2$ on the right axis.

Results. Results for experiments on CIFAR-10 are shown in Fig. 2. The left panel shows the mean test accuracy over five independent training sessions for ResNets, VAN, VAN ($\lambda = 0$) and plain networks. While plain networks provide competitive results for networks with fewer than 30 layers, their performance quickly deteriorates thereafter. We note that a similar phenomenon is observed in VAN networks but the effect is not as dramatic. In particular, the performance of VANs is similar to ResNets for networks with up to 40 layers. Beyond this depth, ResNets outperform VAN by an increasing margin. This holds true for both VAN and VAN ($\lambda = 0$) networks, however, the difference is reduced in magnitude in the case of VAN ($\lambda = 0$) networks. These results are in line with [11], who argue that scalar modulated skip-connections (as is the case in VANs where the scalar is $\mathbf{1} - \boldsymbol{\alpha}_l$) will either vanish or explode in very deep networks whenever the scalar is not the identity.

The right panel of Fig. 2 shows the training and test error for a 26 layer network. We note that throughout all iterations, both the test and train accuracy of the VAN network dominates that of the plain network. The thick gold line indicates the mean residuals of the $\boldsymbol{\alpha}_l$ parameters across all layers. This is defined as $\frac{1}{L}\sum_{l=1}^{L}(\mathbf{1} - \boldsymbol{\alpha}_l)^2$ and is a measure of the extent to which skip-connections are present in the network. Recall that if all $\boldsymbol{\alpha}_l$ values are set to one then all skip-connections are removed (see Eq. (4)). From Fig. 2, it follows that skip-connections are fully removed from the VAN network at approximately the 120th iteration.

A comparison of the performance of VAN networks in provided in Table 1. We note that while VAN networks do not outperform ResNets, they do outperform other alternatives such as Highway networks when networks of similar depths considered. However, it is important to note that Highway networks did not employ batch-normalization, which is a strong regularizer. In the case of both VAN and VAN ($\lambda = 0$) networks, the best performance is obtained with networks of 26 layers while ResNets continue to improve their performance as depth increases. Finally, current state-of-the-art performance, obtained by Wide ResNets [23] and DenseNets [13], are also provided in Table 1.

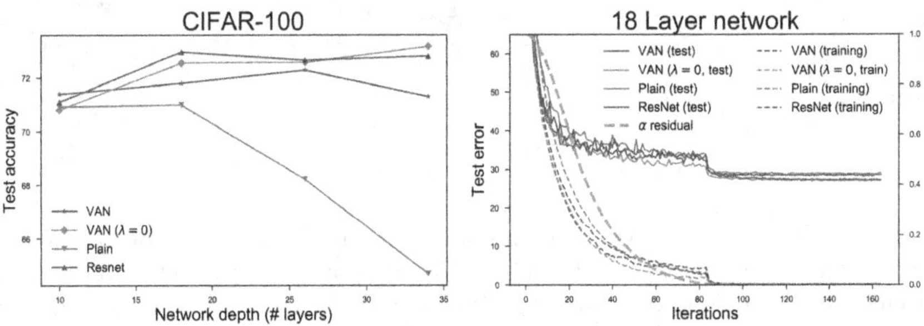

Fig. 3. Left: Results on CIFAR-100 dataset are shown as the depth increases from 10 to 34 layers. We note that the performance of both VAN and plain networks deteriorates as the depth increases, but the effect is far less pronounced for plain networks. **Right:** Training and test error curves are shown for VAN and plain networks with 18 layers. The mean α residuals, $\frac{1}{L}\sum_{l=1}^{L}(\mathbf{1} - \boldsymbol{\alpha}_l)^2$, are shown in gold along the right axis.

Figure 3 provides results on the CIFAR-100 dataset. This dataset is considerably more challenging as it consists of a larger number of classes as well as fewer examples per class. As in the case of CIFAR-10, we observe a fall in the performance of both VAN and plain networks beyond a certain depth; in this case approximately 20 layers for plain networks and 30 layers for VANs. Despite this drop in performance, Table 1 indicates that the performance of VAN networks with both 18 and 26 layers are competitive with many alternatives proposed in the literature. Furthermore, we note that the performance of VAN ($\lambda = 0$) networks is competitive with ResNets in the context of the CIFAR-100 dataset.

Training curves are shown on the right hand side of Fig. 3. As in the equivalent plot for CIFAR-10, the introduction and subsequent removal of skip-connections during training leads to improvements in generalization error.

Table 1. Comparison of VAN networks results (test error %) on CIFAR-10 and CIFAR-100. For VAN networks we report the best value as well as the mean and standard deviation over five independent training runs. We add a * to denote results which did not employ batch-normalization.

Architecture	# Layers	CIFAR-10	CIFAR-100
Highway Network*	32	8.80	-
Highway Network*	19	7.54	32.39
DiracNet (width-1)	34	7.10	-
ELU*	18	6.55	24.28
VAN ($\lambda = 0$)	26	6.29 (6.40 ± 0.16)	27.04 (27.42 ± 0.26)
VAN ($\lambda = 0$)	34	6.28 (6.45 ± 0.14)	26.46 (26.81 ± 0.31)
VAN	18	6.23 (6.49 ± 0.16)	28.20 (28.42 ± 0.36)
VAN	26	6.08 (6.35 ± 0.21)	27.70 (28.01 ± 0.39)
DiracNet (width-2)	34	5.60	26.72
ResNet	164	5.46	24.33
Wide ResNet (width-10)	28	4.00	19.25
DenseNet	160	3.46	17.18

5 Discussion

This manuscript presents a simple method for training deep feed-forward networks which greatly reduces the degradation problem. In the past, the degradation issue has been successfully addressed via the introduction of skip-connections. As such, the goal of this work is to propose a new training regime which retains the optimization benefits associated with ResNets while ultimately phasing out skip-connections. This is achieved by posing network training as a constrained optimization problem where skip-connections are introduced during the early stages of training and subsequently phased out in a principled manner using Lagrange multipliers. Throughout a series of experiments we demonstrate that the proposed training strategy greatly reduces the degradation problem, providing an alternative to ResNets.

References

1. Balduzzi, D., et al.: The shattered gradients problem: If ResNets are the answer, then what is the question? In: ICML (2017)
2. Bengio, Y., et al.: Learning deep architectures for AI. Found. Trends Mach. Learn. **2**(1), 1–127 (2009)
3. Bengio, Y.: Representation learning: a review and new perspectives. IEEE Trans. Pattern Anal. Mach. Intell. **35**(8), 1798–1828 (2013)
4. Boyd, S., Vandenberghe, L.: Convex Optimization. Cambridge University Press, New York (2004)
5. Clevert, D., et al.: Fast and accurate deep network learning by exponential linear units (ELUs). In: ICLR (2016)
6. Glorot, X., Bengio Y.: Understanding the difficulty of training deep feedforward neural networks. In: AISTATS (2010)
7. Goodfellow, I., et al.: Deep Learning. MIT Press, Cambridge (2016)
8. Greff, K., et al.: Highway and residual networks learn unrolled iterative estimation. In: ICLR (2017)
9. He, K., et al.: Delving deep into rectifiers: surpassing human-level performance on imagenet classification. In: ICCV (2015)
10. He, K., et al.: Deep residual learning for image recognition. In: CVPR (2016)
11. He, K., Zhang, X., Ren, S., Sun, J.: Identity mappings in deep residual networks. In: Leibe, B., Matas, J., Sebe, N., Welling, M. (eds.) ECCV 2016. LNCS, vol. 9908, pp. 630–645. Springer, Cham (2016). https://doi.org/10.1007/978-3-319-46493-0_38
12. Hochreiter, S., et al.: Gradient flow in recurrent nets: the difficulty of learning long-term dependencies (2001)
13. Huang, G., et al.: Densely connected convolutional networks. In: CVPR (2016)
14. Hubel, D., Wiesel, T.: Receptive fields, binocular interaction and functional architecture in the cat's visual cortex. J. Physiol. **160**(1), 106–154 (1962)
15. Ioffe, S., Szegedy, C.: Batch normalization: accelerating deep network training by reducing internal covariate shift. In: ICML (2015)
16. Klambauer, G., et al.: Self-normalizing neural networks. In: NIPS (2017)
17. Krizhevsky, A., Hinton, G.: Learning multiple layers of features from tiny images (2009)
18. Lee, C.-Y., et al.: Deeply-supervised nets. In: AISTATS (2015)
19. Raiko, T., et al.: Deep learning made easier by linear transformations in perceptrons. In: AISTATS (2012)
20. Schraudolph, N.N.: Centering neural network gradient factors. In: Orr, G.B., Müller, K.-R. (eds.) Neural Networks: Tricks of the Trade. LNCS, vol. 1524, pp. 207–226. Springer, Heidelberg (1998). https://doi.org/10.1007/3-540-49430-8_11
21. Srivastava, R., et al.: Training very deep networks. In: NIPS (2015)
22. Xiao, H., et al.: Fashion-MNIST: A Novel Image Dataset for Benchmarking Machine Learning Algorithms (2017)
23. Zagoruyko, S., Komodakis, N.: Wide residual networks. In: BMCV (2016)
24. Zagoruyko, S., Komodakis, N.: DiracNets: training very deep neural networks without skip-connections. arXiv preprint arXiv:1706.00388 (2017)
25. Zeiler, M.D., Fergus, R.: Visualizing and understanding convolutional networks. In: Fleet, D., Pajdla, T., Schiele, B., Tuytelaars, T. (eds.) ECCV 2014. LNCS, vol. 8689, pp. 818–833. Springer, Cham (2014). https://doi.org/10.1007/978-3-319-10590-1_53

A Deep Predictive Coding Network for Inferring Hierarchical Causes Underlying Sensory Inputs

Shirin Dora[1(✉)], Cyriel Pennartz[1], and Sander Bohte[2]

[1] University of Amsterdam, Amsterdam, Netherlands
shirin.dora@gmail.com, c.m.a.pennartz@uva.nl
[2] Centrum Wiskunde and Informatica, Amsterdam, Netherlands
S.M.Bohte@cwi.nl

Abstract. Predictive coding has been argued as a mechanism underlying sensory processing in the brain. In computational models of predictive coding, the brain is described as a machine that constructs and continuously adapts a generative model based on the stimuli received from external environment. It uses this model to infer causes that generated the received stimuli. However, it is not clear how predictive coding can be used to construct deep neural network models of the brain while complying with the architectural constraints imposed by the brain. Here, we describe an algorithm to construct a deep generative model that can be used to infer causes behind the stimuli received from external environment. Specifically, we train a deep neural network on real-world images in an unsupervised learning paradigm. To understand the capacity of the network with regards to modeling the external environment, we studied the causes inferred using the trained model on images of objects that are not used in training. Despite the novel features of these objects the model is able to infer the causes for them. Furthermore, the reconstructions of the original images obtained from the generative model using these inferred causes preserve important details of these objects.

Keywords: Predictive coding · Deep generative models

1 Introductions

Predictive coding has been proposed as a theory of sensory information processing in which the brain infers causes that generated a sensory stimulus [1, 2]. It postulates that the top-down flow of information in the brain serve as predictions of the inferred causes of a stimulus at a lower level and the bottom-up flow of information conveys the errors in these predictions to the higher areas. Rao and Ballard [3] proposed the first neural network model of predictive coding for the processing of visual information in the brain. Their model consisted of a recurrently connected neural network with three layers.

Several studies have focused on the biological plausibility of the initial model of predictive coding that was proposed by Rao and Ballard (hereafter, referred simply as predictive coding) and its relation with other existing approaches. In [4], Spratling

V. Kůrková et al. (Eds.): ICANN 2018, LNCS 11141, pp. 457–467, 2018.
https://doi.org/10.1007/978-3-030-01424-7_45

showed that a model of biased competition [5] that uses lateral inhibition to suppress the input of other nodes is equivalent to the linear model of predictive coding. An extension to predictive coding has been proposed in [6] that relaxes the requirement of symmetric weights between two adjacent layers in the network. In a similar study, it was shown that error-backpropagation and predictive coding use similar forms of weight changes during learning [7].

From the perspective of training deep neural networks, predictive coding is an approach that is widely supported by neurophysiological data [8] and adheres to the locality (in terms of learning) constraints [3] imposed by the brain. Previous studies on predictive coding focused on small neural network models to study the development of orientation selective receptive fields in primary visual cortex [3, 6]. It is unclear how predictive coding can be used to build deep neural network models of the brain to study more complicated brain processes like perception, attention, memory, etc. An important question in this regard is how to comply with the architectural constraints applicable in the brain like the retinotopic arrangement of receptive fields that is found in the sensory cortical areas. At present, mostly neural networks with fully connected layers are used, which implies that all neurons have the same receptive field which encompasses the entire input stimulus. To overcome this, predictive coding models are often trained on patches from real world images. This approach works well when training small neural network models but it is difficult to extend it for training deep neural networks.

In this paper, we present a systematic approach for training deep neural networks using predictive coding in a biologically plausible manner. Our goal is to construct a deep neural network model to infer hierarchical (here, hierarchical refers to causes inferred at each layer in the network) causes for a given input stimulus. The architecture of these neural networks is inspired by convolutional neural network. However, to comply with the retinotopic arrangement of receptive fields observed in sensory areas, we employ neural networks in which filters are *not* applied across the entire layer. Instead, filters are applied only to a small receptive field which allows us to train the filters associated with different receptive fields independently. This approach can be easily scaled to construct deep predictive coding models for information processing along the sensory processing pathways.

We trained a deep neural network using predictive coding on 1000 real-world images of horses and ships from the CIFAR-10 data set. The model is trained in an unsupervised learning paradigm to build a generative model for real-world images. To estimate the capacity of the network in modeling real-world images, we used the model to infer hierarchical causes for new images of horses and ships as well as objects that had never been presented before to the network during training. The causes inferred by the model can be used to reconstruct the original real-world images while retaining the important features of the objects in these images. This shows that the model is able to capture the statistical regularities generally present in the real-world images. This allows the trained network to infer causes for images with objects that have never been presented before to the network. This attribute of the network also enables it to infer causes for images that are translated versions of images of horses and ships used in training as well as images of new objects.

The paper is organized as follows: Sect. 2 describes the architecture and the predictive coding based learning algorithm used for training deep neural networks.

Section 3 describes the results of studies conducted using the trained models. Section 4 discusses the computational implications of deep predictive coding and its relationship with other approaches in machine learning. Section 5 summarizes the conclusions from our modelling work and experiments.

2 Model

Suppose, we have a set of training images $(\boldsymbol{x}_1, \ldots \boldsymbol{x}_i, \ldots)$ where $\boldsymbol{x}_i \in \boldsymbol{R}^{W \times H \times C}$. The aim of the learning algorithm is to construct a deep neural network that can be used to infer causes for real-world images presented to the network.

2.1 Architecture

Consider a neural network with $(N+1)$ layers with 0 being the input layer and N being the topmost layer in the network. The input layer is used to present the training images to the network. Figure 1 shows a section of this network that depicts the recurrent connections between layer l and layers above $(l+1)$ and below $(l-1)$ it. The neurons in a given layer l are arranged in a 3-dimensional block of shape $Y_l \times X_l \times K_l$. Here, Y_l, X_l and K_l denote the height, width and the number of channels in layer l, respectively. The neurons in layers l and $(l+1)$ are connected through K_{l+1} filters of size D_l and a stride of s_l. Based on this, the height and width of layer $(l+1)$ are given as

$$Y_{l+1} = (\mathrm{Y_l} - \mathrm{D_l})/s_l + 1 \tag{1}$$

$$X_{l+1} = (X_l - D_l)/s_l + 1 \tag{2}$$

The number of channels in layer $(l+1)$ is equal to the number of filters between layers l and $(l+1)$.

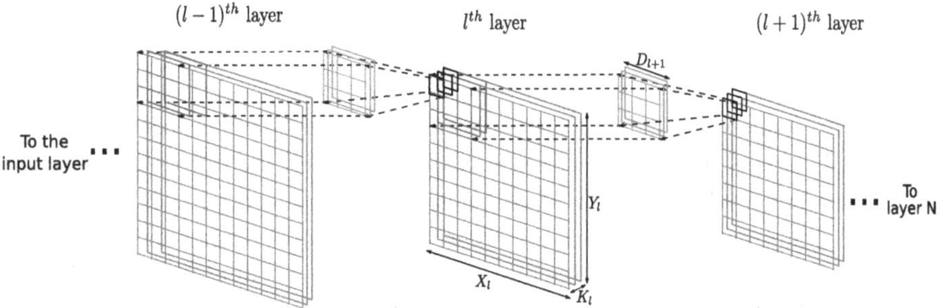

Fig. 1. Architecture of the deep predictive coding network

The architecture of the network in Fig. 1 bears some resemblance to the architecture of Convolutional Neural Networks (CNNs). However, there are two important differences between CNNs and the neural network used in this paper:

- The neurons in a given layer in the network, shown in Fig. 1, are recurrently connected to the neurons only in the corresponding receptive field. This implies that the filters for all the receptive fields in a particular layer are learnt independently.
- The most important difference with respect to CNNs lies in the direction of information propagation. In a conventional CNN, the information propagates from layer 0 to layer N and during learning the error gradients propagate from layer N to layer 0. In contrast, in our predictive coding network the predictive information (Fig. 2) propagates from layer N to layer 0 in the network and the error gradients propagate in the opposite direction. Furthermore, in a CNN both information and error gradients propagate serially (layer-by-layer) whereas in the deep predictive coding network these two processes occur in parallel across all layers in the network. Each layer in the network transmits predictions along the feedback pathway to the layer below and receives the prediction errors from the layer below along the feedforward pathway.

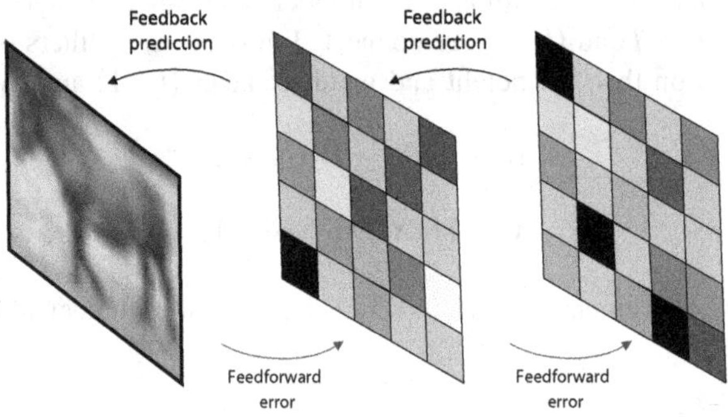

Fig. 2. Direction of information propagation and error gradients in the deep predictive coding network

To better understand the structure of recurrent connections between layer l and layer $(l-1)$, let us denote the activities of the neurons in the mth row and the nth column (here, referred to as (m, n)) of layer l as $y^{(l)}_{m,n}$ which is a vector with K_l elements. Here, the activities of neurons in layer l represent the causes behind the activities of neurons in layer $(l-1)$. Based on this, the feedback predictions generated by the neurons in layer l for the activities of neurons in layer $(l-1)$ are given as

$$\hat{y}^{(l-1)}_{(s_{l-1}m+i),(s_{l-1}n+j)} = \phi\left(w^{(l)}_{m,n,i,j} y^{(l)}_{m,n}\right), \quad \begin{array}{c} i,j \in \{1,\ldots,D_{(l-1)}\}, \\ m \in \{1,\ldots,Y_l\}, n \in \{1,\ldots,X_l\} \end{array} \tag{3}$$

where $w^{(l)}_{m,n,i,j}$ denotes the filters through which the neurons at position (m, n) in layer l project to the position $(s_{l-1}m + i, s_{l-1}n + j)$ in layer $(l - 1)$. The filter $w^{(l)}_{m,n,i,j}$ will be a matrix with dimensions $K_{l-1} \times K_l$. ϕ represents a non-linear vector-valued activation function with K_{l-1} elements.

It may be noted that when the stride is less than the filter size, this results in an architecture with overlapping receptive fields. As a result, neurons in layer l generate predictions for overlapping receptive fields in layer $(l - 1)$. Therefore, the predicted activity of neurons in layer $(l - 1)$ is computed by taking the mean of the predictions across overlapping receptive fields.

2.2 Learning Algorithm

We use the classical methodology of predictive coding [3] to train a deep neural network model that can be used to infer the hierarchical causes of a given input image. For a given input image $(\boldsymbol{x}_i)$, the activities of the neurons in layer l of the network are inferred such that they can predict (using Eq. 3) the activities of the neurons in layer $(l - 1)$. The activities inferred in layer l of the network serve as target for inferring the activities in layer $(l + 1)$ of the network.

Suppose y_l and $\hat{y}_l$ represent the actual and predicted activities of the neurons in layer l of the network, then the total error (E) for all layers in the network is given as

$$E = \sum_{l=0}^{N} \left(\ell_p(\boldsymbol{y}^{(l)} - \hat{\boldsymbol{y}}^{(l)}) + \ell_p(\boldsymbol{y}^{(l)}) + \sum_{m,n,i,j} \ell_p\left(w^{(l)}_{m,n,i,j}\right) \right) \tag{4}$$

where $\ell_p(.)$ denotes the error computed in accordance with p-norm. The total error in Eq. 4 includes both errors, the prediction error and the regularization error.

The total error in Eq. 4 is minimized in order to simultaneously infer the activities and learn the synaptic weights in the network. This implies that the neuronal activities inferred at a particular layer in the network represent the causes behind activities of neurons in the layer below. This allows us to infer hierarchical causes for a given image presented to the network. To explicitly include the aspect of retinotopic arrangement of receptive fields, the total error in Eq. 4 is expanded as

$$E = \sum_{l=0}^{N} \left(\sum_{\mathrm{m,n}}^{\mathrm{Y_l,X_l}} \ell_p\left(y^{(l)}_{\mathrm{m,n}} - \hat{y}^{(l)}_{m,n}\right) + \sum_{\mathrm{m,n}}^{\mathrm{Y_l,X_l}} \ell_p\left(y^{(l)}_{m,n}\right) + \sum_{\mathrm{m,n,i,j}} \ell_p\left(w^{(l)}_{m,n,i,j}\right) \right) \tag{5}$$

Using gradient descent on the error function in Eq. 5, the activities of neurons at a given position (m, n) in layer l are adapted as

$$\Delta y^{(l)}_{m,n} = \epsilon_{bu} \left(\sum_{i=1,j=1}^{D_{(l-1)}} \ell'_p\left(y^{(l-1)}_{(m+i),(n+j)} - \hat{y}^{(l-1)}_{(m+i),(n+j)}\right) \phi'\left(\boldsymbol{w}^{(l)}_{m,n,i,j} y^{(l)}_{m,n}\right) \left(\boldsymbol{w}^{(l)}_{m,n,i,j}\right)^T \right) \\ - \epsilon_{td}\left(y^{(l)}_{m,n} - \hat{y}^{(l)}_{m,n}\right) - \epsilon_p \ell'_p\left(y^{(l)}_{m,n}\right) \tag{6}$$

where $\ell'_p(.)$ denotes partial differentiation of p-norm. ϵ_{bu} is the bottom-up learning rate, ϵ_{td} is the top-down learning rate and ϵ_p is the learning rate for regularization. For a given layer l, the bottom-up learning rate helps in inferring activities that can make better predictions about the activities of the neurons in layer $(l-1)$ and the top-down learning rate helps in ensuring that the inferred activities can be easily predicted by layer $(l+1)$. Together with regularization, these update terms help in inferring causes with sparsely active neurons and provide numerical stability to the learning algorithm.

The filters in the network are also learnt by performing gradient descent along the error function in Eq. 5. The filters are adapted using the learning rule below

$$\Delta w^{(l)}_{m,n,i,j} = \epsilon_w \left(\ell^{\varepsilon}_{p}\left(y^{(l-1)}_{(m+i),(n+j)} - \hat{y}^{(l-1)}_{(m+i),(n+j)}\right) \phi'\left(w^{(l)}_{m,n,i,j} y^{(l)}_{m,n}\right) \left(y^{(l)}_{m,n}\right)^T \right) - \epsilon_p \left(w^{(l)}_{m,n,i,j}\right) \quad (7)$$

where ϵ_w is the learning rate.

For adapting the neuronal activities and the filters simultaneously, we employ the approach described in [3]. At first the filters are held constant and the neuronal activities are adapted using κ update steps in accordance with Eq. 6 and then we update filters once using the update rule in Eq. 7.

3 Experiments

In this section, we study the capabilities of the network in inferring the hierarchical causes for a given input image. First, we will study the capabilities of the generative model in reconstructing the original images from the inferred causes. Second, we analyze the model's abilities in inferring the causes for a new image that was not used in training. Finally, we study the capability of the model to infer causes for an image that is a translated version of the original image. For this purpose, we trained a 6-layered

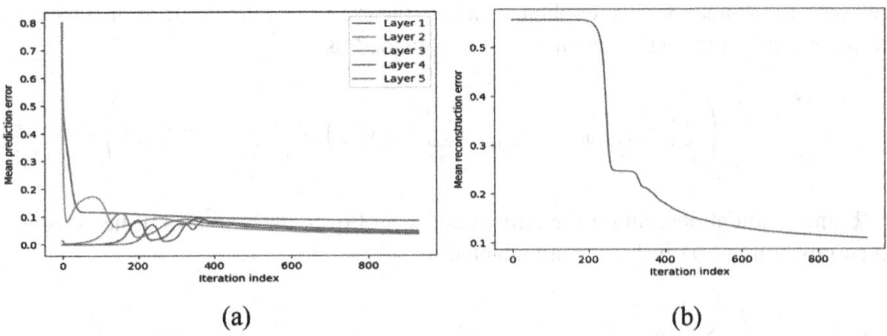

Fig. 3. (a) Mean prediction error at each layer in the network during training. (b) Mean reconstruction error during training. The reconstruction error is based on the images reconstructed by the model using the causes inferred at the topmost layer (as described in Sect. 3.1).

(including the input layer which is referred as the 0th layer in the following sections) neural network on 1000 images of horses and ships from the CIFAR-10 data set. Figure 3 shows the mean prediction error at each layer in the network as well as the mean reconstruction error during training.

3.1 Generative Model

In this section, we study whether the causes inferred at different layers in the network are able to capture the information present in the input image. For a given layer l, we set the activities of the neurons in that layer to the inferred causes. Then, the neurons in layer l predict the activities of neurons in layer $(l-1)$ through the feedback pathways (see Fig. 2). The predicted activities of neurons in layer $(l-1)$ are used to compute the activities of neurons in layer $(l-2)$. This process is repeated across all layers below layer l to compute the activities of neurons in layer 0. If the inferred activations are able to capture the information in the input images then the activities of neurons in layer 0 will provide a closer reconstruction of the original image.

Figure 4 presents some examples of the images reconstructed using the inferred causes at each layer in the network. It can be observed that the images reconstructed by the model are blurry. This is a known problem with the mean square error for computing the error [9]. It may be possible to obtain visually better images using l1-norm, as suggested in [10]. This will be a future direction of research.

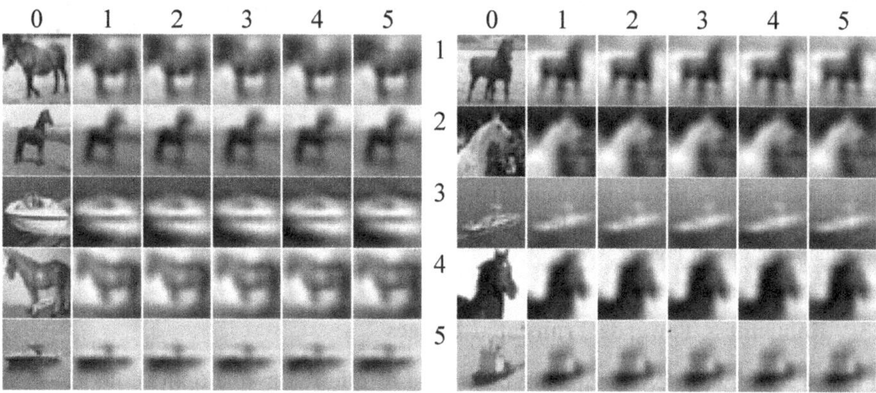

Fig. 4. Examples of images reconstructed by the network when the activities of neurons in different layers of the network have been set to the inferred causes. Each panel (left and right) contains 5 rows. Each row contains six images. The first image in each row is the original image and the following 5 images are reconstructed using the causes inferred in 5 layers of the network. The layer in which the activities of the neurons were set to the inferred causes is shown at the top. The numbers in the center denote the index of the example in the left and right panels.

3.2 Capacity to Represent Novel Input Patterns

To understand, whether the trained model can truly capture the statistical regularities of the real-world images, we used the trained network to infer causes of images from the CIFAR-10 data set that were not used in training. The set of images used included images of objects like airplanes, dogs, birds, etc. which were never presented to the network during training. Note that we used the trained network only for inferring the causes. The filters are no longer adapted in this network.

The inferred causes for the new images are used to reconstruct the original images as described in Sect. 3.1. Figure 5 presents some examples of the images reconstructed from the causes inferred using predictive coding. It can be seen that the network can infer causes even for images that contain objects which were never presented before to the network. This clearly shows the model captures the statistical regularities present in real-world images.

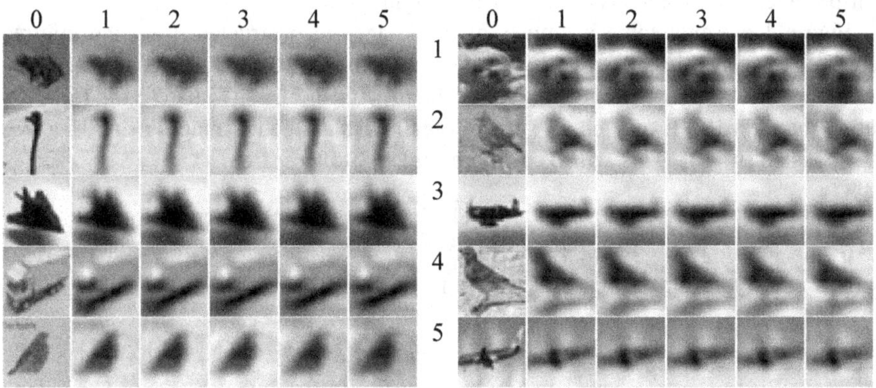

Fig. 5. Non-training images reconstructed by the network using the causes inferred for these images. These images are also arranged in 2 panels, each containing 5 examples. We have used the same layout as in Fig. 4.

3.3 Robustness Towards Translated Images

In this section, we study the quality of the causes inferred by the trained model when translated versions of the original images in the CIFAR-10 data set are presented to the network. This problem is important because the network was trained on only 1000 images of horses and ships without any data augmentation. Convolutional Neural Networks rely on data augmentation to train models that are invariant towards various transformations like translations, rotations, etc. [11]. Here, we study the effect of a specific transformation i.e. translation on the robustness of the causes inferred by the trained network. Note that, again, we do not adapt the filters of the trained network.

The translated versions of the original images are obtained by shifted the content in the images to right and down by 4 pixels. The boundary pixels on the left and top of the original images are used in place of the pixels introduced as a result of shifting the image. For this study, we used images of horses and ships that are used for training as well as images of other objects that are never used in training. These translated images are then presented to the trained network and the inferred causes are used to reconstruct the translated versions of the original images as described in Sect. 3.1.

Figure 6 shows some examples of images reconstructed by the network using the inferred causes for the translated images. It can be observed that, even after presenting translated versions of the image, the information in the input images is well represented in the inferred causes. This may be attributed towards the retinotopic arrangement of receptive fields in the network but further analysis is needed to identify the reason behind this behavior of the network.

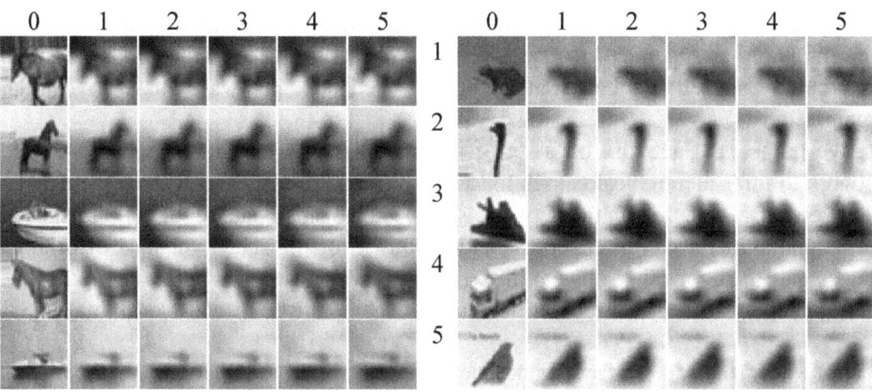

Fig. 6. Translated images reconstructed by the network using the inferred causes. As before, the images are arranged in 2 panels, each containing five rows. Note that the left panel contains translated versions of the images in the left panel of Fig. 4 and the right panel contains translated versions of the images in the left panel of Fig. 5.

4 Discussion

In this section, we discuss the computational implications of the algorithm presented in this paper and the similarities it has with existing approaches in machine learning.

Error-backpropagation is an important algorithm for training deep neural networks. It requires systematic propagation of information through the network in forward direction and during learning, backward propagation of error gradients. This makes it difficult to update all the network parameters in parallel. In this respect, predictive coding can be easily parallelized. It may be seen from Eqs. 6 and 7 that causes and filters can be adapted for all positions in a given layer parallelly due to the retinotopic arrangement of receptive fields. Furthermore, it is also possible to adapt causes and filters across all layers parallelly due to formulation of the error function (Eq. 5).

Another interesting aspect of predictive coding is its proximity to Deconvolutional Neural Networks (DNNs) [12]. DNNs are used to infer hierarchical neuronal activities for a given image. This problem is inherently ill-posed as there is no unique solution. To handle this issue DNNs optimize auxiliary variables and the neuronal activities alternately. A continuation parameter (β) is continuously increased during learning until the inferred neuronal activities are clamped to the auxiliary variables. This requires carefully controlling the learning process and higher computational power due to an extra optimization step on auxiliary variables. Alternatively, in predictive coding the update term associated with ϵ_{td} constrains the algorithm to infer activities that can be easily predicted by successive layers in the network (Eq. 6). This allows predictive coding to infer neuronal activities without using an extra optimization step.

5 Conclusion

In this paper, we describe a method to train deep neural networks using predictive coding. The approach uses network in which neurons the feedforward pathways obey the retinotopic arrangement of receptive fields observed in the brain. More empirical research is needed to determine whether feedback pathways have a similar organization.

We trained the network on a set of real-world images and then used the trained network to infer hierarchical causes for a different set of images as well as their translated versions. Even though the network is trained on a small data set of 1000 images of horses and ships, it can infer representative causes for translated versions of original images and those of other objects like sparrows, dogs, cars, etc. This shows that the network captures statistical regularities that are characteristic of real-world images.

Acknowledgement. The research work reported in this paper is carried out under European Union Horizon 2020 Program under Grant Agreement 720270-Human Brain Project SGA1 to C. M.A. Pennartz.

References

1. Mumford, D.: On the computational architecture of the neocortex - II the role of cortico-cortical loops. Biol. Cybern. **66**(3), 241–251 (1992)
2. Pennartz, C.M.A.: The Brain's Representational Power: On Consciousness and the Integration of Modalities. MIT Press, Cambridge (2015)
3. Rao, R.P.N., Ballard, D.H.: Predictive coding in the visual cortex: a functional interpretation of some extra-classical receptive-field effects. Nat. Neurosci. **2**(1), 79–87 (1999)
4. Spratling, M.W.: Reconciling predictive coding and biased competition models of cortical function. Front. Comput. Neurosci. **2**, 4 (2008)
5. Desimone, R., Duncan, J.: Neural mechanisms of selective visual attention. Annu. Rev. Neurosci. **18**(1), 193–222 (1995)
6. Spratling, M.W.: Unsupervised learning of generative and discriminative weights encoding elementary image components in a predictive coding model of cortical function. Neural Comput. **24**(1), 60–103 (2012)
7. Whittington, J.C.R., Bogacz, R.: An approximation of the error backpropagation algorithm in a predictive coding network with local hebbian synaptic plasticity. Neural Comput. **29**(5), 1229–1262 (2017)

8. Jehee, J.F.M., Ballard, D.H.: Predictive feedback can account for biphasic responses in the lateral geniculate nucleus. PLoS Comput. Biol. **5**(5), e1000373 (2009)
9. Ledig, C., et al.: Photo-Realistic Single Image Super-Resolution Using a Generative Adversarial Network, pp. 1–14. arXiv (2016)
10. Michael Mathieu, Y.L., Couprie, C.: Deep multi-scale video prediction beyond mean square error. arXiv (2015)
11. Kauderer-Abrams, E.: Quantifying Translation-Invariance in Convolutional Neural Networks. arXiv (2017)
12. Zeiler, M.D., Krishnan, D., Taylor, G.W., Fergus, R.: Deconvolutional networks. In: Proceedings of the IEEE Computer Society Conference on Computer Vision and Pattern Recognition, pp. 2528–2535 (2010)

Type-2 Diabetes Mellitus Diagnosis from Time Series Clinical Data Using Deep Learning Models

Zakhriya Alhassan[1,2(✉)], A. Stephen McGough[3], Riyad Alshammari[4], Tahani Daghstani[4], David Budgen[1], and Noura Al Moubayed[1]

[1] Computer Science, Durham University, Durham, UK
{zakhriya.n.alhassan,noura.al-moubayed,david.budgen}@durham.ac.uk
[2] Computing and Information Technology, University of Jeddah, Jeddah, Kingdom of Saudi Arabia
[3] School of Computing, Newcastle University, Newcastle upon Tyne, UK
stephen.mcgough@newcastle.ac.uk
[4] King Saud Bin Abdulaziz University for Health Sciences, Riyadh, Kingdom of Saudi Arabia
{alshammariri,daghistanita}@ngha.med.sa

Abstract. Clinical data is usually observed and recorded at irregular intervals and includes: evaluations, treatments, vital sign and lab test results. These provide an invaluable source of information to help diagnose and understand medical conditions. In this work, we introduce the largest patient records dataset in diabetes research: King Abdullah International Research Centre Diabetes (KAIMRCD) which includes over 14k patient data. KAIMRCD contains detailed information about the patient's visit and have been labelled against T2DM by clinicians. The data is processed as time series and then investigated using temporal predictive Deep Learning models with the goal of diagnosing Type 2 Diabetes Mellitus (T2DM). Long Short-Term Memory (LSTM) and Gated-Recurrent Unit (GRU) are trained on KAIMRCD and are demonstrated here to outperform classical machine learning approaches in the literature with over 97% accuracy.

Keywords: Type 2 diabetes mellitus · Deep learning
Long short-term memory · Gated-recurrent unit
King abdullah international research centre diabetes

1 Introduction

Diabetes is an increasingly growing medical condition worldwide. The estimated number of diabetic patients globally was 415 million in 2015 and is expected to affect one person in 10 by 2040 [6]. The number of people who are borderline diabetic is rapidly increasing. The latest estimates indicate that 35.3% of the adults in the UK are pre-diabetic [17]. Patients suffering from diabetes develop

V. Kůrková et al. (Eds.): ICANN 2018, LNCS 11141, pp. 468–478, 2018.
https://doi.org/10.1007/978-3-030-01424-7_46

serious and complicated health problems to vital organs such as the kidneys, eyes, as well as the heart. By the end of 2015, there were 5 million deaths caused by diabetes worldwide [6].

There are three types of diabetes: (I) Type 1 Diabetes occurs when the body's defence system attacks the pancreas cells, causing it to stop producing the needed insulin. (II) Type 2 Diabetes occurs when the body fails to respond to the insulin produced. (III) Gestational Diabetes which happens when hormonal changes during pregnancy make the body resistant to the insulin [18].

Type 2 Diabetes Mellitus (T2DM) is the most common form accounting for 91% to 95% of all cases [6]. It is the main contributor to causes of death from diabetes and its associated cost. Furthermore, T2DM is difficult to diagnose because it does not have clear clinical symptoms. It often stays undetected for a long time as a result of the slow development of its symptoms [1]. Thus, an early diagnosis of T2DM can assist with delaying any long-term complications.

In many hospital systems, patient data, such as vital signs and lab tests, are routinely collected and stored with an associated time stamp which we will refer to as "Clinical Time Series Data". Patient clinical data is usually carried out at irregular times and stored in the hospital record systems. The frequency of taking these measurements is different for each patient, based on the physician's decisions. In addition, patients differ in their visit patterns (e.g., in-patient or emergency visits), therefore the stay length for each patient varies from few hours to days, weeks or even months.

In this study, we use King Abdullah International Research Centre Diabetes (KAIMRCD) dataset. KAIMRCD is a unique dataset of 14,609 patient visits which have been clinically tested against T2DM. It contains the personal details of every patient such as age and gender along with the vital signs and lab test results for every visit. The availability of such large dataset makes it possible to train advance machine learning techniques, e.g. deep learning models to predict T2DM.

The use of Recurrent Neural Networks (RNNs) has recently redefined the standards for several research areas involiving sequential data such as speech recognition, natural language processing and machine translation [8,11]. Despite their success, RNNs are not usually fit for problems with long temporal dependencies due to the exploding gradients problem [7]. Long Short-Term Memory (LSTM) [9] and Gated-Recurrent Unit (GRU) [3,5], were specifically developed to model problems that involve both long and short temporal dependencies. Thus, LSTM and GRU have demonstrated the ability to model complex clinical data in variety of medical applications such as diseases diagnosis [13,14].

The main contributions of this paper are: (I) Introducing the largest diabetes patients time series data. (II) Applying temporal deep learning models: LSTM and GRU to predict chronic disease, T2DM. (III) Integrating non-sequential risk factors into the time series data such as gender and age. (IV) Investigating the effect of input size on the performance of the built LSTM and GRU models.

Table 1. Neural network models for T2DM diagnosis

Study	Dataset	No of Features	No of Records	Data availability	Accuracy
Venkatesan et al. [21]	Private Date	9	1800	No	91.3%
Meng et al. [15]	Private Date	12	1487	No	72.59%
Temurtas et al. [20]	PPID	8	768	Yes	82.37%
Motka et al. [16]					90.49%
Karegowda et al. [10]					84.71%
Polat et al. [19]					89.47%
GRU	KAIMRCD	30	14,609	Upon request	97.3%

2 Related Work

Machine learning has been successfully applied to clinical data and have been demonstrated in tasks such as the prediction of patient progress and length of stay. Disease diagnosis prediction using time series data is a growing field of research for machine learning. Several neural network models have been applied for T2DM diagnosis prediction, summarised in Table 1. Multi-Layer Perceptron models were applied on various datasets [15,20,21]. Motka et al. [16] and Polat et al. [19] used Artificial Neural Fuzzy Inference Systems (ANFIS). Genetic Algorithms (GA) with Back-propagation Neural Network were also applied [10]. It is important to note that the majority of these models were applied to the Pima Indian Diabetes Data (PIDD) [12] and used small datasets that had no temporal information with a small number of features.

To the best of our knowledge, there are no studies that looked at the T2DM diagnosis from a time-series perspective. We are the first to apply deep learning, LSTM and GRU in particular, for classification in T2DM diagnosis as a time series (vital signs or lab test results) data. There are a few recent studies that are related to our work. These studies used RNN models together with general clinical time series datasets for multi-disease (T2DM was not among them) diagnosis classification [13,14]. However, the time series datasets used in these studies were not specifically collected for the purpose of diabetes diagnosis.

Lipton et al. [13] proposed the first model that applied LSTM on a clinical dataset. The authors used LSTM on a Children's Intensive Care Unit (ICU) dataset to predict multiple diseases diagnosis (such as Asthma, Hypertension and Anemia) using 13 lab test results. The LSTM model was built to classify 128 diseases with competitive accuracy. Another study [4], applied GRU on larger and longitudinal patient data extracted from the general patients clinical records. Similar to Lipton's study, the aim of the study was mainly to predict disease diagnosis. However, The features used in this study are different in type than the ones used in Lipton's study. The authors did not make use of patient's observation records (vital signs or lab test results). Instead, they used previous patient's diagnoses as input to predict future diseases. However, it was not clear how many and what diseases have been examined for evaluating the model.

Both LSTM models as applied in [13,14], and GRU model as applied in [4], have shown promising results with regard to multi-disease diagnosis. The number of samples for each disease, on which the models were trained, was not reported in either studies.

The work is motivated by the temporal nature of clinical data which would potentially be better modelled by a model that directly models sequential/temporal data similar to GRU/LSTM. This is particularly relevant given the size of our dataset, KAIMRCD, which considerably larger than any reported in the literature for the diagnosis of T2DM. Our models incorporate not only the clinical vital signs and lab test results, but also non-sequential data such as age and gender, which are important risk factors for T2DM [6].

3 Dataset

King Abdullah International Medical Research Center (KAIMRC) is one of the leading institutions in health research in the Middle East. The KAIMRCD[1] dataset was collected by Ministry of National Guard Health Affairs (NGHA) from the main National Guard Hospitals located in three populated regions[2]. It is part of the hospital care service procedures to clinically diagnose visitors against T2DM. The collected data contains records of clinical diagnosis of T2DM from the full visits history of 14,609 patient visits.

KAIMRCD dataset was collected over the period between 2010 and 2015. It contains 41 million time-stamped results for lab tests, such as Blood Urea Nitrogin (BUN), cholesterol (Chol) and Mean Corpuscular Hemoglobin (MCH). It also holds time-stamped data about patient vital signs such as Body Mass Index (BMI) and Hypertension. Other important features are also included, such as visit type (inpatient, outpatient or emergency), discharge type (home, referred to another hospital, patient died), gender, patient's age at the visit, service type (e.g. Cardiology, Neurology, Endocrinology) and stay length[3]. The data is imbalanced with 62% of the patients are diagnosed with diabetes, hence F1 measure is used as an evaluation metric rather than accuracy. Figure 1 shows the distribution of the data projected on a two-dimensional space using t-SNE.

Due to the variety of clinical procedures involved in different patient visits, irregularities in data is expected. The frequency and the order of the clinical procedures varies from one patient to another. Hence the episodes of patient data vary with different sets of measures and their frequencies, pre-processing the data for the purpose of this analysis is critical.

[1] Access to KAIMRCD dataset can be obtained upon official request to KAIMRC.

[2] Western, Central and Eastern regions of Saudi Arabia.

[3] For space reasons the full list of features can not be listed here .

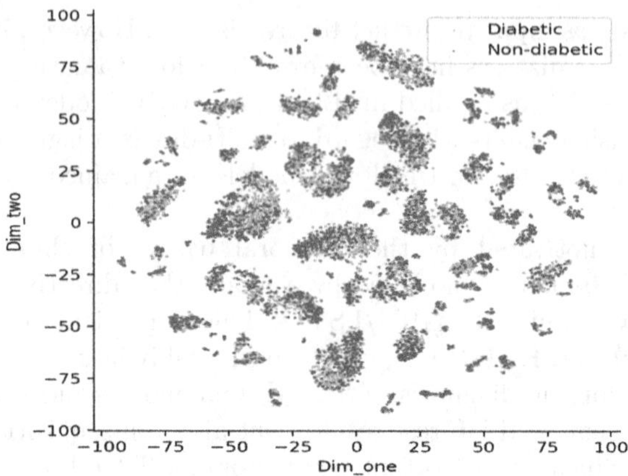

Fig. 1. KAIMRCD dataset distribution.

3.1 Data Pre-processing

Each patient visit is described by a set of measures. These measures are represented as episodes. An episode contains irregular time-stamped vital signs and lab results. In addition, the non-sequential data (gender and age) is also integrated into the episodes.

Every sequence element consists of 30 features (gender, age and 28 vital signs and lab readings)[3]. The interval between the sequences is one day. There are three types of features, starting with constant features which do not change during a patient's visit, such as age and gender. Frequently changing features are collected on a daily basis, or the average of multiple daily measures, such as vital signs. Finally, the infrequently changing features are collected on an interval of more than a day. As a result, features that may be unavailable for some patients are considered to be missing. The representation of an episode of patient x for our proposed solution is defined as:

$$Episode_x = \begin{Bmatrix} t_1 : R_{11} \; R_{12} \; ... \; R_{1m} \\ t_2 : R_{21} \; R_{22} \; ... \; R_{2m} \\ ... \quad\quad ... \; ... \; ... \\ ... \quad\quad ... \; ... \; ... \\ t_n : R_{n1} \; R_{n2} \; ... \; R_{nm} \end{Bmatrix}$$

where R_{ij}: is the reading values (risk factors) at day i for vital signs, lab test results and the embedded non-sequential values (gender and visit age) j. n is the length of the sequence (the input size). m is the number of readings for each sequence.

Patient visit (*Episode*) consists of a sequence length n (based on the length of stay in hospital) at time t. If the number of days for a patient's visit is less than n, zero padding technique is applied to compensate for the missing sequences. For each sequence there are m reading values (R). If R_{ij} is missing then it is assigned the value from the previous day ($R_{ij} = R_{(i-1)j}$). In the case that there was no previous reading, R_{ij} is replaced with zero.

4 Methods

Recurrent neural networks, and its variants, have achieved unprecedented accuracy in many domains with sequential data [11]. Unlike other deep learning methods, RNNs have memory cells allowing the previous output to influence the state for the next output, which proved to be a useful feature for sequential data.

Here, we investigate the performance of temporal models: LSTM and GRU, in diagnosing T2DM from time-stamped sequences of patient observations. Given a sequence of observations for a patient $x_t : R_1, R_2, ...R_m$ at time t, the activation function of a recurrent hidden unit h_t is:

$$h_t = \nu(U_{x_t} + W_{h_{(t-1)}}), \tag{1}$$

where ν is a nonlinear function for the sum of the hidden state, U, matrix of the current patient's sequences, and W is a matrix of the weight input of the previous sequence.

In the experiments, we use n previous sequences of patient's observations (series) to explore the impact of previous dependencies in influencing the classification decision of T2DM. In practice, RNNs have demonstrated a limited performance when learning from sequences with long-term dependencies [2]. This is mainly caused by limitations in the gradient decent approach, as the gradient tends to either vanish or explode when modelling long dependencies. Hochreiter and Schmidhuber addressed this problem by introducing LSTM [9]. LSTM, uses a sophisticated structure with multiple cell and gated unites (forget and input) to cope with learning from long-term dependencies, described by:

$$f_t = \sigma(W_f.[h_{(t-1)}, x_t] + b_f) \tag{2}$$

$$i_t = \sigma(W_i.[h_{(t-1)}, x_t] + b_i) \tag{3}$$

$$\tilde{C}_t = tanh(W_C.[h_{(t-1)}, x_t] + b_C) \tag{4}$$

$$C_t = f_t \times C_{(t-1)} + i_t \times \tilde{C}_t \tag{5}$$

$$o_t = \sigma(W_o[h_{(t-1)}, x_t] + b_o) \tag{6}$$

$$h_t = o_t \times tanh(C_t), \tag{7}$$

where f represents the forget gate of the cell with a sigmoid activation function σ and the weight W and the learned bias b (Eq. 2). i is the input gate (Eq. 3) which is used in combination with a non-linear(tanh) layer $\tilde{C}$. $\tilde{C}$ is the new value for cell state (Eq. 4). The update state value C is then the sum of the multiplication of the old state $C_{(t-1)}$ by f_t, which decides on what to forget, and the new value $\tilde{C}$ multiplied by the input gate value i_t (Eq. 5). Finally o is the output of the sigmoid gate which is used with the cell state C to produce the final decision (Eqs. 6 and 7) whether the patient x is diabetic or not.

Similar to LSTMs, GRU is used to deal with long-term dependencies. The main difference is that GRU merges the forget and input gates in one unit gate called the update gate. This means that previous memory is kept based on the size of the new dependencies (input). GRUs do not have a protected hidden cell state which gives full access to the corresponding allocated memory content. GRU is formally defined as follows:

$$z_t = \sigma(W_f \times [h_{(t-1)}, x_t]) \tag{8}$$

$$r_t = \sigma(W_r.[h_{(t-1)}, x_t]) \tag{9}$$

$$\tilde{h}_t = tanh(W_C.[r_t \times h_{(t-1)}, x_t]) \tag{10}$$

$$h_t = (1 - z_t) \times h_{(t-1)} + z_t \times \tilde{h}_t, \tag{11}$$

where z and r represent the update gate and the reset gate values. These gates are calculated in a similar way to calculating the input gate and the forget gate of LSTM, except that GRU does not consider adding these values in the formula (Eq. 8) and (Eq. 9). The other difference is that instead of changing the current hidden layer h as in the LSTM method, the input x and the previous layer $h_{(t-1)}$ modify the update gate and the reset gate values in the GRU method. Then the current layer is updated accordingly by z and r (Eq. 11) [4].

5 Experimental Setup

Both LSTM and GRU models were implemented, to allow for comparison between their performance in predicting the diagnosis of T2DM. The neural networks of both models have similar architectures. The model contains two LSTM/ GRU layers and two dense layers. The first hidden layer has 128 neurons with a sigmoid activation function, while the second contains 64 neurons with ReLU activation function. The two dense layers also use the ReLU and sigmoid activation functions, with 16 and 1 neurons respectively.

LSTM and GRU are trained using 90% of the data. The remaining 10% is then used for testing. The models use adam optimizer with 0.001 learning rate. The optimisation score function used in both models is root mean squared error. Before preforming the prediction on the test data, the models were trained for 100 epochs. In our experiments, we investigated the performance of each model for six different variations of input sizes (3, 5, 8, 10, 12, and 15). The models are trained and tested using 10-folds cross-validation approach. We report the macro, micro and weighted-averaged F1 scores to compare and evaluate the performance of the classifiers.

Baseline Models. We compared our results against three commonly used baseline models: Logistic Regression (LR), Support Vector Machine (SVM), and Multi-Layer Perceptron (MLP). These models do not model temporal dynamics in the data, hence the patient visits are assumed independent. Only sequences with fewer missing readings are considered. MLP has similar architecture to LSTM/GRU and uses the same optimiser settings.

6 Results

Table 2 shows the performance metrics obtained using LSTM, GRU and baseline models. In Table 2, the results show that all of the neural network models, including MLP, with all of the different number of input sizes, achieved better performance than the models identified in the related work section (Table 1), and the baseline shallow models (LR and SVM).

Table 2. Models performance in T2DM diagnosis

Input size	Model	F1 Weighted	F1 Macro	F1 Micro
1 Sequence*	LR	0.7790	0.7517	0.8041
	SVM	0.7452	0.7194	0.7576
3 Sequences	MLP	0.9409	0.9371	0.9411
	LSTM	0.9631	0.9649	0.9670
	GRU	**0.9706**	**0.9689**	**0.9705**
5 Sequences	MLP	0.9442	0.9406	0.9443
	LSTM	0.9592	0.9566	0.9596
	GRU	0.9634	0.9612	0.9634
8 Sequences	MLP	0.9452	0.9417	0.9451
	LSTM	0.9565	0.9536	0.9567
	GRU	0.9714	0.9694	0.9715
10 Sequences	MLP	0.9508	0.9476	0.9509
	LSTM	0.9512	0.9485	0.9508
	GRU	**0.9729**	**0.9711**	**0.9730**
12 Sequences	MLP	0.9440	0.9403	0.9440
	LSTM	0.9646	0.9623	0.9646
	GRU	0.9624	0.9598	0.9627
15 Sequences	MLP	0.9454	0.9421	0.9451
	LSTM	0.9669	0.9650	0.9667
	GRU	0.9656	0.9632	0.9657

Table 2: shows the performance metrics for LSTM and GRU and baseline classifiers.

* Most complete sequence with fewer missing data among the whole patient's visit.

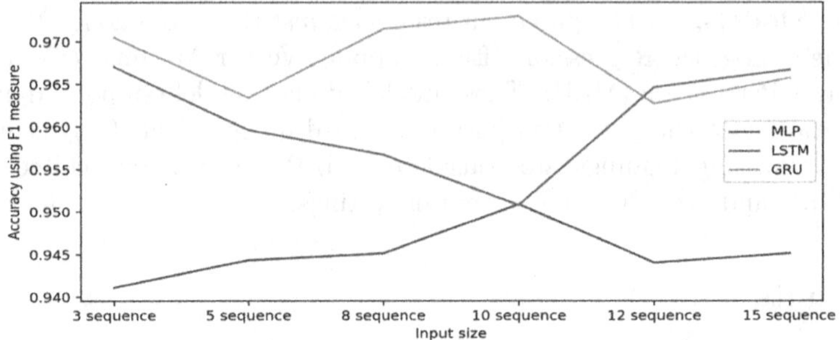

Fig. 2. Change of F1 measure with the length of the input size.

Both LSTM and GRU outperformed MLP models and achieved promising results using different input sizes (from 3 to 15). GRU with 10 input sequence length is the best performing model with regard to the reported measures (results in bold), but with insignificant difference to GRU with only 3 sequences. Table 2 also shows that GRU models with 3 and 10 sequence length, have better results compared to the same model with larger input size. This is not the same for the LSTM models, which show better results with longer dependencies. Figure 2 shows the performance trend of LSTM, GRU and MLP against the input sizes. Figure 3 demonstrates the models performance results. Figure 3 shows that GRU results are distributed in smaller areas to LSTM, which indicates that GRU approach can have more consistent results when used for predicting T2DM.

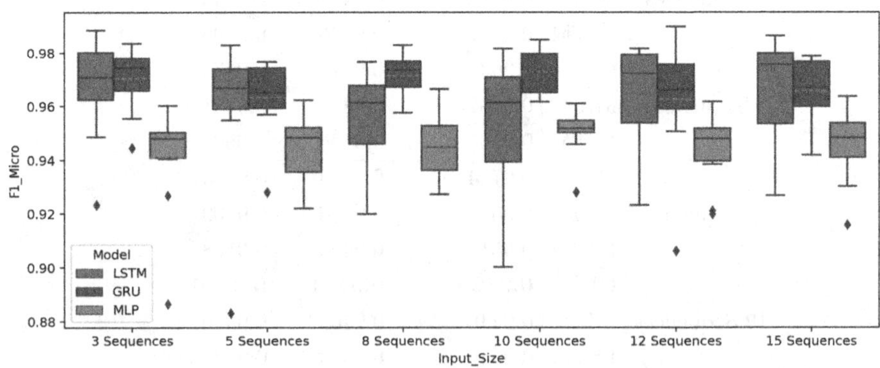

Fig. 3. F1 Micro result for LSTM, GRU and MLP Models

6.1 Discussion and Conclusion

In this paper, we investigated the use of temporal predictive deep neural network models for the diagnosis of T2DM. The proposed models (LSTM and GRU), using clinical time-stamped data and without intensive feature engineering can achieve very high accuracy with as short as 3 sequences. The models were trained and tested with different input sizes using unique and large dataset (KAIMRCD). The results were compared to common baseline classifiers (LR, SVM and MLP) using the same dataset. LSTM and GRU models outperformed the baseline classifiers and achieved 97.3% accuracy. Due to the lack of datasets that are specific to T2DM, replicating this work using different datasets can be difficult.

The models were able to predict with a high accuracy 97% even with a 3-day length sequence. This is very significant finding as it would reduce the time and associated cost required to perform further tests and delivers early diagnosis. Further work may investigate the impact of applying different techniques for handling the missing data on KAIMRCD data.

References

1. Beagley, J., Guariguata, L., Weil, C., Motala, A.A.: Global estimates of undiagnosed diabetes in adults. Diabetes Res. Clin. Pract. **103**(2), 150–160 (2014)
2. Bengio, Y., Simard, P., Frasconi, P.: Learning long-term dependencies with gradient descent is difficult. IEEE Trans. Neural Netw. **5**(2), 157–166 (1994)
3. Cho, K., et al.: Learning phrase representations using rnn encoder-decoder for statistical machine translation. arXiv preprint arXiv:1406.1078 (2014)
4. Choi, E., Bahadori, M.T., Schuetz, A., Stewart, W.F., Sun, J.: Doctor AI: predicting clinical events via recurrent neural networks. In: Machine Learning for Healthcare Conference, pp. 301–318 (2016)
5. Chung, J., Gulcehre, C., Cho, K., Bengio, Y.: Empirical evaluation of gated recurrent neural networks on sequence modeling. arXiv preprint arXiv:1412.3555 (2014)
6. Federation, I.D.: IDF diabetes atlas (2015). http://www.diabetesatlas.org
7. Gers, F.A., Schmidhuber, J., Cummins, F.: Learning to forget: continual prediction with LSTM (1999)
8. Goodfellow, I., Bengio, Y., Courville, A.: Deep Learning. MIT press, Cambridge (2016)
9. Hochreiter, S., Schmidhuber, J.: Long short-term memory. Neural Comput. **9**(8), 1735–1780 (1997)
10. Karegowda, A.G., Manjunath, A., Jayaram, M.: Application of genetic algorithm optimized neural network connection weights for medical diagnosis of pima indians diabetes. Int. J. Soft Comput. **2**(2), 15–23 (2011)
11. LeCun, Y., Bengio, Y., Hinton, G.: Deep learning. Nature **521**(7553), 436–444 (2015)
12. Lichman, M.: UCI machine learning repository (2013). http://archive.ics.uci.edu/ml
13. Lipton, Z.C., Kale, D.C., Elkan, C., Wetzell, R.: Learning to diagnose with LSTM recurrent neural networks. arXiv preprint arXiv:1511.03677 (2015)
14. Lipton, Z.C., Kale, D.C., Wetzel, R.: Modeling missing data in clinical time series with RNNs. Machine Learning for Healthcare (2016)
15. Meng, X.H., Huang, Y.X., Rao, D.P., Zhang, Q., Liu, Q.: Comparison of three data mining models for predicting diabetes or prediabetes by risk factors. Kaohsiung J. Med. Sci. **29**(2), 93–99 (2013)
16. Motka, R., Parmarl, V., Kumar, B., Verma, A.: Diabetes mellitus forecast using different data mining techniques. In: 2013 4th International Conference on Computer and Communication Technology (ICCCT), pp. 99–103. IEEE (2013)

17. (NHS), U.N.H.S.: http://www.nhs.uk
18. World Health Orgnization: Global report on diabetes (2016). http://www.who.int/diabetes/global-report/en/
19. Polat, K., Güneş, S.: An expert system approach based on principal component analysis and adaptive neuro-fuzzy inference system to diagnosis of diabetes disease. Digit. Signal Process. **17**(4), 702–710 (2007)
20. Temurtas, H., Yumusak, N., Temurtas, F.: A comparative study on diabetes disease diagnosis using neural networks. Expert. Syst. Appl. **36**(4), 8610–8615 (2009)
21. Venkatesan, P., Anitha, S.: Application of a radial basis function neural network for diagnosis of diabetes mellitus. Curr. Sci. **91**(9), 1195–1199 (2006)

A Deep Learning Approach for Sentence Classification of Scientific Abstracts

Sérgio Gonçalves[1], Paulo Cortez[1(✉)], and Sérgio Moro[2]

[1] ALGORITMI Centre, Department of Information Systems, University of Minho, Guimarães, Portugal
a72886@alunos.uminho.pt, pcortez@dsi.uminho.pt
[2] Instituto Universitário de Lisboa (ISCTE-IUL), ISTAR-IUL, Lisboa, Portugal
sergio.moro@iscte-iul.pt

Abstract. The classification of abstract sentences is a valuable tool to support scientific database querying, to summarize relevant literature works and to assist in the writing of new abstracts. This study proposes a novel deep learning approach based on a convolutional layer and a bi-directional gated recurrent unit to classify sentences of abstracts. The proposed neural network was tested on a sample of 20 thousand abstracts from the biomedical domain. Competitive results were achieved, with weight-averaged precision, recall and F1-score values around 91%, which are higher when compared to a state-of-the-art neural network.

Keywords: Bi-directional gated recurrent unit
Sentence classification · Scientific articles · Text mining · Deep learning

1 Introduction

In the last decades, there has been a rise in the number of scholarly publications [14]. For instance, around 114 million of English scholarly documents were accessible on the Web in 2014 [9]. Such volume makes it difficult to quickly select relevant scientific documents. Scientific abstracts summarize the most important elements of a paper and thus those are valuable sources for filtering the most relevant papers during a literature review process [1].

The classification of scientific abstracts is a particular instance of the sequential classification task, considering there is a typical order in the classes (e.g., the 'Objective' label tends to appear after the 'Background'). This classification transforms unstructured text into a more information manageable structure [6]. This is acknowledged by the Emerald publisher, which requires all submissions to include a structured abstract [4]. In effect, the automatic classification of abstract sentences presents several advantages. It is a valuable tool for general scientific database querying (e.g., using Web of Science, Scopus). Also, it can assist in manual [11] or text mining [15] systematic literature review processes, as well as other bibliometric analyses. Moreover, it can help in the writing of new paper abstracts [13].

V. Kůrková et al. (Eds.): ICANN 2018, LNCS 11141, pp. 479–488, 2018.
https://doi.org/10.1007/978-3-030-01424-7_47

In this study, we present a deep learning neural network architecture for the sequential classification of abstract sentences. The architecture uses a word embedding layer, a convolutional layer, a bi-directional Gated Recurrent Unit (GNU) and a final concatenation layer. The proposed deep learning model is compared with a recently proposed bi-directional Long Short-Term Memory (LSTM) based model [6], showing an interesting performance on a large 20 K abstract corpus that assumes five sentence classes: 'Background', 'Objectives', 'Methods', 'Results' and 'Conclusions'. This paper is organized as follows. First, the related work is introduced in Sect. 2. Next, the abstract corpus and methods are described in Sect. 3. Then, the experimental results are presented and analyzed in Sect. 4. Finally, the main conclusions are discussed in Sect. 5.

2 Related Work

As pointed out in [6], most sequential sentence classification methods are based on 'shallow' methods (e.g., naive Bayes, Support Vector Machines (SVM)) that require a manual feature engineering based on lexical (e.g., bag of words, n-grams), semantic (e.g, synonyms), structural (e.g., part-of-speech tags) or sequential (e.g., sentence position) information. The advantage of using deep learning is that the neural networks do not require such manual design of features. Also, deep learning often achieves competitive results in text classification [8].

Regarding abstract sentence classification, this topic has been scarcely researched when compared to other text classification tasks (e.g., sentiment analysis). The main reason for this reduced attention is the restricted availability of publicly datasets. In 2010 [2], the manual engineering approach was used to set nine features (e.g., bi-grams) and train five classifiers (e.g., SVM) that were combined to classify four main elements of medical abstracts. In 2013 [13], a private corpus with 4550 abstracts from different scientific fields was collected from ScienceDirect. The abstract sentences were manually labeled into four categories: 'Background', 'Goal', 'Methods' and 'Results'. The authors also used the conventional manual feature design approach (e.g., n-grams) and a transductive SVM. More recently, in 2017 [5], a large abstract corpus was made publicly available. Using this dataset, a deep learning model, based on one bi-directional LSTM, was proposed for a five class sentence prediction, outperforming four other approaches (e.g., n-gram logistic regression, multilayer perceptron) [6].

In this paper, we propose a different deep learning architecture, mainly composed by a convolutional layer and a bi-directional GRU layer to classify the sentences from abstracts, which uses word embeddings instead of character embeddings. By taking into consideration the position of the sentences, as well as encoding contextual information on the vector of each sentence, we expect that the proposed architecture can potentially achieve better results when compared with the study by [6].

3 Materials and Methods

3.1 Abstract Corpus

We adopted the abstract corpus first analyzed by [5], which sets the baseline for comparison purposes. The corpus includes open access papers from the PubMed biomedical database and related with Randomized Controlled Trials (RCT). The sentences were classified by the authors of the articles into the five standardized labels.

The full corpus has a total of 200 K abstracts. A smaller subset, with 20 K most recent abstracts, was also made available for a faster experimentation of sequential sentence classification methods. Considering the 20 K subset was used in the work of [6], we also adopt the same dataset, to facilitate the experimental comparison. Table 1 presents the class frequencies and train, validation and test split sizes. This is an unbalanced dataset, with most sentences being related with 'Methods' or 'Results' (around 30%).

Table 1. Class distribution and train, validation and test sizes (PubMed 20K corpus).

	Background	Objective	Methods	Results	Conclusions
#sentences	28,797	18,548	79,214	77,507	36,321
percentage	12.0%	7.7%	33.0%	32.2%	15.1%

	Train	Validation	Test
#abstracts	15.0K	2.5K	2.5K
#sentences	180.0K	30.0K	30.0 K

3.2 Neural Networks Models

In the last years, there has been remarkable developments in deep learning [8]. Architectures such as Convolutional Neural Network (CNN), LSTM and GRU have obtained competitive results in several competitions (e.g., computer vision, signal and natural language processing).

The CNN is a network mainly composed by convolutional layers. The purpose of the convolutional layers is to extract features that preserve relevant information from the inputs [12]. To obtain the features, a convolutional layer receives a matrix as input, to which a matrix with a set of weights, known as a filter, is applied using a sliding window approach and, at each of the sliding window steps, a convolution is calculated, resulting in a feature. The size of the filter is a relevant hyperparameter.

Although CNNs have been widely used in computer vision, they can also be used in sentence classification [10]. The use of convolutional layers enables the extraction of features from a window of words, which is useful because word embeddings alone are not able to detect specific nuances, such as double negation, which is important for sentiment classification. The width of the filter, represented by h, determines the length of the n-grams. The number of filters is also a hyperparameter, making it possible to use multiple filters with varying lengths [10]. The filters are initialized with random weights and, during the training of the network, the weights are learned for the specific task of the network, through backpropagation. Since each filter produces its own feature map, there is a need to reduce the dimensionality caused by using multiple filters. A sentence can be encoded as a single vector by applying a max pooling layer after the convolutional layer, which takes the maximum value for each position, from all the feature maps, keeping only the most important features.

Recurrent Neural Networks (RNN) are relevant for sequential data, such as the words that appear in a sentence. Consider the words $(x_1, ..., x_t)$ from a given sentence (sequence of words). The hidden state s_t of the word x_t depends on the hidden state s_{t-1}, which in turn is the hidden state of the word x_{t-1} and, for this reason, the order in which words appear over the sequence also influence the various hidden states of the RNN.

The LSTM network is a particular RNN that uses an internal memory to keep information between distant time steps to model long-term dependencies of the sequence. It uses two gating mechanisms, update gate and forget gate, which controls what information should be updated into the memory, and what information should be erased from the memory, respectively. The GRU [3] was recently introduced and it can be used as an alternative to the LSTM model. The GRU uses a reset and update gate, which are able to control how much information should be kept from previous time steps. Both GRU and LSTM are solutions that help mitigate the vanishing gradient problem of conventional RNNs.

A deep learning model was used in [6] for abstract sentence classification. The model uses character embeddings that are then concatenated with word embeddings and used as input for a bi-directional LSTM layer, which outputs a sentence vector based on those hybrid embeddings. The sentence vector is used to predict the probabilities of the labels for that sentence. The authors also use a sequence optimization layer, which has the objective of optimizing the classification of a sequence of sentences, exploiting existing dependencies between labels.

3.3 Proposed Architecture

The proposed word embedding, convolutional and bi-directional GRU (Word-BiGRU) architecture is shown in Fig. 1. We assume that each abstract has i sentences $(S_1, ..., S_i)$ and each individual sentence has n words $(x_1^1, ..., x_n^i)$, where x_n^i is the nth word from the ith sentence. The various words from the sentences are mapped to their respective word embeddings, and those embedding are used to create a sentence matrix $E \in R^{m \times d}$, where d equals to the dimensionality of the embeddings. We use word embeddings pre-trained on English Wikipedia, provided by Glove (with $d = 200$) [16].

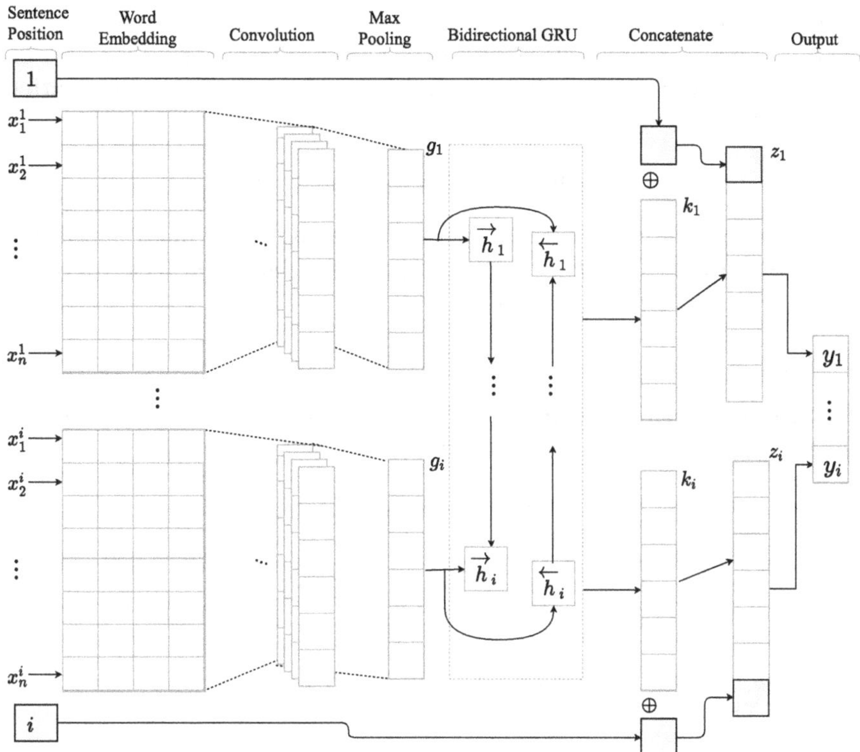

Fig. 1. Schematic of the proposed Word-BiGRU deep learning architecture.

Then, a convolutional layer is used with a sliding window approach that extracts the most important features from the sentences. Let $E \in R^{m \times d}$ denote the sentence matrix, $w \in R^{h \times d}$ a filter, and $E[i : j]$ the sub-matrix from row i to j. The single feature o_i is obtained using:

$$o_i = w * E[i : i + h - 1] \,. \tag{1}$$

In this study, we use a filter with a size of $h = 5$. To add nonlinearity to the output, an activation function applied to every single feature. For the feature o_i, it is obtained by:

$$c_i = f(o_i + b); \tag{2}$$

where f is the activation function and b is the bias. We use ReLU as the activation function in our model because it tends to present a faster convergence [7].

Next, we take the various features maps obtained from the convolutional layer, and feed them into a max pooling layer to encode the most important features extracted by the convolutional layer into a single vector representation that can be used by the next layers. Let $g_1, ..., g_i$ denote several vectors, each one encoding a particular sentence of the abstract. The vectors are then fed to bi-directional GRU layer, where the hidden states for each time step are calculated.

We will use $\odot$ to denote the Hadamard Product, while using W and U to denote weight matrices of the GRU layer. Let h_{i-1} be the hidden state of the previous sentence from the same abstract, the candidate hidden state $\tilde{h}_i$ for the current sentence is given by:

$$\tilde{h}_i = \tanh(W_h g_i + U_h(r_i \odot h_{i-1}) + b_h)\ . \tag{3}$$

The reset gate $r_i \in [0, 1]$ has the purpose of controlling how much information of the past hidden state, h_{t-1} will be kept. Let σ be the sigmoid activation function. The reset gate r_i is calculated by:

$$r_i = \sigma(W_r g_i + U_r h_{i-1} + b_r)\ . \tag{4}$$

To control how much new information will be stored in the hidden state, an update gate $z_i \in [0, 1]$ is used, given by:

$$z_i = \sigma(W_z g_i + U_z h_{i-1} + b_z)\ . \tag{5}$$

The hidden state h_i, which is the hidden state of the sentence i, is obtained by:

$$h_i = z_i \odot \tilde{h}_i + (1 - z_i) \odot h_{i-1}\ . \tag{6}$$

Since we use a bi-directional GRU layer, there is a forward pass and a backward pass. The hidden states resulting from the forward pass are:

$$(\overrightarrow{h_1}, ..., \overrightarrow{h_i})\ . \tag{7}$$

where h_i is the hidden state of the ith sentence of the abstract. Similarly, the hidden states resulting from the backward pass are:

$$(\overleftarrow{h_1}, ..., \overleftarrow{h_i})\ . \tag{8}$$

By using a bi-directional GRU, we want to capture contextual information about each sentence of the abstract, by taking into consideration the sentences that appear before and after it. For the ith sentence of the abstract, the individual vector k_i, which encodes the sentence with contextual information captured using the bi-directional GRU layer, is obtained by concatenating ($\oplus$ operator) the forward and backward hidden states:

$$k_i = [\overrightarrow{h_i} \oplus \overleftarrow{h_i}]\ . \tag{9}$$

Each encoded sentence k_i is then concatenated with an integer value indicating the position of that sentence in the abstract, resulting in z_i:

$$z_i = [k_i \oplus i]\ . \tag{10}$$

Finally, a softmax layer is used, such that the outputs can be interpreted as class probabilities.

3.4 Evaluation

Classification accuracy is often measured using a confusion matrix, which maps predicted versus desired labels. From this matrix, several metrics can be computed, such as: [17]: Precision, Recall, F1-score. For a class c, these metrics are obtained using:

$$\begin{aligned} \text{Precision}_c &= \frac{TP_c}{TP_c+FP_c} \\ \text{Recall}_c &= \frac{TP_c}{TP_c+FN_c} \\ \text{F1-score}_c &= 2 \times \frac{\text{Precision}_c \times \text{Recall}_c}{\text{Precision}_c+\text{Recall}_c} \ . \end{aligned} \tag{11}$$

where TP_c, FP_c, FN_c denote the number of true positives, false positives and false negatives for class c.

To combine all five class results into a single measure, we adopt two aggregation methods: macro-averaging and weight-averaging. The macro-averaging computes first the metric (e.g., Precision using Eq. 11) for each class and then averages the overall result. The weight-averaging is computed in a similar way except that each class metric is weighted proportionally to its prevalence in the data. In [6] only the weight-averaging method was used.

For comparison purposes, we adopt the same train, validation and test sets used in [6] (Table 1). When fitting the deep learning architecture, we adjusted different combinations of its main hyperparameters, namely: the number of filters (128 or 256) in the convolutional layer and the number of units ($\in \{25, 50, 75, 100\}$) in the bi-directional GRU Layer. The validation set was used to select the best configuration, when monitoring the macro-averaging Precision metric. In the test set comparison, we computed all classification metrics.

4 Results

The deep learning models were trained on the p2.xlarge instance from Amazon Elastic Compute Cloud, which has an Intel Xeon E5-2686 v4 2.30 GHz, Nvidia Tesla K80 and 61 GB of RAM. The experiments were implemented in Python using the Keras and Scikit packages. The selected hyperparameters (using validation metrics) are shown in Table 2. Figure 2 shows the normalized confusion matrix of the proposed model. The matrix confirms that a very good classification was achieved, in particular for the 'Methods', 'Conclusions' and 'Results' labels and that correspond to the most frequent classes.

The proposed Word-BiGRU deep learning architecture is compared with two other approaches: a similar model that does not include the bi-directional GRU layer (CNN model), and with the results provided in [6] (Char-BiLSTM). Table 3 shows the test results for each class. Word-BiGRU shows competitive results when compared with Char-BiLSTM. Specifically, it achieves the best Precision and Recall values for three classes and the best F1-scores for all classes. Furthermore, the deep learning model provides the highest classification improvement (11.3% points) for the least frequent class ('Objectives'). The averaged class

Table 2. Selected hyperparameters of the proposed model.

Common parameters			
Embedding dimension	200		
Maximum Length	100		
Dropout	0.35		
Loss Function	Categorical Cross-entropy		
Optimizer	Adam		
Convolutional Layer		**Bi-directional GRU Layer**	
Activation function(s)	ReLU	Activation function	Tanh
Filter size	5	Number of units	50
Number of Filters	128		

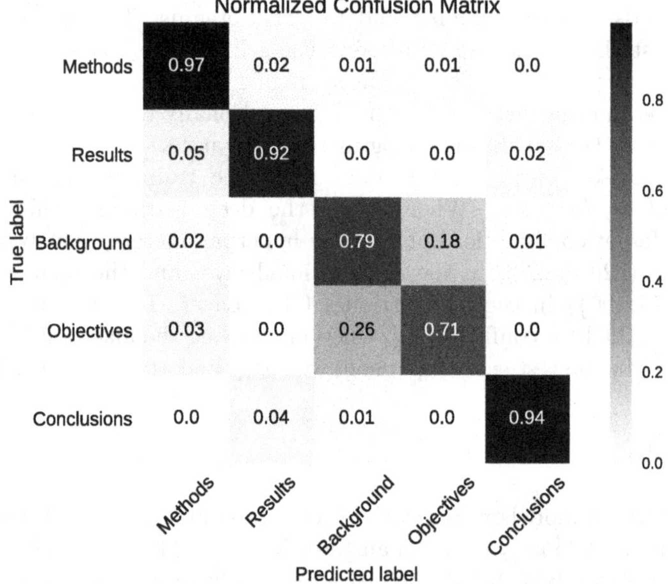

Fig. 2. Normalized confusion matrix.

results are detailed in Table 4. Word-BiGRU provides better results in all metrics when compared with the other models. The improvement ranges: from 6.0 to 9.1% points, when compared with CNN, confirming the value of the bi-directional GRU layer; and from 0.3 to 3.0% points when compared with Char-BiLSTM. Finally, we note that the Word-BiGRU model requires more computation than the simpler CNN model. On average, the proposed architecture requires 880 s per epoch while CNN requires 182 s.

Table 3. Test results for each class (in %, best values in **bold**).

		Background	Objective	Methods	Results	Conclusions
Precision	Word-BiGRU	**79.7**	70.5	93.3	**95.9**	**94.2**
	Char-BiLSTM [6]	71.8	**78.2**	**93.7**	94.8	93.5
Recall	Word-BiGRU	78.7	**71.4**	**96.7**	92.3	**94.5**
	Char-BiLSTM [6]	**88.2**	48.1	96.2	**93.1**	92.9
F1-Score	Word-BiGRU	**79.2**	**70.9**	**95.0**	**94.1**	**94.3**
	Char-BiLSTM [6]	79.1	59.6	94.9	93.9	93.2

Table 4. Averaged test results (in %, best values in **bold**).

Metric	Averaged	Char-BiLSTM [6]	CNN	Word-BiGRU
Precision	Macro-Averaged	86.4	80.7	**86.7**
	Weight-Averaged	90.1	83.6	**90.9**
Recall	Macro-Averaged	83.7	77.6	**86.7**
	Weight-Averaged	89.9	83.5	**90.8**
F1-score	Macro-Averaged	85.0	78.5	**86.7**
	Weight-Averaged	90.0	83.5	**90.8**

5 Conclusions

Abstract sentence classification is a key element to assist in scientific database querying, performing literature reviews and to support the writing of new abstracts. In this paper, we present a novel deep learning architecture for abstract sentence classification. The proposed Word-BiGRU architecture assumes word embeddings, a convolutional layer and a bi-directional Gated Recurrent Unit (GRU). Using a large sentence corpus, related with 20 thousand abstracts from the biomedical domain, we have obtaining high quality classification performances, with weight-average Precision, Recall and F1-score values around 91%. These results compare favourably against a state-of-the-art bi-directional Long Short-Term Memory (LSTM) model. In future work, we wish to enlarge the experimentation of the proposed deep learning architecture to classify abstract corpus from other scientific domains and also to other sequential tasks.

Acknowledgements. This work was supported by COMPETE: POCI-01-0145-FEDER-007043 and FCT Fundação para a Ciência e Tecnologia within the Project Scope: UID/CEC/00319/2013.

References

1. Atanassova, I., Bertin, M., Larivière, V.: On the composition of scientific abstracts. J. Doc. **72**(4), 636–647 (2016)
2. Boudin, F., Nie, J.Y., Bartlett, J.C., Grad, R., Pluye, P., Dawes, M.: Combining classifiers for robust pico element detection. BMC Med. Inform. Decis. Mak. **10**(1), 29 (2010)
3. Cho, K., van Merrienboer, B., Gulcehre, C., Bahdanau, D., Bougares, F., Schwenk, H., Bengio, Y.: Learning phrase representations using rnn encoder-decoder for statistical machine translation. In: Proceedings of the 2014 Conference on Empirical Methods in Natural Language Processing (EMNLP), pp. 1724–1734. Association for Computational Linguistics, Doha, Qatar, October 2014
4. Cornuel, E.: A vision for Business Schools, vol. 24. Emerald Group Publishing (2005)
5. Dernoncourt, F., Lee, J.Y.: Pubmed 200k rct: a dataset for sequential sentence classification in medical abstracts. In: Proceedings of the Eighth International Joint Conference on Natural Language Processing, vol. 2, pp. 308–313 (2017)
6. Dernoncourt, F., Lee, J.Y., Szolovits, P.: Neural networks for joint sentence classification in medical paper abstracts. In: Proceedings of the 15th Conference of the European Chapter of the Association for Computational Linguistics, vol. 2, pp. 694–700 (2017)
7. Glorot, X., Bordes, A., Bengio, Y.: Deep sparse rectifier neural networks. In: Proceedings of the Fourteenth International Conference on Artificial Intelligence and Statistics, pp. 315–323 (2011)
8. Goodfellow, I., Bengio, Y., Courville, A., Bengio, Y.: Deep Learning, vol. 1. MIT press, Cambridge (2016)
9. Khabsa, M., Giles, C.L.: The number of scholarly documents on the public web. PloS One **9**(5), e93949 (2014)
10. Kim, Y.: Convolutional neural networks for sentence classification. In: Proceedings of the 2014 Conference on Empirical Methods in Natural Language Processing (EMNLP), pp. 1746–1751 (2014)
11. Kitchenham, B., Brereton, P.: A systematic review of systematic review process research in software engineering. Inf. Softw. Technol. **55**(12), 2049–2075 (2013)
12. LeCun, Y., Kavukcuoglu, K., Farabet, C.: Convolutional networks and applications in vision. Proceedings of 2010 IEEE International Symposium on Circuits and Systems, pp. 253–256 (2010)
13. Liu, Y., Wu, F., Liu, M., Liu, B.: Abstract sentence classification for scientific papers based on transductive SVM. Comput. Inf. Sci. **6**(4), 125 (2013)
14. Michalska-Smith, M.J., Allesina, S.: And, not or: quality, quantity in scientific publishing. PloS One **12**(6), e0178074 (2017)
15. Moro, S., Cortez, P., Rita, P.: Business intelligence in banking: a literature analysis from 2002 to 2013 using text mining and latent dirichlet allocation. Expert. Syst. Appl. **42**(3), 1314–1324 (2015)
16. Pennington, J., Socher, R., Manning, C.: Glove: global vectors for word representation. In: Proceedings of the 2014 conference on empirical methods in natural language processing (EMNLP), pp. 1532–1543 (2014)
17. Witten, I., Frank, E., Hall, M., Pal, C.: Data Mining: Practical Machine Learning Tools and Techniques, 4th edn. Morgan Kaufmann, San Franscico (2017)

Weighted Multi-view Deep Neural Networks for Weather Forecasting

Zahra Karevan(✉), Lynn Houthuys, and Johan A. K. Suykens

KU Leuven, ESAT-STADIUS Kasteelpark Arenberg 10, 3001 Leuven, Belgium
{zahra.karevan,lynn.houthuys,johan.suykens}@esat.kuleuven.be

Abstract. In multi-view regression the information from multiple representations of the input data is combined to improve the prediction. Inspired by the success of deep learning, this paper proposes a novel model called Weighted Multi-view Deep Neural Networks (MV-DNN) regression. The objective function used is a weighted version of the primal formulation of the existing Multi-View Least Squares Support Vector Machines method, where both the objectives from all different views, as well as the coupling term, are weighted. This work is motivated by the challenging application of weather forecasting. To predict the temperature, the weather variables from several previous days are taken into account. Each feature vector belonging to a previous day (delay) is regarded as a different view. Experimental results on the minimum and maximum temperature prediction in Brussels, reveal the merit of the weighting and show promising results when compared to existing the state-of-the-art methods in weather prediction.

Keywords: Multi-view learning · Neural networks · Deep learning Weather forecasting

1 Introduction

Accurate weather prediction is one of the most challenging tasks in climate informatics. The prediction task is being complicated due to various environmental issues like topography of surrounding structures, the chaotic characteristics of the atmosphere, the influence of human behavior and many more. State-of-the-art methods usually apply the Numerical Weather Prediction (NWP) to get a decent prediction. Because this method is very computationally intensive [3], there is an increasing interest in data-driven methods which uses historical data to do the prediction.

Multi-view learning denotes a group of learning techniques that are applied when the data is described through multiple representations, or views. By using the information available from all views, multi-view learning aims to improve the performance over only using a single view. This could be achieved by simply concatenating the features from all views, like e.g. the work done by Zilca and

V. Kůrková et al. (Eds.): ICANN 2018, LNCS 11141, pp. 489–499, 2018.
https://doi.org/10.1007/978-3-030-01424-7_48

Bistritz [22]. This approach is a typical example of early fusion, as the information from all views is fused early on in the training process. However, as this increases the dimensionality greatly and it ignores the statistical properties of each individual view, most state-of-the-art multi-view methods aim to jointly optimize the objectives of each view [5,19,20]. Liu et al. [13] propose a multi-task multi-view method to predict Urban Water Quality where the spatial and temporal features are considered as two views. Houthuys et al. [10] propose a multi-view kernel-based method to predict temperature by considering the neighboring cities as different views.

Inspired by the success of deep learning in feature learning research [4,7,12], several deep multi-view methods have recently been proposed. These techniques are usually based on one of the two main approaches [18]. The first approach is based on autoencoders, like e.g. the work done by Ngiam et al. [14], the second is based on a Deep Neural Network (DNN) extension to CCA-like [9] methods, e.g. the deep CCA method proposed by Andrew et al. [2].

In this paper a novel DNN-based multi-view method is proposed and its performance is evaluated on the application of temperature prediction. The model follows the second deep multi-view approach, where the novelty lies in the weighting of the view-specific objectives and the coupling term. These weights can be tailored to the needs of each application. They can be determined through e.g. the similarity to the prediction task, some expert knowledge about the application, and so on. For our application we have chosen to weight according to the performance of each view on the validation set when used separately. Temperature prediction is a multi-variate time-series forecasting application, and hence the prediction of a certain day depends on the features of the previous days. To have a reliable prediction, one may use a large feature vector which is the concatenation of the weather features from the previous days. However, instead of simply concatenating these feature vectors, this paper regards each previous day, or *delay*, as a separate view.

We will denote matrices as bold uppercase letters and vectors as bold lowercase letters. The superscript $^{[v]}$ will denote the vth view for the multi-view method.

2 Background: Multi-View LS-SVM Regression

This section summarizes the Multi-View LS-SVM Regression (MV LS-SVM) [10] model. This model is a multi-view extension of the well known Least Squares Support Vector Machine (LS-SVM) [16], where the primal formulation contains the summation of the objective functions corresponding to each view plus a coupling term. The coupling term takes into account the correlation between the different views.

Given a number of V views and training data $\{y_k, \mathbf{x}_k^{[v]}\}_{k=1}^N$ for $v = 1, \ldots, V$, where $\mathbf{x}_k^{[v]} \in \mathbb{R}^{d^{[v]}}$ denotes the k-th input sample and $y_k \in \mathbb{R}$ the k-th target value, the primal formulation of the MV LS-SVM model is stated as follows:

$$\min_{\mathbf{w}^{[v]},\mathbf{e}^{[v]},\, b^{[v]}} \frac{1}{2}\sum_{v=1}^{V} \mathbf{w}^{[v]^T}\mathbf{w}^{[v]} + \frac{1}{2}\sum_{v=1}^{V} \gamma^{[v]}\mathbf{e}^{[v]^T}\mathbf{e}^{[v]} + \rho \sum_{v,u=1;v\neq u}^{V} \mathbf{e}^{[v]^T}\mathbf{e}^{[u]} \tag{1}$$

$$\text{s.t. } \mathbf{y} = \boldsymbol{\Phi}^{[v]}\mathbf{w}^{[v]} + b^{[v]}\mathbf{1}_N + \mathbf{e}^{[v]} \quad \text{for } v = 1, \ldots, V$$

where $\mathbf{y} = [y_1; \ldots; y_N]$, $b^{[v]}$ are bias terms, $\gamma^{[v]}$ are positive real constants and $\mathbf{e}^{[v]} \in \mathbb{R}^N$ are error variables for each view v. The term $\rho \sum_{v,u=1;v\neq u}^{V} \mathbf{e}^{[v]^T}\mathbf{e}^{[u]}$ is defined as the coupling term and the regularization parameter $\rho > 0$ as the coupling parameter.

$\boldsymbol{\Phi}^{[v]} \in \mathbb{R}^{N\times d_h^{[v]}}$ is defined as $\boldsymbol{\Phi}^{[v]} = [\varphi^{[v]}(\mathbf{x}_1^{[v]})^T; \ldots; \varphi^{[v]}(\mathbf{x}_N^{[v]})^T]$ where $\varphi^{[v]} : \mathbb{R}^{d^{[v]}} \rightarrow \mathbb{R}^{d_h^{[v]}}$ are the feature maps, related to the vth view, which map the $d^{[v]}$-dimensional input to a high dimensional feature space. Since this feature space is high dimensional, and can even be infinite dimensional, the function $\varphi^{[v]}(\cdot)$ is usually not explicitly defined. Instead, the dual model [10, Eq.(10)] is derived where the function is implicitly defined trough the use of a positive kernel function $K^{[v]} : \mathbb{R}^{d^{[v]}} \times \mathbb{R}^{d^{[v]}} \rightarrow \mathbb{R}$ where $K^{[v]}(\mathbf{x}_i^{[v]}, \mathbf{x}_j^{[v]}) = \varphi^{[v]}(\mathbf{x}_i^{[v]})^T\varphi^{[v]}(\mathbf{x}_j^{[v]})$.

However, this primal formulation can be used by a Neural Network (NN) as a loss function to optimize the parameters. Hence, an NN could be used to solve the problem in the primal, as shown by the neural networks interpretation in primal and dual by Suykens et al. [16] and as was previously done for kernel methods e.g. by Zhong and Ghosh [21] for the SVM model [17].

3 Proposed Method

In this section the Weighted Multi-view DNN model (Weighted MV-DNN) is introduced. The loss function of the proposed DNN is based on the primal formulation of MV LS-SVM (Eq. (1)) where the objectives of different views are weighted, as well as the coupling term.

The loss function optimized by the Weighted MV-DNN is stated as follows:

$$\min_{\mathbf{w}^{[v]},\mathbf{e}^{[v]}} \frac{1}{2}\sum_{v=1}^{V} s^{[v]}\left(\mathbf{w}^{[v]^T}\mathbf{w}^{[v]} + \gamma^{[v]}\mathbf{e}^{[v]^T}\mathbf{e}^{[v]}\right) + \sum_{v,u=1;v\neq u}^{V} \rho^{[v,u]}\sqrt{s^{[v]}}\sqrt{s^{[u]}}\ \mathbf{e}^{[v]^T}\mathbf{e}^{[u]} \tag{2}$$

where $\rho^{[v,u]}$ denotes the coupling parameter which can be different for each pairwise combination of views v and u and for which should hold that $0 \leq \rho^{[v,u]} \leq \min(\gamma^{[v]}, \gamma^{[u]})$. The reason for this upper bound on the coupling parameter is to ensure that the objective function does not converge to $-\infty$ for error variables $\mathbf{e}^{[v]}$ belonging to a certain view v, which can happen when $\rho^{[v,u]}$ is significantly larger than $\gamma^{[v]}$. Notice that $\mathbf{w}^{[v]}$ are the parameter vectors for the whole DNN.

The proposed model is graphically represented in Fig. 1 and compared to a graphical representation of the early fusion DNN approach, where the features from all views are simply concatenated. Notice that it is possible to use another model and learning mechanism instead of DNN like e.g. LS-SVM, Convolutional Neural Networks [11], Deep Belief Networks [8], Restricted Kernel Machines [15] and so on.

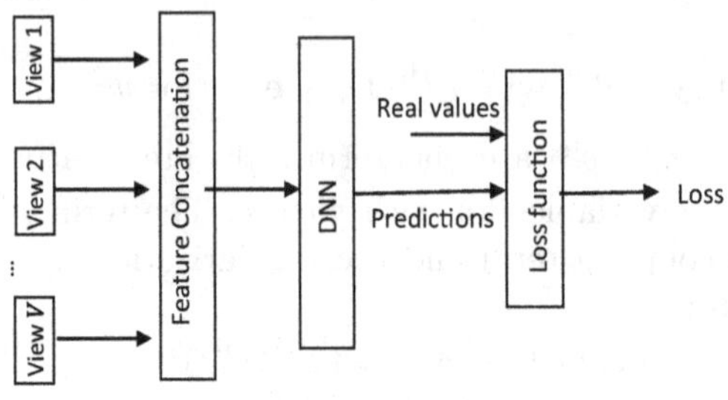

(a) Early fusion DNN

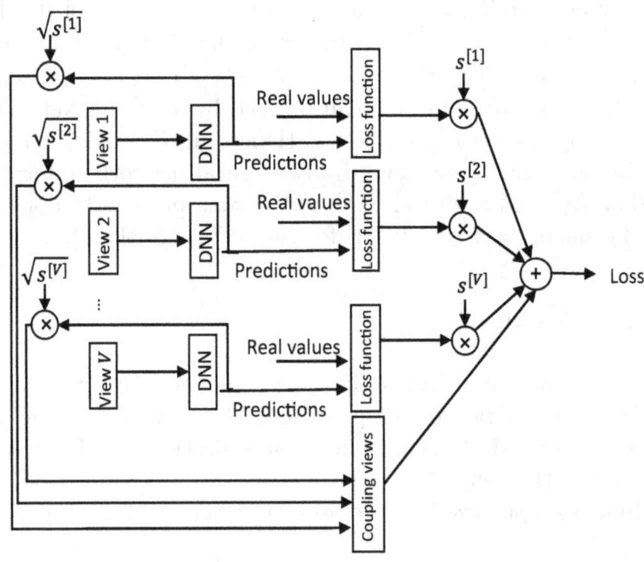

(b) Weighted Multi-view DNN

Fig. 1. General schemes of early fusion and the proposed method

The weights $s^{[v]}$ for $v = 1, \ldots, V$ are added to control the influence of each view. These weights can be tailored to each specific application and can be manually determined by an expert, or calculated during a pre-processing step. Take for example the application of temperature prediction where the different views represent different neighboring cities. In this example the weights could be determined by means of the similarity of different cities (views) to the target city, which could be calculated through a similarity function on the features of each city. Another example for temperature prediction is where each view represents a different weather variable (temperature, wind speed, humidity, etc.). In this example one might have some expert knowledge about which weather variables influence temperature more than others. In case this expert knowledge is not available another way to determine the weights is by looking at the performance of each individual view. In this way the views that have a weak performance can have a smaller weight than the views that perform well.

The resulting regressor $\hat{y}(\cdot)$ for an unseen test point $\mathbf{x_t}$, with representations ${\mathbf{x_t}}^{[v]}$ for all views $v = 1, \ldots, V$, is defined as

$$\hat{y}(\mathbf{x_t}) = \frac{1}{V}\sum_{v=1}^{V} \beta^{[v]}\hat{y}^{[v]}({\mathbf{x_t}}^{[v]}) \tag{3}$$

where $\hat{y}^{[v]}(\cdot)$ is the view-specific function estimation based on the obtained $\mathbf{w}^{[v]}$ and $\mathbf{e}^{[v]}$. This last prediction step thus includes another weighting, where the weighs can be equal to the weights from the training phase, i.e. $\beta^{[v]} = s^{[v]}$, or equal to 1 in order to obtain an unweighted averaged prediction.

4 Experiments

4.1 Weather Data

In this paper the data are collected from the Weather Underground website [1] which is one of the popular ones in weather forecasting. The data include real measurements for weather elements such as minimum and maximum temperature, dew point and pressure from the beginning of 2007 until mid 2014 and for 5 cities including Brussels, Liege, Antwerp, Amsterdam and Eindhoven (Fig. 2).

Fig. 2. Weather stations (from Google maps)

To assess the performance of the proposed method in different weather conditions, the experiments are conducted on two different test sets: one from mid-November 2013 until mid-December 2013 and the other one from mid-April 2014 to mid-May 2014. The prediction is done on a daily basis and for each test set, the training data includes daily weather variables of all of the five cities from the beginning of 2007 until the previous day of the test set. For each location there are 18 measured weather variables per day.

4.2 Model Selection

As it was mentioned, in this study we consider each delay as a view. This was inspired by the fact that Recurrent Neural Networks (RNN) [6], which is a well-known approach in time-series prediction, splits the features based on the time delay and take into account each delay as separate input. In this study, the number of delays that has been taken into account is five; hence the number of views V is equal to five. By concatenation of the features (early fusion), the total number of features is equal to 450 (*number of views* × *number of cities* × *number of features per day per location*). Note that the number of features in each view is equal to 90 (*number of cities* × *number of features per day per location*).

To find a proper baseline, we evaluated the performance of LS-SVM, RNN and DNN with two hidden layers. For the experiments we use LSSVMlab[1] (in MATLAB) to deploy LS-SVM as a learning approach and TensorFlow[2] (in Python) to implement basic RNN [6] and DNN. The results in Tables 1 and 2 suggest that the DNN approach outperforms RNN and LS-SVM in most of the cases. Thus, we deploy DNN as our baseline approach. Note that for LS-SVM, the tuning hyperparameters are the regularization parameter and the RBF kernel bandwidth which are tuned using cross validation. In RNN and DNN, the tuning parameters are the number of neurons and the regularization parameters. To decrease the weighted MV-DNN tuning complexity, the number of neurons in each layer and the regularization parameter $\gamma^{[v]}$ for each view is tuned independently on each view. Afterwards, the views are coupled based on Eq. (2) and the $\rho^{[v,u]}$ values for each couple of views are tuned. Note that all parameters are tuned based on a validation set. The validation set for each test set is defined to include the data from last year prior to the corresponding test set. Moreover, to avoid local minima problem, we did the experiments five times. LS-SVM does not have the local minima problem; nevertheless, we did the experiments five times to tune the hyperparameters. The results are reported based on the median and the standard deviation of the Mean Absolute Error (MAE) on the test sets.

In this study we define the weights of the views based on their performance on the validation set independently. Assuming $mse_{val}^{[v]}$ to be the Mean Squared Error of the view v on the validation set, the weight of this view is defined as $\exp(-mse_{val}^{[v]})$. The weights are further rescaled so that $\sum_{v=1}^{V} s^{[v]} = V$. Thus, a view that performs well will have a higher corresponding weight. In Fig. 3, the average weight values for different delays in one to six days ahead prediction are shown. It can be seen that for short term prediction smaller delays have higher impact on the prediction while for long term prediction the weights of the views are more similar.

In Tables 3 and 4 the performance of different multi-view methods are compared. The last two columns show the performance of the proposed method where *weighted average* refers to taking a weighted averaged prediction and *aver-*

[1] https://www.esat.kuleuven.be/sista/lssvmlab/.

[2] www.tensorflow.org.

Table 1. Median MAE of the predictions in Weather LS-SVM, RNN and DNN with two hidden layers on Nov/Dec test set

Step ahead	Temp.	LS-SVM	RNN	DNN
1	Min	1.84 ± 0.05	$\mathbf{1.71 \pm 0.01}$	$\mathbf{1.71 \pm 0.02}$
	Max	1.52 ± 0.01	1.62 ± 0.05	$\mathbf{1.37 \pm 0.07}$
2	Min	1.84 ± 0.02	1.85 ± 0.04	$\mathbf{1.81 \pm 0.04}$
	Max	1.85 ± 0.01	$\mathbf{1.67 \pm 0.1}$	1.78 ± 0.08
3	Min	2.23 ± 0.04	1.98 ± 0.02	$\mathbf{1.85 \pm 0.011}$
	Max	2.03 ± 0.007	2.06 ± 0.2	$\mathbf{1.93 \pm 0.1}$
4	Min	2.01 ± 0.04	1.76 ± 0.01	$\mathbf{1.70 \pm 0.01}$
	Max	2.07 ± 0.009	1.99 ± 0.03	$\mathbf{1.73 \pm 0.09}$
5	Min	2.26 ± 0.1	$\mathbf{1.84 \pm 0.008}$	$\mathbf{1.84 \pm 0.08}$
	Max	2.06 ± 0.01	2.17 ± 0.3	$\mathbf{1.67 \pm 0.09}$
6	Min	2.18 ± 0.05	$\mathbf{1.89 \pm 0.02}$	1.95 ± 0.02
	Max	2.02 ± 0.01	1.93 ± 0.3	$\mathbf{1.76 \pm 0.1}$

Table 2. Median MAE of the predictions in LS-SVM, RNN and DNN with two hidden layers on Apr/May test set

Step ahead	Temp.	LS-SVM	RNN	DNN
1	Min	1.63 ± 0.007	1.67 ± 0.04	$\mathbf{1.60 \pm 0.01}$
	Max	$\mathbf{2.18 \pm 0.001}$	2.25 ± 0.07	2.37 ± 0.03
2	Min	$\mathbf{2.17 \pm 0.002}$	2.59 ± 0.1	2.10 ± 0.06
	Max	$\mathbf{2.40 \pm 0.008}$	2.58 ± 0.02	$\mathbf{2.40 \pm 0.08}$
3	Min	2.37 ± 0.003	2.24 ± 0.01	$\mathbf{2.10 \pm 0.02}$
	Max	2.50 ± 0.01	$\mathbf{2.46 \pm 0.01}$	2.54 ± 0.06
4	Min	2.59 ± 0.002	2.29 ± 0.01	$\mathbf{2.17 \pm 0.03}$
	Max	3.00 ± 0.003	$\mathbf{2.52 \pm 0.01}$	2.67 ± 0.01
5	Min	2.87 ± 0.004	2.46 ± 0.02	$\mathbf{2.33 \pm 0.03}$
	Max	2.94 ± 0.009	$\mathbf{2.51 \pm 0.03}$	2.70 ± 0.06
6	Min	3.16 ± 0.003	2.77 ± 0.02	$\mathbf{2.56 \pm 0.06}$
	Max	2.76 ± 0.002	$\mathbf{2.71 \pm 0.02}$	2.89 ± 0.06

age to taking an unweighted one (i.e. $\beta^{[v]} = s^{[v]}$ and $\beta^{[v]} = 1$, respectively, for all $v = 1, \ldots, V$ in Eq. (3)). The results yield that Weighted MV-DNN outperforms the unweighted version in most test cases. This suggests that considering weights for different delays can improve the temperature prediction performance. Unweighted MV-DNN refers to the proposed method with all weights equal to one. In Fig. 4, the overall performance of Weather Underground, Early fusion DNN and MV-DNN on both test sets together are compared. The results reveal

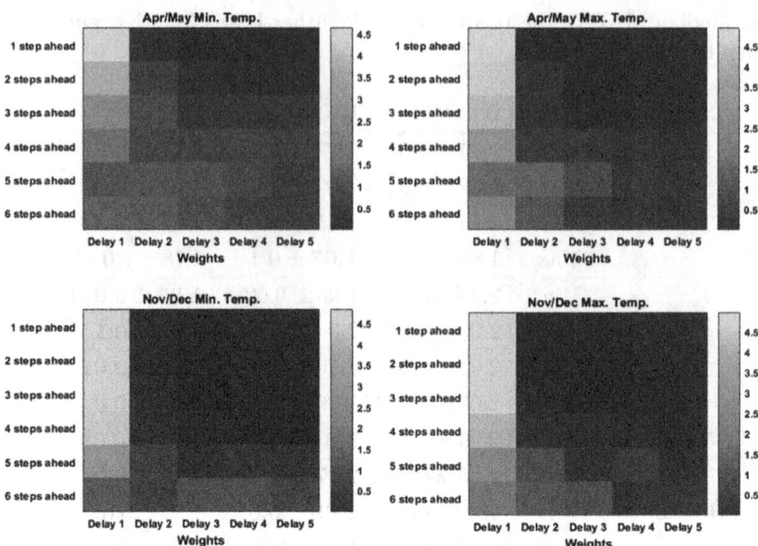

Fig. 3. Weights of different views (delays) for 1 to 6 days ahead in Nov/Dec and Apr/May data sets

Table 3. Median MAE of the predictions in Unweighted MV-DNN and Weighted MV-DNN with two hidden layers on Nov/Dec test set

Step ahead	Temp.	Unweighted MV-DNN	Weighted MV-DNN *(average)*	Weighted MV-DNN *(weighted average)*
1	Min	1.58 ± 0.01	**1.51 ± 0.01**	1.63 ± 0.02
	Max	1.39 ± 0.01	1.59 ± 0.002	**1.35 ± 0.02**
2	Min	**1.64 ± 0.01**	1.69 ± 0.002	1.80 ± 0.02
	Max	**1.76 ± 0.007**	2.00 ± 0.01	1.89 ± 0.02
3	Min	**1.78 ± 0.005**	**1.78 ± 0.003**	2.07 ± 0.01
	Max	2.06 ± 0.03	**1.97 ± 0.01**	**1.97 ± 0.006**
4	Min	**1.79 ± 0.02**	1.84 ± 0.005	1.85 ± 0.009
	Max	**1.80 ± 0.06**	1.88 ± 0.02	**1.80 ± 0.03**
5	Min	1.90 ± 0.02	**1.75 ± 0.04**	1.84 ± 0.04
	Max	1.93 ± 0.04	**1.77 ± 0.01**	1.87 ± 0.1
6	Min	2.18 ± 0.01	**1.88 ± 0.08**	1.90 ± 0.06
	Max	1.94 ± 0.008	**1.85 ± 0.07**	1.90 ± 0.05

that the black-box methods are competitive with the state-of-the-art method used by Weather Underground. Moreover, it is shown that taking into account each delay as a view and deploying multi-view learning can improve the performance.

Table 4. Median MAE of the predictions in Unweighted MV-DNN and Weighted MV-DNN with two hidden layers on Apr/May test set

Step ahead	Temp.	Unweighted MV-DNN	Weighted MV-DNN *(average)*	Weighted MV-DNN *(weighted average)*
1	Min	1.89 ± 0.002	2.01 ± 0.0001	$\mathbf{1.67 \pm 0.01}$
	Max	2.41 ± 0.01	2.52 ± 0.01	$\mathbf{2.11 \pm 0.009}$
2	Min	2.22 ± 0.004	2.17 ± 0.03	$\mathbf{1.96 \pm 0.02}$
	Max	2.53 ± 0.02	2.49 ± 0.03	$\mathbf{2.47 \pm 0.02}$
3	Min	2.29 ± 0.01	2.28 ± 0.002	$\mathbf{2.06 \pm 0.01}$
	Max	2.66 ± 0.01	2.60 ± 0.006	$\mathbf{2.42 \pm 0.0008}$
4	Min	2.28 ± 0.006	2.26 ± 0.02	$\mathbf{2.17 \pm 0.01}$
	Max	2.65 ± 0.005	2.74 ± 0.03	$\mathbf{2.56 \pm 0.01}$
5	Min	$\mathbf{2.46 \pm 0.0006}$	$\mathbf{2.46 \pm 0.0002}$	2.49 ± 0.004
	Max	2.78 ± 0.01	2.83 ± 0.03	$\mathbf{2.73 \pm 0.02}$
6	Min	2.64 ± 0.002	2.60 ± 0.01	$\mathbf{2.59 \pm 0.002}$
	Max	2.85 ± 0.01	2.87 ± 0.03	$\mathbf{2.75 \pm 0.03}$

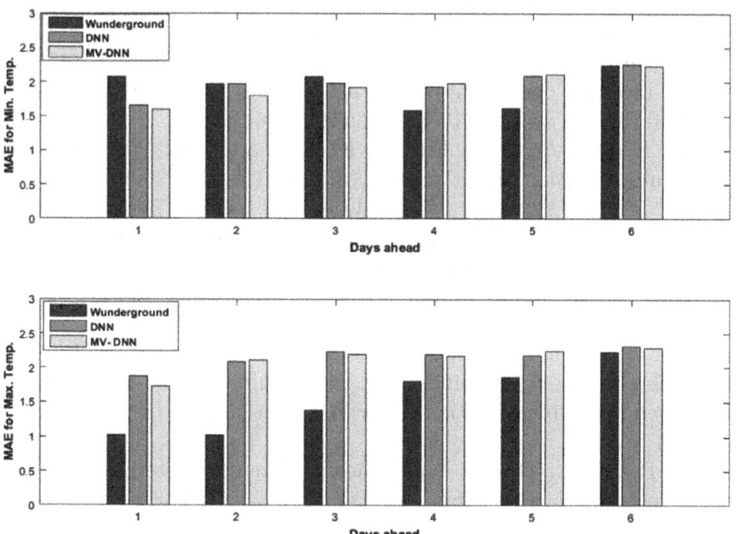

Fig. 4. Average MAE of the predictions for Weather Underground, DNN and MV-DNN on both test set

5 Conclusion

In this paper we proposed a DNN-based multi-view method which is based on the weighting of the view-specific objectives and the coupling term. These weights can be determined by different approaches. In this paper we defined each view to be the weather variables on a specific delay in the time series. The weights are determined based on the performance of each view on the validation set, independently. The results on an application of temperature prediction show the improvement of the proposed MV-DNN method over an unweighted version as well as over the early fusion approach.

Acknowledgments. Research supported by Research Council KUL: CoE PFV/10/002 (OPTEC), PhD/Postdoc grants Flemish Government; FWO: projects: G0A4917N (Deep restricted kernel machines), G.088114N (Tensor based data similarity), ERC Advanced Grant E-DUALITY (787960).

References

1. www.wunderground.com. Accessed: 10 July 2018
2. Andrew, G., Arora, R., Bilmes, J., Livescu, K.: Deep canonical correlation analysis. In: ICML, pp. 1247–1255 (2013)
3. Bauer, P., Thorpe, A., Brunet, G.: The quiet revolution of numerical weather prediction. Nature **525**(7567), 47–55 (2015)
4. Bengio, Y.: Learning deep architectures for AI. Found. Trends Mach. Learn. **2**(1), 1–127 (2009). https://doi.org/10.1561/2200000006
5. Chaudhuri, K., Kakade, S.M., Livescu, K., Sridharan, K.: Multi-view clustering via canonical correlation analysis. In: ICML, pp. 129–136 (2009)
6. Elman, J.L.: Finding structure in time. Cogn. Sci. **14**(2), 179–211 (1990)
7. Hinton, G., Salakhutdinov, R.: Reducing the dimensionality of data with neural networks. Science **313**, 504–507 (2006)
8. Hinton, G.E.: What kind of a graphical model is the brain? In: IJCAI, pp. 1765–1775 (2005)
9. Hotelling, H.: Relations between two sets of variates. Biometrica **28**, 321–377 (1936)
10. Houthuys, L., Karevan, Z., Suykens, J.A.K.: Multi-view LS-SVM regression for black-box temperature prediction in weather forecasting. In: IJCNN, pp. 1102–1108 (2017)
11. LeCun, Y., Bottou, L., Bengio, Y., Haffner, P.: Gradient-based learning applied to document recognition. Proc. IEEE **86**(11), 2278–2324 (1998). https://doi.org/10.1109/5.726791
12. LeCun, Y., Bengio, Y., Hinton, G.: Deep learning. Nature **521**, 436–44 (2015)
13. Liu, Y., Zheng, Y., Liang, Y., Liu, S., Rosenblum, D.S.: Urban water quality prediction based on multi-task multi-view learning. In: IJCAI, pp. 2576–2582 (2016)
14. Ngiam, J., Khosla, A., Kim, M., Nam, J., Lee, H., Ng, A.Y.: Multimodal deep learning. In: ICML, pp. 689–696 (2011)
15. Suykens, J.A.K.: Deep restricted kernel machines using conjugate feature duality. Neural Comput. **29**(8), 2123–2163 (2017)
16. Suykens, J.A.K., Van Gestel, T., De Brabanter, J., De Moor, B., Vandewalle, J.: Least Squares Support Vector Machines. World Scientific (2002)

17. Vapnik, V.: The Nature of Statistical Learning Theory. Springer-Verlag, New-York (1995). https://doi.org/10.1007/978-1-4757-3264-1
18. Wang, W., Arora, R., Livescu, K., Bilmes, J.: On deep multi-view representation learning. In: ICML, pp. 1083–1092 (2015)
19. Xu, C., Tao, D., Xu, C.: A survey on multi-view learning. eprint arXiv:1304.5634, April 2013
20. Zhao, J., Xie, X., Xu, X., Sun, S.: Multi-view learning overview: recent progress and new challenges. Inf. Fusion **38**, 43–54 (2017). https://doi.org/10.1016/j.inffus.2017.02.007
21. Zhong, S., Ghosh, J.: Decision boundary focused neural network classifier. Intelligent Engineering Systems Through Articial Neural Networks (2000)
22. Zilca, R.D., Bistritz, Y.: Feature concatenation for speaker identification. In: EUSIPCO pp. 1–4, September 2000

Combining Articulatory Features with End-to-End Learning in Speech Recognition

Leyuan Qu(✉), Cornelius Weber, Egor Lakomkin, Johannes Twiefel, and Stefan Wermter

Department of Informatics, University of Hamburg, Vogt-Koelln-Str. 30, 22527 Hamburg, Germany
{qu, weber, lakomkin, twiefel, wermter}@informatik.uni-hamburg.de
http://www.informatik.uni-hamburg.de/WTM

Abstract. End-to-end neural networks have shown promising results on large vocabulary continuous speech recognition (LVCSR) systems. However, it is challenging to integrate domain knowledge into such systems. Specifically, articulatory features (AFs) which are inspired by the human speech production mechanism can help in speech recognition. This paper presents two approaches to incorporate domain knowledge into end-to-end training: (a) fine-tuning networks which reuse hidden layer representations of AF extractors as input for ASR tasks; (b) progressive networks which combine articulatory knowledge by lateral connections from AF extractors. We evaluate the proposed approaches on the speech Wall Street Journal corpus and test on the eval92 standard evaluation dataset. Results show that both fine-tuning and progressive networks can integrate articulatory information into end-to-end learning and outperform previous systems.

Keywords: Articulatory features · Automatic speech recognition
Deep neural networks (DNN) · End-to-end learning

1 Introduction

End-to-end learning has been successfully applied in many domains, such as handwriting recognition [1], neural machine translation [2], scene text recognition [3], and so on. Furthermore, end-to-end models have become popular in automatic speech recognition (ASR) tasks. The conventional ASR pipeline consists of many different components: the acoustic model, pronunciation model and language model. These components are separate and require lots of human expertise, e.g. a handcrafted pronunciation dictionary and designed senone states for Hidden Markov Models (HMMs). Additionally, the training targets and alignment information needed for neural networks in a DNN-HMM paradigm can only be obtained from another GMM-HMMs (GMM is short for Gaussian Mixture Model) model which is trained beforehand. Such a pipeline requires not only multiple training stages but also different optimization functions [4].

V. Kůrková et al. (Eds.): ICANN 2018, LNCS 11141, pp. 500–510, 2018.
https://doi.org/10.1007/978-3-030-01424-7_49

To simplify this complex paradigm, end-to-end learning approaches [4–6, 11–13] have been proposed to replace hand-designed feature engineering and jointly learn all components in a single architecture. These approaches can be transformed into computational flow graphs which can be optimized by backpropagation in a simple end-to-end training process. End-to-end models are able to naturally handle sequences of arbitrary lengths and directly optimize the word error rate. However, it is challenging to integrate domain knowledge into these models. Therefore, the goal of this study is to combine articulatory features into end-to-end learning.

Articulatory features (AFs), also known as phonological features, phonological attributes or distinctive phonetic features, are used to represent the movement of different articulators, such as lips and tongue, during speech production. AFs can be robustly estimated from speech by statistical classifiers, such as GMM and neural networks [7]. A series of studies have demonstrated that AFs can improve the performance of ASR systems by systematically accounting for coarticulation, speaking styles and other variability, especially in a noisy scenario [8]. Conventional methods to extract AFs from speech require precise boundary transcription. To get this boundary information, the usual practice is using forced alignments generated by a GMM-HMMs model [9], or labeling data manually at a frame-level [10], which are complex and time-consuming.

Our hypothesis in this paper is that AFs can provide useful and complementary representations that cannot be learned automatically by an end-to-end architecture. This paper explores two approaches to integrate domain knowledge to improve end-to-end model performance. Our contribution is two-fold: In the first step, we train a bank of AF extractors using Connectionist Temporal Classification (CTC) in an end-to-end way, which does not require precise phone or frame-level boundary information; In the second step, we propose two approaches (fine-tuning networks and progressive networks) to integrate domain knowledge (articulatory features) into end-to-end learning in speech recognition tasks.

2 Related Work

2.1 End-to-End Learning in Speech Recognition

At present, end-to-end learning in ASR can be mainly divided into two parts: CTC-based approaches and encoder-decoder models. For the CTC, Graves et al. [5] introduced the CTC loss function which removes the alignment constraint by introducing a "blank" label and allows to train a sequence labeling task directly without alignment and pre-segmentation. Miao et al. [4] explored a weighted finite-state transducers-decoding method to incorporate lexicons and language models in CTC objective function-based models. Recently, Zweig et al. [6] presented an iterated CTC approach on the NIST 2000 conversational telephone speech evaluation set which significantly improved performance over previous systems. For the encoder-decoder, Chorowski et al. [11] introduced an attention mechanism into speech recognition, in which the authors combined both content and localization information to recognize a longer utterance. Bahdanau et al. [12] replaced HMMs with an attention-based recurrent sequence generator (ARSG) on the LVCSR task. Unlike CTC-based methods, the ARSG system can learn a language model implicitly. Chan et al. [13] presented a Listen, Attend and Spell system to transcribe speech to characters directly. They reported 10.3% word error rate (WER) with rescoring compared to the-state-of-the-art WER of 8.0% achieved by a convolutional neural network and long short-term memory DNN-HMMs model [20] on 2000 h Google voice search dataset.

2.2 Domain Knowledge Integration in Speech Recognition

There are lots of approaches focusing on integrating domain knowledge to improve ASR performance, such as in feature engineering: mel-frequency cepstral coefficients [25] and vocal tract length normalization [26], and in algorithm optimization: sequence-discriminative training [27]. Here, we only consider studies that involve linguistic and phonetic knowledge.

Lee et al. [14] proposed automatic speech attribute transcription (ASAT) which is a new detected-based speech recognition paradigm. Compared to conventional ASR top-down paradigms, ASAT is bottom-up and coincident with the mechanism of humans perceiving and producing speech. To further improve phonological feature detection accuracy, Yu et al. [9] replaced one hidden layer multi-layer perceptrons by DNNs when building attribute detectors. Based on the high attribute detection precision, excellent phoneme estimate accuracy was obtained on the WSJ0 benchmark. Siniscalchi et al. [15] integrated acoustic-phonetic information into lattice rescoring. Inspired by shared phonetic knowledge among different languages, Siniscalchi et al. [16] designed a universal set of phones and used the set to improve the performance of cross-language phone recognition. Pitch accent was proposed by Ananthakrishnan et al. [17] to re-score the N-best results outputted from a standard ASR system. At present, the works integrating knowledge into ASR are mostly based on HMM hybrid architectures. Our approaches mainly focus on combining domain knowledge with neural end-to-end ASR systems.

3 Model Architecture

In this section, we present the details of AF extractors, fine-tuning networks and progressive networks.

3.1 AF Extractor

Figure 1 shows the flow diagram to get AF-level transcriptions. First, we split words into phonemes according to the CMU dict[1]. Then, we generate AFs transcriptions according to the mapping [9] (see Table 3 in the Appendix). The AF-level transcriptions will be used as training targets to build the AF extractors.

[1] http://www.speech.cs.cmu.edu/cgi-bin/cmudict.

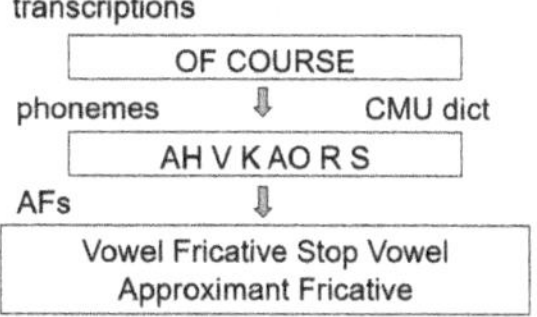

Fig. 1. Flowchart to convert word-level transcriptions of the phrase "of course" to AF labels.

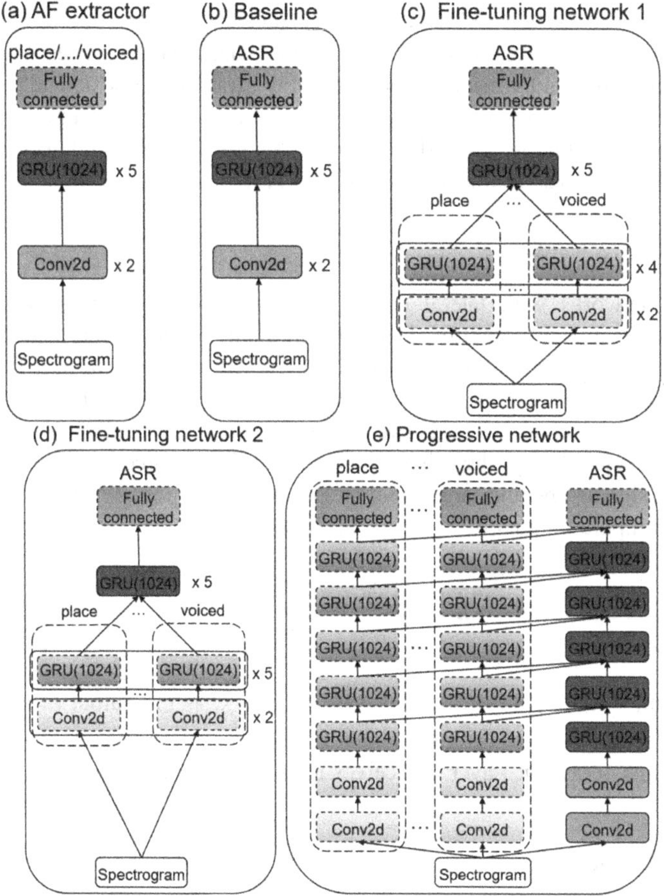

Fig. 2. Illustration of (a) AF extractor, (b) ASR baseline system, (c) and (d) fine-tuning networks and (e) progressive networks. The ASR baseline system is based on Deep Speech 2 [19]. Note: frozen (dotted line) without backpropagation and weight updating.

Eight AF extractors were built: place, manner, anterior, back, continuant, round, tense and voiced. The AF extractor architecture is shown in Fig. 2(a), which begins with two layers of 2D convolutions, followed by five layers of gated recurrent units (GRU), and the output layer is a fully connected layer. We train each extractor with the

CTC and additional two symbols (blank and space). For example, for 'voiced', the target labels are {voiced, other, space, blank}.

3.2 Fine-Tuning Networks

Fine-tuning is a process to transfer what a neural network learned on a given task to a second task. In this paper, AF extractors that have been learnt in a first task can be treated as a fixed front-end which transforms spectrograms to AFs. Hidden layer outputs from different AF extractors will be combined, then fed into another neural network for the second task (ASR). Figure 2 (c) and (d) show the fine-tuning networks used in this study. The details of AF extractors (place, manner, anterior, back, continuant, round, tense and voiced) are shown in Fig. 2(a). We concatenate the fourth or fifth GRU layer output of all extractors as a vector, namely fine-tuning networks 1 (Fig. 2(c)) and fine-tuning networks 2 (Fig. 2(d)) respectively, and feed it into a 5 bidirectional GRU-layer neural network for the ASR task.

3.3 Progressive Networks

Progressive networks with lateral connections from previous tasks can accelerate learning speed and avoid forgetting [18]. They not only learn relevant features but also acquire different representations from previous learned tasks, which may be irrelevant to the target task. The scheme of progressive networks is shown in Fig. 2(e). In this paper, there are no connections between the AF extractors and they are trained in parallel and independently, then linearly combined. The source task is AF extraction from speech signals and the target task is speech recognition. We use the following formula to compute outputs of layer i in ASR tasks:

$$h_i = W_i(h_{i-1} + \sum_{j=1}^{8} k_{i-1}^{j}) \tag{1}$$

where h_i is the output of layer i of the ASR system, k_i^j is the output of layer i of AF extractor j, $W_i \in R^{n_i \times n_{i-1}}$ is the weight matrix of layer i of ASR systems, with n_i the number of units at layer i. Layer h_i receives input from both h_{i-1} and k_{i-1}^{j} via Eq. (1).

4 Experiments

In this section, we present the dataset and the experimental setup.

4.1 Evaluation Metric

In this paper, we use the word error rate (WER) to evaluate model performance. WER quantifies how many elementary operations are required to transform the generated output sequence of the network into the correct target sequence. It is calculated as follows:

$$WER = \frac{S + D + I}{N} \tag{2}$$

where S is the number of substitutions, D is the number of deletions and I is the number of insertions. N is the total number of words in the reference.

4.2 Data

We used the Wall Street Journal (WSJ) [22] speech corpus both for AF and ASR experiments. The training set is the 81 h ‘train-si284’ with about 37 K sentences. We used the ‘dev93’ development set for validation and hyper-parameter optimization and report the final performance on the ‘eval92’ test set.

4.3 Training

The baseline ASR system (shown in Fig. 2(b)) used in this paper is similar to the Deep Speech 2 system [19]. The first two layers of all architectures are 2D (frequency and time domains) convolutions. The convolution layers not only reduce temporal variability in the time domain but also normalize speaker variance in the frequency domain [23]. These are followed by GRU layers. It has been shown that GRU cells achieve comparable performance to Long Short-Term Memory (LSTM) but GRU cells are faster and easier to train [21]. Finally, we pass the output from the GRU cells to a fully-connected layer.

The input features for all models are spectrograms derived from the raw audio files, with 20 ms window size and 10 ms window stride. All neural networks are trained with the CTC, using the stochastic gradient descent optimization strategy along with a mini-batches of 20 utterances per batch. We use 40 epochs and pick the model that performs best on the development set to evaluate on the test set. Learning rates are chosen from [1e−4, 6e−4], and a learning rate annealing algorithm is used by the value of 1.1 after each epoch. The momentum is 0.9. Batch normalization is used to optimize models and accelerate training on hidden layers. All architectures described in this paper do not use language models and add ‘space’ to segment outputs into words. The output alphabet for ASR experiments consists of 29 classes (a, b, c, …, z, space, apostrophe, blank). Once all AF extractors have been built, we freeze all extractor weights during ASR training. All models are trained on the corpus described in Sect. 4.1.

5 Results and Discussion

In this section, we present the performance of AF extractors and ASR systems using fine-tuning networks and progressive networks. Table 1 shows the error rate of different AF extractors trained on the 81 h ‘train-si284’ training set. All error rates are less

Table 1. Results of articulatory feature extractors at a phoneme-level.

	Articulatory Features		Error Rate (%)
Place	Vowel Fricative Nasal	Stop Approximant	9.4
Manner	Coronal High Dental Glottal Labial	Low Mid Retroflex Velar	8.6
Others	Anterior		5.2
	Back		9.2
	Continuant		4.0
	Round		9.1
	Tense		8.7
	Voiced		4.0

Table 2. Word Error Rate (WER) on the Wall Street Journal Corpus "eval92 20 k" evaluation set. All models are trained with CTC loss function. No language models are used but the CTC-lexicon model [4] uses a lexicon.

Model	WER (%)
RNN-CTC [5]	30.1
BDRNN-CTC [24]	35.8
CTC-lexicon [4]	26.9
Baseline	32.4
Fine-tuning network 1	33.2
Fine-tuning network 2	31.6
Progressive network	28.6

than 10%, from which we conclude that articulatory features can be robustly detected from speech signals using the CTC loss function without requiring boundary alignment information.

Table 2 lists the results from our ASR experiments and some results as reported in previous approaches using the CTC loss function on the WSJ benchmark. The fine-tuning network 1 (using 4-layer GRU from AF extractors) achieves a 33.2% WER which is worse than the baseline model (32.4%). However, when concatenating 5 layers of output from all AF extractors, the fine-tuning network 2 performs both better than the fine-tuning network 1 and the baseline system. We hypothesize that the deeper fine-tuning network 2 can capture more invariant and effective articulatory representation than the architecture with shallow layers.

Table 3. The mapping of articulatory features and phonemes used in this paper [9].

AF extractor number	Output units	Category	Attribute	Phonemes
1	39	Manner	Vowel	iy ih eh ey ae aa aw ay ah ao oy ow uh uw er
			Fricative	jh ch s sh z zh f th v dh hh
			Nasal	m n ng
			Stop	b d g p t k
			Approximant	w y l r
2	41	Place	Coronal	d l n s t z
			High	ch ih iy jh sh uh uw y ow g k ng
			Dental	dh th
			Glottal	hh
			Labial	b f m p v w
			Low	aa ae aw ay oy
			Mid	ah eh ey ow
			Retroflex	er r
			Velar	g k ng
3	14	Other	Anterior	b d dh f l m n p s t th v z w
4	11		Back	ay aa ah ao aw ow oy uh uw g k
5	26		Continuant	aa ae ah ao aw ay dh eh er r ey l f ih iy oy ow s sh th uh uw v w y z
6	10		Round	aw ow uw ao uh v y oy r w
7	19		Tense	aa ae ao aw ay ey iy ow oy uw ch s sh f th p t k hh
8	29		Voiced	aa ae ah aw ay ao b d dh eh er ey g ih iy jh l m n ng ow oy r uh uw v w y z

The progressive network performs best in all our approaches achieving 28.6% WER. The progressive network can avoid forgetting and provide some complementary articulatory representations which can be learned by end-to-end architectures.

Table 3 shows the details of eight AF extractors (Manner, Place, Anterior, Back, Continuant, Round, Tense, Voiced). Output units states the number of units in each AF extractor output layer. The phoneme-level transcriptions shown in the last column can be transformed into AF-level labels according to the flow diagram shown in Fig. 1 when building AF extractors.

To examine the approaches we proposed and make a fair comparison, we cite some previous approaches which use CTC and an end-to-end architecture, and only compare the ASR performance without additional language models. Compared to prior approaches, the final performance of our progressive network (28.6%) is better than the bidirectional RNN model [19] (35.8%) and the RNN-CTC approach (30.1%). It is not as good as the CTC lexicon system [4] (26.9%) which uses a lexicon in decoding and the lexicon helps to correct the output to correctly spelled words but we do not.

6 Conclusions and Future Work

In this work, we have presented two approaches to combine domain knowledge AFs into end-to-end learning. First, fine-tuning neural networks are proposed to concatenate hidden layer outputs of AF extractors as inputs to another RNN for ASR. Second, a progressive neural network with lateral connections from AF extractors is proposed to integrate articulatory knowledge into an end-to-end architecture. Results show that both approaches can effectively incorporate articulatory information into end-to-end learning. Furthermore, the progressive neural network brings a significant improvement compared to the baseline system and to previous works.

Different speech attributes play different roles during speech production. Future work will investigate the weighted combination approach to automatically learn the contributions of different speech attributes. Furthermore, we are interested to integrate more domain knowledge into end-to-end learning under noisy and reverberation scenarios. The integration of AF improves ASR performance while increasing computation and time complexity. Future work will also focus on jointly training different AF extractors with one network to decrease computation and time complexity.

Acknowledgements. The authors gratefully acknowledge partial support from the China Scholarship Council (CSC), the German Research Foundation DFG under project CML (TRR 169), and the European Union under project SECURE (No. 642667).

References

1. LeCun, Y., Bottou, L., Bengio, Y., Haffner, P.: Gradient-based learning applied to document recognition. Proc. IEEE **86**(11), 2278–2324 (1998)
2. Bahdanau, D., Cho, K., Bengio, Y.: Neural machine translation by jointly learning to align and translate. In: Proceedings of the ICLR (2015)
3. Wang, K., Babenko, B., Belongie, S.: End-to-end scene text recognition. In: Proceedings of ICCV-2011, pp. 1457–1464 (2011)
4. Miao, Y., Metze, F.: End-to-End Architectures for Speech Recognition. In: Watanabe, S., Delcroix, M., Metze, F., Hershey, J. (eds.) New Era for Robust Speech Recognition, pp. 299–323. Springer, Cham (2017). https://doi.org/10.1007/978-3-319-64680-0_13
5. Graves, A., Fernández, S., Gomez, F., et al.: Connectionist temporal classification: labelling unsegmented sequence data with recurrent neural networks. In: Proceedings of ICML-2006, pp. 369–376 (2006)

6. Zweig, G., Yu, C., Droppo, J., et al.: Advances in all-neural speech recognition. In: Proceedings of ICASSP-2017, pp. 4805–4809 (2017)
7. King, S., Taylor, P.: Detection of phonological features in continuous speech using neural networks. Comput. Speech Lang. **14**(4), 333–353 (2000)
8. Kirchhoff, K.: Robust speech recognition using articulatory information. Ph.D. thesis, University of Bielefeld (1999)
9. Yu, D., Siniscalchi, S.M., Deng, L., et al.: Boosting attribute and phone estimation accuracies with deep neural networks for detection-based speech recognition. In: Proceedings of ICASSP-2012, pp. 4169–4172 (2012)
10. Sak, H., Senior, A., Rao, K., et al.: Learning acoustic frame labelling for speech recognition with recurrent neural networks. In: Proceedings of ICASSP-2015, pp. 4280–4284 (2015)
11. Chorowski, J.K., Bahdanau, D., Serdyuk, D., et al.: Attention-based models for speech recognition. In: Advances in Neural Information Processing Systems, pp. 577–585 (2015)
12. Bahdanau, D., Chorowski, J., Serdyuk, D., et al.: End-to-end attention-based large vocabulary speech recognition. In: Proceedings of ICASSP-2016, pp. 4945–4949 (2016)
13. Chan, W., Jaitly, N., Le, Q., et al.: Listen, attend and spell: a neural network for large vocabulary conversational speech recognition. In: Proceedings of ICASSP-2016, pp. 4960–4964 (2016)
14. Lee, C.-H., et al.: An overview on automatic speech attribute transcription (ASAT). In: Proceedings of INTERSPEECH-2007, pp. 1825–1828 (2007)
15. Siniscalchi, S.M., Lee, C.-H.: A study on integrating acoustic-phonetic information into lattice rescoring for automatic speech recognition. Speech Commun. **51**, 1139–1153 (2009)
16. Siniscalchi, S.M., Lyu, D.C., Svendsen, T., et al.: Experiments on cross-language attribute detection and phone recognition with minimal target-specific training data. IEEE Trans. Audio Speech Lang. Process. **20**(3), 875–887 (2012)
17. Ananthakrishnan, S., Narayanan, S.: Improved speech recognition using acoustic and lexical correlates of pitch accent in a n-best rescoring framework. In: Proceedings of ICASSP-2007, vol. 4, pp. IV-873–IV-876 (2007)
18. Rusu, A.A., Rabinowitz, N.C., Desjardins, G., et al.: Progressive neural networks. arXiv preprint arXiv:1606.04671 (2016)
19. Amodei, D., Ananthanarayanan, S., Anubhai, R., et al.: Deep speech 2: end-to-end speech recognition in English and Mandarin. In: Proceedings of ICML-2016, pp. 173–182 (2016)
20. Sainath, T.N., Vinyals,. O., Senior, A., et al.: Convolutional, long short-term memory, fully connected deep neural networks. In: Proceedings of ICASSP-2015, pp. 4580–4584 (2015)
21. Jozefowicz, R., Zaremba, W., Sutskever, I.: An empirical exploration of recurrent network architectures. In: Proceedings of ICML-2015, pp. 2342–2350 (2015)
22. Paul, D.B., Baker, J.M.: The design for the wall street journal-based CSR corpus. In: Proceedings of the Workshop on Speech and Natural Language, pp. 357–362 (1992)
23. Abdel-Hamid, O., Mohamed, A., Jiang, H., et al.: Applying convolutional neural networks concepts to hybrid NN-HMM model for speech recognition. In: Proceedings of ICASSP-2012, pp. 4277–4280 (2012)
24. Hannun, A.Y., Maas, A.L., Jurafsky, D., et al.: First-pass large vocabulary continuous speech recognition using bi-directional recurrent DNNs. arXiv preprint arXiv:1408.2873 (2014)

25. Davis, S., Mermelstein, P.: Comparison of parametric representations for monosyllabic word recognition in continuously spoken sentences. In: Proceedings of ICASSP-2015, pp. 357–366 (1980)
26. Lee, L., Rose, R.: A frequency warping approach to speaker normalization. IEEE Trans. Speech Audio Process. **6**(1), 49–60 (1998)
27. Veselý, K., Ghoshal, A., Burget, L., et al.: Sequence-discriminative training of deep neural networks. In: Proceedings of INTERSPEECH-2013, pp. 2345–2349 (2013)

Estimation of Air Quality Index from Seasonal Trends Using Deep Neural Network

Arjun Sharma, Anirban Mitra, Sumit Sharma, and Sudip Roy(✉)

CoDA Laboratory, Department of Computer Science and Engineering, IIT Roorkee, Roorkee, India
arjunjamdagni@gmail.com, anbanmta@gmail.com, sumitsharma1825@gmail.com, sudiproy.fcs@iitr.ac.in

Abstract. Growing economy of a country is actually leading to harm for its atmosphere. Due to increase in the number of vehicles and industrial development in or around a city, air pollution has also escalated, which has started affecting health of the citizens. Therefore, the level of air pollution of a city needs to be monitored regularly in real-time to maintain the air quality. The state of the air of a city is described by a dimensionless value known as air quality index (AQI). In order to find a pattern from the time-series data, several techniques have been reported in literature such as linear regression, support vector machine, neural network. In this paper, we propose a method based on deep neural network architecture namely recurrent neural network (RNN) and memory cell called as long-short-term-memory (LSTM) for estimation of AQI of a city on future dates using the seasonal trends of the recorded time-series data. Simulation results confirm that the proposed method outperforms in terms of both root mean square error and Min/Max aggregation of AQI values compared to a state-of-the-art technique of AQI estimation.

Keywords: Air pollution · Air quality index · Deep neural network Long-short-term-memory · Recurrent neural network

1 Introduction

Air pollution occurs when harmful and/or excessive quantities of gases and particulates are released into the atmosphere of a city. Particularly, the excessive presence of NO, CO, O_3, SO_2, NH_4, NO_x, PM_{10}, $PM_{2.5}$, etc. in the air causes air pollution in a city. There are many hazardous biological and ecological effects of air pollution like lung-cancer, asthma, skin-diseases, allergic reactions, smog, acid-rain, etc. [6,7,12,19]. A report of world health organization (WHO) in 2000 states that nearly 2.5% to 11% of annual death in Europe happened due to air pollution [1]. Another survey by Numbeo revealed that New Delhi in India is one of the most polluted cities in the world ranking at 14 [4]. It was also reported that around eight people die every day in New Delhi due to air pollution [2].

V. Kůrková et al. (Eds.): ICANN 2018, LNCS 11141, pp. 511–521, 2018.
https://doi.org/10.1007/978-3-030-01424-7_50

A significant increase in the number of vehicles and the number of factories is observed in recent years and this trend is expected to persist in near future.

In order to reduce the atmospheric pollution level of a region, it is required to develop a reliable monitoring system. Among different indices used in air-quality monitoring systems, air quality index (AQI) [17] is widely used as a metric based on some specific pollutants to estimate the air pollution level of a city. The higher the value of AQI, the higher is the air pollution level. There are different methods to calculate the AQI of a city using the choice of pollutants (parameters) and the methods to combine their concentration levels.

In this paper, we present a method for estimation of AQI of a city using a recurrent neural network (RNN) based model and further it is integrated with a long-short-term-memory (LSTM) for better prediction of AQI, where LSTM is used to memorize the already 'seen' data. As a case study, we choose a location called R. K. Puram of New Delhi, India, for which we got some available data of concentration levels of 10 pollutants to estimate the AQI.

The remainder of the paper is organized as follows. Sect. 2 provides a brief survey of related previous work. Motivation and problem statement are presented in Sect. 3. The proposed method for AQI estimation is discussed in Sect. 4. Simulation results for performance evaluation are provided in Sect. 5 and finally, the paper is concluded in Sect. 6.

2 Related Previous Work

In literature, it is found that AQI is computed using the concentration levels of different pollutants and those pollutants are called as parameters. A recent work on calculating AQI from the concentrations of various parameters is reported by Youping *et al.* [23]. In order to study the adverse effects of air pollution on human health, Georgieva *et al.* [11] provided a relationship between AQI and human health with the help of some health descriptors. Furthermore, some efforts have also been reported on different learning based techniques to predict the value of AQI from the available concentration levels of some parameters. Kumar *et al.* [16] proposed a linear regression based technique for predicting AQI from the available concentration levels of some parameters. Zhang *et al.* [24] purposed another technique based on random forest to predict the AQI from the voting of each and every tree present in the forest. A support vector machine (SVM) based technique has been proposed by Saxena *et al.* [20] to predict the concentration levels of SO_2, NO_2, $PM_{2.5}$ and/or PM_{10} as SVM can segregate the datasets by the best hyperplane. Ganesh *et al.* [8] presented a multiple linear regression based technique to build the relationship between dependent variables and independent variables of AQI estimation, in which support vector regression analysis is used for forecasting the AQI. Song *et al.* [21] provided the decision and correlation coefficients to predict the AQI values considering some relationships among the parameters. Ganesh *et al.* [9] presented a fuzzy interface system to predict the AQI. Kang *et al.* [14] proposed a three-tier neural network optimized by annealing algorithm to predict the AQI. Yang *et al.* [22] described a Gaussian Plume model on the basis of neural network, in which they used multi-layer neural network to estimate the AQI in real-time. Kok *et al.* [15] proposed a

SVM regression and LSTM based classification technique for AQI prediction, whereas Hajek *et al.* [18] proposed hierarchical regression models to predict AQIs to achieve low prediction errors.

3 Motivation and Problem Statement

Here, we discuss about the motivation and the problem statement of this work.

3.1 Motivation

So far, all the previous work are based on the some AQI values known beforehand, which basically depends on the supervised learning technique. However, no integrated approach has been reported to estimate the necessary parameter values for AQI estimation from its time-series data followed by estimating AQI from the predicted concentration levels of the parameters. Hence, the research question is how to predict the future values of the AQI given the input parameters as well as the previous trends of AQIs of the same location.

Recurrent neural network (RNN) has been found to be impressive in processing the sequential data, which exhibits some temporal sequence and whose value at each time-step depends on the context and requires remembering the context present in the data at the previous time-steps [10]. Unlike the feed-forward neural network, in which output of the network depends only on the current input values, in recurrent nets the output value at each time-step depends on the current input as well as the internal state of the network, which is a function of the data seen so far in the previous time-steps [10]. In this context, long-short-term-memory (LSTM) was introduced by Hochreiter and Schmidhuber to primarily solve the long-term dependency problems [10]. It is a popular variant of recurrent nets and facilitates learning as well as forgetting of the context present in the data using its gating mechanism, which fits perfectly well for modeling our aforementioned task [10]. Hence, we found LSTMs are suitable for learning the time-series pattern present in the data and predicting the future values of the AQI of a city. This motivates us to consider the following problem statement.

3.2 Problem Statement

Consider that the concentration levels of ten atmospheric pollutants (parameters) namely ammonia (NH_4), benzene (C_6H_6), carbon monoxide (CO), nitric oxide (NO), nitrogen dioxide (NO_2), oxides of nitrogen (NO_x), ozone(O_3), PM_{10}, $PM_{2.5}$ and sulfur dioxide (SO_2) are given as the inputs. We need to the predict the AQIs for one month after training the model by the transformed input AQIs obtained from the input concentration levels of the parameters considered. The problem is to develop such a model using RNN and LSTM to predict the future values of the AQI of a city. The main objective of this work is to achieve more precise AQI value of a location by considering seasonal pattern and targeted number of memory cells of LSTM along with a particularly suitable number of neurons.

4 Proposed Method for Estimation of AQI

Air quality index (AQI) is the measure of air pollution present in the environment in a city and its impact on the lives of citizens. AQI is calculated from the concentration levels of the pollutants and the corresponding sub-indices. Estimation of AQI is a quantification that converts air pollution parameters (concentration levels of pollutants) into a single number. The final calculation of AQI (I) involves two steps (a) formation of sub-indices and (b) aggregation of calculated sub-indices, as depicted in Fig. 1.

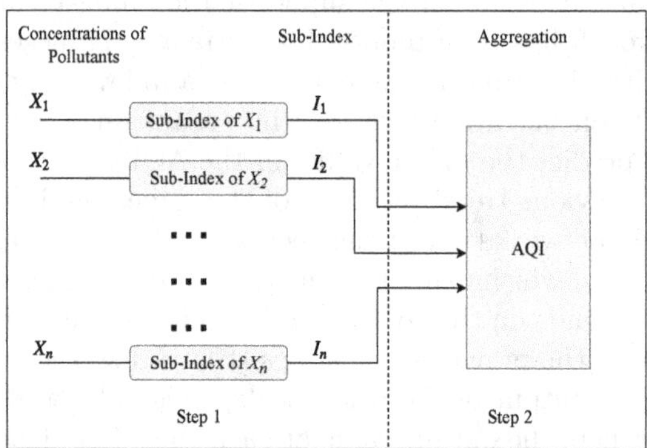

Fig. 1. Estimation of Air Quality Index (AQI).

4.1 Formation of Sub-indices (Step 1)

A sub-index of a pollutant is the weight calculated from the concentration levels of the pollutant (C_p). The sub-index I_i [13,17] of a pollutant X_i is calculated as $I_i = \left[\frac{I_{HI}-I_{LO}}{B_{HI}-B_{LO}}(C_p - B_{LO})\right] + I_{LO}$, where B_{HI} is a breakpoint concentration level of the pollutant X_i, which can be greater or equal to C_p, B_{LO} is another breakpoint concentration level of the same pollutant X_i that can be smaller or equal to C_p, I_{HI} is the AQI value corresponding to B_{HI} and I_{LO} is the AQI value corresponding to B_{LO}.

4.2 Aggregation of Sub-indices (Step 2)

The calculated sub-indices for each of the pollutants are aggregated to obtain the overall AQI. There are two different ways for this aggregation to estimate the AQI (I) value as mentioned below.

a Root Mean-Squared Error (RMSE): Here, first, the squares of all sub-indices are calculated and then the mean of all these squared values is obtained followed by the square-root over that mean is taken. This root value is the overall AQI (I) estimated as $I = \sqrt{\sum_{i=1}^{n} I_i}$, where I_i is the sub-index of pollutant X_i and there are n such pollutants.

b Min/Max Operator: Here, the overall AQI (I) is calculated either by taking maximum or minimum among the sub-indices of the n parameters. Hence, $I = Max(I_1, I_2, I_3, \ldots, I_n)$ or $I = Min(I_1, I_2, I_3, \ldots, I_n)$, where I_i is the sub-index of pollutant X_i.

After the second step (Step 2), the overall AQI of that place is estimated. This AQI is used to find the air quality status of that place and to decide whether it is polluted or not.

4.3 Proposed Models

In this paper, we propose two methods to predict the AQI values of a location. One method is called auto-regressive integrated moving average model (ARIMA model) to calculate the RMSE value of AQI. Whereas, the other one uses a modified recurrent neural network (RNN with 120 LSTM layers) for calculating the RMSE value of AQI and called as RNN-based model.

4.4 ARIMA Model

The auto-regressive integrated moving average (ARIMA) model is a well-used time-series prediction model for non-stationary and non-seasonal time-series data. The auto-regressive (AR) part expresses the next outcome of the time-series as a linear regression of previous observations and an error term. The moving average (MA) part considers the errors in predicting past outcomes as a linear combination to estimate the next step. Whereas, the term 'integrated' refers to the adding of error terms and differentiated value in the prediction of next step. It is often expressed as ARIMA(p, d, q), where p and q are orders of AR and MA models, respectively, while d is the degree of differentiation. We keep the values of p, d and q as 1, 1 and 0, respectively, and use auto-correlation function to estimate the values of p and q. Logarithmic function is used to scale down the original concentration levels. Only the months from the seasonal cycles are used in this prediction of AQI values.

4.5 RNN-Based Model

The recurrent neural network (RNN) has been used to feed the time-series data of certain pollutant concentration levels with specific architecture to obtain the concentration levels for future. This will, in turn, be used to evaluate the estimated values of AQI for future.

4.6 Seasonal Data Re-configuring

As a case study, we have considered New Delhi, India as the region of interest and hence, the weather pattern is split into some clear partitions. As there are primarily three seasons in India, this work considers parameters mentioned for R. K. Puram, New Delhi in the year of 2016, while taking the monthly average of those parameters. It was observed that the patterns of the concentration levels of the pollutants are similar in the seasonal groups as follows: (a) winter consists of

November, December, January, February; (b) neutral consists of March, April, September, October; and (c) summer consists of May, June, July, August.

Figure 2(a) and (b) demonstrate the monthly average trends of two pollutants CO and $PM_{2.5}$, respectively, for R. K. Puram, New Delhi, India in 2016. It is reflected that winter months exhibit the high concentration levels; neutral season follows moderate concentrations and summer observes low values of both these parameters (CO and $PM_{2.5}$). Similar patterns are observed for other parameters as well as mentioned in Sect. 3.2, where the concentration trends are clearly differentiable. Based on these observations, seasons are primarily tuned into well-formed-cycles. Then the concentration levels of all the parameters on the days of a month are estimated based on the corresponding previous cycle(s).

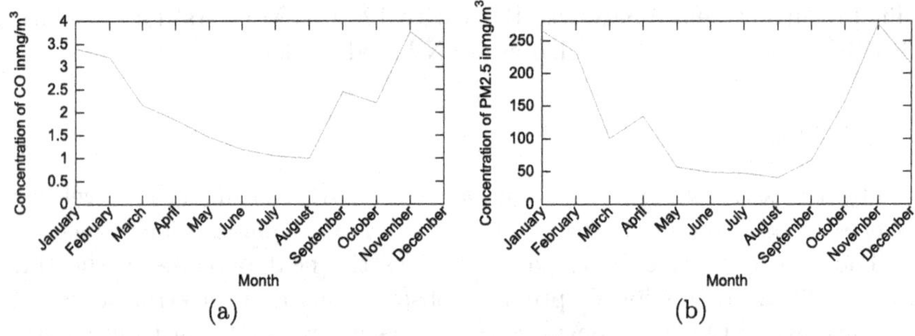

Fig. 2. Monthly average trends of (a) CO and (b) $PM_{2.5}$ for R. K. Puram, New Delhi, India in 2016.

4.7 Architecture of RNN-Layer

The recurrent neural network (RNN) is a widely used approach in time-series forecasting, where some trend is repeated. It excels, especially, where inputs and/or outputs are inter-dependent by maintaining a sequence of memory referred to as long-short-term-memory (LSTM) of the trend calculated (or 'seen') so far. LSTM adds the capability of keeping or losing information to/from series of data passed on RNNs using three types of gates namely input, forget and output. They add up the weighted multiplications of input data and output of the previous cell passed through the sigmoid function. Weights and biases are specific to the type of the gates. An input gate (I_t) is defined as $I_t = g(W_{xi}x_t + W_{hi}P_{t-1} + b_i)$, a forget gate ($F_t$) is defined as $F_t = g(W_{xf}x_t + W_{hf}P_{t-1} + b_f)$ and an output gate (O_t) is defined as $O_t = g(W_{xo}x_t + W_{ho}P_{t-1} + b_o)$, where I_t, F_t and O_t are input, forget and output gate outputs, respectively, g is a sigmoid function, P_{t-1} is the $(t-1)^{th}$ cell output and x_t is t^{th} input. The new cell state is achieved by $S_t = F_t S_{t-1} + I_t S_{in_t}$, where $S_{in_t} = tanh(W_{xc}x_t + W_{hc}P_{t-1} + b_{S_{in}})$, S_{t-1} is previous cell state, W_{x*} is input weight, W_{h*} is previous layer weight, b_* is bias. The current cell output is obtained as $P_t = O_t tanh(S_t)$.

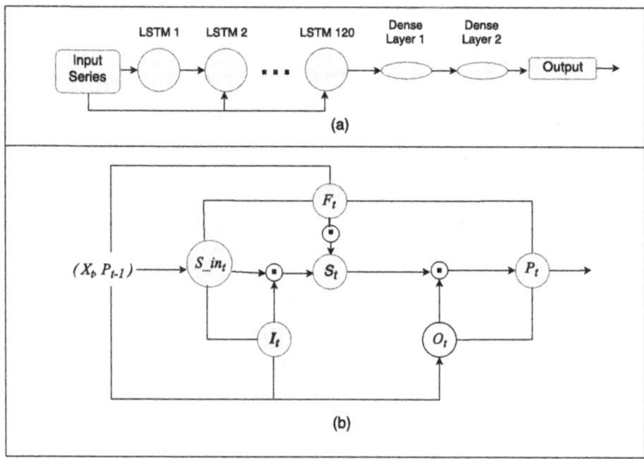

Fig. 3. (a) Overall architecture of RNN-based model and (b) LSTM cell architecture.

Figure 3(a) shows the entire architecture of the RNN-LSTM model, while Fig. 3(b) presents the architecture of a LSTM cell. As shown in Fig. 3(a), a sequential model is built having around 120 LSTM cells (one for each day of training data cycle of four months in a season), one hidden layer, one dense layer at the end. The output of the RNN-based model is then passed into the first step of AQI estimation (Step 1), which computes the sub-indices for the same place. Then the second step of AQI estimation (Step 2) is performed to compute the overall AQI of the place. The mean error is optimized using RMSProp optimizer [5]. The other specifications of the proposed RNN-LSTM model used to predict the AQI of the next month of a place are given in Table 1.

Table 1. Specifications of the proposed RNN-LSTM model.

Specification	Values
# LSTM units	120
# Hidden layer	1
# Dense layer	1
# Output layers	1
Batch size	30
# Epoch	50

5 Simulation Results

In this section, we discuss about the input data used for training and testing of the proposed model and the comparative analysis of the simulation results followed by discussions.

5.1 Input Dataset

The central pollution control board (CPCB) of India acquires the data from the sub-station of R. K. Puram New Delhi, during the period starting from 1st January 2015 to 31st December 2017 [3]. This data has been collected for all the ten parameters for AQI estimation as mentioned in Sect. 3.2. The used units for concentration levels of each of these parameters are as follows: CO is expressed in mg/m^3 and NO, NO_2, NO_x, O_3, PM_{10}, $PM_{2.5}$, SO_2, C_6H_6 and NH_4 are expressed in $\mu g/m^3$. The data of all these parameters of the same place for two years 2015 and 2016 are used as training, while each month of 2017 individually is used as the testing data with corresponding cycle of seasons.

5.2 Comparative Results and Discussions

Here we discuss about our simulation experiment for comparative analysis of performance of the proposed method with two other methods. All the methods for AQI estimation are implemented in Python programming language using NumPy, SciPy and CSV as the necessary packages along with TensorFlow and simulated in an Ubuntu 16.04 operating system environment having an Intel i5 core processor and 8 GB RAM.

Out of three seasonal cycles observed in India the summer cycle (May-June-July-August) is considered for this evaluation. The dataset of all these parameters of the same place for two years 2015 and 2016 are used as training, while the dataset of May, 2017 is used as the testing data. For this case, RNN-LSTM method for AQI estimation provide the root mean-squared error (RMSE) value as 40.

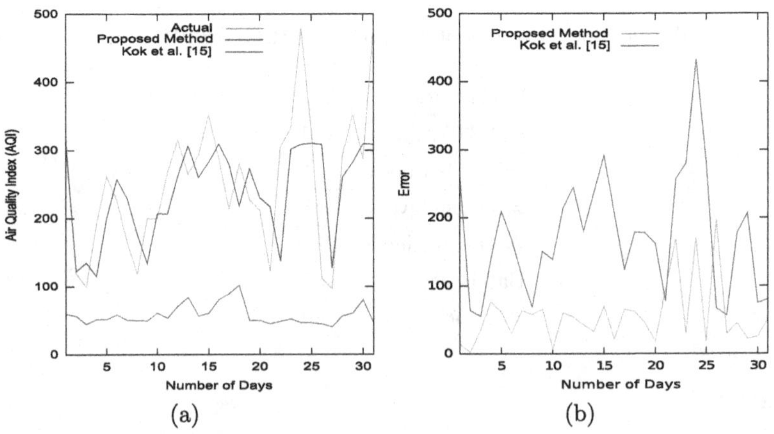

Fig. 4. Comparative results for (a) Max-AQI and (b) error analysis of AQI using Min/Max aggregation technique.

The AQI value is calculated using RMSE and Min/Max as the aggregation techniques and the results are compared with Kok *et al.* [15] on the same dataset. Prediction curve for Max-AQI value obtained by the proposed method are very close to actual AQI value curve as shown in Fig. 4(a). Figure 4(b) shows the comparison of errors in the calculation of AQI values by the proposed method and the previous method by Kok *et al.* [15] on the same dataset. As the error in prediction is less for the proposed model, hence a better prediction accuracy is achieved by the proposed method compared to the previous method [15] on the same dataset.

The RMSE is used as the aggregation technique in order to aggregate the sub-indices to obtain overall AQI and the simulation results are compared with Kok *et al.* [15] using the RMSE as the aggregation method. Figure 5(a) shows a comparison of the overall RMSE-AQI values obtained by the proposed method and by Kok *et al.* [15] along with the actual AQI for the same dataset. It is observed from Fig. 5(b) that the prediction by the proposed method is close to the actual AQI and it has less error compared to the method by Kok *et al.* [15].

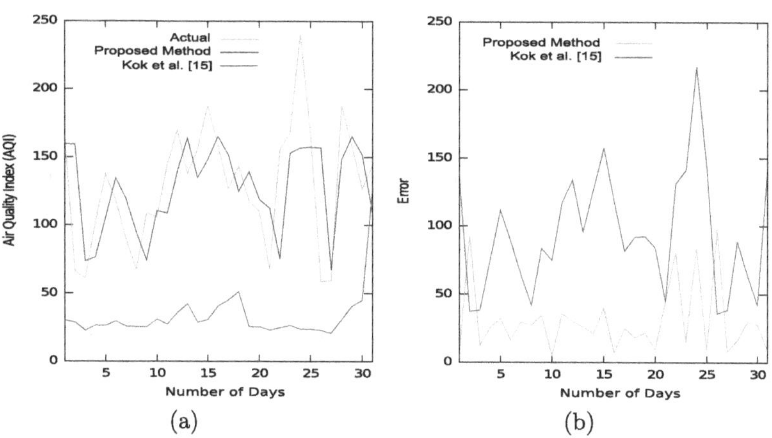

Fig. 5. Comparative results for (a) RMSE-AQI and (b) error analysis of AQI using RMSE aggregation technique.

In another study, the Min/Max aggregation technique is used in simulation of the proposed RNN-LSTM method in order to aggregate the sub-indices to obtain the overall AQI values and the simulation results are compared with Kok *et al.* [15] using the Min/Max aggregation as the aggregation method on the same dataset. In case of Min/Max aggregation technique, overall the prediction error is 2.7%, while it is 0.37% for the RMSE aggregation technique. This suggests that RMSE aggregation technique is better to use than Min/Max aggregation technique in order to predict the AQI values from the trained data by the proposed method.

A comparative analysis among the proposed method, the ARIMA model and the previous work by Kok *et al.* [15] shows RMSE by the proposed method based on RNN-LSTM model using seasonal trends outperforms the other two. For the testing data of the input dataset, the RMSE value of AQIs is obtained as 75 by the proposed method based on RNN-LSTM model and 204 by the previous method by Kok *et al.* [15] with the Min/Max aggregation technique. Whereas for the same dataset, the RMSE value of AQIs is obtained as 40 by the proposed method based on RNN-LSTM model and 105 by the previous method by Kok *et al.* [15] with the RMSE aggregation technique. For the same testing data of the input dataset, the RMSE value of AQIs is obtained as 40 by the proposed method based on RNN-LSTM model with the RSME aggregation technique, whereas it is 114 obtained by the ARIMA model. It confirms that the proposed method with RMSE aggregation technique outperforms and hence, it can be used to predict the future AQI values of a city.

These simulation results confirm that the proposed method based on RNN-LSTM model with the RMSE aggregation technique performs better than ARIMA model and the state-of-the-art method reported by Kok *et al.* [15] for AQI estimation of a city.

6 Conclusions

In this paper, we propose a method based on RNN-LSTM model with the RMSE aggregation technique that can predict the actual value of AQI of a location with less RMSE compared to the state-of-the-art technique for AQI estimation and another method based on ARIMA model. As an added advantage, compared to the supervised learning techniques, RNN provides higher ability for learning and higher capability of parallel computing. Hence, further research may be done in this direction for more accurate and time-efficient model using LSTM to calculate the AQI value of a location in real-time.

References

1. The World Health Report 2000: Health Systems - Improving Performance (2000). http://www.who.int/whr/2000/en/
2. 8 People Die in Delhi Every Day due to Pollution (2018). http://www.thehindu.com/news/cities/Delhi/8-people-die-in-Delhi-every-day-due-to-pollution-SC/article17205973.ece
3. CPCB: Average Report Criteria (2018). http://www.cpcb.gov.in/caaqm/Auth/frmViewReportNew.aspx
4. Pollution Index by City 2018 (2018). https://www.numbeo.com/pollution/rankings.jsp
5. RMSPropOptimizer (2018). https://www.tensorflow.org/api_docs/python/tf/train/RMSPropOptimizer
6. Chen, T.-M., Kuschner, W.G., Gokhale, J., Shofer, S.: Outdoor air pollution: nitrogen dioxide, sulfur dioxide, and carbon monoxide health effects. Am. J. Med. Sci. **333**(4), 249–256 (2007)

7. Chen, B., Kan, H.: Air pollution and population health: a global challenge. Environ. Health Prev. Med. **13**(2), 94–101 (2008)
8. Ganesh, S.S., Modali, S.H., Palreddy, S.R., Arulmozhivarman, P.: Forecasting air quality index using regression models: a case study on Delhi and Houston. In: Proceedings of the ICEI, pp. 248–254 (2017)
9. Ganesh, S.S., Reddy, N.B., Arulmozhivarman, P.: Forecasting air quality index based on Mamdani fuzzy inference system. In: Proceedings of the ICEI, pp. 338–341 (2017)
10. Goodfellow, I., Bengio, Y., Courville, A.: Deep Learning. MIT Press (2016). http://www.deeplearningbook.org
11. Ivanov, V., Georgieva, I.: Air quality index evaluations for Sofia City. In: Proceedings of the IEEE EUROCON, pp. 920–925 (2017)
12. Kampa, M., Castanas, E.: Human health effects of air pollution. Environ. Pollut. **151**(2), 362–367 (2008)
13. Kanchan, K., Goyal, P.: A review on air quality indexing system. Asian J. Atmos. Environ. **9**(4), 101–113 (2015)
14. Kang, Z., Qu, Z.: Application of BP neural network optimized by genetic simulated annealing algorithm to prediction of air quality index in Lanzhou. In: Proceedings of the IEEE ICCIA, pp. 155–160 (2017)
15. Kök, İ., Şimşek, M.U., Özdemir, S.: A deep learning model for air quality prediction in smart cities. In: Proceedings of the IEEE International Conference on Big Data, pp. 1983–1990 (2017)
16. Kumar, A., Goyal, P.: Forecasting of air quality in Delhi using principal component regression technique. Atmos. Pollut. Res. **2**(4), 436–444 (2011)
17. Kyrkilis, G., Chaloulakou, A., Kassomenos, P.A.: Development of an aggregate air quality index for an urban Mediterranean agglomeration: relation to potential health effects. Environ. Int. **33**(5), 670–676 (2007)
18. Petr, H., Olej, V.: Predicting common air quality index - the case of Czech Microregions. Aerosol Air Qual. Res. **15**, 544–555 (2015)
19. Puri, P., Kumar, S., Kathuria, S., Ramesh, V.: Effects of air pollution on the skin: a review. Indian J. Derm.Logy, Venereol., Leprol. **3**(4), 415 (2017)
20. Saxena, A., Shekhawat, S.: Ambient air quality classification by Grey Wolf optimizer based support vector machine. J. Environ. Public Health **2017**(3131083), 12 (2017)
21. Song, L.: Impact analysis of air pollutants on the air quality index in jinan winter. In: Proceedings of the IEEE CSE-EUC, pp. 471–474 (2017)
22. Yang, Y., Zheng, Z., Bian, K., Song, L., Han, Z.: Real-time profiling of fine-grained air quality index distribution using UAV sensing. IEEE Internet Things J. **5**(1), 186–198 (2018)
23. Youping, L., Ya, T., Zhongyu, F., Hong, Z., Zhengzheng, Y.: Assessment and comparison of three different air quality indices in China. Environ. Eng. Res. **23**(1), 21–27 (2017)
24. Zhang, C., Yuan, D.: Fast fine-grained air quality index level prediction using random forest algorithm on cluster computing of spark. In: Proceedings of the IEEE, pp. 929–934 (2015)

A Deep Learning Approach to Bacterial Colony Segmentation

Paolo Andreini, Simone Bonechi(✉), Monica Bianchini, Alessandro Mecocci, and Franco Scarselli

DIISM, University of Siena, Via Roma 56, Siena, Italy
bonechi@diism.unisi.it

Abstract. In this paper, we introduce a new method for the segmentation of bacterial colonies in solid agar plate images. The proposed approach comprises two contributions. First, a simple but nonetheless effective engine is devised to generate synthetic plate images. This engine overlays bacterial colony patches to existing background images, taking into account both the local appearance of the background and the intrinsic opacity of the bacterial colonies. Therefore, a scalable alternative to the human ground–truth supervision—often difficult to obtain in medical imaging, due to privacy issues and scarcity of data—is provided. Then, synthetic generated data, together with few annotated images, were used to train a Fully–Convolutional Network. Such network is actually effective in separating bacterial colonies from the background. Finally, we discuss the role of the generation of synthetic images, conducting experiments that show how their inclusion improves the performances of the segmentation network, producing very encouraging results.

Keywords: Computer vision · Deep learning · Synthetic image generation · Semantic segmentation · Agar plates · Bacterial cultures

1 Introduction

Agar plates are used for bacterial cultures, which are employed in a wide variety of microbiological tests, that range from food and beverage safety assessments to environmental control, and to many specific clinical analyses (i.e. urinoculture). In the standard protocol, the biological sample is sown on a Petri dish that holds a culture substrate, used to artificially recreate the environment required for the bacterial growth. After an incubation period, each dish is typically examined by a human expert. This visual inspection is time consuming and prone to errors. In this work, we introduce a new method for the segmentation of bacterial colonies in solid agar plate images, based on deep learning techniques. Indeed, in recent years, deep learning has pushed the state of the art in many visual recognition tasks, achieving outstanding results [1–3]. Nevertheless, most of these improvements rely on fully annotated data, being the annotation procedure

V. Kůrková et al. (Eds.): ICANN 2018, LNCS 11141, pp. 522–533, 2018.
https://doi.org/10.1007/978-3-030-01424-7_51

inherently difficult and costly. This is especially true for semantic segmentation, which requires pixel–wise annotations. Moreover, in biological and medical applications, the problem of collecting large set of annotated samples is even more crucial, due to privacy issues and scarcity of data. In fact, dealing with a reduced number of fully annotated data, without significantly affecting the recognition performances, is one of the most active research field in computer vision, and has a great relevance, in particular, for the automatic Petri plate analysis, where:

- The data distribution is unbalanced, with a small number of bacterial species found with high frequency and a lot of very rare infections; hence, it is usually necessary to deal with under–represented classes with a reduced number of available samples;
- The bacterial growth is supported by a variety of different substrates, used either to isolate a specific strain or a multitude of different bacteria (i.e., for screening tests); the complete characterization of the whole variability of substrates and species would require a considerable amount of resources.

In order to address these problems, we propose a new method for generating synthetic images of Petri plates, which naturally blend bacterial colonies in existing images of empty dishes. A simple heuristic also allows us to deal with the natural differences in the reflectance within the colonies (Sect. 2.4). The generated images are then used to train a Fully–Convolutional Network, called *Pyramid Scene Parsing Network* (PSP) [4], a state–of–the–art architecture for semantic segmentation.

The paper is organized as follows. After a brief review of related works, in Sect. 2, the process for generating synthetic Petri plate images is outlined, whereas, in Sect. 3.3, we show how the injection of synthetic data improves the PSP training. The segmentation method is then evaluated on the recently released MicrobIA Haemolysis Dataset [5] (described in Sect. 3.2). Finally, conclusions and future research are collected in Sect. 4.

1.1 Related Works

The proposed method is related to three main research topics, namely automatic agar plate analysis, synthetic data generation, and image segmentation by Convolutional Neural Networks (CNNs), whose literature is reviewed in the following.

Agar Plate Analysis. The automatic agar plate analysis has a long history. Specialized recording and processing systems for automatic bacterial counting were originally proposed in the late fifties by [6,7]. Later on, a distance transform on binarized images was used by [8], whereas the watershed transform on grayscale images was firstly employed in [9,10]. A grayscale morphological analysis was also proposed by [11]. A particular lighting technique was presented in [12], aimed at producing highlights on the colonies to simplify their counting. In [13], a method based on segment classification has been proposed for the segmentation of images, whereas the OpenCFU free software [14] employs a multiple threshold segmentation method and a watershed transform for the separation of confluent segments. More recently, a bacterial count and classification approach, based on a custom background subtraction procedure and shallow feedforward neural networks, was proposed in [15,16], while a background subtraction technique based on a mixture of gaussians (MOG) is used in [17]. Moreover, a bag–of–word approach for infected plate detection and colony classification was used in [18]. Finally, [19] exploits a proprietary image processing method for the colony segmentation on blood agar plates, employing CNNs on the obtained segments for the bacterial count. Indeed, to the best of our knowledge, our approach is the first in proposing the use of convolutional neural networks for the colony segmentation problem.

Synthetic Data. Synthetic datasets are a cheap and scalable alternative to the human ground–truth supervision in machine learning. In recent years, several works in computer vision have used synthetic data to face a variety of different problems. For instance, in [20,21], virtual environments have been exploited for the pedestrian detection problem, addressed by neural networks. Synthetic data have also been used for text detection [22,23] and pose estimation [24,25]. Moreover, also in the field of semantic segmentation, some approaches have been recently proposed. Large collections of synthetic images of driving scenes in urban environments were generated in [26,27], while synthetic indoor scenes have been exploited by [28].

Semantic Segmentation with CNNs. Image semantic segmentation aims at making dense predictions, inferring the class of objects represented by each pixel of an image. A lot of efforts have recently been spent in semantic segmentation of natural scenes [2,4,29]. Relatively large datasets have been created with this purpose: for example, PASCAL VOC 2012 [30] and MS–COCO [31], which contain altogether more than 100,000 images with full pixel–wise annotations. In medical imaging, the number of available samples is generally smaller, making small networks, with a reduced number of parameters, the only viable approach. Indeed, one of the most successful deep learning method is constituted by the U–net architecture [32], which uses a standard convolutional network, followed by an upsampling part of up–convolutions combined with skip–connections. In this paper, we advocate the use of synthetically generated images to train more complex architectures, such as the Pyramid Scene Parsing Network.

2 Synthetic Petri Plate Generation

Supervised training of deep convolutional neural networks, which contain millions of parameters, requires a significant number of labeled training data. The generation of pixel–level annotations by a human expert is very costly in term of both time and money. Therefore, segmentation datasets are generally quite smaller compared with the large scale classification collections, such as ImageNet [33]. Moreover, almost all these datasets collect common objects in natural scenes and are not suitable for more specific tasks, that often suffer for the lack of a sufficient amount of data to be tackled with deep learning approaches. This is just the case of the Petri plate analysis, for which, to the best of our knowledge, the only publicly available dataset is the MicrobIA Dataset, released by the University of Brescia. Such dataset only contains a segmentation ground–truth for a small set of blood agar plates (see Sect. 3.2), being barely sufficient to train a large CNN and totally inadequate to represent the huge variety of different growing media and species that can be found on Petri plates. For this reason, we propose a new synthetic image generator, which can be used to cheaply produce large datasets of fully annotated images of Petri plates. The engine constructs a huge variety of realistic images that can be used to train a deep neural network capable of generalizing to real data. The generator pipeline (see Fig. 1) can be described as follows:

- A suitable set of background images and colony prototypes is collected (Sect. 2.1);
- For each colony prototype, a generation model is built (Sect. 2.2);
- A seeding procedure is simulated (Sect. 2.3);
- Randomly selected patches are blended onto the background images, following the seeding simulation (Sect. 2.4).

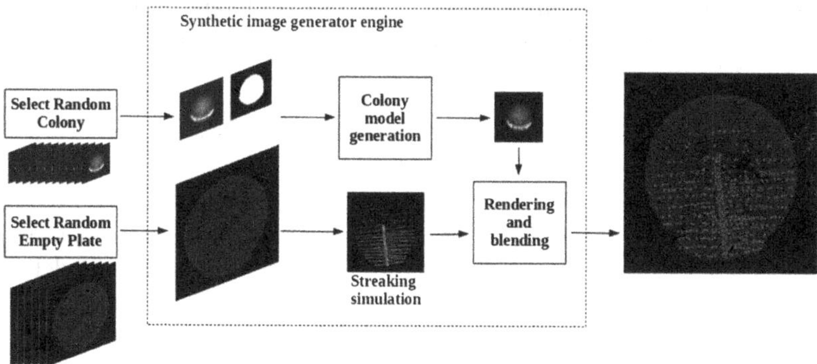

Fig. 1. Scheme of the synthetic agar plate image generation.

Using the proposed engine, a dataset of 120000 simulated blood agar plate images has been generated; some examples of synthetic images are shown in Fig. 2.

2.1 Background and Token Collection

The first step of the generation procedure is the collection of bacterial colony patches (tokens) and empty plate images. From the MicrobIA image dataset, we extracted a set of single bacterial colony prototypes. Each token includes a background/foreground mask that allows us to recognize if a pixel belongs to

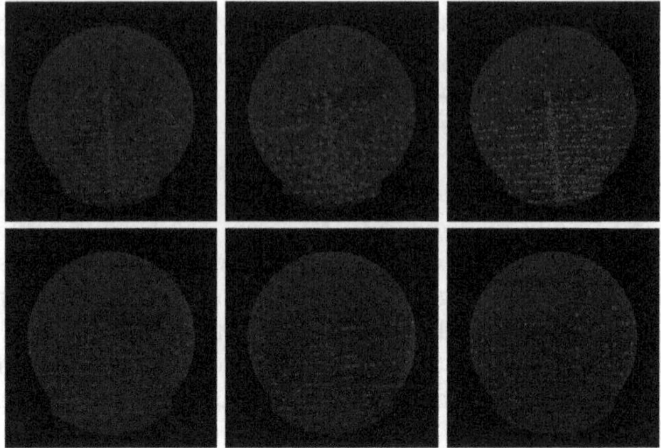

Fig. 2. Some examples of synthetically generated blood agar plate images (top row); images taken from the MicrobIA Haemolysis dataset (bottom row).

the culture ground or to the colony, and a small image crop which contains the colony. Using the MicrobIA dataset, the extraction procedure is straightforward since tokens can be easily isolated exploiting the provided annotations. We also gathered a small set of images of empty plates, representing Petri dishes free of infections, on which colonies are blended. A set of 16 different background images and 30 tokens are used in our simulations, both augmented using different scale, rotations and lightness in order to increase variability.

2.2 Colony Models

The generation of the colony model consists of two steps (see Fig. 3). First, each token is analyzed to generate a model of the background that will be used as a reference. Then, this reference is exploited to produce a generative model of the colony that is independent from the background. The procedure is summarized by the following steps.

- Background model generation – the background colors of each token are quantized in a fixed number of **k** clusters through k–means, to speed–up the

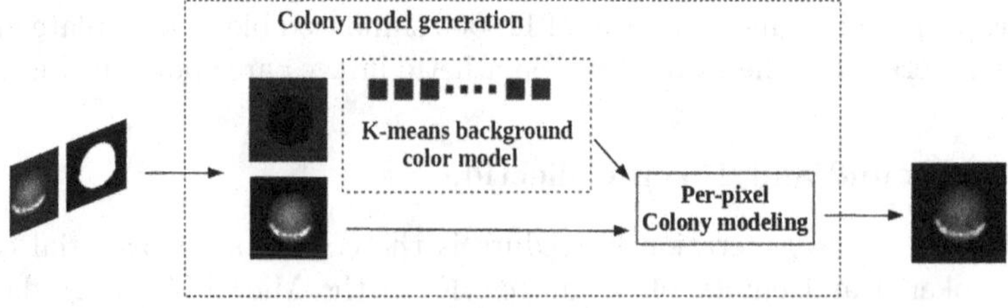

Fig. 3. Colony model generation scheme.

algorithm and smooth the model, removing small changes in the appearance of the substrate. Then, for each pixel $\mathbf{p_{x,y}}$ belonging to a colony, the centroid $\mathbf{r_k}$ with the minimum L_2 distance in the Lab space is chosen, to represent the background reference for the current pixel.

- Colony model – the generative model of the colony, which will be used during the blending procedure, is calculated, subtracting from each colony pixel $\mathbf{p_{x,y}}$ the corresponding reference value:

$$\mathbf{m_{x,y}} = \mathbf{p_{x,y}} - \underset{\mathbf{r_k}}{\operatorname{argmin}} \left(||\mathbf{p_{x,y}} - \mathbf{r_k}|| \right) \tag{1}$$

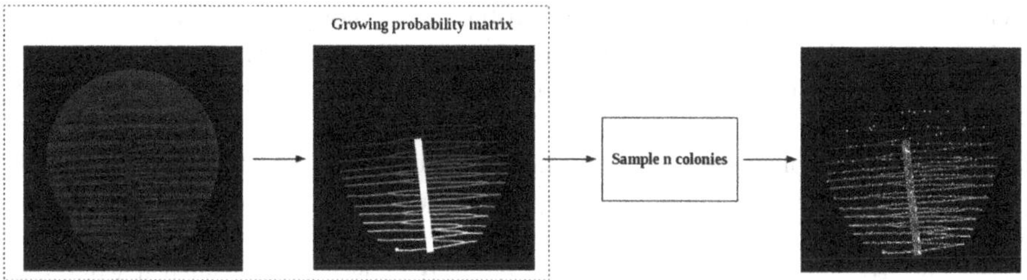

Fig. 4. The streaking simulation scheme.

2.3 Streaking Simulation

In microbiology, several methods are available to plate out cells. The plate streaking procedure consists in inoculating the surface of an agar plate with a high dilution of a biological sample. As a result, after the inoculation, individual cells grow increasingly far apart from each other, on the surface of the agar medium. The sample streaking can be manual or automatic and it can follow different patterns, leading to a variety of topologies for the distribution of the bacterial colonies over the agar plates. In this paper, we simulate the streaking procedure of the WASPLab automation system[1] used in the MicrobIA dataset. Nevertheless, the same approach can be applied to any kind of streaking method. A scheme of the simulation procedure is depicted in Fig. 4. First of all, in order to deduce the streaking path[2], we selected a plate image in which the bacterial growth covers almost the entire surface of the substrate. The sowing procedure generally starts by inoculating the diluted sample from an initial position on the agar and spreading it over the substrate surface. Hence, the concentration of bacteria is greater at the starting point, while it decreases progressively during sowing. Based on this intuition, a probability matrix is constructed, with p_{ij} representing the probability that, in a certain position (i, j), a bacterial colony will

[1] http://www.copanusa.com/products/automation/wasplab//%7Bpath=.

[2] If the path is known *a priori*, this step can be avoided.

grow. We suppose such probability to decrease linearly from the starting point to the end of the streaking path. Although this hypothesis is not completely realistic in certain situations, it looks empirically significant in our experimental set–up (some examples are reported in Fig. 2). Then, the streaking simulation proceeds by selecting n random points within the streaking path, each of which will produce a bacterial colony with probability p.

2.4 Rendering and Blending Procedure

The rendering procedure takes a set of colony models as input and blend them on a background image (i.e. an agar plate without any bacterial growth), following the topology provided by the seeding simulator. Our proposed method is also devised to tackle with the following problem: a colony is a conglomerate of bacterial cells with a three–dimensional structure and with the most inner part which is generally more voluminous than the outer. Hence, from an optical point of view, the center of the colony is much more opaque (i.e. there is a greater concentration of molecules absorbing the light radiation). The following approach is used to simulate this behavior. A specific blurring is initially applied to the background image in the regions where the colony models will be attached. In particular, for such regions, every pixel color $\mathbf{b}'_{\mathbf{x,y}}$ is replaced with a weighted sum of $\overline{\mathbf{b}}$ and $\mathbf{b}_{\mathbf{x,y}}$, where $\overline{\mathbf{b}}$ is the average color of background pixels inside the region, and $\mathbf{b}_{\mathbf{x,y}}$ is the actual pixel value (see Eq. 2). The weighting factor $\alpha_{x,y}$ follows a normal distribution, enhancing the blurring effect in the innermost part of the patch:

$$\mathbf{b}'_{\mathbf{x,y}} = \alpha_{x,y}(\overline{\mathbf{b}}) + (1 - \alpha_{x,y})\mathbf{b}_{\mathbf{x,y}} \quad \text{with} \quad \alpha_{x,y} = \frac{1}{2\pi\sigma^2} e^{-\frac{(x-x_0)^2+(y-y_0)^2}{2\sigma^2}} \tag{2}$$

where (x, y) are the spatial coordinates of the patch and (x_0, y_0) are the coordinates of its center. The colony models are then added to the blurred background image, producing the final result. A dedicated procedure also accounts for the overlapping of different colonies. Indeed, in the overlapping regions, each pixel is associated with the colony with the nearest centroid, and the area near the contours is Gaussian–smoothed to avoid a crisp visual separation.

3 Experiments

In the following Sect. 3.1, the semantic segmentation network employed in our experiments is described, while Sect. 3.2 illustrates the used dataset, and Sect. 3.3 reports our experimental setup and results.

3.1 Semantic Segmentation Network

The segmentation of bacterial colonies is performed through the Pyramid Scene Parsing (PSP) Network. This is a deep fully convolutional neural network, built on the ResNet model [34] for image classification. To enlarge the receptive field of the neural network, a set of dilated convolutions [29] replaces standard convolutions in the ResNet part of the network. Then, a pyramid pooling module is used to gather context information, followed by both an upsampling and a concatenation layer, to form the final feature representation. This representation is then fed into a convolutional layer, to get the expected per–pixel prediction.

3.2 Dataset

The segmentation network has been evaluated on the MicrobIA Haemolysis Dataset, collecting 324 images of blood agar plates. This dataset contains a segmentation ground–truth labeling obtained following the procedure reported in [19]. The dataset has been randomly split, using 221 images for training the network and the remaining 103 images for testing its generalization ability.

3.3 Segmentation Experiments

Training and Evaluation. A dataset containing 119000 synthetic blood agar images, of size 800×800, was used to pre–train the PSP Network. More precisely, random crops of 233×233 pixels were employed during training, whereas a sliding window approach was used for the evaluation. The Adam optimizer, based on a learning rate of 10^{-6} and a mini–batch of 15 examples, has been used to train the network, with a validation set of 1000 synthetic images used for early stopping. Finally, the network has been fine–tuned on the MicrobIA Haemolysis Dataset.

Ablation Study. To evaluate the contribution of the injection of synthetic data during training, we proceed with the following experimental setup:

- Synthetic images – training on synthetic data only;
- Real images – training on real data from the MicrobIA dataset only;
- Synthetic and real images – training on synthetic data and fine–tune on real data from the MicrobIA dataset.

Table 1 collects the obtained experimental results. The segmentation model, trained on the real images of the MicrobIA dataset, produces a mean intersection over union (mean IoU) of 85,30%, which can be considered our baseline. When the network is pre–trained on artificial examples and fine–tuned on the real data, an improvement of 1,03% on the mean IoU is obtained on the test set. Instead, when only synthetic data are used during training, the mean IoU drops down by 2,51%. Both these results prove the importance of the injection of synthetic data during training. In particular, the small difference between performances obtained using only real or only synthetic data is an interesting result. This suggests that, when real agar plate images are not available (with respect to different culture grounds or bacterial species), a deep segmentation network can be used anyway, based on synthetic data only (a hypothesis that is worth proving as a future matter of research). In Fig. 5 a qualitative comparison of the results is shown. In the first row, we can observe that, using only synthetic images, the network learns to segment correctly the isolated colonies but fails to identify the confluent growth. This behavior can be observed in almost all the images in the test set. We can also note that the network is able to recognize the colony shape more accurately when trained on both real and synthetic data, although it is not clear if this is due to the augmented number of available examples or to the rough annotation often provided in the MicrobIA dataset (see (e) in the first row of Fig. 5). Instead, in the second row, an example in which synthetic images suffice to obtain the correct result is depicted.

Table 1. Segmentation results, obtained using the three different experimental setups.

Experimental setup	Mean IoU	Pixel accuracy
Synthetic images	82,79%	98,29%
Real images	85,30%	99,19%
Synthetic and real images	86,33%	99,26%

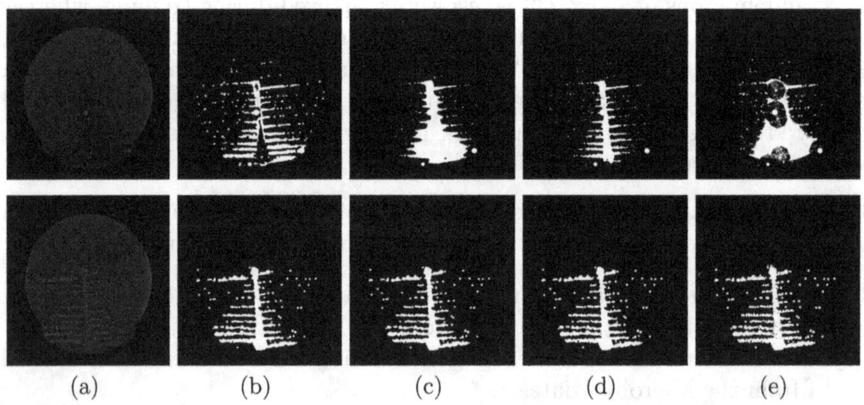

Fig. 5. Original images (a). Results obtained with synthetic images, real images and both real and synthetic images, respectively, in (b)–(d). Ground–Truth images (e).

4 Conclusions

In this paper, we trained a deep convolutional neural network for bacterial colony segmentation in agar plate images. Despite the huge variety of growing media and bacterial species that can be found on Petri dishes, public datasets do not exist accounting for such a variability. For this reason, we propose a new synthetic image generator, which can be used to cheaply produce large datasets of fully annotated images of Petri plates. The synthetically generated data can be employed to train a convolutional neural network for semantic image segmentation, which we proved to be capable to generalize to real images. Actually, the network trained based only on artificial examples achieves comparable results with respect to using real data, whereas a significant improvement in performances can be observed when both types of data are used for training. It is a matter of future research to obtain a more accurate estimation of the probability matrix for the streaking simulation and to improve the quality of synthetic images in the region of the confluent growth.

References

1. Krizhevsky, A., Sustkever, I., Hinton, G.E.: ImageNet classification with deep convolutional neural networks. In: Advances in Neural Information Processing Systems, pp. 1097–1105 (2012)
2. Shelhamer, E., Long, J., Darrell, T.: Fully convolutional networks for semantic segmentation. IEEE Trans. Pattern Anal. Mach. Learn. **39**(4), 640–651 (2017)
3. Girshick, R.B., Donahue, J., Darrell, T., Malik, J.: Rich feature hierarchies for accurate object detection and semantic segmentation. In: Proceedings of CVPR 2014, pp. 580–587 (2014)
4. Zhao, H., Shi, J., Qi, X., Wang, X., Jia, J.: Pyramid scene parsing network. In: Proceedings of CVPR 2017, pp. 6230–6239 (2017)
5. Savardi, M., Ferrari, A., Signoroni, A.: Automatic hemolysis identification on aligned dual-lighting images of cultured blood agar plates. Comput. Methods Programs Biomed. **156**, 13–24 (2018)
6. Mansberg, H.P.: Automatic particle and bacterial colony counter. Science **126**(3278), 823–827 (1957)
7. Alexander, N., Glick, D.: Automatic counting of bacterial cultures – a new machine. IRE Trans. Med. Electron. PGME-12, 89–92 (1958)
8. Mukherjee, D., Pal, A., Sarma, S.E., Majumder, D.D.: Bacterial colony counting using distance transform. Int. J. Biomed. Comput. **38**, 131–140 (1995)
9. Zhang, C., Chen, W., Liu, W., Chen, C.: An automated bacterial colony counting system. In: IEEE International Conference on Sensor Networks, Ubiquitous, and Trustworthy Computing (SUTC), pp. 233–240 (2008)
10. Brugger, S., Baumberger, C., Jost, M., Jenni, W., Brugger, U., Mühlemann, K.: Automated counting of bacterial colony forming units on agar plates. PLoS ONE **7**(3), e33695 (2012)
11. Liu, A., Liu, Z., Song, L., Han, D.: Adaptive ideal image reconstruction for bacteria colony detection. In: Zhu, E., Sambath, S. (eds.) Information Technology and Agricultural Engineering, vol. 134, pp. 353–360. Springer, Heidelberg (2012). https://doi.org/10.1007/978-3-642-27537-1_44
12. Corkidi, G., Diaz-Uribe, R., Folch-Mallol, J., Nieto-Sotelo, J.: COVASIAM: an image analysis method that allows detection of confluent microbial colonies and colonies of various sizes for automated counting. Appl. Environ. Microbiol. **64**(4), 1400–1404 (1998)
13. Masala, G.L., Bottigli, U., Brunetti, A., Carpinelli, M., Diaz, N., Fiori, P.L., Oliva, P., Stegel, G.: Automatic cell colony counting by region-growing approach. Nuovo Cimento C **30**(6), 633–644 (2008)
14. Geissmann, Q.: OpenCFU: a new free and open-source software to count cell colonies and other circular objects. PLoS ONE **8**(2), e54072 (2013)
15. Andreini, P., Bonechi, S., Bianchini, M., Garzelli, A., Mecocci, A.: Automatic image classification for the urinoculture screening. Comput. Biol. Med. **70**, 12–22 (2016)

16. Andreini, P., Bonechi, S., Bianchini, M., Mecocci, A., Di Massa, V.: Automatic image classification for the urinoculture screening. In: Neves-Silva, R., Jain, L.C., Howlett, R.J. (eds.) Intelligent Decision Technologies. SIST, vol. 39, pp. 31–42. Springer, Cham (2015). https://doi.org/10.1007/978-3-319-19857-6_4
17. Andreini, P., Bonechi, S., Bianchini, M., Garzelli, A., Mecocci, A.: ABLE: an automated bacterial load estimator for the urinoculture screening. In: Proceedings of ICPRAM 2016, pp. 573–580 (2016)
18. Andreini, P., et al.: Extraction of high level visual features for the automatic recognition of UTIs. In: Petrosino, A., Loia, V., Pedrycz, W. (eds.) WILF 2016. LNCS (LNAI), vol. 10147, pp. 249–259. Springer, Cham (2017). https://doi.org/10.1007/978-3-319-52962-2_22
19. Ferrari, A., Lombardi, S., Signoroni, A.: Bacterial colony counting with convolutional neural networks in digital microbiology imaging. Pattern Recogn. **61**, 629–640 (2016)
20. Marin, J., Vazquez, D., Geronimo, D., Lopez, A.: Learning appearance in virtual scenarios for pedestrian detection. In: Proceeding of CVPR 2010, pp. 137–144 (2010)
21. Hattori, H., Boddeti, V.N., Kitani, K.M., Kanade, T.: Learning scene-specific pedestrian detectors without real data. In: Proceedings of CVPR 2015, pp. 3819–3827 (2015)
22. Jaderberg, M., Simonyan, K., Vedaldi, A., Zisserman, A.: Reading text in the wild with convolutional neural networks. Int. J. Comput. Vis. **116**(1), 1–20 (2016)
23. Gupta, A., Vedaldi, A., Zisserman, A.: Synthetic data for text localisation in natural images. In: Proceedings of CVPR 2016, pp. 2315–2324 (2016)
24. Busto, P., Liebelt, J., Gall, J.: Adaptation of synthetic data for coarse-to-fine viewpoint refinement. In: Proceedings of BMVC, pp. 14.1–14.12 (2015)
25. Papon, J., Schoeler, M.: Semantic pose using deep networks trained on synthetic RGB-D. In: Proceedings of ICCV 2015, pp. 774–782 (2015)
26. Richter, S.R., Vineet, V., Roth, S., Koltun, V.: Playing for data: ground truth from computer games. In: Leibe, B., Matas, J., Sebe, N., Welling, M. (eds.) ECCV 2016. LNCS, vol. 9906, pp. 102–118. Springer, Cham (2016). https://doi.org/10.1007/978-3-319-46475-6_7
27. Ros, G., Sellart, L., Materzynska, J., Vazquez, D., Lopez, A.M.: The SYNTHIA dataset: a large collection of synthetic images for semantic segmentation of urban scenes. In: Proceedings of CVPR 2016, pp. 3234–3243 (2016)
28. Handa, A., Patraucean, V., Badrinarayanan, V., Stent, S., Cipolla, R.: Synthcam3d: semantic understanding with synthetic indoor scenes. arXiv preprint abs/1505.00171 (2015)
29. Chen, L., Papandreou, G., Kokkinos, I., Murphy, K., Yuille, A.: Semantic image segmentation with deep convolutional nets and fully connected CRFs. In: Proceedings of ICLR (2015)
30. Everingham, M., Eslami, S.M.A., Van Gool, L., Williams, C.K.I., Winn, J., Zisserman, A.: The PASCAL visual object classes challenge: a retrospective. Int. J. Comput. Vis. **111**(1), 98–136 (2015)
31. Lin, T.-Y., et al.: Microsoft COCO: common objects in context. In: Fleet, D., Pajdla, T., Schiele, B., Tuytelaars, T. (eds.) ECCV 2014. LNCS, vol. 8693, pp. 740–755. Springer, Cham (2014). https://doi.org/10.1007/978-3-319-10602-1_48

32. Ronneberger, O., Fischer, P., Brox, T.: U-Net: convolutional networks for biomedical image segmentation. In: Navab, N., Hornegger, J., Wells, W.M., Frangi, A.F. (eds.) MICCAI 2015. LNCS, vol. 9351, pp. 234–241. Springer, Cham (2015). https://doi.org/10.1007/978-3-319-24574-4_28
33. Deng, J., Dong, W., Socher, R., Li, L.-J., Li, K., Fei-Fei, L.: ImageNet: a large-scale hierarchical image database. In: Proceedings of CVPR 2009, pp. 248–255 (2009)
34. He, K., Zhang, X., Ren, S., Sun, J.: Deep residual learning for image recognition. In: Proceedings of CVPR 2016, pp. 770–778 (2016)

Sparsity and Complexity of Networks Computing Highly-Varying Functions

Věra Kůrková(✉)

Czech Academy of Sciences, Institute of Computer Science, Pod Vodárenskou věží 2, 18207 Prague, Czech Republic
vera@cs.cas.cz

Abstract. Approximative measures of network sparsity in terms of norms tailored to dictionaries of computational units are investigated. Lower bounds on these norms of real-valued functions on finite domains are derived. The bounds are proven by combining the concentration of measure property of high-dimensional spaces with characterization of dictionaries of computational units in terms of their capacities and coherence measured by their covering numbers. The results are applied to dictionaries used in neurocomputing which have power-type covering numbers. Probabilistic results are illustrated by a concrete construction of a class of functions, computation of which by perceptron networks requires large number of units or it is unstable due to large output weights.

Keywords: Shallow and deep networks · Model complexity
Sparsity · l_1-norm · Highly-varying functions · Covering numbers
Dictionaries of computational units · Perceptrons

1 Introduction

Although neural networks were introduced as multilayer computational systems, shallow networks with one hidden layer have been the standard type of feedforward network architecture until the recent renewal of interest in deep networks. Successes of deep networks led to the conjecture that "most functions that can be represented compactly by deep architectures cannot be represented by a compact shallow architecture" [1]. On the other hand, an empirical study [2] demonstrated that shallow networks can learn some functions previously learned by deep ones using the same numbers of parameters as the original deep networks. Characterization of tasks, which can be computed by deep networks of smaller model complexities than shallow ones, is an important area of research, which is still in its early stages.

An application of the topological approach for obtaining lower bounds on complexity of shallow networks exhibiting the "curse of dimensionality" (i.e., an exponential dependence on the number of parameters [3]) from [4] was recently in [5] proposed as a potential tool for comparison of deep and shallow networks. However, its applicability is limited to classes of networks where best or near

V. Kůrková et al. (Eds.): ICANN 2018, LNCS 11141, pp. 534–543, 2018.
https://doi.org/10.1007/978-3-030-01424-7_52

best approximation of functions can be obtained by a continuous selection of network parameters. We proved in [6–8] that in many common classes of networks such continuous selection is not possible due their nonlinear and non-convex nature. Generally, derivation of lower bounds on network complexity is much more difficult than estimates of upper ones. Moreover, minimization of network sparsity measured by the number of units formalized as "l_0-pseudonorm" is a difficult non convex optimization problem.

In [9], it was suggested that a cause of large model complexities of shallow networks might be in the "amount of variations" of functions to be computed. As an example of a highly-varying function, the parity function on the Boolean cube was presented and it was proven that classification of points from the d-dimensional Boolean cube by Gaussian SVM requires at least 2^{d-1} support vectors. In [10], we showed that the concept of a highly-varying function has to be studied in dependence on a type of computational units. We proposed to formalize it using a concept of variational norm tailored to a type of computational units. These norms have been used as a tool for estimating rates of approximation by neural networks [11–13]. Using probabilistic arguments based on Chernoff-Hoeffding bound, we derived in [10] lower bounds on variational norms and in [14] on errors of approximation of binary-valued functions (representing binary classification tasks) by shallow networks. In [15] we complemented probabilistic results by constructive ones showing that a class of functions induced by Hadamard matrices has large variational norms with respect to the dictionary of perceptrons.

In this paper, we investigate network complexity and sparsity in terms of the l_1-norms of output-weight vectors. Minimization of the number of hidden units in a shallow network or in the last hidden layer of a deep one is a difficult non convex optimization problem and thus we focus on investigation of minima of l_1-norms of output-weight vectors. l_1-norm is a good approximation of convexification of "l_0-pseudonorm" formalizing the concept of network sparsity and it plays a role of a stabilizer in weight-decay regularization [16]. The l_1-norms of output-weight vectors of all networks with units from a given dictionary computing a given function are bounded from below by the variational norm with respect to the dictioary. We derive lower bounds on minima of l_1-norms of output-weight vectors of networks computing real-valued functions on finite domains. Sets of such functions are isomorphic to Euclidean spaces of dimensions equal to the sizes of the domains. Thus for large domains, geometrical properties of high-dimensional spaces influence distribution of variational norms of real-valued functions on these domains. Combining concentration of measure property of high-dimensional spaces with characterization of dictionaries of computational units in terms of their capacity and coherence described by their covering numbers, we derive lower bounds on variational norms of real-valued functions on finite domains and on l_1-norms of output-weight vectors of networks computing these functions. Applying these estimates to dictionaries with power-type covering numbers, we prove that on large domains almost any uniformly randomly chosen function has large variation with respect to such dictionary and thus its computation requires either large number of units or it is unstable as some output weights are large. We illustrate our probabilistic results by a concrete construction of a class of functions induced by matrices with orthogonal rows which have large variational norms with respect to the dictionary of perceptrons.

The paper is organized as follows. Section 2 contains basic concepts and notations on feedforward networks and dictionaries of computational units. In Sect. 3, approximative measures of network sparsity in terms of l_1 and variational norms are investigated. In Sect. 4, probabilistic lower bounds on distribution of variational norms are derived in terms of covering numbers of dictionaries and sizes of the domains. In Sect. 5, probabilistic results are complemented by constructive ones. Section 6 is a brief discussion.

2 Preliminaries

A *feedforward network with a single linear output* can compute input-output functions from the set

$$\operatorname{span} G := \left\{ \sum_{i=1}^{n} w_i g_i \,\middle|\, w_i \in \mathbb{R},\ g_i \in G,\ n \in \mathbb{N} \right\},$$

where G, called a *dictionary*, is a parameterized family of functions. In *shallow (one-hidden-layer) networks*, G is formed by functions computable by a given type of computational units, whereas in *deep networks* with several hidden layers, it is formed by combinations and compositions of functions representing units from lower layers. By $\operatorname{span}_n G := \left\{ \sum_{i=1}^{n} w_i g_i \,\middle|\, w_i \in \mathbb{R},\ g_i \in G \right\}$ we denote the set of functions computable by networks with at most n units in the last hidden layer.

For $X \subset \mathbb{R}^d$, we denote by $\mathcal{F}(X) := \{f \mid f : X \to \mathbb{R}\}$ the *set of all real-valued functions on* X. In practical applications, domains $X \subset \mathbb{R}^d$ are finite, but their sizes $\operatorname{card} X$ and/or input dimensions d can be quite large. Fixing a linear ordering $\{x_1, \ldots, x_m\}$ of elements of X we define an isomorphism $\iota : \mathcal{F}(X) \to \mathbb{R}^m$ as $\iota(f) := (f(x_1), \ldots, f(x_m))$ and thus we identify $\mathcal{F}(X)$ with the finite dimensional Euclidean space $\mathbb{R}^m$. On $\mathcal{F}(X)$ we denote the induced inner product by $\langle f, g \rangle := \sum_{u \in X} f(u)g(u)$ and the Euclidean norm $\|f\|_2 := \sqrt{\langle f, f \rangle}$. We denote by $\mathcal{B}(X) := \{f \mid f : X \to \{-1, 1\}\}$ the *set of all functions on* X *with values in* $\{-1, 1\}$. It is convenient to consider binary-valued functions with the range $\{-1, 1\}$ instead of $\{0, 1\}$ as all functions in $\mathcal{B}(X)$ have norms equal to $\sqrt{\operatorname{card} X}$.

Dictionaries are parameterized families of functions of the form

$$G(X) = G_\phi(X, Y) := \{\phi(\cdot, y) : X \to \mathbb{R} \mid y \in Y\},$$

where $\phi : X \times Y \to \mathbb{R}$ is a function of two variables: an input vector $x \in X \subseteq \mathbb{R}^d$ and a parameter vector $y \in Y \subseteq \mathbb{R}^s$. We denote by

$$P(X) := \{\operatorname{sgn}(v \cdot . + b) : X \to \{-1, 1\} \mid v \in \mathbb{R}^d, b \in \mathbb{R}\}$$

the dictionary of *signum perceptrons*, where $\operatorname{sgn}(t) = -1$ for $t < 0$ and $\operatorname{sgn}(t) = 1$ for $t \geq 0$. Note that it is more convenient to consider the dictionary of signum perceptrons instead of Heaviside ones because all signum perceptrons have the same norms equal to $\sqrt{m}$, where m is the size of the domain X. Another important class of dictionaries is formed by sets of kernel units. For $X, U \subseteq \mathbb{R}^d$ and a symmetric positive semidefinite kernel $K : \mathbb{R}^d \times \mathbb{R}^d \to \mathbb{R}$, we denote by $K(X,U) := \{K(.,u) : X \to \mathbb{R} \,|\, u \in U\}$ the *dictionary of kernel units on X with parameters (centers) in U*. In the Support Vector Machine (SVM) algorithm, the set $U = \{u_i, \,|\, i = 1, \ldots, l\}$ is the set of points to be classified, among which some play roles of support vectors.

3 Sparsity, Variational Norm, and Correlation

In this section, we investigate approximate measures of network sparsity in terms of l_1-norm and variational norms tailored to computational units.

Formally, the number of hidden units in a shallow network or in the last hidden layer of a deep one can be described as the *number of non zero entries* of the vector of output weights of the network. In applied mathematics, the number of non zero entries of a vector $w \in \mathbb{R}^n$, denoted $\|w\|_0$, is called "*l_0-pseudonorm*" because it satisfies the equation $\|w\|_0 = \sum_{i=1}^n w_i^0$. The quotation marks are used because $\|w\|_0$ is neither a norm nor a pseudonorm. Minimization of "l_0-pseudonorm" is a difficult non convex problem as l_0 lacks the homogeneity property of a norm and its "unit ball" is not convex.

In neurocomputing, instead of "l_0-pseudonorm", l_1 and l_2-norms have been used as stabilizers in weight-decay regularization methods [16]. Acting as a stabilizer, l_2-norm penalizes even a small number of large output weights but it can tolerate many small ones, which are penalized by l_1-norm stabilizers. This can be illustrated by a simple example of a weight vector $w \in \mathbb{R}^m$, with $w_i = \frac{c}{m}$ for all $i = 1, \ldots, m$ and m large. Then $\|w\|_1 = c$, while $\|w\|_2 = \frac{c}{\sqrt{m}}$.

Networks with large l_1-norms of output-weight vectors have either large numbers of units or some of the weights are large. Both are not desirable: implementation of networks with large numbers of units might not be feasible and large output weights might lead to instability of computation. The following lemma from [17] shows that when we restrict l_2-norms of weight vectors, then balls in l_1-norm are good approximations of convexifications of balls in "l_0-pseudonorm". For any norm or "pseudonorm" $\|.\|$, we denote by $B_r(\|.\|) = \{w \in \mathbb{R}^n \,|\, \|w\| \le r\}$ the ball of radius r in $\|.\|$.

Lemma 1. *For every positive integer m and every $r > 0$,*
$\mathrm{conv}\,(B_r(\|.\|_0) \cap B_1(\|.\|_2)) \subset B_{\sqrt{r}}(\|.\|_1) \cap B_1(\|.\|_2) \subset 2\,\mathrm{conv}\,(B_r(\|.\|_0) \cap B_1(\|.\|_2))$.

It should be noted that in contrast to "l_0-pseudonorm", any norm can be made arbitrarily large or small by multiplying a function by a suitable scalar. Also errors in approximation of scalar multiples of a given function can be made arbitrarily large or small with proper choices of scalars. Indeed, for every $c > 0$, $\|cf - \mathrm{span}_n\, G\|_2 = c\|f - \mathrm{span}_n G\|_2$. Thus, approximation and representation of functions by sets of the form $\mathrm{span}_n\, G$ have to be studied either for sets of normalized functions or for sets of functions of a given fixed ambient (typically l_2) norm. In particular, large l_1-norms have to be considered relatively to the norms of elements of a dictionary.

For a function $f \in \mathcal{F}(X)$ and a dictionary G, we denote by

$$W_f(G) = \{w = (w_1, \dots, w_n) \mid f = \sum_{i=1}^{k} w_i g_i, g_i \in G, n \in \mathbb{N}\}$$

the set of output-weight vectors of networks with units from G representing f. Many dictionaries G of computational units used in neurocomputing satisfy the *universal representation property*, i.e., every function on a finite domain can be exactly represented as an element of span G (see, e.g., [14,18]). Such universality type results guarantee representations of all $f \in \mathcal{F}(X)$ by networks with the number of units equal to the size of the domain X, i.e., they prove that $\mathcal{F}(X) \subset \mathrm{span}_m G$, where $m = \mathrm{card}\, X$. Thus from universality type results, we can conclude that sets $W_f(G)$ are non empty.

Proposition 1. *Let $X \subset \mathbb{R}^d$, $f \in \mathcal{F}(X)$, and $G = \{g_1, \dots, g_k\} \subset \mathcal{F}(X)$ be a finite dictionary. Then*

(i) $W_f(G) = \{w = (w_1, \dots, w_k) \in \mathbb{R}^k \mid f = \sum_{i=1}^{k} w_i g_i\}$ is convex;
(ii) if $W_f(G)$ is non empty, then $W_f(G)^* = \{w^* \in W_f \mid \|w^*\|_1 = \min_{w \in W_f} \|w\|_1\}$

is non empty and convex.

Proof. Convexity of both sets follows directly from their definitions. As l_1-norm is a continuous functional and every continuous function on a convex set achieves its minimum, (ii) holds. □

Note that due to its strict convexity, l_2-norm does not satisfy (ii). Thus Proposition 1 (ii) shows an advantage of l_1-norm.

Some insight into efficiency of networks with units from G can be obtained from investigation of minima of l_1-norms of vectors from sets $W_f(G)$. These minima can be investigated in terms of a norm of f tailored to a dictionary G called *G-variation*. It is defined for a bounded subset G of a normed linear space $(\mathcal{X}, \|.\|)$ as

$$\|f\|_G := \inf \left\{ c \in \mathbb{R}_+ \;\middle|\; f/c \in \mathrm{cl}_{\mathcal{X}} \, \mathrm{conv}\, (G \cup -G) \right\},$$

where $-G := \{-g \mid g \in G\}$, $\mathrm{cl}_{\mathcal{X}}$ denotes the closure with respect to the topology induced by the norm $\| \cdot \|_{\mathcal{X}}$, and conv is the convex hull. Variation with respect to Heaviside perceptrons (called *variation with respect to half-spaces*) was introduced in [11] and extended to general dictionaries in [12]. Functions with large G-variations can be seen as *highly-varying with respect to the dictionary G*.

The next proposition showing the relationship between G-variation and l_1-norm follows easily from the definition.

Proposition 2. *Let G be a bounded subset of $(\mathcal{X}, \|.\|)$. Then, for every $f \in \mathcal{X}$*

(i) $\|f\|_G \leq \min \left\{ \sum_{i=1}^{n} |w_i| \;\middle|\; f = \sum_{i=1}^{n} w_i\, g_i\,,\, w_i \in \mathbb{R},\, g_i \in G, n \in \mathbb{N} \right\}$;

(ii) for G finite with $\operatorname{card} G = k$,
$\|f\|_G \le \min\left\{\|w\|_1 \,|\, w = (w_1, \dots, w_k), f = \sum_{i=1}^k w_i\, g_i\, g_i \in G\right\}$.

To derive lower bounds on minima of l_1-norms of output weight vectors we take advantage of geometric characterization of variational norm. The following theorem is a special case formulated for finite dimensional space $\mathcal{F}(X)$ of a theorem from [13]. By $G^\perp$ is denoted the *orthogonal complement of* G in the Hilbert space $\mathcal{F}(X)$.

Theorem 1. *Let X be a finite subset of $\mathbb{R}^d$ and G be a bounded subset of $\mathcal{F}(X)$. Then for every $f \in \mathcal{F}(X) \setminus G^\perp$, $\|f\|_G \ge \frac{\|f\|^2}{\sup_{g\in G}|\langle g,f\rangle|}$.*

Theorem 1 shows that lower bounds on G-variation of a function f can be obtained by estimating correlations of f with functions from the dictionary G. When f is nearly orthogonal to all elements of G, then f has large G-variation (it is highly-varying with respect to G). On the other hand when f is correlated with an element of G, then f can be well approximated by this element. As mentioned above about norms and approximation errors, also G-variation has to be studied for sets of normalized functions or for sets of functions of a given fixed norm.

4 Lower Bounds on l_1 and Variational Norms

In this section, we prove a probabilistic lower bound on distribution of variational norms in terms of covering numbers of dictionaries and sizes of their domains.

Covering numbers were introduced in [19] as a way to measure sizes of subsets of metric spaces using as measuring units small balls. For $\varepsilon > 0$, an *ε-net in G* is a set $\{g_1, \dots, g_n\} \subseteq G$ such that the family of the closed balls $B_\varepsilon(g_i)$ of radii ε centered at g_i covers G. The *ε-covering number* denoted $\mathcal{N}_\varepsilon(G)$ of a subset G of a metric space $\mathcal{S}$ is the cardinality of a minimal ε-net in G, i.e.,

$$\mathcal{N}_\varepsilon(G) = \min\{n \in \mathbb{N}_+ \,|\, G \subseteq \bigcup_{i=1}^n B_\varepsilon(f_i),\ (\forall i = 1, \dots, n)(f_i \in G)\}.$$

When the set over which the minimum is taken is empty, $\mathcal{N}_\varepsilon(G) = +\infty$. Covering numbers are related to *packing numbers* defined as the maximal numbers of disjoint balls that fit in a set.

We consider covering numbers of normalized dictionaries as subsets of the unit sphere $S_1(X) = \{f \in \mathcal{F}(X) \,|\, \|f\|_2 = 1\}$ endowed with the angular pseudo-metrics $\rho(f,g) = \arccos|\langle f,g\rangle|$. So the angular distance between f and g is α, where $\cos\alpha = |\langle f,g\rangle|$. The proof of the following theorem is based on the *concentration of measure on high-dimensional spheres* which states that most values of a Lipschitz function on a high-dimensional sphere are concentrated around their median [20, p. 337].

Theorem 2. *Let d be a positive integer, $X \subset \mathbb{R}^d$ with* $\operatorname{card} X = m$, *$\mu$ be a uniform probability measure on $S_1(X)$, $b > 0$, and $G(X) \subset S_1(X)$ has finite covering numbers. Then*

$$\mu(\{f \in S_1(X) \,|\, \|f\|_{G(X)} \geq b\}) \geq 1 - 2\mathcal{N}_{\arccos(2/b)}(G(X))\, e^{-\frac{2m}{b^2}}.$$

Proof. Let $C(g, \varepsilon) = \{f \in S_1(X) \,|\, |\langle f, g\rangle| \geq \varepsilon\} = \{f \in S_1(X) \,|\, \rho(f, g) \leq \alpha\}$, where $\alpha = \arccos(\varepsilon)$. By Theorem 1, $\|f\|_{G(X)} \geq \frac{1}{\sup_{g \in G} |\langle f, g\rangle|}$. Thus $\{f \in S_1(X) \,|\, \|f\|_G \geq b\} = S_1(X) \setminus 2\bigcup_{g \in G} C(g, 1/b)$. Let $\alpha = \arccos(2/b)$ and $\{g_1, \ldots, g_n\}$ be a minimal α-net in G in the angular pseudometrics ρ. Then $\bigcup_{i=1}^n C(g_i, 2/b) \supseteqq \bigcup_{g \in G} C(g, 1/b)$.

For every $g \in G$, the inner product with g is Lipschitz continuous on $S_1(X)$ and the median of the inner products of g with uniformly randomly chosen functions $f \in S_1(X)$ is zero. Thus by the concentration of measure property [20, p. 28], we have $\mu(C(g, 1/b) \leq e^{-\frac{2m}{b^2}}$. Thus $\mu(S_1(X)) \setminus \bigcup_{i=1}^n C(g_i, 2/b) \geq 1 - 2\mathcal{N}_\alpha(G) e^{-\frac{2m}{b^2}}$ and so the statement follows. □

Theorem 2 implies that for dictionaries with covering numbers $\mathcal{N}_\alpha(G(X))$ which do not outweigh the factor $e^{-\frac{m(\cos\alpha)^2}{2}}$, almost any uniformly randomly chosen function has variation larger than $\frac{1}{\cos\alpha}$.

Combining Theorem 2 with Proposition 2 we obtain the following lower bound on the l_1-norm of the output-weight vector of any network with units from G computing a uniformly randomly chosen real-valued function on X.

Corollary 1. *Let d be a positive integer, $X \subset \mathbb{R}^d$ with* $\operatorname{card} X = m$, *$b > 0$, $G(X) \subset S_1(X)$ has finite covering numbers, and f be a function uniformly randomly chosen from $S_1(X)$. Then for any representation of f as an input-output function $f = \sum_{i=1}^n w_i g_i$, the l_1-norm of the output weight vector $w = (w_1, \ldots, w_n)$ satisfies*

$$\Pr(\|w\|_1 \geq b) \geq 1 - 2\mathcal{N}_{\arccos(2/b)}(G(X))\, e^{-\frac{2m}{b^2}}.$$

For finite dictionaries G, all covering numbers are bounded from above by $\operatorname{card} G$. Dictionaries formed by functions on finite domains with finite ranges are finite. An example of such dictionary is the dictionary $P(X)$ of signum perceptrons. Its size is bounded from above by $2\frac{m^d}{d!}$, where $X \subset \mathbb{R}^d$ with $\operatorname{card} X = m$ [21]. Thus its size grows with m only polynomially with the polynomial degree equal to d. Some dictionaries with infinite ranges have finite sets of parameters and thus they are finite. Kernel dictionaries $K(X, U)$ used in SVM has sizes equal to $\operatorname{card} U$. Note that for some values of ε, covering numbers of finite dictionaries can be even smaller than their sizes. This can happen when a dictionary is highly coherent.

Also some infinite dictionaries have *power-type covering numbers*, i.e., there exists $c > 0$ and a positive integer s such that $\mathcal{N}_\varepsilon(G) \leq \left(\frac{c}{\varepsilon}\right)^{2s}$. It was shown in [22] that for any Lipschitz continuous sigmoidal function, $\mathcal{L}^2$-covering numbers of the dictionary of sigmoidal perceptrons on any bounded domain $\Omega \subset \mathbb{R}^d$ grow as $\left(\frac{1}{\varepsilon}\right)^{\beta}$, where $\beta > 0$. Note that covering numbers in angular pseudometrics are related to covering numbers in l_2. Indeed, for $f, g \in S_1(X)$ with $\alpha = \rho(f, g)$, we have $\|f - g\|_2 = 2\sin(\alpha/2)$. Various estimates of covering numbers in l_2-norm are known. For example, any subset G of the set of functions on a finite domain X with range $\{0, 1\}$ which has a finite VC-dimension has power-type covering numbers in l_2 [23].

On the other hand, covering numbers of the whole set of all normalized functions on X (the unit sphere $S_1(X)$ in $\mathcal{F}(X)$) are growing exponentially with m. It follows from a lower bound on $\lceil e^{\frac{m\varepsilon^2}{2}} \rceil$ on the *quasiorthogonal dimension* $\dim_\varepsilon m$ of $\mathbb{R}^m$ proven in [24,25]. It is defined as the maximal number of vectors such that each pair of distinct ones has inner product at most ε and thus it is related to the packing number. Many dictionaries occupy only fractions of the sphere $S_1(X)$ and their covering numbers grow much more slowly than those of $S_1(X)$. Theorem 2 implies that on a sufficiently large domain almost any uniformly randomly chosen function has large variation with respect to a dictionary with power-type covering numbers.

5 Construction of Functions with Large Variations with Respect to Perceptrons

In this section, we complement probabilistic results from the previous section by constructive ones. We describe a construction of class of functions on square domains whose elements can be seen as pixels.

A function f on a square domain of the form $X = \{x_i \,|\, i = 1, \ldots, n\} \times \{y_j \,|\, j = 1, \ldots, n\}$ can be described by a matrix $M(f)$ defined as $M(f)_{i,j} = f(x_i, y_j)$. The following theorem gives a lower bound on variation with respect to signum perceptrons for a class of real-valued functions defined by matrices with orthogonal rows. It is an extension of our result from [15] constructing classifiers (functions with values in $\{-1, 1\}$) to real-valued functions.

Theorem 3. *Let* $d = d_1 + d_2$, $\{x_i \,|\, i = 1, \ldots, n\} \subset \mathbb{R}^{d_1}$, $\{y_j \,|\, j = 1, \ldots, n\} \subset \mathbb{R}^{d_2}$, $X = \{x_i \,|\, i = 1, \ldots, n\} \times \{y_j \,|\, j = 1, \ldots, n\} \subset \mathbb{R}^d$, $a > 0$, *and* $f_M : X \to \{-1, 1\}$ *be defined as* $f_M(x_i, y_j) = M_{i,j}$, *where* M *is an* $n \times n$ *matrix with orthogonal rows such that the* l_2*-norm of each row vector is bounded from above by* a. *Then* $\|f_M\|_{P(X)} \geq \frac{\sqrt{a}}{\lceil \log_2 n \rceil}$.

The proof of Theorem 3 proceeds in a similar way as our proof of [15, Theorem 5] with replacing Lindsay lemma holding for Hadamard matrices with the following lemma holding for matrices with orthogonal rows with any real-valued entries.

Lemma 2. *Let* n, m *be a positive integers,* M *be an* $m \times n$ *matrix,* $v_1, \ldots, v_m$ *be its row vectors, and* $a = \max_{i=1,\ldots,m} \|v_i\|_2^2$. *If each pair of distinct row vectors is orthogonal, then for any subset* I *of the set of indices of rows and any subset* J *of the set of indices of columns of* M, $\left| b \sum_{i \in I} \sum_{j \in J} M_{i,j} \right| \leq \sqrt{a \, \mathrm{card}\, I \; \mathrm{card}\, J}$.

Proof. Without loss of generality, we can assume that $J = \{1, \ldots, k\}$. Let $\bar{v_i} = (v_{i1}, \ldots, v_{ik})$ and set $u = \sum_{i=I} \bar{v_i}$. Then $\left|\sum_{i \in I} \sum_{j \in J} M_{i,j}\right| = |\langle u, (1, \ldots, 1)\rangle|$. By the Cauchy-Schwartz Inequality, it is bounded from above by $\|u\| \sqrt{\text{card}\, J}$. By orthogonality of the row vectors, $\langle u, u \rangle = \sum_{i \in I} \sum_{l=1}^{k} \langle u_i, u_l \rangle = \sum_{i \in I} \sum_{l=1}^{k} \langle u_i, u_l \rangle = \sum_{i \in I} \|u_i\|^2 \leq a \text{card} I$ and so the statement follows. □

Theorem 3 provides a method of constructing functions on square domains, whose computation by signum perceptrons can be only achieved by networks with large l_1-norms of output weights. Such functions can be defined by $n \times n$ matrices having as rows elements of any orthogonal basis of $\mathbb{R}^n$. For example, the basis of $\mathbb{R}^n$ with $n = 2^d$ formed by *generalized parities* $\{p_u \,|\, u \in \{0,1\}^d\}$, where $p_u(x) = -1^{x \cdot u}$ (normalized generalized parities form the Fourier basis).

6 Discussion

Minimization of "l_0-pseudonorm" formalizing the concept of network sparsity measured by the number of units in the last hidden layer is a difficult non convex problem. Thus we focused on l_1-norm of output-weight vectors, which is a good approximation of convexification of"l_0", has been used in weight-decay regularization [16], and in statistical learning in the Lasso method [26]. We investigated minima of l_1-norms of output-weight vectors of networks computing a given function using variational norms tailored to dictionaries of computational units. Applying geometrical properties of high-dimensional Euclidean spaces (the concentration of measure) we derived probabilistic lower bounds on minima of variational and l_1-norms of output-weight vectors in terms of covering numbers of dictionaries. Combining our results with known estimates of sizes of finite dictionaries of signum or Heaviside perceptrons and kernel units used in SVM, we proved that large lower bounds hold for almost any uniformly randomly chosen function. Estimates of covering numbers of dictionaries consisting of compositions of functions computed in several hidden layers and probabilistic bounds holding for non uniform distributions are subject of our future research.

Acknowledgments. V.K. was partially supported by the Czech Grant Foundation grant GA18-23827S and institutional support of the Institute of Computer Science RVO 67985807.

References

1. Bengio, Y., LeCun, Y.: Scaling learning algorithms towards AI. In: Bottou, L., Chapelle, O., DeCoste, D., Weston, J. (eds.) Large-Scale Kernel Machines. MIT Press, Cambridge (2007)
2. Ba, L.J., Caruana, R.: Do deep networks really need to be deep? In: Ghahrani, Z., et al. (eds.) Advances in Neural Information Processing Systems, vol. 27, pp. 1–9 (2014)
3. Bellman, R.: Dynamic Programming. Princeton University Press, Princeton (1957)
4. DeVore, R.A., Howard, R., Micchelli, C.: Optimal nonlinear approximation. Manuscripta Mathematica **63**, 469–478 (1989)

5. Poggio, T., Mhaskar, H., Rosasco, L., Miranda, B., Liao, Q.: Why and when can deep-but not shallow-networks avoid the curse of dimensionality: a review. Int. J. Autom. Comput. https://doi.org/10.1007/s11633-017-1054-2
6. Kainen, P.C., Kůrková, V., Vogt, A.: Approximation by neural networks is not continuous. Neurocomputing **29**, 47–56 (1999)
7. Kainen, P.C., Kůrková, V., Vogt, A.: Geometry and topology of continuous best and near best approximations. J. Approx. Theor. **105**, 252–262 (2000)
8. Kainen, P.C., Kůrková, V., Vogt, A.: Continuity of approximation by neural networks in L_p-spaces. Ann. Oper. Res. **101**, 143–147 (2001)
9. Bengio, Y., Delalleau, O., Roux, N.L.: The curse of highly variable functions for local kernel machines. In: Advances in Neural Information Processing Systems, vol. 18, pp. 107–114. MIT Press, Cambridge (2006)
10. Kůrková, V., Sanguineti, M.: Model complexities of shallow networks representing highly varying functions. Neurocomputing **171**, 598–604 (2016)
11. Barron, A.R.: Neural net approximation. In: Narendra, K.S. (ed.) Proceedings of 7th Yale Workshop on Adaptive and Learning Systems, pp. 69–72. Yale University Press (1992)
12. Kůrková, V.: Dimension-independent rates of approximation by neural networks. In: Warwick, K., Kárný, M. (eds.) Computer-Intensive Methods in Control and Signal Processing. The Curse of Dimensionality, pp. 261–270. Birkhäuser, Boston (1997)
13. Kůrková, V.: Complexity estimates based on integral transforms induced by computational units. Neural Netw. **33**, 160–167 (2012)
14. Kůrková, V., Sanguineti, M.: Probabilistic lower bounds for approximation by shallow perceptron networks. Neural Netw. **91**, 34–41 (2017)
15. Kůrková, V.: Constructive lower bounds on model complexity of shallow perceptron networks. Neural Comput. Appl. **29**, 305–315 (2018)
16. Fine, T.L.: Feedforward Neural Network Methodology. Springer, Heidelberg (1999). https://doi.org/10.1007/b97705
17. Plan, Y., Vershynin, R.: One-bit compressed sensing by linear programming. Commun. Pure Appl. Math. **66**, 1275–1297 (2013)
18. Ito, Y.: Finite mapping by neural networks and truth functions. Math. Sci. **17**, 69–77 (1992)
19. Kolmogorov, A.: Asymptotic characteristics of some completely bounded metric spaces. Dokl. Akad. Nauk. SSSR **108**, 585–589 (1956)
20. Matoušek, J.: Lectures on Discrete Geometry. Springer, New York (2002). https://doi.org/10.1007/978-1-4613-0039-7
21. Schläfli, L.: Gesamelte Mathematische Abhandlungen, vol. 1. Birkhäuser, Basel (1950)
22. Makovoz, Y.: Random approximants and neural networks. J. Approx. Theor. **85**, 98–109 (1996)
23. Haussler, D.: Sphere packing numbers for subsets of the Boolean n-cube with bounded Vapnik-Chervonenkis dimension. J. Comb. Theor. A **69**(2), 217–232 (1995)
24. Kainen, P.C., Kůrková, V.: Quasiorthogonal dimension of Euclidean spaces. Appl. Math. Lett. **6**(3), 7–10 (1993)
25. Kainen, P.C., Kůrková, V.: Quasiorthogonal dimension. In: Kosheleva, O., Shary, S., Xiang, G., Zapatrin, R. (eds.) Beyond Traditional Probabilistic Data Processing Techniques: Interval, Fuzzy, etc. Methods and Their Applications. Springer (2018, to appear)
26. Tibshirani, R.: Regression shrinkage and selection via the Lasso. J. Roy. Stat. Soc. B **58**, 267–288 (1996)

Deep Learning Based Vehicle Make-Model Classification

Burak Satar[1] and Ahmet Emir Dirik[2(✉)]

[1] Department of Electrical-Electronics Engineering, Uludag University, Bursa, Turkey
buraksatar@gmail.com

[2] Department of Computer Engineering, Uludag University, Bursa, Turkey
edirik@uludag.edu.tr

Abstract. This paper studies the problem of vehicle make & model classification. Some of the main challenges are reaching high classification accuracy and reducing the annotation time of the images. To address these problems, we have created a fine-grained database using online vehicle marketplaces of Turkey. A pipeline is proposed to combine an SSD (Single Shot Multibox Detector) model with a CNN (Convolutional Neural Network) model to train on the database. In the pipeline, we first detect the vehicles by following an algorithm which reduces the time for annotation. Then, we feed them into the CNN model. It is reached approximately 4% better classification accuracy result than using a conventional CNN model. Next, we propose to use the detected vehicles as ground truth bounding box (GTBB) of the images and feed them into an SSD model in another pipeline. At this stage, it is reached reasonable classification accuracy result without using perfectly shaped GTBB. Lastly, an application is implemented in a use case by using our proposed pipelines which detects the unauthorized vehicles by comparing their license plate numbers and make & models. It is assumed that license plates are readable.

Keywords: Deep learning · Vehicle · Model · Classification · CNN ResNet · Detection · SSD · Fraud · License plate

1 Introduction

Numerous researches have been performed on make & model classification of vehicles [8,14,15]. This paper studies some of the main issues of these researches. First of all, there are only a few open source databases which include various vehicles. However, they generally either contain fewer images per class or don't include commonly used vehicles. In this study, a country-specific database is created to address this issue. Tables 1 and 2 explain its content. Images are collected through online sources such as vehicle marketplace websites. A script is used as a web crawler to gather the images.

V. Kůrková et al. (Eds.): ICANN 2018, LNCS 11141, pp. 544–553, 2018.
https://doi.org/10.1007/978-3-030-01424-7_53

On the other hand, plenty of related studies use only CNN [10] based architectures. Thus, they can't reach high classification accuracy results. We implement three different experiments in our database to approach this problem. As a first pipeline, normalization and data-augmentation processes are applied to the database. Then, we feed the images into a ResNet (Residual Network) [9] model for classification. This is called Experiment I. As a second pipeline, the vehicles are detected by an SSD [12] model which pre-trained on MS COCO [11] and PASCAL VOC [7] databases. Detected vehicles pass through the same pre-processing methods. They are fed into the same ResNet model for classification. We call it Experiment II. It is shown that Experiment II reaches a higher classification accuracy result than Experiment I.

Moreover, annotation of the GTBB is another issue. Using manual annotation tools [3] requires a considerable amount of time when a database is immense. For instance, three million images should be annotated manually in some studies [5]. Using methods like Amazon Mechanical Turk also would be possible; however, it could cost a lot of money when the database contains a relatively high volume of the data. For those reasons, we use the pre-trained SSD model for annotation which we already use in Experiment II. Algorithm 1 explains how we implement the annotation semi-autonomously in our database. Therefore, the coordinates of detected vehicles are picked as GTBB of the images. We fine-tune the VGG [13] based SSD model on our database. This pipeline is called Experiment III. It is reached a relatively close classification accuracy result when comparing to Experiment I. It is seen that Experiment III achieves this score without having perfectly shaped GTBB.

Besides, we propose an application to implement this study in a use case. The use case is regarding the detection of an illegal vehicle. Plenty of studies handle detecting the license plates [2,6]. However, it is challenging to understand which vehicle uses a fraudulent license plate when a recurrent license plate is recognized. For this reason, we suggest using our vehicle make & model classification methods to detect the unauthorized license plates assuming that license plates are readable. Reading the license plates is out of the scope of this study. Thus, an open source project is used to fulfill the need [4].

The remainder of this paper is organized as follows. Section 2 provides all the details of our system: data gathering, annotation, testing models, classification and detection architectures respectively. Section 3 describes the experiments with results. Section 4 presents the conclusions and future studies.

2 Vehicle Make-Model Classification

Firstly, this part explains the details about the database. Then, it introduces an algorithm to annotate the database for detection purposes. Lastly, the components of the testing models are explained.

2.1 Data Gathering

We do all experiments in the database; therefore it has a crucial effect on the results. Table 1 shows the distribution of the database. We take into account the statistical works of TurkStat (Turkish Statistical Institute) [1] to form the database. The Institute monthly declares the number of vehicle brands which are registered in Turkey. According to the top 5 list which is composed of between 2015 and 2017, we choose Volkswagen since it is at the top of the list. We choose the models of Renault and Fiat because they manufacture local models in our town. They are also on top 5 of the list. It is also needed to indicate that Fiat Dogan SLX and Renault R12 Toros are manufactured in Turkey and only sold in Turkey. For the seventh class which stands for make & models of other vehicle brands other than Volkswagen, Renault, Fiat; the statistical data of TurkStat is also taken into account. Therefore, this work becomes more focused on country-specific data.

Several focused keywords are used to gather the classes of the images. We eliminate the ones that have inappropriate features such as showing the inside of the vehicle, containing not the main part of the vehicle, etc. As a result, the database includes 27887 number of images of the vehicles.

Table 1. Distribution of the dataset

Make	Model	Year	Feature	# of Images
Volkswagen	Passat	2015	1.6 TDi BlueMotion Comfortline	4024
Renault	Fluence	2016	1.5 dCi Touch	4293
Fiat	Linea	2013	1.3 Multijet Active Plus	4234
Volkswagen	Polo	1999	1.6	3208
Renault	Toros	2000	R12	3783
Fiat	Dogan	1996	SLX	4183
Other Class				4162

Table 2 shows the distribution of the seventh class which refers to the other cars in general. It is composed of seven different make & models, other than the first six classes.

2.2 Annotation

We follow Algorithm 1 to reduce the annotation time. It defines the GTBB and classes of the images from the database with the help of predicted outcomes of pre-trained SSD model. In this case, we assume that the images usually include a car which is bigger than a certain size. Annotation takes a work day long when this algorithm is implemented in our database.

Table 2. Distribution of the other class

Make	Model	Year	Feature	# of Images
Toyota	Corolla	2016	1.4 D-4D Advance	663
Volvo	S60	2014	1.6 D Premium	707
Peugeot	206	2001	1.4 XR	468
Ford	Focus	2017	1.6 TDCi Trend X	693
Mercedes-Benz	C	2015	CLA 180d	608
Nissan	Micra	2016	1.2 Match	533
Audi	A3 Sedan	2017	1.6 TDI	490

Algorithm 1. Annotating ground truth bounding boxes and classes

```
Require: certainSize ← a threshold value, classId ← zero,
  for all images of that class do
      read the image and pass it through the pre-trained SSD to detect only cars;
      carSize ← the size of the detected car;
      if carSize ≥ certainSize then
          classOfDetectedCar ← classId;
      else
          ask annotator to give a label or delete it;
      end if
      save the annotation to a .csv file;
  end for
  increase the classID by one if any and run again;
```

2.3 Model Training and Testing

Figure 1 presents the three main experiments. It shows the differences among classification results of using a custom ResNet model only, a pre-trained SSD with the ResNet model and a fine-tuned SSD only.

Figure 2 shows the custom designed ResNet model which has 30 layers. It is used in Experiment I and II for classification by one difference. In Experiment I, the model takes the images to implement the pre-processing methods on them. Pre-processing methods include normalization, zero padding, resizing and data augmentation. The images are resized to the shape of (300,300,3). Data augmentation is done by flipping, adding Gaussian blur, adding Gaussian noise and zooming. Later, they are fed into the model for training. In Experiment II images are processed through an SSD model, which has weights pre-trained on MS COCO and fine-tuned on PASCAL VOC07 & VOC12 database, to only detect cars. Then, the same pre-processing methods are applied to the images of the detected vehicles. They are fed into the same ResNet model for training. Therefore we give only the vehicles to the model in Experiment II instead of giving the whole image to the model.

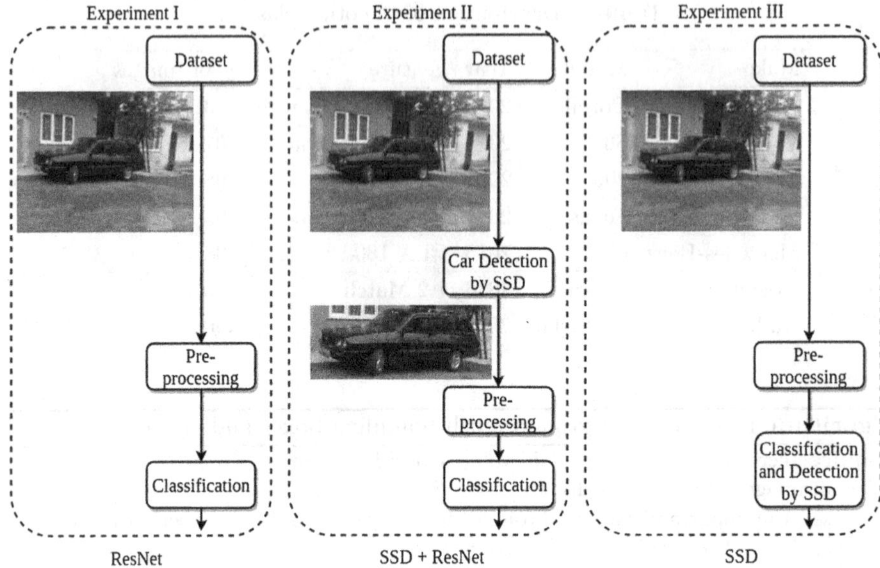

Fig. 1. Overview of experiments

The coordinates of the vehicles are detected in Experiment II. They are used as ground truth bounding boxes of the database in Experiment III. We take VGG based weights for the SDD model which are pre-trained on ImageNet. Then, the SSD model is fine-tuned on our database for classification and detection purposes.

$$y_{predict}^{I,II} = [[class_1 : prob_1], [class_2 : prob_2], ..., [class_7 : prob_7]] \tag{1}$$

$$y_{predict}^{III} = [[prob, class, x_{min}, y_{min}, x_{max}, y_{max}], [...]] \tag{2}$$

Equation 1 refers to the outcome of Experiment I and II. However, Eq. 2 refers to the output of Experiment III. Probability can be in a range between 0 and 1.

The number of trainable parameters which we use in the architecture is equal to 1,132,775. (1,1) is used as stride values in convolutional sections of Identical Blocks. Thus, heights and widths keep their shapes the same. The filter sizes are also not changed. Equation 3 shows the output of the block.

In Convolutional Block, the first section and shortcut section have a stride of (2,2) while other sections have a stride of (1,1). Besides, the first and second section of the main branch has equal filter number. However, the third section on Main Branch has same filter number with the shortcut section. Equation 4 shows the output of the block.

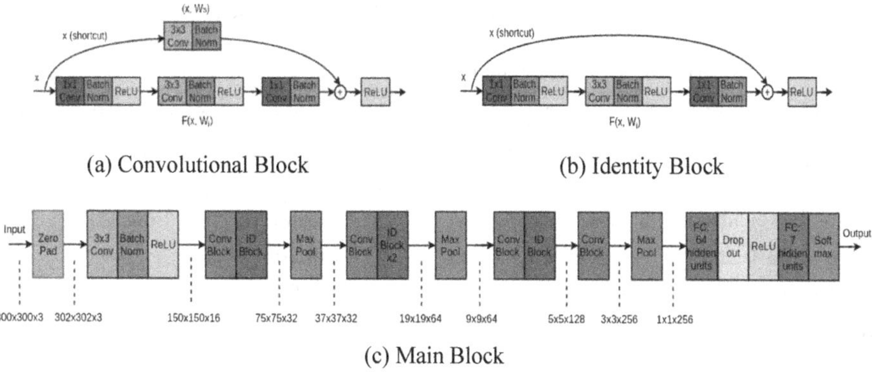

Fig. 2. The architecture of the ResNet based classification model

$$y_{identity\_block} = F(x, W_i) + x. \tag{3}$$

$$y_{conv\_block} = F(x, W_i) + W_s x. \tag{4}$$

Figure 3 shows the architecture of the SSD model. It is consist of series of convolutional blocks. Detections are made on certain levels. The number of detections is equal to 8732 per class. Then, a Non-Maximum Suppression method is implemented to eliminate predictions that have low Intersection over Union (IoU) ratio with GTBB.

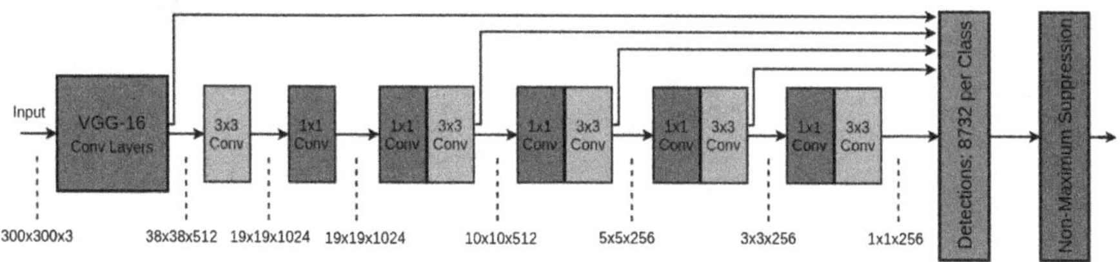

Fig. 3. The architecture of the SSD model for detection

3 Experimental Results

In this part, we examine the results with the help of Table 3, confusion matrices, sample outcomes. Training-validation-test sets are distributed based on 80%-10%-10% rule in Experiment I and II. We implement the distribution of 80%-20% on training-test sets in Experiment III. NVIDIA GT 730 with 2 GB RAM is used for Experiment I and II. However, Tesla K80 is used with the help of Google Colab for Experiment III because it needs a lot more computation.

Table 3 and Fig. 4 show that Experiment I and II reach 91.27% and 95.10% accuracy scores respectively. It can be said that giving only the vehicles in a

Table 3. Comparing the results of experiments

	Experiment I	Experiment II	Experiment III
Method	Only ResNet	Pre-trained SSD + ResNet	SSD with VGG based weights
Batch size	32		32
Epoch	100		30
Loss	Categorical cross entropy		Smooth L1 + Softmax
Train score	0.9635	0.9836	0.9071
Valid score	0.9052	0.9376	0.9057
Test score	0.9127	0.9510	

well-centered way to the model helps to increase accuracy significantly. It is interesting to see that Experiment II generalizes the Other Class 10% better. Fiat Polo Class has less amount of images comparing to the other classes. However, Experiment II also generalizes it 11% better than Experiment I.

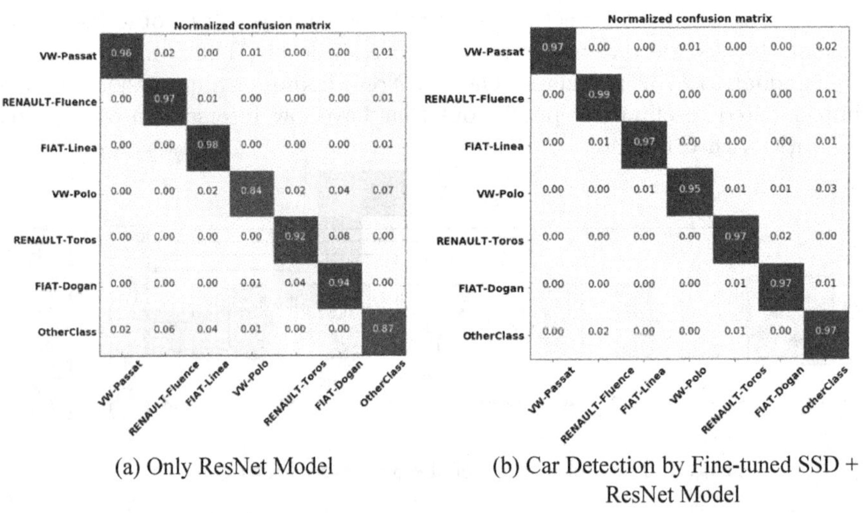

(a) Only ResNet Model

(b) Car Detection by Fine-tuned SSD + ResNet Model

Fig. 4. Confusion matrices: overall accuracy results of Experiment I and Experiment II

Less number of epochs are used in Experiment III than the others. The original SSD model has a VGG base which pre-trained on ImageNet first. Therefore, no need to train further. It is also seen that there is a significant difference between train and validation score. It indicates that we especially need more data and a bit of a change in our model.

Figure 5 shows that we reach 90.57% mAP (Mean Average Precision) score on the test set. It is seen that Experiment III has almost the same and even better classification scores for several classes. We should note that GTBB of images is defined by an algorithm which uses a pre-trained SSD model. The Other Class has the lowest accuracy result. Finally, it reaches 70.34% detection accuracy on the test set. Localization loss is also included in calculating this accuracy.

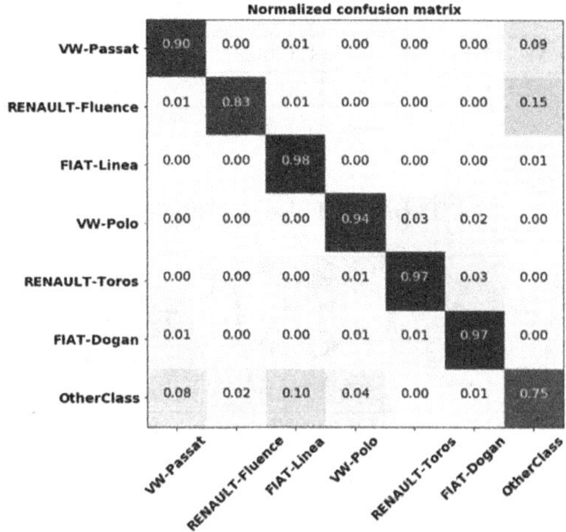

Fig. 5. Overall accuracy result of Experiment III, VGG based weights of SSD

We also tested the SSD based model on some videos. It can detect the vehicles with 12 FPS using Tesla K80. When we compare the power of GPUs with the one used in the original paper, it is very reasonable to get this FPS score. The results can be found in the author's repository. https://goo.gl/EB6vyF.

Tables 4 and 5 show the certain positive and negative outcomes respectively. Green lines refer to the correct predictions. The first image shows that the model can predict the vehicle better in spite of not having perfectly shaped GTBB. The other samples show that having a well-centered position in an image have well effects on detection.

Red lines refer to false predictions in Table 5. The samples show that if the vehicles have a relatively small size in the image, it causes to be detected wrongly. Oppositely, having a relatively big size in the image also causes false detection.

3.1 A Use Case

This study also introduces an application for detecting fraudulent license plates in Fig. 6. Middleware first takes the detected license plate number and predicted class by using our make & model detection method. Then it assigns them to a dictionary value which is composed of a key and value. Finally, it compares them with the values of the database.

It is assumed that every license plate number is matched with the class of a car and the database is set manually from the beginning. Then, if the license plate numbers are matched but make & models of a car not, it means there

Table 4. True decisions

Sample				
Predicted Class	VW. Polo	Other Class	Fiat Linea	Fiat Dogan
Probability	1.00	1.00	1.00	1.00

Ground Truth ▭ Predicted True ▬

Table 5. False decisions

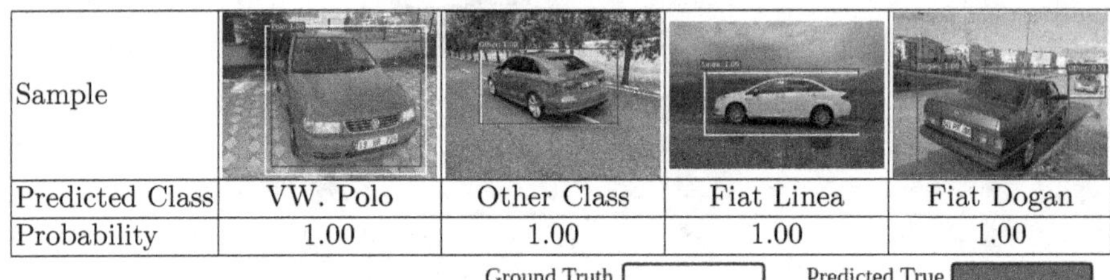

Sample				
Predicted Class	VW. Polo	Other Class	Fiat Linea	Fiat Dogan
Probability	1.00	1.00	1.00	1.00

Ground Truth ▭ Predicted True ▬

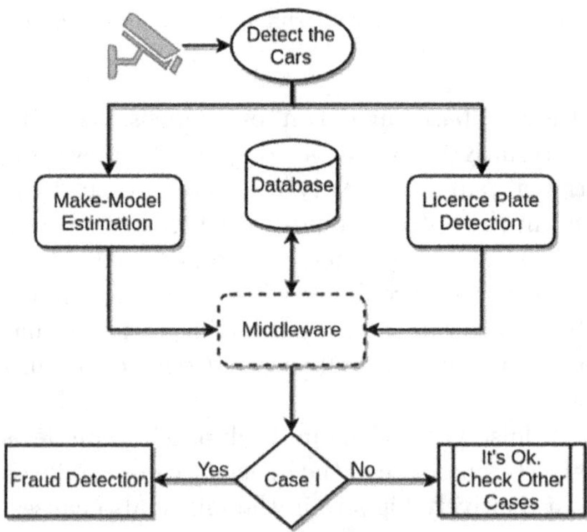

Fig. 6. A use case diagram, the case I: license plates match, but models don't

is a fraud. Meaning that the license plates are recurrent and the detected car uses an illegal license plate. The performance of the application depends on how accurate and fast the detection and the prediction are made.

4 Conclusions and Future Works

This study deals with the problems of vehicle make & model classification. At first, a fine-grained database is created to gather a large number of samples specific to Turkey. It is used in the test experiments. As a first outcome of this paper, we see that combining a CNN based model with an SSD model could increase the classification score. This paper also introduces an algorithm to reduce the annotation time; however, it causes not to have perfectly shaped GTTB of the images. Nevertheless, we reach an acceptable classification score. For future work, it requires a change in the filter sizes of the SSD model architecture to fix false detection results. Besides, this study shows that implementing this model on fraud detection of license plates is considerably possible in certain use cases. The application could be extended to further use cases for future works. For instance, it is quite hard to detect an illegal car when the license plates cannot be recognized to read. However, security providers easily improve their chance to catch the unapproved vehicles by knowing the make & model of them.

References

1. Road motor vehicles (2018). https://goo.gl/svnzXN. Accessed 5 May 2018
2. Chang, S.L., Chen, L.S., Chung, Y.C., Chen, S.W.: Automatic license plate recognition. IEEE Trans. ITS **5**(1), 42–53 (2004)
3. Ciocca, G., Napoletano, P., Schettini, R.: IAT - image annotation tool: Manual. CoRR (2015)
4. Dahms, C.: LPR. https://goo.gl/Wk6GFT. Accessed 5 May 2018
5. Dehghan, A., Masood, S.Z., Shu, G., Ortiz, E.G.: View independent vehicle make, model and color recognition using convolutional neural network. CoRR (2017)
6. Du, S., Ibrahim, M., Shehata, M., Badawy, W.: Automatic license plate recognition (ALPR): a state-of-the-art review. TCSVT **23**(2), 311–325 (2013)
7. Everingham, M., Eslami, S.M.A., Van Gool, L., Williams, C.K.I., Winn, J.: The pascal visual object classes challenge: a retrospective. IJCV **111**(1), 98–136 (2015)
8. Gupte, S., Masoud, O., Martin, R.F.K., Papanikolopoulos, N.P.: Detection and classification of vehicles. IEEE Trans. ITS **3**(1), 37–47 (2002)
9. He, K., Zhang, X., Ren, S., Sun, J.: Deep residual learning for image recognition. In: 2016 IEEE Conference on CVPR, pp. 770–778 (2016)
10. LeCun, Y., Bengio, Y.: ConvNets for images, speech, and time series. In: The Handbook of Brain Theory and Neural Networks, pp. 255–258. MIT Press (1998)
11. Lin, T.-Y., et al.: Microsoft COCO: common objects in context. In: Fleet, D., Pajdla, T., Schiele, B., Tuytelaars, T. (eds.) ECCV 2014. LNCS, vol. 8693, pp. 740–755. Springer, Cham (2014). https://doi.org/10.1007/978-3-319-10602-1_48
12. Liu, W., et al.: SSD: single shot multibox detector. In: Leibe, B., Matas, J., Sebe, N., Welling, M. (eds.) ECCV 2016. LNCS, vol. 9905, pp. 21–37. Springer, Cham (2016). https://doi.org/10.1007/978-3-319-46448-0_2
13. Simonyan, K., Zisserman, A.: Very deep convolutional networks for large-scale image recognition. CoRR (2014)
14. Tafazzoli, F., Frigui, H., Nishiyama, K.: A large and diverse dataset for improved vehicle make and model recognition. In: CVPRW, pp. 874–881 (2017)
15. Zhou, Y., Cheung, N.M.: Vehicle classification using transferable deep neural network features. CoRR (2016)

Detection and Recognition of Badgers Using Deep Learning

Emmanuel Okafor[1(✉)], Gerard Berendsen[2], Lambert Schomaker[1], and Marco Wiering[1]

[1] Bernoulli Institute for Mathematics, Computer Science, and Artificial Intelligence, University of Groningen, Groningen, The Netherlands
{e.okafor,l.r.b.schomaker,m.a.wiering}@rug.nl
[2] Twente Quality Centre (TQC), Enschede Area, The Netherlands

Abstract. This paper describes the use of two different deep-learning algorithms for object detection to recognize different badgers. We use recordings of four different badgers under varying background illuminations. In total four different object detection algorithms based on deep neural networks are compared: The single shot multi-box detector (SSD) with the Inception-V2 or MobileNet as a backbone, and the faster region-based convolutional neural network (Faster R-CNN) combined with Inception-V2 or residual networks. Furthermore, two different activation functions are compared to compute probabilities that some badger is in the detected region: the softmax and sigmoid functions. The results of all eight models show that SSD obtains higher recognition accuracies (97.8%–98.6%) than Faster R-CNN (84.8%–91.7%). However, the training time of Faster R-CNN is much shorter than that of SSD. The use of different output activation functions seems not to matter much.

Keywords: Image recognition · Object detection · Deep learning
Badger classification

1 Introduction

Badgers are short-legged omnivores and wild animals, and their existence is in danger in some parts of the world. To control this threat, some countries in Europe: United Kingdom, France, Republic of Ireland, Northern Ireland, and the Netherlands formed the Eurobadger collaboration with the objective to protect the existence of badgers. To assist this protection, there is a need to deploy computer vision systems that can aid in detecting and recognizing these animals, whose habitat is often a network of underground tunnels (setts). This paper describes the use of several deep neural network approaches to detect and classify different badgers.

Previous research [10] suggests that the human eye is an efficient and reliable method for animal detection. However, the effectiveness of the human eye reduces due to tiredness and a human is not able to focus on an animal for 24 h a day. Therefore, it is more efficient to apply computer-vision techniques for detecting and recognizing animals. Early research in [1] detects animal faces using Haar-like features and the Adaboost classifier, while tracking the animals was done using the Kanade-Lucas-Tomasi

V. Kůrková et al. (Eds.): ICANN 2018, LNCS 11141, pp. 554–563, 2018.
https://doi.org/10.1007/978-3-030-01424-7_54

method. Researchers have investigated different approaches to detect animals or humans: detection of humans in motion using background subtraction (BG) [2], using frame differences with the W4 algorithm [20], using background frame differences based on Gaussian functions [12], and the combination of BG and three-frame differencing [13].

Since the emergence of deep neural networks in the computer vision community, they have gained a lot of attention and successes for solving different learning tasks such as classification of objects, plants, and animals [11, 21, 6], classifying wild-animals [16], and recognizing cows with unmanned aerial vehicles (UAVs) using data-augmented images [18, 17]. Concerning wildlife monitoring and conservation, the authors in [3] investigated an automated detection and classification method of animals or non-animals using thermal images. Their method is based on the discrete cosine transform for feature extraction and k-nearest neighbors for classification. The research in [5] approaches wildlife monitoring using UAVs that use thermal image acquisition and a video processing pipeline to provide automatic detection, classification, and tracking of wildlife in a forest or open area. Recent research in [7] unites some scientists with the objective of monitoring wildlife. Their study showed that convolutional neural networks outperform a more classical technique based on the bag of visual words with a support vector machine in their wildlife detection challenge.

To the best of our knowledge, no research has been done concerning the detection and recognition of different badgers. The challenge is that some of the examined badgers have very similar color appearances, and therefore accurately discriminating the various badgers could be a difficult problem for computer vision algorithms.

Contributions: This research proposes the use of several object detection algorithms based on deep neural networks for detecting and recognizing badgers from video data. For this, a comparison is made between two neural network-based detectors: SSD [14] and Faster R-CNN [19]. SSD is combined with the Inception-V2 [9] or MobileNet [8] as a backbone and the Faster R-CNN detector is combined with either Inception-V2 or Residual networks [6] with 50 layers (ResNet-50) as feature extractors. Furthermore, we compare the use of two output activation functions: the softmax and sigmoid function. For the experiments, we use several videos recorded with a low-resolution camera. The results show that most of the trained SSD detectors significantly outperform the different variants of the Faster R-CNN detector. All the Faster R-CNN methods are computationally much faster than the SSD techniques for training the system, although for testing SSD is a bit faster.

Paper Outline: Section 2 describes the dataset used and the preprocessing steps. Section 3 explains the detection algorithms and the experimental setup for training the models. Section 4 presents the results. Section 5 concludes the paper and provides directions for future research.

2 Dataset and Preprocessing

The dataset is based on videos of different badgers collected by the foundation of Das and Boom[1]. The dataset contains four individual instances of badgers with a total number of 51 videos. The badger classes (identities) are: *badger_esp, badger_iaco, badger_looi,* and *badger_strik.* The badgers were recorded in 2016 and 2017 at the Badger Rescue Center of Das & Boom in the Netherlands. Additionally, some videos and photos were made at release locations for badger rehabilitation purposes. To identify each badger, they are micro-chipped, so the animal can be tracked during captivity and identified after release. The streaming lengths (Ts) of the videos vary in the range between 15 and 60 s. We extracted approximately a frame per second, for which we developed a script that extracts (Ts $\pm$ 2) video frames. We remark that some frames do not contain the existence of badgers and such frames are not used in our experiments. The details of the used dataset are shown in Table 1. Some example images of the used dataset are shown in Fig. 1.

Table 1. Dataset description

Dataset class	No. of videos	Dataset-Split (frames)		Ts (s)
		Train	Test	
Badger_esp	7	328	28	59
Badger_iaco	28	323	30	15
Badger_looi	9	437	61	59
Badger_strik	7	372	62	60
Total	51	1460	181	

We now describe how we made the ground truth annotations for the detection task. We used one video to create the images for the test set for each of the classes except for *Badger_iaco* where two videos are used in the test set. The remaining videos are used to create the train set. Manual extraction of the bounding box containing the existence of a badger was done using the LabelImg[2] tool. The used tool provides the annotation of a given image, and it is saved in the.xml file format. Each of the annotation files contains 4 coordinates representing the location of the bounding box surrounding the badger, the label and the file path to the images. We employed the Pascal VOC format.

[1] http://www.dasenboom.nl/.

[2] http://www.github.com/tzutalin/labelImg.

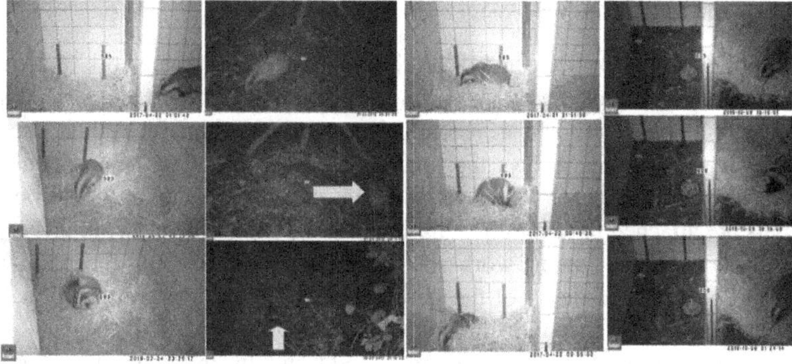

Fig. 1. Example images present in the Badger dataset; where each column represents: *Badger_esp*, *Badger_iaco*, *Badger_looi*, and *Badger_strik* respectively. The yellow arrows in column two indicate the existence of *badger_iaco* under poor illumination conditions (environment). Note that most videos were shot while the badgers were in captivity for a while, although some videos were shot in the wild.

3 Methods

This section describes the used deep neural network detection frameworks. Figure 2 shows the overall network pipeline that consists of data preprocessing as presented in Sect. 2, training the CNN to obtain the different detection models and their corresponding real-time deployment.

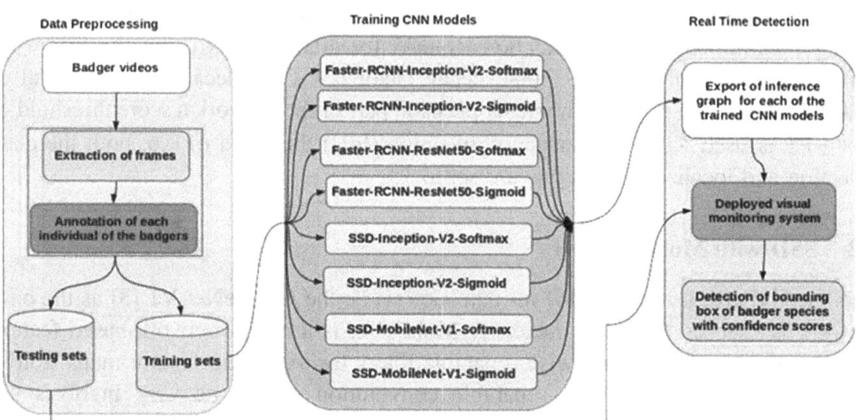

Fig. 2. Overall pipeline for the real-time detection systems; the first box accounts for the data-preprocessing, the second box represents the training of the CNN detection system, and the last box provides the network the inference generator and visual monitoring deployment system in the testing phase.

3.1 SSD with Inception-V2

The Single Shot multi-box-Detector (SSD) [14] is a detection framework that employs feed-forward convolutional neural networks for prediction of object classes and anchor offsets, with no consideration for second phase classification. Instead, it uses non-maximum suppression that allows the final detection of the objects in a single pass. A unique characteristic of this framework is that multi-scale convolutional bounding box outputs are attached to several feature maps at the top of the network layer. At the bottom or base portion of the network, the feature extraction method Inception-V2 [9] increases the breadth and depth of the network with a quite low computational complexity due to the used inception modules. The Inception-V2 extracts feature maps from the input images. The combination of SSD and Inception-V2 is called SSD-Inception-V2 [15]. We examine two forms of classification activation functions; sigmoid and softmax. This results in two variants of this approach.

Network Setup: we have trained the network using pre-trained weights ssd_inception v2_coco_2017_11_17, originally trained by a group of Google researchers. The pre-trained weights contain information from a subset of the Microsoft common object in context (COCO) dataset containing a total of approximately 328 K images with different object classes. We further trained the network using badger images with bounding boxes and class labels as input to the training algorithm. This use of pre-trained weights has the benefit of less training time compared to training random weights from scratch that demands longer computing times. During training of the network, we adopted a similar experimental setup as in [14] because it yields good performances. The network parameters include; the original input image frames contain 427×240 pixels and are resized online to 300×300 pixels, the convolutional box predictor uses a prediction dropout probability 0.8, kernel size 3×3 and a box-code size set to 4. The root mean square propagation (RMSprop) optimization algorithm is used for optimizing the loss functions trained for 40,000 steps using the following parameters; a learning rate of 0.004, decay factor 0.95, and decays at an interval of 16,000 steps. At the non-maximum suppression part of the network a score threshold of 1×10^{-8} is used with an intersection of union (IoU) threshold of 0.6, both the classification and localization weights are set to 1.

3.2 SSD with MobileNet-V1

This method also uses SSD [14] for detection while the MobileNet-V1 [8] as the base network is used as feature extractor. A MobileNet is a neural network-based feature extractor that employs depth-wise separable filters for extracting feature maps from a given image. The depth-wise separable convolution in this network involves the integration of depth-wise convolution and 1×1 point-wise convolution. The merit of this approach is that it reduces computational cost compared to standard convolution [8]. The output from the MobileNet is further processed using SSD. The method is referred to as SSD-MobileNet-V1. Additionally, we consider two forms of classification activation functions: sigmoid and softmax. This results in two variants of this method.

Network Setup: we have trained the network using pre-trained weights ssd_mobilenet_v1_coco_2017_11_17 from the COCO dataset as was explained in the previous subsection, and further trained our custom network using the badger images as input to the SSD-MobileNet-V1 system. The training process uses similar hyperparameters as described in the previous subsection.

3.3 Faster R-CNN with ResNet-50

The Faster R-CNN algorithm [19] is an improvement of Fast R-CNN [4]. In this system, the working operation of the Faster R-CNN involves two phases. The first phase requires the use of a region proposal network (RPN) which allows concurrent prediction of object anchors and confidence (objectiveness) from some intermediate layers. Note that a feature extraction network can be used for this purpose, in this case, a residual network with a depth of 50 layers (ResNet-50) [6] is used. The second phase requires information from the first phase to make an accurate prediction of the class label and its bounding box refinement. Additionally, we made consideration of the classification activation functions that were earlier discussed in the previous subsections. Hence this results in two variants of this network.

Network Setup: We have trained the network using pre-trained weights faster_rcnn_resnet50_coco_2018_01_28 from the COCO dataset. The training of the network factored in some modified experimental setups as in [19]. The original input image (badger) to the network contains 427×240 pixels and is resized online with an aspect ratio of min-max dimensions [600, 1024] during training. As earlier discussed the network comprises of two phases. The first phase initiates a grid-anchor of size 16×16 pixels with scales [0.25, 0.5, 1.0, 2.0], a nonmaximum-suppression-IoU-threshold set to 0.7, the localization loss weight 2.0, objectiveness weight 1.0 with an initial crop size of 14×14 pixels, kernel size 2×2 with strides set to 2. The second phase computes the prediction score with the IoU-threshold set to 0.6; the SGD optimizer optimizes the loss functions using an initial learning rate 0.0002 and momentum value 0.9. Again, the network was trained for 40,000 steps.

3.4 Faster R-CNN with Inception-V2

The Faster R-CNN detector employs an Inception V2 feature extractor for extracting useful feature maps from an input image. The intermediate layer from the Inception module uses the RPN component of the network for prediction of object anchors and confidences. Similar procedures as explained in [19] were followed.

Network Setup: we have trained the network using pre-trained weights faster_rcnn_inception_v2_coco_2018_01_28 from the COCO dataset. The training of our custom network employs the badger images as input to the Faster-RCNN-InceptionV2 system. The training process uses similar hyperparameters as described in the previous subsection.

All the experiments were carried out using the Tensorflow object detection API framework on a Ge-Force GTX 960 GPU model, and the operating system platform employed is Ubuntu 16.0. We modified the deployment script in the Tensorflow object detection API, by providing the possibility to evaluate all images in the test directory instead of applying restrictions. Moreover, we also use our own script to compute the performance index metrics of the used methods. The next section discusses the performance and overall training time for each of the methods.

4 Experimental Results

The overall training time for each of the used methods is reported in Table 2. The table shows that the training time of Faster R-CNN is much shorter than the training time of SSD, and the use of Inception-V2 leads to the shortest training times. The frame rates show that most of the methods can analyze 0.8–1.5 images per second using our hardware, and SSD is a bit faster than Faster R-CNN for deployment.

Table 2. Average time evaluation for the different detection systems

Methods (CNN models)	Training time	Time improvement	Testing time	Frame rate (f/s)
Faster_RCNN-Inception_V2_Sigmoid	3 h, 21 m	×3.0	222 s	0.82
Faster_RCNN-Inception_V2_Softmax	3 h, 23 m	×2.9	211 s	0.86
Faster_RCNN-ResNet-50-Sigmoid	5 h, 37 m	×1.4	268 s	0.68
Faster_RCNN-ResNet-50-Softmax	5 h, 44 m	×1.3	267 s	0.68
SSD_Inception_V2_Softmax	10 h, 45 m	×0.24	162 s	1.12
SSD_Inception_V2_Sigmoid	10 h, 46 m	×0.24	163 s	1.11
SSD_MobileNet_V1_Softmax	13 h, 16 m	×0.01	120 s	1.51
SSD_MobileNet_V1_Sigmoid (Baseline)	13 h, 21 m	− − −	122 s	1.48

We have carried out two experimental runs and computed the average precision, recall and accuracy, based on the predicted class label in a detected box. The standard deviations for all the methods are $\leq 1.4\%$, which indicates that the performances of the techniques are consistent. The summary of the average performance indices and the standard deviations for each of the methods is presented in Table 3. From this table, we draw the conclusion that SSD-Inception-V2 for both output functions and the SSDMobileNet-V1-Sigmoid outperforms all the Faster R-CNN variants with $p < 0.05$ significance level.

The performance index from the SSD-network variants provides a more precise detection compared to the Faster R-CNN network variants. The lower precision in the

Table 3. Average performances for the different detection and recognition systems

Methods (CNN models)	Performance index		
	Precision	Recall	Accuracy
SSD_Inception_V2_Softmax	0.988 ± 0.012	0.986 ± 0.014	0.986 ± 0.014
SSD_Inception_V2_Sigmoid	0.986 ± 0.003	0.986 ± 0.004	0.986 ± 0.004
SSD_MobileNet_V1_Sigmoid	0.985 ± 0.005	0.983 ± 0.006	0.983 ± 0.006
SSD_MobileNet_V1_Softmax	0.978 ± 0.011	0.978 ± 0.011	0.978 ± 0.011
Faster_RCNN-Inception_V2_Softmax	0.942 ± 0.009	0.917 ± 0.011	0.917 ± 0.011
Faster_RCNN-Inception_V2_Sigmoid	0.945 ± 0.003	0.914 ± 0.008	0.914 ± 0.008
Faster_RCNN-ResNet-50-Sigmoid	0.936 ± 0.000	0.890 ± 0.000	0.890 ± 0.000
Faster_RCNN-ResNet-50-Softmax	0.921 ± 0.003	0.848 ± 0.003	0.848 ± 0.003

Fig. 3. Testing detection confidence prediction of the badger individual instances using different neural network detection methods: the first row indicates detection using ssd_mobilenet_v1_-softmax, the second row shows the detection using ssd_inception_ v2_sigmoid, the third row shows the detection using faster_rcnn_inception_v2_softmax, and the last row shows the detection using faster_rcnn_resnet50_sigmoid. Note that each of the columns represents the badger individual instances in the order; *Badger_esp, Badger_strik, Badger_looi,* and *Badger_iaco* respectively. (Color figure online)

Faster R-CNN may have arisen due to localization bias problems. Figure 3 shows some examples of the detection scores of badgers within a given image during testing evaluation. From this figure, we observe that the Faster R-CNN methods misclassified this particular example of badger_strik (gray box) as badger_esp (green box) as shown in sub-images within cells (3, 2) and (4, 2). Hence, this explains the lower performance index using the Faster R-CNN methods compared to the SSD network variants. From an application standpoint, it could be profitable to use Inception-V2 as the backbone for the SSD detector since it presents more precise detections of the objects of interest.

Additionally, the results suggest that SSD-based networks are useful in handling localization bias problems.

5 Conclusion

Real-time detection using deep learning can be used for many localization and identification tasks. In this paper, several deep neural networks were used to detect and classify different badgers using a novel animal dataset. We compared the single shot multi-box detector (SSD) combined with Inception-V2 or MobileNet, to faster-region-based convolutional neural network (Faster R-CNN) combined with Inception-V2 or residual networks (ResNet). We used the pre-trained networks and further trained them on our dataset. The four detectors were combined with either a softmax or sigmoid function for computing the output probability scores, hence resulting in eight different models.

The results showed that SSD with the Inception-V2 as a backbone obtains the highest mean accuracy performance (98.6%). Furthermore, we noticed that during testing, SSD has a higher frame rate than Faster R-CNN, although its training time is longer. Our analyses suggest that the examined SSD methods tackle the problem of localization bias much better than Faster R-CNN during prediction of the bounding boxes. Finally, we noticed that the use of the sigmoid or softmax output activation functions led to comparable results.

Future work will be directed at the scalability in the number of classes and environments, using a much larger dataset. We also suggest that the best found model, SSD-Inception-V2-Softmax, could be improved and deployed into UAVs or thermal acquisition cameras, as this can help to detect badgers in environments where they are endangered.

References

1. Burghardt, T., Calic, J.: Real-time face detection and tracking of animals. In: 8th Seminar on Neural Network Applications in Electrical Engineering, NEUREL 2006, pp. 27–32. IEEE (2006)
2. Chen, P.: Moving object detection based on background extraction. In: International Symposium on Computer Network and Multimedia Technology, CNMT 2009, pp. 1–4. IEEE (2009)
3. Christiansen, P., Kragh, M., Steen, K.A., Karstoft, H., Jørgensen, R.N.: Platform for evaluating sensors and human detection in autonomous mowing operations. Precis. Agric. **18**(3), 350–365 (2017)
4. Girshick, R.: Fast R-CNN. arXiv preprint arXiv:1504.08083 (2015)
5. Gonzalez, L.F., Montes, G.A., Puig, E., Johnson, S., Mengersen, K., Gaston, K.J.: Unmanned aerial vehicles (UAVs) and artificial intelligence revolutionizing wildlife monitoring and conservation. Sensors **16**(1), 97 (2016)
6. He, K., Zhang, X., Ren, S., Sun, J.: Deep residual learning for image recognition. In: Proceedings of the IEEE Conference on Computer Vision and Pattern Recognition, pp. 770–778 (2016)

7. He, Z., Kays, R., Zhang, Z., Ning, G., Huang, C., Han, T.X., Millspaugh, J., Forrester, T., McShea, W.: Visual informatics tools for supporting large-scale collaborative wildlife monitoring with citizen scientists. IEEE Circ. Syst. Mag. **16**(1), 73–86 (2016)
8. Howard, A.G., et al.: Mobilenets: efficient convolutional neural networks for mobile vision applications. arXiv preprint arXiv:1704.04861 (2017)
9. Ioffe, S., Szegedy, C.: Batch normalization: accelerating deep network training by reducing internal covariate shift. arXiv preprint arXiv:1502.03167 (2015)
10. Koik, B.T., Ibrahim, H.: A literature survey on animal detection methods in digital images. Int. J. Futur. Comput. Commun. **1**(1), 24 (2012)
11. Krizhevsky, A., Sutskever, I., Hinton, G.E.: Imagenet classification with deep convolutional neural networks. In: Advances in Neural Information Processing Systems, pp. 1097–1105 (2012)
12. Liu, H., Hou, X.: Moving detection research of background frame difference based on Gaussian model. In: 2012 International Conference on Computer Science & Service System (CSSS), pp. 258–261. IEEE (2012)
13. Liu, H., Dai, J., Wang, R., Zheng, H., Zheng, B.: Combining background subtraction and three-frame difference to detect moving object from underwater video. In: OCEANS 2016-Shanghai, pp. 1–5. IEEE (2016)
14. Liu, Wei, et al.: SSD: single shot multibox detector. In: Leibe, Bastian, Matas, Jiri, Sebe, Nicu, Welling, Max (eds.) ECCV 2016. LNCS, vol. 9905, pp. 21–37. Springer, Cham (2016). https://doi.org/10.1007/978-3-319-46448-0_2
15. Maeda, H., Sekimoto, Y., Seto, T., Kashiyama, T., Omata, H.: Road damage detection using deep neural networks with images captured through a smartphone. arXiv preprint arXiv: 1801.09454 (2018)
16. Okafor, E., et al.: Comparative study between deep learning and bag of visual words for wild-animal recognition. In: 2016 IEEE Symposium Series on Computational Intelligence (SSCI), pp. 1–8. IEEE (2016)
17. Okafor, E., Schomaker, L., Wiering, M.A.: An analysis of rotation matrix and colour constancy data augmentation in classifying images of animals. J. Inf. Telecommun., 1–27 (2018)
18. Okafor, E., Smit, R., Schomaker, L., Wiering, M.: Operational data augmentation in classifying single aerial images of animals. In: 2017 IEEE International Conference on INnovations in Intelligent SysTems and Applications (INISTA), pp. 354–360. IEEE (2017)
19. Ren, S., He, K., Girshick, R., Sun, J.: Faster R-CNN: towards real-time object detection with region proposal networks. In: Advances in Neural Information Processing Systems, pp. 91–99 (2015)
20. Sengar, S.S., Mukhopadhyay, S.: Moving object detection based on frame difference and W4. Signal, Image Video Process. **11**(7), 1357–1364 (2017)
21. Szegedy, C., et al.: Going deeper with convolutions. In: CVPR (2015)

SPSA for Layer-Wise Training of Deep Networks

Benjamin Wulff[1,2(✉)], Jannis Schuecker[1,2], and Christian Bauckhage[1,2,3]

[1] Fraunhofer Center for Machine Learning, Sankt Augustin, Germany
[2] Fraunhofer IAIS, Sankt Augustin, Germany
benjamin.wulff@iais.fraunhofer.de
[3] B-IT, University of Bonn, Bonn, Germany

Abstract. Concerned with neural learning *without* backpropagation, we investigate variants of the simultaneous perturbation stochastic approximation (SPSA) algorithm. Experimental results suggest that these allow for the successful training of deep feed-forward neural networks using forward passes only. In particular, we find that SPSA-based algorithms which update network parameters in a layer-wise manner are superior to variants which update all weights simultaneously.

1 Introduction

Error backpropagation [19] is the de facto algorithm for neural network training, and, given its success especially in deep learning, one can hardly argue against its utility. Nevertheless, a growing number of voices worries about its dominance in neurocomputing.

Some of the criticism points to the fact that, in biological brains, backward communication channels among neurons have not yet been identified that would allow for the backpropagation of gradient information [1]. In fact, for artificial feed-forward neural networks, there is growing evidence that parameters can be learned without having to propagate precise error signals from the output to the input layer [1,5,11,14,18]. Others criticize that gradient-based learning frequently suffers from slow convergence or saturation effects due to vanishing or exploding gradients, saddle points in the error landscape, or poor conditioning of weight matrices [25]. However, it is known that backpropagation-free, layer-wise training, where the parameters of all but one layer of a network are kept fixed during updates, can provide a remedy [3,7,25].

In this paper, we, too, investigate neural learning without backpropagation. Contrary to the work cited so far, we resort to derivative-free optimization and thus avoid the computation of analytical, chain rule based gradients altogether.

In particular, we propose to learn the parameters of deeply layered networks using Spall's *simultaneous perturbation stochastic approximation (SPSA)* [23,24]. The basic idea is to create two random perturbations of the set of weights and biases of a randomly initialized network, to evaluate the network's performance under these perturbed parameters, to apply information gathered thusly in order

V. Kůrková et al. (Eds.): ICANN 2018, LNCS 11141, pp. 564–573, 2018.
https://doi.org/10.1007/978-3-030-01424-7_55

to update the current estimates, and to iterate this process until convergence. This way, learning happens by means of forward passes only and there is no need for elaborate backward communication through the layers of the network.

Our idea of SPSA-based neural network training is not entirely novel since it has previously been applied to train recurrent neural networks for control tasks [4,20,22,27]. While these contributions validate SPSA-based learning, the networks considered there were comparatively small and weights and biases were updated simultaneously. Yet, for larger networks with much more parameters this intuitive approach may suffer from the curse of dimensionality.

Here, we therefore consider layer-wise SPSA updates of network parameters. We propose an algorithm which, in each training epoch, cycles through the layers of a network and updates only the weights in the layer currently considered while keeping the others fixed. Experiments on didactic and real-world classification problems show this to be a viable neural network training algorithm.

2 Derivative-Free Optimization and SPSA

Next, we briefly review derivative-free optimization in general and the SPSA algorithm in particular. Readers familiar with these topics may safely skip ahead.

Assume we need to find the minimizer

$$\boldsymbol{x}^* = \underset{\boldsymbol{x}}{\operatorname{argmin}}\ f(\boldsymbol{x}) \tag{1}$$

of some multivariate function $f : \mathbb{R}^m \to \mathbb{R}$ that may be non-convex, non-smooth, or even non-continuous. For complicated functions like this, solutions to (1) are typically determined iteratively. That is, we first guess an initial solution $\boldsymbol{x}_{t=0}$ and then repeatedly apply an oracle or optimization procedure $o : \mathbb{R}^m \to \mathbb{R}^m$ to create a sequence of improved guesses

$$\boldsymbol{x}_{t+1} = o(\boldsymbol{x}_t) \tag{2}$$

hoping that it approaches $\boldsymbol{x}^*$. For this procedure to work, we have to require that the optimizer achieves $f(\boldsymbol{x}_{t+1}) \leq f(\boldsymbol{x}_t)$ and that the sequence in (2) converges, because only then will it lead to at least a local minimum.

Note that gradient descend is but a specific instance of this general idea, because here we have $o(\boldsymbol{x}_t) = \boldsymbol{x}_t - \eta_t \nabla f(\boldsymbol{x}_t)$ which will meet our requirements if the step sizes η_t are chosen appropriately. However, for gradient descend to be applicable, $f(\boldsymbol{x}_t)$ must be differentiable, and, in order for it to work well, $\nabla f(\boldsymbol{x}_t)$ should neither vanish nor explode.

Derivative-free optimization techniques such as the Nelder-Mead method [16] or pattern search [9] avoid potential limitations of gradient-based techniques. Instead of computing $\nabla f(\boldsymbol{x}_t)$, they merely probe f at several points $\boldsymbol{x}$ in the vicinity of the current estimate $\boldsymbol{x}_t$ and use information gathered this way to compute the next estimate $\boldsymbol{x}_{t+1}$. In other words, derivative-free optimization relies on evaluations of f rather than on evaluations of ∇f.

Algorithm 1. SPSA for solving (1)

function SPSA($f, \boldsymbol{x}_0, a, \alpha, c, \gamma$)
  for all $t = 1, \ldots, t_{\max}$ **do**
    set $a_t = \frac{a}{t^\alpha}$
    set $c_t = \frac{c}{t^\gamma}$
    randomly sample a perturbation vector $\boldsymbol{\delta}$ where $\delta_i \sim \mathcal{U}\{-1, +1\}$
    set $\boldsymbol{x}^+ = \boldsymbol{x}_t + c_t \, \boldsymbol{\delta}$
    set $\boldsymbol{x}^- = \boldsymbol{x}_t - c_t \, \boldsymbol{\delta}$
    compute an approximated gradient $\hat{\boldsymbol{g}}(\boldsymbol{x}_t)$ where $\hat{g}_i(\boldsymbol{x}_t) = \frac{f(x_i^+) - f(x_i^-)}{2 \, c_t \, \delta_i}$
    compute an improved solution estimate such that $\boldsymbol{x}_{t+1} = \boldsymbol{x}_t - a_t \, \hat{\boldsymbol{g}}(\boldsymbol{x}_t)$
  return $\boldsymbol{x}_{t_{\max}}$

Simultaneous perturbation stochastic approximation (SPSA) is a derivative-free optimization procedure that closely resembles gradient descend. Since the components $g_i(\boldsymbol{x})$ of the gradient $\boldsymbol{g}(\boldsymbol{x}) = \nabla f(\boldsymbol{x})$ of f at $\boldsymbol{x}$ can be defined as

$$g_i(\boldsymbol{x}) = \lim_{\epsilon \to 0} \frac{f(x_i + \epsilon) - f(x_i - \epsilon)}{2 \, \epsilon} \tag{3}$$

we can compute a rough, stochastic approximation $\hat{\boldsymbol{g}}(\boldsymbol{x})$ of $\boldsymbol{g}(\boldsymbol{x})$ using

$$\hat{g}_i(\boldsymbol{x}) = \frac{f(x_i + \delta_i) - f(x_i - \delta_i)}{2 \, \delta_i} \tag{4}$$

where $\boldsymbol{\delta}$ is a random perturbation vector. SPSA as summarized in Algorithm 1 utilizes this observation to improve on the older Kiefer-Wolfowitz scheme [12]. It realizes iterative optimization by creating two perturbations $\boldsymbol{x}^+$ and $\boldsymbol{x}^-$ of the current best solution $\boldsymbol{x}_t$ which are used to compute a stochastic approximation of a gradient and to descend accordingly.

To guarantee convergence to a (local) minimum, gradient approximations must become more and more refined in each iteration; this is achieved via the scaling factors a_t and c_t which must obey the Robbins-Monro conditions [17]. Common choices are therefore $a_t = \frac{a}{t^\alpha}$ where $a > 0$ and $\alpha \geq 1$ and $c_t = \frac{c}{t^\gamma}$ where $c > 0$ and $\gamma \in \left[\frac{1}{6}, \frac{1}{2}\right]$.

The perturbation vector $\boldsymbol{\delta}$, too, has to obey certain conditions. Its elements δ_i must be mutually independent zero-mean random variables and their inverse first and second moments (i.e. $\mathbb{E}\left[\delta_i^{-1}\right]$ and $\mathrm{var}\left[\delta_i^{-1}\right]$) must be finite. Note that the latter is explicitly *not* the case if the δ_i are sampled from a zero-mean Gaussian. A good and popular choice for the δ_i is thus to sample them from the uniform distribution over $\{-1, +1\}$.

3 SPSA-Based Neural Network Training

In this section, we discuss how to adapt SPSA-based parameter estimation to neural network training. We focus on feed-forward architectures, i.e. deep or multi-layered networks consisting of L layers of neurons.

Letting the vector $\boldsymbol{a}^{l-1}$ denote the activations computed by the neurons in layer $l-1$ of such a network, neuron i in layer l computes

$$a_i^l = h_i^l\Big(\langle \boldsymbol{w}_i^l, \boldsymbol{a}^{l-1}\rangle\Big) \tag{5}$$

where $h_i^l(\cdot)$ is a non-linear activation function, $\langle\cdot,\cdot\rangle$ denotes the inner product, and the vector $\boldsymbol{w}_i^l$ represents the synaptic weights of the neuron (for notational simplicity, we subsume bias terms into synaptic summations). The collective output of layer l can then be expressed as

$$\boldsymbol{a}^l = \boldsymbol{h}^l\big(\boldsymbol{W}^l\boldsymbol{a}^{l-1}\big) \tag{6}$$

where $\boldsymbol{h}^l(\cdot)$ now denotes a vector-valued activation function and the matrix $\boldsymbol{W}^l$ contains all input weights of the layer. If the network has M input neurons and m output neurons, it computes a function $\boldsymbol{y} : \mathbb{R}^M \to \mathbb{R}^m$ given by

$$\boldsymbol{y}(\boldsymbol{x} \mid \mathcal{W}) = \boldsymbol{h}^L\Bigg(\boldsymbol{W}^L\boldsymbol{h}^{L-1}\Bigg(\boldsymbol{W}^{L-1}\ldots\boldsymbol{h}^2\Big(\boldsymbol{W}^2\boldsymbol{h}^1\big(\boldsymbol{W}^1\boldsymbol{x}\big)\Big)\Bigg)\Bigg) \tag{7}$$

where $\mathcal{W} = \{\boldsymbol{W}^1, \ldots, \boldsymbol{W}^L\}$ represents the set of all weight parameters of the network.

In order to train this model to act as a classifier, we assume that we are given labeled training data

$$\mathcal{D} = \Big\{(\boldsymbol{x}_i, \boldsymbol{y}_i)\Big\}_{i=1}^n \tag{8}$$

where the $\boldsymbol{x}_i \in \mathbb{R}^M$ are data points and the $\boldsymbol{y}_i \in \{-1,+1\}^m$ are corresponding label vectors. Proceeding as usual, we consider minimization of the sum of squared residuals

$$E(\mathcal{D}, \mathcal{W}) = \sum_{i=1}^n \|\boldsymbol{y}(\boldsymbol{x}_i \mid \mathcal{W}) - \boldsymbol{y}_i\|^2 \tag{9}$$

as the learning objective. Training the network therefore amounts to solving

$$\mathcal{W}^* = \underset{\mathcal{W}}{\operatorname{argmin}}\; E(\mathcal{D}, \mathcal{W}) \tag{10}$$

which we recognize as a specific instance of the general problem in (1). This then suggests that SPSA or Algorithm 1 should allow for deep learning.

Indeed, work [4,20,22,27] shows that, at least for small networks, it is viable to compute perturbations $\mathcal{W}^+ = \mathcal{W}_t + c_t\,\boldsymbol{\delta}$ and $\mathcal{W}^- = \mathcal{W}_t - c_t\,\boldsymbol{\delta}$ to approximate the gradient of E in order to update the current parameter estimate $\mathcal{W}_t$.

However, if the network is large, holistic or simultaneous updates of $\mathcal{W}$ may suffer from the curse of dimensionality since, in very high dimensional parameter spaces, two random perturbations can not be guaranteed to sample the vicinity of $\mathcal{W}_t$ comprehensively enough to obtain "useful" gradient approximations. In other words, holistic SPSA-based training may converge slowly as random perturbations in high dimensions might approximate gradients only poorly.

Algorithm 2. SPSA-based, layer-wise neural network training

initialize $\mathcal{W}_0 = \{\boldsymbol{W}_0^1, \ldots, \boldsymbol{W}_0^L\}$

// perform $e_{\max}$ epochs of training
for all $e = 1, \ldots, e_{\max}$ **do**

  // iterate over all layers of the network
  for all $l \in \mathcal{L}$ **do**

    // keeping weight matrices $\boldsymbol{W}_e^{k \neq l}$ fixed, use SPSA to update
    // weight matrix $\boldsymbol{W}_e^l$; the objective function to be evaluated
    // by Algorithm 1 is $E(\mathcal{D}, \mathcal{W})$ in equation (9)
    $\boldsymbol{W}_{e+1}^l = \text{SPSA}(E, \boldsymbol{W}_e^l)$

Yet, experience with hierarchical factor models [2,26] and work on layer-wise neural network training [3,7,25] suggest a solution. Due to the hierarchical nature of the network function in (7), we may just as well proceed in an alternating fashion where weights are updated one layer at a time.

This idea is summarized in Algorithm 2. Having randomly initialized the network weights $\mathcal{W}_0$, we adhere to common custom and perform $e_{\max}$ epochs of training. In each epoch e, we iterate over the layers of the network. Denoting the current layer by l, we keep the weight matrices $\boldsymbol{W}_e^{k \neq l}$ of the other layers fixed and use SPSA to optimize $E(\mathcal{D}, \mathcal{W}_e)$ w.r.t. the weights in matrix $\boldsymbol{W}_e^l$. This way, the dimensions of the parameter spaces that have to be probed become much smaller and perturbation based gradients stand a better chance to well approximate the corresponding analytical gradients. Indeed, our practical experiments in the next section show that layer-wise SPSA updates of network weights find suitable solutions but converge or learn considerably faster than holistic updates.

An open question at this point is in which sequence to iterate over the network layers during training? Three approaches seem possible: top-down from the output to the input layer

$$l \in \mathcal{L}_{\text{td}} = \{L, L-1, \ldots, 2, 1\}, \tag{11}$$

bottom-up from the input to the output layer

$$l \in \mathcal{L}_{\text{bu}} = \{1, 2, \ldots, L-1, L\}, \tag{12}$$

or in a random order

$$l \in \mathcal{L}_{\text{rnd}} = \text{random permutation}\big(\{1, 2, \ldots, L-1, L\}\big). \tag{13}$$

In our experiments reported below, we consider all three possibilities and find that neither training time nor training success seem to depend on the order in which layer-wise learning happens.

Regardless of the update strategy (holistic or layer-wise), however, SPSA-based training only requires forward passes through a network. That is, weight updates based on approximated gradients only require direct evaluations of (9) and thus of (7) but no backward communication among neurons in different layers. In other words, Algorithm 2 accomplishes neural network training without backpropagation.

4 Practical Experiments

Next, we discuss baseline experiments to evaluate the practical performance of (layer-wise) SPSA-based neural network training. For experimentation, we implemented the SPSA method as an Optimizer in the TensorFlow framework; readers interested in this implementation can retrieve it from github.com/fraunhofer-iais.

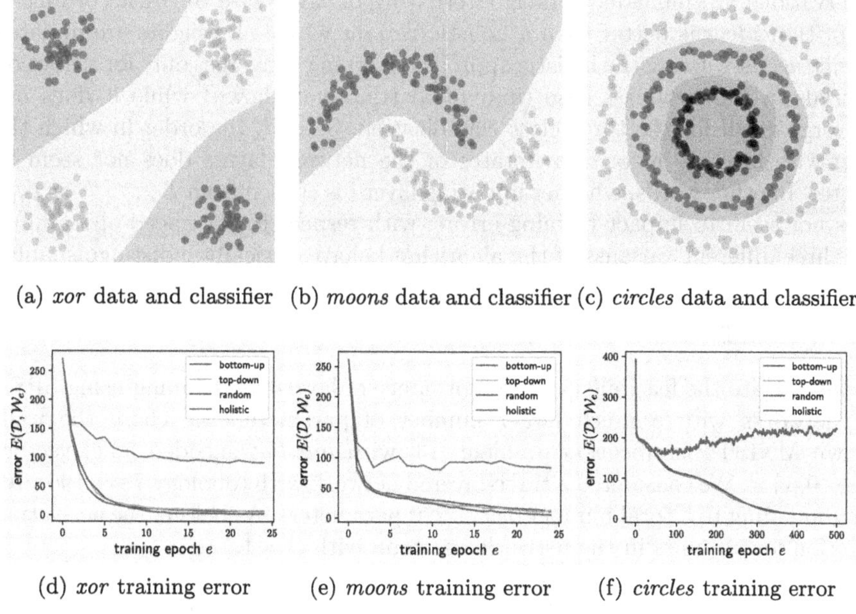

(a) *xor* data and classifier (b) *moons* data and classifier (c) *circles* data and classifier

(d) *xor* training error (e) *moons* training error (f) *circles* training error

Fig. 1. Didactic classification problems. The upper row shows training data for two- and three-class classification problems together with decision boundaries learned by a neural network. The lower row visualizes progressions of training errors (averaged over 100 trials) for network training using the SPSA variants discussed in the text; in each case, the alternating, layer-wise training variants behave almost identical and are superior to the holistic approach.

4.1 Low-Dimensional Classification Problems

The upper row of Fig. 1 shows three sets of two-dimensional training data for simple classification problems together with visualizations of the decision boundaries obtained from training neural networks to classify these data.

For the two-class classification problems in Figs. 1a and b, we considered labels $y_i \in \{-1, +1\}$ and trained five-layered networks of the following topology $2 \times 5 \times 5 \times 5 \times 1$ where each layer also included an additional bias unit; the number of parameters to be learned during training thus was 81. For the three-class classification problem in Fig. 1c, we considered label vectors $\boldsymbol{y}_i \in \{-1, +1\}^3$ and trained a seven-layered $2 \times 10 \times 10 \times 10 \times 10 \times 10 \times 3$ network again with bias units; the number of parameters to be learned in this task was thus 503. The activation functions of all computational units of these networks were chosen to be $h_i^l(\langle \boldsymbol{w}_i^l, \boldsymbol{a}^{l-1} \rangle) = \tanh(\beta \cdot \langle \boldsymbol{w}_i^l, \boldsymbol{a}^{l-1} \rangle)$ with $\beta = 0.5$ for the two-class classification problems and $\beta = 0.25$ for the three-class classification problem.

The lower row of Fig. 1 shows corresponding average evolutions of training errors using holistic and layer-wise SPSA where averages were computed from 100 trials with different random initializations of the network parameters. Two observations are immediate: first, alternating or layer-wise SPSA according to Algorithm 2 learns better than a holistic variant where all weights are updated simultaneously. Using the holistic approach, learning converges only for a fraction of trials in the two-class case (individual trials not shown) while it does not converge at all for the three-class classification. Second, the order in which the layer-wise learning algorithm iterates of the network layers does not seem to matter. In other words, whether updating layer l is chosen from $\mathcal{L}_{\text{td}}$, $\mathcal{L}_{\text{bu}}$, or $\mathcal{L}_{\text{rnd}}$ does not seem to impact training errors; with respect to the speed of learning, the three different variants of the algorithm behave basically indistinguishably.

4.2 MNIST

To investigate the feasibility and performance of layer-wise training using SPSA for networks with a much larger number of parameters we chose the well-known MNIST classification problem [13] with *one-hot* encoded label vectors $y_i \in \{0, 1\}^{10}$. We considered a three-layered network with topology $784 \times 196 \times 10$, corresponding to a total number of 771,270 parameters. As before, the activation function for all units in the network was tanh with $\beta = 1$.

As in the case of the three-class classification example, the holistic variant of SPSA failed to learn the MNIST task. Therefore we trained the network using the bottom-up variant of Algorithm 2 with $a = 0.1$, $c = 0.1$ and $t_{max} = 50$, however, with the following modification. For each layer we first apply the SPSA Algorithm 2 to the weights and afterwards to the biases, which is inspired by our previous findings that a partial perturbation of the network is superior to a holistic one (Sect. 4.1). Without this modification we did not observe any learning behavior of the network. For comparison we also trained the network with standard Gradient Descent (GD) (`tf.train.GradientDescentOptimizer` in TensorFlow) with a learning rate of $l = 0.01$.

In most of the runs, SPSA training was successful. Figure 2 shows the learning curves averaged over three successful runs in comparison to GD training. While GD achieves a higher accuracy after additional training epochs, SPSA already learns within the first twelve epochs. Note, however, that during one epoch, extended Algorithm 2 contains additional iterations over weights and biases compared to GD. Furthermore, each application of SPSA (Algorithm 1) entails t_{max} partial weight updates, while GD only contains one update of all parameters per batch. Anyway, we neither aim for a quantitative comparison between the two approaches nor for achieving state of the art results (<1% error rate). Our goal is rather to show that SPSA training is feasible even for a total number of parameters close to a million.

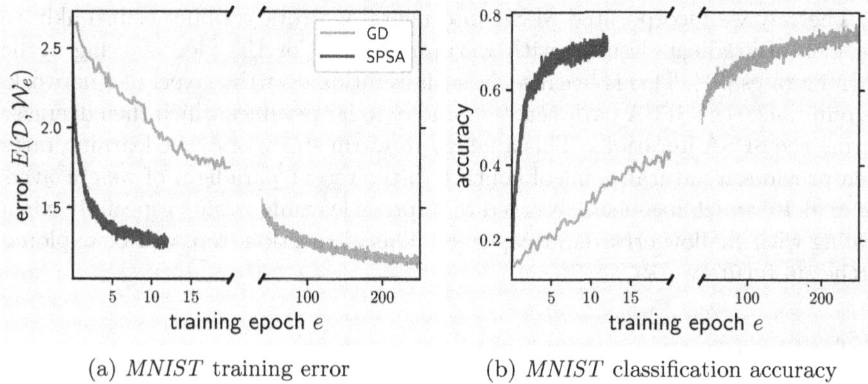

(a) *MNIST* training error (b) *MNIST* classification accuracy

Fig. 2. MNIST classification. The left panel compares the training error for SPSA and gradient descent. The right panel shows the corresponding accuracies evaluated on a test set. While SPSA training learns within the first twelve epochs, gradient descent achieves a higher accuracy in the end.

5 Conclusion

In this paper, we were concerned with the idea of neural network training without backpropagation. To accomplish this, we considered Spall's SPSA algorithm, a derivative-free optimization procedure, and proposed different variants as to how to adopt it towards training feed-forward networks. In particular, we proposed to carry out training in a layer wise manner, where we iterate over the layers of a network and only update the weights of the current layer while the others are kept fixed.

In practical experiments on didactic classification problems, we found that layer-wise training is superior compared to the holistic approach. In other words, sequentially choosing sub-sets of updated parameters is beneficial, presumably because a holistic perturbation is error-prone to the curse of dimensionality. In addition we find that the sequence in which the subsets are perturbed does not influence training performance.

In experiments with larger networks applied to the MNIST classification problem we found the holistic variant to be failing. The bottom-up approach proved to be working after further modification that adjusts weights and biases subsequently. Here, we do not attempt to achieve state of the art results but rather show a proof of concept that SPSA can be used to train multi-layered networks with almost a million of parameters.

From an abstract point of view, the approach studied in this paper is loosely reminiscent of the idea of connectionist reinforcement learning [28]. This is because each individual neuron of the network learns based on immediate feedback as to their collective performance. This opens up auspicious directions for future research.

The way we incorporated SPSA into neural network training is also akin to the idea of gradient descend with warm starts [15] or the idea of using cyclic learning rates [21]. This is because, in each iteration over the layers of a network, we reinitialize the SPSA parameters a_t and c_t to large values which then decrease during the SPSA iterations. This analogy to warm starts or cyclic learning rates then provides a natural point of contact to the recent paradigm of weight averaging [6,10] which has been observed to improve learning results especially when dealing with shallow error landscapes [8]. This connection, too, will be explored further in future work.

References

1. Baldi, P., Sadowski, P., Lu, Z.: Learning in the machine: random backpropagation and the deep learning channel. arXiv:1612.02734 [cs.LG] (2016)
2. Bauckhage, C., Thurau, C.: Making archetypal analysis practical. In: Denzler, J., Notni, G., Süße, H. (eds.) DAGM 2009. LNCS, vol. 5748, pp. 272–281. Springer, Heidelberg (2009). https://doi.org/10.1007/978-3-642-03798-6_28
3. Bengio, Y., Lamblin, P., Popovic, D., Larochelle, H.: Greedy layer-wise training of deep networks. In: Proceedings NIPS (2006)
4. Choy, M., Srinivasan, D., Cheu, R.: Neural networks for continuous online learning and control. IEEE Trans. Neural Netw. **17**(6), 2006 (2006)
5. Courbariaux, M., Bengio, Y., David, J.P.: Training deep neural networks with low precision multiplications. arXiv:1412.7024 [cs.LG] (2014)
6. Garipov, T., Izmailov, P., Podoprikhin, D., Vetrov, D., Wilson, A.: Loss surfaces, mode connectivity, and fast ensembling of DNNs. arXiv:1802.10026 [stat.ML] (2018)
7. Hinton, G., Osindero, S., Teh, Y.: A fast learning algorithm for deep belief nets. In: Proceedings NIPS (2006)
8. Hochreiter, S., Schmidhuber, J.: Flat minima. Neural Comput. **9**(1), 1–42 (1997)
9. Hooke, R., Jeeves, T.: Direct search solution of numerical and statistical problems. J. ACM **8**(2), 212–229 (1961)
10. Izmailov, P., Garipov, D.P.T., Vetrov, D., Wilson, A.: Averaging weights leads to wider optima and better generalization. arXiv:1803.05407 [cs.LG] (2018)
11. Jaderberg, M., et al.: Decoupled neural interfaces using synthetic gradients. arXiv:1608.05343 [cs.LG] (2016)
12. Kiefer, J., Wolfowitz, J.: Estimation of the maximum of a regression function. Ann. Math. Stat. **23**(3), 462–466 (1952)
13. LeCun, Y., Bottou, L., Bengio, Y., Haffner, P.: Gradient-based learning applied to document recognition. Proc. IEEE **86**, 2278–2324 (1998)

14. Lillicrap, T., Cownden, D., Tweed, D., Akerman, J.: Random synaptic feedback weights support error backpropagation for deep learning. Nat. Commun. **7**(13276) (2016)
15. Loshchilov, I., Hutter, F.: SGDR: stochastic gradient descent with warm restarts. In: Proceedings ICLR (2017)
16. Nelder, J., Mead, R.: A simplex method for function minimization. Comput. J. **7**(4), 308–313 (1965)
17. Robbins, H., Monro, S.: A stochastic approximation method. Ann. Math. Stat. **22**(3), 400–407 (1951)
18. Rosenfeld, A., Tsotsos, J.: Intriguing properties of randomly weighted networks: generalizing while learning next to nothing. arXiv:1802.00844 [cs.LG] (2018)
19. Rummelhart, D., Hinton, G., Williams, R.: Learning representations by back-propagating errors. Nature **323**(6088), 533–536 (1986)
20. Sehnke, F., Osendorfer, C., Rückstieß, T., Graves, A., Peters, J., Schmidhuber, J.: Policy gradients with parameter-based exploration for control. In: Kůrková, V., Neruda, R., Koutník, J. (eds.) ICANN 2008. LNCS, vol. 5163, pp. 387–396. Springer, Heidelberg (2008). https://doi.org/10.1007/978-3-540-87536-9_40
21. Smith, L.: Cyclical learning rates for training neural networks. In: Proceedings Winter Conference on Applications of Computer Vision. IEEE (2017)
22. Song, Q., Spall, J., Soh, Y.C., Nie, J.: Robust neural network tracking controller using simultaneous perturbation stochastic approximation. IEEE Trans. Neural Netw. **19**(5), 817–835 (2008)
23. Spall, J.: Multivariate stochastic approximation using a simultaneous perturbation gradient approximation. IEEE Trans. Autom. Control **37**(3), 332–341 (1992)
24. Spall, J.: Introduction to Stochastic Search and Optimization: Estimation, Simulation, and Control. Wiley, Hoboken (2003)
25. Taylor, G., Burmeister, R., Xu, Z., Singh, B., Patel, A., Goldstein, T.: Training neural networks without gradients: a scalable ADMM approach. In: Proceedings ICML (2016)
26. Thurau, C., Kersting, K., Wahabzada, M., Bauckhage, C.: Convex non-negative matrix factorization for massive datasets. Knowl. Inf. Syst. **29**(2), 457–478 (2011)
27. Vande Wouver, A., Renotte, C., Remy, M.: On the use of simultaneuous perturbation stochastic approximation for neural network training. In: Proceedings American Control Conference. IEEE (1999)
28. Williams, R.: Simple statistical gradient-following algorithms for connectionist reinforcement learning. Mach. Learn. **8**(3–4), 229–256 (1992)

Dipolar Data Aggregation in the Context of Deep Learning

Leon Bobrowski[1,2(✉)] and Magdalena Topczewska[1]

[1] Faculty of Computer Science, Bialystok University of Technology, Wiejska 45A Street, Bialystok, Poland
{l.bobrowski,m.topczewska}@pb.edu.pl

[2] Institute of Biocybernetics and Biomedical Engineering, PAS, Trojdena 4 Street, Warsaw, Poland

Abstract. Separable data aggregation processes can be analyzed and realized with models of multilayer neuronal networks. Deep learning techniques can be engaged in forming hierarchical neuronal structures with such powerful properties.

Data processing through hierarchical, multilayer structure may result in a replacement of many feature vectors of the same category by a single output vector in an upper layer. Separable data aggregation in the dipolar layers of binary classifiers allows reaching such goal.

Keywords: Univariate binary classifiers · Separable data aggregation Dipolar aggregation strategies · Deep learning · Designing hierarchical networks

1 Introduction

Data sets used in classifiers designing can be composed of a large number of multivariate feature vectors [1]. It is assumed that particular feature vectors represent objects (patients, events, etc.) [2]. We are considering a situation where a given data set has been divided into separable learning subsets in accordance with additional knowledge about particular objects categories (classes). As an example, separable clinical learning sets may contain such feature vectors which represent patients with only one, particular disease [3].

Different types of classifiers can be designed (trained) on feature vectors contained in learning data sets according to a variety of pattern recognition goals and methods [2]. A classifier allocates each feature vector to one of categories in accordance with the decision (classification) rule designed on the basis of the learning sets. The designed classification rule should have a generalization property. It means, that the designed classifier should reasonably allocate not only elements of the learning sets but also similar feature vectors which are not contained in the learning sets.

A binary classifier transforms a given feature vector into the number equal to one or to zero. The formal neuron is an example of a binary classifier [3]. The output of the formal neuron is equal to one if and only if the weighted sum of input signals is greater or equal to some threshold. If this sum is less than the threshold, then the output is

V. Kůrková et al. (Eds.): ICANN 2018, LNCS 11141, pp. 574–583, 2018.
https://doi.org/10.1007/978-3-030-01424-7_56

equal to zero. Univariate binary classifiers (logical elements) can be treated as formal neurons only with single input signals.

A given layer of L binary classifiers transforms feature vectors into output vectors with L binary components. The layer of binary classifiers aggregates input data sets if some feature vectors are transformed into the same output vector. The aggregation is separable if and only if some of the feature vectors belonging to the same class are aggregated into a single output vector. In other words, there are no two feature vectors belonging to different learning sets (*mixed dipole*) that are transformed (aggregated) into the same output vector [4].

Complex, hierarchical networks can be designed from binary classifiers. The concept of separable layers has been proposed for this purpose [3]. It was demonstrated that the separable layers can be built from binary classifiers in accordance with the ranked strategy [5, 6]. Possibility of separable layer designing from univariate binary classifiers in accordance with the dipolar strategy is examined in the presented paper. Multilayer networks of dipolar separable layers can successively aggregate given data set. This technique can be used, among others, in the deep learning tasks [7].

2 Partially Structured Data Sets

Let us assume, that each of given m objects (patients) O_j ($j = 1,\ldots, m$) can be characterized by n features x_i ($i = 1,\ldots, n$) from the fixed, given a priori set of features $F(n) = \{x_1,\ldots, x_n\}$. If the i-th feature x_i of the j-th object O_j has been measured, then the numerical result $x_{j,i}$ of this measurement is represented as the real number ($x_{j,i} \in R$) or as the binary number ($x_{j,i} \in \{0,1\}$). If the i-th feature x_i of the j-th object O_j remains unmeasured (undefined), then the number $x_{j,i}$ is assumed to be equal to zero ($x_{j,i} = 0$). In result, all the objects O_j can be represented in the n-dimensional feature space $\boldsymbol{F}(n)$ as the feature vector $\mathbf{x}_j$ ($\mathbf{x}_j \in \boldsymbol{F}(n)$):

$$(\forall j \in \{1,\ldots,m\})\ \mathbf{x}_j = \left[x_{j,1},\ldots,x_{j,n}\right]^T \tag{1}$$

For each object O_j ($j = 1,\ldots, m$) we define the subset F_j ($F_j \subset F(n)$) of such features x_i that the i-th component of the j-th feature vector (1) is not equal to zero ($x_{j,i} \neq 0$):

$$(\forall j \in \{1,\ldots,m\})\ F_j = \left\{x_i : x_{j,i} \neq 0\right\} \tag{2}$$

Definition 1. The feature vector $\mathbf{x}_j = \left[x_{j,1},\ldots,x_{j,n}\right]^T$ (1) which represents the j-th object O_j is *partially structured* when a part of the n features x_i ($x_i \in F(n)$) of this object have been not defined and corresponding components $x_{j,i}$ are equal to zero ($x_{j,i} = 0$) (2).

The m feature vector $\mathbf{x}_j$ can be represented as the data matrix $\boldsymbol{X}$ of the dimension $m \times n$:

$$X = [\mathbf{x}_1, \ldots, \mathbf{x}_m]^T \tag{3}$$

The data matrix X is *sparse*, if many of elements $x_{j,i} = 0$ is equal to zero ($x_{j,i} = 0$) [8].

Let us assume, that each of m objects O_j ($j = 1,\ldots, m$) has been assigned by experts to one of K categories (*classes*) ω_k ($k = 1,\ldots, K$). For example, clinical doctors assigned the j-th patients O_j to one of diseases ω_k on the basis of their knowledge and diagnostic examination of this patient. The data matrix X (3) can be divided into K learning sets C_k on the basis of experts' knowledge about objects O_j (*data labelling*):

$$(\forall k \in \{1, \ldots, K\})\ C_k = \{\mathbf{x}_j : O_j \in \omega_k\} = \{\mathbf{x}_j : j \in J_k\} \tag{4}$$

where it is assumed that $J_k = \{ j\colon O_j \in \omega_k\}$ are disjoined sets of m_k indices j:

$$(\forall k \in \{1, \ldots, K\})(\forall k' \in \{1, \ldots, K : k' \neq k\})\quad J_{k'} \cap J_k = \varnothing \tag{5}$$

Definition 2. The disjoined learning set C_k (4) is *partially structured* if it contains *partially* structured feature vectors $\mathbf{x}_j = [x_{j,1}, \ldots, x_{j,n}]^T$ (Definition 1).

Such components $x_{j,i}$ of the feature vector $\mathbf{x}_j = [x_{j,1}, \ldots, x_{j,n}]^T$ (1) which have not been defined should not be used in decision rules and can often be reduced. The reduced vector $\mathbf{x}_j'$ can be obtained from the feature vector $\mathbf{x}_j$ by neglecting such components $x_{j,i}$ which are equal to zero ($x_{j,i} = 0$). The reduced feature vectors $\mathbf{x}_j'$ have different dimensionality n_j equal to the number of such components $x_{j,i}$ which are not equal to zero ($0 < n_j < n$). The partially structured data sets are composed of such reduced feature vectors $\mathbf{x}_j'$ which can have different dimensionality n_j. Partially structured data often occurs in practice, for example, in the deep learning tasks [7]. Special mathematical and computational techniques are needed for exploring such large data sets which are partially structured.

Definition 3. Two learning sets C_k and $C_{k'}$ (4) are separable, if such elements $\mathbf{x}_j$ which belong to different sets ($\mathbf{x}_j \in C_k$ and $\mathbf{x}_{j'} \in C_{k'}$) are not equal:

$$if\,(k' \neq k), then\ (\forall j' \in J_{k'})\ and\ (\forall j \in J_k)\ \ \mathbf{x}_{j'} \neq \mathbf{x}_j \tag{6}$$

where the inequality $\mathbf{x}_{j'} \neq \mathbf{x}_j$ of the vectors $\mathbf{x}_{j'} = [x_{j',1}, \ldots, x_{j',n}]^T$ and $\mathbf{x}_j = [x_{j,1}, \ldots, x_{j,n}]^T$ means that there exists at least one feature x_i ($x_i \in F_{j'}$ and $x_i \in F_j$) which was measured in both objects $O_{j'}$ and O_j and gave different measurement results ($x_{j',i} \neq x_{j,i}$).

The assumption of the learning sets C_k (4) separability (6) is connected to some constraints in the structure of the features subsets F_j (2). Only such partially structured data sets C_k (4) are considered in the paper in which the separability property (6) is fulfilled. The proposed dipolar strategy of separable layers designing is based on the concept of the *mixed dipoles* and the *clear dipoles* [4].

Definition 4. Two feature vectors $\mathbf{x}_j$ and $\mathbf{x}_{j'}$ ($\mathbf{x}_{j'} \neq \mathbf{x}_j$) which belong to different learning sets C_k ($\mathbf{x}_j \in C_k$) and $C_{k'}\left(\mathbf{x}_{j'} \in C_{k'}\right)$ (4) constitute the *mixed* dipole $\{\mathbf{x}_j, \mathbf{x}_{j'}\}$.

Definition 5. Two feature vectors $\mathbf{x}_j$ and $\mathbf{x}_{j'}$ which belong to the same learning sets C_k ($\mathbf{x}_j \in C_k$ and $\mathbf{x}_{j'} \in C_k$) (4) constitute the *clear dipole* $\{\mathbf{x}_j, \mathbf{x}_{j'}\}$.

3 Separable Layers of Univariate Binary Classifiers

The univariate binary classifier $BC_i(\theta_l)$ based on the i-th feature x_i and the l-th threshold θ_l ($\theta_l \in R^1$) can be characterized by the bellow decision rule $r_{i,l} = r_i(\theta_l; \mathbf{x}_j)$: ($\forall i \in \{1,\ldots, n\}$) ($\forall l \in \{1,\ldots, L'\}$)

$$r_{i,l} = r_i(\theta_l; \mathbf{x}_j) = \begin{matrix} 1 \text{ } if \text{ } x_{j,i} \geq \theta_l \\ 0 \text{ } if \text{ } x_{j,i} < \theta_l \end{matrix} \tag{7}$$

where $\mathbf{x}_j = [x_{j,1},\ldots, x_{j,n}]^T$ is the j-th feature vector with n components $x_{j,i}$.

The layer of L binary classifiers $BC_i(\theta_l)$ (7) transforms each of the m input feature vectors $\mathbf{x}_j = [x_{j,1},\ldots,x_{j,n}]^T$ from the data matrix $\boldsymbol{X}$ (3) into the output vector $\mathbf{r}_{j'} = \left[r_{j',1},\ldots,r_{j',L}\right]^T$ with L binary components $r_{j',l}\left(r_{j',l} \in \{0,1\}\right)$, where $j' = j'(j)$ is some *index function* which links the j-th feature vector $\mathbf{x}_j$ to the j'-th output vector $\mathbf{r}_{j'}$:

$$(\forall j \in \{1,\ldots,m\}) \; \mathbf{r}_{j'} = \left[r_{j',1},\ldots,r_{j',L}\right]^T, \; where \; (\forall l \in \{1,\ldots,L\}) \; r_{j',l} \in \{0,1\} \tag{8}$$

We assume, that the index function $j' = j'(j)$ fulfills the below separability condition:

$$(\forall j' \neq j'') \;\; \mathbf{r}_{j'} \neq \mathbf{r}_{j''} \tag{9}$$

Definition 6. The layer of L binary classifiers $BC_i(\theta_l)$ (7) is *separable* in respect to the learning sets $\boldsymbol{C}_k$ (4) if and only if elements $\mathbf{x}_j$ and $\mathbf{x}_{j'}$ of each *mixed* dipole $\{\mathbf{x}_j, \mathbf{x}_{j'}\}$ (Definition 2) are transformed (8) into different vectors $\mathbf{r}_j$ and $\mathbf{r}_{j'}\left(\mathbf{r}_j \neq \mathbf{r}_{j'}\right)$.

Remark 1. The l-th binary classifier $BC_i(\theta_l)$ (7) of the layer divides the dipole $\{\mathbf{x}_j, \mathbf{x}_{j'}\}$ if and only if one of the below two pairs of inequalities is fulfilled [3]:

$$(x_{j,i} > \theta_l \; and \; x_{j',i} < \theta_l) \; or \; (x_{j,i} < \theta_l \; and \; x_{j',i} > \theta_l) \tag{10}$$

In accordance with the decision rule (7), the inequalities (10) mean that only one vector $\mathbf{x}_j$ or $\mathbf{x}_{j'}$ from each mixed dipole $\{\mathbf{x}_j, \mathbf{x}_{j'}\}$ gives the output $r_{i,l} = 1$.

Remark 2. The layer of L binary classifiers $BC_i(\theta_l)$ (7) is *separable* in respect to the learning sets C_k (4) if and only if each *mixed* dipole $\left\{\mathbf{x}_j, \mathbf{x}'_j\right\}$ is divided in accordance with the rules (10) by at least one binary classifier of this layer [4].

4 Separation of Selected Data Subsets by Dipolar Layers of Univariate Binary Classifiers

Let us consider the layer of L_k binary classifiers $BC_i(\theta_l)$ (7) ($i = 1,\ldots, L_k$) designed for extraction of selected data subset $\boldsymbol{C}_k$ from the data matrix $\boldsymbol{X}$ (3). In this case, it is useful to consider for each index k two data subsets $\boldsymbol{C}_k$ and $\boldsymbol{C}_k^c (k = 1,\ldots, K)$. The k-th subset $\boldsymbol{C}_k = \{\mathbf{x}_j: j \in J_k\}$ (4) is composed of m_k feature vectors $\mathbf{x}_j = [x_{j,1},\ldots,x_{j,n}]^T$ (1) and the subset $\boldsymbol{C}_k^c$ is composed from the remaining $m - m_k$ vectors $\mathbf{x}_j$ from the matrix $\boldsymbol{X}$ (3):

$$C_k = \{\mathbf{x}_j : j \in J_k\}, and\, \boldsymbol{C}_k^c = \{\mathbf{x}_j : j \in J_{k'},\ where\ \ k' \neq k\} \tag{11}$$

We can infer on the basis of the Remark 3, that the dipolar separation of the data subset $\boldsymbol{C}_k$ (4) from the *complementary subset* $\boldsymbol{C}_k^c$ by the layer of L_k binary classifiers $BC_i(\theta_l)$ (7) can be based on the division (10) of all the mixed dipoles $\{\mathbf{x}_j,\mathbf{x}_{j'}\}$ [4]:

$$if\,(\mathbf{x}_j \in C_k,\ and\, \mathbf{x}_{j'} \in \boldsymbol{C}_k^c),\ then\ \{\mathbf{x}_j,\mathbf{x}_{j'}\}\ is\ a\ mixed\ dipole \tag{12}$$

Remark 3. The number m_d of the mixed dipoles $\{\mathbf{x}_j,\mathbf{x}_{j'}\}$ (12) depends on the numbers m_k and $m - m_k$ of the elements $\mathbf{x}_j$ of the subsets $\boldsymbol{C}_k$ and $\boldsymbol{C}_k^c$ (12), adequately:

$$m_d = m_k * (m - m_k) \tag{13}$$

The k-th layer of L_k binary classifiers $BC_i(\theta_l)$ (7) allows extracting the subset $\boldsymbol{C}_k$ (4) from the data matrix $\boldsymbol{X}$ (3) if and only if each mixed dipole $\{\mathbf{x}_j,\mathbf{x}_{j'}\}$ (12) is divided in accordance with (10) by at least one of the L_k classifiers from this layer [3].

The optimization of the separable layers designing is aimed at decreasing the numbers L_k of binary classifiers $BC_i(\theta_l)$ (7) in the layers. This postulate can lead also to decreasing dimensionality L_k of the transformed vectors $\mathbf{r}_j$ (8). A merging of possible large number feature vectors $\mathbf{x}_j$ from the same subset $\boldsymbol{C}_k$ (4) is recommended in order to decrease the number of different transformed vectors $\mathbf{r}_j$ (8).

The proposed strategy of the separable layer designing from binary classifiers $BC_i(\theta_l)$ (7) is based on finding the values $\theta_{i,l}$ of the threshold on the i-th axis (feature) x_i. Let us consider for a moment the ordered sequence of the values $x_{j(l),i}$ of the i-th components $x_{j(l),i}$ of the vector $\mathbf{x}_{j(l)} = [x_{j(l),,1},\ldots, x_{j(l),n}]^T \in \boldsymbol{X}$ (3):

$$x_{j(1),i} \leq x_{j(2),i} \leq \ldots \leq x_{j(n),i} \tag{14}$$

Separating values $\theta_{i,l}$ of the threshold θ_l (7) have been located in the centers of such intervals $[x_{j(l),i}, x_{j(l+1),i}]$ on the i-th axis x_i which have been defined by mixed dipoles $\{x_{j(l),i}, x_{j(l+1),i}\}$ (Fig. 1) [5]:

$$\theta_{i,l} = (x_{j(l),i} + x_{j(l+1),i})/2 \tag{15}$$

where $\mathbf{x}_{j(l+1)} = [x_{j(l+1),1},\ldots, x_{j(l+1),n}]^T$, and $x_{j(l+1),i} - x_{j(l),i} > 0$.

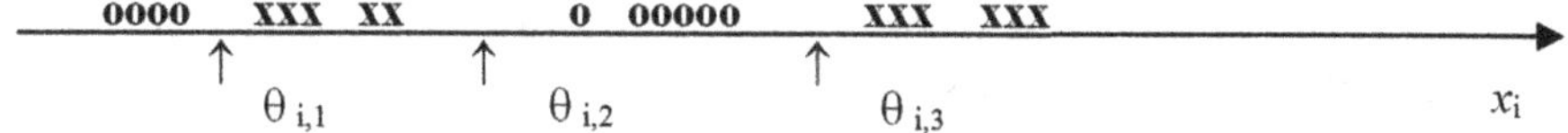

Fig. 1. Example of mixed dipoles $\{\mathbf{x}_j,\mathbf{x}_{j'}\}$ division (11) on the i-th axis x_i

Remark 4. If the i-th feature x_i is binary ($x_i \in \{0,1\}$), then the separating thresholds θ_i can be defined similarly to (15) in the below manner:

$$\theta_i = 0.5 \tag{16}$$

The example shown in Fig. 1 contains 11 objects O_j marked as "**o**" and 11 objects O_j marked as "**x**". These objects O_j (j = 1,..., 22) could be represented by high dimensional feature vectors $\mathbf{x}_j$ (1) belonging to the learning sets C_1 and C_2 (4). All mixed dipoles $\{\mathbf{x}_j,\mathbf{x}_{j'}\}$ constituted by feature vectors $\mathbf{x}_j$ (1) have been divided based on the i-th feature x_i by three binary classifiers $BC_i(\theta_l)$ (7) (l = 1, 2, 3) with the thresholds $\theta_{i,1}$, $\theta_{i,2}$, and $\theta_{i,3}$ adequately to the decision rule (7). The numbers m_l of mixed dipoles $\{\mathbf{x}_j,\mathbf{x}_{j'}\}$ divided by particular classifier $BC_i(\theta_l)$ (7) shown in the figure are equal to: m_1 = 44, m_2 = 54, and m_3 = 60.

It is assumed here that the quality of the classifier $BC_i(\theta_l)$ (7) increases with the number $m_{i,l}$ of the mixed dipoles $\{\mathbf{x}_j,\mathbf{x}_{j'}\}$ divided by this classifier. The optimal binary classifiers $BC_{i*}(\theta_{l*})$ (7) can be found on the basis of the below inequalities:

$$(\forall i \in \{1,\ldots,n\})(\forall l \in \{1,\ldots,L'\})\; m_{i*,l*} \geq m_{i,l} \tag{17}$$

where $m_{i,l}$ is the number of the divided mixed dipoles $\{\mathbf{x}_j,\mathbf{x}_{j'}\}$ by the classifier $BC_i(\theta_l)$.

The optimal feature (axis) x_{i*} is characterized by the largest number $m_{i*,l*}$ (17) of the divided mixed dipoles $\left\{\mathbf{x}_j,\mathbf{x}_j'\right\}$. The optimal threshold $\theta_{i*,l*}$ specified by the inequalities (17) allows defining the optimal classifiers $BC_{i*}(\theta_{l*})$ (7):

$$\textit{\textbf{if}}\; x_{i*} \geq \theta_{i*,l*},\; \textit{\textbf{then}}\; r_{i*,l*} = 1\; \textit{\textbf{else}}\; r_{i*,l*} = 0 \tag{18}$$

where x_{i*} is the i^*-th component of the input feature vector $\mathbf{x} = [x_1,\ldots,x_n]^T$.

The optimal binary classifier $BC_{i*}(\theta_{l*})$ (18) which is based on the i^*-th feature x_{i*} divides the maximal number $m_{i*,l*}$ (17) of mixed dipoles $\{\mathbf{x}_j,\mathbf{x}_{j'}\}$. Usually not all the mixed dipoles $\{\mathbf{x}_j,\mathbf{x}_{j'}\}$ are divided in accordance with the inequalities (18). The below procedure is aimed at division (10) of all mixed dipoles $\{\mathbf{x}_j,\mathbf{x}_{j'}\}$ (12) [5].

Designing separable layer on the basis of the data subsets $\mathbf{C}_k$ and $\mathbf{C}_k^c$(12) (19)

The designing procedure includes L_k steps. During the first step of the procedure, the $m_{i(I),l(I)}$ mixed dipoles $\{\mathbf{x}_j,\mathbf{x}_{j'}\}$ (14) are divided (18) by the first optimal classifier

$BC_{i(I)}(\theta_{l(I)})$ (7) of the layer. The dipole $\{\mathbf{x}_j, \mathbf{x}_{j'}\}$ is divided by the classifier $BC_{i(I)}(\theta_{l(I)})$ (7) if one of the below inequalities (10) is fulfilled:

$$(x_{j,i(I)} > \theta_{l(I)} \; and \; x_{j',i(I)} < \theta_{l(I)}) \; or \; (x_{j,i(I)} < \theta_{l(I)} \; and \; x_{j',i(I)} > \theta_{l(I)}) \tag{20}$$

Such mixed dipoles $\{\mathbf{x}_j, \mathbf{x}_{j'}\}$ (12) which have been divided (20) by the classifier $BC_{i(I)}(\theta_{l(I)})$ (7) are removed from further considerations. The remaining, yet undivided mixed dipoles $\{\mathbf{x}_j, \mathbf{x}_{j'}\}$ are used in the second stage to design the second optimal classifier $BC_{i(II)}(\theta_{l(II)})$ (7) of the layer, and so on. The described scheme is repeated in successive steps l ($l = 1, \ldots, L_k$) until all mixed dipoles $\{\mathbf{x}_j, \mathbf{x}_{j'}\}$ (12) are divided or the number of the undivided mixed dipoles $\{\mathbf{x}_j, \mathbf{x}_{j'}\}$ it's small enough.

Theorem 1. If the subsets $\boldsymbol{C}_k$ and $\boldsymbol{C}_k^c$ (11) are separable (6), then all mixed dipoles $\{\mathbf{x}_j, \mathbf{x}_{j'}\}$ (12) can be divided after a finite number L_k of the steps of the procedure (19).

The proof of a similar theorem can be found in the paper [4].

5 Hierarchical Networks of Separable Layers

During the k-the stage of the procedure (19) all the mixed dipoles $\{\mathbf{x}_j, \mathbf{x}_{j'}\}$ with elements from the two data subsets $\boldsymbol{C}_k$ and $\boldsymbol{C}_k^c$ (11) can be divided (20). The separation of the subsets $\boldsymbol{C}_k$ and $\boldsymbol{C}_k^c$ (11) is assured if all considered mixed dipoles $\{\mathbf{x}_j, \mathbf{x}_{j'}\}$ (12) with one element $\mathbf{x}_j$ from the subset $\boldsymbol{C}_k$ (4) are divided. For each pair of the data subsets $\boldsymbol{C}_k$ and $\boldsymbol{C}_k^c$ (12) the separable sublayer SL_k of L_k optimal binary classifiers $BC_{i*}(\theta_{l*})$ (7) can be designed in accordance with the procedure (19).The sublayer SL_k transforms (8) each of the m input feature vectors $\mathbf{x}_j = [x_{j,1}, \ldots, x_{j,n}]^T$ from the data matrix $\boldsymbol{X}$ (3) into the output vector $\mathbf{r}_{j'} = [r_{j',1}, \ldots, r_{j',L_k}]^T$ with L_k binary components $r_{j',l} (r_{j',l} \in \{0, 1\})$, where $j' = j_k'(j)$ is the index function (9).

The k-th sublayer SL_k of the L_k optimal classifiers $BC_{i*}(\theta_{l*})$ (7) allows transforming the learning set C_k (4) of the m_k feature vectors $\mathbf{x}_j$ (1) into the set $\boldsymbol{R}_k$ composed of $m_k'(m_k' \leq m_k)$ transformed vectors $\mathbf{r}_{j'} = [r_{j',1}, \ldots, r_{j',Lk}]^T$ (8):

$$(\forall k \in \{1, \ldots, K\}) \quad \boldsymbol{R}_k = \{\mathbf{r}_{j'} : j' = j_k'(j) \; (9) \; and \; \mathbf{x}_j \in C_k(4)\} \tag{21}$$

Remark 5. The separable sublayers SL_k ($k = 1, \ldots, K$) of the binary classifiers $BC_i(\theta_l)$ (7) transform the separable learning sets C_k (4) into the disjoined sets $\boldsymbol{R}_k$ (21):

$$(\forall k \in \{1, \ldots, K\})(\forall k' \in \{1, \ldots, K : k' \neq k\}) \boldsymbol{R}_{k'} \cap \boldsymbol{R}_k = \varnothing \tag{22}$$

The separable layer SL_k of binary classifiers $BC_i(\theta_l)$ (7) can be used as a tool for the *separable aggregation* of the learning set C_k (4) with m_k elements $\mathbf{x}_j = [x_{j,1}, \ldots, x_{j,n}]^T$.

Definition 7. The sublayer SL_k of the L_k classifiers $BC_i(\theta_l)$ (7) aggregates the k-th learning set C_k (4) if and only if the number m'_k of the transformed vectors $\mathbf{r}_{j'}$ (8) is less than the number $m_k (m'_k < m_k)$ of the feature vectors $\mathbf{x}_j$ (1) in the subset C_k (4).

The *aggregation coefficient* η_k of the k-th separable sublayer SL_k can be defined as:

$$\eta_k = (m_k - m'_k)/(m_k - 1) \tag{23}$$

where, m_k is the number of the input vectors $\mathbf{x}_j$ from the learning set C_k (4), and m'_k is the number of different output vectors $\mathbf{r}_{j'}$ (9) of the k-th sublayer SL_k.

It can be seen, that the minimal number m'_k of the different output vectors $\mathbf{r}_{j'}$ (9) from the k-th separable sublayer SL_k is equal to one $\left(m'_k = 1\right)$. The aggregation coefficient η_k (23) takes the maximal value equal to one ($\eta_k = 1$) in this ideal situation. The maximal value of the number m'_k is equal to m_k. There is no aggregation in this case and the aggregation coefficient η_k (23) is equal to zero ($\eta_k = 0$). As a result:

$$0 \leq \eta_k \leq 1 \tag{24}$$

Remark 6. If the aggregation coefficient η_k (24) of the k-th separable sublayer SL_k is greater than zero ($\eta_k > 0$), then the number m'_k of the transformed vectors $\mathbf{r}_{j'}$ (8) in the set $\boldsymbol{R}_k(\mathbf{r}_{j'} \in \boldsymbol{R}_k(21))$ is less than the number m_k of the feature vectors $\mathbf{x}_j$ (1) in the learning set $\boldsymbol{C}_k$ (4) ($\mathbf{x}_j \in \boldsymbol{C}_k$).

Remark 7. Each separable data subset $\boldsymbol{C}_k$ (6) ($k \in \{1,\ldots, K\}$) can be aggregated in one vector $\mathbf{r}_{j'}$ by a hierarchical network of separable sublayers SL_k.

If the aggregation coefficient η_k (23) of a given sublayer SL_k is equal to one ($\eta_k = 1$), then such sublayer transforms all feature vectors $\mathbf{x}_j$ from the learning set $\boldsymbol{C}_k$ (4) into one vector $\mathbf{r}_{j'}$ (8) only. In this case, the network with only one layer can fully aggregate the data subset $\boldsymbol{C}_k$ (4). Let us consider now a hierarchical network of L ($L > 1$) separable sublayers SL_k with the aggregation coefficients η_k (24) greater than zero and smaller than one ($0 < \eta_k < 1$). Each such sublayer SL_k causes reduction of the number m'_k of the transformed vectors $\mathbf{r}_{i'}$ (8). So, after gradual inclusion of L layers the number m'_k of the transformed vectors $\mathbf{r}_{j'}$ (8) can be reduced to one.

In order to design hierarchical networks with a small number L of separable sublayers SL_k, the aggregation coefficients η_k (23) of particular sublayers should have large values. It is assumed that the sublayer of binary classifiers $BC_i(\theta_l)$ (7) is enlarged gradually. An additional classifier $BC_{i(k)}(\theta_{l(k)})$ (7) is added to the sublayer during the k-th step of the procedure ($k = 1,\ldots, K$). The below designing postulate can be applied during each step k of a given sublayer enlargement [4]:

The designing postulate : (25)

An additional classifier $BC_i(\theta_l)$ (7) should divide the highest number of the yet undivided mixed dipoles $\{\mathbf{x}_j, \mathbf{x}_{j'}\}$ and the lowest number of the yet undivided clear dipoles.

6 Experimental Results

The synthetic data set of m = 1165 two dimensional feature vectors $\mathbf{x}_j = [x_{j,1}, x_{j,2}]^T$ (1) was generated (Fig. 2). The selected data subset C_1 (11) contained 541 points $\mathbf{x}_j$ (*circles*) and the complementary subset C_1^c contained 624 points $\mathbf{x}_j$ (*crosses*). The number of the mixed dipoles $\{\mathbf{x}_j, \mathbf{x}_{j'}\}$ (12) was equal to 337584, and the number of clear dipoles was equal to 678030.

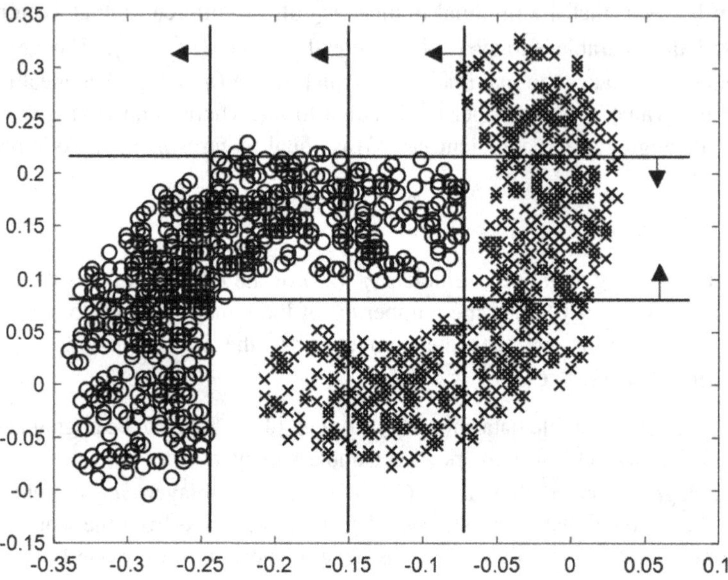

Fig. 2. An example of the division of all mixed dipoles $\{\mathbf{x}_j, \mathbf{x}_{j'}\}$ from two sets C_1 and C_1^c (11)

All mixed dipoles $\{\mathbf{x}_j, \mathbf{x}_{j'}\}$ (12) were divided by the separable layer of five univariate classifiers $BC_i(\theta_l)$ (7). As a result, all 541 points $\mathbf{x}_j$ were transformed into below five vectors $\mathbf{r}_{j'} = [r_{j',1}, \ldots, r_{j',5}]^T$ (8) with five binary components $r_{j',i}(j', i = 1, \ldots, 5)$:

$$\begin{aligned}
\mathbf{r}_1 &= [1,0,1,1,1], \text{with } m_1 = 177 \\
\mathbf{r}_2 &= [1,1,1,1,1], \text{with } m_2 = 121 \\
\mathbf{r}_3 &= [1,1,1,0,1], \text{with } m_3 = 154 \\
\mathbf{r}_4 &= [0,1,1,0,1], \text{with } m_4 = 85 \\
\mathbf{r}_5 &= [1,1,1,0,0], \text{with } m_5 = 4
\end{aligned}$$

where the symbol $m_{j'}$ means the number of points $\mathbf{x}_j$ transformed into the vector $\mathbf{r}_{j'}$ (8). The aggregation coefficient (23) has a high value η_1 = 536/540 in this example.

7 Concluding Remarks

Multilayer hierarchical networks can be designed from univariate, binary classifiers on the basis of the dipolar separability technique described in the paper. This approach to hierarchical networks designing could be an alternative to current methods of deep learning [7].

Dipolar technique described in the presented paper allows designing multilayer hierarchical networks from binary classifiers while preserving learning data separability. Multilayer network of dipolar separable layers can successively aggregate a given data set in one vector only. This technique can enrich the arsenal of tools used in the deep learning tasks.

Dipolar designing allows to obtain separable layers from binary classifiers. The dipolar approach described in the paper can be treated as a completion of the ranked method used in designing linearly separable layers [6]. The ranked approach can be treated as a basic possibility to design linearly separable layers from binary classifiers [6]. The aggregation of given family of separable data sets in one vector only is possible by only two linearly separable layers.

Univariate binary classifiers used in separable aggregating layers of are based on single features only. For this reason the proposed dipolar designing is relatively low costly. This type of classifiers could be particularly useful in processing such large data sets which are only partially structured (Definition 1). Many big data sets encountered in practice have such property.

Acknowledgments. The presented study was supported by the grant S/WI/2/2013 from Bialystok University of Technology and funded from the resources for research by Polish Ministry of Science and Higher Education.

References

1. Hand, D., Smyth, P., Mannila, H.: Principles of Data Mining. MIT Press, Cambridge (2001)
2. Duda, O.R., Hart, P.E., Stork, D.G.: Pattern Classification. Wiley, New York (2001)
3. Bobrowski, L.: Data Mining Based on Convex and Piecewise Linear Criterion Functions (in Polish). Bialystok University of Technology, Bialystok (2005)
4. Bobrowski, L.: Piecewise-linear classifiers, formal neurons and separability of the learning sets. In: Proceedings of ICPR 1996 13th International Conference on Pattern Recognition, Vienna, Austria, pp. 224–228 (1996)
5. Bobrowski, L.: Dipolar data integration through univariate, binary classifiers. In: Nguyen, N. T., Papadopoulos, G.A., Jędrzejowicz, P., Trawiński, B., Vossen, G. (eds.) ICCCI 2017. LNCS (LNAI), vol. 10448, pp. 73–82. Springer, Cham (2017). https://doi.org/10.1007/978-3-319-67074-4_8
6. Bobrowski, L., Topczewska, M.: Linearizing layers of radial binary classifiers with movable centers. Pattern Anal. Appl. **18**(4), 771–781 (2015)
7. Arel, I., Rose, D.C., Karnowski, T.P.: Deep machine learning– a new frontier in artificial intelligence – a survey paper. IEEE Comput. Intell. Mag. (2013)
8. Wang, Z., et al.: Sparse Coding and Its Applications in Computer Vision. World Scientific, New Jersey (2016)

Video Surveillance of Highway Traffic Events by Deep Learning Architectures

Matteo Tiezzi[1(✉)], Stefano Melacci[1], Marco Maggini[1], and Angelo Frosini[2]

[1] Department of Information Engineering and Mathematics, University of Siena, Siena, Italy
{mtiezzi,mela,maggini}@diism.unisi.it
[2] IsTech s.r.l., Pistoia, Italy
a.frosini@istech.it
http://sailab.diism.unisi.it

Abstract. In this paper we describe a video surveillance system able to detect traffic events in videos acquired by fixed videocameras on highways. The events of interest consist in a specific sequence of situations that occur in the video, as for instance a vehicle stopping on the emergency lane. Hence, the detection of these events requires to analyze a temporal sequence in the video stream. We compare different approaches that exploit architectures based on Recurrent Neural Networks (RNNs) and Convolutional Neural Networks (CNNs). A first approach extracts vectors of features, mostly related to motion, from each video frame and exploits a RNN fed with the resulting sequence of vectors. The other approaches are based directly on the sequence of frames, that are eventually enriched with pixel-wise motion information. The obtained stream is processed by an architecture that stacks a CNN and a RNN, and we also investigate a transfer-learning-based model. The results are very promising and the best architecture will be tested online in real operative conditions.

Keywords: Convolutional Neural Networks · Recurrent Neural Networks · Deep learning · Video surveillance · Highway traffic

1 Introduction

The progressive growth of the number of vehicles, that nowadays are traveling on roads and highways, has created high interest in the research areas related to the development of techniques needed in automatic instruments for traffic monitoring. These systems are generically referred to as Intelligent Transportation Systems (ITSs). Basic tasks, that are to be accomplished by ITSs, are the identification of vehicles and of their behaviour from video streams, captured by surveillance cameras installed along the road connections. The automatic detection of specific events happening in the traffic flow, such as accidents, dangerous

V. Kůrková et al. (Eds.): ICANN 2018, LNCS 11141, pp. 584–593, 2018.
https://doi.org/10.1007/978-3-030-01424-7_57

driving, and traffic congestions, has become an indispensable functionality of ITSs since it is impractical to employ human operators both for the number of control points and the need of a continuous attention. Automatic notifications guarantee an immediate response to exceptional events such as car crashes or wrong-way driving. At the same time, the estimation of road congestion allows us to notify drivers and to provide information for optimizing the itineraries computed by navigation devices. This field of research began to be particularly active in the '80, with projects funded by governments, industries and universities, in Europe (PROMETHEUS [12]), Japan (RACS [10]) and the USA (IVHS [1]). These studies included autonomous cars, inter-vehicle communication systems [7], surveillance and monitoring of traffic events [3,8].

Among the general ITSs, the Advanced Traffic Management Systems (ATMS) are aimed at exploiting all the information coming from cameras, sensors and other instruments, positioned along highways and main routes, to provide an analysis of the current state of traffic and to respond in real time to specific conditions. Signals from all devices are gathered at a central Transportation Management Center that must implement technologies capable of analyzing the huge amounts of data coming from all the sensors and cameras.

In this context, Machine Learning provides tools to tackle many problems faced in the design of the ATMS modules. In particular, Deep Neural Network architectures are able to yield state-of-the-art performances in many computer vision tasks [4] and are currently applied in real systems, such those for autonomous driving [2]. Hence, most of current video surveillance modules are based on deep learning techniques, that allow us to tune the system just by providing enough examples of the objects or events of interest [13]. The wide use of these approaches has also be driven by the availability of pre-trained architectures for computer vision tasks that can be adapted to new problems by transfer learning [9].

The objective of this work is the creation of an instrument capable to perform a real time/on-line analysis of data coming from cameras, in order to detect automatically significant events occurring in the traffic flow. We analyze the results obtained by different approaches on real videos of traffic on highways. In particular we compare an approach based on precomputed motion features processed by a Recurrent Neural Network (RNN) with a technique exploiting the original video augmented by channels to encode the optical flow. The latter is based on an architecture composed by a Convolutional Neural Network (CNN), processing each input frame, stacked with a RNN. We consider both the cases in which the CNN is learned from our traffic videos and when it is a pre-trained CNN in a transfer learning scheme.

The paper is organized as follows. The next Section describes the considered problem, while our dataset and the feature representation are described in Sect. 2. In Sect. 4 we introduce the selected deep neural network architectures, while Sect. 5 reports the results. Finally, Sect. 6 concludes the paper.

2 Video Surveillance of Highway Traffic

We focus on a system that processes videos acquired by fixed cameras on highways. Cameras can be positioned in very different environments (e.g. tunnels or outdoor) and can have many different settings for the point of view (e.g. long or short range, wide or narrow span). Moreover, videos are captured in different environmental and weather conditions (daylight, night, fog, rain, etc.). The system is expected to detect specific events of interest happening in the scene for a variable time interval. In particular, we consider four different classes of events, collected in the set $\mathcal{E}$ (see Fig. 1):

- **Stationary vehicle**, a vehicle stops inside the field of the camera;
- **Departing vehicle**, a vehicle, previously stationary, departs from his position;
- **Wrong-way vehicle**, a vehicle moves in the wrong direction;
- **Car crash**, accident involving one or more vehicles.

Fig. 1. The four different classes of events. (a) Stationary. (b) Departing. (c) Wrong-way. (d) Car crash.

As already stated, all the videos are captured by cameras positioned in different places and settings on highways, including tunnels and high-speed stretches. This fact entails several issues that can deteriorate the prediction performances. For instance, cameras are exposed to all kind of weather conditions, including fog, rain or strong wind. Another relevant problem is due to variations in brightness caused by tunnel lamps activation, clouds passing by, and sun movement (see Fig. 2 for examples).

3 Data Description and Representation

Video surveillance cameras provide a continuous stream of a given view of the highway along the direction of the traffic flow. Due to the nature of the events we are trying to detect, it was difficult to collect a large dataset of examples[1]. For instance, some events like wrong-way driving are quite rare.

[1] The dataset was collected thanks to IsTech srl and was based only on a limited number of fixed cameras.

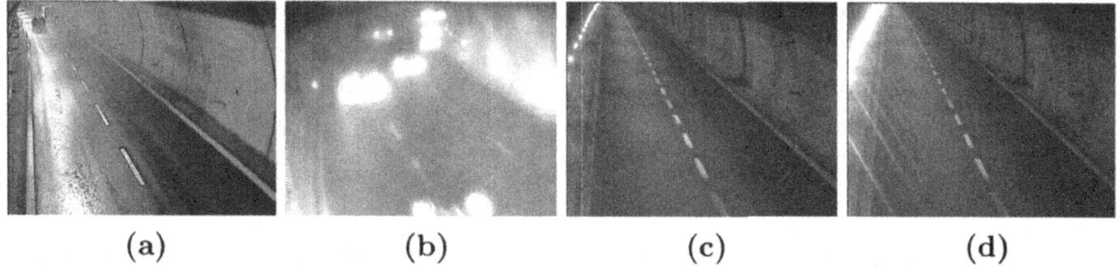

Fig. 2. Conditions causing difficulties in video analysis. (a) Rain. (b) Fog. (c)–(d) Brightness variation, before and after.

Videos were captured in colors in two standard resolutions (352×288 and 640×320 pixels, depending on the camera type) at 25 frames per second. In some cases the videocamera includes the lanes in both directions in its field. Hence, in order to remove potential sources of misleading information (for instance, related to wrong-way vehicles) each frame is masked with a template that keeps only the portion related to the lanes to be considered (see Fig. 4).

Fig. 3. (a) Original frame. (b) Mask. (c) Masked frame.

We down-sampled the available videos at 2 frames per second, and extracted clips of 125 frames (1 min), containing instances of the events $\mathcal{E}$ listed in Sect. 2, as well as clips with normal traffic conditions. To avoid artificial regularities that may hinder the generalization, the clips are generated such that events can happen in every instant inside the 125 frame interval, apart from the very beginning or ending. The statistics of the available dataset used in training and testing are reported in Table 1. The optical flow algorithm[2] was exploited to compute the motion field for each input frame. Each frame was resized and cropped to 160×120 pixels. We represented the input frames in three different ways, using *i.* pre-designed motion features, *ii.* appearance, or *iii.* appearance and motion, as described in the following.

Representation by Motion Features. Due to the effect of perspective, moving objects closer to the camera position have an apparent motion larger than distant objects. Therefore, we decided to split each frame into four horizontal

[2] We used the default implementation in the OpenCV library https://opencv.org/, based on the Farneback's algorithm.

Table 1. Statistics of the dataset used in the paper.

	No Event	Stationary	Departing	Wrong-way	Car crash	Total
# Clips	281	111	56	131	16	595

stripes as shown in Fig. 4a. For each stripe the directions and modules of the optical flow are quantized, building a histogram of the distribution of the motion vectors. In the implementation we considered 32 bins based on 8 directions and 4 levels for the module (Fig. 4b). This scheme yields 128 values (32 bins for each stripe) collected into a vector for each frame. In order to provide evidence for stationary vehicles, we computed an additional feature for each stripe as follows. We applied and manually tuned a Background Subtraction [6] method to extract the pixels not belonging to the static background of the video (see Fig. 4c). The additional feature per stripe is the count of non-background pixels having null motion. Hence, each frame is represented by a vector of 132 entries.

Representations by Appearance and Motion. The appearance-based representation consists of the raw frame converted to grayscale to reduce the image variability. Another representation is obtained by adding two additional channels for each frame corresponding to the horizontal and vertical components of the motion field provided by the optical flow, leading to a $160 \times 120 \times 3$ tensor.

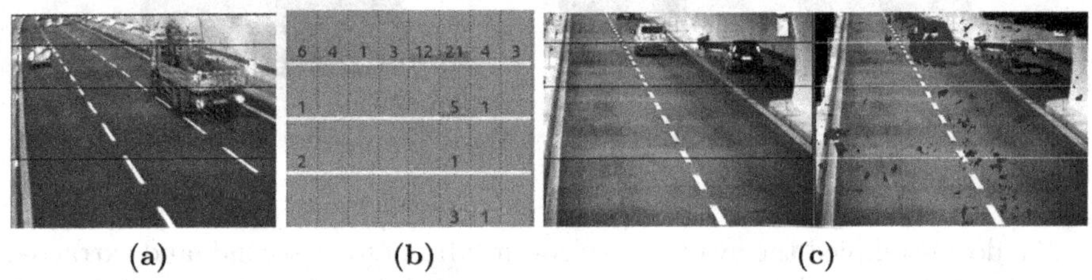

Fig. 4. (a) Motion vectors, frame partitioned into 4 stripes. (b) Histogram computed in one stripe. (c) Background subtraction (original frame on the left, estimated not-background objects on the right).

4 Deep Architectures

We are given a video stream $\mathcal{V}$ that produces frames at each time instant t. At a certain $t > 0$, we have access to the sequence of frames up to time t, that we indicate with $\mathcal{S}_t = \{\mathcal{I}_i,\ i = 1, \ldots, t\}$, where $\mathcal{I}_i$ is the i-th frame of the sequence. We implemented multiple deep architectures that learn to predict the set of events Y_t that characterize frame $\mathcal{I}_t$, given the sequence $\mathcal{S}_t$. Formally, if $f(\cdot)$ is a generic deep neural network, we have

$$Y_t = f(t|\mathcal{S}_t),$$

where $Y_t = \{y_{t,h},\ h = 1, \ldots, |\mathcal{E}|\}$ is a set of predictions of the considered events $\mathcal{E}$ (in this work, $|\mathcal{E}| = 4$). In particular, $y_{t,h} \in \{0, 1\}$, where $y_{t,h} = 1$ means that the h-th event is predicted at time t.

Before being processed by the network, each frame $\mathcal{I}_i$ is converted into one of the three representations that we described in Sect. 3, generically indicated here with r_i,

$$r_i = \texttt{frame\_representation}(\mathcal{I}_i). \tag{1}$$

Our deep architecture $f(\cdot)$ is then composed of four computational stages, and each of them projects its input into a new latent representation. Stages consist of a feature extraction module `feature_extraction`$(\cdot)$, a sequence representation module `sequence_representation`$(\cdot)$, a prediction layer `predictor`$(\cdot)$, and a decision function `decision`$(\cdot)$ that outputs Y_t,

$$q_t = \texttt{feature\_extraction}(r_t) \tag{2}$$

$$s_t = \texttt{sequence\_representation}(q_t,\ s_{t-1}) \tag{3}$$

$$p_t = \texttt{predictor}(s_t) \tag{4}$$

$$Y_t = \texttt{decision}(p_t). \tag{5}$$

Equation (2) is responsible of extracting features from r_t, building a new representation q_t of the current frame. We implemented multiple extractors, in function of the method selected to produce r_t (we postpone their description). Equation (3) encodes the sequence of frames observed so far. The sequence representation s_t is computed by updating the previous representation s_{t-1} with the current input r_t. This is implemented with a Recurrent Neural Network (RNN), where s is the hidden state of the RNN. In particular, we used a Long Short Term Memory RNN (LSTM) [5], and we also experienced multiple layers of recurrence (2 layers). Equation (4) is a fully connected layer with sigmoidal activation units, that computes the event prediction scores $p_t \in [0, 1]^{|\mathcal{E}|}$. We indicate with $p_{t,h}$ the h-th component of p_t, and Eq. (5) converts it into the binary decision $y_{t,h}$. We implemented each decision $y_{t,h}$ to be the outcome of a thresholding operation on $p_{t,h}$, so that

$$y_{t,h} = \begin{cases} 1, \text{ if } p_{t,h} \geq \gamma_h \\ 0, \text{ otherwise} \end{cases}$$

where $\gamma_h \in (0, 1)$ is the threshold associated to the h-th event.

We are given a training set composed of fully labeled video clips, so that we have a ground truth label $\hat{Y}_t = \{\hat{y}_{t,h}, h = 1, \ldots, |\mathcal{E}|\}$ on each frame. For each sequence, the time index t spans from 1 to the length of the sequence itself, and we set s_0 to be a vector of zeros. We trained our network by computing a loss function that, at each time instant, consists of the cross-entropy between the event-related output values and the ground truth,

$$\mathcal{L}_t = \sum_{h=1}^{|\mathcal{E}|} \{w_h \cdot [-\hat{y}_{t,h} \cdot \log(p_{t,h})] - (1 - \hat{y}_{t,h}) \cdot \log(1 - p_{t,h})\}\ .$$

Notice that we introduced the scalar $w_h > 0$ to weigh the contribute of the positive examples of class h. As a matter of fact, it is crucial to give larger weight to those events that are rarely represented in the training data, and our experience with the data of Sect. 3 suggests that an even weighing scheme frequently leads to not promising results (we choose $w_1 = 10$, $w_2 = 40$, $w_3 = 30$, $w_4 = 100$, following the event ordering of Sect. 2).

We evaluated four different deep networks that follow the aforementioned computations, and that are depicted in Fig. 5, together with several numerical details. The networks differ in the frame representation r_t that they process (Eq. (1)) and in the way they implement the `feature_extraction` function of Eq. (2). The first network, referred to as *hist*, processes the histogram of the motion features in the input frame, that are fed to the RNN without further processing ($q_t = r_t$). The second network, *conv*, is based on the appearance-only representation of each frame, i.e. $r_t = \texttt{gray}(\mathcal{I}_t)$, and it extracts features using a Convolutional Neural Network (CNN) with 3 layers (we also tested configurations with 2 layers). When the frame representation consists of the appearance $\texttt{gray}(\mathcal{I}_t)$ paired with the motion field (v_x, v_y), then *conv* becomes the *convFlow* network. Finally, we also considered the effects of transfer learning in the *convPre* model, where we modified the *conv* net by plugging a pre-trained VGG-19 convolutional network [11] in Eq. (2). VGG-19 is composed of 19 layers and trained using the ImageNet database, so r_t is first rescaled/tiled to $224 \times 224 \times 3$ to match the size of the ImageNet data.

5 Experimental Results

We divided our dataset sets of video clips into three groups for fitting, validating and testing our models, with a ratio of 70%, 20%, 10%, keeping the original distribution of events in each split. We selected the F1 measure to evaluate the models of Sect. 4, and since some events occur very rarely in the data (see Sect. 3), we computed the F1 for each single event class. In particular, for every tested architecture, we selected the optimal value of the decision threshold γ_h ensuring the best performances on the validation set (testing multiple values in $[0.1, 0.9]$). We trained our networks with stochastic gradient-based updates that occur after having processed each video clip, and we used the Adam optimizer with a learning rate of $3 \cdot 10^{-5}$, processing the training data for 350 epochs. The training times are reported in Table 2, considering a system equipped with an NVidia GTX Titan GPU (recall that the CNN of *convPre* is pre-trained).

Table 2. Avg training times (hours). Frame representations were precomputed.

	hist	conv	convFlow	convPre
1 Layer RNN	2.03	15.12	17.05	3.91
2 Layers RNN	3.06	21.96	22.44	6.41

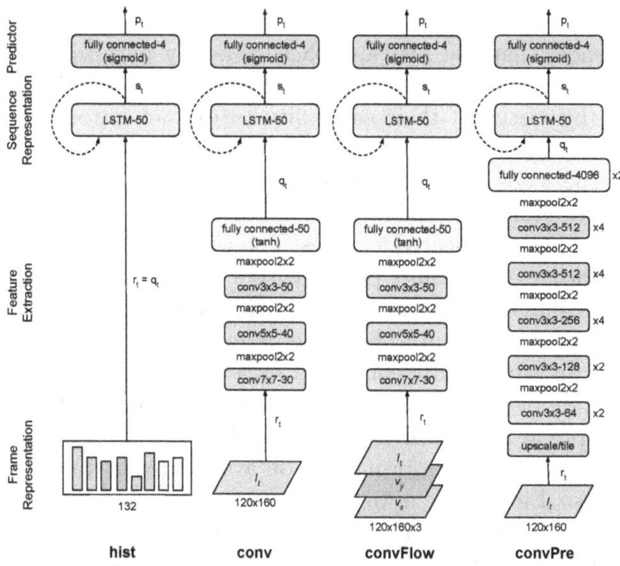

Fig. 5. Deep architectures applied to our task. Layer names are followed by the suffix -n, where n is the number of output units (or the size of the hidden state in LSTM). We use the ReLu activation, unless differently indicated in brackets. In convolutional and pooling layers we report the size of their spatial coverage (e.g., $k \times k$). In Sect. 5 we evaluate several variants of these nets.

Table 3. Performances (F1) of the compared models.

		hist			conv		convFlow		convPre		
		$h = 20$	50	132	$\ell = 2$	3	$\ell = 2$	3	$h = 30$	50	200
(stationary)	1 Layer RNN	0.63	0.89	0.86	**0.98**	0.94	0.91	0.79	0.95	0.92	0.90
	2 Layers RNN	0.87	0.85	0.87	0.87	0.91	0.76	0.82	0.95	0.91	0.89
(departing)	1 Layer RNN	0.56	0.63	0.73	0.61	0.79	0.63	0.57	0.59	0.63	0.58
	2 Layers RNN	0.48	0.66	0.72	0.74	**0.82**	0.52	0.63	0.74	0.81	0.68
(wrong-way)	1 Layer RNN	0.59	0.84	0.89	0.92	0.93	0.89	0.92	**0.96**	0.93	0.94
	2 Layers RNN	0.83	0.87	0.89	0.86	0.88	0.86	0.88	0.94	0.93	0.91
(car crash)	1 Layer RNN	0.65	0.61	0.70	0.85	0.64	0.79	0.78	0.80	0.78	0.77
	2 Layers RNN	0.56	0.33	0.91	0.75	0.50	0.74	0.74	**0.95**	0.86	0.90
(*average*)	1 Layer RNN	0.61	0.74	0.80	0.84	0.83	0.81	0.77	0.83	0.82	0.80
	2 Layers RNN	0.69	0.68	0.85	0.81	0.78	0.72	0.77	**0.90**	0.88	0.85

We summarize in Table 3 the best performances obtained, for each class of event, by the *hist, conv, convFlow, convPre* models of Fig. 5 with multiple layers or recurrence. Depending on the model, we also evaluated different sizes of the recurrent state dimension h (20, 50, 132 for *hist*, 30, 50, 200 for *convPre*), or number of convolutional layers ℓ (2 or 3 layers for both *conv* and *convFlow*). These results show that the *hist* approach generally performs worse than the other models, and that convolutional architectures are a better solution to the proposed task, by virtue of their capability to extract autonomously relevant representation from images. When using 2 layers of RNNs, the configuration of *hist* with $h = 132$ leads to more competitive results, that, however, are paired with a larger computational burden than the CNN-based models due to the cost of computing its hand-engineered features. The *conv* model with only two convolutional layers shows good results paired with a computational cost that can be tolerated in real-time applications. The addition of the motion related information (*convFlow*) does not seem to help the performances. This can be explained by the fact that an architecture composed by a combination of a CNN together with a RNN is able by itself to grasp the temporal dynamics of a video, making an addition of optical flow features worthless. The use of a pre-trained network (*convPre*) leads to the best performances, on average, even if with a more costly inferential process. Finally, we notice that using 2 layers of RNNs does not add useful information to the *conv* model, while it always helps in *convPre*, mostly due to larger number of high-level features that are extracted by the CNN, where the system seems to find longer-term regularities (more easily captured by multiple layers of recurrence). The event class where all the models have shown worse performances is "departing", that we explain by the larger incoherence in the training data in defining the beginning and, mostly, the ending frames of the event. In Fig. 6 we report an example that compares a prediction and the ground truth (test set), showing the mismatch in the ending-part of the event.

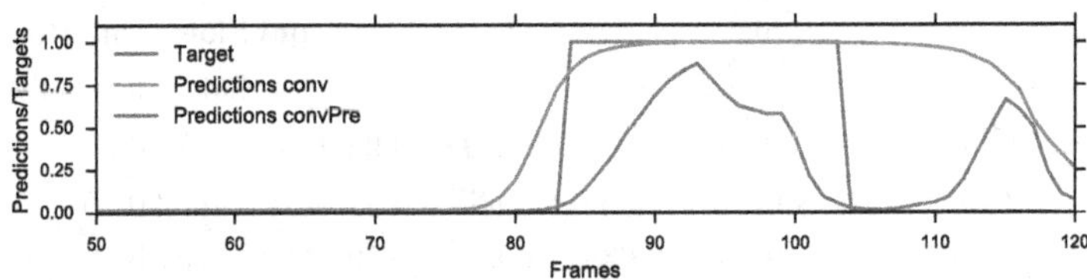

Fig. 6. Comparing predictions and ground truth in a "departing" event.

6 Conclusions

We described a deep-network-based implementation of an ATMS (Advanced Traffic Management System) that predicts a set of events while processing videos of traffic on highways. We performed a detailed analysis of a real-world video data collection, investigating four classes of traffic events. We reported the results of an experimental evaluation that involved multiple representations of the input data and different deep architectures composed of a stack of convolutional and recurrent networks. Our results have shown that these networks can efficiently learn the temporal information from the video stream, simplifying the feature engineering process and making very promising predictions. We also proved the benefits of transferring the representations learned on a generic image classification task. Our best architectures will be tested online in real operative conditions.

References

1. Betsold, R.: Intelligent vehicle highway systems for the united states - an emerging national program. In: JSK International Symposium - Technological Innovations for Tomorrow's Automobile Traffic and Driving Information Systems, pp. 53–59 (1989)
2. Chen, C., Seff, A., Kornhauser, A., Xiao, J.: Deepdriving: learning affordance for direct perception in autonomous driving. In: ICCV, pp. 2722–2730. IEEE (2015)
3. Coifman, B., Beymer, D., McLauchlan, P., Malik, J.: A real-time computer vision system for vehicle tracking and traffic surveillance. Transp. Res. Part C Emerg. Technol. **6**(4), 271–288 (1998)
4. He, K., Zhang, X., Ren, S., Sun, J.: Deep residual learning for image recognition. In: Proceedings of CVPR, pp. 770–778 (2016)
5. Hochreiter, S., Schmidhuber, J.: Long short-term memory. Neural Comput. **9**(8), 1735–1780 (1997)
6. KaewTraKulPong, P., Bowden, R.: An improved adaptive background mixture model for real-time tracking with shadow detection. In: Remagnino, P., Jones, G.A., Paragios, N., Regazzoni, C.S. (eds.) Video-Based Surveillance Systems, pp. 135–144. Springer, Boston (2002). https://doi.org/10.1007/978-1-4615-0913-4_11
7. Lee, W.H., Tseng, S.S., Shieh, W.Y.: Collaborative real-time traffic information generation and sharing framework for the intelligent transportation system. Inf. Sci. **180**(1), 62–70 (2010)
8. Michalopoulos, P.G., Fundakowski, R.A., Geokezas, M., Fitch, R.C.: Vehicle detection through image processing for traffic surveillance and control. Patent (US) 4,847,772, 11 July 1989
9. Oquab, M., Bottou, L., Laptev, I., Sivic, J.: Learning and transferring mid-level image representations using convolutional neural networks. In: Proceedings of CVPR, pp. 1717–1724. IEEE (2014)
10. Shibata, M.: Road traffic management in Japan and development of the RAC system. In: JSK International Symposium - Technological Innovations for Tomorrow's Automobile Traffic and driving Information Systems, pp. 29–27 (1989)
11. Simonyan, K., Zisserman, A.: Very deep convolutional networks for large-scale image recognition. arXiv preprint arXiv:1409.1556 (2014)
12. Williams, M.: PROMETHEUS-the European research programme for optimising the road transport system in Europe, pp. 1–9, January 1989
13. Xu, D., Yan, Y., Ricci, E., Sebe, N.: Detecting anomalous events in videos by learning deep representations of appearance and motion. Comput. Vis. Image Underst. **156**, 117–127 (2017)

Augmenting Image Classifiers Using Data Augmentation Generative Adversarial Networks

Antreas Antoniou[1(✉)], Amos Storkey[1(✉)], and Harrison Edwards[1,2(✉)]

[1] University of Edinburgh, Edinburgh, UK
{a.antoniou,a.storkey,h.l.edwards}@sms.ed.ac.uk
[2] Open AI, San Francisco, USA
https://www.ed.ac.uk/
https://openai.com/

Abstract. Effective training of neural networks requires much data. In the low-data regime, parameters are underdetermined, and learnt networks generalise poorly. Data Augmentation alleviates this by using existing data more effectively, but standard data augmentation produces only limited plausible alternative data. Given the potential to generate a much broader set of augmentations, we design and train a generative model to do data augmentation. The model, based on image conditional Generative Adversarial Networks, uses data from a source domain and learns to take a data item and augment it by generating other within-class data items. As this generative process does not depend on the classes themselves, it can be applied to novel unseen classes. We demonstrate that a Data Augmentation Generative Adversarial Network (DAGAN) augments classifiers well on Omniglot, EMNIST and VGG-Face.

1 Introduction

Over the last decade Deep Neural Networks have enabled unprecedented performance on a number of tasks. They have been demonstrated in many domains [12] including image classification [16–18,21,25], machine translation [44], natural language processing [12], speech recognition [19], and synthesis [42], learning from human play [6] and reinforcement learning [10,13,27,35,40] among others. In all cases, very large datasets have been utilized, or in the case of reinforcement learning, extensive play. In many realistic settings we need to achieve goals with limited datasets; in those cases deep neural networks seem to fall short, overfitting on the training set and producing poor generalisation on the test set.

Techniques have been developed over the years to help combat overfitting such as L1/L2 reqularization [28], dropout [20], batch normalization [23], batch renormalisation [22] or layer normalization [2]. However in low data regimes, even these techniques fall short, since the flexibility of the network is so high. These methods are not able to capitalise on known input invariances that might form good prior knowledge for informing the parameter learning.

V. Kůrková et al. (Eds.): ICANN 2018, LNCS 11141, pp. 594–603, 2018.
https://doi.org/10.1007/978-3-030-01424-7_58

It is also possible to generate more data from existing data by applying various transformations [25] to the original dataset. These transformations include random translations, rotations and flips as well as addition of Gaussian noise. Such methods capitalize on transformations that we know should not affect the class. This technique seems to be vital, not only for the low-data cases but for any size of dataset, in fact even models trained on some of the largest datasets such as Imagenet [7] can benefit from this practice.

Typical data augmentation techniques use a limited set of known invariances that are easy to invoke. Here, we recognize that we can learn a model of a much larger invariance space through training a form of conditional generative adversarial network (GAN) in some *source domain*. This can then be applied in the low-data domain of interest, the *target domain*. We show that such a Data Augmentation Generative Adversarial Network (DAGAN) enables effective neural network training even in low-data target domains. As the DAGAN does not depend on the classes themselves it captures the cross-class transformations, moving data-points to other points of equivalent class.

In this paper we train a DAGAN and then evaluate its performance on low-data tasks using standard stochastic gradient descent neural network training. We use 3 datasets, the Omniglot dataset, the EMNIST dataset and the more complex VGG-Face dataset. The DAGAN trained on Omniglot was used for augmenting both the Omniglot and EMNIST classifiers to demonstrate benefit even when transferring between substantially different domains. The VGG-Face dataset provides a considerably more challenging test for the DAGAN. VGG-Face was used to evaluate whether the DAGAN training scheme could work on human faces, which are notoriously hard to model using a generator. Furthermore the usefulness of the generated faces was measured when used as augmentation data in the classification training.

2 Background

Transfer Learning and Dataset Shift: The term *dataset shift* [36] generalises the concept of covariate shift [33,37,38] to multiple cases of changes between domains. For data augmentation, we may learn a generative distribution that maintains class consistency on one set of classes and apply that consistency transformation to new unseen classes, on the understanding the the transformations that maintain consistency generalise across classes.

Generative Adversarial Networks: GANs [11], and specifically Deep Convolutional GANs (DCGAN) [29] use the ability to discriminate between true and generated examples as a learning objective for generative models. GAN approaches can learn complex joint densities. Recent improvements in the optimization process [1,3,14] have reduced some of the failure modes of the GAN learning process as well as produced objectives that correlate well with sample quality [1,14]. Furthermore image conditional GANs have been used to achieve image to image translation [24], as well as augment datasets [5,34,45]. However the work relating to the enhancement of datasets only uses the GAN to either fine tune simulated data or generate data by attempting to reconstruct existing data points. Whereas our model is explicitly trained to produce data augmentations as a manifold of samples around real data samples.

As demonstrated in [14], the Wasserstein formulation for training GANs has shown superior sample diversity and quality in multiple instances. Additionally the Wasserstein GANs (WGAN) with Gradient Penalty (GP) have the additional benefit of being trainable using advanced architectures such as ResNets [16]. This is especially important since most GAN formulations can only be successfully trained using very specific and often less expressive model architectures. Furthermore WGAN with GP discriminator losses have been empirically observed to correlate with sample quality. Taking into consideration available state of the art methods including standard GAN, LS-GAN, WGAN with clipping and WGAN with Spectral normalization, we focus on the use WGAN with GP training in this paper due to its versatility in terms of architectures and its superior qualitative performance. Our own experiments with other approaches confirm the stated benefits; we found WGAN with GP to produce the most stable models with the best sample quality both qualitatively and quantitatively.

Data Augmentation: Data augmentation similar to [25] is routinely used in classification problems. Often it is non-trivial to encode known invariances in a model. It can be easier to encode those invariances in the data instead by generating additional data items through transformations from existing data items. For example the labels of handwritten characters should be invariant to small shifts in location, small rotations or shears, changes in intensity, changes in stroke thickness, changes in size etc. Almost all cases of data augmentation are from a priori known invariance. Various attempts at augmenting *features* instead of data are investigated in [8,39]. Moreover, the effectiveness of data augmentation has also been shown in other domains except images. Two such domains is sound [32] and text [31]. There has been little previous work that attempts to learn data augmentation strategies. One paper that is worthy of note is the work of [15], where the authors learn augmentation strategies on a class by class basis. Additional papers that attempt to learn models for data augmentation include [4,9,30]. These approaches do not transfer to the setting where completely new classes are considered.

3 Model

If we know that a class label should be invariant to a particular transformation then we can apply that transformation to generate additional data. If we do not know what transformations might be valid, but we have other data from related problems, we can attempt to learn valid transformations from those related problems that we can apply to our setting. This is an example of meta-learning; we learn on other problems how to improve learning for our target problem.

3.1 Model Overview

Consider a collection of datasets $[(x_i^c|i = 1, 2, \dots N^c)|c \in C]$, with each dataset labelled by c, the class, taken from the set of classes C, and with each element in a dataset c indexed by i and denoted by x_i^c. Let $x_i^c \in X$, the space of inputs. In this paper X will be a space of input images.

The goal is to learn a mapping between a conditional sample x_i^c of a certain class c to other samples x_j^c from that same class, using training data $[(x_i^c|i = 1, 2, \dots N^c)|c \in C]$. To do so we learn a differentiable function G which we call a generator. Given some random standard Gaussian vector z, we require a mapping $G : (x_i^c, z)$ such that, $\forall j$, x_j^c has high probability under the density of z mapped through G. Since G is differentiable, z maps out a whole manifold in X space associated with input x_i^c in a class consistent way. Yet G does not have access to the class c itself, thus enabling the DAGAN to generalize to unseen classes. We parameterize our generator function $\tilde{x} = G(x_i^c, z)$ as a neural network and we train it as a GAN using the WGAN with GP formulation. Training a GAN also requires a discriminator network, denoted as D, to be trained along with the generator network. The discriminator network attempts to discriminate between real and fake samples whilst the generator attempts to minimize the discriminator's performance in guessing real from fake.

3.2 Model Objective Definition

We modify the WGAN with GP formulation to account for the fact that we are using an image-conditional GAN with a discriminator that takes as input 2 images, instead of 1. Figure 1 shows the high level overview of our training setup. Our generator and discriminator objectives can be expressed as:

$$L_{discr} = \mathop{\mathbb{E}}_{\tilde{x} \sim P_g}[D(x_i^c, \tilde{x})] - \mathop{\mathbb{E}}_{X \sim P_r}[D(x_i^c, x_j^c)] + \lambda \mathop{\mathbb{E}}_{\hat{x} \sim P_{\hat{x}}}(||\nabla_{\hat{x}} D(x_i^c, \hat{x})||_2 - 1) \quad (1)$$

$$L_{gen} = - \mathop{\mathbb{E}}_{\tilde{x} \sim P_g}[D(x_i^c, \tilde{x})], \quad (2)$$

where x represents real samples, x_i^c and x_j^c represent two separate instances of samples from class c, $\tilde{x}$ represents generated samples from the generator G. $\hat{x}$ is, as defined in [14], randomly sampled points on linear interpolations between the samples of the real distribution P_r and generated distribution P_g. The only difference from the original WGAN with GP formulation is the use of 2 entries in the discriminator arguments, one for the conditional sample x_i^c and one for the target sample x_j^c (for real case) or $\tilde{x}$ (for fake case).

3.3 Architectures

We chose to use a state of the art Densenet discriminator and, for the generator, a powerful combination of two standard networks, UNet and ResNet, which we henceforth call a UResNet. The code for this paper is available[1], and

[1] https://github.com/AntreasAntoniou/DAGAN.

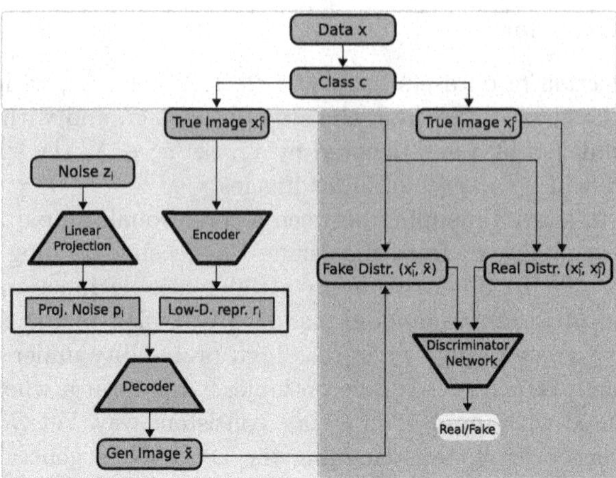

Fig. 1. DAGAN Architecture. Left: the generator network is composed of an encoder taking an input image and projecting it to a lower dimensional manifold. A random vector (z) is transformed and concatenated with the bottleneck vector; these are both passed to the decoder network which generates a within-class image. Right: the adversarial discriminator network is trained to discriminate between the samples from the *real* distribution (two real images from the same class) and the *fake* distribution (a real sample and a generated sample). Adversarial training enables the network to generate within-class images that look different enough to be considered a different sample.

that provides the full implementation of the networks. However we describe the implementational details here.

The UResNet generator has a total of 8 blocks, each block having 4 convolutional layers (with leaky rectified linear (ReLU) activations and batch renormalisation (batchrenorm) [22]) followed by one downscaling or upscaling layer. Downscaling layers (in blocks 1–4) were convolutions with stride 2 followed by leaky ReLU, batch normalisation and dropout. Upscaling layers were implemented by employing a nearest neighbour upscale, followed by a convolution, leaky ReLU, batch renormalisation and dropout. For Omniglot and EMNIST experiments, all layers had 64 filters. For the VGG-Face experiments the first 2 blocks of the encoder and the last 2 blocks of the decoder had 64 filters and the last 2 blocks of the encoder and the first 2 blocks of the decoder 128 filters.

In addition each block of the UResNet generator had skip connections. As with a standard ResNet, we used either a summation skip connection between layers with equivalent spacial dimensions or a strided 1×1 convolution for between layers with different spacial dimensions, thus bypassing the between block non-linearity to help gradient flow. Finally skip connections were introduced between equivalent sized filters at each end of the network (as with UNet).

We used a DenseNet [21] discriminator, using layer normalization instead of batch normalization; the latter would break the assumptions of the WGAN objective function (as mentioned in [14, Chap. 4]). The DenseNet was composed of 4 Dense Blocks and 4 Transition Layers, as defined in [21]. We used a growth rate of $k = 64$ and each Dense Block had 5 convolutional layers. We removed the 1×1 convolutions usually before the 3×3 convolutions as we observed this improved sample quality. For the discriminator we used dropout at the last convolutional layer of each Dense Block; this too improved sample quality.

For each classification experiment we used a DenseNet classifier composed of 4 Dense Blocks and 4 Transition Layers with a $k = 64$, each Dense Block had 3 convolutional layers within it. The classifiers were a total of 17 layers (i.e. 16 layers and 1 softmax layer). Furthermore we applied a dropout of 0.5 on the last convolutional layer in each Dense Block.

4 Datasets and Experiments

We tested the DAGAN augmentation on 3 datasets: Omniglot, EMNIST, and VGG-Face. All datasets were split randomly into source domain sets, validation domain sets and test domain sets.

For classifier networks, data for each character (handwritten or person) was further split into 2 test cases (for all datasets), 3 validation cases and a varying number of training cases depending on the experiment. Classifier training was done on the training cases for all examples in all domains; hyperparameter choice used validation cases. Test performance was reported only on the test cases for the target domain set. Case splits were randomized across each test run.

The Omniglot data [26] was split into source domain and target domain similarly to the split in [41]. The class ids were sorted in an increasing manner. The first 1200 were used as a source domain set, 1201–1412 as a validation domain set and 1412–1623 as a target domain test set.

The EMNIST data was split into a source domain that included classes 0–34 (after random shuffling of the classes), the validation domain set included classes 35–42 and the test domain set included classes 42–47. Since the EMNIST dataset has thousands of samples per class we chose only a subset of 100 for each class, so that we could make our task a low-data one.

In the VGG-Face dataset case, we randomly chose 100 samples from each class that had 100 or more, uncorrupted images, resulting in 2396 of the full 2622 classes available in the dataset. After shuffling, we split the resulting dataset into a source domain that included the first 1802 classes. The test domain set included classes 1803–2300 and the validation domain set included classes 2300–2396.

4.1 Training of DAGAN in Source Domain

A DAGAN was trained on Source Omniglot domains using a variety of architectures: standard VGG, U-Net, and ResNet inspired architectures. Increasingly powerful networks proved better generators, with the UResNet described in Sect. 3.3 generator being our model of choice. Examples of generated data are given in Fig. 2. We trained each DAGAN for 200K iterations, using a learning rate of 0.0001, and an Adam optimizer with Adam parameters of $\beta_1 = 0$ and

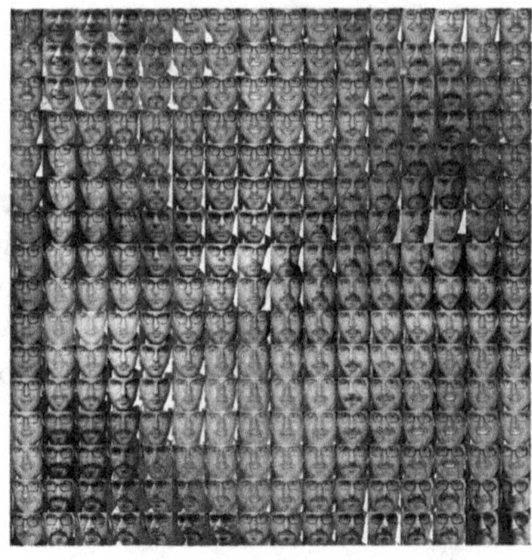

Fig. 2. An Interpolated spherical subspace [43] of the GAN generation space on Omniglot and VGG-Face respectively. The only real image (x_i^c) in each figure is the one in the top-left corner, the rest are generated to augment that example using a DAGAN.

$\beta_2 = 0.9$. We used a pretrained DenseNet classifier to quantify the performance of the generated data in terms of how well they classify in real classes. We chose the model that had the best validation accuracy performance on this classifier.

4.2 Classifiers

The primary question of this paper is how well the DAGAN can augment vanilla classifiers trained on each target domain. A DenseNet classifier (as described in Sect. 3.3) was trained first on just real data (with standard data augmentation) with 5 to 100 examples per class (depending on dataset). In the second case, the classifier was also trained on DAGAN generated data. The real or fake label was also passed to the network, via adding 1 filter before each convolution of either zeros (fake) or ones (real) to enable the network to learn how best to emphasise true over generated data. This last step proved crucial to maximizing the potential of the DAGAN augmentations. In each training cycle, varying numbers of augmented samples were provided for each real example (ranging from 1–10). The best hyperparameters were selected via performance on the validation domain. The classifier was trained with standard augmentation: random Gaussian noise was added to images (with 50% probability), random shifts along x and y axis (with 50% probability), and random 90 degree rotations (all with equal probability of being chosen). Classifiers were trained for 200 epochs, with a learning rate of 0.001, and an Adam optimizer with $\beta_1 = 0.9$ and $\beta_2 = 0.99$. The results on the held out test cases from the target domain is given in Table 1. In every case the augmentation improves the classification.

Table 1. Classification Results: All results are averages over 5 independent runs. The DAGAN augmentation improves the classifier performance in all cases. Test accuracy is the result on the test cases in the test domain. Here for the purposes of compactness we omit the *number of generated samples per real sample* hyperparameter since that would produce more than 100 rows of data. We should note however that the optimal number of generated samples per real image was found to be 3.

Samples per class	Augment with DAGAN	Omniglot	EMNIST	VGG-Face
5	False	68.99%	–	04.47%
5	True	**82.13%**	–	**12.59%**
10	False	79.41%	–	–
10	True	**86.22%**	–	–
15	False	81.97%	73.93%	39.33%
15	True	**87.42%**	**76.07%**	**42.93%**
25	False	–	78.35%	57.99%
25	True	–	**80.26%**	**58.46%**
50	False	–	81.51%	–
50	True	–	**82.78%**	–
100	False	–	83.78%	–
100	True	–	**84.80%**	–

5 Conclusions

Data augmentation is a widely applicable approach to improving performance in low-data settings. The DAGAN is a flexible model to automatically learn to augment data. We demonstrate that a DAGAN can improve performance of classifiers even after standard data-augmentation. Furthermore, it is worth noting that a DAGAN can be easily combined with other model types, including few shot learning models. Further work is needed to evaluate the usefulness in the few shot learning. However the flexibility of the DAGAN makes it a powerful means of enhancing models working with a small amount of data.

Acknowledgements. This work was supported in by the EPSRC Centre for Doctoral Training in Data Science, funded by the UK Engineering and Physical Sciences Research Council and the University of Edinburgh as well as by the European Union's Horizon 2020 research and innovation programme under grant agreement No 732204 (Bonseyes) and by the Swiss State Secretariat for Education, Research and Innovation (SERI) under contract number 16.0159. The opinions expressed and arguments employed herein do not necessarily reflect the official views of these funding bodies.

References

1. Arjovsky, M., Chintala, S., Bottou, L.: Wasserstein GAN. arXiv:1701.07875 (2017)
2. Ba, J.L., Kiros, J.R., Hinton, G.E.: Layer normalization. arXiv:1607.06450 (2016)
3. Berthelot, D., Schumm, T., Metz, L.: BEGAN: boundary equilibrium generative adversarial networks. arXiv:1703.10717 (2017)
4. Bloice, M.D., Stocker, C., Holzinger, A.: Augmentor: an image augmentation library for machine learning. arXiv:1708.04680 (2017)
5. Choe, J., Park, S., Kim, K., Park, J.H., Kim, D., Shim, H.: Face generation for low-shot learning using generative adversarial networks. In: 2017 IEEE International Conference on Computer Vision Workshop (ICCVW). IEEE (2017)
6. Clark, C., Storkey, A.: Training deep convolutional networks to play Go. In: Proceedings of 32nd International Conference on Machine Learning (ICML2015) (2015). (arxiv 2014)
7. Deng, J., Dong, W., Socher, R., Li, L.J., Li, K., Fei-Fei, L.: Imagenet: a large-scale hierarchical image database. In: Computer Vision and Pattern Recognition. IEEE (2009)
8. Dixit, M., Kwitt, R., Niethammer, M., Vasconcelos, N.: AGA: attribute-guided augmentation. In: Proceedings of the IEEE Conference on Computer Vision and Pattern Recognition (2017)
9. Fawzi, A., Samulowitz, H., Turaga, D., Frossard, P.: Adaptive data augmentation for image classification. In: 2013 International Conference on Image Processing (ICIP). IEEE (2016)
10. Foerster, J., Assael, Y.M., de Freitas, N., Whiteson, S.: Learning to communicate with deep multi-agent reinforcement learning (2016)
11. Goodfellow, I.J., et al.: Generative adversarial networks, June 2014
12. Gu, J., et al.: Recent advances in convolutional neural networks (2015)
13. Gu, S., Lillicrap, T., Sutskever, I., Levine, S.: Continuous deep q-learning with model-based acceleration. In: International Conference on Machine Learning (2016)
14. Gulrajani, I., Ahmed, F., Arjovsky, M., Dumoulin, V., Courville, A.: Improved training of wasserstein GANs. arXiv:1704.00028 (2017)
15. Hauberg, S., Freifeld, O., Larsen, A.B.L., Fisher, J., Hansen, L.: Dreaming more data: class-dependent distributions over diffeomorphisms for learned data augmentation. In: Artificial Intelligence and Statistics (2016)
16. He, K., Zhang, X., Ren, S., Sun, J.: Deep residual learning for image recognition, December 2015
17. He, K., Zhang, X., Ren, S., Sun, J.: Delving deep into rectifiers: surpassing human-level performance on ImageNet classification (2015)
18. He, K., Zhang, X., Ren, S., Sun, J.: Identity mappings in deep residual networks. In: Leibe, B., Matas, J., Sebe, N., Welling, M. (eds.) ECCV 2016. LNCS, vol. 9908, pp. 630–645. Springer, Cham (2016). https://doi.org/10.1007/978-3-319-46493-0_38
19. Hinton, G., et al.: Deep neural networks for acoustic modeling in speech recognition: the shared views of four research groups. IEEE Sig. Process. Mag. **29**, 82–97 (2012)
20. Hinton, G.E., Srivastava, N., Krizhevsky, A., Sutskever, I., Salakhutdinov, R.R.: Improving neural networks by preventing co-adaptation of feature detectors (2012)
21. Huang, G., Liu, Z., Weinberger, K.Q., van der Maaten, L.: Densely connected convolutional networks. arXiv:1608.06993 (2016)
22. Ioffe, S.: Batch renormalization: towards reducing minibatch dependence in batch-normalized models (2017)

23. Ioffe, S., Szegedy, C.: Batch normalization: accelerating deep network training by reducing internal covariate shift (2015)
24. Isola, P., Zhu, J.Y., Zhou, T., Efros, A.A.: Image-to-image translation with conditional adversarial networks (2016)
25. Krizhevsky, A., Sutskever, I., Hinton, G.E.: Imagenet classification with deep convolutional neural networks. In: Advances in Neural Information Processing Systems (2012)
26. Lake, B.M., Salakhutdinov, R., Tenenbaum, J.B.: Human-level concept learning through probabilistic program induction. Science **350**, 1332–1338 (2015)
27. Mnih, V., et al.: Human-level control through deep reinforcement learning. Nature **518**, 529 (2015)
28. Nowlan, S.J., Hinton, G.E.: Simplifying neural networks by soft weight-sharing. Neural Comput. **4**, 473–493 (1992). https://doi.org/10.1162/neco.1992.4.4.473
29. Radford, A., Metz, L., Chintala, S.: Unsupervised representation learning with deep convolutional generative adversarial networks. In: Proceedings of ICLR 2016 (2015)
30. Ratner, A.J., Ehrenberg, H., Hussain, Z., Dunnmon, J., Ré, C.: Learning to compose domain-specific transformations for data augmentation. In: Advances in Neural Information Processing Systems, vol. 30 (2017)
31. Rosén, B.: Asymptotic theory for order sampling. J. Stat. Plan. Infer. **62**, 135–158 (1997)
32. Salamon, J., Bello, J.P.: Deep convolutional neural networks and data augmentation for environmental sound classification. IEEE Sig. Process. Lett. **24**, 279–283 (2017)
33. Shimodaira, H.: Improving predictive inference under covariate shift by weighting the log-likelihood function. J. Stat. Plan. Infer. **90**, 227–244 (2000)
34. Shrivastava, A., Pfister, T., Tuzel, O., Susskind, J., Wang, W., Webb, R.: Learning from simulated and unsupervised images through adversarial training. In: The IEEE Conference on Computer Vision and Pattern Recognition (CVPR) (2017)
35. Silver, D., et al.: Mastering the game of go with deep neural networks and tree search. Nature **529**, 484 (2016)
36. Storkey, A.: When training and test sets are different: characterising learning transfer. In: Lawrence, C.S.S. (ed.) Dataset Shift in Machine Learning, Chap. 1. MIT Press (2009)
37. Storkey, A., Sugiyama, M.: Mixture regression for covariate shift. In: Advances in Neural Information Processing Systems (NIPS2006), vol. 19 (2007)
38. Sugiyama, M., Müller, K.R.: Input-dependent estimation of generalisation error under covariate shift. Stat. Decis. **23**, 249–279 (2005)
39. Takeki, A., Ikami, D., Irie, G., Aizawa, K.: Parallel grid pooling for data augmentation. arXiv:1803.11370 (2018)
40. Van Hasselt, H., Guez, A., Silver, D.: Deep reinforcement learning with double Q-learning. In: AAAI (2016)
41. Vinyals, O., Blundell, C., Lillicrap, T., Wierstra, D., et al.: Matching networks for one shot learning. In: Advances in Neural Information Processing Systems (2016)
42. Wang, Y., et al.: Tacotron: a fully end-to-end text-to-speech synthesis model. CoRR abs/1703.10135 (2017)
43. White, T.: Sampling generative networks, September 2016
44. Wu, Y., et al.: Google's neural machine translation system: bridging the gap between human and machine translation. arXiv:1609.08144 (2016)
45. Xian, Y., Lorenz, T., Schiele, B., Akata, Z.: Feature generating networks for zero-shot learning. arXiv preprint arXiv:1712.00981 (2017)

DeepEthnic: Multi-label Ethnic Classification from Face Images

Katia Huri[1(✉)], Eli (Omid) David[1], and Nathan S. Netanyahu[1,2]

[1] Department of Computer Science, Bar-Ilan University, 5290002 Ramat-Gan, Israel
katiahuri@gmail.com, mail@elidavid.com, nathan@cs.biu.ac.il
[2] Center for Automation Research, University of Maryland,
College Park, MD 20742, USA
nathan@cfar.umd.edu

Abstract. Ethnic group classification is a well-researched problem, which has been pursued mainly during the past two decades via traditional approaches of image processing and machine learning. In this paper, we propose a method of classifying an image face into an ethnic group by applying *transfer learning* from a previously trained classification network for large-scale data recognition. Our proposed method yields state-of-the-art success rates of 99.02%, 99.76%, 99.2%, and 96.7%, respectively, for the four ethnic groups: African, Asian, Caucasian, and Indian.

1 Introduction

Ethnic classification from facial images has been studied for the past two decades with the purpose of understanding how humans perceive and determine an ethnic group from a given image. The motivation stems, for example, from the fact that (gender and) ethnicity play an important role in face-related applications, such as advertising, social insensitive-based systems, etc. Furthermore, while facial features are subject to change (due to aging, for example), ethnicity is of interest due to its invariance over time.

Recent works on demographic classification are divided conceptually into appearance based methods (using, e.g., eigenface methods, fisherface methods, etc.) and geometry-based methods (relying, e.g., on geometric parameters, such as the distance between the eyes, face width and length, nose thickness, etc.). One of the main challenges of automatic demographic classification is to avoid any "noise", such as illumination, background distortion, and a subject's pose.

In this paper, we introduce a deep learning-based method, that achieves state-of-the-art results for facial image representations and classification for the four ethnic groups: African, Asian, Caucasian, and Indian.

V. Kůrková et al. (Eds.): ICANN 2018, LNCS 11141, pp. 604–612, 2018.
https://doi.org/10.1007/978-3-030-01424-7_59

2 Related Work

2.1 Traditional ML-Based Techniques

During the past two decades, there has been enormous progress on the topic of ethnic group classification, using various classical Machine Learning methods. These approaches are based mainly on feature extraction and training classifiers; see Table 1 below.

Hosoi et al. [6] were among the first to achieve promising results. They employed Gabor wavelet transformations for extracting key facial features, and then applied SVM classification. They reported classification accuracies of 94.3%, 96.3%, and 93.1%, respectively, for the three ethnic groups: African, Asian, and Caucasian.

Table 1. Previous work on ethnic group classification using traditional Machine Learning methods

Authors	Approaches	Databases	Ethnic groups	Success rate
Hosoi et al. [6]	Gabor Wavelet and SVM	1,991 face photos	African, Asian, Caucasian	94.3%, 96.3%, 93.1%
Lu et al. [11]	LDA	Union of DB (2,630 photos of 263 objects)	Asian, non-Asian	96.3% (Avg)
Yang et al. [26]	Real Adaboost (Haar, LBPH)	FERET and PIE (11,680 Asian and 1,016 non-Asian)	Asian, non-Asian	92.1%, 93.2%
Lyle et al. [12]	Perioucular regions, LBP, SVM	FRGC (4,232 faces, 404 objects)	Asian, non-Asian	92% (Avg)
Guo et al. [5]	Biologically inspired features	MORPH-II (10,530 Africans, 10,530 Caucasians)	African, Caucasian	99.1% (Avg)
Xie et al. [25]	Kernal class dependent feature analysis (KCFA)	MBGC DB (10,000 African, 10,000 Asian, 20,000 Caucasian)	African, Asian, Caucasian	97%, 95%, 97%

Lu et al. [11] constructed an *ensemble framework*, which integrates LDA applied to the input face images at different scales. The combination strategy in the ensemble is the product rule [9] to combine the outputs of individual classifiers at these different scales. Their binary classifier of Asian and non-Asian classes obtained success rates of 96.3%, on average.

Yang et al. [26] used LBPH[1] [4] to extract features of texture descriptions, in order to enhance considerably the human detection algorithm that was previously suggested by Xiaoyu et al. [22]. Real AdaBoost was then used iteratively to learn a sequence of best local features to create a strong classifier. Their binary classifier of Asian and non-Asian classes had success rates of 92.1% and 93.2%, respectively.

Lyle et al. [12] extracted ethnicity information from the *periocular region images*[2] using grayscale pixel intensities and periocular texture features computed by LBP. Their binary SVM classifier of Asian and non-Asian classes yields success rates of 93% and 91%, respectively.

Guo et al. [5] proposed using *biologically-inspired features* for ethnic classification, by applying a battery of linear filters to an image and using the filtered images as primary features [8]). Their binary classifier to Africans and Caucasians achieved 99.1% success rate, on average. However, integrating the three ethnic groups: Asian, Hispanic, and Indian, result in a sharp success rate decrease. Specifically, the accuracies recorded were African: 98.3%, Caucasian: 97.1%, Hispanic: 59.5%, Asian: 74.2%, and Indian: 6.9%.

Xie et al. [25] used *kernel class-dependent feature analysis* for generating nonlinear features (by mapping them onto a higher-dimensional feature space which allows higher order correlations [23]) and facial color-based features to classify large-scale face databases. Their classifier achieved success rates of 97%, 95%, and 97%, respectively, for the three ethnic groups: African, Asian, and Caucasian.

To summarize, although some of the surveyed methods yield high classification results, it appears that they are limited to laboratory conditions, i.e., they may not perform as well on a diverse, large-scale database, consisting of face images of different gender, pose, age, illumination conditions, etc. In contrast, we create in this work a diverse face image database for training and testing.

2.2 Recent Deep Learning Techniques

Ethnic group classification has improved significantly in recent years, due to the use of deep learning techniques, e.g., CNN architectures, enhanced feature extraction, etc. (See Table 2 for an overview.)

Ahmed et al. [1] were the first to apply transfer learning for ethnic classification. Their classifier achieved a success rate of 95.4%, on average, for the ethnic groups: Asian, Caucasian and "Other", using the FRGC 2.0 and FERET databases for training data.

Inzamam et al. [2] performed the classification by extracting features from a deep neural network followed by SVM classification on 10 datasets (13,394 images in total, including different variations of the FERET, CASPEAL, and

[1] LBPH is a combination of *local binary pattern* (LBP) with the *histogram of oriented gradients* (HOG) techniques.

[2] A periocular region includes the iris, eyes, eyelids, eye lashes, and part of the eyebrows.

Table 2. DL-based methods for ethnic group classification

Authors	Approach	Databases	Ethnic groups	Success rate
Ahmed et al. [1]	Transfer learning from pseudo tasks (CNN + transfer learning)	FRGC 2.0, FERET	Asian, Caucasian, Other	95.4% (avg.)
Inzamam et al. [2]	Feature extraction due to ANN and SVM classification	10 different DBs	African, Asian, Caucasian	99.66%, 98.28%, 99.05%
Wang et al. [21]	CNN	Variety of DBs	African, Caucasian Chinese, non-Chinese Han, Uyghur, non-Chinese	99.4%, 100%, 99.62%, 99.38% 99% (avg.)

Yale databases). Their classifier achieved success rates of 99.66%, 98.28%, and 99.05%, respectively, for the ethnic groups: African, Asian, and Caucasian.

Wang et al. [21] used deep CNNs to extract features and classify them simultaneously. Three different classifiers were created: (1) The first binary classifier for African and Caucasian classes, achieving success rates of 99.4% and 100%, respectively; (2) a binary classifier for Chinese and non-Chinese classes, achieving success rates of 99.62% and 99.38%, respectively; and (3) a 3-way classifier for Han, Uyghur, and non-Chinese classes, achieving an average success rate of 99%.

3 Proposed Method

3.1 Data Source

As previously indicated, the purpose of this research is to distinguish between the four ethnic groups: African. Asian, Caucasian, and Indian. We created our dataset by combining 10 different databases, originally proposed for the problem of *face recognition*, and then sorting them into the ethnic groups of interest. The databases included IMFDB [16], CNBC [20], Labeled Faces in the Wild (LFW) [7], the Essex face dataset [18], Face Tracer [10], the Yale face database [3], SCUT5000 [24], and additional collected image datasets. We also used the well-known FERET database [14,15], which contains facial images collected under the FERET program, sponsored at the time by the U.S. Department of Defense (DoD).

Altogether, the collected dataset contains images of various sizes.

3.2 Facial Image Preprocessing

As part of preprocessing, the data should be normalized to be compatible with the network's architecture. Also, it is denoised to make it as clean as possible. Thus, we first convert every RGB image to a grayscale one to create a homogeneous dataset of grayscale images.

Note that our collection also contains datasets (such as AT&T and CAS-PEAL) of only grayscale face images. We then use the Face Cascade detector (part of the OpenCV library), to detect and crop the faces. After detecting and cropping the faces, the cropped images are downscaled to 80 × 80 pixels and are denoised using a non-local means denoising algorithm (implemented by the OpenCV function, fastNlMeansDenoising).

Finally, (grayscale) images are duplicated to create an image size of $80 \times 80 \times 3$. This is done to be compatible with the VGG-16 network, which receives three-channel images as input.

After preprocessing, the face images were sorted manually into the four ethnic groups of interest (i.e., African, Asian, Caucasian, and Indian), creating a labeled face database for ethnic group classification. See Fig. 1 for specific face images per each ethnic group.

Fig. 1. Examples of preprocessed face images and their ethnic group labels (from left to right): African, Asian, Caucasian, and Indian.

Since the number of images acquired was rather imbalanced over the four ethnic groups, we perturbed each image in the smaller training samples with a minor Gaussian noise, so as to augment these training samples with slightly different duplicates.

3.3 Transfer Learning

Due to the challenging problems DL has to solve, it takes enormous resources (mostly training time, but also fast computers, training data storage, and human expertise) to train such models.

Transfer learning is an ML technique that helps to overcome those issues by using a model that was trained on a specific task (without any changes to the weights) to solve other tasks.

Yosinski et al. [27] showed that using transfer learning can solve all of these issues and create more efficient and accurate models for solving additional problems. It is important to note that transfer learning only works if the model features learned from the first task are sufficiently generic.

A pretrained model has been previously trained on a dataset and contains the weights and biases that represent the features of the data it has seen during training. The most commonly used pre-trained models are VGG16, VGG19 [17], and Inception V3 [19], due to their high success rate and improvement on the ImageNet dataset classification problem.

VGG16 is a classification model with 16 layers, which is based on the ImageNet dataset and can classify 1,000 different image types (including animals, buildings, and humans). The model's weight file size is 528 MB, and it can be easily accessed for free.

3.4 Network Architecture

Figure 2 shows the original VGG-16 architecture and our modified architecture, which inputs a preprocessed $80 \times 80 \times 3$ image and outputs its predicted ethnic group.

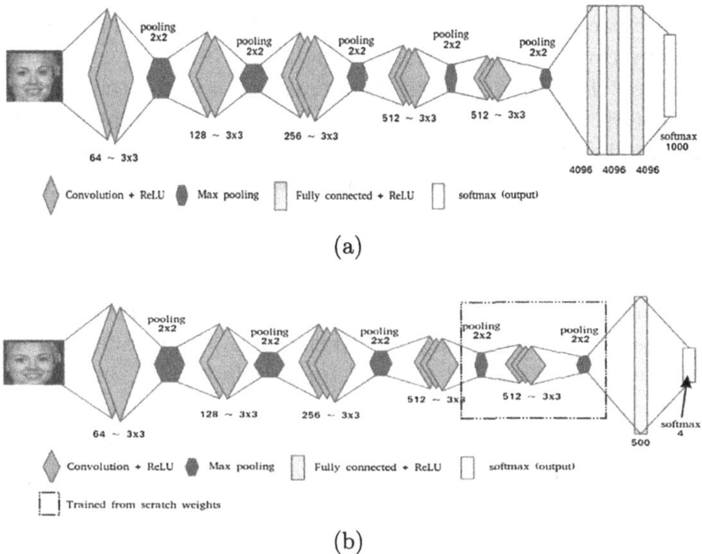

Fig. 2. (a) Original version of VGG-16, and (b) our modified architecture for partial transfer learning from VGG-16.

The modified architecture contains the original, previously trained VGG-16 network, without the final three fully-connected layers and the original softmax layer.

The five layers of the remained network (i.e., max pooling layer, three convolution layers and activation layers, and the final max pooling layer) were selected after experimenting extensively with a large number of possibilities for retraining the entire network. Note that running on the original network "as-is" would have given very poor results. Instead, the idea is to capture universal features (like curves and edges), and further refine these features due to the above modified layers, by retraining the entire network in the context of our problem.

Specifically, the classification softmax layer was replaced by a fully-connected layer of size $n = 500$ and a softmax layer (of size $p = 4$), which outputs a probability distribution for the ethnic group classification.

The output of the softmax layer is the probability distribution for the classification problem. We train the network with the purpose of minimizing the cross-entropy loss function. The network is trained using *stochastic gradient descent* (SGD), as part of the backpropagation phase.

4 Experiments and Results

We present the datasets used in the experiments, and give detailed empirical results of the 10-fold cross validation for the four-class ethnic group classification.

To increase the classification success rate, we first experimented with different network hyper-parameters, e.g., number of epochs, type of activation function, size of the fully-connected layer to add, type of loss function, etc. After running a grid search on the hyper parameters options, we selected the following set of hyper-parameters, which provided the best performance: 50 epochs, a ReLu [13] activation function (an element-wise operation applied per pixel), an additional fully-connected layer of 500 neurons, and a categorical cross-entropy loss function.

We trained and tested the model for each fold, by allocating each time 75%, 10%, and 15% of the data, respectively, to training, validation, and testing.

The training time using TensorFlow and Keras infrastructure on GeForce GTX 1070 was roughly 4.5 h (compared to nearly 11.5 h for training from scratch on the same architecture), and the real-time evaluation of an image is about 10 ms.

We ran a 10-fold cross validation using the selected base model, and obtained classification accuracies of 99.02%, 99.76%, 99.18%, and 96.72%, respectively, for the categories, African, Asian, Caucasian, and Indian. Bottom-line accuracies and loss for the Ethnic classes are summarized in Table 3.

Table 3. Summary of total success rate and loss over entire experiments

African	Asian	Caucasian	Indian	Total success rate	Total loss
99.02%	99.76%	99.18%	96.72%	99.18%	0.03518

5 Conclusions

In this paper we presented a novel approach to the ethnic group classification problem. By modifying a previously trained classification network (namely VGG-16) for transfer learning we achieved state-of-the-art performance with respect to four ethnic classes: African, Asian, Caucasian, and Indian. Specifically, we obtained higher success rate levels for a larger number of classes, while working with a more diverse dataset than previously reported. Also, our derived scheme exhibits faster training time then training from scratch with similar results.

Our future work will focus on extending the number of classes, and improving the robustness of the proposed method to different image conditions, such as different head poses, illumination change, etc.

References

1. Ahmed, A., Yu, K., Xu, W., Gong, Y., Xing, E.: Training hierarchical feed-forward visual recognition models using transfer learning from pseudo-tasks. In: Forsyth, D., Torr, P., Zisserman, A. (eds.) ECCV 2008. LNCS, vol. 5304, pp. 69–82. Springer, Heidelberg (2008). https://doi.org/10.1007/978-3-540-88690-7_6
2. Anwar, I., Islam, N.U.: Learned features are better for ethnicity classification. CoRR 1709.07429 (2017)
3. Belhumeur, P.N., Hespanha, J.P., Kriegman, D.J.: Eigenfaces vs. fisherfaces: recognition using class specific linear projection. IEEE Trans. Pattern Anal. Mach. Intell. **19**(7), 711–720 (1997)
4. Dalal, N., Triggs, B.: Histograms of oriented gradients for human detection. In: IEEE Computer Society Conference on Computer Vision and Pattern Recognition (CVPR), vol. 1, pp. 886–893 (2005)
5. Guo, G., Mu, G.: A study of large-scale ethnicity estimation with gender and age variations. In: IEEE Computer Society Conference on Computer Vision and Pattern Recognition - Workshops, pp. 79–86 (2010)
6. Hosoi, S., Takikawa, E., Kawade, M.: Ethnicity estimation with facial images. In: 6th IEEE International Conference on Automatic Face and Gesture Recognition, pp. 195–200 (2004)
7. Huang, G.B., Mattar, M., Berg, T., Learned-Miller, E.: Labeled faces in the wild: a database for studying face recognition in unconstrained environments. In: Workshop on Faces in 'Real-Life' Images: Detection, Alignment, and Recognition (2008). https://hal.inria.fr/inria-00321923
8. Jarrett, K., Kavukcuoglu, K., Ranzato, M., LeCun, Y.: What is the best multi-stage architecture for object recognition? In: 12th IEEE International Conference on Computer Vision, pp. 2146–2153 (2009)
9. Kittler, J., Hatef, M., Duin, R.P.W., Matas, J.: On combining classifiers. IEEE Trans. Pattern Anal. Mach. Intell. **20**(3), 226–239 (1998)
10. Kumar, N., Belhumeur, P., Nayar, S.: FaceTracer: a search engine for large collections of images with faces. In: Forsyth, D., Torr, P., Zisserman, A. (eds.) ECCV 2008. LNCS, vol. 5305, pp. 340–353. Springer, Heidelberg (2008). https://doi.org/10.1007/978-3-540-88693-8_25
11. Lu, X., Jain, A.K.: Ethnicity identification from face images. In: SPIE, vol. 5404 (2004)
12. Lyle, J.R., Miller, P.E., Pundlik, S.J., Woodard, D.L.: Soft biometric classification using periocular region features. In: 4th IEEE International Conference on Biometrics: Theory, Applications and Systems-BTAS, pp. 1–7 (2010)
13. Nair, V., Hinton, G.E.: Rectified linear units improve restricted boltzmann machines. In: Proceedings of ICML, vol. 27, pp. 807–814 (2010)

14. Phillips, P.J., Moon, H., Rauss, P., Rizvi, S.A.: The FERET evaluation methodology for face-recognition algorithms. In: Proceedings of IEEE Computer Society Conference on Computer Vision and Pattern Recognition, pp. 137–143 (1997)
15. Phillips, P.J., Wechsler, H., Huang, J., Rauss, P.J.: The FERET database and evaluation procedure for face-recognition algorithms. Image Vis. Comput. **16**(5), 295–306 (1998). http://www.sciencedirect.com/science/article/pii/S026288569700070X
16. Setty, S., et al.: Indian movie face database: a benchmark for face recognition under wide variations. In: 4th National Conference on Computer Vision, Pattern Recognition, Image Processing and Graphics - NCVPRIPG, pp. 1–5 (2013)
17. Simonyan, K., Zisserman, A.: Very deep convolutional networks for large-scale image recognition. CoRR 1409.1556 (2014)
18. Spacek, L.: University of Essex Collection of Facial Images (1996). http://cswww.essex.ac.uk/mv/allfaces/index.html
19. Szegedy, C., Vanhoucke, V., Ioffe, S., Shlens, J., Wojna, Z.: Rethinking the inception architecture for computer vision. CoRR 1512.00567 (2015)
20. Tarr, M.J.: CNBC - stimulus image. In: Center for the Neural Basis of Cognition and Department of Psychology. Carnegie Mellon University. Funding provided by NSF award 0339122. http://www.tarrlab.org/
21. Wang, W., He, F., Zhao, Q.: Facial ethnicity classification with deep convolutional neural networks. In: You, Z., et al. (eds.) CCBR 2016. LNCS, vol. 9967, pp. 176–185. Springer, Cham (2016). https://doi.org/10.1007/978-3-319-46654-5_20
22. Wang, X., Han, T.X., Yan, S.: An HOG-LBP human detector with partial occlusion handling. In: 12th IEEE International Conference on Computer Vision, pp. 32–39 (2009)
23. Xie, C., Savvides, M., VijayaKumar, B.V.K.: Kernel correlation filter based redundant class-dependence feature analysis (KCFA) on FRGC2.0 data. In: Zhao, W., Gong, S., Tang, X. (eds.) AMFG 2005. LNCS, vol. 3723, pp. 32–43. Springer, Heidelberg (2005). https://doi.org/10.1007/11564386_4
24. Xie, D., Liang, L., Jin, L., Xu, J., Li, M.: SCUT-FBP: a benchmark dataset for facial beauty perception. In: IEEE International Conference on Systems, Man, and Cybernetics, pp. 1821–1826 (2015)
25. Xie, Y., Luu, K., Savvides, M.: A robust approach to facial ethnicity classification on large scale face databases. In: 5th IEEE International Conference on Biometrics: Theory, Applications and Systems (BTAS), pp. 143–149 (2012)
26. Yang, Z., Ai, H.: Demographic classification with local binary patterns. In: Lee, S.-W., Li, S.Z. (eds.) ICB 2007. LNCS, vol. 4642, pp. 464–473. Springer, Heidelberg (2007). https://doi.org/10.1007/978-3-540-74549-5_49
27. Yosinski, J., Clune, J., Bengio, Y., Lipson, H.: How transferable are features in deep neural networks? CoRR (2014)

Handwriting-Based Gender Classification Using End-to-End Deep Neural Networks

Evyatar Illouz[1], Eli (Omid) David[1(✉)], and Nathan S. Netanyahu[1,2]

[1] Department of Computer Science, Bar-Ilan University, 52900 Ramat-Gan, Israel
iluz101@gmail.com, mail@elidavid.com, nathan@cs.biu.ac.il
[2] Center for Automation Research, University of Maryland,
College Park, MD 20742, USA
nathan@cfar.umd.edu

Abstract. Handwriting-based gender classification is a well-researched problem that has been approached mainly by traditional machine learning techniques. In this paper, we propose a novel deep learning-based approach for this task. Specifically, we present a *convolutional neural network* (CNN), which performs automatic feature extraction from a given handwritten image, followed by classification of the writer's gender. Also, we introduce a new dataset of labeled handwritten samples, in Hebrew and English, of 405 participants. Comparing the gender classification accuracy on this dataset against human examiners, our results show that the proposed deep learning-based approach is substantially more accurate than that of humans.

Keywords: Gender classification · Offline handwriting
HEBIU handwriting dataset · Deep neural network
Convolutional neural network

1 Introduction

Gender classification by handwriting is a well-studied problem, assuming that one's gender can be predicted based on their handwriting. Although there has been a considerable amount of research on this subject, it is still considered a challenging problem. In fact, neither computerized analysis nor humans, have achieved highly-accurate results for this task, as of yet.

The common assumption is that various demographic properties can be learned by studying the discriminative features of a person's handwriting, e.g., gender, handedness (i.e., whether the person is left-/right-handed), age bracket, ethnicity, etc. Indeed, human handwriting is used to examine and investigate human characteristics in a variety of applications, such as mail sorting [6], bank check verification [5,6], personality profiling [12,19], historical document analysis [1], and criminological/forensic investigations [6,7].

Most of the recent approaches to gender classification by handwriting have evolved mainly around the same few datasets, i.e., the training and testing of

V. Kůrková et al. (Eds.): ICANN 2018, LNCS 11141, pp. 613–621, 2018.
https://doi.org/10.1007/978-3-030-01424-7_60

these methods have been confined typically to a handful of datasets, such as the IAM on-line [15], QUWI [3], KHATT [14], and MSHD [9] datasets. The motivation in this paper is mainly twofold: (1) Propose an improved gender classification method, and (2) augment the current pool of handwriting datasets in a significant manner. Specifically, we propose a new *convolutional neural network* (CNN) variant for the gender classification task, which is relatively simple, efficient, and accurate. Also, we present a fairly large and diverse dataset, the *Hebrew-English Bar-Ilan University* (HEBIU) offline handwriting dataset, which consists of 810 Hebrew and English handwriting samples, collected from a group of 405 participants. The newly-generated dataset would allow for extended research and comparative studies, regarding the classification of various attributes of interest. Our results are comparable to those reported by previous methods, and they are substantially better than the accuracy rates obtained by human examiners on our HEBIU dataset.

2 Related Work

Several machine learning techniques have been applied during the past two decades to the handwriting gender classification task. These approaches are based typically on feature extraction and training classifier; see Table 1 below (extended from Gattal et al. [10]), for an overview.

Cha et al. [8] trained an *artificial neural network* (ANN) in order to classify demographic sub-categories (such as gender, handedness, and age group) by using their own uppercase letter dataset. Later, they extended their work [5] to train a feed-forward neural network for feature extraction and classification, using enhancement techniques as bagging and boosting. Their improved gender classifier achieved an accuracy rate of 77.5% using 800 writing samples for training and 400 samples for testing.

Liwicki et al. [13] applied *support vector machines* (SVM) and *Gaussian mixture models* (GMM) to gender classification on the IAM-OnDB handwriting dataset. Their classifier achieved accuracy rates of 62% and 67%, respectively, using SVM and GMM.

Youssef et al. [21] proposed using *wavelet domain local binary patterns* (WD-LBP) to train several SVM classifiers on both English and Arabic handwritings. Their classifier achieved an accuracy rate of 74.3% on (a subset of) the QUWI dataset.

Al-Maadeed et al. [4] proposed using geometric features to classify age, gender, and nationality. Their proposed method applies *random forests* and *kernel discriminant analysis* for both *text-dependent* and *text-independent* classifications (i.e., same/different texts, respectively, of different writers are used for training and testing). Their classifier achieved an overall accuracy of 73% on the QUWI dataset.

Bouadjenek et al. [6] proposed extracting local descriptors, such as *histogram of oriented gradients* (HoG), *local binary patterns* (LBP), and grid features for offline handwriting, and then classifying them by SVM. Their method achieved

Table 1. Overview of handwriting gender classification techniques.

Research	Features	Classifier	Dataset	Accuracy
Cha et al. [8]	A set of macro and micro features	ANN	CEDAR [11]	70.20%
Liwicki et al. [13]	Combination of online & offline features	GMM	IAM-OnDB [15]	65.57%
Youssef et al. [21]	Gradient & WD-LBP	SVM	QUWI [3]	74.30%
Al-Maadeed et al. [4]	Geometric	Random forests	QUWI [3]	73%
Bouadjenek et al. [6]	HoG & LBP	SVM	IAM-OnDB [15]	74%
Siddiqi et al. [20]	Orientation curvature & legibility	SVM	QUWI [3] & MSHD [9]	68.75%/73.02%
Mirza et al. [16]	Gabor filters & Fourier transform	ANN	QUWI [3]	70%
Akbari et al. [2]	Wavelet sub-hands	SVM/ANN	QUWI [3] & MSHD [9]	80%
Ahmed et al. [1]	Textural	Ensemble of classifiers	QUWI [3]	79%–85%
Gattal et al. [10]	Oriented basic image features	SVM	QUWI [3]	68%–76%
Morera et al. [17]	Word separation	CNN	IAM [15] & KHATT [14]	80.72%/68.9%

an accuracy rate of 74% on the IAM offline dataset. Likewise, Bouadjenek et al. [7] used local descriptors, such as *gradient local binary patterns* (GLBP) and HoG to train an SVM classifier to predict age, gender, and handedness. Their classifier achieved accuracy rates in the range of 69%–74% on the IAM-OnDB and KHATT datasets.

Similarly, Siddiqi et al. [20] enhanced handwriting features by computing local and global features (e.g., inclination, texture, curvature, legibility, etc.), which are then used in ANN and SVM classifiers to distinguish between genders. Their classifier achieved accuracy rates of 68.75% and 73.02%, respectively, on the QUWI and MSHD datasets.

Mirza et al. [16] concentrated on the visual appearance of handwriting to investigate its effect on a writer's gender. They extract textural information by applying a bank of *Gabor filters* to handwriting images from the QUWI dataset. They then use the mean and standard deviation of each handwriting plus its Fourier transform as input features for a feed-forward neural network. Their classifier achieved an accuracy rate of 70% on the QUWI dataset.

Akbari et al. [2] extracted a feature vector based on a series of wavelet sub-bands quantized to produce a *probabilistic finite state automaton.* This feature vector is then used to train ANN and SVM classifiers on the QUWI and MSHD datasets, and perform text-dependent and text-independent, as well as *script-dependent* and *script-independent* classifications (i.e., same/different languages, respectively, used for training and testing). They also introduced cross-database evaluations.

To enhance accuracy rates on the gender task, Ahmed et al. [1] used bagging, voting, and stacking of various classifiers based on some of the textural features mentioned earlier. They achieved accuracy rates in the range of 79%–85% on (a subset of) the QUWI dataset.

Gattal et al. [10] proposed using textural information from handwriting as the discriminative attribute between genders. They used image binarization and *oriented basic image features.* Their classifier achieved accuracy rates of 71%, 76%, and 68% on the QUWI dataset, according to the protocols of ICDAR 2013, ICDAR 2015, and ICFHR 2016, respectively.

Finally, Morera et al. [17] were the first to apply a deep CNN for classifying a writer's demographics. They proposed the same architecture for both gender and handedness, as well as an architecture for the combined 4-class problem. Their gender classifier achieved accuracy rates of 80.72% and 68.9%, respectively, on the IAM-OnDB and KHATT datasets.

To summarize, most of the surveyed methods exploit knowledge about the domain to extract certain features from the above datasets, and then train a machine learning module to classify these extracted features. In contrast, we present in this work a deep learning module, which performs essentially *automated* feature extraction and classification, in a rather simple and efficient manner (requires no tedious preprocessing, and is far less complex than the system reported, e.g., by Morera et al. [17]).

3 Proposed Method

3.1 The HEBIU Offline Handwriting Dataset

Our newly generated dataset, the Hebrew-English Bar-Ilan University (HEBIU) offline handwriting dataset, contains 810 Hebrew and English handwriting samples of 405 participants from Israel. Each participant received a standard form, and was asked to write certain texts in Hebrew and English without any writing restrictions (e.g., pen type, pressure, etc.). In addition, each contributer was asked to provide personal data, such as gender, age, height, handedness, native language, country of birth, religion, education level, and profession.

Each such form was scanned by a 300dpi HP OfficeJet Pro 8710, in color mode and JPEG format, at a high resolution of 2480 × 3504.

The added value of our newly presented HEBIU dataset lies in the fact that it contains (also) hundreds of labeled writing samples in Hebrew, as well as diverse personal information per each participant. Thus, additional tasks, such as writer identification/verification and the classification of various demographic characteristics from handwriting samples, can be further pursued with such data.

3.2 Handwriting Preprocessing

As previously mentioned, our HEBIU dataset contains 810 Hebrew and English handwriting samples of 214 males and 191 females (i.e., of a total of 405 participants). Thus, to keep the data balanced, we excluded from the dataset, as part of preprocessing, 23 of the male forms.

In addition, the data should be normalized to be compatible with the network's architecture. Therefore, the first step was to extract a portion of the page which contains handwritten text, and convert it to a grayscale image. Afterwards, in order to enhance our data, we generated N random patches for each form, of size $K \times M$, with (possible) overlaps between patches. A patch can be either a square or a rectangle. A square patch is meant to extract a whole subsection of words, while a rectangular patch is used to extract a line of text (or part of it), a single word, a writing sequence, etc. Both cases are illustrated in Fig. 1.

Having experimented extensively with the number of patches, as well as patch types and patch sizes, we converged eventually on $N = 200$ patches per handwritten sample and squared patches of size 400×400 pixels (i.e., $K = M = 400$). To keep the computational effort feasible, the patches were downscaled by 75% to 100×100 pixels. (Similarly, the originally extracted rectangular patches of size 150×500 were downscaled to 30×100.)

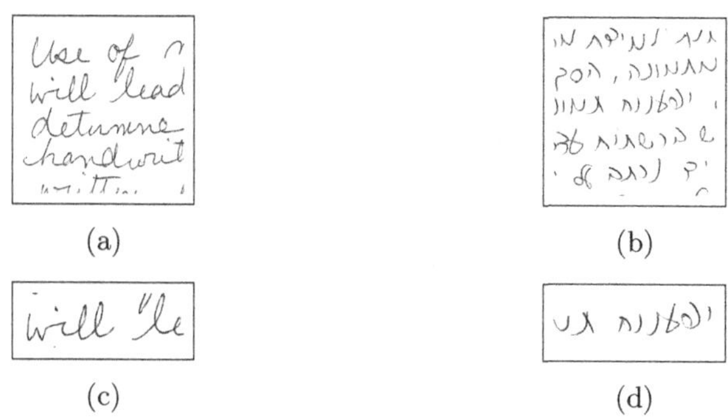

Fig. 1. Examples of resized text patches: (a) + (b) 100×100 English and Hebrew squared patches, and (c) + (d) 30×100 English and Hebrew rectangular patches.

Naturally, some of the generated patches were blank or contained small amounts of data. To overcome the selection of sparse text patches, we conducted a series of experiments to determine a threshold, based on a minimum ratio between black pixels and the total amount of pixels in a given patch. This was then used to select patches which contained a sufficient amount of data. Note that eventually we extracted 200 valid patches per each form.

3.3 Network Architecture

Our proposed network architecture is a CNN variant which inputs a grayscale, 100×100 patch and outputs the gender prediction. It is comprised of a total of four convolutional layers, followed by a single fully-connected layer and a softmax output layer, where all of the filters used are of size 3×3. More precisely, the first two layers consist of 64 and 128 filters, respectively, followed by a max pooling layer of 2×2 with a dropout of 0.4. The next two layers have the same structure, followed by a 2×2 max pooling layer with a dropout of 0.6. Finally, a fully-connected layer with 128 neurons was added with a dropout of 0.5. The following network's hyper-parameters were picked: 20 epochs, a *rectified linear unit* (ReLu) activation function [18], an *Adadelta* optimizer, and a binary cross entropy loss function.

3.4 Accuracy Evaluation by Patch Aggregation

We considered the following two classification measures, for a given handwriting sample:

1. *Majority vote*: The gender class is determined based on the majority of classified patches, where the classification of each patch depends on whether the corresponding softmax value exceeds 0.5.
2. *Average softmax*: The form is classified according to the average softmax value over the form's 200 patches.

4 Experimental Results

We divided the gender classification problem, in the context of this work, into three main types: (1) *Intra-language* classification, where training and testing are conducted on the same language, (2) *inter-language* classification, where training is conducted on one language and testing on the other, and (3) *mixed language* classification, where both training and testing are conducted on both languages. For each type, we ran a 10-fold cross validation as follows. A fixed 20% of the data (i.e., the same 76 forms) were set aside for testing, and 70% (i.e., 268 forms) and 10% (i.e., 38 forms) of the data, respectively, were allocated at random (from the remaining 80%) for training and validation.

4.1 Intra-language Classification

Regarding intra-language classification, we obtained average accuracy rates of 73.02% and 75.26%, respectively, in the case of Hebrew-Hebrew (i.e., training and testing performed on Hebrew texts) and English-English (i.e., both training and testing done on English texts).

4.2 Inter-language Classification

For inter-language classification, we achieved accuracy rates of 75.65% and 58.29%, respectively, in the case of Hebrew-English classification (i.e., training on a Hebrew handwriting and testing on an English one) and English-Hebrew classification (i.e., training on an English handwriting and testing on a Hebrew one).

One attempt to explain this anomaly might be that since English is a second natural language in Israel (after Hebrew), the discriminative features between gender handwritings are less prominent (than in Hebrew), so generalizing becomes more challenging.

4.3 Mixed Language Classification

Enhancing our data by combining the texts of both languages yields an overall test accuracy of 77% for both languages; in particular, 74.61% and 79.34% accuracy rates when tested on Hebrew and English texts, respectively.

4.4 Summary of Results

Table 2 summarizes the results, providing average accuracy rates and standard deviations for each method.

Table 2. Accuracy for gender classification types with 10-fold cross-validation ("HE" stands for Hebrew, and "EN" stands for English).

Experiment	Train	Test	Accuracy method	Avg	Std Dev	Min accuracy	Max accuracy
Intra-language	HE	HE	Majority vote	73.02%	2.42	67.10%	75.00%
			Avg. softmax	72.89%	2.34	67.10%	75.00%
	EN	EN	Majority vote	74.47%	2.65	69.74%	77.63%
			Avg. softmax	75.26%	2.47	71.05%	77.63%
Inter-language	HE	EN	Majority vote	75.52%	6.86	60.52%	82.89%
			Avg. softmax	75.65%	7.40	57.89%	82.89%
	EN	HE	Majority vote	58.29%	5.89	48.68%	65.79%
			Avg. softmax	58.29%	6.20	48.68%	68.42%
Mixed-language	HE+EN	HE	Majority vote	74.61%	2.06	72.37%	77.63%
			Avg. softmax	73.82%	2.36	68.42%	76.32%
	HE+EN	EN	Majority vote	79.34%	3.29	73.68%	82.89%
			Avg. softmax	79.21%	3.15	73.68%	81.58%
	HE+EN	HE+EN	Majority vote	75.13%	2.52	71.05%	78.95%
			Avg. softmax	75.13%	2.10	71.05%	77.63%

4.5 Human Test Results

In order to compare our results with those of human examiners, we developed a mobile application that tests the accuracy of humans on the same task. The application was distributed among 153 females and 147 males; each of the 300 participants received 15 Hebrew handwritings and 15 English handwritings chosen at random (from our HEBIU dataset), and was asked to predict the writer's gender of each examined text. The average classification accuracy for English and Hebrew handwritings were 63.6% and 66.2%, respectively (both with a standard deviation of 0.13). Females achieved slightly better results than males in both cases. Specifically, they obtained an accuracy of 64.8% (vs. 62.2%) for English, and an accuracy of 67.4% (vs. 65%) for Hebrew. No correlations between the accuracy and either age group or education level were observed.

5 Concluding Remarks

In this paper, we proposed an automatic deep learning scheme for binary gender classification from handwriting images. Specifically, we presented a CNN variant for this task without "manual" feature selection/extraction. Our module is relatively simple, yet efficient, in terms of training speed and running time. We considered seven cross-language cases, including training on a Semitic language (Hebrew) and validation on a non-Semitic one (English), and vice versa. Our classification results are comparable to those of previous methods, and are significantly better than those obtained by human examiners on the same dataset.

In addition, we presented a new offline handwriting dataset (the HEBIU dataset), which contains hundreds of labeled handwriting samples in both Hebrew and English, including diverse demographic information.

Our future work will focus on predicting additional attributes of a given writer, e.g., handedness, age group, whether the text is written in the subject's mother tongue, etc. In addition, we plan to apply our approach to other existing handwriting datasets and aim to enlarge our dataset by collecting more handwriting samples, possibly in additional languages.

References

1. Ahmed, M., Rasool, A.G., Afzal, H., Siddiqi, I.: Improving handwriting based gender classification using ensemble classifiers. Expert Syst. Appl. **85**, 158–168 (2017)
2. Akbari, Y., Nouri, K., Sadri, J., Djeddi, C., Siddiqi, I.: Wavelet-based gender detection on off-line handwritten documents using probabilistic finite state automata. Image Vis. Comput. **59**, 17–30 (2017)
3. Al Maadeed, S., Ayouby, W., Hassaïne, A., Aljaam, J.M.: QUWI: An Arabic and English handwriting dataset for offline writer identification. In: International Conference on Frontiers in Handwriting Recognition, pp. 746–751. IEEE (2012)
4. Al Maadeed, S., Hassaine, A.: Automatic prediction of age, gender, and nationality in offline handwriting. EURASIP J. Image Video Process. **2014**(1), 10 (2014)

5. Bandi, K.R., Srihari, S.N.: Writer demographic classification using bagging and boosting. In: Proceedings of the 12th International Graphonomics Society Conference, pp. 133–137 (2005)
6. Bouadjenek, N., Nemmour, H., Chibani, Y.: Local descriptors to improve off-line handwriting-based gender prediction. In: 6th International Conference of Soft Computing and Pattern Recognition, pp. 43–47. IEEE (2014)
7. Bouadjenek, N., Nemmour, H., Chibani, Y.: Age, gender and handedness prediction from handwriting using gradient features. In: 13th International Conference on Document Analysis and Recognition, pp. 1116–1120. IEEE (2015)
8. Cha, S.H., Srihari, S.N.: A priori algorithm for sub-category classification analysis of handwriting. In: Proceedings of the Sixth International Conference on Document Analysis and Recognition, pp. 1022–1025. IEEE (2001)
9. Djeddi, C., Gattal, A., Souici-Meslati, L., Siddiqi, I., Chibani, Y., El Abed, H.: LAMIS-MSHD: a multi-script offline handwriting database. In: 14th International Conference on Frontiers in Handwriting Recognition, pp. 93–97. IEEE (2014)
10. Gattal, A., Djeddi, C., Siddiqi, I., Chibani, Y.: Gender classification from offline multi-script handwriting images using oriented basic iimage features. Expert Syst. Appl. **99**, 155–167 (2018)
11. Hull, J.J.: A database for handwritten text recognition research. IEEE Trans. Pattern Anal. Mach. Intell. **16**(5), 550–554 (1994)
12. King, R.N., Koehler, D.J.: Illusory correlations in graphological inference. J. Exp. Psychol. Appl. **6**(4), 336 (2000)
13. Liwicki, M., Schlapbach, A., Loretan, P., Bunke, H.: Automatic detection of gender and handedness from on-line handwriting. In: Proceedings of the 13th Conference of the Graphonomics Society, pp. 179–183 (2007)
14. Mahmoud, S.A., et al.: KHATT: an open arabic offline handwritten text database. Pattern Recogn. **47**(3), 1096–1112 (2014)
15. Marti, U., Bunke, H.: The IAM-database: an English sentence database for off-line handwriting recognition. Int. J. Doc. Anal. Recogn. **5**, 39–46 (2002)
16. Mirza, A., Moetesum, M., Siddiqi, I., Djeddi, C.: Gender classification from offline handwriting images using textural features. In: 15th International Conference on Frontiers in Handwriting Recognition (ICFHR), pp. 395–398. IEEE (2016)
17. Morera, Á., Sánchez, Á., Vélez, J.F., Moreno, A.B.: Gender and handedness prediction from offline handwriting using convolutional neural networks. Complexity (2018). https://www.hindawi.com/journals/complexity/2018/3891624/
18. Nair, V., Hinton, G.E.: Rectified linear units improve restricted Boltzmann machines. In: Proceedings of the 27th International Conference on Machine Learning, pp. 807–814 (2010)
19. Shackleton, V., Newell, S.: European management selection methods: a comparison of five countries. Int. J. Sel. Assess. **2**(2), 91–102 (1994)
20. Siddiqi, I., Djeddi, C., Raza, A., Souici-Meslati, L.: Automatic analysis of handwriting for gender classification. Pattern Anal. Appl. **18**(4), 887–899 (2015)
21. Youssef, A.E., Ibrahim, A.S., Abbott, A.L.: Automated gender identification for Arabic and English handwriting (2013)

A Deep Learning Approach for Sentiment Analysis in Spanish Tweets

Gerson Vizcarra[1(✉)], Antoni Mauricio[1], and Leonidas Mauricio[2]

[1] Research and Innovation Center in Computer Science, Universidad Católica San Pablo, Arequipa, Peru
{gerson.vizcarra,manasses.mauricio}@ucsp.edu.pe

[2] Department of Mechanical Engineering, Artificial Intelligence, Image Processing and Robotic Lab, Universidad Nacional de Ingeniería, Bldg. A - Off. A1-221, 210 Tupac Amaru Ave., Lima, Peru
lmauricioc@uni.pe

Abstract. Sentiment Analysis at Document Level is a well-known problem in Natural Language Processing (NLP), being considered as a reference in NLP, over which new architectures and models are tested in order to compare metrics that are also referents in other issues. This problem has been solved in good enough terms for English language, but its metrics are still quite low in other languages. In addition, architectures which are successful in a language do not necessarily works in another. In the case of Spanish, data quantity and quality become a problem during data preparation and architecture design, due to the few labeled data available including not-textual elements (like emoticons or expressions).

This work presents an approach to solve the sentiment analysis problem in Spanish tweets and compares it with the state of art. To do so, a preprocessing algorithm is performed based on interpretation of colloquial expressions and emoticons, and trivial words elimination. Processed sentences turn into matrices using the 3 most successful methods of word embeddings (GloVe, FastText and Word2Vec), then the 3 matrices merge into a 3-channels matrix which is used to feed our CNN-based model. The proposed architecture uses parallel convolution layers as k-grams, by this way the value of each word and their contexts are weighted, to predict the sentiment polarity among 4 possible classes. After several tests, the optimal tuple which improves the accuracy were <1, 2>. Finally, our model presents %61.58 and %71.14 of accuracy in InterTASS and General Corpus respectively.

Keywords: Convolutional neural network (CNN) · Sentiment analysis Spanish tweets

The present work was supported by grant 234-2015-FONDECYT (Master Program) from Cienciactiva of the National Council for Science, Technology and Technological Innovation (CONCYTEC-PERU) and the Office Research of Universidad Nacional de Ingeniería (VRI - UNI).

V. Kůrková et al. (Eds.): ICANN 2018, LNCS 11141, pp. 622–629, 2018.
https://doi.org/10.1007/978-3-030-01424-7_61

1 Introduction

Semantic analysis has opened up several fields of research in NLP. In turn, these new fields have helped the development of comprehension systems, which include, as is explained in [1], cross- and multi-domain sentiment analysis, aspect-based sentiment analysis, fake news identification, classification of semantic relations, question answering of non-factoid questions among others. Liu [9] defines sentiment analysis or opinion mining as the computational study of people's opinions, sentiments, emotions, appraisals, and attitudes towards entities such as products, services, organizations, individuals, events, topics, and their attributes.

In sentiment analysis tasks, tweets analysis at document level is highlighted and long addressed one due to the large amounts of information about multiple topics generated in short time and its easy access (unlabeled data). Specific tasks linked to this problem has raised the interest of NLP community for several years [16]. The automatic sentiment detection in tweets is a powerful and useful tool for social networks analysis or advertising analysis and many other applications.

In this paper, we propose a CNN-based model that automatically processes short texts obtained from task 1 proposed in TASS 2017 [1] using tweets in Spanish and detects if a tweet expresses any polarity (positive, negative, neutral or none) about an specific topic. The next sections will be as follows. Section 2, covers related works in the area. Section 3, exposes our proposals (preprocessing method and architecture design) in detail. Section 4, includes final results and their analysis, and Sect. 5 presents our conclusions and future works.

2 Related Studies

Pang et al. [13] and Liu [8] provided an introduction to Sentiment Analysis area. Zhang et al. [20] have published a very complete state of art in Sentiment Analysis using deep learning approaches. They explained that sentiment analysis could be represented as a classification problem (classifying a text document on a bunch of predefined categories) and therefore addressed with different methods, Zhang et al. also mentions that black-box models such as neuronal networks and deep neuronal networks have become increasingly popular. About short texts analysis there are many papers which shows relevant results in real life applications using tweets in different languages.

Rodrigues Barbosa et al. [15] evaluates Twitter hashtags in sentiment analysis for Brazilian presidential elections in 2010. To do so, they analyzed 10,173,382 tweets labeled in 4 labels: Positive, Negative, Ambiguous and Neutral, for hashtags about candidates or events around the election day. They finally conclude that trends in Twitter over time were in accordance with the general feeling of the population. They also verified that information spreads on Twitter following a social graph model and people make their decisions consciously or not, depending on the feelings and choices of their contacts in Twitter.

Go et al. [3] introduced a method to classify Twitter messages. Positive and negative tweets are separated using emoticons labels: ":) /:-)" or ":(/:-(.". They collected 80,000 positive and 80,000 negative tweets as a training set. In preprocessing step, emoticons were removed on training process because the negative impact on precisions on the SVM and Maximum Entropy (ME) classifiers, but has insignificant effects on Naive-Bayes based classifier. Then, they segmented sentences by unigrams (word by word), bigrams (two words), unigram-bigram, and the Speech features extracted by well-known descriptors. Their results in accuracy using SVM and unigrams were 82.9%, while using unigram-bigram in ME and Naive-Bayes were 82.7%, being considered in both cases the best results for each method.

Kin [7] and Wang et al. [19] presented respectively their attempts to use convolutional (CNN) and recursive (RNN) neural networks for polarity classification in short texts, achieving quite inspiring results that define standard architectures to solve the problem. CNN architecture allows to get a fast convergence and presents, in most of cases, a remarkable performance on sentence classification. By other hand, RNN usually converges slow but it can interpret sequences of words better, that is more useful applied to text due to it could capture the context in a sentence. Lost memory or vanishing gradient is a problem for RNN. So a residual network or recurrent Long-Short Term Memory network (LSTM) [19] is capable of capturing the special functions of words avoiding lost memory problem.

In sentiment analysis of tweets at document level, Hassan et al. [5] pro- posed to merge CNN and LSTM-RNN models for shorts texts due LSTM avoid vanishing gradient problem but depending on the text size while CNN works better for very short texts, which are normally the tweets size. For IMDB opinions database, they achieved 88.3% using a single word embedding channel in binary classification. While Severyn et al. [17] explored CNN solutions using Twitter database, getting 84.79% in accuracy for phases and 64.59% in message level.

As can be seen most of works come from English datasets. In Spanish there are few works which define the state of art on TASS datasets. Navas-Loro et al. [12], and Martínez-Cámara et al. [10] resume most of works and methods developed during TASS 2017 competition. In TASS 2017, best results were obtained by neural network models. Hurtado Oliver et al. [6] obtained 60.70% in accuracy InterTASS corpus and 72.50% in General Corpus using a fully connected neural network with ReLU functions, dropout layer (p = 0.3) and polarity-specific embeddings.

3 The Problem and Data Description

Sentiment analysis task can be summarized as multi-class classification problem, considering the polarities as classes (none, neutral, positive or negative attitude expressed in a tweet). We have used the TASS 2017 database [1] in our experiments. This database was employed in the 'Workshop on Semantic Analysis' during the International Conference of the Spanish Society for Natural Language Processing (SEPLN). The competition goal were to classify four types of tweets polarities in task 1, which are: N - negative; P - positive; NEU - neutral and NONE - none classified. Training data is composed as follows: InterTASS (1008 tweets), General TASS (7219 tweets) and InterTASS development corpus (506 tweets), while testing data contains InterTASS test (1899 tweets) and General-TASS test (60798 tweets).

4 Methodology

In this section, we present the pre-processing methodology realized and the architecture designed.

4.1 Preprocessing

Based on Severyn et al. [17] and Navas-Loro and Rodríguez-Doncel [12], we create a tokenizer to handle trivial terms and repeated words following this steps:

- Delete URLs, extra blank spaces, special characters and repeated words.
- Change words to lowercase.
- Replace laugh expressions (like 'jajaja', 'haha', 'LOL', etc.) by 'ja'.
- Replace colloquialisms by formal expressions (e.g. 'por' instead of 'x').
- Create a stop words dictionary to delete trivial words.

In addition, we replaced emoticons by words based on emoticons-clusters model proposed by Wang and Castanon [18], which statistically represents the meaning of emoticons. Table 1 plots the statistical representation of emoticons.

Table 1. Emoticons clusters and its statistical meaning from [18]

Cluster	Emoticons	Statistical meaning
A	:) :D =)	Good thanks happy fantastic lovely wonderful amazing…
B	;) :-) ;-) :-D = D ; P =] XD	Smile friends face music favorite pic kind coffee pleasure positive exciting healthy …
C	:(:/ :') :'(:-(D: ;(:-/ :— :/	Miss sorry bad hate sad omg sick late mad ugh ugly broke
D	:P ;D :-P :] :p	What lol don't no know think can't why ever never look…
E	(:	Love follow please hey wish goodnight…
F	XP	Stuck shoot fatally
H	8)	Best fun coming week playing top happiness weekend…

4.2 Word Vectors

Word vectors are the numerical representation of words, which are encoded using different criteria. The most successful criteria are based on training of networks using a corpus. For our case, the corpus for embedding training is composed by "General Corpus", "Social TV", "STOMPOL", and "InterTASS" datasets [1], and encoded using GloVe [14], Word2Vec [11], and FastText [2] models. The three models we selected are considered as top representations which means that related words are close at vector level.

4.3 Convolutional Neural Network

Convolutional neural networks (CNN) are networks divided into two sections: convolution and fully connected section. According to Goodfellow et al. [4], the convolutional section trains to obtain best features which represent input using linear and non-linear activation functions in ReLU or pooling layers, the last output layer in the convolution stage is the feature map (a set of complex and hard to interpret descriptors) which is used by the classifier (the fully connected section). Normally, the fully connected layer is build using a Multilayer Perceptron (MLP).

Preprocessed data is composed by keywords which implies the unigram representation (1 × N convolution) of each keyword in global polarity evaluation. Word vector models are merged into a 3-channels matrix <GloVe, FastText, Word2Vec>, which is the input of our model.

Figure 1 shows the architecture implemented. The input has <D × E> dimension, where D is the dictionary size and E is the encoding size. To obtain the k-gram analysis we apply 4 convolution layers (<k × E> dimension) in parallel. Each convolution layer needs 100 kernels to train and generates 400 feature maps. MaxPooling layer returns the maximum value per each feature map, then all outputs are flattening into a 400 × 1 vector, which is used as input for the fully connected layer. In the fully connected layer, we used a MLP with 200 neurons and ReLU activation function in the hidden layer, 4 neurons with logistic activation function in the output layer. For training, we apply a categorical cross-entropy loss to maximize the separation between classes, the ADAM training and a dropout layer (p = 0.25) to reduce complexity and avoid over-fitting.

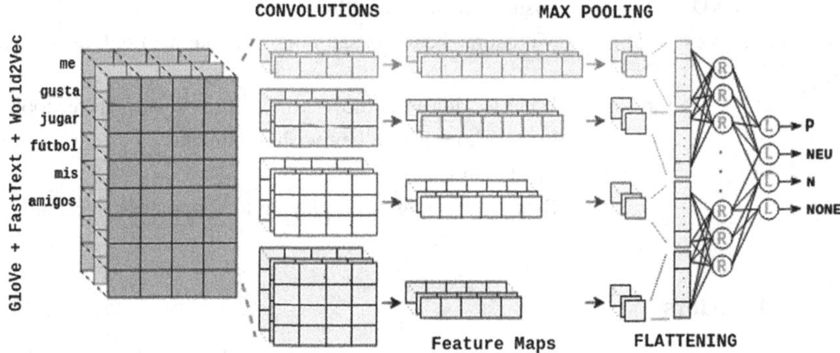

Fig. 1. Assuming that the dictionary size (D) is 8, the encoding size (E) is 4 and the four convolution layers are <<1, 2, 3, 4> × E>. Then, the preprocessed tweet 'me gusta jugar fútbol mis amigos' is classified following the pipeline

5 Experiments and Results

To run experiments, we used a PC with the following settings: 3,6 GHz Intel Core i7 processor, 16 GB 3000 MHz DDR4 memory and NVIDIA GTX 1070 and for implementation we used TensorFlow-1.5 Framework.

5.1 Filters Setting

To define the convolution filters size we performed 2 experiments. In the first one, we combine parallel filters (<<1, 2, 3, 4, 5> × E> dimensions) without repetition into groups of different sizes. To test all combinations we executed each tuple of filters with same conditions. The first experiment results are listed in Table 2.

Table 2. Best three accuracies per run using InterTASS corpus

Run	First		Second		Third	
	Combination	Result	Combination	Result	Combination	Result
1	<1, 2>	0.6182	<2, 4>	0.6131	<1, 2, 3, 4>	0.6125
2	<1, 2, 3>	0.6124	<1, 2, 4>	0.6112	<1, 2>	0.6099
3	<1, 2>	0.6163	<1, 4>	0.6128	<1, 3>	0.6118
4	<1, 2>	0.6156	<1, 3>	0.6120	<1, 2, 3, 5>	0.6114
5	<1, 2>	0.6214	<1, 2, 3, 4>	0.6144	<1, 2>	0.6134

On the second one, we selected the best tuples based on Table 2, then we tuned parameters per each tuple to get optimal results. We run ten times each tuple in order to obtain the best, worst and average accuracies. The second experiment results are showed in Table 3.

Table 3. Statistical results per tuple using InterTASS corpus

Filters	Best run	Worst run	Average
<1, 2>	**0.6219**	**0.6124**	**0.6158**
<1, 3>	0.6163	0.6035	0.6094
<1, 2, 3>	0.6175	0.6029	0.6126
<1, 2, 3, 4>	0.6118	0.5908	0.6008

5.2 Sentiment Analysis

Table 4 expose results for InterTASS and General corpus. In the contest, testing and training data were available in different packages, so results presented in Table 4 refers the testing precision, then we compare our results (CNN-EMOTIC) before the state of art (*).

Table 4. Comparative results in TASS-2017 for sentiment analysis from [1], (*) are best results in the contest and our results are in bold

Proposed system	Corpus	
	InterTASS	General
CNN-EMOTIC	**0.618**	**0.743**
ELiRF-UPV-run1	0.607	0.666
RETUYT-svm cnn	0.596	0.674
ELiRF-UPV-run3	0.597	0.725*
jacerong-run-2	0.602	0.701
jacerong-run-1	0.608*	0.706
INGEOTECevodag-001	0.507	0.514

6 Conclusions and Future Works

The results presented in this paper show that the proposed approach is efficient in sentiment analysis of tweets at document level in Spanish. Based on experiments, our CNN-based model presents an accuracy of 61.82% and 73.22% in testing for InterTASS and General Corpus. During architecture design, we used a well-known CNN-based model of the state of the art but setting a different convolutional tuples. After many runs we concluded that <1, 2> tuple is the best combination, this could be explained if we consider unigram (<1>) representation as the weight of each word and bi-gram (<2>) representation as the weight of context for short texts. The 3-channels input allows a more accurate word- vector representation of the tweet. Also this improvement was possible importing the emoticons statistical meaning [18] to our preprocessing step. During tests, those factors meant a slight but important improvement (from 59.3%–70.7% to 61.58%–74.14% in InterTASS and General corpus respectively). To improve our current results we have to integrate a semantic windows and entropy-based model for large texts, considering to break the words/emoticons according to context (not just for sentiment analysis but aspect-based sentiment analysis).

References

1. Tass 2017 homepage. http://www.sepln.org/workshops/tass/. Accessed 20 May 2018
2. Bojanowski, P., Grave, E., Joulin, A., Mikolov, T.: Enriching word vectors with subword information. arXiv preprint arXiv:1607.04606 (2016)
3. Go, A., Bhayani, R., Huang, L.: Twitter sentiment classification using distant supervision. CS224N Project Report, Stanford **1**(12) (2009)
4. Goodfellow, I., Bengio, Y., Courville, A., Bengio, Y.: Deep Learning, vol. 1. MIT Press, Cambridge (2016)
5. Hassan, A., Mahmood, A.: Deep learning approach for sentiment analysis of short texts. In: 2017 3rd International Conference on Control, Automation and Robotics (ICCAR), pp. 705–710. IEEE (2017)

6. Hurtado Oliver, L., Pla, F., González Barba, J.: Elirf-upv en tass 2017: Análisis de sentimientos en twitter basado en aprendizaje profundo, p. 6, September 2017
7. Kim, Y.: Convolutional neural networks for sentence classification. arXiv preprint arXiv: 1408.5882 (2014)
8. Liu, B.: Sentiment analysis and opinion mining. Synth. Lect. Hum. Lang. Technol. **5**(1), 1–167 (2012)
9. Liu, B.: Sentiment Analysis: Mining Opinions, Sentiments, and Emotions. Cambridge University Press, Cambridge (2015)
10. Martınez-Cámara, E., Díaz-Galiano, M., García-Cumbreras, M., Garcıa-Vega, M., Villena-Román, J.: Overview of TASS 2017. In: Proceedings of TASS 2017: Workshop on Semantic Analysis at SEPLN (TASS 2017), vol. 1896 (2017)
11. Mikolov, T., Chen, K., Corrado, G., Dean, J.: Efficient estimation of word representations in vector space. arXiv preprint arXiv:1301.3781 (2013)
12. Navas-Loro, M., Rodríguez-Doncel, V.: OEG at TASS 2017: Spanish sentiment analysis of tweets at document level
13. Pang, B., et al.: Opinion mining and sentiment analysis. Foundations and Trends ®. Inf. Retrieval **2**(1–2), 1–135 (2008)
14. Pennington, J., Socher, R., Manning, C.: Glove: global vectors for word representation. In: Proceedings of the 2014 Conference on Empirical Methods in Natural Language Processing (EMNLP), pp. 1532–1543 (2014)
15. Rodrigues Barbosa, G.A., Silva, I.S., Zaki, M., Meira Jr., W., Prates, R.O., Veloso, A.: Characterizing the effectiveness of twitter hashtags to detect and track online population sentiment. In: CHI 2012 Extended Abstracts on Human Factors in Computing Systems, pp. 2621–2626. ACM (2012)
16. Rosá, A., Chiruzzo, L., Etcheverry, M., Castro, S.: Retuyt en tass 2017: Análisis de sentimientos de tweets en español utilizando svm y cnn. In: Proceedings of TASS (2017)
17. Severyn, A., Moschitti, A.: Twitter sentiment analysis with deep convolutional neural networks. In: Proceedings of the 38th International ACM SIGIR Conference on Research and Development in Information Retrieval, pp. 959–962. ACM (2015)
18. Wang, H., Castanon, J.A.: Sentiment expression via emoticons on social media. arXiv preprint arXiv:1511.02556 (2015)
19. Wang, X., Liu, Y., Chengjie, S., Wang, B., Wang, X.: Predicting polarities of tweets by composing word embeddings with long short-term memory. In: Proceedings of the 53rd Annual Meeting of the Association for Computational Linguistics and the 7th International Joint Conference on Natural Language Processing (Volume 1: Long Papers), vol. 1, pp. 1343–1353 (2015)
20. Zhang, L., Wang, S., Liu, B.: Deep learning for sentiment analysis: a survey. Wiley Interdisc. Rev. Data Min. Knowl. Discov., e1253 (2018)

Location Dependency in Video Prediction

Niloofar Azizi, Hafez Farazi(✉), and Sven Behnke

Computer Science Department, Bonn University, Endenicher Allee 19a, 53115 Bonn, Germany
niloofarazizi37@gmail.com, {farazi,behnke}@ais.uni-bonn.de

Abstract. Deep convolutional neural networks are used to address many computer vision problems, including video prediction. The task of video prediction requires analyzing the video frames, temporally and spatially, and constructing a model of how the environment evolves. Convolutional neural networks are spatially invariant, though, which prevents them from modeling location-dependent patterns. In this work, the authors propose location-biased convolutional layers to overcome this limitation. The effectiveness of location bias is evaluated on two architectures: Video Ladder Network (VLN) and Convolutional Predictive Gating Pyramid (Conv-PGP). The results indicate that encoding location-dependent features is crucial for the task of video prediction. Our proposed methods significantly outperform spatially invariant models.

Keywords: Video prediction · Deep learning
Location-dependent bias

1 Introduction

The task of video prediction consists of predicting a set of successor frames, given a sequence of video frames. It is challenging, because the predictor needs to understand both contents and motion of the scene in order to make good predictions. In recent years, deep learning approaches became popular for video prediction. They analyze the video both spatially and temporally and learn hierarchical representations, which model the image evolution in terms of its content and dynamics [1,2]. The learned representations can be used for a variety of applications, including action recognition and anticipating future actions, which can be utilized for instance in human-robot interaction scenarios.

Convolutional deep learning architectures cannot recognize location-dependent features, however, due to the location-invariant nature of convolutions. In the task of the video prediction, for instance, learning the location of static obstacles in the environment leads to better frame forecasting. In this work, the authors propose three different methods to overcome this limitation:

N. Azizi and H. Farazi—Contributed equally to this work.

V. Kůrková et al. (Eds.): ICANN 2018, LNCS 11141, pp. 630–638, 2018.
https://doi.org/10.1007/978-3-030-01424-7_62

(a) encoding location features in separate channels of the input,
(b) convolutional layers with learnable location-dependent biases, and
(c) convolutional layers with learnable location-dependent biases and predefined location encodings.

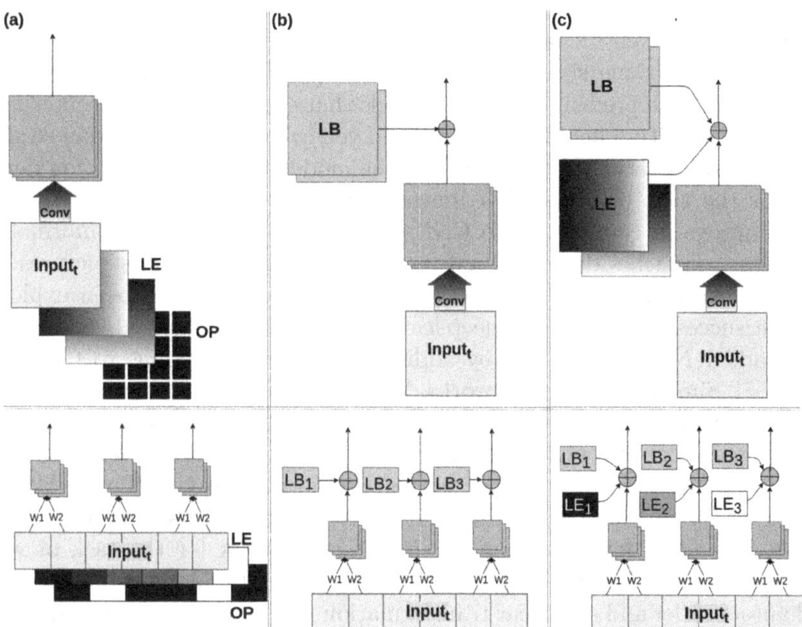

Fig. 1. Proposed methods for location-dependency. Top row 2D and bottom row 1D. (a) Three additional input channels, two of which encode location by gradients in x and y directions (LE); the third contains the occlusion pattern (OP). (b) Learnable location-dependent biases (LB) are added to the output of convolutions. (c) Learnable location-dependent biases and predefined location encodings use combined.

These methods are illustrated in Fig. 1 for 1D and two-dimensional convolutions.

We demonstrate the utility of our approach using two datasets that contain location dependencies. The code and datasets of this paper are publicly available.[1]

2 Related Work

Convolutional deep learning architectures are spatially invariant, which leads to the constraint of not being able to model location-dependent patterns.

[1] https://github.com/AIS-Bonn/LocDepVideoPrediction.

To address this issue in various computer vision tasks, different approaches have been explored. Utilizing fully connected layers leads to learning location-dependent features, but this has the drawbacks of many parameters and no spatial weight sharing. In the PixelCNN architecture for conditional image generation, Oord et al. [3] applied 1×1 convolutions to map a hidden representation into a spatial representation. The disadvantage of this approach is that to extract the spatial features, a very large number of parameters is needed. In saliency prediction, Kruthiventi et al. [4] proposed adding another set of convolutional weights with the same size of the original filters. They convolved these additional weights with predefined fixed channels that encode the image center using Gaussian blobs with different horizontal and vertical extent. Ghafoorian et al. [5] applied specific location features to train the model and utilized location dependency for the task of brain MRI image segmentation. They showed that the results improve in comparison to CNNs that do not use location information. The above approaches depend all on predefined location feature structures.

For the task of video prediction, different approaches have been explored. The most successful ones utilize deep learning methods. Cricri et al. [6] proposed Video Ladder Networks (VLN) by adding recurrent connections to the ladder network [7]. Similar to ladder networks, VLN employs shortcut connections from the encoder to the respective decoder part, whereby it relieves the deeper layers from modeling details. The VLN architecture achieves a result competitive to VPN [8] which is the state-of-the-art on the synthetic dataset of Moving MNIST. However, the VLN architecture due to its convolutional layers, cannot deal with location-dependent features. Another recurrent network for the task of video prediction was proposed by Michalski et al. [9]. Their PGP network is based on a gated autoencoder and a bilinear transformation model, to learn transformations between pairs of consecutive images ([10,11]). PGP is fully connected, which results in a large number of parameters. Its convolutional variant Conv-PGP reduces the number of parameters significantly [12], but looses the ability to learn location-dependent features. For the evaluation of Conv-PGP, the authors augmented one-pixel padding to the input to learn a bouncing ball motion in their synthetic dataset.

While VLN and Conv-PGP have shown impressive performance in the task of video prediction, the above analysis shows that the effect of location-dependent features on these two architectures requires further investigation.

3 Location Dependency in VLN Model

The VLN model [6] is a neural network architecture that predicts future frames by encoding the temporal and spatial features of a video. Although it achieves a competitive result in comparison to the state-of-the-art on Moving MNIST, due to the location invariant property of convolution operation, it cannot learn location-dependent features present in the dataset. The network would become unreasonably huge if we wanted to utilize a fully connected layer to allow for learning location-dependent features. Using a fully connected layer would also violate the assumption of weight sharing in the VLN architecture. The same-padding property around the border, which is not analyzed in the original paper, is the reason which allows the network to learn where to mirror digit velocity despite using only convolutional operations. Such a behavior is accidental, though, and should not be treated as a feature.

To demonstrate this limitation of the VLN architecture, we modified the Moving MNIST dataset to Occluded Moving MNIST, similar to what is used by Prémont-Schwarz et al. [13]. As demonstrated in the experiment section, we tested the original one-layer VLN with this dataset and it did not achieve an acceptable result.

To solve this issue, we propose three methods for providing location information to the network. In the first method illustrated in Fig. 1(a), we provide three additional input channels to the network: two gradient channels in x and y direction, starting from 0 and ending with 1, as well as one channel containing the occlusion grid pattern. The occlusion channel is 1 in the occlusion areas and 0 elsewhere. These additional input channels allow the network to infer the location-dependent feature of the border and to utilize the occlusion pattern. In contrast to encoding location features in the original input channel, having additional channels does not alter the original input. Encooding occlusions in a separate channel can be useful, for example, when they are inferred from modalities other than a camera, like a laser scanner.

In the second method (Figs. 1(b) and 2), we replace the first convolutional layer in the encoder block with a location-dependent convolutional layer:

$$LC(x,y) = A\Bigg(\sum_{i,j} \Big(I(x+i, y+j) * W(i,j) + b \Big) + W_1'(x,y) + W_2'(x,y) \Bigg) \quad (1)$$

where A is the activation function. W and b are the weight and bias of the specified layer, respectively. Note that b can be omitted, but we kept it to make the proposed layer easy to implement on top of an existing convolution layer. $I(x, y)$ is the input vector at the Cartesian position (x, y) and $*$ represents the convolution operator. Note that W_1' and W_2' are location-dependent weights that are learned through the training procedure. W_1' and W_2' are shared for all convolutional filters, which is done by broadcasting over channel dimension.

In the third method, illustrated in Fig. 1(c), we added location-dependent gradients to the W_1' and W_2':

$$LC(x,y) = A\Big(\textstyle\sum_{i,j} \big(I(x+i,y+j) * W(i,j) + b \big) + \big(L_x(x,y) + W_1'(x,y) \big) + \big(L_y(x,y) + W_2'(x,y) \big) \Big) \quad (2)$$

where similar to additional input channels, $L_x(x, y)$ and $L_y(x, y)$ encode location by gradients in x and y directions, respectively. Providing these facilitates the learning of more complex location-dependent biases.

4 Location Dependency in Conv-PGP Model

PGP [9] is designed based on the assumption that two temporally consecutive frames can be described as a linear transformation of each other. In the PGP

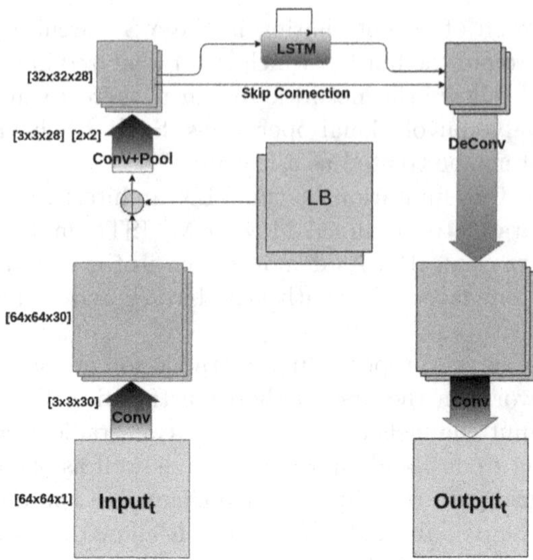

Fig. 2. One-layer location-dependent VLN architecture consisting of two convolution layers in the encoder block, a Conv-LSTM block, and one deconvolution followed by a convolution layer in the decoder part. The trainable location-dependent bias (LB) is applied after the first convolution layer.

architecture, by using a Gated AutoEncoder (GAE) as bi-linear model, the hidden layer of mapping units m encodes the transformation.

The fully connected PGP architecture contains a significant number of parameters. To deal with this issue, we utilized its convolutional variant (Conv-PGP), similar to [12], where fully connected layers are replaced by convolutions.

While Conv-PGP reduces the number of parameters significantly, it cannot learn location-dependent features such as the image border anymore. Using valid convolutions prevents, e.g., learning the mirroring motion in the Bouncing Ball dataset. As shown in the experiment section, in the Conv-PGP model, the balls disappear instead of being reflected at the border which indicates that the model is incapable of predicting location-dependent motions.

To demonstrate this limitation more clearly, we modified the Bouncing Ball dataset. In the Occluded Bouncing Ball dataset, we augmented fixed strides of three pixels to occlude the moving balls as well as invisible lines to mirror the velocity. As shown in the following section, we trained the Conv-PGP with this dataset, and it did not achieve a satisfactory result. To resolve this issue, we applied the three proposed methods for modeling location dependency to Conv-PGP.

5 Experiment

We tested our modified VLN architectures on the Occluded Moving MNIST dataset. Each video in the Occluded Moving MNIST dataset contains 10 frames, with one MNIST digit moving inside a 64×64 patch. Digits are chosen randomly from the training set and placed initially at random locations inside the patch with a random velocity. The frames are filled with occluding vertical and horizontal bars; the distance between them is eight pixels. In addition to that, we added invisible lines to mirror the velocity at a distance of ten pixels from the border.

In our first experiment, we compare the one-layer original VLN architecture on Occluded Moving MNIST with our three proposed solutions:

- VLN-AI: Two location gradient channels and one occlusion channel as additional location encoding inputs (Fig. 1(a)),
- VLN-LDC: Location-dependent bias in the encoder block (Fig. 1(b)), and
- VLN-LDCAI: Location-dependent bias in the encoder block and location gradient channels (Fig. 1(c)).

In our experiment, the first eight frames are predicted using the given frame from the dataset. The last two frames are predicted using the previous network output. Sample results of one-layer original VLN and VLN-LDCAI are depicted in Fig. 3. Sample activations of the Conv-LSTM and the encoder block for both the original VLN and the VLN-LDCAI are shown in Fig. 4. These activations demonstrate that the original VLN cannot infer the location-dependent features while the VLN-LDCAI can learn location-dependent features including the border and the occlusion grid.

Table 1 reports the prediction loss and the number of parameters for the evaluated model variant. It can be observed that all methods to model location dependencies improve performance.

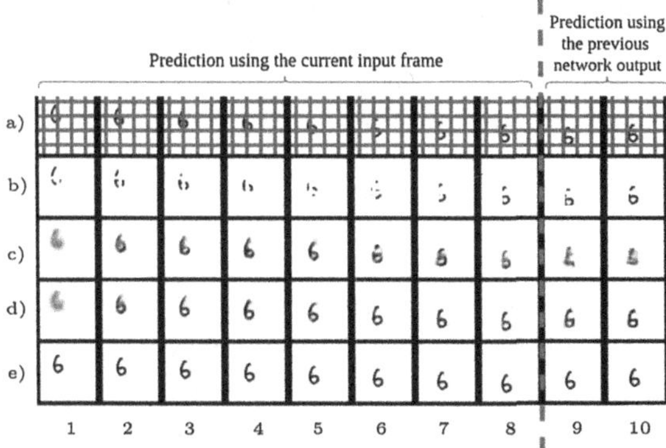

Fig. 3. Occluded Moving MNIST. (a) Input frames with visualized occlusion. (b) Frames given to the network. (c) Predicted frames with the one-layer original VLN. (d) Predicted frames with VLN-LDCAI. (e) Expected ground truth frames.

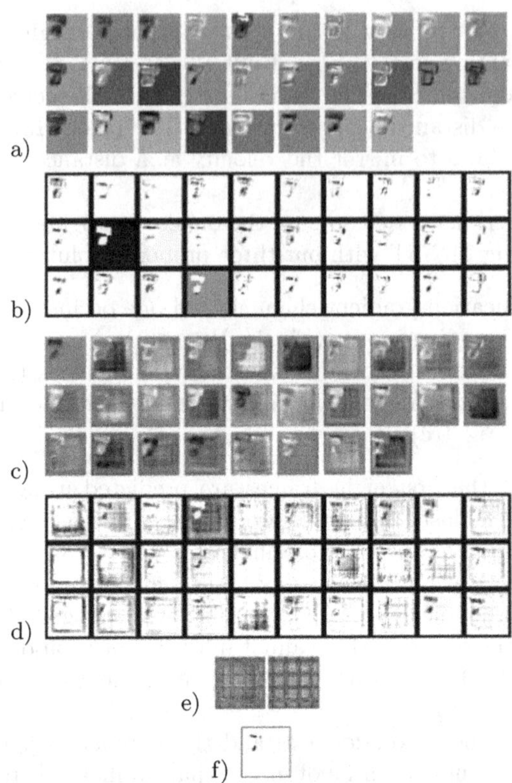

Fig. 4. Occluded Moving MNIST activities. (a) Activation layers of Conv-LSTM block in original VLN. (b) Activation layers of the encoder block in original VLN. Note that none of the channels can detect the location-dependent features. (c) Activation layers of Conv-LSTM block in VLN-LDCAI. (d) Activation layers of the encoder block in VLN-LDCAI. (e) Learned location-bias channels in VLN-LDCAI. (f) Input frame. Note that the VLN-LDCAI automatically inferred location-dependent features.

Table 1. Results of VLN models on Occluded Moving MNIST test dataset.

Model	Prediction test loss (BCE)	Number of parameters
VLN	165.9	90K
VLN-AI	150.7	91K
VLN-LDC	154.7	103K
VLN-LDCAI	153.2	103K

In a second experiment, we compared a one-layer Conv-PGP network with and without the border on the Occluded Bouncing Ball dataset, which is constructed similar to Occluded Moving MNIST. In our experiment, the first three frames are predicted using the given frame from the dataset. The last seven frames are predicted using the previous network output. As illustrated in Fig. 5, learning the location-dependent features is crucial for the prediction task. The prediction losses reported in Table 2 show that our proposed one-layer location-dependent Conv-PGP can solve the Occluded Bouncing Ball dataset and yields a much better result than one-layer Conv-PGP.

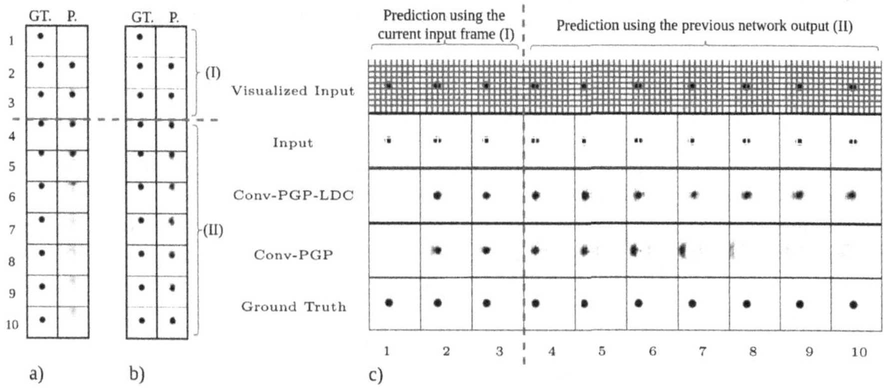

Fig. 5. Bouncing Ball results. (a) Conv-PGP. (b) Conv-PGP-AI. (c) Conv-PGP-LDC and Conv-PGP on Occluded Bouncing Ball dataset.

Table 2. Results of Conv-PGP models on Occluded Bouncing Ball test dataset.

Model	Prediction test loss (BCE)	Number of parameters
Conv-PGP	266.9	39k
Conv-PGP-AI	148.7	40k
Conv-PGP-LDC	139.4	56k
Conv-PGP-LDCAI	143.3	56k

6 Conclusion

Our experiments indicate that location information is a necessity in convolutional architectures for video prediction tasks as, for example, dealing with occlusions in the environment is challenging. To test three proposed variants of learning location-dependent features, we utilized the Occluded Moving MNIST and Occluded Bouncing Ball datasets which mimic occlusions in the real world. The proposed location-dependent inputs and biases allow the VLN and Conv-PGP models to learn more complex location-dependent features than just mirroring velocity at the borders. In contrast to previous approaches, our proposed learnable location-dependent biases do not assume any predefined underlying feature structure. Our proposed location-dependent convolution layers significantly improve on the results of both one-layer VLN and one-layer Conv-PGP architectures.

In future work, we will explore the proposed methods for general deep convolutional neural network architectures, and test the performance on real-world datasets.

Acknowledgment. This work was funded by grant BE 2556/16-1 (Research Unit FOR 2535 Anticipating Human Behavior) of the German Research Foundation (DFG).

References

1. Mathieu, M., Couprie, C., LeCun, Y.: Deep multi-scale video prediction beyond mean square error. Preprint arXiv:1511.05440 (2015)
2. Wagner, J., Fischer, V., Herman, M., Behnke, S.: Learning semantic prediction using pretrained deep feedforward networks. In: 26th European Symposium on Artificial Neural Networks (ESANN) (2017)
3. van den Oord, A., Kalchbrenner, N., Espeholt, L., Vinyals, O., Graves, A., Kavukcuoglu, K.: Conditional image generation with PixelCNN decoders. In: Advances in Neural Information Processing Systems (NIPS) (2016)
4. Srinivas, S.S., Kruthiventi, K.A., Babu, R.V.: DeepFix: a fully convolutional neural network for predicting human eye fixations. Preprint arXiv:1510.02927 (2015)
5. Ghafoorian, M. et al.: Location sensitive deep convolutional neural networks for segmentation of white matter hyperintensities. Sci. Reports **7**(1), 5110 (2017)
6. Cricri, F., Ni, X., Honkala, M., Aksu, E., Gabbouj, M.: Video ladder networks. Preprint arXiv:1612.01756 (2016)
7. Rasmus, A., Berglund, M., Honkala, M., Valpola, H., Raiko, T.: Semi-supervised learning with ladder networks. In: Advances in Neural Information Processing Systems (NIPS), pp. 3546–3554 (2015)
8. Kalchbrenner, N., et al.: Video pixel networks. Preprint arXiv:1610.00527 (2016)
9. Michalski, V., Memisevic, R., Konda, K.: Modeling deep temporal dependencies with recurrent grammar cells. In: Advances in Neural Information Processing Systems (NIPS), pp. 1925–1933 (2014)
10. Memisevic, R.: Learning to relate images. IEEE Trans. Pattern Anal. Mach. Intell. **35**(8), 1829–1846 (2013)
11. Memisevic, R., Hinton, G.E., Roland Memisevic and Geoffrey: Learning to represent spatial transformations with factored higher-order Boltzmann machines. Neural Comput. **22**(6), 1473–1492 (2010)
12. De Roos, F.: Modeling spatiotemporal information with convolutional gated networks. Master thesis, Chalmers University of Technology (2016)
13. Ilin, A., Prémont-Schwarz, I., Hao, T.H., Rasmus, A., Valpola, H.: Recurrent ladder networks. Preprint arXiv:1707.09219 (2017)

Brain Neurocomputing Modeling

State-Space Analysis of an Ising Model Reveals Contributions of Pairwise Interactions to Sparseness, Fluctuation, and Stimulus Coding of Monkey V1 Neurons

Jimmy Gaudreault[1] and Hideaki Shimazaki[2,3](✉)

[1] Polytechnique Montreal, Montreal, QC, Canada
jimmy.gaudreault@polymtl.ca
[2] Graduate School of Informatics, Kyoto University, Kyoto, Japan
h.shimazaki@kyoto-u.ac.jp
[3] Honda Research Institute Japan, Wako, Japan

Abstract. In this study, we analyzed the activity of monkey V1 neurons responding to grating stimuli of different orientations using inference methods for a time-dependent Ising model. The method provides optimal estimation of time-dependent neural interactions with credible intervals according to the sequential Bayes estimation algorithm. Furthermore, it allows us to trace dynamics of macroscopic network properties such as entropy, sparseness, and fluctuation. Here we report that, in all examined stimulus conditions, pairwise interactions contribute to increasing sparseness and fluctuation. We then demonstrate that the orientation of the grating stimulus is in part encoded in the pairwise interactions of the neural populations. These results demonstrate the utility of the state-space Ising model in assessing contributions of neural interactions during stimulus processing.

Keywords: Neural interactions · Neural coding
Macroscopic network properties
Bayesian inference · Binary time-series

1 Introduction

Since neural population activity is constrained by external stimuli and biophysical mechanisms of the neural networks, understanding the statistical regularity of the population activity is an important step toward revealing these underlying mechanisms and further elucidating stimulus coding strategies by the populations of neurons. In order to understand their complex activity patterns, an Ising model has been applied frequently (see [5,8,14] and references therein). This model originally developed in statistical mechanics to describe interacting

V. Kůrková et al. (Eds.): ICANN 2018, LNCS 11141, pp. 641–651, 2018.
https://doi.org/10.1007/978-3-030-01424-7_63

magnetic spins is suitable for analyzing the collective behavior of binary patterns. It is also used in machine learning applications as the Botlzmann machine.

Most of the analyses using the Ising model assumed stationary data in which firing rates and correlations are expected to be constant in time. The static model prohibited analyses of in-vivo data, in which firing rates and even correlations are known to evolve over time [1,15]. As a solution, a state-space model was developed that augmented the stationary Ising model to one that considers dynamics in both firing rates and correlations [4,9,10]. However, the utility of the method has not been fully demonstrated yet.

In this study, we analyzed the activity of V1 neurons using the state-space Ising model. We report that pairwise interactions contribute to increasing temporal sparseness and fluctuation, and encoding stimulus information.

2 Methods

2.1 Data Description and Preprocessing

Population activity of V1 neurons of 3 anesthetized macaque monkeys exposed to visual stimulus was analyzed. It was recorded by Smith and Kohn [12]. The data is available at CRCNS.org [6]. The experimental methods used to perform recordings are briefly explained in [12] and are detailed in [3]. To summarize, an array of 100 microelectrodes was used to perform simultaneous recordings of approximately 100 neurons per monkey. The electrodes were implanted in the primary visual area (V1). The stimuli shown to the monkeys consisted of sinusoidal gratings at 12 different equally separated orientations from 0° (vertical gratings) to 330°. The spike data for each trial lasted 1.28 s. During a trial, a monkey was shown gratings of only one orientation. An isoluminant gray screen was presented during 1.5 s between trials. Temporal and spacial frequencies of the gratings were set to those typically preferred by parafoveal V1 neurons. The experiment was repeated 200 times for every stimulus orientation and for every monkey.

The timing of spikes of different single neurons in this data set was obtained by spike sorting based on a mixture decomposition method [11], allowing to discriminate waveforms from different neurons simultaneously measured by the microelectrodes. To consider only recordings of good quality, we excluded neurons with a signal-to-noise ratio lower than 2.75 and neurons with a firing rate lower than 2 spikes/s for all stimuli, as suggested by Smith and Kohn [12]. This left approximately 40 neurons per monkey.

In the present study, we analyzed nearly simultaneous activity of the neural populations. For this goal, we constructed binary spike trains by binning the spike timing sequences. Time bins (Δt) of 10 ms were used, giving a total of 128 time bins (T) for the duration of the stimulus presentation. For a given trial and neuron, if one or more spikes occurred between times $(i-1)\Delta t$ and $i\Delta t$ s, the value 1 is attributed to the ith time bin. Otherwise, the value 0 is attributed.

2.2 The State-Space Ising Model for a Neural Population

The model used to analyze neural activity is the Ising model (or the Boltzmann machine), a model frequently used in statistical physics and machine learning. For a binary vector of length N, the Ising model is a probability distribution of all 2^N possible patterns. By considering up to pairwise interactions, the Ising model is given by

$$p(x_1, x_2, \ldots, x_N|\boldsymbol{\theta}) = \exp\left[\sum_i \theta_i x_i + \sum_{i<j} \theta_{ij} x_i x_j - \psi(\boldsymbol{\theta})\right]. \tag{1}$$

For a neural system, N is the number of neurons and the binary vector $\mathbf{x} = (x_1, x_2, \ldots, x_N)'$ is the activity of the population, where each binary variable x_i is the activity of the ith neuron (1 if the neuron exhibits a spike and 0 if it is silent). $\boldsymbol{\theta} = (\theta_1, \theta_2, \ldots, \theta_N, \theta_{12}, \ldots, \theta_{N-1,N})'$ is a parameter vector of the Ising model. The second-order parameters θ_{ij} represent pairwise interactions between neurons. ψ is a log normalization function which serves to ensure the sum of all probabilities equals to 1. The model in this form is not dependent on time. Hence fitting this model to the data assumes that samples are generated from the same distribution independently at every time step. However, since neuronal activity of in-vivo animals is dynamic [1,15], it is necessary to augment the model by allowing $\boldsymbol{\theta}$ to vary in time. Naively fitting the Ising model at each time step would result in overfitted models unless we had an excessive amount of data. To avoid the issue, we used a sequential Bayesian algorithm to estimate the time-varying parameters. In this framework, we assume the following dynamics for the state $\boldsymbol{\theta}_t$:

$$\boldsymbol{\theta}_t = \boldsymbol{\theta}_{t-1} + \boldsymbol{\xi}_t(\mathbf{Q}), \tag{2}$$

for $t = 2, \ldots, T$. At the first time bin, we consider a Gaussian prior defined by $\boldsymbol{\theta}_1 \sim \mathcal{N}(\boldsymbol{\mu}, \boldsymbol{\Sigma})$. $\xi_t(\mathbf{Q})$ is a 0-mean Gaussian noise added at every time step to obtain stochastic dynamics. The covariance matrix of the noise is given by $\mathbf{Q} = \lambda^{-1}\mathbf{I}$, where λ is the precision and $\mathbf{I}$ is the identity matrix. Under the principle of maximizing the marginal log likelihood, it is possible to obtain the optimal set of hyperparameters $\mathbf{w} = [\boldsymbol{\mu}, \boldsymbol{\Sigma}, \mathbf{Q}]$ by using the expectation-maximization (EM) algorithm. The EM algorithm also provides the posterior density of the state $\boldsymbol{\theta}_t$ for all time bins given the observed data, namely a distribution of the underlying process $\boldsymbol{\theta}_{1:T}$:

$$p(\boldsymbol{\theta}_{1:T}|\mathbf{x}_{1:T}, \mathbf{w}) = \frac{p(\mathbf{x}_{1:T}|\boldsymbol{\theta}_{1:T})p(\boldsymbol{\theta}_{1:T}|\mathbf{w})}{p(\mathbf{x}_{1:T}|\mathbf{w})}. \tag{3}$$

This posterior density is approximated by a Gaussian distribution. The uncertainty for the parameter estimation is then assessed by its covariance matrix. See [9,10] for details of the EM algorithm and sequential Bayes method.

We randomly selected 3 populations of 12 neurons for each monkey (a total of 9 populations). A separate dynamic state-space Ising model was fitted for each stimulus orientation for each population. To quantitatively determine the effect of pairwise interactions, we compared models fitted to the original data with models fitted to surrogate data (surrogate models). The surrogate data was constructed by randomizing the order of the trials for every neuron. This shuffling of the data destroys correlations between neurons, but preserves their spike rate dynamics. Thus, by comparing original models with surrogate models, we can determine if the observed interactions have significant contributions.

2.3 Macroscopic Properties of the Dynamic Ising Model

After fitting the models, we can investigate the dynamics of the macroscopic properties of the populations during the stimulus exposition. First, the entropy, or the expectation of the information content, is given by

$$S_{pair}(t) = \langle -\log p(\mathbf{x}|\boldsymbol{\theta}_t)\rangle_{\mathbf{x}|\boldsymbol{\theta}_t}, \tag{4}$$

where the brackets indicate the expectation by the observation density $p(\mathbf{x}|\boldsymbol{\theta}_t)$. The model containing N binary elements with the maximal entropy is the uniform model where each element has a firing rate of 0.5. Such a model has entropy $S_0 = N \log 2$. By adding information about the firing rates, we reduce the entropy by constraining the model. We call S_{ind} the entropy of the Ising model projected to an independent model which considers the firing rates of individual neurons, but does not exhibit any correlation ($\theta_{ij} = 0$ for $i < j$). Considering pairwise interactions also decreases entropy as it constrains the model even more (S_{pair}). To assess the contribution of the pairwise interactions in the information content of the population activity, we can compute the fraction of the entropy reduction caused by considering pairwise interactions in the model as

$$\gamma(t) = \frac{S_{ind}(t) - S_{pair}(t)}{S_0 - S_{pair}(t)}. \tag{5}$$

Next, the probability that all neurons are silent, i.e., the sparseness, is given by

$$p_{silence}(t) = p(0, 0, \ldots, 0|\boldsymbol{\theta}_t) = \exp\left[-\psi(\boldsymbol{\theta}_t)\right]. \tag{6}$$

Finally, the fluctuation of a population, or heat capacity, is the variance of the information content. It represents the sensitivity of the model to changes in the state vector $\boldsymbol{\theta}_t$. It is defined as

$$C(t) = \langle \{-\log p(\mathbf{x}|\boldsymbol{\theta}_t)\}^2\rangle_{\mathbf{x}|\boldsymbol{\theta}_t} - \{\langle -\log p(\mathbf{x}|\boldsymbol{\theta}_t)\rangle_{\mathbf{x}|\boldsymbol{\theta}_t}\}^2. \tag{7}$$

2.4 Assessment of Stimulus Coding

We also assessed the contribution of pairwise interactions in encoding the stimulus orientation by comparing the neural responses to different stimulus orientations. To do so, we compared the parameters of Ising models fitted to the neural activity of monkeys exposed to gratings of different orientations. Since the EM algorithm provides the posterior density of the state vector approximated as a Gaussian, we computed the Bhattacharyya distance between the posterior densities. The Bhattacharyya distance between two Gaussians $\mathcal{N}(\boldsymbol{\mu}_1, \boldsymbol{\Sigma}_1)$ and $\mathcal{N}(\boldsymbol{\mu}_2, \boldsymbol{\Sigma}_2)$ is given as

$$D_B = \frac{1}{8}(\boldsymbol{\mu}_1 - \boldsymbol{\mu}_2)'\boldsymbol{\Sigma}^{-1}(\boldsymbol{\mu}_1 - \boldsymbol{\mu}_2) + \frac{1}{2}\log\left(\frac{\det \boldsymbol{\Sigma}}{\sqrt{\det \boldsymbol{\Sigma}_1 \det \boldsymbol{\Sigma}_2}}\right), \quad (8)$$

where $\boldsymbol{\Sigma} = \frac{\boldsymbol{\Sigma}_1 + \boldsymbol{\Sigma}_2}{2}$. We computed this distance at each time bin. The difference in neural responses is quantified by summing the distances at every time bin.

3 Results

3.1 Contributions of Interactions to Macroscopic Network Properties

Using the time-dependent Ising model, we analyzed the population activity of monkey V1 neurons exposed to an oriented grating stimulus. In total, 9 populations (3 per monkey) were separately analyzed. Results with time bins of 10 ms will be shown here, but we found similar results with 5 and 20 ms. The Bayesian algorithm used to fit the model gives the Gaussian-approximated posterior density of the parameters of the Ising model (Eq. 1) given the data, which allows us to obtain the most probable state, or a maximum a posteriori (MAP) estimate, and the credible interval of the estimate (Eq. 3). The fitted model can be used to calculate dynamics of macroscopic properties of the neural populations.

Figure 1 shows results from one exemplary population of 12 neurons. The spike data was recorded 200 times from the same neurons under the same stimulus conditions (here the stimulus orientation (ϕ) is 300°). Figure 1A Top shows the time-steps (x-axis) during which each neuron of the population (y-axis) exhibited spikes (black marks) for 3 exemplary trials. The average spike rate of this population transiently increased about 60 ms after the stimulus onset, as expected for V1 neurons [13], and exhibited oscillatory activity in response to the grating stimulus (Fig. 1A Bottom). It is thus important to take the rate dynamics into account to assess the correlations among neurons. The state-space Ising model adequately estimated the rate dynamics. Similar rates were observed for other stimulus orientations and populations.

Snapshots of the estimated parameters of the Ising model are shown in Fig. 1B Top. The colors of the nodes and edges show the values of the MAP estimates for the first-order parameters (θ_i) and the second-order parameters (θ_{ij}), respectively. Only significant edges are shown, for which the value 0 is outside of the 95% credible interval of the posterior density. The average MAP estimates of the first and second order parameters of the dynamic Ising model can be observed in Fig. 1B Bottom (black lines). While the first order parameters follow a similar dynamic to that of the firing rate, the interaction parameters only vary on a small scale and with no apparent oscillation.

Macroscopic measures of the population are shown in Fig. 1C. The black lines are computed from the MAP estimates of the model parameters. The pale

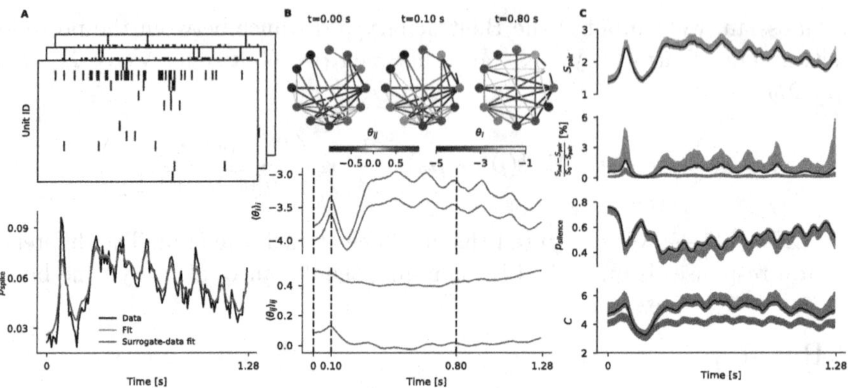

Fig. 1. A (*Top*) Simultaneous activity of 12 neurons with a 10 ms bin size at exemplary trials from the total 200 trials. The stimulus ($\phi = 300°$) is presented from 0 s to 1.28 s (*Bottom*) Empirical and estimated population spiking probability. **B** (*Top*) Snapshots of the estimated parameters of the Ising model. The color of the nodes and edges represent θ_i and θ_{ij}. (*Bottom*) First-order time-dependent parameters averaged over neurons (*Top panel, black line*), and second-order parameters averaged over all pairs (*Bottom panel, black line*). *Red lines* correspond to trial-shuffled data. Vertical dashed bars correspond to the timings of the snapshots. **C** (*From top to bottom*) Estimates of the entropy, entropy reduction due to interactions, sparseness, and heat capacity (*Black lines*) and their 90% credible intervals (*Pale shaded area*). The dark shaded areas correspond to the 90% credible intervals obtained for trial-shuffled data.

shaded areas correspond to the interval between the 5% and 95% quantiles. To compute the quantiles, we sampled $\boldsymbol{\theta}_t$ at every time bin 1000 times from the posterior and computed the macroscopic properties for every sample.

First, the entropy of the pairwise model (S_{pair}) quantifies the information that the population can carry using rates and pairwise interactions. That is to say, the effective number of spiking patterns they can represent is $2^{\frac{1}{log2} S_{pair}}$. Typically, the entropy increases as the probability of spiking increases toward 0.5 (maximum entropy for independent neurons). However, the population activity is constrained by pairwise interactions, which leads to a reduction of the entropy from the independent assumption. In order to examine the contribution of pairwise interactions in the entropy, we computed the fraction of the entropy reduction caused by considering pairwise interactions in the model $\gamma(t)$ (Eq. 5). We found that the pairwise interactions explain approximately 2% of the difference of entropy between the pairwise Ising model and the uniform distribution.

To determine if the observed fraction of entropy γ is significant, we fitted Ising models to surrogate data. In the surrogate data, the order of the experimental trials was randomized for every neuron in order to destroy interactions. Results are reported by the red lines and the dark shaded areas. The average of the θ_{ij} parameters (Fig. 1B Bottom) and the γ of the surrogate model being close to 0 confirms that shuffling the trials effectively removed pairwise interactions.

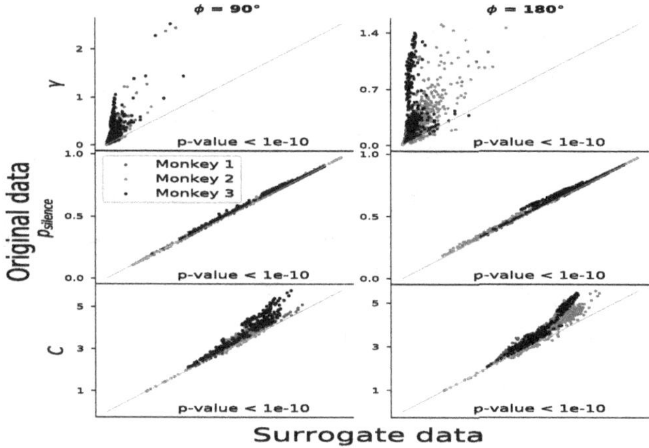

Fig. 2. Comparison between the properties obtained with original data (*y-axis*) and trial-shuffled data (*x-axis*) from 3 monkeys exposed to gratings at 90° and 180°. (*From top to bottom*) Entropy reduction due to interactions, sparseness, and heat capacity.

The surrogate model also accurately estimated the firing rates (see Fig. 1A Bottom). By comparing the γ obtained with the original and surrogate data, we conclude that there are significant pairwise interactions during the stimulus presentation, as the credible intervals do not coincide.

We then examined how the pairwise interactions contribute to other macroscopic quantities of the population. The third panel of Fig. 1C displays the sparseness, i.e., the probability of an all silent pattern (Eq. 6), and the fourth panel displays the heat capacity (Eq. 7). In this example, the heat capacity was clearly greater for the original model, indicating that interactions of neurons significantly contribute to increasing the sensitivity of the population activity. However, the effect on sparseness may not be obvious. To clarify, next we examined these macroscopic values using all populations.

Figure 2 compares the macroscopic properties computed with the original and surrogate data. Data points for every populations at every time step are displayed on this figure. As expected, the original models had a bigger γ. This is because interactions were destroyed in the surrogate data. The original models also displayed significantly bigger sparseness and heat capacity (signed-rank tests). Only results at $\phi = 90°$ and $\phi = 180°$ are shown, but the sparseness and fluctuation were significantly greater for the original data for all orientations.

3.2 Differences in Neural Responses Caused by Different Stimuli

Next we compared models obtained for different stimulus orientations. This should give an idea of how differently the neurons respond to different gratings orientations. To measure the difference, we computed the Bhattacharyya distance (Eq. 8) between the estimated distributions of the Ising model parameters fitted to neural activity of monkeys when exposed to two different stimulus

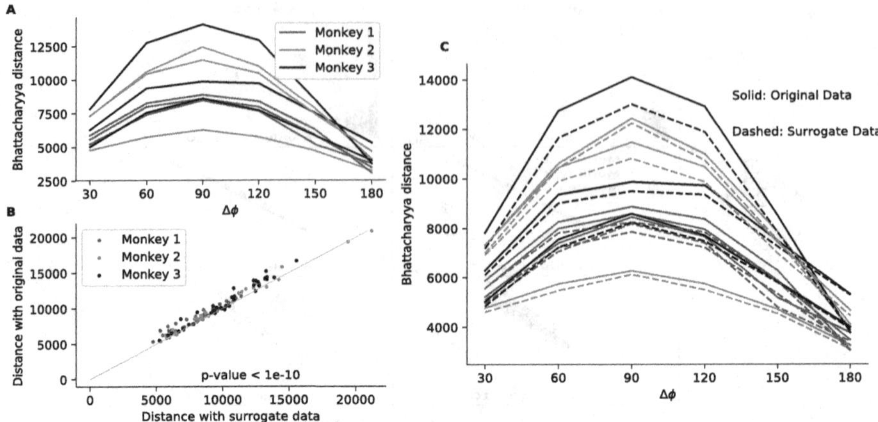

Fig. 3. A Average Bhattacharyya distance between distributions of parameters of Ising models fitted to monkey V1 neural activity when exposed to sinusoidal gratings at different orientations with respect to the difference of orientation ($\Delta\phi$). **B** Comparison of the Bhattacharyya distances obtained with models fitted to original data (*y-axis*) and trial-shuffled data (*x-axis*) for all pairs of stimulus orientations separated by 90°. **C** Average Bhattacharyya distances with respect to the difference of orientation for original data (*full lines*) and trial-shuffled data (*dashed lines*).

orientations. For a given population, we summed the distances between the Ising models computed at each time step for all possible pairs of stimulus orientations. We represent the summed Bhattacharyya distance as a function of the difference between stimulus orientations ($\Delta\phi$). We repeated the computations for all populations (Fig. 3A). The distances exhibited a maximum at $\Delta\phi = 90°$ and a minimum at $\Delta\phi = 180$. This means that the population activities were maximally different for two perpendicular stimuli. The stimuli separated by 180° have the same spacial alignment, but their gratings move in opposite directions (e.g., right to left or left to right). Hence the minimum distances at 180° indicate less sensitivity of the population activity to the direction of the stimulus gratings, which is expected from a population of simple cells.

In order to examine contributions of pairwise interactions to the Bhattacharyya distances, the above procedure was also done for surrogate data. Figure 3B shows a comparison of the distances obtained at $\Delta\phi = 90°$ for original and surrogate data. The distances between original models are significantly greater (signed-rank test). Significant increases of the distances were found for all $\Delta\phi$. Figure 3C displays the Bhattacharyya distances computed from original and surrogate models for all $\Delta\phi$. The distances from original data (full lines) are consistently larger than their corresponding surrogate result (dashed line). From this, we conclude that the interactions contributed to increasing the differences in neural activity when the monkeys are exposed to different stimuli. We repeated the same analysis with the Kullback-Leibler divergence between the estimated observation models at different orientations and reached the same conclusions.

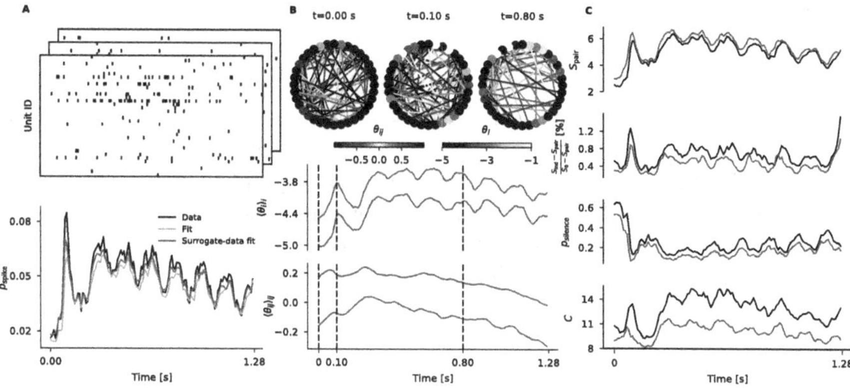

Fig. 4. **A** (*Top*) Simultaneous activity of 36 neurons with a 10 ms bin size at exemplary trials from the total 200 trials. The stimulus ($\phi = 300°$) is presented from 0 s to 1.28 s (*Bottom*) Empirical and estimated population spiking probability. **B** (*Top*) Snapshots of the estimated parameters of the Ising model. The color of the nodes and edges represent θ_i and θ_{ij}. (*Bottom*) First-order time-dependent parameters averaged over neurons (*Top panel*), and second-order parameters averaged over all pairs (*Bottom panel*). Vertical dashed bars correspond to the timings of the snapshots. **C** (*From top to bottom*) Estimates of the entropy, entropy reduction due to interactions, sparseness, and heat capacity. *Black and red lines* correspond to original and trial-shuffled data.

4 Discussion

We found a significant contribution of pairwise interactions to stimulus encoding. Since the neural population activity is more different with respect to the stimulus in the presence of pairwise interactions, the interactions should improve the decoding of stimulus information. However, we found a small percentage of entropy due to pairwise interactions ($\sim 2\%$). While this may be caused by the small number of neurons or by the use of a simple Gabor artificial stimuli instead of correlated natural stimuli [5], considering the firing rate dynamics might have successfully removed spurious correlations. Previous analyses based on the stationary model may suffer from the spurious spike correlations caused by rate covariations. Our analysis reveals that neurons exhibit near-independent activity during stimulus presentation. This result is consistent with the efficient use of population activity expected from the efficient coding hypothesis [2,7].

Donner et al. [4] introduced approximation methods (pseudo-likelihood combined with TAP or Bethe approximation) to fit the state-space Ising model to larger networks. We used these methods to fit models to 1 population of 36 neurons per monkey (Fig. 4, the same monkey and stimulus orientations as shown in Fig. 1). The results were consistent with those obtained in the exact analysis: pairwise interactions had significant contributions to increasing sparseness and sensitivity for all monkeys and orientations (signed-rank test). We chose to provide the results of an analysis without the approximations, but our conclusions regarding sparseness and heat capacity are robust to the network size.

5 Conclusion

The neural interactions significantly contributed to shaping the activity of monkey V1 neurons when exposed to sinusoidal gratings. Neuron populations present significant sparseness and sensitivity due to the neurons' interactions. Neural activities are organized differently when neurons respond to different stimulus orientations, and this difference is enhanced by the presence of neural interactions. From this result, we expect that the decoding of the stimulus orientation is facilitated by considering pairwise interactions of the neurons.

References

1. Aertsen, A.M., Gerstein, G.L., Habib, M.K., Palm, G.: Dynamics of neuronal firing correlation: modulation of "effective connectivity". J. Neurophysiol. **61**(5), 900–917 (1989)
2. Barlow, H.B.: Possible Principles Underlying the Transformations of Sensory Messages. Oxford University Press, Cambridge (1961)
3. Cavanaugh, J.R., Bair, W., Movshon, J.A.: Nature and interaction of signals from the receptive field center and surround in macaque v1 neurons. J. Neurophysiol. **88**(5), 2530–2546 (2002)
4. Donner, C., Obermayer, K., Shimazaki, H.: Approximate inference for time-varying interactions and macroscopic dynamics of neural populations. PLoS Comput. Biol. **13**(1), e1005309 (2017)
5. Ganmor, E., Segev, R., Schneidman, E.: Sparse low-order interaction network underlies a highly correlated and learnable neural population code. Proc. Natl. Acad. Sci. USA **108**(23), 9679–9684 (2011)
6. Kohn, A., Smith, M.: Utah array extracellular recordings of spontaneous and visually evoked activity from anesthetized macaque primary visual cortex (v1). CRCNS.org https://doi.org/10.6080/K0NC5Z4X (2016)
7. Olshausen, B.A., Field, D.J.: Sparse coding with an overcomplete basis set: a strategy employed by v1? Vis. Res. **37**(23), 3311–3325 (1997)
8. Schneidman, E., Berry, M.J., Segev, R., Bialek, W.: Weak pairwise correlations imply strongly correlated network states in a neural population. Nature **440**(7087), 1007–1012 (2006)
9. Shimazaki, H., Amari, S.I., Brown, E.N., Grün, S.: State-space analysis on time-varying correlations in parallel spike sequences. In: IEEE International Conference on Acoustics, Speech and Signal Processing, ICASSP 2009 (2009)
10. Shimazaki, H., Amari, S.I., Brown, E.N., Grün, S.: State-space analysis of time-varying higher-order spike correlation for multiple neural spike train data. PLoS Comput. Biol. **8**(3), e1002385 (2012)
11. Shoham, S., Fellows, M.R., Normann, R.A.: Robust, automatic spike sorting using mixtures of multivariate t-distributions. J. Neurosci. Methods **127**(2), 111–122 (2003)
12. Smith, M.A., Kohn, A.: Spatial and temporal scales of neuronal correlation in primary visual cortex. J. Neurosci. **28**(48), 12591–12603 (2008)
13. Thorpe, S.J., Fabre-Thorpe, M.: Seeking categories in the brain. Science **291**(5502), 260–263 (2001)

14. Tkačik, G., Marre, O., Amodei, D., Schneidman, E., Bialek, W., Berry, M.J.: Searching for collective behavior in a large network of sensory neurons. PLoS Comput. Biol. **10**(1), e1003408 (2014)
15. Vaadia, E., et al.: Dynamics of neuronal interactions in monkey cortex in relation to behavioral events. Nature **373**(6514), 515–518 (1995)

Sparse Coding Predicts Optic Flow Specifities of Zebrafish Pretectal Neurons

Gerrit A. Ecke(✉), Fabian A. Mikulasch, Sebastian A. Bruijns, Thede Witschel, Aristides B. Arrenberg, and Hanspeter A. Mallot

Department of Biology, University of Tübingen, Tübingen, Germany
{gerrit.ecke,hanspeter.mallot}@uni-tuebingen.de

Abstract. Zebrafish pretectal neurons exhibit specificities for large-field optic flow patterns associated with rotatory or translatory body motion. We investigate the hypothesis that these specificities reflect the input statistics of natural optic flow. Realistic motion sequences were generated using computer graphics simulating self-motion in an underwater scene. Local retinal motion was estimated with a motion detector and encoded in four populations of directionally tuned retinal ganglion cells, represented as two signed input variables. This activity was then used as input into one of two learning networks: a sparse coding network (competitive learning) and backpropagation network (supervised learning). Both simulations develop specificities for optic flow which are comparable to those found in a neurophysiological study [8], and relative frequencies of the various neuronal responses are best modeled by the sparse coding approach. We conclude that the optic flow neurons in the zebrafish pretectum do reflect the optic flow statistics. The predicted vectorial receptive fields show typical optic flow fields but also "Gabor" and dipole-shaped patterns that likely reflect difference fields needed for reconstruction by linear superposition.

Keywords: Optic flow · Sparse coding · Optimality · Pretectum Egomotion detection

1 Introduction

Optimality of Visual Receptive Fields. In his *"neuron-doctrine for perceptual psychology"*, Horace Barlow [3] suggests that the *"nervous system is organized to achieve as complete a representation of the sensory stimulus as possible with the minimum number of active neurons"*. This idea also underlies a number of theoretical approaches to visual processing, such as independent component analysis, sparse coding, predictive coding, etc.; for an overview see [6]. While the general approach is widely accepted, specific predictions about the optimal processing scheme will depend on the choice of the optimality criterion employed as well as on the information requirements of each species' life-style. Empirical

V. Kůrková et al. (Eds.): ICANN 2018, LNCS 11141, pp. 652–661, 2018.
https://doi.org/10.1007/978-3-030-01424-7_64

tests of optimal coding theories of visual processing are therefore often limited to a qualitative level.

For the case of mammalian V1 cortex, Olshausen and Field [11] have summarized the evidence and concluded that for a full understanding of the system, simultaneous measurements of the activities of a large, unbiased set of neurons in response to natural stimuli would be required. Two-photon calcium imaging allows to record activity from large populations of neurons. In *Drosophila*, simultaneous monitoring of more than 100 cells from the mushroom body has proven robustly sparse, but non-localized responses to varieties of odors [5]. Insights into functional aspects of memory and learning have been gained that extend findings from single cell recordings which show that sparsity is implemented by means of a normalizing feedback loop on a cellular level [14].

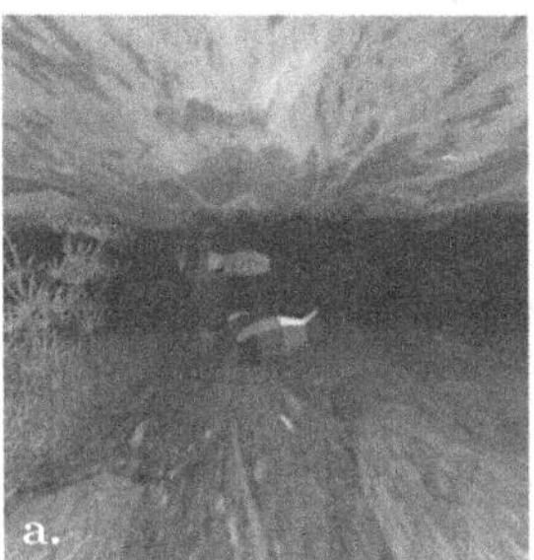
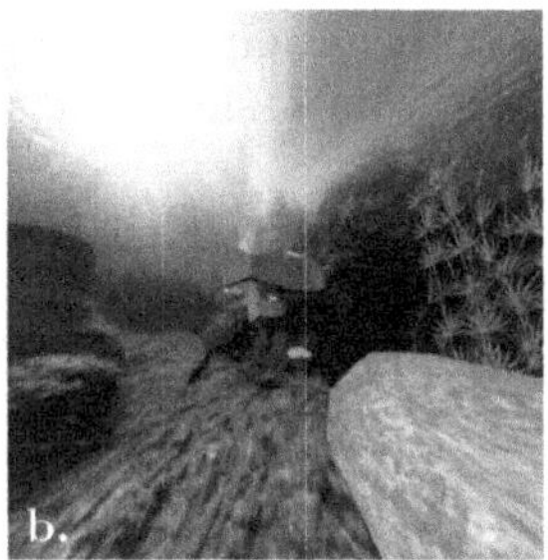
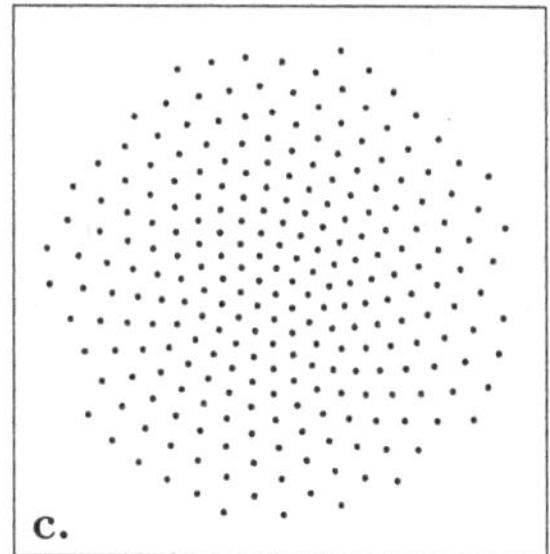

Fig. 1. a. View of the virtual fish tank with muddy water (low viewing distance). Additional fish and plants will generate optic flow discontinuities. **b.** Example with high visibility. **c.** Mosaic of retinal ganglion cells, used to calculate the motion input.

We attempt an analysis of this type for the area pretectalis (APT) of the zebrafish, for which the response of thousands of neurons has indeed been recorded while the fish is presented with optic flow stimuli [8]. Experimentally found response properties from a large, representative sample of neurons will be compared to responses predicted from receptive fields of nodes in a artificial neural network trained with optic flow patterns that were generated by simulating observer movement in a virtual fish tank. The receptive field predictions will be based on two theoretical approaches, (*i*) sparse coding of optic flow patterns (unsupervised) and, for comparison, (*ii*) backpropagation learning of ego-motion parameters from the same optic flow patterns (supervised).

Optic Flow. Like many other animals, zebrafish larvae generate optokinetic responses of the eyes (OKR) and optomotor responses of the body (OMR) when exposed to visual stimuli simulating egomotion of the fish [2,8]. Both eye- and body movements generate space-variant patterns of local motion vectors on the retina which then have to be analyzed by subsequent processing stages. Neural algorithms suggested for optic flow analysis usually consist of at least two components, a local motion detector and a subsequent set of templates or motion models for identifying typical patterns relating to ego-motion maneuvers or encounters with obstacles and self-moving objects such as prey or predator [4,15]. Local motion detection can take place in the retina itself, as is generally the case in lower vertebrates, or in early areas of visual cortex. Higher brain areas analyzing optic flow patterns such as the focus of expansion, rotational vertices, left or right yaw rotations, etc., have been identified in mammalian MST cortex [13] or in the zebrafish area pretectalis, APT [8].

Egomotion estimation from optic flow is subject to a large variety of established approaches derived from geometric considerations [16]. More recently, convolutional neural networks (CNNs) have shown remarkable characteristics, as they can learn depth, motion fields and camera motion altogether in an unsupervised fashion [21,23]. Currently, CNN architectures are state of the art for optic flow estimation [7] while other competitive approaches like [20,22] exist that seek to estimate optic flow from a small (or sparse) number of matched templates.

In our model, local visual motion is encoded in the direction-specific tuning curves of retinal ganglion cells and is not subject to learning. Output from the retinal ganglion cells is then fed into a layer of simulated APT-neurons which develop optic flow analyzers.

Zebrafish Visual System. Zebrafish retinal ganglion cells (RGCs), as well as pretectal cells, exhibit clear tuning to the direction and orientation of drifting gratings [1]. Movement direction is not covered homogeneously, but clustered around three or four major visual field directions [9]. The larval zebrafish retina contains some 4000 ganglion cells with an average angular separation of about 2.5 degrees of visual angle.

RGCs project to APT, among other targets. The response characteristics of APT neurons have been analyzed with visual stripe patterns (drifting gratings) moving either forward or backward and presented to the left, right, or both eyes [8]. Activity of *monocular* neurons depends only on the stimulus delivered to one eye and can therefore be considered to be directly driven from this eye's RGCs. In contrast, *binocular* neurons combine input from both eyes to generate specificities to forward or backward translation as well as to clockwise and counter-clockwise rotation in the horizontal plane.

2 Visual Front End

Realistic optic flow stimuli were generated from a virtual reality simulation of observer motion in a fish tank, programmed in *Blender*[1]. The head of the fish was modeled by two cameras rigidly moving together with a rotation center somewhat behind the eyes. The field of view was 160 by 160° with a binocular overlap of 45° (see [8]). This results in central viewing directions of ±57.5° for the left and right eye.

[1] https://www.blender.org.

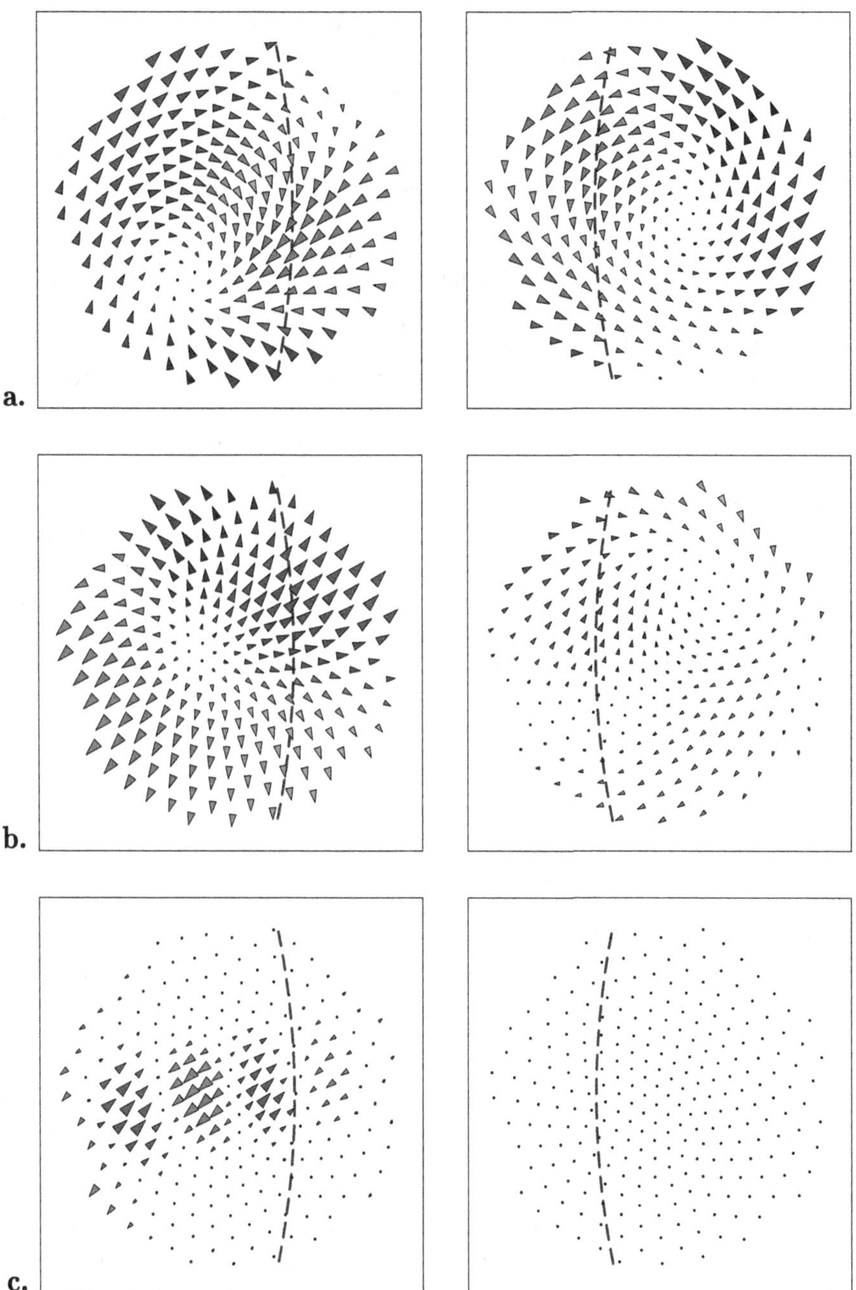

Fig. 2. Sample binocular receptive fields from the sparse coding network. The red dotted lines mark the margin of binocular overlap. **a.** Binocular whole-field neuron with spiral/rotatory characteristic. **b.** Left-dominant whole-field neuron with elliptical focus of expansion in the left eye and a superposition of two curls in the right eye. **c.** Monocular Gabor-field

The virtual fish-tank contained objects at various distances from the observer as well as objects in mid-water (floating plants and passing fish) generating optic flow discontinuities in translational egomotion (Fig. 1a,b). Note that translatory optic flow depends on object distance whereas rotatory optic flow does not. Visibility was set either low (muddy water, Fig. 1a) or high (clear water, Fig. 1b). Overall, the scenery was built to resemble the natural habitat of zebrafish as described in [19].

Virtual fish were placed randomly in the environment and accelerated by a short, random impulse both for translation and rotation. Acceleration for all six degrees of freedom (DoF) were drawn independently from a uniform, zero mean distribution, with an additional scaling factor for the rotatory DoFs introduced in order to equalize the average flow vector lengths of rotatory and translatory flow components. After the acceleration impulse, the motion declined exponentially and a two-frame motion sequence was recorded from the later (slower) parts of this relaxation. Optic flow was calculated with FlowNet 2.0 [7].

The fish retina was modeled as a spherical shell covering 160° in which 256 sampling points were placed using a simple repellence algorithm (Fig. 1c). The planar camera images were warped by stereographic projection and sampled at these points. For each retinal sampling point i the corresponding local motion vector (u_i, v_i) was represented by two signed variables modeling the activity of pairs of RGCs tuned to opposite motion directions (right/left, and up/down).

3 LCA Sparse Coding

For *unsupervised learning*, we used the locally competitive algorithm (LCA) [10, 17] which can be summarized as follows. Let $\boldsymbol{x} = \{x_n\}_{n=1}^{N}$ denote the input signal, i.e. the output of ganglion cells that encode local retinal motion. In sparse coding, the goal is to reconstruct $\boldsymbol{x}$ as a linear combination $\boldsymbol{x} \approx \sum_{k=1}^{K} a_k \varphi_k$ with dictionary elements $\{\varphi_k\}_{k=1}^{K}$, and activation coefficients $\{a_k\}_{k=1}^{K}$, for which sparsity is required [10]. The φ_k are vector fields from which the input vector field can be reconstructed as a linear combination. According to [12,17], each φ_k can also be considered as the receptive field of the k-th output neuron, if a specific activation function with lateral feedback is assumed. In our application, the dictionary elements model the receptive fields of K APT neurons. The vector $\boldsymbol{a} = \{a_k\}$ contains the coefficients needed to reconstruct a given input pattern from the receptive fields. In our simulations, we require $a_k \geq 0$ at all times. If we write the φ_k as columns of a matrix $\boldsymbol{\Phi}$ we obtain the error function $E(\boldsymbol{a}, \boldsymbol{\Phi}) = \frac{1}{2}\left\|\boldsymbol{x} - \boldsymbol{\Phi}\boldsymbol{a}\right\|_2^2 + S(\boldsymbol{a})$, in which the first term penalizes reconstruction errors and $S(\boldsymbol{a})$ penalizes non-sparse vectors $\boldsymbol{a}$. While the original algorithm [10] is based on the ℓ^1-norm, i.e. the total activity of $\boldsymbol{a}$, the locally competitive algorithm (LCA) seeks to minimize the ℓ^0-norm, i.e. the number of non-zero a-values or the number of active units [17]. Since $a_k \geq 0$, this amounts to choosing $S(\boldsymbol{a}) = \sum_{k=1}^{K} \lambda\, \mathcal{H}(a_k - \lambda)$ where $\mathcal{H}$ is the Heaviside function.

For the optimization algorithm see [10,17]. The algorithm was run in Petavision[2] with $K = 512$ APT-neurons and 77,076 motion fields each sampled at 256 retinal points for each eye ($N = 1024$). Examples of the resulting φ_k are displayed as vector fields in Fig. 2.

4 Backpropagation

For comparison, we also implemented a *supervised learning* version of the model that used the same retinal encoding scheme and input data described above. Motion sequences were labeled for egomotion by seven continuous variables, three for the unit-vector of heading (translation), three for the unit vector of the axis of rotation, and a non-negative one for rotational speed. Note that translational speed cannot be recovered from optic flow, so we did not attempt to teach this to the network. The network contained three hidden layers with 1000, 600, and 200 units and an output layer with seven units with the above encoding. Implementation was carried out in TensorFlow[3].

The network was able to recover the heading direction with a mean angular error of about 15° and the axis of rotation with a mean angular error of about 19°.

5 Results

The simulations produce two types of data, i.e. models of vectorial receptive fields, and neuronal responses to optic flow stimuli. Receptive fields will be discussed only for the sparse coding network since no obvious interpretation was found for the backpropagation case.

Figure 2 shows three typical examples out of the set of 512 φ_k fields. Individual vector fields are generally not realizable as optic flow fields in a rigid environment. For example, Fig. 2a approximates a pitch rotation (nose down) in both eyes, but the axes in the two eyes are not properly aligned. Flow vectors are not purely tangential to the pole but involve a spiral component. Figure 2b shows a left-dominant field with an expansion pattern in the left eye. The focus is elongated as might be expected if two nearby foci would superimpose. The right eye field is a superposition of two rotational poles. We conjecture that "dipole" fields of this type are needed to represent multiple axes of heading and rotation as linear combinations of vector fields. The two receptive fields of Fig. 2a,b have high average a_k values (rank 4 and 10 of the entire set). Figure 2c shows a field with low contribution to the reconstruction (a_k rank 130) which is representative of a large number of fields. It is monocular with clearly delineated lobes of motion preferences in opposite directions, resembling Gabor functions for the horizontal and vertical motion components. Comparable, spatial frequency selective but non-localized fields were found by means of a PCA analysis by [22]. Together, these findings mirror typical results when applied to images directly.

[2] https://petavision.github.io and [18].

[3] https://tensorflow.org.

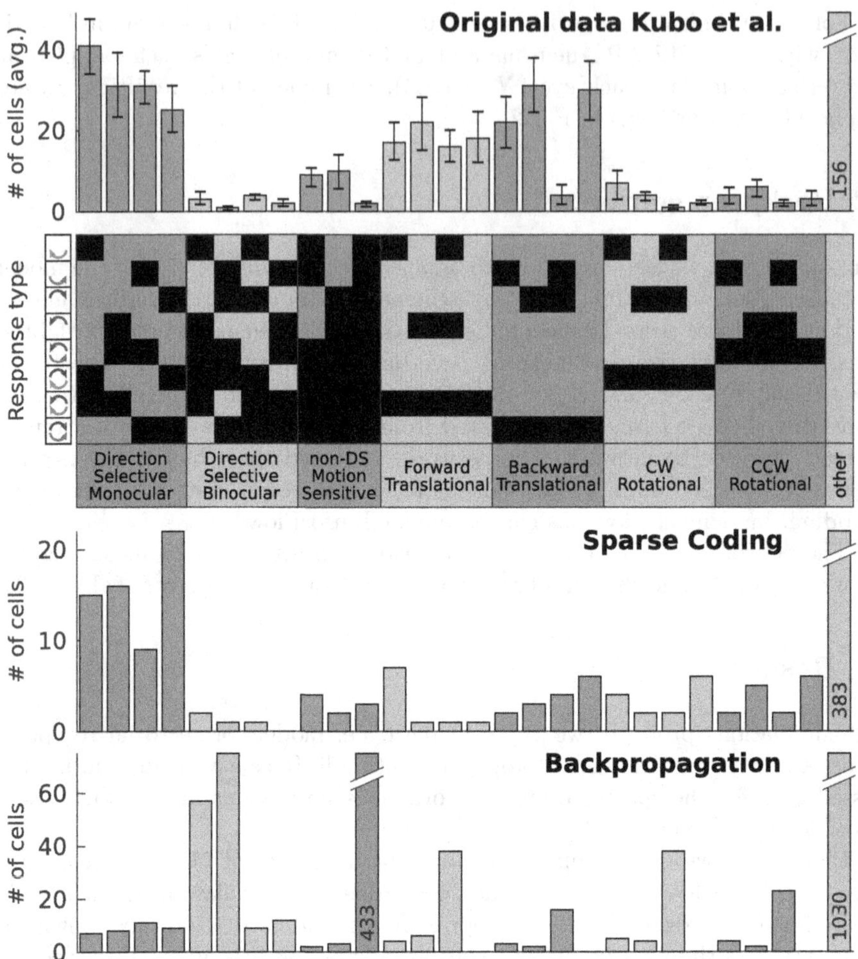

Fig. 3. Summary of neuron response characteristics. The top two panels are redrawn from [8]. On the left of the "**Response type**" panel, the little arrows symbolize optic flow stimulation when the fish is heading towards the left, i.e. the first row shows forward optic flow stimulation to the left eye, the second row backwards stimulation to the left eye and so on. The response types are indicated by the columns of black squares. E.g. the first column refers to neurons responding whenever there is forward stimulation to the left eye, irrespective of the stimulus delivered to the other eye, and so on. The histogram on top ("**Original data**") shows the frequency per fish of neurons of a given response type found in a sample of 3015 cells from six zebrafish larva APT. Most neurons are monocular direction selective (first block). Also, a substantial fraction of neurons specifically responding to global optic flow fields (forward translation etc.) was found. The third panel ("**Sparse Coding**") shows the results of the present study which are in good general agreement with the fish data. The "**Backpropagation**" block shows the responses of the 1,800 units from all three hidden layers of the supervised learning network, which had been trained to classify optic flow patterns for egomotion.

Binocular receptive fields obtained from either learning scheme were further analyzed by calculating their response to spherical rotating or translating grating stimuli as were used for receptive field mapping in the zebrafish study by [8]. Gratings can move either forward or backward and can be presented to the left, right, or both eyes. Altogether, four monocular and four binocular stimulus types can be distinguished, see Fig. 3. Each neuron or model neuron was classified for its reaction to each of the eight stimulus types, resulting in $2^8 = 256$ response types. Of these, 27 optic-flow-related cases are shown in Fig. 3 both for the zebrafish recordings (upper histogram) and for the two network simulations (lower histograms). There is also a substantial number of cells not classified into one of the illustrated 27 response types.

The response-type group "direction selective monocular" is most frequent in the fish as well as in the sparse coding network, but not in the backpropagation network. It includes neurons that react to the stimulation of one eye, but ignore the stimulus of the other eye. On their own, such neurons cannot analyze egomotion because they cannot distinguish between forward translation and rotation to the contralateral side. However, in the reconstruction approach of sparse coding, they do seem to play an important role in describing the binocular motion fields as well.

The next most frequent response type groups comprise binocular neurons reacting to specific types of binocular optic flow such as translation or rotation. The specificity of these responses is established by integrating directional information across both eyes. Again, the sparse coding network seems to fit the data better than the backpropagation network.

6 Discussion

In conclusion, receptive fields of zebrafish APT neurons are clearly related to the statistics of environmental stimuli. The sparse coding network seems to be closer to the data, but does not include a mechanism of egomotion recovery. This recovery is implicit in the backpropagation network, but the behavioral relevance of these patterns is not guaranteed. In any case, more work is needed to identify the detailed objective functions reflecting the information requirements of the behaving fish.

Inspection of the vectorial receptive fields learned in the sparse coding network (Fig. 2) suggests that multiple heading directions and axes of rotation are represented by base fields that are not realizable as optic flow templates but provide a basis for linear combination. This is in contrast to the coding by large field templates in the fly [4] and the piecewise construction of optic flow fields from local templates suggested for mammals [15].

References

1. Antinucci, P.: Neural mechanisms generating orientation selectivity in the retina. Curr. Biol. **26**(14), 1802–1815 (2016). https://doi.org/10.1016/j.cub.2016.05.035
2. Bak-Coleman, J., Smith, D., Coombs, S.: Going with, then against the flow: evidence against the optomotor hypothesis of fish rheotaxis. Anim. Behav. **107**, 7–17 (2015). https://doi.org/10.1016/j.anbehav.2015.06.007
3. Barlow, H.B.: Single units and sensation: a neuron doctrine for perceptual psychology? Perception **1**(4), 371–394 (1972). https://doi.org/10.1068/p010371
4. Franz, M.O., Chahl, J.S., Krapp, H.G.: Insect-inspired estimation of egomotion. Neural Comput. **16**(11), 2245–2260 (2004). https://doi.org/10.1162/0899766041941899
5. Honegger, K.S., Campbell, R.A.A., Turner, G.C.: Cellular-resolution population imaging reveals robust sparse coding in the drosophila mushroom body. J. Neurosci. **31**(33), 11772–11785 (2011). https://doi.org/10.1523/JNEUROSCI.1099-11.2011
6. Hyvärinen, A., Hurri, J., Hoyer, P.O.: Natural Image Statistics. Springer, London (2009). https://doi.org/10.1007/978-1-84882-491-1
7. Ilg, E. et al.: FlowNet 2.0: evolution of optical flow estimation with deep networks. In: 2017 IEEE Conference on Computer Vision and Pattern Recognition (CVPR). IEEE (2017). https://doi.org/10.1109/cvpr.2017.179
8. Kubo, F.: Functional architecture of an optic flow-responsive area that drives horizontal eye movements in zebrafish. Neuron **81**(6), 1344–1359 (2014). https://doi.org/10.1016/j.neuron.2014.02.043
9. Nikolaou, N.: Parametric functional maps of visual inputs to the tectum. Neuron **76**(2), 317–324 (2012). https://doi.org/10.1016/j.neuron.2012.08.040
10. Olshausen, B.A., Field, D.J.: Emergence of simple-cell receptive field properties by learning a sparse code for natural images. Nature **381**(6583), 607–609 (1996). https://doi.org/10.1038/381607a0
11. Olshausen, B.A., Field, D.J.: How close are we to understanding V1? Neural Comput. **17**(8), 1665–1699 (2005). https://doi.org/10.1162/0899766054026639
12. Olshausen, B.A., Field, D.J.: Sparse coding with an overcomplete basis set: a strategy employed by V1? Vis. Res. **37**(23), 3311–3325 (1997). https://doi.org/10.1016/s0042-6989(97)00169-7
13. Orban, G.A.: Higher order visual processing in macaque extrastriate cortex. Physiol. Rev. **88**(1), 59–89 (2008). https://doi.org/10.1152/physrev.00008.2007
14. Papadopoulou, M.: Normalization for sparse encoding of odors by a wide-field interneuron. Science **332**(6030), 721–725 (2011). https://doi.org/10.1126/science.1201835
15. Perrone, J.A.: Model for the computation of self-motion in biological systems. J. Opt. Soc. Am. A **9**(2), 177 (1992). https://doi.org/10.1364/josaa.9.000177
16. Raudies, F., Neumann, H.: A review and evaluation of methods estimating egomotion. Comput. Vis. Image Underst. **116**(5), 606–633 (2012). https://doi.org/10.1016/j.cviu.2011.04.004
17. Rozell, C.J.: Sparse coding via thresholding and local competition in neural circuits. Neural Comput. **20**(10), 2526–2563 (2008). https://doi.org/10.1162/neco.2008.03-07-486
18. Schultz, P.F., et al.: Replicating kernels with a short stride allows sparse reconstructions with fewer independent kernels. In: arXiv preprint arXiv:1406.4205 (2014). http://arxiv.org/abs/1406.4205

19. Spence, R.: The behaviour and ecology of the zebrafish, Danio rerio. Biol. Rev. **83**(1), 13–34 (2007). https://doi.org/10.1111/j.1469-185X.2007.00030.x
20. Timofte, R., Van Gool, L.: Sparse flow: sparse matching for small to large displacement optical flow. In: 2015 IEEE Winter Conference on Applications of Computer Vision, pp. 1100–1106. IEEE (2015). https://doi.org/10.1109/wacv.2015.151
21. Vijayanarasimhan, S., et al.: SfM-Net: learning of structure and motion from video. In: arXiv preprint arXiv:1704.07804 (2017). https://arxiv.org/abs/1704.07804
22. Wulff, J., Black, M.J.: Efficient sparse-to-dense optical ow estimation using a learned basis and layers. In: 2015 IEEE Conference on Computer Vision and Pattern Recognition (CVPR), pp. 120–130. IEEE (2015). https://doi.org/10.1109/cvpr.2015.7298607
23. Zhou, T., et al.: Unsupervised learning of depth and ego-motion from video. In: 2017 IEEE Conference on Computer Vision and Pattern Recognition (CVPR). IEEE (2017). https://doi.org/10.1109/cvpr.2017.700

Brain-Machine Interface for Mechanical Ventilation Using Respiratory-Related Evoked Potential

Sylvain Chevallier[1(✉)], Guillaume Bao[2], Mayssa Hammami[1], Fabienne Marlats[1], Louis Mayaud[3], Djillali Annane[2], Frédéric Lofaso[2], and Eric Azabou[2]

[1] LISV - University of Versailles St Quentin, Versailles, France
sylvain.chevallier@uvsq.fr
[2] Garches Neuro-Physio-Lab, Raymond Poincaré Hospital, AP-HP, Inserm 1173, University of Versailles St Quentin, Versailles, France
eric.azabou@aphp.fr
[3] Mensia Technologies, SA, Paris, France

Abstract. The correct ventilation for patients in intensive care units plays a critical role for the prognostic and the recovery during the stay in the hospital. Desynchronization between the ventilator and the patient is an important source of stress, emphasized by the lack of communication due to intubation or loss of consciousness. This contribution proposes a novel approach based on electroencephalographic (EEG) activity to detect breathing effort. Relying both on recent neuroscience finding on respiratory-related evoked potential and on latest development of information geometry, the proposed approach elaborates on Riemannian distances between EEG covariance matrices to differentiate among different respiratory loads. The results demonstrate that this approach outperform existing state-of-the-art methods quantitatively, in terms of mean accuracy, and qualitatively, being able to predict level of breathing discomfort.

Keywords: Brain-machine interface · Electroencephalography Riemannian geometry · Mechanical ventilation

1 Introduction

Brain-machine interfaces (BMI) allow to interact with a physical system using only cerebral activity and are mostly of interest in situations where muscle activity is not reliable or possible [24]. BMI also offer an opportunity for situations where communication is difficult: it is still possible to measure a brain response to specific stimulus or situation for unconscious patients [19]. Endotracheal ventilation ("intubation") is a commonly used intervention in the ICU [8] that impairs verbal communication. In this context a reliable objective assessment of ventilators performance is of particular importance both for patient's quality of

V. Kůrková et al. (Eds.): ICANN 2018, LNCS 11141, pp. 662–671, 2018.
https://doi.org/10.1007/978-3-030-01424-7_65

stay and clinical outcome. In the case of patient-ventilator asynchrony [6], the ventilator could interfere or impede the autonomous breathing function, which is an automatic and unconscious process, inducing dyspnea. The dyspnea, that is the sensation of shortness of breath, could be the cause of stressful experiences, with psychological or physical consequences [21].

To avoid these situations of asynchrony between a patient and the mechanical ventilation, they should be detected as soon as possible. Common approaches are relying on measurements of physiological signals, such as pressure, flow or blood oxygen saturation, and biosignals, such as electromyography. Several algorithms have been proposed to automatically detect these asynchrony, but they are restricted to certain types of disharmony [2,18]. The cortical networks for breathing control generate an activity observable on EEG [7] and the discomfort level have been reported to be correlated with this neural activity [13]. Two different kinds of neural activity are reported in the literature: preinspiratory potentials that are event-related desynchronization [7,10] and respiratory-related evoked potential which are event-related potential [13].

The detection and classification of these neural activity have been widely explored in the brain-machine interface community. The event-related desynchronization has been studied in the context of motor imagery-based paradigm and the event-related potentials are usually employed with oddball paradigm that elicits a P300 potential. Unfortunately, these signals are difficult to detect because of the poor signal-to-noise ratio and the variability of EEG signal from one subject to another. The most common approach is to design a patient-specific spatial filters to enhance the signal of interest and it is often associated with a reduction of dimensionality of the input. Unfortunately, these highly parametric approaches suffer from various levels of overfitting and underperform on new data [15]. Recent advances and a complete review could be found in [14].

Methods based on Riemannian geometry allows to revisit covariance-based algorithms by considering the spatial covariance matrices in an adequate space. Covariance matrices are symmetric and positive definite, they are elements of manifold with a negative curvature. Euclidean distance is not adequate on these manifolds; specific distances and divergences should be considered [12]. Riemannian methods achieve state-of-the-art results on multiple BCI paradigm, in depth reviews are provided in [4,25]. The study of [10,17] is the first attempt to use Riemannian geometry for the detection of respiratory states, based on preinspiratory potentials. The authors classify two situations, resting unloaded breathing and inspiratory threshold loading, with a variant of the Minimum Distance to Mean inspired by the k-mean algorithm.

The contributions described in this paper are the following:

- this is the first attempt to use Riemannian geometry on respiratory-related evoked potentials (RREP) instead of preinspiratory potentials (PIP),
- classification is done in the tangent space, whereas existing approach use a variation of a Riemannian k-mean,
- the experimental results goes beyond the binary classification (resting vs respiratory load) to perform a multiclass detection of the respiratory load,

- the obtained results outperform previously reported results, in a more challenging setup (multiclass instead of two classes).

The next section describes the existing approaches for detecting respiratory-related evoked potentials and preinspiratory potentials, along the proposed Riemannian framework. Section 3 provides the details concerning the experiment and the dataset. The described approaches are compared in Sect. 3.2 and the classification accuracy is estimated in different setups. These results are discussed in Sect. 4.

2 Methods

We will denote as $X \in \mathbb{R}^{C \times N}$ an EEG signal recorded with C electrodes during N time steps. This EEG signal corresponds to a session containing multiple trials.

2.1 Existing Approaches

When dealing with evoked potentials, XDAWN filters are a robust and widely employed algorithm [20]. It tries to uncover a stimulus $E \in \mathbb{R}^{N_t \times C}$, where N_t is number of time steps of the stimulus, by exploiting the temporal information of the session with $D \in \mathbb{R}^{N \times N_t}$, a Toeplitz matrix with 0 except for stimulus timing. Starting from the model that the EEG is $X^T = DE + \eta$, where $\eta \in \mathbb{R}^{C \times N}$ is non-target signal, the objective of XDAWN is to find a suitable spatial filter $W \in \mathbb{R}^{C \times N_f}$ that enhances the stimulus while reducing the non-target signal. N_f is the number of selected filters. The goal is to find W that maximizes the SSNR:

$$\hat{W} = \text{argmax}_W \frac{\text{tr } W^T \hat{\Sigma}_1 W}{\text{tr } W^T \hat{\Sigma}_X W}, \tag{1}$$

with $\hat{\Sigma}_1 = \hat{E}^T D^T D \hat{E}$, $\hat{X}_X = XX^T$ and $\hat{E} = (D^T D)^{-1} D^T X^T$.

Similarly, for motor imagery, the most common preprocessing technique is to rely on Common Spatial Patterns (CSP) to filter the signal [3]. The EEG signal X should be centered and scaled and it is customary to bandpass filter the signal in the frequency of interest. After epoching the signal, two covariance matrices Σ_1 and Σ_2 are estimated, that correspond to 2 conditions. CSP is obtained by the simultaneous diagonalization of:

$$W^T \Sigma_1 W = \Delta_1 \text{ and } W^T \Sigma_2 W = \Delta_2, \text{ s.t. } \Delta_1 + \Delta_2 = I \tag{2}$$

The common practice is to select only a subset of spatial filters from W.

After this preprocessing, the data are usually well separated, thus a simple classifier such as Fisher Linear Discriminant Analysis is sufficient to achieve very high classification results. In this work, we also consider an SVM classifier using either linear or RBF kernel, chosing the hyperparameters via cross-validation. To ensure the reproducibility of the results and facilitate the comparison with [17], we also consider the One-Class SVM [23] in our experiment. One should note that a direct comparison with [17] is not possible, their study is restricted to a two-class model and rely on AUC estimator whereas our study is multiclass and evaluate models through their accuracy. Accuracy is a basic but correct estimator in this context as the classes are balanced and the classifer are unbiaised [9].

2.2 Riemannian Geometry

Covariances matrices Σ are symmetric and positive-definite (SPD). Spatial covariance matrices could directly be estimated from multivariate EEG signals and we rely on a more robust estimator that sample covariance estimation $\hat{\Sigma} = \frac{1}{N}XX^T$, that is Schäfer-Strimmer estimator [11,22]. Covariance matrices capture well changes of amplitude characteristic of event-related desynchronization, but should be adapted to be suited to evoked potentials detection. So-called extended covariance matrices [5] incorporate evoked potential temple information, here we use XDAWN to build these extended covariance matrices. The covariance matrices are estimated from the extended signal $X_{\text{ext}} = \begin{bmatrix} E^T \\ X \end{bmatrix}$, $X_{\text{ext}} \in \mathbb{R}^{2C \times N_t}$.

It is possible to choose a metric such that the inner product on the tangent space $T_\Sigma\mathcal{M}$ of each point Σ varies smoothly from one point to another. In that case, all the points "glued" together are considered as a differentiable manifold $\mathcal{M}$. For the set of SPD matrices, one could choose the following inner product

$$\langle \Theta | \Theta' \rangle_\Sigma = \text{tr}(\Sigma^{-1}\Theta\Sigma^{-1}\Theta'),$$

for Θ and Θ' in $T_\Sigma\mathcal{M}$. This inner product allows to compute the path between any pair of points from $\mathcal{M}$, this path is called a curve and the shortest path between two points is a geodesic $\gamma(t)$. The length of the geodesic curve between Σ_1 and Σ_2 is the Riemannian distance δ:

$$\delta(\Sigma_1, \Sigma_2) = \left\| \log(\Sigma_1^{-\frac{1}{2}}\Sigma_2\Sigma_1^{-\frac{1}{2}}) \right\|_F . \tag{3}$$

It is known as the affine-invariant Riemannian metric [16].

Any point Θ of the tangent space $T_\Sigma\mathcal{M}$ could be mapped on $\mathcal{M}$ with

$$\Sigma' = \exp_\Sigma(\Theta) = \Sigma^{\frac{1}{2}} \exp(\Sigma^{-\frac{1}{2}}\Theta\Sigma^{-\frac{1}{2}})\Sigma^{\frac{1}{2}}$$

and the reverse mapping, from $\mathcal{M}$ to $T_\Sigma\mathcal{M}$ is

$$\Theta = \log_\Sigma(\Sigma') = \Sigma^{\frac{1}{2}} \log(\Sigma^{-\frac{1}{2}}\Sigma'\Sigma^{-\frac{1}{2}})\Sigma^{\frac{1}{2}} .$$

The geodesic $\gamma(t)$ on the manifold could then be defined as:

$$\gamma(t) = \exp_{\Sigma_1}(t \log_{\Sigma_1}(\Sigma_2)) \tag{4}$$

Another important notion is the mean of Σ_i points, which is computed differently in the context of Riemannian manifold. This is the point minimizing the square of the distance between $\bar{\Sigma}$ and a Σ_i.

$$\bar{\Sigma} = \text{argmin}_{\Sigma} \sum_{i=1}^{N} \delta^2(\Sigma_i, \Sigma). \tag{5}$$

In BMI, two approaches have been proposed for classification. The first one is simply a classification in the tangent space located at the Riemannian mean of the whole session [1]. The main interest of this approach is that all Euclidean algorithm (LDA, SVM and others) could be directly applied in this tangent space. It should be noted that elements of this space are symmetric matrices, thus the dimension of the input is $C(C+1)/2$ instead of C^2.

The other classifier is called *Minimum Distance to Mean* (MDM), introduced in [1], is presented for multi-class classification in the manifold. The classification is decided from the nearest class mean. One of the interest of this approach is that all the computation are made on the manifold, no computation take place on the tangent space.

3 Experiments

The study protocol was approved by the local Ethics committee (CPP): number 11073 on 2011-11-24, and is part of the trial registered in the public trials registry, http://clinicaltrials.gov, number NCT01548586. All study participants gave their informed, written consent.

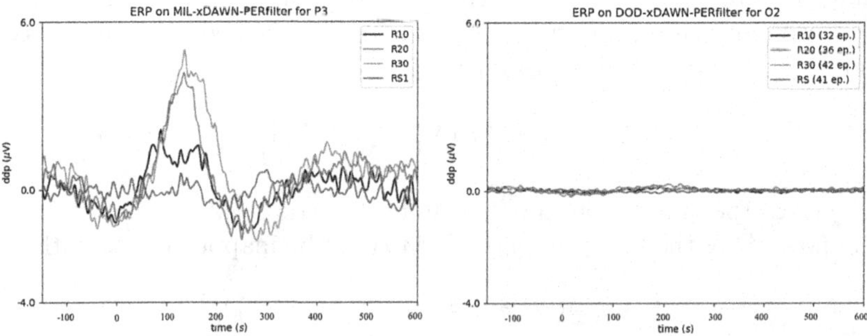

Fig. 1. Evoked potentials found for the subject with the best and the worst classification results, that is MIL and DOD subject. The RREP are filtered with XDAWN to using 8 components.

3.1 Setup and Dataset

The subject was seated comfortably and breathed into a mouthpiece connected to a low-resistance non-rebreathing valve (2600 Medium, Hans Rudolph Inc., St Louis, MO). Respiratory flows were recorded using a pneumotacho-Graph (Fleish no. 2, Lausanne, Switzerland) connected to a differential pressure transducer (TMSi 45 5cmH2O, Holland). Mouth pressure (MP) was measured using a differential pressure transducer (Validyne MP 45 100 cmH2O) and end-tidal pressure of CO2 (PETCO2) using a capnograph (Capnogard 1265, Novametrix, Wallingford, CT). EEG signal was recording synchronously with the breathing using a 19 electrodes Cap (EasyCap, Brain Products GmbH, Germany). Active electrodes were placed in equidistant positions (ActiCap, Brain Products GmbH, Germany) according to the conventional "10–20" topographic system. The ground electrode was positioned at AFz. The EEG signal was digitized at 2000 Hz and recorded using NeuroRT Studio (Mensiatech, Chantepie, France) for subsequent processing.

After an adaptation period during which the subjects breathed quietly through the unloaded circuit, the lowest and highest loads to be investigated were applied during a few respiratory cycles to familiarize the subjects with the load range and evaluation scale. The subjects were then exposed to five levels of inspiratory pressure load conditions (PEEP valve for vital flow 100 set; Vital Signs Inc., Gamida, France):

- Spontaneous breathing through the unloaded circuit (RS)
- Breathing with a resistive load of 10 cmH2O (R10),
- Breathing with a resistive load of 20 cmH2O (R20),
- Breathing with a resistive load of 30 cmH2O (R30).

Each load was applied for 5 min respiratory cycles, after a 3 min rest. To assess that the different loads are generating RREP, Fig. 1 shows the average evoked potentials obtained for each condition (RS, R10, R20 and R30) for two subjects, those with the best and the worst classification results.

3.2 Results

Five methods are evaluated on this dataset: MDM and Tangent Space classification, both introduced in Sect. 2.2, XDAWN+LDA as explained in Eq. (1), One-Class SVM operating on vectorized covariance matrices (SVMeeg), as proposed by [17] and a linear SVM (SVMphy) operating input vectors of 6 features from the MP sensors (peak, average, total volume, flow variance, skewness and kurtosis) [17]. An extensive recursive feature selection process is set up for selecting the best features among the 2^6 possibility for SVMphy classifier. All the methods are evaluated through 10-fold validation using accuracy, as the classes are balanced and the classifer are unbiaised [9].

Figure 2 shows the obtained accuracy for all subjects in the multiclass case. Classification in the tangent space offers the best results and outperform all other methods for all subjects. The second method is the SVM based on physiological parameters which achieves honorable results. The XDAWN+LDA and the MDM classifiers yield comparable results, the MDM displaying a larger variance. The SVM classifying the covariance matrices is performing very poorly, confirming that Euclidean approaches are not suited to deal correctly with curved manifold.

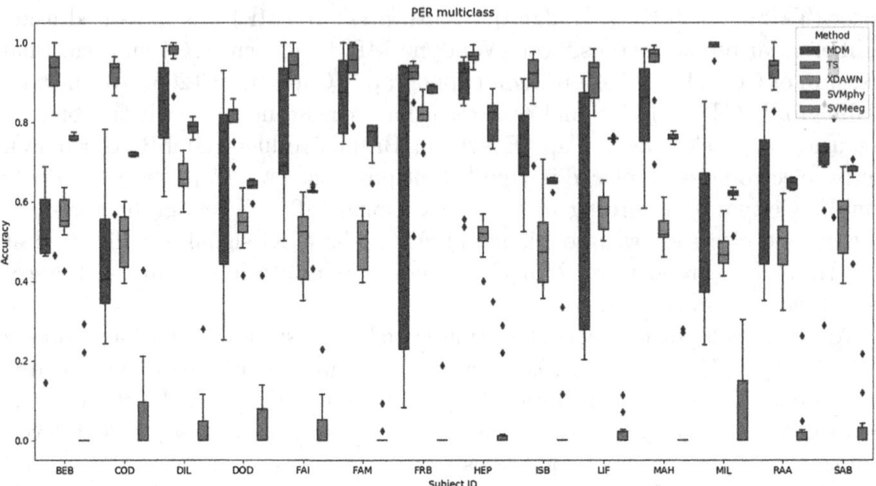

Fig. 2. Comparison of multiclass detection of RREP for each of the 14 subjects with Riemannian approaches Minimum Distance to Mean (MDM) and Tangent Space (TS) and state of the art approaches, that is XDAWN+LDA and SVM based on physiological (SVMphy) or EEG inputs (SVMeeg).

Table 1. Accuracy values for binary classification, that is detection of normal breathing vs respiratory load. The accuracies are compared for the proposed Riemannian approach (Tangent Space on EEG) for both evoked potential (RREP) and pre-inspiratory potential (PIP), and for state-of-the-art approach for physiological input (SVM on pressure sensors).

Method	Input	Accuracy (%)
SVM physiological data	RREP	71.76 ± 9.83%
Tangent space	**RREP**	**93.46 ± 10.04%**
SVM physiological data	PIP	85.17 ± 12.85%
Tangent space	PIP	87.75 ± 12.72%

Figure 3 shows the average accuracy values for the multiclass case (discriminating between RS, R10, R20 and R30) and the two-class case (RS vs R10/R20/R30). The two-class case allows a comparison with the state-of-the-art study of [17]: it could be seen that the results of all the methods are slightly degraded in the multiclass case. Table 1 summarizes the results of the two-class case with RREP and compares with the two best methods for PIP. Tangent space classification on RREP obtains the best results.

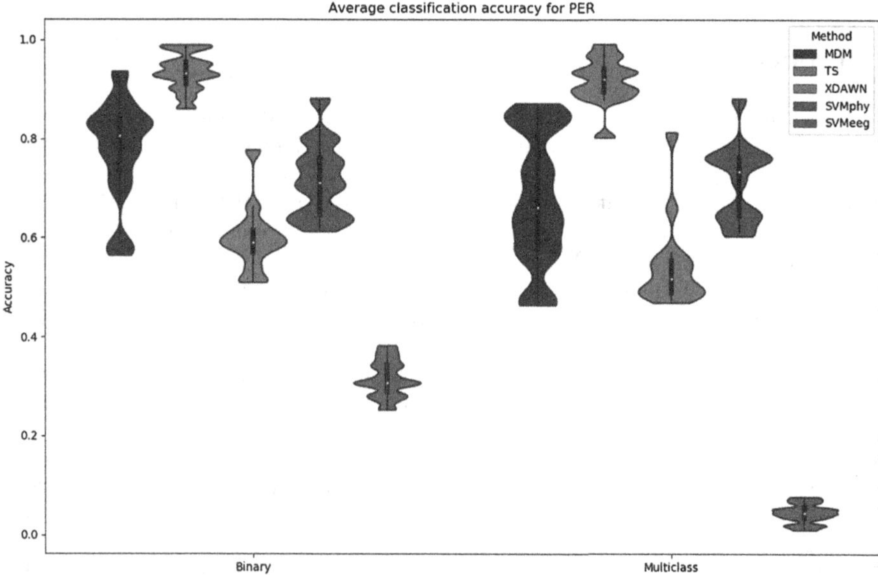

Fig. 3. Mean values for RREP classification for all subjects under 3 increasing respiratory loads and one control condition, for MDM, Tangent Space, XDAWN+LDA, SVM based on physiological and EEG data.

4 Discussion and Conclusion

This paper presents a first step towards a closed-loop BMI ventilator. One current limitation is that EEG is expensive, cumbersome, sensitive to various sources of noise, and not suitable for long-term recordings. Nonetheless, these limitations could be mitigated in a medical and controlled environment. For online processing, the proposed method still needs a physiological channel to extract cues for inspiration and expiration. This drawback is of limited importance as such sensors are cheap and already available on existing ventilator devices.

The existing approaches are relying on physiological or behavioral information, but lack precision to detect certain asynchronous state. A first attempt to use EEG information together with Riemannian geometry yield promising results, but the method proposed by the authors require to tune several parameters and is limited to a two-class case.

The proposed method relies on respiration-related evoked potentials instead of pre-inspiratory potentials and thanks to an appropriate Riemannian classifier outperforms current state of the art. The results are more accurate and allow to detect different respiratory loads, and thus open the possibility quantify the breathing effort.

References

1. Barachant, A., Bonnet, S., Congedo, M., Jutten, C.: Multiclass brain-computer interface classification by Riemannian geometry. IEEE Trans. Biomed. Eng. **59**(4), 920–928 (2012)
2. Blanch, L., et al.: Validation of the better care® system to detect ineffective efforts during expiration in mechanically ventilated patients: a pilot study. Intensiv. Care Med. **38**(5), 772–780 (2012)
3. Blankertz, B., Tomioka, R., Lemm, S., Kawanabe, M., Muller, K.R.: Optimizing spatial filters for robust EEG single-trial analysis. IEEE Signal Process. Mag. **25**(1), 41–56 (2008)
4. Congedo, M., Barachant, A., Bhatia, R.: Riemannian geometry for EEG-based brain-computer interfaces; a primer and a review. Brain-Comput. Interfaces **4**, 1–20 (2017)
5. Congedo, M., Barachant, A., Andreev, A.: A new generation of brain-computer interface based on Riemannian geometry. arXiv preprint arXiv:1310.8115 (2013)
6. Dres, M., Rittayamai, N., Brochard, L.: Monitoring patient-ventilator asynchrony. Curr. Opin. Crit. Care **22**(3), 246–253 (2016)
7. Dubois, M., et al.: Neurophysiological evidence for a cortical contribution to the wakefulness-related drive to breathe explaining hypocapnia-resistant ventilation in humans. J. Neurosci. **36**(41), 10673–10682 (2016)
8. Esteban, A., et al.: How is mechanical ventilation employed in the intensive care unit? An international utilization review. Am. J. Respir. Crit. Care Med. **161**(5), 1450–1458 (2000)
9. Fatourechi, M., Ward, R.K., Mason, S.G., Huggins, J., Schlögl, A., Birch, G.E.: Comparison of evaluation metrics in classification applications with imbalanced datasets. In: International Conference on Machine Learning and Applications (ICMLA), pp. 777–782. IEEE (2008)
10. Hudson, A.L., et al.: Electroencephalographic detection of respiratory-related cortical activity in humans: from event-related approaches to continuous connectivity evaluation. J. Neurophysiol. **115**(4), 2214–2223 (2016)
11. Kalunga, E.K., Chevallier, S., Barthélemy, Q., Djouani, K., Monacelli, E., Hamam, Y.: Online SSVEP-based BCI using riemannian geometry. Neurocomputing **191**, 55–68 (2016)
12. Kalunga, E.K., Chevallier, S., Barthélemy, Q., Djouani, K., Hamam, Y., Monacelli, E.: From euclidean to riemannian means: information geometry for SSVEP classification. In: Nielsen, F., Barbaresco, F. (eds.) GSI 2015. LNCS, vol. 9389, pp. 595–604. Springer, Cham (2015). https://doi.org/10.1007/978-3-319-25040-3_64
13. Knafelc, M., Davenport, P.W.: Relationship between magnitude estimation of resistive loads, inspiratory pressures, and the rrep p1 peak. J. Appl. Physiol. **87**(2), 516–522 (1999)
14. Lotte, F., et al.: A review of classification algorithms for eeg-based brain-computer interfaces: a 10 year update. J. Neural Eng. **15**(3), 031005 (2018). http://stacks.iop.org/1741-2552/15/i=3/a=031005

15. Mayaud, L., et al.: Brain-computer interface for the communication of acute patients: a feasibility study and a randomized controlled trial comparing performance with healthy participants and a traditional assistive device. Brain-Comput. Interfaces **3**(4), 197–215 (2016)
16. Moakher, M.: A differential geometric approach to the geometric mean of symmetric positive-definite matrices. SIAM J. Matrix Anal. Appl. **26**(3), 735–747 (2005)
17. Navarro-Sune, X., et al.: Riemannian geometry applied to detection of respiratory states from EEG signals: the basis for a brain-ventilator interface. IEEE Trans. Biomed. Eng. **64**(5), 1138–1148 (2017)
18. Piquilloud, L., et al.: Neurally adjusted ventilatory assist (NAVA) improves patient-ventilator interaction during non-invasive ventilation delivered by face mask. Intensiv. Care Med. **38**(10), 1624–1631 (2012)
19. Reuter, B., Linke, D., Kurthen, M.: Cognitive processes in unconscious patients? A brain mapping study of the p300 potential. Archiv fur Psychologie **141**(3), 155–173 (1989)
20. Rivet, B., Souloumiac, A., Attina, V., Gibert, G.: xDAWN algorithm to enhance evoked potentials: application to brain-computer interface. IEEE Trans. Biomed. Eng. **56**(8), 2035–2043 (2009)
21. Rotondi, A.J., et al.: Patients' recollections of stressful experiences while receiving prolonged mechanical ventilation in an intensive care unit. Critical Care Med. **30**(4), 746–752 (2002)
22. Schäfer, J., Strimmer, K.: A shrinkage approach to large-scale covariance matrix estimation and implications for functional genomics. Stat. Appl. Genet. Mol. Biol. **4**(1) (2005)
23. Scholkopf, B., Smola, A.J.: Learning with Kernels: Support Vector Machines, Regularization, Optimization, and Beyond. MIT Press, Cambridge (2001)
24. Wolpaw, J., Birbaumer, N., McFarland, D.J., Pfurtscheller, G., Vaughan, T.M.: Brain-computer interfaces for communication and control. Clin. Neurophysiol. **113**(6), 767–791 (2002)
25. Yger, F., Berar, M., Lotte, F.: Riemannian approaches in brain-computer interfaces: a review. IEEE Trans. Neural. Syst. Rehabil. Eng. **25**(10), 1753–1762 (2017)

Effectively Interpreting Electroencephalogram Classification Using the Shapley Sampling Value to Prune a Feature Tree

Kazuki Tachikawa(✉), Yuji Kawai, Jihoon Park, and Minoru Asada

Graduate School of Engineering, Osaka University, 2-1 Yamadaoka, Suita, Osaka 565-0871, Japan
{kazuki.tachikawa,kawai,jihoon.park, asada}@ams.eng.osaka-u.ac.jp

Abstract. Identifying the features that contribute to classification using machine learning remains a challenging problem in terms of the interpretability and computational complexity of the endeavor. Especially in electroencephalogram (EEG) medical applications, it is important for medical doctors and patients to understand the reason for the classification. In this paper, we thus propose a method to quantify contributions of interpretable EEG features on classification using the Shapley sampling value (SSV). In addition, a pruning method is proposed to reduce the SSV computation cost. The pruning is conducted on an EEG feature tree, specifically at the sensor (electrode) level, frequency-band level, and amplitude-phase level. If the contribution of a feature at a high level (e.g., sensor level) is very small, the contributions of features at a lower level (e.g., frequency-band level) should also be small. The proposed method is verified using two EEG datasets: classification of sleep states, and screening of alcoholics. The results show that the method reduces the SSV computational complexity while maintaining high SSV accuracy. Our method will thus increase the importance of data-driven approaches in EEG analysis.

Keywords: Electroencephalogram (EEG) · Shapley sampling value (SSV) Convolutional neural networks (CNN)

1 Introduction

Deep learning, especially via convolutional neural networks (CNNs), is a promising method of classification of electroencephalogram (EEG) signals. CNNs enable identification of brain states from raw EEG signals and provide higher classification accuracy than conventional machine learning techniques [6, 11]. However, understanding how the models classify the signals is difficult because CNNs have highly complex nonlinear functions. Visualization of features, which contribute to their classification, may engender neurophysiological insights and explanations that can be applied to medical diagnoses.

To identify the interpretable features of EEG, bandpass filters are often applied to EEG signals in standard EEG analysis to separate them into five frequency bands: delta, theta, alpha, beta, and gamma. Waves in each band are then analyzed in terms of

V. Kůrková et al. (Eds.): ICANN 2018, LNCS 11141, pp. 672–681, 2018.
https://doi.org/10.1007/978-3-030-01424-7_66

their amplitude and phase. Therefore, it is useful to quantify the contributions of amplitude and phase in a specific frequency band in the EEG classification.

Various methods to interpret classification of learning models have been proposed. They can be categorized into two groups: *backpropagation-based methods,* and *perturbation-based methods* [1]. Backpropagation-based methods, including layer-wise relevance propagation (LRP) [3], deep learning important features (DeepLIFT) [13], integrated gradients (IG) [16], and deep Shapley additive explanations (SHAP) [8], compute the contributions of all input features in accordance with the backpropagation of class information from an output layer to an input one (as denoted in orange characters in Fig. 1). Their computational cost is relatively low. However, these methods show the contributions only in the input feature space, which is not always interpretable.

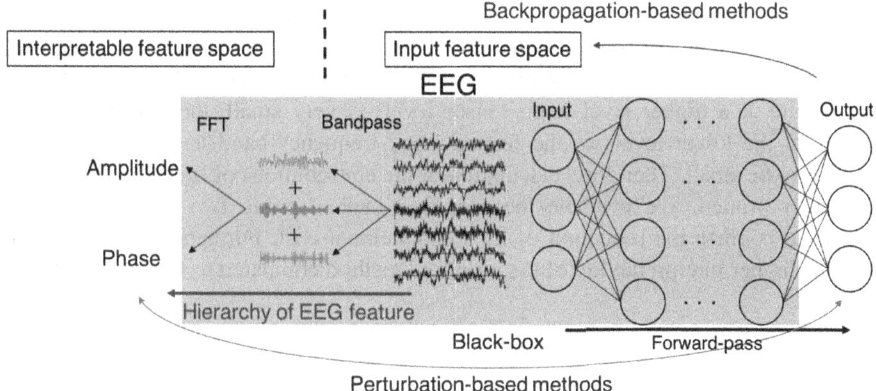

Fig. 1. Overview of methods to interpret EEG classification and a hierarchy of EEG features.

In contrast, perturbation-based methods, including the Shapley sampling value (SSV) [14], local interpretable model-agnostic explanations (LIME) [10], and kernel SHAP [8], regard the classifier as a black-box, i.e., they compute the contributions based on pairs of a perturbed (masked or permuted) input and its output (as denoted in blue characters in Fig. 1). These methods can display the contributions in a space representing the perturbation, which differs from the input feature space. By perturbing the classifiers in an interpretable way, we can obtain the contributions in an interpretive feature space. However, the computational cost becomes drastically higher as the number of features increases.

For visualization of signals contributing to EEG classification, several approaches have been proposed. Sturm et al. [15] applied LRP to EEG classifiers. However, LRP cannot directly reflect the contributions in the amplitude-phase form because it is based on backpropagation. Schirrmeister et al. [11] statistically analyzed EEG classifiers using two methods: input-feature unit-output correlation maps (IFUOCM) and input-perturbation network-prediction correlation maps (IPNPCM). IFUOCM computes correlations between the values of output neurons and the input powers of each frequency. IPNPCM calculates correlations of the output values with variations of the perturbed amplitude or phase [5]. However, the correlations do not always exactly reflect the impact of individual features on the prediction. In addition to the above three methods, two other methods were proposed in [7, 18], respectively. However, they require modifying input features or specifying the classifier architecture.

Recently, IG and SHAP were shown to be theoretically superior to other methods [8, 16] because they are compatible with the Shapley value (SV) that guarantees the equitable attribution of contributions. The SV assigns the contributions according to the impact on the prediction of each feature. In perturbation-based methods, which can quantify the contributions of any classifier in any feature space, the SSV and kernel SHAP also satisfy the SV axioms [8].

Based on the above review, the SSV is apparently a prominent method for interpreting EEG classification because it can display the contributions in an interpretable space and it satisfies the SV axioms. However, its computational cost is relatively high. In this paper, we apply the SSV to EEG classifiers and propose a pruning method to reduce its computational cost. EEG features form a tree structure comprised of a sensor (electrode) level, frequency-band level, and amplitude-phase level. If the contribution of a feature at a higher level (e.g., sensor level) is very small, the contributions of features at the lower levels of the feature (e.g., frequency-band level of the sensor) should also be small. Therefore, calculation of the contributions of such features can be ignored or pruned. We evaluate the proposed method using two benchmark EEG datasets to confirm the reduction of its computational cost. Furthermore, we demonstrate the higher interpretability of the proposed method compared to IG, IPNPCM, and IFUOCM.

2 Method

The SV was originally proposed to fairly assign the gains to players in cooperative game theory [12]. In its application to classification, the contribution $\phi_i(f, x)$ of the i th feature out of input feature x in a classifier, f, is given as:

$$\phi_i(f, x) = \sum_{S \subseteq x \backslash i} \frac{|S|!(M-|S|-1)!}{M!} [f_{S \cup i}(S \cup i) - f_S(S)], \tag{1}$$

where M denotes the number of input features, S denotes all possible subsets of an input feature space except for feature x_i, and $f_S(S)$ indicates the output of classifier f for input S. Basically, the contribution of a feature is defined as how much the output of a classifier is reduced by removal of the feature. The amount of reduction is then averaged over all possible combinations of features. This calculation requires computational cost $\mathcal{O}(2^n)$ for input size n and retraining of the classifier for all possible combinations. The SSV approximates the SV using a sampling method to reduce its computational cost [14].

We apply the SSV to EEG classification to identify the contributions of amplitude and phase in each frequency band in each sensor (electrode). These features, i.e., amplitude phase, frequency bands, and sensors, form a tree structure (left side in Fig. 1).

We contend that pruning of the tree can reduce the SSV computational cost. First, we calculate the SSV at the sensor level, specifically to assess the influence of the elimination of a sensor. The number of features (electrodes) at this level is relatively small. The sensor signals with small contributions do not contribute to the classification at frequency-band or amplitude-phase levels. Therefore, it is not necessary to calculate the contributions of such irrelevant sensors at the lower levels. Similarly, calculation of the contributions of amplitude and phase can be ignored if the frequency bands do not contribute to the classification. The pruning can reduce the computational cost, especially if a few feature branches contribute to the classification.

3 Experimental Settings

We conducted experiments using two EEG datasets to verify the validity of the proposed method. One dataset is the PhysioNet polysomnography (PSG) dataset. It easily shows the raw waves and applies the perturbation-based methods because it includes data of only three sensors. Therefore, we applied the proposed method and IG to this dataset and calculated the computational efficiency of our proposed pruning method. The other dataset was the UCI EEG dataset. This dataset contains much more sensor data. Therefore, we empirically compared the proposed method with IPNPCM and IFUOCM by the input flipping method.

3.1 PhysioNet Polysomnography Dataset

The PhysioNet PSG dataset is a publicly available sleep PSG dataset from PhysioNet [4]. It includes data of 20 healthy subjects (ten males; ten females) of ages ranging from 25 to 34 years. We employed EEG (Fpz-Cz and Pz-Oz electrodes) and electrooculography (EOG) signals in this dataset. Their sampling rates were 100 Hz, and the duration of epochs was 30 s. During the first night of the experiment, PSG was used to train the classifier; during the last night, it was used to test it. We constructed a six-layered CNN, as shown in Fig. 2, to classify the data into five sleep stages: Rem, Wake, N1, N2 and N3. Its classification accuracy for test data is 81%. The sleep stages are officially labeled based on the EEG and EOG signals. For example, the class N3 is defined as the large low-frequency power (delta band) in EEG. Therefore, the power of the delta band is expected to contribute to CNN classification for N3.

We compared the results of our proposed method with those of IG [16]. We applied them to CNN and visualized their results on randomly chosen N3 data. In addition, we evaluated the proposed pruning method in terms of its accuracy and computational cost which is the number of calculations of model outputs. We randomly chose 400 data and computed their SSVs with and without pruning. A branch was pruned when the contribution was smaller than one-fifth that of the most contributed feature. We regarded the SSV of 1,000 samples per feature as the true value, i.e., the SV, and evaluated the difference between the true value and the value estimated by the SSV with pruning.

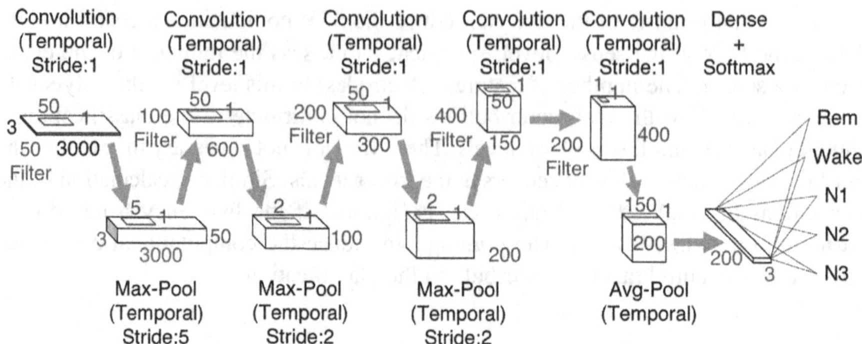

Fig. 2. CNN architecture in the PhysioNet experiment.

3.2 UCI EEG Dataset

The UCI EEG dataset is a publicly available event-related EEG dataset in the UCI Machine Learning Repository [2]. The dataset is comprised of EEG data collected using 64 electrodes at 256 Hz. It contains 120 data items for one subject, each obtained within 1 s and labeled as "alcoholic" or "control." The number of subjects is 122 (77 alcoholics and 45 controls). We evaluated the accuracy of CNN using ten-fold cross-validation, resulting in 75% accuracy, as shown in Fig. 3. We compared the results of the SSV and IPNPCM. We applied them on 30 randomly chosen data items. In addition, we empirically quantified the power of explanation using "frequency-band-level flipping" based on "pixel flipping" [3]. Then, the output values of the classifier were evaluated while removing the most highly contributed features. The output decrease means the power of the explanation.

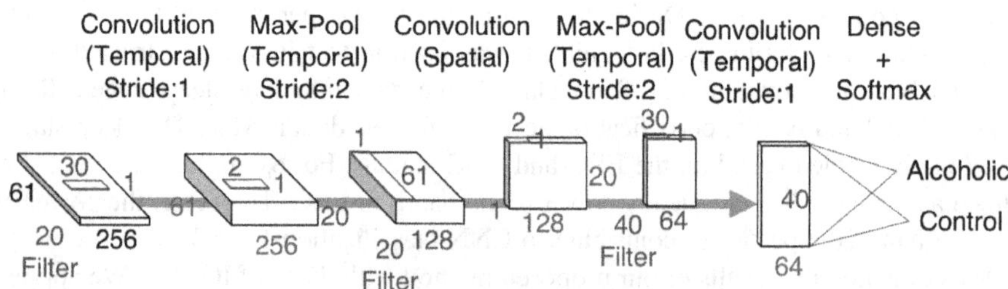

Fig. 3. CNN architecture in the UCI EEG experiment.

4 Results

4.1 Results for the PhysioNet PSG Dataset

An example of the SSV result on the randomly chosen N3 data is shown in Fig. 4. The contributions of features are described as percentages of the SSVs in trees. Orange and blue percentages denote the contributions with and without pruning, respectively.

The figure shows that the power of the delta band in the Fpz-Cz electrode is the most important for this classification, which corresponds to the definition of N3. The percentages of the features are 78% for the SSV with pruning and 76% for the SSV without pruning, suggesting that the pruning effect on the accuracy is minimal. Figure 5 shows an example of the IG result, where the colors on raw EEG signals indicate their contributions. IG shows the contributions in the input space, i.e., raw EEG signals. Therefore, this means of visualization is difficult to interpret and requires additional analysis to identify the important frequency bands.

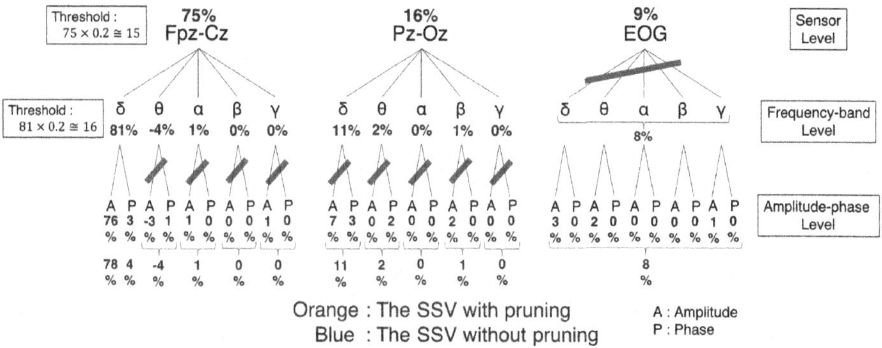

Fig. 4. Example of the results of the Shapley sampling value (SSV). Orange and blue percentages indicate the SSVs with and without pruning, respectively. Orange diagonal lines represent pruning. (Color figure online)

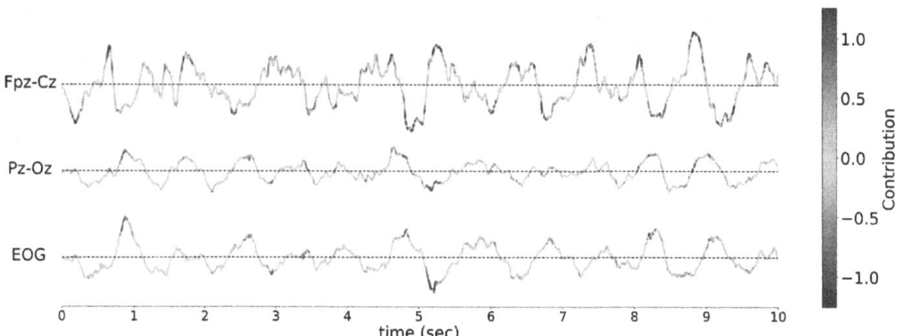

Fig. 5. Example of the results of ingredient gradients [16]. Curves indicate raw EEG signals and their colors represent their contributions at the given time. (Color figure online)

Figure 6 shows the effects of pruning on the accuracy (left panel) and computational cost (right panel). The horizontal axes indicate the number of samplings per feature in both panels. The solid and broken curves indicate the values for the SSV with and without pruning, respectively. The green, red, and blue curves represent the results of classification for the N2 class, all classes, and the N3 class, respectively. The left

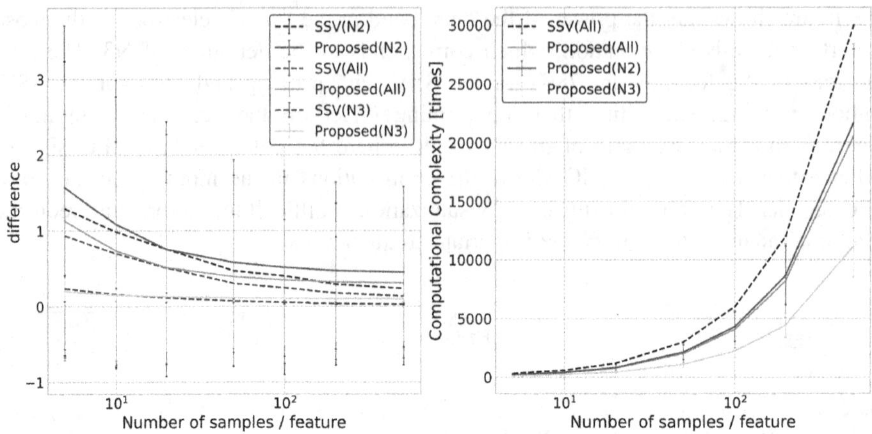

Fig. 6. Comparison of the results of the SSV with and without pruning. Left: difference between the true Shapley value and the SSV. Right: computational cost.

panel shows the approximation errors of the SSVs with respect to the true SVs. The results show that the errors of the SSVs with pruning are the same level as those without pruning, especially in the range of samples per feature from 10 to 50. The right panel shows that pruning reduces the computational cost to approximately two-thirds. These results suggest that the proposed method realizes effective the SV estimation.

4.2 Results for the UCI EEG Dataset

The results of the proposed SSV and IPNPCM are shown in Figs. 7 and 8. The SSV demonstrates significant contributions of amplitude in the delta and gamma bands and of phase in the delta band. IPNPCM contributes amplitude in the beta and gamma bands and phase in the delta band. The beta band was not addressed by the SSV because of the already mentioned problem of the correlation. Figure 9 shows the results

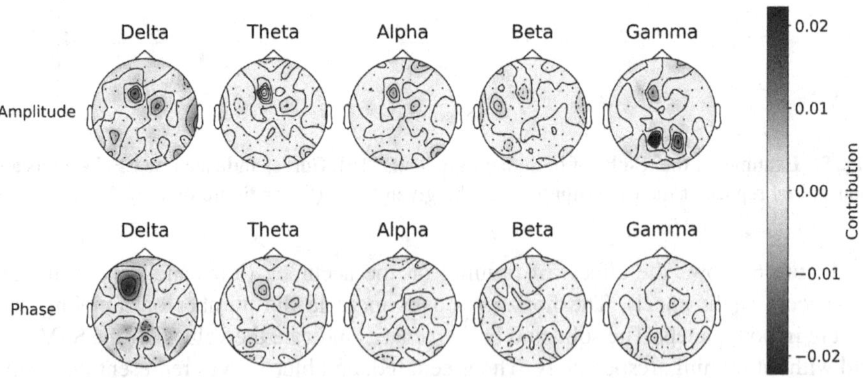

Fig. 7. Averaged contributions for 100 data items, visualized by the SSV with pruning.

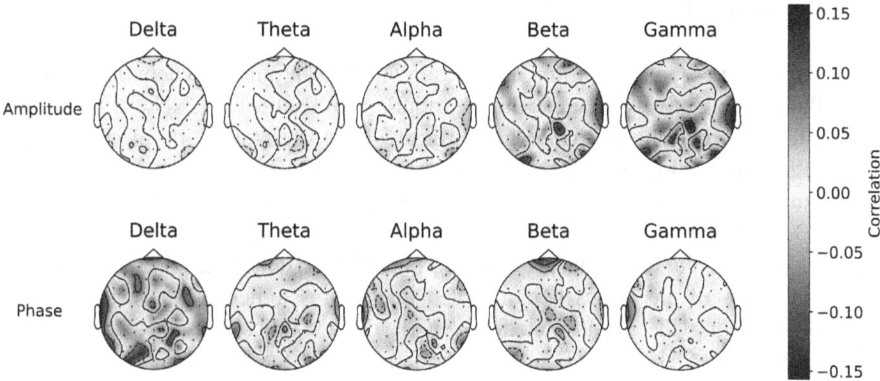

Fig. 8. Averaged contributions for 100 data items, visualized by IPNPCM [11].

of the "frequency-band-level flipping" for the SSV methods with pruning (blue curve), IPNPCM (orange curve), and IFUOCM (green curve). The classification scores of the SSV (with pruning) significantly decreases compared to those of IPNPCM and IFUOCM, suggesting that the proposed SSV more appropriately elucidates the classification.

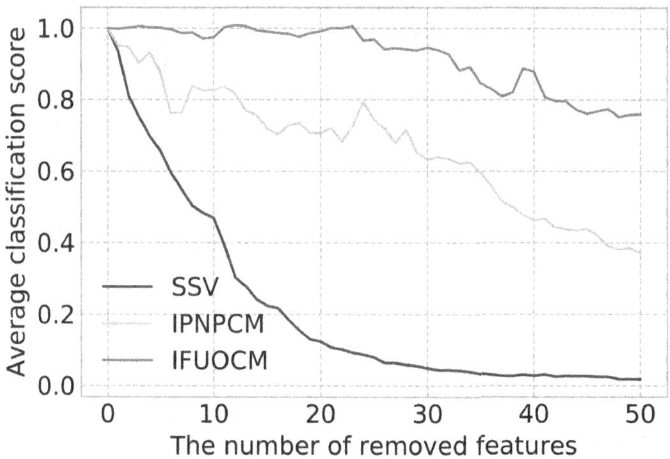

Fig. 9. Result of frequency-band-level flipping for the SSV with pruning, IPNPCM, and IFUOCM [11]. The classification score is normalized so that the scores of the original input are 1.0.

5 Discussion and Conclusion

In this paper, we proposed a pruning method in the SV sampling and demonstrated that the method can effectively quantify the contributions of features in CNN classifiers. We verified the proposed method when applied to two tasks: classification of sleep stages and alcoholic screening. In the first experiment, the SSV assigned the largest contributions to amplitude in the delta band (Fig. 4), which was consistent with the definition of the N3 sleep stage. In the second experiment, the SSV displayed the contributions of amplitude in the delta and gamma bands and phase in the delta band (Fig. 7). A recent review of EEGs of alcoholics demonstrated that many studies focus on the gamma band for screening the event-related potentials of alcoholics [9]. In addition, Tcheslavski and Gonen [17] found significant differences of the power and coherence in the lower frequency bands between alcoholics and controls. These results correspond to our visualization, suggesting that the proposed method can explain the contributing features.

Moreover, the conducted experiments produced the following four results. (1) The proposed method effectively interpreted the EEG classification in the amplitude-phase feature space, while gradient-based methods, including IG, could not explain them in such an interpretable feature space (Fig. 5). (2) Our pruning method reduced the computational cost while maintaining the estimation accuracy (Fig. 6). (3) The SSV explanation is superior to the IPNPCM explanation and IFUOCM explanation in terms of the pixel-flipping evaluation (Fig. 9). (4) The contributions visualized using the proposed method are consistent with previous findings on EEG biomarkers.

Although pruning reduces the SSV computational cost, the cost is still much greater than those of backpropagation-based methods. We must address this problem to apply the SSV to medical data that have a very large number of features. We surmise that combining our method with a backpropagation-based method, such as IG, can enable a more feasible visualization technique.

Acknowledgements. This work was supported by the Center of Innovation Program from Japan Science and Technology Agency and JST CREST Grant Number JPMJCR17A4, Japan.

References

1. Ancona, M., Ceolini, E., Oztireli, C., Gross, M.: Towards better understanding of gradient-based attribution methods for deep neural networks. In: Proceedings of the 6th International Conference on Learning Representations (2018)
2. Asuncion, A., Newman, D.: UCI Machine Learning Repository (2007)
3. Bach, S., Binder, A., Montavon, G., Klauschen, F., Muller, K.R., Samek, W.: On pixel-wise explanations for non-linear classifier decisions by layer-wise relevance propagation. PLoS ONE **10**(7), e0130140 (2015)
4. Goldberger, A.L., et al.: Physiobank, physiotoolkit, and physionet. Circulation **101**(23), e215–e220 (2000)
5. Hartmann, K.G., Schirrmeister, R.T., Ball, T.: Hierarchical internal representation of spectral features in deep convolutional networks trained for EEG decoding. In: Proceedings of the 6th International Conference on Brain-Computer Interface, pp. 1–6 (2018)

6. Lawhern, V.J., Solon, A.J., Waytowich, N.R., Gordon, S.M., Hung, C.P., Lance, B.J.: EEGNet: a compact convolutional network for EEG-based brain-computer interfaces. arXiv: 1611.08024 (2016)
7. Li, Y., et al.: Targeting EEG/LFP synchrony with neural nets. In: Advances in Neural Information Processing Systems, pp. 4623–4633 (2017)
8. Lundberg, S.M., Lee, S.I.: A unified approach to interpreting model predictions. In: Advances in Neural Information Processing Systems, pp. 4768–4777 (2017)
9. Mumtaz, W., Vuong, P.L., Malik, A.S., Rashid, R.B.A.: A review on EEG-based methods for screening and diagnosing alcohol use disorder. Cogn. Neurodynamics, 1–16 (2018)
10. Ribeiro, M.T., Singh, S., Guestrin, C.: Why should I trust you? Explaining the predictions of any classifier. In: Proceedings of the 22nd ACM SIGKDD International Conference on Knowledge Discovery and Data Mining, pp. 1135–1144. ACM (2016)
11. Schirrmeister, R.T., et al.: Deep learning with convolutional neural networks for EEG decoding and visualization. Hum. Brain Mapp. **38**(11), 5391–5420 (2017)
12. Shapley, L.S.: A value for n-person games. Contrib. Theory Games **2**(28), 307–317 (1953)
13. Shrikumar, A., Greenside, P., Kundaje, A.: Learning important features through propagating activation differences. arXiv:1704.02685 (2017)
14. Shtrumbelj, E., Kononenko, I.: Explaining prediction models and individual predictions with feature contributions. Knowl. Inf. Syst. **41**(3), 647–665 (2014)
15. Sturm, I., Lapuschkin, S., Samek, W., Muller, K.R.: Interpretable deep neural networks for single-trial EEG classification. J. Neurosci. Methods **274**, 141–145 (2016)
16. Sundararajan, M., Taly, A., Yan, Q.: Axiomatic attribution for deep networks. arXiv:1703. 01365 (2017)
17. Tcheslavski, G.V., Gonen, F.F.: Alcoholism-related alterations in spectrum, coherence, and phase synchrony of topical electroencephalogram. Comput. Biol. Med. **42**(4), 394–401 (2012)
18. Vilamala, A., Madsen, K.H., Hansen, L.K.: Deep convolutional neural networks for interpretable analysis of EEG sleep stage scoring. arXiv:1710.00633 (2017)

EEG-Based Person Identification Using Rhythmic Brain Activity During Sleep

Athanasios Koutras[1,2(✉)] and George K. Kostopoulos[2]

[1] Department of Informatics and Mass Media, Technical Educational Institute of Western Greece, R. Fereou, 27100 Pyrgos, Greece
koutras@teiwest.gr

[2] Neurophysiology Unit, Department of Physiology, Medical School, University of Patras, Rion, 26504 Patras, Greece

Abstract. In this paper we present a novel approach to the person identification problem using rhythmic brain activity of spindles from whole night EEG recordings. The proposed system consists of a feature extraction module and a K-NN based classifier. Different types of features from time, frequency and wavelet domain are used to highlight the topographic, temporal, morphological, spectral and statistical discriminative information of sleep spindles. The feature set's efficacy is exhaustively tested in order to find the most significant descriptors that maximize intra-subject separability. Extensive experiments resulted in the optimal number of sensors and features that must be used to form the subject-specific unique descriptors. The proposed system showed significant identification accuracy of 99% $\sim$ 90% for 2–20 subjects, and not lower than 86% when identifying 28 persons, indicating that this new type of modality should be further investigated to be used in EEG based identification applications.

Keywords: EEG · Sleep spindles · Person identification · Feature selection

1 Introduction

Recognition of individuals using their unique physiological or behavioral characteristics has already been proposed and examined by many researchers worldwide during the last decade. Person identification is a pattern recognition problem, where a system tries to recognize the identity of a person by comparing a set of his/her personal characteristics with templates already stored in the system's database during an enrollment phase. In the previous years, different types of characteristics have been proposed that include but are not limited to fingerprints, iris, face, emotion, speech, keystroke typing, and walking sequences. [1, 2].

Recently, a new mode of modality has been proposed for labeling an individual which is based on the person's brain signal activity measured by a number of EEG sensors located on the subject's sculp. Using brain signals for person identification has some significant advantages compared to other traditional modalities which are focused mainly on two points: (a) uniqueness of a person's brain signal and (b) difficulty of the on-purpose reproduction of it. During the last years a great number of identification

V. Kůrková et al. (Eds.): ICANN 2018, LNCS 11141, pp. 682–692, 2018.
https://doi.org/10.1007/978-3-030-01424-7_67

systems based on EEG signal acquisition have been proposed [3]. Most of them are based on the extraction of brain activity descriptors in various situations that include relax rest state (eyes open/closed) [4], visually evoked potentials [5], mental tasks [6], emotions [6], and motor imagery [7]. The aim of these systems is to increase the intra-subject separability using feature extraction and pattern recognition algorithms to improve the performance of the identification.

One of the basic problems in EEG based person identification is the acquisition of brain signals which in many cases is not a comfortable situation for subjects. Usually for accurate identification, a great number of EEG electrodes properly placed by an expert on the subject's head is required which increases the complexity of the process. To address this problem, it is crucial to estimate the significance of each sensor and determine an optimal small subset that will be used instead, without affecting the recognition accuracy [8]. Another problem often faced in the EEG based identification task is the dimensionality of the feature vectors that are used to describe the neural activity in various situations. Again, one should also estimate the significance of each feature and reduce their dimensionality, which together with the small number of sensors, will help identification systems to work more efficient [9].

The main contribution of this paper is two-fold: (i) we introduce the problem of person identification using rhythmic brain activity of spindles from EEG recordings during sleep, something that to our knowledge hasn't been presented in the literature (ii) after extensive experiments, we propose the most efficient set of sensors and locations, together with a set of the most significant descriptors that should be used for fast training, low complexity and high accuracy in a person identification system based on the K-NN classifier. Sleep spindles are micro-events in EEG which is characteristic of Nonrapid Eye Movement (NREM) stages of sleep. It is a transient waveform with waxing-waning morphology, particularly present in stage 2 of NREM with frequency in the range 11–16 Hz with duration at least 0.5 s [10].

This paper is organized as follows: In Sect. 2 we present our proposed method for person identification using EEG recordings during sleep. In the same Section, we present the feature extraction module that extracts brain activity descriptors in three different domains: time, frequency, and wavelets. In Sect. 3 the Experimental Setup and the database is presented, while in Sect. 4 we discuss the experimental results. Finally, in Sect. 5 some conclusions are drawn.

2 Method

2.1 Feature Extraction

The main purpose of this work is to examine whether rhythmic brain activity of spindles during sleep presents different characteristics across persons and therefore can be used as template for successful identification of different subjects. To study this, we have selected a set of well-known spindle descriptors extracted from various domains, previously used in the problem of spindle recognition from EEG recordings with great success [11]. The extracted descriptors use time, frequency, and wavelet domain representations of the signal to describe their morphology, topology, spectral characteristics as well as their most important statistical properties.

Time Domain Descriptors (F1-F10). Morphology of sleep spindles in the time domain has proven to play a significant role in the task of automatic spindle recognition in all night multichannel EEG recordings of brain activity during sleep. In our work we have used the following ten (F1 – F10) low level descriptors in the time domain:

F1 - Duration (in sec): Spindle duration is defined as the time between the start point and the end point of the spindle as this is marked by expert annotators of the database.
F2 - Mean: The arithmetic mean of the spindle's amplitude
F3 - Standard deviation: The 2nd order statistical moment (variance) of the spindle's amplitude.
F4 - Skewness: The 3rd central moment of the amplitude's envelope. This feature describes the shift of the spindle's maximal amplitude and is positive when it shows shift towards the left, negative when it is shifted towards the right.
F5 - Kurtosis: The 4th order central moment of the amplitude's envelope. This feature describes the sharpness of the spindle's envelope and it is positive for sharp, negative for flat envelopes compared to the normal distribution.
F6 - Maximum: The maximum peak (positive or negative) of the spindle's amplitude.
F7 - Shape Factor:

$$SF = \frac{x_{rms}}{\frac{1}{N}\sum_{n=1}^{N}\sqrt{|x(n)|}} \tag{1}$$

Among the features extracted from the time domain representation of the signal, the following three main Hjorth features were also extracted and used in the experiments. These parameters were originally proposed by Hjorth [12] and used in many cases of EEG signal analysis as they measure the second moment of first and second differences of the signal:

F8 - Activity: The activity parameter describes the power of the spindle, the variance of the time function. This descriptor indicates the surface of the power spectrum.

$$Activity(x) = \sqrt{\frac{1}{N}\sum_{n=1}^{N} x^2(n)} \tag{2}$$

F9 - Mobility: The mobility parameter represents the mean frequency or the proportion of standard deviation of the power spectrum.

$$Mobility(x) = \frac{Activity(diff(x))}{Activity(x)} \tag{3}$$

F10 - Complexity: The complexity parameter represents the change in frequency by comparing the signal's similarity with a pure sine wave, value converges to 1 when signal is more similar.

$$Complexity(x) = \sqrt{Mobility^2(diff(x)) - Mobility^2(x)} \tag{4}$$

Frequency Domain Descriptors (F11-F27). Spindles like any other rhythmic brain activity carry important information in the frequency domain. For this case we have used the Power Spectral Density (PSD) to extract significant descriptors to be included in our identification task. The PSD was obtained using Welch's averaged periodogram method [in ear]. In this work 17 (F11-F27) features in total were extracted from the frequency domain:

F11 - Peak Frequency in sigma band. We estimate the peak frequency in the sigma band between 12–16 Hz. Peaks are defined as the frequency points where the first derivative of the spectrum changes from a positive to a negative value.
F12 - Intra-spindle frequency change: The rate of frequency change using the instant frequency estimate in the start and the end of the spindle (in Hz/sec).
F13 - Power in lower sigma band: The spindle's energy in the lower sigma band $(9 - 12\,\text{Hz})$ normalized by total signal's power.
F14 - Power in higher sigma band: The spindle's energy descriptors in the higher sigma band $(12 - 16\,\text{Hz})$ normalized by total signal's power.
F15 - Power in the sigma band: The spindle's energy descriptors in the sigma band $[12 - 16\,\text{Hz}]$ normalized by the total signal's power.
F16-20 - Power in basic bands (alpha, beta, gamma, delta, theta): Using the power spectral density, we have estimated the spindle's energy descriptors in five different frequency bands, namely: (i) the *delta* (1–4 Hz) ($F16$), (ii) *theta* (4–8 Hz) ($F17$), (iii) *alpha* (8–12 Hz) ($F18$), (iv) *beta* (13–30 Hz) ($F19$) and (v) *gamma* (30–45 Hz) ($F20$) by calculating the power of the signal in the band of interest normalized by the total power of the signal (normalized in-band spectral density).
F21 - Average inter-spindle frequency: To estimate the average inter-spindle frequency, the S-transform (ST) of the spindle $x(t)$ is used as in [13]. From the s-transformed signal, the time-frequency representation of the spindle $S(t,f)$ is estimated using equation:

$$S(t,f) = \int_{-\infty}^{\infty} x(\tau) \frac{|f|}{\sqrt{2\pi}} e^{-\frac{(t-\tau)^2 f^2}{2}} e^{-i2\pi f\tau} d\tau \tag{5}$$

and the average along the frequency axis is computed for every time point using:

$$f_{aver}(t) = \frac{\int_{-\infty}^{\infty} f|S(t,f)|df}{\int_{-\infty}^{\infty} |S(t,f)|df} \tag{6}$$

Using the $f_{aver}(t)$ we next perform linear regression over the spindle's duration. The frequency value of the regression line at the midpoint of the spindle duration window is the average inter-spindle frequency feature.

F22 - Slope of inter-spindle frequency change: Using the above linear regression, the slope of the calculated line is estimated to describe the inter-spindle frequency change.
F23 - Minimum PSD value: The minimum value of the power spectral density $\widehat{P}_w(f)$
F24 – Maximum PSD value: The maximum value of the power spectral density $\widehat{P}_w(f)$
F25 - Mean PSD value: The mean value of the power spectral density $\widehat{P}_w(f)$
F26 - Standard deviation of the PSD value: The standard deviation of the power spectral density $\widehat{P}_w(f)$
F27 - The Spectral Edge Frequency - 85%: The SEF85 measures the spectral shape and is the frequency f_{SEP85} below which the 85% of the signal's power is present.

Wavelet Domain Descriptors (F28-F32). Wavelet transform has been proposed and proven to be effective for time frequency representation of signals especially in the field of biomedical applications. Its main advantage lies in the fact that it can provide accurate frequency information in low frequencies and at the same time accurate time information in higher frequencies. In this paper we have used the Discrete Wavelet Transform (DWT) to analyze the spindles at different frequency bands of interest, by decomposing the signal using a mother wavelet $\Psi(t)$, low and high pass successive filtering in levels using digital filters followed by a down sampling factor of 2. The detail and approximation decomposition signals carry information of the spindle in different frequency bands (depending on the number of decomposition levels). The signal's energy at level j can be estimated from the energy of the coefficients $d_{j,k}$, while the energy of the signal at decomposition level $N+1$ can be estimated by the energy of the scaling coefficients C_k of the transform.

In our experiments we have used the Daubechies-5 (db-5) wavelet function to decompose the signal in four (4) levels (D1: 22.5–45 Hz, D2: 11.25–22.5 Hz, D3: 5.6–11.25 Hz, D4: 2.8–5.6 Hz, A4: 0.1–2.8 Hz). The energy of the signal at each level is calculated by Eq. 7 for levels 1–4, while the total signal energy is given by Eq. 8:

$$E_j = \sum\nolimits_k \left|d_{j,k}\right|^2, j = 1, 2, \ldots N \qquad E_{N+1} = \sum\nolimits_k |c_k|^2 \tag{7}$$

$$E_{total} = \sum\nolimits_j E_j \tag{8}$$

In this work we have used the Relative wavelet energy ρ_j for every decomposition band given by the following equation (F28–32):

$$\rho_j = \frac{E_j}{E_{total}}, j = 1, 2, \ldots, N+1 \tag{9}$$

Feature extraction was performed in every EEG channel separately, resulting in 56, 32-dimensional vectors. These vectors were concatenated initially to form the 56 * 32 1792-dimension vector that describes every single spindle.

3 Experiments

3.1 The Sleep Spindles Database

For our experiments the NU Sleep Database collected in the Neurophysiology Unit, University of Patras was used. The subset of the database that was used in all experiments consists of 34 whole-night polysomnographic recordings of 28 subjects (16 female/12 male) with no reported psychiatric or neurological conditions, obtained between 2007–2016. The acquired bio signals include 56 channel EEG following the standard 10–20 montage. Original sampling rate of the recordings is 2500 Hz. Sleep scoring, artifact rejection and annotation of sleep spindles have been performed by at least one and usually more than one experts in all cases. The total number of spindles for the 28 subjects is 25784 with a mean value of 920 spindles per subject (minimum number of spindles in a class: 832, maximum number: 1480).

3.2 Data Preprocessing

All acquired data were first down sampled from 2500 Hz to 500 Hz by a down sampling factor of 5 and then a notch filter was applied to eliminate any power line contamination at 50 Hz frequency. Annotated spindles were then band-pass filtered using a fourth order Butterworth band-pass filter with lower and upper cutoff frequencies at 0.1 and 45 Hz since all frequencies of interest in this study lie in this band.

3.3 Experimental Setup

In the identification step, we used the K-NN classifier. K-NN's choice is mainly attributed to its simplicity and feature flexibility, while at the same time it can naturally handle multi-class cases and performs well in practice with enough representative data. K-NN works by comparing the distance between the training and the testing features. In the testing phase, K-NN finds the K-nearest samples in the training feature and the classification is made by the voting scheme within the training samples. In all experiments, we have considered the K-NN classifier at level 3 on the extracted features through all our experiments, as at this level results were constants. For measuring the distance, the cosine distance was used, which was found to perform significantly better than other distance measures.

For the evaluation of the proposed method, we performed a 10-fold cross validation on each subject's data. All results of this paper present the mean accuracy over 10 folds using the randomly created sets. In addition, since testing all possible combinations of the 28 subjects was impossible (the number of possible combinations for n subjects is given by the binomial coefficient $\binom{28}{n}$), all experiments were repeated for 50 randomly chosen combinations of subjects (except for the case of 27 and 28 subjects where all possible combinations were formed and tested) and the mean accuracy was calculated and presented throughout the paper.

4 Results

4.1 Person Identification Using All Channels

In our first set of experiments, we have tested the efficacy of a simple K-NN based classifier in the person identification problem using features extracted from all 56 channels (56 * 32 = 1792 dimensions) for variable number of persons from 2 to 28. In all experiments, 50 different randomly selected combinations of subjects were tested, following the accuracy measure procedure described in Sect. 3.3.

In Fig. 1 (blue line) we present the identification results of the K-NN classifier for the case of 2 to 28 subjects using features extracted from all channels. It is evident that when the number of subjects is small (under 10), the K-NN classifier identifies correctly the subjects with accuracy over 97%. The accuracy drops slightly as the number of subjects increases, but even for the case of 28 subjects, the simple K-NN classifier manages to achieve no less than 92% accuracy.

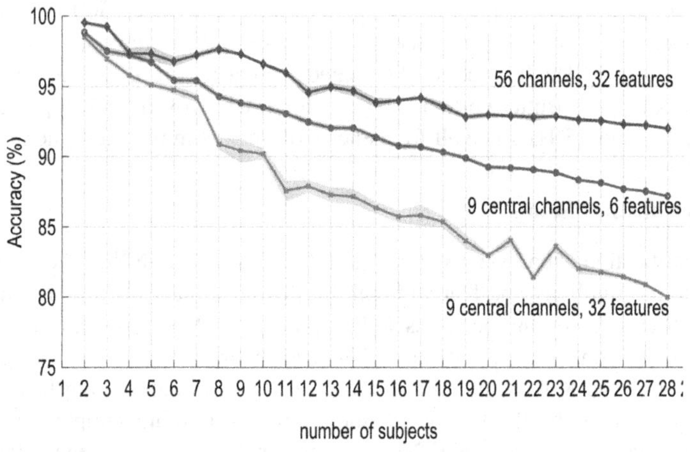

Fig. 1. Mean identification accuracy for (a) 56 EEG channels/32 features/channel (b) 9 central channels, 32 features/channel (c) 9 central channels/6 features/channel (Color figure online)

4.2 Person Identification Using Single Channel

To reduce complexity, we tested the efficacy of the identification system using features extracted from a *single* channel. In this case as Fig. 2A shows, the K-NN classifier's performance drops drastically, indicating that discriminative information lies in more than a single electrode. The accuracy of single channel identification system is higher for the 2-subject case reaching a peak of $\sim$ 99% for a few specific central channels but drops below 65% when most of the remaining channels are used. In average, the single channel system works $\sim$ 27% worse than the case when all channels are used for a small number of subjects (70% for single channel and two subjects – 97% all channels). This decrease is more obvious as the number of subjects increases and surpasses 15, where the identification rate drops under 20% in opposition to the 94% when all channels are used.

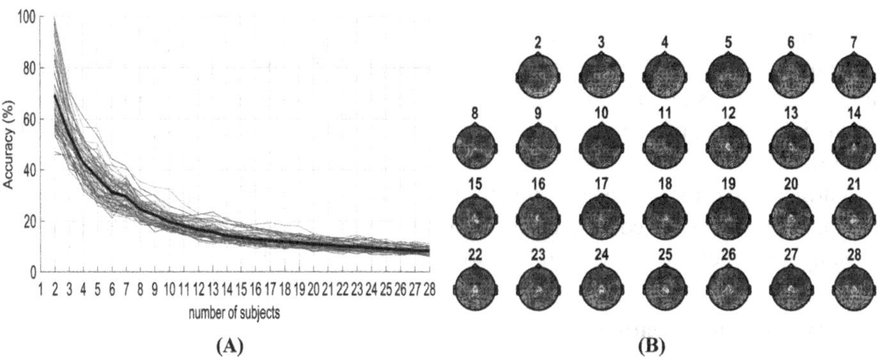

Fig. 2. (A) Identification accuracy using *single channel* feature extraction (black line: mean identification accuracy of all channels, color lines: single channel identification accuracy). (B) topographic plots of single channel accuracy for 2–28 subjects (yellow: higher accuracy, blue: lower accuracy) (Color figure online)

In Fig. 2B we depict the accuracy of the identification system on the electrode space when single channel descriptors are used for the case of 2 to 28 subjects. The figure's color map is relevant to the measured accuracy in the range of 0-(max channel accuracy) for each of the 56 channels (yellow: higher, blue: lower accuracy).

By visual inspection we can see that the electrodes that are located in the central brain regions present the highest accuracy compared to electrodes in the frontal, occipital or parietal regions regardless the number of different subjects under examination. This finding agrees with physiology as spindles are known to be waves initially located in the central part of the brain (fast spindles) moving slowly to frontal areas as they come to end (slow spindles).

4.3 Person Identification Using Significant Channels

Person identification using 56 channels, even though it works well, is very difficult to implement, as the big number of electrodes and features result in vectors with large dimensionality. To reduce the complexity of the problem without compromising the system's accuracy, we considered the previous section's results, and tested several different channel groups to find the most efficient ones. As the central EEG channels showed better identification accuracy compared to frontal, occipital or temporal ones, we started our search by selecting channel CZ as "seed" and formed groups of neighbor electrodes that were tested using the same methodology presented in the previous section.

After examining different groups with variable number of members (3, 4, …25) from the central region, we discovered that the group that is formed by {C1, CZ, C2, C1P, PZA, C2P, C1A, CZA, C2A}, shows top accuracy in the identification task of 2 to 28 subjects (Fig. 1 (red line)). Slightly better results were also measured when considering all central electrodes, but the group size ($\sim$ 21 channels) couldn't compensate for the small increase of the accuracy by a mean value of approximately 2 $\sim$ 3% compared to the group of 9 channels.

Comparing the accuracy of the proposed group with that of a single channel, we measured a mean increase greater than 60% especially for the case of larger number of subjects (20 $\sim$ 28). In these cases, the group formed by the 9 central channels achieves a mean identification accuracy of over 70%, as opposed to single channel that struggles to a low 15%.

Further experiments tested neighborhoods in the frontal, occipital and temporal region, but results showed very low accuracy (increase by only 5 $\sim$ 10% compared to the single channel case) and therefore were not further used.

4.4 Person Identification Using Significant Features

In all previous experiments, features F1-F32 were used. To further test the importance of each individual feature, we have applied the RelieFF [14] feature selection algorithm on the set extracted from the 9-channel group.

Feature selection using the RelieFF algorithm is a well-known technique based on a feature weighting approach that considers the interrelationship among features. The algorithm results in finding a weight factor that is highly correlated to the significance of each feature in the classification task. By considering only those features with significant weighting above a threshold, we can achieve dimensionality reduction of the feature set, thus easing the task of the classifier, while at the same time features with the largest importance can be singled out and could be used to explain characteristics that differentiate sleep spindles across subjects.

By examining the most significant features, we found that the first 100 correspond to a few (6) similar features from different channels and in particular to the Activity, Mobility, Complexity, Power in Sigma, Average inter-spindle frequency, and Slope of inter-spindle frequency change. Using this reduced feature set (F8, F9, F10, F15, F21, F22), we repeated the identification experiments for all subject combinations for the 9-channel group. The experimental results are presented in Fig. 1 (green line). From this Figure it is clear that the use of only 6 features instead of 32, results in a significant improvement of the identifier's accuracy, greater than 6% especially for the difficult case when all 28 subjects were tested compared to the 32 full feature vector. In addition, the proposed combination of features and electrodes approaches the best recognition results measured when all channels and features were used, but with much lower complexity in the electrode (9 instead of 54 channels) as well as the feature space (54 instead of 1792 features). Extensive experiments were further conducted by considering and testing varying number of significant features from the RelieFF step (50 to 200), but results showed that other feature combinations worsen the efficacy of the identification system.

5 Conclusions

In this paper we have investigated an EEG-based person identification system that uses rhythmic brain activity of spindles from sleep to distinguish between 2 to 28 different subjects. Extensive experiments have proven that sleep spindles show characteristics that are different across subjects and can be extracted from a small group of nine EEG channels located in the central region of the subject's head. Additionally, it was found that only six features that describe morphology, power and the basic spindle frequency, include most of the identity's specific information, and achieve high identification accuracy over 90% for 20 subjects, and not lower than 86% when identifying 28 persons using a simple K-NN classifier. As future work, more subjects will be included, while different types of classifiers and feature selection techniques will be tested to fine tune the system's performance and reduce further, if possible, the number of channels, increasing the accuracy at the same time.

References

1. Sivasankari, N., Muthukumar, A.: A review on recent techniques in multimodal biometrics. In: 2016 International Conference on Computer Communication and Informatics, ICCCI 2016 (2016)
2. Faridah, Y., Nasir, H., Kushsairy, A.K., Safie, S.I.: Survey multimodal biometric algorithm: a survey (2016)
3. Del Pozo-Banos, M., Alonso, J.B., Ticay-Rivas, J.R., Travieso, C.M.: Electroencephalogram subject identification: a review (2014)
4. Thomas, K.P., Vinod, A.P.: Toward EEG-based biometric systems: the great potential of brain-wave-based biometrics. IEEE Syst. Man Cybern. Mag. **3**, 6–15 (2017)
5. Reshmi, K.C., Muhammed, P.I., Priya, V.V., Akhila, V.A.: A novel approach to brain biometric user recognition. Procedia Technol. **25**, 240–247 (2016)
6. Vahid, A., Arbabi, E.: Human identification with EEG signals in different emotional states. In: 2016 23rd Iranian Conference on Biomedical Engineering and 2016 1st International Iranian Conference on Biomedical Engineering, ICBME 2016, pp. 242–246 (2017)
7. Jiralerspong, T., Liu, C., Ishikawa, J.: Identification of three mental states using a motor imagery based brain machine interface. In: IEEE Symposium on Computational Intelligence in Brain Computer Interfaces, pp. 2081–2089 (2014)
8. Rodrigues, D., Silva, G.F.A., Papa, J.P., Marana, A.N., Yang, X.S.: EEG-based person identification through binary flower pollination algorithm. Expert Syst. Appl. **62**, 81–90 (2016)
9. Kaur, B., Singh, D.: Neuro signals: a future biomertic approach towards user identification. In: Proceedings 7th International Conference on Cloud Computing, Data Science and Engineering, pp. 112–117 (2017)
10. Iber, C., Ancoli-Israel, S., Chesson, A.: The AASM manual for the scoring of sleep and associated events: rules, terminology and technical specifications (2007)
11. 't Wallant, D.C., Maquet, P., Phillips, C.: Sleep spindles as an electrographic element: description and automatic detection methods. Neural Plast. **2016** (2016)

12. Hjorth, B.: EEG analysis based on time domain properties. Electroencephalogr. Clin. Neurophysiol. (1970)
13. O'Reilly, C., Nielsen, T.: Assessing EEG sleep spindle propagation. Part 2: experimental characterization. J. Neurosci. Methods **221**, 215–227 (2014)
14. Robnik-Šikonja, M., Kononenko, I.: Theoretical and empirical analysis of ReliefF and RReliefF. Mach. Learn. (2003)

An STDP Rule for the Improvement and Stabilization of the Attractor Dynamics of the Basal Ganglia-Thalamocortical Network

Jérémie Cabessa[1(✉)] and Alessandro E. P. Villa[2]

[1] Laboratoire d'économie mathématique et de microéconomie appliquée (LEMMA), University Paris 2 – Panthéon-Assas, 4, Rue Blaise Desgoffe, 75006 Paris, France
jeremie.cabessa@u-paris2.fr

[2] NeuroHeuristic Research Group, University of Lausanne, Quartier UNIL-Dorigny, 1015 Lausanne, Switzerland
alessandro.villa@unil.ch

Abstract. The basal ganglia-thalamocortical (BGT) network has been investigated for many years, in particular in relation to disorders of the motor system and of the sleep-waking cycle. Its attractor dynamics is related to significant aspects of processing and coding of information, the most important of which being associative memories. The consideration of a simplified Boolean model of the BGT network allows for an exhaustive analysis of its attractor dynamics. In this context, it has been shown that both global and local changes in the synaptic weights could strongly influence the attractor-based complexity of the network. We propose a novel adaptive spike-timing dependent plasticity (STDP) rule which allows the network to improve and stabilize its attractor complexity during its computational process. The rule is based on an adaptive learning rate which varies according to the attractor dynamics that the network continuously visits.

Keywords: Boolean recurrent neural networks · Learning
Attractors · STDP · Plasticity · Interactivity
Basal ganglia-thalamocortical circuit · Limbic system

1 Introduction

The basal ganglia-thalamocortical (BGT) network has been investigated for many years, in particular in relation to disorders of the motor system and of the sleep-waking cycle [8,11,13]. Its attractor dynamics is related to significant aspects of processing and coding of information, the most important of which being associative memories [2,10]. The consideration of a simplified Boolean model of the BGT network allows for a complete analysis of its attractor dynamics. Indeed, the attractors of the network correspond precisely to the cycles of

V. Kůrková et al. (Eds.): ICANN 2018, LNCS 11141, pp. 693–702, 2018.
https://doi.org/10.1007/978-3-030-01424-7_68

its corresponding automaton, and therefore, can be computed explicitly and exhaustively.

It has been shown that local and global changes in the synaptic weights could strongly influence the attractor-based complexity of the BGT network. Moreover, modifications of the non-interactive and interactive weights can compensate and/or be combined to each other to drive the network into stable attractor dynamics of high complexity [4–6].

Based on these considerations, we propose a novel adaptive spike-timing dependent plasticity (STDP) rule which allows the BGT network to improve and stabilize its attractor complexity during its computational process. The rule is based on an adaptive learning rate which varies according to the attractor dynamics that the network continuously visits.

2 Boolean Model of the Basal Ganglia-Thalamocortical Network

The basal ganglia-thalamocortical (BGT) network is formed by several parallel and segregated circuits involving different areas of the cerebral cortex, striatum, pallidum, thalamus, subthalamic nucleus and midbrain [1,7]. A characteristic of the pathways of this network is a combination of "open" and "closed" loops, with ascending sensory afferences reaching the thalamus and the midbrain and descending motor efferences from the midbrain (the tectospinal tract) and the cortex (the corticospinal tract).

We consider a Boolean model of the BGT network where each brain area is modeled by a Boolean node. The Boolean model is formed by 9 nodes: the superior colliculus (SC), the thalamus (Thalamus), the thalamic reticular nucleus (NRT), the cerebral cortex (Cerebral Cortex), the striatopallidal and the striatonigral components of the striatum (Str-D1 and Str-D2), the subthalamic nucleus (STN), the external part of the pallidum (GPe), and the output nuclei of the basal ganglia formed by the GABAergic projection neurons of the intermediate part of the pallidum and of the substantia nigra pars reticulata (GPi/SNR). The closed-loop architecture of the network is implemented via feedback connections—or *interactive connections*—from the efferent output (OUT) to the input (IN). The network is illustrated in Fig. 1A and its weight matrix given in Table 1. This pattern of connectivity corresponds to the wealth of data reported in the literature [1,7].

The context of Boolean neural networks, although relatively simple, has the advantage of allowing for a complete analysis of the attractor dynamics of the networks. In fact, Boolean recurrent neural networks are known to be computationally equivalent to finite state automata [9,12], and the attractors of the networks correspond precisely to the cycles in the graphs of their corresponding automata [3]. The attractor dynamics can therefore be computed explicitly and exhaustively. The finite automaton associated to the BGT network of Fig. 1A is illustrated in Fig. 1B [3].

An *attractor-based measure of complexity* for the Boolean model of the BGT network has been introduced [3]. This complexity measure is related to the number of attractors of the network as well as to their classification into meaningful or spurious types. In the present study, we define the attractor-based complexity of the network to be its number of attractors. The BGT network of Fig. 1 with weights of Table 1 has an attractor complexity of 22.

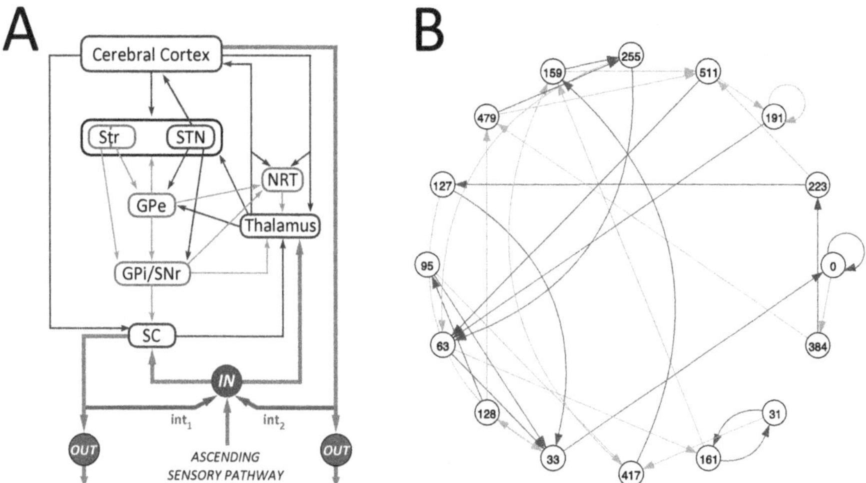

Fig. 1. A. Simplified Boolean model of the BGT network. Each brain area is represented by a single Boolean unit. The network is formed by 9 Boolean nodes: SC, Thalamus, NRT, Cerebral Cortex, Str-D1, Str-D2, STN, GPe, GPi/SNR. The inputs from the ascending sensory pathway (IN) is also a Boolean unit and the efferent outputs (OUT) are coming out of the cerebral cortex and superior colliculus. The excitatory and inhibitory pathways are labeled in blue and orange, respectively. The interactive connections int_1 and int_2 implement the closed-loop architecture. **B.** Finite automaton associated to the Boolean model of the BGT network. Each node of the automaton is a Boolean state of the network. There is a blue or red transition from node i to node j if and only if the network switches from state i to state j when receiving input 0 or 1, respectively. The attractors of the network correspond to the cycles in the automaton.

3 Adaptive STDP Rule

We introduce an adaptive spike-timing dependent plasticity (STDP) rule aimed at improving and stabilizing the attractor-based complexity of the BGT network during its computational process. This STDP rule modifies the connection strengths of the network not only as a function of the timing between the activations of the pre- and post-synaptic neurons, but also as a function of the attractors encountered throughout the computation.

Table 1. Adjacency matrix of the Boolean model of the BGT network of Fig. 1A.

Source		Target Node #									
Node #	Name	0	1	2	3	4	5	6	7	8	9
0	IN	·	1	1	·	·	·	·	·	·	·
1	SC	int_1	·	1	·	·	·	·	·	·	·
2	Thalamus	·	·	·	1	·	1	1	1	1	1
3	NRT	·	·	−1	·	·	·	·	·	·	·
4	GPi/SNr	·	−1	−1	−1	·	·	·	·	·	·
5	STN	·	·	·	·	2	·	2	·	·	2
6	GPe	·	·	·	−1/2	−1/2	−1/2	·	−1/2	−1/2	·
7	Str-D2	·	·	·	·	·	·	−1	·	·	·
8	Str-D1	·	·	·	·	−1/2	·	−1/2	·	·	·
9	C. Cortex	int_2	1/2	1	1/2	·	1/2	·	1/2	1/2	·

Formally, we consider the following *adaptive STDP rule* bounded by a definite weight interval $I = [I_1, I_2]$:

$$a_{ij}(t+1) = \begin{cases} I_1 & \text{if } a_{ij}(t+1) < I_1 \\ R & \text{if } I_1 \leq a_{ij}(t+1) \leq I_2 \\ I_2 & \text{if } a_{ij}(t+1) > I_2 \end{cases}$$

with

$$R = a_{ij}(t) + \lambda(t)\big[x_i(t+1)x_j(t) - C(x_i(t)x_j(t+1))\big] \tag{1}$$

and where $x_i(t)$ and $x_j(t)$ are the activation values of cells x_i and x_j at time t, $a_{ij}(t)$ is the synaptic weight from x_j to x_i at time t, C is a constant modulating the weight decrease (with default value equal to 1), and $\lambda(t)$ is the adaptive learning rate whose evolution is described below.

The adaptive learning rate $\lambda(t)$ remains to be defined. Towards this purpose, given some constant $M > 0$, we let $n(t)$ be the number of attractors of the network at time t, and $n_{min}(t)$ and $n_{max}(t)$ be the minimal and maximal number of attractors that the network has encountered during the last M time steps:

$$\begin{aligned} n(t) &= \text{number of attractors of the network at time } t \\ n_{min}(t) &= \min\{n(t') : \max(0, t-M) < t' \leq t\} \\ n_{max}(t) &= \max\{n(t') : \max(0, t-M) < t' \leq t\}. \end{aligned} \tag{2}$$

The constant M is called the *memory* of the network. It corresponds to the time window during which the network "remembers" the minimum and maximum number of attractors that it has encountered.

The *adaptive learning rate* $\lambda(t)$ is then defined as the image of $n(t)$ by the linear interpolation between the two points $(n_{min}(t), \lambda_{max})$ and $(n_{max}(t), \lambda_{min})$, where $\lambda_{min}, \lambda_{max} \in \mathbb{R}$ are two bounds such that $\lambda_{min} < \lambda_{max}$. Formally,

$$\lambda(t) = \begin{cases} \lambda_{max} + \dfrac{(n(t) - n_{min}(t))(\lambda_{min} - \lambda_{max})}{n_{max}(t) - n_{min}(t)} & \text{if } n_{min}(t) \neq n_{max}(t) \\ \lambda_{max} & \text{otherwise.} \end{cases} \tag{3}$$

The computation of $\lambda(t)$ is illustrated in Fig. 2. The learning rate $\lambda(t)$ has to be understood as follows. If $n(t) = n_{min}(t)$ (resp. $n(t) = n_{max}(t)$), it means that the current number of attractors of the network is at a minimal (resp. maximal) level. In this case, $\lambda(t) = \lambda_{max}$ (resp. $\lambda(t) = \lambda_{min}$). This large (resp. low) learning rate will induce large (resp. low) variations of the synaptic weights (cf. Eq. 1) with the aim of destabilizing (resp. stabilizing) the network's current dynamics. If $n_{min}(t) < n(t) < n_{max}(t)$, then $\lambda_{max} > \lambda(t) > \lambda_{min}$ according to the linear interpolation. The closer $n(t)$ is to $n_{min}(t)$ (resp. to $n_{max}(t)$), the closer $\lambda(t)$ is to $\lambda_{max}(t)$ (resp. to $\lambda_{min}(t)$). If $n_{min}(t) = n_{max}(t)$, the network has settled into the same attractor dynamics during the M last steps. In this case, we set $\lambda(t) = \lambda_{max}$ with the aim of destabilizing the current dynamics.

Observe that, since $n_{min}(t)$ and $n_{max}(t)$ are functions of the memory M (cf. Eq. 2), then so is $\lambda(t)$ (cf. Eq. 3), and hence so is the STDP rule (cf. Eq. 1). Note also that if the network has no memory, i.e. $M = 1$, then $n_{min}(t) = n_{max}(t)$ (cf. Eq. 2), and thus $\lambda(t) = \lambda_{max}$ for all $t > 0$ (cf. Eq. 3), meaning that the network dynamics is driven by a *fixed-rate* STDP rule. By contrast, as soon as the network has a positive memory, i.e. $M > 1$, the learning rate $\lambda(t)$ becomes time dependent, meaning that the network dynamics is driven by an *adaptive* STDP rule. This *adaptive* feature is crucial towards the achievement of reaching a high and stable attractor-based complexity.

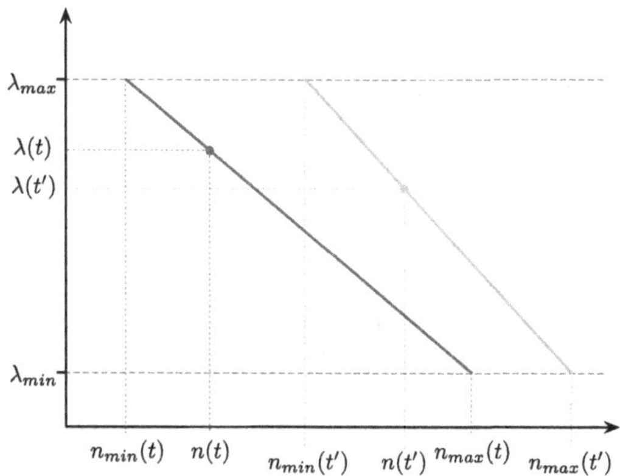

Fig. 2. Computation of the adaptive learning rate $\lambda(.)$ at two different time steps t (blue construction) and t' (red construction). The rate $\lambda(.)$ is defined as the image of $n(.)$ by the linear interpolation between the two points $(n_{min}(.), \lambda_{max})$ and $(n_{max}(.), \lambda_{min})$. (Color figure online)

4 Results

We now study the effect of the adaptive STDP rule on the attractor-based complexity of the BGT network. For this purpose, we implemented the adaptive STDP rule of Eq. 1 for the Boolean BGT network of Fig. 1. The learning interval of each weight a_{ij} of Table 1 was set to $I_{ij} = [a_{ij} - 0.025; a_{ij} + 0.8]$. The bounds of the intervals I_{ij} were chosen on the basis of an empirical analysis. The minimal and maximal learning rates were set to $\lambda_{min} = 0.002$ and $\lambda_{max} = 0.12$. We then performed simulations where we first jittered (each weight of) the matrix of Table 1 by random uniform noise $\epsilon_{ij} \sim \mathcal{U}(-0.025, 0.8)$, and then submitted the network to a random input stream and recorded the variation of its attractor-based complexity throughout its computational process.

In order to emphasise the effect of the network memory on its attractor-based complexity, we performed 10 simulations (of 300 time steps each) where memory $M = 1$, 10 simulations where memory $M = 120$ and 10 simulations where memory $M = 240$. For each lot of 10 simulations, we used the same seed to ensure that the same random jittering and random input streams were considered at each time, and therefore, that the differences observed are entirely due to the variations M. The results are displayed in Fig. 3.

Recall that $M = 1$ means that the network has non memory and the STDP rule is fixed-rate rather than adaptive (cf. Sect. 3). In this case of $M = 1$ (black dotted trace), the attractor-based complexity is usually unstable, with sporadic peaks of higher intensities interspersed by plateaus of lower values. This situation is particularly manifest in simulations 1, 3, 4, 8. Simulations 2, 5. 9, 10 are less peaky, but still unstable. Simulations 6 and 7 are by contrast very stable, with long plateaus of 10 and 1 attractors, respectively. The highest peak of complexity is reached at the beginning of simulation 10, with 154 attractors (pay attention to the x-axis of simulation 10).

For $M = 120$ (blue dashed trace), the attractor complexity is clearly more stable, and in general, it doesn't get stuck into minimal values. Note that the length of the plateaus are of the same order as that of the memory, namely 120 time steps. In all simulations, the network is able to maintain a high complexity during a fairly long period of time. In simulations 2, 6, 7, 9, 10 however, the network also stabilizes into plateaus of low complexity. In simulations 1, 3, 8 (to some extent), 9, the complexity is constantly improving along the computation. Simulations 4 and 5 still alternate between stable and unstable behaviors. The highest complexity of 377 is reached in simulation 10, and it is maintained during exactly 120 time steps.

For $M = 240$ (red solid trace), the attractor complexity is even more stable, and it almost never gets stuck into minimal values. Here again, the length of the plateaus are of the same order as the memory length, namely 240 time steps. In all but the 9-th simulations, the network is able to stabilize in a complexity that is higher than for $M = 120$, and for a longer period of time. However, in simulations 6, 7, 9, 10, the network also stabilizes into plateaus of low complexity. Simulation 4 is the only one to still presents some instability, at its beginning. The highest complexity of 377 is reached in simulation 10, and it is maintained during 193 time steps until the end of the simulation (it but would have probably be maintained for a longer period of time if the simulation would have continued). Overall, we see that as M increases, the network becomes more and more able to stabilize into attractor-based complexities of high intensities.

It has been shown tiny decreases in the weights of the three specific connections (Thalamus, STN), (GPe, STN) and CCortex, STN) (from their original values of Table 1) drastically increases the number of attractors of the BGT network from 22 to 143 [5,6]. Therefore, it is rational to think that a targeted modification of these weights by the adaptive STDP rule might drive the network dynamics into a higher attractor complexity. This hypothesis is explored by implementing a larger decrease-update exclusively for those specific connection strengths. Formally, the value of constant $C = 5$ in Eq. (1) was set to 5 for these connections and kept to its default value of 1 for other connections. The effect of this *targeted adaptive STDP rule* on the attractor-based complexity of the network is illustrated in Fig. 4.

In this case, the attractor-based complexity of the network is indeed drastically higher by few orders of magnitude, but the stabilization process associated with the increase of M has deteriorated. For $M = 1$ (black dotted trace), the complexity is highly unstable, except in simulations 5, 7, 8, where the network gets trapped into a minimal complexity of 1. The highest complexity of 1170 attractors is reached at the beginning of simulation 9. For $M = 120$, the complexity is clearly more stable than for $M = 1$, but the stabilization is not as clear as it was for the previous case of Fig. 3. We less systematically see plateaus of stability that are of the same order as the memory length of 120 time steps. This situation nevertheless occurs in simulations 3 (two plateaus of 25 and 42 attractors of 120 time steps). in simulations 6 (two plateaus of 89 and 198 attractors of 120 and 121 time steps) and in simulation 8(two plateaus of 32 attractors of durations 123 and 129 time steps). The network also sometimes gets trapped into a minimal complexity of 1, like in simulations 9 and 10. The highest complexity of 1735 attractors is reached at the beginning of simulation 10 and is maintained during 11 time steps. For $M = 240$, the complexity is not significantly more stable than for $M = 120$, and this contrasts with the previous case of Fig. 3. However, except for simulation 1, the network is able to reach complexities that are always equal or higher than for $M = 120$. The network remains trapped into a minimal complexity of 1 in simulations 9 and 10. In simulation 6, the huge complexity of 6126 attractors is reached maintained during 17 time steps.

5 Conclusion

We have proposed a novel adaptive STDP rule which allows the BGT network to improve and stabilize its attractor-based complexity during its computational process. The rule is based on an adaptive learning rate which varies according to the attractor dynamics that the network continuously visits. We have shown that the stability of the attractor complexity tends to increase as the network's memory becomes larger. We have also shown that a targeted adaptive STDP

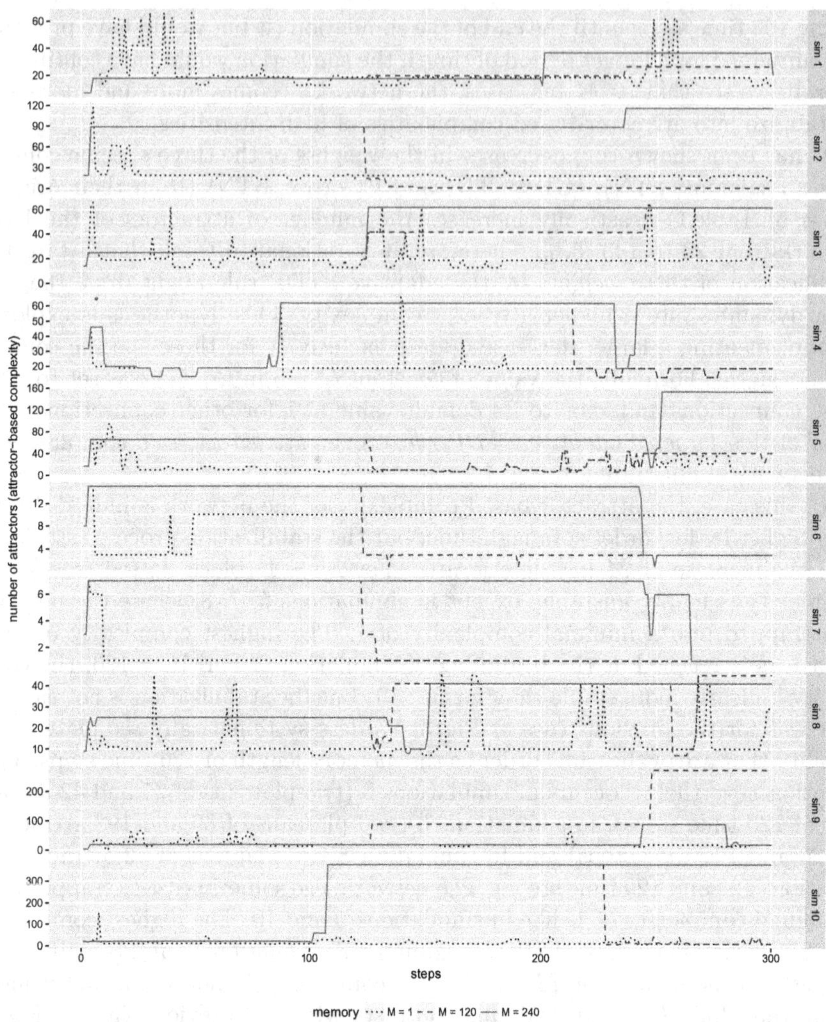

Fig. 3. Results of 10 simulations representing the variations of the attractor-based complexity of the BGT network over time. For each simulation, the weight matrix of the BGT network is initially randomly jittered. Then, the network is subjected to a random input stream and its attractor based complexity computed at each time step. The results for the network memory $M = 1, 120, 240$ are represented.

rule is able to drastically increase the complexity of the network, but at the price of a less stable attractor dynamics.

For future work, the relationship between the synaptic patterns and the attractor dynamics of neural networks is envisioned to be studied in more general architectures, beyond the case study represented by the Boolean BGT network.

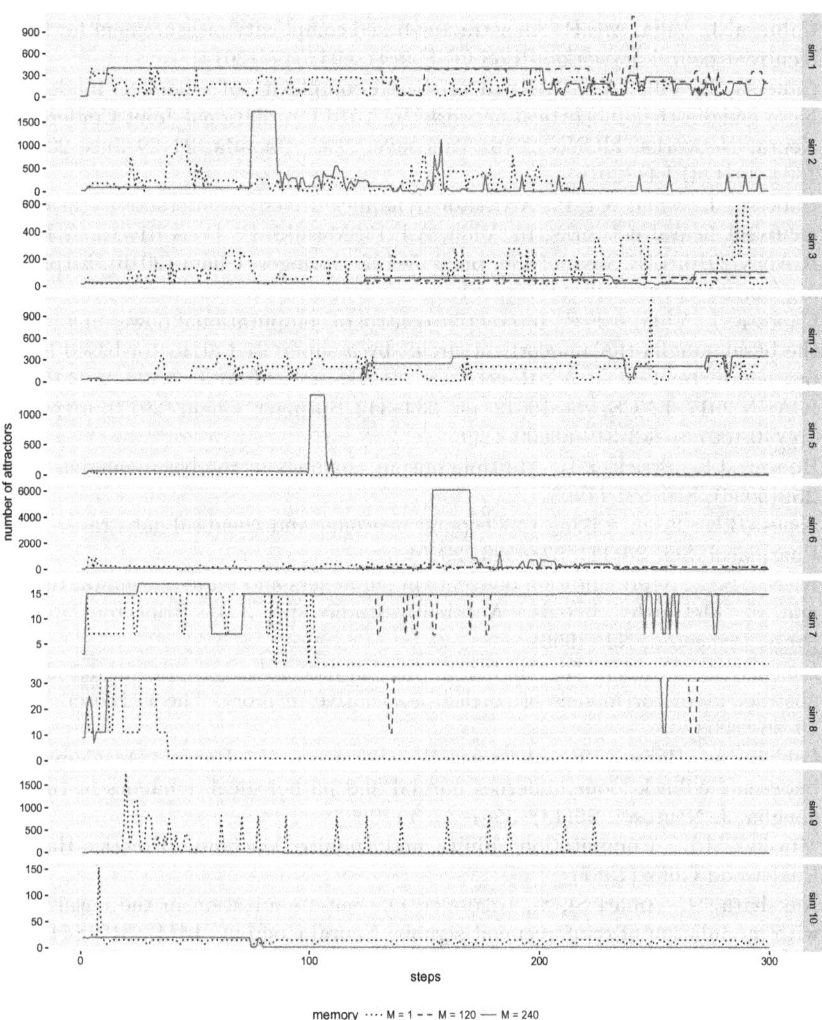

Fig. 4. Results of 10 simulations representing the variations of the attractor-based complexity of the BGT network over time. In this case, the network is subjected to a targeted adaptive STDP rule where constant $C = 5$ for the three weights (Thalamus, STN), (GPe, STN) and CCortex, STN) and $C = 1$ for all other weights (cf. Eq. 1). The results for the network memory $M = 1, 120, 240$ are represented.

References

1. Alexander, G.E., Crutcher, M.D.: Functional architecture of basal ganglia circuits: neural substrates of parallel processing. Trends Neurosci. **13**(7), 266–271 (1990)
2. Beiser, D.G., Hua, S.E., Houk, J.C.: Network models of the basal ganglia. Curr. Opin. Neurobiol. **7**(2), 185–90 (1997)

3. Cabessa, J., Villa, A.E.P.: An attractor-based complexity measurement for boolean recurrent neural networks. PLoS ONE **9**(4), e94204+ (2014)
4. Cabessa, J., Villa, A.E.P.: Attractor-based complexity of a boolean model of the basal ganglia-thalamocortical network. In: 2016 International Joint Conference on Neural Networks, IJCNN 2016, Vancouver, BC, Canada, 24–29 July 2016, pp. 4664–4671. IEEE (2016)
5. Cabessa, J., Villa, A.E.P.: Attractor dynamics driven by interactivity in boolean recurrent neural networks. In: Villa, A.E.P., Masulli, P., Pons Rivero, A.J. (eds.) ICANN 2016. LNCS, vol. 9886, pp. 115–122. Springer, Cham (2016). https://doi.org/10.1007/978-3-319-44778-0_14
6. Cabessa, J., Villa, A.E.P.: Interactive control of computational power in a model of the basal ganglia-thalamocortical circuit by a supervised attractor-based learning procedure. In: Lintas, A., Rovetta, S., Verschure, P.F.M.J., Villa, A.E.P. (eds.) ICANN 2017. LNCS, vol. 10613, pp. 334–342. Springer, Cham (2017). https://doi.org/10.1007/978-3-319-68600-4_39
7. Hoover, J.E., Strick, P.L.: Multiple output channels in the basal ganglia. Science **259**(5096), 819–821 (1993)
8. Jones, B.E.: From waking to sleeping: neuronal and chemical substrates. Trends Pharmacol. Sci. **26**(11), 578–586 (2005)
9. Kleene, S.C.: Representation of events in nerve nets and finite automata. In: Shannon, C., McCarthy, J. (eds.) Automata Studies, pp. 3–41. Princeton University Press, Princeton, NJ (1956)
10. Lansner, A., Fransén, E., Sandberg, A.: Cell assembly dynamics in detailed and abstract attractor models of cortical associative memory. Theor. Biosci. **122**(1), 19–36 (2003)
11. Leblois, A., Boraud, T., Meissner, W., Bergman, H., Hansel, D.: Competition between feedback loops underlies normal and pathological dynamics in the basal ganglia. J. Neurosci. **26**(13), 3567–3583 (2006)
12. Minsky, M.L.: Computation: Finite and Infinite Machines. Prentice-Hall Inc., Englewood Cliffs (1967)
13. Nakahara, H., Amari Si, S., Hikosaka, O.: Self-organization in the basal ganglia with modulation of reinforcement signals. Neural Comput. **14**(4), 819–844 (2002)

Neuronal Asymmetries and Fokker-Planck Dynamics

Vitor Tocci F. de Luca[1], Roseli S. Wedemann[1(✉)], and Angel R. Plastino[2]

[1] Instituto de Matemática e Estatística, Universidade do Estado do Rio de Janeiro, Rua São Francisco Xavier, 524, Rio de Janeiro, RJ 20550-900, Brazil
vitocci_4@hotmail.com, roseli@ime.uerj.br

[2] CeBio, Universidad del Noroeste de la Provincia de Buenos Aires, UNNOBA-Conicet, Roque Saenz Peña 456, Junin, Argentina
arplastino@unnoba.edu.ar

Abstract. Much of our recent work regards the development of schematic, neurocomputational models based on memory associativity to describe some processes associated with basic structures of mental functioning, such as neurosis, creativity, consciousness/unconsciousness, and psychoses. We have emphasized associative memory mechanisms, since they are central in the description of these processes by psychodynamical theories. In memory neural networks, such as the Hopfield or Boltzmann Machine models, the symmetry of synaptic connections is a condition for the existence of stationary states, although this assumption is biologically unrealistic. Many efforts to model stationary states of networks with asymmetric weights are mathematically complex and can usually be applied only to specific cases. We thus further explore a possible new approach to the asymmetry problem, based on studies of some characteristics of the behavior of these networks, which may be modeled by the Fokker-Planck formalism. Besides considering asymmetric interactions, we also relaxed other symmetries of our previous models, enriching the concomitant dynamics. Among other things, we identified the presence of limit cycles.

Keywords: Mental processes · Memory · Asymmetry
Nonlinear Fokker-Planck dynamics · Curl forces

1 Introduction

We have been developing, for some time now, models [1–4] that investigate emergent states of neuronal network mechanisms to describe mental phenomena traditionally studied by psychiatry, psychoanalysis and neuroscience [5–10]. These models are based on two basic hypotheses of neuroscience, that human memory is encoded in the neural net of the brain, and that the capacity to associate is a key element in the description of mental processes, both in normal and pathological functioning. Associative memory mechanisms are therefore important elements of our artificial neural network (ANN) models of memory [2,4,11].

V. Kůrková et al. (Eds.): ICANN 2018, LNCS 11141, pp. 703–713, 2018.
https://doi.org/10.1007/978-3-030-01424-7_69

In ANN memory models, such as the Hopfield or Boltzmann Machine (BM) models [11], the assumption that synaptic connections are symmetric is a necessary mathematical condition for the existence of stationary attractor states, *i.e.* memory [11,12]. This is also the case when one employs more recent approaches, based on the Generalized Simulated Annealing (GSA) algorithm [2,4,13]. As biological neural networks do not comply with the synaptic symmetry condition, the main mathematical models of memory are at odds with biological reality. We have thus been interested in investigating mechanisms where, although the interaction between elements of a physical system may not be symmetrical, the dynamics still guarantees that the system reaches stable (stationary) states [14–16]. Other efforts to model stationary, memory, attractor states with asymmetric weights can be found in the literature [17,18], but they are mathematically complex and usually applicable only to restricted situations. The (a)symmetry issue thus remains as a largely unexplored (and almost forgotten) open problem. This suggests a need to consider alternative approaches to this problem, which has motivated us to explore similarities between the synaptic symmetry problem and some aspects of the nonlinear Fokker-Planck (NLFP) dynamics, and to advance the first steps in the development of a formalism, based on the NLFP equation [14–16].

In our models [2,4], we have used the BM and GSA [13] to simulate memory. Both in the BM and GSA, pattern retrieval is achieved by a simulated annealing (SA) process, where the temperature T is gradually lowered by an annealing schedule. For a BM or GSA network with N nodes, where each node i has a discrete state S_i in $\{-1,1\}$, synaptic weights between nodes i and j must obey $w_{ij} = w_{ji}$, for the network to have stable states. One can then define an Energy function, representing the potential energy corresponding to the interactions between neurons

$$E(\{S_i\}) = -\frac{1}{2}\sum_{ij} w_{ij} S_i S_j\,, \tag{1}$$

and stored memories correspond to minimum energy attractor (stable) states of the memory retrieval, SA mechanism. In the SA process, the energy surface is sampled according to the appropriate transition probabilities [2,4,11,13], which tend to take the system from a current state towards a final, more favorable, minimum energy state, although energy may increase at intermediate steps.

In Sect. 2, we briefly review ANN models in light of the basic theory of Dynamical Systems. We then introduce in Sect. 3, basic aspects of the Fokker-Planck formalism. In Sect. 4, we review work in [14,15], where we introduced a drift (force) term not arising from the gradient of a potential, which is related to asymmetric connections, and the system still evolves to stationary attractor states of the probability density function, in the phase space describing the system. In Sect. 5, we present the original contribution of this paper, where we apply the formalism developed in [14,15] to a system of two different neurons, connected via asymmetric weights (a non-homogeneous system) by a quadratic potential and with a linear drift field. The q-Gaussian solutions of the coupled differential evolution equations reveal individual neural trajectories, exhibiting stationary elliptical limit cycles, caused by the asymmetries of the system. We mention further developments and present our conclusions in the last section.

2 Continuous Neural Networks and Dynamical Systems

For a continuous, deterministic dynamical system with phase space state variables $\boldsymbol{x} = \{x_1, x_2, \cdots, x_N\}$, when there is no noise, the equations of motion can be expressed, for each state variable, x_i as

$$\frac{dx_i}{dt} = K_i(x_1, x_2, \cdots x_N), \tag{2}$$

which in vector notation is expressed as $\frac{d\mathbf{x}}{dt} = \boldsymbol{K}(\boldsymbol{x})$, with $\boldsymbol{x}, \boldsymbol{K} \in \Re^N$. The time evolution of $\boldsymbol{x}$ is thus described by a phase space flux, given by the vectorial field $\boldsymbol{K}$. Neural networks have been widely studied within this framework [11].

In ANN models, the synaptic weight w_{ij} expresses the intensity of the influence of neuron j on neuron i. So the net input signal to neuron i is

$$u_i = \sum_j w_{ij} V_{O_j}, \tag{3}$$

where V_{O_j} is the output signal of neuron j. One can generalize the discrete activation, McCulloch-Pitts neural model, considering continuous state variables [11,12,19], so that in equilibrium V_{O_i} is updated by a continuous activation function $g(u)$ of u_i,

$$V_{O_i}(t + \Delta t) = g(u_i(t)). \tag{4}$$

In Eq. (4), $g(u)$ is usually nonlinear and saturates for large values of $|u|$, such as a sigmoid or $\tanh(u)$. The set of differential equations

$$\frac{dV_{O_i}}{dt} = \frac{-V_{O_i} + g(u_i)}{\tau_i} = K_i(V_{O_1}, V_{O_2}, \ldots), \tag{5}$$

where τ_i are suitable time constants, constitutes a possible continuous-time rule for updating the V_{O_i} [12,19].

In traditional ANN memory models, such as the Hopfield model, BM and GSA, $w_{ij} = w_{ji}$ is a necessary condition for reaching stationary states (memory). This symmetry restriction is not biologically realistic, and we approach this issue, in this contribution, using the NLFP dynamics and extending work in [14,15].

3 Standard Fokker-Planck Dynamics

When we consider an ensemble of identical systems, each consisting of N elements, that evolve from different initial conditions, it is described by a time-dependent probability density in phase space $\mathcal{F}(x_1, \cdots, x_N, t)$ which obeys the Liouville equation

$$\frac{\partial \mathcal{F}}{\partial t} + \boldsymbol{\nabla} \cdot [\mathcal{F}\boldsymbol{K}] = 0. \tag{6}$$

It is necessary to add a new diffusion-like term in Eq. (6), when the system presents noisy behavior, resulting in the Fokker-Planck equation (FPE)

$$\frac{\partial \mathcal{F}}{\partial t} = D\nabla^2\mathcal{F} - \boldsymbol{\nabla}\cdot[\boldsymbol{K}\mathcal{F}], \tag{7}$$

where D is the diffusion coefficient, the term involving the field $\boldsymbol{K}$ is referred to as the *drift* term, and $\boldsymbol{K}$ is called the *drift* field. If

$$\boldsymbol{K} = -\boldsymbol{\nabla}V(\boldsymbol{x}) \tag{8}$$

for some potential function $V(\boldsymbol{x})$, there is a Boltzmann-Gibbs-like stationary solution $\mathcal{F}_{BG}$ to Eq. (7) (satisfying $\frac{\partial \mathcal{F}_{BG}}{\partial t} = 0$), given by

$$\mathcal{F}_{BG} = \frac{1}{Z}\exp\left[-\frac{1}{D}V(\boldsymbol{x})\right], \tag{9}$$

where Z is an appropriate normalization constant. The distribution $\mathcal{F}_{BG}$ maximizes the Boltzmann-Gibbs entropy S_{BG}, under the constraints of normalization and the mean value $\langle V\rangle$ of the potential V.

A dynamical system with a gradient form for the phase space flux, as given by (8), evolves moving *down-hill* along the potential energy surface, minimizing V. For a field $\boldsymbol{K}$ with the form (8) one has

$$\frac{\partial K_i}{\partial x_j} = \frac{\partial K_j}{\partial x_i} = \frac{\partial^2 V}{\partial x_i \partial x_j}. \tag{10}$$

In a Hopfield ANN, if $g(u)$ is linear, for example $K_i \propto \sum_j w_{ij}x_j$ in Eq. (5),

$$\frac{\partial K_i}{\partial x_j} = w_{ij}, \tag{11}$$

corresponding to linear forces and, by Eq. (10), $w_{ij} = w_{ji}$. Condition (10), that guarantees that the Fokker-Planck dynamics evolves towards a stationary Boltzmann-Gibbs distribution (9), is very similar to the synaptic symmetry required so that an ANN evolves towards minima of an energy surface. This similarity is also related to the fact that the SA technique provides an algorithm to find the minima of the network's energy landscape. We have shown [14,15] that, in the Fokker-Planck case, it is possible to relax condition (10), considering more general drift fields, and still have a dynamics that leads to a stationary distribution $\mathcal{F}$. This suggests the relevance of the Fokker-Planck scenario, with non-gradient drift fields, to the treatment of the symmetry problem and, in what follows, we further explore some basic aspects of this scenario.

4 Generalized Fokker-Planck Dynamics

In this Section, we briefly review a more general Fokker-Planck formalism, based on a nonlinear evolution equation. Physical systems characterized by long-range interactions and/or spatial disorder seem to be natural candidates for this formalism, which is recently attracting considerable attention from the complex systems research community [14–16, 20–22].

We thus use the nonlinear Fokker-Planck equation (NLFPE)

$$\frac{\partial \mathcal{F}}{\partial t} = D\nabla^2[\mathcal{F}^{2-q}] - \boldsymbol{\nabla} \cdot [\mathcal{F}\boldsymbol{K}] , \tag{12}$$

to study systems which may deviate from the linear description. Since we need to model stable properties of interesting physical systems, such as the stored memory states in an ANN, we search for possible stationary solutions to Eq. (12).

4.1 Stationary Solution for Drift Fields of Gradient Form

In the most frequently studied case, where the field $\boldsymbol{K}$ is of the gradient form (8), the stationary solution of the NLFPE is found by solving

$$D\nabla^2[\mathcal{F}^{2-q}] - \boldsymbol{\nabla} \cdot [\mathcal{F}\boldsymbol{K}] = 0 , \tag{13}$$

considering the Tsallis ansatz [22]

$$\mathcal{F}_q = A[1 - (1-q)\beta V(\boldsymbol{x})]_+^{\frac{1}{1-q}} , \tag{14}$$

where A and β are constants to be determined, and $\mathcal{F}_q = 0$ when $1 - (1 - q)\beta V(\boldsymbol{x}) < 0$. One finds that the ansatz given by Eq. (14), which we call the q-exponential ansatz, is a stationary solution of the NLFPE, with a $\boldsymbol{K}$ which satisfies Eq. (8), if

$$A = [(2-q)\beta D]^{\frac{1}{q-1}} . \tag{15}$$

The distribution $\mathcal{F}_q$ is also called a q-maxent distribution, because it optimizes the nonextensive q-entropy S_q, under the constraints of normalization and the mean value $< V >$ [20, 22]. In the limit $q \to 1$, the distribution $\mathcal{F}_q$ (14) reduces to $\mathcal{F}_{BG}$ (9), with $\beta = 1/D$.

4.2 Stationary Solution for *K* with Non-Gradient Components

Now we consider the NLFPE, with a drift term not arising from the gradient of a potential and with the form

$$\boldsymbol{K} = \boldsymbol{G} + \tilde{\boldsymbol{K}} , \tag{16}$$

where $\boldsymbol{G}$ is equal to minus the gradient of some potential $V(\boldsymbol{x})$, while $\tilde{\boldsymbol{K}}$ does not come from a potential function (that is, we have $\partial \tilde{K}_i/\partial x_j \neq \partial \tilde{K}_j/\partial x_i$). The force $\boldsymbol{K}$ is thus referred to as a *curl force*. We then substitute this $\boldsymbol{K}$ (16) and $\mathcal{F}_q$ (14) in the stationary NLFP Eq. (13) and obtain

$$D\nabla^2[\mathcal{F}_q^{2-q}] + \boldsymbol{\nabla} \cdot [(\boldsymbol{\nabla} V)\mathcal{F}_q] - \boldsymbol{\nabla}[\tilde{\boldsymbol{K}}\mathcal{F}_q] = 0 . \tag{17}$$

The first two terms in Eq. (17) vanish, because we know that $\mathcal{F}_q$ is a stationary solution of Eq. (13), when only the gradient field $\boldsymbol{G}$ is present. In order for $\mathcal{F}_q$ to satisfy (17), we then require $\boldsymbol{\nabla}[\tilde{\boldsymbol{K}}F_q] = 0$. If this relation is satisfied, then $\mathcal{F}_q$ is also a stationary solution of the full NLFPE, including the non-gradient term corresponding to $\tilde{\boldsymbol{K}}$. We therefore require

$$\boldsymbol{\nabla}\left(\tilde{\boldsymbol{K}}A[1-(1-q)\beta V]^{\frac{1}{1-q}}\right) = 0\,, \tag{18}$$

This equation constitutes a consistency requirement that the potential V, the non-gradient field $\tilde{\boldsymbol{K}}$, β, and the entropic parameter q have to satisfy in order that the NLFPE admits a stationary solution of the q-maxent form. In the most general β-dependent situation, the condition given by Eq. (18) leads to a rather complicated relation between $\tilde{\boldsymbol{K}}$ and V. However, there are cases where a β-independent set of constraints can be obtained. We illustrate this with a two-dimensional example.

5 A Two-Neuron System Admitting Time-Dependent q-Gaussian Solutions

In a commonly used framework for neural network modeling (as in the Hopfield and BM models), flow in phase-space arises from a potential energy function given by Eq. (1), *i.e.* the flow is equal to the gradient of a potential. Expanding the treatment of noisy dynamical systems which can be modeled by the NLFPE advanced in [14,15], the flow $\boldsymbol{K}$ (16) can be expressed in a more general form, arising from a potential V and a non-gradient drift $\tilde{\boldsymbol{K}}$

$$V(\boldsymbol{x}) = \sum_{ij} a_{ij}x_i x_j\,, \tag{19a}$$

$$\tilde{K}_i(\boldsymbol{x}) = \sum_{j} c_{ij}x_j\,, \tag{19b}$$

where $\tilde{K}_i(\boldsymbol{x})$ is the ith component of $\tilde{\boldsymbol{K}}(\boldsymbol{x})$ and the a_{ij} and c_{ij} are constant coefficients, representing synaptic interactions among neurons. We can assume $a_{ij} = a_{ji}$, since $G = -\boldsymbol{\nabla}V$, although the c_{ij} are not necessarily symmetric. Equation (18) leads to constraints on these coefficients, thus defining $V(\boldsymbol{x})$ and $\tilde{\boldsymbol{K}}(\boldsymbol{x})$.

As an example of a time-dependent solution of a NLFPE with a $\tilde{\boldsymbol{K}}$ not arising from a potential, admitting a q-maxent stationary solution, we consider here a two-neuron system, submitted to the following elliptical potential and nongradient linear drift term, which are an instance of Eqs. (19a) and (19b). Phase-space state variables x_1 and x_2 represent the continuous valued output signal (activation function) of neurons 1 and 2, respectively. In order to simplify the notation, we name the state variables $x \equiv x_1$ and $y \equiv x_2$, and the potential and drift field are given by

$$V(\boldsymbol{x}) = a_1x^2 + a_2y^2\,, \tag{20}$$

$$\tilde{\boldsymbol{K}}(\boldsymbol{x}) = (-by, +bx)\,, \tag{21}$$

where a_1, a_2 and b are real constants. This form for the potential $V(\boldsymbol{x})$ and drift field $\tilde{\boldsymbol{K}}$ can be interpreted, within the usual neural network modeling framework (Eqs. (19a) and (19b)), as a two-neuron system, where the network energy (Eqs. (19a) and (1)) has only the self-interacting terms and the drift generates asymmetric interactions between the pair. Since the self-interaction terms are such that $a_1 \neq a_2$, in this work we are actually considering *a system of two different types of neurons, connected by asymmetric synapses*, which are biologically realistic assumptions. According to Eq. (16), the total drift is thus

$$\boldsymbol{K} = -\boldsymbol{\nabla} V + \tilde{\boldsymbol{K}} = (-2a_1 x - by, -2a_2 y + bx) . \tag{22}$$

The resulting NLFPE (12) for this example can then be written as

$$\frac{\partial \mathcal{F}}{\partial t} = D\nabla^2[\mathcal{F}^{2-q}] + \frac{\partial[(2a_1 x + by)\mathcal{F}]}{\partial x} + \frac{\partial[(2a_2 y - bx)\mathcal{F}]}{\partial y} . \tag{23}$$

When we consider the Tsallis ansatz with q-maxent form (see also [14,15])

$$\mathcal{F}_q(x, y, t) = \eta(t) \left[1 - (1-q)(\alpha(t)x^2 + \delta(t)xy + \gamma(t)y^2)\right]_+^{\frac{1}{(1-q)}} , \tag{24}$$

where $\eta(t)$, $\alpha(t)$, $\delta(t)$ and $\gamma(t)$ are time-dependent parameters, it is possible to show, after some algebra, that it is a solution to Eq. (23), given that these parameters satisfy an appropriate set of coupled ordinary differential equations, that we solve numerically.

When we interpret a solution $\mathcal{F}(x_1, \cdots, x_N, t)$ of the NLFPE (12) as a probability density in phase space, or as a physical density of particles or other entities, we can express the NLFPE so that it has the form of a Liouville continuity Eq. (6). In fact, Eq. (12) can be expressed in the form

$$\frac{\partial \mathcal{F}}{\partial t} + \boldsymbol{\nabla} \left[\mathcal{F}\left(\boldsymbol{K} + D\left(\frac{q-2}{1-q}\right) \boldsymbol{\nabla}(\mathcal{F}^{1-q})\right)\right] = 0 . \tag{25}$$

We then define

$$\boldsymbol{\mathcal{K}} = \boldsymbol{K} + D\left(\frac{q-2}{1-q}\right) \boldsymbol{\nabla}(\mathcal{F}^{1-q}) , \tag{26}$$

and rewrite Eq. (25) as

$$\frac{\partial \mathcal{F}}{\partial t} + \boldsymbol{\nabla} [\mathcal{F}\boldsymbol{\mathcal{K}}] = 0 . \tag{27}$$

In Eq. (27), $\mathcal{F}$ is a solution of the NLFPE and $\boldsymbol{\mathcal{K}}$ can be interpreted as the effective force field experienced by the constituents of the system. In our two-neuron system, Eq. (27) corresponds to the equations of motion, governing the dynamics of the activation functions of the neurons.

We can then substitute (22) and the expression for the ansatz (24) in (26) to obtain the components of $\boldsymbol{\mathcal{K}} = (\mathcal{K}_x, \mathcal{K}_y)$ as

$$\mathcal{K}_x = 2[(2-q)D\eta^{1-q}\alpha - a_1]x + [(2-q)D\eta^{1-q}\delta - b]y , \tag{28a}$$

$$\mathcal{K}_y = 2[(2-q)D\eta^{1-q}\gamma - a_2]y + [(2-q)D\eta^{1-q}\delta + b]x . \tag{28b}$$

The dynamics of the activation functions of our two-neuron system can then be expressed, following Eqs. (2), as

$$\frac{dx}{dt} = \mathcal{K}_x = 2[(2-q)D\eta^{1-q}\alpha - a_1]x + [(2-q)D\eta^{1-q}\delta - b]y\,, \tag{29a}$$

$$\frac{dy}{dt} = \mathcal{K}_y = 2[(2-q)D\eta^{1-q}\gamma - a_2]y + [(2-q)D\eta^{1-q}\delta + b]x\,. \tag{29b}$$

It can be verified, after some algebra, that the q-maxent distributions given by the form (24), evolving according to Eqs. (23), lead to stationary solutions of the NLFPE.

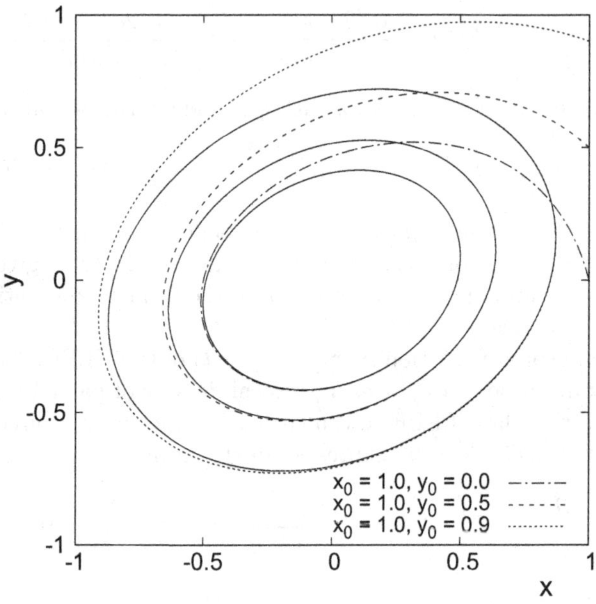

Fig. 1. Dynamical evolution of activation states x and y of two neurons. The initial parameters for the integration of differential Eqs. (29) are: $\alpha_0 = 1$, $\gamma_0 = 2.5$, $\delta_0 = 0$, $D = 0.5$, $q = 1.3$, $a_1 = 1$, $a_2 = 2.5$, $b = 4$.

We then have a family of noisy dynamical systems (described by the NLFPE) that have q-maxent stationary solutions, characterized by the parameters η, α, γ, δ, D, q, a_1, a_2, and b, in spite of having a drift field not necessarily arising from a potential and that therefore does not necessarily comply with the symmetry restriction described by Eq. (10), which is akin to the standard symmetry condition in ANNs. Figure 1 illustrates the numerical solution of the coupled differential Eqs. (29) for $D = 0.5$, $q = 1.3$, $a_1 = 1$, $a_2 = 2.5$, $b = 4$, the set of initial values of parameters $\alpha_0 = 1$, $\gamma_0 = 2.5$, $\delta_0 = 0$, and different initial conditions x_0 and y_0. The initial value of parameter η (η_0) is obtained from the condition that $\mathcal{F}_q$, given by Eq. (24), is normalized to one. This figure shows that the activation functions of the two neurons spiral into limit cycles so that, in a stationary equilibrium situation, the activation values of the two neurons rotate in the phase-space plane (x_1, x_2), following an elliptical orbit. The presence of these limit cycles constitutes a notable manifestation of the new types of dynamics arising from the asymmetric interactions.

We are preparing an extended manuscript with a more detailed and general discussion of the ideas that we presented here briefly, due to space limitations.

6 Conclusions

Still messy, after all these years, is the relationship between theoretical neural network models and the biological brain. A notorious instance of this situation is the assumption of symmetric neural synapses, usually made in neural memory models, which clearly does not correspond to biological reality. Motivated by this symmetry problem, we reported here some recent advances made on the investigation of a nonlinear Fokker-Planck formalism, exhibiting some intriguing parallelisms with neural dynamics, that may contribute to clarify the (a)symmetry issue.

We investigated the NLFPE, with drift fields having a gradient component arising from a potential function, and a curl component which does not originate from a potential. In contrast to our previous work [14,15], where we treated homogeneous networks ($a_1 = a_2$), we considered here a non-symmetrical potential function. This corresponds to networks with different types of neurons. The curl component of the drift field corresponds to non-symmetric interactions between the system's constituents. We also studied individual orbits of the system under consideration (as opposed to statistical densities in phase space). We have shown that these resulting individual trajectories exhibit limit cycles of elliptical shape.

The present developments suggest that the NLFP formalism provides a quite versatile and potentially useful approach to study some aspects of neural dynamics. This approach is still at an embryonic stage and much work remains to be done. One possible line of further development is to explore connections between this approach and the empirical and computational evidence for Tsallis q-maxent distributions in avalanches of neural activity [4]. Any further progress along these or related lines will be very welcome.

Acknowledgments. We acknowledge financial support from the Brazilian National Research Council (CNPq), the Rio de Janeiro State Research Foundation (FAPERJ) and the Brazilian agency which funds graduate studies (CAPES).

References

1. de Carvalho, L.A.V., Mendes, D.Q., Wedemann, R.S.: Creativity and delusions: the dopaminergic modulation of cortical maps. In: Sloot, P.M.A., Abramson, D., Bogdanov, A.V., Dongarra, J.J., Zomaya, A.Y., Gorbachev, Y.E. (eds.) ICCS 2003. LNCS, vol. 2657, pp. 511–520. Springer, Heidelberg (2003). https://doi.org/10.1007/3-540-44860-8_53
2. Wedemann, R.S., Donangelo, R., Carvalho, L.A.V.: Generalized Memory Associativity in a Network Model for the Neuroses. Chaos **19**, 015116-(1–11) (2009)
3. Wedemann, R.S., de Carvalho, L.A.V.: Some things psychopathologies can tell Us about consciousness. In: Villa, A.E.P., Duch, W., Érdi, P., Masulli, F., Palm, G. (eds.) ICANN 2012. LNCS, vol. 7552, pp. 379–386. Springer, Heidelberg (2012). https://doi.org/10.1007/978-3-642-33269-2_48
4. Siddiqui, M., Wedemann, R.S., Jensen, H.J.: Avalanches and generalized memory associativity in a network model for conscious and unconscious mental functioning. Physica A **490**, 127–138 (2018)
5. Freud, S.: Introductory Lectures on Psycho-Analysis. Standard Edition. W. W. Norton and Company, New York - London (1966). First German edition (1917)
6. Kandel, E.: Psychiatry, Psychoanalysis, and the New Biology of Mind. American Psychiatric Publishing Inc., Washington D.C., London (2005)
7. Shedler, J.: The efficacy of psychodynamic psychotherapy. Am. Psychol. **65**(2), 98–109 (2010)
8. Cleeremans, A., Timmermans, B., Pasquali, A.: Consciousness and metarepresentation: a computational sketch. Neural Netw. **20**, 1032–1039 (2007)
9. Taylor, J.G., Villa, A.E.P.: The "Conscious I": a neuroheuristic approach to the Mind. In: Baltimore, D., Dulbecco, R., Francois, J., Levi-Montalcini, R. (eds.) Frontiers of Life, pp. 349–368. Academic Press (2001)
10. Taylor, J.G.: A neural model of the loss of self in schizophrenia. Schizophrenia Bull. **37**(6), 1229–1247 (2011)
11. Hertz, J.A., Krogh, A., Palmer, R.G. (eds.): Introduction to the Theory of Neural Computation. Lecture Notes, vol. I. Perseus Books, Cambridge (1991)
12. Cohen, M.A., Grossberg, S.: Absolute stability of global pattern formation and parallel memory storage by competitive neural networks. IEEE Trans. Syst., Man, Cybern. **13**, 815–826 (1983)
13. Tsallis, C., Stariolo, D.A.: Generalized simulated annealing. Physica A **233**, 395–406 (1996)
14. Wedemann, R.S., Plastino, A.R.: Asymmetries in synaptic connections and the nonlinear fokker-planck formalism. In: Villa, A.E.P., Masulli, P., Pons Rivero, A.J. (eds.) ICANN 2016. LNCS, vol. 9886, pp. 19–27. Springer, Cham (2016). https://doi.org/10.1007/978-3-319-44778-0_3
15. Wedemann, R.S., Plastino, A.R., Tsallis, C.: Curl forces and the nonlinear Fokker-Planck equation. Phys. Rev. E **94**, 062105-1-10 (2016)
16. Wedemann, R.S., Plastino, A.R.: q-Maximum entropy distributions and memory neural networks. In: Lintas, A., Rovetta, S., Verschure, P.F.M.J., Villa, A.E.P. (eds.) ICANN 2017. LNCS, vol. 10613, pp. 300–308. Springer, Cham (2017). https://doi.org/10.1007/978-3-319-68600-4_35
17. Parisi, G.: Asymmetric neural networks and the process of learning. J. Phys. A: Math. Gen. **19**, L675–L680 (1986)
18. Xu, Z.B., Hu, G.Q., Kwong, C.P.: Asymmetric hopfield-type networks: theory and applications. Neural Netw. **9**(3), 483–501 (1996)

19. Hopfield, J.J.: Neurons with graded responses have collective computational properties like those of two-state neurons. Proc. Natl. Acad. Sci., USA **81**, 3088–3092 (1988)
20. Martinez, S., Plastino, A.R., Plastino, A.: Nonlinear Fokker-Planck equations and generalized entropies. Physica A **259**(1–2), 183–192 (1998)
21. Franck, T.D.: Nonlinear Fokker-Planck Equations: Fundamentals and Applications. Springer, Heidelberg (2005). https://doi.org/10.1007/b137680
22. Tsallis, C.: Introduction to Nonextensive Statistical Mechanics, Approaching a Complex World. Springer, New York (2009). https://doi.org/10.1007/978-0-387-85359-8

Robotics/Motion Detection

Learning-While Controlling RBF-NN for Robot Dynamics Approximation in Neuro-Inspired Control of Switched Nonlinear Systems

Sophie Klecker(✉), Bassem Hichri, and Peter Plapper

Faculty of Science, Technology and Communication, University of Luxembourg, 6, rue Richard Coudenhove-Kalergi, 1359 Luxembourg, Luxembourg
sophie.klecker@uni.lu

Abstract. Radial Basis Function-Neural Networks are well-established function approximators. This paper presents an adaptive Gaussian RBF-NN with an extended learning-while controlling behaviour. The weights, function centres and widths are updated online based on a sliding mode control element. In this way, the need for fixing parameters a priori is overcome and the network is able to adapt to dynamically changing systems. The aim of this work is to present an extended adaptive neuro-controller for trajectory tracking of serial robots with unknown dynamics. The adaptive RBF-NN is used to approximate the unknown robot manipulator dynamics-function. It is combined with a conventional controller and a bio-inspired extension for the control of a robot in the presence of switching constraints and discontinuous inputs. The controller-extension increases the robustness and adaptability of the system. Its learned goal-directed output results from the complementary action of an actuator, A, and a preventer, P. The trigger is an incentive, I, based on the weighted perception of the environment. The concept is validated through simulations and implementation on a KUKA LWR4-robot.

Keywords: RBF-NN · Learning-while controlling · Switching constraints

1 Introduction

Radial Basis Functions, RBFs, were presented as technique for interpolation in multidimensional space by [1]. Their implementation as activation functions in neural networks is known as a 3-layer network under the acronym RBF-NN. Its first layer, i.e. the input layer performs a nonlinear transformation mapping the input signals to the hidden layer. The single hidden layer consists of an array of computing units, i.e. hidden nodes which are activated by RBF activation functions. The output layer consists of linear summing nodes which allow the network's output to range over a significant range of values. Compared to multilayer neural networks, their structure is less coherent with the natural neural network but their advantages include: faster convergence, more straightforward training and analysis due to a simpler topology and

V. Kůrková et al. (Eds.): ICANN 2018, LNCS 11141, pp. 717–727, 2018.
https://doi.org/10.1007/978-3-030-01424-7_70

easier implementation due to fewer interconnections [2, 3]. [4, 5] i.e. have shown the universal approximation-capabilities of RBF-NNs.

The choice of the network parameters, i.e. the node-centres and widths of the function is essential for the accurate performance of the RBF-NN. The network is locally responsive, i.e. inputs which are close to the centre in the Euclidean sense strongly affect this node but not the others. The centres should be well selected according to the scope of the inputs, i.e. the values of the centres are to be suitably fixed and appropriately distributed in the input domain. The selected width influences the range over which a node is to have a significant activation. In the vast majority of research works, a priori selected centres and width are kept fixed. Although it simplifies the analysis in dynamic systems, this approach presents some drawbacks [2, 5, 6]. First, fixed parameters and therewith the mapping behaviour of the network do not reflect changes in the system which leads to suboptimal performance in dynamically changing environments. Because the parameters of the system under consideration may change over time, the neural network should be adapted online [2]. Second, the initialization of the parameters is not straightforward. The arbitrary selection of values often practiced does not guarantee satisfactory performance. Real-time computation of parameters based on observed data could be extended from weights to function parameters [3].

One of the challenges of the implementation of neural networks is guaranteeing stability. Several research works addressed this issue through combinations of neural networks and robustifying elements. Using sliding mode control to stabilize a neural network was suggested. The downsides were the occurrence of chattering, i.e. undesired oscillations, high control efforts and the need for a priori knowledge of system limits [2, 3]. As an extension, [7] suggested merging a neural network with a combination of a PD- and a sliding mode controller (SMC). The aim of the PD and the SMC was to first bring the system's output into the targeted regions and to second provide robustness. The multilayer feedforward NN with input modification was used to approximate the system's desired output and improve its global performance.

As serial robot manipulators are illustrative examples of nonlinear and time varying MIMO-plants, they are at the focus of a number of research works on neural networks [4, 8]. Also the stabilizing extension for neural networks was applied to robot manipulators with unknown dynamics [7, 9, 10].

Although the mentioned publications showed promising results for robotic control, the results have mainly exclusively been obtained in numerical simulations. The majority of simulations have been performed for n-link-robot arms with $n = 2$. However, for $n > 2$, the parameters affect the performance of the system more considerably and their initialization becomes even more critical [4, 11].

This work presents an extended adaptive neuro-controller for trajectory tracking by robot manipulators with unknown dynamics. The rest of the paper is structured as follows: In Sect. 2, the considered application, the experimental setup as well as the contributions of this work are described. In Sect. 3, the controller is designed. Section 4 presents the validation-results. The paper ends with a discussion and conclusion Sect. 5.

2 Methodology

In this work, the control problem for trajectory tracking of serial robots with unknown dynamics is addressed. The combination of a Gaussian RBF-NN with a biomimetic controller based on SMC enables tracking discontinuous trajectories while guaranteeing robustness and stability despite uncertainties. Figure 1 graphically summarizes the suggested control concept.

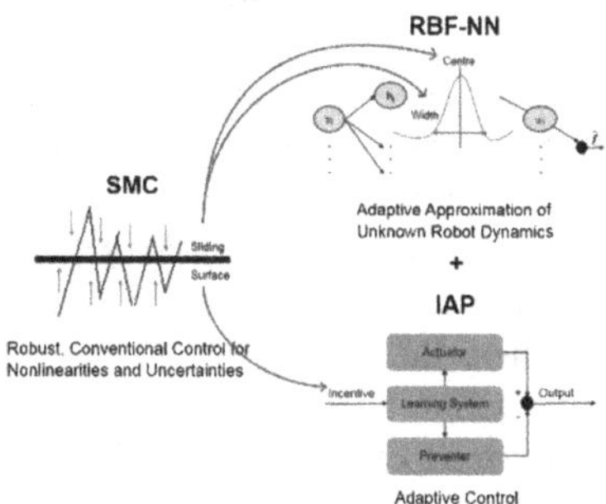

Fig. 1. Combination and interconnection of SMC, RBF-NN and IAP.

The RBF-NN is used to estimate the unknown nonlinear robot dynamics-function. The implementation of adaptive weights, centres and widths enhances the performance of the system in uncertain dynamically changing environments. No offline training phase nor any a priori knowledge is needed. The network exhibits a learning-while controlling behaviour with the online computation of the parameters based on real-time sensor data. The intelligent extension is based on the biomimetic interplay of an actuator (A) and a preventer (P) triggered by an incentive (I) based on the environmental perception. This extension, IAP, increases the robustness as well as the adaptability of the system.

As an illustrative example of a nonlinear, time varying MIMO-system, an n-link robot arm is considered. Its dynamics in the presence of disturbances and varying constraints are expressed in Lagrange form 1.

$$\boldsymbol{M}(\boldsymbol{q})\ddot{\boldsymbol{q}} + \boldsymbol{C}(\boldsymbol{q}, \dot{\boldsymbol{q}})\dot{\boldsymbol{q}} + \boldsymbol{G}(\boldsymbol{q}) = \boldsymbol{u} + \boldsymbol{d} + \boldsymbol{Q}_i \tag{1}$$

with $\boldsymbol{q}, \dot{\boldsymbol{q}}, \ddot{\boldsymbol{q}} \in R^n$ link position, velocity and acceleration with index d for the desired values. $\boldsymbol{M}(\boldsymbol{q}) \in R^{nxn}$ is the inertia matrix, $\boldsymbol{C}(\boldsymbol{q}, \dot{\boldsymbol{q}}) \in R^{nxn}$ the centripetal/Coriolis terms, $\boldsymbol{G}(\boldsymbol{q}) \in R^n$ the gravitational torque-vector. $\boldsymbol{u} \in R^n$ is the applied control-input torque. External disturbances are represented by the bounded term $\boldsymbol{d} \in R^n$. $\boldsymbol{Q}_i \in R^n$ is the global constraint force, $\boldsymbol{Q}_i = \boldsymbol{J}^T(\boldsymbol{q})\boldsymbol{D}_i^T(\boldsymbol{\vartheta})\boldsymbol{\lambda}$ where $\boldsymbol{J}(\boldsymbol{q}) \in R^{nx6}$ is the manipulator's Jacobian, $\boldsymbol{\lambda} \in R^z$ is the vector of Lagrange multipliers and $\boldsymbol{D}_i^T(\boldsymbol{\vartheta}) = \delta(\phi)_i(\boldsymbol{\vartheta})/\delta(\boldsymbol{\vartheta})$ is the gradient of the task space constraints with $\phi_i(\boldsymbol{\vartheta}) \in R^6$ the ith kinematic constraint. $\boldsymbol{\vartheta} \in R^6$ stands for the Cartesian pose and $\boldsymbol{i} = 1, 2, \ldots z$ denotes the index of constraints for the case of multiple switching constraints with z the total number of constraints. The introduced dynamics have the following two relevant properties [12]:

- $\boldsymbol{M}(\boldsymbol{q})$ is a positive definite matrix,
- $\boldsymbol{M}(\boldsymbol{q}) - 2\boldsymbol{C}(\boldsymbol{q}, \dot{\boldsymbol{q}})$ is a skew symmetric matrix, i.e. $\boldsymbol{x}^T\boldsymbol{M}(\boldsymbol{q}) - 2\boldsymbol{C}(\boldsymbol{q}, \dot{\boldsymbol{q}})\boldsymbol{x} = 0$ for all $\boldsymbol{x} \neq 0$.

The robot dynamics can be grouped and expressed as a nonlinear function $\boldsymbol{f}$ 2.

$$\boldsymbol{f} = \boldsymbol{M}(\boldsymbol{q})\ddot{\boldsymbol{q}}_r + \boldsymbol{C}(\boldsymbol{q}, \dot{\boldsymbol{q}})\dot{\boldsymbol{q}}_r + \boldsymbol{G} \tag{2}$$

with $\dot{\boldsymbol{q}}_r = \dot{\boldsymbol{q}}_d - \boldsymbol{q}_{error}$ and $\boldsymbol{q}_{error} = \boldsymbol{q} - \boldsymbol{q}_d$. Because of the manufacturers' reticence about their robots, their kinematics and dynamics, i.e. $\boldsymbol{M}(\boldsymbol{q})$, $\boldsymbol{C}(\boldsymbol{q}, \dot{\boldsymbol{q}})$ and $\boldsymbol{G}(\boldsymbol{q})$ from 1 are not known in practice. As a consequence the need for approximating robot dynamics arises. With the idea to avoid estimating $\boldsymbol{M}(\boldsymbol{q})$, $\boldsymbol{C}(\boldsymbol{q}, \dot{\boldsymbol{q}})$ and $\boldsymbol{G}(\boldsymbol{q})$ separately, the robot function $\boldsymbol{f}$ as defined in 2 is approximated. The considered application is a trajectory tracking use case where the inputs, i.e. the desired positions are fed to the system in a discontinuous manner.

The validation of the developed control concept is done through simulation and experimental work. The simulation is performed on a planar robot with two revolute joints in the Matlab/Simulink environment. The inputs for the considered path following application are two .csv-files, i.e. lists of successive desired joint positions in radians. The parameter-values were consciously and arbitrarily selected small and simple to demonstrate the controller-performance independently of specific parameter-values. The experiments are performed on a 7 DOF-KUKA LWR 4-robot. The controller is implemented in C++ on an external PC. The communication between the robot and the PC is assured through UDP-packages in the framework of the Fast Research Interface, a software add-on provided by KUKA [13]. The inputs for the goal-reaching application are desired angular positions for all 7 joints.

Compared to previous work, the contributions are:

- In the Gaussian RBF-NN, the learning-while-controlling behaviour is extended. Adaptive laws are not limited to the online computation of the weights, but are also implemented to adapt the centres and widths based on real-time sensor data. In this way, first, the problem of parameter-initialization and required a priori knowledge is eliminated. Second, the network is able to adapt in case of dynamically changing systems.
- The biomimetic extension IAP provides adaptive performance. The algorithm of an actuator-preventer interplay which is triggered by a sensory data-based incentive signal is intuitive.
- The control concept is applied to switching constraints. Changes in the interactions between robotic end-effector and surrounding environment result in a switched nonlinear system. The introduction of switching constraints compared to fixed constraints severely impacts the global system performance [14]. The tracking application for robot manipulators with unknown dynamics is extended from continuous inputs to discontinuous inputs, i.e. lists (.csv-files) of successive desired joint positions.

- Next to a validation through simulation on a 2-link robot, the controller is implemented on a 7-DOF KUKA LWR4-robot manipulator.

3 Controller

The suggested control concept 3 is composed of a conventional controller $\boldsymbol{u}_c$ and an adaptive biomimetic controller-extension $\boldsymbol{u}_e$ to enhance the system-performance as well as its robustness.

$$\boldsymbol{u} = \boldsymbol{u}_c + \boldsymbol{u}_e \tag{3}$$

Sliding mode control is at the base of the suggested controller. The sliding surface $\boldsymbol{s} \in R^n$ is defined in 4.

$$\boldsymbol{s} = \dot{\boldsymbol{q}}_{error} + \boldsymbol{q}_{error} \tag{4}$$

The conventional controller $\boldsymbol{u}_c \in R^n$ is formalized in 5.

$$\boldsymbol{u}_c = \boldsymbol{f} + \boldsymbol{c}_c \boldsymbol{s} \tag{5}$$

where $\boldsymbol{c}_c > 0$ is a constant gain factor.

The conventional controller is complemented by a biomimetic, adaptive control-extension. $\boldsymbol{u}_e \in R^n$ is inspired on the human learning process based on adaptive motivation-lifecycles. Neuroscientific foundations as well as computational models of motivations, rewards and reinforcement learning which inspired this work, can be found in literature. [15] presented the neuroscientific foundations of model-free and model-based reward learning. [16] 's work was on the neurosciences of motivation. The authors studied the key roles of motivation in learning processes. [17] presented a computational model of the interplay between amygdala and orbito-prefrontal cortex in emotional learning of mammalians. [18] studied the goal-lifecycle in reinforcement learning.

The key-elements of the IAP-concept used in this work are

- the incentive, I, based on the weighted perception of the agent's environment and serving as motivation for a learning system,
- the complementary action of an actuator, A, and a preventer, P, resulting in an adapted goal-directed output.

The structure of the IAP-concept is illustrated in Fig. 2. In equation-form, the ILAP-concept is expressed by 6–12. The weighted perception of the agent's environment is defined as the positional error 6.

$$\boldsymbol{w}_{state} = \boldsymbol{q}_{error} = \boldsymbol{q} - \boldsymbol{q}_d \tag{6}$$

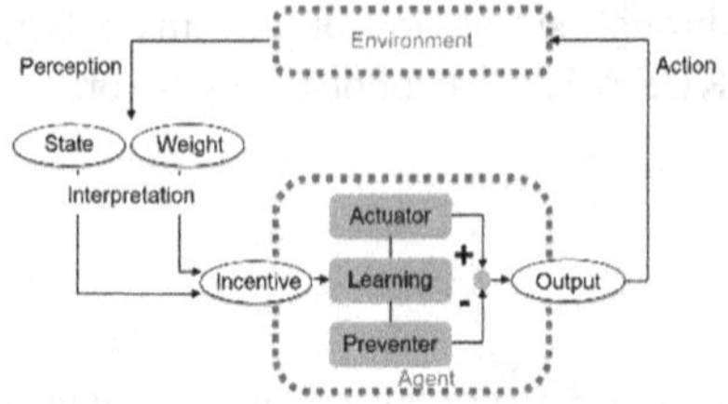

Fig. 2. Structure of the IAP-concept.

The incentive, I, i.e. the motivation which serves as input to the learning system of the agent follows 7. $\boldsymbol{o} \in R^n$ 12, the meaningful learning output is defined as the difference between the outputs of the actuator $\boldsymbol{a} \in R^n$ 8 and the preventer $\boldsymbol{p} \in R^n$ 10. The latter are updated according to the learning rates 9 and 11. Learning can be interpreted as a reorganization of information, as a combination of associating and predicting. The expectancy of a state and the understanding of an action-perception causation are at the base of the algorithm.

$$\boldsymbol{i} = sgn(\boldsymbol{w}_{state})^T \dot{\boldsymbol{w}}_{state} . * (\boldsymbol{s} - \boldsymbol{o}) \tag{7}$$

$$\boldsymbol{a} = \boldsymbol{w}_{state} . * \boldsymbol{\Delta}_a \tag{8}$$

$$\boldsymbol{\Delta}_a = \boldsymbol{c}_a \dot{\boldsymbol{w}}_{state} . * max(0, \boldsymbol{i}) \tag{9}$$

$$\boldsymbol{p} = \boldsymbol{w}_{state} . * \boldsymbol{\Delta}_p \tag{10}$$

$$\boldsymbol{\Delta}_p = \boldsymbol{c}_p \dot{\boldsymbol{w}}_{state} . * (\boldsymbol{o} - \boldsymbol{i}) \tag{11}$$

$$\boldsymbol{o} = \boldsymbol{a} - \boldsymbol{p} \tag{12}$$

where .* denotes element-wise multiplication and $\boldsymbol{c}_a, \boldsymbol{c}_p > 0$ are constant gain factors. The output of the controller-extension $\boldsymbol{u}_e$ is expressed in 13.

$$\boldsymbol{u}_e = \boldsymbol{f}\left((\boldsymbol{s})\, \boldsymbol{sats} + \int_0^T \boldsymbol{o}(t)\ \mathrm{d}t\right) \tag{13}$$

The saturation function $\boldsymbol{sats} \in R^n$ was introduced by [12] to increase the resistance to chattering of a sliding mode controller. T is the total time of the process under consideration. The output of the ILAP-concept is time-dependent in the sense that it changes as time passes and the robotic manipulator moves.

The stability of the system is proven through Lyapunov theory. The candidate function and its derivative are chosen in 14 and 15, respectively.

$$V = 0.5\boldsymbol{s}^T \boldsymbol{M}\boldsymbol{s} \tag{14}$$

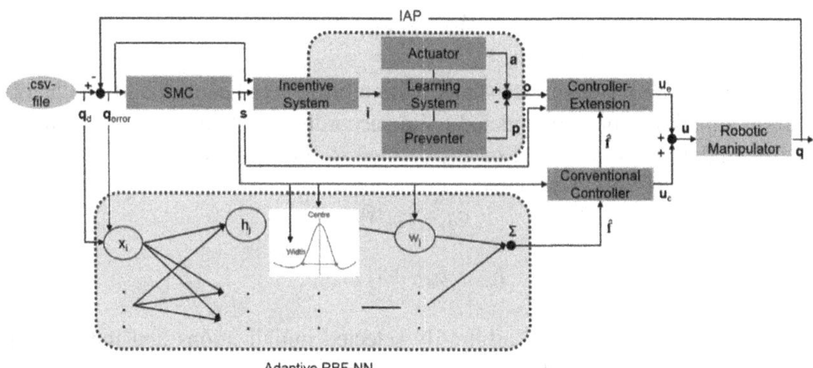

Fig. 3. Structure of the suggested controller with the interplay of SMC, ILAP and adaptive RBF-NN.

$$\dot{V} = \boldsymbol{s}^T \boldsymbol{M} \dot{\boldsymbol{s}} + 0.5 \boldsymbol{s}^T \dot{\boldsymbol{M}} \boldsymbol{s} \tag{15}$$

Making use of the definitions of $\boldsymbol{q}_{error}$ and $\boldsymbol{q}_r$, the skew-symmetry property (2), combining with 4, 2, 5, 13 and a reformulation of 1, 15 becomes:

$$\dot{V} = -\boldsymbol{s}^T \boldsymbol{c}_c \boldsymbol{s} - \boldsymbol{s}^T \boldsymbol{f}(\boldsymbol{sats})\boldsymbol{s} - \boldsymbol{s}^T \boldsymbol{f} \int_0^T \boldsymbol{o}(t)\ \mathrm{d}t - \boldsymbol{s}^T \boldsymbol{Q}_i - \boldsymbol{s}^T \boldsymbol{d} \tag{16}$$

To guarantee stability 16 has to be negative. The first term of the right side of 16 is always negative. For the remaining terms, there are 2 cases to consider. If $s_n > 0$, then $f_n(sats_n)s_n + f_n \int_0^T o_n(t)\ \mathrm{d}t + Q_{i,n} + d_n > 0$. If $s_n < 0$, then $f_n(sats_n)s_n + f_n \int_0^T o_n(t)\ \mathrm{d}t + Q_{i,n} + d_n < 0$ with n the respective manipulator-link. In both cases, $\dot{V} < 0$ which guarantees the stability of the analysed system.

$\boldsymbol{f}$, however is hardly ever known in practice and therefore controllers as developed in 5 and 13 are not directly implementable. To address this problem, an adaptive RBF-NN with j nodes is implemented to approximate the unknown non-linear robot function $\boldsymbol{f}$. The non-linear Gaussian activation function for node j of network input i is defined in 17.

$$h_j(\boldsymbol{x}) = e^{-\|\boldsymbol{x} - c_{ij}\|^2 / \boldsymbol{b}_j^2} \tag{17}$$

with $\boldsymbol{x} = \left[\boldsymbol{q}_{error}^T, \dot{\boldsymbol{q}}_{error}^T, \boldsymbol{q}_d^T, \dot{\boldsymbol{q}}_d^T,\ \ddot{\boldsymbol{q}}_d^T\right]$ the input of the network selected in the scope of $\boldsymbol{f}$, the to be approximated function. $\boldsymbol{c}_{ij}$ is the coordinate value of node j's Gaussian function's centre point for input i and $\boldsymbol{b}_j$ is the Gaussian function's width. The approximation of $\boldsymbol{f}, \hat{\boldsymbol{f}}$ is computed as output of the RBF-NN 18.

$$\hat{\boldsymbol{f}} = \boldsymbol{W} \boldsymbol{h}(\boldsymbol{x}) \tag{18}$$

where $\boldsymbol{W} \in R^j$ is the weight matrix which is adapted according to the update law 19.

$$\dot{W} = h(x)s^T \tag{19}$$

To overcome the problems associated with a priori fixed centres and widths of the radial basis functions, they are updated online according to 20 and 21. As illustrated in Fig. 1, the update laws are based on the defined sliding surface.

$$\dot{c}_{ij} = c_{0,j}|s| \tag{20}$$

$$b_n = b_{n,0} + |1/s_n| \tag{21}$$

where $b_0 \in R^n$ and $c_0 \in R^{jxi}$ are arbitrarily selected initializations and index n representing the respective manipulator-link.

The structure of the suggested controller with the interplay of sliding mode control, adaptive RBF-NN and ILAP is graphically summarized in Fig. 3.

4 Results

For the simulation, the parameters are chosen as follows $c_c = [10, 10], c_a = 5, c_p = 5$ and for the initialization of c, b:

$c_{0,j} = [-0.999, -0.666, -0.333, 0, 0.333, 0.666, 0.999]$ and $b_0 = [1, 1]$.The simulation results for the path following application are depicted in Figs. 4 and 5. They show the position tracking error for both robot links and the approximation error of the norm of the non-linear robot function.

In a next step, the controller is validated for a goal reaching application on a KUKA LWR 4+ -robot. Figure 6 shows the position error for the joints over time.

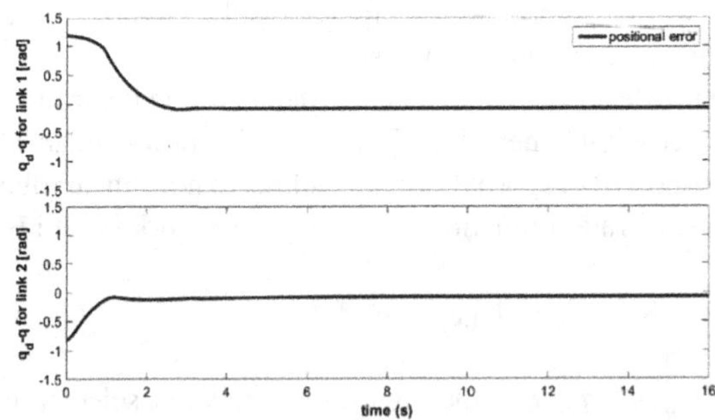

Fig. 4. Position tracking error for link 1 (top) and link 2 (bottom).

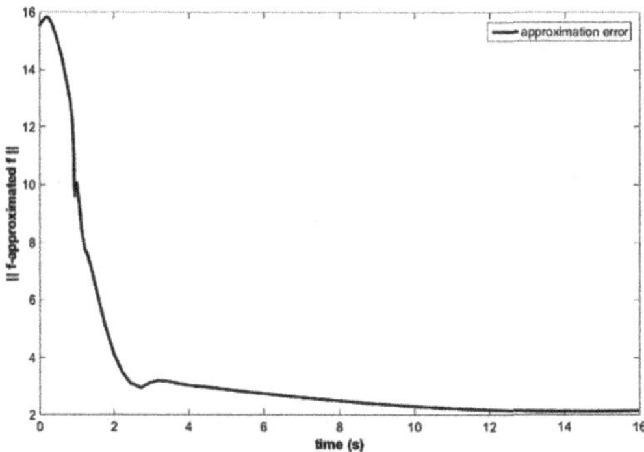

Fig. 5. Approximation error of the norm of the non-linear robot function.

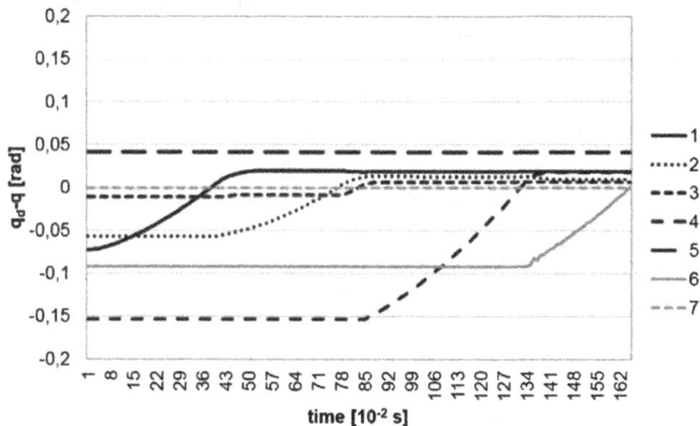

Fig. 6. Position tracking error for the 7 robot joints.

5 Discussion and Conclusion

In this paper, an extended adaptive neuro-inspired controller for trajectory tracking of serial robots with unknown dynamics is designed. The suggested control concept is based on robust sliding mode control and combines an adaptive Gaussian RBF-NN with a biomimetic controller-extension. First, the implementation of adaptive laws for updating not only the weights of the RBF-NN, but also the centres and widths of the function is a promising approach for approximating unknown functions without a priori determination of fixed parameters. Second, the combination of conventional robust with adaptive bio-inspired control-elements is a promising approach for robot control in the presence of varying constraints and uncertainties. It exhibits robustness and adaptability. The results presented in this paper show promising first experimental validations of the suggested concept. To fully validate the control scheme however, more and more advanced experiments should be performed. Examples are path following applications with various input densities and switching between free-space and in-contact positions. Possible extensions of the suggested concept include the addition of desired force-signals as inputs or the combination with a Programming by Demonstration-step to obtain the.csv-files used as inputs [19].

Acknowledgments. This work has been done in the framework of the European Union supported INTERREG GR-project "ROBOTIX-Academy".

References

1. Micchelli, C.A.: Interpolation of scattered data: distance matrices and conditionally positive definite functions. Constr. Approximation **2**, 11–22 (1986)
2. Bass, E., Lee, K.Y.: Robust control of nonlinear systems using norm-bounded neural networks. In: IEEE World Congress Computer Intelligence (Neural Networks part), pp. 2524–2529 (1994)
3. Van Cuong, P., Nan, W.Y.: Adaptive trajectory tracking neural network control with robust compensator for robot manipulators. Neural Comput. Appl. **27**(2), 525–536 (2015). https://doi.org/10.1007/s00521-015-1873-4
4. Yu, L., Fei, S., Huang, J., Gao, Y.: Trajectory switching control of robotic manipulators based on RBF neural networks. Circuits Syst. Signal Process. **33**, 1119–1133 (2014)
5. Tao, Y., Zheng, J., Lin, Y.: A sliding mode control-based on a RBF neural network for deburring industry robotic systems. Int. J. Adv. Robotic Syst. **13**(1), 13–18 (2016). https://doi.org/10.5772/62002
6. Wang, L., Chai, T., Zhai, L.: Neural-network-based terminal sliding-mode control of robotic manipulators including actuator dynamics. IEEE Trans. Ind. Electron. **56**(9), 3296–3304 (2009)
7. Ren, X., Rad, A.B., Lewis, F.L.: Neural network-based compensation control of robot manipulators with unknown dynamics. In: American Control Conference, pp. 13–18 (2007)
8. Otte, S., Zwiener, A., Butz, M.V.: Inherently constraint-aware control of many-joint robot arms with inverse recurrent models. In: Lintas, A., Rovetta, S., Verschure, P.F.M.J., Villa, Alessandro E.P. (eds.) ICANN 2017. LNCS, vol. 10613, pp. 262–270. Springer, Cham (2017). https://doi.org/10.1007/978-3-319-68600-4_31
9. He, W., Dong, Y.: Adaptive fuzzy neural network control for a constrained robot using impedance learning. IEEE Trans. Neural Netw. Learn. Syst. **29**(4), 1174–1186 (2018)
10. Klecker, S., Hichri, B., Plapper, P.: Neuro-inspired reward-based tracking control for robotic manipulators with unknown dynamics. In: 2nd International Conference on Robotics and Automation Engineering, pp. 21–25 (2017)
11. Krabbes, M., Döschner, C.: Modelling of robot dynamics based on a multi-dimensional RBF-like neural network. In: IEEE International Conference on Information, Intelligence, and Systems (1999)
12. Slotine, J.E., Li, W.: Applied Nonlinear Control. Prentice Hall, Englewood Cliffs (1991)
13. KUKA System Technology, KUKA Roboter GmbH: KUKA FastResearchInterface 1.0 For KUKA System Software 5.6 lr Version: KUKA FRI 1.0 V2 en. (2011)
14. Liberzon, D.: Switching in Systems and Control. Birkauser, Boston (2003)
15. Dayan, P., Berridge, K.C.: Model-based and model-free pavlovian reward learning: revaluation, revision and revelation. Cogn. Affect. Behav. Neurosci. **14**(2), 473–492 (2014)
16. Kringelbach, M.L., Berridge, K.C.: Neuroscience of reward, motivation, and drive. In: Recent Developments in Neuroscience Research on Human Motivation, Advances in Motivation and Achievement, vol. 19, pp. 23–35 (2017)

17. Balkenius, C., Moren, J.: Emotional learning: a computational model of the amygdala. Int. J. Cybern. Syst. **32**(6), 611–636 (2001)
18. Merrick, K.E.: Intrinsic motivation and introspection in reinforcement learning. IEEE Trans. Auton. Mental Develop. **4**, 315–329 (2012)
19. Racca, M., Pajarinen, J., Montebelli, A., Kyrki, V.: Learning in-contact control strategies from demonstration. In: IROS (2016)

A Feedback Neural Network for Small Target Motion Detection in Cluttered Backgrounds

Hongxin Wang[1], Jigen Peng[2], and Shigang Yue[1(✉)]

[1] The Computational Intelligence Lab (CIL), School of Computer Science, University of Lincoln, Lincoln LN6 7TS, UK
syue@lincoln.ac.uk

[2] School of Mathematics and Information Science, Guangzhou University, Guangzhou 510006, China
jgpeng@gzhu.edu.cn

Abstract. Small target motion detection is critical for insects to search for and track mates or prey which always appear as small dim speckles in the visual field. A class of specific neurons, called small target motion detectors (STMDs), has been characterized by exquisite sensitivity for small target motion. Understanding and analyzing visual pathway of STMD neurons are beneficial to design artificial visual systems for small target motion detection. Feedback loops have been widely identified in visual neural circuits and play an important role in target detection. However, if there exists a feedback loop in the STMD visual pathway or if a feedback loop could significantly improve the detection performance of STMD neurons, is unclear. In this paper, we propose a feedback neural network for small target motion detection against naturally cluttered backgrounds. In order to form a feedback loop, model output is temporally delayed and relayed to previous neural layer as feedback signal. Extensive experiments showed that the significant improvement of the proposed feedback neural network over the existing STMD-based models for small target motion detection.

Keywords: Small target motion detection · Feedback loop
Neural modeling · Naturally cluttered backgrounds

1 Introduction

In dynamic visual world, the observer (an animal) are more interested in moving objects, since they are more likely to be mates, predators or prey. Being able to detect moving objects in a distance and early could endow the observer with stronger competitiveness for survival. However, when an object is far away from the observer, it often appears as a small dim speckle whose size may vary from one pixel to a few pixels in the visual field. Detecting such small targets in visual cluttered backgrounds has been considered as a challenging problem for artificial

V. Kůrková et al. (Eds.): ICANN 2018, LNCS 11141, pp. 728–737, 2018.
https://doi.org/10.1007/978-3-030-01424-7_71

visual systems. This is not only because shape, color and texture information of small targets cannot be used for motion detection, but also because the cluttered background, such as bushes, trees and/or rocks, always contains a great number of small-target-like features (called background noise). Small target motion detection means detecting small moving targets, meanwhile discriminating them from background noise.

Insects exhibit exquisite sensitivity for small target motion [6] and can pursue small flying targets, such as mates or prey, with high capture rates [7]. As revealed in biological research [5,6], the exquisite sensitivity is coming from a class of specific neurons in the insects' visual system, called small target motion detectors (STMDs). STMD neurons give peak responses to targets subtending $1 - 3°$ of the visual field, with no response to larger bars (typically $>10°$) or to wide-field grating stimuli. The electrophysiological knowledge about STMD neurons and their afferent pathways is helpful for designing artificial visual systems for small target motion detection.

A few STMD-based models have been proposed for detecting small target motion in naturally cluttered backgrounds. Elementary small target motion detector (ESTMD) which was proposed by Wiederman *et al.* [12], can detect the presence of small moving targets, but not the motion direction. To detect small moving targets and their motion directions, three directionally selective models have been proposed, including EMD-ESTMD [1,11], ESTMD-EMD [1,11] and directionally selective small target motion detector (DSTMD) [9]. Although these existing STMD-based models can detect small moving targets, their detection results often contain a great number of background noise. Further improvement is needed for filtering out background noise.

Feedback loops exist extensively in animals' visual systems and can optimize motion estimation [3,4]. Biological research reveals that feedback loops are able to simultaneously mediate the synthesis of motion representations and cancellation of distracting signals [3]. However, it is still unclear if a feedback loop exist in the visual pathway of STMD neurons or if a feedback loop can significantly improve detection performance of STMD neurons. In this paper, we investigate that if a feedback loop exists, can it improve detection performance of STMD neurons. To answer this question, we propose a feedback neural network (**feedback ESTMD**) based on the existing ESTMD model [12] for small target motion detection. In order to form a feedback loop, model output is firstly temporally delayed and then relayed to previous neural layer (medulla layer) as feedback signal. The feedback signal is added on the output of medulla layer for weakening responses to background noise. Systematic experiments demonstrate that the feedback loop can significantly improve detection performance of the existing STMD-based models.

The remainder of this paper is organized as follows. In Sect. 2, the proposed feedback neural network is introduced in details. In Sect. 3, experiments are carried out to test the performance of the proposed feedback neural network. Discussion is also given in this section. In Sect. 4, we give conclusions and perspectives.

2 Formulation of the Model

In this section, we elaborate on the proposed feedback model, called **Feedback ESTMD**. Its schematic illustration is shown in Fig. 1. As can be seen, $I(x, y, t)$ is the model input, denoting an image sequence where x, y and t are spatial and temporal field positions, respectively. Model input $I(x, y, t)$ is successively processed by four neural layers including retina, lamina, medulla and lobula. Through the process of four neural layers, we can obtain a model output $F(x, y, t)$. The output $F(x, y, t)$ is firstly temporally delayed and then relayed to medulla layer so as to form a feedback loop. The proposed feedback loop can weaken responses to background noise and significantly improve detection performance. In the following, functionalities of four neural layers and the feedback loop will be introduced in details.

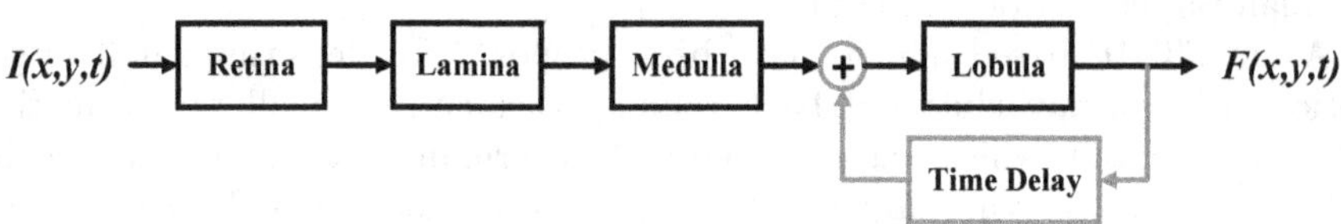

Fig. 1. Schematic illustration of the proposed feedback model.

2.1 Retina Layer

In the insect's visual system, retina layer contains a great number of ommatidia [10]. These ommatidia are able to receive luminance signals from the natural world and relay signals to downstream neurons for further process. The received luminance signal are always highly blurred, due to the extremely low resolution of ommatidia.

In the proposed feedback neural network, each ommatidium is modeled as a spatial Gaussian filter for simulating ommatidium's blur effect. Let $I(x, y, t) \in \mathbf{R}$ denote the input image sequence where x, y and t are spatial and temporal field positions. Then, the output of ommatidium with visual field centered at (x, y) denoted by $P(x, y, t)$ is defined as,

$$P(x, y, t) = \iint I(u, v, t) G_{\sigma_1}(x - u, y - v) du dv \tag{1}$$

where $G_{\sigma_1}(x, y)$ is a Gaussian function, given by

$$G_{\sigma_1}(x, y) = \frac{1}{2\pi\sigma_1^2} \exp(-\frac{x^2 + y^2}{2\sigma_1^2}). \tag{2}$$

2.2 Lamina Layer

In the insect's visual system, lamina layer contains a great number of large monopolar cells (LMCs) [2]. LMCs receive signals from ommatidia and are able to extract motion information from ommatidium output. To be more precise, LMCs show strong responses to brightness increments and decrements, i.e., luminance changes.

In the proposed feedback neural network, each LMC is modeled as a temporal high-pass filter extracting luminance changes, i.e., motion information, from ommatidium output $P(x, y, t)$. Let $L(x, y, t)$ denote the output of LMC located at (x, y). Then, $L(x, y, t)$ is defined by convolving ommatidium output $P(x, y, t)$ with a temporal high-pass convolution kernel $H(t)$. That is,

$$L(x, y, t) = \int P(x, y, s)H(t - s)ds \tag{3}$$

$$H(t) = \Gamma_{n_1,\tau_1}(t) - \Gamma_{n_2,\tau_2}(t) \tag{4}$$

where $\Gamma_{n,\tau}(t)$ is a Gamma kernel, defined as

$$\Gamma_{n,\tau}(t) = (nt)^n \frac{\exp(-nt/\tau)}{(n-1)!\tau^{n+1}}. \tag{5}$$

In the insect's visual system, before LMC relays its output to downstream neurons, it receives lateral inhibition from its adjacent neurons. In the proposed neural network, $L(x, y, t)$ is convolved with an inhibition kernel $W_1(x, y, t)$ so as to implement lateral inhibition mechanism. That is,

$$L_I(x, y, t) = \iiint L(u, v, s)W_1(x - u, y - v, t - s)dudvds \tag{6}$$

where $L_I(x, y, t)$ is the signal after lateral inhibition and $W_1(x, y, t)$ is defined by,

$$W_1(x, y, t) = W_S^P(x, y)W_T^P(t) + W_S^N(x, y)W_T^N(t) \tag{7}$$

where $W_S^P(x, y)$, $W_S^N(x, y)$, $W_T^P(t)$, $W_T^N(t)$ are set as

$$W_S^P = [G_{\sigma_2}(x, y) - G_{\sigma_3}(x, y)]^+ \tag{8}$$

$$W_S^N = [G_{\sigma_2}(x, y) - G_{\sigma_3}(x, y)]^-, \ \sigma_3 = 2 \cdot \sigma_2 \tag{9}$$

$$W_T^P = \frac{1}{\lambda_1} \exp(-\frac{t}{\lambda_1}) \tag{10}$$

$$W_T^N = \frac{1}{\lambda_2} \exp(-\frac{t}{\lambda_2}), \ \lambda_2 > \lambda_1. \tag{11}$$

where $[x]^+, [x]^-$ denote $\max(x, 0)$ and $\min(x, 0)$, respectively.

2.3 Medulla Layer

In the insect's visual system, medulla layer contains a great number of medulla neurons, including Tm1, Tm2, Tm3 and Mi1 [2]. These four medulla neurons receive signals from lamina layer and respond strongly to luminance changes. More precisely, Mi1 and Tm3 neurons respond selectively to luminance increases, with the response of Mi1 delayed relative to Tm3. Conversely, Tm1 and Tm2 respond selectively to luminance decreases, with the response of Tm1 delayed relative to Tm2.

Before modeling the four medulla neurons, we first split the LMC neural outputs $L_I(x,y,t)$ into positive and negative parts denoted by $S^{ON}(x,y,t)$ and $S^{OFF}(x,y,t)$, respectively. That is,

$$S^{ON}(x,y,t) = [L_I(x,y,t)]^+ \tag{12}$$

$$S^{OFF}(x,y,t) = -[L_I(x,y,t)]^- \tag{13}$$

where $[x]^+, [x]^-$ denote $\max(x,0)$ and $\min(x,0)$, respectively. S^{ON} and S^{OFF} are also called ON and OFF signals, which are able to reflect luminance increase and decrease, respectively.

Since the Tm3 and Tm2 respond strongly to luminance increases and decreases, we use $S^{ON}(x,y,t)$ and $S^{OFF}(x,y,t)$ to define the outputs of Tm3 and Tm2, respectively. That is,

$$S^{Tm3}(x,y,t) = \Big[\iint S^{ON}(u,v,t)W_2(x-u,y-v)dudv\Big]^+ \tag{14}$$

$$S^{Tm2}(x,y,t) = \Big[\iint S^{OFF}(u,v,t)W_2(x-u,y-v)dudv\Big]^+ \tag{15}$$

where S^{Tm3} and S^{Tm2} denote outputs of Tm3 and Tm2 neurons, respectively; $W_2(x,y)$ is the second-order lateral inhibition kernel, defined as

$$W_2(x,y) = A[g(x,y)]^+ + B[g(x,y)]^- \tag{16}$$

where A, B are constant, and $g(x,y)$ is given by

$$g(x,y) = G_{\sigma_4}(x,y) - e \cdot G_{\sigma_5}(x,y) - \rho \tag{17}$$

where $G_\sigma(x,y)$ is a Gaussian function and e, ρ are constant.

Since the neural response of the Mi1 (or Tm1) is delayed relative to the Tm3 (or Tm2), we define the output of the Mi1 (or Tm1) using the temporally delayed output of the Tm3 (or Tm2). That is,

$$S^{Mi1}(x,y,t) = \int S^{Tm3}(u,v,t) \cdot \Gamma_{n_N,\tau_N}(t-s)ds \tag{18}$$

$$S^{Tm1}(x,y,t) = \int S^{Tm2}(u,v,t) \cdot \Gamma_{n_F,\tau_F}(t-s)ds \tag{19}$$

where S^{Mi1} and S^{Tm1} represent outputs of Mi1 and Tm1, respectively; n_N, n_F are orders of Gamma kernels while τ_N, τ_F are time constants.

2.4 Lobula Layer

In the insect's visual system, STMD neurons integrate signals from medulla neurons and respond selectively to small target motion.

In the existing ESTMD model [12], the output of STMD neuron $F(x, y, t)$ with visual field centered at (x, y) is defined by multiplying the Tm3 neural output $S^{Tm3}(x, y, t)$ with the Tm1 neural output $S^{Tm1}(x, y, t)$. That is,

$$F(x, y, t) = S^{Tm3}(x, y, t) \times S^{Tm1}(x, y, t). \tag{20}$$

In the proposed feedback neural network, the medulla neural outputs and feedback signal are added together to define the output of the STMD neuron (see Fig. 1). The temporally delayed model output is used as the feedback signal, which is obtained by convolving $F(x, y, t)$ with a Gamma kernel. That is,

$$\begin{aligned} F(x, y, t) = &\left\{S^{Tm3}(x, y, t) + \boldsymbol{k} \cdot \int \boldsymbol{F}(\boldsymbol{x}, \boldsymbol{y}, \boldsymbol{s}) \cdot \boldsymbol{\Gamma}_{n_L, \tau_L}(\boldsymbol{t} - \boldsymbol{s}) \boldsymbol{ds}\right\} \\ &\times \left\{S^{Tm1}(x, y, t) + \boldsymbol{k} \cdot \int \boldsymbol{F}(\boldsymbol{x}, \boldsymbol{y}, \boldsymbol{s}) \cdot \boldsymbol{\Gamma}_{n_L, \tau_L}(\boldsymbol{t} - \boldsymbol{s}) \boldsymbol{ds}\right\}. \end{aligned} \tag{21}$$

where n_L and τ_L are the order and time constant of the Gamma kernel, respectively.

3 Results and Discussions

In this section, we test the ability of the proposed feedback neural network (Feedback ESTMD) for detecting small targets against cluttered backgrounds. The proposed neural network is tested on a set of image sequences produced by Vision Egg [8]. The video images are 500 (in horizontal) by 250 (in vertical) pixels and temporal sampling frequency is set as 1000 Hz.

Before performing experiments, we explain how to determine the location of a small moving target using model output $F(x, y, t)$. For a given detection threshold γ, if there is a position (x_0, y_0) and time t_0 which satisfy model output $F(x_0, y_0, t_0) > \gamma$, then we believe that a small target is detected at position (x_0, y_0) and time t_0. Two metrics are defined to evaluate detection performance. That is,

$$D_R = \frac{\text{number of true detections}}{\text{number of actual targets}} \tag{22}$$

$$F_A = \frac{\text{number of false detections}}{\text{number of images}} \tag{23}$$

where D_R and F_A represent the detection rate and false alarm rate, respectively. The detected result is considered correct if the pixel distance between the ground truth and the result is within a threshold (5 pixels).

In the first experiment, we use an image sequence which shows a small dark target moving against the naturally cluttered background, as model input. A representative frame is shown in Fig. 2(a). The background is moving from left

(a)

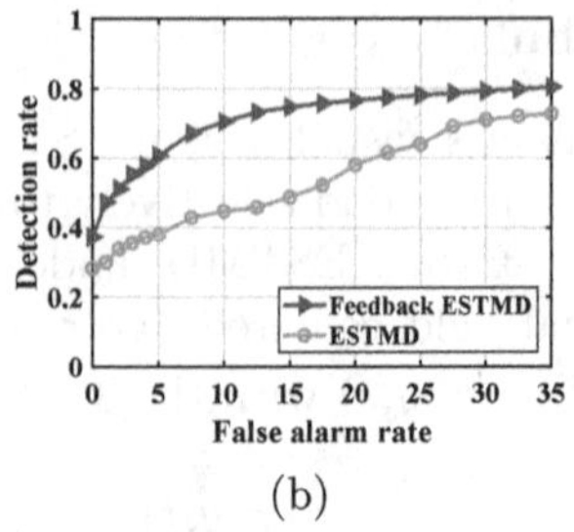

(b)

Fig. 2. (a) A representative frame of the input image sequence. The small target is highlighted by the white circle. Arrow V_B denote motion direction of the background. (b) The receiver operating characteristic (ROC) curve.

to right and its velocity V_B is set as $V_B = 250$ (pixel/second). A small target is moving against the cluttered background and its coordinate at time t is set as $(500 - V_T \cdot \frac{t+300}{1000}, 125 + 15 \cdot \sin(4\pi\frac{t+300}{1000})), t \in [0, 1000]$ ms where V_T denotes target velocity and is set as $V_T = 500$ (pixel/second). The luminance and size of the small target are set as 50 and 5×5 (pixel $\times$ pixel), respectively. The receiver operating characteristic (ROC) curve is presented in Fig. 2(b).

Figure 2(b) is illustrating that the proposed feedback model (Feedback ESTMD) outperforms the existing model (ESTMD) at detecting small targets against naturally cluttered backgrounds. More precisely, for a given false alarm rate, feedback ESTMD has a higher detection rate than ESTMD. This also indicates that the feedback loop can improve detection performance of the existing STMD-based models.

We further test these two models under different parameters of the image sequence, including target luminance, target size, target velocity, background velocity and background motion direction. In order to compare detection performances, we fix false alarm rate F_A as 10 and illustrate detection rates of two models at this false alarm rate. The corresponding results are shown in Fig. 3.

From Fig. 3(a) and (b), we can see that feedback ESTMD has a better detection performance than ESTMD under different target luminance and sizes. To be more precise, the detection rate of feedback ESTMD is much higher than that of ETMD when target luminance varies (see Fig. 3(a)). Similarly in Fig. 3(b), the detection rate of feedback ESTMD is higher than that of ETMD under different target sizes.

From Fig. 3(c), (d) and (e), we can find that detection performance of feedback ESTMD is dependent on velocity difference between the background and the small target. More precisely, as we can see from Fig. 3(c), when target velocity is larger than background velocity $V_B = 250$ (pixel/second), feedback ESTMD has higher detection rates than ESTMD. However, when target velocity is smaller than background velocity, detection rate of feedback ESTMD is slightly lower than that of ESTMD. Similar variation trend can be seen Fig. 3(d) and (e). To be more precise, no matter whether the background and the small target are

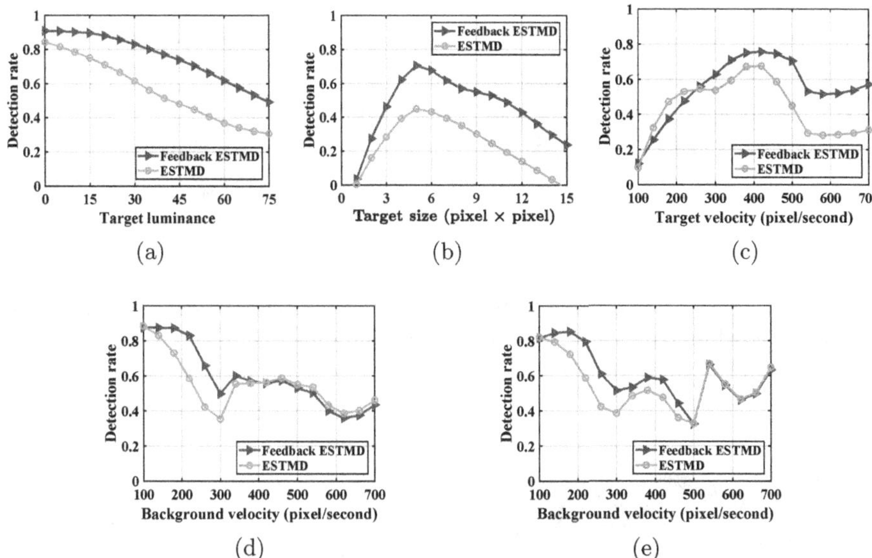

Fig. 3. Detection rates of the proposed feedback model (feedback ESTMD) and the existing model (ESTMD) at a fixed false alarm rate $F_A = 10$ when parameters of image sequences are changed. In each subplot, horizontal axis denotes the varying parameter while vertical axis denotes detection rate D_R. (a) Varying target luminance. (b) Varying target size. (c) Varying target velocity. (d) Varying background velocity when the target and the background are moving along the **opposite direction**. (e) Varying background velocity when the target and the background are moving along the **same direction**.

moving along the same direction or not, the detection rate of feedback ESTMD is higher than that of ESTMD when background velocity is smaller than target velocity $V_T = 500$ (pixel/second). When background velocity is larger than target velocity, detection rates of these two models show no significant difference.

In the second and third experiment, we test the proposed feedback model in different cluttered backgrounds. Two image sequences with different backgrounds are used as model input in these two experiments. Two representative frames are presented in Figs. 4(a) and 5(a), respectively. In these two image sequences, backgrounds are all moving from left to right and their velocities are set as 250 (pixel/second). A small target whose luminance, size are set as 50 and 5×5 (pixel $\times$ pixel), is moving against cluttered backgrounds. The coordinate of the small target at time t equals to $(500 - V_T \frac{t+300}{1000}, 125 + 15 \cdot \sin(4\pi \frac{t+300}{1000})), t \in [0, 1000]$ ms where V_T is set as 500 (pixel/second).

From Figs. 4(b) and 5(b), we can see that feedback ESTMD has a better performance than ESTMD. For a given false alarm rate, the detection rate of feedback ESTMD is higher than that of ESTMD. This indicate that feedback ESTMD performs better than ESTMD in different cluttered backgrounds.

(a)

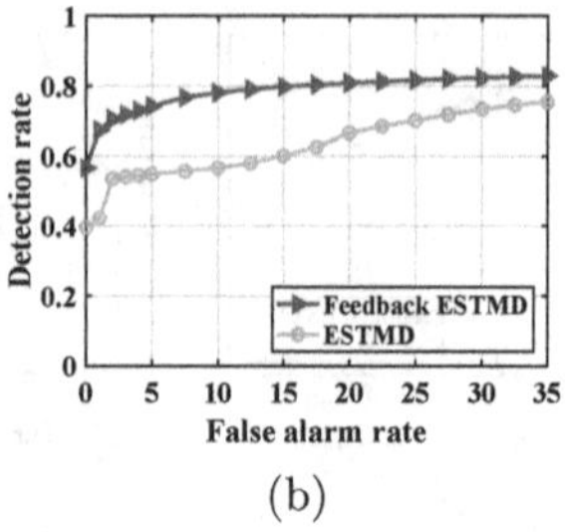

(b)

Fig. 4. (a) A representative frame of the input image sequence. The small target is highlighted by the white circle. Arrow V_B denote motion direction of the background. (b) The receiver operating characteristic (ROC) curves of feedback ESTMD and ESTMD.

(a)

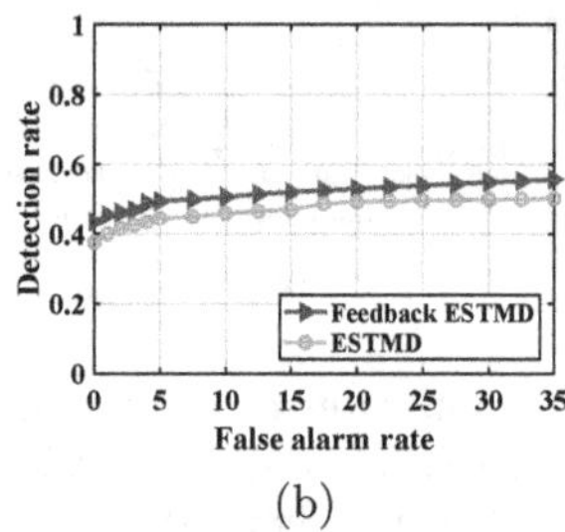

(b)

Fig. 5. (a) A representative frame of the input image sequence. The small target is highlighted by the white circle. Arrow V_B denote motion direction of the background. (b) The receiver operating characteristic (ROC) curves of feedback ESTMD and ESTMD.

4 Conclusion

In this paper, we proposed a feedback neural network for small target detection against naturally cluttered backgrounds. In order to form a feedback loop, network output is temporally delayed and then relayed to middle neural layer as feedback signal. Feedback signal is added on outputs of middle neural layer for weakening responses to background noise. Systematic experiments showed that the proposed feedback neural network has a much better performance than the existing ESTMD model, if there is velocity difference between the background and the small target. In the future, we will further combine feedback loops with visual attention mechanisms for improving detection performances of models.

Acknowledgments. This research was supported by EU FP7 Project HAZCEPT (318907), HORIZON 2020 project STEP2DYNA (691154), ENRICHME (643691) and the National Natural Science Foundation of China under Grant 11771347.

References

1. Bagheri, Z.M., Wiederman, S.D., Cazzolato, B.S., Grainger, S., O'Carroll, D.C.: Performance of an insect-inspired target tracker in natural conditions. Bioinspiration Biomim. **12**(2), 025006 (2017)
2. Behnia, R., Clark, D.A., Carter, A.G., Clandinin, T.R., Desplan, C.: Processing properties of on and off pathways for drosophila motion detection. Nature **512**(7515), 427 (2014)
3. Clarke, S.E., Maler, L.: Feedback synthesizes neural codes for motion. Curr. Biol. **27**(9), 1356–1361 (2017)
4. Kafaligonul, H., Breitmeyer, B.G., Öğmen, H.: Feedforward and feedback processes in vision. Front. Psychol. **6**, 279 (2015)
5. Nordström, K.: Neural specializations for small target detection in insects. Curr. Opin. Neurobiol. **22**(2), 272–278 (2012)
6. Nordström, K., Barnett, P.D., O'Carroll, D.C.: Insect detection of small targets moving in visual clutter. PLoS Biol. **4**(3), e54 (2006)
7. Olberg, R., Worthington, A., Venator, K.: Prey pursuit and interception in dragonflies. J. Comp. Physiol. A Neuroethol. Sens. Neural Behav. Physiol. **186**(2), 155–162 (2000)
8. Straw, A.D.: Vision egg: an open-source library for realtime visual stimulus generation. Front. Neuroinform. **2**, 4 (2008)
9. Wang, H., Peng, J., Yue, S.: A directionally selective small target motion detecting visual neural network in cluttered backgrounds. arXiv preprint arXiv:1801.06687 (2018)
10. Warrant, E.J.: Matched filtering and the ecology of vision in insects. In: von der Emde, G., Warrant, E. (eds.) The Ecology of Animal Senses, pp. 143–167. Springer, Cham (2016). https://doi.org/10.1007/978-3-319-25492-0_6
11. Wiederman, S.D., O'Carroll, D.C.: Biologically inspired feature detection using cascaded correlations of off and on channels. J. Artif. Intell. Soft Comput. Res. **3**(1), 5–14 (2013)
12. Wiederman, S.D., Shoemaker, P.A., O'Carroll, D.C.: A model for the detection of moving targets in visual clutter inspired by insect physiology. PloS one **3**(7), e2784 (2008)

De-noise-GAN: De-noising Images to Improve RoboCup Soccer Ball Detection

Daniel Speck(✉), Pablo Barros, and Stefan Wermter

Department of Informatics, University of Hamburg,
Vogt-Koelln-Strasse 30, 22527 Hamburg, Germany
{2speck,barros,wermter}@informatik.uni-hamburg.de

Abstract. A moving robot or moving camera causes motion blur in the robot's vision and distorts recorded images. We show that motion blur, differing lighting, and other distortions heavily affect the object localization performance of deep learning architectures for RoboCup Humanoid Soccer scenes. The paper proposes deep conditional generative models to apply visual noise filtering. Instead of generating new samples for a specific domain our model is constrained by reconstructing RoboCup soccer images. The conditional DCGAN (deep convolutional generative adversarial network) works semi-supervised. Thus there is no need for labeled training data. We show that object localization architectures significantly drop in accuracy when supplied with noisy input data and that our proposed model can significantly increase the accuracy again.

Keywords: TensorFlow · Neural networks · DCGAN · GAN
De-noising · RoboCup · Robotics

1 Introduction

With an increasing number of devices that are able to record visual data, the available information grows exponentially. Although this growing amount of data covers a huge potential for various fields, it is not very useful without any labels that categorize this information. In the last couple of years, much attention was spent for discriminative models that solve complex classification tasks, especially in deep learning [4,5,10]. However, there is a recent motivation for a more active development of unsupervised models, since labeling data, like marking object positions with bounding boxes, is an expansive task in both resources and time. In this paper we evaluate GANs (generative adversarial networks) for image de-noising.

In RoboCup Humanoid Soccer the movement of the robot itself and also its camera is a severe problem for the robot's vision. Object localization architectures heavily drop in accuracy during such actions, rendering it hard to make use of the camera input. While this problem could be fixed by enforcing the robot to

V. Kůrková et al. (Eds.): ICANN 2018, LNCS 11141, pp. 738–747, 2018.
https://doi.org/10.1007/978-3-030-01424-7_72

stop all actions and just stand still this "hot-fix" is not applicable in RoboCup, since a game of soccer is highly dynamic and robots should continuously move to get the ball, go to the enemy team's goal and get an edge over the enemy team by constantly repositioning on the playfield.

Image De-raining Using a Conditional Generative Adversarial Network by Zhang et al. [11] proposes an architecture for image de-raining. The generator (G) is a composition of convolutional and transposed convolutional layers (sometimes also called *de-convolutional* layers). The network is trained on rainy images, while the discriminator (D) is conditioned with clear images to give G feedback that allows to learn how to de-rain images. Hence, the input can consist of unlabeled, clear images. The only augmentation needed is applying artificial rain to the ground truth, i.e. clear images, in order to produce the conditional input. Another similar approach is the generation of "super-resolution" images out of low-resolution samples with GANs [6].

Our hypothesis is that a deep convolutional generative adversarial network (DCGAN) is able to learn the specific characteristics of RoboCup Humanoid Soccer domain for de-noising real-world images. Due to the fact that real-world scenes out of this domain are highly complex, e.g. they cover different playfields, lighting conditions, presence of audience, different robots and referees, it is difficult to handcraft filter kernels that are able to de-noise high levels of motion blurring. Hence, the model has to learn domain-specific features to be able to reconstruct them in its output. This can be achieved by combining typical de-noising filter kernels and memorizing domain specific features.

Our model, which we call "De-Noise-GAN", is a conditional DCGAN where the generator (G) de-noises artificially noised input and discriminator (D) classifies input images into two different classes"generated" and "real" to supply the adversarial loss to train G. Despite judging the direct output of G, i.e. deciding if it produces reasonable, realistically looking output, we use an evaluation metric: we have a large test dataset for ball localization and use the baseline results of our ball localization model to compare them to the accuracy of (1) artificially noised input and (2) de-noised input generated by G.

2 De-noising Generative Adversarial Network

2.1 Generative Models

Originally proposed in 2014 by Goodfellow et al. [3] *generative adversarial networks* (GANs) recently became a suitable solution for many unsupervised-learning tasks. The idea is to have two networks that train each other instead of one big network for more complex unsupervised learning problems. The discriminator sub-network D tries to categorize input into two classes: *generated* and *real*, where *generated* is an insufficient solution for the problem's domain and should be rejected since it could be distinguished from *real* samples. Thus, *real* is an appropriate solution that fits to the ground truth of the domain. D is trained with real data (unlabeled training data) and generated data by the Generator sub-network G. Hence, G is given the feedback of D in order to try to generate output that is "as good as possible" for a certain task. Therefore D and G efficiently train each other on unlabeled data by playing a two-player min-max game: D tries to minimize its error on distinguishing samples into *real* and *generated* classes and G tries to maximize D's error by generating output that is close to samples of the *real* class, so that D falsely classifies G's generated samples as *real*.

2.2 DCGANs

Radford et al. proposed generative adversarial networks in combination with up-to-date deep learning approaches to build deep convolutional generative adversarial networks (DCGANs) [9]. These models were introduced to move on from tasks like MNIST digit generation to more complex environments. DCGANs are capable of learning certain conditions and specific representations of a domain. For example, when DCGANs are trained with faces and different representations, they can remove or add sunglasses to faces, change the gender of a face and so forth [9].

In comparison to GANs, the convolutional layers in DCGANs are able to learn specific filter kernels in order to alter or generate specific features spatially, while the MLPs used in traditional GANs consist of fully-connected layers, which perform worse at complex, spatial filtering. Basically, it is the descriptive ability of the (de-)convolutional layers that enables DCGANs to go for more complex domains compared to vanilla GANs. It is very similar to standard computer vision tasks, where (deep) CNNs outperform MLPs and other traditional approaches, like at the ImageNet challenge for example [5].

2.3 De-noise-GAN

We propose a conditional DCGAN, called De-Noise-GAN, that is trained with RoboCup Humanoid Soccer samples and artificial noise to have Generator G learn how to detect and remove noise like motion blur and occlusions caused by the robot's walking or camera movements.

G's architecture is illustrated in Fig. 1. The first two layers are 1×1 convolutions to let the network learn its own color representations for our RoboCup domain. Feeding raw RGB images instead of pre-processing or other color spaces like HSV showed interesting results in Mishkin et al.'s work where they evaluated different techniques for comparable network types and discovered that trained color transformation layers could improve results [7]. HSV and other pre-processing steps also covered worse results for our case. The next step is downsampling the dimensionality of the input through two convolutional and max-pooling layers. Instead of pooling and upsampling (nearest-neighbor upscaling), we also evaluated using (de-)convolutions with a stride of 2, but experienced "checkerboard artifacts" in the output [1,8]. Dahl et al. also dealt with this kind of problems in their paper on pixel recursive super-resolution [2]. The pooling and upsampling layers introduce more smoothness for G's output. Using just the upsampling part of the network as output often showed incomplete features

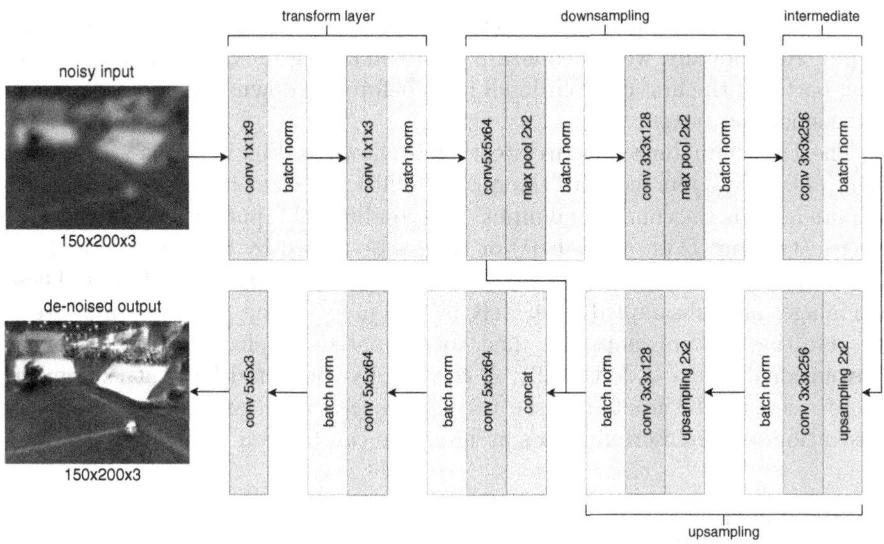

Fig. 1. Generator G of our proposed model. The input image is distorted by random Gaussian noise and translations (to add motion blur effect). Output is a de-noised RGB image. This Figure shows actual training input and output.

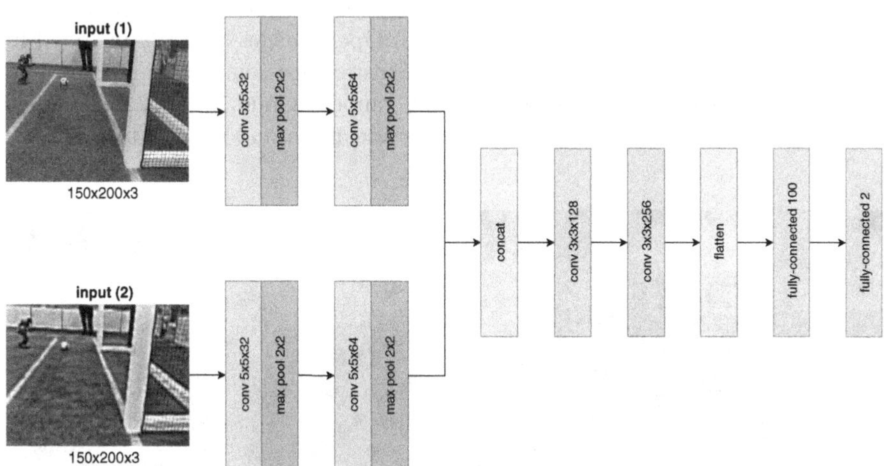

Fig. 2. Discriminator D of our proposed model. The input consists of two images: *input (1)*, which receives clear images, i.e. the *ground truth*, and *input (2)*, which is the conditional input for training. The output layer's two neurons model the probability for "real" and"generated" classes. Training labels are $[0, 1]$ for generated samples and $[1, 0]$ for real samples. This Figure shows an actual training iteration for G, hence *input (1)* is a clear, real training image and *input (2)* the de-noised reconstruction of the noised input for G, which covered a low level of noise for this sample so that the reconstructed output is of high quality.

for bigger objects, so we added two more convolutional layers before the actual output. Additionally, we added a skip layer combining the output of the upsampling part and the first convolutional layer before the downsampling part, which led to smoother output.

The Discriminator's (D) architecture is shown in Fig. 1. It has two inputs: *input (1)* always gets fed with the ground truth, i.e. clear images without noise and *input (2)* is the conditional input. The conditional input either receives clear images (training D on *real* labels) or images de-noised by G. In the case of de-noised input D is trained with *generated* labels and G with *real* labels. These two images are subsampled separately by two independent convolutional layers, the resulting feature maps are then concatenated and fed to the subsequent convolutional layers. Additionally, D has a fully-connected layer at the output level to classify its input into the two classes *generated* and *real.* A graphical illustration of the Discriminator's architecture can be seen in Fig. 2.

3 Experimental Results

3.1 Dataset and Acquisition

Our training dataset consists of 66,623 images and was recorded at three different locations, our old lab, RoboCup 2016, Leipzig, Germany and RoboCup 2017, Nagoya, Japan. The test dataset is composed of 2,177 images from two different locations, RoboCup 2017 and German Open footage. The RoboCup 2017 test images are taken from other games and other playfields than the training images from the same location. The German Open images are *only* included in the test dataset. Therefore this location's features are completely unknown to the network. During the training, we apply random Gaussian noise and image translations to the input image in order to add noise and motion blur effects.

Fig. 3. Left image: **real noise**, right image: **artificial noise**. Both images are taken from a sequence of images at RoboCup 2016, Leipzig, Germany. The left image with real noise was recorded during a sequence with camera movement of the robot's camera, while the right image is the last image of the sequence, where the camera stands still again, and was artificially blurred afterwards.

The image translations (to add the motion effect) and the Gaussian noise kernel are drawn from separated random numbers. This pre-processing to artificially noise the image is done with OpenCV and NumPy. We blend together translated copies of the original image and apply gaussian noise kernels via convolutions using OpenCV. Depending on the random numbers the result of this process ranges from slightly translated, slightly noised images to heavily translated, heavily noised images in order to simulate a broad variety of motion blur effects. A comparison between real and artificial noise of a medium level (non-moving robot, but moving camera) can be seen in Fig. 3. Since a moving robot would not produce *any* clear images, we can not directly compare the high-level artificial noise to the motion blur of a walking robot due to the lack of clear images to apply artificial noise on. However, high-level artificial noise also looks similar to high real-world motion blur caused by walking robots.

3.2 De-noising

Reconstructing noised images in the RoboCup Humanoid Soccer domain is a very complex scenario. The generator has to reconstruct RBG color images of shape 200×150 with a vast amount of variations: different balls, robots, humans, play fields, and so on. Moreover changes in lighting and contrast cause strong differences for various sceneries. Nonetheless, the current architecture shows promising de-noising results. In Fig. 4 four highly noised test images were selected to display the reconstruction abilities of our network. All samples cover a ball and the first and last image also a robot. G learns about common objects in the RoboCup Humanoid soccer domain. Thus small balls, for example, are mostly reconstructed as mostly white spheres. A similar behavior applies for advertis-

Fig. 4. Upper row displays highly **noised test images** and **lower row** the corresponding **de-noised output**. The first image was recorded in the Hamburg Bit-Bots Lab, the next two from a WF Wolves test game at RoboCup German Open, and the last one at RoboCup 2017, Nagoya, Japan. The first two locations are completely unknown to the network since they are only included in test, but not in training data. The last image from RoboCup 2017, Nagoya, Japan, covers actual game footage from a game that is not included in the training data, but other games from RoboCup 2017 are.

ing boards or the audience's clothes: if the noise in the image is too strong, the generator not only reconstructs the original features but often also mixes in common logos, shapes, and other objects that often appear in the training set. We had a significant improvement in accuracy when we moved from our old training dataset (less than 20,000 images) to our current one (66,000 images).

Figure 5 shows an interesting effect of false positives for our DCGAN. Since the DCGAN cannot reconstruct a high-level of detail without memorizing the typical scenery of our domain it sometimes comes to wrong object reconstructions when the DCGAN is fed an image with a very high-level of noise. In the case of Fig. 5 the original image only showed a penalty spot on the playfield, but the network mistakenly classifies this as a ball and therefore reconstructs it accordingly in the output.

3.3 Ball Localization

For our RoboCup Humanoid Soccer robots, we currently use a Fully-Convolutional Neural Network (FCNN) for ball localization in raw camera input. The FCNN maps the raw RGB input onto a heatmap with the same dimensionality as the input, effectively creating a voting for each pixel to be considered "ball" or "no ball". Out of the heatmap, we calculate clusters and find each cluster's center for post-processing the ball's actual location with respect to the robot (camera angle, ...). To allow for easy comparisons, in addition to Jaccard-index (Intersection of Unions) as well as precision and recall, we measure the FCNN by a "radius accuracy", i.e. comparing the center of each cluster with the ground truth in the original image. This is easily comparable for other teams who do not use bounding boxes or heatmaps, but only absolute coordinates for example. Table 1 shows that our FCNN scores accuracies around 90% on our test images, which consist of over 2,000 images from RoboCup 2017, Nagoya, Japan and German Open. The Nagoya pictures are again only covering games that are not included in the training set and German Open data is included in test data *only*. When applying artificial noise to our test data the accuracies drop to less than a third of the original accuracies. After de-noising the noised input with De-Noise-GAN the accuracies increase again to nearly 80%.

Table 1. Results for FCNN ball localization.

Accuracy type	FCNN clear images	FCNN noisy input	FCNN de-noised input
Radius 3	89.8%	22.4%	73.7%
Radius 5	91.5%	28.3%	77.5%
Radius 10	94.3%	32.4%	78.5%

4 Discussion

The results of De-Noise-GAN for de-noising domain specific real-world scenes are promising. As expected, the accuracies of object detection frameworks like our ball localization architecture heavily drop when fed with noisy input. In our case, the accuracies dropped to less than a third (see Table 1), but when fed with our de-noised images from our DCGAN the accuracies more than doubled again, peaking to nearly 80%. In our first models there was still a lot of artifacts, due to the comparably high resolution of our output and the features that need to be reconstructed there, making it easy for D to discriminate, but hard for G to precisely de-noise images. Also, over-sharpening the output happened often. The FCNN's localization accuracy was lower than 70% with these models. Two steps improved the results up to the proposed results: we introduced a skip connection and an addition to the loss function. The skip connection caused smoother output since it keeps some of the more noisy, higher-level features of the early convolutions. This alone increased the accuracies by nearly 5%. The second step was an alteration for the loss function. Originally G was only trained in an adversarial fashion, but we had quite interesting results for (variational) Autoencoders. While all of our Autoencoders did not come close to the level of detail of DCGANs, their output covered considerably fewer artifacts and oversharpening. The output, as expected, was smoother. For our current model, we tried to combine the DCGAN's high-level of detail with the Autoencoder's "smoothness". In addition to the min-max game D and G play during training, we simply added a mean squared error (MSE) to G's error function between G's output and the ground truth (clear image). This approach increased the accuracies by more than 5%, leading to smoother output and fewer artifacts than before. However, there are still artifacts in some images and also false positives like shown in Fig. 5 due to the high reconstruction capability of the GAN (we scale down the MSE to focus on the adversarial loss during learning and only add the MSE to decrease

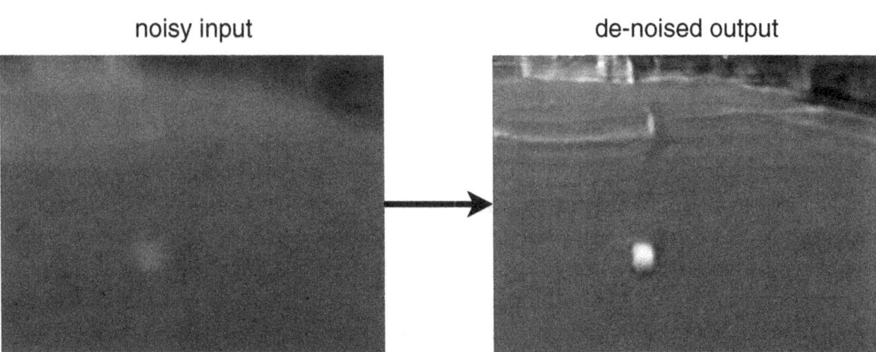

Fig. 5. The **input image (left)** shows a high-level of artificial noise. The **de-noised output (right)** clearly shows a ball, reconstructed by the DCGAN. However, in the input image this object was originally a penalty spot on the playfield, *not* a ball.

oversharpening and artifacts). This behavior suggests that for complex scenes the Generator always also learns which kind of objects appear in the scenery, effectively memorizing the given domain. Given this knowledge G de-noises by a mix of real de-noising and memorizing. This memorizing effect could be observed best for balls and lights in our domain since many training images show a ball and lights on the ceiling. Despite the discussed object mis-classifications G sometimes still has mosaic-like patterns in the output if the scenes get too complex, e.g. when high noise is present in combination with many persons in the background. Especially for the audience's clothes G then usually reconstructs some mix of commonly represented logos, typical clothes, ... of the training set, which looks unrealistic. This might be a problem with our learning procedure or the size of the training dataset: the 66,000 images were only recorded at three different locations: our old Lab, RoboCup 2016 in Leipzig, Germany and RoboCup 2017 in Nagoya, Japan.

5 Conclusion

Our proposed architecture, De-Noise-GAN, showed reasonable and promising results for complex tasks such as de-noising RoboCup Humanoid Soccer images. If supplied with enough training samples, the generator can learn the characteristic features of different objects and reconstruct them in noisy images quite well, including real-world noise. Although the de-noising quality of unknown objects is rather poor, i.e. images look unrealistic to humans, they also show that the generator is not only memorizing different objects but also learning the characteristics of noise in images to generalize de-noising filters. However, the quality of de-noising is significantly better, if the generator has seen the objects in the scene during training, like the ball for example. This *may* suggest that this process is somehow comparable to the reconstruction in biology: e.g. a human most likely recognizes objects behind a window even in heavy rain if the object is well known to the observer, while it is significantly harder to recognize unknown objects.

6 Future Work

We plan to continue our work by evaluating new architectures. The mix-in of MSE to the loss functions, for example, shows interesting results. This suggests that mixing GANs with Autoencoders is doable and can actually decrease the downsides of each of the single approaches. Besides that, a deeper look into the reconstruction abilities of complex scenes could be interesting to understand the importance of well-known domains for the de-noising process. Moreover, this could be compared to similar tasks in neuroscience, which might suggest new alterations for the current architecture to increase the model's robustness.

Acknowledgements. We are grateful to the NVIDIA corporation for supporting our research through the NVIDIA GPU Grant Program (https://developer.nvidia.com/academic_gpu_seeding). We used the donated NVIDIA Titan X (Pascal) to train our models. The work was made in collaboration with the TRR 169 "Crossmodal Learning", funded by the DFG.

References

1. Aitken, A., Ledig, C., Theis, L., Caballero, J., Wang, Z., Shi, W.: Checkerboard artifact free sub-pixel convolution: a note on sub-pixel convolution, resize convolution and convolution resize, July 2017. http://arxiv.org/abs/1707.02937
2. Dahl, R., Norouzi, M., Shlens, J.: Pixel recursive super resolution. arXiv preprint arXiv:1702.00783 (2017)
3. Goodfellow, I., et al.: Generative adversarial nets. In: Advances in Neural Information Processing Systems, vol. 27, pp. 2672–2680 (2014). http://papers.nips.cc/paper/5423-generative-adversarial-nets.pdf
4. Karpathy, A., Leung, T.: Large-scale video classification with convolutional neural networks. In: Proceedings of 2014 IEEE Conference on Computer Vision and Pattern Recognition, pp. 1725–1732 (2014). https://doi.org/10.1109/CVPR.2014.223
5. Krizhevsky, A., Sutskever, I., Hinton, G.E.: ImageNet classification with deep convolutional neural networks. In: Advances In Neural Information Processing Systems, pp. 1–9 (2012)
6. Ledig, C., et al.: Photo-realistic single image super-resolution using a generative adversarial network, September 2016. http://arxiv.org/abs/1609.04802
7. Mishkin, D., Sergievskiy, N., Matas, J.: Systematic evaluation of CNN advances on the ImageNet, June 2016. http://arxiv.org/abs/1606.02228
8. Odena, A., Dumoulin, V., Olah, C.: Deconvolution and checkerboard artifacts. Drill **1**(10), 1–14 (2016). https://doi.org/10.23915/distill.00003
9. Radford, A., Metz, L., Chintala, S.: Unsupervised representation learning with deep convolutional generative adversarial networks. arXiv preprint arXiv:1511.06434, pp. 1–16 (2016)
10. Szegedy, C., Reed, S., Sermanet, P., Vanhoucke, V., Rabinovich, A.: Going deeper with convolutions, pp. 1–12 (2014)
11. Zhang, H., Sindagi, V., Patel, V.M.: Image de-raining using a conditional generative adversarial network. arXiv preprint arXiv:1701.05957, pp. 1–13 (2017)

Integrative Collision Avoidance Within RNN-Driven Many-Joint Robot Arms

Sebastian Otte(✉), Lea Hofmaier, and Martin V. Butz

Cognitive Modeling Group, Computer Science Department, University of Tübingen, Sand 14, 72076 Tübingen, Germany
sebastian.otte@uni-tuebingen.de

Abstract. Robot arm control and motion planning in dynamically changing environments is a challenging task. It requires an adaptive planning algorithm that generates solutions on-the-fly, incorporating the current environmental conditions. This paper explores an alternative approach. Adaptive planning is realized in a generative Recurrent Neural Network (RNN) architecture, which produces goal-directed motor commands by means of active-inference-based, model-predictive control. As the main contribution, in this paper we show how to integrate local collision avoidance gradients into the active inference process. The result is a control mechanism that avoids arm collisions while concurrently pursuing arm goal poses. The RNN processes embodied, sensorimotor dynamics into which proximity signals from locally embedded distance sensors are injected at the respective joint locations. We demonstrate that a 3D trunk-like many-joint robot arm with up to 80 articulated degrees of freedom (DoF) can maneuver collision-free even through very challenging, dynamic obstacle constellations, evading potential collision sources while pursuing goal-directed arm pose and end-effector control.

Keywords: Robot arm control · Inverse kinematics
Collision avoidance · Active inference

1 Introduction

In recent studies [12,13] it has been shown that Recurrent Neural Networks (RNNs) are very well-suited for learning kinematic forward models that can be used to generate goal-directed control even in many-joint robot arms. The employed approximate active inference process [4] is implemented via Back-Propagation Through Time (BPTT) [16]. From the control literature perspective, the implemented algorithm is essentially a model-predictive control approach were the involved, sensorimotor-grounded model is learned by an RNN [3]. A great additional feature of our approach is that all potential target components, including the pose (position and orientation) of the end-effector and all other arm segments, can be selectively turned on and off on-the-fly [12]. Thus, control over the entire arm is possible, allowing the spontaneous, dynamic imposition of arbitrary partial constraints.

V. Kůrková et al. (Eds.): ICANN 2018, LNCS 11141, pp. 748–758, 2018.
https://doi.org/10.1007/978-3-030-01424-7_73

In this paper we address the question of how to integrate collision avoidance mechanisms in environments with complex obstacle constellations and even dynamic obstacles. Traditional control and planning mechanisms, including many other model-predictive control approaches, require additional, sophisticated mechanisms to maneuver a robot arm through obstacle constellations without collisions. In contrast, we pair goal-directed control with local collision avoidance, which is triggered by arm segment-specific distance sensors. This is achieved by integrating both objectives into an approximate active inference process, which is implemented by means of BPTT in a generative RNN. That is, instead of additional, global planning, we exploit the selective constraining capabilities of the RNN-driven robot arm model, integrating locally evasive behavior into goal-directed pose pursuance.

2 Method

We now first recapitulate the selectively constrainable RNN-based inference scheme from [12]. Next, we add local distance sensors and explain how their signals are mapped onto the recurrent active inference-based gradient flow.

2.1 Robot Arm Model and Selective Control

At first, it is required to learn the kinematic forward model M of the robot arm with an RNN. M can be formalized as a mapping from robot arm configuration states, that is, a sequence of angle vectors $\boldsymbol{\varphi}^j$, onto the corresponding pose chain:

$$\boldsymbol{\Phi} = \left(\boldsymbol{\varphi}^1, \ldots, \boldsymbol{\varphi}^n\right) \overset{\mathrm{M}}{\longmapsto} \left({}^0_1\mathbf{A}, \ldots, {}^0_N\mathbf{A}\right), \tag{1}$$

where ${}^0_j\mathbf{A} \in \mathbb{R}^{4\times4}$ refers to the reference frame transformation of the j-th joint and N denotes the end-effector frame. Each ${}^0_j\mathbf{A}$ can be contains the joint's orientation, which is given by the orthonormal base ${}^0_j\mathbf{R} \in SO(3) \subset \mathbb{R}^{3\times3}$, and its translation, that is, its relative position from the base, given by ${}^0_j\mathbf{p} \in \mathbb{R}^3$.

In order to make this mapping well accessible for an RNN, we consider each joint transformation as a "computing time-step" within the RNN, which thus requires only k input neurons, where k is the number of angles per joint. Thus, the computation is fully independent from the number of joints and the length of the arm is reflected by the number of RNN computation steps. The angle vectors $\boldsymbol{\varphi}^j$ are presented to the network in a sequential manner. Consequently, the RNN is forced to use its recurrences to handle the repetitive character of computing kinematic chains of mostly very similar transformations [13]. After the RNN is trained on a sufficiently rich pool of training examples, it is able to predict the pose chain of the arm given a sequence of angle vectors.

To control the arm, it is necessary to compute the inverse mapping, that is, an appropriate angle sequence given a desired pose chain. How this is achieved can best be explained by considering Fig. 1. First, the current arm configuration $\boldsymbol{\Phi}$ is processed by the RNN sequentially, producing corresponding pose chain estimates $({}^0_1\tilde{\mathbf{A}}, \ldots, {}^0_N\tilde{\mathbf{A}})$ (black arrows). The discrepancies (loss) $\mathcal{L}$ between the estimated and desired pose chain $({}^0_1\overset{*}{\mathbf{A}}, \ldots, {}^0_N\overset{*}{\mathbf{A}})$ are back-propagated through the unfolded RNN (blue arrows). The resulting arm pose gradients are thus computed via

$$\frac{\partial \mathcal{L}}{\partial \varphi_i^j} = \sum_{h=1}^{H} \left[\frac{\partial net_h^j}{\partial \varphi_i^j} \frac{\partial \mathcal{L}}{\partial net_h^j} \right] = \sum_{h=1}^{H} w_{ih} \delta_h^j, \tag{2}$$

projecting the loss back onto the static pose sequence of the arm segments, where h indexes the hidden units and net_h^j denotes the weighted sum of inputs (or *net input*) into unit h at computation step j. Starting from any possible arm configuration, by following the negative gradient through the joint space in an iterative manner, a possible solution to the inverse mapping is generated. We thus update the joint angles in the following manner, which is essentially SGD with momentum:

$$\mathbf{\Phi}^{\tau+1} \longleftarrow \mathbf{\Phi}^{\tau} - \eta \nabla_{\mathbf{\Phi}^{\tau}} \mathcal{L} \odot \left[\mathbf{s}^{\tau}\right]^2 + \mu \left[\mathbf{\Phi}^{\tau} - \mathbf{\Phi}^{\tau-1}\right], \tag{3}$$

where τ denotes the current iteration step, $\eta \in \mathbb{R}$ is a gradient scale factor (cf. learning rate in gradient descent learning), and the momentum is scaled with the rate $\mu \in \mathbb{R}$, which accelerates convergence when the gradient signal is weak but stable. $\odot$ is a component-wise multiplication operation. The vector $\left[\mathbf{s}^{\tau}\right]^2$ (component-wise square) realizes a stabilization term that we refer to as *sign damping*. Before each update step, $\mathbf{s}^{\tau}$ is computed by

$$\mathbf{s}^{\tau} = \alpha \mathbf{s}^{\tau-1} + (1 - \alpha) \operatorname{sign}(\nabla_{\mathbf{\Phi}^{\tau}} \mathcal{L}), \tag{4}$$

where $\alpha \in [0, 1]$ is a smoothing factor and the sign operator is applied component-wise as well. Thus, $\left[\mathbf{s}^{\tau}\right]^2$ effectively expresses how strongly the current gradient signal oscillates. The sign damping significantly stabilizes the movement behavior of the robot arm and allows to increase η without causing the arm to oscillate. Note that we also restrict the overall maximum update step size to regularize relatively high gradients, which results in more uniform movements.

During our recent experiments we figured out that simple gradient descent with moderate momentum produces a far more smooth and reliable movement behavior than, e.g., Adam [6] or RMSprop [15]. While the latter mechanisms work better for training, they have a detrimental effect on action inference – at least for high-dimensional arms. This is probably the case, because Adam and RMSprop normalize the individual gradient components independently, whereas the individual magnitudes of the gradient components and their mutual relations are highly relevant when optimizing many-joint arm control commands. Note that this contrasts with findings from [2,11], where Adam was found to significantly stabilize action inference for low-dimensional dynamical systems.

Additionally, we apply a target correction step, compensating the error of the forward model [12,13]. Instead of presenting the desired targets, encoded as vectors $\mathbf{z}_j \in \mathbb{R}^9$, we present "modified" versions $\tilde{\mathbf{z}}_j$ to the network when computing the loss. Let $\mathbf{u}_j \in \mathbb{R}^9$ be the true current pose (obtained from a visual

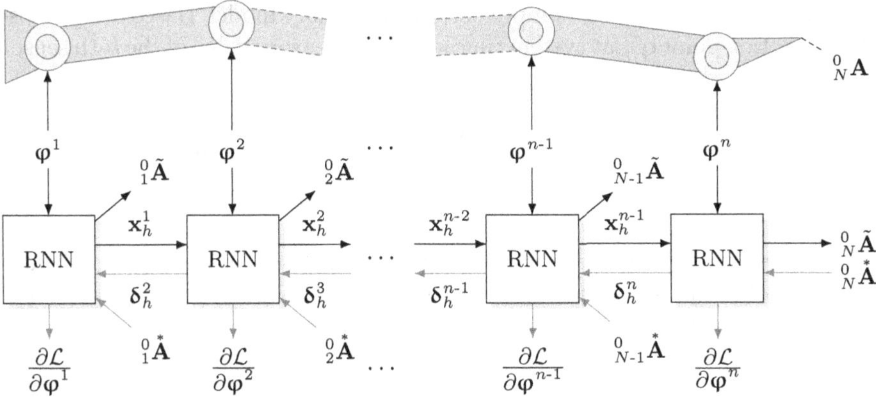

Fig. 1. Illustration of the active inference procedure using BPTT. In the recurrent, unfolded forward pass, arm state inputs generate pose chain estimates. Discrepancies between chain pose estimates and desired chain poses are back-propagated through the network (blue lines), yielding desired arm posture state changes. (Color figure online)

feedback system or a mathematical model) and $\mathbf{y}_j \in \mathbb{R}^9$ the pose prediction of the RNN. We thus compute $\tilde{\mathbf{z}}_j$ with respect to a given $\mathbf{\Phi}$ as follows:

$$\tilde{\mathbf{z}}^j = \begin{bmatrix} [y_{ji} + \gamma_{pos}(z_{ji} - u_{ji})]_{1 \leq i \leq 3} \\ [y_{jk} + \gamma_{rot}(z_{jk} - u_{jk})]_{4 \leq k \leq 9} \end{bmatrix}, \tag{5}$$

where $\gamma_{pos}, \gamma_{rot} \in [0, 1]$ are additional scaling factors, which scale the influence of the positional and the orientation discrepancy, respectively. This modification causes the RNN to converge towards the real target pose with high precision, effectively compensating for remaining forward model errors.

In order to enable the selective induction of constraints, we use "don't care" signals [12], which are defined as the respective zero gradients in the unconstrained components – zero gradients do not induce any additional gradient signals to the backward pass, regardless of their forward pass estimates. As a result, segment-selective control of the robot arm becomes possible.

2.2 Local Distance Sensor Signals

The sensory apparatus of the robot arm consists of several distance sensors distributed over the arm's surface. The distance sensors in turn are simulated using a simple ray-based intersection method, namely, the *Möller-Trumbore intersection algorithm* [7]. Specifically, a ray is cast along the principle axis of a particular sensor and the closest intersection point with possibly surrounding geometry is computed.

Figure 2 depicts some formal components of the sensory model. Based on the closest intersection point $\mathbf{q}^{\tau}_{jk}$ at system time step τ the sensory value of the k-th sensor of joint j is calculated by

$$v^{\tau}_{jk} = \begin{cases} \max\left\{0,\ 1 - \dfrac{|\mathbf{q}^{\tau}_{jk} - \mathbf{o}^{\tau}_{jk}|}{d_{jk}}\right\} & \text{if } \mathbf{q}^{\tau}_{jk} \text{ exists} \\ 0 & \text{otherwise.} \end{cases} \tag{6}$$

Thus, v^{τ}_{jk} effectively represents the strength of a particular sensory signal. It is 0 when no obstacle is detected in the sensor's range, while it converges towards 1 when an obstacle is right in front of the sensor.

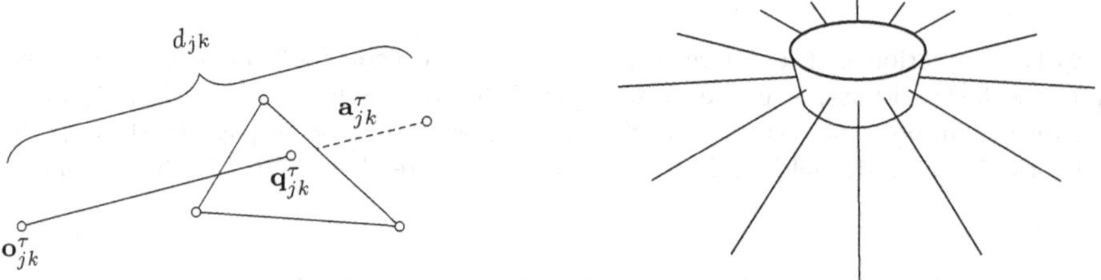

Fig. 2. Illustration of the simple ray-based sensor model (left). Multiple sensors of one arm segment are circularly aligned (right) orthogonal to the segments principled axis providing an all-around collision detection.

2.3 Sensory Gradient Injection

To realized obstacle avoidance of the individual arm segments, we integrated the sensory information into the active inference process as follows: for each sensor k of a joint j it's sensory signal is mapped onto the sensor's main axis in negative direction, which we refer to as *sensory-induced counter vector* (SCV) $\check{\mathbf{s}}^{\tau}_{jk} = -[v^{\tau}_{jk}]^{\beta}\hat{\mathbf{a}}_{jk}{}^{\tau}$, where β (we use $\beta = 3$ throughout all experiments) is an exponential scaling factor. The particular SCVs are summed up per joint/segment

$$\check{\mathbf{s}}^{\tau}_{j} = \lambda\check{\mathbf{s}}^{\tau-1}_{j} + (1-\lambda)\gamma_{sen}\sum_{k}\check{\mathbf{s}}^{\tau}_{jk}, \tag{7}$$

where γ_{sen} is an additional factor weighting the influence of the SCV to the overall gradient and $\lambda \in [0,1]$ is another smoothing factor. For all segments j, ergo, RNN computation steps, the SCVs $\check{\mathbf{s}}^{\tau}_{j}$ are added to the respective target positions, following the selective constraining technique from [12]. As a result, the evasion gradients are injected "locally" where and only when they occur within the model. In conclusion, this procedure pushes the particular components of the robot arm in the opposite direction of the sensory distance signals.

3 Experiments

The experiments in this paper are based on a simulated three dimensional 40-joint robot arm. Each joint can rotate along the x and the y axis. The entire arm thus has $2 \cdot 40 = 80$ DoF. The sensor apparatus, illustrated in Fig. 3, provides twelve radially arranged distance sensors at each of the 40 segments (including the tip). Additionally, the end-effector has four forwardly arranged senors. The entire arm thus has $40 \cdot 12 + 4 = 484$ sensors.

The used RNN architecture consists of two hidden layers with 24 Long Short-Term Memory (LSTM) units [5] with intra-block connected gates [9] each. These additional connections are advantageous in regression tasks [10]. Each hidden block contains three inner cells and has variable biases for cells and gates, which is helpful when the computation involves spatial mappings [13]. Additionally, each hidden layer is not recurrently connected to itself, but both hidden layers are mutually fully connected. All experiments were performed using the JANNLab neural network framework [8].

For training, we applied Adam [6] using the parameters $\beta_1 = 0.9, \beta_2 = 0.999$ (parameterizing the first two moment estimates), and a learning rate of $\eta = 10^{-4}$. In order to achieve the most accurate model, we used ten training episodes, which consisted of respective, randomly generated arm configurations, where the joint angle ranges were limited to 10%, 20%, 30% and so forth of the full range. The first nine sets contained 2 000 training examples each, whereas the tenth set – in which the full angle ranges (here $\pm 45°$) are covered – contained 20 000 examples. In each training episode, 50 epochs were performed. For controlling the robot arm, we used simple gradient descent as described in Sect. 2.1 with $\eta = 0.2$, $\mu = 0.3$, and $\alpha = 0.9$, $\gamma_{pos} = 1.0$ and $\gamma_{rot} = 0.1$ to equalize the magnitude of the position and orientation-induced gradients, as otherwise the orientation gradient would be numerically dominant. The sensor hyper-parameter were $d = 0.1$ (the overall arm length is 1), $\beta = 3$, $\gamma_{sen} = 2$, and $\lambda = 0.5$.

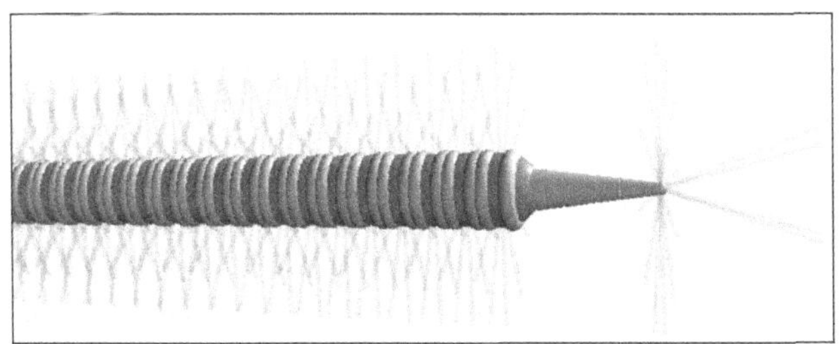
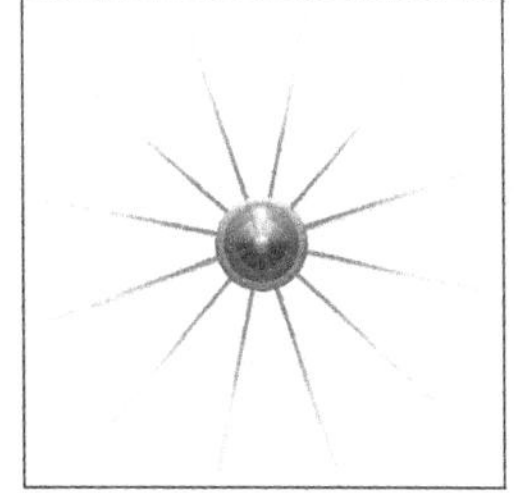

Fig. 3. Sensor apparatus of the 40-joint robot arm. Each segment (including the tip) has twelve radially arranged sensors and the tip has four additional frontal sensors.

3.1 Moving Box

In our first experimental scenario, we positioned a moving box close to the arm within its working area. While the arm tried to approach a target pose with its end-effector, the box followed a wave-like trajectory crossing the postures of the robot arm. We discovered that the robot arm successfully evaded the box, whenever it moved too close towards the arm. Figure 4 shows an image sequence documenting this behavior. As the box enters the detection range of several sensors (top center image; sensor activation indicated by red color), the resulting SCVs push the arm to the right, away from the box, while continuing to reach the target pose of the end effector.

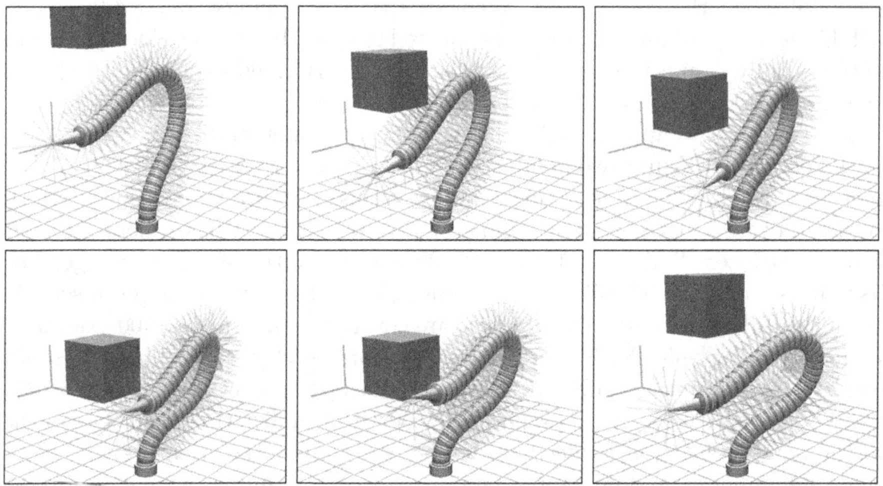

Fig. 4. Image series of the robot arm evading a moving box, which follows a wave-like trajectory that crosses the postures of the robot arm. The blue coordinate system is the target, which is approached by the arm's end-effector.

3.2 Many Boxes

In the second scenario our aim was to study the behavior of the arm in a highly occupied environment. For this purpose we distributed 48 static blocks within the working area of the arm. Due to the obstacles, the arm cannot approach any target pose freely – it has to take the space required for its own "body" into account, while exploiting the partially tight, remaining free space. Again, the arm manages to avoid the obstacles while pursuing end-effector poses. An exemplary image sequence is shown in Fig. 5: to reach the target without collisions, the arm bends it early segments lower, effectively avoiding the central block in front of it while reaching for the target.

In order to analyze this behavior more systematically, we performed 100 trials. In each trial, the particular target was randomly placed into the working area and we recorded the minimal distance (over all 100 trials and 484 sensors) for each time step. The results are depicted in Fig. 6. While the average distance to the target consistently decreased, the sensors responded heavily invoking evasive behavior. No collision occurred (distance < 0) during any of the 100 movements. Note that on average the error does not fully drop to 0, since several random targets were generated within a box, or too close to one, such that these targets were only reached as close as possible, without causing a collision.

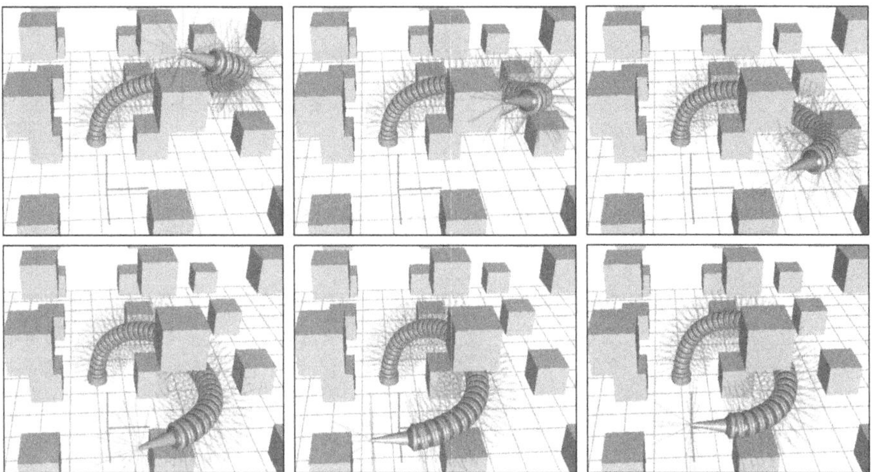

Fig. 5. Image series within a scenario with many boxes. While the robot arm maneuvers towards the target it successfully circumvents collisions with the boxes and exploits the available space.

3.3 Wall Opening

In a last scenario, a wall was placed between the arm and the target. There is no way to circumvent the wall, but there is a small opening within the wall through which the target is reachable.

This scenario can also be handled by the avoidance-integrating arm control mechanism, as can be seen in Fig. 7. The arm is attracted by the target but in turn pushed away from the wall. Since the integrated gradient guides towards the opening along the wall, the arm 'finds' its way through the opening at the bottom of the wall. Note that this would fail, if the target and obstacle-induced gradients would not guide the arm towards the opening, e.g., when the target would be placed far above the opening.

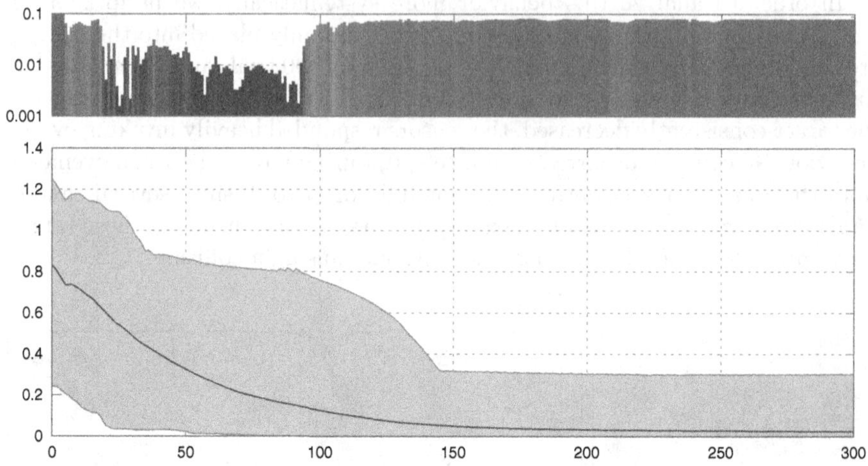

Fig. 6. Minimal detected sensor distance (top) and mean distance to target during 100 runs of approaching a random target in the many blocks scenario.

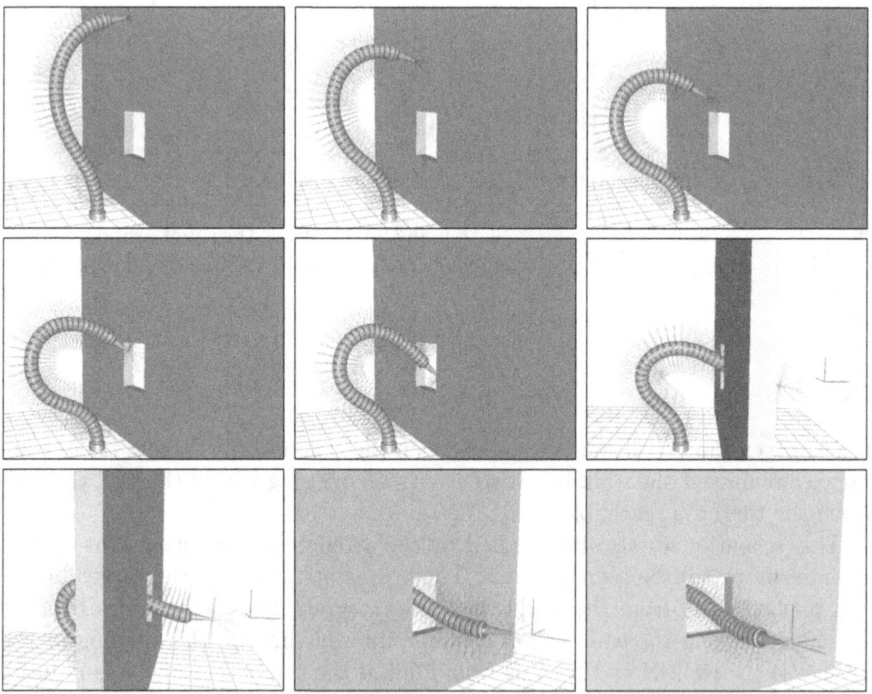

Fig. 7. Image series of the robot arm approaching a target behind a wall. The arm senses the wall opening, maneuvers through it, and reaches the target without any collision.

4 Summary and Conclusion

In this paper we have shown that it is possible to augment RNN-implemented, model-predictive, active inference-approximating control with local distance sensor-based gradients, yielding obstacle avoiding, goal-directed robot arm behavior. As the results have shown, as long as the obstacle signals do not trap the arm into a local gradient optimum, pose goals can be reached while avoiding collisions effectively. Trajectory planning mechanisms on top would be necessary to counteract local optima in behavioral space.

Thus, we intend to combine the model predictive control along the RNN-based kinematic chain model in the near future with temporal dynamic models, which enable trajectory planning. Our recent model on controlling flying objects is a suitable candidate [11]. Moreover, we intend to investigate the option for event-oriented abstractions, such as when the arm interacts with a surface in contrast to moving in free-space. As a result, we expect to enable emergent event-oriented conceptualizations of the experienced environments, as recently put forward elsewhere [1,2], which could enable event-specific optimizations of behavioral policies [14], such as manipulating a surface in a particular manner.

References

1. Butz, M.V.: Towards a unified sub-symbolic computational theory of cognition. Front. Psychol. **7**(925) (2016)
2. Butz, M.V., Bilkey, D., Knott, A., Otte, S.: REPRISE: a retrospective and prospective inference scheme. In: 40th Annual Meeting of the Cognitive Science Society (2018). (Accepted for publication)
3. Camacho, E.F., Bordons, C.: Model Predictive Control. Springer, London (1999). https://doi.org/10.1007/978-0-85729-398-5
4. Friston, K.J., Daunizeau, J., Kilner, J., Kiebel, S.J.: Action and behavior: a free-energy formulation. Biol. Cybern. **102**(3), 227–260 (2010)
5. Hochreiter, S., Schmidhuber, J.: Long short-term memory. Neural Comput. **9**(8), 1735–1780 (1997)
6. Kingma, D.P., Ba, J.L.: Adam: a method for stochastic optimization. In: 3rd International Conference for Learning Representations abs/1412.6980 (2015)
7. Möller, T., Trumbore, B.: Fast, minimum storage ray-triangle intersection. J. Graph. Tools **2**(1), 21–28 (1997)
8. Otte, S., Krechel, D., Liwicki, M.: JANNLab neural network framework for Java. In: Poster Proceedings MLDM 2013, pp. 39–46. ibai-publishing, New York (2013)
9. Otte, S., Liwicki, M., Zell, A.: Dynamic cortex memory: enhancing recurrent neural networks for gradient-based sequence learning. In: Wermter, S., et al. (eds.) ICANN 2014. LNCS, vol. 8681, pp. 1–8. Springer, Cham (2014). https://doi.org/10.1007/978-3-319-11179-7_1
10. Otte, S., Liwicki, M., Zell, A.: An analysis of dynamic cortex memory networks. In: International Joint Conference on Neural Networks (IJCNN), Killarney, Ireland, pp. 3338–3345, July 2015
11. Otte, S., Schmitt, T., Friston, K., Butz, M.V.: Inferring adaptive goal-directed behavior within recurrent neural networks. In: Lintas, A., Rovetta, S., Verschure, P.F.M.J., Villa, A.E.P. (eds.) ICANN 2017. LNCS, vol. 10613, pp. 227–235. Springer, Cham (2017). https://doi.org/10.1007/978-3-319-68600-4_27

12. Otte, S., Zwiener, A., Butz, M.V.: Inherently constraint-aware control of many-joint robot arms with inverse recurrent models. In: Lintas, A., Rovetta, S., Verschure, P.F.M.J., Villa, A.E.P. (eds.) ICANN 2017. LNCS, vol. 10613, pp. 262–270. Springer, Cham (2017). https://doi.org/10.1007/978-3-319-68600-4_31
13. Otte, S., Zwiener, A., Hanten, R., Zell, A.: Inverse recurrent models – an application scenario for many-joint robot arm control. In: Villa, A.E.P., Masulli, P., Pons Rivero, A.J. (eds.) ICANN 2016. LNCS, vol. 9886, pp. 149–157. Springer, Cham (2016). https://doi.org/10.1007/978-3-319-44778-0_18
14. Stulp, F., Sigaud, O.: Robot skill learning: from reinforcement learning to evolution strategies. Paladyn J. Behav. Robot. **4**, 49–61 (2013)
15. Tieleman, T., Hinton, G.: Lecture 6.5-rmsprop: Divide the gradient by a running average of its recent magnitude. In: COURSERA: Neural Networks for Machine Learning (2012)
16. Werbos, P.: Backpropagation through time: what it does and how to do it. Proc. IEEE **78**(10), 1550–1560 (1990)

An Improved Block-Matching Algorithm Based on Chaotic Sine-Cosine Algorithm for Motion Estimation

Bodhisattva Dash(✉) and Suvendu Rup

Image and Video Processing Laboratory, IIIT Bhubaneswar, Bhubaneswar, India
bdash.fac@gmail.com, suvendu@iiit-bh.ac.in

Abstract. Motion estimation (ME) plays an important role in a video coding solution to achieve a low bit rate. The selection of the optimal motion vector (MV) has a significant impact on the quality of the compressed video. Block-matching (BM) algorithm is one of the widely accepted ME techniques to estimate the motion between the successive frames. In any BM technique, the motion vectors (MVs) are obtained for the current frame over a pre-defined search region in the previous frame by minimizing certain matching criterion. However, the computation of these matching criteria is highly expensive (in terms of the computational time). Hence, the block-based ME (BME) can be realized as an optimization problem which aims at finding the best-matched block within a specified search region. In this context, an improved block-matching technique is proposed that incorporates a chaotic-based sine-cosine optimization algorithm along with a fitness approximation (FA) strategy. The proposed approach has been compared with several other BM techniques in terms of different parameters, namely, the peak-signal-to-noise-ratio (PSNR), PSNR degradation ratio (D_{PSNR}), and the number of search points. The analysis of the results obtained demonstrates that the proposed method yields potential improvements over other competent schemes.

Keywords: Block-matching · Optimization · Motion estimation
Sine-Cosine algorithm · Motion vector

1 Introduction

Recently, video coding has been extensively used in various applications like fixed/mobile telephony, video conferencing, HDTV, DVD and so on. Motion estimation (ME) is considered to be a key module in any video coding solution since it can acquire a notable amount of compression by exploiting the temporal correlation that exists between the frames of a video sequence. In this context, various ME techniques have been presented [2,28,33]. Among these, block-matching (BM) is one of the widely used approaches because of its efficacy and ease in implementation (hardware and software) [11]. In BM technique,

V. Kůrková et al. (Eds.): ICANN 2018, LNCS 11141, pp. 759–770, 2018.
https://doi.org/10.1007/978-3-030-01424-7_74

the frames of a video sequence are segregated into a number of non-overlapping blocks. Then, a best-matched block for each of the non-overlapping blocks in the current frame is found within a specified search region in the preceding frame with the aid of certain matching criterion. Though there exist several matching criteria, the sum of absolute difference (SAD) is mostly adopted. However, the evaluation of SAD is highly expensive in terms of the computation time. The displacement of the best-matched block with respect to the preceding block represents the motion vector (MV). Hence, a BM approach can be realized as an optimization problem with the objective of minimizing the SAD value thereby acquiring the most accurate MVs.

The full search algorithm (FSA) [12] is the basic BM algorithm that can produce accurate MVs with minimal SAD values. However, it suffers from extremely high computation time since it matches each block of the current frame with each and every candidate block within the specified search area in the previous frame. To mitigate this issue, many algorithms have been presented which includes three methodologies, namely, use of fixed search pattern [13,15,19,22,36], reducing the number of search locations [16,18,21,24], and minimizing the computational complexity of each search points [15,23,29]. However, these approaches suffer from several limitations like producing false MVs, incapability in matching the diversified motion behavior, and risk of falling in local minima/maxima. On the contrary, evolutionary techniques like genetic algorithm [10], particle swarm optimization (PSO) [14], and differential evolution (DE) [30] are the most popular methods to find the global minima/maxima in a complex optimization problem. In defiance of this, a very few research investigations have been presented using the evolutionary approaches for the problem under consideration [5,17,35].

Albeit these techniques can produce accurate MVs, they end up with high computational complexity since they require their own algorithmic-specific parameters to be defined. To overcome this, some population and parameter-free-based approaches, namely, artificial bee colony-based BM (ABC-BM) [6], harmony search-based BM (HS-BM) [4] have been presented. Further, no free lunch (NFL) theorem [34] suggests that no algorithm can solve all optimization problem specifically with distinct type and characteristics. Therefore, the aforementioned facts motivate the authors to propose a BM algorithm utilizing the principles of a recently developed optimization algorithm referred to as Sine-Cosine algorithm (SCA) by Mirjalili [20]. SCA imitates the mathematical conceptualization of sine and cosine functions. Moreover, Mirjalili has also exhibited that the SCA algorithm shows a faster convergence rate than that of the conventional algorithms like GA, PSO, and so forth. Furthermore, it has already been exploited in several applications and produced satisfactory results [8,9,27]. However, to the best knowledge of the authors, the sine-cosine algorithm has not been exploited for motion estimation.

The rest of the paper is organized as follows. Section 2 presents a brief description of the block-motion technique and sine-cosine algorithm. The proposed approach using improved SCA with FA strategy is presented in Sect. 3. The experimental setup along with the analysis of the results obtained is discussed in Sect. 4. Finally, a conclusive remark is drawn in Sect. 5.

2 Basic Preliminaries

2.1 Motion Estimation and Block-Matching

To estimate the MVs in a BM approach, the current frame (F_T) of a video sequence is partitioned into non-overlapping blocks (T_B) of $P \times P$ pixels. For each T_B, a best-matched block (M_B) within a predefined search area (S_A) of size $(2D+1) \times (2D+1)$ in the preceding frame (F_{T-1}) is obtained where 'D' denotes the given maximum shift in the pixel location. The difference in the position of 'T_B' and 'M_B' represents the motion vector (M_V)(Refer to Fig. 1). Hence, determining the best M_V within the defined S_A can be viewed as an optimization problem. Further, to obtain the accurate M_Vs', various matching criteria like mean square error (MSE), the mean absolute difference (MAD), and SAD are mostly used. In this study, SAD has been used as a matching criterion and can be defined as

$$SAD(\bar{p},\bar{q}) = \sum_{i=0}^{P-1}\sum_{j=0}^{P-1} |G_t(r+i,s+j) - G_{t-1}(r+\bar{p}+i,s+\bar{q}+j)| \tag{1}$$

where $G_t(.)$ and $G_{t-1}(.)$ denote the pixel value (gray-level) in frames F_t and F_{t-1}, respectively. The 'M_V' in $(p,\ q)$ is expressed as

$$(p,\ q) = \underset{(p,q)\epsilon S_A}{\arg\min}\ SAD(\bar{p},\bar{q}), \tag{2}$$

where $S_A = \{A(\bar{p},\bar{q})) \mid -D \leq \bar{p},\bar{q} \leq D\ and\ (r+\bar{p},s+\bar{q})\ is\ a\ valid\ pixel\ location\ in\ F_{T-1})\}$. However, it can be noted that the time consumed to compute the motion vectors is very high which is one of the major drawbacks in a BM approach.

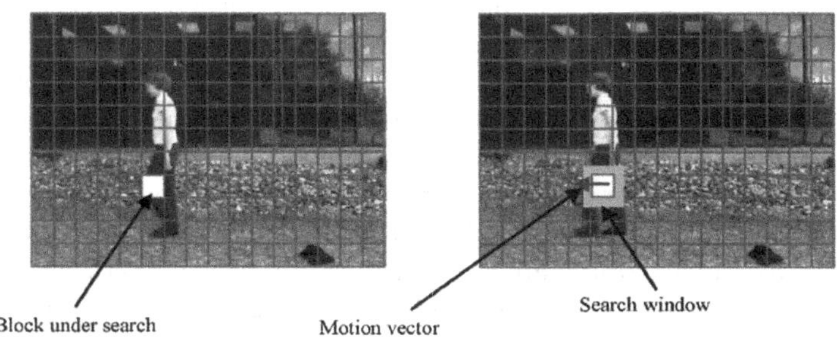

Fig. 1. Block-based motion estimation procedure

2.2 Sine-Cosine Algorithm (SCA)

Sine-Cosine algorithm (SCA) is a population-based optimization technique which utilizes some random variables, sine, and cosine functions to determine the best optimal solution (global optima) [20]. The global optima are obtained by updating a set of randomly initialized candidate population with the help of an objective function over a predefined number of iterations. To update the candidate positions the exploration and exploitation phases of SCA can be mathematically expressed as

$$C_i(g+1) = \begin{cases} C_i(g) + (r_{n1} \times sin(r_{n2}) \times |(r_{n3} \times C_{best}) - C_i(g)|) \; if \; r_{n4} < 0.5 \\ C_i(g) + (r_{n1} \times cos(r_{n2}) \times |(r_{n3} \times C_{best}) - C_i(g)|) \; if \; r_{n4} \geq 0.5 \end{cases} \tag{3}$$

where 'g' denotes the current generation (iteration), '$C(g)$' is the current solution, 'C_{best}' is the best solution obtained so far, '$|.|$' indicates the absolute values. 'r_{n1}, r_{n2}, r_{n3}, r_{n4}' represent the random variables.

The random variable r_{n1} is used to maintain a proper balance between exploration and exploitation phase and can be defined as

$$r_{n1} = C_o - g(\frac{C_o}{M_I}) \tag{4}$$

where C_0 denotes a constant. M_I indicates the total number of generations (iterations).

Similarly, r_{n2} decides the movement of the next solution to/from C_{best}. r_{n3} is used as a random weight for C_{best}. r_{n4} is a random parameter in the range of [0,1] which helps in the transition between the sine and cosine functions. For better understanding of SCA, the readers can refer to [20].

2.3 Chaotic Maps

It is noticed from many observations that the parameters in any meta-heuristic algorithms are randomly initialized with uniform or Gaussian distribution. Since the parameters in a meta-heuristic algorithm are randomly initialized, the algorithm may fall in local optima or have a slow convergence rate. Hence, to further improve the performance of these algorithms in terms of stability, finding the global optima, and converge rate, chaotic maps are introduced. Chaotic maps have the same characteristics as randomness with some inherent properties [31]. The chaotic theory has been employed in various meta-heuristic algorithms and has shown superior performance as compared to the original algorithms [1,32]. There exist various chaotic maps with distinct properties [31]. The prime objective of utilizing the chaotic maps is to further improve the performance of the sine-cosine algorithm by obtaining the global convergence and escaping the local optima.

3 Proposed Chaotic-Based SCA with Fitness Approximation Strategy

Although the sine-cosine algorithm (SCA) is capable of maintaining a proper balance between the exploration and exploitation phases, its performance depends on four random parameters (Eq. 3) thereby it suffers from downsides like falling in local optima, and slow convergence rate [7]. It can also be noticed that r_{n2}, and r_{n3} are the two random parameters which influence the performance of the sine-cosine algorithm. It is also learned from Sect. 2.3 that the chaotic maps help in boosting the performance of any traditional meta-heuristic algorithms. Hence, these facts motivate the authors to employ chaotic maps over the SCA algorithm wherein the two random parameters, namely, r_{n2}, and r_{n3} have been replaced with the logistic chaotic function [25]. In this work, Eq. 3 has been modified as

$$C_i(g+1) = \begin{cases} C_i(g) + (r_{n1} \times sin(\widehat{l_{g+1}}) \times \left|(\widetilde{l_{g+1}} \times C_{best}) - C_i(g)\right|) \; if \; r_{n4} < 0.5 \\ C_i(g) + (r_{n1} \times cos(\widehat{l_{g+1}}) \times \left|(\widetilde{l_{g+1}} \times C_{best}) - C_i(g)\right|) \; if \; r_{n4} \geq 0.5 \end{cases} \tag{5}$$

where $\widehat{l_{g+1}}$ is the modified r_{n2}, and $\widetilde{l_{g+1}}$ denotes the modified r_{n3} using the logistic function defined as

$$l_{g+1} = al_g(1 - l_g), \; a = 4 \tag{6}$$

Moreover, it is also realized that the evaluation of the SAD values (fitness function) in a BM algorithm consumes a lot of computational time. Hence to reduce the overall computational time, the authors utilize a fitness approximation strategy [4] which helps in determining whether to evaluate or estimate the fitness values for a particular search location. It follows three basic rules, namely, exploitation rule, exploration rule, and nearest-neighbor interpolation (NNI) rule [4]. In the exploitation rule, if the current search location (candidate) is found nearer than a distance 'r' with respect to the location of a previously visited search point with best fitness value obtained so far, then the SAD is evaluated for the current search location. In the case of exploration rule, if the current candidate does not have any other pre-visited candidates within a distance 'r', then the SAD is evaluated for the current candidate. In the case of NNI rule, the SAD value for the current candidate is assigned with the SAD value of any one of the previously visited candidates if the current candidate lies nearer than a distance 'r' with respect to the assigned candidate. Additionally, the assigned SAD value must not correspond to the best fitness values obtained so far.

Furthermore, it might be possible that the same search locations might be revisited again and again due to the limited search region. This leads to an increase in the computational time since the same locations will be evaluated repeatedly. Hence to deal with this issue, the current candidate is first searched in a buffer where all the previously visited candidates are stored. If the current candidate is not found in the buffer, then its fitness value will be evaluated else it will be skipped. For a better understanding of the readers, the flowchart and the pseudo-code of the proposed technique are illustrated in Fig. 2 and Algorithm 1, respectively.

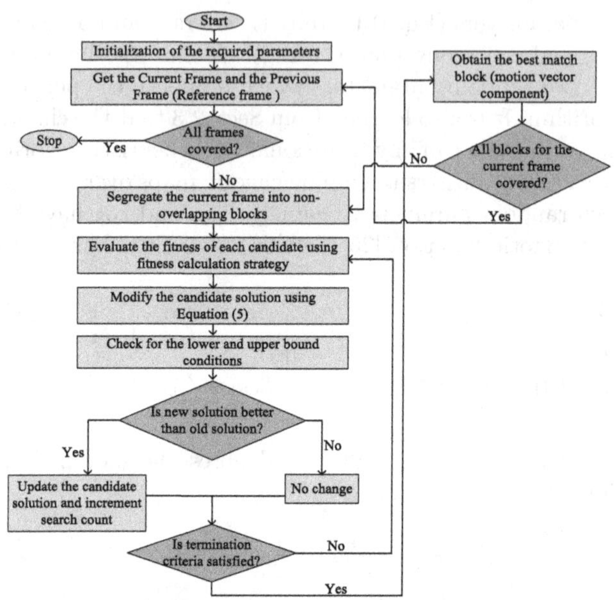

Fig. 2. Flowchart of the proposed technique

4 Discussion and Analysis of the Results

To validate the efficacy of the proposed approach for ME, exhaustive simulations are carried out in MATLAB. Various search algorithms, namely, FSA [12], TSS [13], 4SS [22], NTSS [15], PSO-BM [35], ABC-BM [6], HS-BM [4], and DE-BM [5] have been considered as the benchmarks. The experiments are carried out with some of the standard and widely used video sequences, namely, *Foreman*, *Carphone*, *Akiyo*, *Container*, *Football*, and *Stefan* [3,26]. The details of each of the video sequences are listed in Table 1. It may be noted that only the Luminance component of the sequences is considered. Moreover, the main objective of utilizing all the aforementioned sequences is to demonstrate the efficacy of the proposed algorithm with diversified motion characteristics and varied resolution.

Several performance measures, namely, peak-signal-to-noise-ratio (PSNR), search count, PSNR degradation ratio (D_{PSNR}), and computation time are used to present a detailed comparative analysis of the performance of the proposed approach along with the benchmark schemes. However, due to the constraint in page length, some of the performance measures have been discussed. The various patterns used to obtain the motion vectors are represented in Fig. 3.

Algorithm 1. Pseudocode

input : B_s = block size; $F_f(z)$ = fitness function=SAD(z); $C_k = [-D, D]\ \forall k = 1, 2, ..., N$ (constraints); M_I(max iteration)

output: $F_{s_{min}}$ (minimum location → best matched block)

Begin
  for *each frame* **do**
    Segregate into $(r * c/bs^2)$ non-overlapping blocks. Initialize the candidate population with fixed pattern of different shapes individually (Refer fig...).
    while *stopping criteria is not attained* **do**
      for *each candidate* **do**
        check if available in search history array.
        if *!(found)* **then**
          Evaluate the objective function (SAD).
      if I_C*(current iteration)* == 1 **then**
        Sort the fitness values in ascending order.
        Update the candidate positions with respect to the best solution using Equation 5
        Check the boundary conditions for each of the update candidate solutions.
        Continue.
      else
        if $SAD_{new} < SAD_{old}$ **then**
          update the change and increment the search count.
        Sort the fitness values in ascending order.
        Update the candidate positions with respect to the best solution using Equation 5
        Check the boundary conditions for each of the update candidate solutions.
    Save the motion vector component $(\bar{p}, \bar{q})$ for the current block.
Generate the estimated frames (current frame) using the obtained motion vector.

Table 1. Details of the video sequences

Video sequence	Format	Frame rate	Total frames	Motion characteristic
Container	QCIF	176×144	300	Smooth and Gentle
Akiyo	QCIF	176×144	300	Static background and small motion
Carphone	QCIF	176×144	381	Moderate
Foreman	QCIF	176×144	398	Moderate
Stefan	CIF	352×288	300	High
Football	SIF	352×240	300	High

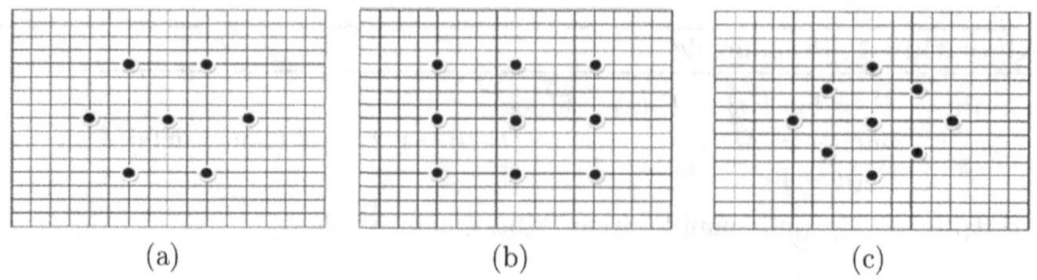

Fig. 3. Patterns : (a) *Hexagon*; (b) *Square*; and (c) *Diamond*.

4.1 Detailed Analysis with Respect to PSNR and D_{PSNR}

This section deals with the detailed analysis of the results obtained with respect to each of the aforementioned measures. As aforementioned, the primary goal of the present work is to estimate accurate motion vectors $(\bar{p}, \bar{q})$ in the reference frame for each of the macro-blocks in the current frame, thereby generating a better quality of the reconstructed frame. In this experiment, the quality of the reconstructed frame is evaluated in terms of the PSNR (in dB) [5]. A comparative analysis of the reconstructed frame quality (in terms of PSNR (in dB)) obtained with the present work and the benchmark schemes are listed in Table 2.

From the Table, it is observed that the proposed approach with different fixed patterns (see Fig. 3) achieves better PSNR values than that of the benchmark schemes except for FSA scheme which is considered to be the state-of-the-art scheme in almost all the literature available. Additionally, a comparison between the proposed algorithm and the benchmark schemes in terms of an alternate metric, namely, PSNR degradation ratio (D_{PSNR}) is depicted in Table 3. D_{PSNR} represents the degree of mismatch (in terms of %) between FSA (reference) and the other techniques (AT) including the present scheme. It is given as

$$D_{PSNR} = -\left(\frac{PSNR_{FSA} - PSNR_{AT}}{PSNR_{FSA}}\right) \times 100\% \tag{7}$$

From the Table, it is noticed that the present scheme results in a maximum of 2% and 3% degradation as compared to that of FSA algorithm for *Foreman* and *Stefan* sequence, respectively.

4.2 Detailed Analysis with Respect to the Number of Search Counts

This section deals with the analysis of the number of search counts made to find the best-matched block in the reference frame. The computational cost of any BM algorithm is assessed in terms of the total number of the search made to find the most accurate MVs. The average number of search counts (SC) made with the proposed approach and the benchmark schemes for all the test video sequences is listed in Table 4. It can be noticed that the present technique makes a significantly less number of search as compared to that of the benchmark schemes.

Table 2. Comparison of PSNR values obtained with the proposed technique and other benchmark schemes

Methods	Video sequences					
	Carphone	*Akiyo*	*Container*	*Foreman*	*Stefan*	*Football*
FSA	31.51	35.51	43.18	32.5	25.95	23.07
TSS	30.27	32.02	43.1	30.12	21.14	20.03
4SS	30.24	25.5	43.12	30.08	21.41	20.1
NTSS	30.35	33.12	43.12	31.34	25.52	25.4
PSO-BM	31.39	35.01	43.15	32.06	25.39	22.88
ABC-BM	31.5	35.44	43.17	32.43	25.9	23.02
DE-BM	31.47	35.15	43.17	-	25.85	-
HS-BM	31.49	35.44	43.16	32.43	25.89	23.01
Proposed method						
SQUARE	31.50	35.51	43.18	32.24	25.9	23.06
DIAMOND	31.51	35.50	43.18	32.15	25.35	23.04
HEXAGON	31.48	35.49	43.18	31.85	25.15	23.02

Table 3. Comparison of D_{PSNR} (in %) of different techniques

Methods	Video sequences					
	Carphone	*Akiyo*	*Container*	*Foreman*	*Stefan*	*Football*
FSA	0	0	0	0	0	0
TSS	−3.94	−9.83	−0.19	−7.32	−18.53	−13.18
4SS	−4.03	−9.83	−0.14	−7.45	−17.49	−12.87
NTSS	−3.68	−6.73	−0.14	−3.57	−13.22	−12.39
PSO-BM	−0.38	−1.41	−0.07	−1.35	−2.16	−0.82
ABC-BM	−0.03	−0.19	−0.02	−0.22	−0.19	−0.22
DE-BM	−0.13	−1.01	−0.02	−0.58	−0.39	-
HS-BM	−0.06	−0.19	−0.05	−0.22	−0.23	−0.26
Proposed method						
SQUARE	−0.031	0	0	−0.8	−0.19	−0.043
DIAMOND	0	−0.031	0	−1.07	−2.31	−0.13
HEXAGON	−0.095	−0.063	0	−2	−3.08	-0.21

Table 4. Average number of search counts made with different BM algorithms

Methods	Video sequences					
	Carphone	*Akiyo*	*Container*	*Foreman*	*Stefan*	*Football*
FSA	289	289	289	289	289	1089
TSS	25	25	25	25	25	25
4SS	25.5	27.3	19	24.8	25.3	25.6
NTSS	21.8	23.5	17.2	22.1	25.4	26.5
PSO-BM	48.5	48.5	32.5	48.1	52.2	52.2
ABC-BM	11.2	12.5	9	10.2	16.1	16.3
HS-BM	12.2	11.5	8	11.2	17.1	15.2
Proposed method						
SQUARE	8.85	5.14	6.38	9.44	15.26	22.47
DIAMOND	9.16	4.77	5.9	11.69	15.56	23.99
HEXAGON	9.62	4.72	5.84	11.51	15.42	18.61

5 Conclusion

This paper proposes an improved block-matching technique embedding the principles of chaotic maps over the sine-cosine algorithm with fitness approximation strategy for block-based motion estimation. The fitness estimation strategy helps to reduce the overall complexity by determining whether the fitness value (SAD) of a particular search location is to be evaluated or estimated. The prime objective of the proposed work is to find the accurate motion vectors(MVs) in the reference frame with reduced fitness evaluations. The analysis of the experimental results obtained reveals that the present scheme produces satisfactory results over the benchmark techniques.

References

1. Arora, S., Anand, P.: Chaotic grasshopper optimization algorithm for global optimization. Neural Comput. Appl. 1–21 (2018)
2. Barron, J.L., Fleet, D.J., Beauchemin, S.S.: Performance of optical flow techniques. Int. J. Comput. Vis. **12**(1), 43–77 (1994)
3. Brites, C.: Advances on distributed video coding. Technical University of Lisbon, MS Thesis, Lisbon, Portugal (2005)
4. Cuevas, E.: Block-matching algorithm based on harmony search optimization for motion estimation. Appl. Intell. **39**(1), 165–183 (2013)
5. Cuevas, E., Zaldivar, D., Pérez-Cisneros, M., Oliva, D.: Block-matching algorithm based on differential evolution for motion estimation. Eng. Appl. Artif. Intell. **26**(1), 488–498 (2013)
6. Cuevas, E., Zaldívar, D., Pérez-Cisneros, M., Sossa, H., Osuna, V.: Block matching algorithm for motion estimation based on artificial bee colony (abc). Appl. Soft Comput. **13**(6), 3047–3059 (2013)

7. Elaziz, M.A., Oliva, D., Xiong, S.: An improved opposition-based sine cosine algorithm for global optimization. Expert Syst. Appl. **90**, 484–500 (2017)
8. Abd Elfattah, M., Abuelenin, S., Hassanien, A.E., Pan, J.-S.: Handwritten arabic manuscript image binarization using sine cosine optimization algorithm. In: Pan, J.-S., Lin, J.C.-W., Wang, C.-H., Jiang, X.H. (eds.) ICGEC 2016. AISC, vol. 536, pp. 273–280. Springer, Cham (2017). https://doi.org/10.1007/978-3-319-48490-7_32
9. Hafez, A.I., Zawbaa, H.M., Emary, E., Hassanien, A.E.: Sine cosine optimization algorithm for feature selection. In: 2016 International Symposium on Innovations in Intelligent Systems and Applications (INISTA), pp. 1–5. IEEE (2016)
10. Holland, J.H.: Adaptation in Natural and Artificial Systems: An Introductory Analysis with Applications to Biology, Control, and Artificial Intelligence. MIT Press, Cambridge (1992)
11. Huang, Y.W., Chen, C.Y., Tsai, C.H., Shen, C.F., Chen, L.G.: Survey on block matching motion estimation algorithms and architectures with new results. J. VLSI Sig. Process. Syst. Sig. Image Video Technol. **42**(3), 297–320 (2006)
12. Jain, J., Jain, A.: Displacement measurement and its application in interframe image coding. IEEE Trans. Commun. **29**(12), 1799–1808 (1981)
13. Jong, H.M., Chen, L.G., Chiueh, T.D.: Accuracy improvement and cost reduction of 3-step search block matching algorithm for video coding. IEEE Trans. Circ. Syst. Video Technol. **4**(1), 88–90 (1994)
14. Kennedy, J.: Particle swarm optimization. In: Encyclopedia of Machine Learning, pp. 760–766. Springer, Boston (2011). https://doi.org/10.1007/978-0-387-30164-8
15. Li, R., Zeng, B., Liou, M.L.: A new three-step search algorithm for block motion estimation. IEEE Trans. Circ. Syst. Video Technol. **4**(4), 438–442 (1994)
16. Liaw, Y.C., Lai, J.Z., Hong, Z.C.: Fast block matching using prediction and rejection criteria. Signal Process. **89**(6), 1115–1120 (2009)
17. Lin, C.I., Wu, J.L.: A lightweight genetic block-matching algorithm for video coding. IEEE Trans. Circ. Syst. Video Technol. **8**(4), 386–392 (1998)
18. Liu, L.K., Feig, E.: A block-based gradient descent search algorithm for block motion estimation in video coding. IEEE Trans. Circ. Syst. Video Technol. **6**(4), 419–422 (1996)
19. Lu, J., Liou, M.L.: A simple and efficient search algorithm for block-matching motion estimation. IEEE Trans. Circ. Syst. Video Technol. **7**(2), 429–433 (1997)
20. Mirjalili, S.: SCA: a sine cosine algorithm for solving optimization problems. Knowl.-Based Syst. **96**, 120–133 (2016)
21. Nie, Y., Ma, K.K.: Adaptive rood pattern search for fast block-matching motion estimation. IEEE Trans. Image Process. **11**(12), 1442–1449 (2002)
22. Po, L.M., Ma, W.C.: A novel four-step search algorithm for fast block motion estimation. IEEE Trans. Circ. Syst. Video Technol. **6**(3), 313–317 (1996)
23. Saha, A., Mukherjee, J., Sural, S.: New pixel-decimation patterns for block matching in motion estimation. Sig. Process.: Image Commun. **23**(10), 725–738 (2008)
24. Saha, A., Mukherjee, J., Sural, S.: A neighborhood elimination approach for block matching in motion estimation. Sig. Process.: Image Commun. **26**(8–9), 438–454 (2011)
25. Sayed, G.I., Khoriba, G., Haggag, M.H.: A novel chaotic salp swarm algorithm for global optimization and feature selection. Appl. Intell. **48**(10), 1–20 (2018)
26. Sequences, S.V.: Standard Video Sequences. https://media.xiph.org/video/derf. Accessed 3 Feb 2018

27. Sindhu, R., Ngadiran, R., Yacob, Y.M., Zahri, N.A.H., Hariharan, M.: Sine-cosine algorithm for feature selection with elitism strategy and new updating mechanism. Neural Comput. Appl. **28**(10), 2947–2958 (2017)
28. Skowronski, J.: Pel recursive motion estimation and compensation in subbands. Sig. Process.: Image Commun. **14**(5), 389–396 (1999)
29. Song, Y., Liu, Z., Ikenaga, T., Goto, S.: Lossy strict multilevel successive elimination algorithm for fast motion estimation. IEICE Trans. Fundam. Electron. Commun. Comput. Sci. **90**(4), 764–770 (2007)
30. Storn, R., Price, K.: Differential evolution-a simple and efficient heuristic for global optimization over continuous spaces. J. Glob. Optim. **11**(4), 341–359 (1997)
31. Tavazoei, M.S., Haeri, M.: An optimization algorithm based on chaotic behavior and fractal nature. J. Comput. Appl. Math. **206**(2), 1070–1081 (2007)
32. Tharwat, A., Hassanien, A.E.: Chaotic antlion algorithm for parameter optimization of support vector machine. Appl. Intell. **48**(3), 670–686 (2018)
33. Tzovaras, D., Kompatsiaris, I., Strintzis, M.G.: 3D object articulation and motion estimation in model-based stereoscopic videoconference image sequence analysis and coding1. Sig. Process.: Image Commun. **14**(10), 817–840 (1999)
34. Wolpert, D.H., Macready, W.G.: No free lunch theorems for optimization. IEEE Trans. Evol. Comput. **1**(1), 67–82 (1997)
35. Yuan, X., Shen, X.: Block matching algorithm based on particle swarm optimization for motion estimation. In: International Conference on Embedded Software and Systems ICESS 2008, pp. 191–195. IEEE (2008)
36. Zhu, S., Ma, K.K.: A new diamond search algorithm for fast block-matching motion estimation. IEEE Trans. Image Process. **9**(2), 287–290 (2000)

Terrain Classification with Crawling Robot Using Long Short-Term Memory Network

Rudolf J. Szadkowski(✉), Jan Drchal, and Jan Faigl

Czech Technical University in Prague, Technicka 2, 16627 Prague, Czech Republic
{szadkrud, drchajan, faiglj}@fel.cvut.cz

Abstract. Terrain classification is a crucial feature for mobile robots operating across multiple terrains. One way to learn a terrain classifier is to use a stream of labeled proprioceptive data recorded during a terrain traversal. In this paper, we propose a new terrain classifier that combines a feature extraction from a data stream with the long short-term memory (LSTM) network. Features are extracted from the information-sparse data stream by applying a sliding window computing three central moments. The feature sequence is continuously classified by the LSTM network into multiple terrain classes. Furthermore, a modified bagging method is used to deal with a limited and unbalanced training set. In comparison to the previous work on terrain classifiers for a hexapod crawling robot using only servo-drive feedback, the proposed classifier provides continuous classification with the F1 score up to 0.88, and thus provide better results than SVM classifier learned on the same input data.

Keywords: Online classification · Proprioception · Recurrent neural networks

1 Introduction

Continuous proprioception processing is essential for crawling robots that adapt their locomotion to particular terrain type. In the animal world, a proprioceptive signal carries information about locomotor organs such as muscle stretch or muscle force output [4, 17]. For multi-legged walking robots, the proprioception describes the state of joint or servomotor actuators, and since the state of actuators is correlated with the robot surrounding environment, it is possible to use the proprioception for a local terrain classification [9, 18]. A terrain classifier can be integrated into locomotion control of a hexapod, a six-legged walking robot, to improve the performance [1] such as speed or stability. The robot is controlled in real time, and therefore, the proprioceptive data must be processed continuously to make the terrain classifier synchronous with the locomotion control.

Two types of terrain classification can be distinguished: local and remote [11]. The remote classification relies on ranged exteroceptive sensors, e.g., camera [1] and range sensors such as LiDARs [7, 19]. The local classification relies on proprioception [10] or local exteroception [12], which measures the environment in the close vicinity of the robot body that can be used to select an appropriate motion gait [13]. On the other hand, the primary function of proprioception is to sense the internal state of the body

V. Kůrková et al. (Eds.): ICANN 2018, LNCS 11141, pp. 771–780, 2018.
https://doi.org/10.1007/978-3-030-01424-7_75

(i.e., muscle stretch pressure or a joint angle) and to participate in the locomotion control. Contrary to local exteroceptive sensors that generate extra costs, the proprioception is usually already on board of multi-legged robots. Therefore proprioceptive signals can be considered as an alternative to the local exteroception for the immediate experience of the robot with the terrain the robot is currently traversing [9, 18].

One of the proprioceptive signals generated by a walking hexapod robot is a sequence of joint angle errors. The joint angle error is a difference between an actual joint angle and desired joint angle which is given by a repetitive locomotion pattern, a gait. In [2], authors classified the terrain using sequences of joint angle errors generated by a simple periodic gait. This simple gait; however, limited the robot to traverse only the flat terrains. To traverse irregular terrains [9] introduces an adaptive gait that adapts the motion to irregularities. Even though the adaptive gait is repetitive, it is not periodic; therefore the adaptive gait cannot be used with classifier [2]. The paper [8] addresses this issue by parsing the gait phases into segments of the same size and then embedded the segments into a feature vector. However, this method relies on prior knowledge about the gait phases, which is not always available. Moreover, SVM-based methods [2, 8] have to wait three gait-cycles to get enough data to produce the feature vector.

We propose to describe the terrain classification as the continuous classification conditioned on a periodic stream of proprioceptive signals. We implemented the continuous classifier as a bagging ensemble [3] combining several Long-Short Term Memory (LSTM) networks [6]. In the ideal case, such a classifier should be trained with a sufficiently large and well-balanced dataset. However, each dataset collection is a costly operation as it requires a complex experimental setup, real robots, and most importantly a human supervisor. Moreover, datasets collected during usual deployments (e.g., exploration) are generally not balanced as it depends on the deployment location. Therefore, in practice, we deal with datasets that are small and unbalanced. We aggregate several LSTM networks into a bagging predictor [3] to address this issue. In particular, we use asymmetric bootstrapping [15] that artificially balances the dataset. We propose a method that exploits the periodic properties of the proprioceptive signal to generate new datasamples, and thus enlarges the dataset. The performance of the proposed predictor is statistically compared with the former SVM-based approach [8]. Regarding the reported results, the proposed method achieves competitive performance while its main benefit is in a continuous prediction.

2 Proprioceptive Signals and Data Collection

The robot classifies the terrain it traverses by processing the stream of proprioceptive signals. We work with the hexapod depicted in Fig. 1(a) which consists of a body and six legs each with three joints connecting body, coxa, femur, and tibia, see Fig. 1(b).

When the hexapod traverses a terrain, it moves its joints in a repetitive pattern called a gait. A single repetition of the pattern is called a gait-cycle. A particular gait is defined by a motion pattern, e.g., a robot walking with a tripod gait always has at least three legs on the ground in the supporting phase, and three legs are simultaneously

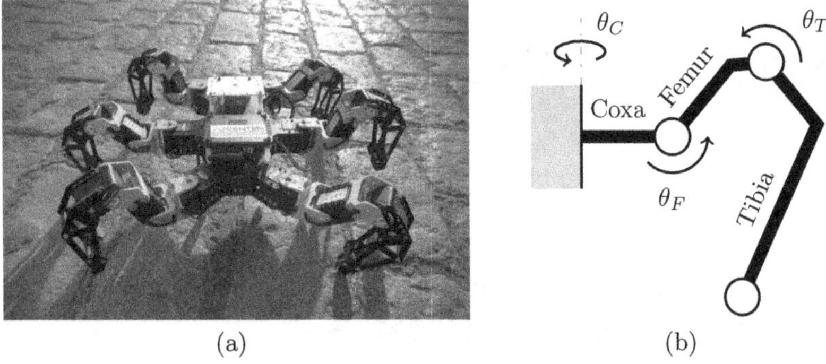

Fig. 1. The utilized hexapod and schema of its leg.

moving forward in the swing phase. The gait rules utilized in this paper are conditioned on the terrain interaction, which makes the gait adaptive [9].

2.1 Adaptive Gait

In [9], the authors take advantage of the proprioceptive signals provided by the servomotors to detect terrain irregularities. During a single gait-cycle, each leg goes through four phases: up, forward, down, and support. For each i-th leg and each j-th joint, two variables are monitored: the current angle $\theta_{i,j}^{cur}$. and the desired angle $\theta_{i,j}^{des}$. The joint angle error is defined as the absolute difference between the current and desired angle

$$\theta_{i,j}^{err} = \left|\theta_{i,j}^{cur} - \theta_{i,j}^{des}\right| \tag{1}$$

During the i-th leg swing-down phase, the error of the body-coxa joint, $\theta_{i,C}^{err}$, is compared with a predefined threshold. If $\theta_{i,C}^{err}$ is above the threshold, it is assumed the deviation is caused by the ground reaction force, and therefore, the motion is stopped and the i-th leg enters into the support phase. Once all moving legs are in the support phase, the body leveling is initiated and move the robot forward. The process is repeated for the next subset of moving legs.

2.2 Data Collection and Preprocessing

The herein proposed approach uses the same data source as in [8] where the SVM classifier processes the angle errors $\theta_{i,j}^{err}$ of the two front legs to classify the terrain. To collect the dataset, we let the hexapod crawl on seven types of terrain: office, asphalt, dirt, bricks, obstacles, stairs, and grass (see Fig. 2).

In each session, the hexapod executes up to ten gait-cycles on a single terrain type. The number of collected gait-cycles for each terrain is shown in Table 1. For each gait-cycle, we recorded the angle errors of the front leg joints, $\boldsymbol{\theta}^{err} \in \mathbb{R}^6$ with the uniform

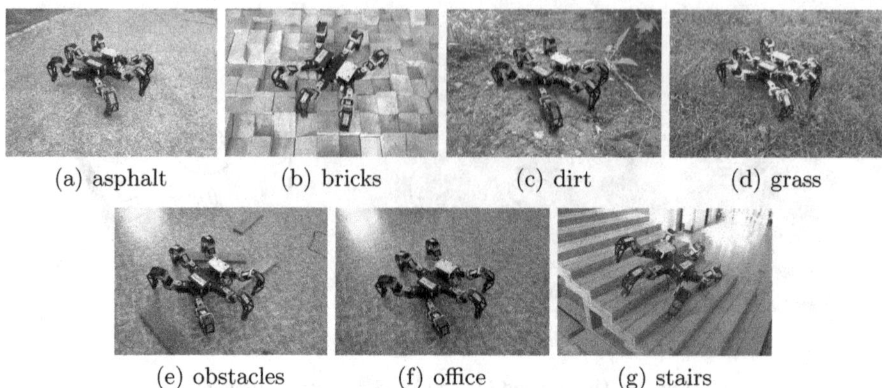

Fig. 2. The hexapod deployed in various terrains for data collection.

sampling rate. Due to the adaptation to the terrain irregularities, the length of each record of errors may differ. Each gait-cycle record is preprocessed by a sliding window method which computed the mean, standard deviation, and skewness. The width of the window is set to 20 units and the window jumps ahead 5 units. Thus, the preprocessing yielded a sequence of feature vectors $\boldsymbol{x}$, where each feature vector has 18 dimensions (2 legs $\times$ 3 joints $\times$ 3 central moments).

Table 1. Numbers of the sampled gait-cycles and division to train and test sets.

Dataset	Asphalt	Bricks	Dirt	Grass	Obstacles	Office	Stairs
Train set	69	26	56	66	61	77	87
Test set	18	9	15	17	16	20	22
Complete set	87	35	71	83	77	97	109

3 Proposed Terrain Predictor

The proposed terrain predictor is based on the basic LSTM model using the bagging extension to deal with the small and unbalanced data. The addressed classification task can be formalized as follows. Let C be a finite set of terrain classes. Our goal is to find a predictor ϕ^* that predicts a distribution over C for each feature vector $\boldsymbol{x}(m)$ in a continuous feature vector stream. Assuming that at the m-th iteration the distribution is conditioned on the sequence $\boldsymbol{x}^m = (\boldsymbol{x}(m), \boldsymbol{x}(m-1), \ldots, \boldsymbol{x}(1))$, we denote the output of the predictor ϕ^* as

$$\boldsymbol{y}(m) = \left(P(C = c_1|\boldsymbol{x}^m), P(C = c_2|\boldsymbol{x}^m), \ldots, P(C = c_{|C|}|\boldsymbol{x}^m)\right), \tag{2}$$

where $P(C = c_i|\boldsymbol{x}^m)$ is probability that the class at the m-th step is $c_i \in C$. The continuous prediction over the sequence $(\boldsymbol{x}(m), \boldsymbol{x}(m-1), \ldots, \boldsymbol{x}(1))$ then yields a sequence of the probability distributions $(\boldsymbol{y}(m), \boldsymbol{y}(m-1), \ldots, \boldsymbol{y}(1))$.

The terrain prediction (3) can be considered as the sequence-to-sequence problem where the input sequence is mapped to the output sequence. We propose to approximate ϕ^* by the neural network ϕ composed of a single LSTM hidden layer (see [6] for equations) with the softmax output layer. In the training phase, each i-th training pair

$$((\boldsymbol{x}_i(M_i), \boldsymbol{x}_i(M_i - 1), \ldots, \boldsymbol{x}_i(1)), d_i), \tag{3}$$

is presented to the neural network ϕ, where M_i is the length of the training sequence. The desired class d_i is time-invariant because the terrain class does not change during the training sequence. For each feature vector $\boldsymbol{x}_i(m)$, we get the output $\boldsymbol{y}_i(m)$ that is compared with the desired class d_i using the loss function $\mathcal{L}(\boldsymbol{y}_i(m), d_i)$. We followed a common practice with neural network classifiers, and we chose the cross-entropy error as the loss function. The loss of the whole i-th training sequence is then evaluated as

$$\mathcal{L}(\mathbf{y}_\mathrm{i}, \mathrm{d}_\mathrm{i}) = \sum\nolimits_{\mathrm{m}=\mathrm{M}_\mathrm{min}}^{\mathrm{M}_\mathrm{i}} \mathcal{L}(\boldsymbol{y}_\mathrm{i}(\mathrm{m}), \mathrm{d}_\mathrm{i}), \tag{4}$$

where M_{min} denotes the offset of the first feature vector in the sequence that is being evaluated. Preliminary experiments showed that it is better to leave several initial samples unevaluated. The length of the i-th sequence M_i determines how much information about the terrain d_i is provided to the predictor.

The problem of small and unbalanced dataset collected by the robot is evident from Table 1 and it is addressed by implementation of the terrain predictor as a bagging ensemble [3] with a modified bootstrapping method. The bagging ensemble is denoted as

$$\phi_\mathrm{B}(\boldsymbol{x}) = \frac{\sum_{j=1}^{S} \phi(\boldsymbol{x}; D^j)}{S}, \tag{5}$$

where D^j is the j-th bootstrap dataset, S is the number of the bootstrap datasets, and $\phi(\boldsymbol{x};D^j)$ is the output of the neural network trained on D^j. The bootstrap datasets are usually generated by taking N random samples with the replacement from the source dataset D. The distribution of the bootstrap datasets then approximates the probability distribution of D [3]. However, in our case, this is undesirable because the source dataset D is unbalanced. Therefore, we propose the modified bootstrapping method described in Algorithm 1. This algorithm uses asymmetric bootstrapping which balances the bootstrap dataset [15]. Then the algorithm creates new samples by combining randomly selected gait-cycle sequences. Note, that by using this random combination we assume that the gait-cycles from the same terrain are independent. After being trained, the proposed predictor does not need to parse the input stream into gait-cycles, i.e., the predictor can work without any knowledge of the gait implementation.

Algorithm 1. Bootstrap dataset generator

```
Input C: classes; G[i]: set of single gait-cycles for
class i in C; L: number of gait-cycles in one sequence;
N: size of the bootstrap dataset.
Output D': bootstrap dataset containing (sequence, class)
training pairs.

  for N times do
    class := random_choice(C)
    sequence := ()
    for L times do
      gaitcycle := random_choice(G[class])
      sequence.concatenate(gaitcycle)
    end for
  trainpair := (sequence, class)
  D'.add(trainpair)
  end for
```

4 Experiments

The dataset collected using the method described in Sect. 2.2 is divided into a training dataset and a testing dataset (see Table 1), the latter is used only for the evaluation. The Algorithm 1 generates bootstrap datasets with $N = 1000$ training pairs, and each training sequence contains $L = 3$ gait-cycles because it should contain enough information to classify the terrain [8]. The average length of the training sequence is 73 and M_{min} is set to 50. We generate 30 bootstrap datasets for 30 neural networks, where each network consists of 20 hidden LSTM units with forget gate [5], the input layer has 18 units, and the output layer has seven units corresponding to the particular terrain classes.

We use the `rmsprop` [16] with the learning rate set to 0.01 and decay rate α set to 0.99 to backpropagate the error. During one epoch, each training sequence is forward-passed and backpropagated. Therefore, the learning algorithm performs 1000 backpropagation iterations per one epoch, and each network is trained on 100 epochs. Finally, all 30 trained networks are aggregated into the bagging predictor. For the evaluation, we generated testing sequences composed of four gait-cycles instead of three gait-cycles that are used during training, because we aim to study the temporal generalization of the networks. Two examples of how the terrain distribution prediction changes in time are shown in Fig. 3.

The performed evolution of the prediction accuracy for each type of the classified terrain is shown in Fig. 4. Based on the results, it seems that for each terrain, the accuracy settles up at a different iteration step, and thus each terrain requires a different amount of the proprioceptive data to be classified with high confidence. Another observation is that after 40 iterations, which roughly corresponds to one and half a single gait-cycle, the prediction accuracy of the grass, office, and stairs terrains is almost perfect. The confusion matrix evaluated on the 70th iteration can be found in Table 2.

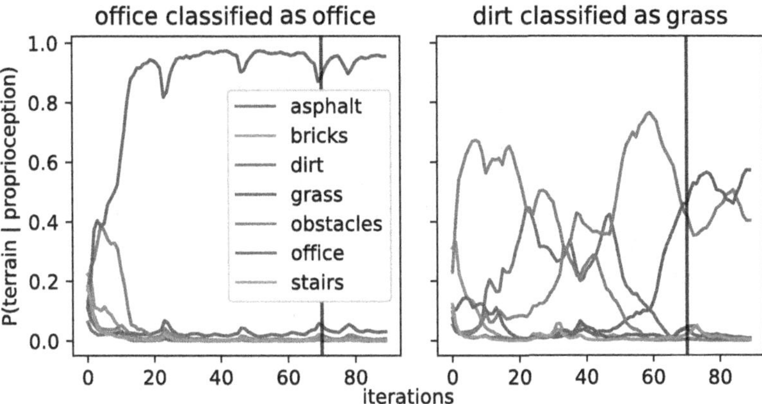

Fig. 3. Example of terrain probability distribution changes generated by the proposed predictor. On the left, the office (brown) is correctly predicted with high certainty, after 20 iterations. On the right, dirt (green) is mispredicted as an obstacle (violet) and then as a grass (red). (Color figure online)

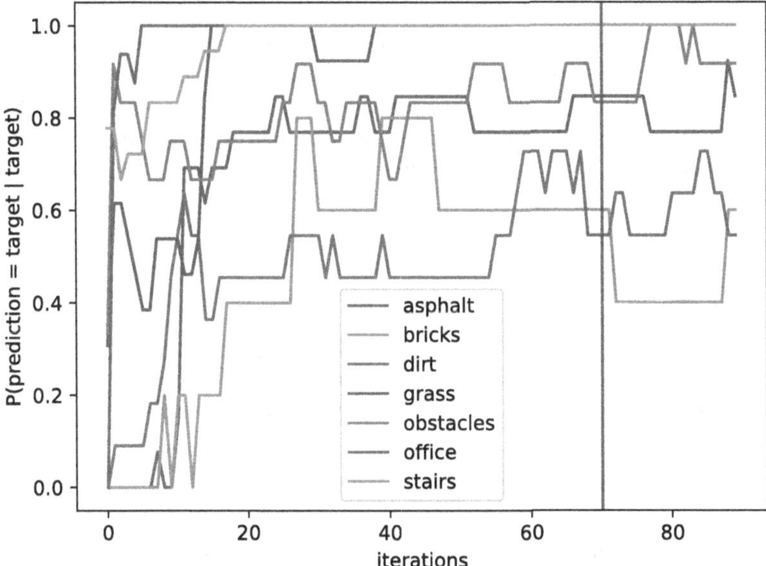

Fig. 4. Evolution of the prediction accuracy for each terrain type. Office floor, stairs, and grass terrain types are classified at almost 100% at the 40th iteration. The accuracy of each terrain settles up around the 70th iteration (marked by the vertical line), which roughly corresponds to the end of the 3rd gait-cycle.

Table 2. Confusion matrix evaluated at the end of the 70th iteration (about the end of 3rd gait-cycle).

	Asphalt	Bricks	Dirt	Grass	Obstacles	Office	Stairs
Asphalt	**12**	0	2	0	0	0	0
Bricks	0	**3**	0	0	0	0	2
Dirt	0	0	**6**	5	0	0	0
Grass	0	0	0	**13**	0	0	0
Obstacles	0	0	2	0	**10**	0	0
Office	0	0	0	0	0	**16**	0
Stairs	0	0	0	0	0	0	**18**

Finally, we compared the bagging ensemble with the SVM classifier utilized in [8]. The comparison is not straightforward because both models are qualitatively different. Our ensemble predicts continuously through iterations as can be seen in Fig. 3 contrary to the SVM classifier [8] that relies on the well defined gait-cycle phases. Therefore, we also consider an uninformed variant of the approach [8] where the feature vector does not contain information about gait-cycle phases. The comparison is shown in Table 3 where we use the weighted F1 score [14] because the testing dataset is unbalanced.

Discussion - The results in Fig. 4 indicate that the prediction accuracy is almost perfect for office, dirt, and stairs terrains. We hypothesize that it is because these three terrains are mutually well distinguishable. From the results in Table 2 we can see that the classifier confuses intuitively similar terrains. An example of such confusion can be seen in Fig. 3. From Fig. 4, it is also evident that for the classification, each terrain needs a different number of iterations. This can be exploited by classifiers that process every feature vector continuously. In that regard, the proposed continuous processing of the proprioceptive data adds a qualitative advantage over non-continuous approaches [2, 8].

Table 3. Predictor comparison using the weighted F1 score [14]. All the predictors are trained and tested using the same training set and test set except for the SVM classifier [8] which uses information about gait-cycle phases. The predictors are considered for the sequences of different lengths up to four gait-cycles.

Predictor	Gait-cycles			
	1	2	3	4
Bagging predictor	**0.83**	**0.86**	0.87	0.88
SVM uninformed	0.63	0.75	0.79	0.77
Single LSTM predictor	0.66	0.78	0.83	0.82
SVM [8]	0.54	0.78	**0.88**	**0.90**

5 Conclusion

In this paper, we report on the proposed LSTM based terrain predictor suitable for a hexapod crawling robot using proprioceptive signals to process a stream of the joint angle errors generated during crawling irregular terrains by the adaptive locomotion. Due to a small and imbalanced dataset, the basic LSTM methods are not directly applicable. Therefore, we propose to wrap multiple LSTM predictors into a bagging ensemble using a modified bootstrapping algorithm to deal with the class imbalance. The proposed modification takes advantage of the periodicity of the input stream to enlarge the dataset artificially. The resulted bagging predictor has been statistically compared with the existing SVM-based predictor utilized in the previous work on the terrain classification using a real hexapod crawling robot. The main advantage of the proposed solution is that, unlike the SVM-based predictor, it can provide prediction each iteration step. The reported results demonstrate that different terrains need a different amount of the input information to get prediction with high confidence. Therefore the proposed formulation of the terrain classification task as the sequence-to-sequence problem seems to be suitable for processing stream of proprioceptive signals.

The main shortcoming of the terrain classification is that it depends on the gait used for the training. Different gaits have different properties such as the servomotor load, and thus the particular gait influences the patterns of the proprioceptive signals. The proposed classifier is designed with the intention to support the locomotion controller, and therefore, we plan to address the influence of the gait to the classification and thus improve the transferability to different gait types in our future work.

Acknowledgments. The presented work has been supported by the Czech Science Foundation (GAČR) under research project No. 18-18858S. The support of grant No. SGS16/235/OHK3/3T/13 to Rudolf Szadkowski is also gratefully acknowledged. Access to computing and storage facilities owned by parties and projects contributing to the National Grid Infrastructure MetaCentrum provided under the programme "Projects of Large Research, Development, and Innovations Infrastructures" (CESNET LM2015042), is greatly appreciated.

References

1. Bartoszyk, S., Kasprzak, P., Belter, D.: Terrain-aware motion planning for a walking robot. In: 2017 11th International Workshop on Robot Motion and Control (RoMoCo), pp. 29–34 (2017)
2. Best, G., Moghadam, P., Kottege, N., Kleeman, L.: Terrain classification using a hexapod robot. In: Australasian Conference on Robotics and Automation (2013)
3. Breiman, L.: Bagging predictors. Mach. Learn. **24**(2), 123–140 (1996)
4. Frigon, A., Rossignol, S.: Experiments and models of sensorimotor interactions during locomotion. Biol. Cybern. **95**(6), 607 (2006)
5. Gers, F.: Long short-term memory in recurrent neural networks. Unpublished Ph.D. dissertation, Ecole Polytechnique Fédérale de Lausanne, Lausanne, Switzerland (2001)
6. Hochreiter, S., Schmidhuber, J.: Long short-term memory. Neural Comput. **9**, 1735–1780 (1997)

7. McDaniel, M.W., Nishihata, T., Brooks, C.A., Salesses, P., Iagnemma, K.: Terrain classification and identification of tree stems using ground based lidar. J. Field Robot. **29**(6), 891–910 (2012)
8. Mrva, J., Faigl, J.: Feature extraction for terrain classification with crawling robots. Inf. Technol. Appl. Theory **1422**, 179–185 (2015)
9. Mrva, J., Faigl, J.: Tactile sensing with servo drives feedback only for blind hexapod walking robot. In: 10th International Workshop on Robot Motion and Control (RoMoCo), pp. 240–245 (2015)
10. Ojeda, L., Borenstein, J., Witus, G., Karlsen, R.: Terrain characterization and classification with a mobile robot. J. Field Robot. **23**(2), 103–122 (2006)
11. Otsu, K., Ono, M., Fuchs, T.J., Baldwin, I., Kubota, T.: Autonomous terrain classification with co- and self-training approach. IEEE Robot. Autom. Lett. **1**(2), 814–819 (2016)
12. Otte, S., Weiss, C., Scherer, T., Zell, A.: Recurrent neural networks for fast and robust vibration-based ground classification on mobile robots. In: IEEE International Conference on Robotics and Automation (ICRA), pp. 5603–5608 (2016)
13. Rebula, J.R., Neuhaus, P.D., Bonnlander, B.V., Johnson, M.J., Pratt, J.E.: A controller for the littledog quadruped walking on rough terrain. In: IEEE International Conference on Robotics and Automation (ICRA), pp. 1467–1473 (2007)
14. Sasaki, Y., et al.: The truth of the F-measure. Teach. Tutor. Mater **1**(5), 1–5 (2007)
15. Tao, D., Tang, X., Li, X., Wu, X.: Asymmetric bagging and random subspace for support vector machines-based relevance feedback in image retrieval. IEEE Trans. Pattern Anal. Mach. Intell. **28**(7), 1088–1099 (2006)
16. Tieleman, T., Hinton, G.: Lecture 6.5-rmsprop: divide the gradient by a running average of its recent magnitude. COURSERA Neural Netw. Mach. Learn. **4**(2), 26–31 (2012)
17. Tóth, T.I., Knops, S., Daun-Gruhn, S.: A neuromechanical model explaining forward and backward stepping in the stick insect. J. Neurophysiol. **107**(12), 3267–3280 (2012)
18. Walas, K., Kanoulas, D., Kryczka, P.: Terrain classification and locomotion parameters adaptation for humanoid robots using force/torque sensing. In: IEEE-RAS 16th International Conference on Humanoid Robots, pp. 133–140 (2016)
19. Walas, K., Nowicki, M.: Terrain classification using laser range finder. In: IEEE/RSJ International Conference on Intelligent Robots and Systems (IROS), pp. 5003–5009 (2014)

Mass-Spring Damper Array as a Mechanical Medium for Computation

Yuki Yamanaka[1(✉)], Takaharu Yaguchi[1,2], Kohei Nakajima[2,3], and Helmut Hauser[4]

[1] Kobe University, Kobe, Hyogo, Japan
y-yamanaka@stu.kobe-u.ac.jp
[2] JST PRESTO, Kawaguchi, Saitama, Japan
yaguchi@pearl.kobe-u.ac.jp
[3] The University of Tokyo, Bunkyo-ku, Tokyo, Japan
k_nakajima@mech.t.u-tokyo.ac.jp
[4] University of Bristol, Bristol, UK
helmut.hauser@bristol.ac.uk

Abstract. Recently, it has been reported that the dynamics of mechanical structures can be used as a computational resource—also referred to as morphological computation. In particular soft materials have been shown to have the potential to be used for time series forecasting. Although most soft materials can be modeled by mass-spring systems, a limited number of researches has been performed on the computational capabilities of such systems. In this paper, we propose an array of masses linked in a grid-like structure by spring-damper connections to investigate systematically the influence of structural (size) and dynamic (stiffness, damping) parameters on the computational capabilities for time series forecasting. In addition, such a structure gives us a good approximation of two-dimensional elastic media, e.g., a rubber sheet, and therefore a direct pathway to potentially implement results in a real system. In particular, we compared the mass-spring array to echo state networks, which are standard machine learning techniques for this kind of problems and are also closely related to the underlying theoretical models applied when exploiting mechanical structures for computation. Our results suggest a clear connection of morphological features to computational capabilities.

Keywords: Soft Robotics · Morphological computation · Reservoir computing Mass-spring system · Recurrent neural network

Supported by JST, PRESTO Grant Number JPMJPR15E7 and JPMJPR16EC, Japan and by the Leverhulme Trust Research Project Grant RPG-2016-345.
Electronic supplementary material The online version of this chapter (https://doi.org/10.1007/978-3-030-01424-7_76) contains supplementary material, which is available to authorized users.

V. Kůrková et al. (Eds.): ICANN 2018, LNCS 11141, pp. 781–794, 2018.
https://doi.org/10.1007/978-3-030-01424-7_76

1 Introduction

In recent years, a new field of robotics, called Soft Robotics, has been risen, see [11]. It uses materials and actuation systems that go beyond conventional building blocks, i.e. rigid body parts and electric motors. This includes a wide range of new, soft materials like silicone, electro-active polymers, gels, and many others, see, e.g. [21]. Despite its success, the field is still struggling to find corresponding control approaches that work with the highly nonlinear dynamics of these materials. One possibility could be to use these, otherwise unwanted morphological features, for our advantage. Instead of controlling every single degree of freedom, we could exploit the underlying complex dynamics as a computational resource. This is often referred to as Morphological Computation, see [19, 20]. Hauser et al. demonstrated with the help of randomly connected networks of nonlinear mass-spring dampers that such dynamics can be indeed used as a computational resource, see [5, 6]. The underlying theoretical framework is provided by a machine learning technique called reservoir computing [8, 12, 13, 23]. It uses a high-dimensional nonlinear dynamical system, i.e. the *reservoir*, as a computational resource by exploiting it as a temporal kernel in the machine learning sense. Only the weights in the output layer are trained while the structure of the reservoir is typically randomly initialized and then fixed. Interestingly, the reservoir can be implemented by a wide range of dynamical systems leading to various types of reservoir computing. Typical examples from simulations include the echo state network [7, 8] and the liquid state machine [13]. Moreover, even real physical systems can serve as reservoirs as long as they have the necessary properties, see [4]. For example, reservoirs have been built with lasers [18] or even with a bucket of water [3].

Hauser et al. [5] showed that mechanical structures can be used as reservoirs as well. Interestingly, the mass-spring damper networks they proposed, are also a good approximation of soft structures, e.g. elastic sheets, silicone structures, or even biological tissue. Nakajima et al. used this insight to exploit the dynamics of an octopus-inspired arm, which was modeled by a mass-spring array, as a computational resource [10, 15, 24, 25]. In addition, they showed that this approach is also transferable to real platforms. They used platforms by using an octopus-inspired robot arm build out of silicone to carry out computation and even control [14, 16, 17]. The same approach has been applied also to other robotics platforms, e.g., in locomotion [26] and in trajectory control of a pneumatic arm [2]. However, in the theoretical frameworks as well the implementations in simulation and real robot platforms, the morphological structures are typically fixed. Nevertheless, it has been speculated that there is a clear connection between the morphological features and the computational capabilities of the reservoir, see [4]. Urbain et al. recently performed studies on the trade-offs between morphology, efficiency of control and the ability as a computational resource [22]; however, so far, to the best of the authors' knowledge, there has been very little work done on systematically investigating of how morphological features (like size and form of the network and dynamic properties like stiffness and damping) have influence on the computational performance.

Therefore, in this paper, we propose a structured mass-spring damper array to investigate this question systematically. As computational benchmark tasks we use the approximation of various nonlinear auto regression moving average models (NARMA models) as proposed and used previously by [16]. Furthermore, we compare the results to a standard echo state network, which is a standard tool in machine learning for these kind of tasks.

2 Mass-Spring Damper Array

In this paper, we employed a simulated mass-spring damper array, see Fig. 1(a), as a reservoir. The use of this mass-spring damper array is motivated by the device that was introduced in [16]. They used a silicone based arm inspired by an octopus arm. They added bending sensors and attached it to a motor to actuate the otherwise passive arm. Using this device, they showed that soft structure can be used as a computational resource.

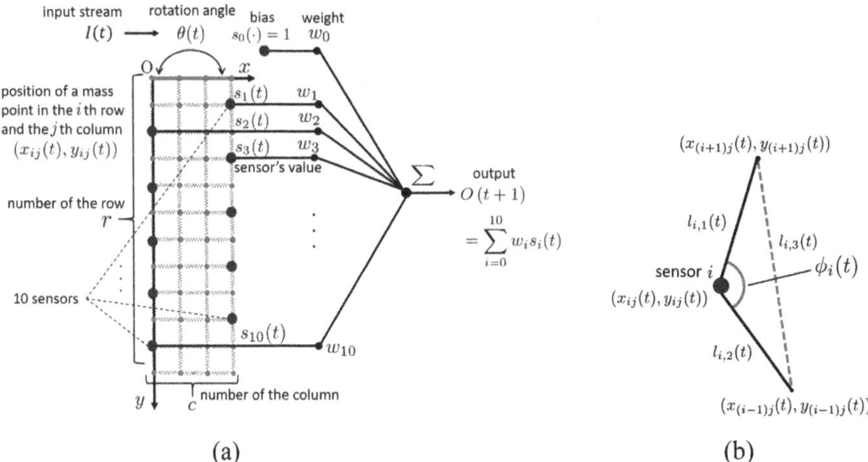

Fig. 1. (a) Is an illustration of the mass-spring damper array. (b) describes the *i*th sensor node. The output $s_i(t)$ of the sensor is expressed as follows: when two springs vertically connected to the node are on a straight line (in this case $\phi_i(t) = \frac{\pi}{2}$), $s_i(t) = 0$; when these bend outside of the mass-spring damper array, $\phi_i(t)$ and $s_i(t)$ take positive values ($s_i(t) = 1$ when $\phi_i(t) = \frac{\pi}{4}$); when these bend inside, $\phi_i(t)$ and $s_i(t)$ take negative values ($s_i(t) = -1$ when $\phi_i(t) = -\frac{\pi}{4}$).

The motor was located on the top of the body and served as an input device. The 5 sensors on each side functioned as outputs. In this paper, we use a similar device by using the model shown in Fig. 2. The body made of the soft material is modeled by the 2-dimensional mass-spring damper grid, which consists of $r \times c$ mass points. The position of a mass point in the *i*th row and the *j*th column is defined as (x_{ij}, y_{ij}). The *i*th sensor output at time t is denoted by $s_i(t)$, where s_0 is assumed to be the bias; $s_0(t) = 1$

for all t. Each $s_i(t)$ is computed from the angle $\phi_i(t)$ between the two springs that are connected to ith sensor in the vertical direction. This angle is obtained by

$$\phi_i(t) = \pm \arccos\left(\frac{l_{i,1}(t)^2 + l_{i,2}(t)^2 - l_{i,3}(t)^2}{2l_{i,1}(t)l_{i,2}(t)}\right) \tag{1}$$

where $l_{i,1}$, $l_{i,2}$ respectively denote the distances from the sensor to the two neighboring mass points in the vertical direction, and $l_{i,3}$ is that between the two neighboring points. The sign of ϕ_i is determined by the positions of the sensor and the two neighboring mass points. Each output $s_i(t)$ is defined as $s_i(t) = \frac{4}{\pi}\phi_i(t)$ to be the normalized value of $\phi_i(t)$ so that $|s_i(t)| = 1$, if $\phi_i(t) = \pm\frac{\pi}{4}$ (see Fig. 1(b)). The output $O_{\mathrm{MS}}(t+1)$ is the weighted sum of the outputs of the sensors

$$O_{\mathrm{MS}}(t+1) = \sum_{i=0}^{10} w_i^{\mathrm{MS}} s_i(t), \tag{2}$$

where $\mathbf{W}^{\mathrm{MS}} = \left[w_0^{\mathrm{MS}}, \ldots, w_{10}^{\mathrm{MS}}\right]^{\mathrm{T}}$ are the weights. The superscript MS on the symbols is the abbreviation of "Mass-Spring." This superscript is used for distinction of these symbols from those by echo state networks, which are introduced in Sect. 4.

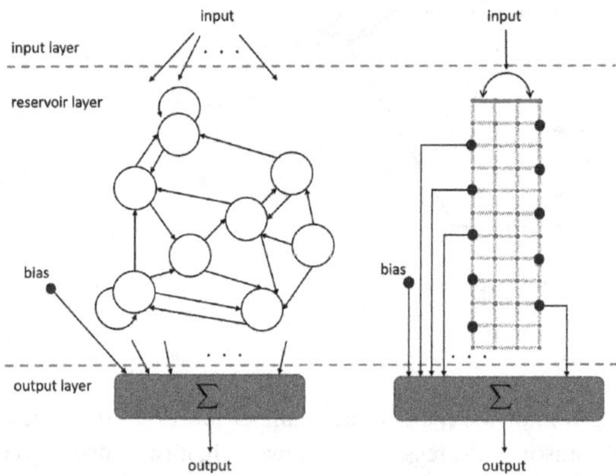

Fig. 2. Correspondence between the mass-spring damper system and echo state networks

We assume that the mass-spring array is under the effect of gravity, which acts in positive y direction. We also assume that a damping force exists between each neighbouring pair of the mass points, and that the mass points $(x_{1j}, y_{1j})(j = 1, \ldots, c)$ are fixed on the top of the device on line by rigid horizontal connections. For the sake of simplicity the masses of the all mass points are assumed to be a same value $m = 1.0$. The springs are also assumed to be uniform, i.e., they all have the same spring constant k and the same equilibrium length l_s and the same damping coefficient γ. Under these assumptions the equation of motion of each x_{ij} is derived in a straightforward way as

$$k\Bigg\{-4x_{ij}+x_{(i+1)j}+x_{(i-1)j}+x_{i(j+1)}+x_{i(j-1)}$$
$$+l\left(\frac{x_{ij}-x_{(i-1)j}}{\sqrt{(x_{ij}-x_{(i-1)j})^2+(y_{ij}-y_{(i-1)j})^2}}+\frac{x_{ij}-x_{(i+1)j}}{\sqrt{(x_{ij}-x_{(i+1)j})^2+(y_{ij}-y_{(i+1)j})^2}}\right. \tag{3}$$
$$\left.+\frac{x_{ij}-x_{i(j-1)}}{\sqrt{(x_{ij}-x_{i(j-1)})^2+(y_{ij}-y_{i(j-1)})^2}}+\frac{x_{ij}-x_{i(j+1)}}{\sqrt{(x_{ij}-x_{i(j+1)})^2+(y_{ij}-y_{i(j+1)})^2}}\right)\Bigg\}-m\ddot{x}_{ij}=\gamma\dot{x}_{ij}$$

and

$$k\Bigg\{-4y_{ij}+y_{(i+1)j}+y_{(i-1)j}+y_{i(j+1)}+y_{i(j-1)}$$
$$+l\left(\frac{y_{ij}-y_{(i-1)j}}{\sqrt{(x_{ij}-x_{(i-1)j})^2+(y_{ij}-y_{(i-1)j})^2}}+\frac{y_{ij}-y_{(i+1)j}}{\sqrt{(x_{ij}-x_{(i+1)j})^2+(y_{ij}-y_{(i+1)j})^2}}\right. \tag{4}$$
$$\left.+\frac{y_{ij}-y_{i(j-1)}}{\sqrt{(x_{ij}-x_{i(j-1)})^2+(y_{ij}-y_{i(j-1)})^2}}+\frac{y_{ij}-y_{i(j+1)}}{\sqrt{(x_{ij}-x_{i(j+1)})^2+(y_{ij}-y_{i(j+1)})^2}}\right)\Bigg\}-m\ddot{y}_{ij}+mg=\gamma\dot{y}_{ij}.$$

3 Approximation of NARMA Models as a Benchmark Test

In order to illustrate the potential effectiveness of the mass-spring damper array as a mechanical medium for computation, we performed the following tests. We used the problem of approximation of outputs of NARMA(n) models for n = 2, 10, 20 as benchmarks:

NARMA2

$$y(t+1)=\begin{cases}0.4y(t)+0.4y(t)y(t-1)+0.6I^3(t)+0.1 & (t\geq 0)\\ 0 & (t\leq -1)\end{cases} \tag{5}$$

NARMA10, 20

$$y(t+1)=\begin{cases}0.3y(t)+0.05y(t)\left(\sum_{j=0}^{n-1}y(t-j)\right)+1.5I(t-n+1)I(t)+0.1 & (t\geq 0)\\ 0 & (t\leq -1)\end{cases} \tag{6}$$

where n = 10, 20 respectively for NARMA10, 20. These models have been proposed and used by [1] for the evaluation of recurrent neural networks. However, they have been used as a benchmark in various other studies, e.g., [5, 7, 16, 23].

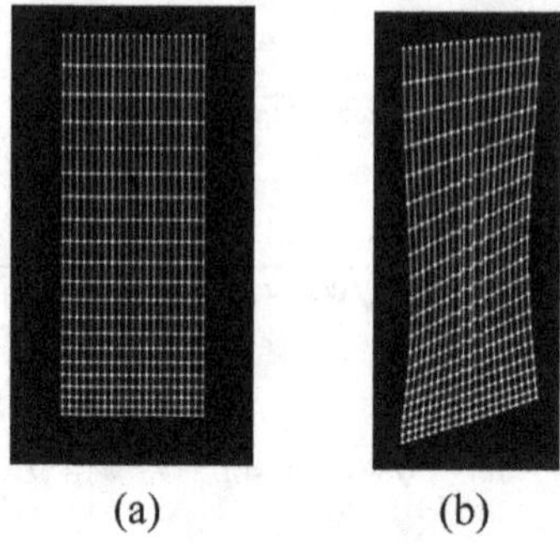

(a) (b)

Fig. 3. Visualization of a mass-spring network using WebGL. (a) is a network under the force of gravity. Note that connections on the top are more stretched as they carry more weight than connections at the bottom. (b) is a snapshot of mass-spring system with the top rotated. The input $I(t)$ is applied to the network as the rotational angle of the top (see [16] for details).

Following [16], we used

$$I(t) = \begin{cases} 0.2\sin\left(2\pi f_1 \frac{t}{T}\right)\sin\left(2\pi f_2 \frac{t}{T}\right)\sin\left(2\pi f_3 \frac{t}{T}\right) & (t \geq 0) \\ 0 & (t \leq -1) \end{cases} \tag{7}$$

with $(f_1, f_2, f_3) = (2.11, 3.73, 4.33)$ as the input sequence. The parameter T controls the rate of change of $I(t)$; actually $I(t)$ is applied to the mass-spring network as the rotation angle of the top (see Figs. 1 and 2). We set $T = 400$ in this paper.

The model Eqs. (3) and (4) are numerically solved by using the 4th order Runge–Kutta method with a step size of $\Delta t = 0.005$. The computational results are visualized by using WebGL, which is an implementation of OpenGL for Java Script, as shown in Fig. 3. Figure 3(a) shows the equilibrium state of the mass-spring array only under the influence of gravity and Fig. 3(b) a snapshot of the typical motion of the array introduced by the input and the effect of gravity. The weights $\mathbf{W}^{\mathrm{MS}} = \left[w_0^{\mathrm{MS}}, \ldots, w_{10}^{\mathrm{MS}}\right]^{\mathrm{T}}$ are determined by minimizing the normalized mean square error with $y(t+1)$ for $1 \leq t \leq 5000$ as the training data. More precisely, first we performed numerical simulations until the mass-spring systems reach an equilibrium state (see Fig. 3(a)) and we set $t = 0$ at this time. Then the weights are determined by minimizing

$$E = \frac{\sum_{t=1}^{5000}\left(y(t+1) - O^{\mathrm{MS}}(t+1)\right)^2}{\sum_{t=1}^{5000} y^2(t+1)} \tag{8}$$

so that the squared error between the output of the system and the NARMA models is minimized. As the output is defined by (2), $\mathbf{W}^{\mathrm{MS}}$ is obtained by

$$\mathbf{W}^{\mathrm{MS}} = S^{+}\mathbf{y} \tag{9}$$

where S is the 5000×11 matrix of which row vectors are $s_0(t), \ldots, s_{10}(t)$ for each $t = 1, \ldots, 5000$, S^{+} is the Moore–Penrose pseudoinverse of S and $\mathbf{y} = [y(2), \ldots, y(5001)]^{\top}$.

4 Pretests with Echo State Networks

To get a better understanding of the computational performance of the proposed mechanical structure we compare it to echo state networks (ESNs), which are standard tools to learn dynamical systems like the chosen NARMA tasks. The ESNs will serve as a baseline for comparison. We performed pretests to determine the appropriate values of the parameters for the ESNs. In what follows, results are evaluated by the normalized error

$$E = \frac{\sum_{t=5001}^{10000} \left(y(t+1) - O(t+1)\right)^2}{\sum_{t=5001}^{10000} y^2(t+1)}. \tag{10}$$

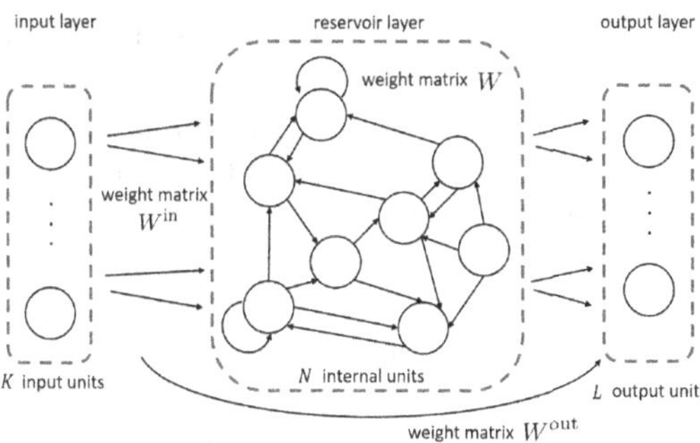

Fig. 4. Echo state network setup. The new input to the internal nodes of the reservoir layer caused by propagation from the input layer and the reservoir layer itself is represented by $\tilde{x}(t)$. $\tilde{x}(t)$ flows into the internal nodes at the leaking rate α, and then values of the internal nodes $x(t)$ is obtained.

Figure 4 is a schematic description of ESNs. We denote the numbers of input nodes, internal nodes and output nodes by K, N and L respectively. We also denote the $N \times (1+K)$ weight matrix from the input layer to the reservoir layer by $W^{\mathrm{in}} = \left[w_{ij}^{\mathrm{in}}\right]$, the weights between the nodes in the reservoir by $N \times N$ matrix $W = \left[w_{ij}^{\mathrm{in}}\right]$, and the

$L \times (1+K+N)$ weight matrix from the reservoir layer to the output layer by $W^{\mathrm{out}} = \left[w_{ij}^{\mathrm{out}}\right]$. The bias is denoted by b. We used leaky integrator echo state networks because the input sequence (7) has low frequency modes and leaky integrator ESNs are suitable for such sequences (see [9]). The output of leaky integrator ESNs is denoted by $O_{\mathrm{ESN}}(t)$ in the following update equations:

$$\tilde{x}(t) = \tanh\left(W^{\mathrm{in}}[b, I(t)]^{\top} + W_x(t-1)\right), \tag{11}$$

$$x(t) = (1-\alpha)x(t-1) + \alpha\tilde{x}(t), \tag{12}$$

$$O_{\mathrm{ESN}}(t) = W^{\mathrm{out}}[b, I(t), x(t)]^{\top}, \tag{13}$$

where the vector $x(t)$ represents the values of the internal nodes and α is the leaking rate, which controls the speed of dynamics, and is fixed to 0.3 for simplicity. We use the hyperbolic tangent function as the activation function, and set $K = 1$ and $L = 1$. Each component of W^{in} is randomly set to one of the three values of 1.0, −1.0, 0 with probabilities 2.5%, 2.5%, 95% respectively. Similarly, the weights in W are set to w, $-w$ or 0 with probabilities 2.5%, 2.5%, 95% and with a fixed $w > 0$.

We performed the benchmark tests, changing the size N of the reservoir (100 or 200 nodes) and the weights. For each choice of the parameters N and w, 20 reservoirs were randomly generated.

The performance of ESNs is dependent on the spectral radius[1] ρ of the matrix W, see [7]. The objective of the first test is investigation of the actual dependence of the performance on the spectral radius. The results of the approximation tests of NARMA2, 10, 20 are shown in Fig. 5. The horizontal axis shows the spectral radius ρ of the weight matrix W, and the vertical axis the normalized squared error. Note that the spectral radius becomes larger as each of N and w takes a larger value.

Figure 5(a), (b), (c) show the results for NARMA2, 10, 20. In these figures, no significant difference in the dependence of the accuracy on the spectral radius ρ is observed. In all of the figures, the performance of the ESNs with $(N, w) = (200, 2.0), (100, 4.0), (200, 4.0)$ was stable in the sense that the accuracy with these parameters was almost the same among the 20 trials. Meanwhile, the ESNs with $(N, w)(100, 0.4), (200, 0.4), (200, 0.5), (200, 1.0), (100, 2.0)$ often show a worse performance. In particular, the deviations of the errors by the networks with $(N, w) = (100, 0.4), (200, 0.4), (200, 0.5)$ are quite large.

The ESN with the best accuracy was obtained when the parameters were set to $(N, w) = (200, 0.4)$, which gave $\rho \simeq 1.32$. The errors in this case were about 10^{-8} for the NARMA2 test, and about 10^{-7} for NARMA10 and NARMA20, while when in most cases with $\rho > 3$ the errors were around 10^{-5} for NARMA2, 10^{-2} for NARMA10

[1] The spectral radius of the matrix is the largest absolute value of the eigenvalues of the matrix. The performance of ESNs strongly depends on if the network has the so-called echo state property, and it is known that the small spectral radius indicates this property. See [7] for detail.

and 10^{-3} for NARMA20. This dependence of the performances on ρ may be due to whether the generated reservoir had the echo state property or not, see [7].

Despite the fact that approximation of NARMA models with higher degree is known to be a difficult task, the accuracy of the networks with $\rho > 3$ was better for NARMA20 than for NARMA10. This implies that networks with a large ρ have a different property from standard ESNs with a small ρ. When the spectral radius is small ($\rho < 2$), the deviation of the order of accuracy was quite large. That for the results for NARMA2, for example, was from 10^{-8} to 10^{3}. Similar results are also reported in [16].

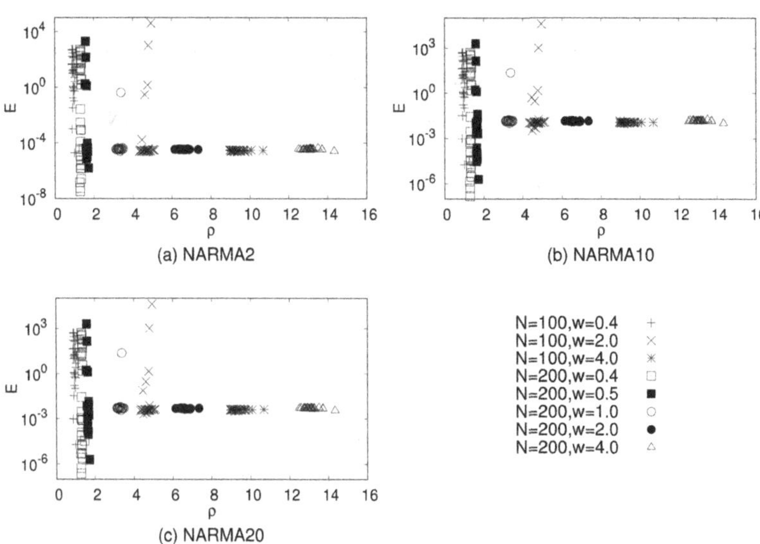

Fig. 5. Results of echo state networks with various N and w

5 Results of the Benchmark Tests of the Mass-Spring Damper Array

First, we compared performances of the mass-spring arrays with averaged errors of 20 randomly generated ESNs with $(N, w) = (200, 4.0)$, which gave the best results in the previous tests. Table 1 shows the averaged errors over all experiments of the mass-spring array performed with various physical parameters and the averaged and the smallest errors of the ESNs with the above parameters. As illustration, we also show in Fig. 6 the input signal and examples of the outputs of the array with the parameters $(r, c, m, l, k, \gamma) = (50, 50, 1.0, 1.0, 3000, 0.05)$ for $5001 \leq t \leq 5500$, along with the results by the ESN with $(N, w) = (200, 4.0)$.

Next, we investigated relations between parameters of the mechanical structure (i.e., the size and the dynamical parameters as well) and the performance of the system through some tests.

Firstly, we observed the dependence of the performance on the size of the mass-spring damper system by performing the tests with various r and c; $r = 10, 20, \ldots, 100$,

$c = 10, 20, \ldots, 100$. The results are shown in Fig. 7(a), (b) and (c). These figures show that there exists a certain dependence between the size of the array and the accuracy of the mass-spring damper system. For example, in the results of the tests for NARMA2 shown in Fig. 7(a), the parameters $r = 40, c = 80, 90, 100$ and $r = 100, c = 90, 100$ gave better results than others. The best accuracy was achieved when $r = 100, c = 100$, and in that case, the error E was about 0.000027. Interestingly there exist two local optima around $r = 40, c = 80, 90, 100$ and $r = 100, c = 90, 100$. A remarkable conclusion is that outputs of larger systems, which have a larger number of degrees of freedom, are not always more accurate than smaller systems.

Table 1. The averaged errors by the mass-spring damper array (MS) and by the echo state networks (ESN) along with the best results of echo state networks

	Average of MS	Average of ESN	Best of ESN
NARMA2	3.93×10^{-5}	3.31×10^{-5}	3.34×10^{-8}
NARMA10	2.65×10^{-3}	1.43×10^{-2}	1.52×10^{-7}
NARMA20	1.93×10^{-3}	4.91×10^{-3}	2.36×10^{-7}

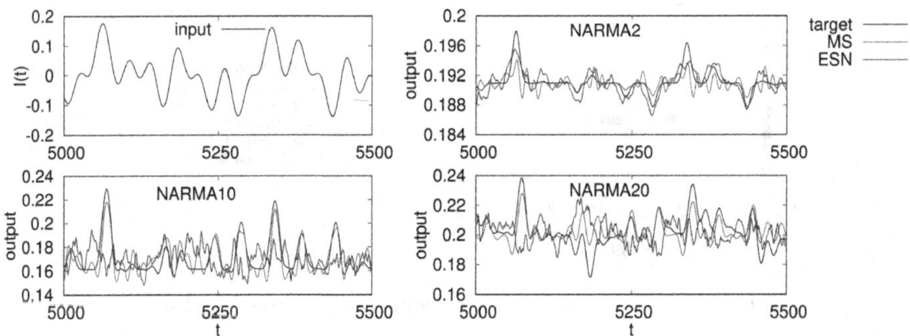

Fig. 6. Examples of the results of the NARMA tasks. In the legend, "target" corresponds to the output of the NARMA model, "MS" to that of the mass- spring array and "ESN" to that of the echo state network.

Secondly, similarly we investigated the dependence of the performance on the spring constant k and the damping coefficient γ. In the tests we tried various values of k and γ with r, c, m, l fixed to $r = 50, c = 50, m = 1.0, l = 1.0$. The results for $k = 500, 1000, \ldots, 10000$ and $\gamma = 0.01, 0.02, \ldots, 0.2$ are shown in Fig. 7(d), (e) and (f). In the results of the NARMA2 test shown in Fig. 7(d), larger γ gives higher accuracy, while the best k was around 3500. Figure 7(e) and (f) show the results for the NARMA10 and NARMA20 tasks.

It is clearly shown in Fig. 7(d), (e) and (f) that smaller k is suitable for these tasks. In particular, optimal values of k for NARMA10 and NARMA20 tasks are possibly less than 500, which is the smallest value of k plotted in Fig. 7(e) and (f). Therefore we performed the additional tests using $k = 50, 100, \ldots, 500$, of which results are shown in Fig. 7(g) and (h).

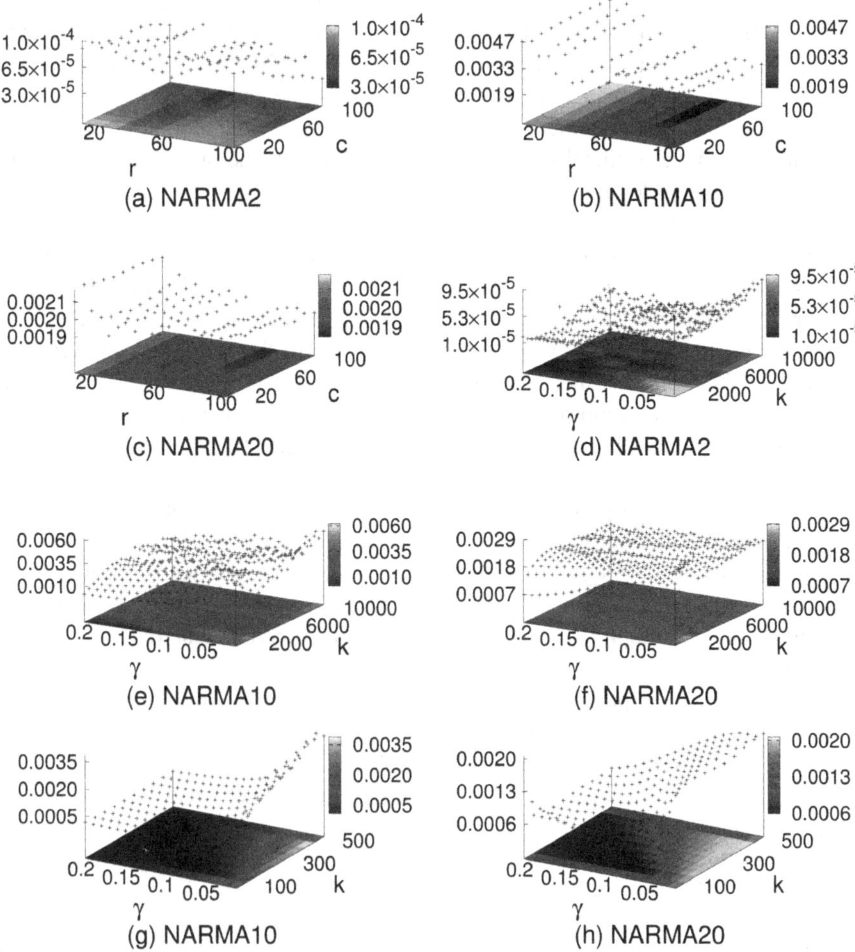

Fig. 7. (a), (b) and (c) are the results by the mass-spring damper array with various r and c. The vertical axis corresponds to the normalized mean squared error between the outputs of the mass-spring damper array and those of the NARMA models. (d), (e) and (f) are the results by the mass-spring damper array with various k and γ. (g) and (h) are enlarged graphs of the results of the mass-spring damper array for smaller k.

6 Discussion

The results presented in Fig. 7(a), (b) and (c) suggest an interesting conclusion. The pure number of mass points is not enough to determinate the performances of the system. For example, the accuracy of the system with $r = 40, c = 100$ was better than that of the system with $r = 100, c = 40$. This implies that the performance of the system depends in some sense on the two dimensional shape of the medium rather than just the size. This is in so far interesting as the theoretical models proposed by Hauser et al. predict that the higher dimensional the reservoir is the more likely the computational power would increases. The difference here could be mainly due to the existence of the gravity force. Because of the gravity force, the motion of the system is larger in the y direction than in the x direction, and hence changes of c, which is the number of the mass points in the y axis, are more affected by the motion of the system. In addition, we have artificially introduced asymmetry in the structure by allowing sensors only on the side and input on the top.

The difference of the dependence of the performance on r and c was also observed in the results in NARMA10 and NARMA20, which are shown in Fig. 7(b), (c). In these tests the systems with $r = 70, 80, c = 60, 70, 80, 90, 100$ yield better results than the others for both the NARMA10 and the NARMA20 tasks. It should be noted that the optimal parameters for NARMA2 are different from those of NARMA10 and NARMA20. This confirms that when the mass-spring array is used as a mechanical medium for computation, morphological parameters related to the size or the shape of the array must be carefully chosen when considering a specific computational task.

Regarding the tests where various k and γ are investigated, for all of the NARMA2, 10, 20 tests, the performance depended on both parameters. In particular, the results in Fig. 7(g), (h) show that outputs of systems with larger γ are more accurate than those with smaller γ, meanwhile systems with smaller k yield more accurate results than those with larger k. Moreover, the values of the error in Fig. 7(g), (h) are smoothly dependent on k and γ, thereby implying existence of a simple function that relates the error function to k and γ.

Because γ is the damping coefficient, the motion of the mass-spring damper system can become unstable when γ is set to a small value. In contrast, when γ is large, the whole systems tends to act as one rigid block. Similarly, larger k makes the motion of the system more dynamic (i.e., can move at higher frequencies), and motions of systems with smaller k are softer (i.e., moves slowly). Hence, for NARMA(n) tasks with higher n mass-spring damper arrays with stiffer behavior (i.e., move rigidly (larger γ) and slowly (smaller k)) are seemingly more suitable than the systems with more dynamic behavior.

In the systems with more active motions, a motion of a mass point wields a great influence on the neighbouring points. In comparison with ESNs, if the mass-spring damper array is in some sense equivalent to the reservoir of an ESN, links between the mass points with greater interaction may correspond to strong links between the neighbouring nodes in the reservoir of the ESN, thereby possibly corresponding to the weight matrix with large weights. Similarly the mass-spring systems with stiffer behavior should correspond to reservoirs with small weights. In the previous tests of ESNs, it was shown that if the spectral radius of the weight matrix is large, the accuracy of outputs of the systems is feasible, but not excellent, while the deviations of the errors are small. The spectral radius is dependent on the size and the weights of the reservoir; in particular large weights yield a large spectral radius. Hence, it is expected that deviations of the errors with large k and small γ must be small, and the outputs are not extremely accurate. The results in Fig. 7(f), (g), (h) are compatible with this expectation.

In this paper, we used the product of three sinusoidal signals as the input, different trends may appear when other input time series are imposed (e.g., random input time series from uniform distribution). These cases with other benchmarks will be investigated in future work.

7 Conclusion

In this paper we have investigated by simulations the performance of the mass-spring damper array as a computational medium, in particular, to what extent the morphological parameters affect the overall computational performance.

The errors of the mass-spring damper array for the NARMA tests were almost same as the averaged errors of the ESNs, but still larger than for the best perform ESNs. However, considering that the deviation of performances of ESNs with small spectral radius was very large, the stable performance of the mass-spring damper system was remarkable. This implies that when the proposed mechanical array can be used as a medium for computation, it should surely work to a certain extent although the accuracy may not be excellent. This stability of the performance of the mass-spring array would be advantageous for real applications in terms of ease-of-use without strict tuning parameters.

References

1. Atiya, A.F., Parlos, A.G.: New results on recurrent network training: unifying the algorithms and accelerating convergence. IEEE Trans. Neural Netw. **11**(3), 697–709 (2000)
2. Eder, M., Hisch, F., Hauser, H.: Morphological computation-based control of a modular, pneumatically driven, soft robotic arm. Adv. Robot. **32**(7), 375–385 (2018). https://doi.org/10.1080/01691864.2017.1402703
3. Fernando, C., Sojakka, S.: Pattern recognition in a bucket. In: Banzhaf, W., Ziegler, J., Christaller, T., Dittrich, P., Kim, J.T. (eds.) ECAL 2003. LNCS (LNAI), vol. 2801, pp. 588–597. Springer, Heidelberg (2003). https://doi.org/10.1007/978-3-540-39432-7_63
4. Hauser, H., Füchslin, R., Nakajima, K.: Morphological computation—the physical body as a computational resource. In: Hauser, H.; Füchslin, R.M., Pfeifer, R. (eds.) Opinions and Outlooks on Morphological Computation, Chap. 20, pp. 226–244 (2014). ISBN 978-3-033-04515-6
5. Hauser, H., Ijspeert, A.J., Füchslin, R.M., Pfeifer, R., Maass, W.: Towards a theoretical foundation for morphological computation with compliant bodies. Biol. Cybern. **105**(5), 355–370 (2011)
6. Hauser, H., Ijspeert, A.J., Füchslin, R.M., Pfeifer, R., Maass, W.: The role of feedback in morphological computation with compliant bodies. Biol. Cybern. **106**(10), 595–613 (2012). https://doi.org/10.1007/s00422-012-0516-4
7. Jaeger, H.: Adaptive nonlinear system identification with echo state networks. In: Advances in Neural Information Processing Systems, pp. 609–616 (2003)
8. Jaeger, H., Haas, H.: Harnessing nonlinearity: predicting chaotic systems and saving energy in wireless communication. Science **304**(5667), 78–80 (2004)

9. Jaeger, H., Lukoševičius, M., Popovici, D., Siewert, U.: Optimization and applications of echo state networks with leaky-integrator neurons. Neural Netw. **20**(3), 335–352 (2007)
10. Kang, R., et al.: Dynamic model of a hyper-redundant, octopus-like manipulator for underwater applications. In: 2011 IEEE/RSJ International Conference on Intelligent Robots and Systems, pp. 4054–4059 (2011). https://doi.org/10.1109/IROS.2011.6094468
11. Laschi, C., Mazzolai, B., Cianchetti, M.: Soft robotics: technologies and systems pushing the boundaries of robot abilities. Sci. Robot. **1**(1), eaah3690 (2016)
12. Lukoševičius, M., Jaeger, H.: Reservoir computing approaches to recurrent neural network training. Comput. Sci. Rev. **3**(3), 127–149 (2009)
13. Maass, W., Natschläger, T., Markram, H.: Real-time computing without stable states: a new framework for neural computation based on perturbations. Neural Comput. **14**(11), 2531–2560 (2002)
14. Nakajima, K., Li, T., Hauser, H., Pfeifer, R.: Exploiting short-term memory in soft body dynamics as a computational resource. J. R. Soc. Interface **11**(100) (2014)
15. Nakajima, K., Hauser, H., Kang, R., Guglielmino, E., Caldwell, D., Pfeifer, R.: A soft body as a reservoir: case studies in a dynamic model of octopus-inspired soft robotic arm. Front. Comput. Neurosci. **7**, 91 (2013). https://doi.org/10.3389/fncom.2013.00091
16. Nakajima, K., Hauser, H., Li, T., Pfeifer, R.: Information processing via physical soft body. Sci. Rep.**5** (2015)
17. Nakajima, K., Hauser, H., Li, T., Pfeifer, R.: Exploiting the dynamics of soft materials for machine learning. Soft Robot. **5**(3), 339–347 (2018)
18. Paquot, Y., et al.: Optoelectronic reservoir computing. Sci. Rep. **2**, 287 (2012)
19. Paul, C., Valero-Cuevas, F.J., Lipson, H.: Design and control of tensegrity robots for locomotion. IEEE Trans. Robot. **22**(5), 944–957 (2006)
20. Pfeifer, R., Gómez, G.: Morphological computation – connecting brain, body, and environment. In: Sendhoff, B., Körner, E., Sporns, O., Ritter, H., Doya, K. (eds.) Creating Brain-Like Intelligence. LNCS (LNAI), vol. 5436, pp. 66–83. Springer, Heidelberg (2009). https://doi.org/10.1007/978-3-642-00616-6_5
21. Rus, D., Tolley, M.T.: Design, fabrication and control of soft robots. Nature **521**(7553), 467–475 (2015)
22. Urbain, G., Degrave, J., Carette, B., Dambre, J., Wyffels, F.: Morphological properties of mass-spring networks for optimal locomotion learning. Front. Neurorobotics **11**, 16 (2017). https://doi.org/10.3389/fnbot.2017.00016
23. Verstraeten, D., Schrauwen, B., d' Haene, M., Stroobandt, D.: An experimental unification of reservoir computing methods. Neural Netw. **20**(3), 391–403 (2007)
24. Yekutieli, Y., Sagiv-Zohar, R., Aharonov, R., Engel, Y., Hochner, B., Flash, T.: Dynamic model of the octopus arm.I. biomechanics of the octopus reaching movement. J. Neurophysiol. **94**, 1443–1458 (2005)
25. Yekutieli, Y., Sagiv-Zohar, R., Aharonov, R., Engel, Y., Hochner, B., Flash, T.: Dynamic model of the octopus arm.II. control of reaching movements. J. Neurophysiol. **94**, 1459–1468 (2005)
26. Zhao, Q., Nakajima, K., Sumioka, H., Hauser, H., Pfeifer, R.: Spine dynamics as a computational resource in spine-driven quadruped locomotion. In: IEEE/RSJ International Conference on Intelligent Robots and Systems (IROS 2013), pp. 1445–1451. IEEE (2013)

Kinematic Estimation with Neural Networks for Robotic Manipulators

Michail Theofanidis(✉), Saif Iftekar Sayed(✉), Joe Cloud, James Brady(✉), and Fillia Makedon(✉)

HERACLEIA Human-Centered Computing Laboratory, Department of Computer Science and Engineering, University of Texas at Arlington, Arlington, USA
{michail.theofanidis,saififtekar.sayed,joe.cloud, james.brady2}@mavs.uta.edu, makedon@uta.edu

Abstract. In this paper, we focus on estimating the forward kinematic equation of robots with multilayer feed-forward neural networks. The effectiveness of this approach is tested on a simulated kinematic model of the 7-DOF Sawyer Robotic Arm. In the initial sections of the paper, we discuss related work that associates with the creation of model agnostic control schemes on a kinematic level. Moreover, we formalize the kinematic problem as a supervised problem and we propose an MLP architecture to solve the problem. Lastly, we present experimental results and discuss the potential and importance to create model agnostic control schemes with machine learning.

Keywords: Robot kinematics · Forward kinematics
Neural networks for engineering

1 Introduction

Kinematics is the branch of classical mechanics, which studies the motion of bodies, without consideration of acting forces or moments. Robot kinematics provide mathematical tools to model and analyze the motion and structure of robotic manipulators, which is a fundamental component of robot control. In general, robotic manipulators are composed by a series of links and joints, followed by a gripper (the end effector). The joints of a robot can be either rotational or prismatic and they can be controlled by a certain actuator, such as an electric motor. To move the robot's end effector along a particular trajectory, actuation must be caused by the motors of the joints. The equations that describe the relationship between the position of the end effector and the position of the joints are addressed as the kinematic equations of the robotic arm.

Specifically, the mapping from the joint space of the robot to the Cartesian space of the robot's end effector is known as forward kinematics, while the inverse of this relationship is addressed as the inverse kinematics. Traditionally, the kinematic equations of a robot are derived from the kinematic model of the

V. Kůrková et al. (Eds.): ICANN 2018, LNCS 11141, pp. 795–802, 2018.
https://doi.org/10.1007/978-3-030-01424-7_77

robot, which describes the spacial relationship of each link and joint of the robot. Spacial relationships can be decomposed into rotational and translational and they can be represented mathematically by homogeneous transformations matrices [3]. In this paper, we focus on estimating the forward kinematic equations of robots with neural networks.

2 Related Work

A considerable amount of research has been conducted in the fields of both machine learning and control theory to try and create reliable control algorithms, that enable robotic arms to perform tasks autonomously and adapt to new environments [1]. Since robotic systems can be abstracted as continuous time systems that moves along a trajectory given a particular control input in the joint domain, it is worthwhile to investigate control frameworks based on neural networks that have the capability to solve nonlinear problems. According to the relevant literature, two different network architectures have been employed successfully to solve control problems in robotics [5]. Feed forward neural networks and recurrent neural networks.

The architecture of the neural network is based on whereas the system has full knowledge, partial knowledge or no knowledge of the robot's plant dynamics [9]. When the system has full or partial knowledge of the dynamics, feed forward neural networks have been used to compensate uncertainties due to modeling or sensor error [6]. In the case of model-free control of robotic systems, neural networks are used as function approximators that estimate the kinematic and dynamic equations of the robot. Note though, that both the forward and inverse kinematic and dynamic equations of robotic arms can not be fully learned by a single feed forward neural network, but they can be partially learned with recurrent neural networks [7].

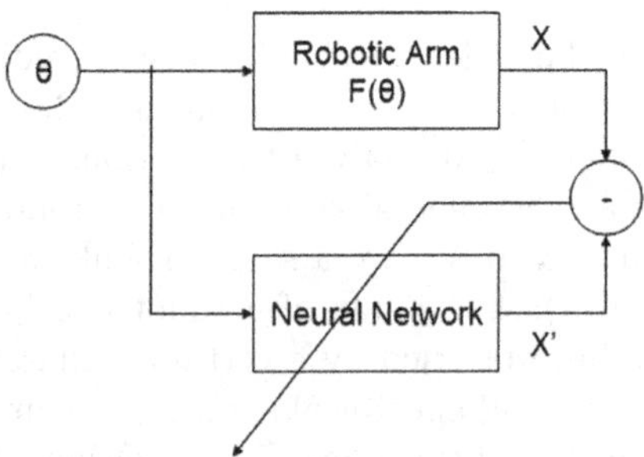

Fig. 1. Learning the forward kinematics with supervised learning.

3 Problem Formulation

As previously explained, the forward kinematics is a function F that connects the vector of joint positions θ with the Cartesian coordinates of the robot's end effector X:

$$X = F(\theta) \quad (1)$$

A very important property of Eq. 1 is that it is a one-to-one function, regardless of the geometrical properties of the robotic arm [7]. This statement holds true for every possible open loop kinematic chain and thus, every possible joint configuration can be uniquely mapped to one and only one end effector Cartesian coordinate [10]. Practically, this means that F can be learned in a supervised manner by a neural network as Fig. 1 suggests.

In addition, Fig. 1 indirectly suggests that the forward kinematics problem is independent of the robot geometry. That is not the case with the inverse kinematics problem, whose goal is to find a set of joint configurations given a particular end-effector position and orientation [3]. The difficulty of the inverse kinematics problem arises from its dependence on the physical configuration of the robot and that is has multiple solutions. Thus, any machine learning algorithm that tries to learn the inverse kinematics problem, will only be able to find one solution per kinematic configuration [4,8,11]. Also, the leaner might learn different inverse kinematics solutions for different kinematic configurations within the same workspace of a particular robot [2].

4 Experimental Testbed

The fact that the forward kinematics problem can be solved with classical supervised learning algorithms, means that the training process can occur off-line with training samples that are collected from measurements. These training samples will constitute a dataset whose input is measured from the robot joint encoders, and the output is the equivalent Cartesian coordinates of the robot end effector. A problem with this approach is that the Cartesian coordinates must be obtained from an external sensor and most mechanical manipulators possess only internal sensors. However, if the geometric characteristics of the robot are known, then the training dataset can be also generated from a simulated kinematic model of the robot. In this section, we present how we derived the kinematics of the 7-DOF Sawyer Robotic arm, and how well a multilayer perceptron neural network can learn to estimate the equation.

4.1 Kinematics of the Sawyer Robot

Figure 2 illustrates the kinematic model of the Sawyer Robotic Arm. The model was constructed by reverse engineering the geometrical properties of the physical robot. According to the homogeneous transformation of the joint frames from Fig. 2, the DH Table 1 of the model was composed. Note though, that in the table we do include the elevation of the robot above the world frame, which is estimated to be 0.3160 m. Based on the DH table, the homogeneous coordinate matrix of the frames can be derived according to matrix (2). Finally, we computed the forward kinematic equations of the robot according to Eq. (2).

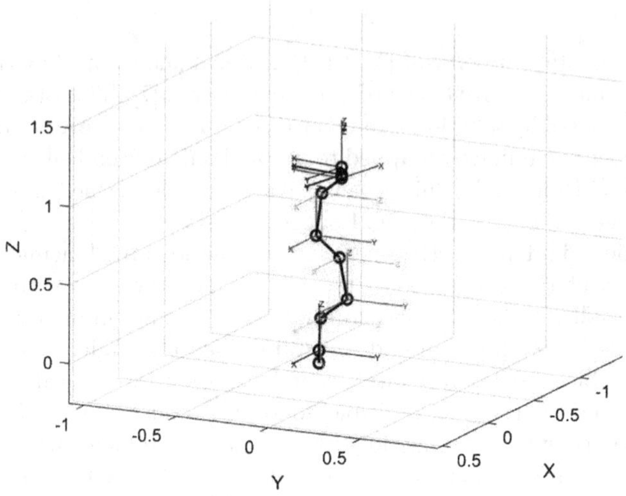

Fig. 2. Kinematic model of the sawyer robot.

Table 1. DH Table for the 7DOF sawyer robotic arm

i	α_i	a_i	d_i	θ_i
1	$-90°$	0.0810	0	θ_1
2	$90°$	0	0.1910	θ_2
3	$-90°$	0	0.3990	θ_3
4	$90°$	0	-0.1683	θ_4
5	$-90°$	0	0.3965	θ_5
6	$90°$	0	0.1360	θ_6
7	0	0	0.1785	θ_7

$$ {}^{i-1}_{i}T = \begin{bmatrix} c\theta_i & -c\alpha_i s\theta_i & s\alpha_i s\theta_i & a_i c\theta_i \\ s\theta_i & c\alpha_i c\theta_i & -s\alpha_i c\theta_i & a_i s\theta_i \\ 0 & s\alpha_i & c\alpha_i & d_i \\ 0 & 0 & 0 & 1 \end{bmatrix} \tag{2} $$

$$ {}^{1}_{7}T = {}^{1}_{2}T * {}^{2}_{3}T * {}^{3}_{4}T * {}^{4}_{5}T * {}^{5}_{6}T * {}^{6}_{7}T \tag{3} $$

$$\begin{cases} -175^\circ \leq \theta_1 \leq 175^\circ \\ -175^\circ \leq \theta_2 \leq 175^\circ \\ -175^\circ \leq \theta_3 \leq 175^\circ \\ -170^\circ \leq \theta_4 \leq 170^\circ \\ -170^\circ \leq \theta_5 \leq 170^\circ \\ -170^\circ \leq \theta_6 \leq 170^\circ \\ -180^\circ \leq \theta_7 \leq 180^\circ \end{cases} \tag{4}$$

4.2 Network Architecture

To solve the forward kinematics problem of Eq. 3 the multi-layered feed-forward neural network of Fig. 3 is proposed. The input layer of the network represents a vector of joint angle values (θ_1, θ_2, θ_3, θ_4, θ_5, θ_6, θ_7), while the output of the network stands for the cartesian coordinates of the robot's end effector. Both the input and output units contain linear units for normalization purposes.

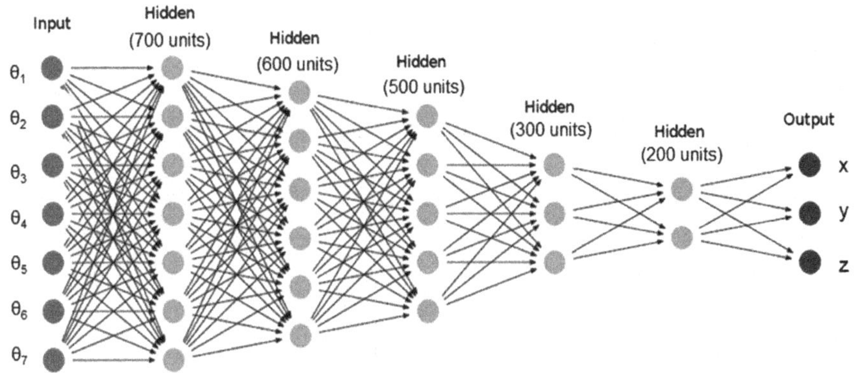

Fig. 3. Network architecture.

The network was trained using the backpropagation algorithm with the mean squared error of the output units as a metric. During the backpropagation process, we used adam optimizer. To produce the training dataset of the network, 4 million random kinematic configurations of joint angles with their equivalent Cartesian positions were utilized. During the creation of the dataset, we made sure that the joint angle values uniformly cover the ranges of Eq. 4. Because of the size of the dataset, the network was trained with a batch size of 100 units and 30 epochs. Also, 10% of the dataset was used for cross validation and 10% was used for testing purposes.

4.3 Experimental Results

After the training was complete, the networks achieved 99.997% validation accuracy. To demonstrate the effectiveness of the network, in this section we will compare the network estimations with the output of the forward equation as computed by Eq. 3 for the same input joint trajectory samples. Figure 4 shows the sample trajectory in joint space.

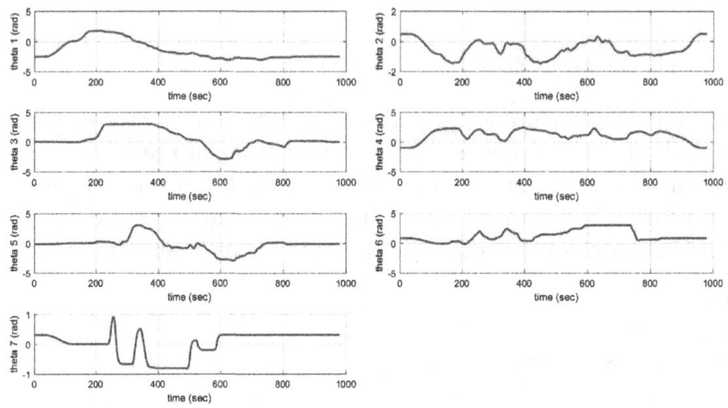

Fig. 4. Experimental joint space trajectories.

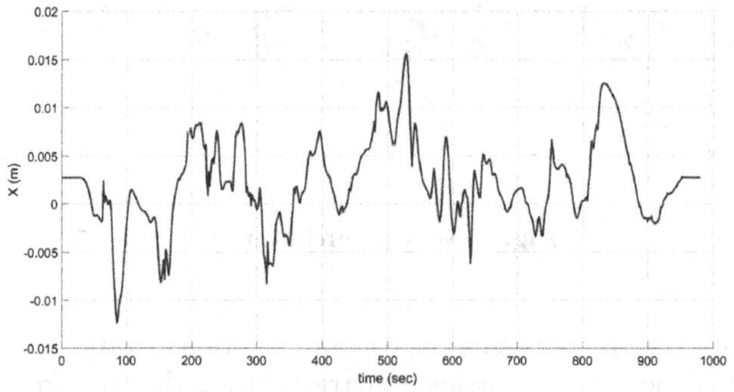

Fig. 5. Error between the forward kinematic equation and the network in the x dimension.

The difference between the estimations of the forward kinematic equations and the proposed network is shown in Figs. 5, 6 and 7, where every figure represents one of the cartesian dimensions of the robot's end effector. Note that the scale in the vertical axis is in meters.

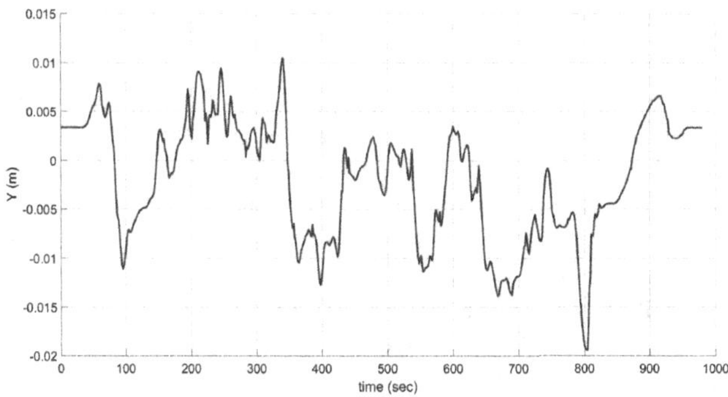

Fig. 6. Error between the forward kinematic equation and the network in the y dimension.

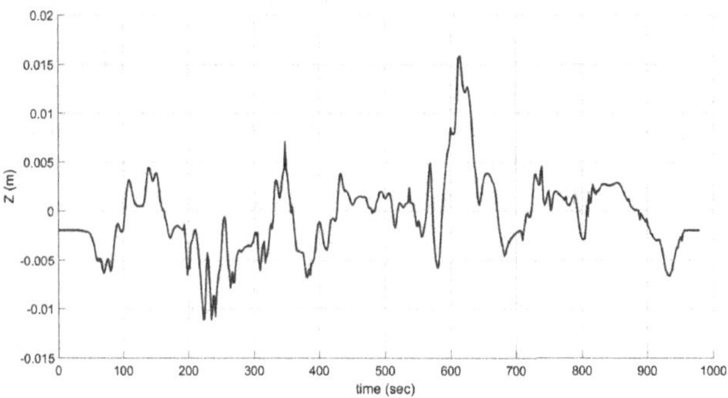

Fig. 7. Error between the forward kinematic equation and the network in the z dimension.

5 Conclusions

In this work, we presented how to estimate the forward kinematic equations of a kinematically redundant robotic arm with a neural network. The proposed network architecture showed promising results between different kinematic configurations. However, it is worthy to mention that although the forward kinematics equations can be estimated algebraically in a simple manner, learning the same equations is an arduous process for a neural network. The proposed architecture was found after training multiple models with different parameters, such as the number of units per level and the number of levels, on the same dataset with different resolution. That was possible to achieve, because the workspace of the robot can not possibly change.

Acknowledgments. This work is supported in part by the National Science Foundation under award numbers 1338118 and 1719031. Any opinions, findings, and conclusions or recommendations expressed in this publication are those of the author(s) and do not necessarily reflect the views of the National Science Foundation.

References

1. Argall, B.D., Chernova, S., Veloso, M., Browning, B.: A survey of robot learning from demonstration. Robot. Auton. Syst. **57**(5), 469–483 (2009)
2. Bingul, Z., Ertunc, H., Oysu, C.: Comparison of inverse kinematics solutions using neural network for 6R robot manipulator with offset. In: 2005 ICSC Congress on Computational Intelligence Methods and Applications, p. 5. IEEE (2005)
3. Craig, J.J.: Introduction to Robotics: Mechanics and Control, vol. 3. Pearson/Prentice Hall, Upper Saddle River (2005)
4. Duka, A.V.: Neural network based inverse kinematics solution for trajectory tracking of a robotic arm. Procedia Technol. **12**, 20–27 (2014)
5. Jin, L., Li, S., Yu, J., He, J.: Robot manipulator control using neural networks: a survey. Neurocomputing **285**, 23–34 (2018)
6. Jin, L., Zhang, Y., Li, S.: Integration-enhanced zhang neural network for real-time-varying matrix inversion in the presence of various kinds of noises. IEEE Trans. Neural Netw. Learn. Syst. **27**(12), 2615–2627 (2016)
7. Jordan, M.I., Rumelhart, D.E.: Forward models: supervised learning with a distal teacher. Cogn. Sci. **16**(3), 307–354 (1992)
8. Karlik, B., Aydin, S.: An improved approach to the solution of inverse kinematics problems for robot manipulators. Eng. Appl. Artif. Intell. **13**(2), 159–164 (2000)
9. Lin, D., Wang, X., Nian, F., Zhang, Y.: Dynamic fuzzy neural networks modeling and adaptive backstepping tracking control of uncertain chaotic systems. Neurocomputing **73**(16–18), 2873–2881 (2010)
10. Nguyen, L., Patel, R., Khorasani, K.: Neural network architectures for the forward kinematics problem in robotics. In: 1990 IJCNN International Joint Conference on Neural Networks, pp. 393–399. IEEE (1990)
11. Tejomurtula, S., Kak, S.: Inverse kinematics in robotics using neural networks. Inf. Sci. **116**(2–4), 147–164 (1999)

Social Media

Hierarchical Attention Networks for User Profile Inference in Social Media Systems

Zhezhou Kang, Xiaoxue Li, Yanan Cao(✉), Yanmin Shang, Yanbing Liu, and Li Guo

Institute of Information Engineering, Chinese Academy of Sciences, Beijing, China
14281111@bjtu.edu.cn,
{lixiaoxue,caoyanan,shangyanmin,liuyanbing,guoli}@iie.ac.cn

Abstract. User profile inference, which aims to portray a user in detail, is one of fundamental tasks in social network analysis. Existing works still suffer from the difficulty in modeling user's explicit attributes and social links, which is mainly caused by the text diversity and complex community structures. In this paper, we propose a hierarchical attention neural network to infer users' missing attributes, which handles the user representation integrating both explicit personal information and social links. The core module is a hierarchical recurrent neural network which encodes both attribute-level and user-level information, and the attention mechanism can adaptively render different attributes and users with different weights. Extensive empirical studies are conducted on two real-world datasets. The experimental results show that our model prominently outperform other comparative deep models in predicting multi-value attributes (especially occupation), verify the effect of using user social links, and reveal different effects of different attention mechanism.

Keywords: Recurrent neural network · Social network analysis
Hierarchical attention networks · Attention mechanism
User attributes inference

1 Introduction

As people's awareness of privacy increases, personal information of social network users becomes more and more difficult to acquire. However, in most cases, if user information can be utilized legally and reasonably, it can significantly improve the quality of user's life. For example, acquiring a user's gender, interest and occupation are very helpful to make more precise advertising or recommendation. Hence, user attributes inference gets more and more attention in both industry and academia.

Existing attribute inference works can be roughly classified into two categories according to the source data. One is based on user content mining and the other is based on social relationship analysis. Content-oriented methods mainly focus on mining user's potential information from their comments on

V. Kůrková et al. (Eds.): ICANN 2018, LNCS 11141, pp. 805–816, 2018.
https://doi.org/10.1007/978-3-030-01424-7_78

the social network platforms. However, a user's comments don't always reflect his/her implicit attributes. Even so, it is difficult to mine the topic from comments precisely. Relationship-oriented works focus on utilizing the social links to propagate or predict unknown labels based on the hypothesis that two linked users may share similar attributes. These methods usually performs poorly in referring multi-value attributes.

In our opinion, user's known attributes and social links are both important information for inferring his/her unknown attributes. So, for each target user u, we build an ego network to integrate u, his/her direct friends and their attributes. In an ego network, a user is represented by an attribute vector, and the ego network is represented by several user vectors (forming a matrix). So, how do we process ego network representation appropriately? How do we figure out the useful users and their attributes exactly? These are still big challenges. To address these problems, we apply hierarchical attention-based Recurrent Neural Network (RNN) to automatically extract important features from an ego-network. Firstly, as the ego network representation consists of users vectors which attributes, the hierarchical structure can observe both attribute-level and user-level information. Secondly, we adopt attribute-level and user level attention mechanism to select relevant users and attributes which contributes more to the target users attribute reference.

In this work, we proposed two different structures of hierarchical attention model. In these two structures, the positions of the attribute-level attention layer are different. In one structure, we add attention on encoded user representation, while in the other one we add inner-attention on original user representation. To evaluate the performance of our different model structures, we carried out several experiments on two real-world datasets. Experimental results show that the hierarchical RNN model with inner-attention mechanism outperforms comparative methods significantly and integrating user links in ego user's representation is very effective.

In summary, our key contributions are as follows: (i) we propose a hierarchical neural network to infer users missing attributes, which handles the user representation integrating both explicit personal information and social links. (ii) We apply two structures of attention mechanism in the hierarchical models to adaptively select relevant friends and attributes, and experimental results verified the effectiveness of our models.

2 Related Work

Existing attribute inference works can roughly divide into content-mining method and social-links analysis method according to the features of source data.

Content-mining methods mainly focus on contents posted by users on social network platforms. They try to extract useful information from user's microblogs and then use it to predict incomplete user attributes. The concept is feasible, but the challenge is how to obtain the exact meaning of these microblogs, which are usually short, emotional, colloquial and diverse. However, machine learning methods have shown great advances in text analysis and image analysis. Work by [1–5] solved this problem by analyzing a large amount of microblogs of a single user. This helps in getting useful information, but it needs a lot computing resources in analyzing a single user. With the rapid growth in social networks, the modality of social data consists of not only texts but also photos and videos, and these data are all used in [3,5]. [3] proposed a semantic attention network based on image for multimodal sentiment analysis and [5] exploited the multimedia information to infer user attributes. These works extend the data which is suitable for user analysis, however, it costs much computing resources, which makes it hard to be applied in large-scale user analysis.

Relationship-based method. [2,4,9,10] considered the contribution of user's social links. Bhattacharya et al. [2] made use of relations between a user and his/her following topics, which helped in getting a better understanding of what the ego user truly expressed without costing too much computing resources. Vidyalakshmi et al. [4] concentrated on the ego network of a certain circle. They inferred ego user attributes by propagating the known attribute value of followers. Work by [2] firstly deduce the topical expertise of popular Twitter users, and then transitively infer the interests of the users who follow them. Li et al. [9] tried to infer user's multi-valued attributes in one trained model. Cao et al. [10] presented an ego-social network model which integrates the target user's attributes, social links and their comments. All of these works get impressive results.

As for models, we apply two structures of hierarchical attention model to our work. Yang et al. proposed a hierarchical attention network for document classification [6]. They designed the model to capture two basic insights about document structure, one at word level and one at the sentence level. Wang et al. proposed an inner attention-based recurrent neural network [7]. They analyzed the deficiency of the traditional attention based RNN models and present three new models which add attention before computing RNN hidden representation. Chen et al. proposed a novel attention-based convolutional neural network (CNN). They applied attention mechanism to CNN [8].

3 Hierarchical Attention Networks

Our work aims to infer a given user's missing attributes (occupation in particular), which is regarded as an attribute classification problem. In order to utilize the user's known attributes and social links, we define an ego-network [9] for each user. The input of our model is the target user's ego-network which is represented as an $(k+1)*m$ matrix. The input matrix and model architecture is shown in Fig. 1. In the input matrix, each column represents one type of attribute and each row represents one user. The first row is the target user and the following k rows represent the target user's friends. Each user has m attributes, such as gender, age, education and etc. In real application, we extend some attributes to multi-dimension, which will be discussed in Sect. 4.2.

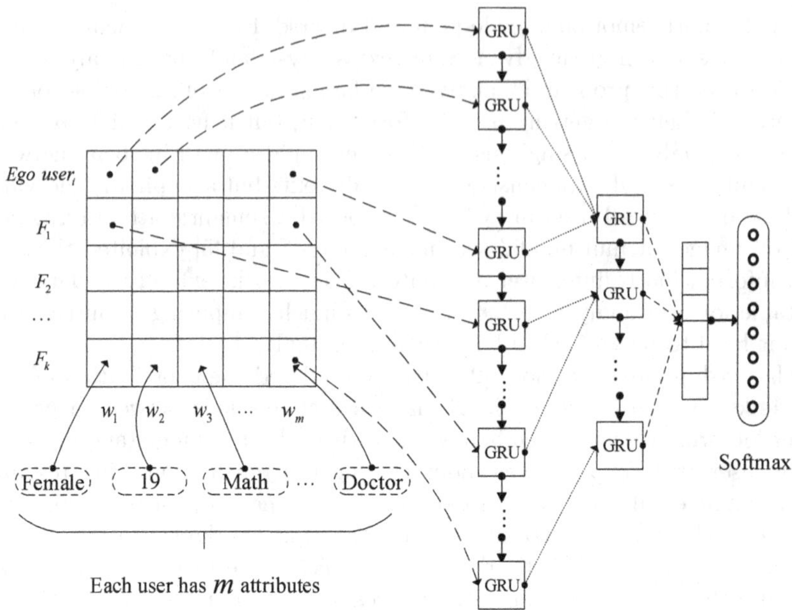

Fig. 1. An example of ego network

Our model contains several recurrent operations, and we take a hierarchical GRU network to extract features of input data. We firstly feed the ego-network matrix to a GRU layer, then we aggregate the representation of all attributes of a single user to form a user vector. Next, we feed all user vectors to the second GRU layer. At last, we get an encoded representation of an ego-network and feed it to the softmax layer to classify the target user to one occupation category.

We design two hierarchical attention network architectures which are respectively shown in Figs. 2 and 3. Both of these architectures consist of several modules: an attribute sequence encoder, an attribute-level attention layer, a user sequence encoder and a user-level attention layer. We describe the details of different components in the following sections.

3.1 GRU-Based Sequence Encoder

Gated recurrent unit (GRU) is a gating mechanism in recurrent neural networks. It can track the state of sequences without using separate memory cells. GRU has fewer parameters than LSTM, because it doesn't contain output gate. GRU has two types of gates: the reset gate r_t and the update gate z_t. The reset gate determines how to combine the new input with the previous memory. The update gate defines how much of the previous memory to keep around and how much new information is added. The idea of using a gating mechanism to learn long-term dependencies is the same as in a LSTM. The GRU computes the new state as follows:

$$h_t = (1 - z_t) \odot h_{t-1} + z_t \odot \tilde{h_t} \quad (1)$$
$$z_t = \sigma(W_z x_t + U_z h_{t-1} + b_z) \quad (2)$$
$$\tilde{h_t} = tanh(W_z x_t + U_z h_{t-1} + b_h) \quad (3)$$
$$r_t = \sigma(W_r x_t + U_r h_{t-1} + b_r) \quad (4)$$

3.2 Hierarchical Attention Based GRU Neural Network

As shown in Fig. 2, given a user u_i ($i \in [0, k]$), we use w_{it} ($t \in [0, m]$) to represent the tth attribute of the ith user. We firstly embed the attribute w_{it} into a vector representation x_{it} through an embedding matrix W_e. Then we use a forward GRU layer f to encode the user attribute x_{it} at time t, and got its hidden status h_{it}.

$$x_{it} = W_e w_{it} \quad (5)$$
$$h_{it} = GRU(x_{it}) \quad (6)$$

In different tasks, we know that not all attributes contribute equally to inferring certain attribute of an ego user. For example, when we aim to predict the

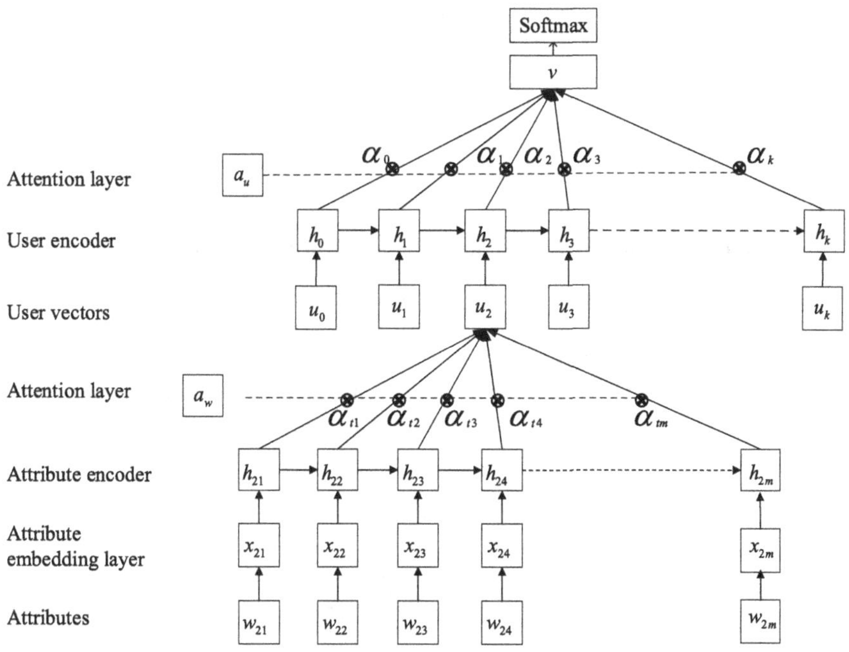

Fig. 2. Structure of hierarchical attention based GRU neural network

ego user's interests, his/her major and gender may contribute more than his/her address. So we applied attention mechanism to self-adaptively pick out important attributes, which is computed as follows.

$$a_{it} = tanh(W_w h_{it} + b_w) \quad (7)$$

$$\alpha_{it} = \frac{\exp(a_{it}^T a_w)}{\Sigma_t \exp(a_{it}^T a_w)} \quad (8)$$

$$u_i = \Sigma_t \alpha_{it} h_{it} \quad (9)$$

In the attention layer, we feed the attribute hidden status h_{it} through a neural network layer to get a_{it} as a hidden representation of h_{it}. Then we measure the importance of an attribute as the similarity of a_{it} with an attribute-level context vector a_w and get a normalized importance weight through a soft-max function. After that, the user vector u_i is computed as a weighted sum of the attribute hidden status.

In the user sequence encoder, we also used a one-layer GRU to encode each user vector u_i:

$$h_i = GRU(u_i) \quad (10)$$

To reward users that contribute more to the ego user's attribute inference, we use attention mechanism again and introduce a user-level context vector a_u which is used to measure the importance of users in the ego-network.

$$a_i = tanh(W_u h_i + b_u) \quad (11)$$

$$\alpha_i = \frac{\exp(a_i^T a_u)}{\Sigma_i exp(a_i^T a_u)} \quad (12)$$

$$v = \Sigma_i \alpha_i h_i \quad (13)$$

Where v represents the ego network that summarizes all information of users in an ego network.

3.3 Hierarchical Inner Attention Based Neural Network

As for inner attention mechanism, we add the attention layer before GRU layer. The structure is shown in Fig. 3. Firstly, we feed attribute vectors x_{it} through a one-layer MLP to get a_{it}. Then we measure the importance of the attributes as the similarity of a_{it} with an attribute-level context vector a_w and get a normalized importance weight through a soft-max function. Then we use GRU to get annotation of attribute.

$$x_{it} = W_e w_{it} \quad (14)$$

$$a_{it} = tanh(W_w x_{it} + b_w) \quad (15)$$

$$\alpha_{it} = \frac{\exp(a_{it}^T a_w)}{\Sigma_t \exp(a_{it}^T a_w)} \quad (16)$$

$$h_{it} = GRU(x_{it} \alpha_{it}) \quad (17)$$

$$u_i = \Sigma_t h_{it} \quad (18)$$

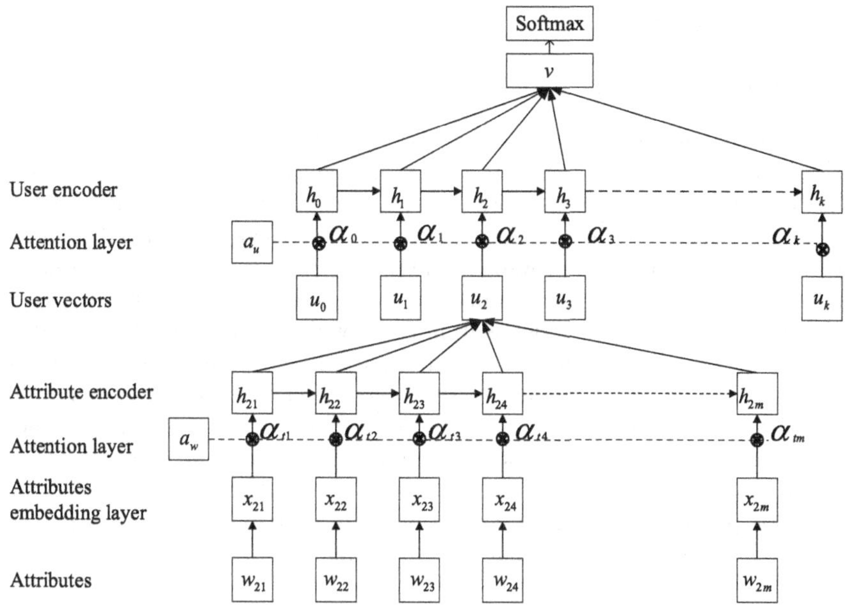

Fig. 3. Structure of hierarchical inner attention based neural network

For user vector u_i, we use attention mechanism and introduce a user-level context vector a_u and use the vector to measure the importance of users.

$$a_i = tanh(W_u u_i + b_u) \tag{19}$$

$$\alpha_i = \frac{\exp(a_i^T a_u)}{\Sigma_i \exp(a_i^T a_u)} \tag{20}$$

$$h_i = GRU(u_i \alpha_i) \tag{21}$$

$$v = \Sigma_i h_i \tag{22}$$

3.4 Ego Network Classification

The ego network vector v is a high level representation of the ego network and can be used as features to infer ego user's attributes.

$$p = softmax(W_c v + b_c) \tag{23}$$

We use the negative log likelihood of the correct labels as training loss:

$$L = -\Sigma_d \log p_{dj} \tag{24}$$

Where j is the label of ego network d.

4 Experiments

4.1 Datasets

In our experiments, we aim to infer the user occupation which is a multi-valued attribute and is more difficult to predict than gender, age and etc. There is no public benchmark in social network user occupation inference problem. So, we evaluate the effect of our model on two real-world datasets constructed from two Chinese online social network website Zhihu and Sina weibo. For each user, we crawled his/her public personal information and social links. For user representation, we randomly select 5 friends from the downloaded datasets for each user. We removed some data with few user information, and preprocess the datasets by deleting special punctuation and symbols. Zhihu dataset consists of 16035 pieces of user information with 9 attributes, including user id, gender, education, major, personal brief introduction and some numerical information like the number of followings, that of followers and etc. Sina Weibo dataset contains 21608 pieces of user basic information with 5 attributes, including gender, address, education, personal signature and company. For both datasets, we use 80% of them for training, 10% for validation and 10% for testing. According to these datasets, we divide occupations into 12 categories in advance.

4.2 User Representation and Dimension Selection

Due to expression diversity in Chinese, these are polysemy and ill-formedness problems, which may result in the sparsity of attribute data. This is a big challenge for training a good supervised model for user profile inference. For example, attributes like university, address, organization commonly has several abbreviations. Taking university as an example, one user's university is "北京交通大学 (Beijing Jiaotong University)" which is a full name, but others may use abbreviations "北京交大 (Beijing Jiao University)" and "北交大 (Bei Jiao University)". In order to identify the similarity between different snippets, there are several relevant methods which solve this problem in grammatical level (such as using q-gram to measure the distance between snippets) or semantic level (such as using topic model or embedding learning to cluster snippets). However, the effectiveness of these methods are limited when the scale of corpus is not large enough.

In this paper, we conduct a shallow processing of users' attributes. We use a matual segmentation tool [11] to divide attribute text into words, and use a word vector to represent one attribute which extend user information dimension. In the above example, we use "北京 (Beijing)", "交通 (Jiaotong)" and "大学 (University) "to be three dimension attributes rather than use "北京交通大学 (Beijing Jiaotong University)" as one attribute. The advantage of this representation is that the full name, abbreviations "北京交大 (Beijing Jiao University)" and "北交大 (Bei Jiao University)" has common words which are represented as independent attribute, as shown in Fig. 4. These common attributes will be utilized to divide users into the same category.

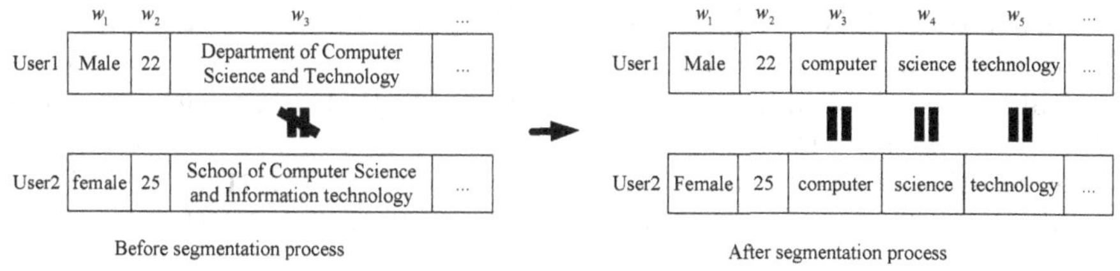

Fig. 4. The preprocessing of user attributes

For each attribute, we choose a fixed number of words as user information. For example, we choose 3 words to represent the user's education and choose 5 for self-introduction. As a result, the attributes of users in Zhihu and Sina are both extended into 21 dimension. Although this method can't solve the similarity measurement problem perfectly, in some way it extend user's information and somehow establishes some connections among users. Most of all, this substantially significantly promotes the prediction precision, although it is. After getting the information that can represent users, we embed this information using word2vec. We set the word embedding dimension to be 256.

4.3 Comparative Methods and Experiment Setting

In our experiments, we test both CNN and RNN model to find out which is more suitable to abstract user features. We also conduct experiments to discuss whether to integrate users' social links with their attributes, whether to use the hierarchical network structure, whether and where to add attention mechanism. For this end, we design different model architectures as comparative methods and baselines in the following.

- **GRU without friends (GRU(NF)).** This model just contains a single layer GRU network followed by a soft-max layer. And the user representation just contains his/her attributes, which doesn't integrate the social links. This representation is denoted as NF for short, and we will not explain it repeatedly in the following.
- **GRU with attention without friends (GRU-ATT(NF)).** This model is used to evaluate the effectiveness of attention in GRU, and it is compared with GRU(UF). This model use an attention mechanism besides the basic GRU network.
- **CNN without attention (CNN(NF)).** This model contains three layers of convolution network which are followed by two max pooling layers. We use filters of three convolution layers with fields 1×3, 1×3 and 1×2. Max-pooling is performed over a 1×2 window, with stride 2. Then it is followed by two layers of fully-connected layer and dropout layer. The final layer is the soft-max layer.
- **CNN with attention (CNN-ATT(NF)).** This model is similar to CNN(NF) but adds an attention layer before the first two max-pooling layers.

- **Hierarchical GRU with friends (HGRU).** In this model, we use the user representation integrating attributes and social links. This model is a hierarchical neural network, it contains two layers of GRU to cope with attribute-level and user-level information respectively.
- **Hierarchical GRU with single layer attention (HGRU-SATT).** It extends HGRU by adding an attention layer to the first GRU layer which cope with attribute-level information.
- **Hierarchical attention-based GRU network (HAGN).** This model contains two layers of GRU network and both of these layers are followed by attention layer.
- **Hierarchical inner attention-based GRU networks (HIAGN).** This model has two GRU layers which are similar with HGRU. The difference is that the attention layer is added before GRU layers.

For each layer of GRU encoder, the dropout is set to be 0.8. For training, the mini batch size is set as 100. We use adam as the optimizer and cross entropy as the loss function. The learning rate is set to be 0.001.

4.4 Result and Analysis

The experimental results of comparative models on two datasets are shown in Table 1. We use accuracy, precision, recall and F1 score as evaluation metrics. These results are analyzed in detail in the following.

Comparison Between CNN and GRU Architecture. To concern on the results of CNN(NF) and CNN-ATT(NF), we can find that the F1 score of CNN architecture is lower than 50%. In comparison, using the same user representation with CNN, both GRU(NF) and GRU-ATT(NF) reached about 70% F1-score, which performed much better. GRU uses gate mechanism to prevent vanishing gradient problem. It can be trained to keep information from long ago, without washing it through time. However, CNN is not suitable for capturing sequence information. It can be greatly affected by user order, representation and users' relevance.

Evaluation of Attention Mechanism. To compare GRU(NF) with GRU-ATT(NF), CNN(NF) with CNN-ATT(NF), results show that the attention mechanism is very useful for both CNN and single-layer GRU. The attention mechanism promotes the effectiveness of CNN more significantly because it can pay attention to important attributes which are more relevant to the user occupation. However, we note that the F1-score of HGRU-SATT is close to or even lower than that of HGRU, which demonstrates that the attention used after the first GRU layer maybe overwhelmed to select from high-dimensional attributes including the target user's attributes and his/her friends' attributes.

Compared with CNN models and GRU baseline models, both HAGN and HIAGN show great advances in our task. For Zhihu corpus, HAGN achieve the

Table 1. Experimental results of comparative models on Zhihu and Sina corpus

Model	Zhihu data				Sina data			
	Accuracy	Precision	Recall	F1 score	Accuracy	Precision	Recall	F1 score
CNN(NF)	73.067	38.384	41.474	39.194	56.840	36.066	22.481	23.368
CNN-ATT(NF)	80.423	55.966	54.469	54.413	70.273	72.162	39.885	46.499
GRU(NF)	90.897	76.412	75.064	75.423	83.150	69.364	68.267	68.585
GRU-ATT(NF)	91.022	77.765	75.884	76.500	86.900	74.696	70.997	72.211
HGRU	92.955	82.888	88.817	84.116	88.523	78.430	79.860	78.666
HGRU-SATT	93.079	85.118	83.837	84.067	88.570	77.756	79.836	78.506
HAGN	*95.137	86.955	83.805	85.186	89.356	78.528	79.142	78.562
HAIGN	92.830	86.250	88.993	*86.050	*91.254	84.134	82.433	*83.169

highest accuracy but HIAGN achieve the highest F1 score, which means HIAGN do well in both positive and negative samples. For Sina corpus, HIAGN achieve highest score in both accuracy and F1 score. In summary, the inner-attention which used before the GRU layer performs better than that used after the GRU layer.

Effectiveness of Using Social Links. In Table 1, the first four methods doesn't utilize the ego user's social links, while the last four regard social links as important information for user profile inference. Experimental results shows that hierarchical GRU networks which use social links always performs better than GRU(NF) and CNN(NF). That is because our hierarchical models have two advantages: (i) we integrate the social friends' information in the input user representation which contributes to portraying the ego user; (ii) the hierarchical GRU networks not only encode the target user's attributes but also encode his/her friends' attributes. In the experiments, we just randomly select 5 social links for each ego user, which may be not very close to the ego user or contain useless information. What's more, integrating friends' attributes in an ego user's representation may cause confusion for the user's original information. However, from the results, it can be seen that HAGN and HAIGN improves the performance of HGRU, which demonstrates that the addition of attention after the second GRU layer make the models pay attention to important users which are close to the ego user.

5 Conclusion

In this paper, we construct the ego network and feed the network to hierarchical attention based model. We use a brief method to processing users' irregular information. We apply two structures of hierarchical attention network to user attribute inference. The models are tested on two datasets and both show great results. For future work, we plan to find an effective method to choose relevant friends that should be added to an ego network. This may contribute to improving the performance.

Acknowledgement. This work was supported by the National Key Research and Development program of China (No. 2016YFB0801300), the National Natural Science Foundation of China grants (No. 61602466, No. 61702234).

References

1. Yo, T., Sasahara, K.: Inference of personal attributes from tweets using machine learning (2017)
2. Bhattacharya, P., Zafar, M.B., Ganguly, N., Ghosh, S., Gummadi, K.P.: Inferring user interests in the twitter social network, pp. 357–360 (2014)
3. Xu, N.: Analyzing multimodal public sentiment based on hierarchical semantic attentional network. In: IEEE International Conference on Intelligence and Security Informatics, pp. 152–154 (2017)
4. Vidyalakshmi, B.S., Wong, R.K., Chi, C.H.: User attribute inference in directed social networks as a service. In: IEEE International Conference on Services Computing, pp. 9–16 (2016)
5. Park, M.-H., Hong, J.-H., Cho, S.-B.: Location-based recommendation system using bayesian user's preference model in mobile devices. In: Indulska, J., Ma, J., Yang, L.T., Ungerer, T., Cao, J. (eds.) UIC 2007. LNCS, vol. 4611, pp. 1130–1139. Springer, Heidelberg (2007). https://doi.org/10.1007/978-3-540-73549-6_110
6. Yang, Z., Yang, D., Dyer, C., He, X., Smola, A., Hovy, E.: Hierarchical attention networks for document classification. In: Conference of the North American Chapter of the Association for Computational Linguistics: Human Language Technologies, pp. 1480–1489 (2017)
7. Wang, B., Liu, K., Zhao, J.: Inner attention based recurrent neural networks for answer selection. In: Meeting of the Association for Computational Linguistics, pp. 1288–1297 (2016)
8. Chen, K., Wang, J., Chen, L.C., Gao, H., Xu, W., Nevatia, R.: ABC-CNN: an attention based convolutional neural network for visual question answering. Comput. Sci. (2015)
9. Li, X., Cao, Y., Shang, Y., Liu, Y., Tan, J., Guo, L.: Inferring user profiles in online social networks based on convolutional neural network. In: Li, G., Ge, Y., Zhang, Z., Jin, Z., Blumenstein, M. (eds.) KSEM 2017. LNCS (LNAI), vol. 10412, pp. 274–286. Springer, Cham (2017). https://doi.org/10.1007/978-3-319-63558-3_23
10. Cao, Y., Wang, S., Li, X., Cao, C., Liu, Y., Tan, J.: Inferring Social Network User's Interest Based on Convolutional Neural Network (2017)
11. Chinese Words Segementation Tool. https://pypi.org/project/jieba/

A Topological k-Anonymity Model Based on Collaborative Multi-view Clustering

Sarah Zouinina[1,2(✉)], Nistor Grozavu[1], Younès Bennani[1], Abdelouahid Lyhyaoui[2], and Nicoleta Rogovschi[3]

[1] Université Paris 13, Sorbonne Paris Cité, LIPN UMR 7030 CNRS, Paris, France
zouinina@lipn.univ-paris13.fr, sarahzouinina1@gmail.com
[2] Ecole Nationale des Sciences Appliqués de Tanger, LTI, Tangier, Morocco
[3] Université Paris 5, Sorbonne Paris Cité, LIPADE, Paris, France

Abstract. Data anonymization is the process of de-identifying sensitive data while preserving its format and data type. The masked data can be a realistic or a random sequence of data, dependent on the technique used for anonymization. Individual privacy can be at risk if a published data set is not properly de-identified. The most known approach of anonymization is k-anonymity that can be viewed as clustering with a constraint of k minimum objects in every cluster. In this paper, we propose a new anonymization approach based on multi-view topological collaborative clustering. The proposed method has the advantage of detecting the k level automatically. The aim of collaborative clustering is to reveal the common structure of data using different views on variables, it allows to take into account other knowledges without recourse to the data in an unsupervised learning frame. The proposed approach has been validated on several data sets, and experimental results have shown very promising performance.

Keywords: Anonymization · Collaborative clustering · Multi-view

1 Introduction

In recent years, with the increase of data volumes created by the social media and intensive internet use, the protection of individuals privacy had become a necessity. Many techniques were introduced to study the risk of identity disclosure and the possibility of data anonymization.

The first approaches were mainly based on the randomization method which consists of adding noise to data [1], this technique was proven to be inefficient and many data reconstruction approaches were presented [10]. The risk of data privacy breach using randomization was overtaken by the emergence of the k-anonymization [17] technique. This group based anonymization method outputs a dataset containing at least k identical records and the anonymization is achieved by firstly removing the key-identifiers like the name and the address and secondly by *generalizing* and/or *suppressing* the pseudo-identifiers which

V. Kůrková et al. (Eds.): ICANN 2018, LNCS 11141, pp. 817–827, 2018.
https://doi.org/10.1007/978-3-030-01424-7_79

are for example: the date of birth, the ZIP code, the gender and the age. The k value should be chosen in a way to preserve the information provided by the database.

The efficiency of this approach was widely studied [2,12,15] and it gave a strong basis to further works on anonymization. Since the k-anonymity is a group based method, clustering was considered as one of its strong assets. Creating small groups of k elements and replacing the data by the group representatives gives a good tradeoff between the information loss and the potential data identification risk [3].

In this paper, we are interested in the unsupervised learning and we will use Kohonen's Self Organizing Maps [11] as a clustering model. This neural network has given rise to numerous practical applications in order to visualize and perform the dimension reduction. At the end of this topological learning, the "similar" data will be collected in clusters, which correspond to the sets of similar patterns. These clusters can be represented by a more concise information, such as their gravity center or different statistical moments. As expected, this information is easier to manipulate than the original data points.

To improve the clustering quality we build a collaborative model combining the results of the SOMs already created. The Collaborative Clustering [16] enables the models to exchange their key indicators with the purpose of making their clustering more performant [8,16].

The approach proposed in this paper is split into three major steps, the first is the collaboration step where we apply the collaborative muliview algorithm. The second is the pre-anonymization step which consists of coding the data set using the BMUs and the third step is the fine-tuning and anonymization step, where the information coded and reconstructed is learned through a global SOM, recoded using the BMUs and evaluated using accuracy.

The rest of this paper is organized as follows: we present the principle of the anonymization and collaborative clustering models in Sect. 2 and the proposed anonymization method with discussion of the results in Sect. 3.

2 Related Works

2.1 Clustering and Anonymization

Anonymizing tabular data is not an automatic process, and it is very problem specific. The k-anonymity model, for example, assumes that person-specific data are stored in a table of attributes and records. To anonymize a dataset, a technique that consists of suppressing or/and generalizing the *quasi-identifiers* was proposed in a way for each record to have at least *(k–1)* similar records. As an example, people in the United States are identified by a set of attributes such as ZIP, gender, date of birth. Each attribute alone is not significant, but the combination of them all may explicit a particular individual that is why they are called *quasi-identifiers.* The goal of the k-anonymity model is to transform a table so that associations of elements become improbable, without compromising the quality of the information enclosed in the dataset.

The first algorithm that combines clustering and anonymization was introduced by Li et al. [13]. The algorithm measures the data distortion caused by generalization using a *weighted hierarchical distance* calculated following the domain generalization hierarchies. The algorithm forms equivalence classes from the database by finding an equivalence class with record's size smaller than k. It measures the distance between the found equivalence class and the other equivalence classes and fuses it with the nearest equivalence class in order to form a cluster of at least k element with minimal information distortion. This method gives good computational results but its very time consuming.

The second algorithm was detailed in [3], it forms intersimilar clusters of at least k records. The value of k is fixed, looks for the record and the cluster with the minimal information loss, adds the record to the cluster and iterates until getting clusters with at least k members. Another approach is the *Clustering based greedy algorithm.* Introduced by Loukides et al. [14], it focuses on capturing the usefulness of the data taking in account the attribute, the tuples diversity and a clustering algorithm. This algorithm is similar to the previous k-member clustering algorithms [3] but with the constraint of maximizing the dissimilarity of sensitive data values (privacy) and minimizing the similarity of the quasi-identifiers (usefulness).

Our approach consists of anonymizing tabular data using multi-view topological collaborative clustering [7], to do so, we start by choosing the number of views to use then, we randomly subset the dataset vertically and we feed each subset to a SOM to get the codebooks. After getting the first results we increase the quality of the coding by making the SOMs collaborate between each other. We code the output data using the codeword parts of each element provided by each map, we reconstruct the dataset and we add a fine-tuning layer using a global SOM clustering and we recode the data once again. Lastly we proceed by evaluating the level of k anonymization and the accuracy of each coded data set to quantify its utility to further analyses.

2.2 Multi-view Topological Collaborative Clustering

Topological learning aims to develop methods grounded on statistics to recover the topological invariants from the observed data points [4]. The models we are interested in are those that both, reduce dimension and achieve clustering. Since SOM models [11] allow projection in small spaces that are generally two dimensional and they are often used for visualization and unsupervised topological clustering. In order to improve the SOM's clustering quality, we use the topological collaboration approach and we study the collaboration between several clustering results, specifically the collaboration between several self-organizing maps outputs. Each dataset is clustered through the SOM approach, and to simplify the formalism, the maps build from various datasets will have the same dimensions (number of neurons) and the same structure (the structural topology).

The main idea of the used collaborations is that if an observation from the ii-th dataset is projected on the j-th neuron in the ii - SOM map, then that same observation in the jj-th dataset will be projected on the same j neuron of the jj-th map or one of its neighboring neurons. In other words, neurons that correspond to different maps should capture the same observations. Therefore we added to the classical SOM objective function an additional term reflecting the principle of collaboration. Based on the works of [8,9], we add a new collaboration step to estimate the importance of the collaboration, during the collaborative learning process. Formally, the objective function is composed of two terms:

$$R^{[ii]}(\chi, w) = R^{[ii]}_{SOM}(\chi, w) + (\lambda^{[jj]}_{[ii]})^2 R^{[ii]}_{Col}(\chi, w) \tag{1}$$

with

$$R^{[ii]}_{SOM}(\chi, w) = \sum_{i=1}^{N}\sum_{j=1}^{|w|} K^{[ii]}_{\sigma(j,\chi(x_i))} \|x^{[ii]}_i - w^{[ii]}_j\|^2 \tag{2}$$

$$R^{[ii]}_{Col}(\chi, w) = \sum_{jj=1, jj\neq ii}^{P} \sum_{i=1}^{N}\sum_{j=1}^{|w|} \left(K^{[ii]}_{\sigma(j,\chi(x_i))} - K^{[jj]}_{\sigma(j,\chi(x_i))}\right)^2 * D_{ij} \tag{3}$$

$$with\ \ D_{ij} = \|x^{[ii]}_i - w^{[ii]}_j\|^2 \tag{4}$$

where P represents the number of views, N - the number of observations, $|w|$ is the number of prototype vectors from the ii SOM (the number of neurons). $\chi(x_i)$ is the assignment function which allows to find the Best Matching Unit (BMU), it selects the neuron with the closest prototype from the data x_i using the Euclidean distance.

The value of the collaboration link λ is determined during the first phase of the collaboration step. This parameter allows to determine the importance of the collaboration between each two SOMs. Its value is in the interval [1–10], 1 - for the neutral link, when no importance to collaboration is given, and 10 for the maximal collaboration within a map. Its value changes for each iteration during the collaboration step. In the case of the collaborative learning, as it is shown in the Algorithm 1, this value depends on topological similarity between both collaboration maps.

This function depends on the distance between two neurons and is defined as follows:

$$K^{[cc]}_{\sigma(i,j)} = exp\left(-\frac{\sigma^2(i,j)}{T^2}\right) \tag{5}$$

$\sigma(i,j)$ represents the distance between two neurons i and j from the map, and it is defined as the length of the shortest path linking cells i and j on the SOM. $K^{[cc]}_{\sigma(i,j)}$ is the neighborhood function on the $SOM[cc]$ between two cells i and j. T is the temperature which allows to control the size of the neighborhood influence of a cell on the map, it decreases with the T parameter. The value of T can be decreased between two values T_{max} and T_{min}.

The nature of the neighborhood function $K^{[cc]}_{\sigma(i,j)}$ is identical for all the maps, but its value changes from one map to another: it depends on the closest prototype to the observation that is not necessarily the same for all the SOM maps.

Algorithm 1: The Topological Collaborative Multi-view Algorithm.

Input : P views dataset $V[ii]$
Output: P SOMs optimized $\{w[ii]\}_{ii=1}^{P}$
1. SOMs building:
for $ii = 1$ **to** P **do**
Build SOM for view $V[ii]$

$$w[ii] \leftarrow \arg, \min_{w} \left[R_{SOM}^{[ii]}(\chi, w) \right]$$

Compute DB index for $SOM[ii]$ where $DB[ii]$ is the Davies Bouldin index [?] computed using $w[ii]$

$$DB_{Beforecollab}[ii] \leftarrow DB[ii]$$

end
2. Collaborative learning:
for $ii = 1$ **to** P **do**
for $jj = 1,\ jj \neq ii$ **to** P **do**

$$\lambda_{[ii]}^{[jj]}(t+1) \leftarrow \lambda_{[ii]}^{[jj]}(t) + \frac{\sum_{i=1}^{N} \sum_{j=1}^{|w|} K_{\sigma(j,\chi(x_i))}^{[ii]}}{2 \sum_{i=1}^{N} \sum_{j=1}^{|w|} \left(K_{\sigma(j,\chi(x_i))}^{[ii]} - K_{\sigma(j,\chi(x_i))}^{[jj]} \right)^2}$$

$$w_{jk}^{[ii]}(t+1) \leftarrow w_{jk}^{[ii]}(t) + \frac{\sum\limits_{i=1}^{N} K_{\sigma(j,\chi(x_i))}^{[ii]} x_{ik}^{[ii]} + \sum\limits_{jj=1, jj \neq ii}^{P} \sum\limits_{i=1}^{N} \lambda_{[ii]}^{[jj]} L_{ij} x_{ik}^{[ii]}}{\sum\limits_{i=1}^{N} K_{\sigma(j,\chi(x_i))}^{[ii]} + \sum\limits_{jj=1, jj \neq ii}^{P} \sum\limits_{i=1}^{N} \lambda_{[ii]}^{[jj]} L_{ij}}$$

$$DB_{AfterCollab}[ii] \leftarrow DB[ii]$$

if *($DB_{AfterCollab}[ii] \geq DB_{BeforeCollab}[ii]$)* **then**

$$w_{jk}^{[ii]}(t+1) \leftarrow w_{jk}^{[ii]}(t)$$

end
end
end

3 Proposed Anonymization Model

3.1 Experimental Protocol

The proposed anonymization method uses the multi-view approach with the purpose of treating complex data and multisources data. This technique is also used to preserve the quality of the dataset to recode and prevent the dimensionality curse. The number of subsets to be used for collaboration is fixed by the user and it depends on the size of the data. The algorithm 1 use classical SOM and collaborative paradigm to form the maps by exchanging the topological information between the collaborated maps. In the pre-anonymization step shown in algorithm 2, the dataset is coded using the prototypes of the best matching units for each data point. At the end of this step, the output is a pre-anonymized dataset that will be fine-tuned using a SOM model where the map size is determined by the Kohonen heuristic [11]. The resulting dataset is recoded using the prototypes of the closest object to the BMU and we examine the anonymity level of the dataset. In the proposed experiences we use a simple decision tree model to classify the original data and the coded data and we compare the accuracy results.

Algorithm 2: The proposed Anonymization approach.

Input : D dataset to anonymize
P number of views $V[ii]$
Output: Anonymized dataset
k anonymity level
Collaboration step:
Randomly generate P views $V[ii]$
Use the collaboration algorithm presented in Algorithm 1 with all $V[ii]$
Pre-Anonymization:
For each $V[ii]$, $ii = 1$ to P :
Find the BMU (Best Matching Unit) for each object in $V[ii]$ using corresponding $w[ii]$
Code the dataset D using all code $V[ii]$, output result in D'
Fine-tuning and anonymization:
Build a global SOM using the pre-anonymized dataset D'
Find the BMU for each object in D'
Recode the dataset, output results in D'' and evaluate the k-anonymity level of D''

3.2 Data Sets

The approach presented earlier was tested on five real world datasets available for public use in the UCI Machine learning repository [6]. The DrivFace data set (606×6400) is an image sequence of subjects while driving in real scenarios, it was acquired over different days from 4 drivers (2 women and 2 men) with several features. Ecoli data (336×8) contains protein localization sites. The third data set is the Glass data set, containing 214 instances and 10 attributes with the aim of determining the types of glass based on their oxide content. The fourth data set which is Waveform (5000×40) describes 3 types of waves with an added noise. The fifth data set is the Wine data that relates to a chemical analysis of wines grown in the same region in Italy but derived from different cultivars. The last experiences were made on Yeast data (1484×8) which is also a protein data.

3.3 Experimental Results

For each dataset we experience the performance of the method by varying the number of views, the maps sizes and the collaboration method. We then test the utility of the anonymized data by learning it by a decision tree model using 10 fold cross validation. We compared the accuracy of the original data with the anonymized one and computed a 95% confidence interval. All these results are represented in Table 1. In most of the cases, we remark that the accuracy of the classification model is getting higher or do not change drastically after the collaboration (it strongly depends on the relevance of the collaborative map). The same analysis can be made for the *DB* index which decreases after the collaboration using a relevant map.

Table 1. Accuracy and confidence interval before and after collaboration with k anonymity level before fine-tuning.

	DrivFace	Ecoli	Glass
Acc-Init-without-anonym	92.24	82.44	69.63
95% confidence interval	[89.86, 94.62]	[77.84, 87.04]	[61.76, 77.50]
Acc-Before-Collab	92.24	79.46	95.79
95% confidence interval	[90.77, 93.71]	[75.14, 83.78]	[93.15, 98.43]
Acc-After-Collab	91.24	82.14	96.26
95% confidence interval	[89.29 , 93.19]	[81.40, 87.64]	[93.60, 98.92]
	Waveform	Wine	Yeast
Acc-Init-without-anonym	76.88	88.76	83.63
95% confidence interval	[75.89, 77.87]	[84.72, 92.80]	[81.66, 85.60]
Acc-Before-Collab	81.98	89.89	86.05
95% confidence interval	[80.37, 83.59]	[85.88, 93.90]	[85.23, 86.87]
Acc-After-Collab	81.94	88.76	84.30
95% confidence interval	[80.67, 83.21]	[85.37, 92.15]	[82.91, 85.69]

Before the fine-tuning, the k-anonymity level was equal to 1 and after adding the last layer of anonymization, the accuracy slightly decreased but we gained in terms of anonymization. The Fig. 1, is a representation of the results of the accuracy at each step of the process.

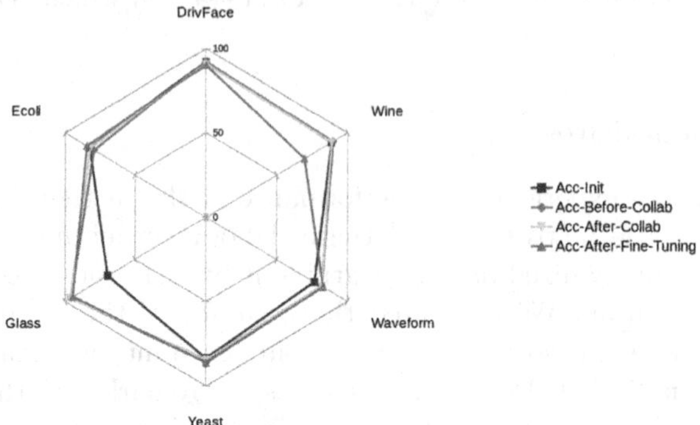

Fig. 1. Comparison of accuracy results before/after collaboration in the pre-anonymization step and accuracy after the last anonymization step

Table 2. DB index before and after collaboration.

	DrivFace	Ecoli	Glass	Waveform	Wine	Yeast
DB-Before-Collab	7.94	4.23	5.16	5.35	18.74	3.97
DB-After-Collab	7.56	4.16	3.70	5.28	16.71	3.94
K-Anonymity-Level	1	1	1	1	1	1

We choose the Davies Bouldin index [5] as an internal index between two clusters, we seek clusterings that minimize the DB, and thus have minimum possible similarity with the clusters. The Table 2 shows that the DB index after collaboration decreases, so, the collaboration impacts the quality of the clustering positively.

The Table 3 shows an amelioration of the anonymization process. Indeed, there is a slight decrease in performance (Accuracy), but a clear improvement in the quality of anonymization. The value of k is no longer a constant equal to 1 but variable according to the datasets and this change guarantees a better quality of data anonymization.

Figure 2 shows a PCA of the Ecoli, Waveform and Yeast data sets before and after anonymization. The goal of these projections is to illustrate how the method of anonymization proposed doesn't change the topological structure of the dataset. The number of points represented after the anonymization look fewer than the number of points presented before the anonymization, this appearance comes from the fact that each point is presented k times, in other

Table 3. Accuracy, confidence interval and k-anonymity level after Fine tuning.

	DrivFace	Ecoli	Glass
Acc-Init (without anonymization)	92.24	82.44	69.63
95% confidence interval	[89.86, 94.62]	[77.84, 87.04]	[61.76, 77.50]
Acc-After-Fine-Tuning	90.26	84.52	94.39
95% confidence interval	[87.43, 93.09]	[81.4, 87.64]	[91.27, 97.51]
K-Anonymity-Level	10	2	5
	Waveform	Wine	Yeast
Acc-Init (without anonymization)	76.88	88.76	83.63
95% confidence interval	[75.89, 77.87]	[84.72, 92.80]	[81.66, 85.60]
Acc-After-Fine-Tuning	83.00	69.66	86.25
95% confidence interval	[82.36, 83.64]	[65.48, 73.84]	[85.02, 87.84]
K-Anonymity-Level	4	3	3

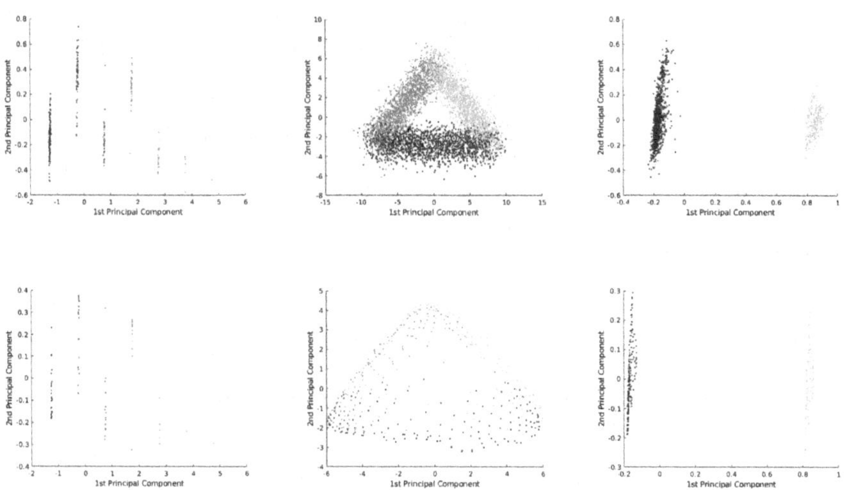

Fig. 2. PCA on data sets from top to bottom before and after anonymization (from left to right representations of Ecoli, Waveform and Yeast data sets).

words, after anonymization, the points projected are k times superposed. Also, in Fig. 2, classes are well defined and the regions are respected before and after anonymization.

4 Conclusion

In this paper we presented a new anonymization approach based on multi-view topological collaborative clustering. The algorithm proposed de-identifies a dataset using multi-view topological collaborative clustering with the purpose of treating complex and multisources data. This technique is also used to preserve the quality of the dataset to recode and prevent the dimensionality curse. In contrast to the k-anonymization models based on clustering, the proposed method has the advantage of detecting the k level automatically, the k value is determined from the size of the elements clustered in the same neuron. Also, it gives good results even with high dimensional datasets. We illustrated the power of this technique using five real datasets and the obtained coded datasets give a good tradeoff between the anonymization level and the accuracy results. As a future work, the collaboration with different datasets can be performed in order to increase the quality of the anonymized dataset by minimizing the loss of information.

References

1. Agrawal, R., Srikant, R.: Privacy-preserving data mining. In: ACM Sigmod Record, vol. 29, pp. 439–450. ACM (2000)
2. Bayardo, R.J., Agrawal, R.: Data privacy through optimal k-anonymization. In: Proceedings of the 21st International Conference on Data Engineering. ICDE 2005, pp. 217–228. IEEE (2005)
3. Byun, J.-W., Kamra, A., Bertino, E., Li, N.: Efficient k-anonymization using clustering techniques. In: Kotagiri, R., Krishna, P.R., Mohania, M., Nantajeewarawat, E. (eds.) DASFAA 2007. LNCS, vol. 4443, pp. 188–200. Springer, Heidelberg (2007). https://doi.org/10.1007/978-3-540-71703-4_18
4. Cornuéjols, A., Wemmert, C., Gançarski, P., Bennani, Y.: Collaborative clustering: why, when, what and how. Inf. Fusion **39**, 81–95 (2018). https://doi.org/10.1016/j.inffus.2017.04.008
5. Davies, D.L., Bouldin, D.W.: A cluster separation measure. IEEE Trans. Pattern Anal. Mach. Intell. PAMI **1**(2), 224–227 (1979). https://doi.org/10.1109/TPAMI.1979.4766909
6. Dheeru, D., Karra Taniskidou, E.: UCI machine learning repository (2017). http://archive.ics.uci.edu/ml
7. Ghassany, M., Grozavu, N., Bennani, Y.: Collaborative multi-view clustering. In: The 2013 International Joint Conference on Neural Networks, IJCNN 2013, Dallas, TX, USA, August 4–9, 2013, pp. 1–8. IEEE (2013). https://doi.org/10.1109/IJCNN.2013.6707037
8. Grozavu, N., Bennani, Y.: Topological Collaborative Clustering. In: 17th International Conference on Neural Information Processing, LNCS. ICONIP 2010. Springer (2010)
9. Grozavu, N., Ghassany, M., Bennani, Y.: Learning confidence exchange in collaborative clustering. In: IJCNN. pp. 872–879 (2011)
10. Huang, Z., Du, W., Chen, B.: Deriving private information from randomized data. In: Proceedings of the 2005 ACM SIGMOD International Conference on Management of Data, pp. 37–48. ACM (2005)
11. Kohonen, T.: Self-organizing Maps. Springer-Verlag, Berlin (1995). https://doi.org/10.1007/978-3-642-97610-0
12. LeFevre, K., DeWitt, D.J., Ramakrishnan, R.: Mondrian multidimensional k-anonymity. In: Proceedings of the 22nd International Conference on Data Engineering. ICDE 2006, pp. 25–25. IEEE (2006)

13. Li, J., Wong, R.C.-W., Fu, A.W.-C., Pei, J.: Achieving k-anonymity by clustering in attribute hierarchical structures. In: Tjoa, A.M., Trujillo, J. (eds.) DaWaK 2006. LNCS, vol. 4081, pp. 405–416. Springer, Heidelberg (2006). https://doi.org/10.1007/11823728_39
14. Loukides, G., Shao, J.: Capturing data usefulness and privacy protection in k-anonymisation. In: Proceedings of the 2007 ACM Symposium on Applied Computing, pp. 370–374. ACM (2007)
15. Machanavajjhala, A., Kifer, D., Gehrke, J., Venkitasubramaniam, M.: l-diversity: Privacy beyond k-anonymity **1**(1), 3. http://dl.acm.org/citation.cfm?id=1217302
16. Pedrycz, W.: Collaborative fuzzy clustering. Pattern Recognit. Lett. **23**(14), 1675–1686 (2002)
17. Sweeney, L.: Achieving k-anonymity privacy protection using generalization and suppression. Int. J. Uncertain. Fuzziness Knowl.-Based Syst. **10**(5), 571–588 (2002)

A Credibility-Based Analysis of Information Diffusion in Social Networks

Sabina-Adriana Floria[1], Florin Leon[1(✉)], and Doina Logofătu[2]

[1] Department of Computer Science and Engineering, "Gheorghe Asachi" Technical University of Iaşi, Iaşi, Romania
{sabina.floria, florin.leon}@tuiasi.ro
[2] Faculty of Computer Science and Engineering, Frankfurt University of Applied Sciences, Frankfurt, Germany
logofatu@fb2.fra-uas.de

Abstract. Social networks have many advantages and they are very popular. The number of people having at least one account on a certain social network has grown considerably. Social networks allow people to connect and interact more easily with one another, leading to a much easier way to obtain information. However one major disadvantage of social networks is that some information may be untrue. In this paper we propose a protocol in which the network becomes more immune to the diffusion of false information. Our approach is based on evidence theory with Dempster-Shafer and Yager's rule which plays an important role in an individual's decision whether to send further the received information or not. We also took into consideration the confidence degree of the neighbours regarding the information which is spread by a specific source node. Furthermore, we propose a simulation algorithm that allows us to observe the diffusion of two contradictory information spread by two different source nodes. The experimental results show that the true information spreads more easily if the ground truth is sometimes revealed, even rarely.

Keywords: Information credibility · Information diffusion · Social networks Confidence degree

1 Introduction

In recent years, social networks have had a quick development and an increase in their diversity, so people can connect and interact with other users in a very easy way. A social network is an efficient way of spreading news and facts, but it also has the disadvantage that some information may be untrue. In this paper we propose a protocol that makes the network more immune to the diffusion of false information based on evidence theory with Dempster-Shafer and Yager's rule. Evidence theory can be considered an extension of the classical probability model because the single value that represents a probability is replaced by confidence intervals.

V. Kůrková et al. (Eds.): ICANN 2018, LNCS 11141, pp. 828–838, 2018.
https://doi.org/10.1007/978-3-030-01424-7_80

1.1 Dempster-Shafer Theory

When we relate to some information, there may be different evidence to support it in different and possibly contradictory degrees. A first way to combine evidence from different sources was developed by Dempster and Shafer [1]. Beliefs from different sources are represented by an interval in which the lower bound is called *Belief* (denoted *Bel*) and the upper bound is called *Plausibility* (denoted *Pl*). For a piece of information A, the plausibility is determined as follows:

$$Pl(A) = 1 - Bel(\overline{A}) \tag{1}$$

The values for A and not A ($\overline{A}$) are computed independently. Both A and $\overline{A}$ have a degree of support between 0 and 1, where 0 means that there is no support and 1 means that there is total support. If we do not have evidence for either A or $\overline{A}$, the confidence interval is [0, 1].

Let θ be the set of all mutually exclusive hypotheses, also called the *frame of discernment*. In this case $\theta = \{A, \overline{A}\}$, i.e. the information is either true or false.

Let m be a function called the *mass function*, $m : \wp(\theta) \to [0, 1]$, where $\wp(\theta)$ is the powerset of θ. The values of $m(A)$ are called basic belief masses (BBM). By applying the properties of the Dempster-Shafer theory, we will always have:

$$m(\phi) = 0 \tag{2}$$

$$\sum_{A \in P(\theta)} m(A) = 1 \tag{3}$$

The Dempster-Shafer fundamental equation for combining two pieces of evidence of m_1 and m_2 into a new one m_3 is:

$$m_3(Z) = \frac{\sum_{X \cap Y = Z} m_1(X) \cdot m_2(Y)}{1 - \sum_{X \cap Y = \varnothing} m_1(X) \cdot m_2(Y)} \tag{4}$$

1.2 Yager's Rule

Unlike Dempster-Shafer rule, $m(\theta) \geq 0$. Yager's rule [2] does not normalize the conflict, instead it adds it to the θ set. The following relations are used in order to combine two pieces of evidence:

$$m_3(Z) = \sum_{X \cap Y = Z \neq \varnothing} m_1(X) \cdot m_2(Y) \tag{5}$$

$$m_3(\theta) = m_1(\theta) \cdot m_2(\theta) + \sum_{X \cap Y = \varnothing} m_1(X) \cdot m_2(Z) \tag{6}$$

When more pieces of evidence are combined, Yager's rule is:

$$m_{n+1}(Z) = \sum m_1(X_1) \cdot \ldots m_n(X_n) \tag{7}$$

2 Related Work

In [3], the authors present a sophisticated Knowledge-Based Trust (KBT) method to evaluate the trustworthiness of web pages with regard to the information they provide. The first step is to parse data to obtain a certain format: (subject, predicate, object). This knowledge triplet is provided by various extractors (i.e. methods for information extraction from web pages). However, this extracted data using the extractors may be erroneous, but also the information published on the web pages may be untrue. KBT is a multi-level probabilistic model that can distinguish between these main sources of error: incorrect data on a web page and incorrect extractions made by the extractor.

A model that evaluates the content of posts posted on a social network, as well as the interest in a post to determine the credibility of the person which distributed the news is proposed in [4].

In [5], Dempster-Shafer theory of combined evidence is used to identify the insider attacker from a wireless sensor network (WSN) by observing the parameters of the neighbour nodes. To identify the insider attacker the authors took into account the observations of the neighbour nodes regarding to the behaviour of the suspected attacker. Data from neighbours is considered evidence. They combined these independent pieces of evidence and made a decision based on the Dempster-Shafer theory.

The authors of [6] describe a way to solve the problem of identifying the credible sources of relevant information in social networks. In order to evaluate the sources of relevant and credible information in social networks, their approach combines the analysis of the link structure of social networks with topic content models of messages. They have developed a method to automatically identify and categorize users based on relevance and knowledge in a particular domain for any given subject.

There are also several approaches to analyze the credibility of information diffusion in social networks. For example, in [7] an algorithm to detect the spreading of false information through the network is presented. It uses the collaborative filtering property of social networks to measure the credibility of sources of information as well as quality of news items. Two aspects regarding to the diffusion of misinformation in social networks are presented in [8]. These problems identify the misinformation sources and limit its diffusion in the network. Paper [9] analyzes the credibility of information in tweets corresponding to fourteen high impact news events of 2011 around the globe. To predict the credibility of information in a tweet, they used regression analysis to identify the most relevant features on the Twitter social network that can help in assessing the credibility of messages. The top relevant features found are content based (unique characters, swear words, pronouns, emoticons) and user-based features (number of followers, length of username). The CredRank algorithm is proposed in [10] to measure the credibility of social media users based on their online behaviour by finding those users with similar behaviour and clustering them.

The factors that influence individuals' perceived information credibility are studied in [11]. Five factors are identified as the most relevant to assess online information: medium dependency, interactivity, medium transparency, argument strength and information quality. A learning method, Information Credibility Evaluation (ICE), to learn representations of information credibility is proposed in [12], where the learning is based on the user credibility, behaviour types, temporal properties, and comment attitudes. Other machine learning or simulation models could be used as well [13–15].

3 Model Description

In this paper we analyze the spreading of information starting simultaneously with two source nodes, but we consider that these nodes will spread two different information. Let I be one of the two pieces of information, and we consider that it is true. Let $\bar{I}$ be the second piece of information that is transmitted by the other source node and which is considered to be false. Because the pieces of information are contradictory, we design a probabilistic decision mechanism based on Dempster-Shafer and Yager's rule for information diffusion and we compute a confidence degree which is held by a node for each of its neighbours. The observation of the two information types flow through the network according to various factors: the credibility of the two messages, the initial confidence degree of the nodes held by their neighbours, the number of simulation rounds where we establish which of the two pieces of information is true. Consequently, we develop a mechanism to suppress the transmission of the false information.

3.1 The Information Diffusion Protocol

The protocol of information diffusion is a cascaded one. We initialize a queue with the two source nodes and update it as follows:

- After a node has transmitted, it is removed from the queue;
- If a node receives a piece of information, it is added to the queue if it is not already contained;
- A node can be re-added to the queue for retransmission if it has received a piece of information that is different from the one which it has previously sent.

The information diffusion process stops when the queue no longer contains any nodes. We will define a round as the action of information diffusion starting with the moment in which the queue is initialized with the two source nodes until the queue becomes empty. We will refer to a simulation as the execution of a certain number of rounds. When a round is completed, the queue is reinitialized with the two source nodes, but the nodes of the network retain the statistical data: the information type (I or $\bar{I}$) and the number of each of these received information from neighbours.

Regarding the transmission probability of the node, we use Dempster-Shafer or Yager's rule together with a Gaussian distribution. When a node sends a type of information, the receiver node retains the fact that its neighbour has sent that specific information as well as its confidence degree. From the point of view of the receiver node, the received confidence degree is taken as a piece of evidence, namely belief.

In our model we have no plausibility evidence, so it will have the default value of 1. In order to keep a statistic for the received information type, some specific counters are incremented.

The beliefs accumulated by a node which must send are transformed into confidence intervals, where only the plausibility is set by default with value 1. Then, we use Dempster-Shafer or Yager's rule to combine the intervals, but only if the node contains two such intervals and the information type is different. If the node contains only one interval, then the combining procedure is ignored.

Once two confidence intervals have been combined, we obtain two more different confidence intervals. At this point we distinguish a few cases in our chosen probabilistic transmission protocol, depending on the newly computed beliefs and plausibilities, as follows:

- If both intervals are equal, the node will transmit the information with the higher generated number based on the Gaussian distribution and this number shall be also higher than the send threshold of value 0.5:

$$I: [0, a, b, 1] \quad G_1 = GenGauss(\frac{a+b}{2}, \sigma)$$
$$\bar{I}: [0, a', b', 1] \quad G_2 = GenGauss(\frac{a'+b'}{2}, \sigma)$$
$$\rightarrow SendInfo(\max(G_1, G_2))\ when(\max(G_1, G_2) > 0.5)$$

- If both the lower and the upper bounds are higher than the other interval limits, the information that has the interval with the larger limits will always be transmitted:

$$I: [0, a, b, 1] \quad G_1 = GenGauss(\frac{a+b}{2}, \sigma) \rightarrow SendInfo(I)\ when(G_1 > 0.5)$$
$$\bar{I}: [0, a', b', 1] \quad Ignored$$

- If the absolute difference of the means from the two interval limits is less or equal to a chosen value ε = 0.05, both intervals have the chance to further send the information. This case is only considered if the above cases are not satisfied:

$$I: [0, a, m, b, 1], \quad \bar{I}: [0, a', m', b', 1]$$
$$when(|m - m'| \leq 0.05): \quad G_1 = GenGauss(m, \sigma) \rightarrow SendInfo(I)\ when(G_1 > 0.5)$$
$$G_2 = GenGauss(m', \sigma) \rightarrow SendInfo(\bar{I})\ when(G_2 > 0.5)$$

For all the above cases, we have chosen the Gaussian distribution to have the variance $\sigma = 0.025$.

3.2 Computing Confidence Degrees

A node contains a list of confidence degrees, one for each neighbour. Thus, each node has its own point of view towards a neighbour. For example, the confidence degree of node 3 towards node 1 may be different from the confidence degree of node 3 towards node 2. This approach fits well with the real behaviour because each individual has his/her own point of view and it is not totally influenced by the opinion of others on the same common friend.

We quantify this confidence degree as a real number in the range of [0, 1]. The higher it is, the higher chance for the receiver node to get information from its transmitting neighbour, to whom this confidence degree is attached. In the first phase of the information diffusion through the network, when it is not yet known which of the two information is true, we consider the confidence degree in all node lists to be initialized with 0.9. At the moment that the round number has reached to the established one, to which the true and false information is specified, the confidence degree in the node lists will be recomputed using the Laplace correction [16].

After the execution of all rounds until the true information is established, each node also stores statistics with the received information type from neighbours as well as their total number.

For the computation of the confidence degrees of each node, the order in which they are processed is relevant. For this reason, before the main simulation, we establish the node transmission order considering the simple case in which the diffusion is permanently possible for all nodes. Thus, we establish a queue in which the nodes are introduced as they transmit information. This queue is initialized with the two source nodes and it will be updated until there are no longer transmitting nodes. We expect the queue to contain all the nodes of the network and we chose to determine it separately, before the start of the main simulation. In this way, we avoid the case in which it is possible that some nodes do not transmit or receive information, thus leading to an incomplete queue.

Once the confidence degree of the nodes has been computed, we let the simulation run further in order to observe how this impacts the information diffusion process.

The simulation algorithm contains three main phases:

- The execution of k rounds with the initial confidence degrees;
- The computation of confidence degrees after k rounds (i.e. when the ground truth about the information is revealed);
- The execution of j rounds with the new confidence degrees to observe the effect of the truth recently found.

4 Simulation Results

To illustrate how the networks become more immune to the diffusion of the false information, we choose three networks with different sizes and topologies. In the studied networks we have chosen two source nodes that contain contradictory types of information. The first network has a very simple topology: 9 chained nodes in which the sources are the two end nodes of the chain. We have chosen this network not only for the initial verification of the protocol, but also to test the collision point of the information, which is easily identified as the mid-chain node. The second network consists of 5 nodes with a random topology. In this case, the small size of the network allows us an easier observation of the computed confidence degrees taking into account the topology of the source nodes. The last network consists of 100 nodes with a scale free topology and we chose the source nodes to be as marginal as possible.

The two selected sources are marked with two different colours: green (S_1) and red (S_2). The initial number of rounds chosen for the diffusion of the two information types through the network is 1000. Source S_1 transmits the information I and source S_2 transmits the information $\bar{I}$. The initial confidence degree of the neighbours is 0.9.

For the visual illustration of the information diffusion we colour the nodes with different gray intensity levels, where the white colour means the node has received only the type I information and black colour only $\bar{I}$. Let X be the total number of the received type I information and Y the total number of the received type $\bar{I}$ information. We applied the following equation to obtain the gray level intensity for a particular node:

$$G = \frac{X}{X+Y} \cdot M \tag{8}$$

The fraction is the normalized quantity of type I information received by a node (in the range of [0, 1]), and M is the maximum allowed value of the pixel colour representation. In our case $M = 255$.

After we obtain the confidence intervals based on Dempster-Shafer or Yager's rule, this information can be transmitted with a probability higher than the transmission threshold of 0.5. Figure 1 shows the initial information diffusion through all the three networks.

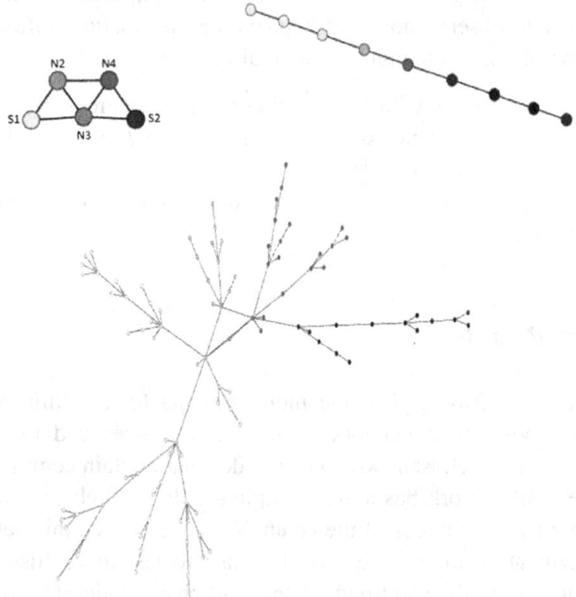

Fig. 1. The initial diffusion of the two information types through the all three networks

After the first 1000 rounds, we establish which of the transmitted information is true. In our simulations, we chose the information *I* to be true. In Fig. 2 it can easily be noticed that the confidence degree of the nodes for this information has increased and it has been more easily spread through the network, i.e. the greyscale level of the nodes containing false information has decreased in intensity.

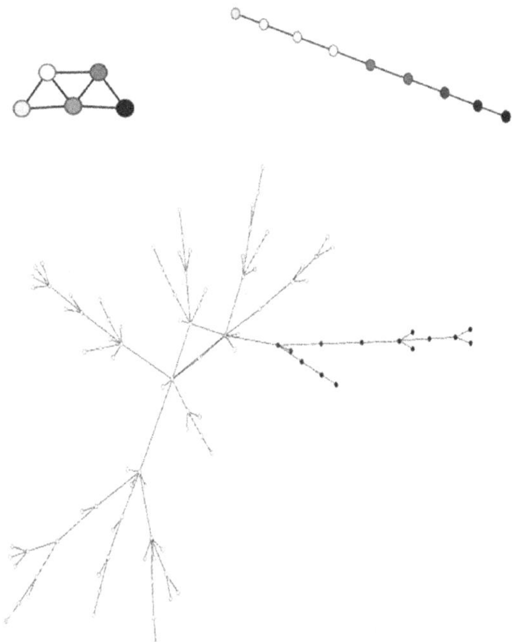

Fig. 2. The diffusion of the two information types after establishing the ground truth

By choosing a higher transmission threshold for the 100-node network of 0.55, it can be seen in Fig. 3 that when the two information types collide, the diffusion of one of them is totally or partially inhibited around the collision nodes. We colour the nodes with orange in case the diffusion of both information types is totally inhibited (Fig. 3a). Once the ground truth is revealed, i.e. the true information has been established, there are no longer nodes with totally inhibited diffusion (Fig. 3b).

From a graphical point of view, we cannot see any difference between the usage of Dempster-Shafer and Yager's rule, but we can see the small numerical differences in computing the confidence degree of neighbours. Table 1 shows these differences for the network with 5 nodes.

These results confirm that those neighbours containing mainly the true information, spread by the source with information *I* (i.e., the green node), have higher confidence degrees.

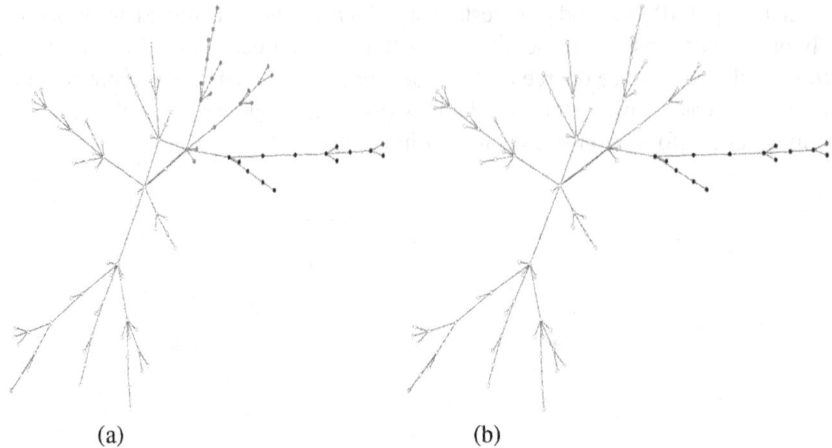

Fig. 3. The information diffusion through the network with a transmission threshold of 0.55: (a) initial diffusion, (b) diffusion after establishing the ground truth

Table 1. Numerical results

Nodes	Confidence degree of neighbour (CD)	
	Dempster- Shafer rule	Yager's rule
N2	CD(S1): 0.99900 CD(N3): 0.77203 CD(N4): 0.69369	CD(S1): 0.99900 CD(N3): 0.76390 CD(N4): 0.68442
N3	CD(S1): 0.77619 CD(N2): 0.79346 CD(N4): 0.75520 CD(S2): 0.64733	CD(S1): 0.76921 CD(N2): 0.78915 CD(N4): 0.75000 CD(S2): 0. 64364
N4	CD(N2): 0.68056 CD(N3): 0.66500 CD(S2): 0.60105	CD(N2): 0. 67802 CD(N3): 0. 66106 CD(S2): 0. 59787

5 Conclusions

In this paper we analyzed a model of information diffusion in social networks based on evidence theory in order to explicitly take into account the credibility of information sources, but also that of regular nodes in the network. By updating the credibility levels, it is possible to block the spread of false information, in time, provided that the ground truth, i.e. whether a piece of information is true or false, is sometimes, even rarely, revealed, after the actual transmission of that information. Once the credibility of a source node is lowered, this creates a phenomenon similar to a positive feedback that begins to gradually block that source, but also the paths used by that source to transmit information.

A future direction of investigation is to validate the information diffusion methods by studying sociological and psychological research about how real users react when exposed to contradictory information.

References

1. Shafer, G.: A Mathematical Theory of Evidence. Princeton University Press, Princeton (1976)
2. Yager, R.: On the Dempster-Shafer framework and new combination rules. Inf. Sci. **41**, 93–137 (1987)
3. Dong, X.L., et al.: Knowledge-based trust: estimating the trustworthiness of web sources. In: Li, C., Markl, V. (eds.) Proceedings of the VLDB Endowment, vol. 8, pp. 938–949. VLDB Endowment (2015)
4. Carchiolo, V., Longheu, A., Malgeri, M., Mangioni, G., Previti, M.: Post sharing-based credibility network for social network. In: Ivanović, M., Bădică, C., Dix, J., Jovanović, Z., Malgeri, M., Savić, M. (eds.) IDC 2017. SCI, vol. 737, pp. 149–158. Springer, Cham (2018). https://doi.org/10.1007/978-3-319-66379-1_14
5. Ahmed, M., Huang, X., Sharma, D.: Dempster-Shafer theory to identify insider attacker in wireless sensor network. In: Park, J.J., Zomaya, A., Yeo, S.-S., Sahni, S. (eds.) NPC 2012. LNCS, vol. 7513, pp. 94–100. Springer, Heidelberg (2012). https://doi.org/10.1007/978-3-642-35606-3_11
6. Canini, K.R., Suh, B., Pirolli, P.L.: Finding credible information sources in social networks based on content and social structure. In: 2011 IEEE Third International Conference on Privacy, Security, Risk and Trust and 2011 IEEE Third International Conference on Social Computing, Boston, vol. 1, pp. 1–8 (2011)
7. Kumar, K.P.K., Geethakumari, G.: Detecting misinformation in online social networks using cognitive psychology. Hum. Centric Comput. Inf. Sci. (2014). 13673
8. Amoruso, M., Anello, D., Auletta, V., Ferraioli, D.: Contrasting the spread of misinformation in online social networks. In: Proceedings of the 16th Conference on Autonomous Agents and MultiAgent Systems AAMAS 2017, pp. 1323–1331. International Foundation for Autonomous Agents and Multiagent Systems Richland, São Paulo (2017)
9. Gupta, A., Kumaraguru, P.: Credibility ranking of tweets during high impact events. In: Proceedings of the 1st Workshop on Privacy and Security in Online Social Media, PSOSM 2012. ACM New York, Lyon (2012)
10. Abbasi, M.-A., Liu, H.: Measuring user credibility in social media. In: Greenberg, A.M., Kennedy, W.G., Bos, N.D. (eds.) SBP 2013. LNCS, vol. 7812, pp. 441–448. Springer, Heidelberg (2013). https://doi.org/10.1007/978-3-642-37210-0_48
11. Li, R., Suh, A.: Factors influencing information credibility on social media platforms: evidence from Facebook pages. Procedia Comput. Sci. **72**, 314–328 (2015)
12. Liu, Q., Wu, S., Yu, F., Wang, L., Tan, T.: ICE: information credibility evaluation on social media via representation learning. arXiv preprint (2016). https://arxiv.org/pdf/1609.09226.pdf
13. Muharemi, F., Logofătu, D., Andersson, C., Leon, F.: Approaches to building a detection model for water quality: a case study. In: Sieminski, A., Kozierkiewicz, A., Nunez, M., Ha, Q.T. (eds.) Modern Approaches for Intelligent Information and Database Systems. SCI, vol. 769, pp. 173–183. Springer, Cham (2018). https://doi.org/10.1007/978-3-319-76081-0_15

14. Curteanu, S., Leon, F., Lupu, A.S., Floria, S.A, Logofatu, D.: An evaluation of regression algorithms performance for the chemical process of naphthalene sublimation. In: Proceedings of the 14th International Conference on Artificial Intelligence Applications and Innovations (AIAI), pp. 219–230 (2018)
15. Balabanov, K., Logofatu, D., Badica, C., Leon, F.: A simulation-based analysis of interdependent populations in a dynamic ecological environment. In: Proceedings of the 14th International Conference on Artificial Intelligence Applications and Innovations (AIAI), pp. 437–448 (2018)
16. Russell, S., Norvig, P.: Artificial Intelligence: A Modern Approach, 2nd edn., p. 863. Pearson Education, Inc., Upper Saddle River (2010)

Author Index

Printed in the United States
By Bookmasters